Valuing Small Businesses and Professional Practices

Valuing Small Businesses and Professional Practices

Third Edition

Shannon P. Pratt, DBA, CFA, FASA, CBA
Managing Director
Willamette Management Associates

Robert F. Reilly, CFA, ASA, CPA
Managing Director
Willamette Management Associates

Robert P. Schweihs, ASA
Managing Director
Willamette Management Associates

McGraw-Hill
New York • San Francisco • Washington, D.C. • Auckland
Bogotá • Caracas • Lisbon • London • Madrid • Mexico City
Milan • Montreal • New Delhi • San Juan • Singapore
Sydney • Tokyo • Toronto

Library of Congress Cataloging-in-Publication Data

Pratt, Shannon P.
    Valuing small businesses and professional practices / Shannon P.
  Pratt : with Robert F. Reilly and Robert P. Schweihs.   --3rd ed.
      p.   cm.
    Includes bibliographical references (p.   ) and index.
    ISBN 1-55623-551-8
    1. Small business--Valuation.   2. Professions--Valuation.
I. Reilly, Robert F.   II. Schweihs, Robert P.   III. Title.
HG4028.V3P73   1998
   658.15—dc21   97-46846
                                              CIP

McGraw-Hill

A Division of The McGraw·Hill Companies

8 9 10 11 12   QWK/QWK   0 9 8 7 6 5 4 3

ISBN 0-7863-1186-X

The sponsoring editor for this book was Roger Marsh, the editing supervisor was John M. Morriss, and the production supervisor was Suzanne W. B. Rapcavage. It was set in Times Roman by Douglas & Gayle Limited.

Printed and bound by Quebecor World / Kingsport.

McGraw-Hill books are available at special quantity discounts to use as premiums and sales promotions, or for use in corporate training programs. For more information, please write to Director of Special Sales, McGraw-Hill, 11 West 19th Street, New York, NY 10011. Or contact your local bookstore.

 This book is printed on recycled, acid-free paper containing a minimum of 50% recycled de-inked fiber.

To our many close friends in the business valuation profession

*Your leadership and efforts have contributed immensely
to developing a body of knowledge
and generally accepted business valuation methodology*

*We sincerely hope that this work
adequately reflects that collective effort*

Preface

The state of the art in small business and professional practice valuation has seen exceptional advancement in the last five years. We have made every attempt to bring readers of this edition to the leading edge of that state of the art.

It is noteworthy that there has been an increased demand for high-quality valuation analyses for small businesses and professional practices in recent years. There is no sign of abatement in this demand.

However, at the same time, valuation analyses that may have been acceptable a few years ago would not stand up under challenge today. We have tried to provide a basic reference both for performing and evaluating business valuation analyses that *will* stand up under challenge.

Data Availability Encourages Market Approach

Perhaps the greatest advancement in the valuation profession has been the recent availability of empirical data for valuing small businesses and professional practices. These empirical data, although still limited, are especially useful in the application of market approach valuation methods. The following are some of the new and expanded empirical data sources that have become available since the last edition:

- *EDGAR* (Electronic Data Gathering and Retrieval System). Over 15,000 publicly traded companies with data available *free* through the Internet; many of these companies have market capitalizations under $5 million.
- *Done Deals*. Over 1,500 transactions between $1 million and $100 million are available on disk.
- *Pratt's Stats*. The official database of the International Business Brokers Association, providing more detail than ever before available regarding small businesses and professional practice transactions.
- *Bizcomps* and *IBA Database*. Both sources have been significantly expanded.
- New *trade association* and *industry comparative* data.

With the emergence of these easily accessible and inexpensive databases on small business and professional practice transactions, there is much more emphasis in this edition on the market approach to valuation. For example, this edition includes the following:

- A new chapter on the comparative transaction method.
- A new chapter on the multiple of discretionary earnings (owner's discretionary cash flow) method.
- Two new chapters on using small public company data.
- A greatly expanded chapter on transaction databases, placed earlier in the book in conjunction with the market approach chapters.

References to scores of new comparative data sources are included as appropriate throughout the book.

Many Advances in Business Valuation Education

Another area of professional advancement has been in business valuation education. This includes courses, seminars, books, articles, unpublished (but available) papers, videotapes, and audiotapes. These greatly expanded general sources of education and information are summarized in Chapter 1. We have placed hundreds of other sources within the various subject chapters and at the ends of chapters.

More Emphasis on Legal Context, Including Divorce

One of the most valuable changes from the second edition is the emphasis throughout the book on the effect of the legal context in which the valuation is being performed. For example, valuation rules and conclusions may be very different for gift and estate taxes than for a marital dissolution or for a dissenting stockholder action.

The chapter on defining the valuation assignment has been completely rewritten and expanded to provide a more valuable road map for the analyst, attorney, or client, in order to address all the critical categories of issues at the outset of an engagement. Throughout the book, citations of judicial precedent document what the courts have found both acceptable and unacceptable in various legal contexts.

In particular, this edition has much more emphasis on valuation for marital dissolution purposes, recognizing that marital dissolution property settlements represent a common reason for valuing small businesses and professional practices. The chapter on valuations for divorce is completely rewritten and updated.

In addition, throughout the chapters, discussion has been added about using the material in the marital dissolution context. Finally, marital dissolution court case citations have been added to illustrate the courts' positions on various issues.

Other New Material in This Edition

- A new chapter on value drivers and their impact on valuation methods.
- A new chapter on discounts for lack of marketability.
- A new sample case and new sample professional practice reports.
- A broadened chapter on alternative dispute resolution, which includes mediation as well as arbitration, and has been retitled Arbitrating or Mediating Disputed Valuations.
- An updated chapter on small company ESOPs.

Keeping Up

Even with all the professional advancement in the last five years, developments in business valuation practice continue to evolve at a rapid pace. Accordingly, we encourage practitioner involvement in the professional associations discussed in this book.

Finally, preparers and users of business appraisals now have a monthly newsletter available to keep up to date: *Shannon Pratt's Business Valuation Update*. Readers may obtain a complimentary sample copy of this newsletter by calling Business Valuation Resources, 888-BUS-VALU (888-287-8268).

Shannon Pratt
Portland, Oregon
January 1998

Acknowledgments

This third edition has benefited from the careful review of all (or parts) of the manuscript by a broad representation of practitioners of the business valuation and business intermediary professions.

Thanks to the unstinting service of the following individuals, we believe this volume truly represents the consensus positions of a broad cross-section of the practitioners from all facets of the business valuation community:

David Bishop
American Business
Appraisers, Inc.

Gary R. Trugman
Trugman Valuation
Associates, Inc.
Member, AICPA Management
Consulting Services Committee

James S. Rigby Jr.
The Financial Valuation Group
Member, AICPA Business
Valuations and Appraisals
Subcommittee

James L. (Butch) Williams
Williams, Taylor & Associates
Chairman, NACVA Executive
Advisory Committee

Portions of the manuscript were also reviewed by the following individuals:

John Bailey
World M&A Network

Jeff Jones
Certified Business Brokers
Chairman, IBBA Standards
Committee

John M. Cahill
Michael P. Carroll
Caroll/Cahill Associates
Co-chairmen, Professional
Practice Valuation Study Group

Brian Knight
Country Business, Inc.
Past President, IBBA

Robert J. Gurrola
Summa Financial Group, Inc.
Past President, International
Business Brokers Association

Ray Miles
Executive Director
Institute of Business Appraisers

Ken Hoganson
Hoganson Venture Group
Chairman, IBBA/Pratt's Stats
Database Committee

Jack Sanders
Bizcomps

Roman Iwanyshyn   Leonard J. Sliwoski
Iwanyshyn & Associates   Small Business Development
                                         Center

Thomas West
Business Brokerage Press
Past Executive Director, IBBA

Several chapters were prepared or updated by members of the professional staff of Willamette Management Associates. Chapter 25, Discount for Lack of Marketability, and Chapter 39, Employee Stock Ownership Plans in Small Companies, were prepared by Jeffrey S. Tarbell, a senior associate in the Willamette Management Associates San Francisco office. The Sample Case and Solution to the Sample Case (Chapters 30 and 31) were prepared by Andrew S. Ward, an associate in the firm's Chicago office. The chapter on Public Company Data (Chapter 17) was drafted by Jan D. Tudor, a former member of the firm's Portland office. Chapter 36, Sample Professional Practice Valuation Report, was prepared by Michelle M. Hartstrom, senior associate, and Charles A. Wilhoite, principal and co-director, of the firm's Portland office. James G. Rabe, a principal of the firm and co-director of the Portland office, prepared Chapter 37, Examples of Professional Practice Valuation Methods. Chapter 38, Buy-Sell Agreements and Estate Planning, was prepared by Curtis R. Kimball, the national director of estate and gift tax services and director of the Atlanta, Georgia, office. The chapter on Marital Dissolutions (Chapter 41) was drafted by Sharon K. Moore, a former member of the firm's Chicago office. Daniel R. Van Vleet, a principal in the Chicago office, prepared the chapter on Litigation (Chapter 46). And, Charles A. Wilhoite, a principal and co-director of the Portland office, prepared the chapter on Damages (Chapter 47).

Daniel P. Callanan, a former senior associate in our Chicago office, checked the accuracy of the mathematical formulas and calculations. Jan D. Tudor, Cynthia K. Stewart-Rinier, and Charlene Blalock prepared the chapter bibliographies. Other members of the Willamette Management Associates staff reviewed or prepared portions of chapters. In particular, we would like to thank Portland office associate Terry G. Whitehead and Portland office research associate Irene Moore.

The authors have reviewed and edited all of the chapters written and updated by others and take final responsibility for their content.

Charlene M. Blalock, a research associate in the Portland office, served as the project manager for this undertaking. This included acting as a liaison and coordinating with the authors, the publisher, and the outside reviewers. She was responsible for obtaining permission to use material reprinted in this book from other sources. Charlene also prepared the index and edited and proofread the manuscript. This book would simply not have been completed without Charlene's dedication and project management.

Mary McAllister and Charlene Blalock were responsible for typing the entire manuscript. This was a monumental task that they performed well under very tight time schedules. Sally Martin provided additional proofreading.

For permission to use material, we especially wish to thank:

The Appraisal Foundation	Prentice Hall
The American Society of Appraisers	Robert Morris Associates
Practitioners Publishing Company	Ibbotson Associates
Mergerstat Review	John Wiley & Sons

We express our gratitude to all of the people singled out above as well as all those unnamed (but not forgotten) people who wrote letters and had discussions with us about many conceptual and technical points since the last edition. As always, final responsibility for all content and judgments rests with the authors.

Shannon Pratt **Robert Reilly** **Robert Schweihs**
Portland, Oregon Chicago, Illinois Chicago, Illinois

About the Authors

Dr. Shannon P. Pratt is a managing director and one of the founders of Willamette Management Associates. Founded in the 1960s, Willamette Management Associates is one of the oldest and largest independent valuation consulting, economic analysis, and financial advisory firms in the country. It has regional offices in Atlanta; McLean, Virginia; Chicago; San Francisco; and Portland, Oregon. Willamette Manage-ment Associates is well known for its extensive research library, which has a constantly updated collection of books, articles, transactional data sources, and court cases involving valuation and economic analysis issues. This book draws heavily on that resource.

In addition to this book, Dr. Pratt is a co-author of *Valuing a Business: The Analysis and Appraisal of Closely Held Companies*, Third Edition (McGraw-Hill, 1996) and a co-author of *Guide to Business Valuations*, Seventh Edition (Practitioners Publishing Company, 1997). He is also editor in chief of *Shannon Pratt's Business Valuation Update*, a monthly newsletter covering current developments in the field of business valuation.

Dr. Pratt holds a doctorate in finance from Indiana University and a bachelor of arts in business administration from the University of Washington. He is a chartered financial analyst, an accredited senior appraiser (certified in business valuation) and fellow of the American Society of Appraisers (the highest designation awarded by that society), and a certified business appraiser of the Institute of Business Appraisers. Dr. Pratt has held many offices of the various professional societies and has served on numerous committees. Currently, he is a life member emeritus of the Business Valuation Committee of the American Society of Appraisers, a life member emeritus of the Valuation Advisory Committee of The ESOP Association, a life member of the Institute of Business Appraisers, and a trustee of The Appraisal Foundation (the entity responsible for establishing, issuing, promoting, and improving the *Uniform Standards of Professional Appraisal Practice* under the auspices of the United States government). He is frequently called upon to testify in disputed business valuation matters.

Robert F. Reilly is a managing director of Willamette Management Associates. He holds a masters of business administration in finance from the Columbia University Graduate School of Business and a bachelor of arts in economics from Columbia College. He is an accredited senior appraiser of the American Society of Appraisers (certified in business valuation), a chartered financial analyst, a certified public accountant, a certified management accountant, an accredited tax advisor, a state certified general appraiser, a certified review appraiser, and a state certified affiliate of the Appraisal Institute.

In addition to this book, Mr. Reilly is a co-author of *Valuing a Business: The Analysis and Appraisal of Closely Held Companies*, Third Edition (McGraw-Hill, 1996). He is also co-author of *Valuing Accounting Practices* (John Wiley & Sons, 1997) and *Valuing Professional Practices: A Practitioner's Guide* (CCH Incorporated, 1997). He is a co-editor of *Financial Valuation: Businesses and Business Interests*, 1997 Update (Warren, Gorham & Lamont, 1997). Mr. Reilly currently serves in an editorial capacity for—and is a regular contributor to—such professional journals as *The American Bankruptcy Institute Journal* and *The Journal of Property Tax Management*.

As an appraiser and economist, he has testified both in domestic and international courts on well over 150 occasions regarding the valuation of intangible assets, businesses, and business interests, and regarding various economic damages issues.

Robert P. Schweihs is a managing director of Willamette Management Associates. He holds a masters of business administration in economics and finance from the University of Chicago Graduate School of Business and a bachelor of science in mechanical engineering from the University of Notre Dame. He is an accredited senior appraiser of the American Society of Appraisers (certified in business valuation). He currently serves as a member of the Industry Advisory Council of The Appraisal Foundation and a Trustee of The Appraisal Foundation.

In addition to this book, Mr. Schweihs is a co-author of *Valuing a Business: The Analysis and Appraisal of Closely Held Companies*, Third Edition (McGraw-Hill, 1996). He is also co-author of *Valuing Accounting Practices* (John Wiley & Sons, 1997) and *Valuing Professional Practices: A Practitioner's Guide* (CCH Incorporated, 1997). He is a co-editor of *Financial Valuation: Businesses and Business Interests*, 1997 Update (Warren, Gorham & Lamont, 1997).

Mr. Schweihs frequently speaks to professional societies and is a prolific author of journal articles regarding various valuation issues. He is often called upon to testify as an expert witness with regard to contested valuation and economic analysis matters.

Notation System Used in This Book

A source of confusion for those trying to understand financial theory and methods is the fact that financial writers have not adopted a standard system of notation. For this edition, we have studied dozens of financial texts and have developed a system of notation that reflects either the most commonly used conventions or ones that seem intuitively easy to understand. If other financial writers adopt this standardized system of notation, we believe it will go a long way toward removing ambiguity, clarifying communication, and making it easier for readers to absorb financial articles and texts.

Value at a Point in Time

PV	=	Present value
FV	=	Future value
MVIC	=	Market value of invested capital
T	=	Terminal value (the expected value at the end of some discrete projection period, used in the discounted economic income method)

Cost of Capital and Rate of Return Variables

k	=	Discount rate (generalized)
k_e	=	Discount rate for common equity capital (cost of common equity capital). Unless otherwise stated, it generally is assumed that this discount rate is applicable to net cash flow available to common equity.
k_p	=	Discount rate for preferred equity capital
k_d	=	Discount rate for debt (Note: for complex capital structures, there could be more than one class of capital in any of the above categories, requiring expanded subscripts.)
$k_{d(pt)}$	=	Cost of debt prior to tax effect
k_{ni}	=	Discount rate for equity capital when net income rather than net cash flow is the measure of economic income being discounted
c	=	Capitalization rate
c_e	=	Capitalization rate for common equity capital (cost of common equity capital). Unless otherwise stated, it generally is assumed that this capitalization rate is applicable to net cash flow available to common equity.
c_{ni}	=	Capitalization rate for net income
c_p	=	Capitalization rate for preferred equity capital

c_d = Capitalization rate for debt (Note: for complex capital structures, there could be more than one class of capital in any of the above categories, requiring expanded subscripts.)

t = Tax rate (expressed as a percentage of pretax income)

R = Rate of return

R_f = Rate of return on a risk-free security

$E(R)$ = Expected rate of return

$E(R_m)$ = Expected rate of return on the "market" (usually used in the context of a market for equity securities, such as the NYSE or S&P 500)

$E(R_i)$ = Expected rate of return on security i

B = Beta (a coefficient, usually used to modify a rate of return variable)

B_L = Levered beta

B_U = Unlevered beta

RP = Risk premium

RP_m = Risk premium for the "market" (usually used in the context of a market for equity securities, such as the NYSE or S&P 500)

RP_s = Risk premium for "small" stocks (average size of lowest quartile of NYSE as measured by market value of common equity) over and above RPm

RP_u = Risk premium for unsystematic risk attributable to the specific company

RP_i = Risk premium for the ith security

$K_1 \ldots K_n$ = Risk premium associated with risk factor 1 through n for the average asset in the market (used in conjunction with Arbitrage Pricing Theory)

WACC = Weighted average cost of capital

Income Variables

E = Expected economic income (in a generalized sense—i.e., could be dividends, any of several possible definitions of cash flows, net income, and so on)

NI = Net income (after entity-level taxes)

NCF_e = Net cash flow to equity

NCF_f = Net cash flow to the firm (to overall invested capital, or entire capital structure, including all equity and long-term debt)

PMT = Payment (interest and principal payment on debt security)

D = Dividends

GCF = Gross cash flow (usually net income plus noncash charges)

EBIT = Earnings before interest and taxes

EBDIT = Earnings before depreciation, interest, and taxes ("Depreciation" in this context usually includes amortization. Some writers use EBDITA to specifically indicate that amortization is included.)

Periods or Variables in a Series

i = The ith period or the ith variable in a series (may be extended to the jth variable, the kth variable, and so on)

n = The number of periods or variables in the series, or the last number in the series

∞ = Infinity

o = Period$_o$, the base period, usually the latest year immediately preceding the valuation date

Weightings

W = Weight

W_e = Weight of common equity in capital structure

W_p = Weight of preferred equity in capital structure

W_d = Weight of debt in capital structure

Note: For purposes of computing a weighted average cost of capital (WACC), it is assumed that above weightings are at market value.

Growth

g = Rate of growth

Mathematical Functions

Σ = Sum of (add up all the variables that follow)

Π = Product of (multiply together all the variables that follow)

$\times$ = Mean average (the sum of the values of the variables divided by the number of variables)

G = Geometric mean (the product of the values of the variables taken to the root of the number of variables)

Contents

Debt-Free Value. Problems in the Application of Gross Revenue Multiples. *Ambiguity about Exactly What Was Sold. Ambiguity about the Terms of the Transaction. A Profit Factor Usually Comes into Play. Differences in Persistence of Revenues. Uniqueness of Each Entity. Multiples Change Considerably over Time. Even Gross Revenue Data May Not Be Reliable.* Multiples of Some Measure of Physical Volume. Using Industry Earnings Data to Check Gross Revenue Multiples. Summary.

Maintenance. Other Investment Needed. Failure to Understand What the Indicated Value Represents. *What Assets and / or Liabilities Are Included? Asset versus Stock Valuation. Ownership Characteristics.* Assuming That the Buyer Will Pay for the Now and the Hereafter. Emphasis on Items Not in Proportion to Their Relative Importance. Inadequate Documentation. Failure to Conduct a Site Visit and/or Management Interviews. Errors Articulated by Tax Court Judges. Common Mistakes Made by CPAs. Summary.

List of Exhibits

Valuing Small Businesses and Professional Practices

Part I

Introduction: Understanding the Valuation Process

Chapter 1

Business Valuation Standards and Professional Associations

Introduction: Professionalization of Business Valuation
Uniform Standards of Professional Appraisal Practice
American Society of Appraisers
Institute of Business Appraisers
National Association of Certified Valuation Analysts
American Institute of Certified Public Accountants
Canadian Institute of Chartered Business Valuators
Internal Revenue Service
Department of Labor
Summary
Bibliography and Resource List

3

Introduction: Professionalization of Business Valuation

The professionalization of the business valuation discipline has progressed significantly since the last edition of this book five years ago.

The typical valuation work product that may have been acceptable five years ago may well be considered substandard today—in comparison to the more sophisticated and comprehensive valuation on the opposite side of a transaction negotiation or of a litigation controversy. Courts, attorneys, business brokers, buyers, and fiduciaries are all becoming increasingly aware of business valuation standards, and they are increasingly demanding that such standards be followed.

It is important, therefore, to start the book with an overview of generally accepted business valuation professional standards, of the organizations that promulgate them, and of the educational resources available to business appraisers and business appraisal users today.

Uniform Standards of Professional Appraisal Practice

The *Uniform Standards of Professional Appraisal Practice* (USPAP) may be regarded as an "umbrella" set of professional standards that is often appropriate for any appraisal, whether the appraisal is of real estate, personal property, a business, a business interest, or an intangible asset.

USPAP is promulgated by the Appraisal Standards Board (ASB) of The Appraisal Foundation. The Appraisal Foundation is a not-for-profit educational organization established in 1987. It was established to foster professionalism in appraising through the establishment and promotion of appraisal standards and appraiser qualifications.

According to the Mission Statement of The Appraisal Foundation, "the Appraisal Standards Board promulgates the generally accepted standards of the appraisal profession." The fact that these standards are, indeed, reaching a position of general acceptance is evidenced by frequent references to USPAP in both judicial decisions and in the professional literature.

The Appraisal Standards Board publishes an updated version of USPAP annually, typically in November. (See the Bibliography and Resource List at the end of the chapter for prices and ordering information.) An outline of the content of the 1998 edition of USPAP is presented in Exhibit 1-1. As of this writing, USPAP has been drafted entirely by real estate appraisers and has not been fully embraced by the business valuation community. Major revisions are planned for the 1999 edition, to be released in November of 1998.

The American Society of Appraisers (ASA) has made compliance with the Uniform Standards of Professional Appraisal Practice mandatory for appraisals prepared by their members. However, in 1997, the ASA Board of Governors approved Business Valuation Advisory Opinion

Exhibit 1–1

TABLE OF CONTENTS

UNIFORM STANDARDS OF PROFESSIONAL APPRAISAL PRACTICE

INTRODUCTION

SOURCE: *Uniform Standards of Professional Appraisal Practice* (Washington, DC: The Appraisal Foundation, 1998). Reprinted with permission of The Appraisal Foundation.

No. 1, limiting the scope of business valuation engagements for which USPAP is considered mandatory:

> It is the opinion of the Business Valuation Committee that the American Society of Appraisers Business Valuation Standards and the Uniform Standards of Professional Appraisal Practice of the Appraisal Foundation, as they apply to business valuation issues, are intended to apply to appraisals that are formally developed and presented opinions of value performed as the primary or ultimate objective of an engagement. These standards are not intended to apply to financial consultation or advisory services including but not limited to fairness opinions, solvency opinions, pricing of securities for public offerings, feasibility studies, transfer pricing studies, lifing studies of intangibles,

estate planning or estate tax services, economic damage analysis and quantification, litigation consulting, royalty rate studies for intangibles, and similar engagements where there is no expression of value opinion or the primary or the ultimate objective is not to express an opinion of value.[1]

The Institute of Business Appraisers generally endorses USPAP but does not require compliance by its members. IBA executive director Ray Miles stated in 1997, "We do not wish to subject our members to a requirement to comply with USPAP, given the existing problems of interpretation and enforcement of USPAP as related to business appraisal."[2]

The Appraisal Foundation also has an Appraiser Qualifications Board (AQB). Its mission is to establish education, experience, and examination criteria for appraisers. As of this writing, the AQB has established qualifications for real estate appraisers, but it has not yet committed to the task of establishing qualifications for business appraisers.

American Society of Appraisers

The American Society of Appraisers (ASA) is a multidisciplinary professional society founded in 1952. It awards accreditations in appraisal of real estate, machinery and equipment, personal property, and business valuation (including intangible assets).

Through its Business Valuation Committee, the ASA issues the American Society of Appraisers Business Valuation Standards. These standards embrace USPAP and provide additional detail on the requirements for performing an acceptable business valuation.

Exhibit 1-2 provides a summary of the ASA business valuation accreditation requirements and educational offerings. (See the Bibliography and Resource List at the end of the chapter for information on ordering ASA materials.)

Institute of Business Appraisers

The Institute of Business Appraisers (IBA), founded in 1978, focuses on the appraisal of small to medium-size businesses. It awards the accreditation of Certified Business Appraiser (CBA). In 1997, it introduced an additional certification, Business Valuation Accredited for Litigation (BVAL).

---

[1]"Financial Consultation and Advisory Services," Advisory Opinion No. 1, *American Society of Appraisers Business Valuation Standards* (Herndon, VA: American Society of Appraisers, 1997), p. 23.

[2] Testimony presented May 2, 1997, at an Appraisal Foundation hearing on the size and composition of the Appraisal Standards Board, quoted in *Shannon Pratt's Business Valuation Update*, June 1997, p. 3.

Exhibit 1–2

AMERICAN SOCIETY OF APPRAISERS (ASA)
P.O. Box 17265, Washington, D.C. 20041, (703) 478-2228

Date formed:	1936	Ownership: Owned by members

Description: Multidisciplinary professional organization offering courses and exams leading to designations in the appraisal of real estate, machinery and equipment, personal property, gems and jewelry, businesses and business interests (including intangible assets), and certain technical specialties.

Designations offered:

AM—Accredited Member:

Educational requirement:	College degree or equivalent
Courses/exams:	Completion of four courses of three days each, with successful completion of one half-day exam following each of the three courses and a full-day exam following BV204, OR successful completion of one all-day challenge exam. In addition, successful completion of an ethics exam is required.
Reports:	Submission of two actual appraisal reports to satisfaction of Board of Examiners
Experience requirement:	Two years full-time or full-time equivalent (e.g., 5 years of 400 hours business appraisal work per year equals one year full-time equivalent).
Related experience offset:	One full year of the experience requirement is granted to anyone who has any of the following three designations with five years of practice in that respective field: Certified Public Accountant (CPA), Chartered Financial Analyst (CFA), or Certified Business Intermediary (CBI).

ASA—Accredited Senior Appraiser:

has met all requirements above plus an additional three years of full-time or full-time equivalent experience.

FASA—Fellow of the American Society of Appraisers:

has met all requirements above plus is voted into the College of Fellows on the basis of technical leadership and contribution to the profession and the Society.

Courses: Each of the core courses (BV201–204) are three days; BV201 through 203 are followed by a half-day exam and BV204 is followed by a full-day exam. BV205 and 206 are two days each.

BV201:	Introduction to business valuation, part one
BV202:	Introduction to business valuation, part two
BV203:	Business valuation case study
BV204:	Business valuation selected advanced topics
BV205:	Appraisal of small businesses and professional practices
BV206:	Employee stock ownership plans: valuing ESOP shares

Seminars and Conferences: Seminars on specialized topics lasting from two hours to two days are sponsored by various groups within the ASA.

Annual interdisciplinary meeting with two and a half days of technical presentations on each of the Society's appraisal disciplines.

Annual Advanced Business Valuation Conference with two or two are a half days of advanced business valuation papers, presentations, and discussion.

Publications: *Business Valuation Review*, quarterly professional journal with articles accepted based on peer review. Published at 2777 South Colorado Boulevard, Suite 200, Denver, Colorado 80222, (303) 758-8818. The other valuation disciplines also have their professional journals, similar to *Business Valuation Review*.

Valuation, published on an irregular basis, contains articles on all of the disciplines of valuation within the ASA. Published at ASA headquarters (see title of exhibit for address).

Local chapters: Chapters with regular monthly meetings in 87 cities throughout the United States and Canada

The IBA has also promulgated a set of business valuation standards. Like the ASA, the IBA business valuation standards embrace USPAP and provide further, more detailed guidance for good business appraisal practice.

Exhibit 1-3 provides a summary of the IBA accreditation requirements and educational offerings. (See the Bibliography and Resource List at the end of the chapter for information on ordering IBA materials.)

National Association of Certified Valuation Analysts

The National Association of Certified Valuation Analysts (NACVA), founded in 1991, focuses on valuations of closely held businesses performed by certified public accountants and other valuation professionals.

NACVA issues a set of standards for both professional practice conduct and valuation report writing. Compliance with USPAP is not a mandatory requirement for valuations performed by NACVA members, although their standards incorporate most business valuation-related USPAP standards.

Exhibit 1-4 provides a summary of the NACVA accreditation requirements and educational offerings (See the Bibliography and Resource List at the end of the chapter for information on ordering NACVA materials.)

American Institute of Certified Public Accountants

In November 1996, the AICPA authorized a specialty designation called Accredited in Business Valuation (ABV). The first exams for this designation were given in November 1997.

Exhibit 1-5 provides a summary of AICPA's ABV accreditation requirements and educational offerings. (See the Bibliography and Resource List at the end of the chapter for information on ordering AICPA materials.)

Canadian Institute of Chartered Business Valuators

The Canadian Institute of Chartered Business Valuators (CICBV) was founded in 1971. It has a Code of Ethics and standards for its members to follow for business valuations in Canada. As of this writing, the Institute has nine standards for business valuation.

Exhibit 1-6 provides a summary of the CICBV accreditation requirements and educational offerings. (See the Bibliography and Resource List at the end of the chapter for information on ordering CICBV materials.)

Exhibit 1–3

INSTITUTE OF BUSINESS APPRAISERS (IBA)
P.O. Box 1447, Boynton Beach, Florida 33425, (407) 732-3202

Date formed:	1978	Ownership:	Florida not-for-profit corporation (privately owned)

Description: Offers programs of interest to members whose business valuation activities are less than full time and/or whose practice includes valuation of small to midsize businesses.

Certification offered: *CBA—Certified Business Appraiser:*

Educational requirement:	Four years of college or equivalent
Courses/exams:	Three and one-half hour exam
Reports:	Submission of two business appraisal reports demonstrating professional level of competence
Experience requirement:	None

FIBA—Fellow of the Institute of Business Appraisers:
has met all requirements above plus is voted into the College of Fellows on the basis of technical leadership and contribution to the profession and to the Institute

Courses:
2001   Fundamentals of valuing mid-size and smaller business (2 days)
2002   Advanced theory and applications of business valuations (2 days)
7001   Litigation support and expert witness training (7 days)
8001   Mastering appraisal skills of the closely held business (8 days)

Seminars and Conferences: One-day seminars on business valuation held at various locations around the United States. Annual conference held in different cities.

Local chapters: A few at present

Internal Revenue Service

The Internal Revenue Service (IRS) issues a number of types of publications that provide various levels of authority or guidance with respect to business valuations.

The U.S. Congress directs the Treasury Department to issue regulations to provide structure for the tax laws it passes. These regulations do not have the force of law, but they present the position of the IRS on various tax matters, including the valuation of businesses, business interests, and related intangible assets. Regulations are actually formulated by the IRS, but they are approved by the Secretary of the Treasury or by his delegate. As an example, the regulations for Chapter 14 of the estate and gift tax laws require appraisers to use a special valuation methodology in certain circumstances with regard to family-owned businesses.

The IRS issues "pronouncements" representing administrative (as opposed to legislative) tax authority. The pronouncements include revenue rulings, revenue procedures, letter rulings, technical advice mem-

Exhibit 1–4

National Association of Certified Valuation Analysits (NACVA)
1245 East Brickyard Road, Suite 110, Salt Lake City, Utah 84106, (801) 486-0600

Date formed	1991 Ownership: Group of shareholders
Description:	NACVA is an association of CPAs, government valuers, and other professionals that perform valuation services. Its purpose is to promulgate the members' status, credentials, and esteem in the field of performing valuations of closely held businesses.

Certification offered:	*CVA—Certified Valuation Analyst*	
	Education requirement:	CPA
	Courses/exams:	60-hour, take-home exam, which includes one case study and report writing requirement.
	Reports:	Only for sample case on exam
	Experience requirement:	Experience required for certification as CPA
	GVA—Government Valuation Analyst	
	Education requirement:	College degree
	Courses/exams:	60-hour, take-home exam, which includes one case study and report writing requirement.
	Reports:	Only for sample case on exam
	Experience requirement:	Employed by government agency, GS-12 or higher, 2 years full-time business valuation experience

Courses:	Five days of training consisting of the following:
	Days 1-2: Fundamentals, Techniques, and Theory
	Days 3: Case Analysis No. 1 and Report Writing
	Day 4: Using Valuation Master 4.0 Software
	Day 5: Working Effectively in the Litigation Environment

Seminars and Conferences:	Two conferences held annually. Semi-annual one and a half day seminar on business valuation topics. Also one- and two-day seminars on key valuations topics, including symposiums.
Publications:	*The Valuation Examiner*, a bimonthly magazine
Local chapters	State chapters presently in 38 states and one in Mexico City

orandums, and general counsel memorandums. These pronouncements illustrate the treatment of certain issues not clearly addressed in the regulations. Over time, many of the positions espoused by the IRS through regulations and revenue rulings come up in court disputes. The resolution of these issues by the courts establishes judicial precedent. Much, but by no means all, of the case law has been supportive of positions taken in the regulations and revenue rulings. The following are the most important of the revenue rulings that relate to business valuation:

59-60	Discusses valuing closely held stock. Theory in Revenue Ruling 59-60 applies to income and other taxes as well as to estate and gift taxes; to business interests of any type, including partnerships and proprietorships; and to intangible assets for all tax purposes.

Exhibit 1–5

AMERICAN INSTITUTE OF CERTIFIED PUBLIC ACCOUNTANTS (AICPA)
201 Plaza Three, Jersey City, New Jersey 07311-3881, (201) 938-3000

Date formed	1887	Ownership:	Organization-sponsored

Description: Recognizes business valuation as a CPA service niche and confers an accreditation credential reflecting this recognition for those in public practice, industry, government, and education.

Certification offered: *ABV—Accredited in Business Valuation*
Prerequisite: AICPA member with current CPA license
Courses/exams: One-day exam
Reports: None
Expertise requirement: Involvement in at least 10 business valuation engagements

Courses: Eight basic one-day courses (NBV1-NBV8) plus five one-day advanced "core" courses and several one-day advanced elective courses; two-day ABV exam review course.

Seminars and Conferences: Annual National Valuation Conference

Publications: *CPA Expert*, a quarterly newsletter
The AICPA also publishes an extensive list of consulting service publications, generally referred to as "practice aids" or "special reports," including practice aids related to consulting with specific industry engagements.

68-609	Discusses the "formula method" for determining fair market value of intangible assets of a business. Supersedes ARM 34.
77-287	Recognizes relevance of restricted stock studies (see Chapter 26) in determining discounts for lack of marketability.
83-120	Discusses valuing preferred stock.
93-12	Allows the application of minority discounts to partial interest transfers even when a family owns overall control of a closely held business. Supersedes and reverses Revenue Ruling 81-253, which disallowed such discounts but was overturned by case law.

Representing less authority than the revenue rulings, the private letter rulings, technical advice memorandums, and general counsel memorandums issued by the IRS are responses to specific inquiries from taxpayers (and/or from IRS field offices). They may not be cited as precedent. Nevertheless, these can be helpful in understanding the IRS's likely position on emerging issues for tax-related appraisals.

The IRS's internal publications and other official materials also provide useful insights. The 1994 *Course Book on Valuation Training for Appeals Officers* is available through Commerce Clearing House and the 1997 edition of this course book is available on-line (see bibliography).

Exhibit 1–6

THE CANADIAN INSTITUTE OF CHARTERED BUSINESS VALUATORS
277, Wellington St. West, Toronto, Ontario, Canada M5V 3H2, (416) 204-3396

Date formed:	1971	Ownership: Non-profit Federally Incorporated Corporation owned by Members

Description: The CICBV is the largest professional valuation organization in Canada. It was established to promote high standards in business and securities valuations. Members are entitled to use the professional designation CBV (Chartered Business Valuator) following completion of rigorous study and practical experience requirements. The Institute's 650 members and 350 students provide a broad range of business valuation services to Canada's business, legal, investment, banking, and governmental communities.

Designation Offered: CBV (Chartered Business Valuator)

Educational Requirement: College degree or equivalent.

Courses/Examinations: Successful completion of a program of six courses including assignments and examinations for each course plus the required experience, followed by the writing of the Membership Entrance Examination. Writing of this examination can be challenged without successful completion of the six courses, provided the applicant has at least five years of full-time experience in the field of business valuations.

Experience Requirement: Two years of full-time experience or the equivalent of part-time obtained over a 5-year period, attested to by a sponsoring CICBV member.

Courses: All courses are provided by correspondence, including mandatory assignments with proctored examinations. Courses are offered twice per year. The courses offered are: Introductory Business & Security Valuations; Law and Valuation; Intermediate Business & Security Valuations; Taxation in Business Valuation; Special Topics; and Litigation.

Subscription: Subscription service is available for a yearly fee, which entitles the subscriber to receive all publications issued by the Institute and to be maintained on a mailing list to receive other mailings.

Seminars & Conferences: Seminars and Workshops offered monthly in major cities across Canada
Biennial National Conferences (2 full days)
Regional Conferences—one to one and one-half days

Publications: *The Valuation Law Review* is published twice yearly with three sections: Corporate Securities Law, Family Law and Taxation.
Business Valuation Digest is published twice yearly and consists of articles on business valuations.
The Journal of Business Valuation contains the proceedings of the Institute's Biennial Conferences.
The Business Valuator is a quarterly publication dealing with the activities of the Institute.

To provide a convenient reference tool for both users and preparers of business and intangible asset appraisals, the revenue rulings listed in this section and also the chapters of the *IRS Valuation Training for Appeals Officers* dealing with valuation of businesses and intangible assets are searchable by key word on *Business Valuation Update Online* and may be downloaded from that site.[3]

---

[3] *Business Valuation Update Online* can be accessed on the Internet at http://www.nvst.com/bvu.

Revenue rulings and other IRS pronouncements often are cited for valuation guidance for purposes other than for income, gift, or estate taxes. They can be useful to the extent that the material contains general valuation guidance. However, as discussed extensively in this book, valuation methods may vary for different purposes. Some aspects of revenue rulings may not be entirely appropriate for non-taxation-related purposes. This is especially true if the appropriate standard of value (or definition of value, as discussed in Chapter 3) is something other than fair market value.

Department of Labor

If a company has an employee stock ownership plan (ESOP), the valuation work must comply not only with IRS regulations but with provisions of the Employee Retirement Income Security Act (ERISA). Regulations under ERISA are issued by the Department of Labor (DOL).

Like the IRS revenue rulings, regulations issued by the Department of Labor (DOL) do not have the force of law. They represent the DOL's position with respect to interpretation of the law as it applies to certain issues.

In May of 1988, the DOL issued a proposed draft of "Regulation Relating to the Definition of Adequate Consideration" (for ESOP-owned stock). Hearings have been held, and written comments have been received. As of this writing, there is no indication as to when they expect to issue a final regulation.

Summary

The business valuation profession has progressed to the point where business valuation standards not only exist but are becoming increasingly recognized by courts, attorneys, fiduciaries, business brokers and other intermediaries, and business owners.

Virtually all business valuations are potentially subject to some sort of contrarian challenge. These challenges may come from the Internal Revenue Service, parties to the proposed transaction, spouses or beneficiaries of parties to the transaction, creditors (in cases of insolvency actions), or the DOL (in cases of ESOP-owned securities).

As is attested to in the many court cases we review every month, the fact that a business or professional practice is small is no excuse for incompetent or inadequate valuation work. In many jurisdictions, lawyers who cross-examine appraisers have progressed to the point where the inadequate or ill-prepared valuation almost always will be exposed.

It behooves all of the parties to a negotiated transaction—and their professional advisors—to insure that their valuation work is performed with the professional competence and adequacy necessary to withstand any potential challenge.

Bibliography and Resource List

This listing covers business valuation resources of a general nature. Additional resources for specific aspects of small business and professional practice valuation are listed at the end of the relevant chapters.

American Institute of Certified Public Accountants

Harborside Financial Center, 201 Plaza III, Jersey City, NJ 07311-3881, (800) 862-4272

- *Business Valuation Videocourse*, moderated by Shannon P. Pratt (New York: American Institute of Certified Public Accountants, 1993; manual updated 1996). The objective of this videocourse is to provide practitioners with an overview of the essentials of business valuation. Joining Dr. Pratt in the two-hour video presentation are Robert F. Reilly, Robert P. Schweihs, and Jay E. Fishman. The videocourse and accompanying course handbook are available from the AICPA, P.O. Box 2209, Jersey City, NJ 07303-2209, (800) 862-4272. The course code number is 350115.
- *Conducting a Valuation of a Closely Held Business*, Consulting Practice Aid 93-3, by Gary R. Trugman (Jersey City: AICPA, Management Consulting Services Division, 1993). A consulting service practice aid available from the AICPA.
- *Understanding Business Valuation: A Practical Approach to Valuing Small and Medium Size Companies*, by Gary R. Trugman (Jersey City: AICPA, Management Consulting Services Division, 1997).
- *CPA Expert*, quarterly newsletter for professionals engaged in business valuation and litigation services.

American Society of Appraisers

P.O. Box 17265, Washington, DC 20041, (703) 478-2228

- "Principles of Appraisal Practice and Code of Ethics." Available free from the ASA.
- "American Society of Appraisers Business Valuation Standards." Single copies available free from the publisher of *Business Valuation Review*.
- *Business Valuation Review*, a quarterly publication of the Business Valuation Committee of the American Society of Appraisers. Subscriptions are available by calling or writing the publisher: P.O. Box 24222, Denver, CO 80224, (303) 758-6148. Back issues are also available.
- *Valuation*, published periodically by the ASA, is multidisciplinary.

- Books recognized as "authoritative references" by the American Society of Appraisers Business Valuation Committee:
  - Campbell, Ian R. *The Valuation and Pricing of Privately-Held Business Interests*. Toronto, Canada: The Canadian Institute of Chartered Accountants, 1990.
  - Fishman, Jay E., Shannon P. Pratt, et al. *Guide to Business Valuations*. 7th ed. Fort Worth: Practitioners Publishing Company, 1997 (updated annually).
  - Mercer, Z. Christopher. *Valuing Financial Institutions*. Burr Ridge, IL: McGraw-Hill, 1992.
  - Pratt, Shannon P, Robert F. Reilly, and Robert P. Schweihs. *Valuing a Business: The Analysis and Appraisal of Closely Held Companies*. 3d ed. Burr Ridge, IL: McGraw-Hill, 1996.
  - Pratt, Shannon P, Robert F. Reilly, and Robert P. Schweihs. *Valuing Small Businesses and Professional Practices*. 3d ed. Burr Ridge, IL: McGraw-Hill, 1998.
  - Smith, Gordon V., and Russell L. Parr. *Valuation of Intellectual Property and Intangible Assets*. 2d ed. New York: John Wiley & Sons, 1994.
  - Zukin, James H., ed. *Financial Valuation: Businesses and Business Interests*. New York: Warren, Gorham & Lamont, 1990, updated annually.

The Appraisal Foundation

1029 Vermont Avenue, N.W., Suite 900, Washington, DC 20005, (202) 347-7722

- *Uniform Standards of Professional Appraisal Practice*, issued annually in November.
- Information Service: The Information Service is designed to provide summary-oriented information to appraisers, users of appraisal services, and others who have an interest in remaining current on the activities of The Appraisal Foundation, the Appraisal Standards Board (ASB), and the Appraiser Qualifications Board (AQB).
- Subscription Service: The Subscription Service is the complete source of information for appraisers, users of appraisal services, and others on the activities of The Appraisal Foundation, the Appraisal Standards Board (ASB), and the Appraiser Qualifications Board (AQB).

Business Brokerage Press

P.O. Box 247, Concord, MA 01742 (508) 369-5254.

Business Reference Guide, annual publication that provides extensive information for appraisers and brokers of small businesses, including 80 pages of "rules of thumb" for valuations in various industries, listings of trade publications and trade associates, and a listing of business brokers specializing in various industries.

Business Valuation Resources

4475 S.W. Scholls Ferry Road, Suite 101, Portland, OR 97225 (888) BUS-VALU.

- *Shannon Pratt's Business Valuation Update*, a monthly newsletter abstracting precedential business valuation court cases, updating business valuation data sources and publications, and providing professional association and company news. Contains a reader/editor exchange; guest articles; and interviews with and by judges, regulators, attorneys, and business valuation leaders; and provides special reports on timely business valuation topics.
- *Business Valuation Update Online*, a library of business valuation references available on the Internet at http://www.nvst.com/bvu. Contains many otherwise unpublished business valuation research papers, especially professional conference presentations; IRS positions on issues including the *Valuation Training Manual for Appeals Officers*, major revenue rulings, TAMs, and letter rulings; the full text of court case opinions abstracted in *Shannon Pratt's Business Valuation Update*; and the complete text of *Shannon Pratt's Business Valuation Update* since its inception in 1995. Material is key word searchable and can be downloaded.
- *Where to Find It: Business Valuation Data and Publications Directory*, annual.
- *Pratt's Stats*, a detailed database on private company transactions (see Chapter 21, Comparative Transaction Databases, for a description of this database).

Canadian Institute of Chartered Business Valuators

277 Wellington Street West, 5th floor, Toronto, Ontario, Canada M5V 3H2, (416) 204-3396.

- *The Valuation Law Review*, published semiannually, summarizes corporate and securities decisions and recent regulatory developments of interest to business valuators.
- *Business Valuation Digest*, published semiannually, contains articles devoted to business valuation and other related matters. It is supplied free of charge to members of the CICBV.
- *The Journal of Business Valuation* contains the proceedings of the Institute's Biennial Conferences (joint with the American Society of Appraisers).
- *The Business Valuator*, published quarterly, is a newsletter covering activities of the CICBV and its members.
- Business Valuation Standards.

The ESOP Association

1100 17th Street, N.W., Suite 210, Washington, DC 20036, (202) 293-2971.

Valuing ESOP Shares, revised edition, 1994.

Harcourt Brace Professional Publishing

6277 Sea Harbor Drive, Orlando, FL 32887 (800) 831-7799.

CPA Litigation Services Counselor, a monthly newsletter providing background information, practice management techniques, marketing help, case studies and technical data to help prepare for a valuation or other litigation engagement.

Institute of Business Appraisers

P.O. Box 1447, Boynton Beach, FL 33425 (407) 732-3202.

- IBA Business Valuation Standards.
- Miles, Ray. *Basic Business Valuation*.
- IBA Market Database (see Chapter 21, Comparative Transaction Databases, for a description of this database).
- *IBA News*, a quarterly newsletter.

Internal Revenue Service

1111 Constitution Avenue, N.W., Washington, DC 20224, (202) 566-5000.

Valuation Training for Appeals Officers, May 1997, available on *Business Valuation Update Online* http://www.nvst.com/bvu. The 1994 edition is available through Commerce Clearing House, (800) 248-3248.

National Association of Certified Valuation Analysts

1245 East Brickyard Road, Suite 110, Salt Lake City, UT 84106 (800) 677-2009.

- *The Valuation Examiner*, a newsletter published six times a year.
- NACVA also publishes a catalog of publications, training aids, and courses available by calling the above number.

Practitioners Publishing Company

3221 Collinsworth, Fort Worth, TX 76107 (800) 323-8724.

- Fishman, Jay E., Shannon P. Pratt, J. Clifford Griffith, and D. Keith Wilson. *Guide to Business Valuations*, updated annually.
- PPC also offers several other publications relevant to business valuation, including *Guide to Buying and Selling a Business*, *Guide to Dealerships* (auto dealers), and others. A complete catalog may be obtained by calling the number above.

Research Institute of America

589 Fifth Avenue, New York, NY 10017 (212) 755-8900.

- Alerding, James R. *Valuation of a Closely Held Business*. Both a softcover book and a 90-minute videotape are available.
- *Valuation Strategies* (bimonthly journal) covers legal, tax, accounting, and finance issues of importance to valuation professionals.

Warren, Gorham & Lamont

31 St. James Avenue, Boston, MA 02116 (800) 999-9336.

- Bogdanski, John A. *Federal Tax Valuation*, 1996, updated twice a year.
- Zukin, James H., ed. *Financial Valuation: Businesses and Business Interests*, 1997. Updated annually.

Chapter 2

Defining the Valuation Assignment

Accepting and Defining the Engagement

It is critical that the appraiser define the assignment as completely and as accurately as possible at the outset of the engagement.

Obtain a Clear Mutual Understanding

This clear mutual understanding will start the valuation assignment out on the right track from the beginning. This process allows the appraiser and the client (or the attorney) to focus on all the key issues. It prevents wasted time, appraiser/client misunderstandings, and misdirected appraisals. In addition to helping ensure that the valuation will be performed properly, it increases the probability that the appraiser will collect all appropriate fees for the analysis performed. If there is an attorney involved, as is often the case, it will help eliminate any attorney/client relationship problems with respect to the appraisal engagement. This is especially critical when the appraisal will be used in litigation because a delay in completing the assignment properly may result in its exclusion at trial.

Conflict of Interest Check

Of course, before accepting the valuation assignment, the analyst should ensure that there are no conflicts of interest. Usually this process is straightforward. But, occasionally, this conflict of interest check results in some ambiguity.[1] Until the appraiser is satisfied on this point, the appraiser should not allow the client or attorney to provide him or her with any confidential information.

Basic Elements of the Valuation Assignment

The appraiser and client (or the attorney) should reach agreement on the following essential elements of the appraisal assignment at the outset of the engagement or as close thereto as possible:

1. Definition (standard) of value.
2. Identification of the property to be valued.
3. Effective valuation date.
4. Relevant ownership characteristics.
5. Intended use or uses of the appraisal.

---

[1] One definitive legal case on the issue of what does or does not constitute a conflict of interest on the part of a business appraiser is *Estate of George S. Halas Sr.* v. *Commissioner*, T.C. Memo 1989-536 (Sept. 28, 1989) and 94 T.C. 33 (April 11, 1990) upholding the 1989 decision in response to plaintiff's motion to reconsider that decision. A more recent (but narrower) case is *Coopers & Lybrand* v. *Sabet*, No. 2373-92, N.Y. Sup. Ct., 1st Dept. (Dec. 4, 1996).

6. Scope of written and/or oral report.
7. Access to information sources and any known limiting conditions.
8. Any special instructions from the client or attorney.
9. Contractual relationship with the client.

The analyst may assist the client (and the attorney, if one is involved) in specifying the exact appraisal assignment. Inadequacies in the specification of the appraisal assignment often result in misdirected efforts and invalid conclusions. There are many cases where misspecification of the assignment relative to the definition of value appropriate in the legal context has resulted in an entire valuation being disregarded in a trial or arbitration. The knowledge and experience of the professional appraiser can be invaluable in helping to assure that the appraisal assignment is specified completely and correctly.

The analyst should make it clear that it is inappropriate for instructions from an attorney to include anything that smacks of advocacy or directs the analyst to reach a particular conclusion. However, occasionally, in a litigation context, the attorney may provide a list of assumptions that the analyst is directed to use in reaching the valuation conclusion. When this occurs, each assumption should be clearly identified in both the engagement letter and the valuation report.

To the greatest extent possible, the information discussed in this chapter should be incorporated into the engagement letter, including assumptions and limiting conditions known at the time of the engagement. A sample valuation assignment checklist is presented as Exhibit 2-1. A sample engagement letter is presented as Exhibit 2-2. These exhibits can both be found at the end of this chapter.

Definition (Standard) of Value

It may come as a surprise to the typical client to find that there can be more than one "value" to a clearly defined item of property at any given effective date of valuation. The potential for value differences arises partly because of differing expectations among different buyers and sellers. The most common reason, however, is that the legal definition (or standard) of value being sought, and the various courts' precedent-setting interpretations of that legal standard, vary greatly from one legal context to another.

For this reason, it is important to understand the legal standard to which the valuation will be subject if challenged. Most valuations are potentially subject to challenge in one way or another.

Chapter 3, Defining Value, describes the commonly encountered standards of value (e.g., fair market value, fair value, investment value, and intrinsic value), as well as the relevant premises of value, such as going-concern versus various premises of liquidation value. Chapter 4, How Valuations Differ for Different Purposes, discusses matching up the use to which the valuation will be put with the appropriate definition of value.

Identification of the Property to Be Valued

Much of the confusion and apparent disagreement among appraisers and appraisal reports arises simply because it is not clear exactly what asset, property, or business interest is to be valued. In order to determine the applicable valuation approaches, methods, and procedures, *exactly* what is to be valued must be made clear. An important determination is whether the stock or the assets of the business are to be valued. More small businesses and professional practices are sold on the basis of an asset sale rather than on the basis of a stock sale. In such cases, it is necessary to specify the assets or liabilities that are being acquired (or assumed) by the buyer and the assets (and liabilities) that are being retained by the seller.

Stock represents an indirect ownership interest in whatever bundle of assets and liabilities (actual or contingent) exists in a corporation. Stock ownership is quite different from the direct ownership of assets and the direct obligation for liabilities.

If stock is to be valued, it should be identified in the appraisal assignment. If assets are to be valued, those assets (and any liabilities to be assumed) should be specified.

If a partial ownership interest in an entity is to be valued, the proportionate relationship of the partial interest to the whole is obviously important.

If special contractual rights are included (e.g., noncompete covenants, employment or consulting agreements, options to sell the shares or buy additional shares), they should be identified. Similarly, any restrictions, such as restrictions on transfer, should be identified. To the extent that it is feasible to include information such as the above in the initial engagement letter, that is desirable. To the extent that some of these factors are learned or decided later, a note to the file (sometimes also a memo modifying the engagement letter) is warranted. And, of course, it is important to ultimately reflect the impact of all the rights and restrictions in the value conclusion and to explain the analyst's thinking (rationale) regarding their impact on the final valuation report.

Identification of the Entity

Name of Company.   It is important to identify the exact legal name of the entity subject to appraisal, such as "Southeast Restaurants, Inc." If the company does business under another name, it is also desirable to indicate that, such as d.b.a. "Grandma's Greatest Gatorburgers." If there are subsidiaries or interests in affiliated entities to be included in the valuation, it is generally helpful to indicate those as well.

Form of the Organization.   It is also important to indicate the form of business organization of the appraisal subject, such as C corporation, S corporation, nonprofit corporation, general partnership, limited partnership, limited liability company (LLC), cooperative, sole proprietorship, and so on.

The form of business organization is likely to have income tax consequences that may impact value. Also, the legal rights and restrictions applicable to the form of business organization are likely to impact value. These factors may have different impacts in different litigation contexts, and it is important for the analyst to understand the impact in the relevant context.

State of Incorporation or Registration. The assignment should also designate the state (or country) in which the entity is incorporated or registered.

Many companies of the same name are incorporated or registered in different states, so identifying the state avoids possible ambiguity from that source.

More importantly, however, different states have different laws affecting the rights and privileges of various types of entities and their owners. These differences arise partly from differences in state statutes and partly from precedent-setting judicial decisions interpreting state statutes. *These state-to-state legal differences can have a major impact on the value of a business or professional practice or an ownership interest in one, depending to a great extent (but not entirely) on the purpose of the valuation.* Again, in a litigation context, the analyst's assumptions and conclusions relative to the applicable law and case precedent are likely to be tested by the opposing attorneys.

Specification of the Ownership Interest to Be Valued

It is important to specify exactly what portion of the subject business entity is to be valued.

If valuing stock, this can be shown as a percentage or (more commonly if less than 100 percent) as the number of shares to be valued out of the number of shares outstanding.

In the case of an asset valuation, the description of the assignment should indicate what assets are included and what liabilities, if any, are to be assumed. In small business and professional practice transactions, it is quite common for the seller to keep the receivables and collect them him- or herself and to pay off all or some of the liabilities. It is also common for the seller to keep the cash.

Noncompete Covenants, Employment Agreements, and Other Rights and Restrictions. The analyst also needs to know whether to assume that the business value includes a noncompete covenant, consulting or employment agreement, or any other rights, obligations, or restrictions in addition to the stock or normal business assets included.

Equity versus Invested Capital

Stated conclusions as to the value of a business or practice are often ambiguous in the sense that it is not clear what part of the "right-hand side" of the balance sheet is intended to be included.

The term *equity* means the ownership interest. In a corporation, equity is represented by stock. If there is more than one class of stock outstanding, the term *equity* by itself usually means the combined value of all classes of stock. If it is intended that the value represents only one class of stock in a multiclass capital structure, there should be a statement as to which class of equity the value purports to represent.

In a partnership, equity is represented by the partners' capital. If it is a multiclass partnership (such as a limited partnership), there should be a statement as to which class or classes of partnership interests the value purports to represent.

In a sole proprietorship, equity is the owner's interest.

The term *invested capital* is not always as clearly defined. Therefore, if the term is used, it should be supplemented by an explanation of exactly what it means in the given valuation assignment.

The most commonly used definition of invested capital is all equity and all interest-bearing long-term debt. Sometimes, it is used to mean all equity and all interest-bearing debt, whether short-term or long-term. (This latter definition often applies in the case of small businesses and professional practices. This is because debt shown on the books as short-term often is actually being used as long-term debt, and in some cases, such short-term debt even represents equity—that is, loans from owners that are never really intended to be repaid.) Another balance sheet category that is occasionally included under the umbrella of invested capital is deferred liabilities. Taken to the extreme, the term *invested capital* has been used occasionally to represent *all* equity and all debt.

It is our hope that this discussion has made it abundantly clear that *the value of the business* is a highly ambiguous term, and it is therefore necessary to clarify exactly what elements of equity and debt are (or are not) intended to be included in that value.

Effective Valuation Date

The date, or dates, at which the business or professional practice is being valued is critical. Even within very short time spans, circumstances can cause values to vary materially from one date to another.

There have been many court cases where the effective date of valuation was a pivotal issue, sometimes having the impact of more than doubling or halving a given value. For example, in a divorce case, the husband who headed a construction company was convicted of sexual molestation of one of the couple's daughters. This conviction resulted in the loss of financing necessary to run the company. Ultimately, the case went to the state's supreme court, which ruled that the valuation should be as of a date *before* the arrest.[2]

Choosing an Applicable Valuation Date

It is usually easier to arrive at the most reliable valuation at the end of an entity's fiscal year. This is because most companies take physical inventories then and also analyze and adjust other accounts in the normal course of business. If a transaction is to take place at the end of a fiscal year, it often involves arriving at a value before the end of the fiscal year. This valuation is then subject to certain adjustments for physical inventory, accounts receivable, and/or certain other accounts, depending on exactly which assets and/or liabilities are being transferred as part of the sale.

Valuations shortly after the end of a fiscal year can often rely on year-end data, in most cases with some minor adjustments. If the effective date of the closing is some other time, it may be necessary to go through a complete year-end closing of the books in order to arrive at the final price. More often, especially in smaller businesses and professional practices, a value can be arrived at without such a complete accounting exercise. But, such a valuation may be subject to adjustment for a physical inventory count, if inventory is a significant item.

Valuations for employee stock ownership plans (ESOPs) are usually pegged to a fiscal year-end, and valuations for some other purposes, such as gifts, charitable contributions, and incentive stock options, can be pegged to a specific date.

Valuation Dates Determined by Law

For many valuation purposes, the effective date for valuation is out of the parties' hands. In most states, the valuation date for inheritance taxes is the date of death. For federal estate taxes, the taxpayer can elect the date of death or an alternative valuation date six months after, whichever is more advantageous. (For estate tax purposes, whichever date is chosen must apply to the entire estate.) For divorces, one common valuation date is the effective date of the divorce, which could be the date of trial or the date the divorce decree was entered. However, this varies from state to state and from situation to situation (see Chapter 41, which addresses divorce litigation). For dissenting stockholder actions, the valuation date is almost always the moment before the stockholders approved the action creating the dissenters' appraisal rights. Relevant valuation dates for damage cases must be determined on a case-by-case basis. Frequently the relevant valuation date may itself be a matter of dispute among the parties.

---

[2]*Quillen* v. *Quillen*, No. 29502-9608-CV-531, Ind. Sup. Ct (Aug. 6, 1996), *aff'g* 659 N.E.2d 566 (Ind. App., Dec. 11, 1995), *aff'g in part, rev'g in part* No. 29C02-9209-DR-533, Ind. Circ. Ct., County of Hamilton. The Supreme Court decision is summarized in *Shannon Pratt's Business Valuation Update*, February 1997, pp. 4-5.

If possible, the valuation date—or alternate possible valuation dates —should be specified in both the engagement letter and in the valuation opinion report.

There are times when the valuation date is not known at the time the appraisal assignment is initially made. This is often a problem in valuations for divorces, where courts in many jurisdictions have discretion to set the valuation date at the date of separation, date of filing, date of trial, or some other date.

If the valuation date is disputed or uncertain, it is generally desirable to try to get it resolved by the court as early as possible. This early resolution will save the cost of various valuation "as of" dates that the court ultimately deems irrelevant. Sometimes, however, the resolution of this issue before trial is not possible. It may be necessary to go to court prepared to present valuations as of two or more different dates.

If the valuation date or dates are changed—or clarified—after the initial valuation assignment, it is desirable to document this in writing with a copy to the client.

Relevant Ownership Characteristics

The two most relevant ownership characteristics that impact value are (1) the *degree of control or lack of it* inherent in the interest and (2) the *degree of marketability* of the interest.

As implied by the word *degree* in the previous sentence, neither of these characteristics necessarily constitute black and white issues. And these ownership characteristics may have to be analyzed, as part of the appraisal engagement, in order to determine where in the spectrum of possibilities the subject ownership interest falls. Nevertheless, these are factual matters that should be specified, at least in broad terms, in the valuation assignment.

Although the control/noncontrol and marketability issues are interrelated, appraisers usually treat them separately. In the last several years, courts have often expressed a preference for treating these two ownership characteristics issues separately. U.S. Tax Court Judge David Laro's statement summarizes this position:

> Appraisers must be careful not to confuse the marketability discount with the minority discount. In certain cases, it is appropriate to apply a combined minority and marketability discount to a particular interest in a corporation. Wherever possible, however, separately derived discounts should be applied.[3]

---

[3]Laro, Hon. David, "A View from the Tax Court Bench," *Shannon Pratt's Business Valuation Update*, December 1995, p. 4.

Control versus Noncontrol

The degree of ownership control—or lack of it—may fall anywhere across a broad spectrum, depending on (1) the percentage ownership, (2) the distribution of other ownership interests, and (3) state laws governing the rights of various percentage ownership interests in circumstances pertinent to the valuation assignment.

The degree of ownership control—or lack of it—may be a very important factor in the estimation of value. In most valuation situations, the degree of ownership control can be stated clearly and unequivocally at the outset. In some cases, however, the degree of control represented in the ownership interest being valued is a matter of controversy.

In some instances, the degree of control/noncontrol to be analyzed by the appraiser is dictated by the legal context. For example, in some states, the courts' interpretations of the *fair value* standard for dissenting owner and minority oppression actions requires the appraiser to value the appraisal subject as a proportionate share of the total equity value. This is true, even though such ownership interests are virtually always noncontrolling—or minority—ownership interests. Many ESOP documents specify whether valuation is to be done on a controlling or a noncontrolling ownership interest basis. Buy-sell and arbitration agreements sometimes address this issue. Family law courts tend to be vague on this issue, and the family law judges usually have wide discretion.

In many instances, the control/noncontrol issue can make a difference of 50 percent or more in the final value. (There are cases of discounts up to 85 percent!) Therefore, this is a critical issue in defining the valuation assignment.

Chapter 24 covers the subject of Valuing Minority Ownership Interests.

Degree of Marketability

All other things being equal, investors prefer to own something that they can turn into cash immediately without any depressing effect on value, rather than owning something that is difficult, time-consuming, and/or costly to liquidate. The benchmark usually used to represent full marketability is an actively traded stock of a publicly owned company. The owner can sell such publicly traded stock at (or very near) the last reported transaction price merely by making a phone call to a broker, with the seller receiving cash within three business days. The premise as to the extent to which the subject entity is or is not marketable is usually considered in relation to this benchmark.

Minority ownership interests in closely held companies are usually discounted substantially for lack of marketability. Such valuation discounts are often an additional 35 percent or more *after* reflecting the valuation discounts for minority ownership interest (i.e., for lack of ownership control). Controlling ownership interests may also suffer from lack of marketability. However, the lack of marketability valuation discounts, if any, are much less—often 10 to 25 percent. Chapter 25 covers discounts for lack of marketability.

Going-Concern or Liquidation Premise

If it is clear at the outset that the business is to be valued on either a going-concern or a liquidation basis, it is also desirable to include that choice in the valuation assignment and engagement letter. Often, however, it is left to the appraiser to opine as to whether all or part of the entity may have greater value on a going-concern or on a liquidation basis. Premises of value are discussed in more detail in the following chapter, Defining Value.

Intended Use or Uses of the Appraisal

This book covers business valuations intended to be used for almost all conceivable purposes. The following are some of them:

- Buying or selling an entire business or a partial interest in a business.
- Marital dissolution.
- Gift, estate, and income taxes.
- Sharcholder disputes.
- Damage cases.
- Employee stock ownership plans (ESOPs).
- Corporate and partnership dissolutions and buyouts.
- Buy-sell agreements.

Valuations for each of these intended uses are impacted by a mass of complex federal and state statutes and precedential judicial decisions. The result is that different standards of value, and different valuation criteria, must be applied in different cases. These differing applications depend both (1) on the use to which the valuation is to be put and (2) on the jurisdiction that controls the legal rules applicable to the valuation.

The potential impact of the differing legal contexts has two important implications:

1. The analyst should thoroughly understand the statutory and case law applicable to each engagement.
2. The use to which the valuation is to be put should be clearly specified in the engagement letter.

We also recommend that the engagement letter include a clause to the effect that the valuation is only applicable for the specified use and only for the stated effective date of the appraisal.

Chapter 4 addresses many details of how valuations differ for different purposes.

Part V contains chapters that address valuations for specific purposes. Part VI discusses topics related to valuation, such as dealing with business appraisers and business brokers. Part VII covers the subjects of litigation and alternative dispute resolution.

Scope of the Written and/or Oral report

The scope of the expected valuation work product should be addressed in the initial engagement letter although it could be subject to change as the engagement progresses. The valuation report could be oral, written, or a combination. It is not uncommon for the client, the attorney, or both to request an oral report concerning a range of value before committing to the expense of a written report.

In most cases, the use to which the valuation will be put will have a major bearing on the expected work product.

If it is expected that the work product conform to the *Uniform Standards of Professional Appraisal Practice* (USPAP), this should be stated in the engagement letter. If the work will be subject to legal challenges, conformance to USPAP at least assures meeting some minimum professional standards.

Written Valuation Reports

USPAP outlines the minimum requirements for a full, formal written report. USPAP also allows for departure from some, but not all, of its requirements for more limited forms of reports. The more limited reports are designed for situations like client decision making, but the complete report is better suited for many litigation purposes.

The full valuation opinion report will typically include the following sections:

1. A valuation opinion letter summarizing the appraisal procedures and the valuation conclusions.
2. Several sections summarizing the relevant valuation theory, methodology, procedures, analyses, and conclusions.
3. A valuation synthesis and conclusion.
4. An exhibit section presenting a summary of the quantitative and qualitative appraisal analyses.
5. A listing of the data and documents the appraiser relied on.
6. A statement of the contingent and limiting conditions of the appraisal.
7. An appraisal certification.
8. The professional qualifications of the principal analysts.

Oral Reports and Testimony

In some cases, the client may require only an oral valuation report. If the engagement calls for conformance to USPAP, there are minimum requirements that must be met in terms of providing support for the opinion. This is true even if the client only requires an oral report.

In many cases, the analyst may be asked to attend one or more client meetings to explain the valuation, whether or not there is a written report.

The question of potential expert testimony should be addressed, where applicable. If expert testimony is expected, the venue should be noted, along with what is known about the schedule. The question should be raised as to whether or not depositions or participation in one or more settlement conferences is expected. While all of these matters may not be resolved at the time of the initial assignment, they should all be addressed so that all parties are aware of the possible expectations and that the scheduling and fee arrangements allow for all of the possibilities.

Access to Information Sources and Any Known Limiting Conditions

In most business valuation engagements, it is expected that the analyst will conduct one or more site visits and management interviews and have virtually unlimited access to relevant books and records. This expectation should be raised at the time of the engagement. To the extent that there will be any limitations on normal information gathering (called "discovery" in the context of litigation), this is a limiting condition that should be disclosed in the valuation report. Most appraisers today consider it necessary to also include such limiting conditions in their engagement letter or to memorialize them as an addendum to the engagement letter if they are discovered in the course of the valuation process.

If there is litigation, many appraisers believe that the less formal the information-gathering process the better. Also, if there is resistance to any element of discovery, courts will typically require compliance with the discovery request when asked. The discovery process is critical, and often the appraiser is key to insuring that the process is adequate. This is a very important reason to bring the appraiser in as early as possible in any case involving litigation or potential litigation. This issue is discussed in more detail in Part VII, Litigation and Dispute Resolution.

Special Instructions from the Client or Attorney

The most common special instructions have to do with confidentiality. Confidentiality agreements are both common and reasonable. A problem may arise occasionally with respect to a request for the return of client documents since USPAP requires the appraiser to retain copies of all documents that were relied upon for a period of several years.

Sometimes, there are restrictions on who the appraiser is allowed to contact, either directly or indirectly. These restrictions should be made clear as part of the engagement process.

Some attorneys and some clients want to see drafts of valuation reports before the final reports are issued. This is usually a very reasonable instruction. It provides the client and/or attorney with an opportunity to check the accuracy of all facts, correct any errors, and bring attention to any material matter that the appraiser may have overlooked.

Contractual Relationship with the Client

Previous sections have addressed the work expected during the assignment. The valuation engagement agreement should also address work product timing and fee arrangements.

Work Product Timing

We cannot stress enough the importance of getting the appraiser involved in the transaction and/or controversy process at the earliest possible time, relying on the appraiser's guidance, and giving the appraiser the maximum possible lead time.

Fee Arrangements

An appraiser may work on a fixed-fee basis, on a range of estimated fees, or on an hourly or daily basis. The more clearly defined the appraisal assignment, the more likely it is that the appraiser will be able to quote a fixed fee or a very close fee estimate. For most types of appraisal assignments, an independent professional appraiser is legally and ethically prohibited from entering into an arrangement that makes the appraiser's fee contingent on completed settlement negotiations or the outcome of a court decision. These points are discussed further in Chapter 44, Working with a Business Appraiser.

The fee arrangements should include the terms of payment, as well as the basis for establishing the fee.

Summary

In summary, the valuation assignment should address all of the following elements:

1. The definition of the value being sought (including reference to any legal or documentary source that governs the applicable standard).
2. Precise and complete description of the property to be valued, including a description of liabilities to be assumed, if any.

3. The effective date—or dates—of the valuation.
4. The relevant ownership characteristics (i.e., the degree of control/noncontrol and marketability or lack thereof).
5. The use or uses to which the valuation work product will be put.
6. The form and extent of the expected oral and/or written valuation work product (appraisal report).
7. Access to information sources and any known limiting conditions.
8. Any special instructions from the client or attorney, including, in a litigation context, any assumptions the appraiser was instructed to use.
9. The expected engagement timing.
10. Fee arrangements.

Exhibit 2-1 is a handy valuation assignment checklist. Since it is a form, readers are welcome to make copies of it to use with clients and attorneys in planning their valuation engagements.

Exhibit 2-2 is a sample professional services agreement (i.e., an abbreviated valuation engagement letter).

Exhibit 2–1

VALUATION ASSIGNMENT CHECKLIST

Definition of value: ☐ Fair market value   ☐ Fair value   ☐ Other _____

      Authority for value definition (statute, buy-sell agreement, etc.) _____

      _____

Property to be valued: Name of entity _____

      State of incorporation or registration _____   Valuation of ☐ stock ☐ partnership ☐ assets

      Form of organization   ☐ C corporation   ☐ S corporation   ☐ Limited partnership
                           ☐ General partnership   ☐ LLC   ☐ Other

      Description of interest to be valued (if asset basis, list assets and liabilities to be assumed, if any)

      _____

      Restrictions on transfer ☐ yes   ☐ no   If yes, describe _____

      Other classes of ownership outstanding ☐ yes   ☐ no   If yes, describe _____

      Covenant not to compete ☐ yes   ☐ no   If yes, describe _____

      Consulting/employment agreement ☐ yes   ☐ no   If yes, describe _____

Effective date or dates of valuation: _____

Ownership characteristics (either actual or assumed for purpose of valuation):

      Minority/control status _____

      Marketability _____

      Going-concern or liquidation premise (if known) _____

Use or uses of the valuation: _____

Work product: Written report ☐ yes   ☐ no   If yes, give scope _____

      Oral report ☐ yes   ☐no   If yes, describe _____

      Deposition testimony ☐yes   ☐ no   Court testimony ☐yes   ☐ no

Exhibit 2–1 (concluded)

VALUATION ASSIGNMENT CHECKLIST (continued)

Comments re work product _____

_____

Limiting conditions: ☐ none, full access ☐ describe any limiting conditions _____

_____

Special instructions: ☐ none ☐ describe any special instructions _____

_____

Engagement timing: Fill in dates for each increment of project:

_____   _____

_____   _____

_____   _____

Fee arrangements: Retainer $_____   Estimated fee $_____

Basis for billing and terms of payment _____

Client: _____

Contact persons names	Title	Telephone	Fax number	E-mail
_____	_____	_____	_____	_____
_____	_____	_____	_____	_____
_____	_____	_____	_____	_____

Address _____

_____

SOURCE: Shannon P. Pratt, Robert F. Reilly, and Robert P. Schweihs, *Valuing Small Businesses and Professional Practices*, 3rd edition (Burr Ridge, Ill.: McGraw-Hill, 1998). Permission is granted to produce copies of this exhibit (2-1) with this source line included, for use by appraisers, attorneys, and clients in formulating business appraisal assignments.

Exhibit 2–2

SAMPLE PROFESSIONAL SERVICES AGREEMENT

Amelia Appraiser & Associates and Estate of Charlie Client agree as follows:

1.   **Description of services.** We agree to perform certain professional services for you, described briefly as follows as to purpose and objective, with the understanding that any modification to the assignment as stated below will be by a letter agreement signed by both parties.

> Estimate the fair market value of a 100% interest in Charlie's Choo Choos, an Illinois corporation, held by the estate of Charlie Client, as of August 30, 1998, for estate tax purposes.

2.   **Date(s) services due.** We will begin performance upon receipt of all information requested of you, and will complete our assignment, unless delayed or prevented by matters beyond our control, according to the following schedule:

> Full, formal appraisal report due within 90 days of receipt of signed agreement and all requested documents.

3.   **Fees.** Our fees for such professional services will be calculated on standard hourly rates in effect at the time services are rendered for staff members assigned to this project, plus out-of-pocket expenses. The fee is estimated at a range of $_____ to $_____, exclusive of expenses such as travel, long distance telephone, purchases of data, copying and printing costs, and clerical time. The fee will not exceed such estimate by more than 25% without prior notification to you.

4.   **Retainer.** $_____ is due as a retainer upon execution of this Agreement. Retainer paid by you will be applied to the **final** billings.

5.   **Payment terms.** You will receive regular twice-monthly invoices, including fees and expenses incurred, for which payments will be due at our offices within 15 days of dates of invoices. Balances which remain unpaid 30 days from dates of invoices will be assessed a finance charge of 1.5% monthly (18% annual percentage rate).

If we are to provide expert witness testimony as part of our assignment, you agree that payment of all fees and expenses invoiced and/or incurred to date will be received at our offices before we provide expert witness testimony, or if travel for testimony is necessary, payment will be received before travel is incurred.

You agree that the fees and expenses invoiced by us must be paid current per the terms of this Agreement before we provide any report or analysis conclusions.

6.   You understand that we will need prompt access to documents, materials, facilities, and/or company personnel in order to perform our services in a timely and professional manner, and you agree to fulfill all such requests in a timely manner and to cooperate fully with us. You further understand and agree that delays in providing data or information may result in a delay of the completion date of the project.

7.   We agree to perform our services in a professional and objective manner. You understand that we do not guarantee the results of any analysis which we may undertake, but only agree that any report or analysis shall represent our professional opinion based on the data given to us or compiled by us. We will attempt to obtain and compile our data from reliable sources, but we cannot guarantee its accuracy or completeness.

8.   You warrant that the information and data you supply to us will be complete and accurate in every respect to the best of your knowledge; that any reports, analysis, or other documents prepared by us will be used only in compliance with all applicable laws and regulations; and that you will hold us harmless for any breach of this warranty.

Exhibit 2–2 (concluded)

9.   You agree to indemnify and hold us harmless against any and all liability, claim, loss, cost, and expense, whatever kind or nature, which we may incur, or be subject to, as a party, expert witness, witness or participant in connection with any dispute or litigation involving you unless such liability, claim, loss, cost, and expense, whatever kind or nature, is due to our wrongdoing and such wrongdoing is not caused by, related to, or the result of information provided to us by you. This indemnity includes all out-of-pocket expenses (including travel costs and attorney fees) and payment for all our staff members' time at standard hourly rates in effect at the time rendered to the extent we attend, prepare for, or participate in meetings, hearings, depositions, trials, and all other proceedings, including travel time. If we must bring legal action to enforce this indemnity, you agree to pay all costs of such action, including any sum as the Court may fix as reasonable attorney fees.

10.   If this Agreement, or any moneys due under the terms hereof, is placed in the hands of an attorney for collection of the account, you promise and agree to pay our attorney fees and collection costs, plus interest at the then legal rate, whether or not any legal action is filed. If any suit or action is brought to enforce, interpret, or collect damages for the breach of this agreement, you agree to pay our reasonable attorney fees and costs of such suit or action, including any appeal as fixed by the applicable Court or Courts.

Dated this 30th day of September, 1998, at Chicago, Illinois.

Estate of Charlie Client   **Amelia Appraiser & Associates**

By: _____   By: _____
Name: Cynthia Client, Executor   Name: Amelia Appraiser, CFA, ASA

Address: 111 South 5th Street, Peoria, Illinois 64444
Telephone: (309) 555-4455
FAX: (309) 555-4456

Chapter 3

Defining Value

Many terms are used to define value . . . Only a few of these terms have some definition. Others have the definition which the parties choose to place upon them.[1]

It comes as a surprise to many clients that there is not just a single value for a property but that there can be different values for the same property—even at the same time—depending on the definition of the value being sought.

The logical place to begin a valuation engagement is to identify and define the standard and premise of value that apply in the specific situation. Many terms are used to describe various notions of value. Unfortunately, such terms mean different things to different people.

The need for a clear delineation of the definition of the value being sought in the particular engagement cannot be overemphasized. Clients rarely give it much thought. Most attorneys do not have enough technical background in business valuation to think through the matter of defining the value and to raise the right questions. One of the most important tasks of the analyst is to work carefully and thoroughly with the client and/or attorney in order to arrive at a definition of value that is appropriate to the specific valuation engagement.

This chapter presents the concepts of value (both the standards and the premises) that are most widely encountered and most useful in business valuation.

Standards (Definitions) of Value

As used in this book, a standard of value is a definition of the type of value being sought. For some valuation situations, the standard of value is legally mandated, either by law or by binding legal documents or contracts. In other cases, it is a function of the wishes of the parties involved. There are numerous horror stories about disputes, situations that often resulted in litigation, that arose because the parties had differing understandings about the standard of value applicable to the situation. Basic standards of value are often further clarified by the various premises relating to the value, as discussed in the next major section.

Fair Market Value

In the United States, the most widely recognized and accepted standard of value is *fair market value*. It is the standard that applies to most federal and state tax matters, such as estate taxes, gift taxes, inheritance taxes, income taxes, and ad valorem taxes. It is also the legal standard of value in many other—although not all—valuation situations.

---

[1]John E. Moye, *Buying and Selling Businesses* (Minneapolis: National Practice Institute, 1983), p. 25.

The ASA definition of fair market value is "the amount at which property would change hands between a willing seller and a willing buyer when neither is acting under compulsion and when both have reasonable knowledge of the relevant facts."[2] This is essentially the same definition as in Revenue Ruling 59-60 (see Appendix B).

There is general agreement that the definition implies that the parties have the ability—as well as the willingness—to buy or to sell. The "market" in this definition can be thought of as all the potential buyers and sellers of like businesses or professional practices.

In the legal interpretations of fair market value, the willing buyer and willing seller are *hypothetical* persons, dealing at arm's length, rather than any *particular* buyer or seller. In other words, a price would not be considered representative of fair market value if it is influenced by special motivations not characteristic of a typical buyer or seller.

That is not to say, however, that the concept of fair market value precludes identifying *groups* of willing participants. Quite the contrary, the valuer should be able to identify categories of willing purchasers. Furthermore, the analyst cannot ignore the *seller.* However, the seller must be willing to sell under conditions that exist as of the valuation date.

The concept of fair market value assumes prevalent economic and market conditions at the date of the particular valuation. You have probably heard it said many times, "I couldn't get anywhere near the value of my house if I put it on the market today," or "The value of XYZ Company stock is really much more (or less) than the price it's selling for on the New York Stock Exchange today." The standard of value that those people have in mind is some standard *other than* fair market value. This is because the concept of fair market value means the price at which a transaction could be expected to take place under *conditions existing at the valuation date.*

The terms *market value* and *cash value* are sometimes used interchangeably with the term *fair market value.* Real estate appraisers generally use the term *market value* rather than *fair market value.* The Appraisal Foundation defines *market value* as follows:

> Market Value: Market value is the major focus of most real property appraisal assignments. Both economic and legal definitions of market value have been developed and refined. A current economic definition agreed upon by agencies that regulate federal financial institutions in the United States of America is: The most probable price which a property should bring in a competitive and open market under all conditions requisite to a fair sale, the buyer and seller each acting prudently and knowledgeably, and assuming the price is not affected by undue stimulus. Implicit in this definition is the consummation of a sale as of a specified date and the passing of title from seller to buyer under conditions whereby:

---

[2]*ASA Business Valuation Standards* (Herndon, VA: American Society of Appraisers, 1997), p. 20.

1. buyer and seller are typically motivated;
2. both parties are well informed or well advised, and acting in what they consider their best interests;
3. a reasonable time is allowed for exposure in the open market;
4. payment is made in terms of cash in United States dollars or in terms of financial arrangements comparable thereto; and
5. the price represents the normal consideration for the property sold unaffected by special or creative financing or sales concessions granted by anyone associated with the sale.

Substitution of another currency for *United States dollars* in the fourth condition is appropriate in other countries or in reports addressed to clients from other countries.[3]

The most salient change in the above definition of market value compared to definitions widely accepted a few years ago is the phrase "the most probable price" in substitution for "the highest price."

In a tax court case, Judge David Laro articulated the following as some of the guiding principles regarding the estimation of fair market value:

1. The willing buyer and the willing seller are hypothetical persons, rather than specific individuals or entities, and the characteristics of these hypothetical persons are not necessarily the same as the personal characteristics of the actual seller or a particular buyer.
2. Fair market value is determined as of the valuation date, and no knowledge of unforeseeable future events which may have affected the value is given to the hypothetical persons.
3. Fair market value equals the highest and best use to which the property could be put on the valuation date, and fair market value takes into account special uses that are realistically available due to the property's adaptability to a particular business. Fair market value is not affected by whether the owner has actually put the property to its highest and best use. The reasonable, realistic, and objective possible uses for the property in the near future control the valuation thereof. Elements affecting value that depend upon events or a combination of occurrences which, while within the realm of possibility, are not reasonably probable, are excluded from this consideration.
4. As typically occurs in a case of valuation, the parties rely primarily on their experts' testimony and reports . . . .Expert testimony sometimes aids the Court in determining valuation. Other times, it does not. For example, expert testimony is not useful to the Court when the expert is merely an advocate for the position argued by the party.[4]

---

[3]*Uniform Standards of Professional Appraisal Practice* (Washington, DC: The Appraisal Foundation, 1998), p. 163. Reprinted with permission of The Appraisal Foundation.

[4]*Pabst Brewing Company* v. *Commissioner*, T.C. Memo 1996-506 (Nov. 12, 1996), summarized in *Shannon Pratt's Business Valuation Update*, January 1997, p. 7.

It is generally understood that fair market value means a value in cash or cash equivalents (as indicated in The Appraisal Foundation definition of *market value*) unless otherwise stated. However, very few small businesses and professional practices actually sell for cash. Consequently, it is common for business brokers to think of the value of a business or practice on the basis of the face value of a transaction—on the terms at which the particular type of business or practice typically sells in the marketplace. The International Business Brokers Association (IBBA) has adopted the term *transaction value* for this concept, defined as follows:

> The total of all consideration passed at any time between the buyer and seller for an ownership interest in a business enterprise and may include, but is not limited to, all remuneration for tangible and intangible assets such as furniture, equipment, supplies, inventory, working capital, noncompetition agreements, employment and/or consultation agreements, licenses, customer lists, franchise fees, assumed liabilities, stock options, stock or stock redemptions, real estate, leases, royalties, earn-outs and future considerations.[5]

Analysts performing business valuations that may be subject to litigation should seek the exact legal definition of fair market value in the relevant jurisdiction. However, this may not be as easy as it sounds. In some states, such as California, family law courts sometimes use the term *fair market value* and then invoke various restrictions on acceptable valuation methods or other departures from the classic definition. It may require careful study of the case law to understand fair market value in such contexts.

For a discussion of converting *transaction value* (or any other price that is not a cash equivalent) to a cash equivalent value, see Chapter 27, Trade-off between Cash and Terms.

Investment Value

In real estate terminology, *investment value* is defined as "the specific value of an investment to a particular investor or class of investors based on individual investment requirements; distinguished from market value, which is impersonal and detached."[6] In real estate appraisal, calculations of investment value conventionally involve discounting an anticipated income stream.

One of the leading real estate appraisal texts makes the following comments regarding the distinction between market value and investment value:

---

[5]International Business Brokers Association, Business Brokerage Glossary, printed in full in *Shannon Pratt's Business Valuation Update*, December 1996, p. 7.

[6]*The Dictionary of Real Estate Appraisal*, 3d ed. (Chicago: Appraisal Institute, 1993), p. 190.

As used in appraisal assignments, investment value is the value of an investment to a particular investor based on his or her investment requirements. In contrast to market value, investment value is value to an individual, not necessarily value in the marketplace.

Investment value reflects the subjective relationship between a particular investor and a given investment. It differs in concept from market value, although investment value and market value indications may be similar. If the investor's requirements are typical of the market, investment value may be the same as market value.[7]

In their well-received text *The Stock Market: Theories and Evidence,* Lorie and Hamilton discuss investment value by reference to the classic work of John Burr Williams:[8]

He considers the appropriate rate of discounting, the effects of stock rights and assessments, risk premiums, the effect of the capital structure of the firm, and the marketability of the security. His treatment of these various subjects leads to the grand conclusion that the investment value of a stock is determined by discounting the "expected" [authors' term] stream of dividends at the discount rate appropriate for the individual investor.[9]

There can be many valid reasons for the investment value to one particular owner or prospective owner to differ from the fair market value. Among these reasons are the following:

1. Differences in estimates of future earning power.
2. Differences in perception of the degree of risk.
3. Differences in income tax status.
4. Synergies with other operations owned or controlled.

In fact, *investment value* is sometimes called *strategic value* because it often incorporates elements of synergistic value inherent in combinations of related companies. Studies show that, on average, strategic buyers pay higher multiples of the acquiree's earnings than do financial buyers.

The discounted economic income method of the income approach (see Chapter 14) is oriented toward developing an investment value if the returns used are those that would be expected by a *particular* owner or investor. Whether or not the value thus developed also represents fair market value depends on whether the projections used would be accepted by a consensus of market participants. If valuing a minority ownership interest, the returns used usually would be based on the projection of the current management remaining in place.

---

[7]*The Appraisal of Real Estate,* 11th ed. (Chicago: Appraisal Institute, 1996), p. 26.

[8]John Burr Williams, *The Theory of Investment Value* (Cambridge, MA: Harvard University Press, 1938). Reprinted in Amsterdam by North Holland Publishing Company, 1956.

[9]James H. Lorie and Mary T. Hamilton, *The Stock Market: Theories and Evidence* (Burr Ridge, IL: Irwin, 1973), pp. 116-17.

If sound analysis leads to a valid conclusion that the investment value to a particular owner exceeded market value at a given time, the rational economic decision for that owner would be not to sell at that time—that is, unless a particular buyer could be found to whom investment value would be higher than the consensus of value among a broader group of typical buyers.

Of course, the concept of investment value as described above is not completely divorced from the concept of fair market value. This is because it is the actions of many specific investors, acting in the manner just described, that eventually lead to a balancing of supply and demand through the establishment of an equilibrium market price that represents the consensus value of the collective investors.

Finally, the term *investment value* has a slightly different meaning when used in the context of dissenting stockholder suits. In this context, it means a value based on earning power, as described above. However, the appropriate present value discount rate or the direct capitalization rate is usually considered to be a consensus rate—rather than a rate peculiarly appropriate for any specific investor.

Intrinsic or Fundamental Value

Intrinsic value (sometimes called *fundamental value*) differs from *investment value* in that it represents an analytical judgment of value based on the perceived characteristics inherent in the investment, not tempered by characteristics peculiar to any one investor. Rather, this value is tempered by how these perceived characteristics are interpreted by one analyst versus another.

Financial Decision Making defines *intrinsic value* as follows:

> A security's *intrinsic value* is the price that is justified for it when the primary factors of value are considered. In other words, it is the *real worth* of the debt or equity instrument as distinguished from the current market price. The financial manager estimates intrinsic value by carefully appraising the following *fundamental factors* that affect security values:
>
> *Value of the Firm's Assets.* The physical assets held by the firm have some market value. They can be liquidated if need be to provide funds to repay debt and distribute to shareholders. In techniques of going concern valuation, asset values are usually omitted.
>
> *Likely Future Interest and Dividends.* For debt, the firm is committed to pay future interest and repay principal. For preferred and common stock, the firm makes attempts to declare and pay dividends. The likelihood of these payments affects present value.
>
> *Likely Future Earnings.* The expected future earnings of the firm are generally viewed as the most important single factor affecting security value. Without a reasonable level of earnings, interest and dividend payments may be in jeopardy.
>
> *Likely Future Growth Rate.* A firm's prospects for future growth are carefully evaluated by investors and creditors and are a factor influencing intrinsic value.[10]

---

[10]John J. Hampton, *Financial Decision Making*, 4th ed. (Upper Saddle River, NJ: Prentice Hall, 1989), pp. 368-69. Adapted by permission of Prentice-Hall, Inc., Upper Saddle River, NJ.

Further concurrence on the meanings of intrinsic value and fundamental value is found in the following definitions from an authoritative reference in the accounting field:

> *Intrinsic value.* The amount that an investor considers, on the basis of an evaluation of available facts, to be the 'true' or 'real' worth of an item, usually an *equity security*. The value that will become the market value when other investors reach the same conclusions. The various approaches to determining intrinsic value of the *finance* literature are based on expectations and discounted cash flows. See *expected value; fundamental analysis; discounted cash flow method.*[11]
>
> *Fundamental analysis.* An approach in security analysis which assumes that a security has an 'intrinsic value' that can be determined through a rigorous evaluation of relevant variables. Expected earnings is usually the most important variable in this analysis, but many other variables, such as dividends, capital structure, management quality, and so on, may also be studied. An analyst estimates the 'intrinsic value' of a security on the basis of those fundamental variables and compares this value with the current market price of this security to arrive at an investment decision.[12]

In the analysis of securities, intrinsic value is generally considered the appropriate price for a stock according to a security analyst who has completed a fundamental analysis of the company's assets, earning power, and other factors. Loric and Hamilton comment on the notion of intrinsic value as follows:

> The purpose of security analysis is to detect differences between the value of a security as determined by the market and a security's "intrinsic value"—that is, the value that the security *ought* to have and will have when other investors have the same insight and knowledge as the analyst.[13]

If the market value is below what the analyst concludes is the intrinsic value, then the analyst considers the stock a "buy." If the market value is above the assumed intrinsic value, the analyst suggests selling the stock.

It is important to note that the concept of intrinsic value cannot be entirely disassociated from the concept of fair market value. This is because the actions of buyers and sellers based on their *specific* perceptions of intrinsic value eventually lead to the *general* consensus market value and the constant and dynamic changes in market value over time.

Case law often refers to the term *intrinsic value*. However, almost universally, such references do not define the term other than by refer-

---

[11]W.W. Cooper and Yuri Ijiri, eds., *Kohler's Dictionary for Accountants*, 6th ed. (Upper Saddle River, NJ: Prentice Hall, 1983), p. 285. Reprinted by permission of Prentice-Hall, Inc., Upper Saddle River, NJ.

[12]Ibid., p. 228.

[13]Lorie and Hamilton, *The Stock Market*, p. 114.

ence to the language in the context in which it appears. Such references to *intrinsic value* can be found both in cases where there is no statutory standard of value and in cases where the statutory standard of value is specified as *fair value* or even *fair market value*. When references to *intrinsic value* appear in the relevant case law, the analyst should heed the notions ascribed to that term as discussed in this section.

Fair Value

The expression *fair value* is an excellent example of ambiguous terminology used in the field of commercial appraisal. In order to understand what the expression means, you have to know the context of its use. The accepted definition of fair value in real estate appraisal terminology is totally different from the interpretation the courts have given to fair value as a statutory standard of value applicable to a business appraisal.

A leading authority on real estate terminology states that fair value is: "A concept that was developed in the 1970s to address specific concerns which have since been satisfied by the evolution of the market value concept in the 1980s."[14]

However, in most states, fair value is the statutory standard of value applicable in cases of dissenting stockholders' appraisal rights. In these states, if a corporation merges, sells out, or takes certain other major actions, and if the owner of a noncontrolling interest believes that he is being forced to receive less than adequate consideration for his stock, he has the right to have his shares appraised and to receive fair value in cash.[15]

> The Revised Model Business Corporation Act (RMBCA) defines fair value as:
> "the value of the shares immediately before the effectuation of the corporate action to which the dissenter objects, excluding any appreciation or depreciation in anticipation of the corporate action unless exclusion would be inequitable."
> The statutory definition of fair value in 26 states is similar to the definition provided by the RMBCA.
> The definition . . . in 14 other states is similar . . . , but without the "unless exclusion would be inequitable" clause . . . . The definition of fair value in Delaware and Oklahoma is similar to that of the 14 states . . . , but includes a clause that states, "in determining such fair value, the court should take into account all relevant factors."[16]

---

[14]*The Dictionary of Real Estate Appraisal*, 3d ed., p. 130.

[15]For a complete listing of states' dissenters' rights statutes, see *Shannon Pratt's Business Valuation Update*, May 1996, p. 6.

[16]Daniel R. Van Vleet, "Fair Value in Dissenting Stockholder Disputes," Chapter 9A, in *Financial Valuation: Businesses and Business Interests*, 1997 Update, James H. Zukin, ed. (New York: Warren, Gorham & Lamont, 1997), p. U9A-6. This chapter lists the definitions of fair value in each state.

The other states have other definitions.

There is no clearly recognized consensus about the definition of fair value in this context. However, the judicial precedents of most states certainly have not equated it to fair market value. When a situation arises of actual or potential stockholder dissent, it is important to carefully research the legal precedents applicable to each case.

The term *fair value* is also found in the dissolution statutes of those few states in which minority stockholders can trigger a corporate dissolution under certain circumstances (e.g., California Corporations Code Section 2000). Even within the same state, however, a study of case law precedents does not necessarily lead one to the same definition of fair value under a dissolution statute as under that state's dissenting stockholder statute.

Ownership Characteristics

The specification of ownership characteristics (minority/control and degree of marketability, as discussed in the previous chapter) is integrally linked with the definition of value. The impact of such characteristics on the value depends on the standard of value and the statutory or precedential case law in the relevant jurisdiction.

Alternative Premises of Value[17]

Virtually all businesses or interests in businesses may be appraised under each of these following four alternative premises of value:

1. *Value as a going concern.* Value in continued use, as a mass assemblage of income producing assets, and as a going-concern business enterprise.
2. *Value as an assemblage of assets.* Value in place, as part of a mass assemblage of assets, but not in current use in the production of income, and not as a going-concern business enterprise.
3. *Value as an orderly disposition.* Value in exchange, on a piecemeal basis (not part of a mass assemblage of assets), as part of an orderly disposition. This premise contemplates that all of the assets of the business enterprise will be sold individually and that they will enjoy normal exposure to their appropriate secondary market.
4. *Value as a forced liquidation.* Value in exchange, on a piecemeal basis (not part of a mass assemblage of assets), as a piece of a forced

---

[17]This section is adapted from Shannon P. Pratt, Robert F. Reilly, and Robert P. Schweihs, *Valuing a Business: The Analysis and Appraisal of Closely Held Companies*, 3d ed. (Burr Ridge,IL: McGraw-Hill, 1996), p. 29.

liquidation. This premise contemplates that the assets of the business enterprise will be sold individually and that they will experience less than normal exposure to their appropriate secondary market.

While virtually any business enterprise may be appraised under each of these four alternative fundamental premises, the value conclusions reached under each premise, for the same business, may be dramatically different.

Each of these alternative premises of value may apply under the same standard, or definition, of value. For example, the fair market value standard calls for a "willing buyer" and a "willing seller." Yet, these willing buyers and willing sellers have to make an informed economic decision as to how they will transact with each other with regard to the subject business. In other words, is the subject business worth more to the buyer and the seller as a going concern that will continue to operate as such or as a collection of individual assets to be put to separate uses? In either case, the buyer and seller are still "willing." And, in both cases, they have concluded a set of transactional circumstances that will maximize the value of the collective assets of the subject business enterprise.

The selection of the appropriate premise of value is an important step in defining the appraisal assignment. Typically, in a controlling ownership interest valuation, the election of the appropriate premise of value is a function of the highest and best use of the collective assets of the subject business enterprise. The decision regarding the appropriate premise of value is usually made by the analyst, based upon experience, judgment, and analysis.

Sometimes, however, the decision regarding the appropriate premise of value is made "for" the appraiser. This occurs when the appraiser knows—or is told—that the subject business enterprise will, in fact, be continued as a going concern or will be sold in a certain set of transactional circumstances. For example, if the business assets are, in fact, going to be sold on a value in exchange basis, it is not relevant for the appraiser to consider the value in continued use—or going-concern—premise of value.

Sometimes premises of value are imposed artificially in a particular legal context. To give an example, under California Corporations Code Section 2000 (the California corporate dissolution statute), the case law is generally interpreted to mean that a minority interest is valued *as if* it were a proportional share of a control value.[18]

In some circumstances, it may be relevant—and, in fact, critical—to appraise the subject business enterprise under several alternative premises of value. For example, it may be extremely important to conclude the value of the same business enterprise under several alternative

---

[18]See, for example, *Roland* v. *4-C's Electronic Packaging*, 168 Cal.App.3d 290 (1985) and *Brown* v. *Allied Corrugated Box Co.*, 91 Cal.App.3d 477 (1979).

premises of value in appraisals performed for bankruptcy and reorganization purposes or for financing securitization and collateralization purposes.

Of course, if appraising a minority ownership interest, one would normally adopt the premise of value that actually exists as of the valuation date (most likely on a going-concern basis), unless given reason to do otherwise.

Sources of Guidance about Applicable Standards and Premises of Value

The expertise and craft of the analyst include the skill to seek out and interpret guidance as to the standard of value and the premise of value that are relevant to the assignment at hand. The following are some of the most important sources of guidance about the applicable standard of value and the premise of value for the given situation:

- Statutory law (state and federal).
- Case law (cases decided under the controlling statutory or common law).
- Administrative regulations (e.g., Internal Revenue Service Revenue Rulings).[19]
- Company documents (e.g., articles of incorporation or partnership, bylaws, meeting minutes, agreements).
- Contracts between the parties (e.g., buy-sell agreements, arbitration agreements).
- Precedent established by prior transactions.
- Directives issued by the court (in some litigated cases where the standards or premises are not clear, the valuer may take the initiative to seek direction from the court regarding the relevant definition of value).
- Discussions with an attorney involved in the valuation matter or experienced in similar matters.
- Legal case documents (e.g., complaint, response, and so forth).
- The analyst's practice experience and professional judgment.

Effect of Terms on Value

As noted earlier in the chapter, most small businesses and professional practices do not sell for cash or cash equivalents. The majority of small businesses and professional practice sales include a cash down pay-

---

[19]Note that administrative rulings do not have the force of law but represent the position of the agency administering the law as to their interpretation of the law and rules for applying it.

ment, typically 20 to 40 percent of what we will call the *transaction value*, with the balance on a contract to be paid over some period of time, usually a few years.

The contracts for the balance of the transaction price are usually interest-bearing contracts, but the rate of interest is frequently below a market rate. In other words, third-party lenders would generally charge higher rates on loans that have comparable collateral and the same terms as those in the contract for the balance of a transaction price. Consequently, the fair market values of such contracts in terms of cash or cash equivalents accepted as part of the consideration in a sale are usually less than their face values. The procedure for converting the face value of such a contract to cash value is the subject of Chapter 27.

Some purchase contracts may include a contingency clause. This makes the full expected amount that the seller will realize dependent on certain future events. Such an event could be the level of future earnings or retention, for some time period, of the clients who were doing business with the seller at the time of the transaction.

Two other major components often are included in *transaction value*: (1) a noncompete agreement and/or (2) an employment agreement. If the objective is to reach a conclusion about the value of the business itself without these components, the value of these components must be subtracted from the "transaction value" as defined earlier.

As discussed more fully in Chapter 27, we know of no other class of transactions whose prices diverge as far from a cash equivalent fair market value as the values of contracts arising from sales of small businesses and professional practices. It is not at all uncommon for the terms of the contract to be such that the cash equivalent value is 20 to 50 percent, or even more, below the transaction value as presented on the face of the transaction documents or as reported in some services.

Summary

This chapter has explained why the notion that there can be only one value is a myth. For reasons either mandated by law or driven by investor objectives and perspectives, different standards of value may be applicable in different circumstances. Various premises, or transactional assumptions, relating to the business or business interest being valued also have an important impact on the valuation methodology and conclusion.

Differing opinions about the appropriate standard of value and/or premise of value may have greater impact on the ultimate conclusion of value than differences in methodology or estimates of figures affecting the value that follow once the standard and premise have been established.

Failure to accord adequate attention to establishing the appropriate standard of value and premise of value historically has been a major contributor to flawed conclusions of value and to wide differences in value between opposing appraisers. This chapter has provided a road map to the alternatives to consider. It has also provided guidance about sources that will help in selecting the appropriate standard and premise for the particular valuation situation.

Chapter 4

How Valuations Differ for Different Purposes

Before you can value a company, you must know the purpose for which you need the valuation. Different purposes will provide differing values and different valuation methods.[1]

When we present papers on valuing businesses and professional practices, we frequently tell the audience that the purpose of the valuation has an important bearing on the valuation process. And in some cases, the purpose of the valuation affects the conclusion that will be reached. This revelation usually surprises at least some of the members of the audience, those who had never realized that different valuation considerations and conclusions can be appropriate for the same interest in a business or professional practice, depending on the purpose of the valuation.

While many people's initial reaction is that there can be only one value for any given property at any one time, it simply isn't so. Various state and federal statutes, regulations, and legal precedents impose different standards of value and different sets of criteria for valuations for different purposes. Also, apart from the valuation process and conclusion, the extent and form in which the valuation should be reported—whether oral, written, or both—is influenced to a considerable extent by the purpose of the valuation.

This chapter moves through various valuation purposes, starting with various types of typical market transactions, then moving on to transfers governed by federal tax law and regulations, and on to transactions frequently involving dispute resolution or litigation.

This grouping is arbitrary and is simply for the reader's convenience. There certainly is overlap between the groups. For example, in the "typical buy and sell transaction" category, a transaction between related parties could be challenged by the Internal Revenue Service as producing gift or income tax consequences. ESOPs certainly are buy and sell transactions, but they are placed under the tax group because the law requires strict adherence to federal tax regulations.

Typical Buy and Sell Transactions

Buying or Selling a Business or Practice

A valuation for a business purchase or sale is subject to all the forces that affect supply and demand. This includes all relevant economic factors prevalent at the time and all the vagaries of the market for the business or practice in question. As noted in the previous chapter, the *market* can be thought of as all the potential buyers and sellers of like businesses or practices.

It is logical for a potential seller to think of value in two ways. The first way is to identify what is acceptable to her, by whatever value cri-

---

[1]Paul B. Baron. *When You Buy or Sell a Company,* rev. ed. (Meriden, CT: The Center for Business Information, Inc., 1983), pp. 8–9.

teria and parameters she chooses. This idea can be expressed as *intrinsic value*, *fundamental value*, or *investment value*, as discussed in the previous chapter. The second way is to identify what potential buyers are willing to pay or what the market will bear, called *market value* or *fair market value*.

There can be many reasons why the owner may place the value of a business or professional practice higher than anyone else is willing to pay. In that case, the logical decision is to keep the business or professional practice. If the market value appears to be at or above the value acceptable to the prospective seller, the objective becomes finding the buyer who is willing to pay the most.

It is logical for a potential buyer to think of value in the same two ways. He may first decide on his own valuation criteria and parameters, given his particular set of circumstances. He would use these criteria and parameters to determine his intrinsic, fundamental, or investment value for any given business or practice in which he might consider investing. He might include in his deliberations of investment value certain strategic advantages associated with acquiring the subject company. He might also survey the prices at which businesses or practices that interest him would be available, and he could think of these prices as the market available to him.

If nothing is available at a price that the prospective buyer would be willing to pay, the logical decision is not to make an investment until market prices are more appealing. If several investments appear to be available at acceptable prices, the objective is to find the one that represents the best value according to that buyer's criteria and parameters.

Market conditions for various types of businesses and practices vary considerably from time to time and from one locality to another. When many buyers are willing to pay prices at or above a typical seller's notion of fundamental value for a given type of business or practice, the condition is called a *seller's market*. When many sellers are willing to sell for an amount at or below a typical buyer's notion of fundamental value, the condition is called a *buyer's market*.

Partly because of these ever-changing market conditions, as well as because of the unique nature of each business and practice and other circumstances that may be unique to certain potential buyers, no formula can ever be devised that will produce a reliable conclusion about the market value of any particular business or practice at any given time.

Chapter 43 discusses the various valuation factors that prospective buyers or sellers should consider. These factors may differ in relative importance from factors relevant for other valuation purposes.

Chapter 21 describes various data sources available for pricing and other data on actual completed business sales. Chapter 45 discusses working with a business or practice broker to buy or sell a business or professional practice.

Buying or Selling a Partial Ownership Interest

A partial ownership interest in a business or practice may or may not be worth a proportionate value of the total entity. Put another way, depending on the circumstances, the sum of the values of the various parts taken individually may or may not add up to the value of the business or professional practice if it were valued as one total entity.

Minority ownership interests are typically (although not always) worth less than their proportion of the total entity value. In some special circumstances, a minority interest may even be worth more than its proportional share of the total entity value. This matter is discussed in some detail in the chapters on valuations for specific purposes, especially Chapter 24, Valuing Minority Ownership Interests.

Leveraged Buyouts

Leveraged buyouts became increasingly popular in the 1980s. But they became subject to more stringent credit criteria in the 1990s. For businesses that have considerable unused borrowing capacity, prospective buyers may arrange to borrow a significant portion of the total purchase price by using the assets, and possibly also the stock, of the business as collateral, thus "cashing out" the seller. Both banks and insurance companies have become involved in leveraged buyouts in recent years.[2] Also, a group of specialized financial institutions has sprung up to participate in this market. These lenders frequently demand some equity participation. A well-documented appraisal of the fair market value of the business can be important to the implementation of a leveraged buyout.

Mergers

A merger involves the combination of two entities so that stock or partnership interests in one are exchanged for stock or assets of another. Some amount of cash may be offered in addition to stock or a partnership interest.

The situation usually requires the valuation of each entity in order to establish an exchange ratio. Sometimes, however, an exchange ratio may be established by some criterion without actually valuing the entities. (Squeeze-out mergers are a special case, addressed later in the chapter.)

Obtaining or Providing Financing

The typical bank lending officer has no conception of the total value of the entity to which he is lending. The banker usually has some notion of the value of assets pledged as collateral but neither has nor avails herself of expertise in the field of business appraisal. Many businesses and professional practices have far greater value than is indicated by their financial statements alone. If this value can be demonstrated convincingly, it may be helpful in obtaining desired financing.

---

[2]At this writing, banks are the primary source of funds for leveraged buyouts for small businesses, while most insurance companies are interested only in multimillion-dollar deals.

There are many sources of *venture capital* today, including venture capital funds, insurance companies, and special venture capital departments or affiliates of some banks. Such sources almost always seek an equity participation, such as convertible debt or warrants. Owners who approach such sources should go in with a soundly based notion of the market value of their business; of course, the question of value will be of prime importance to the providers of the financing. Sources of debt financing for small businesses have also expanded considerably since the early 1990s.

Going Public

While the public market is composed mainly of the stocks of large companies, hundreds of successful public stock offerings were made in the $500,000 to $5,000,000 range in the 1980s and 1990s. That market for small initial public offerings (IPOs) continues to be available as this edition goes to press. Most companies that succeeded in such offerings had innovative products or services offering the prospect of rapid growth and thus a high potential rate of return to the investor in the form of appreciation in the stock price. Most such offerings are sold to the public through small, regional, investment banking firms.

When appraising a company for the purpose of a public stock offering, the analyst should pay special attention to other public offerings that may be considered comparable in some respect. The analyst should also pay special attention to the receptiveness of the public market to the type of offering being considered. These factors are subject to constant change, sometimes changing dramatically in very short periods.

Another variant on the small company public offering sometimes called the *consolidation IPO* became popular in the late 1990s. The idea is that several businesses or practices too small to go public by themselves agree to merge, with the consummation of the merger contingent on a successful IPO for the group. Some recent examples include automobile dealerships and medical practices.

Transactions Governed by Federal Tax Laws

Between statutory law, Internal Revenue Service regulations, and a long history of precedential case law, there is more valuation guidance available for transactions governed by federal tax laws than for any other category of transactions. The Service tends to favor the market approach to valuation. ("Comparable companies" are mentioned seven times in Revenue Ruling 59–60.) Therefore, for taxation-related business valuations, it is important to use the market approach if at all possible, although the Service and the courts have accepted other approaches on many occasions.

Estate, Gift, Inheritance, and Income Taxes

The universal standard of value for estate, gift, and inheritance taxes is *fair market value*, which is defined and interpreted in the previous chapter. Guidelines for federal estate and gift taxes are found in Revenue Ruling 59–60. Revenue Ruling 68–609, which basically is the "excess earnings" ruling, contains important language broadening the application of Revenue Ruling 59–60:

> The general approach, methods, and factors, outlined in Revenue Ruling 59–60 . . . are equally applicable to valuations of corporate stocks for income and other tax purposes as well as for estate and gift tax purposes. They apply also to problems involving the determination of the fair market value of business interests of any type, including partnerships and proprietorships, and of intangible assets for all tax purposes.[3]

Valuation guidelines for state inheritance taxes are generally consistent with federal estate and gift tax guidelines.

Although the standard of value for estate, gift, and inheritance taxes is fair market value, there can be differences between a valuation for tax purposes and a valuation for the sale of a business or for other purposes. For example, estate and gift tax valuations are based on the value of a business to a *hypothetical* buyer, who would have no special synergy with—or relationship to—the seller. In a normal tax valuation, the fact that the seller might be able to command a higher price because of some feature that might be uniquely valuable to a particular buyer would not be considered.

Another distinction between estate and gift tax valuations and valuations for the sale of a business is how much each relies on the historical record, as opposed to projections. Some buyers may be willing to pay for the opportunity for future profits that they envision. However, such projections may not exist or may be considered too speculative to be relied on as a basis of value in a legal context, such as an estate or gift tax valuation.

Revenue Ruling 59–60 specifically recognizes that "valuation of securities is, in essence, a prophecy as to the future. . . . "[4] Nevertheless, as a practical matter, valuations for tax purposes rely relatively more heavily on a company's historical record than do valuations for sales, which are more prone to rely on projections. This difference is a matter of emphasis rather than of concept.

Charitable Contributions

Revenue Ruling 59–60 is also the basic guideline for charitable contributions.

---

[3]Revenue Ruling 68–609 (1968–2, C.B. 327).

[4]Revenue Ruling 59–60 (1959–1 C.B. 237), Section 3. For a detailed discussion of possible transactions triggering income tax consequences, see "Federal Income Tax Reasons to Conduct an Appraisal," in Pratt, Reilly, and Schweihs, *Valuing a Business: The Analysis and Appraisal of Closely Held Companies*, 3d ed., pp. 618-22.

If the claimed value of securities donated is more than $10,000, the Tax Reform Act of 1984 makes it mandatory that the value be supported by a "qualified appraisal" attached to the income tax return. The appraisal must be made by a "qualified appraiser" and must be received by the donor before the due date (including extensions) of the return on which the deduction is claimed.

The 1993 Omnibus Budget Reconciliation Act added considerable documentation and substantiation requirements with regard to the charitable contribution of property.

Internal Revenue Service Form 8283 must be completed by all donors if the aggregate claimed or reported value of such property—and all similar items of property for which charitable deductions are claimed or reported by the same donor for the same tax year (whether or not donated to the same donee)—is more than $5,000. The term *similar types of property* means property of the same generic category or type, such as stamps, books, land, buildings, or nonpublicly traded stock.

In cases where the noncash charitable contributions deduction includes items with a value in excess of $5,000, Form 8283 must include an acknowledgment of receipt signed by the donee charity and a signed appraiser's certification of appraisal, per Regulation Section 1.170A–13(c)(3).

Closely Held Stock.   Qualified appraisals are not required for deductions of $10,000 or less of nonpublicly traded stock. However, a partially completed appraisal summary signed by the donee must be attached to his or her income tax return for charitable contributions of closely held stock valued between $5,000 and $10,000.

Qualified Appraisers.   According to Regulation Section 1.170A–13(c)(5), a qualified appraiser is an individual who:

1. Holds him- or herself out to the public as an appraiser or who regularly performs appraisals.
2. Is qualified to appraise property because of his or her qualifications.
3. Is aware of the appraiser penalties associated with the overvaluation of charitable contributions.

Certain individuals, however, including the following, may not act as qualified appraisers:

1. The property's donor (or the taxpayer who claims the deduction).
2. The property's donee.
3. A party of the property transfer transaction (with certain very specific exceptions).
4. Any person employed by, married to, or related to any of the above persons.
5. An appraiser who regularly appraises for the donor, donee, or party to the transaction and does not perform a majority of his or her appraisals for other persons.[5]

---

[5]For a more extended discussion of qualified appraisals, see "Valuation Requirements for Charitable Contribution Deductions," in Pratt, Reilly & Schweihs, *Valuing a Business: The Analysis and Appraisal of Closely Held Companies*, 3d ed., pp. 622-26.

Employee Stock Ownership Plans

The Tax Reform Act of 1984 substantially enhanced the financial advantages of selling stock to employees through an employee stock ownership plan (ESOP). And the 1986 Tax Reform Act further enhanced the attractiveness of ESOPs. The stock to be sold through an ESOP can range from small minority ownership interests to 100 percent of the company. The income tax advantages of an ESOP make the vehicle attractive to use in conjunction with a leveraged buyout. The income tax advantages of ESOPs, as well as other issues related to this topic, are discussed in Chapter 39, Employee Stock Ownership Plans in Small Companies.

Valuations for ESOPs follow the guidelines of Revenue Ruling 59–60, used for gift and estate tax purposes, with certain special modifications necessary to accommodate the unique nature of ESOPs.

In recent years, many smaller companies have implemented ESOPs, as ownership success with employee involvement has become more widespread. Companies such as *Willamette Capital* have sprung up to help smaller companies obtain ESOP financing. Consequently, in this edition we have expanded the chapter on employee stock ownership plans in small businesses and professional practices (Chapter 39).

Buy-Sell Agreements

Valuations for buy-sell agreements can be based on whatever criteria the parties mutually agree to, and they may or may not bear any relationship to any recognized standard of value. Valuations for this purpose are discussed more fully in the chapter on buy-sell agreements and estate planning (Chapter 38).

The business valuation professional can make an important contribution in consulting on the implications of the buy-sell agreement at the time that it is being set up. The valuation consultant can make another important contribution by being at the meeting when the agreement is finalized, to make sure that all parties to the agreement understand the valuation implications of the language to which they are agreeing.

Determining Life Insurance Needs

Life insurance can serve three important uses in a business or professional practice:

1. To fund the redemption of stock or a partnership interest from the estate of the deceased.
2. To pay estate and inheritance taxes.
3. To provide for the continuity of the business or professional practice for a period of time in the absence of a key person.

Valuation factors to determine the amount of life insurance needed to meet these objectives are discussed in Chapter 38.

Valuations for Litigation and Dispute Resolution

Property Settlements in Divorces

State laws govern property settlements in marital dissolutions. However, state statutes generally fail to specify what standard of value applies to businesses and professional practices in divorces. The law governing various aspects of the valuation of businesses and professional practices in divorces is often established by judicial precedent in each state. The impact of such precedent varies greatly from state to state and can vary from case to case within a state.

On some valuation issues, some state courts have established precedents that are diametrically opposed to those of courts of other states on the same issues.

For some valuation issues, many state courts have established no precedents at all. It is no wonder that the parties and their appraisers frequently find themselves far apart on the matter of valuation of a business or professional practice in a divorce. Added to the confusing and contradictory legal guidance is the acrimony and distrust that frequently accompany matrimonial dissolutions.

Valuations for divorces have become so important to certain valuation practitioners that an entire chapter of this book is devoted to valuations of businesses and professional practices for divorces (Chapter 41).

Damage Cases

The following are the most common damage situations that may require a business valuation to establish the amount of damages:

- Breach of contract.
- Condemnation.
- Lost business opportunity.
- Lost profits.
- Antitrust.
- Personal injury.
- Insurance casualty claims.
- Wrongful termination of a franchise.

Each must be approached with as thorough an understanding as possible of the legal precedents that affect the valuation in the specific case since the precedents vary considerably—not only from one type of damage situation to another, but also from one jurisdiction to another. Chapter 47 presents more detail on valuations for damage actions.

Squeeze-out Mergers and Dissenting Stockholder Actions

In virtually all states, controlling stockholders have the right to effect certain actions that give rise to minority stockholders' appraisal rights. In general, these actions include a merger or sale of the company or the disposition of a major portion of its business or assets.

If controlling stockholders wish to eliminate minority stockholders, they can (1) form a new corporation, (2) sell the stock of the old corporation to the new corporation, and (3) pay off the minority stockholders. This action gives rise to the term *squeeze-out merger* since it forces out the minority stockholders.

If any minority stockholder believes the consideration offered in the transaction is inadequate, he has the right to have his shares appraised and to be paid, in cash, the amount finally determined. Almost all state statutes specify that the standard of value for such actions is *fair value*, as discussed briefly in the previous chapter. A stockholder who exercises his dissenting stockholder rights may end up receiving more than, less than, or the same amount as was originally offered.

A study of the relevant legal precedents is extremely important in a valuation under dissenting stockholder rights. Such valuations are discussed in Chapter 40.

Minority Stockholder Oppression Actions

In several states (notably California, Rhode Island, and Delaware),[6] there are procedures whereby certain minority stockholders who are unable to achieve satisfaction regarding operations can sue for dissolution of the company. In these states, the other stockholders can avoid dissolution of the company by having the stock appraised and paying off the disgruntled stockholders at the appraised value.

The standard of value for these minority stockholder dissolution actions is *fair value*. Note that this is the same phrase used in the dissenting stockholder statutes discussed in the previous section. Do not, however, be misled into thinking that these terms mean the same thing in the two different legal contexts. Within the given state, you may find that case law interprets fair value differently in actions under dissolution statutes than in actions under dissenter statutes. This is a good example of the importance of the analyst's study and understanding of relevant case law.

In general, the rights of minority stockholders are extremely limited,[7] which is a major reason minority stock usually sells at a substantial discount from a pro rata portion of the value of the whole company. However, there has been a trend in the 1990s toward greater protection against abuses of minority stockholders, both in state legislatures and

---

[6]Cal. Corp. Code §§1300, 2000; Del. Code Ann. §262; R.I. Gen. Laws §7–1.1–74.

[7]See F. Hodge O'Neal and Robert B. Thompson, *O'Neal's Oppression of Minority Shareholders*, 2d ed. (Deerfield, IL: Clark Boardman Callaghan, 1991, supplemented in 1997).

in the courts. We have been involved in several situations in the late 1990s where minority stockholders have achieved settlements that would not have been reached a decade ago.

Ad Valorem Taxes

Ad valorem is a Latin expression that has found its way into English dictionaries. It means "according to value" and is the basis for assessing property taxes in virtually all state and local taxing jurisdictions.

Municipal taxing authorities have been hard-pressed to raise adequate funds. Sometimes assessing officers are pressured to be aggressive in their opinions of the values of taxable properties. Many sudden and huge increases in property taxes have been levied on such businesses as manufacturers, shopping centers, and motels. In many cases, the economics of the respective businesses have not justified the increases. Businesses have often been assessed for real estate values that exceeded the entire going-concern value of the total business, *including* the real estate.

Taxpayers can save millions of dollars by properly valuing businesses in which the business and the physical property are interrelated. Fair market value is the legal standard of value in most ad valorem cases.[8] The real-world market values such properties on their ability to produce income, which is this book's primary valuation focus. Proper application of business valuation principles should be able to counteract some methods used in many assessing jurisdictions. These methods sometimes produce values well in excess of the applicable legal standard of fair market value.

On the other hand, in many states, ad valorem taxes are applicable *only* to the value of *tangible* assets. In these cases, taxpayers may save a lot in taxes by having an analyst separate the total value into the tangible and intangible portions, paying tax only on the tangible asset value.[9]

Valuations for Multiple Purposes

The situation can become tricky when the same valuation is intended to be used for two or more different purposes. For example, a valuation for the purpose of selling the company or attracting outside investment capital may contain speculative elements based on future potential that may be acceptable to a risk-oriented investor but not acceptable to a court charged with determining value under some set of statutory standards and legal precedents.

---

[8]For a further discussion of ad valorem valuation issues, see Robert F. Reilly, "Assessing Your Assessment: Valuation Techniques for Finding Out What Your Property's Really Worth," *Commercial Investment Real Estate Journal*, Summer 1995, pp. 30-33.

[9]For more information on this topic, see Robert F. Reilly, "The Valuation of Intangible Assets in Property Tax Assessments," *Journal of Property Tax Management*, Summer 1995, pp. 33–45.

As noted earlier, valuations pursuant to buy-sell agreements can be just as arbitrary as the parties mutually agree to make them, but such valuations will not necessarily (or even usually) be appropriate for determining property settlements in divorces or estate and inheritance taxes.

Setting a value for a tender offer to buy out minority shareholders is quite a different matter from setting a price at which to effect a squeeze-out merger, in which all the stockholders are required to sell, whether they like it or not. A valuation for a tender offer may be at a lower price than a valuation for a squeeze-out merger. If so, and that valuation is subsequently used for a squeeze-out merger, a dissenting stockholder suit is likely to follow.

The material in this book should provide the reader with considerable guidance on when a certain valuation procedure will be suitable for two or more specific contemplated uses and when it will not. When in doubt, seek professional valuation advice.

Considering Alternatives: Estate Planning and Other Types of Choices

An owner may need to find out a range of possible values for the business or professional practice in order to decide what to do. For example, the owner may be considering making charitable contributions, giving gifts within the family, selling stock to employees, and/or initiating an employee stock ownership plan. The decision to implement any of these choices is likely to depend to some extent on the values of the shares or interests to be transferred in each case. In such cases, the valuation process should proceed so that it addresses all of the possible alternatives contemplated. Differences in valuation procedures and/or conclusions that may be applicable, depending on which of the possible alternatives are finally implemented, should be noted and brought to the client's attention.

Summary

Readers of this chapter should now be convinced that the purpose of the valuation has an impact on how (and even whether) certain elements of value will be reflected in the applicable standard of value, valuation procedures, and ultimate conclusion of value. It is always important to determine whether or not the appraisal is governed by a legally mandated standard of value. If it is, then it is also important to gain an understanding of the case law interpretation of that standard of value.

Later chapters present more detail about the specific nuances of valuations for the most commonly encountered valuation purposes: buying or selling a company or a partial interest; buy-sell agreements; divorces, damage cases, and other litigated valuation contexts; gift and estate taxes; and employee stock ownership plans.

Exhibit 4–1 summarizes matching the applicable standard of value with some of the most common valuation purposes.

Exhibit 4–1

MATCHING THE STANDARD OF VALUE
WITH THE PURPOSE OF THE VALUATION

Purpose of Valuation	Applicable Standard of Value
Purchase or sale	Generally fair market value, but in many instances investment value, reflecting unique circumstances or motivations of a particular buyer or seller
Gift, estate, and inheritance taxes and charitable contributions	Fair market value
Divorce	No statutory standards of value. Courts have wide discretion to achieve equitable distribution. Requires careful study of relevant case law.
Buy-sell agreements	Parties can do anything they want. Very important that all parties to the agreement understand the valuation implications of the wording in the agreement.
Dissenting stockholder actions	Fair value in almost all states. Must read both relevant statute and case law to determine how interpreted in the particular state.
Minority oppression action	Generally, fair value in those states that address it at all. Not always interpreted the same as fair value for dissenting stockholder actions.
Employee stock ownership plans (ESOPs)	Fair market value.
Ad valorem (property) taxes	Generally, fair market value with varied nuances of interpretation. In many states, intangible portion of value excluded by statute.

Chapter 5

Differences between the Valuation of Large and Small Businesses

Introduction

Obviously, there are numerous differences between large businesses and small businesses. This is true whether the business is a manufacturing company, a wholesale or retail concern, a service firm, or a professional practice. And these differences affect the valuation of these businesses. This chapter will describe some of the many differences between large and small businesses. This chapter will also summarize many of the ways in which these size differences affect the business valuation process.

While there are noteworthy differences in the valuation of large businesses and small businesses, these differences may be even more salient when comparing large professional practices to small professional practices. Small professional practices are sometimes principally self-employment opportunities. In these cases, it is difficult to distinguish between the subject professional's employment activities and rewards and the subject professional's equity ownership activities and rewards. However, in very large professional practices, it is relatively easy to distinguish between the professional's employment activities and rewards and the professional's equity ownership activities and rewards. Such differences are noteworthy because, in terms of the business size spectrum, professional practices range in size from single professional medical or dental practices to international accounting and law firms.

However, the objective of this chapter is to highlight the differences in the valuation of small and large businesses. Therefore, for purposes of this chapter, we will group smaller commercial firms and professional practices into the category of small businesses, and we will group larger commercial firms and professional firms into the category of large businesses.

Many analysts naively apply the same set of approaches, methods, and procedures to the valuation of small businesses as they do to the valuation of substantial corporations. And they erroneously ignore the many differences between large professional practices and small professional practices.

Because there are numerous differences between the valuation of large and small businesses, analysts should carefully consider these differences in their selection of valuation methods, their application of valuation procedures, their search for and analyses of transactional data, and their synthesis of value indications to reach the final value conclusion. In fact, the recognition of the appraisal subject as either a big business, a small business, a large professional practice, or a small professional practice is an important initial step in the business valuation process.

There are three principal categories of differences between big businesses and small businesses that affect the business valuation process: (1) operational differences—meaning the way businesses are organized (from a legal, taxation, and business formality perspective), the way businesses account for their transactions, and they way businesses finance themselves; (2) transactional differences—meaning the way that such businesses are actually bought and sold in their respective transactional markets; and (3) market dynamics differences—in the data (in terms of both quantity and quality), methodology, and analytical factors that are involved directly in the business valuation process.

It is important to note that there are not formal business valuation rules that recognize the differences between—and the definitions of—big and small businesses. Indeed, in terms of the above-mentioned three categories of differences that affect the valuation process, not all big businesses are the same. Likewise, not all small businesses are the same.

Experienced analysts do, in fact, consider the fundamental differences (operational, transactional, and market dynamics) in their business valuation analyses. So, in one respect, this discussion is directed more to the users (as opposed to the preparers) of business valuation analyses. However, this chapter may prove to be a good review (or provide a convenient checklist) for even the most experienced valuation practitioner.

Definitions and Distinctions

There is no absolute quantitative or qualitative definition of what distinguishes a big business from a small business. The only fact that may be unambiguous when comparing big and small businesses is that the distinctions are based on many factors, not just on size alone.

For purposes of this discussion only, we will classify big businesses as those that generate more than $5 million in revenues and where equity ownership is typically with individuals who are not employed by the company. We will classify smaller businesses as those that generate less than $5 million in revenue and where employees and/or family members are the principal equity owners. Also for definitional purposes, in big businesses, the company is expected to survive the current owners. In small businesses, the company may not survive an ownership transition (or, at least, not without some significant organizational disruption).

Generally, a big business operates as a business institution—with organizational qualities that are distinct from the abilities of the employee/owners. An example of such a big business may be a law firm with 250 lawyers. A small business operates more as a convenient association of individuals/practitioners—with organizational qualities that are directly dependent on the abilities of the employee-owners. An example of such a small business is a law firm with three lawyers. Big businesses usually operate as a separate entity (from legal, accounting, and taxation perspectives) from the owners. But in the typical small business, the business operations are often inseparable (financially, legally, and organizationally) from the employee-owners.

Exhibit 5-1 presents a list of some of the other factors that distinguish big businesses from small businesses from a valuation perspective.

Exhibit 5–1

DEFINITIONAL DIFFERENCES THAT DISTINGUISH
BIG BUSINESSES AND SMALL BUSINESSES

Item	Factor	Large Businesses	Small Businesses
1	Size, in terms of annual revenues	The size is generally greater than $5 million.	The size is generally less than $5 million.
2	Ownership	The owners may have no direct association with the company (e.g., as current or former employees) other than their equity ownership interests.	The owners are often directly associated with the firm— typically as full-time employees.
3	Legal form	Typically, the business operates as a corporation or a partnership— both with limited liability.	The business may be a proprietorship, a partnership, or a corporation—and it may or may not have limited liability.
4	Tax form	It is typically a C corporation or a partnership.	It may be an S corporation (if a corporation), partnership, or a sole proprietorship.
5	Management	Typically, professional executives are hired to handle the administrative and day-to-day management aspects of the company; the equity owners will delegate management responsibility to a board of directors and, through the board, to the professional managers.	Employee-owners generally make all significant management decisions; employee-owners are typically "hands on" (i.e., involved in the company matters on a day-to-day basis).
6	Perceptions of identity of the business (separately consider perceptions of bankers, clients, suppliers, competitors, owner-employees, non-owner-employees, and professional management)	The business operates as a separate organizational entity from the equity owners; it has stability (financial and otherwise) separate from the support (financial and otherwise) of the individual equity owners.	The business operations are often inseparable from the employee-owners; the business stability (financial and otherwise) depends directly upon the stability financial and otherwise) of the individual equity owners.
7	Durability and duration of the business	The business is expected to survive the current equity owners; it has institutional attributes that transcend the departure of any individual equity owners.	The business may not survive beyond the tenure of the current equity owners; it may not have created institutional attributes that allow the business to transcend the departure of the individual equity owners.

Exhibit 5–1 (concluded)

Item	Factor	Large Businesses	Small Businesses
8	Ownership transition	There are mechanisms in place in order to allow for a relatively smooth ownership transition; these mechanisms may be in the form of buy-sell agreements, redemption agreements, or shareholder agreements; the departing employee-owners deal with the company-established management structure in these matters.	There are usually not mechanisms in place in order to allow for a smooth ownership transition; the departing employee-owners have to negotiate with each other in order to arrange for each ownership transition event.
9	Organizational attributes	The company operates as a business institution with a well-defined organizational relationship (1) between employees and (2) between equity owners and nonowner employees.	The company operates more as a convenient association of individuals without a well-defined organizational relationship (1) between employees or (2) between equity owners and nonowner employees.
10	Business locations	Often, there are numerous company locations that may require separate —and fairly autonomous—management teams.	Often, there is one company location—with a single management team.

Operational Differences

The valuation analyst should consider the differences in (1) the organization structure and (2) the accounting, financial, and management operations between large and small businesses. Such differences *do* affect the availability of data for—and the analyses prepared during—the business valuation. Consideration of these operational differences is important because, after all, the analyst needs to understand the workings (both financial and operational) of the business subject to appraisal.

Generally, big businesses have various types of debt financing available to them, regardless of the creditworthiness of the individual equity owners. However, such institutional debt capacity (separate from the creditworthiness of the individual equity owners) is not generally available for smaller businesses. Alternative sources of financing, such as the owner's capital, are typically needed in the case of small businesses. In addition, the personal guarantees of the individual equity holders are typically required for the debt financing for small businesses. These conditions often represent a constraint on the ability of a small business to finance growth or other strategic initiatives.

In a big business, employees are paid market-derived salaries and wages for their services, and the equity owners receive a nonwage return on their equity investment. This return on equity investment comes in the form of dividends or other profit distributions. Accordingly, the compensation for services and the return on equity ownership are separate. This is true even if the same individual is associated with the big business both as an employee and as an equity owner. However, in the smaller business, employees/owners are not always paid market-derived wages. And the equity owners often pay out all of the profits generated by the small business to themselves as some form of compensation bonus. Accordingly, in the case of small businesses, the compensation for employment services and the return on an equity ownership investment may be inseparable.

Concerning operational management, there may be outside board of directors members and outside corporate officers and other senior managers in big businesses. By "outside" in this context, we mean directors and executives who are not themselves substantial equity holders in the business. In contrast, all board of directors members, corporate affiliates, and senior management are insiders at a small business. Within this context, we define *insider* as a substantial equity holder in the business.

With regard to the quality of historical financial data, large businesses typically have financial statements that are prepared in compliance with generally accepted accounting principles (GAAP). These financial statements are often audited by independent certified public accountants. The footnotes to audited financial statements will provide a great deal of supplemental data regarding the company's results of operations and financial position. These supplemental data can be extremely useful to the valuation analyst. And the footnotes to audited financial statements will describe the accounting principles upon which the financial statements were prepared. This description of accounting principles is also extremely useful to the valuation analyst. It allows the analyst to more fully understand the basis for the financial statements that will be used in the valuation.

Small businesses may not have financial statements prepared in accordance with GAAP. And the financial statements are often not audited by independent certified public accountants. To the extent that the small business financial statements are examined at all by certified public accountants, they may be reviewed or compiled rather than audited.

Exhibit 5-2 presents a typical certified public accountant's unqualified opinion. Exhibit 5-3 presents a typical certified public accountant's review opinion. And Exhibit 5-4 presents a typical certified public accountant's compilation opinion. It is obvious from the language of these three opinions that the analyst will assign the greatest reliability to the audited financial statements.

Large businesses often use one set of accounting principles for the preparation of financial statements and another set of accounting principles for the preparation of income tax returns. Small businesses, on

Exhibit 5–2

EXAMPLE OF CERTIFIED PUBLIC ACCOUNTANT'S AUDIT REPORT

Penney and Nichols, CPAs
45789 Beachwood Drive
Centerville, New Jersey 08000

Board of Directors and Stockholders
X Company

We have audited the accompanying balance sheet of X Company as of December 31, 19XX, and the related statements of income, retained earnings, and cash flows for the year then ended. These financial statements are the responsibility of the Company's management. Our responsibility is to express an opinion on these financial statements based on our audit.

We conducted our audit in accordance with generally accepted auditing standards. Those standards require that we plan and perform the audit to obtain reasonable assurance about whether the financial statements are free of material misstatement. An audit includes examining, on a test basis, evidence supporting the amounts and disclosures in the financial statements. An audit also includes assessing the accounting principles used and significant estimates made by management, as well as evaluating the overall financial statement presentation. We believe that our audit provides a reasonable basis for our opinion.

In our opinion, the financial statements referred to above present fairly, in all material respects, the financial position of X Company as of December 31, 19XX, and the results of its operations and its cash flows for the year then ended in conformity with generally accepted accounting principles.

[Report Date]

[Signature]

SOURCE: Excerpt from *GAAS Guide, A Comprehensive Restatement of Standards for Auditing, Attestation, Compilation and Review, and the Code of Professional Conduct*, by Larry P. Bailey, copyright © 1997 by Harcourt Brace & Company, reprinted by permission of the publisher, p. 11.07.

the other hand, may use their income tax accounting principles in the preparation of financial statements for all purposes. In fact, in the case of very small businesses, the business may not prepare financial statements separate from its income tax returns. Often in these cases, the only historical data the analyst has to work with are the historical income tax returns of the business.

With regard to the quantity of historical financial data, large businesses typically have more data than small businesses do for two reasons. First, as mentioned above, there is a considerable amount of

Exhibit 5–3

EXAMPLE OF CERTIFIED PUBLIC ACCOUNTANT'S REVIEW REPORT

Penney and Nichols, CPAs
45789 Beachwood Drive
Centerville, New Jersey 08000

Board of Directors and Stockholders
ABC, Inc.

We have reviewed the accompanying balance sheet of ABC, Inc., as of December 31, 19XX, and the related statements of income, retained earnings, and cash flows for the year then ended, in accordance with Statements on Standards for Accounting and Review Services issued by the American Institute of Certified Public Accountants. All information included in these financial statements is the representation of ABC, Inc.

A review consists principally of inquiries of company personnel and analytical procedures applied to financial data. It is substantially less in scope than an examination in accordance with generally accepted auditing standards, the objective of which is the expression of an opinion regarding the financial statements taken as a whole. Accordingly, we do not express such an opinion.

On the basis of our review, we are not aware of any material modifications that should be made to the accompanying financial statements in order for them to be in conformity with generally accepted accounting principles.

[Report Date]

[Signature]

SOURCE: Excerpt from *GAAS Guide, A Comprehensive Restatement of Standards for Auditing, Attestation, Compilation and Review, and the Code of Professional Conduct*, by Larry P. Bailey, copyright © 1997 by Harcourt Brace & Company, reprinted by permission of the publisher, p. 14.49.

supplemental data presented with audited financial statements. These data are simply not presented with reviewed or compiled financial statements. And with regard to very small businesses for which there are income tax returns only, the quantity of historical financial data will obviously be limited. Second, larger businesses have typically been around longer than smaller businesses. Therefore, the valuation analyst may be able to collect and assimilate 10 years or more of financial data for a large company. On the other hand, the valuation analyst may not be able to collect and assimilate even five years of financial data for a small company.

Exhibit 5–4

EXAMPLE OF CERTIFIED PUBLIC ACCOUNTANT'S COMPILATION REPORT

Penney and Nichols, CPAs
45789 Beachwood Drive
Centerville, New Jersey 08000

Board of Directors and Stockholders
ABC Company

We have compiled the accompanying balance sheet of ABC Company as of December 31, 19XX, and the related statements of income, retained earnings, and cash flows for the year then ended, in accordance with Statements on Standards for Accounting and Review Services issued by the American Institute of Certified Public Accountants.

A compilation is limited to presenting in the form of financial statements information that is the representation of management. We have not audited or reviewed the accompanying financial statements and, accordingly, do not express an opinion or any other form of assurance on them.

[Report Date]

[Signature]

SOURCE: Excerpt from *GAAS Guide, A Comprehensive Restatement of Standards for Auditing, Attestation, Compilation and Review, and the Code of Professional Conduct*, by Larry P. Bailey, copyright © 1997 by Harcourt Brace & Company, reprinted by permission of the publisher, pp. 14.37–14.38.

Exhibit 5-5 presents a nonexhaustive list of additional operational differences between big businesses and small businesses.

Transactional Differences

The valuation analyst should consider the transactional differences between large businesses and small businesses. These differences relate to how the subject business or business interest would sell—if and when it were actually put up for sale. A consideration of these transactional differences is particularly important to the business valuation process. When relying on a transaction approach to business valuation, the analyst is trying to assess the actual market dynamics of buyers and sellers in the business valuation process.

The buyer's economic motivation behind the business acquisition is one of the transactional differences between big business sales and

Exhibit 5–5

OPERATIONAL DIFFERENCES BETWEEN BIG BUSINESSES
AND SMALL BUSINESSES

Item	Factor	Large Businesses	Small Businesses
1	Debt financing availability	Debt financing is generally available—and it is generally independent of the creditworthiness of the individual equity owners.	Significant debt financing may not be available; therefore alternate sources of financing are often used—e.g., the equity owners may contribute capital to the business when needed.
2	Debt financing guarantees	Typically, the personal guarantees of the individual equity owners are not required in order to arrange for business financing.	Typically, the personal guarantees of the individual equity owners are required in order to arrange for business financing.
3	Debt financing from owners	Typically, loans to the business from the equity owners are not a common source of financing.	It is common to find loans to the business from the individual equity owners.
4	Organization	The equity owners are organizationally separate from the direct management of the business.	The equity owners are often the direct management of the business.
5	Quality of accounting	Typically, historical financial statements are prepared in accordance with generally accepted accounting principles (GAAP), and they are audited by independent public accountants.	Often, historical financial statements are internally prepared and may or may not be prepared in accordance with GAAP; when the financial statements are examined by independent public accountants, they may be reviewed or compiled—instead of audited.
6	Separate accounting	Typically, there are relatively few transactions between the company and the individual equity owners; therefore, it is easy to keep the accounting for the company affairs separate from the accounting for the equity owners' affairs.	Often, there are frequent transactions between company and the individual equity owners (e.g., shareholder receivables, shareholder payables, discretionary or personal expenses paid by the company on behalf of the owners, discretionary bonuses paid to the employee-owners, etc.); therefore, it is sometimes difficult to keep a separate accounting between the company's affairs and the equity owners' affairs.
7	Owners' personal expenses	Typically, the owners' personal expenses are not paid by the business.	Often, the equity owners' discretionary expenses are paid by the business.

Exhibit 5–5 (concluded)

Item	Factor	Large Businesses	Small Businesses
8	Management	The business will likely have outside (i.e., nonowner) board members and outside (i.e., nonowner) corporate officers and senior management.	Often, all of the board members and all of the senior management group are the equity owners.
9	Separate commercial transactions	The company has business transactions that are totally separate from those of the equity owners.	The company business transactions are often not easily separable from those of the equity owners.
10	Investment diversification	Typically, the equity owners have other investments with regard to their personal wealth.	Often, all of the equity owners' wealth is tied up in the subject small business.
11	Operational transactions/interactions with the equity owners	Generally, there are very few contractual or other transactions with the equity owners.	The equity owners often own the real estate and other assets used by the subject small business; and the equity owners lease these assets to the company.
12	Capital type	Principally, the capital is in the form of equity from outside (i.e., nonemployee) owners, and in the form of various types of unsecured debt.	Principally, the capital is in the form of equity from inside (i.e., employee) owners, and in the form of various types of secured debt.
13	Capital mix	There is often more debt than equity in the company's capital structure.	There is often more equity than debt in the company's capital structure.
14	Capital cost	There is usually a lower cost of debt and a lower cost of equity—when compared to smaller companies in the same industry.	There is usually a higher cost of debt and a higher cost of equity—when compared to larger companies in the same industry.

small business sales. In the acquisition of big businesses, expected return on investment and/or expected return on equity is the principal economic motivation. In the acquisition of a small business, the buyer is often "buying a job." This source of self-employment is often the principal economic motivation behind the business purchase. In these cases, the new owner's expected salary is often taken into account as part of the total return on the business buyer's investment.

In the typical big business acquisition, lawyers, accountants, investment/merchant bankers, and financial advisors are often involved in the due diligence, valuation, financing, and closing aspects of the transaction. In the typical small business purchase, this level of professional involvement often does not occur.

In addition, big businesses are usually bought or sold for business-related strategic reasons. An example of such a reason would be a corporate parent deciding to reallocate their portfolio of investments. On the other hand, small businesses are often sold for personal reasons, such as the death of a family member/employer. The buyer and unrelated sources (e.g., debt and equity offerings underwritten by an investment banker) usually finance the acquisitions of big businesses. Often, the seller and the subject company's traditional source of financing (e.g., the company's commercial bank) provide the financing for the small business in an acquisition.

Exhibit 5-6 presents a partial list of some of the other differences in the ways that big businesses and small businesses are sold.

Market Dynamics Differences

Finally, when comparing big business valuations and small business valuations, the analyst should consider the differences in the quality and quantity of (1) the actual valuation variables and (2) the market-derived data elements. Clearly, these factors will directly affect the valuation methods selected, the valuation procedures performed, the valuation analyses made, and the overall business valuation synthesis and conclusion.

Market-derived guideline public company pricing data and guideline merged and acquired company pricing data are generally available and applicable for big businesses. See Chapter 21, Comparative Transaction Databases, for a summary of available data on smaller businesses. In addition, subject company prospective financial information (i.e., accounting budgets, projections, or plans) and subject company prospective operational information (i.e., sales or production budgets, forecasts, and plans) are available for use in the valuation of big businesses in most cases. Also, the management of the big business generally has access to a detailed listing of all owned assets (both tangible and intangible) and to estimates of individual asset values (i.e., through management experts, property tax renditions, insurance appraisals, or other prior asset appraisals). In contrast, the management of the typical small business often does not have access to accurate listings of all owned assets. This is because the small company's accounting systems may not be sufficient to collect these data, or it may be that management is familiar enough with the assets and their history that keeping a documented record is not cost-efficient. Likewise, small company management probably will not have access to documented estimates of individual owned asset values.

As explained above, the historical financial data are typically audited for most big businesses. However, historical financial statements may be compiled or even internally prepared in the case of many small businesses. The historical and prospective financial data and operational data are usually adequate for the analyst's purpose in the valuation of a big business. In comparison, analysts must often work with less complete financial and operational information in preparing the valuation of a small business.

Exhibit 5–6

TRANSACTIONAL DIFFERENCES BETWEEN BIG BUSINESSES AND SMALL BUSINESSES

Item	Factor	Large Businesses	Small Businesses
1	Business buyer motivations	The buyer's primary economic motivation is the expected return on equity—excluding personal salary considerations.	The buyer is often "buying a job," so that the equity owner's salary is considered part of the total return on investment analysis made by the business buyer.
2	Type of business broker	Typically, an investment banker or other financial advisor is involved in the transaction.	Often, a small business or professional practice broker is involved in the transaction.
3	Transaction cost	The business sale/purchase transaction costs are relatively lower—as a % of the total business price—compared to small business transactions.	The business sale/purchase transaction costs are relatively higher—as a % of the total business price—compared to large business transactions.
4	Transaction time	When considered in relation to the total dollar size of the transaction, there is a relatively shorter amount of time required to close the business sale.	When considered in relation to the total dollar size of the transaction, there is a relatively longer amount of time required to close the business sale.
5	Professional advisor involvement	Frequently, lawyers, accountants, investment/merchant bankers, and other financial advisors are involved in pricing and structuring the transaction.	Few professional advisors are typically involved in pricing and structuring the transaction.
6	Reasons to buy or sell the business	The reasons are typically business-related.	The reasons are typically personal.
7	Source of acquisition financing	Typically, the acquisition financing is provided by the buyer and from unrelated outside financing sources.	Often, the acquisition financing is provided from the seller and from the subject company's traditional financing source (e.g., the company's commercial bank).
8	Transaction structure: stock versus asset sale	The transaction is typically a stock sale.	The transaction is frequently an asset sale.
9	Properties included in the business sale	The transaction encompasses all business assets that are included in the company stock.	There are often personally owned assets (e.g., equity owner–owned real estate) that must be sold separately from the business operations.

Exhibit 5–6 (concluded)

Item	Factor	Large Businesses	Small Businesses
10	Consideration is paid for	Generally, the consideration is paid for the sale of the company stock only.	Generally, the total consideration encompasses payments for the sale of the business and payments for noncompete and transitional employment agreements.
11	Earn-out provision as part of the consideration	Typically, this is less common in the sale of big businesses.	Typically, this is more common in the sale of small businesses.
12	Types and number of possible business buyers	There are frequently numerous types of buyers—with numerous buyers in each type.	There are frequently few types of buyers—with only a few buyers in each type.
13	Sales of the business conducted	The sale of the business is exposed to the market on a national basis.	The sale of the business is exposed to the market on a local basis.
14	Typical type of business buyer	The buyer could be a passive and/or financial investor.	The buyer will most likely be an active owner/manager (e.g., the buyer may be a current competitor or employee of the subject company.

Relevant industry information is also difficult for the management of small businesses to obtain and to provide to the analyst. In big businesses, management typically has ready access to data on the subject company's competitive position and on the subject company's public competitors. But small business management may not readily have accurate data on the subject company's competitive position and may have no access to verifiable data on the subject company's small, private competitors.

Typically, national and/or regional economic data are applicable to the valuation of big businesses, and these data are readily available. However, the small business valuation generally involves the analysis of local economic data, and these data may not be readily available.

Another difference in market economics is that big business management generally can confer with outside company advisors, such as accountants, lawyers, and consultants. Accordingly, these outside advisors may also be available to the analyst. On the other hand, small business management often does not have such ready access to professional advisors. Accordingly, such professional advisors may not be available to the analyst during the valuation of a small business.

In addition, valuation discounts, such as key person dependence, key customer dependence, key supplier dependence, lack of diversification with regard to products, lack of diversification with regard to location, obsolescence regarding plant, obsolescence regarding technology, and obsolescence regarding products, are typically less applicable to the valuation of many big businesses. However, the identification and quantification of these discounts is often quite relevant to—and is the most complicated aspect of—the valuation of a small business.

Finally, the owners of a big business may have seriously considered the concept of an exit plan (i.e., a plan to liquidate their investment at some future time). At the very least, an exit (with or without a formal plan) is reasonably possible with regard to the typical big business. However, in the case of small businesses, an owner exit plan is not likely to have been rigorously considered by the current equity owners. In addition, an exit plan is typically much more difficult to implement with regard to a small business.

Exhibit 5-7 presents a partial list of some of the market dynamics differences that affect the valuation of big businesses vis-à-vis small businesses.

Summary

The operational, transactional, and market dynamics differences between big and small businesses may be second nature to experienced small business appraisers. However, these differences—and how they affect the business valuation process—may not be intuitively obvious to less experienced small business valuation practitioners. Nonetheless, these three categories of differences deserve serious consideration in the valuation of all businesses—but particularly in the valuation of small, privately owned businesses. Clearly, these differences affect the availability and the reliability of market-derived pricing data, the applicability of valuation methods, the identification of valuation discounts and premiums, the quantification of capitalization rates and pricing multiples, the consideration of transactional comparability, the analysis of a sale transaction's cash equivalency price, and ultimately, the estimation of the value of the privately owned business.

For these reasons, valuing small commercial businesses and small professional practices is often more professionally challenging than valuing larger businesses. This may seem counterintuitive because novice valuation practitioners often start their professional careers assigned to the analysis and appraisal of such smaller businesses. Nonetheless, as the factors outlined in this chapter indicate, the appraisal of small commercial businesses and small professional practices often requires at least as much experience and professional judgment as the appraisal of big businesses. Additional discussion regarding the differing applications of valuation methods to small businesses versus large businesses is presented in Chapter 12, Value Drivers.

Exhibit 5–7

MARKET-DYNAMICS DIFFERENCES BETWEEN BIG BUSINESSES AND SMALL BUSINESSES

Item	Factor	Large Businesses	Small Businesses
1	Guideline public company pricing data	Generally, guideline public companies are available for analysis.	Often, guideline public companies are not available for analysis.
2	Guideline merged and acquired company pricing data	Generally, guideline merged and acquired companies are available for analysis.	Often, guideline merged and acquired companies are not available for analysis.
3	Subject company prospective financial information (e.g., accounting budgets, projections, plans)	Generally, these prospective data are available to the valuation analyst.	Generally, these prospective data are not available to the valuation analyst.
4	Subject company prospective operational information (e.g., sales and/or production budgets, forecasts, plans)	Generally, these prospective data are available to the valuation analyst.	Generally, these prospective data are not available to the valuation analyst.
5	Detailed descriptive listing of all owned assets (both tangible and intangible)	Generally, these data are available.	Generally, these data are not available.
6	Informed estimates of individual asset values (e.g., through management experts, property tax renditions, prior asset appraisals, etc.)	Generally, these data are available.	Generally, these data are not available.
7	Applicability of valuation discounts: key person dependence, key customer dependence, key supplier dependence, lack of diversification in products, lack of diversification in location, obsolescence in plant, obsolescence in technology, obsolescence in products, etc.	Generally, the identification and quantification of these valuation discounts are less applicable.	Generally, the identification and quantification of these valuation discounts are more applicable in smaller businesses than in larger businesses.

Exhibit 5–7 (concluded)

Item	Factor	Large Businesses	Small Businesses
8	Reasonably defined owner exit plan	A reasoned owner exit plan may be in place; at least the exit of the current owner is possible (e.g., through an IPO).	A reasoned owner exit plan is likely not in place; and an efficient exit of the current owner may not be possible.
9	Historical financial data quality	Typically, there are audited financial statements, prepared in compliance with GAAP.	Often, there are compiled or even internally prepared financial statements that are not prepared in compliance with GAAP.
10	Historical financial data quantity	Generally, the data are adequate for the analyst's purposes.	Often, the data are limited and and certain analyses may not be available.
11	Historical operational data	Generally, the data are adequate for the analyst's purposes.	Often, the data are limited and certain analyses may not be available.
12	Ability to confer with ouside company advisors (e.g., accountants, lawyers, etc.)	Generally, the analyst has access to these professionals.	Generally, the analyst does not have access to these professionals.
13	Availability of relevant subject industry data	Typically, the subject company is a member of an industry trade association that can provide relevant data.	The subject company may not be a member of an industry trade association—and the relevant data may be limited.
14	Availability of subject competitive position	Typically, the subject company management has data on the subject's competitive position.	The subject company management may not have accurate data on the subject's competitive position.
15	Availability of relevant competitive data	There are often data available on publicly traded competitors.	There may be no data available on small privately owned competitors.
16	Availability of relevant economic data	Often, national and/or regional economic data apply to the valuation—and these data are readily available.	Often, local economic data apply to the valuation—and these data may not be readily available.

Chapter 6

Comparison between Business Appraisal Practices and Real Estate Appraisal Practices

While both real estate appraisal and business valuation are so-
phisticated professional disciplines with conceptual commonality, the
procedures, language, knowledge, and experience required are very
different. This flows from the fact that what is being appraised is
quite different.

Business valuation has to do with the value of the rights inherent in
ownership of a commercial, industrial, or service organization pursuing
an economic activity. Real estate appraisal involves the valuation of
land, improvements, and associated rights.[1]

The appraisal of small businesses and professional practices and
the appraisal of real estate are both disciplines within the overall
academic study of applied economics. In fact, business appraisal and
real estate appraisal share many conceptual underpinnings. Ultimately, all appraisal analyses represent the practical application of the
theoretical work, both of the classical economists Adam Smith, David
Ricard, and T.R. Malthis, and of the neoclassical economists, such as
J.S. Mill, Leon Walras, Alfred Marshall, Stanley Fischer, and of course
John Maynard Keynes. This is true regardless of the category of asset, property, or business interest to which the appraisal analyses are
applied.

However, the appraisal of small businesses and professional practices differs in significant ways from the appraisal of real estate. The
most important difference relates to the nature of the property subject
to appraisal.

A business is a complex and dynamic entity, involving the interaction of three categories of resources: capital, labor, and coordination.
Real estate, by definition, is a physical property. Real estate, of course,
can be one part of a total business. Within the classical microeconomics
context, real estate is one of the components of the "capital" of a business. Nonetheless, the valuation of a business integrates the total entity,
including (1) all of the assets (i.e., financial assets, real estate, tangible
personal property, and intangible assets—including intangible personal
property and intangible real property interests), (2) all of the liabilities
(i.e., current liabilities and long-term liabilities), and (3) all of the various classes of owners' equity.

Other differences have arisen from the historical development of
these two appraisal disciplines and in the backgrounds and training of
the people who practice them. Some terminology overlaps exist between
these two disciplines, and some terminology contradictions also exist.
Both the terminology similarities and differences often cause confusion
for the readers and users of appraisal reports.

There are also many similarities between business appraisal and
real estate appraisal. The purpose of this chapter is to provide the
reader with some perspective by highlighting some of the differences
and some of the similarities between the two appraisal disciplines.

---

[1] John D. Emory, "Why Business Valuation and Real Estate Appraisal Are Different," *Business Valuation Review*, March 1990, pp. 3-7.

Nature of the Property Rights Subject to Appraisal

Real estate, by definition, is static property. It is immobile and tangible. The leading dictionary in the field of real estate defines real estate as "Physical land and appurtenances attached to the land, e.g., structures."[2]

A business, by contrast, is a complex and dynamic organization of interrelated resources, including (1) capital (which itself encompasses a wide variety of tangible and intangible assets, one of which may be real estate), (2) labor (that is, people at all levels in the organization), and (3) coordination (or the successful management and integration of these resources into one economic unit).

In a real estate appraisal, the property rights may be identified in terms of ownership, legal estates, economic benefits, and financial interests. Real estate ownership, sometimes referred to as "real property," may be held in fee simple or leased fee.[3] When real estate appraisal literature refers to partial or fractional ownership interests, it discusses interests such as (1) vertical interests (such as air rights, surface rights, and subsurface rights), (2) easements, and (3) transferable development rights (TDRs).

By contrast, the appraisal of a business involves an almost limitless amalgam of rights and opportunities, some contractual and others not, including any or all of the bundle of legal rights that may be associated with the ownership or use of one or more parcels of real estate. Furthermore, the valuation of partial or fractional ownership interests in a corporation (or in a partnership) that is dominated by real estate will usually involve the valuation of the business entity's equity on a minority ownership interest basis. The minority ownership equity holder has no direct claim on the overall entity's assets. Therefore, the minority ownership interest value may have little relationship to its pro rata share of the overall entity.

In most cases, especially with respect to properties used by small businesses and professional practices, the real estate is separable from the business. In such cases, as is discussed in Chapters 7 and 22, the real estate and the business may be appraised separately, with the income stream associated with the business charged with an appropriate economic real property rent expense.

Sometimes, the business and the real estate that it occupies are virtually inseparable, as in the case of a special-purpose property, for example. In these cases, the intertwined, or location-dependent, business will have more of the economic characteristics of a business entity than the economic characteristics normally associated with real estate. When the business and real estate are virtually inseparable, valuation ap-

---

[2] *The Dictionary of Real Estate Appraisal*, 3d ed. (Chicago: Appraisal Institute, 1993), p. 292.

[3] For a rigorous discussion of the ownership differences between fee simple and partial interests, the reader is referred to Chapter 7 of *The Appraisal of Real Estate,* 11th ed. (Chicago: Appraisal Institute, 1996), pp. 135-55.

proaches normally associated with business appraisal are likely to lead to a more reliable appraisal result than valuation approaches normally associated with real estate appraisal.

Relative Development of the Discipline

One organization that provides leadership in the discipline of business appraisal is the American Society of Appraisers, a multidisciplinary appraisal society conferring professional certification in several fields, including real estate appraisal. It has nearly a thousand members certified in business appraisal and has several thousand members certified in one or more aspects of real estate appraisal. In addition, in the field of real estate appraisal, the Appraisal Institute offers an extensive array of data sources, publications, continuing education offerings, and programs leading to professional designations—including MAI (Member of the Appraisal Institute).

Real estate appraisal theory and practice have been authoritatively published and taught widely for decades. For example, the first edition of *The Appraisal of Real Estate* was published in 1951. In contrast, much of the organized development of closely held business appraisal theory and practice has taken place since 1980 and has been spearheaded by the Business Valuation Committee of the American Society of Appraisers.

The development of the business appraisal discipline has drawn heavily on the theory and practice of applied microeconomics—and in particular the subdisciplines of corporate finance and security analysis. The use of the theory and knowledge of corporate finance and security analysis is eminently reasonable since the umbrella discipline of microeconomics covers the financing function, the investment function, and the dividend function of all kinds of business entities. This is true, regardless of whether the business entities happen to be corporations, partnerships, or sole proprietorships. The basic thrust of security analysis is the appraisal of an interest in an operating entity. The discipline of security analysis, therefore, is a specialized variation of business appraisal.

The business appraisal discipline combines the relevant elements of these fields of expertise with the requisite understanding of macroeconomics, business management, and accounting. The business appraisal employs a process that incorporates and focuses the considerations necessary to estimate the value of an operating entity within the economic and industry environment prevalent at any given time.

Language Similarities and Differences

A term may have a certain well-accepted definition in the lexicon of finance and security analysis and a different and equally well-accepted definition in the lexicon of real estate appraisal. Similarly, practitioners in business finance and security analysis may label a concept with one name, and practitioners in real estate appraisal may identify the same concept by some other name. The lexicon of business appraisal logically follows the language of finance and security analysis since the common subject matter is operating businesses.

For example, under generally accepted accounting principles (GAAP), the term *net operating income* is typically defined to be income after the deduction of depreciation and amortization, and the literature of finance follows the accounting definition. By contrast, real estate terminology does not include noncash items such as depreciation or amortization in its definition of operating expenses. Therefore, the definition of net operating income as used in real estate terminology is a measure of economic income before deduction of depreciation or amortization expense.[4]

In business finance and security analysis terminology, the term *cash flow* is commonly used to mean net income after all cash expenses, which means after interest costs but before noncash items such as depreciation and amortization.[5] However, in real estate terminology, cash flow is typically defined as net operating income minus annual debt service (with debt service encompassing both principal and interest payments).

It is beyond the scope of this book to provide a comparative lexicon of terminology used in the fields of real estate and business appraisal. Our hope is that the foregoing examples will alert both analysts and appraisal users to the potential for miscommunication. The ambiguities prevalent in current usage are responsible both for miscommunications and for many erroneous appraisal results.

Typically, real estate appraisals estimate the market value of the subject real estate—that is, an estimate of the price of the property if it was sold separately from the existing business. The value of real estate as part of a going-concern business is more accurately defined as *use value*. In fact, *The Appraisal of Real Estate* indicates, "In estimating use value, the appraiser focuses on the value the real estate contributes to the enterprise of which it is part, without regard to the property's highest and best use or the monetary amount that might be realized from its sale."[6]

Accordingly, it is not unusual for the market value of a piece of real estate to be quite different from its use value. An example of this situation would be an old-fashioned factory still in use by the original manufacturing company—to which it has considerable use value—that would require substantial renovation to be productive for another use. In this case, the factory would have a lower market value than it would a use value.

---

[4] *The Dictionary of Real Estate Appraisal*, 3d ed.,p. 243.

[5] For example, the *Dictionary of Banking and Financial Services* defines cash flow as "the reported net income of a corporation, plus amounts charged off for depreciation, depletion, amortization, and extraordinary charges to reserves which are bookkeeping deductions and not actually paid out in cash." (New York: John Wiley & Sons, 1985), p. 121.

[6] *The Appraisal of Real Estate*, 11th ed., p. 24.

Differences in Appraisal Approaches

Real Estate Appraisal Approaches

In the field of real estate appraisal, there are three generally accepted valuation approaches:

1. *Income capitalization approach.* A set of procedures through which an appraiser derives a value indication for an income-producing property by converting its anticipated benefits (cash flows and reversion) into property value. This conversion can be accomplished in two ways. One year's income expectancy can be capitalized at a market-derived capitalization rate or at a capitalization rate that reflects a specified income pattern, return on investment, and change in the value of the investment. Alternatively, the annual cash flows for the holding period and the reversion can be discounted at a specified yield rate.[7]

2. *Sales comparison approach.* A set of procedures in which a value indication is derived by comparing the property being appraised to similar properties that have been sold recently, applying appropriate units of comparison and making adjustments to the sale prices of the comparables based on the elements of comparison. The sales comparison approach may be used to value improved properties, vacant land, or land being considered as though vacant; it is the most common and preferred method of land valuation when comparable sales data are available.[8]

3. *Cost approach.* A set of procedures through which a value indication is derived for the fee simple interest in a property by estimating the current cost to construct a reproduction of, or replacement for, the existing structure; deducting accrued depreciation from the reproduction or replacement cost; and adding the estimated land value plus and entrepreneurial profit. Adjustments may then be made to the indicated fee simple value of the subject property to reflect the value of the property interest being appraised.[9]

Business Appraisal Approaches

In the field of business appraisal, there are also three generally accepted valuation approaches:

1. *Income approach.* A general way of determining a value indication of a business, business ownership interest, or security using one or more methods wherein a value is determined by converting anticipated benefits.[10]

---

[7]*The Dictionary of Real Estate Appraisal*, 3d ed., p. 178.
[8]Ibid., p. 318.
[9]Ibid., p. 81.
[10]*ASA Business Valuation Standards* (Herndon, VA: American Society of Appraisers, 1997), p. p. 20.

2. *Market approach.* A general way of determining a value indication of a business, business ownership interest, or security using one or more methods that compare the subject to similar businesses, business ownership interests, or securities that have been sold.[11]

3. *Asset-based approach.* A general way of determining a value indication of a business's assets and/or equity interest using one or more methods based directly on the value of the assets of the business less liabilities.[12]

Within the income capitalization approach, the real estate appraisal profession recognizes certain analyses that are generally analogous to the income approach used in business appraisal. For example, the method that real estate appraisers call "direct capitalization" is conceptually similar to the income approach method of capitalizing normalized earnings in business valuation. Within the category of direct capitalization, the real estate profession includes gross income multipliers, recognizing—as do business appraisers—that the concept underlying their validity is that a given level of gross income generated by a certain type of property or business should be able to generate a certain level of net income. Also, the method that real estate appraisers call "yield capitalization" is conceptually similar to the income approach method of discounted cash flow analysis in business appraisal.

Income capitalization approach methods are conceptually similar in business appraisal and in real estate appraisal. However, in most cases, estimating an economic income stream for an operating business is much more difficult than estimating an economic income stream for an apartment complex, office building, or some similar income-producing real estate. Furthermore, the risks of an operating business are typically more complex to assess and quantify than are the risks of operating real estate. Therefore, the selection of the appropriate discount rates and/or capitalization rates is often more difficult within the context of business appraisal. To cope with these challenges adequately, the business appraiser needs a broad understanding of relevant economic and industry factors, capital market conditions, business management, and accounting.

As for the sales comparison approach, the real estate appraiser will seek and analyze market-derived data on the sales of comparable properties. Likewise, the business appraiser will seek and analyze market-derived data on transactions involving comparable, or guideline, businesses. The business appraiser will interpret the transactional data for guidance in determining applicable valuation parameters—such as capitalization rates for earnings or cash flow, and gross revenue multipliers —and multiples of the entity's market value to asset value measures, such as book value or adjusted net tangible asset value. One tool the business appraiser has that is not available to the real estate appraiser is an actual public market in the fractional interest securities of many kinds of companies.

---

[11] Ibid., p. 21.

[12] Ibid., p. 19.

The business appraiser's asset-based approach methods have some general similarities to the real estate appraiser's cost approach methods. The asset-based business valuation approach really provides an indication of the value of the business enterprise by developing a fair market value balance sheet. All of the business's assets are identified and their fair market value in use is estimated, and the current value of all of the business liabilities as of the valuation date is estimated. The difference between the fair market value of the assets and the current value of the liabilities is an indication of the business enterprise equity value under this approach.

Similarly, in the various cost approach methods, the real estate appraiser will identify and quantify all of the hard costs, the soft costs, the developer's profit, and the entrepreneurial incentive associated with developing the subject real estate. In a fee simple real estate appraisal, mortgage liabilities are not subtracted by the real estate appraiser.

Exhibit 6-1 presents a brief comparison of the terminology used for the various approaches and methods in the business valuation and real estate appraisal professions.

Exhibit 6–1

COMPARISON BETWEEN BUSINESS VALUATION
AND REAL ESTATE APPRAISAL APPROACHES

BUSINESS VALUATION	REAL ESTATE APPRAISAL

Income Approach
  Discounted economic income
 	
  Capitalization of economic income
	Income Approach
	  Yield capitalization
	
	  Direct capitalization

Market Approach
  Guideline public company method
  (based on analysis of publicly traded
  securities with similar characteristics
  to subject)
 	
  Comparative transaction method
	Sales Comparison Approach
	  No counterpart, because there is no
	  organized market for fractional direct
	  ownership interests in real estate
	
	  Sales comparison method

Asset-Based Approach
  Asset accumulation method
 	
  Excess earnings method
	Cost Approach
	  Cost approach
	
	  No counterpart

Differences in Estimating Capitalization Rates

There is a general tendency for the market for business sale transactions to change more rapidly than the market for real estate sale transactions.[13] One reason for this phenomenon is that a business is typically a collection of tangible and intangible assets, each with its own price volatility and risks of ownership.

Pretax income streams from the direct investment in real estate tend to be capitalized at lower rates of return than comparably defined pretax income streams from investments in non–real estate oriented businesses. One reason for this phenomenon is the income tax advantages of real estate that usually result in a comparably defined pretax income stream translating into a higher after-tax income stream. Another reason is the lower perceived level of risk of ownership in direct real estate investment—compared with the typical investment in a small business.

On a market value basis, real estate investors may accept a lower rate of return from their cash flow stream (i.e., current yield rate) than they would accept from other assets. This is because they expect a rate of return in the form of capital appreciation on the property (i.e., a property value growth rate). This contrasts with a business investment that includes both (1) machinery and equipment that eventually will become worthless through wear and tear and/or obsolescence and (2) intangible assets that will typically become obsolete over time.

Availability of Comparative Transactional Data

Useful comparative transactional data are much harder to obtain for sales of businesses than for sales of real estate. And the problem of obtaining comparative transactional data is greater for small businesses and professional practices than it is for large businesses.

Real estate transactional data are readily available in county courthouses, and the sales of publicly owned companies are reported in great detail. However, there is no requirement for the public reporting of data regarding the sales of closely held companies. As a consequence, unless the business appraiser has access to a private transactional data source, there may be no comparative transactional data readily available for pricing guidance.[14]

---

[13]In the minds of some, this is a controversial statement, because for many types of small businesses, statistical analysis of sale prices over time does not reveal any long-term trend of increasing or decreasing prices. This can be very misleading, however, because long-term trends themselves mask the many sharp upward and downward changes within shorter time periods.

[14]A new database, *Pratt's Stats*, was started in 1997 to address this problem. It is available from Business Valuation Resources, Portland, Oregon, telephone (888) BUS-VALU.

Another problem with the use of comparative sales data for business appraisers is the uniqueness of every business. Each parcel of real estate is also unique, of course. But the large number of variables, many of which are impossible to measure quantitatively, usually makes the matter of comparability a greater problem when using comparative business sale transactional data than when using comparative real estate transactional data.

Summary

As a further reference, the American Society of Appraisers has published a monograph entitled *Business Appraiser or Real Estate Appraiser—Determining Which to Use*.[15] For a further exploration of the similarities and differences between business appraisal and real estate appraisal, this publication is highly recommended.

When performed correctly, real estate appraisal practices and business appraisal practices are totally compatible with each other. In fact, logically, the valuation of income-producing real estate may be considered a special case of business valuation. This is true in the sense that income-producing real estate is logically equivalent to a business that has very limited assets. When each type of appraisal is performed properly, the significant differences in approaches and emphases emerge logically from the basic differences in the nature and scope of the property being appraised.

It is unfortunate, however, that the terminology used by these two appraisal disciplines is not interchangeable. The differences in usage of certain important terms are so ingrained in each discipline that there may be no realistic prospect for developing a set of compatible terms. It is also important to recognize that the complex variables and risk factors involved in business appraisal require a different set of security and financial analysis training and skillls than those required for real estate appraisal.

---

[15]*Business Appraiser or Real Estate Appraiser—Determining Which to Use* (Denver: Business Valuation Committee of the American Society of Appraisers, 1994). Complimentary copies are available from *Business Valuation Review*, P.O. Box 101923, Denver, Colorado 80250, telephone (303) 758-6148.

Part II

Analyzing the Company

Chapter 7

Adjusting the Balance Sheet

*The process of determining the price begins with "normalizing" the com-
pany's financial records. Neither the balance sheets nor the income statements of smaller, privately held companies necessarily bear any relationship to reality.* [1]

The value of most businesses and professional practices generally depends on the assets being transferred and/or how much the business or
practice can earn. The starting place, then, is to adjust the financial
statements so that they reflect *a best estimate of economic reality.*
Making these adjustments is often referred to as "normalizing" the financial statements.

Small business owners have a fair amount of latitude when interpreting and implementing accounting standards. Many small business
owners make their selection among alternative accounting practices depending upon the owner's attitude about paying income taxes.
Therefore, the analyst frequently needs to make a variety of adjustments to historical financial statements, especially for small businesses,
before implementing the selected valuation methods.

Many small businesses and professional practices report financial
results on a cash basis (where revenues are reported when the cash is
received, and expenses are reported when the cash is paid) versus an accrual basis (where revenues are credited to the period in which they are
earned, expenses are recorded when they are actually incurred, and no
consideration is given to when cash is received or disbursed). For companies with financial statements on a cash basis, it is generally necessary for the analyst to convert the reported balance sheets and income
statements to an accrual basis.

This chapter deals with adjusting the balance sheet to get an economically realistic picture of the assets that are part of the business.
The next chapter deals with adjusting the income statement to get a realistic picture of the entity's earnings power. Many of the factors
involved in these adjustments are interrelated: many of them have a
bearing on both the balance sheet and the income statement.

Accounts Receivable

When the assets of a small business or professional practice are sold,
the seller typically collects his accounts receivable. Therefore, accounts
receivable are not part of the transaction. In other cases, a buyer may
agree to collect the accounts on a consignment basis, paying the seller
(for example) 85 percent or so of collections.

If accounts receivable are to be transferred on other than a consignment basis, it should be questioned whether they may be worth more or
less than the net amount at which they are carried on the books.

---

[1]Thomas P. Murphy, "What Price Independence?" *Forbes,* September 27, 1982, pp. 208-9.

Companies using the cash basis of accounting do not normally report accounts receivable. Many professional services firms, for example, do not recognize revenue until payment for services rendered is received. This is a typical procedure used by professional services firms that are paid on a contingency fee basis. The analyst should endeavor to understand this unrecorded "asset."

For companies using accrual accounting, accounts receivable usually are presented on the balance sheet in the following format:

Gross accounts receivable	$100,000
Less: Allowance for doubtful accounts	5,000
Net accounts receivable	$ 95,000

The collectibility of receivables is evaluated based upon many factors. Among the most common factors are:

- Historical experience.
- The state of the economy and its effect on the company's customers.
- The aging of the receivables.
- The financial stability of the customers.
- The company's credit-granting policies.

Some companies are extremely conservative, and they accrue a greater amount for doubtful accounts than will ultimately be necessary to offset uncollectible accounts. At the other extreme, some companies do not accrue any allowance for doubtful accounts. They just write off an account directly against accounts receivable when they determine it to be uncollectible.

An aged accounts receivable schedule (Exhibit 7-1) is the starting place to try to examine whether the net amount shown on the books is really a good estimate of the amount that actually will be collected.

The lower the percentage of receivables in the older categories the better. The percentages can be compared with prior years' results or to industry data in order to better understand collectibility.

Some buyers of businesses value accounts receivable by some arbitrary rule of thumb. For example, they may accept current accounts at face value, discount those over 30 days by 10 percent, those over 60 days by 20 percent, those over 90 days by 30 percent, and allow little or nothing for accounts over 120 days. It is generally possible, however, to get a much more accurate estimate of net collectibility by analyzing each account, looking at the past payment history of any accounts that are sizable or that are more than 30 or 60 days old, and taking into consideration the typical collection period for businesses in the particular industry. (Sources for average collection periods for different types of businesses are discussed in Chapter 9.)

A buyer may be willing to accept most of the accounts receivable, either at face value or at some discount, but will leave some for the seller to try to collect. In other cases, a buyer may accept accounts receivable on a consignment basis, reserving some portion to be paid to the seller when, and if, the accounts are collected.

Exhibit 7–1

PATRICK'S MACHINERY & EQUIPMENT, INC.
AGED ACCOUNTS RECEIVABLE
AS OF DECEMBER 31, 1997

Account Name	Total $	Current $	30-60 Days $	60-90 Days $	90-120 Days $	Over 120 Days $
Ace Widget Co.	1,000	1,000				
A-1 Equipment	20,000					20,000
Best Rentals	5,000				5,000	
Cascade Construction	500			500		
Davidson Machine	6,000			6,000		
E & F Transportation	70,000	35,000	35,000			
Frank Industries	2,000	2,000				
General Equipment	3,000					3,000
Holt Industries	1,500				1,500	
I.K. Industries	12,000					12,000
Jay Manufacturing	500			500		
K Construction	25,000	25,000				
Long's Machinery	6,500				6,500	
Mountain Resources	30,000	15,000	15,000			
Nelson Excavating	2,000					2,000
Power Enterprises	8,000					8,000
Rolling Transportation	25,000	20,000	5,000			
Sam's Equipment	40,000	12,000	20,000	8,000		
T.X. Resources	2,000				2,000	
Vic's Manufacturing	10,000	10,000				
Western Industries	30,000					30,000
TOTAL	300,000	120,000	75,000	15,000	15,000	75,000
	100.0%	40.0%	25.0%	5.0%	5.0%	25.0%

Inventory

Inventory is typically accounted for in three categories: raw material, work in process, and finished goods.

Raw material is generally valued by multiplying the quantity of each useable item on hand by the lower of either the actual cost of the item or by its market value, depending on prevailing accounting policy. Work-in-process value is determined by either adding the costs incurred to bring the item from raw material to its current condition or by subtracting from its finished goods price the costs to be incurred to complete the item. For transactional and/or other valuation purposes, finished goods may be valued at the selling price less the total costs of material, labor, and overhead required to prepare the item for sale (e.g., selling cost, handling, shipping).

Ideally, the inventory account would be estimated by taking a physical inventory count and extending it at current costs. If the existing inventory account must be adjusted by the appraiser (after relying on the physical inventory conducted by others and on the books and records), the two main questions to answer involve the basic accounting policy (generally either FIFO of LIFO) and the write-off and/or write-down policy.

FIFO versus LIFO

FIFO, or *first-in, first-out,* means that the first unit of an inventory item purchased is the first unit considered sold for accounting purposes. LIFO, or *last-in, first-out,* means that the unit of an inventory item purchased last is the first unit considered sold for accounting purposes. The difference between FIFO and LIFO accounting appears in the ending inventory on the balance sheet; this affects the cost of goods sold and thus the earnings on the income statements.

To the extent that prices go up, LIFO results in lower figures for ending inventory, a higher cost of goods sold, and therefore lower earnings than would result with FIFO. Since LIFO accounting is acceptable for federal income tax purposes, there has been a widespread tendency for companies to adopt LIFO rather than FIFO inventory accounting in times of inflation.

Let's consider the simple example of a company that started its accounting period with 30 widgets, purchased for $10 each, then purchased 60 more widgets for $15 each during the accounting period, and ended the period with an inventory of 40 widgets. Using FIFO versus LIFO accounting, let's compute the comparative inventory and cost of goods sold as follows:

	FIFO		LIFO	
Beginning Inventory	30 units @ $10 =	$300	30 units @ $10 =	$300
Purchases	60 units @ $15 =	900	60 units @ $15 =	900
Goods available for sale		$1,200		$1,200
Ending inventory	40 units @ $15 =	$600	30 units @ $10 =	$300
			10 units @ $15 =	150
		$600		$450
Cost of goods sold		$600		$750

In other words, under the LIFO method, the company's accounting assumes that the original units in the inventory are the ones still there. In the case above, under LIFO accounting, the ending inventory would be shown on the balance sheet at $450. Under FIFO accounting, the same ending inventory would be shown on the balance sheet at $600.

Since the FIFO method results in presenting more current value on the balance sheet, that method comes closer to presenting the inventory at an economically realistic current value. Therefore, if the subject company uses LIFO, analysts will often adjust the balance sheet to a FIFO basis. If the company reporting on LIFO has audited statements, the footnotes usually provide the information necessary to adjust the inventory values from LIFO to FIFO. The simple adjustment procedure is to add the balance shown as LIFO reserve to the amount of the inventory account presented on the balance sheet. If the statements of a company reporting on LIFO are not audited, the company's accountant should be able to provide the analyst with the necessary information in order to adjust to a FIFO basis.

Some analysts further reduce this FIFO inventory valuation by the amount of the income tax liability that would result from this LIFO to FIFO inventory revaluation. This income tax adjustment is further discussed in the upcoming section, Income Tax Effect.

Some companies account for inventory on some type of an average cost basis, but that practice is so uncommon that it does not warrant a discussion in this book.

Write-Down and Write-Off Policies

Regardless of whether the FIFO, LIFO, or average-cost inventory method is used, most companies adhere to the "lower-of-cost-or-market" inventory accounting principle. This principle holds that the carrying value should be reduced if the market value is less than the original cost. Market value for this purpose is defined as "current replacement cost except that market shall not be higher than net realizable value, nor should it be lower than net realizable value reduced by the normal profit margin."[2]

Implementation of the lower-of-cost-or-market inventory accounting principle varies from company to company. One company may have a stockroom full of obsolete inventory, while another company may have an aggressive program of automatic write-downs and write-offs of inventory (perhaps on the basis of the number of months it has been in stock). Appropriate adjustments to inventory values may be necessary when a company goes to one extreme or the other in making, or not making, adjustments to inventory values in its implementation of the lower-of-cost-or-market principle. The more extreme the inventory accounting policies, the less the accounting records can be relied on to assist in obtaining an economically realistic inventory value.

Income Tax Effect

If the analyst is valuing a business as a going concern for a transaction involving 100 percent of the equity, he or she should recognize that the cost basis of the inventory for income tax purposes will still be its book value, not its adjusted current market value. Therefore, any adjustment made to the value of inventory should net out the appropriate income tax effect.

For example, if we revalue inventory upward from a book value of $100,000 to an adjusted current market value of $150,000, the $50,000 gain will be taxed to the business at the company's ordinary income tax rate when the inventory is sold. If the company is in the 30 percent tax

---

[2]Leopold A. Bernstein, *Financial Statement Analysis: Theory, Application, and Interpretation,* 5th ed. (Burr Ridge, IL: Richard D. Irwin, 1993).

bracket, the markup of $50,000 in the inventory account should be net of, or offset by, the $15,000 in income taxes that will eventually come out of the $50,000 markup. Therefore, the net markup for the purpose of valuing the company stock should be only $35,000.

If we are valuing a business as a going concern in a transaction involving the purchase of all of the company's assets, no income tax adjustment to the purchase price is required. This is because the buyer will have the benefit of the stepped-up basis in the acquired assets. It will, however, impact the net after-tax proceeds ultimately realized by the business seller.

Prepaid Expenses

The components of the prepaid expense account presented on the accrual-based balance sheet should be examined. The most common components are rent, insurance, and office supplies. If the value of these items is fairly presented and if they will be necessary for the going-concern business, no adjustment may be necessary. However, if they are not necessary, the prepaid expense account should be adjusted accordingly. An example of such an item would be $10,000 worth of stationery and promotional materials that the company buyer will not use because the buyer plans to change the name of the company. Some valuable prepaid expenses may also not show up on the balance sheet because they were charged directly to expense when they were paid; it may be appropriate to make an adjustment for these items.

Other Current Assets

If other current assets are involved in the valuation, such as marketable securities or short-term notes or contracts receivable, they should be adjusted to market values. As with the inventory account adjustment, if equity in a business is being valued, any adjustment to current asset account values should net out the related income tax effect; that is, the income tax that will be incurred when the asset is sold should be recognized in the adjustment.

Real Estate

In valuing most small businesses and professional practices, it is often better to deal with real estate separately from the value of the business or practice. For one thing, many sellers who own the premises being occupied by the business are willing to sell the business or professional practice with or without the real estate. This means that the business has to be valued separately. Since many small businesses and professional practices do not own the real estate they occupy, balance sheet and income statement data usually can best be compared from one entity to another and to industry averages without real estate on the balance sheet. Also, appraisal approaches appropriate for the real estate may be different from those appropriate for the operating entity. Finally, environmental concerns and regulations have affected the transferability of real estate, which can complicate the sale of the business.

Sometimes, appraising the real estate and appraising the business entity separately may lead to more meaningful conclusions than appraising only one or the other.

If the real estate is to be removed from the balance sheet, items related to real estate must also be removed from the income statement and a reasonable rent should be subtracted in the operating expenses. Examples of such items that may be included on the income statement would be interest, property taxes, and insurance related to the property ownership. In some cases, there could also be rental income that may require an adjustment.

If real estate is to be left on the balance sheet, it may be adjusted to fair market value if a current appraisal is available. If the appraisal available is outdated, or if the real estate changed hands a few years ago, the real estate value should be updated.

The Real Estate Appraisal Process

Just as businesses can be valued using several approaches, real estate is appraised by considering the three traditional approaches to asset appraisal: the sales comparison approach, the income capitalization approach, and the cost approach.

Sales Comparison Approach.   The sales comparison approach provides a systematic framework for estimating the value of the subject property based on an analysis and correlation of actual transaction prices reflecting the purchase and sale of properties comparable to the subject property. This approach requires the comparison and correlation of the subject property to comparable properties that have been listed for sale or actually sold in the appropriate secondary market. Considerations such as the location of the comparable properties, the time of the sale, physical characteristics, and special financing or other terms and conditions of the sale are discretely analyzed for each comparable property. These data are appropriately adjusted in the correlation of data used to indicate the current value of the subject property.

Income Capitalization Approach.   The income capitalization approach provides a systematic framework for estimating the value of the subject property based on the capitalization or present value determination of the prospective economic income to be derived from property ownership. In the income capitalization approach, economic income can be defined several ways, including the following:

- Net income.
- Net operating income.
- Gross or net rental income.
- Gross cash flow.
- Net cash flow.

The income capitalization procedure can also be accomplished in several ways, including the following:

- Capitalizing the current year's income.
- Capitalizing a normalized period's income.
- Projecting future income over a discrete time period.
- Determining a present value.

Quantifying the appropriate capitalization rate or discount rate is an essential element of the income capitalization approach to real estate appraisal. The appropriate capitalization rate or discount rate should reflect a fair return on stakeholders' invested capital and should consider the opportunity cost of capital, the time value of money, the term of the investment, and the risk of the investment.

Cost Approach. The cost approach provides a systematic framework for estimating the value of the subject property based on the principle of substitution. A prudent investor would pay no more for a property than the amount necessary to replace the asset with a comparable substitute. Replacement cost new (cost of a new asset with equal utility) typically establishes the maximum amount that a prudent investor would pay for an property.

To the extent that the subject property has less utility than an ideal replacement, the value of the subject property must be adjusted for this measurable decrease in utility. The property's replacement cost new is then adjusted for losses in value due to physical deterioration, functional obsolescence, technological obsolescence (a specific form of functional obsolescence), and external obsolescence (one component of which is economic obsolescence).

Due to budget constraints and other factors, business appraisers often rely on the cost approach to estimate the fair market value of the business operating assets.

Under the cost approach, the typical formula for estimating an asset's fair market value is as follows: *Reproduction cost new less incurable functional and technological obsolescence equals replacement cost new. Replacement cost new, less physical deterioration, less external obsolescence, and less curable functional and technological obsolescence equals fair market value.*

The proper sequencing of the appropriate decrease in asset value due to deterioration, depreciation, and obsolescence is important to the correct application of the cost approach. The previously indicated sequence of cost and obsolescence analyses is appropriate for estimating the fair market value of assets for ad valorem taxation and other purposes. Each of the previously indicated terms will be defined briefly in the following paragraphs.

Reproduction Cost. Reproduction cost is the cost to construct, at current prices, an exact duplicate or replica of the subject asset. This duplicate would be created using the same materials, construction standards, design, layout, and quality of workmanship that were used to create the original asset. Therefore, an asset's reproduction cost will encompass all of the deficiencies, enhancements, and obsolescence that exist in the subject asset. Many of these inadequacies, enhancements, and so on inherent in the subject asset are incurable.

An asset's deficiencies are considered curable when the prospective economic benefit of enhancing or modifying the asset exceeds the current cost—in terms of material, labor, and time—to change the asset. An asset's deficiencies are considered incurable when the current costs of enhancing or modifying the asset—in terms of material, labor, and time —exceed the expected future economic benefits

Replacement Cost. The replacement cost of a subject asset is the cost to create, at current prices, an asset having equal utility to the asset being appraised. The replacement asset, however, would be created with modern materials, current construction standards, state-of-the-art design and layout, and the highest available quality of workmanship.

The difference between an asset's reproduction cost and its replacement cost is, typically, the quantification of incurable functional and technological obsolescence. That is, in an ideal replacement asset, all elements of incurable functional and technological obsolescence have been removed or "reengineered" from the subject asset.

An asset's replacement cost is sometimes quantified using a "green field" approach. That is, the replacement cost of a subject asset or property is the cost to build a redesigned and reengineered ideal replacement from scratch—on a virgin "green field."

Physical Deterioration. Physical deterioration is the reduction in the value of an asset due to physical wear and tear and the impact of continued use and the elements of nature on the subject asset. Physical deterioration affects the value of an asset in two ways. First, an asset experiencing physical deterioration looks old and used. This appearance will impact the value of that asset in its secondary market. Second, continued use or the effect of natural elements on an asset will ultimately reduce its remaining useful life and its anticipated remaining utility. In effect, the asset will be partially "used up." Obviously, this also affects the value of the asset in its secondary market.

Functional Obsolescence. Functional obsolescence is the reduction in the value of an asset due to its inability to perform the function (or yield the periodic utility) for which it was originally designed. Due to structural deficiencies (in the case of real estate) or due to mechanical deficiencies (in the case of tangible personal property), the subject asset can no longer do the job for which it was designed (i.e., perform at design specifications) at the same cost as available replacement assets. Unlike elements of physical deterioration, elements of functional obsolescence may not be visually evident.

An asset manifesting functional obsolescence may not be physically damaged in any way. In fact, the asset may be brand new. However, due to faulty construction or to changes in its use or mechanism, the asset can no longer perform (in terms of a standardized measure of utility produced) as designed. Like physical deterioration, however, elements of functional obsolescence are physically inherent in the subject asset.

Technological Obsolescence. Technological obsolescence is a decrease in the value of the subject asset due to improvements in technology that make the subject asset less than the ideal replacement for itself. Technological obsolescence occurs when, due to improvements in design or engineering technology, a new replacement asset will produce a greater standardized measure of utility production than the subject asset.

For example, due to technological improvements in construction engineering, a replacement building may perform the same function as the subject building, but with 20 percent less square footage. Or due to enhancement in design technology, a replacement machine may produce its output better, cheaper, or faster than the subject machine.

With respect to technological obsolescence and unlike physical deterioration, the subject asset need not be physically damaged at all. Unlike functional obsolescence, the subject asset can be performing exactly to design specification. As a result of technological improvements, however, the design specifications of a replacement asset have materially improved compared with those of the subject asset. Accordingly, the subject asset will have a lower value in its secondary market compared with that of a replacement asset that meets the technologically enhanced specifications.

External Obsolescence. External obsolescence (Economic obsolescence) is a reduction in the value of real property or tangible personal property due to the impact of events or conditions that are external to, and not controlled by, the physical nature or the structural or mechanical operation of the asset. The impact of external obsolescence is typically beyond the control of the subject asset's owner. For that reason, economic obsolescence is typically considered incurable.

Approximations of Real Estate Values

Rather than adopt this rigorous, three-approach process, sometimes a friendly local real estate broker can help. Or an earlier real estate appraisal may be adjusted to an estimate of current market value by using an index of real estate values for the subject property type and locale.

If no better approximation of current market value is available, a tax-assessed value might be helpful. However, even in jurisdictions where tax-assessed values purportedly represent market value, they frequently do not. If there is a way of knowing the typical relationship between tax-assessed values and market values in a particular jurisdiction, the tax-assessed values can be adjusted accordingly.

Incidentally, since Proposition 13, tax-assessed values are often worthless as indicators of market value in California; tax-assessed values there are limited by a formula ceiling, unless the property changes hands.

Income Tax Effect

If equity is being valued, this question arises: Should any tax effects of adjusting real estate values be taken into consideration on the balance sheet? If a sale of the real estate is pending or imminent, income tax effects certainly should be netted out of the real estate value adjustment. (Alternatively, the income tax effects could be recognized by a Deferred Taxes Payable account in the liability section of the balance sheet.)

If a buyer would not be expected to sell the real estate (a premise often used in appraisals for divorce purposes in some jurisdictions, for example), it is debatable whether implied income taxes on the markup should be recognized on the adjusted balance sheet. When recognizing the income tax effect, one method is to account for the capital gains taxes implied in the markup with a deferred tax account. Alternatively, they could be footnoted as a contingent liability.

Tangible Personal Property

Generally speaking, to adjust a balance sheet on a going-concern basis, the furniture, fixtures, and equipment should be adjusted to their current market values. Different analysts, however, have different ideas of what that means for this category of assets. The replacement cost for most used equipment is twice, or several times, as much as could be realized in a liquidation sale if the subject business operation were closed.

Depreciated Replacement Cost

One of the common approaches to valuing the furniture, fixtures, and equipment for an adjusted balance sheet on a going-concern basis is *depreciated replacement cost*. In simple terms, depreciated replacement cost means the current cost to replace the item new, less an allowance for the length of time it has been in service. For example, if a new comparably productive machine would cost $1,000 and could be expected to have a useful economic life of 10 years (with no salvage value) and the present machine had been in use for 4 years and could be expected to last 6 more years, the appraiser could estimate the depreciated replacement cost at $600 (6/10 x $1,000 = $600).

This calculation assumes that the subject equipment has been maintained in reasonably good operating order. If the condition of the equipment is exceptionally good or bad, an upward or downward adjustment would be in order. If the subject equipment suffers from functional obsolescence, a downward adjustment should be made to arrive at a proper value based on the depreciated replacement cost approach. For example, if the subject machine can do the same job as the new replacement machine, but at a higher operating cost (perhaps because of a difference in energy efficiency, for example) a downward adjustment in value should be made to recognize this factor.

The depreciated replacement cost approach is commonly used by industrial equipment appraisers when analyzing asset values.

Liquidation Value

Orderly disposition value is the net amount that could be expected to be received if the assets were sold off in an orderly manner. Estimates of orderly disposition value can be obtained from equipment appraisers or wholesale dealers. Although a creditor might focus heavily on the balance sheet adjusted to liquidation value, that is not normally the primary focus for an adjusted balance sheet on a going-concern basis.

Forced liquidation value is the net amount that could be expected to be received if the assets were sold off piecemeal immediately. Some creditors rely on this value for tangible personal property as a basis for collateral. Estimates of forced liquidation value can be obtained from equipment appraisers or auctioneers.

It should be kept in mind, however, that leasehold improvements usually are worthless in a liquidation sale. Also, most furniture, fixtures, and equipment bring prices in a liquidation sale that are heavily discounted even from used replacement cost.

Approximations of Personal Property Values

In the majority of cases, net book value (cost less depreciation) is a lower limit of reasonable value for equipment on a going-concern basis. This is because most privately held companies write off depreciation at least as fast as the useful economic life of the equipment is used up. For some types of equipment, a reasonable approximation of current value would simply be the undepreciated original cost. The reasoning is that inflation in the cost of new equipment has proceeded at a pace at least fast enough to offset any physical deterioration and/or obsolescence in well-maintained used equipment. That was generally true for several years for most manufacturing equipment. On the other hand, for equipment such as computers, obsolescence rapidly takes its toll.

With a basic knowledge of the condition of the equipment and the general status of the market for equipment in the particular industry, a reasonable adjustment often can be made by adding back some portion of the depreciation account. Another possibility is to use personal property depreciation schedules available from most county assessors' offices. Such schedules give valuation factors as a percentage of cost for each of most major categories of equipment, depending on the date the equipment was placed in service.

Intangible Assets

At this stage of the valuation process, balance sheet adjustments usually are limited to those necessary to arrive at an adjusted net tangible asset value. If the value of the business based on earning capacity is greater than the return required on net tangible asset value, some intangible value is indicated. Frequently, this intangible value is simply called goodwill. However, that may be an improper characterization of the intangible value; and for other reasons, it may be worthwhile to quantify the amount of value attributable to specific intangible assets such as patents, copyrights, customer lists, and many other possibilities. This concept is discussed more fully in Chapter 42.

Liabilities

If equity is being valued or if liabilities are to be assumed in conjunction with an asset sale, then the liability side of the balance sheet also should be examined for possible adjustments. Most liabilities, of course, would be left on an adjusted balance sheet at their face value. An adjustment can be made on an interest-bearing obligation with an interest rate significantly different from current market rates, or on a deferred taxes account, for example.

Interest-Bearing Debt

It is common to read or hear the phrase "assume favorable financing" to make a business more attractive to a potential buyer. Most analysts, however, fail to resolve this important question: In valuing the business in question, how much value is attributable to the favorable financing?

For example, suppose the buyer assumes a mortgage or bond or note with a remaining principal balance of $500,000, payable in 84 equal monthly installments (i.e., seven years), including interest at 8 percent, when the current market rate for comparable debt financing is 14 percent. The payments on the obligation would be $7,793.11 per month. The present value of the mortgage can be computed as follows:

$$PV = \sum_{i=1}^{84} \frac{\$7,793.11}{(1.011667)^i} = \$415,854$$

In other words, the $500,000 face value of the obligation should be adjusted to a present value of $415,854 for the adjusted balance sheet under current economic conditions.

Suppose an adjusted gross asset value is $700,000. Without adjusting the liability, the face amount of $500,000 would be deducted, resulting in an adjusted net asset value of $200,000. Applying the appropriate adjustment to the liability results in a deduction of only about $416,000, leaving an adjusted net asset value of $284,000. In other words, in this example, the ability to use favorable financing to control $700,000 worth of assets makes the business worth $84,000 more than it would if such financing were not available as part of the package.

Deferred Taxes

An item called *deferred taxes* sometimes appears on the balance sheet. This account arises when income taxes have been incurred but they are not yet due to be paid. The analyst should inquire about the likely timing of such payments, or even whether they will have to be paid at all. It frequently is appropriate to reduce the deferred taxes item, or possibly eliminate it entirely, in constructing the adjusted balance sheet from an appraisal viewpoint. (As noted earlier, it is sometimes also appropriate to bring a deferred tax item onto the balance sheet to partly offset certain asset valuation write-ups.)

Contingent or Off-Balance-Sheet Assets and Liabilities

Many items that do not actually appear on the balance sheet should be considered in the course of the balance sheet analysis. These are items for which it has not been established for certain whether or not a payment (complete or partial) actually will be made or received. The factors giving rise to such off-balance-sheet items may already be in place (such as a lawsuit filed, accrued vacation, or pension liabilities), or the item may be dependent on some future event (such as a change in taxation or some aspect of the regulatory environment). Whether or not such items warrant specific attention depends on their potential magnitude and the probability of their actually resulting in future payments or receipts.

In general, one of the reasons that many buyers prefer an asset purchase rather than a stock purchase is to avoid the obligation for any possible contingent liabilities of the selling company. However, under various states' bulk sales laws, this type of contingent liability is likely to be transferred to a new owner even through an asset transaction rather than a stock transaction. If that is a prospect, a buyer should seek an attorney's advice as to what his or her position will be on this matter.

Sometimes, when constructing the adjusted balance sheet, one or more of these contingencies should be added to the line items in the statements at their probable value (e.g., estimated amount after adjusting for taxes × probability of payment × time value factor). More often, because of their uncertain nature, it would be appropriate to call attention to these items in the analysis. The following are a few fairly common examples of off-balance-sheet liabilities and assets.

Product Liability

If a company manufactures or sells widgets, for example, it may have an obligation for repairs, replacements, or other restitution for defective widgets, through express warranty or otherwise. Many small manufacturing companies just charge the expense of such claims against earnings, as they occur. If a company is exposed but does not have a reserve or liability account on its balance sheet to cover it, a good procedure is to estimate the probable cost of such future claims, perhaps from the history of such claims, and establish a liability account on the balance sheet to recognize these obligations.

Lawsuits

Actual or potential lawsuits of all kinds are an area far too broad to treat in any detail; if such possibilities exist, they should be investigated as thoroughly as possible. It is also possible, of course, that the company could have a suit pending against someone else, which could be resolved with a great benefit to the company (i.e., a contingent asset).

Regulatory Compliance

In these days of extensive bureaucratic regulation, often administered with utter disregard for economic consequences to the individual business, community, or nation, the specter of the potential cost of complying with government mandates cannot be ignored.

Some of the most common sources of such mandatory expenditures are asbestos and real estate environmental cleanup, which may not be indemnified away; pollution control requirements; and Occupational Safety and Health Administration (OSHA) requirements. A potential buyer should inquire into possible costs of compliance and should recognize a liability for incurring such costs.

A potential cost could be uncertain, perhaps pending the outcome of an administrative or legal proceeding that may require considerable time to resolve. In these circumstances, the business value is analyzed assuming no compliance problems. Then a transaction could be structured wherein a buyer might establish an escrow account with part of the purchase price reserved for the compliance cost, with the seller entitled to any residual in the reserve not actually required to meet the final compliance mandate.

Past Service Liability

There may be obligations to employees for past services, perhaps in the form of unfunded pension liabilities, accrued vacations, or arrangements with individual employees. These obligations should be quantified, if possible, and presented as a liability on the balance sheet.

Employment Agreements

Some companies may have employment agreements or consulting agreements under which regular payments are made to former owners or employees. When that is the case, from an appraisal viewpoint, unless services of commensurate value are received, the obligations under such agreements should be viewed as liabilities. As will be discussed in Chapter 8, the income statement may need to be adjusted for this non-recurring expense item.

Unrecorded Obligations

The analyst should investigate whether there may be any outstanding obligations for goods or services that are not recorded on the books. In one case, for example, a balance sheet on which a sale of a company was based showed accounts receivable for sales that had been made but did not accrue the liability for the salespeople's commissions that would have to be paid out of the accounts receivable when collected.

Liens

If the company has any of its assets pledged, either to secure its own indebtedness or because it is contingently liable for someone else's indebtedness, such facts should be noted.

Examples of Adjusted Balance Sheets

The following are hypothetical examples of the procedures discussed in this chapter. These examples assume that the respective companies have done their accounting on an accrual basis. It is noteworthy that these adjusted balance sheets do not conclude business values because intangible asset values have not yet been incorporated into the analysis.

Sole Proprietorship Example

Ashley was a good merchandiser and a shrewd businesswoman. When she decided to retire, the apparel shop she had bought a few years before was well maintained and operating profitably. Exhibit 7-2 is the adjusted balance sheet her appraiser prepared in connection with selling her business.

Corporation Example

Patrick's Machinery & Equipment, Inc., distributes and services industrial machinery and equipment. Patrick's is well known for its top-notch mechanics and rebuilding expertise. Patrick wants to sell the business and move to Hawaii for rest and relaxation. The company felt the brunt of the recession for a couple of years, but it returned to profitability in 1997. Exhibit 7-3 is the adjusted balance sheet the company's appraiser prepared in connection with the sale of the business.

Exhibit 7–2

ASHLEY'S APPAREL STORE
ADJUSTED BALANCE SHEET
AS OF DECEMBER 31, 1997

	Balance Sheet as Reported		Adjustments	Balance Sheet as Adjusted	
	$	%	$	$	%
ASSETS					
Current assets:					
Cash	5,000	2.2	(5,000) a	0	0.0
Accounts receivable	30,000	13.2	(3,000) b	27,000	9.6
Inventory	180,000	78.9	40,000 c	220,000	78.6
Prepaid expense	3,000	1.3		3,000	1.1
Total current assets	218,000	95.6		250,000	89.3
Fixed assets:					
Fixtures & equipment	50,000	21.9			
Less: Depreciation	(40,000)	(17.5)			
	10,000	4.4	20,000 d	30,000	10.7
TOTAL ASSETS	228,000	100.0		280,000	100.0
LIABILITIES & OWNER'S EQUITY					
Current liabilities:					
Accounts payable	110,000	48.2	(110,000) e	0	0.0
Notes payable	1,000	0.4	(1,000) e	0	0.0
Accrued payroll	2,000	0.9	(2,000) e	0	0.0
Total current liabilities	113,000	49.5		0	0.0
Long-term debt:					
Contract payable	100,000	43.9	(10,984) f	89,016	31.8
Total liabilities	213,000	93.4		89,016	31.8
Owner's equity	15,000	6.6	175,984 g	190,984	68.2
TOTAL LIABILITIES & EQUITY	228,000	100.0		280,000	100.0

a Cash to be retained by seller.

b It is easier for an ongoing operator to collect accounts receivable--accounts receivable discounted 10% for doubtful accounts and time to collect.

c Aggressive policy in inventory markdowns has been followed. This adjustment results from taking a physical inventory, extending at probable selling prices, and allowing a 45% gross margin, the store's average historical gross margin.

d Adjustment to furniture and fixtures based on talks with dealers--approximate used replacement cost.

e Will pay out of proceeds of sale.

f Buyer will assume remaining balance of 7% note from Ashley's purchase of store--60 payments of $1,980.12, discounted at 12% (See Chapter 27).

g The net amount of adjustments a through f.

Exhibit 7–3

PATRICK'S MACHINERY & EQUIPMENT, INC.
ADJUSTED BALANCE SHEET
AS OF DECEMBER 31, 1997

	Balance Sheet as Reported		Adjustments	Balance Sheet as Adjusted	
	$	%	$	$	%
ASSETS					
Current assets:					
Cash & equivalents	65,000	7.2		65,000	6.0
Accounts receivable	300,000	33.3	(70,000) a	230,000	21.3
Inventory	320,000	35.6	105,000 b	425,000	39.5
Prepaid expense	15,000	1.7		15,000	1.4
Marketable securities	10,000	1.1	7,800 c	17,800	1.7
Other	5,000	0.6		5,000	0.5
Total current assets	715,000	79.5	42,800	757,800	70.4
Furniture, fixtures & equipment:					
Equipment	110,000	12.2			
Furnishings	40,000	4.4			
Vehicles	200,000	22.2			
	350,000	38.8			
Less: Accumulated depreciation	(225,000)	(25.0)			
Net furniture, fixtures & equipment	125,000	13.8	125,000 d	250,000	23.2
Leasehold interest	0	0.0	8,200 e	8,200	0.8
Other assets	60,000	6.7		60,000	5.6
TOTAL ASSETS	900,000	100.0	176,000	1,076,000	100.0
LIABILITIES & STOCKHOLDER'S EQUITY					
Current liabilities:					
Notes payable	50,000	5.7		50,000	4.6
Current maturity long-term debt	40,000	4.4		40,000	3.7
Accounts & notes payable--trade	120,000	13.3		120,000	11.2
Accrued expenses	40,000	4.4		40,000	3.7
Other	30,000	3.3		30,000	2.8
Total current liabilities	280,000	31.1		280,000	26.0
Long-term debt	100,000	11.1	(4,855) f	95,145	8.8
Other liabilities	20,000	2.2		20,000	1.9
Contingent liabilities	0	0.0	50,000 g	50,000	4.6
Total liabilities	400,000	44.4	45,145	445,145	41.4
Stockholder's equity:					
Common stock	25,000	2.8			
Paid-in capital	25,000	2.8			
Retained earnings	525,000	58.3			
	575,000	63.9			
Less: Treasury stock	(75,000)	(8.3)			
Total stockholder's equity	500,000	55.6	130,855 h	630,855	58.6
TOTAL LIABILITIES & STOCKHOLDER'S EQUITY	900,000	100.0	176,000	1,076,000	100.0

Note: Percentages may not total due to rounding.

Exhibit 7–3 (concluded)

a   The following accounts are believed to be uncollectible (see Exhibit 7-1).
    A-1 Equipment $ 20,000
    I.K. Industries   12,000
    Power Enterprises   8,000
    Western Industries   30,000
                                           $ 70,000

b   Inventory needs to be adjusted to a FIFO basis as follows:
    LIFO Reserve $ 110,000

    In addition, the inventory needs to be reduced by $5,000 for obsolete inventory.

c   200 shares of IBM common stock   200
    (closing price 12/31/97) $ 89
                                           $ 17,800

d   Adjustment to furniture, fixtures, and equipment based on talks with dealers--approximate cost to replace
    used, including delivery.

e   Rent paid by Patrick's is approximately $200 per month below fair market rent. Discount this amount at
    Patrick's weighted cost of capital, computed as follows:

    Balance sheet composition: 2/3 debt @ 7.5% after-tax cost of debt   =   5%
                                        1/3 equity @ 27% cost of equity   =   9%
                                        Weighted average cost of capital   16%

    The lease has a five-year term. The present value of $200 per month discounted for 60 months at 16% annually is
    approximately $8,200.

f $50,000 of the long-term debt is at current market interest rates. However, $50,000 is payable in 36 equal
    monthly installments (3 years), including interest at 6%, resulting in monthly payments of $1,521.10. The
    current market rate for comparable debt financing is 13%. The present value of favorable financing is
    $45,144.60, or approximately $45,145, thus reducing the market value of the liability by approximately $4,855.

g   Patrick's is currently involved in a lawsuit for which the probable judgment against the company will amount
    to $50,000.

h   The net amount of adjustments a through g.

Summary

This chapter discussed the most common asset and liability account adjustments that business appraisers frequently make to estimate the balance sheet accounts at current value. This process of adjusting balance sheet asset and liability accounts helps to provide a better perspective on the values of assets employed in the business. Many of the balance sheet adjustments imply related income statement adjustments. Exhibit 7-4 provides a quick summary of the steps in adjusting the balance sheet. The next chapter discusses adjustments to the income statements.

Exhibit 7–4

SUMMARY OF STEPS IN
ADJUSTING THE BALANCE SHEET

Step 1   Obtain a copy of the subject company's balance sheet as of or just before the valuation date.

Step 2   Adjust each of the company's assets from their stated book value to reflect appraised fair market values. Although not considered to be comprehensive, a list of potential adjustments to the company's assets as stated on the balance sheet includes the following:

- Adjust the cash and cash equivalents of the company to that required for normalized operations of the firm, eliminating any nonoperating cash and cash equivalents or including an adjustment for any operating cash deficiency.
- Adjust the accounts receivable as shown on the balance sheet to eliminate any accounts considered uncollectible.
- Review the inventory as stated on the company's balance sheet. Ideally, adjust the inventory through a physical count and extend the inventory at current costs while eliminating any obsolete inventory. Otherwise, review the company's inventory accounting policy and write-off or write-down policy.
- Adjust components of the prepaid expense account if these items will not be necessary for the ongoing operations of the company.
- Adjust other assets as listed on the balance sheet to reflect fair market values.
- Adjust real estate to appraised fair market value using a current appraisal.
- Adjust the furniture, fixtures, and equipment to their market values.
- Adjust any identifiable intangible assets to their appraised values.
- If appropriate, make any adjustments necessary to income taxes to reflect the adjustments made to the assets as stated on the balance sheet.

Step 3   Adjust each of the company's liabilities from their stated book value to reflect appraised fair market values. Although not considered to be comprehensive, a list of potential adjustments to the company's liabilities includes the following:

- Adjust any interest-bearing debt with favorable financing to reflect fair market value at current interest rates.
- Adjust the deferred taxes account to accurately reflect the likelihood and timing of income tax payments.

Step 4   Adjust the balance sheet to include any assets and liabilities of the company that are not stated on the balance sheet, such as contingent or off-balance-sheet assets and liabilities.

Step 5   Compute the adjusted value of the equity by subtracting the liabilities stated at current value from the assets stated at fair market value. If the company has preferred stock, then the common equity should be reduced by the value of those securities.

Chapter 8

Adjusting the Income Statement

The objective of adjusting the income statement to a "normalized" basis is to make the best possible estimate of the true economic earning power of the entity in question. The first set of income statement adjustments generally is performed based on the premise that the entity will continue to operate independently in essentially its current condition. Adjustments under that premise are the subject of this chapter.

The following quote describes the analytical purpose of income statement adjustments:

> The purpose of normalization adjustments is to give the analyst an insight into:
> a. What prior operations might have looked like under normal conditions (and on a consistent basis with comparable companies), or
> b. What a prospective buyer might reasonably be expected to obtain from the company in the future, using history as a guide.
> Normalization adjustments may be affected by the size of the ownership interest, type of entity, definition of value, and purpose of the valuation.[1]

If a particular buyer contemplates changes that will affect revenues, expenses, or both, it is a good idea for the buyer to prepare an income statement as he or she would expect it to look with the change implemented. We will call this a *pro forma* income statement, or a *buyer's* income statement, to distinguish it from an *adjusted* income statement. The *pro forma* or *buyer's* income statement is discussed in Chapter 11.

In this chapter, we will assume the adjustments are being made in order to assist in valuing a controlling ownership interest. Differences in procedures that might be appropriate for valuing noncontrolling ownership interests are discussed in Chapter 24.

Compensation to Owners

The item that most often begs adjustment on the income statements of a privately held entity is the compensation to the owners. Actual compensation tends to be based on what the entity can afford or how the owners desire to be compensated, and may bear little or no relationship to the economic value of the services the owners actually perform.

The general idea of the compensation adjustment is to substitute the cost of hiring and paying a nonowner employee for the compensation actually paid to the owner to perform the same function. Another way to look at it is to compare the actual compensation paid to some average amount that other people normally are compensated for performing similar services. For example, if we are valuing a small restaurant where the owner is being paid $50,000 per year, and if a competent, full-

---

[1]Jay E. Fishman, Shannon P. Pratt, J. Clifford Griffith, and D. Keith Wilson, *Guide to Business Valuations,* 7th ed. (Fort Worth, TX: Practitioners Publishing Co., 1997), pp. 4-23.

charge manager could be hired for $30,000 to perform the same services, the owner's compensation would be adjusted downward by $20,000 on the adjusted income statement, resulting in a $20,000 addition to pretax profit.

Analyzing the Components of Compensation

The adjustment should reflect all components of compensation, many of which may be buried in various expense accounts. Expenses that would be considered discretionary on the owner's part are candidates for adjustment. Many types of expenses that are perfectly legitimate from an income tax viewpoint would not be considered essential by an owner whose objective was to maximize bottom-line profits.

All salary, bonuses, and direct payments to owners are part of the compensation. Payments into pension, profit sharing, or other retirement accounts for the benefit of the owners also should be included. In some cases, substantial life insurance premiums should be included. However, when comparing to industry averages (as discussed in the next chapter), it may be necessary to exclude certain compensation components. For example, neither the *Annual Statement Studies* nor the *Almanac of Business and Industrial Financial Ratios* includes either pension or life insurance payments in compensation.

Some of the most common expense items that may be considered discretionary are automobile expenses, travel and entertainment, and costs of maintaining boats, airplanes, various condominiums, and other residences. When analyzing compensation to owners, the analyst should also consider the relatives of the business owners who may be on the payroll or who may otherwise be receiving benefit from the business.

Sources of Comparative Compensation Data

Employment agencies and executive recruiters are good sources of informal estimates of how much it would cost to fill a particular job. The large compensation consulting firms also maintain data on compensation levels for various positions in various locales. Many trade associations compile data on compensation in their respective industries and publish it.

Three commonly used sources that provide average levels of compensation to owners in various business and professional classifications are the Robert Morris Associates' *Annual Statement Studies*, the *Almanac of Business and Industrial Financial Ratios*, and *Financial Studies of the Small Business*. These sources are discussed more fully, with sample pages of each, in Chapter 9. Additional sources of compensation data include *Source Book Statistics of Income* (Internal Revenue Service, Washington, DC), *Officer Compensation Report* (Panel Publishers, New York), and *Executive Compensation Survey Analysis* (National Institute of Business Management, New York). When relying on these sources of comparative compensation data, the analyst should be careful to note whether the source reports single officer's compensation data or total officers' compensation data.

Depreciation

Depreciation accounting policies differ greatly from one company to another. Large companies often account for depreciation in one way for tax purposes and in another way for financial reporting purposes; smaller businesses and professional practices tend to account for depreciation one way only: in whatever acceptable manner minimizes their income tax burdens. Exhibit 8-1 is a condensed primer on acceptable alternative depreciation methods currently in use.

Depreciation is a noncash charge against earnings; that is, the business makes no cash outlay at the time it charges the depreciation against earnings. (The cash outlay was made at the time the equipment was purchased.)

If the analyst wishes to normalize *net cash flow*, the preferred approach is to add back all the depreciation to earnings and then to deduct a separate charge that is an estimate of the annual average cost to replace the equipment necessary to sustain the level of revenues that the income statement assumes.

Alternatively, if the object is to normalize net income, depreciation may be adjusted to an economically realistic life or to a basis typically used by comparative companies. (The latter procedure typically is appropriate if the guideline publicly traded company method is being used as a valuation method). See Chapter 16 for a discussion of this method.

Cost of Goods Sold

For a merchandising or manufacturing business, the cost of goods obviously is a critical item. Like depreciation, it is an area where accounting practices differ significantly from one company to another. Moreover, it is an area where it is not uncommon to find accounting practices varying significantly from one year to another within the same company. It is desirable, if possible, to analyze statements for several years and to be able to explain any significant differences in the cost of goods sold as a percentage of sales from year to year, as well as any significant departures from the industry average.

Adjustment for Companies Using LIFO Accounting

For companies using the LIFO accounting method for their inventories, both the beginning and ending inventories presented on the income statement should be converted to a FIFO basis in order to conclude a good approximation of the true economic cost of goods sold. This adjustment can be performed by adding back the LIFO reserve provided in the footnotes to the financial statements, as follows:

Exhibit 8–1

ALTERNATIVE DEPRECIATION METHODS

Data used for the following examples:
Piece of equipment, purchased at beginning of Year 1
Cost of equipment $50,000
Estimated useful life   5 years

Year	Computation		Year's Depreciation Charge	Balance Accumulated Depreciation	Book Value Year-End
STRAIGHT-LINE METHOD					
1	1/5 (20%) x	$50,000	$10,000	$10,000	$40,000
2	20% x	50,000	10,000	20,000	30,000
3	20% x	50,000	10,000	30,000	20,000
4	20% x	50,000	10,000	40,000	10,000
5	20% x	50,000	10,000	50,000	0
200% DECLINING BALANCE METHOD					
1	40% x	$50,000 a	$20,000	$20,000	$30,000
2	40% x	30,000	12,000	32,000	18,000
3	40% x	18,000	7,200	39,200	10,800
4	40% x	10,800	4,320	43,520	6,480
5	40% x	6,480	2,592	46,112	3,888

a Based on double the straight-line rate of 20%, multiplied by the undepreciated book value.

Year	Computation		Year's Depreciation Charge	Balance Accumulated Depreciation	Book Value Year-End
SUM OF THE YEARS' DIGITS METHOD					
1	5/15 x	$50,000 b	$16,667	$16,667	$33,333
2	4/15 x	50,000	13,333	30,000	20,000
3	3/15 x	50,000	10,000	40,000	10,000
4	2/15 x	50,000	6,667	46,667	3,333
5	1/15 x	50,000	3,333	50,000	0

b Numerator is the remaining estimated useful life. Denominator is the sum of the years (5 + 4 + 3 + 2 + 1 = 15).

Year	Computation		Year's Depreciation Charge	Balance Accumulated Depreciation	Book Value Year-End
MODIFIED ACCELERATED COST RECOVERY SYSTEM					
1	20.00% x	$50,000 c	$10,000	$10,000	$40,000
2	32.00% x	50,000	16,000	26,000	24,000
3	19.20% x	50,000	9,600	35,600	14,400
4	11.52% x	50,000	5,760	41,360	8,640
5	11.52% x	50,000	5,760	47,120	2,880
6	5.76% x	50,000	2,880	50,000	0

c Statutory percentages for MACRS five-year property used for tax purposes.

Note: The above are examples of the more popular depreciation methods now in use. Salvage value has not been considered in the examples. An introductory accounting text can be consulted for a thorough presentation of potential depreciation methods. The Modified Accelerated Cost Recovery System (MACRS) was enacted as part of the Economic Recovery Tax Act of 1986 and is used for federal tax purposes. One of the periodic tax guides can be consulted for a thorough presentation of the provisions of the MACRS.

	LIFO Basis	Add LIFO Reserve	FIFO Basis
Beginning inventory	$100,000	$40,000	$140,000
Add: purchases	300,000		300,000
Goods available for sale	$400,000		$440,000
Less: ending inventory	120,000	50,000	170,000
Cost of goods sold	$280,000		$270,000

On a LIFO basis, the cost of goods sold was $10,000 more than it was on a FIFO basis, so the LIFO basis would have resulted in $10,000 less pretax earnings than the FIFO basis. (See also the example of the widgets in Chapter 7, where LIFO accounting produced a cost of goods sold of $750, versus $600 by the FIFO method. In that example, if the sales were $1,000, the gross margin would be $400 under FIFO accounting and $250 under LIFO accounting.)

Unconventional but Not Uncommon Practices

When counting and pricing the inventory at the end of a particularly prosperous year, the owner(s) of a company may decide to be less optimistic by taking write-offs or markdowns on slow or questionable inventory in order to avoid paying a higher amount of income tax. If the company counts and prices the inventory in a more optimistic manner in the following year, there will be a pickup in inventory on a comparative basis and a commensurate reduction in cost of goods sold. This will result in a dislocation of gross margin and pretax earnings. One way to recognize and adjust for such erratic practices is to analyze income statements for several years, discounting an abnormally high gross margin in some years, unless there is evidence that such a higher-than-average margin is sustainable in future years.

The notion that unconventional inventory accounting practices exist is reinforced by the following quote:

> Understating year-end inventory is a simple and relatively safe—though improper—means of reducing a profitable concern's taxes. When goods are sold, their cost is deducted from sales revenue to determine taxable profit. Falsely reducing inventory has the effect of falsely increasing that deduction because the hidden goods are presumed to have been sold. . . . Cheating is the little guy's LIFO. . . . The New York garment maker who hides $500,000 of inventory at tax time uses a different fiscal period for financial statements to his bank. After writing down the inventory as of December 31, he writes it up six months later when the financial statement year ends. In this way, he underpays the IRS and impresses his banker. Some describe that kind of inventory accounting as WIFL—Whatever I Feel Like.[2]

---

[2]*Wall Street Journal*, August 4, 1981, quoted in Philip L. Cooley, *How to Value an Oil Jobbership for Purchase or Sale* (Bethesda, MD: Petroleum Marketing Education Foundation, 1982), pp. 3-16.

Occupancy Costs

Occupancy costs are the costs of occupying the premises, primarily rent and utilities. If the premises are owned, the occupancy costs shown on the statements usually would include depreciation, insurance, property taxes, building repairs, and interest on any mortgage balance outstanding, as well as utilities.

Rented or Leased Premises

If the premises are rented or leased, it should be considered whether rent or lease payments are on an arm's-length basis. If the premises are rented from the owner or the owner's affiliates, relatives, or friends at something above or below a market rate of rent, an adjustment to a market rate should be made, unless the existing rate can be expected to prevail for a long period of time under a new, unrelated owner.

If a lease is about to expire, or if an existing arrangement is tenuous, occupancy costs should be adjusted to their anticipated amount under an arm's-length arrangement. If the lessee is responsible for such variable items as taxes, common area maintenance, and/or insurance, the status and possible changes in those items should be investigated and adjusted as appropriate.

Owner-Occupied Premises

As noted elsewhere, and except for certain kinds of special-use or single-use properties, it is often best to treat the valuation of the business occupying the premises separately from the valuation of the premises themselves. To separate the real estate value from the business value, described in Chapter 7, it is necessary to remove from the income statement (and in another manner from the balance sheet) all expenses associated with the property ownership and to substitute a market rate of rent for the premises occupied.

Nonrecurring Items

Since the objective of the adjustment is to get a normalized income estimate, it is necessary to adjust historical income statements for any items that would not be expected to recur in the future. Such items include a much broader spectrum than just those that would meet the narrow definition of extraordinary items under generally accepted accounting principles (GAAP). The following are a few examples of frequently encountered items that would call for an adjustment.

For items that actually occurred over a long time frame, it may be appropriate to adjust for the gain or loss in the actual years in which it occurred.

Business Interruptions

Business interruptions may occur for any of a wide variety of reasons, such as strikes, storm or fire damage to premises, lack of access to premises due to street repair, extended closure for remodeling, interruption in availability of critical supplies, illness of a key person or owner, withdrawal of bank financing, loss of lease, or many other occurrences of a temporary but significant nature.

When such items are identified, their effect should be removed from the historical income stream being used as a basis for estimating a normalized income stream. If the amount of the effect can be reliably estimated, the income figures for that period can be adjusted accordingly. If not, then the period during which the business interruption occurred can be omitted from the historical income statement data being used to derive a normalized statement.

Insurance Proceeds

A business may receive proceeds as a result of some particular event in the company's history such as from life insurance on a key person or from some type of property and casualty claim. The amount of such proceeds can be based on any of a number of factors, and the amount is not likely to be an exact offset to the amount of current earnings lost during the accounting period in which the particular event took place. Consequently, such proceeds usually are removed from the normalized earnings stream calculations.

Lawsuit Settlements

Sometimes, companies have substantial payments or receipts as a result of lawsuits, which can arise from a wide variety of circumstances, including property and casualty losses, breach of contract, patent or copyright infringement, product liability, antitrust actions, and income or property tax disputes. Usually the amount of the settlements paid or received would be removed when calculating a normalized earnings level.

Gains or Losses on Disposal of Assets

Gains or losses on the sale of assets should be adjusted out of the normalized income stream to the extent that they are nonrecurring in nature. If a company sells its only building or airplane, the gain or loss should be removed from computation of normalized earnings. On the other hand, if a construction company, for example, has $20,000 to $50,000 in gains from disposal of equipment almost every year, that would be considered recurring in nature. However, the analyst should be careful not to "double count" earnings by adding back depreciation in excess of the actual economic decrement in value, while at the same time leaving in the earnings stream income from the gain on the depreciated asset that was sold.

Discontinued Operations

If a company had earnings or losses in the past from operations that were discontinued and that consequently are not relevant to the company's expected future earning power, such earnings or losses should be adjusted out when estimating a prospective normalized earnings stream.

Payments on Employment Contracts and Covenants Not to Compete

It is common to find payments to a former owner included in expenses on the income statement that are attributable to an employment contract and/or a covenant not to compete. An analysis should be made of the extent to which such payments were actually for services rendered to the company during the accounting periods in which they were paid. If such payments were not for services rendered, but a hypothetical buyer is going to be liable for such payments, the value of such future payments should be deducted from the value of the business as otherwise determined.

Abnormal Market Conditions

From time to time, businesses experience abnormally high or low profits (or losses) due to abnormal market conditions. For example, some service stations made unprecedented profits because of the very high gross margins they were able to achieve during periods of gasoline shortages in the mid 1970s. Some stations were sold at prices that were very high by historical standards, apparently to buyers who thought the high margins and lack of price competition at the retail level were permanent. Buyers who paid high prices on the basis of that assumption never realized an adequate return on their investments, and many went broke because they couldn't service the debt they had incurred in the purchases.

Governmental regulations can introduce temporary market dislocations. This was evident in the timber industry when the spotted owl was placed on the endangered species list, in the airline and trucking industries when deregulation went into effect, and in the savings and loan industry when minimum capital requirements were changed.

Some industries, such as sawmills, for example, are cyclical by nature and seem to have abnormally good or bad years from time to time; but for some companies, such so-called abnormalities keep recurring over the years. In cyclical industries, statements for several years should be examined to try to normalize the especially good and bad years.

If the analyst is trying to estimate normalized earnings, the problem is to identify what part of the historical record is abnormal. Analysts tend to extrapolate future expectations on the basis of the most recent past, a practice that can be very misleading. Some informed and dispassionate judgment about the economy and the industry and its prospects should be brought to bear on the question of what adjustments, if any, should be made to the historical income statements for abnormal market conditions.

Unrecognized Costs

Sometimes there are actual or potential expenses that have not been recognized on the income statement. If any such items exist, the statements should be adjusted to reflect them. The following are examples of such items that are frequently encountered.

Accrued Expenses

Sometimes companies do not recognize incurred costs as expenses. The previous chapter mentions an occasion when salespeople's commissions, payable when the accounts were collected, were not recorded as expenses, even though the revenues were recorded when the sale was made. This oversight resulted in an overstatement of income since the unrecorded commissions were really a cost of generating the revenue.

Sometimes invoices for purchases may not come in or may not be recorded until after the end of the accounting period, even though the merchandise was received and counted in the ending inventory. This lack of cost recognition would result in an understatement of cost of goods and an overstatement of profit.

The objective of accrual accounting is to match expenses with the associated revenues. Whenever revenues are recognized on the income statement, it is important to also recognize the expense associated with those revenues, and vice versa.

Bad Debts

Most companies and professionals who sell goods or services on credit have some accounts that don't get collected. Recommended accrual accounting practices call for recognizing some bad debt expense on the income statement at the time the revenues are recorded (and an allowance for doubtful accounts as a deduction from accounts receivable on the balance sheet) or when the specific accounts are determined to be uncollectible.

Generally, the appropriate amount of bad debt expense to be charged against revenues at the time the revenues are recognized can be determined by examining the company's historical amount of uncollectible accounts as a percentage of revenues. To the extent that the bad debt expense actually recorded for a period significantly differs from the company's historical bad debt experience, an adjustment to that expense item is indicated.

Insurable Liabilities

Most companies exposed to product liabilities take out insurance to protect themselves against product liability claims. Sometimes, insurance for officers and directors is appropriate. Similarly, most professional practitioners have some type of errors and omissions and/or malpractice liability insurance. If a company or professional with such exposure lacks appropriate liability insurance, an additional expense in the amount of the premiums for the insurance that the company or practice is expected to incur is an appropriate adjustment.

Nonoperating Income and Expenses

When the business or practice has nonoperating items of income, expense, or both, they usually should be removed when creating a normalized income statement. For example, if a company owns some property from which it is deriving income unrelated to the basic business or practice, such nonoperating income and any expenses (including the income tax effects) associated with it should not be included in the normalized income statement. Then the entity can be valued on an operating basis, and the assets not part of the basic operations can be dealt with separately even though they are to be a part of the total package being valued.

Adjusting for Taxes, if Necessary

If obtaining an after-tax rather than a pretax earnings figure is desired, each adjustment to pretax earnings should be accompanied by an adjustment for the applicable income taxes. If the entity is incorporated, the appropriate rate to use is the corporation's marginal income tax rate —that is, the income tax rate applicable to its last dollar of taxable income. State and local income taxes should be included when applicable, as well as federal income taxes. If the subject entity has tax attributes that would carry over to the hypothetical buyer, it may be appropriate to recognize those tax attributes.

If the entity is a sole proprietorship, a partnership, or an S corporation, the normalized income statement usually stops at pretax income. This is because each owner may be subject to a different tax rate. If an estimated after-tax figure is desired, one way to do it is to find out, or make an assumption about, the owner's income tax bracket and use the owner's marginal income tax rate. Another method is to use what the corporate income tax rate would be if it were a corporation since incorporation is usually an available option.

Samples of Adjusted Income Statements

The accompanying examples illustrate the procedures discussed in this chapter. The two examples continue with the same two hypothetical companies used in the previous chapter.

Sole Proprietorship Example

Exhibit 8-2 is an adjusted income statement for Ashley's Apparel Store, a sole proprietorship, which her appraiser prepared when she was ready to sell her business.

Corporation Example

Exhibit 8-3 shows the income statements as reported for Patrick's Machinery & Equipment, Inc., for the years ended December 31, 1993 through 1997. Exhibit 8-4 shows the adjusted income statements for Patrick's over the same time period. Both the reported and adjusted statements were prepared by Patrick's appraisers; the adjusted statements were prepared in connection with the sale of the business.

Summary

This chapter discussed the most common income and expense account adjustments that business appraisers frequently make to bring the income statement accounts close to a presentation of economic reality on a going-concern basis. These are the most commonly needed adjustments, but many others are called for in certain instances.

A summary of these steps is included in Exhibit 8-5. In some cases, income statement adjustments cause related balance sheet adjustments; however, many do not. The adjusted financial statements should show what a hypothetical willing buyer could expect.

Finally, we caution the analyst to carefully explain and justify each adjustment and to be cautious not to overreach in making income statements adjustments.

Exhibit 8–2

ASHLEY'S APPAREL STORE
ADJUSTED INCOME STATEMENT
FOR THE YEAR ENDED DECEMBER 31, 1997

	Income Statement as Reported		Adjustments	Adjusted Income Statement	
	$	%	$	$	%
Sales	1,000,000	100.0		1,000,000	100.0
Cost of goods sold:					
Beginning inventory	170,000		15,000 a	185,000	
Plus: Purchases	570,000			570,000	
	740,000			755,000	
Less: Ending inventory	(180,000)		40,000 b	(140,000)	
Cost of goods sold	560,000	56.0		535,000	53.5
Gross margin	440,000	44.0		465,000	46.5
Expenses:					
Owner's salary	70,000	7.0	(20,000) c	50,000	5.0
Other salaries	150,000	15.0		150,000	15.0
Payroll taxes	30,000	3.0		30,000	3.0
Employee benefits	23,000	2.3		23,000	2.3
Rent	65,000	6.5		65,000	6.5
Utilities	3,000	0.3		3,000	0.3
Telephone	3,000	0.3		3,000	0.3
Insurance	0	0.0	2,000 d	2,000	0.2
Supplies	5,000	0.5		5,000	0.5
Advertising	25,000	2.5		25,000	2.5
Travel & entertainment	25,000	2.5	(20,000) e	5,000	0.5
Automobile expense	5,000	0.5		5,000	0.5
Outside accountants	5,000	0.5		5,000	0.5
Legal	3,000	0.3		3,000	0.3
License, registrations, etc.	2,000	0.2		2,000	0.2
Dues & subscriptions	1,000	0.1		1,000	0.1
Allowance for doubtful accounts	0	0.0	2,400 f	2,400	0.2
Depreciation	13,000	1.3		13,000	1.3
Interest	7,000	0.7		7,000	0.7
Total expenses	435,000	43.5	(35,600) g	399,400	39.9
Pretax income	5,000	0.5		65,600	6.6

a   In order to arrive at a realistic cost of goods sold, we have adjusted the beginning inventory to Ashley's best estimate of what it would have been at the then-current market price.

b   From inventory adjustment made in Exhibit 7-2.

c   According to Robert Morris Associates' *Annual Statement Studies*, 1997 edition, the median officer's compensation/sales ratio for companies with assets of less than $2 million was 4.4%, or approximately $44,000 for a store the size of Ashley's. Since Ashley is such an excellent operator, we felt $50,000 compensation is reasonable.

d   Ashley's should carry fire, casualty, and liability insurance at a cost of approximately $2,000 per year.

e   Ashley has had an above-average amount of travel and entertainment expenses through her business in an amount of approximately $20,000. In fact, a retail store the size of Ashley's might not incur even $5,000 in travel and entertainment expense.

f   About 24%, or $240,000, of Ashley's sales are made on credit. Historically about 1%, or $2,400, has been uncollectible.

g   Summary of adjustments a through f.

Exhibit 8–3

PATRICK'S MACHINERY & EQUIPMENT, INC.
INCOME STATEMENTS
(000s, except per-share data)

	1997 $	1997 %	1996 $	1996 %	1995 $	1995 %	1994 $	1994 %	1993 $	1993 %
Sales	2,400	100.0	2,000	100.0	2,200	100.0	2,400	100.0	2,200	100.0
Cost of goods sold:										
Beginning inventory	300		320		340		320		320	
Plus: Purchases	1,620		1,380		1,480		1,610		1,450	
	1,920		1,700		1,820		1,930		1,770	
Less: Ending inventory	(320)		(300)		(320)		(340)		(320)	
Cost of goods sold	1,600	66.7	1,400	70.0	1,500	68.2	1,590	66.2	1,450	65.9
Gross margin	800	33.3	600	30.0	700	31.8	810	33.8	750	34.1
Operating expenses:										
Officers' compensation	120	5.0	100	5.0	110	5.0	120	5.0	110	5.0
Salaries & wages	230	9.6	210	10.5	220	10.0	230	9.6	220	10.0
Employee benefits	50	2.1	45	2.3	45	2.0	50	2.1	45	2.0
Payroll taxes	50	2.1	40	2.0	45	2.0	50	2.1	45	2.0
Rent	24	1.0	24	1.2	24	1.1	24	1.0	24	1.1
Depreciation	33	1.4	35	1.8	37	1.7	39	1.6	41	1.9
Insurance	20	0.8	20	1.0	20	0.9	20	0.8	20	0.9
Travel & entertainment	30	1.3	25	1.3	25	1.1	30	1.3	25	1.1
Policy adjustments	26	1.1	32	1.6	30	1.4	24	1.0	35	1.6
Transportation vehicles	24	1.0	28	1.4	30	1.4	26	1.1	25	1.1
Prov. for bad debt	13	0.5	21	1.1	15	0.7	13	0.5	10	0.5
Other	90	3.8	100	5.0	95	4.3	92	3.8	100	4.5
Total operating expenses	710	29.7	680	34.2	696	31.6	718	29.9	700	31.7
Operating income	90	3.6	(80)	(4.2)	4	0.2	92	3.9	50	2.4
Other income (expense):										
Interest expense	(15)	(0.6)	(18)	(0.9)	(20)	(0.9)	(18)	(0.8)	(18)	(0.8)
Dividend income	1	Nil	1	Nil	1	Nil	1	Nil	1	Nil
Gain on sale of assets	-	-	10	0.5	-	-	-	-	-	-
Fire damage	-	-	-	-	(15)	(0.7)	-	-	-	-
Discontinued operations	-	-	-	-	-	-	(10)	(0.4)	20	0.9
Total other income (expense)	(14)	(0.6)	(7)	(0.4)	(34)	(1.6)	(27)	(1.2)	3	0.1
Income before taxes	76	3.0	(87)	(4.6)	(30)	(1.4)	65	2.7	53	2.5
Income taxes	16	0.7	-	-	-	-	14	0.6	10	0.5
Net income	60	2.3	(87)	(4.6)	(30)	(1.4)	51	2.1	43	2.0
Average number of shares outstanding	200		200		250		250		250	
Earnings per share	$300		($435)		($120)		$204		$172	
Dividends per share	$50		$0		$0		$50		$50	
Effective tax rate	21.2%		0.0%		0.0%		21.2%		19.1%	

NOTE: Figures may not total due to rounding.

Nil = Inconsequential amount, greater (or less) than zero.

SOURCE: Company financial statements.

Exhibit 8–4

PATRICK'S MACHINERY & EQUIPMENT, INC.
ADJUSTED INCOME STATEMENTS
(000s, except per-share data)

	1997 $	1997 %	1996 $	1996 %	1995 $	1995 %	1994 $	1994 %	1993 $	1993 %
Sales	2,400	100.0	2,000	100.0	2,200	100.0	2,400	100.0	2,200	100.0
Cost of goods sold:										
Beginning inventory	400 a		430 a		460 a		425 a		420 a	
Plus: Purchases	1,620		1,380		1,480		1,610		1,450	
	2,020		1,810		1,940		2,035		1,870	
Less: Ending inventory	(430) a		(400) a		(430) a		(460) a		(425) a	
Cost of goods sold	1,590	66.2	1,410	70.5	1,510	68.6	1,575	65.6	1,445	65.7
Gross margin	810	33.8	590	29.5	690	31.4	825	34.4	755	34.3
Operating expenses:										
Officers' compensation	120	5.0	100	5.0	110	5.0	120	5.0	110	5.0
Salaries & wages	230	9.6	210	10.5	220	10.0	230	9.6	220	10.0
Employee benefits	50	2.1	45	2.3	45	2.0	50	2.1	45	2.0
Payroll taxes	50	2.1	40	2.0	45	2.0	50	2.1	45	2.0
Rent	24	1.0	24	1.2	24	1.1	24	1.0	24	1.1
Depreciation	33	1.4	35	1.8	37	1.7	39	1.6	41	1.9
Insurance	20	0.8	20	1.0	20	0.9	20	0.8	20	0.9
Travel & entertainment	30	1.3	25	1.3	25	1.1	30	1.3	25	1.1
Policy adjustments	26	1.1	32	1.6	30	1.4	24	1.0	35	1.6
Transportation vehicles	24	1.0	28	1.4	30	1.4	26	1.1	25	1.1
Prov. for bad debt	13	0.5	21	1.1	15	0.7	13	0.5	10	0.5
Other	90	3.8	100	5.0	95	4.3	92	3.8	100	4.5
Total operating expenses	710	29.7	680	34.2	696	31.6	718	29.9	700	31.7
Operating income	100	4.1	(90)	(4.7)	(6)	(0.2)	107	4.5	55	2.6
Other income (expense):										
Interest expense	(15)	(0.6)	(18)	(0.9)	(20)	(0.9)	(18)	(0.8)	(18)	(0.8)
Dividend income	1	Nil	1	Nil	1	Nil	1	Nil	1	Nil
Gain on sale of assets	0	0.0	0 b	0.0	0	0.0	0	0.0	0	0.0
Fire damage	0	0.0	0	0.0	0 c	0.0	0	0.0	0	0.0
Discontinued operations	0	0.0	0	0.0	0	0.0	0 d	0.0	0 d	0.0
Total other income (expense)	(14)	(0.6)	(17)	(0.9)	(19)	(0.9)	(17)	(0.8)	(17)	(0.8)
Income before taxes	86	3.5	(107)	(5.6)	(25)	(1.1)	90	3.7	38	1.8
Income taxes	20	0.8	0	0.0	0	0.0	23	1.0	7	0.3
Net income	66	2.7	(107)	(5.6)	(25)	(1.1)	67	2.7	31	1.5
Average number of shares										
outstanding	200		200		250		250		250	
Earnings per share	$330		($535)		($100)		$268		$124	
Dividends per share	$50		$0		$0		$50		$50	
Effective tax rate	23.3%		0.0%		0.0%		25.6%		18.4%	

NOTE: Figures may not total due to rounding.
Nil = Inconsequential amount, greater (or less) than zero.

a

	As of December 31 (000s):					
	1997 $	1996 $	1995 $	1994 $	1993 $	1992 $
Inventory as stated	320	300	320	340	320	320
Add: LIFO reserve	110	100	110	120	105	100
Adjusted inventory	430	400	430	460	425	420

b   The $10,000 gain was from the sale of the company's condominium. Since that was a nonrecurrring item, the gain was eliminated in the
      adjusted income statement.

c   The $45,000 loss was from a fire in the warehouse in 1995. That represented the amount of the loss not recovered from insurance proceeds.
      Since it was a nonrecurring item, it needed to be eliminated from the adjusted income statement.

d   Patrick's discontinued a retail parts store in 1994. Since we are interested only in Patrick's current earning power, those gains were eliminated
      from the adjusted income statement.

Exhibit 8–5

SUMMARY OF STEPS IN
ADJUSTING THE INCOME STATEMENT

Step 1   Obtain copies of the subject company's income statements for the five-year period preceding the valuation date, or for whatever period is considered relevant to the valuation assignment.

Step 2   Adjust the company's historical income statements to a normalized basis to determine the true economic earning power of the company. Although not intended to be comprehensive, a list of potential adjustments to expenses on the company's income statements includes the following:

- Adjust total owner compensation (including salary, bonuses, and profit sharing payments) to reflect the cost of hiring a nonowner employee to perform the same function.
- Adjust depreciation to reflect an economically realistic life or to a basis typically used by comparable companies.
- For companies using LIFO inventory accounting, both the beginning and ending inventories shown on the income statements should be converted to a FIFO basis to get a good approximation of the true economic cost of goods sold.
- Adjust rent expense to reflect the rent expense resulting from an arm's length lease. If the lease is about to expire, adjust occupancy costs to the probable cost under a new lease.

Step 3   Adjust the income statement to exclude any items that are not expected to recur in the future. These nonrecurring items could include the following:

- Eliminate the effect of any business interruptions that are unexpected in the future, such as strikes, fire damage, illness of a key person, etc.
- Adjust the income statement to exclude any insurance proceeds, such as proceeds from life insurance on a key person or a property and casualty claim.
- Eliminate the amount of any lawsuit settlement payments paid or received from the company's income statements.
- To the extent that they are nonrecurring, adjust any gains or losses from the sale of assets out of the historical income stream of the company.
- Eliminate earnings or losses from discontinued operations of the company from the historical income statements.
- Adjust the historical income stream to eliminate abnormally high or low profits or losses due to abnormal market conditions that are considered nonrecurring.

Step 4   Adjust the income statements to include any actual or potential expenses that have not been recognized on the income statements. These expenses may include the following:

- Include any accrued expenses that have not been reflected in the latest income statement.
- Adjust the bad debt expense to reflect the bad debt that was actually recorded if it significantly differs from the company's historical bad debt experience.

Step 5   Adjust the latest income statements prior to the valuation date to reflect any imminent changes in business, such as the expected loss of a major customer.

Step 6   Adjust the historical income statements to eliminate any nonoperating income and expenses.

Step 7   Adjust the income statements for applicable income taxes.

Chapter 9

Comparisons with Industry Averages

One of the benefits of having normalized the balance sheet and income statement is that it makes it possible to make valid comparisons between the subject entity and other entities in the same business or profession. Comparison with peers is a useful step in the valuation process. It can be helpful in several ways, especially for businesses and professional practices for which a good body of comparative data is available. However, care should be exercised in this process in order to be sure that comparison of income statement and balance sheet items are conducted under like accounting treatment and ratio definitions.

Advantages of Comparative Analysis

Comparative analysis provides some insight into how the subject entity compares with its peers. This information is especially useful, of course, for analysts who do not have a great deal of financial experience with the business or profession in question, even though they may have considerable experience with it from other viewpoints. Even the veteran buyer, however, will sharpen his or her perspective on the subject entity by going through a comparative analysis exercise.

Identifying Errors

Comparative analysis highlights the differences between the subject company's historical financial performance and industry averages. This disparity could cause the analyst to recheck balance sheet and/or income statement data for possible errors.

Identifying Strengths and Weaknesses

Comparative analysis points up the relative financial operating strengths and weaknesses of the subject entity compared to its peers, from both a balance sheet and an income statement point of view. It shows where the company outperforms its peers and what financial items need to be improved—and by how much—in order to bring it into line with industry averages.

Identifying Opportunities

Comparative analysis can point out opportunities that become apparent from studying balance sheets, income statements, and ratios that use the two statements together.

For example, if a company has little or no debt compared with others in its line of business, its assets might be used as collateral for borrowing purposes—to help finance the purchase. That is the basic concept of the *leveraged buyout*, or using debt financing, supported by the company's assets, to pay a significant portion of the purchase price. If the bottom line profits fall below industry averages, this suggests further investigation is warranted to isolate a problem or find room for improvement. The income statement comparisons may reveal specific categories of costs that might be reduced to improve profitability. If a retailer's gross margin is below the industry average, profits might be improved considerably by bringing the margin up to, or better than, standard. If the salary costs for a service business are out of line, it suggests that there should be room to generate the same revenue with less labor cost or to generate more revenue with the existing amount of labor.

Ratios that use both the balance sheet and the income statement include, for example, accounts receivable turnover (average collection period) and inventory turnover (average length of time merchandise is held in inventory). Improvements in these ratios would mean a reduction in working capital requirements, thus reducing interest costs if the company is borrowing money to finance receivables and inventory.

Sources of Comparative Industry Data

Sources of comparative industry data can be classified into two broad groups: (1) general sources that provide data for a wide variety of businesses and professional practices, and (2) specialized sources that provide data on some specific category of businesses or professional practices.

General Sources

The most widely used general sources for comparative financial data for small businesses are Robert Morris Associates' *Annual Statement Studies*, *IRS Corporate Ratios*, *IRS Corporate Financial Ratios*, the *Almanac of Business and Industrial Financial Ratios*, *Financial Ratio Analyst*, and *Financial Studies of the Small Business*. Each is published annually. The degree of usefulness of the data varies considerably from one type of business to another. This depends largely on how many reasonably homogeneous businesses exist for which the publications are able to collect data in each category.

RMA Annual Statement Studies. Probably the most popular data source is the RMA *Annual Statement Studies*, which is a product of a national association of bank loan and credit officers. The 1997 edition was based on financial statements of over 138,000 businesses and professional practices that had received bank loans. These financial statements were submitted to Robert Morris Associates by member banks. One reason for the broad appeal of the *Annual Statement Studies* is the over 400 different industries it covers.

Exhibit 9-1 is a typical page from RMA *Annual Statement Studies*, in this case retailers of women's ready-to-wear. Note that each industry group is disaggregated into six size categories, based on total assets. (No figures are presented for the second-to-largest size category in this particular industry group because RMA considers that fewer than 10 financial statements in a particular size category is too small a sample to be considered representative and could be misleading.) Also, data are shown in the aggregate for five years so that year-to-year comparisons can be made.

Each of the ratios given is defined in a section several pages long at the beginning of each RMA annual volume. Note that, according to RMA, "all ratios computed by RMA are based on year-end statement data only." For example, the cost of sales/inventory (inventory turnover ratio) is computed by dividing the cost of goods sold for the year by the ending inventory. A truer picture of inventory may be derived by dividing cost of goods sold by average inventory, but the data on which the RMA ratios are based are not sufficient to make that computation.

IRS Corporate Ratios.   This program, published annually by John Wiley & Sons, allows users to look up and search data numerically by SIC codes and alphabetically by industry type for over 230 industries. Raw data based on a sample of 85,000 out of over 3.7 million public and closely held companies' tax returns have been compiled from the *IRS Source Book, Statistics of Income, Corporation Income Tax Returns*.

The database comes in two versions: professional and standard. The professional version contains data from 1989 through 1993 tax returns, including both "returns with and without net income" and "returns with net income." All 13 asset categories, ranging from $0 to $250 million, are included in the professional version. The standard version includes only "returns with net income," and the 13 asset categories have been combined into five categories. Exhibit 9-2 is a sample printout from the professional version of this program, showing the first six asset size categories.

IRS Corporate Financial Ratios.   Published annually by Schonfeld & Associates, Inc., the 11th edition covers tax returns for fiscal years ending July 1993 through June 1994. There is one page for each of 220 industry groups or aggregations of industry groups. Each page has 10 columns of each of 76 ratios broken into five total asset size groups. For each of the size groups, there is a column for companies with profits and a column for companies with losses.

The book contains detailed descriptions of each ratio. It also gives discussions of the strengths and weaknesses of some of the ratios, based on the Internal Revenue Service procedures for compiling the data. As with *RMA*, all ratios are based on year-end data. Exhibit 9-3 is a sample page from the 1997 edition of this publication presenting the industry category of women's and children's clothing.

Almanac of Business and Industrial Financial Ratios.   The source of all data used in the *Almanac* is also the data compiled from corporate tax returns by the Internal Revenue Service. It is disaggregated into 180 fields of business and industry, about half the number offered by RMA.

Exhibit 9-4 is a typical data presentation from the *Almanac*, in this case apparel and accessory stores. Each industry group is presented in two tables. The first table includes corporations that reported a profit as well as those that did not; the second table includes only those that reported a profit.

Exhibit 9–1

RETAILERS—WOMEN'S READY-TO-WEAR.   SIC# 5621

Current Data Sorted By Assets							Comparative Historical Data	
						# Postretirement Benefits		**5**
						Type of Statement		
1	2	5	8	1	6	Unqualified	35	20
4	16	10	1	1		Reviewed	37	38
31	18					Compiled	99	85
7	2					Tax Returns	7	8
11	16	8	8		5	Other	41	36
	49 (4/1-9/30/96)			112 (10/1/96-3/31/97)			4/1/92-3/31/93	4/1/93-3/31/94
0-500M	500M-2MM	2-10MM	10-50MM	50-100MM	100-250MM		**ALL**	**ALL**
54	54	23	17	2	11	**NUMBER OF STATEMENTS**	219	187
%	%	%	%	%	%	**ASSETS**	%	%
5.7	14.8	6.5	10.5		12.5	Cash & Equivalents	10.5	11.1
8.7	9.1	11.0	6.2		3.9	Trade Receivables - (net)	10.1	10.3
62.1	49.1	52.2	38.9		38.3	Inventory	51.0	52.3
1.0	.7	1.6	1.6		.8	All Other Current	1.4	1.0
77.6	73.7	71.4	57.3		55.6	Total Current	72.9	74.7
15.0	18.2	23.3	25.0		26.9	Fixed Assets (net)	18.8	18.1
4.2	2.3	.8	10.8		12.0	Intangibles (net)	1.8	2.0
3.2	5.8	4.5	6.9		5.5	All Other Non-Current	6.4	5.2
100.0	100.0	100.0	100.0		100.0	Total	100.0	100.0
						LIABILITIES		
12.7	10.8	14.0	6.6		.6	Notes Payable-Short Term	9.2	11.3
5.3	2.5	2.6	1.7		4.9	Cur. Mat.-L/T/D	3.1	3.2
15.4	16.4	19.8	21.8		17.1	Trade Payables	16.6	16.0
.2	.2	.8	.1		.5	Income Taxes Payable	.6	2.5
7.6	8.5	8.8	10.0		9.8	All Other Current	9.7	7.5
41.2	38.3	46.0	40.1		33.0	Total Current	39.1	40.5
17.0	13.0	7.6	12.9		19.5	Long Term Debt	11.8	13.0
.1	.1	.4	.4		.5	Deferred Taxes	.1	.1
3.5	4.4	4.7	8.9		1.3	All Other Non-Current	3.6	4.9
38.2	44.2	41.2	37.7		45.7	Net Worth	45.4	41.5
100.0	100.0	100.0	100.0		100.0	Total Liabilities & Net Worth	100.0	100.0
						INCOME DATA		
100.0	100.0	100.0	100.0		100.0	Net Sales	100.0	100.0
41.4	42.2	43.3	38.8		37.2	Gross Profit	40.4	40.1
35.6	40.5	42.6	37.6		31.9	Operating Expenses	38.2	38.0
5.8	1.7	.7	1.2		5.3	Operating Profit	2.1	2.2
1.3	.6	.7	.8		1.4	All Other Expenses (net)	.7	.7
4.5	1.1	.0	.3		3.8	Profit Before Taxes	1.5	1.4
						RATIOS		
3.4	4.5	2.3	2.1		2.2	Current	3.0	2.9
1.9	2.1	1.7	1.3		1.5		2.0	1.8
1.4	1.2	1.2	1.1		1.4		1.4	1.3
.8	1.5	.7	1.1		1.7	Quick	1.0	1.1
(52) .3	.7	.3	.2	(10) .2	.2		(217) .5	(186) .4
.1	.1	.1	.0		.1		.2	.2
0 UND	0 UND	0 999.8	0 UND		1 267.0	Sales/Receivables	0 735.4	0 UND
2 164.0	3 115.8	2 169.4	2 229.1		4 87.8		4 86.4	4 85.0
17 21.0	21 17.8	33 11.1	4 98.5		7 50.8		26 14.3	23 15.9
85 4.3	65 5.6	63 5.8	51 7.1		68 5.4	Cost of Sales/Inventory	65 5.6	63 5.8
140 2.6	104 3.5	140 2.6	94 3.9		96 3.8		104 3.5	111 3.3
203 1.8	159 2.3	174 2.1	118 3.1		114 3.2		159 2.3	166 2.2
16 22.9	14 26.7	34 10.7	27 13.5		35 10.5	Cost of Sales/Payables	18 20.0	14 26.4
29 12.5	33 11.1	49 7.4	36 10.1		41 8.8		31 11.7	28 12.9
50 7.3	56 6.5	65 5.6	72 5.1		50 7.3		49 7.5	49 7.5
4.7	4.0	5.9	8.9		5.6	Sales/Working Capital	4.8	4.6
8.9	8.0	9.4	15.7		15.1		9.2	10.0
17.8	24.8	51.8	41.2		17.9		17.1	19.9
6.1	5.2	3.7	8.3		7.3	EBIT/Interest	7.6	7.6
(48) 2.7	(46) 2.3	(20) 2.0	(16) 1.6		(10) 3.5		(192) 2.4	(160) 3.0
.9	-1.6	.5	-1.8		2.1		.3	1.1
		4.3				Net Profit + Depr., Dep., Amort./Cur. Mat. L/T/D	4.9	3.4
	(11) 1.2						(53) 1.7	(47) 1.4
		-1.5					1.0	.4
.2	.1	.3	.5		.3	Fixed/Worth	.2	.2
.4	.3	.5	.8		.8		.4	.4
1.1	1.2	1.5	NM		1.1		.7	.9
.8	.4	.6	1.2		.7	Debt/Worth	.6	.6
1.8	1.2	1.3	2.0		1.3		1.1	1.5
8.6	5.9	3.7	NM		2.1		2.5	3.2
77.5	29.9	14.7	16.6			% Profit Before Taxes/Tangible Net Worth	29.7	30.2
(49) 23.7	(51) 8.5	6.4	(13) 2.4				(210) 11.9	(172) 11.9
3.4	-15.9	-10.4	-6.8				.0	1.1
19.7	9.3	5.1	6.4		16.0	% Profit Before Taxes/Total Assets	11.8	11.8
8.6	3.6	2.3	2.7		4.8		4.3	5.5
.9	-6.7	-2.4	-3.6		1.8		-2.0	.0
68.4	48.5	21.3	30.7		11.6	Sales/Net Fixed Assets	51.1	52.8
26.7	23.2	15.2	12.7		9.2		19.6	23.2
11.6	11.8	8.7	6.4		7.5		10.2	11.0
4.0	4.1	3.2	4.4		3.0	Sales/Total Assets	3.9	4.0
2.8	2.7	2.8	2.8		2.3		2.8	2.9
2.1	2.0	2.1	1.7		2.1		2.1	2.1
.4	.5	.7	1.1			% Depr., Dep., Amort./Sales	.6	.6
(48) 1.0	(47) .9	(22) 1.2	(15) 1.7				(187) 1.1	(153) 1.1
1.7	1.6	1.9	2.4				1.9	1.9
4.4	2.5	.8				% Officers', Directors', Owners' Comp/Sales	2.3	1.9
(23) 5.4	(24) 4.8	(10) 1.8					(95) 5.0	(87) 4.9
7.5	7.8	2.3					8.1	9.6
35001M	165730M	353756M	1269619M	346702M	3883226M	Net Sales ($)	4122715M	2966656M
12329M	53202M	123849M	447757M	146994M	1602614M	Total Assets ($)	1579465M	1105719M

© RMA 1997

M = $thousand   MM = $million
See Pages 1 through 20 for Explanation of Ratios and Data

Interpretation of Statement Studies Figures. RMA cautions that the Studies be regarded only as a general guideline and not as an absolute industry norm. This is due to limited samples within categories, the categorization of companies by their primary Standard Industrial Classification (SIC) number only, and different methods of operations by companies within the same industry. For these reasons, RMA recommends that the figures be used only as general guidelines in addition to other methods of financial analysis.

SOURCE: *RMA Annual Statement Studies* (Philadelphia, PA: Robert Morris Associates, 1997), p. 556. Reprinted with permission, copyright, Robert Morris Associates, 1997.

Exhibit 9–2

1993 Financial Statement Percentages and Ratios
Apparel and Accessory Stores

Returns with Net Income, by Asset Size	Total	Zero Assets	1 - 100	100- 250	250- 500	500- 1000	1000- 5000
Number of Returns	10K-25K	100-500	5K-10K	5K-10K	1K-5K	1K-5K	500-1K
Net Sales	3,341,286	1,430,059	237,290	503,000	808,586	1,644,291	4,542,154
Total Assets	1,697,875	0	52,808	159,659	348,097	682,708	1,974,193
Assets							
Cash & Equivalents	5.60%	NA	16.33%	12.89%	13.35%	13.84%	15.56%
Trade Receivables (net)	13.05%	NA	10.08%	9.11%	10.44%	12.55%	5.72%
Inventory	32.34%	NA	62.52%	57.84%	50.49%	48.71%	51.45%
All Other Current	5.34%	NA	2.85%	5.03%	4.91%	5.20%	4.62%
Total Current	56.32%	NA	91.78%	84.86%	79.19%	80.30%	77.35%
Fixed Assets (net)	23.49%	NA	4.63%	8.91%	10.61%	9.91%	15.45%
Intangibles (net)	4.17%	NA	0.07%	2.00%	1.61%	0.18%	0.39%
All Other Non-Current	16.01%	NA	3.52%	4.23%	8.59%	9.61%	6.80%
Total Assets	100.00%	NA	100.00%	100.00%	100.00%	100.00%	100.00%
Liabilities							
Notes Payable-Short Term	5.83%	NA	4.48%	6.30%	3.21%	7.60%	5.77%
Curr. Mat. L/T/D	NA	NA	NA	NA	NA	NA	NA
Trade Payables	16.33%	NA	20.99%	16.59%	16.13%	19.93%	26.79%
Income Taxes Payable	NA	NA	NA	NA	NA	NA	NA
All Other Current	11.28%	NA	9.77%	7.28%	6.83%	5.53%	6.62%
Total Current	33.45%	NA	35.24%	30.17%	26.17%	33.05%	39.18%
Long Term Debt	14.47%	NA	29.17%	24.13%	22.57%	11.99%	12.56%
Deferred Taxes	NA	NA	NA	NA	NA	NA	NA
All Other Non-Current	2.53%	NA	0.00%	0.48%	0.36%	2.44%	1.00%
Net Worth	49.55%	NA	35.59%	45.23%	50.90%	52.53%	47.27%
Total Liab. & Net Worth	100.00%	NA	100.00%	100.00%	100.00%	100.00%	100.00%
Income Data							
Net Sales	100.00%	100.00%	100.00%	100.00%	100.00%	100.00%	100.00%
Cost of Sales and Operations	60.39%	60.00%	58.01%	62.79%	60.82%	60.19%	60.05%
Gross Profit	39.61%	40.00%	41.99%	37.21%	39.18%	39.81%	39.95%
Operating Expenses:							
Compensation of Officers	1.45%	1.07%	6.95%	4.13%	4.22%	5.26%	4.82%
Repairs	0.50%	1.41%	0.24%	0.40%	0.34%	0.49%	0.44%
Bad Debts	0.40%	0.10%	0.28%	0.04%	0.13%	0.10%	0.13%
Rent Paid on Business Property	6.42%	3.63%	9.79%	8.97%	6.21%	4.19%	6.54%
Contributions or gifts	0.06%	0.20%	0.00%	0.01%	0.02%	0.07%	0.04%
Amortization	0.12%	0.72%	0.00%	0.10%	0.03%	0.04%	0.16%
Depreciation	1.92%	1.61%	0.38%	0.64%	0.61%	0.76%	0.84%
Depletion	0.00%	0.00%	0.00%	0.00%	0.00%	0.00%	0.00%
Advertising	2.03%	2.01%	1.89%	2.17%	1.85%	2.16%	2.15%
Pension, Prof Sh. Stock, Annuity	0.28%	0.12%	0.33%	0.00%	0.16%	0.50%	0.31%
Employee Benefit Programs	0.76%	0.91%	0.09%	0.16%	0.14%	0.26%	0.45%
Other Deductions	20.94%	23.17%	16.16%	14.66%	18.10%	21.06%	18.55%
Total Operating Expenses	34.87%	34.94%	36.09%	31.28%	31.80%	34.89%	34.44%
Operating Profit	4.74%	5.06%	5.90%	5.93%	7.39%	4.92%	5.51%
Other Expenses/Revenue:							
Other Revenues	3.36%	4.85%	1.18%	2.97%	1.27%	1.40%	0.82%
Interest Paid	0.99%	0.62%	0.46%	0.44%	0.81%	0.70%	0.63%
Net Loss, Non Capital Assets	0.09%	0.00%	0.00%	0.02%	0.00%	0.03%	0.03%
Total All Other Expenses (net)	-2.28%	-4.23%	-0.71%	-2.51%	-0.46%	-0.67%	-0.17%
Profit Before Taxes	7.02%	9.28%	6.62%	8.44%	7.85%	5.58%	5.68%
Less Taxes Paid	2.20%	2.29%	1.95%	2.16%	3.05%	2.47%	2.64%
Net Income	4.82%	6.99%	4.67%	6.28%	4.79%	3.12%	3.04%
Ratios							
Current	1.68	NA	2.60	2.81	3.03	2.43	1.97
Quick	0.56	NA	0.75	0.73	0.91	0.80	0.54
Net Sales/Trade Receivables (net)	15.08	NA	44.59	34.60	22.25	19.20	40.22
Cost of Sales / Inventory	3.68	NA	4.17	3.42	2.80	2.98	2.69
Cost of Sales / Payables	7.28	NA	12.42	11.92	8.76	7.28	5.16
Sales/Working Capital	8.60	NA	7.95	5.76	4.38	5.10	6.03
EBIT/Interest	8.08	15.94	15.28	20.24	10.66	8.95	10.03
Net Profit + Depr., Dep., Amort/Cur. Mat. L/T,	NA	NA	NA	NA	NA	NA	NA
Net Fixed Assets/Tangible Net Worth	0.52	NA	0.13	0.21	0.22	0.19	0.33
Total Debt/Tangible Net Worth	1.11	NA	1.81	1.27	1.00	0.91	1.12
% Profits Before Taxes / Tangible Net Worth	30.44%	NA	83.68%	61.54%	36.97%	25.68%	27.86%
%Profit Before Taxes / Total Assets	13.81%	NA	29.73%	26.61%	18.22%	13.44%	13.06%
Sales/Net Fixed Assets	8.38	NA	96.99	35.34	21.90	24.30	14.89
Sales/Total Assets	1.97	NA	4.49	3.15	2.32	2.41	2.30
% Depr., Dep., Amort./Sales	2.04%	2.33%	0.38%	0.74%	0.64%	0.80%	1.00%
% Officers', Directors, Owners' Comp/Sales	1.45%	1.07%	6.95%	4.13%	4.22%	5.26%	4.82%

SOURCE: printout from *IRS Corporate Ratios* database and software program (New York: John Wiley & Sons, 1997). Reprinted with permission of John Wiley & Sons, Inc.

Exhibit 9–3

IRS CORPORATE FINANCIAL RATIOS
BY SIZE OF TOTAL ASSETS
FOR PROFITABLE VERSUS UNPROFITABLE COMPANIES
ELEVENTH EDITION

INDUSTRY WOMEN'S & CHILDREN'S CLOTHING
INDUSTRY DIVISION # 40   MAJOR GROUP # 12   MINOR GROUP #2345

	ALL FIRMS PROFIT	LOSS	1M - 999.99M PROFIT	LOSS	1MM - 24.99MM PROFIT	LOSS	25MM - 99.99MM PROFIT	LOSS	100MM & OVER PROFIT	LOSS
*** TURNOVER RATIOS										
RECEIVABLES TURNOVER	7.75	11.48	22.51	17.45	9.77	10.36	8.66	9.83	N/A	5.29
CASH TURNOVER	37.40	47.40	40.54	31.59	48.69	37.33	55.07	243.08	N/A	26.52
INVENT SALES TURNS	6.32	7.14	12.36	12.73	7.08	7.87	5.61	4.16	N/A	5.21
INVENT COST TURNS	4.56	5.61	8.83	9.54	5.24	6.37	4.11	3.12	N/A	3.64
WORKING CAP TURNOVER	5.97	7.34	12.72	8.97	7.45	8.33	5.59	5.47	N/A	4.33
FIXED ASSET TURNOVER	21.91	18.67	54.43	17.78	37.77	30.49	17.99	10.95	N/A	12.76
TOTAL ASSET TURNOVER	2.29	2.33	4.85	3.76	2.95	2.85	2.11	1.47	N/A	1.54
*** EXPENSES PCT.										
C-O-S-O TO SALES	72.09	78.66	71.46	74.94	74.04	80.98	73.40	74.95	N/A	69.87
ADVERTISING TO SALES	1.13	1.04	0.21	0.22	0.64	0.68	1.17	2.23	N/A	2.17
DEPREC TO SALES	0.73	0.92	0.72	0.96	0.48	0.65	0.71	1.31	N/A	1.17
RENTAL EXP TO SALES	1.27	2.46	2.30	4.80	1.01	1.86	0.91	1.44	N/A	1.66
INT EXP TO SALES	1.29	1.51	0.63	0.68	1.04	1.08	1.71	3.21	N/A	1.70
VAR EXP TO SALES	73.45	79.94	71.97	75.55	74.82	81.81	74.76	77.39	N/A	72.41
FIXED COST TO SALES	5.36	6.38	7.45	9.60	6.27	5.18	3.85	7.51	N/A	4.28
OTHER COST TO SALES	16.29	19.98	17.51	23.16	16.32	17.17	15.44	20.78	N/A	17.18
*** COST OF OPER PCT.										
VAR COST TO C-O-S-O	101.89	101.62	100.72	100.81	101.06	101.02	101.86	103.25	N/A	103.63
FIX COST TO C-O-S-O	7.44	8.11	10.42	12.81	8.47	6.40	5.25	10.02	N/A	6.12
*** BAD DEBT & ALLOW PCT										
ALLOW TO RECEIVABLES	2.59	3.17	0.86	0.77	1.30	1.89	2.39	6.67	N/A	3.95
ALLOW TO SALES	0.33	0.28	0.04	0.04	0.13	0.18	0.28	0.68	N/A	0.75
BAD DEBT TO RECEIVE	1.44	5.28	1.99	5.53	2.10	5.90	1.58	3.74	N/A	0.83
BAD DEBT TO SALES	0.19	0.46	0.09	0.32	0.21	0.57	0.18	0.38	N/A	0.16
*** EMPLOYMENT PCT.										
PENSION TO PBIT	3.43	-2.19	0.95	0.00	6.37	-2.16	1.70	-24.95	N/A	3.29
EMP BENEFITS TO PBIT	11.23	-27.06	2.26	-23.56	13.27	-37.58	8.78	-50.91	N/A	15.53
OFFICER COMP TO PBIT	41.99	-55.60	102.87	-50.19	102.69	-68.66	25.65	-297.80	N/A	11.69
*** PROFITABILITY PCT.										
GROSS MARGIN	27.91	21.34	28.54	25.06	25.96	19.02	26.60	25.05	N/A	30.13
OPERATING MARGIN	21.18	13.68	20.58	14.86	18.90	13.01	21.38	15.10	N/A	23.32
NET MARGIN	5.45	-6.30	2.87	-8.31	3.13	-4.27	5.99	-4.61	N/A	6.63
OTHER INC TO SALES	1.88	1.53	0.42	0.68	1.59	1.04	1.78	4.24	N/A	2.30
CASH FLOW TO SALES	8.59	-3.54	5.02	-6.66	5.14	-2.06	9.11	0.53	N/A	11.45
EARNING POWER	12.64	-14.75	13.91	-31.31	9.34	-12.26	12.86	-6.90	N/A	10.41
BEFORE TAX ROTA	14.75	-14.65	17.79	-31.29	10.60	-12.17	13.87	-6.79	N/A	12.82
AFTER TAX ROTA	12.45	-14.65	13.90	-31.29	9.26	-12.17	12.62	-6.79	N/A	10.23
*** TAXES PCT.										
EFFECTIVE TAX RATE	11.29	0.00	2.07	0.00	7.53	0.00	7.99	0.00	N/A	18.51
TAX CREDIT USE	16.28	N/A	0.34	N/A	20.76	N/A	42.96	N/A	N/A	6.82
*** INVESTMENT PCT.										
BEFORE TAX ROE	38.66	-59.69	49.20	-167.17	27.82	-32.05	32.59	-50.69	N/A	38.40
AFTER TAX ROE	32.63	-59.69	38.44	-167.17	24.31	-32.05	29.67	-50.69	N/A	30.66
RETN FROM OPERATIONS	33.08	10.41	26.09	7.08	34.04	16.02	37.18	2.54	N/A	31.10
RETN FROM LEVERAGE	8.71	31.53	0.85	23.23	0.19	28.98	10.34	58.40	N/A	8.31
RETN FROM TAX POLICY	26.91	34.00	40.86	34.00	30.29	34.00	28.57	34.00	N/A	19.40
SUSTAIN GROWTH RATE	25.51	-39.40	32.47	-110.33	18.36	-21.15	21.51	-33.46	N/A	25.34
*** LIQUIDITY RATIOS										
CURRENT RATIO	1.94	1.85	1.94	2.15	1.84	1.73	1.99	1.70	N/A	2.05
QUICK RATIO	0.86	0.66	0.82	0.91	0.76	0.74	0.72	0.38	N/A	1.00
DAYS RECEIVABLE	47.13	31.79	16.21	20.92	37.37	35.23	42.12	37.13	N/A	69.04
DAYS PAYABLE	49.14	33.13	26.86	23.84	42.82	36.24	32.19	37.32	N/A	71.52
DAYS WORKING CAPITAL	61.12	49.73	28.68	40.69	49.00	43.83	65.34	66.72	N/A	84.39
DAYS INVENTORY	57.72	51.14	29.52	28.66	51.58	46.40	65.11	87.67	N/A	70.12
INVENTORY TO C-O-S-O	0.22	0.18	0.11	0.10	0.19	0.16	0.24	0.32	N/A	0.27
*** FIXED ASSETS PCT.										
PL & EQUIP TO SALES	9.81	10.77	7.57	11.15	6.59	9.26	10.92	13.17	N/A	14.72
CAP LEASES TO SALES	4.22	8.21	7.67	16.00	3.35	6.19	3.03	4.80	N/A	5.55
INTAN ASTS TO SALES	0.65	0.29	0.01	0.02	0.29	0.27	0.87	1.08	N/A	1.10
FIXED ASTS TO SALES	4.56	5.36	1.84	5.62	2.65	3.28	5.56	9.13	N/A	7.84
CAP EXP TO SALES	N/A	N/A	N/A	N/A	N/A	N/A	N/A	N/A	N/A	N/A
CAP EXP TO PL&EQUIP	N/A	N/A	N/A	N/A	N/A	N/A	N/A	N/A	N/A	N/A
DEPR/DEPL RATE	7.85	10.70	9.54	8.54	7.40	10.69	6.11	12.91	N/A	9.11
FIXED ASTS CONSUMED	54.26	54.31	76.67	53.49	60.52	67.75	54.20	37.09	N/A	46.30
*** DEBT PCT.										
DEBT RETIRE CAPACITY	172.05	-101.77	805.76	-483.02	99.04	-58.34	91.88	-19.58	N/A	441.78
CUR ASTS TO ST DEBT	943.48	597.63	3634.25	1372.05	796.92	530.34	486.59	322.69	N/A	2466.38
PAYABLES TO CUR LIAB	54.62	44.55	63.08	50.43	54.51	48.74	35.69	29.50	N/A	62.27
PAYABLES TO TOT DEBT	79.16	44.71	120.07	39.16	103.70	78.65	40.84	17.28	N/A	78.04
ST DEBT TO TOT DEBT	29.84	31.07	10.18	12.16	43.98	52.57	46.73	30.92	N/A	10.42
LT DEBT TO TAN ASTS	19.96	25.76	19.08	41.39	13.98	13.92	18.13	45.89	N/A	24.66
LT DEBT TO TOT ASTS	19.66	25.59	19.07	41.35	13.86	13.82	17.80	45.16	N/A	24.24
*** NET WORTH PCT.										
PBT TO TAN WORTH	40.22	-61.38	49.24	-167.88	28.46	-32.70	34.05	-57.56	N/A	40.45
NET INC TO TAN WORTH	33.95	-61.38	38.47	-167.88	24.87	-32.70	31.00	-57.56	N/A	32.30
FIX AST TO TAN WORTH	28.45	52.18	24.66	113.58	21.01	25.12	28.77	114.13	N/A	38.14
CUR LIA TO TAN WORTH	110.78	156.10	111.85	196.17	126.44	126.31	93.89	324.63	N/A	107.03
TOT LIA TO TAN WORTH	168.69	316.09	176.66	436.20	166.27	166.63	141.06	734.30	N/A	210.27
*** INT COVERAGE RATIOS										
INT COVERAGE	6.01	-3.18	6.84	-11.18	4.44	-2.96	4.84	-0.43	N/A	5.89
CASH FLOW COVERAGE	6.67	-2.35	7.99	-9.76	4.94	-1.90	5.32	0.16	N/A	6.74
TOT COVERAGE	4.53	-2.06	3.08	-3.34	3.36	-1.88	4.11	-0.38	N/A	4.44
TOT CASH COVERAGE	5.02	-1.52	3.60	-2.92	3.74	-1.21	4.52	0.14	N/A	5.08
*** WORKING CAP PCT.										
WORK CAP TO SALES	16.75	13.62	7.86	11.15	13.42	12.01	17.90	18.28	N/A	23.12
NET INC TO WORK CAP	32.52	-46.25	36.48	-74.57	23.35	-35.57	33.45	-25.19	N/A	28.69
INVENT TO WORK CAP	94.44	102.85	102.92	70.45	105.26	105.87	99.65	131.39	N/A	83.09
ST DEBT TO WORK CAP	21.85	36.41	5.67	13.64	27.44	44.76	41.37	75.02	N/A	7.91
LT DEBT TO WORK CAP	51.38	80.78	50.05	98.56	34.95	40.38	47.17	167.57	N/A	67.97
*** MISCELLANEOUS										
BASE NO. COMPANIES	2139	2723	1427	2232	631	270	36	14	N/A	12
MEAN ASSETS (M)	4146	986	225	168	4999	3822	48737	44698	N/A	357664
MEAN SALES (M)	9477	2293	1090	631	14769	10893	102749	65891	N/A	551698

N/A INDICATES NO DATA, ACTUAL OR ESTIMATED ARE AVAILABLE FOR THIS VALUE.

SOURCE: *IRS Corporate Financial Ratios* (Lincolnshire, Ill.: Schonfeld & Associates, Inc., 1997), p. 44. Reprinted with permission.

Exhibit 9–4

Table II		RETAIL TRADE
Corporations with Net Income		5600

APPAREL AND ACCESSORY STORES

MONEY AMOUNTS AND SIZE OF ASSETS IN THOUSANDS OF DOLLARS

Item Description for Accounting Period 7/93 Through 6/94	Total	Zero Assets	Under 100	100 to 250	251 to 500	501 to 1,000	1,001 to 5,000	5,001 to 10,000	10,001 to 25,000	25,001 to 50,000	50,001 to 100,000	100,001 to 250,000	250,001 and over
Number of Enterprises 1	22039	236	8423	7721	2703	1828	843	121	84	22	23	20	15
Revenues ($ in Thousands)													
Net Sales 2	73638606	337494	1998695	3883660	2185609	3005764	3829036	1822026	3626234	1851079	3331894	6137447	41629668
Portfolio Income 3	800280	12071	1449	4511	12898	13010	7361	1591	17718	5839	11050	60033	652747
Other Revenues 4	1673786	4286	22090	110828	14825	28943	24025	6900	36988	51278	42445	120682	1210497
Total Revenues 5	76112672	353851	2022234	3998999	2213332	3047717	3860422	1830517	3680940	1908196	3385389	6318162	43492912
Average Total Revenues 6	3454	1499	240	518	819	1667	4579	15128	43821	86736	147191	315908	2899527
Operating Costs/Operating Income (%)													
Cost of Operations 7	60.4	60.0	58.0	62.8	60.8	60.2	60.1	64.2	60.3	62.4	61.3	58.7	60.2
Rent 8	6.4	3.6	9.8	9.0	6.2	4.2	6.6	5.4	7.0	5.0	5.6	5.1	6.5
Taxes Paid 9	2.2	0.2	2.0	2.2	3.1	2.5	2.6	2.3	2.0	1.9	2.0	2.7	2.1
Interest Paid 10	1.0	0.6	0.5	0.4	0.8	0.7	0.6	1.1	0.7	0.6	1.1	0.7	1.2
Depreciation, Depletion, Amortization 11	2.1	2.3	0.4	0.7	0.6	0.8	1.0	1.0	1.4	1.4	1.7	1.7	2.7
Pensions and Other Benefits 12	1.1	1.0	0.4	0.2	0.3	0.8	0.8	0.5	0.8	1.1	1.1	1.1	1.3
Other 13	24.0	26.9	18.6	17.3	20.4	23.9	21.3	18.9	24.5	24.8	23.5	26.8	25.1
Officers Compensation 14	1.5	1.1	7.0	4.1	4.2	5.3	4.8	2.0	2.2	1.3	0.8	0.7	0.3
Operating Margin 15	1.5	2.2	3.5	3.3	3.5	1.7	2.2	4.8	1.3	1.7	2.9	2.4	0.6
Oper. Margin Before Officers Compensation 16	2.9	3.2	10.5	7.5	7.8	7.0	7.1	6.8	3.5	3.0	3.7	3.2	0.9
Selected Average Balance Sheet ($ in Thousands)													
Net Receivables 17	222	•	5	15	36	86	113	966	1170	2448	6358	19016	238803
Inventories 18	549	•	33	92	176	333	1016	3557	7491	13405	26783	49769	413563
Net Property, Plant and Equipment 19	399	•	2	14	37	68	305	1027	3908	8011	18313	42804	418259
Total Assets 20	1698	•	53	160	348	683	1974	6902	15418	34742	65917	153027	1627841
Notes and Loans Payable 21	345	•	18	49	90	134	362	2219	4290	5440	19034	23122	310393
All Other Liabilities 22	512	•	16	39	81	190	679	1821	4316	9644	17223	44855	507610
Net Worth 23	841	•	19	72	177	359	933	2861	6812	19653	30660	85051	809838
Selected Financial Ratios (Times to 1)													
Current Ratio 24	1.7	•	2.6	2.8	3.0	2.4	2.0	2.0	1.9	2.0	2.3	2.3	1.4
Quick Ratio 25	0.6	•	0.8	0.7	0.9	0.8	0.6	0.6	0.5	0.4	0.6	0.8	0.5
Net Sales to Working Capital 26	8.6	•	8.0	5.8	4.4	5.1	6.0	5.5	8.4	7.2	6.6	6.1	12.4
Coverage Ratio 27	5.9	12.3	11.1	•	6.8	5.4	5.8	6.0	5.4	8.8	5.2	8.5	5.2
Total Asset Turnover 28	2.0	•	4.5	3.2	2.3	2.4	2.3	2.2	2.8	2.4	2.2	2.0	1.7
Inventory Turnover 29	3.7	•	4.2	3.4	2.8	3.0	2.7	2.7	3.5	3.9	3.3	3.6	4.1
Receivables Turnover 30	•	•	•	•	•	•	•	•	•	•	•	•	•
Total Liabilities to Net Worth 31	1.0	•	1.8	1.2	1.0	0.9	1.1	1.4	1.3	0.8	1.2	0.8	1.0
Selected Financial Factors (in Percentages)													
Debt Ratio 32	50.5	•	64.4	54.8	49.1	47.5	52.7	58.6	55.8	43.4	53.5	44.4	50.3
Return on Assets 33	11.4	•	23.1	21.2	12.9	9.2	8.4	13.8	9.8	13.0	12.2	12.0	10.8
Return on Equity 34	13.8	•	•	39.1	18.2	12.7	13.0	24.2	15.3	15.7	16.5	12.6	11.5
Return Before Interest on Equity 35	23.1	•	•	•	25.3	17.5	17.8	33.2	22.2	23.0	26.2	21.5	21.6
Profit Margin, Before Income Tax 36	4.8	7.0	4.7	6.3	4.7	3.1	3.0	5.3	2.9	4.8	4.5	5.3	5.1
Profit Margin, After Income Tax 37	3.5	5.3	4.3	5.6	4.0	2.8	2.7	4.6	2.4	3.7	3.5	3.5	3.4

Trends in Selected Ratios and Factors, 1988-1997										
	1988	1989	1990	1991	1992	1993	1994	1995	1996	1997
Cost of Operations (%) 38	58.7	59.1	58.9	59.4	59.3	59.5	59.7	60.4	60.8	60.4
Operating Margin (%) 39	2.5	2.0	2.2	2.4	2.4	2.3	1.6	1.2	1.4	1.5
Oper. Margin Before Officers Comp. (%) 40	4.8	4.3	4.2	4.6	4.3	4.0	3.2	2.5	2.6	2.9
Average Net Receivables ($) 41	112	124	155	138	153	185	177	198	212	222
Average Inventories ($) 42	280	313	348	325	389	417	442	551	595	549
Average Net Worth ($) 43	394	450	500	436	539	608	662	850	953	841
Current Ratio (×1) 44	2.2	2.1	2.2	2.1	2.0	2.0	1.9	1.8	1.8	1.7
Quick Ratio (×1) 45	0.8	0.8	0.8	0.8	0.7	0.7	0.6	0.6	0.5	0.6
Coverage Ratio (×1) 46	5.6	5.3	5.8	5.9	6.2	4.7	4.3	4.4	4.7	5.9
Asset Turnover (×1) 47	2.1	2.0	2.0	2.1	2.1	1.9	1.9	1.9	2.0	2.0
Operating Leverage 48	0.9	0.8	1.1	1.1	1.0	1.0	0.7	0.8	1.2	1.0
Financial Leverage 49	1.1	1.0	1.0	1.1	1.1	0.9	1.0	1.0	1.0	1.0
Total Leverage 50	0.9	0.8	1.1	1.2	1.1	0.9	0.7	0.8	1.2	1.1

SOURCE: *Almanac of Business and Industrial Financial Ratios*, by Leo Troy. Copyright © 1997 by Prentice Hall, p. 254. Reprinted with permission of Prentice Hall.

Each group for which there are sufficient data is disaggregated into 13 asset size categories, compared with 6 in the RMA data. The *Almanac* gives more income statement line items than does RMA, while RMA gives more balance sheet line items and more ratios.

The various ratios used are defined in the front part of the *Almanac*. Computations of some of the ratios differ from computations used by RMA.

Financial Ratio Analyst. Compiled by James R. Hickman and E.W. Lester and published by Warren, Gorham & Lamont, the 1996 second edition of this publication presents ratios based on the IRS's sample of 85,000 federal tax returns. There are eight asset categories. This particular version of the IRS tax return data is available in both book and diskette version, and the software version allows automated comparison of client information with IRS ratios.

Exhibit 9-5 presents a same page from the 1996 edition of this publication.

The biggest drawback to the four publications that rely on the Internal Revenue Service data is the degree to which the information is outdated. The latest (1997) editions cover tax returns for fiscal years ended July 1993 through June 1994, the most recent year for which authoritative figures derived from tax return data of the Internal Revenue Service are available. Nevertheless, operating figures for most industries have at least some degree of stability over time.

Financial Studies of the Small Business. *Financial Studies of the Small Business*, published by Financial Research Associates (FRA), is a compilation from over 30,000 financial statements submitted by over 1,500 independent certified public accountant firms, from all across the country.

Exhibit 9-6 is a typical page from *Financial Studies*, in this case, retail apparel stores with total assets of $100,000 to $250,000. *Financial Studies* differs particularly from *Annual Statement Studies* and the four compilations from tax return data in that it focuses on especially small firms. Within each business or professional services group for which sufficient data are available, four size breakdowns are presented by total assets: $10,000 to $100,000, $100,000 to $250,000, $250,000 to $500,000, and $500,000 to $1,000,000. In addition, an overall presentation from $10,000 to $1,000,000 follows the individual breakdown. If any one breakdown did not contain 10 or more companies, the data were omitted.

Median figures are used for financial statement line items, and it is necessary to read the explanation in order to interpret those figures correctly. Definitions of ratios are included in the front of the loose-leaf book, and most are similar, if not identical, to those used by RMA. As is the case with the RMA ratios, upper and lower quartile figures, as well as medians, are presented.

It is noteworthy that the 1997 edition (as well as earlier editions) offered the following statement:

Again data has revealed noticeable differences when compared to studies including large firms in their sampling. FRA compared data on

Exhibit 9–5

SOI CODE: **5600**	Table One: Financial Information
MAJOR INDUSTRY: **Apparel And Accessory Stores**	Corporations With Net Income
MINOR INDUSTRY: **Apparel And Accessory Stores**	

Accounting Item (Period 7/92 to 6/93)	Group Totals	Under 100	100 to 250	251 to 500	501 to 1000	1001 to 10000	10001 to 25000	Over 25000
Number of Companies	21349	9467	6395	2739	1609	974	84	81
Group Totals in Millions								
Total Revenues	81289	2115	3126	2739	2808	5491	3559	61462
Total Deductions	77697	2006	2940	2623	2692	5261	3427	58727
Net Income (Less Deficit)	0	0	0	0	0	0	0	0
Total Assets	40566	488	971	985	1092	2225	1284	33520
Average Revenue in Thousands								
Net Receipts or Sales	3592	218	488	995	1721	5575	41518	731217
Investment Income	41	1	1	1	5	17	145	10036
Other Income	75	4	0	4	19	46	712	17415
Total Revenues	3808	223	489	1000	1745	5638	42375	758670
Average Operating Costs in Thousands								
Cost of Sales and Operations	2245	133	304	598	1053	3546	24719	442880
Rent	245	19	39	51	89	326	2463	49267
Advertising	77	5	10	18	35	123	1490	14615
Taxes Paid	85	4	11	18	64	122	817	16883
Interest Paid	44	1	2	8	12	53	269	10335
Depletion, Deprec. and Amort.	77	1	3	6	18	52	514	18233
Pension and Related	40	0	3	4	16	40	377	8096
Bad Debt Expense	14	0	0	1	2	12	116	3362
Other Costs	767	44	74	199	313	971	9305	189996
Officers' Comp.	43	5	14	54	76	175	817	3428
Selected Averages in Thousands								
Cash	86	6	19	47	110	340	1585	11082
Net Receivables	212	5	26	41	58	224	1462	46440
Inventories	595	32	74	187	310	1164	6952	113489
Net Plant, Property and Equipment	457	4	13	36	62	347	3360	111478
Total Assets	1900	52	152	359	679	2285	15281	413832
Accounts Payable	272	8	25	71	132	535	3020	54296
Mort. and Notes Less Than a Year	112	2	4	19	29	223	1784	23290
Other Current Liabilities	190	4	14	29	33	129	1375	43694
Mort. and Notes More Than a Year	225	6	14	18	62	216	1736	51641
Loans from Shareholders	42	10	18	57	36	58	203	4892
Other Liabilities	108	4	0	1	10	81	255	25854
Net Worth	953	17	77	185	377	1042	6909	210263

SOI CODE: **5600**	Table Two: Ratios and Percentages
MAJOR INDUSTRY: **Apparel And Accessory Stores**	Corporations With Net Income
MINOR INDUSTRY: **Apparel And Accessory Stores**	

Accounting Item (Period 7/92 to 6/93)	Group Totals	Under 100	100 to 250	251 to 500	501 to 1000	1001 to 10000	10001 to 25000	Over 25000
Number of Companies	21349	9467	6395	2739	1609	974	84	81
Solvency Ratios								
Current Ratio	1.8	3.1	2.9	2.5	2.7	2.0	1.7	1.6
Quick Ratio	0.5	0.8	1.1	0.7	0.9	0.6	0.5	0.5
Liquidation Ratio	0.2	0.4	0.4	0.4	0.6	0.4	0.3	0.1
Total Liabilities to Net Worth	1.0	2.0	1.0	1.2	0.8	1.2	1.2	1.0
Net Sales to Working Capital	8.5	7.2	5.9	5.7	5.1	6.1	9.5	9.7
Coverage Ratio	4.7	14.5	*	6.0	7.0	5.1	6.8	4.3
Leverage Ratios								
Debt Ratio	49.9	66.5	49.3	54.2	44.4	54.4	54.8	49.2
Return on Equity	–	–	–	–	–	–	–	–
Return on Equity Before Interest	4.8	4.9	2.4	5.1	3.1	5.1	3.9	4.9
Profit Margin, Before FIT	0.0	0.0	0.0	0.0	0.0	0.0	0.0	0.0
Profit Margin, After FIT	–	–	–	–	–	–	–	–
Operating Costs as a Percentage of Sales (%)								
Cost of Sales and Operations	60.8	60.7	62.3	60.1	61.2	63.6	59.5	60.6
Rent	6.6	8.7	8.1	5.2	5.1	5.9	5.9	6.7
Advertising	2.1	2.3	2.1	1.8	2.1	2.2	3.5	2.0
Taxes Paid	2.3	1.8	2.2	1.8	3.7	2.2	2.0	2.3
Interest Paid	1.2	0.4	0.4	0.9	0.7	0.9	0.6	1.4
Depletion, Deprec. and Amort.	2.1	0.6	0.7	0.6	0.7	0.9	1.2	2.5
Pension and Related	1.1	0.2	0.5	0.4	1.0	0.7	0.8	1.2
Bad Debt Expense	0.4	0.0	0.0	0.1	0.1	0.2	0.3	0.5
Other Costs	23.3	22.5	17.3	22.0	20.4	19.8	26.2	23.9
Officers' Comp.	1.2	2.2	2.8	5.4	4.5	3.1	2.0	0.5
Profitability Ratios								
Return on Gross Profit	–	–	–	–	–	–	–	–
Gross Profit to Sales	39.2	39.3	37.7	39.9	38.8	36.4	40.5	39.4
Operating Expense to Sales	60.8	60.7	62.3	60.1	61.2	63.6	59.5	60.6
Operating Margin	1.4	3.0	5.7	3.7	2.8	2.7	1.7	0.8
Operating Margin Before Officers' Comp.	2.6	5.2	8.5	9.1	7.3	5.9	3.7	1.3
Operating Margin Before Int. and Deprec.	4.6	3.9	8.7	5.1	4.1	4.5	3.5	4.6
Efficiency Ratios								
Turnover of Assets	1.9	4.2	3.2	2.8	2.5	2.4	2.7	1.8
Income Tax Rate Ratio	–	–	–	–	–	–	–	–
Expenses to Gross Profit	8.3	6.9	5.4	8.5	8.7	8.7	10.2	8.4
Depreciation Expense Ratio	1.9	0.5	0.6	0.5	0.6	0.8	1.2	2.3
Days Sales in Inventory	58.9	53.9	55.6	66.7	65.8	76.3	61.2	58.7

SOURCE: James R. Hickman and E.W. Bud Lester, *Financial Ratio Analyst* (New York: Warren, Gorham & Lamont, 1996), pp. 544–45. Reprinted with permission.

retail establishments to other studies containing a substantial number of firms with larger asset sizes. This comparison revealed the typical FRA firm to be more liquid, employing less debt, and earning a higher return on investment. These differences are significant and we would hope that one in an evaluating position would now be better able to make valid comparisons for the particularly small firm.[1]

Specialized Sources

Many trade and professional associations compile and make available composite financial data on businesses or professions that are members.

---

[1] *Financial Studies of the Small Business*, 20th ed. (Winter Haven, FL: Financial Research Associates, 1997), p. i.

Exhibit 9–6

RETAIL APPAREL TOTAL ASSETS $100000–$ 250000

INCOME DATA

	AS A PCT OF NET SALES
NET SALES (GROSS INCOME)	100.00
COST OF SALES	59.86
GROSS PROFIT	40.14
GENERAL/ADMINISTRATIVE EXP	37.85
OPERATING PROFIT	2.29
INTEREST EXPENSE	0.19
DEPRECIATION	0.47
PROFIT BEFORE TAXES	1.63

ADDITIONAL OPERATING ITEMS

LABOR	10.28
ADVERTISING EXPENSE	1.83
TRAVEL EXPENSE	0.58
RENT	5.46
INSURANCE	0.85
OFFICER/EXECUTIVE SALARIES	7.31

RATIOS

	MEDIAN	UPPER QUARTILE	LOWER QUARTILE	UNITS
CURRENT	3.5	5.6	2.5	TIMES
QUICK	1.1	2.5	0.4	TIMES
CURRENT ASSETS/TOTAL ASSETS	89.5	96.4	80.8	PCT
SHORT TERM DEBT/TOTAL DEBT	57.5	100.0	17.2	PCT
SHORT TERM DEBT/NET WORTH	28.8	107.5	3.9	PCT
TOTAL DEBT/NET WORTH	60.3	302.3	9.0	PCT
SHORT TERM DEBT/TOTAL ASSETS	23.2	32.4	8.3	PCT
LONG TERM DEBT/TOTAL ASSETS	25.3	62.4	0.0	PCT
TOTAL DEBT/TOTAL ASSETS	65.2	91.1	21.2	PCT
SALES/RECEIVABLES	8.8	44.2	0.0	TIMES
AVERAGE COLLECTION PERIOD	2.	16.	0.	DAYS
SALES/INVENTORY	5.9	9.2	3.2	TIMES
SALES/TOTAL ASSETS	2.6	3.4	1.5	TIMES
SALES/NET WORTH	4.2	10.1	2.0	TIMES
PROFIT (PRETAX)/TOTAL ASSETS	4.5	19.1	0.0	PCT
PROFIT (PRETAX)/NET WORTH	15.3	58.9	0.4	PCT

RETAIL APPAREL TOTAL ASSETS $100000–$ 250000

ASSETS

	AS A PCT OF CURRENT ASSETS	AS A PCT OF TOTAL ASSETS
CURRENT ASSETS		
CASH	23.90	20.10
ACCOUNTS RECEIVABLES	1.75	1.65
INVENTORIES	67.36	52.60
OTHER CURRENT ASSETS	0.00	0.00

FIXED ASSETS	AS A PCT OF FIXED ASSETS	AS A PCT OF TOTAL ASSETS
LAND,BUILDINGS,LEASE-HOLD IMPROVEMENTS	0.00	0.00
EQUIPMENT	100.00	2.59
OTHER FIXED ASSETS	0.00	0.00

LIABILITIES & CAPITAL

CURRENT LIABILITIES	AS A PCT OF CURRENT LIABILITIES	AS A PCT OF TOTAL LIABILITIES
ACCOUNTS PAYABLE/TRADE	53.83	17.80
SHORT TERM BANK LOANS	0.00	0.00
OTHER CURRENT DEBT	35.94	10.56

LONG TERM DEBT	AS A PCT OF LONG TERM DEBT	AS A PCT OF TOTAL LIABILITIES
NOTES PAYABLE	0.00	0.00
MORTGAGES PAYABLE	0.00	0.00
LONG TERM BANK LOANS	0.00	0.00
STOCKHOLDER LOANS (DUE TO OWNERS)	0.00	0.00
OTHER LONG TERM DEBT	0.00	0.00

SOURCE: *Financial Studies of the Small Business* (Winter Haven, FL: Financial Research Associates., 1997), pp. 25–26. Reprinted with permission.

Also, some trade and professional publications offer financial data. Each issue of the RMA *Annual Statement Studies* now contains a bibliography listing 261 separate sources of composite financial data for specific lines of business. One advantage of franchise operations is that most franchisers provide comparative financial data. Also, many manufacturers that sell through networks of retail outlets provide comparative financial data to their retailers. Certain accounting firms and management consultants that specialize in particular lines of business provide clients with comparative financial data.

Interpretation of Financial Statement Ratios

Comparisons between financial statement ratios for the subject company and industry averages can indicate both specific opportunities for possible improvement and situations that could cause problems. Financial statement ratios fall into four broad categories:

1. Short-term liquidity measures.
2. Balance sheet leverage ratios.
3. Activity ratios.
4. Profitability ratios.

In addition to the traditional categories of ratios, each line item on the income statement can be compared with industry averages.

Short-Term Liquidity Measures

The two primary short-term liquidity ratios are the *current ratio* and the *acid test ratio* (also called the *quick ratio*). Both of these ratios are discussed in some detail in Chapter 10 in the section on analyzing working capital requirements. Their most important use is to indicate the extent to which a company may have either inadequate or excessive working capital.

Balance Sheet Leverage Ratios

The primary balance sheet leverage ratios are the *equity ratio* (owner's equity as a percent of total assets) and the *long-term debt to equity ratio*. These ratios are one indicator of the degree of risk; the less the equity relative to the total assets and to the long-term debt, the greater the degree of risk. For some companies, these ratios might also indicate borrowing power; leverage ratios well below industry averages may indicate unused borrowing power.

Activity Ratios

The general idea of activity ratios is to measure how efficiently the assets are being employed. The primary activity ratios are *accounts re-*

ceivable turnover, inventory turnover (both discussed in Chapter 10 under working capital analysis), and *asset turnover* (sales divided by total assets).

Profitability Ratios

Profitability ratios fall into two broad categories: income statement profitability ratios and rates of return on some level of investment. Income statement profitability ratios are usually expressed as a percentage of sales. Rate of return ratios are usually expressed either as a percentage of equity or as a percentage of investment, with investment usually defined to mean either equity plus long-term debt, or equity plus all interest-bearing debt. The following measures of profitability are often expressed as a percentage of one or more of the four variables above:

1. *EBDIT.* Earnings before depreciation, interest, and taxes.
2. *EBIT.* Earnings before interest and taxes.
3. *EBT (pretax profit).* Net income before taxes.
4. *EBDT.* Earnings before depreciation and taxes.
5. *Net Income.* Earnings after interest, depreciation, and taxes.

When comparing any ratios with industry averages, it is important to be sure that the comparison is on an apples-to-apples basis; that is, the industry average measures of comparison and the subject company ratios are being computed in exactly the same way. The following section offers some examples that compare company financial statement ratios with industry averages.

Examples of Comparative Industry Analysis

The following hypothetical examples illustrate how the average industry data discussed in this chapter can be compared with data from the entity in which we are interested. The two examples continue to refer to the same two hypothetical companies used in two previous chapters.

Sole Proprietorship Example

Exhibit 9-7 shows how Ashley's Apparel Store compares with other apparel and accessory stores. The *Almanac of Business and Industrial Financial Ratios* is used as the basis of comparison in this example in order to compare as many expense items on the income statement as possible.

It is apparent that Ashley's gross margin is far above the industry average, as is its return on equity. Compensation of officers appears to be a bit higher than the industry average for companies of this size (5.0

Exhibit 9–7

ASHLEY'S APPAREL STORE AND
ALMANAC OF BUSINESS & INDUSTRIAL FINANCIAL RATIOS
RETAIL TRADE: APPAREL AND ACCESSORY STORES
COMPARATIVE ANALYSIS

Asset Size	The Almanac $251,000 - $500,000	Ashley's Apparel a $280,000
Revenues	$819,000 b	$1,000,000
Cost of operations	60.8 %	53.5 %
Compensation of officers	4.2	5.0
Rent on business property	6.2	6.5
Interest	0.8	0.7
Depreciation, depletion, amortization	0.6	1.3
Pension and other benefit plans	0.3	2.3
Other expenses	20.4 c	22.9
Net profit before taxes	4.7	6.6
RATIOS		
Coverage ratio	6.8	12.3
Asset turnover	2.3	3.5
Total liabilities/net worth	1.0	0.5
Return on assets	12.9	25.9
Return on equity	18.2	34.4

a   Figures used are from the adjusted income statement and balance sheet (see Exhibits 7-2 and 8-2).

b   Average revenues for the 2,703 companies in this asset size.

c   Includes repairs, bad debts, contributions, and advertising.

SOURCE: Exhibits 7-2 and 8-2 and *Almanac of Business and Industrial Financial Ratios,* 28th edition (Englewood Cliffs, N.J.: Prentice-Hall, 1997), p. 254.

percent for Ashley's versus 4.2 percent for the industry). Ashley's return on assets is also higher than the industry average. (Because the adjusted balance sheet eliminates the current liabilities for Ashley's, several ratios that normally would be computed are omitted in this example.)

Corporation Example

Exhibit 9-8 shows how Patrick's Machinery & Equipment, Inc., compares with other wholesale machinery and equipment distributors. Robert Morris Associates' *Annual Statement Studies* is used as the basis of comparison in this example.

Many more comparisons are available by comparing Patrick's with the industry averages, as shown in the RMA data.

Patrick's is above the industry average short-term liquidity measures for both the current ratio and the quick ratio. It has less balance sheet leverage, with a debt/equity ratio of only 0.8. This leverage posi-

Exhibit 9–8

PATRICK'S MACHINERY & EQUIPMENT, INC. AND
RMA FINANCIAL STATEMENT STUDIES
COMPARATIVE ANALYSIS

	RMA $500m - $2mm	PATRICK'S
Asset Size:		
Statement Date:	4/1/96 to 9/30/96	1997

COMPOSITION OF THE BALANCE SHEET AND THE INCOME STATEMENT

	%	%
ASSETS:		
Cash & equivalents	7.2	6.0
Accounts & notes receivable	35.3	21.3
Inventory	36.8	39.5
All other current	1.3	3.6
Total current	80.6	70.4
Fixed assets (net)	12.9	23.2
Intangibles	1.4	0.8
All other noncurrent	5.1	5.6
Total assets	100.0	100.0
LIABILITIES AND NET WORTH		
Notes payable--short-term	13.4	4.6
Current maturity long-term debt	2.8	3.7
Accounts & notes payable--trade	23.6	11.2
All other current	8.4	6.5
Total current	48.7	26.0
Long-term debt	8.7	8.8
All other noncurrent	3.8	6.5
Net worth	38.6	58.6
Total liabilities and net worth	100.0	100.0
INCOME STATEMENT DATA		
Net sales	100.0	100.0
Gross profit	29.7	33.8
Operating expenses	26.8	29.7
Operating profit	2.9	4.1
All other expenses (net)	0.3	0.6
Profit before taxes	2.6	3.5

RATIOS

	Upper Quartile	Median	Lower Quartile		Patrick's
Current ratio	2.4	1.7	1.3		2.5
Quick ratio	1.3	0.9	0.6		1.1
Sales/receivables	11.7	8.9	7.0		10.4
Cost of sales/inventory	11.3	6.5	3.7		4.2
Cost of sales/payables	17.9	10.6	6.7		13.3
Sales/working capital	6.1	10.1	19.1		5.7
EBIT/interest	6.8	3.1	1.6		6.7
Fixed assets/net worth	0.1	0.3	0.7	a	0.4
Debt/net worth	0.9	1.6	3.2		0.8
% pretax income/tangible net worth	35.7	15.7	6.1		14.9
% pretax income/total assets	12.0	5.3	1.8		8.3
Sales/net fixed assets	82.8	38.2	17.6	a	9.6
Sales/total assets	3.9	3.1	2.2		2.3
% depreciation, amortization/sales	0.4	0.8	1.4		1.4
% officers' compensation/sales	2.7	4.5	7.3		5.0

a   Patrick's assets have been adjusted upward to reflect replacement cost, while RMA companies' fixed assets are unadjusted; therefore,
     Patrick's ratio would be higher in the case of fixed assets/net worth and lower in the case of sales/fixed assets if they were computed as
     the RMA ratios were.

LTD = Long-term debt

SOURCE: Exhibits 7-3 and 8-4 and *RMA Annual Statement Studies* (Philadelphia, PA: Robert Morris Associates, 1997), p. 498.
         Annual Statement Studies,

tion definitely suggests a very strong financial position and probable borrowing power, if Patrick's wanted to use it.

The activity ratios show that it is above the industry median for accounts receivable turnover, but its inventory turnover is between the industry median and the lower quartile. It is just above the industry lower quartile for sales to total assets. These statistics suggest that Patrick's might be able to use its assets a little more intensively to get a little more sales out of the assets in use.

Most importantly, however, Patrick's is ahead of the industry averages in all categories of profitability ratios. Gross profit, operating profit, and pretax profit as a percent of sales are all above industry averages. Pretax return on equity is just below the industry median.

Each of the various industry comparison services does not necessarily compute all the ratios of interest, but they offer enough to make very useful generalizations in many respects about how the subject company compares with its peers.

Summary

Comparing the subject company with industry averages is a useful and often revealing exercise as part of the valuation process. It may help the analyst to spot errors and/or areas for further inquiry. It helps to reveal the company's strengths, weaknesses, and opportunities.

Several generalized sources of comparative data have been presented. In addition to these, many trade and professional associations and trade and professional publishers generate comparative financial data for their industry or profession.

When using comparative industry data, the analyst should be careful to check definitions of both the financial statement line items and ratios. Different sources use different definitions. The analyst may have to adjust the subject company data to conform to the comparative source's definitions to get an apples-to-apples comparison.

In the course of the analysis, the analyst should think about how any deviations from industry norms impact value. These points should be noted in the ultimate valuation analysis.

Chapter 10

Analyzing Qualitative Factors

Qualitative factors are the characteristics of the business, industry, and the economy as a whole that affect (1) the future of the company and (2) whether its performance will be consistent with past results. Many of these factors are difficult or impossible to quantify, such as the effects of competition or unanticipated upturns or downturns in the economy. Other factors are more easily quantifiable, such as the expected cost of improvement to facilities and future compensation. A thorough analysis of these factors will assist the analyst in assessing the company's ongoing earning power. It will also help the analyst estimate the degree of risk involved in the enterprise, which in turn will have an important bearing on the applicable capitalization rates. And it may bring to light additional capital investment that may be required in order to produce some expected level of income.

One good way of acquiring information on some of the factors discussed in this chapter is to visit the company's operating facilities and talk with current owners, managers, and others, as well as outside sources. In some cases, the potential buyer may be wise to work in the operation for a day, a week, or even longer, to get a good look at the operation from the inside.

The relevance of the various factors will differ from one industry to another and sometimes from one business to another within an industry. The following sections discuss the major categories of qualitative factors that should be considered in valuing a typical business or professional practice. (There is further discussion of certain qualitative factors specific to professional practices in Part IV.) For some companies, some of the factors discussed in this chapter obviously will not apply. For others, these factors (and others) will be relevant.

Relevant Economic Data

The importance of economic data varies greatly from one kind of business or practice to another. As a broad generality, businesses providing goods or services for which demand is highly elastic are more affected by changes in economic conditions than are businesses providing goods or services that people regard as daily necessities. The discretion available to buyers to avoid or postpone purchase of certain goods and services can determine how much broad economic influences affect the enterprise. The analyst should use judgment and experience when considering which economic factors will have a bearing on the fortunes of the business or professional practice being valued.

National Economic Data

Relevant national economic data will provide clues to people's propensity to spend money for the goods or services offered by the business or professional practice being valued, along with anything else that might affect profit margins. Depending on the line of business, the following economic variables could have a bearing on the company's outlook:

1. *Gross Domestic Product (GDP)*[1] The value of all goods and services produced in a country. GDP covers the goods and services produced by labor and property located in the United States.
2. *Gross National Product (GNP).* The value of all goods and services produced in a country plus income earned in foreign countries less income payable to foreign sources. GNP covers the goods and services produced by labor and property supplied by U.S. residents. As long as the labor and property are supplied by U.S. residents, they may be located either in the United States or abroad.
3. *Disposable Personal Income.* The total income received by individuals, available for consumption and savings; this is total personal income less personal taxes.
4. *Business Capital Spending.* The total amount of business expenditures on durable assets, such as plant and equipment, during a specific time period.
5. *Consumer Durable Goods Expenditures.* The total amount of consumer expenditures on such items as appliances and automobiles during a specific time period.
6. *Housing Starts.* The total number of housing units started during a specific time period.
7. *Consumer Price Index (CPI).* The most common means of measuring the price changes of goods and services purchased by the typical household. The CPI indexes the cost of the typical market basket purchased by an urban family against its cost in a base year. The market basket includes such items as food, clothing, shelter, fuels, transportation fares, charges for doctors' and dentists' services, drugs, and other goods and services purchased for daily living.

---

[1] Since 1991, comprehensive revision of the National Income and Product Accounts, the Bureau of Economic Analysis has featured gross domestic product (GDP), rather than gross national product (GNP), as the primary measure of U.S. production. This change in emphasis recognizes that GDP is more appropriate for many purposes for which an aggregate measure of the nation's production is used.

8. *Producer Price Index* (formerly called the Wholesale Price Index). Designed to measure average changes in prices of all commodities, at all stages of processing, produced or imported for sale in primary markets in the United States. It is based on more than three thousand commodities. All prices used in constructing the index are collected from sellers and generally apply to the first significant large-volume transaction for each commodity—for example, the manufacturer's or other producer's selling price.

Unfortunately, economists historically have not been able to predict relevant demand and other economic variables with enough accuracy to be very useful for this purpose. Nevertheless, the analyst must use these imperfect prospective economic data in the valuation process. There are literally thousands of sources of such data. The following are a few readily available sources:

1. Government Publications
    a. The *Federal Reserve Bulletin* (the Board of Governors of the Federal Reserve System in Washington, DC). Published monthly, the *Federal Reserve Bulletin* includes such data as employment, industrial production, housing and construction, consumer and producer prices, GDP, personal income and savings, and key interest rates. Three years of annual historical data are usually presented for each set of statistics, and data for the current year are provided in monthly or quarterly units. It is usually available at public and university libraries. This is the best single service for finding current U.S. banking and monetary statistics.
    b. *Survey of Current Business* (U.S. Department of Commerce). This monthly publication has two sections. The first contains an article, "The Business Situation," which reviews business developments, pointing out relative strengths and weaknesses. The second section contains an extensive compilation of basic statistics on all phases of the economy. This is the most important single source for current U.S. business statistics. It can be found in most major libraries.
    c. *Statistical Abstract of the United States* (U.S. Department of Commerce). This annual publication contains statistics on all phases of U.S. life—economic, social, political, industrial—and some comparative international statistics. It is well-indexed and easy to use, and is available at most public libraries.
    d. *U.S. Industrial Outlook* (U.S. Department of Commerce and McGraw-Hill). Published annually, this publication contains information on recent trends and outlook for about 350 individual industries. Narrative with statistics contains discussions of changes in supply and demand, price changes, employment trends, and capital investment. The *U.S. Industrial Outlook* is helpful not only for its succinct narratives and summary statistics, but also for its highly regarded forecasts.

2. Banks
   a. *Economic Trends* (Federal Reserve Bank of Cleveland). Published monthly by the Federal Reserve Bank of Cleveland, this publication is an excellent source of economic variables, ranging from GDP and its components to money supply aggregates. Economic indicators, such as consumer income, business fixed investment, housing starts, and producer and consumer prices, are usually given on a quarterly or monthly basis. *U.S. Financial Data*, published weekly by the Federal Reserve Bank of St. Louis, is an especially good compilation of statistics on the money supply, commercial paper and business loans, interest rates, and securities yields. *Economic Trends, U.S. Financial Data* and selected publications from the other 11 Federal Reserve Bank Districts, are available at major libraries and on the Internet. For example, the Federal Reserve Bank of Chicago's World Wide Web page contains a large amount of financial data such as bond yields.
   b. *Economic Report* (Security Pacific National Bank). Each quarterly issue highlights one of four aspects of the economy: the U.S. economy and long-term outlook, the short-term outlook, the California economy, and the international economy.
3. Popular Materials
   a. *Barron's*. This weekly newspaper includes a wealth of statistical information. It includes articles covering a wide range of business and financial topics.
   b. *Business Week*. As its name implies, this weekly publication covers all aspects of the business world. One of the strengths of this publication is that it offers intelligent business articles in an easy-to-read magazine format. Each issue contains an index of leading economic indicators, prices, and exchange rates. The first issue of each year gives forecasts on a wide variety of industries.
   c. *Fortune*. Perhaps one of the most comprehensive sources for economic forecasts. In addition to monthly comments in each issue, the magazine makes quarterly and yearly forecasts for nearly all major economic indicators.
   d. *The Wall Street Journal*: This is the daily newspaper of the business world. The paper is divided into three sections: The first covers world news, the second contains prices and information from the financial markets, and the third presents special reports on a particular aspect of business. The highlight of the *Journal* is the daily statistical tables for stock, mutual funds, bonds, and so on. Statistics released by the Federal Reserve on Fridays appear in the next Monday's *Journal*.

Regional and Local Economic Data

Obviously, the more a business or professional practice depends on the economy of some locality, the more relevant the analysis of economic data about that area. An automobile dealership located in a town dependent on an economically troubled industry is not worth nearly as much as a dealership with comparable sales and profits the prior year that is located in a rapidly growing metropolis. Population, employment, and income forecasts are generally the most relevant types of local economic data. If a business depends on a certain industry, such as travel or construction, then estimates of such variables as the level of tourism or the number and dollar amounts of construction starts are relevant.

The primary sources for regional and local economic data are bank economics departments, public utilities, chambers of commerce, and various state agencies, such as departments of economic development and bureaus of labor statistics. Most state government agencies now make a significant amount of information available on the Internet via their World Wide Web pages. Most major local banks publish statistical tabulations of economic indicators, although their availability is limited. Although major libraries usually subscribe to one or more bank economic publications, the selections at libraries are usually limited to those published nearest to the particular library. The best way to obtain regional bank publications is to write or call the particular bank's economic department.

Some universities publish regional and local economic data, sometimes focused on one or a few industries important to the region. Most states and multistate regions now have regular monthly business magazines that give economic statistics, and most metropolitan areas now have weekly newspapers that focus on business developments. Business sections of some metropolitan daily newspapers are offering more economic analysis and statistics, sometimes regularly in Sunday editions and sometimes irregularly in special features that focus on a specific part of the local economic scene. Below is a list of additional data sources for regional and local economic information.

1. *Regional Economies and Markets.* Published quarterly by the Economic and Business Environment Program of the Conference Board, this analysis looks at groups of states in terms of manufacturing production, employment, and income.
2. *The Complete Economic and Demographic Data Source.* Published by Woods & Poole Economics, this is an excellent source for statistical profiles of metropolitan areas, counties, and states. Historical as well as projected data are included in this source. Other publications from Woods & Poole include *State Profiles* and *MSA Profiles*, which currently include statistical economic data and forecasts through the year 2010.
3. The U.S. Census Bureau provides a wealth of data on its World Wide Web page. The data is derived from the Bureau of Economic Analysis and the U.S. Department of Commerce as well as other U.S. government agencies.
4. *Survey of Buying Power.* Published annually in two monthly editions of *Sales & Marketing Management* magazine, this publication breaks down demographic and income data by state, metropolitan area, and county. Retail sales data are presented for store groups and merchandise lines. Also included are population and retail sales forecasts for local areas.

Industry Factors

Knowing something about the prospects and problems of the industry can provide a useful perspective for the valuation process. Quantitative comparisons between the subject company and industry-average operating figures were covered in the previous chapter. This section suggests qualitative aspects to be considered as well as available information sources. The sections Competition and Regulation also address industrywide topics. The sources of information listed below address these topics as well.

Markets

The industry factor most important to the value of most businesses and practices is the market outlook for the products or services being offered. For a given dollar amount of physical asset value, historical sales, or historical profits, a business or practice with a growing market for its products or services would be expected to be worth more than one facing a stagnant or declining market demand, all other things being equal.

Channels of Distribution

For many industries, channels of distribution evolve over time. The most obvious and widespread trend is that of consolidation, which has at least three important aspects: (1) cutting out the intermediary, (2) a trend toward larger business units, and (3) a trend toward more corporate chain and/or franchised units and fewer independent business units.

Independent wholesalers have been getting closer to extinction for many years in such fields as groceries, jewelry, and many (if not most) other consumer goods as more and more manufacturers sell directly to retailers. Manufacturers' representative firms and brokerage firms, such as food brokers, have found the suppliers they represent to be a fickle lot, as accounts they have built successfully are taken away in favor of direct distribution by the manufacturer. Industrial distributors of all kinds are constantly in jeopardy of losing one or more of their leading lines because of the supplier's shift to a direct distribution policy.

Economic efficiencies of scale have been operating for years to increase the average size of such diverse entities as farms and ranches, motels and hotels, and grocery and discount merchandising stores. The effect, of course, has been a dramatic increase in the amount of investment required for such entities. An economies-of-scale strategy pursued by the largest companies opens up opportunities for businesses at the small end of the spectrum. As consolidation provides strategic advantages to the larger entities in a particular industry group, the smaller participants in the industry carefully identify, protect, and promote their niche.

While the impact of consolidation increases the competitive pressure on independent operators, there also can be some advantages. One of the obvious ones is that national and regional acquirers provide an important group of prospective buyers for the owners of businesses and professional practices in lines in which such acquisitions are taking place. Another is that hundreds of chains are expanding through franchising. Some business owners may be able to benefit by becoming local franchise operators. In any case, some understanding of how the channels of distribution of an industry or professional practice area are evolving should add perspective to the valuation of most businesses and professional practices.

Technology

Moore's theorem is that microprocessors will become twice as fast and half as expensive with every succeeding generation of chips. Some products or services will be completely (or nearly) obsolete within a few years. Other products or services will skyrocket in usage as technological advances make them more attractive because of such factors as lower costs, miniaturization, improved performance, and greater compatibility with other related products.

There is hardly a business or profession for which the dynamics of technological change do not have implications for the value of the entity. For some, technology will determine the very viability of the enterprise. For others, such as retail establishments, technological changes will merely mandate capital expenditures for new equipment, such as the latest electronic bar code readers and reading and transmission equipment for the new generation of bank debit cards. The effects of technological change should be considered in terms of their impact on earnings potential, capital expenditure requirements, and risk for the entity being valued.

Sources of Industry Information

Generally, the best sources of industry information are trade and professional associations and publications. The owners of the subject entity usually can direct the analyst to the relevant associations and publications, although many small business owners are unaware of many of the sources of information relating to their own businesses. Several directories for such sources exist. The most comprehensive directory of trade and professional associations is *The Encyclopedia of Associations*, published annually by Gale Research, Inc. Also useful is *National Trade & Professional Associations of the United States*, published annually by Columbia Books, Inc. One of the most comprehensive directories of trade and professional publications is *Encyclopedia of Business Information Sources*, published annually by Gale Research, Inc. Information on these directories can be found in the bibliography at the end of this chapter.

Examples of these sources are found in the bibliography at the end of this chapter. A number of indexing services can also be used to find industry information. These indexing services are listed in *Encyclopedia of Business Information Sources*.

Competition

It should go without saying that a potential buyer trying to place a value on a prospective acquisition would want to check out the existing and potential competition, but this important qualitative factor is often neglected.

Existing Competition

Analysis of the competition takes different forms in different lines of business or professional practice. Therefore, this section offers only broad suggestions. In general, it is desirable to know the number of competitors, their names, their locations, the sizes of their respective operations, and how long they have been in business. One or more significant *new* competitors could be an important factor, since the full effects of their competition probably would not be reflected in the historical financial statements of the entity being valued. It is also desirable to know in what ways the competition is similar or differentiated along product or service lines, pricing policy, marketing methods, and other factors.

The statement, "We have no competition," simply is not adequate. Everyone has competition. The world has finite buying power and infinite demands. There are very few products or services for which there is absolutely no substitute. The analyst should probe the question of competition until a satisfactory picture is developed.

Of course, a certain amount of competition can be healthy. We have all heard the old saw that an attorney in town with no competition will starve to death, but when a second attorney comes to town, they will both prosper. In a shopping mall, competitors are often successful because they collectively draw a good flow of traffic interested in their line of wares. Wineries have found it profitable to be located among groups that collectively promote tours and local wines.

Potential Competition

From the point of view of the person trying to value an operation, the most dangerous competition is the competition that isn't there yet because its effect on the subject entity's earning power is a matter of guesswork. A unit of a large retail chain opening near a small or medium-size independent store can sometimes put the independent out of business completely. Introduction of a technically superior or lower-cost competitive product may damage or even destroy some manufacturers and their distributors. A manufacturer may authorize an additional distributor in the same territory or even open a company store in competition with its distributor. The easier the entry into the line of business, the more likely that new competition may be lurking just around the corner. It is never possible to know all the competitive problems the future will bring, but an effort should be made to avoid being blindsided by new competition that might have been foreseen.

Regulation

Various industries and professional practices are subject to greater or lesser degrees of regulation, mostly from government agencies but sometimes from their own professional associations. From a valuation viewpoint, the regulation can have either positive or negative implications. In any case, it is desirable to understand the regulatory situation.

Present Regulations

The gamut of existing regulations that affect the values of businesses and professional practices defies comprehensive categorization, but a few general groupings deserve special note.

Compliance Requirements. Two major government bodies administering regulations that cost the private sector hundreds of millions of dollars are the Occupational Safety and Health Administration (OSHA) and the Environmental Protection Agency (EPA). The analyst should inquire whether there are any OSHA, EPA, or other compliance requirements that may cost money or market share to satisfy.

Restrictions on Entry. Some protection from excessive competition may be provided by restrictions on others entering the field. These restrictions range from the quasi-monopoly status of some utilities (e.g., gas, electric, water, local telephone, cable TV) to merely passing certain competency tests in order to obtain licenses.

Licenses for many activities, such as paging systems, taxicabs, and (in most states) liquor outlets, are available only in limited numbers. Wherever there are regulatory restrictions to entry, there is likely to be some intangible value to the existing entities.

Potential Changes in Regulatory Environment

The political and social moods of the country and its leaders have been changing rapidly in recent years, causing dramatic changes in regulations that affect businesses and professions, which in turn have had dramatic impacts on the values of businesses and practices in many lines. Generally, the widespread move toward deregulation allows new competition and reduces the premium values that entrenched entities may formerly have commanded.

Costs of regulatory compliance are driving the values of many businesses to zero as they shut down because the costs of compliance are too great. Others sell far below book value because the economic return possible under current conditions is not enough to justify the amount of investment made at an earlier time.

On the other hand, changes in regulatory requirements can create bonanzas for entities in a position to provide products or services to help companies meet newly mandated requirements.

Another area of government regulation that undergoes constant review and change is the amount of federal and state subsidies and reimbursements available for various activities, as well as import restrictions and tariffs. As attitudes vacillate between subsidies and restrictions, businesses dependent on them face considerable risk, and their values are likely to be discounted considerably. Import/export firms may enjoy substantial windfall increments in their values when import restrictions are relaxed for selected goods. The values of nursing homes and other healthcare facilities, for another example, are very sensitive to changes in the government's programs of cost reimbursements available for their patients.

The foregoing comments and examples just scratch the surface of the major problem of anticipating and assessing the effect of a myriad of potential regulatory changes on the values of existing businesses and professional practices.

Product or Service Line

The product or service lines being offered is another qualitative factor that will have varying degrees of impact on value in different situations.

Existing Lines

The analyst can get an understanding of the product or service lines being offered through sales literature, a visit to the premises, and/or interviews with an owner or manager. The analyst should inquire about the relative size of each major product line and how long the company has offered it. The analyst should also ask about any prior lines that may have been discontinued. This information should be analytically useful to the extent to which historical operating information for the company represents a reasonable basis for extrapolating the future.

The more the market demand for a particular product or service, as opposed to others that are merely comparable, the more valuable the entity that sells or distributes it. Good examples of this principle are found in the pricing of soft drink bottlers and beer distributorships, where much of the premium value is associated with the performance or image of the leading brands.

Opportunities for Related Lines

From the potential buyer's point of view, there could be value in the opportunity to add related lines. For example, there may be a perfect opportunity for a professional practice to enhance its position by bringing in someone with a related specialty not adequately represented in the market. A small food packer may have established a strong local brand recognition and a route distribution system for a specialty line, which may provide an opportunity to sell related specialty items under the same brand name through the existing distribution system.

Related lines may be either developed internally or brought in from outside. Even though a potential buyer may recognize opportunities, he or she will be reluctant to pay for opportunities that have not already been seized and developed.

Patents, Copyrights, Trademarks

Like any intangible asset, the value of patents, copyrights, and trademarks lies in their ability to contribute to profits. Specific methods for placing values on each of these items are discussed in Chapter 42. In many small business and professional practice valuation assignments, however, no attempt is made to value each item individually; rather, the items are considered general qualitative factors in the valuation of the overall entity.

The importance of patents, copyrights, and trademarks lies in their ability to contribute to continuity of revenues, hopefully at higher margins of profit than would be possible if such legal protections did not exist. It is only to the extent that they fulfill this function that they genuinely contribute to the value of the enterprise, and their contributions should be reflected in the income approaches to value. To the extent that patents, copyrights, and trademarks are well protected or have been tested in court, and are long-lived, the analyst can have more confidence in the continuity of the income stream associated with them.

If the value of the total entity is determined to be greater than its net tangible asset value, it may be desirable for tax purposes to allocate the value above the tangible asset value to specific intangible assets (see Chapter 23).

Relative Profitability of Lines

Sometimes it is revealing to inquire into the relative profitability of different lines. It is not unusual for a business to have one or more lines that generate impressive gross volume; however, on examination, these business lines are found to be marginal or even negative in contributing to profitability. That may explain why an operation produces profit margins below industry averages. If the business is being valued on an income capitalization basis, the low level of profitability will be reflected in the income stream being capitalized. However, if the business is being valued by some other method, the negative impact of low-margin lines needs somehow to be reflected within that valuation method. For example, if some version of a multiple of gross revenues method is being used in the valuation, the revenues from the underperforming lines may not be included in the revenues to be capitalized, or they could be capitalized at a lower multiplier than other lines.

Service or Warranty Obligations

Obligations to service products sold can be either a positive or a negative influence on value, depending on the situation. If the company is a manufacturer with off-balance-sheet warranty liability, this factor should be recognized, either as a lump-sum deduction from the enterprise value or as an expense deduction from the income stream being capitalized. On the other hand, if a company is a distributor that performs warranty service work and adequate reimbursements come from the manufacturer for such work, the customer traffic generated by warranty service can be a very positive factor in assuring continuity of revenues and profits.

Supplier Relationships

If supplier relationships are important to the entity, this subject should be investigated carefully.

Continuity

The continuity of a supplier relationship is of considerable importance to many businesses. The ultimate disaster would be the single-product distributor facing the loss of the single supplier. Often, there are strong personal relationships between an owner and one or more key suppliers; the potential new owner will need to ascertain whether he can maintain a business relationship with this supplier once the seller's personal relationship is gone or, if that is not possible, whether he can find another supplier. It is important to determine the extent to which continuity of supplier relationships can be assured or is at risk under new ownership.

In addition to keeping the supplier relationship, the issue of price may also be important. The existing owner may have favorable pricing because of existing relationships, either contractual or noncontractual, which may be amended in a relationship with a potential new buyer. If the potential buyer faces this possibility, the effect on profit margins obviously should be assessed.

Degree of Exclusivity

An exclusive relationship for a market generally is more valuable than a nonexclusive relationship because it is more conducive to continuity of revenues and maintenance of profit margins. An example of this would be a fast-food franchise agreement. If the degree of exclusivity is threatened, that may be regarded as a negative factor in the valuation picture. Of course, if the transfer of an exclusive distributorship is contemplated, the willingness of the supplier to maintain the arrangement under potential new ownership should be ascertained.

Contractual Relationships

As a general rule, the strongest type of contractual relationship with a supplier is a franchise. A franchise is often, but not always, transferable. Most distributorship agreements are not actually franchises and are not transferable without the supplier's consent. That may pose a perplexing valuation problem since considerable value may depend on whether or not a potential new owner could take over the distributorship agreement, a decision that may be entirely up to the supplier.

For tax purposes, case histories show there is a reluctance by the courts to accept any value dependent on a relationship that the owner does not have the legal right to transfer. When transferring a business, however, intangible value relating to the supplier relationship usually is included in the price. However, the deal is contingent on the supplier's approval of the new owners. The arguments that go on over this issue in divorces, damage cases, dissenting stockholder suits, and other valuation disputes are voluminous enough to fill a book by themselves.

Market Position

Whether the subject entity is a professional practice, a service business, a retailer, a manufacturer, or any other kind of business, its market position has an important bearing on the amount and certainty of its ability to generate earnings, and thus on its value.

Reputation

Reputation is critical to a professional practice, while it would be less important to a retailer of standard merchandise selling primarily on a price basis. As with many factors, the degree of importance should help to determine how much investigation is warranted. Sources of information can include customers, suppliers, competitors, current and/or former employees, outside consultants of various kinds who may be familiar with the business or practice, and creditors.

Geographic Scope

An understanding of the subject entity should include the geographic scope of the markets its serves. The company's geographic scope can be either a positive or negative factor, depending on costs involved in doing business in the area, competitive factors, opportunities to increase market penetration, and other characteristics of the market.

Method of Marketing and Distribution

The analyst should understand the company's methods of marketing and distribution. If revenues are generated primarily because of referrals or location, the appraiser should assess the potential continuity of the referral sources and the continued availability of the location. If revenues depend on continuous advertising, the business may not be able to continue without the advertising. If marketing is based heavily on personal sales efforts, will existing sales people or adequate replacements be available?

Another factor is whether the distribution system will continue to be available at a reasonable cost. If distribution is by mail, contract delivery service, or freight, will there be significant changes in costs?

In summary, in order to assess the potential continuity of revenues and profit margins, it is important to understand how the revenues are generated, what brings the buyers to the entity, and how the goods and services are delivered.

Pricing Policies

Commodity versus Specialized Products. In general, on the bottom of the value scale is a company that prices on a commodity basis —that sells on a price basis alone—without differentiating between its products or services and those offered by several direct competitors in the market. Such companies' pricing policies are totally subject to the external forces of the marketplace; they have no control over their own destiny in that respect. Their profit depends on their ability to operate more efficiently than their competitors. These companies include those that distribute branded merchandise but compete primarily on a price basis.

At the other end of the spectrum is the company whose product or service is so unusual or so superior that it is insulated from direct competition; such a company has a high degree of discretion over its own pricing policies. Such companies usually are able to maintain consistently high profit margins and returns on investment and usually sell at a premium price over their net tangible asset value, in some cases very handsome premiums.

Most companies and practitioners are, of course, somewhere between these extremes, and the analyst should use professional judgment to assess how the entity's pricing situation bears on the level and reliability of its earning power.

Bid versus Negotiated Contract Prices. For companies that do a large portion of their business on fixed-price contracts (or fixed prices, subject to certain variables), it is desirable to ascertain how much is done on a bid basis instead of on a negotiated basis. In general, companies that have a large portion of their contracts strictly on a bid basis are considered to be in the category of commodity firms in terms of pricing, while those with more contracts on a negotiated basis are considered to be in the category of specialty firms. However, in some lines of business, buyers exercise considerable discretion in accepting bids, with quality and service considered as well as price. In those cases, bidder firms are considered a step removed from commodity firms in pricing.

Customer Base

Several aspects of the customer base are important, including diversification, persistence, and quality.

Diversification. For some companies, diversification or concentration of the customer base is a major factor. The low-value end of the spectrum would be represented by a company performing a single government contract that will be completed soon with no follow-up business presently in sight. (One might even question whether that situation should be classified as a going concern.) At the high-value end of the spectrum is a customer base so broad that losing a few customers would have no perceptible impact on the entity's revenues or profits.

Small businesses, and certain types of professional practices, commonly have one or a few large customers whose loss would deal a serious blow to the entity's earning capacity, or even its viability. In these cases, the continuity of the key customers' business must be analyzed carefully and the risk assessed accordingly All other things being equal, companies with very concentrated customer bases usually sell at discounts compared with other companies of comparable revenues and earnings but with more diversified customer bases.

Persistence. Another aspect of the customer base is *persistence*, the extent to which the same customers tend to repeat. This characteristic has the dimensions of both longevity and frequency. In businesses such as insurance agencies and periodical publications, for example, first-year customers are not considered as valuable as longer-term customers because statistics have shown a positive correlation between longevity and propensity to renew. A service business that provides its services regularly to the same clientele, such as annual audits provided by an accounting firm, is generally worth more per dollar of historical revenues and earnings than the kind of service business in which each service performed is a new piece of business. This is true even though some of the customers may have patronized the firm previously.

Quality

Appraising the quality of the customer base certainly is a very subjective, but nevertheless important, judgment. Some of the measures of quality are customers' ability and willingness to pay their bills on time, their ability to pay the kind of prices the operation would like to charge, their ability to increase their purchases over time, and their ability and propensity to refer other customers of comparable quality.

Customer Relationships

Closely akin to the analysis of the customer base is the analysis of customer relationships. If one or several major customers are family members or have close personal or other business ties with the owner or a key person, the analyst should candidly assess the ability to retain those customers under different ownership.

Another aspect of customer relationships is customer satisfaction. Talks with customers and former customers can help shed some light on this factor. However, the analyst must be sensitive to client confidentiality.

Market Continuity, Growth Opportunities, and Weaknesses

The point of this whole analysis of market position is to assess both the level and the degree of certainty of future revenues, along with the level and degree of certainty of the margins that those revenues will be able to generate in light of the pricing forces the company is subject to. The greater the degree of continuity promised by the market position, the lower the risk. Growth opportunities are more valuable to the extent that they seem likely to evolve naturally from forces already in place than from large doses of entrepreneurial effort and expenditures. Weaknesses should be listed, evaluated, and reflected in the earnings stream and/or capitalization rates used in the valuation.

Management and Employees

The people factor certainly is a key qualitative element in most businesses and professional practices. This is especially true in small businesses, where there typically is substantial owner involvement in management, or the business focuses around one or a few key people.

Size and Composition of Workforce

A basic factor that influences the health of a business is the size and composition of the workforce: the number of employees, their functions, their general backgrounds, their qualifications, their levels of competence, and their basis and level of compensation. Whether the company is adequately staffed, understaffed, or overstaffed will have a bearing on the extent to which the company's long-term earning capacity will conform to its recent history.

Key Employees

The importance of the owner or other key employees to the success of the business is a matter that should be given significant attention in valuing small businesses and professional practices. Information should be acquired as to age, length of service, education, and prior experience of each key employee, whether she works full-time or part-time, whether she has outside work or financial interests that may dilute her efforts or cause any conflict of interest, her level of compensation, including all fringe benefits and discretionary expenses, and how long she intends to stay with the entity.

If key employees' expertise and customer relationships would take some time to transfer to a different owner, the value of the transaction to the hypothetical buyer would depend on the buyer's willingness to enter into an employment contract with the key employees for the ownership-transition period.

Furthermore, if customers would follow the seller if she left and opened a new shop or joined a competitor, the value of the transaction probably also depends on a noncompete agreement. Employment agreements and noncompete agreements, if applicable, usually are calculated in the total value arrived at for the business or practice. However, in negotiating the actual deal, they often are separated and the total value is allocated among the purchase price for the business, for the employment agreements, and for the covenants not to compete. This matter is discussed further in Chapter 43.

Other Employees

It is helpful to have an idea of the nature of the workforce, the extent to which it is unionized—or may be unionized in the future—the history of any strikes or work stoppages, and its general adequacy for the tasks at hand. This analysis may give some indication of necessary or possible changes that may affect profitability.

Compensation

Several sources of comparative compensation data are listed in the bibliography at the end of this chapter. Trade associations in the relevant industry can sometimes also provide compensation data for that particular industry.

Nonowner Employees.   The main consideration with respect to nonowner employees is whether the compensation is adequate, inadequate, or too high. If inadequate, some additional costs should be allowed when estimating earning power. If compensation is too high, there should be room for savings, but perhaps not immediately.

Owner Employees.   If a seller is going to stay on as an employee, the seller's value in his employment role should be estimated. If the seller wants to take out more than the value of his employment in direct compensation and benefits, the purchase price can be adjusted downward accordingly.

Personnel Policies, Satisfaction, Conflict, and Turnover

A prospective owner should know the main features of past personnel policies. Only a small percentage of small businesses and professional practices have personnel policies in writing. And those companies that do have written policies may not follow them closely. Consequently, such information usually needs to be gleaned through interviews. Analyzing personnel policies may also uncover additional cost requirements or possible savings.

Informal discussions with employees give clues about whether they are satisfied or dissatisfied, and about costs that might be necessary for the potential owner to incur in order to correct existing problems. If there are internal conflicts, it may be possible to bring them to light during the valuation process. People do like to talk, especially about things that are bothering them. Sometimes employees are frustrated about being unable to pursue opportunities they envision—opportunities that may be good for the enterprise as well.

A personnel turnover rate below the industry average usually is considered a plus, while a high turnover rate usually is considered a minus. Some businesses, however, intentionally have a high turnover rate in order to avoid the higher direct compensation and benefits that tend to accrue with seniority.

Adequacy of Physical Facility

The physical facility may allow for considerable expansion; it may be just about adequate for current operations; it may require capital expenditures; or it may be so inadequate that a move is imminent. If the physical facility is important, its adequacy or lack of it obviously has a bearing on value.

Condition

As discussed in Chapter 7, an important concern in the valuation of facilities is deferred maintenance, which can include such items as needed painting; repair of leaks; repair of broken or cracked windows, doors, and walls; equipment maintenance; and anything else necessary to put the facility in good operating condition. For retail outlets or service establishments with considerable foot traffic, maintenance can also include modernizing, even when existing equipment and decor are not necessarily in bad condition, in order to keep up with current trends and upscale consumer expectations. For franchised business operations, the analyst should consider if the subject facilities are in compliance with the constraints or requirements of the franchise agreement.

Heat, Light, Plumbing, and Other Systems

Special attention should be paid to the adequacy of all operating systems, including all utility hookups, heating and air conditioning, all electrical systems, burglar alarms, sprinkler system, and plumbing. There may be deferred maintenance, but more importantly, certain systems may be antiquated in their abilities to serve current needs. This is especially true of electrical systems because commercial electrical appliances have placed a much bigger demand on electrical systems than was planned when they were installed. These factors need to be assessed and any cost implications reflected in value.

Size

The size of the facility should be considered, not only in relation to current needs, but also in relation to needs in the foreseeable future. If a move appears necessary, its cost and the likely changes in occupancy cost should be taken into consideration.

Continuity of Occupancy

If it seems preferable to continue occupying the present location, it is important to determine the length of time that the premises will be assured to be available, and at what cost. Any increased costs should be reflected in the valuation.

Operating Efficiencies and Inefficiencies

Any special efficiencies or inefficiencies that may be identified should be helpful in assessing ongoing earning power and future costs. *Efficiency* in this context means getting the job done at the lowest possible cost, and *inefficiency* means any circumstance that would cause higher-than-necessary costs.

Physical Plant

Plant-related efficiency, or lack of it, generally arises from location, size, and layout, and the extent to which the equipment is state-of-the-art. Some causes of plant inefficiency are easily curable, some may be difficult or costly to cure, and some may be incurable. The valuation should consider the impact on earnings power of any inefficiencies not curable, such as extra transportation costs because of remote location, functional obsolescence of equipment, or extra labor costs because of inefficient layout, as well as the costs to cure any existing inefficiencies that will be worthwhile to cure. It is also possible that curing inefficiencies will result in some profitability gains that should be reflected.

Accounting and Other Controls

Accounting systems can be adapted to be very useful tools of management control, but few small businesses and professional practices even approach getting maximum management benefit out of their accounting systems. The extent of controls implemented should be investigated. To the extent that good controls are in place and being used effectively, the risk of an unexpected earnings decline is reduced, although most of the upside profit potential from efficiency may already have been achieved. To the extent that controls are poor, of course, the risk of an unanticipated drop in earnings is increased.

Reason for Sale

It is always desirable to know why a business is being offered for sale. If a sale is under duress, the price is likely to be less than it would be if there is no pressure to sell. If the business is in an estate, in most cases, it is worth less than if the former owner/manager were still living. Usually, some value is lost due to the lack of an orderly transition period. This factor varies considerably, depending on the role of the former owner/manager in the operations of the business and his relationships with its public. The value implications of the many reasons to sell vary greatly, but it is another qualitative item to take into consideration.

Summary

This chapter covered a wide variety of qualitative factors that most frequently have a bearing on the value of a business or professional practice. This chapter has not covered all the vast number of possible factors that might be encountered in any specific case. Exhibit 10-1 summarizes the steps in analyzing qualitative factors.

It should be clear that it is impossible to create any quick fix or formula valuation models or methods that can fully reflect and evaluate all the subjective factors that have a bearing on value. In most individual cases, one or a few subjective or qualitative factors really have a significant influence on value; dozens of others may have a secondary influence.

While the chapter has suggested factors to look for, the analyst will require considerable experience and judgment to put them in perspective and to determine how they will influence the ultimate opinion of value, or the price that a hypothetical buyer would be willing to pay or that a hypothetical seller should be willing to accept.

Exhibit 10–1

SUMMARY OF STEPS IN
ANALYZING QUALITATIVE FACTORS

Step 1   Collect and analyze national economic data that could have a bearing on the subject company's outlook.

Step 2   Collect and review relevant regional and local economic data that could impact the subject company's future profitability.

Step 3   Collect and analyze sources of information on the industry in which the subject company operates.

Step 4   Analyze the existing competitors of the subject company and consider the potential for new entrants into the company's markets.

Step 5   Review government regulations that affect the business, especially with a view toward potential changes.

Step 6   Review the product lines offered by the subject company as of the valuation date and review the following:

- Opportunities for the subject company to add related business lines.
- The extent of the continuity of the income stream associated with any patents, copyrights, or trademarks of the company.
- The relative profitability of each of the company's product lines.

Step 7   Examine the continuity, degree of exclusivity, and contractual relationships of any supplier relationships of the subject company.

Step 8   Evaluate the market position of the company being appraised, including, but not limited to, the following:

- The reputation of the company.
- The geographic scope of the company's operations.
- The company's methods of marketing and distribution.
- The pricing policies of the company.
- The diversification, quality, and persistence of the company's customer base.
- The strengths and weaknesses of the company's overall market position.

Step 9   Review the employees of the subject company, including the following:

- Review the size and composition of the workforce.
- Summarize each of the key employees of the company, including background information, such as age, length of service, education, and prior experience.
- Evaluate the level of owner compensation.
- Review the historical turnover rates of the company's workforce.

Step 10   Analyze the physical facility of the company to determine its condition, adequacy of operating systems, and capacity.

Step 11   Summarize the operating efficiencies and inefficiencies related to the subject company.

Bibliography

General Directories

Business Organizations, Agencies, and Publications Directory, 8th ed. (Detroit: Gale Research, 1996). Gale Research, 645 Griswold Street, Detroit, MI 48226-4094; telephone (800) 877-GALE.

Encyclopedia of Business Information Sources, 1997-98, 11th ed. (Detroit: Gale Research, 1996).

National Trade and Professional Associations of the United States (Washington, DC: Columbia Books, Inc., annual). Columbia Books, Inc., 1212 New York Avenue, N.W., Suite 330, Washington, DC 20005; telephone (888) 265-0600.

Selected Composite Financial Data Sources

Dun's Financial Records Plus
Dun & Bradstreet Business Credit Services
One Diamond Hill Road
Murray Hill, NJ 07974-0027
(800) 362-3425

Selected Manufacturing Industries
Key Ratios of the Folding Carton Industry
Key Ratios of the Rigid Box Industry
National Paperbox Association
801 North Fairfax Street, Suite 211
Alexandria, VA 22314-1757
(703) 684-2212

Printing Industries of America Financial Ratio Studies
Printing Industries of America
100 Dangerfield Road
Alexandria, VA 22314-2888
(703) 519-8138

Statistical Report on Sales, Production, and Profit in
  Men's and Boys Tailored Clothing Industry
Clothing Manufacturers Association of the U.S.A.
730 Broadway
New York, NY 10003
(212) 529-0823

Statistics of Paper, Paperboard & Wood Pulp
American Forest and Paper Association
1111 19th Street, N.W., Suite 800
Washington, DC 20036
(202) 463-2700

Selected Retail Industries

Food Marketing Industry Speaks
Food Marketing Institute
800 Connecticut Avenue, N.W., Suite 500
Washington, DC 20006
(202) 452-8444

Cost of Doing Business Survey
National Association of Retail Dealers of America
10 East 22nd Street, Suite 310
Lombard, IL 60148
(630) 953-8950

Cost of Doing Business Survey
National Sporting Goods Association
1699 Wall Street
Mt. Prospect, IL 60056-5780
(708) 439-4000

Financial Comparison and Performance Benchmarking Guide
Business Products Industry Association
301 N. Fairfax Street
Alexandria, VA 22314-2696
(800) 542-6672

Financial and Operating Results of Department and Specialty Stores
National Retail Federation
325 7th Street, N.W., Suite 1000
Washington, DC 20004-2608
(800) 673-4692

NHFA Operating Expenses
National Home Furnishings Association
Post Office Box 2396
High Point, NC 27261
(919) 883-1650

Restaurant Industry Operations Report
National Restaurant Association
1200 17th Street, N.W.
Washington, DC 20036-3097
(202) 331-5900

Selected Service and Construction Industries

Construction Industry Annual Financial Survey Report
Construction Financial Management Association
707 State Road, Suite 223
Princeton, NJ 08540-1413
(609) 683-5000

Cost of Doing Business Survey
American Rental Association
1900 19th Street
Moline, IL 61265
(309) 764-2475

Financial Performance Report
National Electrical Contractors Association
3 Bethesda Metro Center, Suite 1100
Bethesda, MD 20814-3299
(310) 657-3110

Financial Report of the Hospital Industry
Healthcare Financial Management Association
Two Westbrook Corporate Center, Suite 700
Westchester, IL 60154
(708) 531-9600

Gas Facts
American Gas Association
1515 Wilson Boulevard
Arlington, VA 22209
(703) 841-8400

MGMA Annual Cost and Production Survey Report
Medical Group Management Association
104 Inverness Terrace East
Englewood, CO 80112-5306
(303) 799-1111

Mortgage Banking Financial Statements and Operating Ratios
Mortgage Bankers Association of America
1125 15th Street, N.W.
Washington, DC 20005
(202) 861-6500

Radio Financial Report
Television Financial Report
National Association of Broadcasters
1771 N Street, N.W.
Washington, DC 20036-2891

Railroad Facts
Association of American Railroads
50 F Street, N.W., Room 5401
Washington, DC 20001-1564
(202) 639-2100

Trends in the Hotel Industry
Pannell Kerr Forster
425 California Street, Suite 1650
San Francisco, CA 94104
(415) 421-5378

Selected Wholesale Industries

Operations Performance Report
American Supply Association
222 Merchandise Mart Plaza, Suite 1360
Chicago, IL 60654-1202
(312) 464-0090

Paper Merchant Performance
National Paper Trade Association
111 Great Neck Road
Great Neck, NY 11021
(516) 829-3070

IDA Member Profitability Report
Industrial Distribution Association
Three Corporation Square, Suite 201
Atlanta, GA 30329
(404) 325-2776

Selected Sources of Officer Compensation Data

Almanac of Business and Industrial Financial Ratios (Englewood Cliffs, NJ: Prentice Hall, annual).

RMA Annual Statement Studies (Philadelphia, PA: Robert Morris Associates, annual).

Executive Compensation Survey Results (New York: National Association of Business Management, annual).

Financial Studies of the Small Business (Winter Haven, FL: Financial Research Associates, annual).

The Hay Report (Wellesley, MA: Hay Group, annual).

Officer Compensation Report (Greenvale, NY: Panel Publishers, Inc., annual).

Source Book, Statistics of Income (Washington, DC: Internal Revenue Service, annual).

Selected Electronic Sources of Industry Data[2]

ABI Inform
Vendors: On-line: Dialog (ABI Inform); UMI (Proquest Direct); Nexis.
CD-ROM: UMI
This is one of the oldest and largest electronic sources of business information. The Dialog file indexes more than 1,000 business periodicals. Citations and lengthy abstracts are available for all articles, and a full-text version is available for most articles added to the database in recent years. Limited accessibility is also available through CompuServe.

Business Database Plus
Vendors: On-line: CompuServe
Full text of business and trade journals and industry newsletters. The "Business/Trade Journals" section contains articles from over 750 business periodicals for the past five years.

Trade and Industry Database and PROMT
Vendors: On-line: Dialog; Nexis; DataTimes; Newsnet; Profound
Trade and Industry Database provides indexing, abstracting, and complete text of over 300 trade and industry journals, and selected articles from an additional 1,200 publications.

Intelliseek
Vendors: CD-ROM: Information Access
This product is a subset of PROMT (see above). It offers abstracts and full-text articles from over 400 U.S. trade and industry newsletters, newspapers, and business magazines.

NewsPage
Address: http://www.newspage.com
NewsPage filters over 20,000 news stories from hundreds of sources daily. Basic access includes wire services such as BusinessWire and PR Newswire. The Premium plan allows access to all of the sources. Articles are organized by 25 major industry categories.

ASAE Member Associations Online
Address: http://www.asaenet.org/Gateway/onlineassoclist.html
A free service of the American Society of Association Executives, this internet site contains links to over 1,500 trade associations.

---

[2]This section is adapted from Eva M. Lang and Jan Davis Tudor, "Electronic Sources of Business Valuation Data (BV in Cyberspace)." A version of this information appears in Jay E. Fishman, Shannon P. Pratt, et al., *Guide to Business Valuations* 7th ed. (Fort Worth, TX: Practitioners Publishing Company, 1997). It is used here with the permission of Ms. Lang and Ms. Tudor.

U.S. Census Bureau: The Official Statistics
Address: http://www.census.gov
This free service of the U.S. Census Bureau has a "Subjects A to Z" section to guide users to Census publications such as "Census of Construction Industries.

Business Valuation Update Online
Address: http://www.nvst.com/bvu
Constantly updates new information sources for business valuation from the monthly Data and Publications Department of *Shannon Pratt's Business Valuation Update*. Also includes the annual "Where to Find It—Business Valuation Data Directory." In most cases, this source contains links to the respective publishers' websites.

Chapter 11

The Buyer's Perspective—
Pro Forma Statements

The thrust of this chapter is to step into the buyer's shoes, to consider the financial statements and possible changes from the viewpoint of a buyer. From the buyer's viewpoint, some changes may be necessary or desirable. Before coming to grips with the question of how much to offer, a buyer should take a number of factors into consideration.

Up to this point, we have been looking at the financial statements of the business in question under its current operations and as it stands. Of course, the reader should always have the scope of the valuation assignment in mind. When the assignment's scope includes the fair market value standard, for instance, both the hypothetical buyer's perspective and the hypothetical seller's perspective should be considered. In this chapter, the term *buyer* should be considered based on the valuation assignment's scope. For example, the buyer might be the hypothetical willing buyer who is knowledgeable about relevant facts referred to in the fair market value standard, or the buyer might be the specific buyer referred to in the investment value standard of value.

The buyer looks at the total investment in the business, not just what the buyer pays to the seller. Apart from how much the buyer pays the seller for the business or practice, how much additional financing will be necessary, what its source will be, and what it will cost are important considerations. The analyst should also consider the possibility of the business itself being a source of financing for the purchase.

Analysis of Working Capital Requirements

If it will be necessary to provide additional working capital, the buyer's pro forma balance sheet should reflect the amount needed and the source. If the buyer will be providing extra dollars for working capital, that amount should be reflected in the pro forma balance sheet and recognized as part of the buyer's total investment in the business when deciding how much to offer the seller. If the buyer plans to borrow from a bank to finance working capital needs, the pro forma balance sheet should reflect the average amount of borrowing expected. And the interest should be reflected on the buyer's pro forma income statement. Definitions and examples of working capital and its components are presented in Exhibit 11-1.

Steps in Analyzing Working Capital

If the prospective buyer doesn't know how much working capital it will take to operate the business, the buyer can get some guidance from the industry average data discussed in Chapter 9. For example, Exhibit 9-1 shows that the average ratio of sales to working capital for women's ready-to-wear stores with assets between $500,000 and $2,000,000 is 8 percent. Therefore, among those in the RMA sample, the average women's ready-to-wear store expecting to do $1 million in sales would have about $80,000 in working capital.

Exhibit 11–1

ANALYSIS OF WORKING CAPITAL
AND ITS MAJOR COMPONENTS

Definitions

Working Capital = Current Assets – Current Liabilities

Current Assets: Cash and items expected to be converted to cash or used up in the business within one year. Major items are: cash, marketable securities, accounts receivable, notes receivable within a year, and prepaid expenses.

Current Liabilities. Items expected to be paid within one year. Major items are: accounts payable, notes payable within a year (including any portion of longer-term debt that is due within a year), and accrued expenses.

$$Current\ Ratio = \frac{Current\ Assets}{Current\ Liabilities}$$

$$Quick\ Ratio = \frac{Cash\ \&\ Equivalents + Receivables}{Current\ Liabilities}$$

$$Working\ Capital\ Turnover = \frac{Sales}{Working\ Capital}$$

Preferably, this ratio is computed using *average* working capital as the denominator. However, as a matter of expedience, it often is computed using working capital at the end of the period as the denominator.

$$Accounts\ Receivable\ Turnover = \frac{Sales}{Accounts\ Receivable}$$

Preferably computed using *average* accounts receivable; for expedience, often computed using ending accounts receivable.

$$Average\ Collection\ Period\ (Days) = \frac{365}{Accounts\ Receivable\ Turnover}$$

$$Inventory\ Turnover = \frac{Cost\ of\ Goods\ Sold}{Inventory}$$

Preferably computed using *average* inventory; for expedience, often computed using ending inventory. Many companies have unusually low inventories at the end of their fiscal periods because they let the inventories run down to make it easier to take the physical inventory count and/or because they set the end of the fiscal year to coincide with a seasonally slow time, when inventories would normally be low. In such cases, doing the computation on the basis of ending inventory will overstate the true inventory turnover.

$$Average\ Day's\ Inventory = \frac{365}{Inventory\ Turnover}$$

Exhibit 11–1 (concluded)

Example of Working Capital Analysis

Sales	$100,000	Cost of goods sold	$ 60,000
Current Assets:		Current liabilities:	
Cash	$ 1,000	Accounts payable	$ 8,000
Accounts receivable	10,000	Bank note payable	12,000
Inventory	15,000		
Prepaid expenses	2,000		
Total current assets	$ 28,000	Total current liabilities	$ 20,000

Working Capital = $28,000 − $20,000 = $8,000

$$Current\ Ratio\ =\ \frac{\$28,000}{\$20,000}\ =\ 1.4$$

$$Quick\ Ratio\ =\ \frac{\$11,000}{\$20,000}\ =\ 0.55$$

$$Working\ Capital\ Turnover\ =\ \frac{\$100,000}{\$8,000}\ =\ 12.5$$

$$Accounts\ Receivable\ Turnover\ =\ \frac{\$100,000}{\$10,000}\ =\ 10$$

$$Average\ Collection\ Period\ (Days)\ =\ \frac{365}{10}\ =\ 36.5\ Days$$

$$Inventory\ Turnover\ =\ \frac{\$60,000}{\$15,000}\ =\ 4.0\ times\ per\ year$$

$$Average\ Day's\ Inventory\ =\ \frac{365}{4.0}\ =\ 91\ Days$$

Note, however, that in Exhibit 9-1 the sales to working capital range is quite wide. The upper quartile figure is 24.8 percent ($248,000 working capital to support $1 million sales), and the lower quartile is 4.0 percent ($40,000 working capital to support $1 million).

One of the biggest variables, of course, would be whether or not the company has a policy of selling on credit. The other major variables on the asset side are how often the inventory turns over (average length of time the merchandise stays in inventory) and, if the company sells on credit, the average length of time it takes to collect accounts receivable. On the liability side, the two main variables are the trade terms available from suppliers and the terms under which other financing (usually bank borrowing) can be arranged.

To summarize, the buyer's analysis of the business's working capital needs consists of the following steps:

1. Estimate sales volume.
2. Decide on credit policy and estimate the average amount of accounts receivable on the basis of the average estimated collection period.
3. Estimate the amount of inventory needed on the basis of estimated average inventory turnover.
4. Estimate the amount of prepaid expenses needed.
5. Estimate the average amount of accounts payable on the basis of trade terms available from suppliers.
6. Estimate the average amount of bank financing on the basis of the terms of the bank financing available.
7. Allow for some extra cash because the steps above are estimates and averages; there may not be enough cash at peak periods. (If the business is highly seasonal, this analysis should be done on the basis of the high seasonal requirements rather than on averages.)
8. From the steps above, compute the amount of working capital that will be necessary.
9. As a check, compute the current ratio, quick ratio, and working capital turnover based on the results of steps 1 through 8 and compare them with industry averages.

An Example of Working Capital Analysis

1. Ashley's Apparel has been generating $1 million in sales volume. Industry sources expect retail selling prices to go up by about 5 percent this year. The shopping center's consultant has predicted a 4 percent increase in foot traffic. Considering these factors, and assuming no major changes in the operation, an estimated sales volume of approximately $1.1 million seems reasonable.
2. Ashley's accounts receivable turnover has been 33 times per year because she has extended only very limited credit. If the new buyer follows the same policy, on $1.1 million sales, average accounts receivable would be estimated at about $35,000.
3. Using the adjusted balance sheet (Exhibit 7-2), the inventory value at current prices is $220,000. Using the adjusted income statement (Exhibit 8-2), the cost of goods sold was $535,000. If the buyer can maintain the same gross margin, the cost of goods sold will be about $589,000 (0.56 × $1,100,000 = $589,000). Inventory turnover last year was 2.6 times. If the same inventory turnover is maintained, Ashley's will need about $227,000 average inventory.

4. Ashley's $3,000 of prepaid expenses includes a rental deposit only. The buyer will need to pay a rent advance of $5,000 immediately. Also, as noted in Exhibit 8-2, Ashley's has not been carrying any fire, theft, or liability insurance. The buyer will need to take out a policy with a $2,000 annual premium, bringing total prepaid expenses to $10,000.

5. Trade credit is on a 30-day basis. With estimated purchases of $589,000 (from step 3 above), average estimated trade accounts payable would be about $49,000.

6. Ashley's can get a bank line of credit of $200,000 based on 60 percent of inventory and accounts receivable under 90 days old. At $227,000 average inventory and an average of $30,000 eligible accounts receivable (under 90 days old), average bank financing would be about $155,000 (0.6 x $257,000 = $155,000).

7. There is not a great deal of seasonality to the business, and some flexibility is available in suppliers' trade terms at peak periods, so $10,000 extra cash is a reasonable reserve to cover fluctuations and contingencies.

8. On the basis of steps 1 through 7, working capital requirements can be estimated as follows:

Current Assets:		Current Liabilities:	
Cash	$ 10,000	Accounts payable	$ 49,000
Accounts receivable	35,000	Bank note payable	155,000
Inventory	227,000		
Prepaid expenses	10,000		
Total current assets	$282,000	Total current liabilities	$204,000

Working capital: $282,000 - $204,000 = $78,000

$$\text{Current ratio} = \frac{\$282,000}{\$204,000} = 1.4$$

$$\text{Quick ratio} = \frac{\$10,000 + \$35,000}{\$204,000} = .22$$

$$\text{Working capital turnover} = \frac{\$1,100,000}{\$78,000} = 14.1$$

9. Exhibit 9-1 shows that the average current ratio for women's ready-to-wear stores with total assets of $500,000 to $2,000,000 is 2.1, but the lower quartile is 1.2, a little lower than our estimate. The average quick ratio is 0.7, with a lower quartile of 0.1, also fairly close to our estimate. The median sales/working capital (working capital turnover) ratio is 8.0, with a lower quartile of 24.8, so our estimate falls close to the median. The result is that Ashley's is in the bottom 30 percent of similar companies in short-term liquidity. This is within a reasonable operating range and isn't necessarily alarming. The buyer will have to exercise cash flow controls.

In summary, the above analysis suggests a balance sheet that will include $282,000 of current assets, of which $49,000 will be financed by trade payables, $155,000 by short-term bank borrowings, and $78,000 by long-term debt and/or owner's equity.

This analysis of Ashley's assumes that business will be pretty much as usual, based on recent history. It should be noted that the inventory turnover of 2.6 times per year is near the bottom quartile of the industry average (from Exhibit 9-1), considerably below the median of 3.5. It would appear that there might be room for improvement in inventory turnover. On the other hand, Ashley's gross margin of 44 percent is slightly above the industry average of 42.2 percent, which may be partly due to a merchandise mix that turns more slowly than the industry's average merchandise mix.

Analysis of Fixed Assets

The buyer should analyze the fixed assets to determine whether an additional investment in fixed assets will be necessary or whether any existing assets are above the needs of the business and could be sold without affecting the entity's earning power.

Deferred Maintenance and Replacement Requirements

It is not at all uncommon to find that physical premises and equipment have not been kept up to the standard necessary to continue to perform their jobs effectively. Owners may have deferred normal maintenance and equipment for a wide variety of reasons, anything from inadequate capital to just plain apathy.

When such conditions are present, the buyer should estimate the cost of the deferred maintenance and replacements and consider that cost as part of the required investment in the business. Generally, if a buyer would pay $100,000 for a business with equipment in average condition but it will cost $20,000 in repairs and replacements to bring the equipment in the subject business to average condition, the buyer might be willing to pay only $80,000 for the business "as is."

Compliance Requirements

As noted in Chapter 7, there may be some off-balance-sheet liabilities, such as costs of equipment to comply with environmental clean-up regulations, OSHA, pollution control, zoning standards, building codes, or other governmental requirements. A buyer should make provision for any such costs as part of his investment.

Other Asset Inadequacies

Sometimes a company has simply outgrown its physical capacity to do its job because of inadequate space and/or equipment. Costs of moving, or any capital additions necessary to maintain the level of revenues on which the valuation analysis is based, should be provided for as part of the buyer's investment.

Excess Assets

In some cases, businesses have assets that are not really needed in the operations, usually excess equipment and/or real estate. Any net proceeds a buyer could expect to receive from disposals of such assets could be used to reduce the amount of permanent investment she might otherwise require. If disposal of excess assets is contemplated, any revenues and/or expenses associated with such assets should be removed when compiling the buyer's pro forma income statement.

Contingent Liabilities

It is important that the buyer analyze any contingent liabilities that may carry forward into new ownership and determine what provision needs to be made for them. As noted in Chapter 7, they may be recognized on the balance sheet by either a line item in the liability section or a footnote.

Structure of Long-Term Liabilities

When preparing to make an offer to buy a business or practice, the buyer should take into consideration the likely structure of his long-term liabilities. The structure of the buyer's financing has a bearing on the cost of capital, which in turn may influence the price offered for a business. This interrelationship is discussed in Chapter 13. The structure of the long-term liabilities also affects the buyer's ability to service the debt, as discussed in Chapter 28.

A buyer may elect to pay off some existing long-term liabilities because he or she considers the financing cost high and either doesn't need it or can get it cheaper elsewhere. The buyer may be forced to pay off certain long-term liabilities because they are not assumable, a matter that must be checked in each case if a buyer is considering assuming any existing liabilities.

A buyer who has the desire and ability to obtain long-term financing for the purchase should investigate the probable amount and terms and reflect them in his pro forma balance sheet and income statement.

One option, which is very popular in sales of small businesses and professional practices, is to have the seller carry a long-term contract for a significant portion of the transaction price. Whether this contract will be technically the obligation of the business under the new owner or a personal obligation of the new owner, putting the obligation on pro forma financial statements of the business makes clear the amounts that will have to be paid, one way or another, relative to the other financial variables of the business. As a practical matter, if it is technically a personal obligation of the buyer, the resources of the business probably will be pledged to secure its payment anyway.

The Buyer's Income Statement

A sophisticated buyer will make a pro forma income statement for an entity she is considering purchasing, based on how that specific buyer thinks she will operate the business.

Broadly speaking, a buyer's income statement might differ from the adjusted (normalized) income statements, as developed in Chapter 8, as a result of three factors:

1. Changes in the prospects for the business that the buyer anticipates while still viewing the operation as a stand-alone, independent entity, with no basic changes in its business.
2. Changes the buyer contemplates as a result of effecting some change in the nature or in the operations of the business, but still viewing it as an independent entity.
3. Synergies and efficiencies that arise as a result of combining the entity income in some way with other entities controlled by the buyer.

This categorization of possible changes is somewhat arbitrary. And the categories are not mutually exclusive. In most cases, the changes would sooner or later make the business worth more to the specific buyer than the business would be worth if it were assumed it would continue to operate as it had in the past. Obviously, such considerations have a bearing on how much any specific buyer might be willing and able to pay. Since these items are predicated on the specific buyer's perception of her ability to improve operations, the specific buyer wants as little as possible of the potential benefit of such changes reflected in the transaction price. Consequently, in most cases, the seller and her representatives don't see the specific buyer's pro forma income statement.

Changes in Existing Operations

Revenues.   The buyer may believe that revenues can be increased, perhaps significantly, without major changes in the basic nature of the business. These improvements could result from a number of things, such as changes in the promotional theme, changes in the merchandise mix, or improved service to increase repeat business. Obviously, the buyer's pro forma statement must reflect any increased costs associated with the hypothetical increases in revenues.

Operating Expenses.   The buyer should analyze all the operating expenses to determine whether he would anticipate their being higher or lower than in the past. The buyer's analysis may be based on personal experience or on industry averages, as developed in Chapter 9. Some of the items most likely to be adjusted might be wage costs and promotional expense items.

At this point in the analysis, the new owner/manager should set his own salary at something approximating a market rate for his services, regardless of what he actually thinks he may or may not take out of the business in salary and perks.

Interest Expense.   If the buyer would finance the operation differently than it was financed in the past, there would be a difference in interest cost. The buyer's pro forma income statement should reflect interest based on how the buyer contemplates financing the business.

Sensitivity Analysis.   Often, the buyer will consider several "states of the world" in order to understand the sensitivity of various factors. For example, the buyer might analyze the required changes in the operations of the business (and the resulting change in purchase price) due to a decrease or increase in revenues of 20 percent.

New Business Directions

The potential for this category of change is so vast that it almost defies any comprehensive discussion of the possibilities. The buyer may plan to turn a conventional retailer into a discounter. She may add entire new product lines. She may eliminate or implement a credit policy. She may discontinue a losing or marginal aspect of the operation. In any case, the buyer's income statement should reflect the anticipated consequences of the contemplated changes.

Synergies and Efficiencies

A particular buyer may be in a unique position to effect changes because of other related operations under his control. The buyer may benefit from eliminating a competitor, controlling a source of supply, controlling a distribution outlet, or reducing costs by combining activities. No two potential buyers' pro forma statements will be alike, but it is in the category of synergies where they are likely to differ the most. From the strategic buyer's perspective, the most important aspects of the potential acquisition might be the synergies, without which he might have little or no interest in the seller's operation. The buyer will want to see what the income statement would look like when the benefits of the available synergies appear.

Samples of Buyer's Pro Forma Statements

The following are hypothetical examples of buyers' pro forma income statements that illustrate the considerations from the buyer's perspective discussed in this chapter. The two examples use the same two hypothetical companies used in the last three chapters.

Purchase of a Sole Proprietorship

Exhibit 11-2 is a buyer's pro forma income statement for Ashley's Apparel Store from the perspective of one hypothetical buyer. The prospective buyer of Ashley's Apparel Store is Rags, Inc. Rags operates a chain of 10 women's ready-to-wear stores. Rags plans to continue to operate the new store as Ashley's Apparel Store, although the merchandising mix will change somewhat, and thus the gross margins will probably be more in line with the 40 percent experienced by most of the Rags Stores. However, Rags does expect operating expenses to be lower due to efficiencies effected through combining the stores. Such expenses as legal, accounting, insurance, automobile, trade and entertainment, and supplies should be lower. Rags projects that Ashley's sales will increase 10 percent due to a more effective advertising campaign, which will be less expensive than the one Ashley's used. Rags' employee benefit program is not as generous as Ashley's and will be less expensive.

Purchase of Corporate Stock

Exhibit 11-3 is a buyer's pro forma income statement for Patrick's Machinery & Equipment, Inc., from the perspective of Barney Backhoe, who has been working as general manager for Patrick's. Mr. Backhoe and two associates want to purchase Patrick's.

Mr. Backhoe plans to keep the name of the business as it is because Patrick's has a reputation for good quality and service. He expects to be able to maintain sales at their current level. Mr. Backhoe does want to emphasize the service end of the business more because Patrick's has an excellent team of mechanics and service people. That should cause margins to improve slightly.

Summary

It is typical for a knowledgeable buyer to make up a pro forma balance sheet and income statement for the business or practice under consideration reflecting the buyer's plans and expectations. This chapter addressed the pro forma statements on a single-year basis, but many buyers will project three to five years of the future operations with pro forma statements. This analysis helps the buyer quantify and assess expectations for the business.

Exhibit 11–2

ASHLEY'S APPAREL STORE
BUYER'S PRO FORMA INCOME STATEMENT

	Income Statement as Reported 1997		Adjusted Income Statement 1997		Pro Forma Income Statement	
	$	%	$	%	$	%
Sales	1,000,000	100.0	1,000,000	100.0	1,100,000	100.0
Cost of goods sold:						
Beginning inventory	170,000		185,000		185,000	
Plus: Purchases	570,000		570,000		695,000	
	740,000		755,000		880,000	
Less: Ending inventory	180,000		220,000		220,000	
Cost of goods sold	560,000	56.0	535,000	53.5	660,000	60.0
Gross margin	440,000	44.0	465,000	46.5	440,000	40.0
Expenses:						
Owner's salary	70,000	7.0	50,000	5.0	50,000	4.5
Other salaries	150,000	15.0	150,000	15.0	150,000	13.6
Payroll taxes	30,000	3.0	30,000	3.0	30,000	2.7
Employee benefits	23,000	2.3	23,000	2.3	20,000	1.8
Rent	65,000	6.5	65,000	6.5	65,000	5.9
Utilities	3,000	0.3	3,000	0.3	3,000	0.3
Telephone	3,000	0.3	3,000	0.3	3,000	0.3
Insurance	-	-	2,000	0.2	1,000	0.1
Supplies	5,000	0.5	5,000	0.5	4,000	0.4
Advertising	25,000	2.5	25,000	2.5	20,000	1.8
Travel & entertainment	25,000	2.5	5,000	0.5	3,000	0.3
Automobile expense	5,000	0.5	5,000	0.5	3,000	0.3
Outside accountants	5,000	0.5	5,000	0.5	3,000	0.3
Legal	3,000	0.3	3,000	0.3	1,500	0.1
License, registrations, etc.	2,000	0.2	2,000	0.2	2,000	0.2
Dues & subscriptions	1,000	0.1	1,000	0.1	1,000	0.1
Allowance for doubtful accounts	0.00		2,400	0.2	3,500	0.3
Depreciation	13,000	1.3	13,000	1.3	13,000	1.2
Interest	7,000	0.7	7,000	0.7	7,000	0.6
Total expenses	435,000	43.5	399,400	39.9	383,000	34.8
Pretax income	5,000	0.5	65,600	6.6	57,000	5.2

NOTE: Figures may not total due to rounding.
SOURCE: Exhibit 8-2.

Almost all buyers expect businesses to perform *better* under their ownership than they did historically. Generally, this is due to the buyer's plans to improve operations. Thus, the buyer's pro forma results, if translated into a value, would result in what we defined as *investment value* (value to that particular buyer) in Chapter 3. This may set an absolute upper limit on what the buyer is willing to pay. The buyer, of course, wants little if any of the value resulting from future changes to be reflected in the purchase price. However, buyers sometimes are willing to pay *something* over the value indicated by historical results in order to get access to the business opportunity.

Exhibit 11-4 presents a summary of the steps in preparing pro forma statements.

Exhibit 11–3

PATRICK'S MACHINERY & EQUIPMENT, INC.
BUYER'S PRO FORMA INCOME STATEMENT

	Income Statement as Reported 1997		Adjusted Income Statement 1997		Pro Forma Income Statement	
	$	%	$	%	$	%
Sales	2,400,000	100.0	2,400,000	100.0	2,400,000	100.0
Cost of goods sold:						
Beginning inventory	300,000		400,000		400,000	
Plus: Purchases	1,620,000		1,620,000		1,590,000	
	1,920,000		2,020,000		1,990,000	
Less: Ending inventory	320,000		430,000		430,000	
Cost of goods sold	1,600,000	66.7	1,590,000	66.2	1,560,000	65.0
Gross margin	800,000	33.3	810,000	33.8	840,000	35.0
Expenses:						
Officers' compensation	120,000	5.0	120,000	5.0	110,000	4.6
Salaries & wages	230,000	9.6	230,000	9.6	230,000	9.6
Employee benefits	50,000	2.1	50,000	2.1	50,000	2.1
Payroll taxes	50,000	2.1	50,000	2.1	50,000	2.1
Rent	24,000	1.0	24,000	1.0	24,000	1.0
Depreciation	33,000	1.4	33,000	1.4	33,000	1.4
Insurance	20,000	0.8	20,000	0.8	20,000	0.8
Travel & entertainment	30,000	1.3	30,000	1.3	25,000	1.0
Maintenace & repair	0.0		0.0		20,000	0.8
Policy adjustments	26,000	1.1	26,000	1.1	26,000	1.1
Transportation vehicles	24,000	1.0	24,000	1.0	29,000	1.2
Provision for bad debt	13,000	0.5	13,000	0.5	13,000	0.5
Other	90,000	3.8	90,000	3.8	90,000	3.8
Total expenses	710,000	29.7	710,000	29.7	720,000	30.0
Operating income	90,000	3.6	100,000	4.1	120,000	5.0
Other income (expense):						
Interest expense	(15,000)	(0.6)	(15,000)	(0.6)	(20,000)	(0.8)
Dividend income	1,000	Nil	1,000	Nil	0	0.0
Total other income (expense)	(14,000)	(0.6)	(14,000)	(0.6)	(20,000)	(0.8)
Income before taxes	76,000	3.0	86,000	3.5	100,000	4.2
Income taxes	16,000	0.7	20,000	0.8	25,750	1.1
Net income	60,000	2.3	66,000	2.7	74,250	3.1

NOTE: Figures may not total due to rounding.

Nil = Inconsequential amount, greater (or less) than zero.

SOURCE: Exhibits 8-3 and 8-4.

Exhibit 11–4

SUMMARY OF STEPS IN
PREPARING PRO FORMA STATEMENTS

Step 1   Analyze the working capital requirements of the business based on industry sources.

Step 2   Analyze the fixed assets of the company to determine whether an additional investment in fixed assets is necessary, or whether any existing assets are above the needs of the business and could be sold without affecting the entity's earning power.

Step 3   Review any contingent liabilities and determine what provision needs to be made for them.

Step 4   Determine the desired structure of long-term liabilities.

Step 5   Summarize a pro forma income statement for the subject company.

Part III

Reaching the Value Conclusion

Chapter 12

Value Drivers

Different factors "drive," or impact, the values of different kinds and sizes of small businesses and professional practices. The next several chapters address the broad approaches to value (income, market, and asset-based) and the commonly used methods within these three fundamental business valuation approaches.

In the process of selecting which valuation approaches and methods to use, the analyst should first consider the factors that motivate people to invest in different situations. Then the analyst should consider how those motivations translate into what investors would be willing to pay or receive in a transaction.

An analysis of investment motivations will not only affect the business valuation methods selected, it will also affect the valuation procedures and the variables that will be considered most important within each method. In some cases, the value drivers are influenced primarily by the type of industry that the appraisal subject participates in. For some industries, the primary value drivers may change over time.

In other cases, the value drivers may be influenced heavily by the circumstances of a particular transaction. This may be due to the type of the transaction (e.g., a squeeze-out merger is a totally different type of transaction than a simple offer to buy out a minority stockholder). The value drivers may also be influenced by the circumstances—or motivations—of one (or a group or class of) potential buyer(s) or seller(s).

Buyer/Seller Motivations

The following are some of the typical motivations to buy or sell a small business or professional practice:

1. To buy a job.
2. To realize certain nonfinancial benefits (e.g., involvement with something of personal interest).
3. To realize a desired rate of return on investment.
4. To achieve a targeted market position (e.g., eliminate a competitor).
5. To achieve critical mass (for cost savings, access to capital, or many other reasons).
6. To liquidate the business.

Elements That Influence Value Drivers

Size

Size certainly comes into play with buyer/seller motivations. In general, the larger the business, the more it is viewed as an investment, with return on investment being a major value driver. Conversely, the smaller the business, the more the personal motivations of buyers and sellers, such as "buying a job" drive value.

Leonard Sliwoski, director of the Small Business Development Center at Moorhead State University, categorizes small businesses by value of total assets, including intangible assets, as "very small," "medium small," and "larger small."

He classifies "very small" as "less than $50,000 to $100,000." Sliwoski explains:

> These are often small retail or service businesses which have been started by the owner/operator. If the owner/operator earns a reasonable salary, many times these businesses will reflect little profit, if any. In many instances, the prices at which these businesses sell are greater than what is economically rational based upon the income they generate. This is because the purchaser for this type of business is primarily interested in buying a job, and not buying the business as an investment. The purchaser is willing to pay for the job, and the job is valued differently by different purchasers.[1]

Sliwoski classifies "medium small" as those "from $50,000 to $100,000 on the low end and $300,000 to $400,000 on the high end. Regarding this size category, he says:

> As businesses approach this size, they begin to take on characteristics of an economic entity, separate and distinct from their owners. Also, as businesses approach this size, the sophistication of a potential purchaser's economic analysis becomes greater, and the emotional value of the business diminishes. In many instances, these businesses are viewed by purchasers as part job and part business.[2]

He opines that a business starting at $300,000 to $400,000 "is typically viewed by a potential purchaser as an independent investment, as opposed to part job and part business."[3]

Persistence of Customer, Supplier, and Employee Base

The more persistent and predictable the customer, supplier, and employee base, the more the value is driven by the established income stream. This is especially true if the persistence and predictability are not tied to the professional capability, reputation, or personality of one or a few individuals. Such businesses lend themselves well to valuation by the income approach, particularly by the discounted economic income method.

---

[1]Leonard J. Sliwoski and Maggie Jorgenson, "Acquiring a Small Business: How Much Can Your Client Afford?" *National Public Accountant*, October 1996, pp. 16-17.

[2]Ibid., p. 17.

[3]Ibid.

Three examples of businesses that are especially noted for customer persistency are insurance agencies, newsletters, and funeral homes. People have a strong tendency to renew policies with the same insurance agency, even when ownership and personnel change. Agencies that have been in business for a while usually have good records of renewal rates. This information usually provides a valid basis for the extrapolation of a renewal revenue stream. The same tends to be true of newsletters. While many people don't think of funeral homes as an industry with a high level of repeat business, the fact is that families tend to use the same funeral home generation after generation.

Stable and dependable supplier and employee bases are also value drivers in many businesses. Even within an industry, the persistence of these two elements will be more important to some buyers than to others. To the extent that these factors are important, sellers may consider establishing contractual relationships to insure continuity.

Ease of Entry

As a generality, the easier it is to enter a business, the more the value will be driven by its tangible assets. As barriers to entry increase, value is driven more by the intangible assets of the business and the importance of its income-producing ability increases.

Licenses, Franchise Agreements, or Permits

Closely related to ease of entry is the question of whether or not any licenses, franchise agreements, or permits are required. Licenses, franchise agreements, and permits may be considered a special form of barrier to entry. Licenses, franchise agreements, or permits are intangible assets of the business and may be required for any or all of the following reasons:

- To insure that a licensee has a minimum level of knowledge or competency.
- To regulate; that is, a license or permit may be renewed or withdrawn based on compliance with laws, regulations, or expected standards of performance.
- To limit competition, thereby maintaining an economically viable number of participants.
- To collect taxes in the form of license or permit fees.

Where a license, franchise agreement, or permit is involved, the analyst should understand (1) the reasons for it, and (2) the ability to transfer it, either as part of a going concern or separately from the business. If the license, franchise agreement, or permit is an integral and inseparable part of a going concern, it may be difficult to value it as a separate intangible asset. In such cases, an asset-based valuation approach may not be appropriate, and an income and/or market valuation approach may be called for.

On the other hand, if the license, franchise agreement, or permit can be separated from the business or practice, it may be appropriate to value it separately and use an asset-based approach as one valuation indicator. Incidentally, in marital dissolutions in New York and in some other states, family law courts *require* a professional license to be valued separately from the practice, no matter how long the practice has been established.[4]

Competition

The more competitive the market, the greater the value of an established customer base and an established market share, and the more emphasis should be placed on the ongoing income-generating capacity of the business.

Buyouts of competitors often are driven by special motivations unique to the particular combination. Such special motivations may include eliminating a competitor, spreading fixed marketing costs over a larger revenue base, eliminating duplicative expenses, expanding into a contiguous territory, and achieving greater buying power or other economies of scale. In such cases, the buyer needs to assess the value of such synergies. This analysis usually incorporates a discounted economic income exercise. The value of the synergies added to the value of the target as a stand-alone entity should establish a ceiling that the buyer would consider paying. The extent to which the seller or the buyer benefits from the synergies depends to a great extent on the relative number of potential buyers or sellers that could take advantage of the potential synergies and the negotiating ability of the particular seller and buyer.

In any case, such special motivations introduce an element of *investment value* into the negotiation process. Such an investment value analysis recognizes the special circumstances of the business combination, which does not occur in a traditional analysis of *fair market value* on a stand-alone basis. Whenever investment value considerations are involved, this suggests greater attention to income approach and asset-based approach valuation methods, compared with market approach valuation methods.

Classification of Valuation Methods

The business appraisal profession generally thinks of valuation methods as falling within three basic categories of analytical approaches:

1. Income.
2. Market.
3. Asset-based (cost).

---

[4]*McSparron v. McSparron*, 639 N.Y.S.2d 265 (N.Y. App., Dec. 7, 1995).

These valuation approaches are not entirely independent or discrete. For example, we use market-derived empirical data to estimate required rates of return in the income approach. Within the market approach, value measures observed are multiples of either some economic income variable or some measure of asset value. In the asset-based approach, we use market-derived empirical data in order to estimate asset values.

There is not a "right" or a "wrong" way to classify valuation methods. We have basically classified the methods by a consensus of the classifications used in the various professional business valuation curriculums. We also believe that most practitioners on the leading edge of the profession are classifying these valuation methods in a similar manner.

Historically, many people have classified the capitalization of almost any kind of an economic income variable under the income approach. However, there is a growing recognition that net cash flow, as defined in the next chapter, is the economic income variable that investors focus on most if return on investment is the primary value driver. Thus, the income approach, as most widely applied today, focuses on discounting or capitalizing net cash flow.

The income approach may also include use of some other economic income measure, such as net income, where the discount rate or capitalization rate for that variable can be reconciled with the rate applicable to net cash flow. There are two reasons for the emphasis on net cash flow in the income approach:

1. Conceptually, it represents what the owner can take out (in addition to normal compensation) without jeopardizing the ongoing operation of the business.
2. Empirically, it is the economic income variable for which there are the most data available to support development of the required cost of capital (i.e., required rate of return) for the particular investment.

These points are developed more fully in the three chapters that discuss the income approach.

We discuss the capitalization of financial fundamentals other than economic income, such as gross revenue or book value, under the market approach because these procedures tend to rely on empirical evidence derived from transactions occurring in the market.

Historically, most people have viewed the capitalized excess earnings method as a "hybrid approach." That is, the capitalized excess earnings method was considered an asset-based approach with respect to the tangible assets and an income approach with respect to the capitalization of excess earnings. This view certainly makes sense in a way. However, the basic thrust of the capitalized excess earnings method is to develop a total value for the goodwill and other intangible assets of the company. So the analysis really focuses on the valuation of all of the assets of the business. In consideration of this view, the current trend seems to be to classify the capitalized excess earnings method under the umbrella of the asset-based approach.

Many authors, including ourselves, have classified these methods differently for presentation purposes in the past. However, we believe that the classification as presented here represents the current consensus of the leadership of the business valuation profession. And we believe it makes conceptual sense.

Again, the classification of valuation methods does not have the dimension of being "right" or "wrong." The idea is to make the presentation of the valuation work product comprehensive—that is, to recognize all methods that are generally used in the profession today in a way that is (1) conveniently organized, (2) easily understandable, and (3) conceptually correct. The organization we have used, along with some brief explanatory notes, is summarized in Exhibit 12-1.

Summary

When considered in the aggregate, motivations of buyers and sellers may be typical within certain categories of businesses or practices. The greater the extent to which motivations are driven by something other than return on investment, the greater the extent to which the market approach becomes more relevant—as compared with the income approach or the asset-based approach. (For example, although income plays some role, sports franchises are often valued principally by the market approach.)

Elements to be considered in assessing what the primary value drivers (and thus the appropriate valuation methods) are for a particular business include, among others, the size, the persistence of the customer base independent of a particular owner, ease of entry, required licenses and/or permits, and the competitive situation as it may affect the particular business.

There is not a "right" or "wrong" way to classify valuation methods. However, some consensus has developed among business valuation practitioners over recent years, which we believe this edition reflects. This classification is basically as follows:

Valuation Approach	**Valuation Methods**
Income approach	Discounted economic income method
	Capitalized economic income method
Market approach	Guideline publicly traded company method
	Guideline comparative transaction (sale of an entire company) method
Asset-based approach	Asset accumulation method
	Capitalized excess earnings method

The next 11 chapters of the book, which discuss valuation methods, are organized in accordance with this classification.

Exhibit 12–1

ORGANIZATION OF VALUATION METHODS IN THIS TEXT

	<u>Chapter(s)</u>

Income Approach   **13–15**

Understanding Discount Rates and Capitalization Rates   13

This chapter sets up the income approach in general. It explains discount rates (used in the discounting method) and capitalization rates (used in the direct capitalization method). As used within the income approach, direct capitalization rates are derived from present value discount rates. Methods involving the extraction of direct capitalization rates by direct observation in the marketplace are classified under market approach methods.

Discounted Economic Income Method   14

Capitalized Economic Income Method   15

Market Approach   **13, 16–21**

Understanding Discount and Capitalization Rates   13

Portions of this chapter describe how capitalization rates for various income variables are observed directly in guideline companies in the market and applied to the subject company as part of the market approach.

Guideline Publicly Traded Company Method   16–17

Chapter 16 explains the guideline publicly traded company method, using minority ownership transactions in publicly traded stocks, and Chapter 17 describes the available data and ease of accessibility to it.

Guideline Comparative Transaction Method   18–21

The guideline comparative transaction method generally means the sale of entire companies, although both controlling and noncontrolling past transactions in the subject company are included here. Chapter 18 sets up the method in general and includes discussion of the use of rules of thumb. Chapters 19 and 20 focus on the two variables most commonly available and used in the market approach to valuing small businesses and professional practices: (1) multiples of gross revenues and (2) multiples of discretionary earnings, respectively. Chapter 21 describes available data to implement the guideline comparative transaction method.

Asset-Based Approach   **22–23**

Asset Accumulation Method   22

Capitalized Excess Earnings Method   23

These methods identify all assets—both tangible and intangible, and both on or off the balance sheet—add the assets, and subtract the liabilities in order to arrive at an indicated value. In the capitalized excess earnings method, various intangible assets are usually not individually identified. Rather, all intangible value is included in one "big pot" and measured by capitalizing economic income over and above the levels needed to support the value of the subject's tangible assets.

Chapter 13

Understanding Discount and Capitalization Rates

Discount Rate. A rate of return used to convert a monetary sum [or series of monetary sums], payable or receivable in the future, into present value.[1]

Capitalization Rate. Any divisor (usually expressed as a percentage) that is used to convert income into value.[2]

Converting expected income into value, this is the core of valuation of small businesses and professional practices. Obviously, this chapter is one of the most critical in the book.

The most common methods for valuing most going-concern businesses or practices encompass the discounting or capitalization of some measure of economic income. Whether we classify the many discounting and capitalization methods under the "income approach," the "asset-based approach," or the "market approach" is irrelevant. In each of the discounting and capitalizing methods, the analyst converts one or more measures of historical or estimated economic income to an indication of value, using discount or capitalization rates derived from market data.

An understanding of the nature of discount rates and capitalization rates and the selection of the applicable rate for a given situation is probably the most difficult problem in the entire process of business valuation.

Perfectly valid methods of valuation will produce perfectly meaningless results, unless one uses valid numbers. The ability to select appropriate discount and capitalization rates in a wide variety of situations is an indispensable skill of the business appraiser. It is also one of the most difficult skills to understand and implement thoroughly. Mistakes and poor judgment in the selection of discount and capitalization rates are probably the most common sources of error in business valuation.

"Discounting" versus "Capitalizing"

In the paragraphs above, the terms *discounting and capitalizing methods* and *discount and capitalization rates* were used several times. Before proceeding, we need to understand the difference between a discounting method and a capitalizing method. With this understanding, we can then proceed to understand the difference between discount rates and capitalization rates.

As we will see in the next sections, discounting is a procedure that is applied to one or a series of economic income flows expected in the future, while capitalizing is a procedure that can be applied to an historical, current, or expected future level of economic income flows.

---

[1] American Society of Appraisers, Business Valuation Standards, "Definitions" (American Society of Appraisers, June 1994) (parenthetical note supplied).
[2] Ibid.

Note that up to this point, we have talked about discounting or capitalizing *economic income*—a generic terms with no specific meaning. Later we will deal with the critical matter of exact definitions of the many measurements of economic income that may be discounted or capitalized.

Discounting

Mathematically, *discounting* is the exact opposite of *compounding*. In compounding, we ask the question, "If I invest a dollar today at x percent interest for a period of y years, how much will it be worth at the end of y years?" In discounting, we ask the opposite question, "In order to receive a dollar y years in the future, based on x percent assumed compound rate of return, how much do I have to invest today?" Exhibit 13–1 presents the basic arithmetic of discounting.

Discounting is a procedure that converts an expected future flow, or a series of expected future flows, to a present value, using a present value discount rate. The present value discount rate is the assumed periodic compound total rate of return on the investment over the life of that investment. The total flow is comprised of one, or both, of two components:

1. *Income.* Amounts received by the investor while holding the investment (usually in the form of interest on debt, dividends on stock, or withdrawals from a partnership or sole proprietorship).
2. *Appreciation (or depreciation).* The incremental (or decremental) amount received by the investor at the time of liquidating the investment, over and above (or below) the amount paid for the investment.

Perhaps the purest form of discounting a lump sum future payment to a present value is found in zero-coupon U.S. Treasury bonds. An investor buys a bond that pays a lump sum of $1,000 at some specified date in the future. The term *zero coupon* means that they pay the investor no interest along the way. Instead, the bonds are sold at a discounted price to give the investor the annually compounded rate of return that the market requires to attract investment in those bonds at the time that the bonds are issued. For example, if current market conditions require a rate of return of 8 percent on a 10-year "zero," the present market value would be computed as follows (using the arithmetic shown in Exhibit 13–1):

$$PV = \frac{\$1,000}{(1 + .08)^{10}}$$
$$= \$463.19$$

An investor can look in *Barron's* or other financial publications and see the current price and rate of return, assuming the bond is held to maturity, for all maturities of zero coupon U.S. Treasury bonds.

Exhibit 13–1

ARITHMETIC OF DISCOUNTING VS. COMPOUNDING

COMPOUNDING

The formula to determine the future value of an amount invested at annually compounded rate of return for a certain number of years is as follows:

$$FV = PV(1 + k)^i$$

where:

FV = future value
PV = present value
k = rate of return
i = ith year (the number of years into the future that the principal plus the compound rate of return will be received)

Example

Assume that we invest $1,000 for 3 years at a 10% rate of interest. Substituting in the above formula gives us the following:

$$
\begin{aligned}
FV &= \$1,000(1 + .10)^3 \\
&= \$1,000(1.10 \times 1.10 \times 1.10) \\
&= \$1,000(1.331) \\
&= \$1,331
\end{aligned}
$$

DISCOUNTING

Start with the formula for compounding:

$$FV = PV(1 + k)^i$$

As we learned in basic algebra, we can divide both sides of an equation by the same factor:

$$\frac{FV}{(1+k)^i} = \frac{PV(1+k)^i}{(1+k)^i}$$

Also, if the same factor appears in both the numerator and the denominator of an expression, we can cancel them out:

$$\frac{FV}{(1+k)^i} = \frac{PV\cancel{(1+k)^i}}{\cancel{(1+k)^i}}$$

We then have the formula for discounting from a future value to a present value! Since it is customary to put the dependent variable (the value we are solving for) on the left hand side, the basic formula for discounting is written as follows:

$$PV = \frac{FV}{(1+k)^i}$$

Exhibit 13–1 (concluded)

Example

If we can earn a 10% annually compounded rate of interest, how much do we have to invest today to get a lump sum payment of $1,331 exactly 3 years from now? Substituting in the above formula gives us the following:

$$PV = \frac{\$1,331}{(1+.10)^3}$$
$$= \frac{\$1,331}{1.331}$$
$$= \$1,000$$

DISCOUNTING A SERIES OF FUTURE ECONOMIC INCOME FLOWS

Discounting a series of future economic income flows simply involves discounting each individual future flow, and adding up the present values of each flow to get a total present value for the series of flows. The formula for discounting a series of future economic income flows may be written as follows:

$$PV = \sum \frac{FV_i}{(1+k)^i}$$

The capital Greek letter Sigma (Σ) stands for "sum of." It means to add up each of the components that follow, in this case the present values of each of the expected future amounts.

Example

Let's assume that a bond pays $100 interest at the end of each year for 3 years, and pays $1,000 principal at the bond's maturity date at the end of 3 years. If the market requires a 10% total rate of return on bonds of this quality and maturity at this time, what is the present value of the bond? Substituting in the above formula gives us the following:

$$PV = \frac{\$100}{(1+.10)} + \frac{\$100}{(1+.10)^2} + \frac{\$100}{(1+.10)^3} + \frac{\$1,000}{(1+.10)^3}$$

$$= \frac{\$100}{1.10} + \frac{\$100}{(1.10\times1.10)} + \frac{\$100}{(1.10\times1.10\times1.10)} + \frac{\$1,000}{(1.10\times110\times1.10)}$$
$$= \$90.90 + \$82.64 + \$75.13 + \$751.31$$
$$= \$1,000$$

It can readily be seen from the above that if the discount rate (i.e., the rate of return required to attract capital to the investment) goes up, then the present value goes down, and vice versa.

Note: In all the examples in this book, unless otherwise indicated, for simplicity it is assumed that compounding is on an annual basis, and that all returns are received at the end of each year. With minor adjustments in the arithmetic, assumptions of semiannual, quarterly, monthly, daily, or even continuous compounding can be accommodated. It can also be assumed that proceeds are received at some time other than the end of the year. For example, proceeds received at the middle of the year, or more or less evenly throughout the year, may be accommodated by the "mid-year discounting convention," discussed later in this chapter.

Exhibit 13–1 presents an example using a bond that pays regular interest plus returns its face value at maturity.

Many measures of expected future economic income can be discounted when valuing a business or professional practice. The following are some of the most commonly used:

1. Net cash flow available to all invested capital.
2. Net cash flow available to common equity.
3. Net income.
4. Dividends or other withdrawals.

Obviously, it is essential that the present value discount rate selected be appropriate for the future measure of economic income that is to be discounted. More on selecting present value discount rates will be presented in future sections.

Capitalizing

Capitalizing is a procedure that converts a single flow of economic income into an indication of value. The arithmetic of direct capitalization is very simple: the economic income flow to be capitalized is divided by the capitalization rate. The formula to determine indicated value by direct capitalization is as follows:

$$PV = \frac{E}{c}$$

where:
  PV = Present value
  E = Amount of economic income flow to be capitalized (usually expressed as dollars per annum)
  c = Capitalization rate (usually expressed as a percentage)

Let's assume that a stock paid $.48 per share annual dividend and that we believe that 4 percent is an appropriate direct capitalization rate for that stock's dividend. The indicated value of that share of stock, based on capitalizing its dividend, would be as follows:

$$PV = \frac{\$.48}{.04}$$

$$= \$12$$

Note that the direct capitalization rate is the reciprocal of the valuation multiple. In other words, to convert a valuation multiple into a direct capitalization rate, the analyst divides 1 by the multiple.

Let's assume that the aforementioned stock had earned net income of $1.00 per share in the last 12 months and that we determined that an appropriate P/E (price/earnings) multiple is 12. The stock should be worth 12 × $1.00 = $12.00. Another way to say the same thing is to say that we will capitalize the latest 12 months' earnings. Since the direct capitalization rate is the reciprocal of the valuation multiple,

$$\text{Cap rate (for latest 12 months' earnings)} = \frac{1}{12}$$

$$= .0833$$

Using the direct capitalization of earnings procedure, the indicated value of the stock based on capitalizing its latest 12 months' earnings would be:

$$PV = \frac{\$1.00}{.0833}$$

$$= \$12$$

Note that virtually any measure of economic income can be capitalized. The following are examples:

1. Revenues (gross or net).
2. Earnings (any of many definitions).
3. Cash flow (any of many definitions).
4. Dividends (or interest or partnership withdrawals).

Note also that any of the above economic income variables can be measured over any of an almost infinite variety of time periods in determining the level of return to be capitalized. The time periods for measurement could include the following, for example:

1. Latest fiscal year.
2. Latest available 12 months.
3. Simple or weighted average of last three years, five years, or any other historical period.
4. Projection for current or following fiscal year.
5. Projection for next 12 months.
6. A "normalized" estimate of the economic income variable to be capitalized.

Quite obviously, it is essential that the direct capitalization rate selected be appropriate for the return variable to be capitalized, both in terms of the definition of the return variable and the time period for which it is measured or estimated.

After understanding the basic methodologies of discounting and capitalizing, the analyst should realize that a discount rate and a direct capitalization rate clearly are not the same thing. They are two different concepts that should not be confused. The relationship between discount rates and direct capitalization rates is discussed in subsequent sections. Within the income approach, the capitalization rate is a derivative of the discount rate, so we will first address developing a present value discount rate.

Components of a Discount Rate

The present value discount rate is the expected total rate of return required to attract capital to the particular investment. The *total return* includes all the financial benefit the investor expects to receive from the investment. The total return includes both income and capital appreciation, if any is expected. As noted earlier, this includes payouts (interest, dividends, withdrawals) plus or minus any change from the purchase price of the investment to the proceeds expected to be realized on its sale.

In the appraisal literature (especially in the real estate appraisal literature), the discount rate is sometimes referred to as the *yield capitalization rate*. However, the yield capitalization (or present value discount rate) should not be confused with the direct capitalization rate.

The *discount rate* is the total required rate of return, expressed as a periodic compounded percentage of the amount to be invested to produce that return over the life of the investment. Put another way, the discount rate (required total rate of return) is the *cost of capital* for a particular category of investment. It is the expected total rate of return that the market requires in order to attract money to any category of investment, considering the risks and other characteristics of the investment. In other words, the discount rate (i.e., the required total rate of return) is the rate of return available in the market on other investments comparable in terms of risk, liquidity,[3] and other characteristics of importance to investors. In economic terms, it can be thought of as an *opportunity cost* (the cost of giving up the opportunity to do something else with the same money).

A simple example of the total rate of return available in the market on one category of investment is a bond that is only one year away from maturity, at which time the issuer would pay back the face value (usually $1,000 per bond) to the holder, along with any interest due. If the bond carried an interest rate of 10 percent, the interest would be $100 per year. This is because interest is computed on the face value of the bond ($1,000 × .10 = $100). If an investor bought the bond for $950, the investor would also expect to earn $50 in capital appreciation ($1,000 - $950 = $50), which would also be part of this total expected return. These two components of expected return would be expressed as a total expected rate of return by dividing the total expected return by the amount invested, as follows:

$$\frac{\$100 \ (interest) \ + \ \$50 \ (capital \ appreciation)}{\$950 \ (amount \ paid \ for \ bond)}$$

In the example above, the total expected rate of return is 15.8 percent. (In bond terminology, the total expected rate of return is called the *yield to maturity*.)

---

[3] In venture capital situations, the liquidity factor often is built into the discount rate. It is more common, however, to develop a discount rate assuming liquidity and to handle the lack of liquidity at the end of the process as a "discount for lack of marketability" (see Chapter 25).

The present value discount rate (i.e., the required total rate of return) for an investment in the ownership of a closely held business or professional practice is comprised of the following five components:

1. The rate of return available in the market on investments that are essentially free of risk, highly liquid, and virtually free of any administrative costs associated with ownership.
2. The premium that is required to compensate the investor for risk in an investment in equity.
3. The premium that is required to adjust for the additional risk associated with smaller companies.
4. The premium that is required to compensate the investor for illiquidity.
5. The premium required to compensate the investor for administrative costs.

These five components of the required rate of return are discussed in the following five subsections.

Risk-Free Rate of Return

The concept that underlies the risk-free investment is that the investor can be sure to get back the exact amount of money promised, exactly when it is promised. The investor can count on receiving the principal at a certain time, along with a stated amount of interest. To make it even sweeter, if he decides he wants his money before the principal is due, there is a ready liquid market in which he can instantly sell the investment to someone else, paying only a nominal commission cost.

The *risk-free rate* is the rate of return available to an investor at any given time on such an investment, such as U.S. Treasury bills or the highest quality money market funds. The rates of return available on such investments usually cover the expected rate of inflation plus a "real" rate of return, that is, something for renting out the money for a period of time. For example, if U.S. Treasury bills yielded 6 percent, and economists' expectations were that inflation was running at an annual rate of about 4 percent, the investor in T-bills would get enough interest to keep up with inflation, plus a real rate of return of about 2 percent for loaning the money on a risk-free basis.

For reasons discussed in a later section, the total rate of return available on long-term (20-year) U.S. Government bonds frequently is used as a proxy for the risk-free rate when developing a required total rate of return for an equity investment.

Premium for Risk

Risk is the uncertainty about exactly when or how much return an investor will receive on a given investment. In order to induce an investor to put her money into something with risk, the investor must have a reasonable expectation that she will earn a higher rate of return than that available on a risk-free basis.

There are two categories of risk factors inherent in investing in a small business or professional practice: (1) risk factors peculiar to the specific business or practice, including those peculiar to the particular industry or profession within which it operates; (2) risk factors arising from general and local economic conditions, such as interest rates, availability of credit, and expansionary or recessionary conditions.

Premium for Size

In recent years, a significant amount of research has shown that a great deal of a company's risk can be accounted for by its size. Even better for appraisers of small companies, a number of studies have shown success in *quantifying* the impact of size on the discount rate.

Ibbotson Associates now shows equity risk premiums for the smallest size decile on the New York Stock Exchange (NYSE). In their 1997 *Stocks, Bonds, Bills and Inflation* (SBBI), the 10th decile size premium over the general equity risk premium was 5.78 percent, significantly higher than the 3.47 percent "micro-capitalization equity size premium," which combines the 9th and 10th deciles (the smallest 20 percent of the New York Stock Exchange). In the 1997 *SBBI Yearbook*, the size of the 10th decile was below $94 million in terms of market value of equity capital, still above the range this book addresses but certainly helpful in estimating a reasonable discount rate.

The accounting firm of Price Waterhouse performed further studies on the size phenomenon. They took the NYSE to four percentage point size breakdowns (25 size groups in all). In addition to the traditional market value of equity capital, they used seven other measures of size. The results across the eight size measures are remarkably consistent. A summary of the Price Waterhouse study is presented in Exhibit 13–2.

To carry the size phenomenon down to an even smaller size level, an analysis of data from *Bizcomps* shows that companies that sell for over $500,000 command a significantly higher ratio of sale price to seller's discretionary cash flow than companies that sell for less.

An analysis done on the IBA Market Database showed that there was a positive correlation between size and P/E multiples for small companies. The results of this analysis are summarized as follows:

Range of Company Size $000s	Mean P/E Multiple
0 to 49	1.66
50 to 99	2.11
100 to 149	2.44
150 to 199	2.74
200 to 249	3.06
250 to 499	3.44
500 to 1000	4.26

Exhibit 13–2

EQUITY RISK PREMIUM STUDY
FOR VARIOUS SIZE MEASURES

Prior research has demonstrated a significant "size effect" in the sense that smaller companies have higher equity risk premiums than would be explained by their betas (in the context of the Capital Asset Pricing Model). The size used in these prior studies has been the aggregate market value of common equity.

This study extends the prior research in several ways, most importantly by testing the comparative results using several different measures of size. As can be seen in the table below, the size effect is quite strong regardless of which size measure is used.

Readers can approximate an equity required rate of return reflecting various size measures by adding the appropriate equity risk premium from the table below to the 20-year Treasury bond rate. Information to use the data along with a beta in the context of CAPM is contained in the full paper.

| Size Rank | Market Value of Equity | | Book Value of Equity | | 5-Year Avg. Net Income | | Mkt. Value of Inv. Capital | |
	Average Size	Arithmetic Equity Risk Premium	Average Size	Arithmetic Equity Risk Premium	Average Size	Arithmetic Equity Risk Premium	Average Size	Arithmetic Equity Premium
	$000	%	$000	%	$000	%	$000	%
1	30,323	3.81	10,219	4.52	1,446	4.42	45,992	3.59
2	10,958	2.83	4,538	3.86	552	4.81	16,718	2.46
3	6,883	2.81	2,937	4.90	354	3.79	10,784	3.90
4	5,227	5.13	2,179	5.16	248	5.01	7,860	3.68
5	4,179	3.86	1,693	5.70	191	5.23	5,952	4.89
6	3,164	5.51	1,389	6.46	147	7.23	4,753	7.24
7	2,726	5.97	1,104	6.11	117	6.57	3,749	6.65
8	2,132	7.05	860	5.45	97	6.90	3,213	6.15
9	1,860	6.36	744	5.31	76	6.91	2,459	6.26
10	1,494	6.62	631	7.25	66	5.67	2,085	6.70
11	1,283	7.68	534	6.69	54	9.25	1,789	5.23
12	1,093	7.28	474	9.06	45	7.81	1,556	7.63
13	922	6.92	393	7.59	39	9.24	1,363	8.42
14	809	7.91	347	8.72	30	7.47	1,127	9.14
15	678	8.70	282	9.76	27	9.76	908	9.03
16	564	8.99	251	9.37	23	9.36	799	9.21
17	502	9.30	205	8.12	18	10.28	657	9.50
18	394	10.65	192	8.50	16	10.71	549	8.24
19	319	9.15	163	9.97	13	9.77	456	9.27
20	256	9.56	136	10.15	11	10.72	367	11.15
21	211	10.69	112	9.94	8	10.61	286	10.21
22	170	10.21	86	11.84	6	11.65	233	11.03
23	123	11.53	71	10.13	4	11.00	172	10.08
24	77	12.19	46	11.31	3	12.31	108	11.86
25	30	15.79	19	13.89	1	13.38	41	15.51

| Size Rank | Book Val. of Inv. Cap. | | 5-Year Average EBITDA | | Sales | | Number of Employees | |
	Average Size	Arithmetic Equity Risk Premium	Average Size	Arithmetic Equity Risk Premium	Average Size	Arithmetic Equity Risk Premium	Average Size	Arithmetic Equity Premium
	$000	%	$000	%	$000	%	$000	%
1	27,352	3.63	5,123	5.04	29,270	5.32	165,775	4.74
2	10,106	3.79	1,793	4.49	10,825	4.50	63,742	6.20
3	6,758	3.69	1,129	4.81	7,356	5.78	41,822	6.94
4	4,457	5.92	835	5.11	5,144	7.62	31,991	6.67
5	3,242	4.94	619	5.91	3,968	8.25	24,545	8.19
6	2,598	6.78	470	7.25	3,200	6.81	19,609	8.06
7	2,046	6.10	368	8.02	2,640	6.34	15,756	6.84
8	1,575	5.79	309	5.24	2,194	7.04	13,416	7.03
9	1,379	5.35	251	6.20	1,726	6.06	10,482	8.54
10	1,153	7.51	212	7.10	1,468	7.39	8,943	8.34
11	952	7.18	176	8.15	1,200	8.36	7,407	8.52
12	831	8.32	149	9.68	1,060	10.46	6,334	9.12
13	687	7.65	137	8.63	916	11.72	5,358	8.69
14	604	9.70	109	8.02	773	8.33	4,668	8.37
15	499	9.42	83	9.02	653	8.84	4,077	10.15
16	410	9.00	74	9.91	550	8.25	3,506	8.96
17	347	8.25	63	10.40	498	9.64	2,821	8.07
18	306	11.84	56	9.87	446	9.25	2,341	8.52
19	255	9.09	45	10.64	369	9.72	1,958	8.22
20	213	10.73	37	9.00	287	8.83	1,644	10.21
21	174	9.48	30	10.00	245	9.25	1,371	9.98
22	141	9.61	23	11.22	191	10.00	1,015	10.22
23	103	10.16	18	12.54	148	12.41	748	11.20
24	75	11.95	12	12.15	100	11.17	475	10.23
25	31	13.88	5	13.09	37	13.34	156	13.14

SOURCE: Roger Grabowski and David King, "New Evidence on Size Effects and Rates of Return," *Business Valuation Review*, September 1996, pp. 103–115, summarized in *Shannon Pratt's Business Valuation Update*, June 1996, p. 11.

While there is a definite correlation, the standard deviations for the various size groups run from about 40 percent to 60 percent of the mean, and the correlation coefficient is only about 0.3.[4]

A new database, *Pratt's Stats*, will be investigating this phenomenon in considerable detail. This and other databases are described in Chapter 21, Comparative Transaction Databases.

Premium for Illiquidity

In contrast to the ready marketability noted as a hallmark of the risk-free investment, small businesses and professional practices are relatively illiquid. The sale of a small business usually requires a few months to accomplish, during which time the seller usually expends considerable time and effort on the sale. The seller will either pay a brokerage commission or incur other direct selling costs. It is difficult to predict how long it will take to sell or what the price will be relative to either what the owner paid for it or what his notion of its intrinsic value may be. When the owner does sell the business, more often than not he will receive only part of the price in cash and the balance on a contract over some extended period of time.

In the practice of valuing businesses and business interests, there are two common procedures for dealing with the adverse characteristic of illiquidity. Either procedure is acceptable if properly applied. However, the procedures typically used for large businesses differ from those typically used for small businesses. In valuing interests in large businesses for which a liquid public trading market is not readily available, the typical procedure is to reach a value as if a public trading market existed and then take a percentage discount for the lack of ready marketability. This procedure is attractive in valuing illiquid interests in large companies because there is considerable market evidence available to help one quantify the discount for illiquidity (lack of immediate marketability).[5]

In valuing small businesses and professional practices, however, it is a common procedure to build the adverse characteristic of illiquidity into the discount rate. The relative impact of this factor is somewhat subjective, since little empirical evidence has been developed up to this point to quantify this factor as it applies to small businesses and professional practices. Also, the analyst should avoid the double-counting associated with building the illiquidity factor into the discount rate and then taking another discount for lack of marketability.

In any case, it obviously requires a fairly high expected rate of return to induce investors to accept the risks and illiquidity of small businesses compared with available risk-free investments.

---

[4]Raymond C. Miles, "Price/Earnings Ratios and Company Size Data for Small Businesses," *Business Valuation Review*, September 1992, pp. 135–39.

[5]For a discussion of this procedure and related market data, see Chapter 15, "Discounts for Lack of Marketability," in Pratt, Reilly, and Schweihs, *Valuing a Business: The Analysis and Appraisal of Closely Held Companies*, 3d ed. (Burr Ridge, IL: McGraw-Hill, 1996), pp. 331–365.

Premium for Administrative Costs

Some analysts also recognize that the total required rate of return contains a component for the cost of administering the investment. This is separate from any compensation for services in managing the business. This component would be analogous to a bank's custodial fee for collecting, depositing, and accounting for receipts and expenditures from a client's investments. Such administrative costs tend to be higher for direct proprietary investments in small businesses or practices, even if the investment is made as a silent partner, than for passive holdings in such things as publicly traded securities. Usually time is spent communicating with people active in the business. And the tax aspects are usually more complicated than they are for a securities investment.

Relationship between Discount Rates and Direct Capitalization Rates

A *discount rate* converts *all* of the expected future return on investment (however defined) to an indicated present value. It is generally accepted that the discounted economic income method is the most theoretically correct way to value income-producing investments, including small businesses and professional practices.

In contrast to the more comprehensive method of discounting *all* of the expected returns, a *direct capitalization rate* converts *only a single return flow number* to an indicated present value.

This leads us to the logical answer to the difference between the discount rate and the direct capitalization rate: *For an investment with perpetual life, the difference between the discount rate and the cap rate is the average annually compounded percentage rate of growth or decline in perpetuity in the economic income variable being discounted or capitalized.*

The above relationship can be expressed as a formula very simply:[6]

$$c = k - g$$

where:

   c = direct capitalization rate (a rate to be used as a divisor to convert an economic income flow variable, such as net cash flow, to an indication of value)

   k = present value discount rate

   g = annually compounded rate of growth in the economic income variable being capitalized over the life of the investment (If there is an expected rate of decline, the g is negative, so the effect is that the rate of decline is *added* to the discount rate in order to estimate the direct capitalization rate.)

---

[6]For further discussions of this concept and step-by-step mathematical proofs showing that the cap rate equals the discount rate less growth as defined above, see Greg Gilbert, "Discount Rates and Capitalization Rates—Where Are We?" *Business Valuation Review*, December 1990, pp. 108–113, and Philip L. Cooley, *How to Value an Oil Jobbership for Purchase or Sale* (Bethesda, MD: Petroleum Marketing Education Foundation, 1982), pp. 7-34–7-37.

Reflecting Growth or Decline in Expected Returns

If the economic income stream to be capitalized does not include all of the total return expected on the investment, the rate of return expected from some source other than the amount of the current economic income stream being capitalized must be subtracted from the required total rate of return (discount rate) in order to get an applicable rate at which to capitalize the current economic income stream. For example, let's assume that the required total rate of return on an equity investment has been estimated to be 30 percent. Let's also assume that the investment is expected to produce an income stream of $10,000 in the coming year. And let's assume that the income stream is expected to increase at a rate of 3 percent per year. In that case, the 3 percent incremental expected return can be subtracted from the 30 percent total required rate of return in determining the applicable rate at which to capitalize the $10,000 expected next year's income. In this case, the capitalized value would be computed as follows:

$$\frac{\$10,000}{(.30 - .03)} = \frac{\$10,000}{.27} = \$37,037$$

Note that in the above example, the dollar amount that we capitalized was the amount expected in the year *immediately forthcoming*. If the $10,000 was last year's actual dollar amount, and we expected 3 percent annual growth from that base, the formula and computation would be as follows:

$$PV = \frac{E_0(1 + g)}{k - g}$$

where

E_0 = economic income in year 0 (the year just ended)
g = annually compounded growth rate of E
k = present value discount rate

This is often called the "Gordon Growth Model." Using the same example as above, we substitute the numbers in the formula as follows:

$$\frac{\$10,000(1 + .03)}{.30 - .03} = \frac{\$10,300}{.27} = \$38,148$$

Regardless of whether the analyst plans to use the required rate of return (i.e., discount rate) directly to develop a direct capitalization rate in one of the valuation methods, it is important that she have a pretty good idea of what the required total rate of return should be for the specific type of investment. Knowledge of the required total rate of return enables one to judge reasonably whether the capitalization rates used for certain streams of income, plus other elements of the total expected rate of return not reflected in the income stream, will actually sum up to the required total rate of return for the type of investment.

Guidance as to developing required total rates of return (i.e., discount rates) and direct capitalization rates is presented in a later section.

The above discussion shows that there is one unique situation where the discount rate and the direct capitalization rate are equal to each other: where the economic income flow to be discounted or capitalized is constant in perpetuity. The best example of this is a U.S. preferred stock with a constant dividend in perpetuity and no sinking fund or redemption provision. If the stock pays a $5 annual dividend and the market requires a 10 percent total rate of return, the stock can be valued by dividing the annual dividend by the market required rate of return, which in this unique situation can correctly be characterized as *both* the discount rate and the direct capitalization rate:

$$\frac{\$5.00}{.10} = \$50.00$$

In summary, the consensus of current professional appraisal thinking is that the direct capitalization rate impounds all the components of the present value discount rate (assuming that the two rates are to be applied to the return variable in exactly the same way except for the time period of measurement or estimation). For any given valuation date, values of the components of the discount rate (risk-free rate, risk premiums, etc.) are the same for the direct capitalization rate as for the discount rate. The difference is that the direct capitalization rate impounds one additional component: the annually compounded expected rate of change in the return variable being capitalized over the life of the investment, plus any increment or decrement to the value of the investment not reflected in the return variable being capitalized. (The following paragraphs illustrate the development of a cap rate where the value of the investment goes to zero over the life of the investment.)

Return *on* Investment versus Return *on and of* Investment

In business appraisal, direct capitalization rates are usually stated in the form of some variation of return on investment. For example, if an investor were willing to invest $100,000 to receive an annual return of $25,000, we would say that the *return on investment* is 25 percent ($25,000 ÷ $100,000 = .25). In reverse, we would say that the $25,000 income flow was capitalized at a rate of 25 percent, meaning that the income stream was valued at $100,000 ($25,000 ÷ .25 = $100,000).

In some cases, however (more often in real estate appraisal, but occasionally in business appraisal), a direct capitalization rate is stated in a form that represents a return *on and of* investment. We encountered an example of this method in a business appraisal in which a broker was valuing a restaurant by a variation of the capitalized excess earnings method (described in Chapter 23). He capitalized earnings before depreciation. However, he assumed that the used restaurant equipment would have an average remaining life of five years. He accounted for this finite life by using a direct capitalization rate that gave him an 18 percent return on his investment in the equipment plus enough additional return to amortize his investment completely in five years. In other words, he used a rate that yielded an 18 percent return on his investment plus the return of his investment in five years.[7]

In the example above, the direct capitalization rate worked out to be 30.5 percent, or 12.5 percent over that investor's required return on capital. The additional amount was built into the capitalization rate instead of recognizing either depreciation or a reserve for replacements as an expense. This form of direct capitalization rate, in lieu of depreciation expense, is used quite commonly in the appraisal of buildings and of certain limited life intangible assets. But it is not used frequently in business appraisals.

Distinguishing between *Return on Equity* (ROE) and *Return on Invested Capital* (ROI)

Much confusion arises among different people involved in valuing businesses because of failure to distinguish between return on equity and return on total investment (or invested capital). *Equity* is the ownership interest. If the business is financed entirely by equity, then equity and invested capital are one and the same. However, *investment* (also frequently called *invested capital*) is a broader term, including long-term debt as well as owners' equity. Therefore, if the business is financed by long-term, interest-bearing debt as well as by owners' equity, equity is a subset, or only a portion, of the total investment.

Return on Equity

Return on equity (ROE) is defined as follows:

$$\frac{\text{Earnings}}{\text{Equity}}$$

For example, if a company had earnings of $10,000 and equity of $50,000, the return on equity would be computed as follows:

$$\frac{\$10,000}{\$50,000} = .20$$

Return on Invested Capital

Return on investment (ROI) is a term used more ambiguously than *return on equity*. In some contexts, *investment* (or *invested capital*) is defined to be synonymous with *capital*, that is, all equity plus long-term,

---

[7]Dick Fraser, "How Much Is Your Business Worth?" *Restaurant Business*, August 1, 1981, pp. 85–88.

interest-bearing debt.[8] In other contexts, *investment* is defined to include all equity and interest-bearing debt, including short-term debt.

None of these ways of defining return on equity or return on investment is necessarily right or wrong. The point of this discussion is that it is necessary to be explicit about the exact meaning of these expressions in any given context.

The following is one of many formulas for return on investment:

$$\frac{\text{Earnings before interest and taxes (EBIT)}}{\text{Investment}}$$

For example, if a company had $75,000 worth of long-term, interest-bearing debt and $50,000 equity, and it paid $7,500 in interest on the debt and had $10,000 worth of pretax earnings, the pretax return on investment would be computed as follows:

$$\frac{\$7,500 + \$10,000}{\$75,000 + \$50,000} = \frac{\$17,500}{\$125,000} = .14$$

Implication for Discount and Capitalization Rates

If the economic income flow being discounted or capitalized is that available to common equity (after any payments of interest or preferred dividends), the discount rate or direct capitalization rate is strictly a common equity rate. The discount rate should represent the best available approximation of the cost of equity capital for the subject enterprise as of the valuation date.

If, on the other hand, the economic income flow being capitalized represents income available to *both* debt holders and equity holders, the discount rate should reflect a blending of the cost of debt capital and the cost of equity capital. This blending is based on the assumed proportions of long-term debt and equity capital. The blended rate is called the *weighted average cost of capital* (WACC). The development of a weighted average cost of capital is discussed in a subsequent section of this chapter. And its application in discounted or capitalized economic income valuation methods is discussed in the following two chapters.

Relating Discount or Capitalization Rate to Economic Income Flow

Economic income flows can be defined in many ways. It is essential to understand the nature of the economic income flow being capitalized and to select a capitalization rate that is applicable to that particular income flow.

---

[8]If the balance sheet also has deferred items in the long-term liability section, such as deferred taxes or unearned subscription revenues, such items are sometimes included in "capital" and sometimes not.

Exhibit 13–3

SALLY'S SALONS, INC.
INCOME STATEMENT
For the Year Ended December 31, 1997

Sales	$ 1,000,000
Operating expenses (excluding depreciation and owner's compensation	730,000
Owner's discretionary cash (discretionary earnings)	270,000
Owner's compensation	150,000
Earnings before interest, taxes, and depreciation (EBITDA)	120,000
Depreciation expense	40,000
Earnings before interest and taxes (EBIT)	80,000
Interest expense	50,000
Earnings before taxes (EBT)	30,000
Income taxes	5,000
Net income	$ 25,000

To appreciate this problem, consider the simple example of Sally's Salons, a small chain of hairdressing shops, well established in upscale apartment and hotel locations. As illustrated in Exhibit 13–3, the following are several common ways of defining economic income:

1. *Discretionary earnings* (sometimes called *seller's discretionary cash flow* (SDCF) or *owner's discretionary cash*). Earnings before owner's compensation (as discussed in Chapter 8), depreciation, interest, and taxes.[9]
2. *EBITDA.* Earnings before interest, taxes and noncash charges (depreciation and amortization) but after owner's compensation.
3. *EBIT.* Earnings before interest and taxes but after owner's compensation and depreciation.
4. *EBT.* Earnings before taxes but after owner's compensation, depreciation, and interest.
5. *Net income.* The bottom line, earnings after all expenses, including income taxes if incorporated.

---

[9]In October 1996, the International Business Brokers Association created a Business Brokerage Glossary that included the term *discretionary earnings*, defined as "The earnings of a business enterprise prior to income taxes, nonoperating income and expenses, nonrecurring income and expenses, depreciation and amortization, interest expense or income, and owner's total compensation for those services which could be provided by a sole owner/manager."

When Sally asks a business broker what price she can expect to get for her business and he replies, "Businesses like yours in this metropolis usually sell for net assets at market value plus one year's earnings," what does he mean by *earnings*? He may be referring to any of the five definitions above or any of many possible variations. For example, as discussed in Chapter 8, depreciation may be included in expenses but at an adjusted amount. Or earnings may be stated before depreciation but after an allowance for replacements. Similarly, the owner's compensation may be deducted from sales as an expense but at an adjusted amount.

Another variation sometimes encountered is the treatment of principal repayments on borrowed funds as an expense in determining the earnings variable to capitalize. That procedure is performed in order to estimate a direct capitalization rate in the form of a return on a cash-on-cash basis. A *cash-on-cash* return is the amount of cash per year expected to be available to the investor, divided by the amount of cash invested. In real estate appraisal, this concept is called the *equity dividend rate*.

In summary, there are many ways to define the economic income flow, no single one of which is universally right or wrong. No matter how the economic income flow is defined, it is essential that the discount rate or direct capitalization rate selected be the rate that is appropriate to the particular definition of the economic income flow being discounted or capitalized.

Several levels of economic income flows that may be discounted or capitalized are shown in Exhibit 13–4, along with the distinctions as to (1) which economic income flows represent return to equity and (2) which economic income flows represent return to all invested capital.

Exhibit 13–4

LEVELS OF ECONOMIC INCOME THAT MAY BE DISCOUNTED OR CAPITALIZED

Level of Economic Income	Returns to Equity	Returns to Total Invested Capital
Gross or net revenues	X	X
Discretionary earnings (owner's discretionary cash)		X
EBITDA		X
EBIT		X
EBT	X	
Net income	X	
Net cash flow to invested capital		X
Net cash flow to equity	X	

Note: With the exception of gross or net revenues, the levels of economic income falling in the "Returns to Invested Capital" column by definition include returns available to long-term debt holders as well as to equity holders.

Developing a Discount Rate

Methods directly employing direct capitalization rates are used more frequently in valuing small businesses and professional practices than methods directly employing present value discount rates. We present the development of present value discount rates first, however, because in theory, as noted in an earlier section, the direct capitalization rate should reflect all the elements of the discount rate plus one or two others. The analyst should be able to mentally reconcile the reasonableness of the direct capitalization rates used with the reasonableness of the levels of discount rates theoretically impounded in them.

Discount Rates for Debt

Discount rates for debt instruments are widely observable in the marketplace. If a company borrows, its actual cost of borrowing provides significant evidence as to its cost of debt. If it does not borrow but is in a position to do so, the cost of borrowing for other companies of comparable risk can be used to develop a cost of debt for the subject company.[10]

An often overlooked component of the cost of debt for small businesses and professional practices is *personal guarantees*. If an owner were to obtain a third-party guarantor on an arm's-length basis, there would be a charge for that service. There is not much data on this factor because few guarantees actually are arm's-length. However, it seems reasonable to recognize a premium of upwards of three percentage points to the face value interest rate if personal guarantees are required.

Discount Rate for Net Cash Flow to Equity

Unlike discount rates for debt, discount rates for equity are *not* directly observable in the marketplace. Therefore, the cost of equity capital generally has to be pieced together or "built up" by adding the components of the discount rate, as discussed in an earlier section of this chapter.

The economic income variable for which an equity discount rate is most frequently built up is *net cash flow*. There are two reasons for this. One is conceptual; the other is a matter of empirical expediency (ready availability of data). The conceptual reason is that net cash flow represents the return on the investment that the investor has completely available to take out of the business or to do with as he wishes with absolutely no impairment of the ongoing ability of the business to continue to produce the expected level of cash flows in the future. The empirical reason to prefer discounting net cash flow over other measures of eco-

---

[10]For step-by-step direction on costs of debt capital, see Chapter 20, "Valuing Debt Securities" in Pratt, Reilly, and Schweihs, *Valuing a Business*, 3d ed., pp. 479–491.

nomic income is the availability and acceptance of market data to help quantify the discount rate applicable to net cash flow.

Definition of Net Cash Flow.   For the purpose of developing and applying an equity discount or capitalization rate, net cash flow may be defined as follows:

	Net income (after taxes)
+	Noncash charges
−	Capital expenditures (the net changes in fixed and other noncurrent assets)*
−	Changes in working capital*
±	Net changes in long-term debt*
=	Net cash flow

*Assumes amounts are those necessary to support projected operations.

If there are preferred dividends, they would have to be subtracted, of course, if the objective is to determine cash flow available to the common equity.

Risk-Free Rate of Return.   The truly risk-free benchmark rate of return is the short-term Treasury bill rate. Longer maturities have some risk inherent in them because the market prices of the bonds fluctuate with changes in interest rates.

It is intuitively appealing, however, to use long-term government bond rates as the base from which to build an equity discount rate for two related reasons:

1. The long-term bonds come closer to matching the expected life of most equity investments.
2. Long-term interest rates fluctuate less over time. This lesser fluctuation seems more consistent with the fluctuations of required rates of return on equity investments.

Fortunately, data now have been developed allowing the 20-year government bond rate to be used as the risk-free base in developing an equity discount rate for net cash flow. These data are described in the following section.

Premium for Risk

The annual yearbook, *Stocks, Bonds, Bills, and Inflation,*[11] publishes several series that quantify data on rates of return on equity over and above rates of return on government securities. The two series of greatest usefulness in this context are the long-horizon expected equity risk premium and the expected small stock premium. Exhibit 13–5 presents these series for the 1997 yearbook.

---

[11] *Stocks, Bonds, Bills, and Inflation: 1997 Yearbook* (Chicago: Ibbotson Associates, annual).

Exhibit 13–5

Key Variables in Estimating
the Cost of Capital

	Value
Yields (Riskless Rates)*	
Long-term (20-year) U.S. Treasury Coupon Bond Yield	6.7%
Intermediate-term (5-year) U.S. Treasury Coupon Note Yield	6.2
Short-term (30-day) U.S. Treasury Bill Yield	5.2
Risk Premia**	
Long-horizon expected equity risk premium: large company stock total returns minus long-term government bond income returns	7.5
Intermediate-horizon expected equity risk premium: large company stock total returns minus intermediate-term government bond income returns	7.9
Short-horizon expected equity risk premium: large company stock total returns minus U.S. Treasury bill total returns[†]	8.9
Expected default premium: long-term corporate bond total returns minus long-term government bond total returns	0.5
Expected long-term horizon premium: long-term government bond income returns minus U.S. Treasury bill total returns[†]	1.4
Expected intermediate-term horizon premium: intermediate-term government bond income returns minus U.S. Treasury bill total returns[†]	1.0
Size Premia***	
Expected mid-capitalization equity size premium: capitalization between $755 and $3,242 million	1.0
Expected low-capitalization equity size premium: capitalization between $197 and $755 million	1.7
Expected micro-capitalization equity size premium: capitalization below $197 million	3.5

* As of December 31, 1996. Maturities are approximate.
** Expected risk premia for equities are based on the differences of historical arithmetic mean returns from 1926–1996. Expected risk premia for fixed income are based on the differences of historical arithmetic mean returns from 1970–1996.
***See Chapter 7 for complete methodology.
† For U.S. Treasury bills, the income return and total return are the same.

Note: An example of how these variables can be used is found with equation (35).

SOURCE: *Stocks, Bonds, Bills, and Inflation 1997 Yearbook™* (Chicago: Ibbotson Associates, 1997), p. 161. Annual updates work by Roger G. Ibbotson and Rex A. Sinquefield. Used with permission. All rights reserved.

The market value of the common equity for the stocks comprising the "micro-capitalization" group at year-end 1996 was below $197 million. Small stocks as we have defined them in this book are much smaller than these.

Premium for Size.   As mentioned earlier, much research has been performed in the mid-1990s in order to quantify the effect of size as a component of risk. Some analysts use a general equity risk premium and then add a premium for size. Others use a single figure that incorporates the general equity risk premium and size premium into a single figure (as in Exhibit 13–2, for example).

Premium for Illiquidity.   The equity risk premium and size premium data referred to above are from publicly traded minority ownership interests. Investors as a whole cherish liquidity and loathe illiquidity. Certainly, if one is valuing a minority ownership interest in a closely held company, some discount for the illiquidity of the subject securities is warranted. When valuing a small business or practice overall, there is still an illiquidity factor associated with the closely held nature of the business. When valuing a closely held company, the illiquidity factor is usually reflected in a separate step at the end of the process. However, some appraisers of smaller companies like to reflect the illiquidity factor in the discount rate. (It is also common for venture capitalists to impound the illiquidity factor into their discount or cap rate.)

When one is dealing with direct capitalization rates, impounding the discount for illiquidity into the cap rate is a matter of very simple arithmetic. The cap rate before the discount for illiquidity is multiplied by one divided by one minus the discount for illiquidity. For example, let's assume that the cap rate is 20 percent before the discount for illiquidity, and the discount for illiquidity is determined to be 30 percent. The arithmetic would be as follows:

$$.20 \left(\frac{1}{1 - .30} \right)$$

$$= .20 \left(\frac{1}{.70} \right)$$

$$= .20(1.43)$$

$$= .286 \text{ cap rate adjusted for illiquidity}$$

Note that this adjustment is only applicable when the cap rate itself is derived from publicly traded company data. If the cap rate is derived from closely held company data, this adjustment is not applicable. When dealing with discount rates instead of cap rates, there is no simple arithmetic for impounding the discount for illiquidity into the discount rate. For this reason, we still prefer to take a discount for illiquidity as a separate step when valuing minority ownership interests in small businesses and professional practices. Discounts for lack of marketability of minority ownership interests in closely held businesses can cover a very wide range, but most fall in the area of about 25 to 45 percent, trending toward the higher end of the range for smaller companies. See Chapter 25, Discounts for Lack of Marketability, for more information.

Controlling ownership interests are generally much easier to sell than minority ownership interests and may not require any discount for lack of marketability. If the facts and circumstances of the case suggest that there should be any discount for lack of marketability for a controlling ownership interest, it would usually be a smaller discount, more like 10 to 25 percent. This subject is also covered in Chapter 25.

Weighted Average Cost of Capital (WACC)

When developing a discount rate to apply to an economic income flow available to all invested capital (equity plus long-term, interest-bearing debt), the present value discount rate is a weighted average of the costs of debt and equity based on the assumed relative proportions of each in the capital structure at market values (not book values).

When valuing a minority ownership interest, the assumed weighting of debt and equity should normally be the actual weighting in the capital structure as it exists because the minority stockholder generally would not have the ability to change it. When valuing a controlling ownership interest, an industry average capital structure is often used, based on the theory that a control owner would have the ability to put an optimal capital structure in place.[12]

When computing the cost of debt, its cost is normally calculated on an after-tax basis—that is, reduced by the tax savings—since interest is a deductible business expense for income tax purposes. The formula for this is as follows:

$$k_d = k_{d(pt)} \left(1 - t\right)$$

where:

k_d = after-tax cost of debt
$k_{d(pt)}$ = pretax cost of debt
t = effective income tax rate

As an example, let's assume that a company has 40 percent debt at a 10 percent borrowing rate, 60 percent equity at a 20 percent cost of equity, and an effective income tax rate of 30 percent. The weighted average cost of capital would be computed as follows.

Capital Component	Cost of Capital Component		Proportion of Capital Component in Capital Structure		Weighted Cost of Capital
Debt {.10 × (1.0 − .3)} =	.07	×	.40	=	.028
Equity	.20	×	.60	=	.120
Weighted average cost of capital					.148

Data on industry-average leverage (market value weighted proportions of debt and equity) for many industry groups are contained in

---

[12]Since the market value of equity often is what we are solving for, this tends to require an iterative process. Estimate a market-weighted capital structure and then see how it works out. This is fairly easy mechanically with today's computer capabilities.

Ibbotson Associates' *Cost of Capital Quarterly*. Most other sources provide weightings based only on book value, which can be misleading if the market value of equity differs significantly from the book value of equity.

Discount Rate for Other Return Variables

Defensible discount rates for economic income measures other than net cash flow are difficult (but not impossible) to develop. The measure of economic income most commonly discounted other than net cash flow is net income. There are two basic methods for developing a discount rate for an economic income measure other than net cash flow:

1. Convert a discount rate developed for net cash flow to a discount rate applicable to some other economic income measure.
2. Attempt to develop a discount rate for the desired economic income measure from directly observed market data for that variable.

Converting a Net Cash Flow Discount Rate. The key to converting a net cash flow discount rate to a discount rate for some other economic income measure is to estimate the typical percentage difference between the two measures and adjust the net cash flow discount rate accordingly. One way is to compute the historical percentage difference between net cash flow and the desired economic income measure (such as net income) for the subject company. Another way is to research public companies in the industry to estimate the percentage difference.

Net cash flow is usually lower than net income or any other economic income measures that the appraiser is likely to discount or capitalize. Therefore, the discount rate applicable to other measures is usually higher than the discount rate applicable to net cash flow.

Developing a Discount Rate Directly from Market Data. Sometimes a discount rate can be estimated from market data by converting observed market capitalization rates to discount rates. The most likely economic income measure to lend itself to this exercise is net income.

Recall that we said that the primary difference between the present value discount rate and the direct capitalization rate is growth. For some companies, earnings growth estimates can be obtained for as much as five years ahead.[13] Adding the growth rate to the capitalization rate (the reciprocal of the P/E multiple in the case of net income) provides a rough estimate of the implied discount rate. There are at least two problems with this method. First, to be valid, the growth rate used in the conversion should be an expected growth rate in perpetuity. The five-year growth rate could differ considerably from the longer-term growth rate. Secondly, the five-year projected growth rates found in such

---

[13]*Value Line Investment Survey* is one source of such estimates.

publications leave much to be desired in terms of accuracy. Nevertheless, in some cases the method provides at least a useful rough estimate.

Developing A Direct Capitalization Rate

Unlike present value discount rates, direct capitalization rates for almost any level of return to either equity or overall invested capital (except net cash flow)[14] are directly observable in the market. If enough reliable guideline company transaction data are available, the direct market comparison method (often called the "guideline company method") may be the easiest and most reliable way to develop direct capitalization rates to apply to various income variables for the subject company. Alternatively, for some income variables, it is possible to convert a discount rate to a capitalization rate.

Direct Market Comparison Method

The direct market comparison method of developing a capitalization rate consists of (1) finding transactions in the market involving the sale of entities with comparative economic income flows and (2) computing the capitalization rates implied in the prices at which the transactions took place. The example familiar to most people is price/earnings multiples in the public stock market.

For example, if a small restaurant chain wants to value shares of its stock for the purpose of selling shares to the public (going public), the analyst will look at the prices at which similar small restaurant chain stocks are selling in the public market in relation to various measures of earning power, one of which will be the latest 12 months' earnings per share. The price/earnings multiple reported in daily newspapers is the current market price of a stock, divided by the latest reported 12 months' earnings per share. In the public market, price/earnings multiples are quoted on the basis of after-tax earnings. If the analyst finds that most similar stocks are selling between six and nine times their latest 12 months' earnings, that information provides a ballpark within which to capitalize the subject company's latest 12 months' earnings to determine a public offering price. The analyst will then very carefully examine all the guideline companies' characteristics relative to the subject company and make an estimate of just where within that ballpark the subject company belongs.

Then, using the guideline companies' financial statements, the analyst will conduct the same exercise to develop market-derived capitalization rates for several other measures of earning power. Such measures could include, for example, the last three and five years' straight and/or weighted average earnings, projected next year's earn-

---

[14]Net cash flow can be computed from most public company financial statements, but it is hard to discern how much capital expenditures and changes in working capital are discretionary rather than necessary in the normal course of business.

ings, and perhaps one or several measures of cash flow. In other words, for each of several measures of economic income, the market will provide a range of capitalization rates for various guideline companies. And the analyst will have to exercise her judgment to determine where in each range the subject company best fits.

The most important thing about the above example is that the analyst derives a different applicable capitalization rate from the public market for each different measure of economic income considered for the subject company. Direct capitalization rates derived directly from transaction data should be based on the same measure of economic income as the measure of the subject company's economic income to which that capitalization rate will be applied. Otherwise, adjustments must be made. And such adjustments may be difficult to support.

It is obvious from the above example that the analyst could conceivably develop quite a wide array of capitalization rates. These capitalization rates could include those based on each of several definitions of economic income, each involving several historical and/or projected time periods. The analyst should judge which measure or measures of economic income, along with the respective indicated capitalization rate(s), most realistically indicate value in each case. Any capitalization rate found in a market transaction reflects expectations of the level and risk of future earnings. In order for capitalization rates found in the market to be realistic guides for valuing the subject company, there must be a reasonable basis for expecting the subject company's economic income flow to be at least approximately parallel to what was expected from the economic income flows from which the capitalization rates were derived.

In the small restaurant chain example, if the average stock was selling at 12 times last year's earnings, the market is capitalizing *last year's earnings* at 8.33 percent (1 ÷ 12 = .0833). The market is certainly not buying those stocks because it expects their future earnings to be only 8.33 percent of the current stock price. The market obviously expects earnings growth since earnings of 8.33 percent are available on much safer investments. To realistically capitalize the subject company's latest year's earnings at the market-derived direct capitalization rate of 8.33 percent, the analyst must reasonably expect the growth and risk characteristics of the subject company's future earnings to be somewhat similar to the industry or, more specifically, to that subset of the industry from which the capitalization rate was derived.

The point of the example above is to stress the need for comparability between the subject company and the comparative companies from which the capitalization rate is derived. The comparability should be reflected in the definition of the economic income being capitalized and also in the assumptions regarding it.

Also, note that the purpose of the valuation clearly influences the analyst's choice of data. Since the purpose is a public offering, public market data are used for comparison. That is not to say that public market data cannot be used at all for other purposes for which small business valuations may be undertaken but, as discussed in Chapter 5 and elsewhere in this book, it is much more difficult to make useful comparisons between public companies and small private companies than between public companies and medium-size to larger private companies.

The same kind of exercise can be used to derive direct capitalization rates from closely held company market transaction data. The problem is that the data themselves are much harder to obtain because there is no requirement for public reporting of most private transaction data. Sources of such data that do exist are discussed in Chapter 21, Comparative Transaction Databases.

The direct market comparison method is generally considered the best valuation method if a sufficient number of directly comparative transactions are available for comparison. But that is a big "if." As noted above, comparative data are not always readily available. Moreover, because of the unique nature of each business, the analyst must exercise a great deal of analytical judgment to ascertain the degree of comparability between the subject company and the comparative transactions found in the market.

Converting a Discount Rate to a Direct Capitalization Rate

As discussed in an earlier section in this chapter (Relationship between Discount Rates and Direct Capitalization Rates), one way to develop a cap rate is to start with a discount rate and subtract from the discount rate a number that represents the expected annually compounded growth in perpetuity of the variable to be capitalized.

Warning! Historical Industry Returns Not Reliable for Discount and Capitalization Rates

We have said consistently that discount rates and capitalization rates are determined by the market. Also, some type of market *transaction data* is the proper type of source for developing such rates. A common error is to use some source of industry historical data (such as *RMA Annual Statement Studies*) as a basis for such rates. If the sawmill industry returned 5 percent on equity over the last five years, would you buy equity in a sawmill for an expected 5 percent long-term total expected return? Of course not! Only expected future economic income flows count. Recent historical economic income for an industry may provide some information to the analyst, but this income is often not representative of expected future economic income. Therefore, historical industry data are generally not a valid source of discount rates and capitalization rates.

Relationship between Payback Period and the Direct Capitalization Rate

Some purchasers of businesses use the *payback period* as a criterion to determine the maximum amount they will be willing to pay. The payback period is based on cash flow and can be defined as follows:

> The time required (usually in years) for estimated future net cash receipts to equal the initial cash outlay for a project. If the estimated receipts are the same amount each year, the payback period is equal to the investment outlay divided by this annual amount.[15]

Since the payback period is a cash flow concept, income before depreciation expense but after allowance for replacements should be used to compute the payback period. If the expected cash flow thus defined was $30,000 each year and the asking price for the business was $120,000, the payback period could be computed as follows:

$$\frac{\$120,000}{\$30,000} = 4 \text{ years}$$

If a buyer sets a maximum payback period as a limit to the amount she would consider paying and the expected cash flow is an even amount each year, the maximum price becomes the payback period times the expected annual cash flow. In the example with the $30,000 expected cash flow each year, if the buyer set a maximum payback period of three years, the maximum price she would pay would be computed as follows:

$$\$30,000 \times 3 \text{ years} = \$90,000$$

When the expected cash flow is an even amount each year, the reciprocal of the payback period could be regarded as the capitalization rate applicable to cash flow. In other words, a three-year payback period would be equivalent to a 33.33 percent direct capitalization rate applicable to cash flow ($1 \div 3 = .3333$), in the same manner that the reciprocal of the price/earnings multiple is a capitalization rate for the earnings stream on which the price/earnings multiple is based.

The payback period becomes most relevant when returns beyond a relatively short time horizon are highly uncertain. For example, during the housing boom of the 1970s, we encountered a company buying small sawmills on the basis of a maximum payback period of three years, recognizing that the industry was highly cyclical and its future very uncertain.

---

[15]W.W. Cooper and Yuji Ijiri, eds. *Kohler's Dictionary for Accountants*, 6th ed. (Englewood Cliffs, NJ: Prentice Hall, 1983), p. 375.

The *payback period method* sometimes is referred to as the *LBO model* because it relates to the time period within which the company is expected to pay back the debt incurred in a leveraged buyout. In this context, it is viewed by some as the *justification to purchase*. Since most small business and professional practice transactions involve seller financing, the payback period can be thought of as the time required to retire the seller financing. This can be a useful reality check on the reasonableness of the estimated value of the business or practice.

The primary disadvantage of the payback period is that it gives no recognition whatsoever to expected economic income beyond the payback period. For example, depreciation during the payback period may exceed capital expenditures, a most unlikely occurrence in a perpetual model. Another, less important, criticism of the payback period is that it gives no recognition to the timing of the cash flows within the payback period. The payback period can be a useful supplemental tool, but it should not be used alone.

Different Rates for Different Buyers

The cost of capital, either debt or equity, is different from one potential buyer to another. For an individual buying a sole proprietorship from another individual, the cost of capital would probably be about the same for the buyer as for the seller. On the other hand, the cost of capital to a sizable public company is probably somewhat less than the cost of capital to the typical small entrepreneur.

The buyer will often use a capitalization rate based on that buyer's own cost of capital. This is a questionable procedure if the buyer's company actually has lower risk than the acquiree. However, the seller should consider the cost of capital to the likely classes of buyers and estimate the capitalization rates that they are likely to use.

As discussed earlier, when *fair market value* is the applicable standard of value, direct capitalization rates used should be representative of a market consensus. However, when estimating *investment value* of a business to a particular party, the applicable discount rates or capitalization rates are those based on that party's cost of capital, risk perceptions, and other relevant factors.

Summary

Discount rates and capitalization rates are two different concepts. But there is a clearly identifiable relationship between the two. The direct capitalization rate is, in effect, a variable rooted in the discount rate. But direct capitalization rates also reflect other factors. The discount rate is applied to *all* the economic income expected by the investor. The capitalization rate is applied to a single amount of economic income at some point in time. Therefore, the direct capitalization rate must differ from the discount rate by the amount necessary to reflect in the indicated value any expected return not impounded directly in the economic income flow being capitalized. The most common such element is expected growth in the economic income flow being capitalized. Another element, in the case of a limited life investment, is any increase or decrease in the value of the investment from purchase to sale or liquidation.

Discount rates or capitalization rates are meaningless until we define the investment base to which they apply. The most common investment bases are either the equity of the company or all the invested capital of the company, generally including equity plus long-term, interest-bearing debt.

There are a wide variety of definitions of economic income flows that may be discounted or capitalized. A discount rate or capitalization rate is meaningless until there is a clear definition of the economic income flow to which it is applicable. *It is absolutely critical to properly match the discount or capitalization rate to the economic income flow being discounted or capitalized.* In the income approach, discount and capitalization rates are most often applied to net cash flow. In the market approach, capitalization rates usually are matched to other economic income variables, such as net income, pretax income, or gross cash flow.

Finally, discount rates and capitalization rates are determined by the market. They reflect economic and industry conditions as well as internal company conditions at the time of the valuation. These conditions particularly include interest rates, inflation expectations, the industry and company outlook, and investor perceptions of the risk of the prospective investment as of the valuation date. All of these factors are subject to constant change and must be analyzed by the analyst as of the valuation date as part of the process of estimating the appropriate present value discount and/or direct capitalization rates.

Bibliography

Abrams, Jay B. "A Breakthrough in Calculating Reliable Discount Rates." *ASA Valuation*, August 1994, pp. 8–24.

_____. "Discount Rates as a Function of Log Size and Valuation Error Measurement." *The Valuation Examiner*, February/March 1997, pp. 19–21.

Annin, Michael. "Fama-French and Small Company Cost of Equity Calculations." *Business Valuation Review*, March 1997, pp. 3–13.

_____. "The Right Tools Can Simplify Company Valuation." *Accounting Today*, November 6, 1995, pp. 14, 35.

_____. "Using Ibbotson Associates' Data to Develop Minority Discount Rates." *CPA Expert*, Winter 1997, pp. 1–4.

Annin, Michael E., and Dominic A. Falaschetti. "Equity Risk Premium Still Produces Debate." *Valuation Strategies*, January/February 1998, pp. 17–44.

Arneson, George S. "Capitalization Rates for Valuing Closely Held Companies." *TAXES*, May 1981, pp. 310–17.

Boykin, James H. "Seeking the Elusive Discount Rate." *Appraisal Journal*, July 1990, pp. 328–33.

Brock, Thomas. "More on Capitalization Rates." *ASA Valuation*, June 1986, pp. 68–71.

Dietrich, William C. "Capitalization Rates—Seeing Is Believing." *Business Valuation News*, December 1985, pp. 3–4.

Gilbert, Gregory A. "Discount Rates and Capitalization Rates—Where Are We?" *Business Valuation Review*, December 1990, pp. 108–113.

Grabowski, Roger, and David King. "New Evidence on Size Effects and Rates of Return," *Business Valuation Review*, September 1996, pp. 103–115.

Greer, Willis R. "The Growth Rate Term in the Capitalization Model." *Business Valuation Review*, June 1996, pp. 72–79.

Hawkins, George B. "Critically Assessing a Business Valuation: Is the Capitalization Rate Used Reasonable?" *Internet: http://www.cris.com/~banister/caprates.htm*, 1996, pp. 1–6.

Honnold, Keith L. "The Link between Discount Rates and Capitalization Rates: Revisited." *Appraisal Journal*, April 1990, pp. 190–95.

Ibbotson, Roger G. "Equity Risk Premium: Where We Stand Today." *Proceedings of the Equity Risk Premium Conference*, University of Chicago, June 6, 1996.

Joyce, Allyn A. "Why the Expected Rate of Return is a Geometric Mean." *Business Valuation Review*, March 1996, pp. 17–19.

Julius, J. Michael. "Market Returns In Rolling Multi-Year Holding Periods: An Alternative Interpretation of the Ibbotson Data." *Business Valuation Review*, June 1996, pp. 57–71.

Kaplan, Paul D. "Why the Expected Rate of Return is an Arithmetic Mean." *Business Valuation Review*, September 1995, pp.126–29.

Kenny, Thomas J. "Closely Held Corporation Valuation: Determining a Proper Discount Rate." *Business Valuation Review*, March 1992, pp. 22–30.

King, David W. "Recent Evidence on Discount Rates." *Proceedings of the AICPA 1995 National Business Valuation Conference*, New Orleans, LA, December 1995, pp. 12·i–12·13.

Lally, Martin. "The Accuracy of CAPM Proxies for Estimating a Firm's Cost of Equity." *Accounting & Finance*, May 1995, pp. 63–72.

Leung, Tony T.S. "Myths about Capitalization Rate and Risk Premium." *Business Valuation News*, March 1986, pp. 6–10.

Ling, David C. "Implementing Discounted Cash Flow Valuation Models: What Is the Correct Discount Rate?" *Appraisal Journal*, April 1992, pp. 267–74.

Lippitt, Jeffrey W., and Nicholas J. Mastriacchio. "Developing Capitalization Rates for Valuing a Business." *The CPA Journal*, November 1995, pp. 24–28.

Mard, Michael J., and James S. Rigby. "New Research to Estimate Cost of Capital." *CPA Expert,* Fall 1995, pp. 9–12.

McMullin, Scott G. "Discount Rate Selection." *Business Valuation News*, September 1986, pp. 16–19.

Meyer, James E., Patrick Fitzgerald, and Mostafa Moini. "Loss of Business Profits, Risk, and the Appropriate Discount Rate." *Journal of Legal Economics*, Winter 1994, pp. 27–42.

Miles, Raymond C. "Price/Earnings Ratios and Company Size Data for Small Businesses." *Business Valuation Review*, September 1992, pp. 135–39.

Moyer, R. Charles, and Ajay Patel. "The Equity Market Risk Premium: A Critical Look at Alternative Ex Ante Estimates." *Proceedings of the Equity Risk Premium Conference*, University of Chicago, June 6, 1996.

Nevers, Thomas J. "Capitalization Rates." *Business Valuation News*, June 1985, pp. 3–6.

Pratt, Shannon P. *Cost of Capital: Theory and Applications*. New York: John Wiley & Sons, 1998.

_____. "Evidence Suggests Equity Risk Premium Lower than Conventional Wisdom Thinks." *Shannon Pratt's Business Valuation Update*, July 1996, pp. 1–5.

_____. "Alternative Equity Risk Premium Measures Unstable; Lack Robust Predictive Power." *Shannon Pratt's Business Valuation Update*, August 1996, pp. 1–2.

Raabe, William A., and Gerald E. Whittenburg. "Is the Capital Asset Pricing Model Appropriate in Tax Litigation?" *Valuation Strategies*, January/February 1998, pp. 10–15, 36–37.

Rigby, Jim, and Michael J. Mattson. "Capitalization and Discount Rates: Mathematically Related, but Conceptually Different." *CPA Expert*, Fall 1996, pp. 1–3.

Schilt, James H. "Selection of Capitalization Rates—Revisited." *Business Valuation Review*, June 1991, pp. 51–52.

Slay, Kelley D. "The Capitalization Rate, the Discount Rate, and Projected Growth in Value." *Appraisal Journal*, July 1990, pp. 324–27.

Swad, Randy. "Discount and Capitalization Rates in Business Valuations." *CPA Journal*, October 1994, pp. 40–46.

Wincott, D. Richard. "Terminal Capitalization Rates and Reasonableness." *The Appraisal Journal*, April 1991, pp. 253–260.

Chapter 14

The Discounted Economic Income Method

Value today always equals future cash flow discounted at the opportunity cost of capital.[1]

The discounted economic income method is presented as the first of all the small business and professional practice valuation methods. This is because, for an investor whose objective is return on investment, it is the most theoretically correct of all valuation methods. Arguably, this method is used more commonly in the valuation of larger businesses than in the valuation of smaller businesses. This is partly because it is generally easier to develop reliable economic income projections for larger businesses than for smaller businesses.[2] However, it is important that every analyst understand this fundamental valuation method. This is because value indications from any other valuation method should be realistically reconcilable with value indications from the discounted economic income method. Furthermore, as discussed later, the use of the discounted economic income method for valuing smaller businesses and professional practices is increasing.

The Essentials of the Discounted Economic Income Method

The essence of the discounted economic income method is twofold:

1. *Projecting prospective economic income.* The first step is to project the amount and timing of all the economic income that the business is expected to produce for its owner(s) in the future (the *numerator* in the arithmetic formula).
2. *Discounting prospective economic income to present value.* The second step is to discount each flow of economic income back to a present value at a rate that reflects the risk (degree of certainty or uncertainty) of receiving that economic benefit in the amount and at the time anticipated in the projection (the *denominator* in the arithmetic formula).

The Discounted Economic Income Formula

The basic formula for valuing an entity by the discounted economic income method is as follows:

---

[1] Richard A. Brealey and Stewart C. Myers, *Principles of Corporate Finance*, 4th ed. (New York: McGraw-Hill, 1991), p. 63.

[2] Because the discounted economic income method is used more in larger than in smaller businesses, the chapter on it in this book is relatively short, presenting the rudiments. For a more compete exposition of the discounted economic income method, see Chapter 9 in Pratt, Reilly, and Schweihs, *Valuing a Business: The Analysis and Appraisal of Closely Held Companies*, 3d ed. (Burr Ridge, IL: McGraw-Hill, 1996).

$$PV = \sum_{i=1}^{\infty} \frac{E_i}{(l+k)^i}$$

where:

PV = Present value

Σ = Sum of

E_i = Expected economic income in the ith period in the future

k = Present value discount rate

i = The period (usually stated as a number of years) in the future in which the economic income to be discounted is expected to be received

Note that, as presented above, this is a *very generalized* formula. To actually use this valuation method, the analyst should be specific about the following points:

1. Are we valuing *all invested capital* or just the *common equity* with these calculations?
2. What is the measure of economic income that we are projecting to be used in the numerator (e.g., net cash flow, net income, or some other economic income measure)?
3. The present value discount rate (k) represents the cost of what kind of capital (e.g., weighted average for cash flow to invested capital, cash flow available to equity, or something else)? *The answer to this question depends on the answers to questions 1 and 2. The present value discount rate must be appropriate for the definition of economic income being discounted.*

Valuing Equity versus Invested Capital

The *value of the business* is an ambiguous term until it is clearly defined as to exactly what elements of equity and debt are to be included in that value.

Equity means the ownership interest. In a corporation, equity is represented by stock. If there is more than one class of stock, the term *equity* by itself usually means the combined value of all classes of stock. If it is intended that the value represents only one class of stock in a multiclass capital structure, there should be a statement as to which class of equity the value purports to represent.

In a partnership, equity is represented by partners' capital. If it is a multiclass partnership (such as a limited partnership), there should be a statement as to which class or classes of partnership interests the value purports to represent.

In a sole proprietorship, equity is the owner's interest.

Invested capital is not always as clearly defined. Therefore, if the term is used, it should be supplemented by a definition of exactly what it means in the given valuation context.

Often, invested capital means all owners' equity and interest-bearing debt, whether short-term or long-term. Also, invested capital often means all equity and only long-term debt. However, there are so many variations that it is essential to pin down *exactly* what is and is not to be included on both the left and right sides of the valuation balance sheet.

Whichever valuation objective is selected, equity or invested capital, all of the economic income accruing to that class of capital must be included in the numerator.

Selecting the Measure of Economic Income

Within the scope of the income approach, most valuation professionals today prefer to use *net cash flow* as the measure of economic income to be discounted. This is true whether (1) valuing equity only or (2) valuing all invested capital.

Net Cash Flow to Equity. Net cash flow to equity (*NCFe* in the notation used in this book) is defined as follows:

    Net income (after taxes)
  + Noncash charges (e.g., depreciation, amortization, deferred income
    taxes)
  - Net capital expenditures (the net changes in fixed and other non-
    current assets)*
  - Changes in net working capital*
  + Net changes in long-term debt*
  = Net cash flow to equity

   *Assumes that these amounts are the levels necessary to support projected business operations.

If there are preferred dividends, they would have to be subtracted if the objective is to estimate net cash flow available to common equity holders.

Net Cash Flow to Invested Capital. Net cash flow to invested capital (*NCF$_f$* in the notation used in this book) is defined as follows:

    Net income (after taxes)
  + Noncash charges
  − Net capital expenditures (the net change in fixed and other non-
    current assets)*
  − Changes in working capital*
  + Interest expense, net of the income tax effect (i.e., interest expense
    × [1 - tax rate])
  + Preferred dividends, if any
  = Net cash flow to overall invested capital

   *Assumes that these amounts are those necessary to support projected business operations.

Other Measures of Economic Income. If net income approximates net cash flow, some analysts use net income as the economic income measure to discount. If this measure of economic income is used, the analyst's report should explain why it is expected that net income will approximate net cash flow. Normally, this would be the case only when the company's capital expenditure and net working capital requirements to support its future operations are minimal.

Alternatively, there is a formula for converting a discount rate applicable to net cash flow to a discount rate applicable to net income.[3] However, we do not recommend this procedure because the critical assumptions necessary to make this conversion formula applicable rarely are actually met in real-life situations. This is especially true in the case of small businesses and professional practices.

Finally, cursory analysis of public company data suggests a typical differential of three to six additional percentage points for a discount rate applicable to net income compared with a discount rate applicable to net cash flow.[4] However, if such an approximation is to be considered, the analyst should present evidence that this range is warranted for the particular subject company.

Other measures of economic income (e.g., operating gross cash flow, seller's discretionary cash flow, earnings before interest and taxes, and so on) are treated in this book under the market approach. This is because such economic income measures are usually capitalized based on pricing multiples extracted from the transactional market for comparative companies.

Why Net Cash Flow?   There are two reasons why net cash flow is the preferred measure of economic income in the application of the income approach: (1) It is conceptually preferable, and (2) It is easier to develop an empirically defensible discount rate for net cash flow.

1. *Conceptual preference.* Net cash flow is considered conceptually preferable because it represents what most investors are after: what they can get out of the business. As Greg Gilbert succinctly put it: "It represents cash that may be permanently removed from the business and used by the owner for other purposes."[5]
2. *Empirical basis.* Most of the capital market and other empirical data that are used to derive a present value discount rate, such as the Ibbotson Associates data, are data that relate to net cash flow as the measure of economic income.

---

[3] See Pratt, Reilly, and Schweihs, *Valuing a Business: The Analysis and Appraisal of Closely Held Companies*, 3d ed., pp. 192-94.

[4] Jay E. Fishman, Shannon P. Pratt, J. Clifford Griffith, and D. Keith Wilson, *Guide to Business Valuations*, 7th ed. (Fort Worth, TX: Practitioners Publishing Company, 1997), pp. 5-9.

[5] Gregory A. Gilbert, "Discounted Future Benefits Methods—An Income Approach," in *Handbook of Business Valuation*, Thomas L. West and Jeffrey D. Jones, eds. (New York: John Wiley & Sons, 1992), p. 202.

Projecting Prospective Economic Income

Projecting prospective economic income is really a matter of carrying out the adjusted income statement exercises discussed in Chapter 8 and Chapter 11. Of course, if the measure of economic income is to be net cash flow, the adjustments to reach that figure (as defined earlier in this chapter) must also be made.

It is noteworthy that the discounted economic income method is a forward-looking exercise. Buyers don't invest in a business based on what the seller got out of the business in the past unless they believe they will get similar results in the future. Pure extrapolations of past results usually are inadequate for the discounted economic income method. And usually they are wrong.

For example, ESOPs often use the discounted economic income method of valuation, and more small companies are adopting ESOPs (see Chapter 39). A small company's CPA firm valued the company's ESOP stock using the discounted economic income method based on "past performance extended into the future." The company failed, and the employees sued both the CPA firm that prepared the valuation report and the controlling stockholder. The CPA firm settled with the plaintiffs for an undisclosed amount before the case against the controlling stockholder was litigated. During the trial against the controlling stockholder, the court stated that the projections were "negligently prepared," and the controlling stockholder was held liable for all accrued benefits plus interest, attorney's fees, and costs.[6]

Period of the Projection

There is no *right* answer to the question of how far into the future one should try to prepare the projections. Theoretically, the further the better. As a practical matter, for most small operations, it is not possible to project earnings very far before the projections become so unreliable that they are useless.

If the cash flows are stabilized and if they are expected to remain constant (or to increase or decrease at a constant rate in perpetuity), all one has to do is to capitalize a single number. The premise underlying this analytical procedure is addressed in the following chapter, The Capitalized Economic Income Method.

The best guidance that can be offered is that the analyst should project as many years into the future as he has a realistic basis for predicting. At the end of that period, the analyst may estimate a *terminal value* to be discounted back to a present value (discussed later in this chapter).

---

[6] *Davis v. Torvick, Inc.*, No. C-93-1343 CW, 1996 WL 266127 (N.D.Cal., May 2, 1996).

Constant Real Dollars or Nominal Dollars?

One question that frequently arises is whether the projections should be performed on the basis of constant dollars (1999 dollars, for example, if the projection is being performed in 1999) or whether an estimate of the effects of inflation should be included in the projected cash flow or earnings figures. The answer is that the projection can be based on either measure of purchasing power. However, the selection of constant or inflation-adjusted dollars affects the selection of the appropriate present value discount rate, as discussed in a later section.

Who Prepares the Projections?

Another question that frequently arises is "Who should prepare the projections, the analyst or the company?" A related question is "If the company prepares the projections, what is the analyst's role in assessing the credibility of the projections?" In some cases, the analyst will develop projections with the assistance of management input. Sometimes, the company (or the buyer) will make the projections. When the analyst does not prepare the projections, there often is an opportunity to review the underlying projection variables with management. In this case, the analyst may make some adjustments based on an evaluation of the reliability of the projection variables. In any case, the source of the projections should be disclosed in any written or oral report that uses them. The analyst's evaluation of the credibility of the projections will be a factor in the judgment about the weight to be accorded to the discounted economic income method in concluding the final opinion of value of the subject entity.

Selecting the Present Value Discount Rate

The appropriate present value discount rate to use in the denominator is the rate of return that the market requires for comparable investments, as discussed in Chapter 13. If the economic income projection is the economic returns available to equity, the analyst should use the discount rate that applies to an equity investment. If the projection is for the economic returns available to a total investment that includes borrowed funds, the analyst should use a discount rate applicable to the overall investment (i.e., weighted average cost of capital).

Recall that Chapter 13 pointed out that one component of the discount rate is inflation. This component is intended to compensate the investor for the decreased buying power of future dollars, when she receives them. If the economic income projections are in dollars that include the effects of inflation ("nominal dollars"), a discount rate that includes the inflation component (as described in Chapter 13) should be used. If the earnings or cash flow projections are in constant dollars, the inflation component should be subtracted out of the total required rate of return to arrive at the appropriate discount rate.[7]

Please refer to Chapter 13 for more detail on developing the present value discount rate (or, as it is sometimes called in the real estate appraisal literature, the yield capitalization rate).

Cash Flows Plus a Terminal Value

Assuming that a steady state is not the appropriate expectation, the common procedure is to project specific cash flows for some discrete number of years followed by a *terminal value*. The terminal value could be an expected liquidation value, the expected proceeds from a sale of the business, or a value based on capitalization of cash flow starting when the business has reached a stabilized state.

The formula for discounting discrete projected cash flows plus a terminal value is as follows:

$$PV = \frac{NCF_1}{(1+k)} + \frac{NCF_2}{(1+k)^2} + \cdots + \frac{NCF_n}{(1+k)^n} + \frac{T}{(1+k)^n}$$

where:

PV	=	Present value
$NCF_{1,2,\cdots n}$	=	Net cash flows for the first through the nth periods
k	=	Cost of capital appropriate to the cash flows being discounted (e.g., the cost of equity capital if for equity, the weighted average if for invested capital, etc.)
T	=	Terminal value (value as of the end of the nth period in the discrete projection period)

We noted earlier that there are several ways to develop the terminal value. If the discrete projection period is short, or if the cash flows during the discrete projection period are quite low, most of the present value can be a result of the discounted terminal value. Our preference is to calculate the terminal value based on capitalization of sustainable cash flows, as presented in the following example. A further explanation of this procedure is presented in the following chapter, The Capitalized Economic Income Method.

If the analyst uses a market-derived pricing multiple of some other economic income variable to develop the terminal value, the analyst is really mixing a market approach with the income approach. We prefer to see one or more market approach methods performed separately, with the income approach confined to discounting or capitalizing, as discussed in this and the following chapter.

---

[7] A long-term inflation forecast is included in each month's Cost of Capital department in *Shannon Pratt's Business Valuation Update*.

An Example

The Ace Widget Company has developed an outstanding patented widget. Its market acceptance has increased steadily over the last few years. The market potential for continued growth in sales and earnings seems assured. However, Mr. Ace himself has decided to sell out and seek new challenges.

We carefully prepared a set of pro forma adjusted income statements for the next five years (prepared in accordance with Chapters 8 and 11), which indicate the following projected net cash flow:

Projection Period:	**Year 1**	**Year 2**	**Year 3**	**Year 4**	**Year 5**
Net Cash Flow:	$20,000	$30,000	$40,000	$50,000	$60,000

For years 6 and beyond, it appears that the market will have reached saturation and that net cash flow will level off at around $65,000 per year.

The potential buyer has great confidence in the future of the Ace widgets. She has decided that it would be worthwhile to buy the business from Ace at a price that would provide her a rate of return on her investment of 20 percent or more (i.e., our estimate of the company's weighted average cost of capital developed in accordance with Chapter 13).

Using the discounted economic income formula presented earlier, the present value of the cash flows for the first five years can be computed as follows:

$$PV = \frac{\$20,000}{(1 + .20)} + \frac{\$30,000}{(1 + .20)^2} + \frac{\$40,000}{(1 + .20)^3} + \frac{\$50,000}{(1 + .20)^4} + \frac{\$60,000}{(1 + .20)^5}$$

At the end of five years, we projected a business with net cash flows of $65,000 per year. If we capitalize $65,000 per year at 20 percent, the value of that projected cash flow stream starting at the end of the fifth year can be computed as follows:[8]

$$\frac{\$65,000}{.20} = \$325,000$$

However, that value is five years away, and it has to be discounted back to a present value. The present value of the cash flow stream starting five years from now can be computed as follows:

$$\frac{\$325,000}{(1 + .20)^5}$$

Putting the whole thing together, we can compute the value of Ace Widget Company as follows:

---

[8] Note that we *capitalize* the expected cash flow for year 6 and beyond because of the assumption that it is a constant expected amount in perpetuity.

$$\frac{\$20,000}{(1+.20)} + \frac{\$30,000}{(1+.20)^2} + \frac{\$40,000}{(1+.20)^3} + \frac{\$50,000}{(1+.20)^4} + \frac{\$60,000}{(1+.20)^5} + \frac{(\$65,000 \div .20)}{(1+.20)^5}$$

$$= \$16,667 + \$20,833 + \$23,148 + \$24,113 + \$24,113 + \$130,610$$

$$= \$239,484 \text{ (or } \$240,000, \text{ rounded)}$$

On the basis of this analysis, the buyer would decide to purchase Ace Widget if she can negotiate a deal with Mr. Ace at less than $240,000, cash or cash equivalent. (As we will see in Chapter 27, she can afford to pay Mr. Ace a price of $300,000 or more if he is willing to take a substantial portion of it in a long-term contract at a low interest rate. But that is another story.)

The calculations above can be performed using present value tables, or they can be performed easily on an inexpensive pocket calculator. For example, computing the present value of $325,000 five years from now, discounted at 20 percent compounded annually, will result in $130,610.

In the above example, we simplified the calculations by assuming there would be no more growth in net cash flows beyond the sixth year. A more common assumption is that there will be some level of growth continuing, perhaps just at the expected rate of inflation. If that is the expectation, the capitalization rate for the sixth year's projected cash flow would be the discount rate *minus* the expected long-term growth rate. In the above example, if the expected continued growth rate was 4 percent, the capitalization rate for the sixth year's projected cash flow would be .16(.20 − .04 = .16). In that case, the computation would be as follows:

$$\frac{\$20,000}{(1+.20)} + \frac{\$30,000}{(1+.20)^2} + \frac{\$40,000}{(1+.20)^3} + \frac{\$50,000}{(1+.20)^4} + \frac{\$60,000}{(1+.20)^5} + \frac{(\$65,000/(.20-.04))}{(1+.20)^5}$$

$$= \$16,667 + \$20,833 + \$23,148 + \$24,113 + \$24,113 + \$163.263$$

$$= \$272,137$$

In this case, the assumption of a continued 4 percent compound growth rate into perpetuity adds a little over $30,000 to the indicated value.

Values calculated using the discounted economic income method can fall within a wide range, depending on the cash flow or earnings projections used and the present value discount rate selected. Exhibit 14-1 shows how the indicated value can vary (1) using pessimistic, most likely, and optimistic earnings projections; and (2) varying the discount rate from 16 to 24 percent. By varying the cash flow projections up or down by 20 percent and varying the discount rates up or down by 4 percent, we get a range of values from a high of about $380,000 to a low of about $150,000. This represents a differential of well over 2 to 1 on the indicated value of the business.

No wonder different people can have wide disagreements about the value of any particular business!

Exhibit 14–1

PRESENT VALUE OF ACE WIDGET COMPANY
By the Discounted Economic Income Method

Optimistic Projection

Year	Projected Cash Flow		Present Value Discounted At				
		16	18%	20%	22%	24%
1	$ 24,000	$ 20,690	$ 20,339	$ 20,000	$ 19,672	$ 19,355
2	36,000	26,754	25,855	25,000	24,187	23,413
3	48,000	30,752	29,214	27,778	26,434	25,175
4	60,000	33,137	30,947	28,935	27,084	25,378
5	72,000	34,280	31,472	28,935	26,640	24,560
6 on	78,000	232,105	189,414	156,732	131,182	110,860
Total Value		$ 377,718	$ 327,241	$ 287,380	$ 255,199	$ 228,741

Most Likely Projection

Year	Projected Cash Flow		Present Value Discounted At				
		16%	18%	20%	22%	24%
1	$ 20,000	$ 17,241	$ 16,949	$ 16,667	$ 16,393	$ 16,129
2	30,000	22,295	21,546	20,833	20,156	19,511
3	40,000	25,626	24,345	23,148	22,028	20,979
4	50,000	27,615	25,789	24,113	22,570	21,149
5	60,000	28,567	26,227	24,113	22,200	20,466
6 on	65,000	193,421	157,845	130,610	109,318	92,383
Total Value		$ 314,765	$ 272,701	$ 239,484	$ 212,665	$ 190,617

Pessimistic Projection

Year	Projected Cash Flow		Present Value Discounted At				
		16%	18%	20%	22%	24%
1	$ 16,000	$ 13,793	$ 13,559	$ 13,333	$ 13,115	$ 12,903
2	24,000	17,836	17,236	16,667	16,125	15,609
3	32,000	20,501	19,476	18,519	17,623	16,784
4	40,000	22,092	20,632	19,290	18,056	16,919
5	48,000	22,853	20,981	19,290	17,760	16,373
6 on	52,000	154,737	126,276	104,488	87,454	73,907
Total Value		$ 251,812	$ 218,160	$ 191,587	$ 170,133	$ 152,495

The "Midyear Discounting Convention"[9]

In the formulas presented up to this point, we have implied (by using whole integer exponents) that the cash flows (or other economic income) are expected to be received at the *end* of each period. This is reasonable since many closely held companies wait until the end of their fiscal year to assess capital requirements and decide on shareholder distributions.

On the other hand, sometimes it seems more reasonable to project that cash flows are received (or at least available) more or less evenly throughout the year. This projection can be reflected in the discounted economic income model by using the "midyear discounting convention." This convention projects cash flows being received at the middle rather than the end of each year, thus more or less approximating the valuation effect of even cash flows throughout the year.

The formula using the perpetual growth model and the mid-year discounting convention is as follows:

$$PV = \frac{E_1}{(1 + k)^{.5}} + \frac{E_2}{(1 + k)^{1.5}} + \ldots + \frac{E_n}{(1 + k)^{n-5}} + \frac{\dfrac{E_n(1 + g)(1 + k)^{.5}}{k - g}}{(1 + k)^n}$$

where:

PV = Present value

$E_1 \ldots E_n$ = Expected amounts of the economic income (often net cash flow) in each of periods E_1 through E_n

k = Present value discount rate

n = Number of periods in the discrete projection period

g = Annually compounded growth rate projected in perpetuity for the prospective economic income, beyond the discrete projection period

Note that use of the perpetual growth model in the final term of the above formula reflects the midyear convention with respect to the terminal value. This term of the formula is explained in the following chapter, The Capitalized Economic Income Method.

Of course, the midyear discounting convention increases the indicated present value since it projects that the cash flows will be received earlier on average than the more common year-end discounting model assumes.

The model can be varied to accommodate any projections about the timing of cash flows, such as monthly, quarterly, or irregularly. The calculations for any such variations can be done on any modern, inexpensive pocket financial calculator.

---

[9] This section is taken from Pratt, Reilly, and Schweihs, *Valuing a Business: The Analysis and Appraisal of Closely Held Companies*, 3d ed., p. 186.

Does the Discounted Economic Income Model Produce a Control Value or a Minority Value?[10]

The discounted economic income model can produce either a control value or a minority value, depending primarily on the model inputs regarding the valuation variables. Generally, if the inputs in the valuation model reflect changes that only a control owner would (or could) make (e.g., changed capital structure, reduced owner's compensation, and so on), the model would be expected to produce a control value.

If the economic income projections merely reflect the continuation of present policies, the model would be expected to produce a minority value. If every facet of the company is being so well optimized that a control owner could not improve on it, there may be little or no difference between a control value and a minority value.

The argument is often made that because discount rates typically are developed from minority trades in publicly traded stocks, the discount rate is a minority interest discount rate and the value indicated by a discounted economic income model must, therefore, be a minority value. There are at least three problems with this argument. First, *most, if not all, of the difference between a control value and a minority value in a discounted economic income model results from differences in the projected economic income (the numerator), not from differences in the discount rate.* Second, the cost of equity capital used in deriving the WACC is based on the opportunity cost of equity capital, as illustrated every day in stock market transactions. The opportunity cost of equity capital is similar for both the investor in a control position and for the minority interest investor. Third, while the costs of equity capital are estimated from trades of minority ownership interests, the capital structure (i.e., the percent of debt versus percent of equity) of the subject company is clearly influenced by the controlling stockholder. And the capital structure mix is at least as important as the cost of equity capital in the estimation of a company's overall WACC—that is, the discount rate associated with net cash flow. In other words, the cost of equity capital may be the same, or nearly the same, whether a control or a minority interest is being transacted. However, the controlling owner (and, generally, not the minority owner) influences the projection of economic income (the numerator in the model) and the capital structure component of the WACC (the denominator in the model).

What Standard of Value Does a Discounted Economic Income Model Produce?

As with the control/minority ownership issue, the answer to this question depends to some extent on the individual valuation variable inputs that go into the model.

---

[10] This section is taken from Pratt, Reilly, and Schweihs, *Valuing a Business: The Analysis and Appraisal of Closely Held Companies*, 3d edition, pp. 194-95.

If valuing a company on a stand-alone basis, use of that company's own economic income projections and a market-derived cost of capital as the discount rate would be expected to estimate *fair market value*. If, on the other hand, a particular acquirer with a lower cost of capital would discount an economic income projection at that acquirer's lower cost of capital, the result would be *investment value*, the value of the subject— but only to that individual acquirer. Similarly, if a particular acquirer were to include synergistic benefits or other enhancements in the economic income projections, the result would be *investment value* rather than *fair market value*.

Growing Acceptance of the Discounted Economic Income Method[11]

Since the previous (1993) edition of this book, there has been a growing acceptance and use of the discounted economic income method for valuing small businesses and professional practices. This is partly because of its increasing emphasis in MBA and other business school programs and partly due to increasing sophistication on the part of business appraisers. For example, there have been more participants in the business valuation education courses offered by the professional organizations discussed in Chapter 1 in the last five years than in all the time cumulatively leading up to the most recent five years.

Many appraisers have presented and explained the method to the point of being acceptable to various courts in recent years. In the second edition of this book, we reported a somewhat unusual example of the Delaware Chancery Court accepting the discounted economic method in valuing a radiology practice.[12] Since then, the method has been accepted much more frequently in a wide variety of courts.

Marital Dissolution

An Ohio 11th District Appellate case affirmed a trial court's decision that accepted the discounted economic income method over the capitalized excess earnings method for a small S corporation whose primary business was operating and renting out a railroad passenger car for excursions.[13] An Ohio 9th District Appellate case also affirmed a trial court decision based on one expert's discounted economic income method as opposed to the other expert's capitalized excess earnings method.[14] In that case, the trial judge stated that the discounted economic income method had never been used before within her family law jurisdiction. She was willing to consider it based on testimony that

---

[11] Many of the court cases cited as recent examples in this section are discussed in greater detail in the monthly issues of *Shannon Pratt's Business Valuation Update*.

[12] *In re Radiology Associates, Inc.*, No. 9001, 1991 Del. Ch. Lexis 175 (November 1, 1991).

[13] *Giuffre v. Baker*, No. 95-G-1904, 1996 WL 535254 (Ohio App. 11th Dist., Aug. 30, 1996).

[14] *Sergi v. Sergi*, No. 17476, 1996 WL 425914 (Ohio App. 9th Dist., July 31, 1996).

members of the professional financial community would be likely to use the method in valuing a company of that type. It goes to show that, "We haven't used that method here before" is not adequate cause for rejection. This is true as long as it is a method generally accepted in the financial community, which the discounted economic income method certainly is.

In yet another Ohio case, the trial court accepted the conclusion of a special master who used the discounted economic income method to reach his final estimation of value. The wife appealed, and the trial court's acceptance of the discounted economic income value was upheld.[15]

Some analysts are reluctant to use the discounted economic income method in marital dissolution matters because they are afraid that it impounds the results of future efforts of the operating spouse (which are not marital property) into the present value of the business. If this is a potential issue, the analyst should be careful when using the discounted economic income method to reflect only the cash flows that would reasonably be expected from running the business with an employed, nonowner manager. This procedure would not reflect the potential contribution of extra efforts or special talents of the owner/manager.

Damage Cases

One area of disputes where courts have historically accepted discounted economic income analysis is in damage cases. As a recent example, in a 1997 case, a jury awarded $1,525,000 in damages for termination of a small forklift truck distributorship based on a discounted economic income analysis. In approving the jury's award, the judge described the amount as "far-fetched," and suggested that it might have been less than a fifth as much if the defendant's expert had presented reasonable rebuttal to the plaintiff's expert.[16] This seems to be an example where the defendant would have been well served to use an expert with strong abilities in applying the discounted economic income method to small businesses.

Legal Malpractice

In another 1997 case, the court awarded $15 million in damages against a law firm whose client was forced to discontinue franchising fitness salons because it was in violation of the Connecticut Business Opportunities Act. While the defendant's expert claimed that the company was insolvent and worthless, the plaintiff's expert developed a

---

[15] *Oatey* v. *Oatey*, Nos. 67809, 67973, 1996 WL 200273 (Ohio App. 8th Dist., April 25, 1996).

[16] *TO-AM Equipment Company, Inc.* v. *Mitsubishi Caterpillar Forklift America, Inc., et al.*, No. 95 C 0836, 1997 WL 29520 (N.D. Ill., Jan. 24, 1997).

12-year projection showing lost profits of $22,209,834. The court arrived at a value of $15,931,280 in damages.[17]

Gift and Estate Taxes

In a 1996 case, the U.S. Tax Court accepted a mathematical weighting of a value based on the discounted economic income method and a value based on the market approach. Both methods were used by the expert for the Internal Revenue Service in this case.[18] Although the Service does have some tendency to favor the market approach, experts retained by the Service often do rely on the discounted economic income method.[19]

Dissenting Stockholder Actions

The Delaware courts have accepted the discounted economic income method in dissenting stockholder actions since the landmark *Weinberger* case in 1983.[20] In a recent case, a company's board valued a company at $563,000 ($.98 per share) based on their historical dollar investment. The court concluded a value of $5.11 per share based on plaintiffs' expert's discounted economic income method, using cash flow as the measure of economic income. In reaching its conclusion, the court noted, "The discounted cash flow valuation model is well-accepted and established in the financial community."[21]

Summary

There are two principal variables in the discounted economic income method:

1. The projected future economic income (i.e., the numerator).
2. The present value discount rate (i.e., the denominator).

The projected economic income can be either (1) that available to equity or (2) that available to overall invested capital (usually defined to include equity plus interest-bearing debt, although other definitions sometimes are used).

The economic income that is projected is usually net cash flow, although other definitions of economic income are sometimes used.

---

[17] *Beverly Hills Concepts, Inc.* v. *Schatz & Schatz, Ribicoff & Kotkin, et al.*, No. CV-890369864S, 1997 WL 41224 (Conn. Super. Ct., Jan. 27, 1997).

[18] *Estate of Ross H. Freeman* v. *Commissioner*, T.C. Memo 1996-372 (August 13, 1996).

[19] *Kosman* v. *Commissioner*, T.C. Memo 1996-112 (March 11, 1996).

[20] *Weinberger* v. *UOP, Inc.*, 457 A.2d 701 (Del. Sup. Ct. 1983).

[21] *Ryan* v. *Tad's Enterprises, Inc.*, Nos. 10229, 11977, 1996 WL 204502 (Del. Ch., April 24, 1996).

The economic income may be projected either in the actual expected dollars in the year received (including inflation) or in "constant" or "real" dollars (today's dollars, *not* including inflation).

The present value discount rate includes a riskless rate of return (usually based on yields on U.S. Government Treasury bonds or bills yield to maturity as of the valuation date) plus a premium for the risk incurred in the investment. Sometimes a premium is added to the rate to reflect illiquidity (or lack of marketability). However, in other cases, the matter of illiquidity (if significant) is handled as a separate discount at the end of the valuation process.

If the projected economic income is that income available to equity holders, the present value discount rate applicable to equity should be used. If the projected economic income includes what is available to cover interest on debt, a weighted average cost of capital is an appropriate present value discount rate.

The "riskless rate" (government bond yield) includes investors' expectations of inflation over the life of the bond. If the economic income projections are in constant dollars ("real" dollars—today's dollars without inflation), the expected inflation must be subtracted from the present value discount rate.

In any written or oral presentation, the definition of the projected economic income should be clearly spelled out. The derivation of the present value discount rate should also be explained so that it can be understood.

The critical element of this valuation method is that the present value discount rate used be an appropriate rate that is matched to the definition of the projected economic income. One of the most common errors in the application of the discounted economic income method is using a present value discount rate that is not appropriate for the particular level of economic income used in the projection.

Bibliography

Annin, Michael. "The Right Tools Can Simplify Company Valuation." *Accounting Today*, November 6, 1995, pp. 14, 35.

Bielinski, Daniel W. "The Debt-Free DCF Model: A Fix on Intrinsic Values." *Mergers & Acquisitions*, September/October 1989, pp. 43–47.

_____. "How to Capture Equity Value in Pricing a Target." *Mergers & Acquisitions* , November/December 1991, pp. 26–31.

Black, Fischer. "A Simple Discounting Rule." *Financial Management,* Summer 1988, pp. 7–11.

Cassiere, George C. "Geometric Mean Return Premium versus the Arithmetic Mean Return Premium—Expanding on the SBBI 1995 Yearbook Examples." *Business Valuation Review*, March 1996, pp. 20–23.

Colborn, Asli F. "Estimating a Firm's Continuing Value." *Business Valuation Review* , December 1991, pp. 157–62.

Cornell, Bradford. "The Discounted Cash Flow Approach" (Chapter 5), "Estimating the Continuing Value at the Terminal Date" (Chapter 6), and "The Cost of Capital" (Chapter 7). In *Corporate Valuation: Tools for Effective Appraisal and Decision Making*. Burr Ridge, IL: McGraw-Hill, 1993.

Damodaran, Aswath. *Damodaran on Valuation: Security Analysis for Investment and Corporate Finance*. New York: John Wiley & Sons, 1993.

"Discounted Future Earnings" and "Discounted Future Cash Flow" in *IRS Valuation Guide for Income, Estate and Gift Taxes: Valuation Training for Appeals Officers* . Chicago: Commerce Clearing House, 1994, pp. 7-16–7-18.

Evans, Frank C. "Recognizing the Key Factors in the Income Approach to Business Valuation." *Business Valuation Review*, June 1996, pp. 80–87.

Fowler, Bradley A. "Venture Capital Rates of Return Revisited." *Business Valuation Review*, March 1996, pp. 13–16.

Gilbert, Gregory A. "Discounted Future Benefits Methods—An Income Approach" (Chapter 18). In *Handbook of Business Valuation*. New York: John Wiley & Sons, 1992, pp. 201–209.

Hartl, Robert J. "DCF Analysis: The Special Case of Risky Cash Outflows." *Real Estate Appraiser & Analyst* , Summer 1990, pp. 67–72.

Hempstead, John E. "Delaware Court Embraces Cash Flow Valuation Method with Both Arms." *Business Valuation Review*, December 1991, pp. 182–83.

Kaltman, Todd A. "Capitalization Using a Mid-Year Convention." *Business Valuation Review*, December 1995, pp. 178–182.

Kane, Walter M. "Discounted Cash Flow Analysis and Newton's Apple." *Appraisal Journal,* July 1991, pp. 328–37.

Pratt, Shannon P., and Ralph Arnold. "Misuse of the Discounted Future Returns Valuation Method." *FAIR$HARE*, March 1990, pp. 3–5.

Wincott, D. Richard. "Terminal Capitalization Rates and Reasonableness." *Appraisal Journal*, April 1991, pp. 253–60.

Chapter 15

The Capitalized Economic Income Method

Capitalization—A method used to convert an estimate of a single year's income expectancy into an indication of value in one direct step, either by dividing the income estimate by an appropriate rate or by multiplying the income estimate by an appropriate factor.[1]

In real estate terminology, the above definition is called *direct capitalization*, the basic subject matter of this chapter. It is distinguished from what real estate appraisers call *yield capitalization*, which is comparable to the business appraiser's *discounted economic income*, the subject of the previous chapter.

The capitalized economic income method means the application of one divisor (or multiple) to one economic income measure. The result is an indication of value derived from that single division or multiplication.

For example, let's assume that the next year's net cash flow is expected to be $200,000 and the appropriate direct capitalization rate is 25 percent. In this case, the indicated value of the business is $800,000:

$$\frac{\$200,000}{.25} = \$800,000$$

Note from the opening quote above that the method is based on *expectancies*. Like the discounted economic income method, it is a method to convert *anticipated* income to a present value.

The capitalized economic income method actually is used more in the valuation of small businesses and professional practices than the discounted economic income method is. So why did we put the discounted economic income method first? Because, *the capitalized economic income method is simply an abridged version of the discounted economic income method.* We presented the discounted economic income method first because the valuation theory that is applied in the discounted economic income method is more comprehensive. And once the analyst has a grasp of the discounted economic income method, the valuation theory that is applied in the capitalized income method can be grasped more easily.

Exhibit 15-1 shows that, with the same set of assumptions, the discounted economic income method and the capitalized economic income method will produce an identical valuation indication. Therefore, an analyst using the capitalized economic income method should understand its parent method (the discounted economic income method) and think through, as a form of mental verification of reasonableness, "If I carried out the full discounting procedure, would I get approximately the same answer?" If not, the valuation variables used in the capitalization method should be reexamined.

---

[1] *The Dictionary of Real Estate Appraisal*, 3d ed. (Chicago: Appraisal Institute, 1993), p. 100.

Exhibit 15–1

EQUIVALENCE OF DISCOUNTED ECONOMIC INCOME METHOD AND CAPITALIZED ECONOMIC INCOME METHOD UNDER CONSTANT GROWTH RATE SCENARIO

Projection scenario: $80,000 net cash flow in Year 1, 5 percent perpetual annual growth rate from Year 1 forward, and a 25 percent present value discount rate.

Discounted Economic Income Method

Projection period:	Year 1	Year 2	Year 3	Terminal Value

$$\text{Indicated value of business entity} = \frac{\$80,000}{(1+.25)} + \frac{\$84,000}{(1+.25)^2} + \frac{\$88,200}{(1+.25)^3} + \frac{\frac{\$88,200(1.05)}{.25-.05}}{(1+.25)^3}$$

$$= \frac{\$80,000}{1.25} + \frac{\$84,000}{(1.25)^2} + \frac{\$88,200}{(1.25)^3} + \frac{\frac{\$92,610}{.20}}{(1.25)^3}$$

$$= \$64,000 + \$53,760 + \$45,158 + \frac{\$463,050}{(1.25)^3}$$

$$= \$64,000 + \$53,760 + \$45,158 + \$237,082$$

Indicated value of business entity = $400,000

Capitalized Economic Income Method

Projection period:	Year 1
Economic income to equity	$ 80,000
Present value discount rate minus expected long-term growth rate	.25 – .05
Indicated value of business entity	$400,000

The Essentials of the Capitalized Economic Income Method

Like the discounted economic income method, the essence of the capitalized income method is twofold:

1. *Projecting an anticipated economic income stream.* As opposed to projecting the amount and timing of each individual economic income flow the business is expected to produce for its owner, the direct capitalization method requires projecting a single, normalized amount of economic income (the *numerator* in the arithmetic formula).

2. *Capitalizing the expected economic income amount to produce a present value.* This second step involves dividing the expected economic income by a rate that reflects the risk (degree of certainty or uncertainty) of receiving that expected amount on a regular basis. In other words, the starting point is the *present value discount rate*, as discussed in the previous chapter. However, the numerator reflects only a *single period* of economic income, not any future changes. Therefore, if changes are expected, the present value discount rate should be modified by adding or subtracting the anticipated rate of growth (or decline) in the economic income flow to convert the present value discount rate into a direct capitalization rate (the *denominator* in the arithmetic formula).

The Capitalized Economic Income Formula

The basic formula for valuing a business by the capitalization of economic income method is as follows:

$$PV = \frac{E}{c}$$

where:

PV = Present value

E = Expected economic income, usually a normalized expectation for the period immediately following the valuation date, in which case we would label it E_1

c = Direct capitalization rate (derived as $k-g$, or the present value discount rate minus the annually compounded expected long-term rate of growth in E, as explained in Chapter 13)

It is noteworthy that, as presented above, this is a *very generalized* formula. To actually use this valuation method, the analyst should be specific about the same points as in the discounted economic income method:

1. Is the analyst valuing *all invested capital* or just the *common equity* with these calculations?

2. What measure of economic income is being projected to be used as the numerator (e.g., net cash flow, net income, or some other economic income measure)?

3. The direct capitalization rate (c) represents the cost of what kind of capital (e.g., weighted average for net cash flow to invested capital, net cash flow available to equity, or something else)? In other words, the direct capitalization rate is a single figure representing the cost of a certain type of capital (the present value discount rate), modified by the projected annual percentage growth (or decline) in the economic income flow available to the capital structure being valued. *The direct capitalization rate must be appropriate for the definition of economic income being capitalized.*

Essential Difference between the Discounting Model and the Capitalization Model

The obvious implication of all this, when one stops to think about it simplistically, is that *the difference between the discounting model and the capitalization model is how one treats anticipated changes in future income over time*:

1. In discounting, *changes over time in the expected economic income are treated specifically in the terms of the numerator of the present value equation.*
2. In capitalizing, *changes over time in the expected economic income are treated as a single average percentage change, and that annualized percentage is subtracted (assuming it is positive) from the cost of capital in the denominator.*

As noted in Chapter 13, the important conceptual underpinning of the capitalized economic income valuation model is that there is a constant annualized rate of growth (or decline) in the economic income variable being capitalized in perpetuity. Obviously, this constant growth rate projection is rarely met in the real world.

Unlike the discounted economic income model, the capitalization model does not take into consideration the timing of future changes in expected economic income. The greater the differences in the anticipated changes over time, especially in the early years, the more the analyst is encouraged to apply the discounted economic income method rather than the capitalized income method.

This leads to some generalizations about the relative attractiveness of the two basic income approach valuation methods:

1. *Stable or evenly growing economic income flow.* If the economic income flow is either stable or growing (or declining) at a fairly even rate, the capitalized economic income method should conclude as accurate a value indication as the discounted economic income method.
2. *Predictable but uneven changes.* If there are reasons to believe that changes will be significant but predictable, even though uneven, the discounted economic income model should produce a more accurate valuation.
3. *Short- or intermediate-term supergrowth.* If growth is expected to be quite high in the immediate future, the discounted economic income model should produce a more accurate valuation. One of the

most common mistakes in the application of this method is to use a 10 percent growth for the first few years (even though it may not be sustainable over the long term) and then subtract that 10 percent from the present value discount rate. This mistake will result in a low capitalization rate and in an overvaluation of the subject company.

4. *Changes that are erratic and unpredictable as to timing.* If the company's economic income is unstable and also more or less random as to timing, the company's risk increases, and thus the present value discount rate increases. However, the discounted economic income method may not be able to produce any more accurate a value indication than the direct capitalization method.

Valuing Equity versus Invested Capital

The same fundamental principles apply with regard to the valuation of equity versus invested capital as those that apply in the discounting method.

Whichever measure of capital is selected as the appraisal subject owners' equity or invested capital—all of the economic income accruing to that class of capital should be included in the numerator.

It is noteworthy, however, that the direct capitalization model is much more sensitive to the projected rate of growth when it is applied to all invested capital than when it is applied only to owners' equity. This is because the present value discount rate is a weighted average cost of capital for invested capital (blended debt rate and equity rate). And that rate is lower than the cost of equity capital alone. If the same percentage growth rate is projected on economic income available to invested capital as to owners' equity, the growth rate will have a greater impact on the resulting value of the invested capital.

Selecting the Appropriate Measure of Economic Income

As with the discounted economic income method, most valuation professionals today prefer to use *net cash flow* whether valuing equity or invested capital, for the same reasons as discussed in the previous chapter.

If you are considering using *net income*, the entire discussion in the previous chapter applies and should be read and applied in conjunction with this chapter.

We believe that capitalization of other income variables (such as gross revenue; owner's discretionary earnings; gross cash flow; earnings before interest, taxes, depreciation and amortization; and so on) are better handled within the scope of the market approach. That is because capitalization rates for those economic income variables are better developed by direct observations of transactions in the market than by modifications to a built-up or CAPM present value discount rate.

Projecting the Basic Economic Income Level and the Growth Rate

The projections needed for the capitalized economic income method are twofold:

1. The normalized expected base economic income.
2. The expected long-term growth rate.

These projections may be prepared by the company or by the valuation analyst, ideally with some involvement by both. The arithmetic of this valuation method could not be more simple. However, this fact implies the extreme importance of the realism of the expectations impounded in the base expected income estimate and the long-term growth estimate.

Start with Normalized Expected Economic Income

In order for the capitalized economic income method to produce a realistic value indication, the numerator should be a realistic normalized base of expected economic income. The expected economic income should be either stable or expected to change at a somewhat constant average rate over a long period of time.

As with the discounted economic income method, this method requires carrying out the adjusted income statement procedures discussed in Chapters 8 and 11. Of course, if the operational economic income variable is net cash flow, the adjustments to reach that measure (as defined in the previous chapter) should also be made.

Again, it is noteworthy that the capitalized economic income method is a forward-looking analysis, just as the discounted economic income method is. The number capitalized should represent *expected* future economic income. A simple average—or a weighted average—of past operating results is not an adequate procedure in and of itself to develop this number. The historical average should be used only if the analyst is able to justify the notion that this past average is indeed a reasonable proxy for future economic income expectations.

The Projected Long-Term Growth Rate

Treating the Impact of Inflation. If the build-up procedure or the capital asset pricing model (CAPM) procedure is used to develop the present value discount rate from which the growth rate is to be subtracted in order to derive a direct capitalization rate, that discount rate should incorporate the expected rate of inflation as part of the required rate of return. The implication is that the selected long-term growth rate should also reflect the impact of expected inflation on the economic income variable being capitalized.

For example, if the projection of the financial performance for the company assumes no real growth, but it is expected that the economic income will grow enough to keep up with the general level of expected inflation, the consensus long-term inflation rate should be subtracted from the present value discount rate in order to arrive at the appropriate direct capitalization rate.

Sustainability. It is noteworthy that the economic income capitalization method has impounded in it the implied projection that the growth rate used to arrive at the direct capitalization rate is a long-term sustainable growth rate. In fact, technically, it is a growth rate expected *in perpetuity*.

As a practical matter, discount rates and capitalization rates for investments in small businesses and professional practices are relatively high compared to most other investments. Therefore, changes in the growth rate after 15 or 20 years would have almost no impact on the present value. However, misspecification of the projected growth rate during the first 10 years or so can have a major impact on the indicated value.

As suggested earlier, if significant changes in the growth rate are expected within the first 10 years, the discounted economic income method probably is preferable to the capitalization of economic income method. The capitalization of economic income method can be incorporated to estimate the terminal value in the discounted economic income calculations, as explained further in a subsequent section.

If some changes in the growth rate are expected but are either too minimal or too unpredictable as to timing to justify using the discounted economic income method, some subjective adjustment to the projected growth rate using the capitalized economic income method might be an acceptable compromise. To the extent that the higher growth is expected in the early years, the long-term average growth rate used might be raised slightly, and vice versa.

The Gordon Growth Model

As noted earlier, the direct capitalization model assumes that the base level of normalized economic income to be capitalized is the expected income in the period *immediately following* the effective valuation date (i.e., E_1 in our notation system).

If the normalized economic income for the period *immediately preceding* the effective valuation date is considered a reasonable base level from which to project sustainable growth, the *Gordon Growth Model* version of the capitalized economic income method is appropriate. Using net cash flow as the economic income measure, the formula for the Gordon Growth Model is as follows:

$$PV = \frac{NCF_0 \, (1 + g)}{k - g}$$

where:

PV = Present value

NCF_0 = Net cash flow for period 0, the period immediately preceding the effective valuation date (It is assumed that this has been normalized by whatever adjustments are appropriate, such as eliminating nonrecurring items and so on.)

g = Projected long-term growth rate (annually compounded, sustainable in perpetuity)

k = Present value discount rate (cost of capital applicable to definition of the economic income variable being capitalized)

The Gordon Growth Model version of the capitalized economic income method is often used to derive the terminal value in the discounted economic income method, as discussed in a subsequent section.

Modification of the Capitalized Economic Income Method to Reflect the Midyear Discounting Convention

The basic capitalized economic income method as presented so far reflects the implicit assumption that the income becomes available to the owners of the subject business at the end of each period (usually assumed to be a year). This is a reasonable assumption for some small businesses and professional practices. This is because, at the end of the year, the owners assess the operating results and capital requirements, and distribute income in some form—such as dividends, partner withdrawals, or bonuses to owners.

If a more realistic scenario is that business income will be available to the business owners more or less evenly throughout the year, a simple modification to the capitalized economic income formula can reflect this assumption:

$$PV = \frac{E_1 (1 + k)^{.5}}{k - g}$$

where:

PV = Present value

E_1 = Expected economic income in the full period immediately following the effective valuation date

k = Present value discount rate (i.e., the cost of capital)

g = Expected long-term growth rate in E

Similarly, if the Gordon Growth Model version of the capitalized economic income method is used, the modified formula is as follows:

$$PV = \frac{E_0\,(1 + g)(1 + k)^{.5}}{k - g}$$

where:

    PV =   Present value

    E_0 =   Expected economic income in the full period immediately preceding the effective valuation date

    k =   Present value discount rate (i.e., the cost of capital)

    g =   Expected long-term growth rate in E

This modified formula for the economic income capitalization method accomplishes the same result as the midyear discounting convention described in the previous chapter on the discounted economic income method.[2] Since this convention reflects earlier availability of economic income to the business owners, it slightly raises the indicated value of the business from what it would be using the end-of-the-year convention.

Using the Capitalized Economic Income Method to Develop a Terminal Value for the Discounted Economic Income Method

Why the Capitalized Economic Income Method Is Preferable

As noted in the previous chapter, the discounted economic income method often involves projecting cash flows for some discrete time period, followed by a *terminal value* as of the end of the discrete projection period. It is not uncommon for the present value of the terminal value to be 50 percent or more of the total value indicated by the discounted economic income method.

It is noteworthy that there are a variety of ways to develop a terminal value. The most common methods are (1) the capitalized economic income method or (2) a multiple of some economic income variable, such as EBIT or EBITDA. Between these two methods, we recommend the capitalized economic income method.

One reason for this recommendation is that multiples of EBIT, EBITDA, and other economic income variables used in estimating a terminal value should be market derived. That is, they should be dependent on observing those multiples in actual market transactions rather than developing the multiples by modifying a discount rate or capitalization rate to be applicable to that economic income variable. Such pricing multiples are best developed through the use of the market approach, for which several chapters have been added in this edition.

---

[2] Proof of the accuracy of this method was presented in Todd A. Kaltman, "Capitalization Using a Mid-Year Convention," *Business Valuation Review*, December 1995, pp. 178–82.

If the terminal value is estimated for the discounted economic income method using a market-derived pricing multiple of some economic income variable other than that used for the interim economic income flows, the analysis is not a pure income approach. Rather, the analysis is a mixture of a market approach and income approach. The greater the impact of the terminal value on the total present value, the more important this distinction becomes.

We have seen valuations where the present value of the interim cash flows was zero or even negative, and the terminal value was based on a market-derived multiple of EBIT or EBITDA. Such an analysis should in no way be classified as an income approach (as we've described it). Rather, such an analysis is driven entirely by what we have classified as a market approach.

A major problem with using a market-derived pricing multiple method to estimate the terminal value is estimating what that multiple will be 3 to 10 years from now. Unlike the current pricing multiples used in the market approach, that future multiple can't be directly observed in the marketplace. Rather, it must be estimated. The procedure most commonly used is to naively assume that the future multiple will be the same as the current multiple. However, current pricing multiples impound investors' expectations about future changes, especially expectations regarding growth. Industries often sell at high multiples reflecting high short-term growth expectations. If the expected future growth will be less following the terminal value date, using the current pricing multiple will reflect too high a growth expectation following the terminal value date. This will have the effect of overstating the terminal value. We suspect that using a market-derived pricing multiple for estimating the terminal value, on balance, has a tendency to upwardly bias the valuation indication.

One of the primary objectives of using market price methods is to weight and check the results of each multiple against each other for reasonableness. When using a multiple of only a single variable, any possible benefit of comparing the indicated results from using multiples of several variables is lost. For the reasons discussed, we believe that this differentiation of methods is best accomplished by using the economic income capitalization method rather than a market multiple method to estimate the terminal value within the discounted economic income method.

Implementation of the Capitalized Economic Income Method to Estimate the Terminal Value

The *terminal value* is the expected value of the entity *as of the end of the discrete projection period*.

Constant Income Scenario. If the economic income is expected to be constant following the discrete projection period, the formula for the terminal value is as follows:

$$PV = \frac{E_{(n+1)}}{c}$$

where:

PV = Present value

$E_{(n+1)}$ = Expected economic income in the period immediately following the end of the discrete projections

c = Direct capitalization rate (which is equal to k, the present value discount rate, when the expected economic income is a constant amount in perpetuity)

Constant Growth Scenario. A more common projection is that the economic income is expected to increase at some long-term sustainable rate following the discrete projection period. In this case, the Gordon Growth Model typically is used:

$$PV = \frac{E_n(1 + g)}{k - g}$$

where:

PV = Present value

E_n = Expected economic income in the last (nth) increment of the discrete projection period

g = Long-term sustainable growth rate in E

k = Present value discount rate (i.e., the cost of capital)

Midyear Discounting Scenario. If the economic income for the discrete projection period was discounted using the midyear discounting convention, consistency would suggest using the direct capitalization formula modified to reflect the midyear convention. This procedure was presented in the immediately prior section.

$$PV = \frac{E_n(1 + g)(1 + k)^{.5}}{k - g}$$

where:

PV = Present value

E_n = Expected economic income in the final (nth) increment of the discrete projection period

g = Long-term sustainable growth rate in E

k = Present value discount rate (i.e., the cost of capital)

Number of Periods by Which to Discount Terminal Value. In all of the above formulations, the terminal value is then discounted back to a present value at the present value discount rate (k) for n periods, the same number of periods for which the final increment of the discrete projection period was discounted. This is because the terminal value is the value *at the beginning* of the time immediately following the discrete projection period. This is exactly the same point in time as *the* *end* of the discrete projection period. (A common error is to discount the terminal value for $n + 1$ periods instead of n periods.)[3]

Does the Capitalized Economic Income Method Produce a Control Value or a Minority Value?

The answer to this question is the same as was presented for the discounted economic income method (the value indication can be either a control value or a minority value, depending primarily on the normalization adjustments made to the economic income flow being capitalized). If the adjustments include changes that only a control owner could make, such as normalization of compensation, then the value generally would represent a control ownership position. If such adjustments are not made, the value generally would represent a minority ownership position. If adjustments are not reasonably available for a control owner to make, it is possible that there may be little difference between a control value and a minority value—at least before consideration of marketability factors. (For example, the more the minority stockholder's access to the business's net cash flow is restricted, the greater the discount for lack of marketability. See Chapter 25 for more discussion of this topic.)

What Standard of Value Does the Capitalized Economic Income Model Produce?

The answer to this question is also essentially the same as was presented for the discounted economic income method.

If the economic income capitalized and the direct capitalization rate used reflect the condition of the company as it is on a stand-alone basis, the value indication should be *fair market value*. If synergies or circumstances peculiar to a particular investor are reflected in the economic income stream or in the direct capitalization rate, the value indication would reflect those elements of *investment value*.

Since the capitalized economic income method can be used to develop either fair market value or investment value, and most family law courts lean toward one or the other of those two standards of value, the capitalized economic income method is often used in appraisals for purposes of marital dissolution.[4]

---

[3] If midyear discounting is used, a mathematical equivalent to using the modified (midyear) capitalization model is (1) to use the standard capitalization model (typically the Gordon Growth version) and (2) to discount the indicated terminal value by n -.5 periods. While this procedure produces exactly the same answer, it seems that using the modified capitalization formula is a conceptually preferable presentation. This is because the modified formula, along with explanatory text, would make it easier for the appraisal reader to understand the calculations.

[4] See, for example, DeLucia v. DeLucia, No. FA950249319s, 1997 WL 16832 (Conn. Super. Ct., Jan. 10, 1997), and Backhaus v. Backhaus, No. A-94-1083, 1996 WL 737590 (Neb. App., Dec. 17, 1996).

Summary

There are three principal variables in the direct capitalization of economic income method:

1. The projected base-level economic income flow.
2. The present value discount rate (i.e., the cost of capital).
3. The expected long-term growth rate by which the present value discount rate is to be modified to derive the direct capitalization rate.

The capitalized economic income method is essentially an abridged version of the discounted economic income method. The primary difference is in the treatment of future changes in the expected economic income. In the discounted economic income method, future changes in economic income are specifically reflected in the discrete income projections in the numerator of the arithmetic equation. In the capitalized economic income method, future changes in economic income are combined into a single growth rate. This single growth rate is subtracted from the present value discount rate in the denominator of the arithmetic equation.

The economic income flow to be capitalized can be either the amount available to equity or the amount available to all invested capital (usually defined to include owners' equity plus long-term interest-bearing debt, although other definitions are sometimes used).

The economic income flow that is projected is usually net cash flow (at least that is the preference of a consensus of valuation professionals), although other definitions of economic income are sometimes used.

Like the discounted economic income method, the capitalized economic income method is a forward-looking exercise. Using some average of actual past economic income is only appropriate if that average does, in fact, represent the expected level of economic income in the future.

The projected base-level economic income flow is divided by a direct capitalization rate, which is comprised of the present value discount rate less a rate of growth in the variable being capitalized. This long-term growth rate is assumed to be constant in perpetuity. The development of the present value discount rate is the same as for the discounted economic income method, as discussed in Chapters 13 and 14. If either a build-up procedure or the CAPM procedure is used to develop the discount rate, that rate includes expected inflation. Therefore, the growth rate used should also reflect inflation—to the extent that it impacts the economic income variable being capitalized. The results are extremely sensitive to changes in the growth rate factor, especially when valuing invested capital. This is because the analysis of invested capital starts with a lower present value discount rate than for straight equity.

It is essential that the direct capitalization rate be developed so that it is appropriate for the definition of the economic income flow being cap-

italized. One of the most common errors in implementing the capitalized economic income method is using a direct capitalization rate that is not appropriate for the particular definition of economic income that is being capitalized.

The capitalized economic income method is also an excellent method for developing the terminal value in the discounted economic income method.

Bibliography

Agiato, Joseph A., and Thomas L. Johnston. "The Relationship between the Earnings Yield and the Cash Flow Yield." *CPA Expert*, Winter 1996, pp. 6–9.

Bakken, John E. "Capitalization of Earnings—an Income Approach." Chapter 17 in *Handbook of Business Valuation*, Thomas L. West and Jeffrey D. Jones, eds. New York: John Wiley & Sons, 1992, pp. 192–200.

Evans, Frank C. "Recognizing the Key Factors in the Income Approach to Business Valuation." *Business Valuation Review*, June 1996, pp. 80–86.

Kaltman, Todd A. "Capitalization Using a Mid-Year Convention." *Business Valuation Review*, December 1995, pp. 178–82.

Lippitt, Jeffrey W., and Nicholas J. Mastrachhio Jr. "Developing Capitalization Rates for Valuing a Business." *The CPA Journal*, November 1995, pp. 24–28.

Chapter 16

The Guideline Publicly Traded Company Method

The use of the guideline publicly traded company method to value stocks of closely held companies has been significantly enhanced in the late 1980s and in the 1990s by three important developments:

1. A vastly increased number of available actively traded public companies for the analyst to select from. This is especially true with regard to smaller companies, which may be more comparative in many respects to many small, closely held companies than those traded in the public markets a decade ago.

2. Development of EDGAR (Electronic Data Gathering and Retrieval). By May 1996, all of the approximately 16,000 companies required to report to the SEC were required to file electronically. Where it had been expensive to obtain these filings from sources such as *Disclosure*, they now are available *at no charge* on the Internet. Accessing these filings is discussed in the next chapter.

3. Development of extensive new databases that provide empirical guidance (not previously available) to assist in quantifying the discount for lack of marketability between (1) a publicly traded security equivalent value and (2) an otherwise similar closely held security value. These data are described in detail in Chapter 25, Discounts for Lack of Marketability.

While there are significant differences between the manner in which small businesses and large businesses operate, actual market transaction data can provide compelling empirical evidence of value. This is especially true if the relevant standard of value is fair market value.

The size requirements for an initial public offering and public stock trading are far less than many analysts realize. Many small companies that analysts naively believe are too small are actually large enough to trade on public stock exchanges. However, it is not necessary for a company to be a candidate for an initial public offering in order for the analyst to obtain useful valuation guidance from capital market data. The capital market provides general guidance as to how securities in many industries are being priced.

Public stock markets in the United States (as well as in other countries) reprice thousands of stocks every day. This pricing of securities takes place through transactions among financial buyers and sellers who (1) are well-informed (because of stringent disclosure laws, at least in the United States) and (2) have no special motivations or compulsions to buy or to sell. This constant transactional repricing provides contemporaneous evidence of prices that buyers and sellers agree on for stocks in all kinds of industries. These security prices may be analyzed relative to the financial fundamental pricing variables perceived to drive their values, such as dividends, cash flows, and earnings. Multiples of these—and other—relevant financial fundamental variables are important investor valuation guidelines.

It is noteworthy that companies whose shares are already publicly traded are themselves potential acquirers for many small companies.

And the pricing parameters of the potential acquirers' stock certainly will influence the pricing that the public company can pay for a potential acquiree. Of course, if the subject small company *could* be a candidate to go public, this factor makes the guideline publicly traded company method even more directly relevant.

The analysts who disparage the use of this vast, empirical database for pricing guidance in the valuation of small closely held companies tend to be those who are least schooled in its use. This chapter is designed to help both the veteran analyst and the neophyte make the best possible use of capital market transaction data. It should also be helpful to those reviewing a business appraisal work product in order to evaluate its thoroughness and appropriateness.

Introduction to the Guideline Publicly Traded Company Method

The purpose of compiling guideline publicly traded company tables is to develop value measures based on the prices at which stocks of companies with similar characteristics exchange. The value measures thus developed will be applied to the subject company's fundamental financial data. And these value measures will be correlated in order to reach an estimate of value for the subject company (or for its shares or for other ownership interests).

A "value measure" is usually a multiple derived from the price of the guideline companies' stock as of the valuation date. The stock price is divided by some relevant economic variable observed or calculated from the guideline companies' financial statements. Some financial variables, such as projections of next year's economic income, may be estimated by security analysts. The reciprocal of the calculated pricing multiple is the direct capitalization rate applicable for that financial variable.

The following are some of the income statement financial variables most often used to develop equity value measures from guideline companies:

- Gross or net revenue.
- Net income.
- Gross cash flow (net income plus noncash charges).
- Net income before taxes.
- Operating cash flow (earnings before depreciation, other noncash charges, and taxes, sometimes called EBDT).
- Dividends or dividend-paying capacity.

In addition to value measures that use only the value of the guideline common stock to develop the pricing multiple, some value measures include the value of *all* the invested capital. In this case, the numerator for the value measure pricing multiple is called market value of invested capital (MVIC). The MVIC includes the market value of all classes of stock and all long-term, interest-bearing debt. In these cases, the denominator used to compute the value measure should include all of the economic returns available to all classes of capital reflected in the numerator. For example, preferred dividends and interest would be included as economic returns available to the total capital of the subject small business.

The following are some of the income statement financial variables most often used to develop value measures for MVIC:

- Gross or net revenue.
- Earnings before interest and taxes (EBIT).
- Earnings before depreciation, interest, and taxes (EBDIT).
- Operating cash flow (net income plus interest and noncash charges) available to invested capital.
- Debt-free net income (net income plus interest)

Any of the above financial variables may be measured for any or all of a variety of time periods to create the denominator for a value measure. The following are some of the typical time periods used:

- Latest 12 months.
- Latest fiscal year.
- Straight average of some number of past years.
- Weighted average of some number of past years.
- Estimates for the forthcoming year.

All of the above financial performance variables and time periods may have various other permutations, depending on the availability and the relevance of data.

It is noteworthy that *net cash flow* (defined in Chapters 13–15, the chapters on the income approach) is *not* one of the economic income variables normally used in the market approach. Recall that the definition of net cash flow required estimates of capital expenditures and changes in net working capital in amounts necessary to support the level of operations being discounted or capitalized. In the market approach, there is no way to determine whether actual capital expenditures or changes in working capital in a period were the amounts actually necessary to support the level of operations resulting in the other income variables for which market multiples are observed. Therefore, while net cash flow is the economic income variable *preferred* in the income approach, it normally is *not* one of the income variables used in the market approach.

Value measures also may be developed based on balance sheet financial data. Such measures normally are derived from public stock prices as of the valuation date. The stock prices are divided by the balance sheet financial variables as of a date as close as possible preceding the valuation date for which the guideline company and the subject company data are both available. The following are some of the typical balance sheet financial variables:

- Book value.
- Tangible book value.
- Adjusted book value.
- Adjusted tangible book value.

As with value measures derived from income statement financial data, value measures based on balance sheet financial data may also be calculated on an MVIC basis. In such cases, the market values of the senior equity and the long-term, interest-bearing liabilities generally are added into both the numerator and the denominator when deriving the value measure.

It is noteworthy that income statement financial variables are measured over one or more *periods* of time. On the other hand, balance sheet financial variables normally are measured only at the latest practical *point* in time.

The actual value measure applied to the subject company may be anywhere within (or sometimes even outside) the range of value measures extracted from the capital market data. Where each value measure should fall will depend on the quantitative and qualitative analyses of the subject company—relative to corresponding analyses of the companies that comprise the capital market transaction data.

When Is the Guideline Publicly Traded Company Method Most Useful?

The initial value derived from the guideline publicly traded company method, before adjustment for shareholder level factors (such as size of the block and degree of marketability or lack of it), is often called a *publicly traded equivalent value* or *as if freely traded value*. That is, the initial value derived by this method is the price at which the subject company stock would be expected to trade if it were traded publicly. In other words, the level of value represents marketable, noncontrolling ownership interests. Values estimated from this method are almost always on a going-concern basis.

This valuation method can be used in conjunction with an appraisal for any standard of value, certainly most importantly for fair market value. Use of this valuation method in conjunction with each of the standards of value is discussed in the next subsection.

The necessary adjustments to make when this method is used to value (1) a nonmarketable, noncontrolling ownership interest or (2) a controlling ownership interest are discussed in a subsequent subsection.

Finally, we will consider the impact of the quantity and quality of available data on the use of this valuation method.

Standard of Value

Fair Market Value. While the guideline publicly traded company method can be used in conjunction with any standard of value, it generally is most useful when the standard of value is fair market value. By definition, this valuation method is based on making comparisons between the subject stock and active market transactions in guideline stocks.

Fair market value is the standard of value in most taxation-related valuations. For example, Revenue Ruling 59-60 references the public capital markets no fewer than seven times. Fair market value is also the standard of value for most ESOP-related valuations.

As a practical matter, fair market value is *de facto* the standard of value for initial public offerings (IPOs) and for arm's-length private placements to raise capital. This is because the pricing of such transactions should be guided by what the market is willing to pay.

Fair Value. As noted in Chapter 3, fair value is a statutorily defined standard of value. In the United States, it is applicable in almost all states with respect to dissenting stockholder actions. It is also applicable in the few states that have corporate and partnership dissolution statutes. It is interpreted differently by the judicial precedent in each state. Generally, in most states, it is a broader standard that incorporates the market approach value, as well as values indicated by the income and asset-based approaches. Therefore, a guideline publicly traded company method is normally one part of the analysis when fair value is the desired standard of value.

Investment Value. This is the standard of value that may depart the most from the value indicated by a strict application of the guideline publicly traded company method. The guideline publicly traded company method would be expected to indicate a value based on a *consensus* of market participants, as evidenced by their transactions. Investment value, by definition, is the value to a *particular* buyer or seller. Therefore, income approach valuation methods provide more opportunity for a specific party to (1) project owner-specific economic income flows and (2) use discount rates and capitalization rates that are appropriate to their specific individual investment criteria.

Even a party primarily interested in investment value, however, generally would want to have some notion of what a capital market-derived consensus value would be. Furthermore, the analyst interested in investment value can always adjust the financial variables on a *pro forma* basis. These adjustments would be made in order to (1) reflect anticipated changes in the subject company and (2) use the guideline publicly traded company method to assess the sensitivity of market value to various possible changes in the financial variables.

Levels of Value

Control versus Lack of Control. Since guideline publicly traded company transactions are, by definition, noncontrolling (or minority) ownership interests, they are most directly relevant for valuation of other minority ownership interests.

In applying the guideline publicly traded company method, qualitative and quantitative differences between the guideline companies and the subject company are reflected in arriving at the publicly traded equivalent value of the subject stock. These differences are usually in the selection of pricing multiples applied to the subject company's financial fundamental data—relative to the guideline companies' pricing multiples. In arriving at a publicly traded equivalent value, adjustments may also be made for other factors, such as relative excess assets or deficiencies. Thus, having arrived at a publicly traded equivalent value, the only remaining adjustment necessary for a minority ownership interest value is the shareholder-level attribute of lack of marketability. As already noted, there are a plethora of empirical data on which to base this value adjustment.

When valuing controlling ownership interests, it may be preferable to apply the market approach by using only guideline controlling ownership interest transactions. This is the subject of Chapter 18. However, the practical reality is that there are far more reliable guideline public company minority transaction data available than data on controlling ownership interest transactions. Therefore, it is often useful to use the guideline publicly traded company method even when valuing controlling ownership interests. This usually requires some adjustment from the publicly traded minority stock equivalent value in order to account for the element of control. This may be offset—in part or even fully—by a value adjustment for lack of marketability. (In the valuation of a controlling ownership interest, some analysts call this value adjustment a discount for lack of liquidity, to distinguish it from the lack of marketability adjustment appropriate to minority interests.) This is a complicated issue. It is addressed briefly toward the end of this chapter in the section "Typical Adjustments to Reach a Value Conclusion" and in considerable detail in Chapter 25, Discounts for Lack of Marketability.

Marketable versus Nonmarketable. The guideline publicly traded company method is most appropriate, of course, when valuing marketable shares by direct comparison with marketable shares. The most obvious application of this valuation method is when pricing an IPO.

Like most shareholder level attributes of securities, marketability (or lack of it) is often not a totally black or white issue. For example, private placements of stocks that already have a public market generally will be restricted for a period of time, then they will enjoy full marketability. Most ESOP-owned stock, by law, enjoys the right of a *put*. The put guarantees a market for the ESOP-owned stock at the appraised price at the occurrence of specified triggering events. There is much empirical data and procedural precedent for making value adjustments for the limited marketability in such situations. As noted at the beginning of this chapter, much of these data have been developed in recent years. The data are described in Chapter 25, Discounts for Lack of Marketability.

Going-Concern Value versus Liquidation Value. In almost all cases, the public capital market prices a stock based on the premise that the publicly traded company will continue to operate as a going concern. Unless there is evidence to the contrary, the guideline publicly traded company method would be expected to produce a value indication consistent with the premise that the subject company will continue to operate as a going concern. The premises of value related to liquidation value (i.e., orderly disposition premise and forced liquidation premise) are introduced in Chapter 22, The Asset Accumulation Method.

Quantity and Quality of Available Data

As with any valuation method, the quantity and quality of relevant available data will have an important bearing on the usefulness of the method. As noted earlier, there are more publicly traded companies, especially smaller ones, than most analysts realize.

First, we will discuss the criteria for the selection of guideline companies. Second, we will address the question of how many guideline companies should be analyzed in the application of this valuation method. We would not totally reject this valuation method just because we are not completely satisfied with either (1) the number or (2) the degree of comparability of the available guideline publicly traded companies. In the final analysis, the quantity and quality of the guideline company data —compared to the quantity and quality of data available for other valuation methods—will be one factor in concluding the weight to be accorded to this method in (1) correlating the results of various valuation methods and (2) reaching a final value estimate.

It is not necessary for the analyst to use each selected guideline publicly trade company for every value measure included in the analysis. For example, one of the selected guideline companies may have negative net income. Therefore, that guideline company can not be used to derive the appropriate price to net income value measure. However, that same guideline company may have a meaningful amount of operating cash flow. Therefore, it could be quite useful in deriving the appropriate price to operating cash flow value measure.

Sometimes an industry segment may include a good guideline company that went public recently, say within the last two or three years. Therefore, this guideline company would not be available for the derivation of the price to five-year average value measures. However, this guideline company would be available for the derivation of the price to latest 12 months value measures. The analyst should exercise caution and careful judgment, however, to ensure that the use of certain guideline companies for some value measures (and not for others) does not introduce bias or distortion into the value indications.

Criteria for Guideline Publicly Traded Company Selection

The following question succinctly summarizes the essence of the key characteristic analysts look for in a guideline company: Do the underlying economics driving this comparable company match those that drive our company?[1]

In Revenue Ruling 59-60, the Internal Revenue Service makes the following observation:

> Although the only restrictive requirement as to comparable corporations specified in the statute is that their lines of business be the same or similar, yet it is obvious that consideration must be given to other relevant factors in order that the most valid comparison possible will be obtained.[2]

In analyzing whether a particular publicly traded company may be considered as a guideline company with respect to the subject company, the following are some of the factors analysts often consider:

1. Products.
2. Markets.
3. Management.
4. Earnings.
5. Dividend-paying capacity.
6. Book value.
7. Position of the company in its industry.
8. Capital structure.
9. Credit status.
10. Depth of management.
11. Personnel experience.
12. Nature of the competition.
13. Maturity of the business.

Depending on the individual circumstances of the appraisal subject, the analyst may need to consider additional factors. These factors may include the number and size of retail outlets, sales volume, product mix, territory of operations, and customer mix. Clearly, it is not possible to present an exhaustive list of comparability criteria. And the necessity of tailoring the list of comparability criteria to be considered in each individual valuation cannot be overemphasized.

Much of the information needed to assess comparability can be gath-

---

[1] Daniel W. Bielinski, "The Comparable-Company Approach: Measuring the True Value of Privately Held Firms," *Corporate Cashflow Magazine*, October 1990, pp. 64-66.

[2] Revenue Ruling 59-60 (1959-1 C.B. 237), Section 4(h).

ered in a thorough review of each public company's Form 10-K to the Securities and Exchange Commission (SEC). However, in order to assess comparability, it may sometimes be necessary to consult additional sources—such as industry and trade publications (discussed in Chapter 10, Analyzing Qualitative Factors)—or to call the company for additional information.

With regard to assessing comparability, it is also useful to analyze the financial statements of both the subject company and the selected guideline publicly traded companies. This analytical procedure is intended to uncover both the similarities and the differences to consider in the subject company valuation. Bearing in mind the company being valued and the nature of the industry, the performance of the subject company may be compared to the selected guideline companies by analyzing financial ratios that measure liquidity, leverage, activity, and profitability, as well as historical trends in revenues, expenses, and profitability. This type of financial ratio analysis is illustrated in Chapter 9, Comparisons with Industry Averages. In particular, if this financial ratio analysis indicates that the guideline companies' capital structures differ significantly from that of the subject company, this difference can be mitigated using the market value of invested capital (MVIC) procedures referred to earlier.

In some valuation situations, the subject company is so unusual that it is difficult to find a set of truly useful guideline publicly traded companies. In these cases, the analyst may find a group of companies that can provide some general valuation guidance. However, of that group, only one or two companies may be considered truly comparative. In such cases, the analyst may tabulate data for the entire group of guideline companies; however, the analyst may elect to accord more weight to the data for those public companies considered to be the most comparative.

Sometimes, the subject company appears to be so unusual that even an exhaustive search for guideline publicly traded companies produces no companies that provide useful valuation guidance. In such cases, the analyst should remember that over 30,000 small public companies have sold stock through public offerings at one time or another. Also, if the valuation is for federal gift and estate taxes, Revenue Ruling 59-60 states that the selected companies may be in the same "or similar" industries. This phrase gives the analyst latitude to exercise reasonable judgment in selecting publicly traded companies from related industries if the analyst is unable to find guideline companies in the subject company's specific industry group.

When analyzing what industry segments qualify as "the same or similar lines of business," the analyst should consider underlying economic factors that influence the subject company. This consideration may uncover some potential guideline companies. Important economic factors for consideration include the market(s) into which the company sells, its brand acceptance (or lack of it), and the raw material supply conditions.

A problem may also arise if the analyst establishes comparability criteria that are too restrictive. By unnecessarily limiting the number of guideline companies considered, the analyst may miss relevant capital market pricing evidence—pricing evidence that would otherwise be important to the valuation process.

How Many Guideline Publicly Traded Companies?

The answer to this guideline company selection question depends on a number of factors, including the following:

1. *Similarity to the appraisal subject.* The more similar the guideline companies, the fewer guideline companies are needed for a meaningful analysis.
2. *Trading activity.* The more actively traded the guideline companies are, the fewer guideline companies are needed for a meaningful analysis.
3. *Dispersion of value measure data points.* The wider the range of relevant value measure data points, the more guideline companies are needed in order to identify a pricing pattern relevant to the subject company.

Sometimes, a sample of as few as two or three guideline publicly traded companies is adequate for a meaningful analysis. The analyst's level of confidence, however, rises sharply when he or she finds four or more good guideline publicly traded companies. In those rare instances where it seems there are a dozen or more good guideline publicly traded companies in terms of line of business, analysts may narrow down the comparability criteria—in terms of size, earnings pattern, and other factors—in order to select the most meaningful of the guideline companies.

Time Period for Analysis

In the absence of a compelling reason to do otherwise, the time period most commonly used for the analysis of subject company operating data is five years. This conventional time period should not, however, be naively used. The operative phrase in this part of the valuation process is "relevant time period."

For a cyclical industry, a complete economic cycle may be considered the relevant time period from which to develop average operating performance results to be used as the basis for value measures. This complete economic cycle criteria sometimes leads the analyst to use averages of operating performance data for periods of as long as 10 years.

Sometimes, the relevant time period for analysis is constrained by structural economic changes that affect either the subject company or the subject industry as a whole. Such structural economic changes may render otherwise comparative financial data useless for valuation purposes. In these cases, it may only be appropriate for the analyst to use one (or a very few) years of comparative data for analytical purposes.

Once in a while, the historical data may include an aberration that is clearly nonrecurring for either the subject company or for the subject industry. In such instances, the best thing to do may be to just omit that year of data when computing the relevant value measures. In such cases, however, the aberrational data normally are tabulated and presented in the valuation report. The reason for the omission of the aberrational historical data from the value measure calculations should be explained.

Typically, the same time period that is selected for gathering and presenting historical data is used for both the income statement and the balance sheet data. Value measures based on income statement data typically are computed by dividing the valuation date price by the income statement financial variables for one—or a number of—prior period(s). Value measures based on balance sheet financial variables (e.g., price to book value measures) typically are computed by dividing the valuation date price by the most recent balance sheet financial variable. The reason for collecting and presenting several years of balance sheet financial information is to (1) identify and (2) interpret comparative trends among the guideline companies and the subject company. However, the earlier years' balance sheet financial data are usually not used directly in the computation of subject company value measures.

Compiling Guideline Publicly Traded Company Tables

The purpose of gathering data on guideline publicly traded companies is to extract some pricing benchmarks by which to value the subject privately held company. The process of compiling a comprehensive list of guideline publicly traded companies is not simple. No single source provides an exhaustive list. And it is much easier to find good guideline publicly traded companies in some industries than in others. A complete search requires creativity, ingenuity, and experience. In addition to searching traditional print sources and electronic sources for guideline publicly traded companies, the analyst may consult (1) trade association membership lists and (2) regional investment publications. Or the analyst may ask the management of the subject company about the comparability of the potential guideline companies identified through the conventional search for additional guideline prospects.

Of all the comparability criteria by which the different companies may be judged, the one criterion that typically receives the most attention is the industry in which the subject company operates. Therefore, the starting point in compiling a list of guideline publicly traded companies is to create a list of the public companies that operate in the subject company's industry group. The most widely accepted categorization of industry groups is the U.S. government's *Standard Industrial Classification Manual*. This manual publishes and defines Standard Industry Classification (SIC) codes. The SIC code is the statistical classification standard underlying all establishment-based federal economic statistics classified by industry. The latest edition of the manual was published in 1987. It was revised in 1987 to take into account (1) technological changes; (2) institutional changes, such as deregulation in the banking, communications, and transportation industries; and (3) the tremendous expansion in the service sector.

The search for guideline publicly traded companies should be as exhaustive as the scope of the particular valuation case permits. Frequently, the most obvious public companies in an industry are the largest ones. However, because of this size factor alone, such companies may be less comparable to the small, subject company than some smaller, but more obscure, public companies. Another reason to conduct a comprehensive search for guideline companies is for the analyst to demonstrate that (1) he considered all companies that may be considered reasonably comparable and (2) he selected for analysis only the most comparative companies available. The analyst should establish, document, and adhere to an objective set of selection criteria. Because of this objective set of selection criteria, the final list of selected guideline companies will not bias the valuation result either upward or downward.

Developing a List of Guideline Publicly Traded Companies

Data concerning publicly traded companies by SIC group are found in a number of sources, including printed material, CD-ROM technology, and on-line databases. These sources are discussed in the following chapter, Public Company Data.

Financial Statement Adjustments to Guideline Publicly Traded Companies

In general, the same types of adjustments should be made to the financial statements of the guideline publicly traded companies as are made to the financial statements of the subject company. The following are some of the main categories of financial statement adjustments:

- Remove nonrecurring items from income statements.
- Put the guideline companies and the subject company on a comparable accounting basis (e.g., adjust any companies accounting for inventory on a LIFO basis to a FIFO basis, use consistent depreciation methods and lives, etc.).
- Adjust for nonoperating items.
- Adjust for the results of discontinued operations.

Comparative Ratio Analysis

For purposes of comparative performance and other ratio analysis between the subject company and the guideline publicly traded companies, the comparisons will be most meaningful if the ratios are computed *after* the adjustments to the financial statements of the guideline companies as well as the subject company.

On the other hand, it is both faster and less expensive to use ratios for publicly traded companies from one of the many handy on-line or CD-ROM services, such as Standard & Poor's Compustat, Disclosure's Compact D/SEC, or Media General Plus. The decision of whether to use ratios computed by a service or to compute them oneself depends on the analyst's judgment about the extent to which the difference in results is likely to justify the cost. Such a judgment is made on a case-by-case basis.

Typically, the comparative ratio procedure is performed only for the latest available comparative year. This is true even if the value measures are based on several years' average financial performance results. If the comparative ratio analysis is used to conclude where the subject's value measures should be (relative to the guideline companies' value measures), the analyst should be careful to recognize any abnormalities in the year for which the ratios were calculated. Such abnormalities may cause the ratios to be misleading for use in concluding the relevant value measure.

Obtaining the Guideline Publicly Traded Company Market Pricing Data

If the value measures to be used are only those that relate to common equity, all that is needed is the market price for each guideline company's stock as of the valuation date.

If value measures based on the market value of invested capital (MVIC) are to be used, the market values of all the components of the invested capital need to be determined. Some of the guideline company senior securities (e.g., debt and/or preferred stock) may not be publicly traded. In that case, book values of those securities are often used as a proxy for their market values. If, however, the analyst suspects that the book value may be far enough apart from market value to create a significant distortion in the value measure computed, the senior securities should be revalued to market value.[3]

---

[3] If this is necessary, we refer the reader to Chapter 20, "Debt Securities" and/or Chapter 21, "Preferred Stock," in Pratt, Reilly, and Schweihs, *Valuing a Business: The Analysis and Appraisal of Closely Held Companies*, 3d ed.

Presenting Guideline Publicly Traded Company Tables

Guideline company tables are typically presented on a per share basis. They usually show (1) the name of the guideline company, (2) the market in which it is traded (e.g., New York Stock Exchange, American Stock Exchange, Nasdaq, and so on), (3) the per share market price as of the valuation date, (4) the fundamental financial variable (e.g., earnings per share, operating cash flow per share, and so on), and (5) the resulting valuation pricing multiple (i.e., the price divided by the financial fundamental variable). If space permits, there may be columns for more than one fundamental financial variable and for the corresponding valuation ratio on the same table. The table typically presents the comparable financial fundamental data for the subject company.

For each valuation ratio presented, the table typically presents a mean average, median, standard deviation, coefficient of variation, and (sometimes) a range of pricing data. The sample case in Chapters 30 and 31 presents guideline publicly traded company tables for a variety of financial fundamental value measures.

A question often arises about the extent to which value measures that were not ultimately used in reaching the final value estimate should be presented in the valuation report tables. There is no clear-cut right or wrong answer to this. We suggest that there is not much point in presenting value measures that are never seriously considered. If, however, a value measure was considered but discarded because of the nature of the data (i.e., perhaps a very wide dispersion of value ratios), it might be worthwhile to present it. In that way, the appraisal report reader can see the data that was discarded in the final valuation analysis.

Selecting and Weighting Pricing Multiples Based on Guideline Publicly Traded Companies

The result of the guideline publicly traded company tables is an array of pricing multiples for each of several value measures. At this point, it is necessary to again visit the questions of (1) which value measures to use in reaching an indication of value and (2) the relative weight to be accorded to each of the value measures used.

For each value measure used, it is also necessary to decide what the pricing multiple for the subject company should be—relative to the observed pricing multiples for the guideline publicly traded companies.

Impact of Guideline Publicly Traded Company Data Evaluation

The same general thought processes and decision criteria apply both to (1) deciding whether or not to rely on any particular value measure and

(2) deciding on the relative weight to be accorded each value measure that is ultimately used. A study of the actual pricing data may lead to greater or lesser reliance on certain value measures than the analyst may have expected prior to compiling the pricing data.

Number of Data Points Available.   If it turns out that very few data points are available for a particular value measure, this problem may lead the analyst (1) to abandon that measure or (2) to put relatively little weight on it. This is true even though the value measure might be conceptually significant if there were more data. A common example is price to latest 12 months' earnings. If only two of seven guideline companies had meaningful positive earnings, the analyst has to decide whether those two companies convey enough information to be accorded weight in the final analysis. For example, the analyst may decide to use a price to operating cash flow multiple—or some other pricing measure —instead of the price to earnings measure.

Comparability of Data Measurement.   Another issue to consider is the extent to which the analyst is satisfied that the adjustments, if any, to the subject company and guideline companies' financial fundamental data have resulted in stating the data on a comparable basis. The level of confidence regarding the comparability of financial fundamental data may influence the analyst's judgment regarding the use of (or weight accorded to) value measures based on that particular financial fundamental variable.

Comparability of Data Patterns.   Another factor in assessing comparability is the extent to which the data for the subject company "tracks" with the data for the guideline publicly traded companies. For example, if the subject company and six of the seven guideline companies had a generally upward earnings trend but one guideline company had a downward trend, the analyst may omit the maverick company when selecting appropriate value measures relative to earnings.

Apparent Market Reliance.   The extent to which the value measures are tightly clustered—or widely dispersed—tends to indicate the extent to which the market tends to focus on that particular measure in pricing stocks in that particular industry. For this reason, it is helpful if the guideline publicly traded company tables present not only measures of central tendency (such as mean and median) but also measures of dispersion (such as standard deviation and coefficient of variation).

In general, the lower the dispersion of the value measure, the greater the weight the analyst may accord to that measure. In some cases, the guideline publicly traded company table may lead the analyst to the conclusion that the value measures based on some particular financial fundamental variable are so widely dispersed that the value measure has no usefulness as to valuation guidance.

Multiples of Earnings or Cash Flow

Multiples of economic income variables (e.g., price/earnings multiples, price/cash flow multiples, and so on) are the reciprocals of the direct capitalization rates applicable to those financial fundamental variables. Therefore, pricing multiples are influenced by the same forces that influence direct capitalization rates. The two most important of these influences are:

1. Risk.
2. Expected growth in the financial fundamental variable being capitalized.

In order to make an intelligent estimate of what pricing multiple is appropriate for the subject company—relative to the pricing multiples observed for the guideline companies—the analyst should make some judgments as to the relative risk and growth prospects of the subject compared with the guideline companies.

Size Factor. The size factor has also been shown to be an important indicator of risk. We presented data in Chapter 13 that showed that companies of the size of the smallest decile of the New York Stock Exchange required a present value discount rate more than five points above the average for all securities traded on the New York Stock Exchange. This differential in the present value discount rate will translate directly into a difference in the direct capitalization rate.

Relative Growth. As shown in Chapter 15, the expected growth rate in perpetuity for an economic income variable (e.g., earnings or cash flow) translates—point for point—into the direct capitalization rate applicable for that variable. Therefore, if the subject company has very long-term growth prospects above or below those of the subject company, each percentage point of such differential should be subtracted from or added to the capitalization rates observed for the guideline companies. Analysts should be careful, however, not to make a simple point-for-point adjustment to the capitalization rate for growth prospect differences that are only short- or intermediate-term.

Capitalization of Dividends or Dividend-Paying Capacity

Dividends from operations ultimately are possible only as a result of earnings and adequate available cash flow. Therefore, capitalization of dividends or dividend-paying capacity may be analyzed as a valuation method separate from the capitalization of earnings and/or cash flow. This depends on the circumstances and the purpose of the valuation.

If the valuation is of a controlling ownership interest, dividend-paying capacity is a more important factor than actual dividends paid. This is because the controlling stockholder has the discretion to pay—or not to pay—cash dividends as long as the company has the capacity to do so. In valuing a minority ownership interest, however, the actual dividends the company pays usually are more important than its dividend-paying capacity. This is because the minority stockholder generally cannot force the company to pay dividends even if the company unquestionably has the capacity to do so.

When the direct capitalization of dividends method is used as a method in the valuation, it usually is by reference to dividend yields on guideline publicly traded companies. For example, let's assume that (1) the guideline publicly traded companies were found to have an average dividend yield (i.e., market price per share divided by annual dividends per share) of 5 percent and (2) the subject company paid dividends or was determined to have a dividend-paying capacity of $1 per share. The direct capitalization of dividends method would be used to simply divide the dividend-paying capacity per share by the appropriate direct capitalization rate (or dividend yield). In this case, the appropriate direct capitalization rate would be 0.05. This direct capitalization rate of 0.05 implies a $20 per share value by the direct capitalization of dividends method.

An estimate of dividend-paying capacity may be based, in part, on the typical payout ratios of publicly traded companies in the subject company's industry. For example, if public companies in that industry typically pay out 30 percent of their net income in dividends, then 30 percent of net income may be a good starting point from which to estimate the subject company's dividend-paying capacity. However, it is noteworthy that the typical small, closely held company is less well capitalized than its publicly traded counterpart and has less access to additional debt and equity capital. Therefore, the subject company may have less dividend-paying capacity per dollar of net income than do most of the publicly traded companies with which it is comparative. This factor should also be considered when estimating the subject company's dividend-paying capacity.

Multiples of Revenue

Valuation pricing multiples of revenue tend to be most highly correlated with the financial fundamental measure return on sales. However, the strength of this correlation varies greatly from one industry to another. Therefore, when considering using a pricing multiple of revenue, it is useful for the analyst to determine whether the guideline companies' multiples of revenue are well correlated with the guideline companies' return on sales. This value measure tends to be more useful for those industries where such a correlation is high as compared to those industries where it is not. In a way, the capitalization of revenues may be considered a "shortcut" application of the capitalization of economic income valuation method. This is true because there is generally an implicit assumption that a certain level of revenues should be able to generate a specific economic income level in a given type of business.

The capitalization of revenues method is applied most frequently to the valuation of service businesses. Such businesses include advertising agencies, insurance agencies, mortuaries, professional practices, and some types of publishing operations. The capitalization of revenues method tends not to work very well in the valuation of manufacturing companies.

Analysts can find guidance in deriving an appropriate pricing multiple of revenues for a particular business in both empirical public stock market data and empirical merger and acquisition data. There are quite a few publicly traded companies in most service business categories, such as insurance agencies, advertising and public relations firms, and securities brokers. If the subject company's actual return on revenue financial fundamental measure is known, an estimate of a reasonable price to revenue pricing multiple can be extracted by simple regression analysis using the guideline companies' empirical price to revenue multiples and returns on revenue historical financial fundamental data.

It is noteworthy that valuations performed by the multiple of revenue method are particularly susceptible to distortion. This is, in large part, because of the differences in the capital structure between the subject company and the guideline publicly traded companies. Therefore, the multiple of revenue pricing multiple is often extracted on a market value of invested capital (MVIC) basis, as discussed in a later section.

One step removed from a multiple of revenue method is a valuation method based on a multiple of some measure of unit volume or capacity. Examples of this type of valuation method include nursing homes priced at so much per bed, forest products plants priced at so much per thousand board feet of production, service stations and fuel distributors priced at so much per gallon sold per month, and so on. The implication of this valuation method, of course, is that so much volume can be expected to translate into some anticipated amount of revenues and economic income.

Multiple of Stock Value to Asset Value

When the analyst has determined that either (1) book value or (2) adjusted book value provides a useful representation of the company's underlying net asset value, the next procedure in this method is to translate that book value into its implication for the market value of the subject shares of stock or partnership interest. This procedure is usually performed by referring to the relationship of the price of guideline companies' stocks to their respective underlying net asset values. The pricing multiple data for the guideline companies may be based on (1) the empirical prices of stocks traded on organized capital markets, (2) transactional prices paid in mergers and acquisitions, or (3) both. Which data source will be used depends on several factors, including the ownership percentage of the subject business interest.

Market Price to Book Value Pricing Multiple. It may be possible (1) to compute the multiple of market price to book value for a group of guideline companies that have stock publicly trading in the capital markets and (2) to apply a multiple somewhere within the range of such market-derived multiples to the subject company's book value. If (1) the book values of the subject company and the guideline companies were computed on comparable bases and if (2) the asset composition of the subject company and the guideline companies is comparative, this procedure may provide a reasonably realistic estimate of the value of the subject business interest.

If accounting methods for the subject company and the guideline companies differ significantly, the analyst should make appropriate adjustments before (1) computing the market price to book value pricing multiples and (2) applying these derived multiples to the subject valuation. There can be additional significant differences, such as differences in asset mix, that challenge the validity of using the market price to book value pricing multiple method.

In this valuation method, often the value measure pricing multiples are computed based only on *tangible* book value. This procedure may help to avoid distortions. This is because some companies may have created their own intangible assets (and thus expensed them for accounting purposes), while other companies may have acquired their intangible assets (and thus carry them on the balance sheet).

As common sense would suggest, empirical tests indicate a significant degree of correlation between market price to book value multiples and return on equity—for both publicly traded stocks and for acquisition prices paid in most industries. As a consequence, an analysis of the relationship between (1) market price to book value multiples and (2) return on equity financial fundamental for the guideline companies can often provide objective guidance when extracting the appropriate market price to book value pricing multiple for the subject company.

Market Price to Adjusted Net Asset Value Pricing Multiple.
For a limited number of industries, empirical data on the market values of underlying net assets are available. Where this is the case, it is possible to extract multiples of the public company stock's price to adjusted net asset value.

In particular, market values for the net asset values of some real estate companies are provided in *Realty Stock Review* and for many partnerships in *Partnership Profiles*. Also, estimates of the market values of the timber owned by many forest products companies are available from brokerage house analysts. When using multiples of market price to adjusted net asset value, it is important to make the same kinds of adjustments to the subject company as have been made to the net asset values for the guideline companies. For example, some real estate company adjusted net asset values are reported net of the impounded capital gains taxes and some are not.

Typical Adjustments to Reach a Value Conclusion

As discussed earlier, the guideline publicly traded company method is based on minority ownership interest, day-to-day transactions in publicly traded stocks. Therefore, if valuing a closely held minority ownership interest, it would not be appropriate to take a lack of control (or minority ownership interest) discount. However, it would be appropriate to take a discount for lack of marketability (discussed in Chapter 25, Discounts for Lack of Marketability).

If a controlling ownership interest is being valued, it may or may not be appropriate to apply a valuation premium for ownership control.

Also, a control premium may be fully—or partially—offset by a discount for lack of marketability.

Disadvantages of the Guideline Publicly Traded Company Method

The business owners, brokers, and analysts of very small closely held businesses will sometimes refuse to recognize the valuation guidance available from public capital markets. Besides the typical observation about how the subject company cannot be compared to any publicly traded company, small business owners and analysts realize there are fundamental differences between large and small companies (see Chapter 5). The analyst should take all of these factors into consideration before relying on the guideline publicly traded company method.

Shares traded on public stock market exchanges are marketable, minority (i.e., noncontrolling) ownership interests. Therefore, significant adjustments to the value indicators are required in order to arrive at a reasonable value indicator for a nonmarketable ownership interest (on either a controlling or a minority basis) for the subject privately owned company.

Public companies are run by boards of directors and professional managers. These executives make operating decisions based on a different set of corporate objectives than private companies typically have. Private companies are more likely to have relationships with family members, employees, suppliers, customers, and the local community that have developed over a long period of time. These relationships can present the board and the management of the private company with corporate objectives that are different than a strict duty to maximize shareholder value. As an additional example, in private companies, the analyst is more likely to observe a strategy that is designed to minimize income taxes, compared with the strategies of public companies.

Small, private companies do not maintain management information systems to the same degree as public companies. Small, private companies tend to have less management information documented in writing. For example, it is rare for a small business to maintain a detailed projection of next year's financial performance. It is even more rare for a small, private company to develop a five-year strategic plan such as is often an integral part of the public company's management information policy.

Closely held companies do not have the access to capital that public companies do. The small, private company may have its growth potential or diversification opportunities frustrated by the lack of access to capital. Or the small company may simply manage its growth prospects or its scope of operations with that capital constraint in mind. In either case, the potential for growth of small, private companies makes them fundamentally different from public companies.

Investment analysts can not readily scrutinize the financial performance of private companies because of their confidential nature.

Therefore, unlike public companies, private companies do not react to investment analyst reports. Accordingly, private company management does not try to operate in a manner that is implicitly designed to post impressive quarterly financial performance statistics.

The private company does not need to incur the costs of filing reports with the Securities and Exchange Commission, conducting annual audits, preparing quarterly reports to shareholders, or staffing an "investor relations" department like most public companies do.

Many analysts believe there is an inherent lack of comparability between small private businesses and companies whose shares are traded on public stock exchanges. Of course, no two companies are the same, not even two publicly traded companies. Most analysts believe that adjustments can be made to the empirical pricing evidence developed from the analysis of large publicly traded companies. However, these adjustments are often made in an attempt to derive legitimate indications of value for large privately owned companies. The fundamental differences in required rates of return, which have been attributed primarily to the difference in size (even between large publicly owned companies and small publicly owned companies), illustrates the challenge of applying capital market pricing evidence to the small, private company.

As with any business valuation method, the disadvantages associated with applying the guideline publicly traded company method may be significant in any given valuation assignment. Therefore, they should not be ignored by the analyst. As with other methods, however, the experienced analyst may be able to make reasonable use of the value indications available from a rigorous application of this method, even for small businesses.

Common Errors

The guideline company method can be a powerful and useful tool in the valuation of closely held business interests. Proper application of it, however, requires some expertise in the analysis of publicly traded, capital market securities. This section discusses a few of the most common categories of errors in the use of the guideline publicly traded company valuation method.

Failure to Conduct an Adequate Search for Guideline Transaction Data

As noted early in the chapter, there are thousands of publicly traded stocks. Some capital market reporting services only report on a fraction of them, usually the largest ones. It is common to see valuation reports that assert something to the effect that, "We searched for guideline publicly traded companies in the industry, but there were none." However, in fact, a more rigorous search for guideline publicly traded companies would unearth several. A related error is to select only companies reported in a capital market reporting service such as *Value Line*, which generally covers only the larger companies. However, smaller publicly traded companies not included in *Value Line* may be more comparative to the subject company.

Failure to Make Appropriate Financial Statement Adjustments to Guideline Companies

Analysts often adequately make adjustments to the subject company financial statements, but they give little or no consideration to possible appropriate adjustments to the guideline companies' financial statements. It is important that the analyst peruse the financial statements of the guideline companies in order to determine whether adjustments may be appropriate for one or more of the companies in order to put them on a basis as comparable as possible to the subject company.

Along the same line, we recommend using the guideline companies' original financial statements and SEC filings rather than secondary reporting sources. This is especially true if the guideline publicly traded company method is to be the primary valuation method relied on. Secondary reporting sources often do not provide the requisite level of detail of the financial data needed for certain adjustments. Also, analysts are sometimes not careful to understand the definition a secondary reporting source may use for certain financial data. Therefore, they may get caught in a mismatch when using the secondary reporting source data to value the subject company.

Multiples that Mismatch Numerator and Denominator

There are many ways to mismatch the numerator in a value multiple (i.e., the multiple selected on the basis of guideline publicly traded company market evidence) with the denominator (i.e., the financial fundamental data for the subject company to which the numerator is applied to arrive at an indication of value). Two of the most common are mismatched time periods and mismatched definitions.

Mismatched Time Periods. It is not uncommon to find value multiples computed from guideline publicly traded company data for one time period applied to the subject company data for a different time period. This inconsistency can result in serious distortions, especially if industry conditions differed significantly between the two sets of time periods. At a market turning point for a cyclical industry, a single quarter period of time difference in the financial fundamental data used between the guideline companies and the subject company can result in seriously misleading value multiples.

In order to avoid such distortion, it often is necessary to work with interim (versus fiscal year-end) data for the guideline companies. This procedure is performed in order to match time periods as closely as possible with the available subject company data closest to the effective date of the valuation. This usually requires more work on the part of the analyst. But this procedure is worth the effort in order to produce a more reliable value indication.

Mismatched Definitions of Valuation Variables. If a valuation multiple is computed based on guideline company data defined in a certain way, that multiple should be applied to the financial fundamental data defined the same way for the subject company. Looking at the same point another way, if subject company data are defined in a certain way, the same definition should be used for the guideline publicly traded company data from which the valuation multiple is computed.

Elementary as this sounds, we have seen many instances of data mismatches. The following are a few of the most often encountered instances of this type of error:

- Fully diluted per share data used for the guideline publicly traded companies or for the subject company, but not for both.
- Subject company data— but not guideline publicly traded company data—adjusted for nonrecurring items.
- After-tax pricing multiples for the guideline publicly traded companies applied to pretax financial fundamental data for the subject company.
- Economic income data after officers' compensation for the guideline publicly traded companies applied to subject company economic income data before owner/officer compensation.

These are just a few examples of typical mismatches. Mismatch possibilities are innumerable.

Naive Reliance on Average of Guideline Publicly Traded Company Multiples without Comparative Analysis

Unless the guideline companies and the subject company are homogenous in their financial characteristics, the mean or median of the guideline publicly traded company pricing multiples may not be the most appropriate valuation multiples for the subject company. Nonetheless, we frequently see the mean or median pricing multiple used with no explanation—to justify the implied notion that the subject company's financial characteristics indicate it should be valued right at the average of the pricing multiples extracted from the guideline publicly traded companies.

A section of this chapter was devoted to selecting the valuation multiple for the subject company relative to the guideline publicly traded company pricing multiples. Such analysis is little more than common sense. Nonetheless, it is surprising how often analysts totally ignore such a fundamental analysis.

Summary

This chapter has presented the methodology and sources for implementing the guideline publicly traded company method of valuation of business ownership interests. It is a widely used and generally accepted small business valuation method. However, this valuation method should be implemented vary carefully.

Exhibit 16-1 summarizes the procedures in carrying out the guideline publicly traded company valuation method.

The guideline publicly traded company method usually uses measures that give an indication of the value of the equity directly, such as price to economic income multiples. However, sometimes the market value of the total invested capital (MVIC) is estimated and then the value of the interest-bearing, long-term debt is subtracted in order to estimate the indicated value for the subject equity.

Because the guideline publicly traded company method usually relies on publicly traded minority ownership interest stock transaction data, the value estimated usually is a minority ownership interest value—on a fully marketable basis. If the analyst is valuing a minority ownership interest in a private company, it normally requires the procedure of applying a valuation discount for lack of marketability. If the analyst is valuing a controlling ownership interest, a valuation premium for ownership control may or may not be appropriate. And such a valuation premium may be fully—or partially—offset by a valuation discount for the illiquidity of the privately held company controlling ownership interest.

This chapter should be helpful both for analysts performing a valuation by using the guideline publicly traded company method and for those individuals responsible for reviewing and evaluating a valuation report that has used this valuation method.

Bibliography

Alford, Andrew W. "The Effect of the Set of Comparable Firms on the Accuracy of the Price-Earnings Valuation Method." *Journal of Accounting Research*, Spring 1992, pp. 94–108.

Barron, Michael S. "When Will the Tax Court Allow a Discount for Lack of Marketability?" *Journal of Taxation*, January 1997, pp. 46–50.

Bielinski, Daniel W. "The Comparable-Company Approach: Measuring the True Value of Privately Held Firms." *Corporate Cashflow Magazine*, October 1990, pp. 64–68.

Bjorklund, Victoria B., and Susan A. Meisel. "Valuation: When Are Comparables Comparable Enough?" *Practical Tax Lawyer*, Spring 1991, pp. 45–47.

Cowhey, Gregory J., and Sandra A. Rodio. "Is One Market Multiple Better than Any Other?" *Proceedings of the ASA International Appraisal Conference Business Valuation Program*, New Orleans, June 30, 1992.

Exhibit 16–1

PROCEDURES IN THE GUIDELINE PUBLICLY TRADED COMPANY METHOD

1. Set criteria for selection of guideline publicly traded companies.

2. Search for and identify the companies that meet the criteria.

3. Decide on the relevant time period for comparative analysis of the subject company and the guideline companies.

4. Obtain the guideline companies' financial statements for the time period decided in Step 3.

5. Broaden or narrow the criteria, if necessary, to provide the best group of guideline companies, adding or deleting companies according to the revised criteria.

6. Analyze and adjust the subject and/or guideline company financial statements as appropriate (Chapters 7 and 8).

7. Compile comparative financial multiples for the subject and guideline companies (Chapter 9).

8. Decide which guideline company value measures to use.

9. Obtain the market price of each guideline company's stock as of the valuation date. (If market value of invested capital is used in any of the value measures, it is necessary to obtain the market value of all the guideline companies' securities that are included in their invested capital.)

10. Compile guideline company value measure tables for the value measures decided in Step 8.

11. Based on analysis of the value measure tables in conjunction with the comparative financial analysis of the subject and guideline companies, decide on the appropriate multiple for the subject company for each value measure to be used.

12. Multiply each value measure to be used by the relevant financial variable for the subject company to get indications of value according to each value measure.

13. Weight or otherwise correlate the indications of value from Step 12 to reach an estimate of "value as if publicly traded" (a marketable, minority ownership interest value).

14. Make adjustments to this value, if appropriate, for factors in the definition of value but not reflected in the value as if publicly traded, such as discount for lack of marketability and/or premium for control. Also, adjust any other elements of value, if appropriate, that were adjusted out of the guideline company analysis, such as nonoperating assets.

Fishman, Jay E. "The Alternate Market Comparison Approach in Valuing Closely Held Enterprises." *FAIR$HARE: The Matrimonial Law Monthly*, October 1988. pp. 7–8.

Fowler, Bradley A. "How Do You Handle It?" *Business Valuation Review*, September 1996, pp. 136–37.

_____. "The Problem with Rules of Thumb in the Valuation of Closely Held Entities." *FAIR$HARE: The Matrimonial Law Monthly*, October 1984, pp. 13–15.

Graham, Michael D. "Selection of Market Multiples in Business Valuation." *Business Valuation Review*, March 1990, pp. 8–12.

Hickman, Kent, and Glenn H. Petry. "A Comparison of Stock Price Predictions Using Court Accepted Formulas, Dividend Discount, and P/E Models." *Financial Management*, Summer 1990, pp. 76–87.

McCarter, Mary B., and Kathryn F. Aschwald. "The Market Comparable Approach Using Public Market Data" (Chapter 14). In *Handbook of Business Valuation*, Thomas L. West and Jeffrey D. Jones, eds. New York: John Wiley & Sons, 1992, pp. 145–65.

McDonagh, Christopher S., and John M. McDonagh. "Valuing a Target's Ability to Compete in the Market." *Mergers & Acquisitions*, September/October 1995, pp. 22–25.

Mercer, Z. Christopher. "Public Multiples/Private Companies: Grappling with the Fundamental Issues." *Proceedings of the 1996 IBA National Conference*, Orlando, FL, January 25–26, 1996.

Randisi, Martin P. "Comparable Company Method of Valuing a Closely-Held Business." *FAIR$HARE: The Matrimonial Law Monthly*, January 1991, pp. 3–5.

Schreier, W. Terrance, and O. Maurice Joy. "Judicial Valuation of 'Close' Corporation Stock: *Alice in Wonderland* Revisited." *Oklahoma Law Review* 31 (1978), pp. 853–85.

Summers, S. Chris. "The Myth of Public Company Comparisons." *Business Valuation Review*, June 1992, pp. 59–62.

Taub, Maxwell J. "Can Market Comparables Be Used in Valuing Small Businesses? *IBBA Journal*, October 1991, pp. 10–14.

Trugman, Gary R. "Using the Market Approach to Value Small and Medium-Sized Businesses." *Proceedings of the Institute of Business Appraisers' 1996 National Conference*, Orlando, FL, January 25–26, 1996.

_____. "Mid-Size Companies—How Do They Differ from Small Businesses and Publicly Held Firms?" *IBBA Journal*, Fall 1993, pp. 25–32.

West, Thomas L. "Pricing Businesses: The Use of Comparables." *The Business Broker*, June 1992, pp. 1–4.

Chapter 17

Public Company Data: What's Available and How to Get It Easily and Inexpensively

Ready access to public company capital market data is essential for business appraisers. This is because several valuation methods use fundamental financial data from guideline publicly traded companies. A careful analysis of the fundamental financial information of public companies is necessary in order to develop meaningful comparisons between publicly traded companies and privately held companies.

There are more relatively small public companies available for comparison than most people realize. For example, of the 12,000 public companies covered by Disclosure, in March of 1997 there were almost 2,500 with market capitalization under $50 million. We often use companies up to 10 times the size of the subject in the guideline publicly traded company method. Gary Trugman suggests that up to 25 times the size of the subject still provides a meaningful comparison.[1] The following table presents the number of companies in various size categories included in the Disclosure database.

| Market Capitalization | Number of Companies | |
(Shares Outstanding × Closing Price)	March 1997	March 1996
Under $5 million	317	246
$5 to $10 million	382	358
$10 to $25 million	854	839
$25 to $50 million	901	863
$50 to $100 million	1,172	1,064

In addition to the increasing number of small public companies available, the other factor facilitating greater use of the guideline publicly traded company method for valuing smaller businesses is the greatly reduced cost of getting the information. This is due to the requirement, starting in 1996, that all companies filing with the SEC must do so on the Electronic Data Gathering and Retrieval System (EDGAR), discussed below. While it used to cost thousands of dollars per year to access SEC filings, access to all EDGAR filings is *free* through the Internet. Several vendors also offer inexpensive packages to facilitate the use of EDGAR.

The fundamental financial data of publicly traded companies is available from an assortment of sources in a variety of formats. The Securities and Exchange Commission (SEC) EDGAR database and financial reporting publishers, such as Moody's Investors Service, Standard & Poor's Corporation, Disclosure Incorporated, and Global Securities Inc., provide access to capital market data. When selecting a source of public company financial data, analysts should be aware of the difference between "as reported" data and "recast" data. For example, an SEC Form 10-K purchased from Disclosure or accessed from the EDGAR database provides the exact financial information "as reported" by the company to the SEC. On the other hand, many financial reporting services "recast" the company financial data in order to provide consistency within their database. For instance, Disclosure "templates" fi-

---

[1]Gary Trugman, "Using the Market Approach to Value Small and Medium-Sized Businesses," presentation at the 1996 Annual Conference of the Institute of Business Appraisers.

nancial data from company statements of operations and balance sheets. As an example, if a company reports their research and development expense in five separate line items, Disclosure will add all five line items and state the expense as one item. In this way, Disclosure attempts to consistently present research and development costs of all companies in its database.

EDGAR

With the arrival of the EDGAR system, analysts can now access "as reported" financial data from over 15,000 companies. There is no charge for the data when accessed directly through the Internet. The EDGAR database, conceptualized by SEC Chairman John Shad in 1983 and started in 1984, is an effort to improve the speed and collection of financial documents required by the various U.S. securities laws and regulations. Starting in 1996, all public companies subject to the Securities Act or the Exchange Act must file specific documents electronically. Although EDGAR does not hold every single type of disclosure document, it does contain the disclosure documents most valuable to analysts, such as Forms 10-K, 10-Q, and 8-K.

The EDGAR database provides benefits not only to investors, filers, and the SEC staff, but also to analysts. With EDGAR, analysts have a quick and economical means of obtaining disclosure information, using fairly advanced search and retrieval capabilities.

The EDGAR database is accessible from the Internet, as well as from a variety of commercial vendors. With an Internet connection, analysts can access disclosure documents free of charge from both the SEC and New York University (NYU) Stern School of Business Internet home pages. The formatting is not good, but there is freeware available to convert the documents to a more convenient format. Several companies provide EDGAR documents with value-added features, such as Boolean search capabilities or preformatted documents.

Because analysts who download documents from the NYU and SEC Internet sites often experience formatting problems that require time to correct, they may find it more cost-effective to use a commercial service that sells EDGAR documents for a low fee, such as Global Securities' GSI On-line. GSI On-line's *LivEDGAR* database allows users to download specific pages of a document without formatting problems or to search across the entire EDGAR database using key words. As of this writing, *LivEDGAR* costs only $10 to access plus $1 per minute; an experienced researcher can retrieve a 10-K in a few minutes.

To take the value-added features a step further, commercial vendors such as Disclosure have added all sorts of bells and whistles to their traditional database products in order to maintain their market share in selling public company financial data. For example, Disclosure developed a product called *Global Access,* which indexes EDGAR documents so that analysts can perform sophisticated searches and obtain selected portions of documents in a short amount of time. In other words, when analysts access the EDGAR database from the SEC site or *LivEDGAR*, they cannot limit the printout to specific portions of a 10-K, such as company, name, ticker symbol, Standard Industrial Classification (SIC) Code, balance sheet, and statement of operations. With Disclosure's *Global Access*, researchers can essentially perform a guideline publicly traded company search and download only the portions of the source documents of the selected guideline companies that are needed. However, this value-added database comes with a price, and analysts need to consider the costs associated with using such a service.

There is another important distinction between EDGAR via the SEC or NYU Internet sites and EDGAR via a commercial vendor. The SEC will only provide a two-year archive, plus the current year, of public disclosure documents. Commercial vendors will maintain a much longer historical archive. For example, in March 1999, analysts will find Forms 10-K from 1997, 1998, and January through March of 1999 from the SEC and NYU Internet sites. On the other hand, analysts will find Forms 10-K from 1995 through March of 1999 from the commercial vendors, such as Global Securities, Inc.

Additional Sources of Financial Data

Disclosure Incorporated, Moody's Investors Service, and Standard & Poor's Corporation are the most well-known commercial publishers of financial data with respect to publicly traded companies. While each publisher provides the same fundamental information, the manner in which they present the data varies. Publishers are continually seeking to provide value-added products that contain not only financial information but also flexible search capabilities for their electronic products, or additional data such as debt ratings or earnings estimates.

Most of the publishers of financial data make the data available in both electronic (on-line and CD-ROM) and print formats. In general, on-line products tend to be the most frequently updated sources, with CD-ROM and print sources coming in second and third. CD-ROMs are often more flexible to use than on-line sources. CD-ROMs are usually designed for the novice database searcher, while on-line sources tend to require more sophisticated search experience.

The most cost-effective source depends on the user's skill, knowledge of the database, and frequency of use. It may be less expensive per search for an analyst with excellent database skills to use an on-line service such as Dialog. However, if the analyst uses the database several times a day, the cost per search may be lower with a CD-ROM product. With the user-friendly, powerful electronic sources of financial data available, it is difficult to imagine a situation where the print equivalent would be the least expensive alternative, except when the data required is not available electronically. The selection of sources depends on the user's level of skill and on the availability of time and money.

Disclosure Incorporated

Disclosure has been selling public company financial data for 30 years. Disclosure provides this data through a variety of sources, including its own clearinghouse of publicly available documents in print form. Disclosure also provides research services for a fee. The *Disclosure SEC Database* contains financial statement information for more than 12,000 publicly traded companies. The *SEC Database* is available in several versions and through a variety of on-line and CD-ROM products. The following commercial vendors offer this database, although versions and prices of the database may differ from vendor to vendor:

- Dialog Information Services.
- Compuserve.
- America Online.
- Microsoft Network.
- DataTimes.
- LEXIS/NEXIS.
- Profound.
- Dow Jones News Retrieval.

For example, an abridged version of the database is available on Compuserve for a price much lower than that charged from the major on-line services such as LEXIS/NEXIS. Two versions of the database are available on CD-ROM: they are called *Compact D/SEC* and *Laser D/SEC*.

Two features that distinguish Disclosure from its competitors are (1) the availability of Zack's earnings estimates for most of the companies listed and (2) stock ownership profiles. On the other hand, the Disclosure business descriptions are not as comprehensive as those found on Moody's and Standard & Poor's.

Disclosure recently introduced its powerful *Global Access* (described above) and *EdgarPlus* databases, which integrate EDGAR documents with their archive of SEC documents.

Moody's Investors Service

In addition to its databases of U.S. and International public company financial data, Moody's Investors Service is well-known for its corporate bond ratings: *Moody's Manuals* and *Investment Guides*.

Electronic. Moody's Company Data CD-ROM product contains business and financial information on over 10,000 public companies. The database is also available on-line from Dialog. The distinguishing features of the *Moody's Company Database* are (1) the detailed company business descriptions and history and (2) corporate bond rating actions. Moody's provides enhanced access to EDGAR filings to the subscribers of its CD-ROM product.

Print. *Moody's Manuals* are comprehensive guides to public companies divided into eight volumes. A subscription also includes a twice-weekly *News Reports* that keeps readers up-to-date on mergers and acquisitions, new products and contracts, new issues, financing, and other significant events. There is a master index to identify the industry volume in which each of the over 15,000 public companies is included.

Standard & Poor's Corporation

Electronic. *Standard & Poor's Corporation Records* provides financial and descriptive information on over 12,000 public companies. The database is available on CD-ROM. An on-line version of the database, *Corporate Descriptions plus News*, is available on Dialog and on Compuserve. The on-line version also provides business and financial news along with each company record. Both on-line and CD-ROM versions of the product provide S&P issue-by-issue debt ratings, as well as detailed stock data and excellent company descriptions. The CD-ROM version also contains data on 45,000 private companies, extracted from the *S&P Register of Corporations*, as well as data on 70,000 executives extracted from the *S&P Register of Executives and Directors*.

Compustat is Standard & Poor's "Cadillac" source of public company financial data in a CD-ROM format. Although it carries a hefty price tag, *Compustat* is one of the few sources of significant historical coverage available electronically. It not only contains 20 years of annual financial data on approximately 12,000 companies, it also includes 12 years of quarterly information and 240 months of stock prices.

Print. *Standard & Poor's Corporation Records* is also available in a six-volume set. Companies are arranged alphabetically. A Classified Index of Industrial Companies is published annually as part of the *Standard & Poor's Corporation Records*. This index is classified by SIC code and includes every public company that appears in the *S&P Corporation Records*. A *Daily News* volume, containing current and archival business and financial news on the companies listed in the set, is also available.

The *Standard & Poor's Register* is perhaps the most comprehensive directory of companies by SIC group. It does not distinguish, however, between public and private companies. Nonetheless, if a company is public and it has been quoted in the *National Daily Quotation Service*, it will be listed in the *National Quotation Bureau Monthly Stock Summary*. Therefore, the *S&P Register* and the *National Quotation Bureau Monthly Stock Summary* can be used together to develop a list of possible guideline publicly traded companies within a particular SIC group.

Other Sources of Data

Directory of Companies Required to File Annual Reports with the Securities and Exchange Commission under the Securities Exchange Act of 1934. This annual publication lists companies alphabetically and classified by industry group according to the Standard Industrial Classification (SIC) Manual. The latest edition (September 30, 1996) lists 12,977 companies required to file annual reports with the SEC.

Company Intelligence is an on-line combined directory and company news file published by Information Access Company. It contains current address, and financial and marketing information on more than 160,000 private and public U.S. companies. Over 130,000 of these companies are listed in the five-volume set of *Ward's Business Directory*. A search by primary SIC code on public companies can be accomplished in command-based language. This database is available on Dialog, File 479.

Media General Plus provides timely and detailed financial and stock price information on approximately 9,000 public companies. This on-line data source covers all New York Stock Exchange and American Stock Exchange companies, plus all Nasdaq companies and selected over-the-counter companies. This database is available on Dialog, File 546.

Summary

Time will tell if EDGAR will replace many of the traditional sources of public company financial data. After a shaky start due to budgetary constraints, the SEC is committed to maintaining and enhancing the EDGAR database. In a recent speech, SEC Commission Chairman Arthur Levitt called on Wall Street to expand its use of the Internet for prospectus delivery. The chairman also stated that the SEC is moving rapidly to modernize EDGAR, including enhancements such as graphics capabilities that would include charts and photos.

While the SEC is continuing its commitment to public access of public company financial data via the EDGAR database, commercial publishers are vying for the public's dollars for information that was once exclusively in their domain. Exhibit 17-1 is a summary reference table of electronic sources of public data. This table provides a quick overview of the sources discussed in this chapter, as well as the price (as of press time) of the various products. We expect better and more cost-effective means of obtaining SEC disclosure documents in the future, thus ensuring an excellent source of public company financial documents for analysts.

Exhibit 17–1

ELECTRONIC SOURCES OF PUBLIC COMPANY DATA

Vendor	Product	Format	Scope	Special Features	Cost
Disclosure Incorporated 1-800-843-7747 http://www.disclosure.com	SEC Database	CD-ROM and on-line	Financial statements for over 12,000 public companies trading in 3 major exchanges	I/B/E/S earnings estimates; stock ownership profiles	$6000/year w/monthly updates
	Global Access	Internet	EDGAR filings	A "high-end" product; extensive search capabilities; filings are indexed for quick, precise retrieval	Price varies; contact Disclosure
	EDGAR Access	Internet	EDGAR filings	Free, personalized alerts	$4.95 per month for 25 EDGAR filings; add'l reports $2.00
Global Securities Information, Inc. 1-800-669-1154 http://www.gsionline.com	LIVEDGAR	Internet or Dial-up	EDGAR filings	Preformatted searches; ability to download or print a list of filings at once w/o additional formatting	$10 initial log-on fee; $1.00 per minute thereafter
Moody's Investors Service 1-800-342-5647 http://www.moodys.com	Moody's Company Data	CD-ROM or on-line	Business descriptions and complete financial statements on over 10,000 public companies trading in 4 major exchanges	Good company descriptions and histories; credit/debt ratings	$4500/year w/monthly updates
	Moody's Company Data with EDGAR	CD-ROM w/dial-up connection	Same as above, but includes EDGAR filings	A "high-end" product; ability to perform complex searches on CD-ROM, then dial in to an SEC feed to obtain the source documents; ability to create an archive of EDGAR documents on CD-ROM; no add'l formatting required	Contact Moody's
Securities and Exchange Commission http://www.sec.gov	EDGAR	Internet	EDGAR filings	No charge for filings	Cost of an Internet connection
Standard & Poor's Corporation 1-800-221-5277 http://www.stockinfo. standardpoor.com	S&P Corporations	CD-ROM and on-line	Financial and descriptive information on over 12,000 public companies	Excellent business descriptions; vital statistics on 45,000 private companies	$4000/year w/monthly updates
	Compustat PC-Plus	CD-ROM	A numeric database containing historical financial and statistical data on over 13,000 companies	A "high-end" source; excellent source of historical data	Contact Standard & Poor's

Bibliography

Bates, Mary Ellen. "Where's EDGAR Today? Finding SEC Filings Online." *Database,* June 1996, pp. 41–50.

DiVittorio, Martha Montes. "Evaluating Sources of U.S. Company Data." *Database,* August 1994, pp. 39–44.

"Enhanced EDGAR Site Has Email Capabilities and Itegrates with Microsoft Excel 97." *Shannon Pratt's Business Valuation Update,* September 1997, p. 5.

Jefferson, Mozette. "Through EDGAR on the Internet: How to Access SEC Filings Cheaply and Easily." *Shannon Pratt's Business Valuation Update*, November 1995, pp. 6–7.

_____. "Convert Raw Internet Filings into Easy-to-Read Formatting." *Shannon Pratt's Business Valuation Update*, December 1995, p. 7.

Lang, Eva, and Jan Tudor. "Electronic Sources of Business Valuation Data." An appendix in *Guide to Business Valuations*, 7th ed., by Jay E. Fishman, Shannon P. Pratt, J. Clifford Griffith, and D. Keith Wilson. Fort Worth, TX: Practitioners Publishing Company, 1997, pp. 4-55–4-72.

O'Leary, Mick. "The Many Faces of Disclosure." *Database,* October/November 1996, pp. 91–92.

Penhollow, John, and Gary Purnhagen. "EDGAR." In *Securities Filings 1996,* by Alan K. Austin. New York: Practicing Law Institute, 1996, pp. 33–131.

Tudor, Jan Davis. "For Free SEC Documents, Call EDGAR." *Business Valuation Review*, December 1995, pp. 174–77.

Resource List: Publicly Traded Company Financial Data

Major Sources

EDGAR Database
Securities and Exchange Commission
http://www.sec.gov/cgi-gin/srch-edgar

New York University Stern School of Business
http://www.edgar.stern.nyu.edu

EDGAR Conversion Software (freeware)
Available from the above two sources, as well as from
Business Valuation Resources
http://www.transport.com/~shannonp

Standard & Poor's Corporation
25 Broadway, 16th Floor
New York, NY 10004
(800) 221-5277

Compustat
7400 South Alton Court
Englewood, CO 80112
(800) 523-4534

Disclosure Incorporated
888 Seventh Avenue, 44th Floor
New York, NY 10106
(800) 846-0365

Moody's Investors Service
1 Sansome St., Suite 3100
San Francisco, CA 94104
(800) 700-1709

Additional Sources

IRIN Company Database
Investor Relations Information Network
http://www.irin.com/colist/html
Contains brief company information, some press releases, and an-
nual/quarterly reports for selected companies.

Corporate Financials Online
Corporate Financials Online, Inc.
http://www.cfonews.com
Corporate Financials Online, Inc. (CFO) provides news announcements
and investor information issued by public companies. News is posted on-
line by CFO customers using CFO software. News announcements are
posted on-line after distribution to the financial news wires and other
media.

Market Guide Investment Center
Market Guide, Inc.
http://www.marketguide.com
This investment bank's site provides financial and investment information for over 8,300 publicly traded companies. Subscriptions to some
forms of information are available.

On-line Service Providers

Knight-Ridder Information
Dialog
2440 W. El Camino Real
Mountain View, CA 94040
(800) 3DIALOG

CompuServe Information Service
5000 Arlington Centre Blvd.
PO Box 20212
Columbus, OH 43220
(800) 848-8990

Dow Jones News Retrieval
Dow Jones Business Information Services
PO Box 300
Princeton, NJ 08543-0300
(609) 452-1511

Lexis-Nexis
9393 Springboro Pike
PO Box 933-NR
Dayton, OH 45401
(800) 544-7390

Datatimes
14000 Quail Springs Parkway
Oklahoma City, OK 73134
(405) 751-6400

Profound, Inc.
1100 Regency Parkway, 4th Floor
Cary, NC 27511
(800) HELP-560

Chapter 18

The Comparative Transaction Method

The conceptual underpinnings of the comparative transaction method are the same as those for the guideline publicly traded company method. That is, the analyst relates the price at which the transaction was consummated to the financial fundamentals of the business that was sold. Under the comparative transaction method, the analyst estimates the value of the subject business by relying on information gathered from transactions where most (or all) of the ownership of comparative companies has changed hands. This method is categorized as a market approach method. This is because the transactions that are used as valuation evidence come from "the market." That market is where willing buyers and willing sellers, each looking out for their own economic self-interests, exchange property at a negotiated price.

The ownership interest transferred in these transactions often includes the entire capital structure—not necessarily just the equity—of the business. The company being sold may have been either publicly owned or privately owned prior to the transaction. The nature of the transaction—and the nature and availability of transactional data about it—varies much more than public market guideline company transactional data.

There may be different value conclusions indicated based on different valuation criteria and under different circumstances. Merger and acquisition transactions should be examined as carefully as possible when they are used for guidance in the market approach to valuing a company. When the data have been interpreted carefully, this method may provide compelling evidence of value for small businesses and professional practices.

Overview of the Comparative Transaction Method

The analyst can derive indications of value (1) from data on the prices at which entire companies—or operating units of companies—have been sold or (2) from the prices at which significant ownership interests in companies changed hands. Again, this market approach method emphasizes the economic principle of substitution; that is, a buyer will pay no more for something than for a substitute that provides equivalent economic utility. Data from arm's-length transactions involving comparative companies are used to develop relationships—or value measures—between the price paid for the company and the underlying financial fundamental performance of the property. Then, the analyst applies these relationships to the underlying financial fundamental data regarding the subject business.

This method of valuation begins with identifying and analyzing negotiated, arm's-length transfers of comparative, or guideline, transactions. In this way, this method is similar to the guideline publicly traded company method described in Chapter 16. Also, the underlying financial fundamental data of the guideline companies used in this method are similar to the data used in the guideline publicly traded company method. Namely, the analyst develops value measures by comparing the price paid for an acquisition to the target company's income statement variables and balance sheet variables, such as the following:

- Gross or net revenue.
- Earnings before interest and taxes (EBIT).
- Earnings before depreciation, interest, and taxes (EBDIT).
- Gross cash flow (net income plus interest and noncash charges) available to invested capital.
- Debt-free net income (net income plus interest)
- Discretionary earnings (see Chapter 19).
- Book value.
- Tangible book value.
- Adjusted book value.
- Adjusted tangible book value.

Gross revenue multiples are used often enough in valuing small businesses and professional practices that a separate chapter, Chapter 20, has been devoted to that topic. Also, discretionary earnings has had wide enough recognition and usage that a new, separate chapter (Chapter 19) has been devoted to that topic.

When the value pricing multiple used is a measure of economic income, such as EBIT, EBDIT, net cash flow, gross cash flow, or debt-free net income, this method is sometimes referred to as an income approach method (or a capitalization of economic income method). In Chapter 15, we discussed the capitalized economic income method. When the valuation pricing multiple is derived from a present value discount rate, in this book, we call that an income approach method. When the valuation pricing multiple is derived from empirical market transactions, we categorize the method as a market approach method.

Reliable transactional data on sales of all or most of the ownership of public or private companies is generally difficult to locate. Most of the transactional data on small businesses and professional practices are gathered from business and practice brokers and merger and acquisition intermediaries. The databases that provide this information are the subject of Chapter 21, Comparative Transaction Databases. Experienced analysts recognize that imperfect information will have to be analyzed and adjusted, if necessary, before being put to use.

In contrast to the guideline publicly traded company method, comparative transactions involve all or most of the target company's invested capital—rather than the target company's equity alone. This is because the transactions often involve the entire capital structure. Or if they do not, at least the acquiring control owner usually has the power to change the target company's capital structure.

Also, it is common to consider comparative transactions over a fairly long time period. This might involve analyzing transactions over several years in the subject company's industry or similar industries. This is partly because there are fewer transactions. However, this is also because acquisition pricing multiples seem to fluctuate somewhat less over time than do public stock market valuation multiples.

Generally speaking, the criteria used for selection of merger and acquisition guideline transactions are similar to those used for selecting guideline publicly traded companies. However, because of the fewer companies available, the criteria may have to be broadened somewhat.

General Framework of the Comparative Transaction Method

There is a general systematic process—or framework—to applying market approach methods to the valuation of small businesses and professional practices. The basic steps of this systematic process are summarized as follows:

1. Research the appropriate market in order to obtain as much information as possible on recent sale or merger transactions involving similar small businesses or practices that may be comparative to the subject company.
2. From the information on consummated merger and sale transactions gathered in step 1, select a sample of "guideline" companies (i.e., companies that are similar from a risk/expected return investment perspective or from an operational perspective) that are comparative enough to the subject company—in terms of characteristics such as industry, product line specialization, geographic markets served, historical and prospective growth, and so forth—to provide meaningful valuation guidance.
3. To the extent possible, verify the information by confirming that the transactional data obtained are factually accurate and that the sale or merger transactions reflect arm's-length market considerations. (If the guideline transactions were not at arm's-length market conditions, adjustments to the transactional data may be necessary.) This verification procedure may also elicit additional information about the current market conditions for the possible sale or merger of the subject business.
4. Select relevant units of pricing comparison or valuation pricing multiples (e.g., price to gross revenue, EBIT, EBDIT, etc.).
5. Compare the guideline company sale or merger transactions with the subject small business or practice using the basic elements of comparison and then adjust the sale or merger price of each guideline transaction appropriately to the subject business—or eliminate the sale or merger transaction as a guideline for future consideration.
6. Reconcile the various value indications produced from the analysis of the guideline transactions into a single value indication or into a range of values. In an imprecise market—subject to varying economics—a range of values may sometimes be a better conclusion for the subject business than a single value estimate.

When is the Comparative Transaction Method Most Useful?

The initial value derived from the merger and acquisition method, before adjustment for factors such as size of the subject block and degree of marketability, is an indication of transaction prices of substantial ownership interests, usually controlling ownership interests. The characteristics of each transaction need to be analyzed carefully in order for the analyst to make judgments about what adjustments may be necessary in order to use the transaction value multiples as guidance in a specific valuation assignment.

Standard of Value

Merger and acquisition transaction prices may be representative of *fair market value*, *investment value*, or something in between. At one end of the spectrum, a sale to a pure financial buyer (i.e., a buyer who is buying strictly for a return on investment from the company as a stand-alone entity) usually would be representative of fair market value. At the other end of the spectrum, the more unique the synergies between the acquirer and the acquiree, the more the transaction is representative of investment value rather than fair market value. This is because the pricing may reflect the synergistic benefits to a *particular* buyer rather than the price a typical *hypothetical* buyer would pay (as required in the definition of fair market value).

When the comparative transactions include the presumption that the buyer will become an owner/operator, the normal cost of compensation for the operator of the business should be one of the factors taken into consideration when analyzing the comparative transactions, except when the value measure used is the multiple of discretionary cash flow, which is *before* owners' compensation, as discussed in Chapter 19.

There is no formula to sort out the amount by which a price that was paid reflected synergistic value over and above a strict fair market value price. This is a continuing source of contention in using such transactional data for resolution of disputed valuations and a challenge to the analyst's judgment.

Characteristics of Value

Control Ownership versus Minority Ownership.   Since mergers and acquisitions usually represent control transactions, they are most directly relevant for valuation of other controlling ownership interests.

If valuing a noncontrolling (or minority) ownership interest, it usually is necessary to apply a minority ownership interest discount to a value indicated by merger and acquisition data. It may also be appropriate to apply an additional valuation discount for lack of marketability.

Marketable versus Nonmarketable Ownership Interests.
The issue of adjustments for marketability—or the lack of marketability—relative to actual control transactions is a subject of continuing debate among business valuation professionals.

In many respects, this controversy is more semantic than real. Analysts recognize that a controlling (or substantial) ownership interest in a company obviously is not as marketable as is a publicly traded stock. Publicly traded stock can be sold in seconds at (or very near) a recently established and known price, with cash delivered to the seller within three business days. Thus, if merger and acquisition transactional data are used as guidance to estimate fair market value—that is, a cash equivalent value as of a certain date—certain adjustments may be appropriate.

The illiquidity of small businesses is illustrated when one recognizes that, in many situations, small business transactions simply could not be agreed to without creative payment structures, such as seller financing or earn-out provisions. These creative transactional structures facilitate a more active market for the target company's ownership interest than there would be if the only transactional structure available was a one-time cash payment to the seller. Even making the necessary adjustments to the comparative transactions to account for their creative transactional structures may not completely capture the illiquidity of many small businesses.

Premise of Value

Sometimes, but not always, it is possible to analyze a transaction in order to estimate the extent to which a price represents a going-concern premise of value or a liquidation premise of value. Often, a transaction price reflects some combination of the two. In these instances, some of the assets acquired will be liquidated, while other required assets will be operated as a going concern. This is a matter that varies on a case-to-case basis.

Prior Subject Company Transactions

Past sale transactions involving the subject company may be fruitful subjects to analyze in order to obtain guidance about value.

Prior Subject Company Transfers

When the subject company has a history of ownership transfers between shareholders, those transactions should be analyzed in order to determine the extent to which they provide an indication of value. Of course, that indication of value should be applicable to the specific ownership interest that is the objective and purpose of the current valuation assignment. Some prior transactions in the company's shares may involve unique circumstances that do not fit the typical conditions that are indicative of fair market value.

Many small businesses and professional practices have share-holder agreements or partnership agreements that include what are known as "buy-sell" provisions. These provisions are designed to smooth the potential disruption in the operation of the company when ownership interests change hands. The structure of these provisions vary from company to company. Some of these provisions are accommodating to—and some are restrictive of—ownership transfers. Prior transactions in the subject company's capital accounts may provide evidence of value. However, as with other transactional data, the analyst should not rely on prices paid in prior subject company transfers without considering the circumstances surrounding the transactions.

Subject Company Prior Changes of Control

If the subject company itself has had a change of ownership control in the last several years, the transaction may be an excellent source of value measures. The value measures used would generally be the same as those discussed earlier. The value measures indicated by the prior transaction may need some adjustment in order to reflect (1) internal changes in the company or (2) changes in merger and acquisition market conditions for companies in the industry.

Prior Acquisitions by the Subject Company

If the company has made one or more acquisitions in the last several years, such transactions may prove to be excellent sources of value measures. Again, adjustments may be necessary for changes between the dates of the acquisitions and the relevant valuation date.

It may be easy for the analyst to overlook such acquisitions because they may not come to light in any of the search procedures normally used to identify merger and acquisition transactions. The subject company may be the *only* source for such data. However, it is typically a very comprehensive and reliable source. Therefore, if considering using a merger and acquisition comparative transaction method at all, it often is a good idea to ask the subject company management whether they have made any acquisitions.

Elements of Comparison

A number of elements of comparison should be considered, to the extent the information is available, when selecting and analyzing each comparative transaction in the market approach valuation of a small business or professional practice. Some of the potentially important elements of comparison are summarized below:

1. The legal rights of business ownership or business equity (whether invested capital, stock ownership, or partnership units) that were conveyed in the guideline transaction.

2. The existence of any special financing terms or arrangements between the buyer and the seller. These may include short-term or interim employment agreements with the seller and (quite frequently) earn-out provisions with regard to the payment of the purchase price.

3. Whether the elements of arm's-length sale conditions existed; whether the transaction was, in any way, a distress sale; or whether there were any transferability restrictions related to the ownership interest that would indicate anything other than an arm's-length, independent sale.

4. The economic conditions that existed in the appropriate secondary market at the time of the sale or merger transaction. This includes consideration of the local economic conditions in the geographic area principally served by the business or practice—and of the economic conditions in the industry principally served by the business or practice.

5. The degree of industry specialization of the comparative company —and the particular industry in which the business specializes (e.g., is that industry on the incline or the decline?).

6. The physical characteristics of the comparative company—in terms of number of operating locations, offices, favorable versus unfavorable leases, short-term versus long-term leases, new/modern offices versus old/antiquated operations, and so on.

7. The functional characteristics of the comparative company—in terms of product lines and specializations.

8. The human capital characteristics of the comparative company— such as number of key managers, age and credentials of key managers, business development effectiveness of owners, employment agreements with managers, age and qualifications of staff, annual turnover at the manager and/or staff levels, and so forth.

9. The economic characteristics of the comparative company—such as average billing rates for each level of professional (in a professional practice), strength of client relationships, current backlog of client work, and so forth.

10. The inclusion of other assets in the comparative company sale transaction. This may include the sale of a bundle—or a portfolio —of assets, which could include owned real estate (and/or below-market leases on real estate owned by the owners), noncompete agreements from the selling owners, and so on.

11. The extent to which employment and/or noncompete agreements were included in the guideline transaction.

Formulas or Rules of Thumb

Some industries have rules of thumb (sometimes given an aura of credibility by being referred to as "industry valuation formulas") about how companies in their industry are valued for transfer of controlling ownership interests. On the one hand, if such rules of thumb are widely disseminated and referenced in the industry, they probably should not be totally ignored. On the other hand, there is rarely credible evidence as to how such rules were developed or how well they actually relate to empirical transactional data.

Rules of thumb usually are quite simplistic. Consequently, they fail to recognize how differences in either operating characteristics or assets from one company to another affect the valuation. They also fail to recognize changes in conditions for companies in various industries from one time period to another. Furthermore, it is common for companies in many industries to sell on terms other than cash. In this way, the "prices" generated by the rules of thumb often are not cash equivalent values. Consequently, they rarely, if ever, should be used without other, more reliable and more rigorous valuation methods.

At times, it seems that sources of rules of thumb are everywhere. There are many anecdotes about the prices of certain businesses. Some trade associations publish compilations of transactions and "How to Value Your Business" articles. Business brokers and other industry sources will occasionally be available with helpful observations about standard yardsticks.

Under a heading "Cautions about Using Formulas" in his book *Handbook of Small Business Valuation Formulas and Rules of Thumb*, Glenn Desmond makes the following observations:

Formulas Are General in Nature
Formulas are general in nature. Adjustments must be made to account for variations in revenue and cash-flow trends; location; lease; condition of the plant, fixtures, and equipment; reputation with customers, suppliers, bankers, and others; special skills required; difficulty in starting the business; and so forth.

There Is No Single, All-Purpose Formula
There is no single formula that will work for every business. Formula multipliers offer ease of calculation, but they also obscure details. This can be misleading. Net revenue multipliers are particularly troublesome because they are blind to the business's expense and profit history. It is easy to see how two businesses in any given industry group might have the same annual net revenue (ANR), yet show very different cash flows. A proper valuation will go beyond formulas and include a full financial analysis whenever possible.[1]

Adjustments to Comparative Transactions

In general, the same types of adjustments should be made to the financial statements of companies involved in the comparative transactions as are made to the financial statements of the subject company. As described in more detail in the guideline publicly traded company method

---

[1]Glenn M. Desmond, *Handbook of Small Business Valuation Formulas and Rules of Thumb*, 3d ed. (Camden, ME: Valuation Press, 1993), p. 12.

discussion (Chapter 16), some main categories of adjustments include the following:

- Remove nonrecurring items from the income statements.
- Put comparative companies and the subject company on a comparable accounting basis (e.g., adjust any companies accounting for inventory on LIFO basis to FIFO basis, use consistent depreciation methods and lives).
- Adjust for nonoperating items such as excess assets or asset deficiencies.
- Adjust for the results of discontinued operations.

Adjust for the Terms and Conditions of the Comparative Transactions

Implicit within the ultimate transaction "price" are assumptions regarding time value of money considerations, as well as future owners' compensation and related ownership benefits. Further, issues relating to owning versus leasing the existing premises, the duration of the existing office lease, and the impact on future earnings of relocating the purchased business or practice are considered during the purchase price negotiation process.

Time Value of Money Considerations

With regard to many types of small businesses and professional practices, it is not unusual for transactions to be structured such that the payout (often called the earn-out) for the transfer of the business or practice will occur over a period of time. For example, with regard to the sale of a practice, it is very common for the seller to agree to transfer his or her practice to the buyer based on the terms that the buyer will remit to the seller 20 percent of estimated collected fees over a five-year period.

Normally, the buyer will not be required to compensate the seller for the opportunity costs relating to the seller's time value of money considerations. In other words, the buyer effectively obtains interest-free financing.

Because the analyst is often faced with the task of estimating fair market value for the subject company, time value of money issues should be taken into consideration when analyzing market transactions. Those transactions that are structured in a manner requiring payment over time should be analyzed in order to reflect the implications that time value of money considerations present with regard to the ultimate transaction price.

Obviously, discounting a stream of payments to be received over a five-year period to a present value, and assuming a reasonable required rate of return, will result in a fair market value that is lower than the total "gross" payments estimated to be received over the five-year term of the earn-out agreement.

This scenario presents a clear example of why the terms of a particular transaction should be analyzed carefully before the actual price, or the estimated fair market value, of the business transferred is clear.

Once the "true" cash price—often called the "cash equivalency value" —for the transaction has been established, it can be used to estimate valuation pricing indicators. Then these pricing indicators can be applied to the financial fundamentals of the subject business. This topic is addressed in more detail in Chapter 27, Tradeoff between Cash and Terms.

Owners' Compensation and Related Benefits

Typically, one of the first considerations that enters the buyer's mind when facing a potential acquisition is the level of economic income the investment will provide. To the extent that the buyer's financial analysis of historical operations reported by the target company indicates that the discretionary cash flow will exceed her expectations, she will be willing to "give" more during the negotiation process. The opposite is true when the buyer anticipates that future discretionary cash flows will simply meet, or be slightly lower than, her expectations.

Because an analyst is normally hired to estimate fair market value, he is usually required to assume a "hypothetical willing" buyer rather than an individual specific buyer. Therefore, the analyst should adjust the economic income for the purchased business to a level that reasonably could be expected by a typical potential buyer. Consequently, comparing a reasonable expectation of economic income with the transaction sale price will result in a valuation pricing indicator more reflective of economic reality.

Facilities Ownership versus Facilities Lease

Many small- to medium-size businesses are operated from premises owned by the partners of the business. Consequently, all of the costs associated with the ownership of real property (i.e., land and buildings) are included in the company's operating expenses. Related costs might include property taxes, interest expense on the outstanding mortgage balances, significant repairs and maintenance expenses, insurance costs, and other charges resulting from excess operating space.

The analyst may adjust the earnings fundamentals reported by an acquired business operating from owned real property to reflect expenses (and consequently, earnings) at levels more commensurate with the level expected if the subject company leases its real property.

Along the same lines, "sweetheart" leasing arrangements that exist for the current business may not be available to the new owners after a sale transaction. Thus, the analyst should analyze all leasing terms reported by an acquired business. This procedure is performed in order to estimate whether its buyer will experience similar lease-related expenses in future operating periods.

Similar to the adjustments relating to compensation and benefits discussed above, operating expense adjustments relating to facilities are made in order to estimate the true economic benefits of ownership that a buyer should expect in future operating periods. Comparing these adjusted levels of economic benefits with the business sale price (adjusted by time value of money and other appropriate considerations) should result in relevant valuation pricing indicators.

Comparative Ratio Analysis

For purposes of comparative performance and other ratios between the subject company and the guideline companies, the comparisons will be most relevant if the ratios are computed *after* the adjustments to the financial statements of the guideline companies—as well as the subject company.

Typically, the comparative ratio analysis is performed only for the latest available comparative year. This is true even if value measures are based on several years' average results. If the comparative ratio analysis is used to decide where the subject company's value measures should be relative to the guideline companies' value measures, the analyst should be careful to recognize any distortions or abnormalities in the year for which the ratios were calculated. These distortions or abnormalities could cause the ratios to be misleading for use in extracting a relevant value measure.

Time Period to Consider

In the absence of a compelling reason to do otherwise, the time period most commonly used for analysis of comparative transactions is one year. This conventional time period should not, however, be blindly and mechanistically adopted. The operative phrase is "relevant time period."

If there is stability in the operating environment in the industry under examination, it may be appropriate to consider transactions that took place over a much longer period of time. In certain industries, patterns of transaction prices have been established that are not highly sensitive to any specific time horizon. It may be helpful to study older transactions in order (1) to identify any pricing changes that have taken place over a longer period of time and (2) to understand whether those older transactions provide any information about industry pricing factors.

Sometimes the relevant time period is constrained by major changes that affected either the subject company or the industry as a whole. Such events may render comparative financial data before such changes irrelevant for valuation purposes.

Treating Nonoperating Assets, Excess Assets, and Asset Deficiencies

If the subject company has significant nonoperating assets, excess assets, or asset deficiencies that distinguish it from the guideline companies, adjustments for those items may be appropriate.

Nonoperating Assets

Many privately held companies own assets that are not part of their operations. Such assets may add some value to the closely held stock over and above the values indicated by the ratios of guideline company stock prices to their underlying financial fundamentals.

If nonoperating assets are to be given separate consideration, they should be separated from the operating company data. Any income they generate (or expenses incurred on behalf of their maintenance) should be removed from earnings or cash flows capitalized. If a price/asset value multiple is used based on guideline companies, nonoperating assets should be removed from the asset value that is being capitalized. These financial statement adjustments should be made prior to the ratio analysis of the financial statements if such analysis is to be used to help select multiples relative to guideline company multiples.

The question then becomes, "How much extra value do these nonoperating assets contribute to the stock?"

The theory of valuing nonoperating assets separately from operating assets rests on the assumption that the nonoperating assets could be liquidated without impairing operations. Thus, if the market value of nonoperating assets is higher than their book value, and if the analyst is going to mark the nonoperating assets up to the market value to make the valuation, the analyst should also consider offsetting factors. These factors include (1) the capital gains or ordinary income tax that the company would have to pay if it liquidated the assets, (2) any costs of liquidation, and (3) any discounts that would be appropriate to reflect the estimated time required to liquidate and the selling price risk related to the liquidation.

From there, it often makes a significant difference whether one is valuing a minority ownership interest or a controlling ownership interest. It also is important to know, if possible, the likelihood of sale of the assets. The market attributes very little weight to non-income-producing, nonoperating assets, unless they are likely to be sold, because their existence provides little, if any, benefit to the noncontrolling stockholder. Even when valuing a controlling ownership interest, these assets might be discounted from their net realizable value because most control buyers would rather buy a pure operating company and not have to deal with disposing of nonoperating assets.

Marginal Operating Real Estate

An issue that often is a gray area in stock valuations is whether certain real estate should be valued separately when using the comparative transaction valuation method.

One factor is the degree of comparability. If the subject company owns its real estate and the guideline companies do not, it often is appropriate to value the real estate separately. This is more true for controlling ownership interests than for noncontrolling ownership interests for the same reasons discussed in connection with nonoperating assets.

Real estate used in operations at a level far below its highest and best use may be a controversial issue. This becomes a matter of the analyst's judgment. Certainly, if prospective development or sale of the real estate is imminent, that would play a role in making the judgment.

Excess Assets or Asset Deficiencies

An often controversial area for possible adjustment may arise when the subject company has significantly greater amounts of some assets relative to its operations than do the guideline companies. The most common assets giving rise to such a potential adjustment are cash and marketable securities.

If it appears that some assets may be held in excessive amounts, the analyst should ask the company officials if there is a reason why such apparent excesses may be necessary for operations. If they are not necessary, adjustment may be appropriate. The same reasoning regarding control versus lack of control ownership characteristics discussed earlier also applies here.

It is also common to find the reverse situation, one in which it might be appropriate to value the company by a capitalization of economic income method but then to subtract an amount reflecting an inadequate reserve of operating assets. This can easily be the case if net working capital is inadequate to support the level of business or if certain plant and equipment items are in imminent need of replacement or major repair. Evaluating such inadequacies may require more subjective judgment than would assessing excess or nonoperating assets, but the potential problem of measurement does not render recognition of the concept of asset inadequacy any less important.

Typical Adjustments to Reach a Value Conclusion

As discussed earlier, the comparative transaction method is based on transactions of controlling (or substantial) ownership interests in companies. Therefore, if valuing a minority ownership interest in the subject company by using the comparative transaction method, it would be appropriate to take a minority ownership interest discount. It may also be appropriate to take a valuation discount for lack of marketability (discussed in Chapter 25, Discounts for Lack of Marketability).

Selecting and Weighting Multiples for the Subject Company Based on Comparative Transactions

The result of the comparative transaction analysis is an array of pricing multiples for each of several value measures. At this point, it is necessary to again visit the questions of (1) which measures to use in reaching an indication of value and (2) the relative weight to be accorded to each of the measures used.

For each value measure used, it is also necessary to decide what the pricing multiple for the subject company should be relative to the observed multiples for the comparative transaction companies.

Impact of Comparative Transactional Data Evaluation

The same general thought processes and decision criteria apply to (1) both deciding on whether or not to rely on any particular value measure at all and (2) deciding on the relative weight to be accorded each value measure ultimately used in reaching the opinion of value. A study of the transactional data may lead to greater or lesser reliance on certain value measures than one might have expected prior to compiling the data.

Number of Data Points Available. If it turns out that very few data points are available for a particular value measure, that problem may lead one to abandon that measure or to put relatively little weight on it. This is true even though it might be quite conceptually significant if there were more data. A common example is the pricing multiple of price to the latest 12 months' earnings. If only two of seven comparative transaction companies had meaningful positive earnings (and thus meaningful price to earnings multiples), the analyst has to decide whether the two convey enough information to be accorded weight in the final analysis. The analyst may, for example, decide instead to use a price to cash flow pricing multiple or a price to some number of years average earnings pricing multiple.

Comparability of Data Measurement. Another issue to consider is the extent to which the analyst is satisfied that the adjustments, if any, to the subject company and to the guideline companies' financial fundamental data have resulted in stating the data on a comparative basis. The analyst's confidence regarding the comparability of financial fundamental data may influence the analyst's judgment regarding the use of or weight accorded to value measures based on that particular financial fundamental variable.

Comparability of Data Patterns. Another factor in assessing comparability is the extent to which the data for the subject company "tracks" with the data for the guideline transaction companies. For example, if the subject company and six of the seven comparative transaction companies had a generally upward earnings trend but one comparative transaction company had a downward trend, the analyst may omit the maverick company when deciding on appropriate value measures relative to earnings.

Apparent Market Reliance.   The extent to which the value measures are tightly clustered or widely dispersed tends to indicate the extent to which the market tends to focus on that particular value measure in pricing companies in the particular industry.

Multiple of Stock Value to Asset Value

When the analyst has determined that either book value or some adjusted book value figure provides a useful representation of the subject company's underlying net asset values, the next step is to translate that figure into its implication for the value of the shares of stock or partnership interest being valued. This transaction usually is made by referring to the relationship of the transactional prices of the guideline companies to their respective underlying net asset values.

It may be possible to compute the multiple of market price to book value for a group of comparative transaction companies and to apply a multiple somewhere within the range of such multiples to the subject company book value. If (1) the book values of the subject company and comparative transaction companies were computed on comparable bases, and (2) if the asset composition is comparable, this procedure may provide a reasonably realistic estimate for the value of the subject business interest.

If accounting methods for the subject company and for the guideline companies differ significantly, the analyst should make appropriate adjustments before (1) computing the market price to book value multiples and (2) applying them in the subject valuation. There can be additional significant differences, such as in asset mix, that challenge the validity of using one company's price to book value multiple in valuing another company's stock.

Many of the private company sale transactions in the *Pratt's Stats* database show balance sheet information at adjusted net asset value. This enables the analyst to compute price to adjusted net asset value for those companies. At this writing, this is the only database for which adjusted net asset values are available for control transactions.

Reaching the Value Indication

The relative weighting of valuation multiples is similar to that used in the guideline publicly traded company method. The exception is that multiples of an asset fundamental (such as MVIC to tangible book value) may get a little more weight in a valuation of a controlling ownership position. This is because the control owner has discretion over the assets' use or disposal. The same observations apply to nonoperating assets, excess assets, and asset deficiencies. (See Chapter 16, The Guideline Publicly Traded Company Method, for a detailed discussion of these topics.)

Since merger and acquisition transaction analysis usually focuses on market value of invested capital, the market value of the debt must be subtracted in order to estimate the market value of equity.

If a minority ownership interest is being valued, both the minority ownership interest discount and the lack of marketability discount should be considered. Even in the case of a controlling ownership interest, it may be appropriate to make some adjustment for lack of marketability (or "illiquidity") relative to the values indicated from actual consummated transactions. This topic is discussed in Chapter 25, Discounts for Lack of Marketability.

Summary

The comparative transaction method is similar in concept to the guideline publicly traded company method. Both methods seek valuation guidance from actual transactions in the market. Since the transactional data used usually are controlling ownership interests, this method is most directly applicable for valuing other controlling ownership interests. Nonetheless, this method can be used for minority ownership interest valuations—when proper adjustments are made.

Merger and acquisition transactional data come from diverse sources, and these transactional data are less consistent (and sometimes less reliable) than transactional data related to day-to-day public stock market transactions. Sometimes, past transactions involving the subject company are a good source of value measures.

Since merger and acquisition transaction dates almost always differ from the subject company effective valuation date, adjustments often are needed to reflect differences in economic and industry conditions between the dates.

Merger and acquisition transactional prices often to some extent reflect synergies between acquirer and acquiree. To the extent that this is true, a transaction may be more reflective of *investment value* (i.e., value to that particular buyer) than *fair market value* (i.e., the value to a hypothetical, typically motivated buyer). For this reason, the circumstances of the merger and acquisition transactions must be carefully analyzed.

Bibliography

Articles

Graham, Michael D. "Selection of Market Multiples in Business Valuation." *Business Valuation Review*, March 1990, pp. 8–12.

McDonagh, Christopher S., and John M. McDonagh. "Valuing a Target's Ability to Compete in the Market." *Mergers & Acquisitions*, September/October 1995, pp. 22–25.

Mercer, Z. Christopher. "Public Multiples/Private Companies: Grappling with the Fundamental Issues." *Proceedings of the 1996 IBA National Conference*, Orlando, Florida, January 25–26, 1996.

Books

Albo, Wayne P., and A. Randal Henderson. *Mergers & Acquisitions of Privately-Held Businesses*, 2d ed. Toronto: Canadian Institute of Chartered Accountants, 1989.

Kuhn, Robert Lawrence, ed. *Mergers, Acquisitions, and Leveraged Buyouts*, Vol. 4. Burr Ridge, IL: McGraw-Hill, 1990.

Marren, Joseph H. *Mergers & Acquisitions: A Valuation Handbook*. Burr Ridge, IL: McGraw-Hill, 1993.

Rood, Stanley F., and Lane and Edson, P.C. *The Art of M&A: A Merger Acquisition Buyout Guide*, 2d ed. Burr Ridge, IL: McGraw-Hill, 1994.

Rock, Milton L., ed. *The Mergers and Acquisitions Handbook*, 2d ed. New York: McGraw-Hill Book Company, 1993.

West, Thomas L. *Business Reference Guide*. Concord, MA: Business Brokerage Press, annual.

West, Thomas L., and Jeffrey D. Jones. *Mergers and Acquisitions Handbook for Small and Midsized Companies*. New York: John Wiley & Sons, 1997.

Chapter 19

The Multiple of Discretionary Earnings (Seller's Discretionary Cash) Method

There is a growing group of business appraisers who use Seller's Discretionary Cash as a valuation method. We applaud this group and feel that in valuing small businesses, it just may be the method of the future.[1]

This chapter has been added to this edition because many business brokers use a multiple of "discretionary earnings" as the primary (or as a significant) method of pricing small businesses.

Also, the International Business Brokers Association (IBBA), the largest professional association of business brokers in the United States, teaches this pricing method in its two-day course on business valuation. It is one of the core courses required for the IBBA's Certified Business Intermediary (CBI) professional designation.

Leonard Sliwoski, a professor of accounting and director of the Small Business Development Center at Moorhead State University, also supports the method. As Sliwoski explains:

> This method is based on a cash payback concept. The discretionary cash flow is the cash flow available to the prospective purchaser to service acquisition debt associated with the business purchase and to pay himself or herself a salary. This number is the focus of small business owners.[2]

Another endorsement comes from Ray Miles, Executive Director of the Institute of Business Appraisers: "The use of buyer's discretionary cash makes a lot of sense for valuing closely-held businesses whose owners are also likely to be the working management."[3] However, Brian Knight, president of Country Business, Inc., and a past president of the International Business Brokers Association, cautions that "This approach really applies to the truly smaller business," such as where buying a job, rather than a return on investment, is the major consideration.

An important factor that helps make this method a viable tool for business appraisers is that considerable empirical data on multiples of business sale price to discretionary earnings have been collected in the last few years. Extracts from these data sources are presented later in the chapter.

As with most valuation methods, and especially with most small business valuation methods, we generally do not recommend using this method alone. However, this method is now in wide enough use—and there are enough empirical pricing data available—to make it worth considering in many small business valuation engagements.

---

[1] Thomas L. West, ed., *The 1997 Business Reference Guide* (Concord, MA: Business Brokerage Press, 1997), p. 354.

[2] Leonard J. Sliwoski and Maggie Jorgenson, "Acquiring a Small Business: How Much Can Your Client Afford?" *National Public Accountant*, October 1996, p. 17.

[3] *1997 Business Reference Guide*, p. 326.

Defining Discretionary Earnings

The International Business Brokers Association defines *discretionary earnings* as the earnings of a business enterprise prior to the following items:

- Income taxes.
- Nonoperating income and expenses.
- Nonrecurring income and expenses.
- Depreciation and amortization.
- Interest expense or income.
- Owner's total compensation for those services that could be provided by a sole owner/manager.

It is obvious from the above definition that "discretionary earnings" is a cash flow concept. The *Handbook of Small Business Valuation Formulas* calls this financial fundamental variable "annual owner's cash flow" and defines this variable essentially the same as above.[4]

Sliwoski uses the same definition, except that he subtracts expected capital expenditures necessary to maintain the existing fixed-asset base.[5]

Selecting the Appropriate Multiple

Pricing Multiples from Empirical Evidence

A very large proportion of the empirical pricing multiples fall in the range of .75 times to 2.75 times. Nonetheless, the empirical pricing multiples sometimes range all the way from .4 times to 5.8 times.[6] An analysis of over 500 transactions prepared by Certified Business Brokers of Houston shows an overall average pricing multiple of 1.67 times.

Jeff Jones, chairman of Certified Business Brokers, Inc., and Certified Business Appraisers, Inc., as well as chairman of the Standards Committee of the IBBA, states, "Selecting the multiplier is unquestionably the most difficult step in applying the Multiple of Discretionary Earnings Method."[7] He goes on to explain:

---

[4] Glenn M. Desmond, *Handbook of Small Business Valuation Formulas and Rules of Thumb*, 3d edition (Camden, ME: Valuation Press, 1993), p. 7.

[5] Sliwoski and Jorgenson, "Acquiring a Small Business: How Much Can Your Client Afford?," p. 17.

[6] Of course, empirical pricing multiples are even higher in special situations, such as where a business had virtually no historical discretionary earnings but considerable potential.

[7] Thomas L. West and Jeffrey D. Jones, eds., *Handbook of Business Valuation* (New York: John Wiley & Sons, 1992), p. 184.

The range of multipliers that make economic sense, when applied to discretionary earnings, will be zero to three. This range of multipliers is not determined arbitrarily. It is based on factors that set the minimum and maximum economic limits given the reality of the market place. The selection of the specific multiplier will be based on the appraiser's review of the subjective and objective risk and economic factors pertaining to the subject company. While the consideration of any one factor could result in a multiplier of less than one, the weighted average of all factors will normally result in selecting a multiplier that is at least one. There is the economic reality that an owner is not likely to sell at a price that is less than one year's discretionary earnings. Thus, the final selected multiplier will usually be somewhere between one and three, which if stated as the reciprocal would result in a range of capitalization rates of 33.3 percent to 100 percent.[8]

Jack Sanders, publisher of *Bizcomps* and an experienced business broker, says "the ultimate sale price of a business sold should be . . . from 1.5 to 3.5 times Seller's Discretionary Cash Flow."[9]

Exhibit 19-1 presents a summary of typical pricing multiples for certain industry groups developed from data in the *Pratt's Stats* database and from the *Bizcomps* data. It is noteworthy that the *Bizcomps* pricing multiples represent business sale prices that do *not* include inventory, while the *Pratt's Stats* pricing multiples represent business sale prices that *do* include inventory.

Note also that many of the medians in *Pratt's Stats* are lower than those in *Bizcomps*, even though the *Pratt's Stats* prices include inventory and *Bizcomps* prices do not. This probably is due to differences in the sources of the data and emphasizes the point that the data provide only ranges unless there is enough detail on each transaction to make a direct comparison with the subject.

It is noteworthy that for *every* industry group presented in Exhibit 19-1, the average pricing multiple is higher than the median pricing multiple, some by a considerable amount. This is because, when dealing with empirical pricing multiples, a few outliers on the high end tend to upwardly influence the average more than a few outliers on the low end tend to downwardly influence the average. For this reason, when dealing with empirical pricing multiples, the median usually is a better measure of central tendency than the mean.

Exhibit 19-2 presents ranges of pricing multiples for selected industry groups from the *Handbook of Small Business Formulas and Rules of Thumb*.[10] While the ranges presented in the exhibit are fairly wide, the book offers some discussion for each industry as to factors affecting the selection of pricing multiples in that industry.

---

[8] Ibid., p. 187.

[9] Jack R. Sanders, *Bizcomps 96: Western States Edition of Recent Small Business Sales* (San Diego: Asset Business Appraisal, 1997), p. 6.

[10] Glenn M. Desmond, p. 7.

Exhibit 19–1

MULTIPLES OF SELLING PRICE TO DISCRETIONARY EARNINGS DEVELOPED FROM THE PRATT'S STATS DATABASE*

Industry Group	Average Multiple	Median Multiple
Auto repair	1.39	1.25
Beauty salons	1.55	1.23
Card and gift shops	2.66	2.23
Coin laundries	2.07	1.83
Deli and sandwich shops	1.35	1.31
Dry cleaners	2.08	2.00
Florists	1.25	0.89
Grocery and convenience stores	1.75	1.55
Ice cream shops	2.10	2.05
Liquor stores	1.31	1.09
Printing shops	1.76	1.71
Service stations	1.34	1.23
Video stores	1.62	1.53

* Transaction prices include inventory.

SOURCE: *Pratt's Stats* (Portland, OR: Business Valuation Resources, 1997).

MULTIPLES FROM BIZCOMPS**

Type of Business	Eastern States	Central States	Western States
Automotive repair	1.6	2.0	1.9
Beauty salons	1.8	1.4	1.8
Cocktail lounges	1.6	1.5	2.6
Coin laundries	2.0	2.0	2.8
Convenience stores	1.8	1.2	2.6
Delicatessens	1.8	1.2	1.9
Day care centers	2.4	2.0	1.9
Dry cleaners	2.5	2.7	3.2
Florists	1.6	1.6	n/a
Food markets	1.6	1.9	2.6
Liquor stores	1.9	1.6	3.8
Printing	2.2	2.2	2.2
Restaurant/family	2.2	2.0	2.3
Service stations	1.4	2.0	2.1
Service stations w/mini-marts	1.9	1.5	n/a
Video stores	1.8	1.8	2.3

** Transaction prices exclude inventory.

SOURCE: Thomas L. West, *The 1997 Business Reference Guide* (Concord, Mass.: Business Brokerage Press, 1997), p. 323. See bibliography at the end of this chapter for information on *Bizcomps*.

Exhibit 19–2

RANGES OF OWNERS CASH FLOW (DISCRETIONARY EARNINGS) SUGGESTED IN HANDBOOK OF SMALL BUSINESS FORMULAS

Industry Group	Range of Multiples
Appraisal practices	1.5 to 4.0
Auto repair	1.0 to 3.0
Beauty salons and barbershops	1.0 to 2.0
Card and gift shops	1.0 to 3.0
Coin laundries	1.5 to 3.0
Convenience stores	2.0 to 5.0
Delicatessens	2.0 to 3.5
Drugstores	2.0 to 4.0
Dry cleaners	1.5 to 2.0
Fast food establishments	1.0 to 3.5
Fitness centers	1.5 to 4.0
Florists	1.0 to 3.0
Funeral services and mortuaries	3.0 to 5.0
Ice cream shops	1.0 to 3.0
Insurance agencies	2.0 to 5.0
Optometric practices	1.0 to 2.0
Printing shops	1.5 to 3.5
Real estate brokers	0.75 to 1.5
Restaurants	1.0 to 3.0
Service stations	1.5 to 3.5
Veterinary practices	1.25 to 3.5

SOURCE: Compiled from Glenn M. Desmond, *Handbook of Small Business Valuation Formulas and Rules of Thumb* (Camden, ME: Valuation Press, 1993).

Analytical Development of a Pricing Multiple

Most business brokers that use the multiple of discretionary earnings method have some kind of a worksheet listing the factors that affect the multiple. In addition, there is some type of rating and weighting system for each factor. The factors and rating and weighting schemes may vary considerably from one broker to another. This variability depends to a great extent on the types of businesses the brokers specialize in or typically tend to sell.

There is general recognition that the factors and the ratings and weightings are quite subjective. However, brokers who have the experience of selling certain types of businesses several times a year tend to develop a "feel" for how buyers are perceiving those businesses in the particular market at the particular time. This ongoing connection with the transactional market helps the brokers use their respective analytical systems in advising sellers and buyers about prices that the market is likely to accept.

The most publicized such analytical framework is that developed by Certified Business Brokers. It is generalized to apply to most types of small businesses typically selling in the $50,000 to $500,000 price range. The Certified Business Brokers Appraiser's Analysis Table is presented as Exhibit 19-3. The multiple developed is applied to discretionary earnings, as defined earlier. This would produce an indicated value for the intangible and operating assets, which include furniture, fixtures, and equipment and inventory at a normalized amount. If any other elements of working capital or other assets were included in the sale, or any liabilities assumed, the indicated value would be adjusted accordingly.

What Is Being Valued?

Most small business transactions are structured as asset sales. As noted in Chapter 2, it is important to define exactly what assets the valuation is intended to encompass. No matter how carefully the discretionary earnings are measured and the pricing multiple selected, the value indication is meaningless until it is clear what assets are—and are not—included in the resulting indication of value.

There is general agreement that the value indicated from the multiple of discretionary earnings method includes the following:

1. Furniture, fixtures, and equipment.
2. The lease, if one exists.
3. Goodwill and intangible assets customarily found in the type of business.

There is also agreement that the indicated value derived from this method excludes the following:

1. Cash and cash equivalents.
2. Accounts receivable.
3. Prepaid expenses.
4. Real estate.
5. Nonoperating assets.
6. Liabilities.

The major item of disagreement is whether or not the indicated value includes inventory. In the *Handbook of Small Business Valuation Formulas and Rules of Thumb*, inventory is *not* included—but it is "added separately to the 'formula' assets where applicable."[11] However, according to Jeff Jones, the indicated value *does* include the normal amount of inventory expected to be on hand to operate the business. Jones explains:

---

[11] Ibid., p. 10.

Exhibit 19–3

APPRAISER'S ANALYSIS TABLE

Rating Scale	Description	Selected Multiple	Weight	Weighted Value
Historical Profits		1.25	10	12.50
0.1–1.0	Negative to break-even			
1.1–2.0	Positive, but below industry norm			
2.1–3.0	Industry norm or above			
Income Risk		1.00	9	9.00
0.1–1.0	Continuity of income at risk			
1.1–2.0	Steady income likely/3–5 years old			
2.1–3.0	Profitability assured/5+ years old			
Terms of Sale		1.50	8	12.00
0.1–1.0	Seller requires all cash			
1.1–2.0	Reasonable terms available			
2.1–3.0	Exceptional terms available			
Business Type		1.50	7	10.50
0.1–1.0	Service business with few assets			
1.1–2.0	Equipment and/or inventory are significant component of total value			
2.1–3.0	High cost of entry, equipment and/or inventory major component of total value			
Business Growth		0.50	6	3.00
0.1–1.0	Declining and further decline likely			
1.1–2.0	Flat or at inflationary levels			
2.1–3.0	Rapid growth with more expected			
Location/Facilities		2.50	5	12.50
0.1–1.0	Less than desirable to tolerable			
1.1–2.0	Acceptable to average			
2.1–3.0	Above average to superior			
Marketability		1.00	4	4.00
0.1–1.0	Limited market—special skills required			
1.1–2.0	Normal market—needed skills available			
2.1–3.0	Large market—many qualified buyers			
Desirability		1.00	3	3.00
0.1–1.0	No status, rough or dirty work			
1.1–2.0	Respectable and satisfactory			
2.1–3.0	Challenging and attractive environment			
Competition		2.00	2	4.00
0.1–1.0	Highly competitive or unstable market			
1.1–2.0	Normal competitive conditions			
2.1–3.0	Little competition/high startup cost			
Industry		2.00	1	2.00
0.1–1.0	Declining and further decline likely			
1.1–2.0	Flat or at inflationary levels			
2.1–3.0	Rapid growth with more expected			

SUMMARY OF APPRAISER'S ANALYSIS TABLE

Categories	Selected Multiple	Weight	Weighted Values
Historical earnings	1.25	10	12.50
Income risk	1.00	9	9.00
Terms of sale	1.50	8	12.00
Business type	1.50	7	10.50
Business growth	0.50	6	3.00
Location/facilities	2.50	5	12.50
Marketability	1.00	4	4.00
Desirability	1.00	3	3.00
Competition	2.00	2	4.00
Industry	2.00	1	2.00
Total		55	72.50
Selected Weighted			1.32

SOURCE: Thomas L. West and Jeffrey D. Jones, *Handbook of Business Valuation* (New York: John Wiley & Sons, 1992), pp. 186, 189. Reprinted with permission of John Wiley & Sons, Inc.

It is important to understand that the capitalized value obtained by multiplying the selected multiplier by the discretionary earnings includes all of the operating assets including inventory, if any, at normalized level. If at the date of the appraisal, the inventory is more or less than the normalized level needed to support the current level of sales, then the price needs to be adjusted up or down to account for the variance.[12]

Of the two major data sources that report pricing multiples of discretionary earnings for current transactions, the *Bizcomps* multiple does *not* include inventory and the *Pratt's Stats* multiple *does* include inventory. Both services report the amount of inventory associated with the business sale transaction if those data are available. Therefore, the pricing multiple can be adjusted if desired.

For many types of small businesses, of course, the matter of inventory is inconsequential to the business value. However, for businesses where it does matter, such as retailing and wholesaling, be sure to note whether the source of published price to discretionary earnings multiples does—or does not—include inventory.

An intangible asset that often is created to facilitate the sale of a small business or professional practice is a *covenant not to compete*. If this is the case, the covenant usually is included in the purchase price, and therefore also in the price to discretionary earnings multiple. More discussion on this point is included later in this chapter.

Multiple of Discretionary Earnings Method Produces a Control Value

The multiple of discretionary earnings method clearly is designed to produce an indicated value for a controlling owner. As discussed earlier, the calculation of the discretionary earnings base *includes* compensation to a controlling owner.

Furthermore, the method was developed by the business brokerage community as an aid to pricing entire businesses for sale. These brokers virtually never sell fractional ownership interests. Accordingly, there have been no mechanics developed to modify the indicated value from this method in order to estimate a minority ownership interest value.

What Standard of Value Does the Multiple of Discretionary Earnings Method Produce?

The answer as to the standard of value that the multiple of discretionary earnings method produces is not clear-cut.

---

[12] West and Jones, *Handbook of Business Valuations*, p. 188.

Desmond says, "The valuation standard of the formulas and their illustrations in this text is fair market value as a going concern."[13] He adds, "the valuation formulas set forth in this book are market-derived."[14] Yet Desmond recognizes that fair market value represents a price in cash or terms equivalent to cash and that many small business transactions don't meet this criterion. Where they do not, he suggests making appropriate adjustments. These adjustments are addressed in Chapter 27, Tradeoff between Cash and Terms.

Perhaps more troublesome is the fact that Desmond lists, under a section called "Common Elements That May Influence Value," the issue of a covenant not to compete.[15] This typically is an intangible asset that is created specifically to facilitate the sale of the business. Without this intangible asset, the subject business may be worth much less or even be unsalable.

But the covenant restricts the personal activities of the seller. For this reason, in marital dissolution cases, family law courts have often taken the position that the value of a covenant not to compete is the property of the operating spouse, not part of the marital estate.[16]

Consequently, if the multiple of discretionary earnings method is used in a valuation performed for divorce purposes, the analyst should try to check the comparative transactions used. This check is performed in order to attempt to determine the extent to which, if any, the multiple may reflect a covenant (or other personal services or restraints) that the court may consider nonmarital property. To the extent that the information is available, *Pratt's Stats* indicates (1) whether or not a covenant not to compete was included and (2) if it is included, how much of the purchase price was allocated to it.

Summary

The multiple of discretionary earnings method was developed by the business brokerage community to be used with buyers, sellers, and brokers of small businesses. It is widely used in the business brokerage community. This method is taught in the core business valuation course required to achieve the Certified Business Intermediary professional designation offered by the International Business Brokers Association.

Discretionary earnings (also called owner's, buyer's, or seller's discretionary cash flow) is defined as earnings prior to taxes, interest, noncash charges, all aspects of compensation to one owner, and nonoperating and nonrecurring items.

---

[13] Desmond, p. 7.

[14] Ibid., p. 11.

[15] Ibid., p. 15.

[16] See, for example, *In re the Marriage of Delores A. Monaghan and Robert D. Monaghan*, No. 16508-2-11, 78 Wash. App. 918, 899 P.2d 841 (Aug. 9, 1995); *Sweere* v. *Gilbert-Sweere*, 534 N.W.2d 294 (Minn. App., July 18, 1995); and *Williams* v. *Williams*, No. 95-00577, 1996 WL 47675 (Fla. Dist. Ct. App., Feb. 7, 1996).

The earnings thus defined are multiplied by a pricing multiple that typically is in the range between .75 times and 2.75 times. Data sources are available that present this pricing multiple for hundreds of specific transactions and that summarize the averages and ranges of the multiples for typical small business industry groups.

The value thus derived typically includes the assets needed to operate the business, including typical intangibles, but not necessarily all elements of working capital. For example, some practitioners and data reporting services include inventory and some do not.

Clearly, this method is used primarily for the purpose of developing a controlling ownership interest value, not a minority ownership interest value.

Since the guideline transactions contained in the transactional data sources are market derived, the method would tend to be representative of fair market value. However, adjustments may be needed to convert guideline transactions made on terms to a cash equivalent value. Also, some guideline sales may need to be adjusted for items included such as a covenant not to compete, which may be separate from the value of the business itself.

Bibliography

Books and Articles

Desmond, Glenn M. *Handbook of Small Business Formulas and Rules of Thumb,* 3d ed. Camden, ME: Valuation Press, 1993.

Jones, Jeffrey D. "Multiple of Discretionary Earnings Method," Chapter 16 in *Handbook of Business Valuation*, Thomas L. West and Jeffrey D. Jones, eds. New York: John Wiley & Sons, 1992, pp. 177–92.

Sliwoski, Leonard J., and Maggie Jorgenson. "Acquiring a Small Business: How Much Can Your Client Afford?" *National Public Accountant*, October 1996, pp. 16–20.

West, Thomas L. *The 1997 Business Reference Guide*. Concord, MA: Business Brokerage Press, 1997. *See especially* "Multiple of Discretionary Earnings," pp. 321–26.

Sources of Current Price/Discretionary Earnings Ratios

Bizcomps, published annually in four separate editions (Western, Eastern, Central, and National Industrial) by Jack R. Sanders, Asset Business Appraisal, PO Box 711777, San Diego, CA 92171, phone (619) 457-0366, web page www.bizcomps.com.

Pratt's Stats, compiled and published by Business Valuation Resources, 4475 S.W. Scholls Ferry Road, Suite 101, Portland, OR 97225, phone (503) 291-7963, web page www.transport.com/~shannonp/.

Chapter 20

The Gross Revenue Multiples Method

A commonly used method for the valuation of small businesses and professional practices is gross revenue pricing multiples. Gross revenue pricing multiples can be useful in the valuation process. However, as an analytical tool, this method has several limitations. When gross revenue pricing multiples are used naively in the valuation process, without the analyst completely understanding the limitations that apply to each case, the result can be an erroneous estimate of value.

The Basic Concept of this Method

Another, and perhaps more descriptive, name for the gross revenue pricing multiple is the *price-to-sales multiple*. In other words, the basic concept is that the value of the business is some multiple of the amount of revenue that the subject business generates.

For example, let's assume that empirical transactional data on the sales of a certain type of business or practice indicate that the particular type of business almost always sells in a range of .40 to .75 times annual revenue. Let's also assume that the appraisal subject is a business or practice that generates $200,000 in annual revenues. The range of multiples of sales would indicate that the subject business should be worth somewhere between $80,000 and $150,000 (i.e., .40 × $200,000 = $80,000 and .75 × $200,000 = $150,000). Where our subject business would fall within that range of indicated values would depend on its profitability (if that information is available) and on a variety of other factors.

The gross revenue pricing multiple method is a market approach valuation method. This is because the pricing multiples are derived from the marketplace. That is, the multiples are extracted from market-derived empirical data, with respect to the actual sales of businesses that are reasonable valuation guidelines to the subject business. Accordingly, this valuation method is commonly used by business brokers and industry participants. This is because this method is—at least conceptually—based on actual, current, market-derived transactional data.

When Gross Revenue Multiples May Be Useful

As a broad generalization, gross revenue pricing multiples may be useful with regard to the following objectives:

1. To approximate a range of possible values with a minimum of time and effort.
2. To conclude an estimate of value when other data are unavailable or inadequate.
3. As one indicator of a value—or of a range of values—used in conjunction with other, more rigorous, valuation methods.

The following sections discuss some of the situations in which the application of gross revenue pricing multiples may be useful.

When Gross Sales Are the Only Reliable Income Data Available

For many entities, especially small sole proprietorships, a record of profitability may be impossible, or nearly impossible, to construct. This is either because there have never been complete records, they have not been saved, or because personal and business receipts and expenditures are difficult to clearly separate from each other. In these situations, no other accounts on the income statement of the business provide a reliable indication of its historic profitability, and the analyst may be forced to rely on the accuracy of the historical reported gross revenue of the business as the only indication of its financial performance.

For Companies with Losses or Erratic Earnings

For many reasons, a business may not have demonstrable earnings to capitalize. This may be true even though the business has considerable potential. This may be (1) because of adverse economic conditions that are expected to improve, (2) because the company is in a start-up or research and development stage, or (3) because of significant nonrecurring factors. In cases such as these, most buyers would construct a pro forma income statement for one or several years into the future. However, multiples of price to revenues at which actual sales of comparative companies were consummated may offer one indication of value.

Earnings of some businesses may be highly erratic. This is either (1) because of economic factors affecting the industry or (2) because of special factors affecting the particular company. Attempts to normalize the earnings may require a great deal of subjective judgment about what level of historical economic income is the best indication of prospective economic income. Gross revenue pricing multiples derived from recent sales of guideline businesses or practices may give some indication of how others assess the future of the industry or the profession.

Finally, recent earnings may have experienced a "spike," an unprecedented upward thrust that may or may not be sustainable. In this case, a rigorous analysis of the gross revenue pricing multiples of other recent sales of guideline businesses may prevent a buyer from paying too much by basing the pricing strictly upon an unsustainable earnings level.

For Highly Homogeneous Industries and Professions

The more similar many businesses or practices within an identifiable industry are, the more valid the indication of value provided by the gross revenue pricing multiple method. If an industry or profession tends to have a fairly standard cost structure, a given level of revenue should be expected to produce a somewhat predictable amount of economic income. In the limited number of industry or professional segments for which this homogeneity is characteristic, entities may sell within a fairly tight range of prices—in terms of multiples of revenue.

Even for relatively homogeneous industry or professional practice segments, gross revenue pricing multiples usually can be expected to vary quite a bit at any given time from one geographical region to another.

Estimating Value of Intangible and/or Other Assets

A method used by some professional practice analysts is to appraise the practice tangible assets on a market value basis and then estimate the practice intangible value based on a multiple of practice revenue. As with other gross revenue pricing multiples, the multiple to be used may be developed on the basis of some expected level of future economic income per dollar of revenue. Or it may be developed on the basis of reported multiples of revenue actually paid for goodwill and/or for other intangible assets in comparative practice sale transactions.

Some wholesalers that help to finance franchised retailer customers (or to facilitate the sales of franchises) use a gross revenue pricing multiple method to set a value on fixtures and intangible assets. Typically, they take the view that a store should be worth the value of its inventory plus x weeks' sales for its fixtures and intangibles. Where the particular store falls within the range of the high and low boundaries of the number of weeks' sales should be based, at least in part, on its historical profitability. In the limited instances where the analyst can obtain actual empirical data on comparative transactions priced this way, the gross revenue multiple method can be useful.

Where There Is a High Industry Correlation between Price and Return on Sales

In some industries, there is a high degree of correlation between the sale price of a business and its percentage return on sales. In other industries, no such correlation exists. If there is such a correlation evident (although not necessarily to an extremely high degree of statistical significance), the industry transaction data can be helpful in developing an appropriate gross revenue pricing multiple for the subject business.

Consider the data tabulated and graphed in Exhibit 20-1 for illustrative industries A and B. In industry A, there is a smooth progression (i.e., a high degree of correlation) between return on sales and gross revenue pricing multiples. If the analyst knows or can make a good estimate of the return on sales for the subject business, it is possible to estimate what gross revenue pricing multiple is appropriate for the subject business. This can be developed either visually on the graph or statistically. For industry B, return on sales provides virtually no guidance as to selection of an appropriate gross revenue pricing multiple.

Exhibit 20–1

CORRELATION BETWEEN PRICE AND RETURN ON SALES

Company	Industry A		Industry B	
	Return on Sales %	Price per $ of Sales	Return on Sales %	Price per $ of Sales
1	1.190	0.235	1.169	0.475
2	2.010	0.355	2.01	0.245
3	2.830	0.385	2.79	0.630
4	3.650	0.510	3.83	0.325
5	4.780	0.485	4.57	0.445
6	5.750	0.615	5.77	0.419
7	6.800	0.665	6.77	0.555

Industry A

Regression Output		Regression Line	
		ROS	P/R
Constant	0.186357445	1.190	0.272
Standard error of Y estimate	0.040195190	2.010	0.331
R squared	0.940741036	2.830	0.390
Number of observations	7	3.650	0.449
		4.780	0.531
X coefficient(s)	0.072028799	5.750	0.601
Standard error of coefficient	0.008084696	6.800	0.676

Price/revenues multiple = 0.1864 + 0.0720 x Return on sales

Correlation = 96.99%

Industry B

Regression Output		Regression Line	
		ROS	P/R
Constant	0.384834717	1.169	0.402
Standard error of Y estimate	0.139181500	2.019	0.415
R squared	0.052756267	2.790	0.426
Number of observations	7	3.830	0.442
		4.579	0.453
X coefficient(s)	0.148397460	5.779	0.471
Standard error of coefficient	0.028121296	6.779	0.485

Price/revenues multiple = 0.3848 + 0.0148 x Return on sales

Correlation = 22.97%

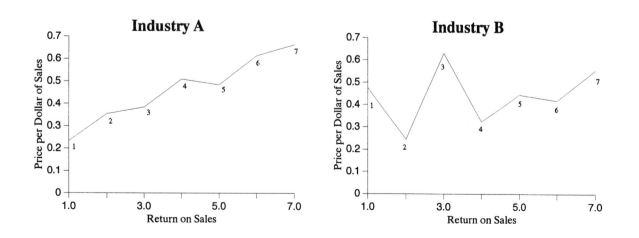

Gross Revenue Multiples Generally Indicate Debt-Free Value

Gross revenue pricing multiples generally lend themselves better to developing an indication of the total value of invested capital (i.e., the total of long-term, interest-bearing debt and of owners' equity) than of a straight equity value. If all the businesses in the industry are essentially unleveraged (i.e., financed all or mostly by owners' equity), or if all the businesses have essentially similar capital structures, it doesn't much matter whether the gross revenue pricing multiple is used to indicate (1) the value of invested capital or (2) the value of equity. However, if capital structures vary, analysts should perform the valuation analysis on a total invested capital basis and then subtract the amount of long-term debt outstanding in order to estimate the residual value of the owners' equity.

Let's consider Company A and Company B, with equal revenues and equal EBITs. However, Company A has debt while Company B has no debt. If the analyst naively assumes that the equity of each is worth the same multiple of gross revenue, the analyst would erroneously conclude that the equity of the business burdened with debt was worth as much as the business with no debt outstanding. The application of a valuation analysis on an invested capital basis would produce a more plausible value conclusion.

Problems in the Application of Gross Revenue Multiples

Analysts using gross revenue pricing multiples as indicators of value should do so with considerable caution. Careful analysis should be performed in order to assess the impact on value of whatever differences there may be between (1) the subject business and (2) the transactional population from which the range of gross revenue pricing multiples was extracted. Even after being as thorough as possible, the analyst should realize that there still may be considerable latitude in the indicated range of reasonable values. The following sections present some of the problems with the naïve application of gross revenue pricing multiples as an indicator of value.

Ambiguity about Exactly What Was Sold

As noted in Chapter 2, value is meaningless until what is being valued is clearly defined. Some industry participants report figures purported to be market-derived gross revenue pricing multiples, without making it clear just what they supposedly represent. Do the reported pricing multiples value only the intangible assets? Intangible assets and fixed assets? Inventory? Other assets? Liabilities? When a gross revenue pricing multiple is reported, the analyst should take care to understand what the pricing multiple is supposed to represent before judging its meaningfulness.

Ambiguity about the Terms of the Transaction

Is the gross revenue pricing multiple at issue supposed to represent a cash value, or does it relate to a price on some noncash terms that may be typical for sales of entities in the particular business or profession? The cash equivalency value of a transaction price on long, easy terms may be half as much as a transaction price paid in cash. (This topic is discussed in Chapter 27.)

When gross revenue pricing multiples are discussed, they more often than not relate to the terms of sale typical in the business or profession rather than to cash values or to cash equivalency values for the business or practice.

A Profit Factor Usually Comes into Play

For most kinds of businesses or industries for which gross revenue pricing multiples are used, the assumption of some level of profitability is inherent in the range of market-derived pricing multiples generally reported. To apply the gross revenue pricing multiple method correctly, the analyst should have some idea about (1) what level of profitability is implicit in the multiple and (2) what the chances are that the subject entity will achieve the implied level of profitability.

Differences in Persistence of Revenues

Another factor implied in any industry average gross revenue pricing multiple is some industry average persistence of the revenues to which it is applied. In other words, if a buyer thinks of the value of an entity in terms of a multiple of its revenues, he is thinking in terms of "buying a book of business." The buyer must have some implicit idea about how much of that business is likely to stay with the entity after he buys it, and for how long.

In order to use gross revenue pricing multiples correctly, the analyst should have some idea of (1) the degree of expected persistence on which the industry average multiple is based and (2) the likelihood that the persistence for the subject entity will be better or worse than the industry standard expectation.

Uniqueness of Each Entity

The validity of gross revenue pricing multiples as indicators of value depends on some degree of homogeneity. Typically, homogeneity is not characteristic among diverse entrepreneurs and professional practitioners. The historical developments of different entities, as well as the unique personalities and preferences of the personally managed operations, may create a uniqueness not characteristic of real estate or other commercial investments. The analyst may have great difficulty selecting from a range of multiples that were derived from a group of unique entities so that the multiple reasonably represents the unique characteristics of the subject entity.

Multiples Change Considerably over Time

A business broker recently reported that the multiples of revenue at which sales of businesses through his office were being consummated were running 30 percent lower than a year earlier. In other words, at the time of the report, the business broker would have expected to sell at 70 percent of a year's revenues the same business that would have sold for 100 percent of a year's revenues a year earlier.

Even when gross revenue pricing multiples may be useful, analysts should recognize that they are volatile and change over time for several reasons.

Ease of Entry.   The degree to which it is easy, or even feasible, to start one's own operation may vary over time. This is either (1) because of changes in the supply and demand relationship of the business or practice category or (2) because of changes in the regulatory environment, such as the amount or method of allocating licenses for a certain activity. These factors obviously influence what buyers will pay to get into an established business or practice.

Consider an extreme but very real example. Assume that a city had for a long time limited the number of taxicab licenses it issued. Then, suddenly, the city changed its historical practice in order to allow licensing of an unlimited number of cabs. The value of a taxi company per dollar of historical revenue would be expected to drop dramatically. As another example, municipalities differ greatly from one another in the way they allocate trash collection routes. And municipalities occasionally make changes in their allocation procedure. These changes usually would impact gross revenue pricing multiples for such trash collection companies.

Fashions, Fads, and Fantasies.   Certain types of businesses and practices may be in or out of fashion in the market at any given time. This phenomenon occurs just as certain groups of stocks can be the "darlings" of the market one year and the "dogs" the next. Innovative ideas and scarce opportunities are the kinds of things that drive gross revenue multiples up. Fading glitter and a glut of participants can move gross revenue multiples down.

Economic and Industry Conditions.   Economic and industry conditions can considerably influence the outlook for persistence of revenues for both the near-term and the long-term future. They can also affect the profit margins that those revenues can generate. Obviously, these factors will have an impact on what a buyer will be willing to pay per dollar of revenues currently being generated by a business.

Even Gross Revenue Data May Not Be Reliable

For some businesses, it is not even possible to obtain reliable data on the amount of gross revenues being generated. That is especially true of cash businesses, including many types of retail and service establishments. This fact poses a dilemma. Will the buyer rely on someone's oral estimate of revenues, or will she consider only those data that can be independently verified? There is no single correct answer to that question. Different buyers have different criteria by which they judge the reliability of the data they may be willing to accept.

Multiples of Some Measure of Physical Volume

In a few industries, some buyers look at some measure of physical volume in determining how much they are willing to pay. For example, the cable TV industry looks at the number of cable system subscribers. Funeral homes are priced partly on the basis of the average number of services per year, although that pricing method is less dominant today than it used to be. Buyers of soft drink bottlers and beer distributors often look at the number of cases sold, with most of the value related to the premium brands. Taverns sometimes are priced on the basis of the monthly volume of draft beer purchased from the distributor.

But even gross physical volume measures are not always reliable. A business broker reported a business owner who bought and sold taverns frequently and usually owned two or more at any one time. When the business owner planned to sell a tavern, the purchase invoices showed that the tavern bought a lot of kegs of beer from the distributor during the months prior to his offering the tavern for sale. What the prospective buyer didn't know was that some of the kegs went out the back door of the subject tavern and were actually sold through one of the owner's other taverns.

Using Industry Earnings Data to Check Gross Revenue Multiples

Logically, the multiple of revenue at which a business should sell would be the business's profits (expressed as a percentage of sales), divided by the applicable rate at which its economic income should be capitalized. For example, let's assume that a manufacturing company earned an average of 5 percent on its sales, and that buyers of companies in that industry demanded a 20 percent return on their investment. Therefore, the buyers would be willing to pay:

$$\frac{.05}{.20} = .25, \text{ or 25 percent of sales}$$

If an analyst proposes to price a company or group of companies in an industry on the basis of a gross revenue multiple, the average return on sales for the industry can be estimated by using trade association statistics if they are available. So, as part of a verification process, if the average profit on sales divided by an appropriate direct capitalization rate comes out somewhere near the suggested gross revenue multiple, the gross revenue multiple would appear reasonable.

Summary

The gross revenue pricing multiple method of valuation is used much more with small businesses and professional practices than with larger businesses. This is primarily because reliable data on other measures of economic income for both the subject business and for comparative businesses tend to be less readily available than is typically the case for larger companies.

The premise of a gross revenue pricing multiple for valuation is that the subject business or practice is about equally profitable—with about the same level of risk—as the population or sample of comparative companies from which the gross revenue pricing multiple is extracted. If this is not the case, the analyst should adjust the market-derived pricing multiple appropriately in order to reflect any differences. Another premise of the gross revenue pricing multiple method is that the assets being valued are similar in nature—relative to the revenue level—as the population or sample from which the market-derived pricing multiple is extracted.

The multiple of gross revenue (or of physical volume) is less than an ideal business valuation method. However, it is useful when other reliable data are not available or as a reasonableness check on the validity of the results of more rigorous business valuation methods.

See Chapter 21, Comparative Transaction Databases, for sources of actual sale gross revenue multiples for small business and professional practices.

Chapter 21

Comparative Transaction Databases

One frustration that constantly plagues appraisers of small businesses and professional practices is the lack of comparative transactional data. Unlike transactions in either real estate or publicly traded securities, there are no legal requirements that the transfers of ownership of most closely held businesses be publicly reported.

It is noteworthy that, since the last edition of this book, considerable progress has been made in the collection and availability of small business transaction data.

Two of the transaction databases that were discussed in the last edition have expanded considerably:

1. *The IBA Market Database.* The Institute of Business Appraisers has more than doubled the number of transactions in its database, which now number over 11,500.
2. *Bizcomps.* With only a two-year track record at the time of the previous edition of this book (1993), *Bizcomps* planned to have 1,300 transactions by the end of 1993. As of the end of 1997, it has over 2,700 transactions.

In addition, two databases have emerged that didn't exist at the time of the previous edition of this book:

1. *Done Deals Data.* Started in 1996, *Done Deals* has been growing at a rate of 200 transactions per quarter. At current levels of activity, *Done Deals* is expected to have nearly 2,000 by the end of 1997. Most transactions are in the $1 million to $100 million price range.
2. *Pratt's Stats.* Started in 1997 with the cooperation of the International Business Brokers Association, *Pratt's Stats* has folded in what began as the M&A Source Sold Company Database. As of this writing, it has approximately 500 transactions and is growing rapidly.

This chapter presents descriptions and samples of these transactional databases. While these databases do not yet encompass enough transactions to make a market approach analysis feasible for every small business and professional practice valuation, they come a lot closer to that objective than was the case five years ago. Furthermore, these transaction databases are all relatively inexpensive. Based on the prices in effect as of this writing, analysts starting from scratch could have access to a year's service and all the back data in *all four* of these databases for a total cost of under $1,000.

The IBA Market Database

The Institute of Business Appraisers (IBA) maintains an empirical database of information on the actual sales of closely held businesses. Exhibit

Exhibit 21-1

THE INSTITUTE OF BUSINESS APPRAISERS, INC.
MARKET DATABASE SAMPLE PAGE

The information below is supplied in response to your request for data to be used in applying the "market data approach" to business appraisal. Because of the nature of the sources from which the information is obtained, we are not able to guarantee its accuracy. Neither do we make any representation as to applicability of the information to any specific appraisal situation.

Following is an explanation of the entries in the data table:

Business Type	= Principal line of business.
SIC No.	= Principal Standard Industrial Classification number applicable to business sold.
Ann. Gr.	= Reported annual sales volume of business sold.
Ann. Earn.	= Reported annual earnings before owner's compensation, interest and taxes.
Own. Comp.	= Reported owner's compensation.
Sale Price	= Total reported consideration, i.e. cash, notes, liabilities assumed, etc., excluding real estate.
Sales Pr./Gross	= Ratio of total consideration to reported annual gross.
Price/Ann. Earn.	= Ratio of total consideration to reported annual earnings.
Yr/Mo of Sale	= Month and year during which transaction was consummated.

DATA FOR MARKET COMPARISON

Business Type	SIC	Ann. Gr. $000s	Ann. Earn. $000s	Own. Comp. $000s	Sale Price $000s	Sale Pr./ Gross	Price/ Ann. Earn.	Geographical Location	Yr/Mo of Sale
Lawn service	0782	44	20		19	0.43	0.95	Midwest	90/04
Lawn maint./snow removal	0782	44	35	30	39	0.89	1.11	Montana	96/04
Landscape maintenance	0782	49	37		35	0.71	0.95	Oregon	92/04
Lawn care	0782	60	26		40	0.67	1.54	Texas	85/09
Lawn care	0782	65	20		33	0.51	1.65	Midwest	89/03
Lawn care maintenance	0782	106	52		100	0.94	1.92	Ohio	92/01
Lawn care maintenance	0782	113	35		40	0.35	1.14	Minnesota	91/03
Lawn care	0782	115	34		49	0.43	1.44	Texas	86/07
Lawn care	0782	126			60	0.48		Florida	95/06
Lawn/snow	0782	126			30	0.24		Midwest	
Lawn care	0782	150			160	1.07		Texas	84/09
Landscape management	0782	150	76		45	0.30	0.59	Cal/Ariz/Nev	88/10
Lawn care	0782	161	62	11	64	0.40	1.03	Iowa	93/12
Lawn & landscaping	0782	300	81	81	280	0.93	3.46	Florida	90/01
Lawn maintenance	0782	300	100	50	48	0.16	0.48	Florida	90/09
Lawn maintenance	0782	436	187		370	0.85	1.98	Texas	93/01
Lawn care maintenance	0782	451	249		375	0.83	1.51	Florida	93/06
Landscape nursery	0782	507	98		165	0.33	1.68	Tennessee	87/08
Lanscape contractor	0782	525	120		225	0.43	1.88		88/08
Lawn care	0782	636	48		150	0.24	3.13	Cal/Ariz/Nev	84/09
Lawn service	0782	661	172		300	0.45	1.74	Cal/Ariz/Nev	88/07
Landscape maintenance	0782	680	81		240	0.35	2.96	New Mexico	92/02
Tree and landscape service	0782	800			141	0.18		California	90/02
Landscape contractor	0782	1100	60		248	0.23	4.13	Colorado	94/01

SOURCE: IBA Market Database   (Boynton Beach, FL: The Institute of Business Appraisers, Inc., 1997).

21-1 is a printout of the data included for SIC Code 0782, lawn service. Definitions of the variables are presented at the top of Exhibit 21-1.

Information for the *IBA Market Database* is obtained from IBA members and other sources having actual knowledge of the subject sales. The amount of information about each sale is limited by practical considerations such as (1) the amount of information that IBA sources have about the sale of a closely held business and (2) the willingness of IBA members to take the time to record transactional data and to submit them to the IBA.

The IBA database contains at least one transaction in each of more than 600 SIC code groups, a total of over 11,500 transactions that span a period over the last 15 years. The following list presents the number of SIC codes in the IBA database with at least the minimum number of transactions tabulated.

1 or more transactions	=	628
5 or more transactions	=	308
20 or more transactions	=	90
50 or more transactions	=	36
100 or more transactions	=	29

The *IBA Market Database* is available from the Institute of Business Appraisers, PO Box 1447, Boynton Beach, Florida 33425, phone (561) 732-3202, fax (561) 732-4304. Printouts by SIC code, as presented in Exhibit 21-1, are available to IBA members as part of their membership dues. Membership is open to anyone interested. As of this writing, IBA membership dues were $250 for the first year and $200 for each year thereafter.

The IBA also offers its members an enhanced service called *Market Data Plus*. It includes some market analysis tables and charts for the industry group; rules of thumb, if available; and optional "common size" financial information from Robert Morris Associates data (see Chapter 9).

Bizcomps

The *Bizcomps* database is published in a series of four editions, each issued once a year. There are three geographical editions: Western, Central, and Eastern. In addition, there is a National Industrial Edition, which includes larger transactions drawn as a subset from the other three editions. The combined data are also available on disk, updated annually at the beginning of each year.

A sample page from the *Bizcomps* 1996 Western Edition is presented as Exhibit 21-2. Besides the breakdown by four-digit SIC code, each geographical edition also presents transactions grouped by other criteria. These groupings include all businesses sold for cash, businesses sold for over $500,000 (of which there are a limited number), and five broad industry groups: manufacturing, wholesale and distribution, food service, retail, and service.

The information is gathered from about 20 business brokers in each region. The 1996 Western Edition includes 950 transactions. The latest Eastern Edition included 735 transactions. The 1997 Central Edition included 950 transactions. The 1997 National Industrial Edition, including larger businesses taken from the other three editions, included 345 transactions. A new restaurant edition has 503 transactions.

Jack Sanders explains, "All sales are shown as asset transactions and do not include cash, accounts receivable, or accounts payable. Inventory also has been excluded but the actual amount of inventory at the time of sale is shown for each business sale."[1]

---

[1]Jack R. Sanders, *Bizcomps 96: Western States Edition of Recent Small Business Sales* (San Diego: Asset Business Appraisal, 1996), p. 6.

Exhibit 21–2

BIZCOMPS 1996 WESTERN EDITION
SAMPLE PAGE

EXHIBIT #52 - All Mail Box, Copying & Shipping Businesses in Data Base

SIC #	BUS TYPE	ASK PRICE (000)	ANN GROSS (000)	SDCF (000)	SALE DATE	SALE PR(000)	% DOWN	TERMS	SALE/ SALES	SALE/ SDCF	INV AMT (000)	FF&E	RENT/ SALES	AREA
7389	Mail Boxes/Copying	140	148	66	11/30/96	95	34%	5 Yrs @ 7%	0.64	1.4	0	N/A	8%	North Rocky Mtns.
7389	Mail Box Rentals	125	180	60	2/28/96	90	55%	3 Yrs @ 10%	0.50	1.5	1	15	11%	Orange Cty, CA
7389	Mail Box Rentals	55	124	27	1/31/96	50	100%	N/A	0.40	1.9	2	15	10.6%	Northern Calif.
7389	Mail Box Rental	64	929	23	11/20/95	55	83%	2 Yrs @ 0%	0.06	2.4	5	40	N/A	Murrieta, CA
7389	Copy Center	125	181	63	10/2/95	110	80%	1 Yr @ 10%	0.61	1.7	4	N/A	8.5%	Belmont, CA
7389	Mail Box Franchise	145	1,172	48	4/28/95	125	46%	6 Yrs @ 9%	0.11	2.6	5	N/A	2%	San Jose, CA
7389	Mail Box Franchise	160	293	67	11/30/94	140	100%	N/A	0.48	2.1	10	N/A	N/A	Huntington Beach, CA
7389	Mailing & Shipping	100	193	73	5/20/94	100	100%	N/A	0.52	1.4	0	25	N/A	Corona Del Mar, CA
7389	Mail & Shipping Service	63	130	31	3/31/94	48	46%	5 Yrs @ 9%	0.37	1.5	7	30	8%	Tucson, AZ
7389	Mail Box Rental	70	133	25	9/30/93	58	50%	2.5 Yr @ 9%	0.44	2.3	1	N/A	14%	Newark, CA
7389	Mail & Shipping Service	110	N/A	50	8/31/93	70	64%	5 Yrs @ 10%	#ERRC	1.4	5	23	N/A	Tempe, AZ
7389	Mail & Shipping Service	150	N/A	67	8/31/93	150	33%	10 Yrs @ 10%	#ERRC	2.2	3	42	N/A	Phoenix, AZ
7389	Mail Service & Check	105	N/A	65	4/30/93	53	100%	N/A	#ERRC	0.8	5	23	N/A	Phoenix, AZ
7389	Mail Box Rentals	51	168	40	11/30/92	51	49%	5 Yrs @ 10%	0.30	1.3	4	10	18%	Lakewood, CA
7389	Mail Boxes & Shipping	34	120	30	10/31/92	28	50%	5 Yrs @ 10%	0.23	0.9	2	8	16%	Long Beach, CA
7389	Mail Box rentals	37	110	18	7/31/92	34	100%	N/A	0.31	1.9	1	12	13%	Las Vegas, NV
7389	Postal Services	80	150	55	2/28/92	70	40%	3 Yrs @ 10%	0.47	1.3	5	30	16%	Long Beach, CA
7389	Mail Boxes & Shipping	57	75	42	1/31/91	53	48%	4.5 Yr @ 10%	0.71	1.3	3	20	16.4%	Albuquerque, NM
7389	Mail Boxes/Copying	245	202	N/A	10/31/90	200	100%	N/A	0.99	#ERRC	-0-	25	N/A	Santa Barbara, CA

All Mail Box Businesses In Data Base Sold For An Average of 82.5% of Asking Price.

Average Sale Price Divided By Gross Sales = .45 (ie: Sale Price Was 45% of Gross Sales)

Median = .46

Average Sale Price Divided By SDCF = 1.7 (ie: Sale Price Was 1.7 Times SDCF)

Median = 1.5

SOURCE: *Bizcomps ™ 1996 Western Edition* (San Diego: Asset Business Appraisal, 1996), p. 118.

Seller's discretionary cash flow (SDCF) is essentially defined the same way as *discretionary earnings,* as discussed in Chapter 19, The Multiple of Discretionary Earnings (Seller's Discretionary Cash) Method. It is defined as net profit before taxes and before any compensation to the business owner (normally one working owner), plus all noncash expenses and non-business-related expenses.

Bizcomps is available from Jack R. Sanders, Asset Business Appraisal, PO Box 711777, San Diego, California 92171, phone (619) 457-0366. *Bizcomps* informational web page may be found at www.bizcomps.com. As of this writing, the four print editions were $95 each.

The combined database is also available on disk. It is searchable by SIC code, word, sale size, and geographical area. It has the capability to export the data into a spreadsheet, a database, or a word processing program; to filter the records among any of the column headings; and to reconfigure tables to include only selected information among selected records.

The disk version is compatible with Wiley's *ValuSource* software and is available for $195 from Asset Business Appraisal at the address above and from John Wiley & Sons, Inc., 7222 Commerce Center Drive, Suite 210, Colorado Springs, Colorado 80919-2632, phone (800) 825-8763 or (719) 548-4455, fax (719) 548-1212, e-mail softwsale@wiley.com.

Bizcomps subscribers may make special inquiries for updated business sale information by calling (619) 457-0366. The charge is $30 for the first SIC code or category requested and $10 for each additional SIC code or category.

Done Deals Data

In 1996, the World M&A Network started a database called *Done Deals Data*. It is available on disk. Subscribers receive an updated disk quarterly from which they can print all or selected transactions. Exhibit 21-3 is a sample printed page.

Unlike the other three databases discussed in this chapter, the *Done Deals* data are collected from public documents rather than from business brokers and M&A intermediaries. This gives the *Done Deals* database the advantage of specifying the name of the buyer and seller in each transaction. Approximately 20 percent of the sellers are private companies acquired by public companies.

Done Deals intends to cover transactions valued at $1 million to $100 million plus emerging growth companies on track to soon reach this range. An analysis of a sampling of the 1,400 transactions reported between January 1995 and January 1997 includes the following breakdown by transaction size.

Acquisition Transaction Price	Percent of Reported Transactions
Under $1 million	8%
$1 million–$9 million	54
$10 million–$49 million	29
$50 million–$99 million	8
Over $100 million	1

The disk includes a user-friendly software program, *Deal Navigator*, that allows the user to search by closing date, SIC code (28 fairly broad industry categories), key word (as a substitute for precise industry codes), price, buyer, seller, and location. It includes printout capability by company, by industry, or by location. All transactions include five financial indicators of size and profitability (e.g., cash flow from operations) and five price ratios.

Done Deals Data is available from the World M&A Network, 717 D Street, N.W., Suite 300, Washington, DC 20004, phone (800) 809-0666, fax (202) 628-6618. As of this writing, the price is $195 for all industries or $95 for a single industry. This price includes the current database plus three quarterly updates.

Exhibit 21–3

DONE DEALS DATA
SAMPLE PAGE

World M&A Network

Mid-Market M&A Deals Completed

Closing	Description						
11/18/96	*Buyer* Reunion Industries, Inc. 62 Southfield Avenue Stamford, CT 06902 Richard L. Evans, Exec. VP 203-324-8858	*Seller* Quality Molded Products, Inc. (NC)		*Seller Description* xxCUSTOM INJECTION MOLDER serving customers in the housewares, office equipment, consumer products, transportation and construction industries in the southeastern U.S., located in Siler City, NC		*Terms* $3MM cash within 90 days + $3.1MM bank debt assumed + $2.7MM other liabilities assumed	*SIC* 30

	Price	*Assets*	*Stk. Equity*	*Revenue*	*Income*	*Cash Flow*	*P/A*	*P/SE*	*P/R*	*P/E*	*P/CF*
	8.80MM	$8.2MM (12/95)	$3.3MM (12/95)	$16.5MM (1995)	$693.3M (1995)	$1.6MM (1995)	1.1	2.7	0.5	12.7	5.5

Closing	Description						
1/3/97	*Buyer* Maxco Inc. 1118 Centennial Way Lansing, MI 48917 Vincent Shunsky, VP Finance 517-321-3130	*Seller* Atmosphere Annealing, Inc. (MI)		*Seller Description* xxLansing, MI based privately-owned by four individuals, provider of METAL HEAT TREATING to Midwestern industrial users with approximately 370 people in Lansing, MI, Canton, OH, and North Vernon, IN		*Terms* $3.2MM cash + $3.2MM sub-ordinated note + $6.4MM debt assumption	*SIC* 33

	Price	*Assets*	*Stk. Equity*	*Revenue*	*Income*	*Cash Flow*	*P/A*	*P/SE*	*P/R*	*P/E*	*P/CF*
	12.80MM	$11.9MM (12/96)	$2.7MM (12/96)	$27.7MM (1996)	$1.7MM (1996)	$4.0MM (1996)	1.1	10.1	0.5	7.5	3.2

Closing	Description						
2/3/97	*Buyer* Hi-Rise Recycling Systems, Inc. 16255 N.W. 54th Avenue Miami, FL 33014 Donald Engel, CEO 305-624-9222	*Seller* Wilkinson Company, Inc. (OH), (a wholly owned subsidiary of EFCO, Inc.)		*Seller Description* xxMfr., distribute & installs SHEET METAL FABRICATION PRODUCTS, including metal kick plates, corner guards, door edge protectors, lighted hand rails, bumper rail systems, and conveyor systems		*Terms* $2.5MM cash (funded by loan from Ocean Bank) + $305M in Hi-Rise Recycling Systems common stock	*SIC* 34

	Price	*Assets*	*Stk. Equity*	*Revenue*	*Income*	*Cash Flow*	*P/A*	*P/SE*	*P/R*	*P/E*	*P/CF*
	2.80MM	$3.4MM (9/96)	$2.8MM (9/96)	$4MM (FYE 9/96)	$475M(FYE9/96)	$704M (FYE 9/96)	0.8	1.0	0.7	5.9	4.0

Closing	Description						
6/3/96	*Buyer* Unit Instruments, Inc. 22600 Savi Ranch Parkway Yorba Linda, CA 92687 Gary N. Patten, CFO 714-921-2640	*Seller* Control Systems, Inc. (NM)		*Seller Description* xxA privately held company based in Rio Rancho, NM, that manufactures gas isolation boxes, gas panels and other ultra high purity GAS DELIVERY SYSTEMS for the semiconductor industry		*Terms* $1.2MM cash + $4MM in UII common stock	*SIC* 35

	Price	*Assets*	*Stk. Equity*	*Revenue*	*Income*	*Cash Flow*	*P/A*	*P/SE*	*P/R*	*P/E*	*P/CF*
	5.20MM	$4MM (12/95)	$448.9M (12/95)	$10.4MM (1995)	$589.5M (1995)	$2.0MM (1995)	1.3	11.6	0.5	8.8	2.6

Closing	Description						
7/1/96	*Buyer* AirSensors, Inc. 16804 Gridley Place Cerritos, CA 90703 Thomas M. Costales, CFO 810-860-6666	*Seller* Ateco Automotive Pty. Ltd. (Australia)		*Seller Description* xxA private company that distributed AirSensors, Inc.'s GASEOUS FUEL CARBURETION SYSTEMS and devices for use with internal combustion engines		*Terms* $6.5MM cash ($4MM financed by Bank of America, $1.9MM by A/R)	*SIC* 50

	Price	*Assets*	*Stk. Equity*	*Revenue*	*Income*	*Cash Flow*	*P/A*	*P/SE*	*P/R*	*P/E*	*P/CF*
	6.50MM	$4.7MM (6/96)	$2.6MM (6/96)	$6.4MM (FYE 6/96)	$360.5M(FYE6/96)	$1.1MM (FYE 6/96)	1.4	2.5	1.0	18.0	5.9

SOURCE: *Done Deals Data* (Washington, D.C.: World M&A Network, 1997).

Pratt's Stats

The newest entrant in the field, *Pratt's Stats*, is being developed by Business Valuation Resources in conjunction with the International Business Brokers Association. *Pratt's Stats* incorporates the M&A Source Sold Company Database (which had been started at the time of the previous edition of this book, but was never completed). The M&A Source is a subsidiary of the International Business Brokers Association, composed of intermediaries involved in transactions priced primarily in the $500,000 to $50 million range. Formerly oriented only to transactions priced over $500,000, under *Pratt's Stats* management, this database is now being broadened to encompass transactions of all sizes.

In addition, *Pratt's Stats* will encompass the other four databases referred to in the previous edition of this book: the Geneva Business Sale Database, United Business Investments (UBI) *Analyx* database, the Carroll/Cahill Dental Practice Transaction Database, and the Professional Practice Valuation Study Group Transaction Database. The *Geneva Business Sale Database* was never available to independent analysts for analytical use. Now the Geneva Companies, headquartered in Irvine, California, and one of the nation's largest middle-market business intermediaries, will make its transactional data available through *Pratt's Stats*.

United Business Investments (UBI) for many years kept up the UBI business sale database, known as *Analyx*. That database was only available to UBI franchisees. Now UBI has been disbanded as a franchise organization, with each former office now owned and operated as an independent entity. David Scribner, former UBI president, now handles middle-market transactions through his new entity, Blue Chip Financial in Los Angeles, and is reporting all Blue Chip transactions through *Pratt's Stats*. Other former UBI franchisees, some of which are also members of IBBA, are also reporting their transactions to *Pratt's Stats*.

The Carroll/Cahill database of dental practice transactions in the San Francisco Bay Area, developed by Carroll/Cahill Associates of San Francisco (a dental practice broker), was never commercially available. They are now reporting their transactions through *Pratt's Stats*.

Finally, the Professional Practice Valuation Study Group transaction database was never fully developed. The transactions included in this database are 70 to 80 percent dental practices and 20 to 30 percent medical practices. The leadership of the Professional Practice Valuation Study Group has encouraged members to participate in the *Pratt's Stats* database, and many members have begun to do so.

Information for the *Pratt's Stats* database is collected from transactions completed by M&A intermediaries and business brokers. Although as of this writing it has been in operation for less than a year, the database already has approximately 500 transactions.

Exhibit 21-4 is a sample page from *Pratt's Stats*. The sale prices presented *include* inventory, the amount of which is presented as a balance sheet line item. As presented, the level of detail is much greater than for any of the other databases. However, not all of the transactions have the desired level of detail.

Exhibit 21-5 is the transaction input form for *Pratt's Stats*. *Pratt's Stats* is available from Business Valuation Resources, 4475 S.W. Scholls Ferry Road, Suite 101, Portland, Oregon 97225, phone (888) BUS-VALU, fax (503) 291-7955, e-mail shannonp@transport.com. As of this writing, the database was priced at $375 per year, including both print form and disk quarterly updates. Subscribers will soon have real-time custom access and search capabilities as well. As of this writing, the cost for these capabilities has not been determined.

As of December 1997, the distribution of the "deal value" in the *Pratt's Stats* database was as follows:

	Size of Pratt's Stats Transactions 4th Quarter 1997	
	Average Sell Price	% of Total Observations
$0—$500,000	$ 225,812	18.5%
$500,001—$1,000,000	$ 692,439	6.3%
$1,000,001—$5,000,000	$ 2,941,828	29.3%
$5,000,001—$10,000,000	$ 7,497,554	12.4%
$10,000,001—$20,000,000	$ 14,088,219	12.4%
$20,000,001—$50,000,000	$ 31,494,196	12.4%
$50,000,001—$100,000,000	$ 64,149,325	7.8%
$100,000,001+	$111,945,355	0.7%

How Does Business Value Vary with Time?

A study conducted by the IBA on its database addressed the significance of the time of the sale by correlating pricing multiples with the date of sale. Specifically, the IBA performed a linear regression of the price/earnings multiple ("earnings" as defined in Exhibit 21-1) on the date of sale for the years 1982 through 1991. They also regressed the price/sales multiple on the date of sale for the same years. The results of this analysis indicate that "price to net and price to gross ratios of closely held businesses sold during the period 1982 through 1991 show essentially zero correlation with date of sale."[2]

From the results of the above analysis, the following conclusion is stated:

> The variation of business value with time does not appear to be significant in comparison with other influences affecting business value. Consequently, there is no need to restrict choice of 'comparables' to sales within the very recent past.[3]

---

[2]Raymond C. Miles, "Business Appraising in the Real World: Evidence from the IBA Market Database," presentation to The Institute of Business Appraisers 1992 National Conference, February 6–7, 1992, in Orlando, Florida.

[3]Ibid.

Exhibit 21–4

PRATT'S STATS TRANSACTION TABLE
SAMPLE PAGE

Pratt's Stats Combination Report

Intermediary Name: Cuff, Terry & King, Lori		Firm Name: Business Exchange Center, Inc.	
SIC Code: 3425	Business Description: Manufacturing, Saw Blades and Construction Supplies		
Sale Location: Bellevue , WA	Company Type: C Corporation	Number of Employees: 32	Company Age: 15

☒ Data is "Latest Full Year" Reported	☒ Data is "Latest Full Year" Reported	Asking Price:	$1,750,000.00
☐ Data is "Purchase Price Allocation"	☐ Data is "Restated"	Selling Price:	$1,350,000.00
Cash and Equivalents: $288,000.00	Net Sales: $3,400,000.00	Amount of Down Payment:	$500,000.00
Trade Receivables: $270,000.00	COGS: $2,215,000.00	Stock or Asset Sale:	Asset
Inventory: $248,000.00	Gross Profit: $1,185,000.00	Date of Sale:	3/1/97
Other Current Assets: $4,000.00	Yearly Rent: $31,000.00	Months on Market:	2.3
Total Current Assets: $810,000.00	Owner's Compensation: $160,000.00	Price/Net Sales:	0.40
Fixed Assets: $177,000.00	Other Operating Exp.: $643,500.00	Price/Net Income:	4.30
Real Estate: $0.00	Noncash Charges: $36,500.00	Price/Gross Cash Flow:	3.83
Intangibles: $0.00	Total Operating Exp.: $871,000.00	Price/EBITDA:	3.85
Other Noncurrent Assets: $0.00	Operating Profit: $314,000.00	Price/EBIT:	4.30
Total Assets: $987,000.00	Interest Expense: $0.00	Price/EBT:	4.30
Liabilities Assumed: $70,000.00	EBT: $314,000.00	Price/Discretionary Earnings:	2.64
Emplymnt/ConsltAgrmnt: $100,000.00	Taxes: $0.00	Discretionary Earnings:	$510,500.00
Noncompete Value: $250,000.00	Net Income: $314,000.00		

Noncompete Length: (Months) 60   Noncompete Description: United States

Terms of Loan: 13%, 120 Months, $12,691.41/Month

Employment/Consulting Agrmnt: 120 Days maximum of 25 hours/week. Seller available for another 240 days at $30/hour for a maximum of 25 hours/week.

Notes: Purchase price allocation: Trade Receivables $200,000, Inventory $200,000, Other Current Assets $4,000, Fixed Assets $188,000, Intangibles $408,000.

Intermediary Name: Miles, Richard		Firm Name: March Group, LLC, The	
SIC Code: 8021 02	Business Description: Dental Clinics		
Sale Location: Indianapolis IN	Company Type: S Corporation	Number of Employees: 58	Company Age: 15

☐ Data is "Latest Full Year" Reported	☒ Data is "Latest Full Year" Reported	Asking Price:	
☒ Data is "Purchase Price Allocation"	☐ Data is "Restated"	Selling Price:	$4,900,000.00
Cash and Equivalents: $0.00	Net Sales: $3,153,000.00	Amount of Down Payment:	$3,600,000.00
Trade Receivables: $195,000.00	COGS:	Stock or Asset Sale:	Stock
Inventory: $0.00	Gross Profit: $3,153,000.00	Date of Sale:	8/1/97
Other Current Assets: $0.00	Yearly Rent: $100,000.00	Months on Market:	0.0
Total Current Assets: $195,000.00	Owner's Compensation: $313,000.00	Price/Net Sales:	1.55
Fixed Assets: $249,000.00	Other Operating Exp.: $1,985,000.00	Price/Net Income:	6.49
Real Estate:	Noncash Charges: $0.00	Price/Gross Cash Flow:	6.49
Intangibles:	Total Operating Exp.: $2,398,000.00	Price/EBITDA:	6.49
Other Noncurrent Assets: $1,000.00	Operating Profit: $755,000.00	Price/EBIT:	6.49
Total Assets: $445,000.00	Interest Expense: $0.00	Price/EBT:	6.49
Liabilities Assumed: $164,000.00	EBT: $755,000.00	Price/Discretionary Earnings:	4.59
Emplymnt/ConsltAgrmnt:	Taxes: $0.00	Discretionary Earnings:	$1,068,000.00
Noncompete Value:	Net Income: $755,000.00		

Noncompete Length: (Months) 36   Noncompete Description: Indiana

Terms of Loan:

Employment/Consulting Agrmnt: 3 Years (Management and Performance agreement)

Notes: Acquired in conjunction with IPO. $4,619,000 allocated to Goodwill.

SOURCE: *Pratt's Stats* (Portland, OR: Business Valuation Resources, 1997).

Exhibit 21–5

Pratt's Stats Submittal Form

Do you wish to have your name and firm associated with the reported information? Yes ☐ No ☐ Date of Report: _____

Intermediary Name: _____ Firm Name: _____

Location of Firm, City: _____ State: ___ Phone: _____

Product/Service Description of Company Sold: _____

SIC Code: ___ SIC Sub Code: ___ Company Name: _____

Years in Business: ___ Number of Employees: ___ City of Sale: _____ State of Sale: ___

Income Data	**Asset Data**	**Transaction Data**
☐ Data is "Latest Full Year" Reported	☐ Data is "Latest Full Year" Reported	"Latest Full Year" Financial Report Date: _____
☐ Data is Restated (See Notes field for any additional explanation)	☐ Data is "Purchase Price Allocation agreed upon by Buyer and Seller"	Date Sale Initiated: _____
Net Sales: _____	Cash and Equivalents: _____	Date of Sale: _____
COGS: _____	Trade Receivables: _____	Asking Price: _____
Gross Profit: _____	Inventory: _____	Selling Price: _____
Yearly Rent: _____	Other Current Assets: _____	Amount of Down Payment: _____
Owner's Compensation: _____	Total Current Assets: _____	Stock or Asset Sale _____
Other Operating Exp.: _____	Fixed Assets: _____	Company Type: (C or S Corp., LLC, LLP, Sole Prop., etc.) _____
Noncash Charges: _____	Real Estate: _____	
Total Operating Exp.: _____	Intangibles: _____	Was there an Employment/Consulting Agrmnt?
Operating Profit: _____	Other Noncurrent Assets: _____	Yes ☐ No ☐
Interest Expense: _____	Total Assets: _____	Was there an Assumed Lease in the sale?
EBT: _____	Liabilities Assumed: _____	Yes ☐ No ☐
Taxes: _____	Emplymnt/ConsltAgrmnt: _____	Is there a Renewal Option with the Lease?
Net Income: _____	Noncompete Value: _____	Yes ☐ No ☐

Additional Transaction Information

Was there a Note in the consideration paid? Yes ☐ No ☐ Was there a personal guarantee on the Note? Yes ☐ No ☐

Terms of Loan Balance or Financing Information: (Length, Rate, Payment, Baloon Payment, etc.)

_____

Balance of Assumed Lease: (Months) _____ Terms of Lease: _____

Noncompete Length: (Months) _____ Noncompete Description: (Miles Radius, etc.) _____

Employment/Consulting Agreement Description: (Obligation, Length of Time, Services Required, etc.)

_____

Additional Notes:

_____

Please send completed form to:
Business Valuation Resources, 4475 SW Scholls Ferry Rd, Suite 101, Portland, OR 97225; Fax to (503) 291-7955
If your have any questions please call Jim Jordon, Chad Phillips or Doug Twitchell toll free at (888) BUS-VALU   Revised 11/97

SOURCE: *Pratt's Stats* (Portland, OR: Business Valuation Resources, 1997).

However, the above conclusion may be misleading. Often, important information contained in subsets of data is masked by analyzing the data only on a mass basis. This phenomenon is particularly true of linear regression statistics. In this case, two of the significant data subsets that are masked are (1) time periods that are characterized by significantly different economic circumstances, such as interest rates and the availability of capital, and (2) differing patterns of pricing of the businesses over time among different industry groups.

The above factors suggest that further study is appropriate before applying this conclusion broadly. For example, if one compared the average pricing multiples during the period of highest capital costs with the pricing multiples during the periods of lowest capital costs or made comparisons between different phases of the economic cycle (recession versus expansion), one would be surprised if there were not differences. (One would need to be careful, however, in analyzing terms of sale because sellers tend to counter high interest rates with "creative financing." Creative financing is a euphemism for a discount in the form of a contract for a larger balance, for a longer time, and further below general market interest rate levels.)

It is also reasonable to believe that pricing multiples for industry groups tend to rise and fall with the relative popularity of investing in different industry groups at different times.

One prominent restaurant broker once reported that average pricing multiples (such as the price to gross sales multiple) dropped fully a third within a six-month period in his market. This decline was due to a combination of (1) tight and expensive financing and (2) some detrimental publicity regarding restaurant investments.

Glenn Desmond makes the point that small businesses are not isolated from economic and industry trends and that their values *do* fluctuate over time:

> Formulas and rule-of-thumb multiplier ranges change because of new forms of competition, influences from regional or national inflation or recession, changes in popularity and marketability of businesses, and refinements in valuation methodology and data sources.[4]
>
> Small businesses today are affected by the regional, national, and even international economies as well as the local economy. There are "outside" forces that the independent small business can do little about. The economic recession which began in 1990 in the United States is a perfect example; it appears that many businesses were hurt, and surveys indicate that businesses in many industries suffered declines in value of 25% to 30% or more.
>
> What has been said regarding the general economy also goes for the industry of which the small business is a part. However, a particular industry may have different trends and a different outlook from the general economy. The economy may be performing well or poorly, but that does not always mean that a specific industry will follow suit.[5]

---

[4]Glenn M. Desmond, *Handbook of Small Business Valuation Formulas and Rules of Thumb,* 3d ed. (Camden, ME: Valuation Press, 1993), p. *x.*

[5]Ibid., pp. 15–16.

How Is Price Affected by Terms?

There are at least a half dozen significant elements in the terms of payment that influence the price of a small business or professional practice transaction:

1. Down payment percentage.
2. Length of contract payout.
3. Extent to which contract payout is fixed or dependent on contingencies.
4. Interest rate (especially relative to market rates at the time of the transaction).
5. Strength of contract, collateral, covenants, and remedies in case of default.
6. Other consideration (employment contracts, covenants not to compete, and so on).

It is important to know as much about these items as possible for each sale that is considered a possible guideline transaction in the market approach to valuation. Guidance on adjusting for these differences from one sale to another is found in Chapter 27, Tradeoff between Cash and Terms.

Using the Databases in the Market Approach

The progress in private transaction databases, especially in the last year or two, has made valuation by the market approach using these data much more feasible than it was a few years ago.

An important limitation compared to using guideline publicly traded companies is that, in most cases, the specific company involved is not disclosed. This precludes verification of the data from the transaction source or analysis of special motivations or circumstances that may have affected the price of a given transaction.

Because of this important limitation, it generally is necessary to have more transactions in the subject industry group in order to develop a reasonably reliable range of value. The less detailed the data per transaction, the more transactions necessary to develop a range of value for the subject company in which one would have confidence. In this regard, at their present stages of development, the *IBA Market Database* and *Bizcomps* have the advantage in terms of number of transactions, while *Done Deals* and *Pratt's Stats* have the advantage of more detailed information per transaction.

To the extent the data are available, the following valuation multiples can be developed, much as in the application of the guideline publicly traded company method:

- Price/sales.
- Price/earnings (after-tax).
- Price/pretax earnings.
- Price/discretionary earnings (owner's or seller's cash flow).
- Price/gross cash flow.
- Price/cash flow from operations.
- Price/EBITDA.
- Price/net asset value.

As with the guideline publicly traded company method, relative emphasis with respect to these value measures will vary in importance from one type of company to another. As with guideline publicly traded companies, the tightness or dispersion of the ranges of multiples for each value indicator is an indication of its relevance in the particular industry. The tighter the measures of dispersion, the greater the indication that buyers and sellers tend to put weight on that particular value measure. For comparing dispersion of various valuation multiples within an industry, a good measure of dispersion is the coefficient of variation (the standard deviation divided by the mean).

The relative emphasis on different valuation multiples also will be influenced by the relative quantity and quality of data available for each. Even if the analyst believes that multiples of EBIT are most important in the market for companies in the industry, if there are 10 transactions with price/discretionary earnings multiples and only 3 with price/EBIT multiples, the analyst probably won't put as much weight on the price/EBIT multiples as would be the case if there were more price/EBIT data.

Size of the company is also a factor in the relative importance of different valuation multiples. The smaller the company, the greater the emphasis on pretax valuation measures. Also, for smaller companies, the focus of the pricing tends to be more on the basis of discretionary earnings and/or price/revenue ratios, while relative emphasis tends to shift to multiples such as price/EBIT as we move up the size scale.

There are some differences in definitions of variables among the databases. For example, *Done Deals* and *Pratt's Stats* include inventory in the deal price. *Bizcomps* excludes inventory from the reported deal price, and the *IBA Market Database* is silent on this point. *Bizcomps* defines what it calls *seller's discretionary cash flow* and *Pratt's Stats* defines what it calls *discretionary earnings* essentially the same way: earnings before taxes, interest, compensation to one working owner, and noncash charges. The *IBA Market Database* uses the term *annual earnings*: earnings before taxes, interest, and owner's compensation but not before noncash charges. It is important that the analyst using these databases understands these differences in definitions so that data used from each database can be applied to variables defined in the same way for the subject company.

Virtually all of the transactions represent an actual sale of the entire invested capital of a business. Therefore, adjustments to the indicated values derived from these databases may be necessary for liabilities assumed, minority interest, and/or marketability.

To the extent that data are available, of course, it is always desirable to combine market approach methods using these databases with other valuation approaches and methods.

Summary

This chapter has described four databases covering private transactions in small to middle-market sized companies.

Two of these databases, *Done Deals Data* and *Pratt's Stats*, are new since the previous edition of this book. These two databases provide more detail per transaction than was previously available. They also have more emphasis on transactions over $500,000 in deal value.

Each of the two databases that were discussed in the last edition, the *IBA Market Database* and *Bizcomps*, have roughly doubled the number of transactions they contain. These developments combine to make using private transaction databases potentially much more of a factor in the valuation of small businesses and professional practices.

These databases are relatively inexpensive, especially compared to typical databases on larger company transactions. As of this writing, one could obtain all of the back data and a year's subscription to all current data for all four of the described databases for a combined cost of less than $1,000.

Definitions of the variables used in the different databases vary somewhat. It is important that the analyst using the databases understand the definitions of the variables used and apply the data to identically defined variables for the subject company.

The deal prices in the databases described all are reported to be based on actual sales of all the invested capital of a business or practice and often include covenants not to compete and/or employment contracts. Therefore, adjustments to values indicated by multiples from these databases may need to be made where appropriate for liabilities assumed, minority interest, marketability, and items not included in the subject business value, such as covenants not to compete or employment contracts.

For convenience, the addresses and telephone numbers of the four database sources are repeated below:

1. *IBA Market Database*, Institute of Business Appraisers, PO Box 1447, Boynton Beach, Florida 33425, phone (561) 732-3202, fax (561) 732-4304. Available in print only.
2. *Bizcomps,* Jack R. Sanders, Asset Business Appraisal, PO Box 711777, San Diego, California 92171, phone (619) 457-0366. Available in both print and disk. Disk version also available from John Wiley & Sons, 7222 Commerce Center Drive, Suite 210, Colorado Springs, Colorado 80919-2632, phone (800) 825-8763 or (719) 548-4455, fax (719) 548-1212, e-mail softwsale@wiley.com.

3. *Done Deals Data,* World M&A Network, 717 D Street, N.W., Suite 300, Washington, DC 20004, phone (800) 809-0666, fax (202) 628-6618. Available on disk only.

4. *Pratt's Stats*, Business Valuation Resources, 4475 S.W. Scholls Ferry Road, Suite 101, Portland, Oregon 97225, phone (888) BUS-VALU, fax (503) 291-7955, e-mail shannonp@transport.com. Available in both print and disk.

Chapter 22

The Asset Accumulation Method

Business financial statements prepared in accordance with generally accepted accounting principles (GAAP) are prepared based on the historical cost principle. That is, almost all assets and liabilities recognized on a company's balance sheet are recorded at their historical acquisition price (i.e., their historical cost). Wasting assets, such as real estate (other than land) and tangible personal property, are depreciated over their expected useful life. Therefore, at any point in time, the balance sheet presents the depreciated historical cost for these types of tangible assets. This GAAP-based, historical cost–accounting principle allows for conservatism, consistency, and cost-efficiency in the preparation of periodic financial statements.

Under GAAP, the depreciated historical cost of assets recorded on the balance sheet is referred to (in the vernacular) as book value. Also under GAAP, the total depreciated historical cost of the recorded assets minus the total historical values of the recorded liabilities is referred to (in the vernacular) as the book value of the owners' equity in the business.

Arguably, the most fundamental *accounting* principle is this: The book value of assets minus the book value of liabilities equals the book value of owners' equity. This formula is an accounting identity.

Also arguably, the most fundamental business *valuation* principle is this: The current value of assets minus the current value of liabilities equals the current value of owners' equity. This formula is an economics identity.

From a business valuation perspective, the relevant standard (or definition) of value is the one that is appropriate given the purpose and objective of the appraisal. Chapter 3 presented several alternative standards of value, including fair market value, fair value, intrinsic or fundamental value, and investment value. These (and other) similar standards of value are the appropriate value definitions to use in a small business or professional practice valuation assignment that is performed using asset-based valuation approach methods.

Accordingly, based on the purpose and objective of the appraisal, the analyst will first select the appropriate standard of value to apply to the equity interest subject to appraisal. If an asset-based valuation approach is used, the analyst will apply an appropriate standard of value to all of the assets and liabilities of the subject company. It is noteworthy that the standard of value for the assets and liabilities may be fair market value, even if the standard for the subject equity interest is ultimately a different standard of value.

In other words, the analyst will restate all of the assets and liabilities of the subject company from their historical cost values to, for example, fair market value. After the revaluation of all asset and liability accounts from their historical cost to fair market value, the analyst can then apply the axiomatic "assets minus liabilities" formula to conclude the fair market value of the subject owners' equity.

At this point, the business appraiser has typically concluded the value of 100 percent of the subject company's equity, on a marketable, controlling ownership interest basis. If the appraisal subject is something other than 100 percent of the company's equity (e.g., the value of a nonmarketable, minority ownership interest), several valuation discounts and/or premiums may need to be considered.

In some cases, a discount for lack of marketability and/or other valuation discounts or premiums will be appropriate even when valuing 100 percent of the company's equity. Such valuation discounts or premiums often are affected by the standard of value applicable to the subject equity interest.

Fundamentals of the Asset-Based Approach

If properly applied, asset-based approach valuation methods are, arguably, the most complex and rigorous small business and professional practice valuation analyses. The costs and benefits of using asset-based approach valuation methods are described below. Before we consider these costs and benefits, or the various asset-based approach valuation methods, several important fundamentals should be reiterated.

First, in properly applying asset-based methods, historical cost–based financial statements are a starting point, not an ending point, in the business appraisal.

Analysts use the company's GAAP-based balance sheet only as a point of departure from which to begin their valuation analyses. While the final format of the valuation-basis balance sheet is usually similar to the historical cost–basis balance sheet (e.g., the assets may be on the left-hand side and the liabilities may be on the right-hand side), it usually differs significantly in content.

The valuation-basis balance sheet is materially different from the historical cost–basis balance sheet in at least two ways: (1) The balances in the asset and liability accounts have been revalued as of the valuation date, and (2) several new asset and liability accounts are likely to be added.

Second, in applying asset-based valuation methods, all assets and liabilities should be restated to an appropriate standard of value consistent with the standard of value selected for the business valuation. As described below, if certain asset and liability accounts are immaterial or if the revaluation change is immaterial, the analyst may elect to leave those account balances at their historical cost value. Otherwise, the analyst will separately consider and analyze each asset and liability account, either item by item or by category.

The analyst will then conclude the defined value (e.g., fair market value) of each asset and liability, in the process of ultimately concluding the defined value (e.g., fair market value) of the subject company's equity structure. It is generally inappropriate to conclude that the value of the company's assets and liabilities—and of the company's equity value —is "net book value."

Third, in applying asset-based valuation methods, *all* of the company's assets and *all* of the company's liabilities should be considered for revaluation to the selected appropriate standard of value. In many cases, the business appraiser may need to rely on experts in real estate appraisal, in machinery and equipment appraisal, or in other appraisal disciplines.

Many of a company's most valuable assets are not recorded on the company's historical cost–basis balance sheet. This includes the whole category of the company's intangible assets. These intangible assets are typically not included on a historical cost, GAAP-basis balance sheet (unless the intangible assets were acquired as part of a business acquisition, accounted for under the purchase method of accounting).

Also, many of the company's most significant liabilities are not recorded on the company's historical cost–basis balance sheet. This includes the whole category of the company's contingent liabilities. Accordingly, as part of the asset-based approach valuation, new asset and, possibly, new liability accounts will be recorded on the company's valuation-basis balance sheet.

Asset-Based Approach versus Book Value

It is important to distinguish between the application of asset-based approach valuation methods and the naïve reliance on accounting "book value" to reach a valuation conclusion. Under any standard of value, the economic value of a business enterprise equals the company's accounting book value only by chance and happenstance. More likely than not, the true value of the company will be either higher or lower than book value.

There is no theoretical support, conceptual reasoning, or empirical data to suggest that the value of a business enterprise (under any standard of value) would equal the company's historical cost–basis book value.

The terms *book value* or *net book value* are unfortunate accounting jargon from a valuation perspective. This is because book value is not related to economic value or to the valuation process at all. As an accounting convention, the book value of a company is the historical cost of all of the company's assets—less total accumulated depreciation. Net book value is the company's book value less the recorded liabilities. Net book value (often called book value, in the vernacular) is synonymous with the company's recorded owners' equity. Therefore, net book value can also be calculated as the sum of the owners' equity investments in the company plus the cumulative amount of the company's retained earnings.

In any event, accounting book value is not a rigorous business valuation method. In fact, book value is not a business valuation method at all. Book value is not a conceptually sound asset-based valuation method. It is naïve and generally inappropriate to conclude a business valuation based exclusively on book value. The values presented on the GAAP-based balance sheet are not representative of an appropriate value for business valuation purposes. Also, there may be one or several important asset and/or liability accounts not presented on the historical cost, GAAP-basis balance sheet at all.

Asset-Based Approach Valuation Methods

In the appraisal literature, there are several names for very similar asset-based valuation methods. These methods are interchangeably referred to as the net asset value method, the adjusted net worth method, the adjusted book value method, the asset build-up method, or the asset accumulation method. In fact, these are all different names for the same method within the asset-based valuation approach.

Accordingly, only as a notation convention, these different names for the same method will be referred to as the *asset accumulation method* for the remainder of this chapter.

The asset accumulation method is a balance-sheet oriented valuation method. Essentially, the company's balance sheet is restated to current value (as defined). This typically involves the identification and valuation of otherwise unrecorded tangible and intangible assets and liabilities, as well as the revaluation of the assets and liabilities already recorded on the balance sheet.

There are two alternatives in the application of the asset-based approach to business valuation:

1. The collective revaluation of all of the company's assets and liabilities.
2. The discrete (individual) revaluation of all of the company's assets and liabilities.

Each of these methods is described briefly below. In most cases, procedural practicality will dictate which asset-based valuation method will be used.

Collective Revaluation of Assets and Liabilities

In the collective revaluation method (often referred to as the *capitalized excess earnings method*), revaluation of all of the company's assets and liabilities (and, hence, the company's owners' equity) is made—collectively —in one analysis and calculation. Typically, this collective revaluation quantifies all of the company's incremental value over and above the book value of its recorded net assets.

Using this method, the company's intangible value in the nature of goodwill is collectively defined as all of the appreciation (or depreciation) in the value of the company, as compared to the recorded book value of the company.

Under the capitalized excess earnings method, the value of the company's equity is the value of the company's net tangible assets plus the value of the company's total intangible value, in the nature of goodwill. This total intangible value (or total appreciation in the value of the business over its book value) is quantified using the capitalized excess earnings method. This method is discussed in Chapter 23.

When viewed from the perspective of the asset-based valuation approach, the capitalized excess earnings method is one application of the asset-based approach (where all asset revaluation is concluded on a collective basis).

It should be noted, however, that in the strictest application of the capitalized excess earnings method (as discussed in Chapter 23 and in Internal Revenue Service Revenue Ruling 68-609), (1) all tangible assets are revalued to fair market value and (2) the capitalized excess earnings method is used to quantify only the company's collective intangible value in the nature of goodwill.

Discrete (Individual) Revaluation of Assets and Liabilities

In the discrete revaluation method (often referred to as the *asset accumulation method*), all of the company's asset and liability accounts are analyzed and appraised individually.

This involves a separate identification and revaluation of the company's:

1. Financial assets (e.g., cash, accounts receivables, prepaid expenses, inventory, and so on).
2. Tangible personal property (e.g., machinery and equipment, furniture and fixtures, trucks and automobiles, and so on).
3. Real estate (e.g., land, land improvements, buildings, building improvements, and so on).
4. Intangible real property (e.g., leasehold interests, easements, mineral exploitation rights, air and water rights, development rights, and so on).
5. Intangible personal property (e.g., patents, trademarks, copyrights, computer software, trade secrets, customer relationships, going-concern value, goodwill, and so on).
6. Current liabilities (e.g., accounts payable, taxes payable, salaries payable, accrued expenses, and so on).
7. Long-term liabilities (e.g., bonds, notes, mortgages, and debentures payable, and so on).
8. Contingent liabilities (e.g., pending tax disputes, pending litigation, pending environmental concerns, and so on).
9. Special obligations (e.g., unfunded pensions, earned vacations or other leaves of absence, ESOP repurchase liabilities, and so on).

Under this application, the value of the discretely appraised assets (both tangible and intangible) less the value of the discretely appraised liabilities (both recorded and contingent) represents the business value of the company.

Theoretically and practically, the business value concluded under the collective revaluation method (i.e., the capitalized excess earnings method) should equal the business value concluded under the discrete revaluation method (e.g., the asset accumulation method).

The determination of which application to use in a given appraisal should be a function of:

1. The experience and judgment of the business appraiser.
2. The quantity and quality of available data.
3. The purpose and objective of the business appraisal.
4. The scope and timing of the appraisal assignment.

As will be discussed below, there are both costs and benefits associated with the discrete application of the asset accumulation method.

Partial Revaluation of Individual Assets and Liabilities

Very often, it is practical to revalue some of—but not all of—the company's specific assets and liabilities before using the capitalized excess earnings method to quantify the balance of the remaining increment (or decrement) to the company's total equity value. When selecting a capitalization rate to apply to the subject company's "excess earnings," the analyst should consider the extent to which the "excess earnings" are the result of intangible assets and the extent to which the "excess earnings" are the result of appreciated tangible asset values.

Since the collective revaluation method of the asset-based valuation approach will be discussed in detail in Chapter 23 (with regard to the capitalized excess earnings method), the remainder of this chapter will focus on the discrete revaluation method of the asset-based approach.

Steps in the Application of the Asset Accumulation Method

This section lists and briefly discusses the application of the asset accumulation method, as divided into the following six steps:

1. Obtain or develop a GAAP-basis balance sheet.
2. Determine which assets and liabilities on the GAAP-basis balance sheet require revaluation adjustment.
3. Identify off-balance-sheet intangible assets that should be recognized and valued.
4. Identify off-balance-sheet or contingent liabilities that should be recognized and valued.
5. Value the various asset and liability accounts identified in steps 2 through 4.
6. Construct a valuation-basis balance sheet, based on the results of steps 1 through 5.

Obtain or Develop a GAAP-Basis Balance Sheet

As mentioned above, first, the analyst starts with a GAAP- or historical cost–basis balance sheet for the subject small business or professional practice. Ideally, this balance sheet will be prepared as of the valuation date. If a historical cost-basis balance sheet is not available because the valuation is being conducted as of an interim date, the analyst has three options:

1. The client (or an accountant retained by the client) may prepare a historical cost–basis balance sheet as of the valuation date and give it to the analyst as the basic tool from which to begin the appraisal.
2. The analyst may prepare a historical cost–basis balance sheet as of the valuation date, assuming that the business appraiser has the requisite basic accounting expertise to prepare such a financial statement.
3. The analyst may rely on the most recent historical cost–basis balance sheet prepared at the fiscal period end just prior to the valuation date. It is noteworthy that a recent fiscal period end balance sheet usually will require more revaluation adjustments than a valuation date balance sheet. However, using a recent fiscal period end balance sheet is typically better than not having a starting point at all.

Identify Recorded Assets and Liabilities to Be Revalued

Second, the analyst will carefully analyze and understand each material recorded asset account and liability account of the subject company. The objective of this analysis is to determine which recorded assets and liabilities will need to be revalued—according to the selected standard of value appropriate for the subject business valuation.

As a convention throughout the remainder of this discussion, we will assume that fair market value is the appropriate standard of value for the subject business valuation. Accordingly, in this step, the analyst will analyze which material recorded asset accounts and liability accounts of the company should be revalued in order to estimate fair market value.

Identify Off-Balance-Sheet Assets That Should Be Recognized

Third, the analyst will identify which unrecorded (sometimes called "off-balance-sheet") assets need to be recognized on the valuation balance sheet. For example, while intangible assets are not normally recorded on financial statements prepared under GAAP, they often represent the largest component of economic value for a small business or professional practice.

The company's tangible and intangible assets represent the allocation of the elements of the overall business value into specific assets.

They represent the identification of the specific factors (i.e., the specific asset accounts or asset groups) responsible for the company's earning capacity, cash flow–generating capacity, and dividend-paying capacity. Intangible assets normally do not appear on the balance sheet if they are developed internally. They are only recorded on the balance sheet if they are acquired in a purchase.

Some tangible assets may have been expensed rather than capitalized when they were acquired. Other tangible assets may be fully depreciated in the financial statements even though they still have remaining useful life and a material economic value. For these reasons, the analyst should look for unrecorded tangible assets as well as unrecorded intangible assets.

Identify Off-Balance-Sheet and Contingent Liabilities That Should Be Recognized

Fourth, the analyst will identify which unrecorded material contingent liabilities, if any, need to be recognized on the valuation balance sheet. If there are potential environmental liabilities, a specialized expert opinion may be needed.

Under GAAP accounting, contingent liabilities are not recorded on a historical cost–basis balance sheet. However, in audited and reviewed financial statements, material contingent liabilities are subject to footnote disclosure.

The identification and valuation of contingent liabilities is a relatively less common step in the asset accumulation method. Typically, this is only because most small businesses and professional practices do not have material contingent liabilities. However, the business appraiser should consider this procedure in the application of the asset accumulation method.

Certainly, for those companies that have material pending litigation against them, income or property tax claims against them, environmental claims against them, and so forth, these contingent liabilities have a significant (and often quantifiable) effect on the risk of the business. Therefore, these material contingent liabilities have a significant effect on the company's business enterprise value.

Value the Items Identified Above

Fifth, after the analysis of recorded assets and liabilities and the identification of unrecorded assets and liabilities, the analyst will begin the quantitative process of revaluing each of the company's asset accounts and, if necessary, each of the company's liability accounts.

Typically, the analyst will perform these valuation analyses by category of assets. The standard categorization of assets, for purposes of applying the asset accumulation method, was described above. These standard categories of assets are (1) financial assets, (2) tangible personal property, (3) real estate, (4) intangible real property, and (5) intangible personal property. For some of these categories, the business appraiser may need to rely on specialized appraisal experts.

The general valuation approaches, methods, and procedures for appraising these asset categories (and the component tangible and intangible assets) will be summarized later in this chapter.

Construct a Valuation-Basis Balance Sheet

Sixth, after concluding the value for all of the company's tangible and intangible assets—and for all of the company's recorded and contingent liabilities—the analyst will construct a valuation-basis balance sheet, as of the valuation date.

From this valuation-basis (as opposed to historical cost–basis) balance sheet, it is a mathematically direct procedure for the analyst to subtract the value of the company's liabilities (recorded and contingent) from the value of the company's assets (tangible and intangible). The remainder of this subtraction procedure is the value of a 100 percent ownership interest in the company's equity structure (typically on a marketable, controlling ownership basis).

At this point, the asset accumulation method has estimated the value of the total owners' equity of the company. Of course, if the company has several classes of equity securities outstanding, additional valuation and value allocation procedures may be required.

In addition, if the appraisal assignment relates to something less than the overall business equity value (e.g., to a nonmarketable, noncontrolling ownership interest in the class B nonvoting common stock of the company), additional valuation discount and/or premium analyses are required. Also, if foreseeable sales of appreciated assets are contemplated, the income tax liability on the potential gain may have to be recognized.

Valuation Premises for Individual Assets

Before considering the various valuation methods with respect to the individual assets of a company, the analyst should first consider both the appropriate standard (or definition) of value and the appropriate premise of value for each asset category. Usually (but not always), the appropriate standard of value selected for each asset category should be the same standard of value as selected for the overall business valation.

With regard to the individual asset appraisal, analysts will select from among four alternative premises of value. Each of these four premises of value may apply under each of the standards of value.

The standard (or definition) of value answers the general question "Value to whom?" The premise of value answers the general question "Value under what set of hypothetical market transaction conditions?" For example, under the fair market value standard of value, the same asset category may be appraised under each of the four premises of value.

Under the fair market value standard, the question of "Value to whom?" is answered by "a hypothetical willing buyer and a hypothetical willing seller." The selected premise of value answers the question "In what type of market transaction will these two willing parties interact?"

The four alternative premises of value for individual asset appraisal are (1) value in continued use, as part of a going concern; (2) value in place, as part of a mass assemblage of assets; (3) value in exchange, in an orderly disposition; and (4) value in exchange, in a forced liquidation.

Value in Continued Use, as Part of a Going Concern

Under this premise, it is assumed that the subject assets are sold (1) as a mass assemblage and (2) as part of an income-producing business enterprise.

This premise of value contemplates the mutually synergistic relationships (i.e., the value enhancement) (1) of the company's tangible assets to the intangible assets and (2) of the intangible assets to the tangible assets.

Value in Place, as Part of a Mass Assemblage of Assets

Under this premise, it is assumed that the subject assets are sold as a mass assemblage. And it is assumed that the mass assemblage is capable of being, but is not currently operating as, an income-producing business enterprise.

This premise of value contemplates some of the mutual contributory value (i.e., value enhancement) (1) of the tangible assets to the intangible assets and (2) of the intangible assets to the tangible assets. However, while there is a value in place component to the subject assets, this premise may exclude some of the contributory value of such common intangible assets as a trained and assembled workforce, going-concern value, and intangible value in the nature of goodwill.

Value in Exchange, in an Orderly Disposition

Under this premise, it is assumed that the subject assets are sold piecemeal, not as part of a mass assemblage. It is assumed that the assets are given an adequate level of exposure in their normal secondary market.

However, due to the orderly disposition market transaction assumption, this premise does not contemplate any contributory value effect of the subject tangible assets on the intangible assets or of the subject intangible assets on the tangible assets.

Value in Exchange, in a Forced Liquidation

Under this premise, it is assumed that the subject assets are sold piecemeal, not as part of a mass assemblage. It is also assumed that the assets are not allowed a normal level of exposure to their normal secondary market. Rather, the assets are permitted an abbreviated level of exposure to a market of the highest bidders present (who may or may not represent the collective demand-side marketplace for such assets), as in an auction environment.

Due to the forced liquidation market transaction assumption, this premise assumes no contributory value (or other economic interrelationships) from the subject tangible assets to the subject intangible assets, or vice versa.

Selecting the Appropriate Premise of Value

Any of the four premises of value described above may be applied to the same asset (or category of assets) being appraised under the same standard of value. For example, an analyst may select the fair market value standard and assume that a willing buyer and a willing seller will transact to exchange an asset.

The selected premise of value describes the assumed market conditions under which this willing buyer and willing seller will meet and transact—that is, (1) during the sale of an up-and-running business, (2) during the sale of a temporarily closed business, (3) during the brokered sale of individual assets, or (4) during the auction sale of individual assets.

The analyst will select the appropriate premise or premises of value (1) based on the purpose and objective of the appraisal and (2) based on the most likely form of the ultimate sale of the subject business (and, accordingly, of the assets of the subject business).

Two other factors directly influence the selection of the appropriate premise of value:

1. The actual condition and operation of the subject assets. That is, whether the subject assets are in use, in place, or held out for sale (in an orderly disposition or forced liquidation environment).
2. *The highest and best use of the subject assets.* That is, the premise of value that will result in the greatest estimated value for the subject business enterprise.

Needless to say, the selection of the appropriate premise or premises of value is a critical decision in the application of the asset accumulation method of business valuation. This is because even under the same standard of value, the subject business can have materially different value conclusions—given the premise or premises of value selected for valuing the various assets.

Individual Asset Valuation Approaches, Methods, and Procedures

After the appropriate premise of value is selected, the next step in the asset accumulation method is to apply one or more generally accepted appraisal approaches to each asset category.

The conceptual cornerstone of the asset accumulation method is the identification and valuation of all of the company's assets. This includes the financial assets, the tangible assets (real and personal), and the intangible assets (real and personal).

In Chapter 7, the procedures related to adjusting the balance sheet were discussed. Those adjustment procedures should be considered when analyzing the company's balance sheet in preparation for the application of *any* business valuation approach or method. It is noteworthy that the procedures discussed below are generally accepted asset appraisal procedures, as compared to common balance sheet adjustment procedures. These asset appraisal procedures should be considered when using the asset accumulation method.

Since this is not a text devoted to individual asset appraisal, this discussion will be introductory in nature. In the bibliography to this chapter, appropriate references to articles and books regarding the appraisal of individual tangible assets are presented. Business appraisers may wish to study these subjects in detail. References to specialized texts and articles on appraising intangible assets are included in the bibliography at the end of Chapter 42.

Financial Assets

The most common assets included in this category include cash, accounts and notes receivable, and prepaid expenses.

With regard to cash, no revaluation procedures need to be performed, of course.

In the sale of a small business, it is common for the seller to retain some or all of the cash balances on hand. This is true in a transaction involving the sale of stock as well as in a transaction involving the sale of assets. Accordingly, the business appraiser should verify the amount of cash, if any, that will actually be transferred with the business enterprise.

With regard to accounts and notes receivable, the analyst may estimate the net realizable value of these receivables. The net realizable value is, essentially, the present value of the expected realization of (i.e., collection of) the receivables.

For businesses with audited or reviewed financial statements (or more sophisticated accounting systems), a reserve for uncollectible accounts is typically established as a contra-asset valuation account. Particularly if the valuation date is other than a fiscal period end, the analyst may assess the adequacy of this reserve for uncollectible accounts.

For smaller businesses that have not established reserves for uncollectible accounts, the analyst may assess the ultimate collectibility of the gross receivables.

Based on this assessment of historical collection patterns, the analyst will typically discount the gross accounts receivable in order to conclude an estimate of net cash collections.

Finally, if the expected realization of the receivables is anticipated to occur over an extended period of time (i.e., longer than the normal collection cycle), the analyst may also apply a present value analysis to the longer-term receivables.

The net balance of the accounts and notes receivable, after the analysis for uncollectible accounts and the present value of extended period receivables (if applicable), represents the net realizable value of this asset category.

With regard to prepaid expenses, the analyst may estimate the net realizable value of this asset category. Prepaid expenses typically include deposits and prepaid rent, insurance, utilities expenses, and so forth.

Normally, the business expects to realize the economic benefit of these assets within the normal course of one business cycle. Therefore, normally, no revaluation adjustment is required with respect to recorded prepaid expenses.

However, if the analyst determines that the company will not enjoy an economic benefit from a prepaid expense during a normal business cycle, a revaluation adjustment may be appropriate. For example, if the company has recorded prepaid rent expense on a facility it is no longer using, that asset will likely have little economic value.

The expected realization of the prepaid expenses represents the net realizable value of this asset category.

Real Estate

Real estate includes such assets as owned land, land improvements, buildings, and building improvements.

Technically, in the appraisal literature, real estate represents the tangible element of real property ownership. Real estate is distinguished from intangible real property. Intangible real property represents the bundle of legal rights associated with real estate. For example, a real property interest would be a limited legal interest (i.e., less than a fee simple ownership interest)—such as a leasehold estate—in real estate.

There is a prodigious body of literature with respect to the appraisal of real estate. And both the appraisal regulatory agencies and the various professional appraisal membership organizations have promulgated professional standards with respect to the valuation of real estate.

Nonetheless, all real estate is valued by reference to these three generally accepted appraisal approaches: (1) the cost approach, (2) the income capitalization approach, and (3) the sales comparison approach. However, each of these three approaches represents a general category of several discrete appraisal methods. Each of these approaches is described briefly below.

Cost Approach.   The cost approach is based on the economic principle of substitution. That is, no one would pay more for an asset than the price required to obtain (by purchase or by construction) a substitute asset of comparable utility. This assumes, of course, that the subject asset is fungible.

In other words, the cost approach assumes that substitute properties of comparable utility may be obtained. If, in fact, the subject asset is unique in one or more respects, the cost approach may not be a viable appraisal approach.

Using the cost approach, the value of land is appraised separately from the value of all appurtenances to land. The subject land is valued as if vacant and unimproved. The subject land is also valued at its highest and best use. The value of vacant land is determined by reference to the sale of comparable land parcels in the reasonably proximate marketplace.

The analyst collects and analyzes data with respect to recent sales of vacant land parcels. If necessary, quantitative adjustments are made for important factors such as size, access, services, frontage, topography, distance, time of sale, and special terms of sale. Based on an analysis of these adjusted comparable property sales data, the analyst estimates the value of the subject land.

The subject buildings and improvements are valued by reference to the current cost to recreate their functional utility. There are several commonly used cost approach methods. One of the common methods is the depreciated reproduction cost method.

This method is algebraically described as follows:

	Reproduction cost new of buildings and improvements
Less:	Allowances for incurable functional obsolescence
equals:	Replacement cost
less:	Allowance for physical deterioration
equals:	Depreciated replacement cost
less:	Allowance for economic or external obsolescence
less:	Allowances for curable functional obsolescence
equals:	Market value of buildings and improvements

To complete the cost approach, the value of the land is added to the value of the buildings and improvements. The sum of these two values estimates the market value of the subject real estate.

Income Capitalization Approach. The income capitalization approach is based on the economic principles of (1) risk and expected return investment analysis and (2) anticipation. Using this approach, the value of the real estate is the present value of the expected economic income that could be earned through the ownership of the subject asset.

There are two categories of valuation methods under the income capitalization approach: (1) the direct capitalization method and (2) the yield capitalization method.

From an investment analysis perspective, these two methods are conceptually similar. Therefore, from a theoretical perspective, both methods should conclude identical values for the same parcel of real estate.

Using the direct capitalization method, the analyst first estimates the normalized economic income that would be earned from the rental (whether hypothetical or actual) of the subject real estate. Economic income may be defined many ways (i.e., before tax, after tax, before interest expense, after interest expense, and so on).

The most common definition of economic income used in the direct capitalization method of real estate is (before-tax) net operating income.

This estimate of economic income is normalized to represent an average or typical period's rental income (including normal rental rates and occupancy levels) and operating expenses (including normal repairs, maintenance, etc.).

The normalized economic income is capitalized, typically, as an annuity in perpetuity, by a capitalization rate (1) commensurate with the risk of investment and (2) consistent with the measurement of economic income. For example, if projected economic income is measured on an after-tax basis, the capitalization rate should be derived on an after-tax basis. If economic income is measured before tax, the capitalization rate should be derived before tax, and so forth.

Consistent with the definition of economic income as before-tax net operating income, the most common derivation of the direct capitalization rate is a blended debt and equity rate (or a weighted average cost of capital).

The equity component of this blended rate represents the typical real estate investor's current income yield expectation for similar rental properties. It excludes the investor's derived long-term capital appreciation expectation for the subject property. The debt component of this blended rate represents the typical mortgage debt rate for similar rental properties. It includes a yield component for the amortization of mortgage principal as well as the payment of mortgage interest.

The debt component and the equity component are blended, or weighted together, based on the typical loan-to-value ratio for new mortgages offered on comparable rental properties. The result of this analysis is the direct capitalization rate.

Using the direct capitalization method, the value of the subject real estate is presented algebraically, as follows:

$$Value = \frac{Normalized\ economic\ income}{Direct\ capitalization\ rate}$$

Using the yield capitalization method, the value of the subject real estate is the present value of the projected economic income to be derived from the property over a discrete period of time. While there is no absolutely correct project period, discrete projection periods of from 5 to 10 years are common.

The analyst projects the economic income to be derived from the rental of the subject property for each year in the discrete projection period. Again, before-tax net operating income is the most common measurement of economic income.

The analyst next derives a present value discount rate to calculate the present value of the discrete projection of economic income. This present value discount rate is often called the *going-in capitalization rate*. The analyst then estimates the normalized economic income to be generated by the property after the conclusion of the discrete projection period. This is sometimes called an estimate of the residual value (or reversionary period) income. This is the average or typical level of income to be generated by the property after the end of the projection period.

The analyst next derives a capitalization rate consistent with this estimate of residual value (or reversionary period) income. This rate is often called the *residual (or reversionary) capitalization rate*. It is sometimes called the *coming-out capitalization rate*. The coming-out capitalization rate is often different from the going-in capitalization rate due to the changing relative remaining life of the property and the different risk positions of the two investment periods.

The estimate of residual normalized economic income is capitalized by the residual capitalization rate. The result is the estimated value of the property at the end of the discrete projection period. This residual value is brought back to its present value, using the discrete projection period present value discount rate.

Finally, under the income capitalization approach, the value of the subject real estate is the sum of discrete projection period present value plus the residual value present value.

Sales Comparison Approach. The sales comparison approach is based on the economic principles of (1) efficient markets and (2) supply and demand. That is, when there is a relatively efficient and unrestricted secondary market for comparable properties and when that market accurately depicts the activities of a representative number of willing buyers and willing sellers, the market is most determinative of the value of the subject property.

Using the sales comparison approach, the analyst first collects data with regard to relatively recent sales of comparable real estate properties. Next, the analyst analyzes each of these sale transactions to determine if any quantitative adjustments are necessary due to the lack of comparability of the subject property when compared to the comparable properties.

The analyst would consider these factors, among others, when determining if quantitative adjustments to the sales comparison data are necessary:

1. Age of each transaction (i.e., elapsed time from the valuation date).
2. Land-to-building ratio of each property.
3. Absolute location and relative location of each property compared to population centers, highways, and so forth.
4. Age of each property.
5. Physical condition of each property.
6. Municipal and other services available to each property.
7. Frontage and access of each property.
8. Topography of land and soil type of each comparable property.
9. Environmental aspects of each property.
10. Special financing or other terms regarding each sales transaction.

Accordingly, if necessary, the analyst adjusts the sales comparison data to make each transaction as comparable to the subject property as possible. Based on these adjusted sales comparison data, the analyst will conclude a market-derived valuation multiple. This multiple is often expressed in terms of value per square foot of improved building space.

Next, the analyst applies the market-derived valuation multiple to the size characteristics of the subject property. The resulting product is the estimate of value of the subject real estate, per the sales comparison approach.

Final Value Reconciliation.   To reach a final valuation synthesis and conclusion regarding the subject real estate, the analyst will carefully consider the quantitative results of each of the three appraisal approaches used. In reaching the valuation conclusion, the analyst will consider the quantity and quality of available data used in each appraisal approach.

The analyst will also assess the appropriate degree of confidence in the applicability and validity of each approach with respect to unique characteristics of the subject real estate. Based on these factors, the analyst will synthesize the results of each approach and conclude an overall value for the subject real estate.

Tangible Personal Property

The tangible personal property category of assets include such assets as inventory, office furniture and fixtures, computer and office automation equipment, store racks and fixtures, manufacturing machinery and equipment, processing equipment, tools and dies, trucks and automobiles, and material handling and transportation equipment.

There is a considerable body of literature with regard to the appraisal of industrial and commercial tangible personal property. There is also authoritative literature regarding the appraisal of special purpose and technical tangible personal property, such as scientific and laboratory equipment, medical and healthcare equipment, mining and extraction equipment, and so forth.

Nonetheless, all of the various tangible personal property appraisal methods and procedures can be grouped into three generally accepted appraisal approaches: (1) the cost approach, (2) the income approach, and (3) the market approach.

Inventory.   With regard to inventory, the analyst should distinguish between the work-in-process inventory of a professional service firm (e.g., accounting firms, law firms, and so on) and the merchandise inventory of a manufacturer or a wholesale/retail company.

The work-in-process inventory of a professional service firm is essentially the unbilled receivables of the firm. Therefore, the same net realizable value rules discussed with respect to accounts and notes receivable would apply to this asset as well.

With regard to tangible merchandise inventory, there are at least three common valuation methods: (1) the cost of reproduction method, (2) the comparative sales method, and (3) the income method. These valuation methods apply equally to raw material, work-in-process, and finished goods inventory.

While these three inventory valuation methods are discussed elsewhere in the appraisal literature, they are concisely summarized in Internal Revenue Service Revenue Procedure 77-12, 1977-1 C.B. 569.

Revenue Procedure 77-12 (Exhibit 22-1) was originally issued with respect to the valuation of merchandise inventory for purchase price allocation purposes. Nonetheless, these valuation methods provide reasonable guidelines for the appraisal of merchandise inventory for business valuation purposes, as well.

The cost of reproduction valuation method generally provides a good indication of fair market value if the inventory is readily replaceable in the volume and in the mix equal to the subject quantity on hand. In valuing inventory under this method, however, other factors may be relevant. For example, a well-balanced inventory available to fill customers' orders in the ordinary course of business may have a fair market value in excess of its cost of reproduction. This is because such an inventory provides a continuity of business. However, an inventory containing obsolete merchandise unsuitable for customers might have a fair market value of less than the cost of reproduction.

The comparative sales valuation method uses the actual or expected selling prices of finished goods to customers as a basis of determining the fair market value of that inventory. When the expected selling price is used as a basis for valuing inventory, consideration should be given to the time that would be required to dispose of this inventory, the expenses that would be expected to be incurred in such disposition, applicable discounts (including those for quantity), sales commissions, and freight and shipping charges, and a profit commensurate with the amount of investment and degree of risk.

Whether the quantity of inventory to be valued is a larger than normal trading volume should also be recognized. Also, the expected selling price can be a valid starting point only if customers' orders are filled in the ordinary course of business.

The income valuation method when applied to the fair market value estimation of inventory recognizes that the subject inventory must generally be valued in a profit-motivated business. Since the amount of inventory may be large in relation to the normal trading volume, the highest and best use of the inventory will be to provide for a continuity of the marketing operation of the going-concern business.

Additionally, the subject inventory will usually provide the only source of revenue of the subject business during the period it is being used to fill customers' orders. The historical financial data of the subject company can be used to estimate the amount that could be attributed to inventory in order to pay all costs of disposition and provide a return on the investment during the period of disposition.

The analyst will apply one or more of these inventory valuation methods (1) based on the quantity and quality of available data and (2) based on the most likely ultimate disposition of the subject inventory. The analyst will estimate the value of the subject inventory based on the results concluded from one or more of these inventory valuation methods.

Exhibit 22–1

Revenue Procedure 77-12

26 CFR 601.105: Examination of returns and claims for refund, credit or abatement; determination of correct tax liability. (Also Part I, Section 334; 1.334-1.)

Rev. Proc. 77-12

SECTION 1. PURPOSE.

The purpose of this Revenue Procedure is to set forth guidelines for use by taxpayers and Service personnel in making fair market value determinations in situations where a corporation purchases the assets of a business containing inventory items for a lump sum or where a corporation acquires assets including inventory items by the liquidation of a subsidiary pursuant to the provisions of section 332 of the Internal Revenue Code of 1954 and the basis of the inventory received in liquidation is determined under section 334(b)(2). These guidelines are designed to assist taxpayers and Service personnel in assigning a fair market value to such assets.

SEC. 2. BACKGROUND.

If the assets of a business are purchased for a lump sum, or if the stock of a corporation is purchased and that corporation is liquidated under section 332 of the Code and the basis is determined under section 334(b)(2), the purchase price must be allocated among the assets acquired to determine the basis of each of such assets. In making such determinations, it is necessary to determine the fair market value of any inventory items involved. This Revenue Procedure describes methods that may be used to determine the fair market value of inventory items.

In determining the fair market value of inventory under the situations set forth in this Revenue Procedure, the amount of inventory generally would be different from the amounts usually purchased. In addition, the goods in process and finished goods on hand must be considered in light of what a willing purchaser would pay and a willing seller would accept for the inventory at the various stages of completion, when the former is not under any com-

pulsion to buy and the latter is not under any compulsion to sell, both parties having reasonable knowledge of relevant facts.

SEC. 3. PROCEDURES FOR DETERMINATION OF FAIR MARKET VALUE.

Three basic methods an appraiser may use to determine the fair market value of inventory are the cost of reproduction method, the comparative sales method, and the income method. All methods of valuation are based on one or a combination of these three methods.

.01 The cost of reproduction method generally provides a good indication of fair market value if inventory is readily replaceable in a wholesale or retail business, but generally should not be used in establishing the fair market value of the finished goods of a manufacturing concern. In valuing a particular inventory under this method, however, other factors may be relevant. For example, a well balanced inventory available to fill customers' orders in the ordinary course of business may have a fair market value in excess of its cost of reproduction because it provides a continuity of business, whereas an inventory containing obsolete merchandise unsuitable for customers might have a fair market value of less than the cost of reproduction.

.02 The comparative sales method utilizes the actual or expected selling prices of finished goods to customers as a basis of determining fair market values of those finished goods. When the expected selling price is used as a basis for valuing finished goods inventory, consideration should be given to the time that would be required to dispose of this inventory, the expenses that would be expected to be incurred in such disposition, for example, all costs of disposition, applicable discounts (including those for quantity), sales commissions, and freight and shipping charges, and a profit commensurate with the amount of investment and degree of risk. It should also be recognized that the inventory to be valued may represent a larger quantity than the

normal trading volume and the expected selling price can be a valid starting point only if customers' orders are filled in the ordinary course of business.

.03 The income method, when applied to fair market value determinations for finished goods, recognizes that finished goods must generally be valued in a profit motivated business. Since the amount of inventory may be large in relation to normal trading volume the highest and best use of the inventory will be to provide for a continuity of the marketing operation of the going business. Additionally, the finished goods inventory will usually provide the only source of revenue of an acquired business during the period it is being used to fill customers' orders. The historical financial data of an acquired company can be used to determine the amount that could be attributed to finished goods in order to pay all costs of disposition and provide a return on the investment during the period of disposition.

.04 The fair market value of work in process should be based on the same factors used to determine the fair market value of finished goods reduced by the expected costs of completion, including a reasonable profit allowance for the completion and selling effort of the acquiring corporation. In determining the fair market value of raw materials, the current costs of replacing the inventory in the quantities to be valued generally provides the most reliable standard.

SEC. 4. CONCLUSION.

Because valuing inventory is an inherently factual determination, no rigid formulas can be applied. Consequently, the methods outlined above can only serve as guidelines for determining the fair market value of inventories.

SOURCE: Rev. Proc. 77-12, 1977-1 C.B. 569.

Other Tangible Personal Property. The conceptual underpinnings of the cost approach for tangible personal property are essentially identical to those for real estate. Again, the cost approach is based on the economic principle of substitution.

Particularly with respect to tangible personal property, a willing buyer will pay no more to a willing seller than the cost associated with replacing the subject asset with an asset of comparable functional utility.

As with real estate, there are several common cost approach methods. These methods include the depreciated reproduction cost method, the depreciated replacement cost method, the creation cost method, and the recreation cost method.

For special-purpose tangible personal property (which may experience a considerable amount of incurable obsolescence), the depreciated reproduction cost method is one common valuation method. However, for most general-purpose tangible personal property, the depreciated replacement cost method is the more common valuation method.

The depreciated replacement cost method for tangible personal property is presented algebraically below:

	Replacement cost new, of the subject asset
less:	Allowance for physical deterioration
equals:	Depreciated replacement cost
less:	Allowance for economic or external obsolescence
less:	Allowance for curable functional and technological obsolescence
equals:	Fair market value of the subject asset

If the subject asset is no longer produced, the replacement cost of the most comparable available substitute asset is used as the starting point in the cost approach (and, specifically, in the depreciated replacement cost method).

Using the income approach, the value of the tangible personal property is often quantified as the present value of the rental income from the hypothetical rental of the subject property over its remaining useful life.

First, the analyst estimates the remaining useful life of the subject asset. This is typically the shortest of the asset's remaining physical, functional, technological, or economic lives.

Second, the analyst estimates a fair rental rate for the subject asset. This gross rental income is reduced by insurance, maintenance, and other expenses that are the responsibility of the lessor. The result is a projection of the net rental income (real or hypothetical) to be derived from the subject asset over the asset's expected remaining life.

Next, the analyst derives an appropriate present value discount rate. This discount rate is intended to provide for a fair, risk-adjusted rate of return to the property lessor over the term of the lease. The present value of the projected rental income over the expected remaining life of the property represents the value of the subject asset, per the income approach. (Since tangible personal property has a finite life, analysts typically do not have to consider a residual value to tangible personal property—as would be appropriate with regard to real estate.)

Using the market approach, the value of the subject asset is the price that it would command in its appropriate secondary market. This valuation approach is based on the economic principle of efficient markets. In using this approach, one assumes that an efficient secondary market exists with regard to the exchange of the subject asset. One also assumes that reliable information is available regarding this tangible personal property exchange market.

Using this approach, the analyst first obtains data regarding secondary transactions with respect to comparable assets. Next, the analyst analyzes these data with regard to a set of reasonable comparability criteria. The market transactional data are adjusted, if necessary, to enhance their comparability and applicability to the subject asset.

Based on the adjusted transactional database, the analyst selects comparable sales most indicative of a hypothetical transaction involving the subject asset. These adjusted sales data are used to conclude the value of the subject asset.

Finally, the analyst concludes an overall value of the subject asset based on a synthesis of the results of the various appraisal approaches used. Based on the analyst's perceived reliability of, and confidence in, the various approaches, the analyst will reach a final value estimate for the subject tangible personal property.

Intangible Real Property

Intangible real property assets represent intangible legal claims on tangible real estate. The type of assets encompassed by this category of assets includes leasehold interests (and various other leasehold estates), possessory interests (associated with franchise ordinances or other permits), exploration rights, air rights, water rights, land rights, mineral exploitation rights, use rights, development rights, easements (including scenic easements), and other intangible rights and privileges related to the use or exploitation of real estate. As intangible claims on real estate, the value of these assets is generally a subset of, or a derivative of, the value of the associated real estate.

As with real estate, there are many individual methods and techniques to appraise intangible real property. However, as with real estate, all of these methods can be conveniently grouped into three generally accepted appraisal approaches: (1) the cost approach, (2) the income capitalization approach, and (3) the sales comparison approach.

Each of these approaches (and some associated methods) were discussed above with respect to the value of real estate. Those general discussions will not be repeated here.

It is noteworthy, however, that the cost approach is not usually relied on to value intangible real property. Intangible real property typically represents a legal claim on the use of, exploitation of, development of, or forbearance of real estate. Accordingly, the cost of the underlying real estate is generally irrelevant to the intangible property right holder.

Rather, the income approach is typically the most widely used approach with respect to the appraisal of intangible real estate interests.

The sales comparison approach is also used to value certain intangible real estate interests. For example, there is a reasonable sales transaction secondary market for certain intangible real estate interests—such as the unexpired portion of assignable below-market industrial and commercial leases (i.e., leasehold interests).

As with the appraisal of real estate, the appraisal of intangible real property interests is based on (1) a synthesis of all available appraisal data and (2) the conclusions of whatever appraisal approaches were used. The analyst considers and synthesizes the results of the various appraisal approaches and estimates the value for the subject intangible real property interests.

Intangible Personal Property

Intangible personal property assets include most of the assets generally called intangible assets and intellectual properties. There are, arguably, over 100 different types of intangible assets and intellectual properties. However, many of these individual intangible assets are industry-specific.

Generally, all intangible assets can be conveniently grouped into the following 10 categories:

1. Customer-related (e.g., customer lists).
2. Contract-related (e.g., favorable supplier contracts).
3. Location-related (e.g., certificates of need).
4. Marketing-related (e.g., trademarks and trade names).
5. Data processing-related (e.g., computer software).
6. Technology-related (e.g., engineering drawings and technical documentation).
7. Employee-related (e.g., employment agreements).
8. Goodwill-related (e.g., going-concern value).
9. Engineering-related (e.g., patents and trade secrets).
10. Literary-related (e.g., literary copyrights, musical composition copyrights).

In addition, there is a special subgroup of intangible assets called intellectual properties. All intellectual properties (which are themselves part of the 10 categories of intangible assets) can be conveniently grouped into the following two categories:

1. Creative (e.g., copyrights).
2. Innovative (e.g., patents).

Chapter 42 will discuss in detail the identification, valuation, and remaining useful life analysis of intangible assets. Therefore, these issues will not be expanded on here.

As with other assets, intangible personal property assets are valued by the application of three generally accepted appraisal approaches: (1) the cost approach, (2) the income approach, and (3) the market approach.

The analyst will apply one or more of these approaches to the appraisal of each intangible personal property asset. Then, the analyst will derive a conclusion of value based on a synthesis of the results of the various intangible personal property appraisal approaches used.

Although the discussion of intangible asset appraisal is deferred to Chapter 42, the identification, valuation, and remaining useful life analysis of intangible personal property assets is the conceptual cornerstone of the asset accumulation method.

It is noteworthy that, in any particular business valuation, a rigorous and thorough analysis of intangible personal property assets may indicate a nominal or even a zero economic value for the subject intangible assets.

It is also noteworthy that, in any particular business valuation, a rigorous and thorough analysis of intangible personal property assets may even indicate a negative economic value for the subject intangible assets. In such a case, the overall valuation of the company cannot generate adequate economic support for the values assigned to the discrete tangible real and personal property assets.

When that situation occurs, the valuation phenomenon of economic obsolescence exists. Economic obsolescence is defined as the amount, if any, of negative intangible asset value calculated in an asset accumulation method valuation (given the indicated values for the real and personal property assets).

When economic obsolescence is indicated by the asset accumulation method, the indicated values of the tangible real and personal property assets are overstated—from an economic perspective—and must be reduced. In fact, the indicated values of the real and personal property assets may be reduced (i.e., allocated down, typically in direct proportion to their indicated values) until the final concluded values for these assets indicate no economic obsolescence.

At that value conclusion, no positive intangible personal property value may be indicated by the intangible asset valuation. But neither will negative intangible personal property value be indicated by the intangible asset valuation. In other words, after any calculated economic obsolescence is allocated to the subject company's real and personal property assets, the remaining amount of unidentified intangible asset value in the subject company will be zero.

Of course, based on the standard of value and the premise of value applied, based on the industry in which the company operates, and based on the microeconomic dynamics of the company, the analysis and appraisal of the subject assets of any subject company may indicate little or no (or even negative) intangible asset value. Nonetheless, such an analysis and appraisal should be performed as an integral part of any asset-based method business valuation.

As mentioned above, when using the asset-based approach, the company's intangible assets may be valued collectively (e.g., using the capitalized excess earnings method) or individually and discretely (e.g., using the asset accumulation method). However, the company's intangible assets should be appraised as part of the valuation process.

As will be discussed in Chapter 42, several important concepts with regard to the valuation of intangible assets are part of the asset accumulation method. Several of these concepts are introduced briefly below.

First, it is important to understand and follow the flow (or funnel) of economic income from customers/clients/patients into the firm. The intangible assets most affected by this economic income flow should be identified and considered for separate valuation.

Second, the identification and valuation of intangible assets should be correctly prioritized. Typically, intangible assets appraised using a market approach are valued first, intangible assets appraised using a cost approach are valued second, and intangible assets appraised using an income approach are valued last.

Third, it is important to carefully avoid double counting (or overcounting) of economic value when appraising intangible assets. For example, the analyst should procedurally avoid identifying one component of economic value and then, inadvertently through various appraisal techniques, assigning some or all of the same economic value to more than one of the company's assets.

Fourth, like tangible assets, intangible assets may be valued using a cost approach, an income approach, or a market approach. If several intangible assets are identified as part of the asset accumulation method, it is quite likely that (1) some intangible assets will be valued using a cost approach, (2) others will be valued using an income approach, and (3) others may be valued using a market approach. Clearly, given the function and purpose of each intangible asset, the analyst should use the valuation approach (or approaches) that is (are) most determinative of the true economic value of the subject intangible asset.

Nonetheless, as a general rule, at least one intangible asset should be valued using an income approach as part of each asset accumulation method valuation. In this way, the appraisal will verify and validate the economic income-generating capacity of the subject assets. The intangible assets valued using the income approach confirm the economic support for the tangible real and personal property assets (and other intangible assets) of the company. And the intangible assets valued using the income approach confirm that there is no (or that there is) economic obsolescence associated with the tangible real and personal property assets of the company.

Example

To illustrate the general application of the asset accumulation method, let's create a hypothetical small business. Let's call this small business Illustrative Client Company, Inc.

Illustrative Client Company, Inc., is a successful, family-owned widget manufacturing company. To make this example relatively simple, let's assume that the owners of Illustrative Client Company, Inc., are contemplating the sale of this going-concern business enterprise.

Therefore, the objective of this appraisal is to estimate the fair market value of the overall business enterprise. In other words, for purposes of this example, we can eliminate from consideration the identification and quantification of valuation discounts and premiums. The purpose of this appraisal is to provide an independent valuation opinion to the current owners to allow them to assess the most likely transaction price regarding the sale of the company.

In order to more finitely identify the components of the Illustrative Client Company, Inc., business value for the selling family members and for potential buyers, we have elected to use the asset-based approach. Specifically, we will use the asset accumulation method (i.e., we will perform the analysis on a discrete asset valuation basis—as opposed to a collective asset valuation basis).

Given the purpose and objective of the appraisal, we will estimate the fair market value (as the standard of value) of all of the tangible and intangible assets of Illustrative Client Company, Inc., as of the valuation date.

Given the successful historical operations of the company and management's plans to sell the business as an ongoing business, we have selected the individual asset valuation premise of value in continued use, as a going-concern business enterprise.

Exhibit 22-2 presents the statement of financial position (i.e., balance sheet) of Illustrative Client Company, Inc., as of the December 31, 1997, valuation date. Let's assume that this statement of financial position is prepared in accordance with generally accepted accounting principles. In other words, the Exhibit 22-2 statement of financial position is prepared on a GAAP, historical-cost basis. Exhibit 22-2, then, is the basic working document that is the point of departure for the asset accumulation method analysis.

Exhibit 22-3 presents the final summary of the asset accumulation method valuation for Illustrative Client Company, Inc.

Exhibit 22-3 presents both the historical cost–basis values for all recorded asset and liability accounts of Illustrative Client Company, Inc. (just slightly rearranged from the GAAP-basis balance sheet) and the fair market values for all of the asset (both tangible and intangible) and liability accounts of the company.

Let's review each of the asset and liability fair market value conclusions in Exhibit 22-3. The following paragraphs describe an illustrative appraisal analysis for each asset and liability account.

The cash balance remains at its historical cost value. The analyst would confirm whether or not the cash balances would be transferred to the new owner when the business was sold.

The accounts and notes receivable assets remain at their historical cost value. This conclusion was reached after an assessment of the timing and collectibility of the receivables.

Prepaid expenses remain at their historical cost value. This conclusion was reached after an assessment of the value of the prepaid expenses to the going-concern business.

Exhibit 22–2

ILLUSTRATIVE CLIENT COMPANY, INC.
STATEMENT OF FINANCIAL POSITION
AS OF DECEMBER 31, 1997

ASSETS

Current assets:

Cash	$ 200,000
Accounts and notes receivable	500,000
Prepaid expenses	200,000
Inventory	600,000
Total current assets	1,500,000

Noncurrent assets:

	200,000
Buildings and improvements	1,200,000
Office furniture and fixtures	300,000
Machinery and equipment	500,000
Tools and dies	300,000
Total plant, property, and equipment	2,500,000
Less: Accumulated depreciation	1,000,000
Net plant, property and equipment	1,500,000

Other noncurrent assets:

Long-term notes receivable	250,000
Note receivable from supplier	250,000
Total other noncurrent assets	500,000
TOTAL ASSETS	$ 3,500,000

LIABILITIES AND OWNERS' EQUITY

Current liabilities:

Accounts payable	$ 400,000
Wages payable	200,000
Taxes payable	100,000
Accrued liabilties	300,000
Total current liabilities	1,000,000

Noncurrent liabilities:

Bonds payable	200,000
Notes payable	200,000
Mortgages payable	700,000
Debentures payable	200,000
Total noncurrent liabilities	1,300,000

Owners' equity:

Capital stock	200,000
Additional paid-in capital	500,000
Retained earnings	500,000
Total owners' equity	1,200,000
TOTAL LIABILITIES AND OWNERS' EQUITY	$ 3,500,000

Exhibit 22–3

ILLUSTRATIVE CLIENT COMPANY, INC.
BUSINESS ENTERPRISE VALUATION
ASSET-BASED APPROACH
ASSET ACCUMULATION METHOD
AS OF DECEMBER 31, 1997

	At Historical Cost	At Fair Market Value
ASSETS		
Financial assets:		
Cash	$ 200,000	$ 200,000
Accounts and notes receivable	500,000	500,000
Prepaid expenses	200,000	200,000
Inventory	600,000	700,000
Long-term notes receivable	250,000	250,000
Note receivable from supplier	250,000	150,000
Total financial assets	2,000,000	2,000,000
Real estate:		
Land	200,000	300,000
Buildings and improvements	1,200,000	1,000,000
Less: Accumulated depreciation	400,000	
Net real estate	1,000,000	1,300,000
Tangible personal property:		
Office furniture and fixtures	300,000	200,000
Machinery and equipment	500,000	300,000
Tools and dies	300,000	200,000
Less: Accumulated depreciation	600,000	
Net tangible personal property	500,000	700,000
Intangible real property:		
Leasehold interests	0	100,000
Net Intangible real property	0	100,000
Intangible personal property:		
Trademarks and trade names	0	200,000
Computer software	0	150,000
Patents	0	150,000
Favorable supplier contracts	0	100,000
Goodwill	0	100,000
Net intangible personal property	0	700,000
TOTAL ASSETS	$ 3,500,000	$ 4,800,000
LIABILITIES AND OWNERS' EQUITY		
Current liabilities:		
Accounts payable	$ 400,000	$ 400,000
Wages payable	200,000	200,000
Taxes payable	100,000	100,000
Accrued liabilties	300,000	300,000
Total current liabilities	1,000,000	1,000,000
Noncurrent liabilities:		
Bonds payable	200,000	200,000
Notes payable	200,000	200,000
Mortgages payable	700,000	650,000
Debentures payable	200,000	200,000
Total noncurrent liabilities	1,300,000	1,250,000
Contingent liabilities:		
Contingent claims	0	150,000
Total contingent liabilities	0	150,000
TOTAL LIABILITIES	2,300,000	2,400,000
TOTAL LIABILITIES AND OWNERS' EQUITY	$ 3,500,000	$ 4,800,000
TOTAL OWNERS' EQUITY	$ 1,200,000	$ 2,400,000

Inventory is revalued upward. This revaluation is based on the sales comparison method described in Internal Revenue Service Revenue Procedure 77-12.

Long-term notes receivable are valued at their historical cost. This conclusion is based on (1) an analysis of the stated interest rate versus current interest rates for similar risk notes and (2) the historical and likely prospective payment pattern regarding the notes.

The note receivable from a supplier is revalued downward. Some years ago, this business extended a loan to one of its key suppliers. This decremental revaluation was based on an analysis of (1) the below-market interest rate on the note and (2) the erratic historical payment history from the supplier on the note.

Land is revalued upward. This incremental revaluation is based on a market value appraisal of the land, as if vacant and unimproved, and at its highest and best use, using the sales comparison approach.

Buildings and improvements are revalued incrementally, as market value exceeds the (depreciated) historical cost of these properties. This appraisal is based on depreciated reproduction cost analysis of the subject properties.

Office furniture and fixtures, machinery and equipment, and tools and dies are revalued incrementally; that is, the market value conclusions for each asset category exceed their (depreciated) historical cost. The depreciated replacement cost method would be a typical valuation method for the appraisal of these assets.

A leasehold interest is identified and capitalized on the valuation-basis balance sheet. In this example, Illustrative Client Company, Inc., enjoys a favorable rental advantage (i.e., below-market rental rates) on some warehouse space that it leases. The analyst used the income capitalization approach to project and capitalize this favorable (below-market) lease rate advantage and to conclude the market value of the leasehold interest. This leasehold interest intangible asset was not previously recorded on the historical cost-basis balance sheet.

The entire category of intangible personal property would not be recorded on a GAAP, historical cost-basis balance sheet. However, these intangible assets are identified and appraised for business valuation purposes.

Trademarks and trade names are an important intangible asset for Illustrative Client Company, Inc. Company management spends a great deal of time and money promoting the company's name: They advertise, send promotional announcements, sponsor booths at trade shows, and so forth.

The analyst used the recreation cost method to quantify the value of this intangible asset. The analyst estimated the current cost required for the company to recreate its current level of customer awareness, brand recognition, and consumer loyalty. The estimated cost to recreate this level of name awareness is capitalized as the value of this intangible asset.

Computer software is an important intangible asset for Illustrative Client Company, Inc. This computer software was internally developed, instead of externally purchased. Accordingly, the value of this computer software typically will not be recorded on a GAAP-basis balance sheet.

The systems analyst at Illustrative Client Company, Inc., has developed and implemented an automated materials requirement planning (MRP) system. This system is extremely useful to the company with regard to material purchasing, labor scheduling, and production planning.

The analyst used the market approach to estimate the value of this intangible asset, as there is a relatively similar (in terms of functionality) MRP system available on the market from a commercial software vendor. After consideration of the market value of a comparable commercial system, and after including the costs of customization, installation, testing, and training, the analyst concluded the market value of the Illustrative Client Company, Inc., computer software.

The patent that Illustrative Client Company, Inc., holds is a valuable intangible asset to them. The widgets that Illustrative Client Company, Inc., manufactures have certain unique and proprietary technological feature advancements compared to the widgets manufactured by competitors. And other manufacturers cannot reverse-engineer and copy the Illustrative Client Company, Inc., advanced features because the subject product is protected by a U.S. product patent.

Because of the advanced features (protected by the patent), Illustrative Client Company, Inc., management estimates that it sells more widgets than it would otherwise and that its average selling price per widget is higher than its competitors' prices. Accordingly, the analyst used the income approach to value the intangible value of the Illustrative Client Company, Inc., patent.

Illustrative Client Company, Inc., has a favorable supply contract with a key supplier. The materials buyer for Illustrative Client Company, Inc., is a skilled negotiator. Using these superior negotiating skills, the materials buyer convinced the key supplier to agree to supply an essential raw material to Illustrative Client Company, Inc., at 20 percent below the prices that the supplier normally charges to its other, similar-sized customers. This agreement is documented in a written three-year-term supply contract.

The analyst used the income approach to estimate the economic value of the Illustrative Client Company, Inc., favorable supply contract.

Goodwill is sometimes considered the accumulation of all the other economic value of the company not specifically identified with (or allocated to) individual tangible and intangible assets. The analysis and quantification of goodwill (or the lack of goodwill) is an important component in the application of the asset accumulation method to a company like Illustrative Client Company, Inc.

With respect to the subject company, the analyst used a capitalized excess earnings method to identify and value goodwill. First, the analyst identified and valued all of the other individual assets of Illustrative Client Company, Inc.—both tangible and intangible. Second, the analyst assigned a fair rate of return against each asset of the company—both tangible and intangible. Third, the analyst compared the total calculated fair return on the total tangible and intangible assets to the total economic income actually earned by the company. Fourth, any excess economic income (above a fair return on all identified tangible and intangible assets) was capitalized as an annuity in perpetuity.

This capitalization conclusion, then, is the indicated value of the Illustrative Client Company, Inc., intangible value in the nature of goodwill.

The current liabilities of Illustrative Client Company, Inc., were also analyzed. Given the short-term nature of these monetary liabilities, the analyst estimated their fair market value at their historical cost carrying amounts.

The noncurrent liabilities were also analyzed. Given the term of these liabilities and their stated (or implied) interest rates, the analyst estimated the fair market value of the bonds, notes, and debentures at their historical cost carrying amounts.

The mortgage payable, however, has a substantial remaining term and an interest rate that is considerably below current market rates. The analyst confirmed with the mortgage bank that they would allow Illustrative Client Company, Inc., to pay off the mortgage at a discount compared to the principal balance. The analyst estimated this discount and concluded the fair market value of the mortgage payable.

There is an outstanding lawsuit against Illustrative Client Company, Inc., The plaintiff, a former employee, alleges that Illustrative Client Company, Inc., violated the employee's exclusive marketing territory agreement. Although there were extenuating circumstances, Illustrative Client Company, Inc., management realized that it did violate the agreement and that it owes damages to the former employee.

While the trial is not yet scheduled, and no one can predict the court's decision regarding either liability or damages, Illustrative Client Company, Inc., management believes that an offer of $150,000 will be adequate to settle the case and satisfy all future liability to the plaintiff.

The analyst reviewed this estimate and used it to capitalize a contingent liability on the Illustrative Client Company, Inc., valuation balance sheet.

In the final step, the analyst summed the estimated fair market values for all of the tangible and intangible assets of Illustrative Client Company, Inc., and summed the estimated fair market values for all of the recorded and contingent liabilities of Illustrative Client Company, Inc. The analyst subtracted the total liability value from the total asset value. The remainder is an indication of the fair market value of the total owners' equity of Illustrative Client Company, Inc., according to the asset accumulation method.

Advantages of the Asset Accumulation Method

As should be apparent from the above discussion of the theoretical concepts and the practical applications of this method, there are a number of advantages of the asset accumulation method of the asset-based approach.

First, the results of the asset accumulation method are presented in a traditional balance sheet format. This format should be comfortable and familiar to anyone who has ever worked with basic financial statements.

Second, this method componentizes all of the business value of the company. In the example above, the valuation conclusion was exactly two times book value for Illustrative Client Company, Inc. Other business valuation methods would, presumably, reach the same valuation conclusion. But those methods would not explain why the subject company is worth two times book value. The asset accumulation method identifies exactly which assets (tangible and intangible) are contributing value to the company and how much value each asset is contributing.

Third, this method is useful when structuring the sale of a business. This method can immediately quantify the effects on business value of many common seller structural considerations, such as these:

1. What if the seller retains the company's cash on hand or accounts receivable?
2. What if the seller retains (or leases back to the company) the operating real estate facilities?
3. What if the seller personally retains title to the patent or to some other valuable intangible assets of the company?
4. What if the seller personally retains any or all of the debt instruments of the company?

Fourth, this method is useful to the seller when negotiating the sale of the company. If the buyer offers a lower price than the asset accumulation method indicates, the seller can ask, "Since you're not willing to pay for all of the assets of the business, which of these assets don't you want me to sell you as part of the transaction?"

Fifth, this method is useful to the buyer when negotiating the purchase of the company. If the seller wants a higher price than the value indication of the asset accumulation method, the buyer can ask, "What other assets are you willing to sell to me—in addition to what has already been appraised on this valuation balance sheet—to justify the price you are asking?"

Sixth, after the sale transaction is consummated, this business valuation method allows for a ready and reasonable allocation of the lump-sum purchase price among the assets acquired. This purchase price allocation is often required for both financial accounting purposes and tax accounting purposes. This is important because the tangible assets are subject to depreciation cost recovery—and the intangible assets are subject to amortization cost recovery—for both financial accounting and federal income tax purposes.

Seventh, this method is useful with regard to financing the subject transaction. Typically, all categories of lenders (secured, unsecured, mezzanine, etc.) will want to know the value of the company's assets—both tangible and intangible—before they will commit to financing the business purchase deal. This business valuation method generally provides lenders with the information they need.

Eighth, this method is particularly useful in litigation support and dispute resolution matters. Since it identifies the individual value components of the individual assets of the company, it allows for the easy measurement of the impact of certain alleged actions (or lack of actions) on the overall value of the company. Also, this method can be used to allocate assets (as well as—or instead of—stock) in a stockholder/partner dissolution dispute or in a marital dissolution dispute.

Ninth, this method can be used with virtually any standard of value or with any premise of value. In other words, using the same comparative balance sheet format, analysts can value the same business under several alternative standards (i.e., definitions) of value. Likewise, using the same comparative balance sheet format, analysts can value the same business under several alternative premises of value. Therefore, the impact of changing standards of value or premises of value can be immediately identified and quickly quantified.

Tenth, this method requires the most rigorous analysis and thorough understanding of company operations on the part of the analyst. Such required rigorous analyses can only help enhance the quality of the valuation. Also, this method generally requires much more active participation of company management in the valuation process. This active interest and participation can only help enhance the quality of the business valuation.

Disadvantages of the Asset Accumulation Method

The primary disadvantage of the asset accumulation method is that, if taken to its ultimate extreme, it can be very expensive and time-consuming. It also may necessitate the involvement of appraisal specialists in several appraisal disciplines. The costs and efforts of these appraisal specialists may be more suitable for larger businesses than for small businesses and professional practices.

Also, as described in this chapter, this method requires the valuation of all of the company assets—including the intangible as well as tangible assets. Many intangible asset values depend, in good measure, on the income valuation approach. Therefore, taken to its extreme, the asset accumulation method may ultimately depend as much on economic income capitalization variables as it does on the values of tangible assets. This is especially true for small businesses and professional practices. Of course, ultimately, the value of all assets, properties, or business interests depends on their economic income-generating capacity.

Summary

The asset accumulation method is a common asset-based approach valuation method. The theoretical underpinning of this method is simple: The value of the business is the value of the business assets (both tangible and intangible) less the value of the business liabilities (both recorded and contingent). Basically, this method recognizes that all of the economic value of a business has to come from—and can be identified with—the productive assets of the subject business.

The asset-based valuation approach can be applied on a collective basis, where all of the economic value of the company greater than the tangible asset value is aggregated and generally called "intangible value in the nature of goodwill." A common implementation of this collective revaluation basis of the asset-based approach is the capitalized excess earnings method. The capitalized excess earnings will be the focus of the next chapter of this book.

Also, the asset-based valuation approach can be applied on a discrete basis, where all of the company's tangible assets and intangible assets are individually identified and appraised. The discrete application of the asset-based approach is often called the asset accumulation method, which was the focus of this chapter.

It is naïve and conceptually incorrect to automatically conclude that the value of a business is based only on the value of the tangible assets of the business. Likewise, it is also naïve and conceptually incorrect to conclude that the value of a business is equal to its accounting "book value"—without the use of substantial valuation procedures and rigorous fundamental analysis to support that conclusion.

The intangible assets of the company may contribute substantial economic value. Or they may contribute little or no economic value. Or they may contribute negative economic value, which is recognized as economic (or external) obsolescence. Economic (or external) obsolescence is recognized as a decrease in the value of the tangible assets of the company. Again, the ultimate application of an asset-based approach valuation method requires a structured, rigorous, and comprehensive valuation analysis of all the company's assets.

There are numerous advantages to the asset accumulation method of business valuation, particularly with regard to valuations of small businesses and professional practices. These advantages include application to transaction pricing and structuring, deal negotiation, acquisition financing, purchase accounting, and dispute resolution.

However, there are "costs" associated with the application of the asset accumulation method of business valuation. This method requires more time and effort on the part of the business appraiser than many other business valuation methods. It requires more access to company facilities and to management than many other business valuation methods. It requires more access to company data, particularly operational data, than many other business valuation methods. And it requires more time and effort on the part of company management and more involvement of company management in the valuation process.

Finally, the asset accumulation method requires that the business appraiser have expertise in the identification and valuation of both the tangible assets and the intangible assets of a company. Certainly, this method is only recommended for analysts who have adequate experience and expertise in the appraisal of the individual component assets of a business enterprise. The use of supporting analysts with the requisite experience and qualifications may fill the void for a particular asset type for which the business appraiser lacks technical expertise.

Bibliography

Alico, John, ed. *Appraising Machinery and Equipment.* Herndon, VA: American Society of Appraisers, 1989.

Altman, Edward I. "Mark-to-Market and Present Value Disclosure: An Opportunity or a Costly Annoyance?" *Financial Analysts Journal,* March-April 1993, pp. 14–16.

The Appraisal of Real Estate, 11th ed. Chicago: Appraisal Institute, 1996.

Baxter, William. "Asset and Liability Values (Complexities of Current Value Accounting)." *Accountancy,* April 1994, pp. 135–37.

Cheung, Joseph K., and Mandy Li. "Income Tax Effects on Asset Valuation and Managerial Analysis." *Abacus*, March 1992, pp. 98–106.

Churchill, Michael. "Asset Valuation." *Australian Accountant,* April 1992, pp. 35–39.

Crawford, Robert G., and Gary C. Cornia. "The Problem of Appraising Specialized Assets." *Appraisal Journal*, January 1994, pp. 75–85.

Dandekar, Manoj P. "Analytical Problems with the Weibull Distribution: In Defense of the Iowa-Type Survivor Curves." *Valuation*, June 1996, pp. 3–13.

Dandekar, Manoj P., and Pamela Garland. "Tangible Personal Property Remaining Useful Life Estimation Analysis." *Willamette Management Associates Insights*, Winter 1996, pp. 13–20.

Dandekar, Manoj P., and Robert F. Reilly. "Tangible Personal Property Valuation Approaches, Methods, and Procedures." *Willamette Management Associates Insights*, Winter 1996, pp. 1–12.

DeThomas, Arthur R., and Robert R. Neyland. "Asset Valuation: A Practical Approach for Decision Making." *CPA Journal*, September 1991, pp. 82–83.

Fowler, Bradley A., and Edward C. Fowler. "Coordinating 'Business Valuation Overlay' with Asset Based Valuations." *Business Valuation Review*, December 1996, pp. 171–73.

Godfrey, Austin E. "The Valuation of Assets Subject to Lease Transaction." *Secured Lender*, September/October 1993, pp. 62–64+.

Huffaker, John B. "Oil and Gas Sold before Alternate Valuation Date Is Valued in Place." *Journal of Taxation*, September 1995, p. 161.

Jacoby, Henry D., and David G. Laughton. "Project Evaluation: A Practical Asset Pricing Method." *Energy Journal*, 1992, pp. 19–47.

Jones, P. C., W. J. Hopp, and J. L. Zydiak. "Capital Asset Valuation and Depreciation for Stochastically Deteriorating Equipment." *Engineering Economist*, Fall 1992, pp. 19–30.

Lynn, Daniel M., and Robert R. Neyland. "Asset Valuation: Softening the Bankruptcy Blow." *Bank Management*, April 1992, pp. 48–49.

McCrodan, Andrew. "Tackling Tax-Related Troubles." *CA Magazine*, April 1993, pp. 45–48.

Schmidt, Richard M. "Valuing the Assets of a Manufacturing Company." *The Appraisal Journal*, April 1997, pp. 120–23.

Tole, Thomas M., Sammy O. McCord, and Charles P. Edmonds. "How Much Is the Business Worth?" *Real Estate Review*, Summer 1993, pp. 39–43.

Chapter 23

The Capitalized Excess Earnings Method

As was discussed in the previous chapter, the asset-based approach can be applied on either a collective basis or a discrete basis. When this approach is applied on a collective basis, all of the intangible value of the company—in excess of its tangible asset value—is estimated in the aggregate. When it is applied on a discrete basis, the individual intangible asset components of the company's business enterprise value are identified and quantified. The capitalized excess earnings method is the most commonly used method for estimating a company's intangible value in the nature of goodwill on a collective (or aggregate) basis. Therefore, this chapter will focus on the capitalized excess earnings method of the asset-based valuation approach.

Some analysts categorize the excess earnings method as an income approach valuation method. In truth, the categorization of any valuation method is purely a semantic matter. The categorization of a particular valuation method in no way affects the applicability (or lack of applicability) of that method.

As a notational convention, we will categorize the capitalized excess earnings method as an asset-based approach method. That is because the conclusion of the application of the capitalized excess earnings method is an indication of the value of an asset: the company's intangible value in the nature of goodwill. Of course, goodwill is an intangible asset of the company. And the valuation of a company by reference to its component assets (both tangible and intangible)—whether on a collective or a discrete basis is the very definition of an asset-based approach.

Some analysts disparage the use of the capitalized excess earnings method. They allege that this method is archaic and that it is formulaistic and mechanistic.

First, the fact that a valuation method is old does not make it invalid. As we recall, John Marshall first published a description of the three generally accepted valuation approaches (i.e., the cost approach, the market approach, and the income approach) in 1890 in his landmark text, *Economics*. The fact that an analytical method is old means that it has passed the test of time. It does not necessarily mean that it is outdated and inapplicable.

Second, it is true that the capitalized excess earnings method is sometimes referred to as "the formula method." This does not mean that it is formulaistic or mechanical. Rather, it may be argued that the application of the capitalized excess earnings method requires a great deal of analysis and judgment. In fact, one conclusion of this chapter is that the capitalized excess earnings method (if it is to be applied correctly) requires as much (or more) analysis and judgment on the part of the analyst as do other business valuation methods.

Some analysts assert that the capitalized excess earnings method—while often used—is often misused. It is sometimes applied by analysts who do not appreciate the subtle complexities of this method. That allegation may be true. The objective of this chapter is to educate readers about how to deal with these subtle complexities.

History of the Capitalized Excess Earnings Method

The capitalized excess earnings method is sometimes called the *Treasury method*. This is because this valuation method originally appeared in a 1920 publication by the U.S. Treasury Department, Appeals and Review Memorandum Number 34 (ARM 34). It was adopted in order to estimate the intangible value of goodwill that breweries and distilleries lost because of the legal imposition of prohibition in the U.S. Treasury Department laws.

Since then, both taxpayers and the Internal Revenue Service have widely used (and often misused) this valuation method in connection with business valuations for gift tax, estate tax, and other taxation purposes. Also, (1) perhaps partly because of its fairly wide dissemination and (2) partly because of its apparent simplistic nature, this valuation method has been widely adopted in one form or another for pricing small businesses and professional practices. Perhaps for the same reasons, it is also frequently used for valuing businesses and practices for marital dissolutions.

In 1968, the Service updated and restated the ARM 34 valuation method. This occurred with the publication of Internal Revenue Service Revenue Ruling 68-609. This revenue ruling is reproduced as Exhibit 23-1. It is noteworthy that Revenue Ruling 68-609 is still in effect today.

The reader should keep in mind the fact that the excess earnings method originally was created for the purpose of valuing intangible assets, *not* for the purpose of valuing the company as a whole. Consequently, perhaps the most appropriate application of the excess earnings method is for the purpose of *allocating* total value between tangible and intangible assets. Examples of this include:

- Divorce cases, in jurisdictions where personal goodwill value is considered a personal rather than a marital asset and therefore needs to be separated from the value of the business or practice.
- Conversions from C corporations to S corporations.
- Eminent domain cases, where the tangible and intangible values need to be recognized separately.
- Property tax cases, where a company's tangible assets are subject to property tax but its intangible assets are not.
- Damage cases, such as a breach of a patent or trademark.

Exhibit 23–1

Revenue Ruling 68-609

The "formula" approach may be used in determining the fair market value of intangible assets of a business only if there is no better basis available for making the determination; A.R.M. 34, A.R.M. 68, O.D. 937, and Revenue Ruling 65-192 superseded.

SECTION 1001.—DETERMINATION OF AMOUNT OF AND RECOGNITION OF GAIN OR LOSS

26 CFR 1.1001-1: Computation of gain or loss.   Rev. Rul. 68-609[1]
(Also Section 167; 1.167(a)-3.)

The purpose of this Revenue Ruling is to update and restate, under the current statute and regulations, the currently outstanding portions of A.R.M. 34, C.B. 2, 31 (1920), A.R.M. 68, C.B. 3, 43 (1920), and O.D. 937, C.B. 4, 43 (1921).

The question presented is whether the "formula" approach, the capitalization of earnings in excess of a fair rate of return on net tangible assets, may be used to determine the fair market value of the intangible assets of a business.

The "formula" approach may be stated as follows:

A percentage return on the average annual value of the tangible assets used in a business is determined, using a period of years (preferably not less than five) immediately prior to the valuation date. The amount of the percentage return on tangible assets, thus determined, is deducted from the average earnings of the business for such period and the remainder, if any, is considered to be the amount of the average annual earnings from the intangible assets of the business for the period. This amount (considered as the average annual earnings from intangibles), capitalized at a percentage of, say, 15 to 20 percent, is the value of the intangible assets of the business determined under the "formula" approach.

The percentage of return on the average annual value of the tangible assets used should be the percentage prevailing in the industry involved at the date of valuation, or (when the industry percentage is not available) a percentage of 8 to 10 percent may be used.

The 8 percent rate of return and the 15 percent rate of capitalization are applied to tangibles and intangibles, respectively, of businesses with a small risk factor and stable and regular earnings; the 10 percent rate of return and 20 percent rate of capitalization are applied to businesses in which the hazards of business are relatively high.

The above rates are used as examples and are not appropriate in all cases. In applying the "formula" approach, the average earnings period and the capitalization rates are dependent upon the facts pertinent thereto in each case.

SOURCE: Rev. Rul. 68-609, 1968-2, C.B. 327.

The past earnings to which the formula is applied should fairly reflect the probable future earnings. Ordinarily, the period should not be less than five years, and abnormal years, whether above or below the average, should be eliminated. If the business is a sole proprietorship or partnership, there should be deducted from the earnings of the business a reasonable amount for services performed by the owner or partners engaged in the business. See *Lloyd B. Sanderson Estate* v. *Commissioner*, 42 F. 2d 160 (1930). Further, only the tangible assets entering into net worth, including accounts and bills receivable in excess of accounts and bills payable, are used for determining earnings on the tangible assets. Factors that influence the capitalization rate include (1) the nature of the business, (2) the risk involved, and (3) the stability or irregularity of earnings.

The "formula" approach should not be used if there is better evidence available from which the value of intangibles can be determined. If the assets of a going business are sold upon the basis of a rate of capitalization that can be substantiated as being realistic, though it is not within the range of figures indicated here as the ones ordinarily to be adopted, the same rate of capitalization should be used in determining the value of intangibles.

Accordingly, the "formula" approach may be used for determining the fair market value of intangible assets of a business only if there is no better basis therefor available.

See also Revenue Ruling 59-60, C.B. 1959-1, 237, as modified by Revenue Ruling 65-193, C.B. 1965-2, 370, which sets forth the proper approach to use in the valuation of closely-held corporate stocks for estate and gift tax purposes. The general approach, methods, and factors, outlined in Revenue Ruling 59-60, as modified, are equally applicable to valuations of corporate stocks for income and other tax purposes as well as for estate and gift tax purposes. They apply also to problems involving the determination of the fair market value of business interests of any type, including partnerships and proprietorships, and of intangible assets for all tax purposes.

A.R.M. 34, A.R.M. 68, and O.D. 937 are superseded, since the positions set forth therein are restated to the extent applicable under current law in this Revenue Ruling. Revenue Ruling 65-192, C.B. 1965-2, 259, which contained restatements of A.R.M. 34 and A.R.M. 68, is also superseded.

---

[1]Prepared pursuant to Rev. Proc. 67-6, C.B. 1967-1, 576.

How This Valuation Method Works

Application of This Method

While there are several variations in the application of this business valuation method, the typical procedures in the capitalized excess earnings method are summarized as follows:

1. Estimate the net tangible asset value for the subject company. This procedure was discussed in Chapter 7. It is noteworthy that this es-

timated value is for the net tangible assets of the company only. As we will see, net tangible assets may or may not include such discrete intangible items as leasehold interests, patents, trademarks, copyrights, and so on.

2. Estimate a normalized level of economic earnings. There are many alternative definitions of economic earnings, as was discussed in Chapter 8 and elsewhere.

3. Quantify excess earnings. First, estimate an appropriate (percentage) fair rate of return on the estimated net tangible asset value of the subject company. Next, multiply the estimated net tangible asset value (from Step 1) by the estimated fair rate of return in order to estimate the amount of economic earnings that would be attributable to the company's net tangible assets. Next, subtract that fair return on net tangible assets amount from the estimated normalized earnings developed in Step 2. The result of this procedure is sometimes called the *excess earnings* or the *excess economic income* (that is, this is the amount of economic earnings above a fair rate of return on the net tangible asset value of the subject company).

4. Estimate an appropriate direct capitalization rate to apply to the excess economic earnings. These excess earnings are (presumably) the economic earnings attributable to goodwill or other intangible asset values—as opposed to the net tangible asset values for the subject company.

5. Capitalize the excess economic earnings at that estimated direct capitalization rate.

6. Add the values from Steps 1 (i.e., the net tangible asset values) and 5 (i.e., the intangible value in the nature of goodwill).

The Apparent Simplicity of This Method

In a subsequent section, we will examine the many appraisal decisions and judgments encountered in each of the above analytical procedures. The discussion will indicate that the application of this valuation method is anything but simple. But first, let's look at an illustration of the application of the capitalized excess earnings method.

An Illustration

For purposes of this illustration, let's assume that Flora's Flower Shop has a net tangible asset value of $20,000. Let's also assume that, after an allowance for a reasonable salary for Flora, the flower shop earns about $8,000 of net income per year. For the purpose of this example, we will use an estimated fair rate of return of 15 percent on the net tangible assets of Flora's Flower Shop. Also, for purposes of this illustration only, we will capitalize the excess economic earnings of Flora's Flower Shop at a 20 percent direct capitalization rate. (The matter of estimating applicable direct capitalization rates is discussed later in the chapter.) In this simplified application of the capitalized excess earnings method, the value of Flora's Flower Shop would be estimated as follows:

Net tangible asset value	$20,000
Normalized economic earnings	$8,000
Economic earnings attributable to net tangible assets ($20,000 × .15) =	3,000
"Excess" economic earnings	$5,000
Indicated value of capitalized excess economic earnings ($5,000 ÷ .20) =	25,000
Indicated total value of Flora's Flower Shop business enterprise	$45,000

A Popular Version

Exhibit 23-2 is typical of the summaries of the capitalized excess earnings valuation method as they are applied in popular usage. The appraisal report text accompanying the "formula method" often offers comments such as the following:

> The buyer looks at the business for its ability to earn a fair return on investment, after deducting his or her salary. The present and future earning power of the business is of prime importance. If the business is not at least equal in earning power to an outside investment in a comparable business or in securities, the buyer usually will not be willing to pay more than the price of tangibles. In fact, the buyer may not want to buy the tangible assets—even at bargain prices—if the business is not profitable. . . .
>
> Goodwill can be thought of as the difference between an established successful business and one that has yet to establish itself and achieve success. The price the buyer should be willing to pay for goodwill depends on the earning power and potential of the business.
>
> The price the seller should be content with is the amount considered as compensation for the transfer of intangible values and for the surrender of the expected earning power of the business. The seller should base the value of goodwill on the actual condition and earning power of the business. If past efforts and capital were used effectively, the current earning power of the business should be above average. If earnings are low, the buyer probably will resist paying any amount for intangibles. . . .
>
> Because each business and sales transaction is different, the formula should be used only to indicate some of the major considerations in pricing a business.[1]

Analysis of the Capitalized Excess Earnings Method

One of the most widely used small business valuation methods today certainly deserves some additional analysis.

---

[1]*How to Buy or Sell a Business*, Small Business Reporter series (San Francisco: Bank of America, 1982), p. 8.

Exhibit 23–2

A Popular Version of the Excess Earnings Method

The Pricing Formula	Example:	Business A	Business B
Step 1. Determine the adjusted tangible net worth of the business. (The total market value of all current and long-term assets less liabilities.)	1. Adjusted value of tangible net worth (assets less liabilities).	$100,000	$100,000
Step 2. Estimate how much the buyer could earn annually with an amount equal to the value of the tangible net worth invested elsewhere.	2. Earning power at 10%* of an amount equal to the adjusted tangible net worth, if invested in a comparable risk business.	10,000	10,000
Step 3. Add to this a salary normal for an owner-operator of the business. This combined figure provides a reasonable estimate of the income the buyer can earn elsewhere with the investment and effort involved in working in the business.	3. Reasonable salary for owner-operator in the business.	18,000	18,000
Step 4. Determine the average annual net earnings of the business (net profit before subtracting owner's salary) over the past few years. This is before income taxes, to make it comparable with earnings from other sources or by individuals in different tax brackets. (The tax implications of alternate investments should be carefully considered.) The trend of earnings is a key factor. Have they been rising steadily, falling steadily, remaining constant, or fluctuating widely? The earnings figure should be adjusted to reflect these trends.	4. Net earnings of the business over recent years (net profit before subtracting owner's salary).	30,000	23,350
Step 5. Subtract the total of earning power (2) and reasonable salary (3) from this average net earnings figure (4). This gives the extra earning power of the business.	5. Extra earning power of the business (line 4 minus lines 2 and 3).	2,000	(4,650)
Step 6. Use this extra, or excess, earning figure to estimate the value of the intangibles. This is done by multiplying the extra earnings by what is termed the "years-of-profit" figure. This "years-of-profit" multiplier pivots on these points. How unique are the intangibles offered by the firm? How long would it take to set up a similar business and bring it to this stage of development? What expenses and risks would be involved? What is the price of goodwill in similar firms? Will the seller be signing an agreement with a covenant not to compete? If the business is well established, a factor of five or more might be used, especially if the firm has a valuable name, patent, or location. A multiplier of three might be reasonable for a moderately seasoned firm. A younger, but profitable, firm might merely have a one-year profit figure.	6. Value of intangibles —using three-year profit figure for moderately well-established firm (3 times line 5).	6,000	None
Step 7. Final Price equals Adjusted Tangible Net Worth plus Value of Intangibles. (Extra Earnings times "Years of Profit.")	7. Final price (lines 1 and 6).	$106,000	$100,000 (or less)

In example A, the seller receives a value for goodwill because the business is moderately well established and earning more than the buyer could earn elsewhere with similar risks and effort. Within three years, the buyer should have recovered the amount paid for goodwill in this example.

In example B, the seller receives no value for goodwill because the business, even though it may have existed for a considerable time, is not earning as much as the buyer could through outside investment and effort. In fact, the buyer may feel that even an investment of $100,000— the current appraised value of net assets—is too much because it cannot earn sufficient return.

* This is an arbitrary figure, used for illustration. A reasonable figure depends on the stability and relative risks of the business and the investment picture generally. The rate of return should be similar to that which could be earned elsewhere with the same approximate risk.

SOURCE: *How to Buy or Sell a Business*, Small Business Reporter Series (San Francisco: Bank of America, 1982), p. 8.

First of all, it is noteworthy that the Treasury Department did not initiate this valuation method to estimate the value of the total business enterprise. Rather, this valuation method was developed to value the goodwill or other intangible value, if any, above the net tangible asset values of the brewery or other companies affected by the Prohibition of the 1920s. However, since it seems logical that any intangible value identified by the capitalized excess earnings valuation method should be added to the tangible value of the subject company in order to estimate the total business enterprise value, this valuation method has attained popularity for valuing the total small business or professional practice enterprise.

Unfortunately for business appraisers, Internal Revenue Service Revenue Ruling 68-609 contains many ambiguities and leaves many unanswered questions. Various valuation practitioners have adopted a wide variety of interpretations to these ambiguities and a wide variety of answers to the unanswered questions.

In the following section, we will discuss these ambiguities and open questions in the same order as they were presented in the "Application of This Method" section above.

Estimating the "Net Tangible Asset Value"

The first procedure in the capitalized excess earnings method is to estimate a net tangible asset value for the subject company. Unfortunately, Revenue Ruling 68-609 does not specifically define what it means by *net tangible asset value*. For example, the Revenue Ruling is not very specific with respect to the important question "net of what?"

Defining Net Tangible Asset Value. Revenue Ruling 68-609 offers little guidance to analysts as to either the appropriate standard or the appropriate premise of value that should be used when estimating *net tangible asset value*. This lack of specificity may be purposeful, however. In other words, the Revenue Ruling may imply that there is no single answer as to the appropriate standard of value or premise of value. Rather, these determinations may have to be made on a subject-specific basis.

As with the application of other business valuation methods, the questions of standard of value and premise of value with respect to applying the capitalized excess earnings method may only be answered after careful consideration of (1) the purpose and objective of the individual appraisal, (2) the quantity and quality of available data, and (3) the highest and best use of the subject small business or professional practice.

There is some agreement among valuation practitioners that the most common interpretation of the phrase *net tangible asset value* in this context is fair market value, estimated on a value in continued use premise. Typically, this standard of value and premise of value would be measured by one or more of the generally accepted asset appraisal approaches discussed in the previous chapter.

It is noteworthy that IRS Private Letter Ruling 79-05013 (also promulgated as an IRS National Office Technical Advice Memorandum) takes a fairly firm position that the appropriate standard of value for the net tangible assets should be fair market value:

> Rev. Rul. 68-609 addresses the determination of fair market value of intangible assets by the formula approach, and for this reason it is proper

that all terms used in the formula be consistent. The formula uses value in terms of fair market value, so the term '. . . value of the tangible assets used in a business,' in the formula, should be in terms of fair market values, as defined in Rev. Rul. 59-60.

As a practical matter, it is rare that the analyst will engage in such a rigorous appraisal of the tangible assets of a small business or professional practice. Typically, the analyst will estimate the fair market value of the net tangible assets on a value in continued use premise.

Often, the analyst resorts to using the book value of the subject tangible assets simply because there are no readily available data to aid in reaching a better estimate of tangible asset value. This use of book value for estimating the value of the subject net tangible assets is not preferred. However, tangible assets are typically not a major component of the business value of most small businesses and professional practices. Therefore, this simplifying assumption regarding net tangible asset values is often adequate for such purposes.

Should Asset Value Adjustments be Tax-Affected?

Because the objective of the analysis is to estimate the value of subject net tangible assets on a continued use basis—on which a reasonable rate of return should be earned—the analyst normally does not make any adjustment to recognize the income tax effect of unrealized (built-in) gains or losses. However, analysts should not just ignore income tax considerations. For example, there could be cases (e.g., a large inventory write-up where a tax payment on the sale of the inventory is imminent) where an income tax adjustment may be appropriate.

Are Intangible Assets Included or Excluded?

Typically, as the phrase *net tangible asset value* implies, intangible asset values should be removed from the subject company balance sheet before performing the capitalized excess earnings analysis. However, some practitioners leave on the balance sheet those intangible assets that are already capitalized on the subject company financial statements. Examples of such intangible assets already recognized on the company's financial statements would include purchased goodwill, purchased computer software, computer software internally developed in anticipation of resale, and so forth.

It is noteworthy that, so far, this discussion assumes the application of the capitalized excess earnings method to estimate the company's total intangible value in the nature of goodwill (i.e., the collective valuation of intangible assets). If the subject company's intangible assets are valued discretely (using, for example, the asset accumulation method), this conclusion would be different. In that case, the capitalized excess earnings method is used to estimate the residual value of the company's goodwill—after all of its individual intangible assets have been valued and included in the amount of net assets subject to the capitalized excess earnings analysis.

Treatment of Nonoperating Assets.

There is general agreement that it is preferable to remove nonoperating and/or excess assets from the balance sheet (and related revenue from the income statement) and to treat such items separately in the capitalized excess earnings method.

Treatment of Real Estate Owned. In the appraisal of those small businesses or professional practices where real estate is not usually owned by the company, some valuation practitioners remove the owned real estate from the company's balance sheet and impute a fair market rental expense on the company's income statement. The objective of this adjustment, when appropriate, is to analyze what the company would actually look like if it were sold—that is, with the real estate likely being sold separately from the business.

Estimating Net Tangible Asset Value. There is no universally accepted conclusion as to what accounts should be "netted out" in the estimation of net tangible asset value. For example, net tangible assets could be interpreted to mean any one of the following:

1. Gross assets net of accumulated depreciation (i.e., net current value of the tangible assets).
2. Net current value of the financial and tangible assets less current liabilities.
3. Net current value of the tangible assets minus all liabilities.

The most common interpretation of net tangible asset value is alternative 2, net current value of the financial and tangible assets less current liabilities. However, alternative interpretations may be equally relevant and equally applicable.

In fact, this determination is not particularly important to the application of the capitalized excess earnings method. That is, the final product of this method (the indicated value of the owners' equity in the subject business) should be unaffected by the definition of net tangible asset value.

This is because there could be a different fair rate of return and a different direct capitalization rate for each measure of net tangible asset value. The most important aspect of this method is not an academic debate over the conceptually correct definition of net asset value. Rather, the most important aspect of this method is consistency. That is, the measure of net tangible asset value has to be consistent with (1) the measure of fair rate of return and (2) the measure of the direct capitalization rate. As long as all of the capitalized excess earnings method variables are applied consistently, this method will provide a valid estimate of value.

Estimating the Value of Debt. The conceptual answer to the question of the amount of debt to be included is that it depends on when the debt is likely to be paid. If payment at face value is imminent (e.g., if a payment is triggered by the very transaction for which the valuation is being performed), it is appropriate to value the subject debt at face value. If the debt may remain outstanding for a period of time, many practitioners would value the subject debt at its fair market value.

Estimating a "Normalized Level of Earnings"

Step 2 in the capitalized excess earnings method is to estimate a normalized level of earnings. This is also called a normalized level of economic income. This more generic description is particularly appropriate because Revenue Ruling 68-609 does not specifically define the term *earnings*. It does, however, make the key statement that the earnings *"should fairly reflect the probable future earnings"* (emphasis supplied). In suggesting the use of past years' earnings as a basis for estimating future earnings, the Revenue Ruling notes that abnormal years should be eliminated from consideration. Practitioners also agree that nonrecurring income and/or expense items should be eliminated from any historical period that is used for the earnings base calculations.

Treatment of Nonoperating Income. Consistent with removing nonoperating assets from the tangible asset base, related nonoperating income is typically removed from the earnings base.

Treatment of Owners' Compensation. Revenue Ruling 68-609 states that "if the business is a sole proprietorship or partnership, there should be deducted from the earnings of the business a reasonable amount for services performed by the owner or partners engaged in the business." Valuation practitioners concur that owner/employee's abnormal compensation should be adjusted to a more normal level of compensation. The "normal level" of compensation is generally considered to be the expense of employing a nonowner/employee to perform the owner/employee's services.

Treatment of Income Taxes. The measure of earnings—or economic income—to be capitalized should normally be net of federal and state income taxes paid by the entity being valued. Most small businesses and professional practices are organized as sole proprietorships, partnerships, or S corporations—entities that normally pay no federal or state income taxes—so the matter may be moot. Even small businesses and professional practices organized as C corporations often manage their affairs in order to minimize—or eliminate—corporate income taxes.

However, there are instances where a case can be made for tax affecting the economic income even where the subject business does not pay income taxes. For example, if the subject business were to be sold to a corporation that would have to pay income taxes on the subject's income, in estimating that buyer's investment value, the buyer almost surely would tax-affect the economic income. If that actual buyer were also the typical "willing buyer," the tax-affected earnings probably would also be the appropriate measure of economic income to use in estimating fair market value. Also, a significant (and not uncommon) problem arises when tax liability flows through to an owner but the earnings giving rise to the tax liability are not paid out. Tax-affecting the subject business's earnings is one of several possible ways to treat this problem for purposes of valuation.

Again, what is most important is consistency in application. That is, the measure of "earnings" or economic income that is selected—whether it is net income, net cash flow, or operating cash flow and whether it is before tax or after tax—should be consistent with (1) the measure of the fair rate of return and (2) the measure of the direct capitalization rate.

Definition of "Earnings."   Revenue Ruling 68-609 does not provide a definition of the term *earnings*. Is it net income? Net cash flow? Or some other measure of economic income?

There is some agreement among valuation practitioners that the variable best suited to represent earnings in the context of the capitalized excess earnings method is cash flow. However, even within this general agreement, there is a difference in opinion about whether (1) net cash flow or (2) operating cash flow are the best measures of economic income. These different measures of economic income were discussed in Chapter 13. The trend among valuation practitioners is to favor net cash flow because that is what the owner can take out of the business without disrupting operations.

For most small businesses and professional practices, the difference between net income and any measure of cash flow is so minimal that it often doesn't matter. Again, there is some discretion in the analyst's treatment of income taxes in the excess earnings method. As long as income taxes are accounted for consistently, this method will provide a valid indication of value. That is, (1) the economic income, (2) the fair rate of return, and (3) the direct capitalization rate should be consistently measured—on either a before-tax basis or an after-tax basis.

Appropriate Rate of Return on Tangible Assets

Several alternative procedures can be used to quantify the appropriate rate of return on the subject company's net tangible assets.[2] Most practitioners agree that the required return is dependent largely on the asset mix. The riskier the assets, the higher the rate of return required to support them.

One common procedure is to use a weighted average of the company's cost of debt and cost of equity, with the weighting based on the proportions of the various asset classes that can be financed by debt. The following is an example of this procedure.

Asset Class	Asset Value	Percent Financible	Borrowing Capacity
Receivables	$100,000	80%	$ 80,000
Inventory	200,000	60%	120,000
Fixtures and equipment	200,000	50%	100,000
	$500,000		$ 300,000

[2]For an extensive discussion of development of the respective capitalization rates for tangible assets and excess earnings, see Jay E. Fishman, Shannon P. Pratt, J. Clifford Griffith, and D. Keith Wilson, *Guide to Business Valuations*, 7th ed. (Fort Worth, TX: Practitioners Publishing Co., 1997), pp. 7-22–7-26.

If the company's borrowing cost is 10 percent and its cost of equity (see Chapter 13) is 20 percent, the weighted average would be as follows:

Debt   @ 10% × 0.6 ($300,000/$500,000)   = 6%
Equity @ 20% × 0.4 ($200,000/$500,000)   = 8%
Weighted average required return on tangible assets = 14%

If the company is a C corporation and subject to paying income taxes, the cost of debt would be tax-affected by multiplying the cost of debt by 1 minus the tax rate. For example, if the company's tax rate is 30 percent, the cost of debt would be 10% × (1 - 0.30) = 10% × 0.7 = 7%.

If the company's borrowing capacity is dependent on personal guarantees, this is an additional debt cost factor. While no empirical support for the amount of this cost factor exists, it would be reasonable to add to the cost of debt if personal guarantees are involved. Such guarantees carry risk to the guarantor and limit the guarantor's borrowing capacity for purposes unrelated to the business.

Some practitioners use historical industry average rates of return. The problem with this is that required rates of return, by definition, are based on the future expectations and alternative opportunity cost of the investor. The historical industry rate of return in many instances is not representative of future expectations.

Appropriate Capitalization Rate for Excess Earnings

Since all of the available debt rate and the safest part of the equity rate were used up for a rate of return for the tangible assets, the capitalization rate applicable to excess earnings normally would have to be higher than the company's overall required equity rate.

Most practitioners agree that the most important force driving the capitalization rate for excess earnings is the perceived persistence of the excess earnings. The longer the time period and the greater the certainty of the expectation of receiving the excess earnings, the lower the applicable capitalization rate. The rate most commonly encountered in the market is 33 1/3 percent, which is the equivalent of paying for three years of excess earnings (1 ÷ 0.3333 = 3). This would assume a solid earnings base expected to continue well into the future. We have seen rates as high as 400 percent—that is, payment for only three months of expected excess earnings. A low capitalization rate would be applicable only for a very long and very predictable persistence of the excess earnings, such as for insurance policy renewals with a long history of demonstrated renewal rates.

It should be obvious that the selection of an excess earnings capitalization rate by these typical considerations is one of the most subjective judgments that must be made within the various business valuation methods. However, ultimately, the weighted average of the capitalization rates for the tangible assets and excess earnings (weighted by the amount of value ascribed to each of the two components) should be the same as the company's overall capitalization rate, as developed and used in Chapter 15, The Capitalized Economic Income Method. The following comprehensive example and related Exhibits 23-3 through 23-8 show how it would all work out in a perfect world.

Comprehensive Example

Exhibit 23-3 presents the historical financial statements for the illustrative company that is subject to appraisal using the capitalized excess earnings method. This illustrative company is named Typical Small Business. Exhibit 23-3 presents a balance sheet, income statement, and cash flow statement for Typical Small Business.

The objective of this business valuation is to estimate the fair market value of 100 percent of the owners' equity of Typical Small Business, as of December 31, 1997.

Exhibit 23-4 presents two alternative measures of (or definitions of) net tangible asset value for Typical Small Business:

1. Book value of net tangible assets.
2. Fair market value of net tangible assets.

Exhibit 23-5 presents, with simplified assumptions, estimates of capitalization rates applicable to the fair market value of tangible assets and the "excess earnings."

Readers should note that the estimation of the capitalization rate applicable to excess earnings is the weakest link in the excess earnings method. It is a matter of subjective estimation and analyst's judgment. There is no generally accepted conceptual method to estimate the capitalization rate without first valuing the whole company, and there is precious little supporting empirical market evidence.

Exhibit 23-6 applies these estimated capitalization rates to Typical Small Business (based on fair market value of net tangible assets) to arrive at an indicated value by the excess earnings method.

We know that the blended, or overall, capitalization rate for the entire capital structure should be equal to the company's weighted cost of capital, less the long-term estimated growth rate in the economic income variable being capitalized. When valuing a controlling interest, we typically value the overall capital as opposed to just the equity.

Exhibit 23-7 illustrates the estimate of the overall required rate of return (WACC) and overall direct capitalization rate for Typical Small Business.

As a "sanity check" or "reasonableness check" on our results from application of the excess earnings method in Exhibit 23-6, we can apply

Exhibit 23–3

TYPICAL SMALL BUSINESS
SUMMARY BALANCE SHEET
(HISTORICAL COST BASIS)
AS OF DECEMBER 31, 1997

ASSETS		LIABILITIES AND OWNERS' EQUITY	
Current assets	$1,000,000	Current liabilities	$1,000,000
(cash, receivables, and inventory)		(payables and accruals)	
Tangible assets	2,000,000	Long-term debt	1,000,000
(real estate and equipment—		Owners' equity	1,000,000
net of accumulated depreciation)			
		TOTAL LIABILITIES AND	
TOTAL ASSETS	$3,000,000	OWNERS' EQUITY	$3,000,000

TYPICAL SMALL BUSINESS
SUMMARY INCOME STATEMENT
FOR THE TWELVE MONTHS ENDED DECEMBER 31, 1997

Net revenues	$5,000,000
Operating expenses	
Cash expenses	3,700,000
Depreciation expense	200,000
Interest expense	100,000
Total expenses	4,000,000
Profit before taxes	1,000,000
Income taxes	400,000
Profit after taxes	$ 600,000

TYPICAL SMALL BUSINESS
SUMMARY RESULTS OF OPERATIONS
FOR THE TWELVE MONTHS ENDED DECEMBER 31, 1997

Net cash flow (debt-free):

	Profit after taxes	$	600,000
Plus:	Tax-affected interest expense ($100,000 interest expense less $40,000 income tax expense)		60,000
Equals:	Profit after taxes—debt free	$	660,000
Plus:	Depreciation expense		200,000
Less:	Capital expenditures (during 1997)		200,000
Less:	Increase in net working capital (from 12/31/96 to 12/31/97)		100,000
Equals:	Net cash flow (debt free)	$	560,000

Operating cash flow (debt-free):

	Profit after taxes	$	600,000
Plus:	Tax-affected interest expense		60,000
Equals:	Profit after taxes—debt-free	$	660,000
Plus:	Depreciation expense		200,000
Equals:	Operating cash flow (debt-free)	$	860,000

Exhibit 23–4

TYPICAL SMALL BUSINESS
APPLICATION OF CAPITALIZED EXCESS EARNINGS METHOD
ALTERNATIVE MEASURES OF NET TANGIBLE ASSET VALUE

Measure #1
Book Value of Net Tangible Assets

		"Book Value" from 12/31/97 Balance Sheet
	Current assets	$ 1,000,000
Minus:	Current liabilities	1,000,000
Equals:	Net working capital	0
Plus:	Tangible assets	2,000,000
Equals:	Book value of net tangible assets	$ 2,000,000

Measure #2
Fair Market Value of Net Tangible Assets

		Fair Market Value as of 12/31/97
	Current assets	$ 1,000,000
Minus:	Current liabilities	1,000,000
Equals:	Net working capital	0
Plus:	Tangible assets	2,500,000
	(based on contemporaneous market value appraisals of real estate and equipment)	
Equals:	Fair market value of net tangible assets	$ 2,500,000

this direct capitalization rate to Typical Small Business's net cash flow, and compare the results:

$$\frac{\$560,000}{.15} = \$3,733,000$$

The result (admittedly a bit contrived) is amazingly close to the $3,740,000 indicated value of Typical Small Business's overall capital as developed in Exhibit 23-6. If the results were not within a reasonable range of each other, it would be appropriate to examine the saaumptions of each method and perhaps make some revisions in order to make one or the other of the two methods more realistic.

The weights assigned to the capital structure components (generally debt and equity) usually should be the "target" weights for the company—that is, "the proportions of debt and equity that the firm targets

Exhibit 23–5

**TYPICAL SMALL BUSINESS
APPLICATION OF CAPITALIZED EXCESS EARNINGS METHOD
ASSET-SPECIFIC REQUIRED RATE OF RETURN AND
ASSET-SPECIFIC DIRECT CAPITALIZATION RATE**

In this application of the capitalized excess earnings method, we use asset-specific required rates of return and asset-specific direct capitalization rates. That is, the required rate of return for each category of Typical Small Business net assets is specific to the investment risk associated with that class of asset investment. Also, the direct capitalization rate to be applied to the excess economic income is a rate that is specific to the risk of that measure of economic income—that is, the risk associated with the intangible goodwill of the subject company.

We could perform this asset-specific capitalized excess earnings analysis based upon any—and all—of the two measures of net tangible asset value illustrated in the previous exhibit. For simplicity, we only illustrate the asset specific application of the capitalized excess earnings method using one measure of net tangible asset value: Measure #2, with net tangible asset value estimated at contemporaneously appraised fair market value, the most common formulation of the method.

From Exhibit 23-3, we recall that the net working capital balance for Typical Small Business is zero (i.e., $1,000,000 current assets minus $1,000,000 current liabilities). This was a conscious simplifying assumption for illustrative purposes only. The asset-specific application of required rates of return and direct capitalization rates can work with any level of positive—or negative—net working capital.

While it will have no impact on our final business value estimate, let's estimate an asset-specific rate of return for the Typical Small Business net working capital. Net working capital is usually considered a very low risk asset investment capital. Accordingly, a short-term, risk-free rate is often used as the asset-specific rate of return for net working capital. For purposes of this illustration, let's assume a short-term, risk-free rate of 6% to be applied against this low risk net investment category.

From Exhibit 23-4, we recall that the fair market value of the Typical Small Business tangible assets (i.e., real estate and equipment) is $2,500,000. This value is based upon a current appraisal of the subject real estate and equipment.

Let's assume that the appropriate asset-specific rate of return on the Typical Small Business tangible assets is 10%. This would be a rate of return specific to the risk and expected return of these tangible assets. For purposes of this illustration, let's assume that this 10% is the cost of financing for these tangible assets. In other words, let's assume that Typical Small Business could borrow funds, using some equity, at a blended rate of 10% for the purposes of purchasing such tangible assets.

It is noteworthy that in the application of the asset-specific rate of return procedure, there could be several asset-specific rates of return: one for land, one for buildings, one for machinery and equipment, and so on.

At this point, we need to estimate an asset-specific capitalization rate for goodwill (on the "big pot" premise that we are subsuming all intangible asset value under "goodwill"). If we believe that a buyer would pay for four years of expected earnings from the company's goodwill (which assumes a rather highly reliable and persistent expected income stream from the goodwill), the capitalization rate would be 25% (1 ÷ 4 = 0.25). The application of these asset-specific capitalization rates is shown in Exhibit 23-6.

for its capital structure over the long-term planning period."[3] This often is based on industry average capital structures.

Let's look back for a moment to other measures of net tangible asset value as shown in Exhibit 23-4. We should consider the implications of these other measures for the estimates of capitalization rates for net tangible asset value and for excess earnings.

In the case of Measure #1, book value, we know that (at least in this case) book value understates the fair market value of the net tangible assets. Consequently, it is reasonable to assume that a higher proprtion of the net tangible assets as measured by book value could be financed by debt, with the result that the required return on net tangible assets would be lower than if measured by fair market value. Similarly, this leaves a higher proportion of the net cash flow attributable to intangible assets, suggesting a higher capitalization rate for that component.

Exhibit 23-8 illustrates the value estimate for Typical Small Business using book value as the net tangible asset base, an 8 percent return on net tangible assets, and a 30 percent capitalization rate on excess earnings.

---

[3]Alfred Rappaport, *Creating Shareholder Value,* rev. ed. (New York: The Free Press, 1998), p. 37.

Exhibit 23–6

**TYPICAL SMALL BUSINESS
APPLICATION OF CAPITALIZED EXCESS EARNINGS METHOD
CAPITALIZATION OF ASSET-SPECIFIC EXCESS EARNINGS
USING FAIR MARKET VALUES OF ASSETS**

Net Tangible Asset Value Measure #2 (Fair Market Value)

Net cash flow (after-tax)		$ 560,000	(from Exhibit 23-3)
Fair market value of net tangible assets	$2,500,000		(from Exhibit 23-4)
Times: Asset-specific required rate of return on net tangible assets	× 10%		(from Exhibit 23-5)
Required level of economic income		$ 250,000	
Excess economic income (i.e., net cash flow less required level of economic income)		$ 310,000	
Divided by: Direct capitalization rate (based upon applying an asset-specific required rate of return on goodwill)		25%	(from Exhibit 23-5)
Equals: Estimate of intangible asset value in the nature of goodwill		$1,240,000	
Add: Fair market value of net tangible assets		2,500,000	
Implied value of Typical Small Business (including existing equity and debt)		$3,740,000	
Less: Existing debt		1,000,000	
Indicated value of equity		**$2,740,000**	

Not surprisingly, since book values bear little relationship to market values, the $3,333,333 from Exhibit 23-8 is not as close to the $3,733,333 as we got using fair market values in Exhibit 23-6. However, most analysts probably would still consider it within a reasonable range of value.

The principal reason the alternative applications of this method appear to yield different value indications is that there are no precise methods for estimating the two capitalization rates, especially the rate for excess earnings.

In the comprehensive example, we did not illustrate the effect of the alternative growth rate projections on the excess economic income, on the direct capitalization rate, and (ultimately) on the estimation of goodwill. This omission was also due to space constraints. The effect of growth rate projections on the estimate of economic income and on the selected direct capitalization rate is discussed in detail in Chapter 13, Understanding Discount and Capitalization Rates.

The Treatment of Negative Goodwill

The capitalized excess earnings method is an asset-based valuation approach method. In the strictest application of this method, all of the subject entity's assets—both tangible and intangible—are valued. However, the actual capitalization of excess economic income procedure values one asset only: the entity's intangible value in the nature of goodwill.

Exhibit 23–7

TYPICAL SMALL BUSINESS
APPLICATION OF CAPITALIZED EXCESS EARNINGS METHOD
OVERALL REQUIRED RATE OF RETURN AND
OVERALL DIRECT CAPITALIZATION RATE

After-Tax Weighted Average Cost of Capital

Assumptions: (a)   Let's assume that the blended interest rate on the Typical Small Business long-term debt is 10%. Let's also assume that the required risk-adjusted rate of return on the owners' equity of Typical Small Business is 24%.

            (b)   As indicated in Exhibit 23-3, the effective income tax rate for Typical Small Business is 40%; the cost of debt capital (i.e., the interest rate) is affected by this income tax rate, where the cost of equity capital is already "paid" from after-tax dollars.

Type of Capital Component in Capital Structure	Before-Tax Cost of Capital Component	After-Tax Cost of Capital Component	Weighting in Capital Structure	Weighted Cost of Capital Component
Long-term debt	10%	6%	50%	3%
Owners' equity	24%	24%	50%	12%
Total			100%	15%

After-tax weighted average cost of capital (rounded)   15%

Direct Capitalization Rate

As explained in Chapter 13, a direct capitalization rate can be mathematically derived as follows:

$$c = k - g$$

where:

    c = direct capitalization rate
    k = present value discount rate
    g = expected long-term growth rate

Also, as explained in Chapter 13, one procedure for estimating a company's present value discount rate is to calculate it's weighted average cost of capital.

     Since we have just claculated the Typical Small Business weighted average cost of capital to be 15%, we use that indication as the appropriate present value discount rate. For purposes of simplicity, we assume a zero percent expected long-term growth rate. Therefore, we use 15% as the direct capitalization for the estimated net cash flow.

This intangible value in the nature of goodwill is the value of the company's economic income (if any) over and above a reasonable rate of return on the company's net tangible assets. A significant conceptual and practical question is: What if the subject company's economic income is less than a reasonable rate of return on the net tangible assets? The result of this phenomenon (i.e., economic income less than a fair rate of return on net tangible assets) is often referred to as *negative goodwill*. Negative goodwill indicates that the collective going-concern value of the total subject entity is less than the sum of the individual values of the entity's total tangible assets.

In such a situation, the subject company's economic income is insufficient to justify buying the business on the basis of the collective value of its individual assets. In such an instance, the collective value of the company's assets (including tangible assets and discrete intangible assets) would have to be reduced to the level of economic value indicated by the conclusion of the capitalized excess earnings analysis. In other words, the negative economic value associated with the company's goodwill would

Exhibit 23–8

TYPICAL SMALL BUSINESS
APPLICATION OF CAPITALIZED EXCESS EARNINGS METHOD
CAPITALIZATION OF ASSET-SPECIFIC EXCESS EARNINGS
USING BOOK VALUES OF ASSETS

Net Tangible Asset Value Measure #1 (Book Value)

Net cash flow (after-tax)		$ 560,000	(from Exhibit 23-3)
Book value of net tangible assets	$2,000,000		(from Exhibit 23-4)
Times: Asset-specific required rate of return on net tangible assets	× 8%		(from text discussion)
Required level of economic income		$ 160,000	
Excess economic income (i.e., net cash flow less required level of economic income)		$ 400,000	
Divided by: Direct capitalization rate (based upon applying an asset-specific required rate of return on goodwill)		30%	(from text discussion)
Equals: Estimate of intangible asset value in the nature of goodwill		$1,333,333	
Add: Book value of net tangible assets		2,000,000	
Implied value of Typical Small Business (including existing equity and debt)		$3,333,333	
Less: Existing debt		1,000,000	
Indicated value of equity		**$2,333,333**	

offset the positive economic value of the company's tangible assets and discrete intangible assets.

Should the adjusted net asset value indicated by the application of the company's negative goodwill fall below the liquidation value of the company's net assets, one might conclude that the business would be worth more dead than alive. That is, a liquidation of the subject business would be a rational economic choice.

Common Errors in Applying the Capitalized Excess Earnings Method

As mentioned previously, the capitalized excess earnings method is often misused in valuing small businesses and professional practices. Some of the most common errors in the application of this valuation method are discussed in the following sections.

Failure to Allow for Owner's Salary

As noted in Revenue Ruling 68-609 (Exhibit 23-1), "If the business is a sole proprietorship or partnership, there should be deducted from the earnings of the business a reasonable amount for services performed by the owner or partners engaged in the business." (This point is also covered in Chapter 8.)

Nonetheless, valuations are often performed using the capitalized excess earnings method without including a reasonable allowance for compensation to the business owners for the services they performed. This error results in an overstatement of the true economic income of the company. This in turn leads to an overstatement of the value of the subject business.

Failure to Use Realistic Normalized Earnings

To the extent that the method is valid, it depends on a reasonable estimate of normalized earnings, as discussed in Chapter 8. As noted in Revenue Ruling 68-609, "The past earnings to which the formula is applied should fairly reflect the probable future earnings."

However, this valuation method is sometimes applied naively to the latest year's earnings or to some simple or weighted average of recent years' earnings without regard to whether or not the earnings base used fairly reflects the probable future earnings. Such a naive use of some historical earnings base usually results in either an undervaluation or an overvaluation.

Errors in Selecting Appropriate Rates

The selection of the two capitalization rates is critical to the validity of the result of the capitalized excess earnings method. A conceptual approach to the selection of the appropriate capitalization rates was suggested in an earlier section. However, one clearly erroneous practice procedure for the selection of the capitalization rates is to use the rates suggested in the ruling itself.

The revenue ruling, written in 1968, suggests rates of 8 to 10 percent on tangible assets, with 15 to 20 percent applied to the excess earnings. However, the revenue ruling states that

> the percentage of return . . . should be the percentage prevailing in the industry involved at the date of the valuation. . . . The above rates are used as examples and are not appropriate in all cases. . . . The capitalization rates are dependent upon the facts pertinent thereto in each case. [4]

Both the wording of the revenue ruling and common sense indicate that the specific rates mentioned in the ruling are illustrative only. The appropriate capitalization rates depend on the facts at the time of the valuation. In spite of that, even in the late 1990s, some analysts use the rates for the excess earnings method published in the ARM 34 example back in 1920, and repeated in Revenue Ruling 68-609 in 1968.

---

[4]Revenue Ruling 68–609, 1968–2 C.B. 327.

Summary

The capitalized excess earnings method (also called the *formula method)* dates back to the period of Prohibition. It was the U.S. Treasury Department method of determining the amount to compensate distilleries for their loss of goodwill as a result of the effects of Prohibition. The Service's current position regarding the valuation method is embodied in Revenue Ruling 68-609 and Private Letter Ruling 79-05013, both referenced in this chapter.

The capitalized excess earnings method is one of the most widely used and misused methods of valuation for small businesses and professional practices. This is because analysts often naively apply the mechanics of this "formula method" without considering the sophisticated nuances of this conceptually elegant methodology. In addition, analysts often ignore the guidance regarding the proper implementation of this method contained in the above three Internal Revenue Service references. Therefore, the result is a plethora of misapplications of a fundamentally sound (and potentially analytically rigorous) valuation method.

This chapter has developed the proper use of the capitalized excess earnings method. It has quoted the relevant guidance provided in each of the Internal Revenue Service references cited above. And it has provided guidance on how to develop the four key variables in the capitalized excess earnings method:

1. Net tangible asset value.
2. Earnings base to be capitalized.
3. Reasonable rate of return on net tangible assets.
4. Direct capitalization rate to be applied to the "excess earnings."

The chapter has concluded with a discussion of several of the more common errors found in attempted implementations of the capitalized excess earnings method. By following the guidance in this chapter, the analyst should be able to properly apply the excess earnings method—and to identify the common errors resulting in the improper application of the capitalized excess earnings method.

Bibliography

Fishman, Jay E., and William J. Morrison. "Capitalization of Excess Earnings for Talent-Based Personal Service Business." *FAIR$HARE: The Matrimonial Law Monthly*, February 1996, p. 13.

Gallinger, George W., and Glenn A. Wilt. "The Excess Earnings Model's Necessary Assumptions." *ASA Valuation*, February 1988, pp. 74–78.

Gomes, Glenn M. "Excess Earnings, Competitive Advantage, and Goodwill Value." *Journal of Small Business Management*, July 1988, pp. 22–31.

Lippitt, Jeffrey W., and Nicholas J. Mastriacchio. "Developing Capitalization Rates for Valuing a Business." *The CPA Journal*, November 1995, pp. 24–28.

Mastracchio, Nicholas J., and Jeffrey W. Lippitt. "A Comparison of the Earnings Capitalization and the Excess Earnings Models." *Journal of Small Business Management*, January 1996, pp. 1–12.

"Practitioners Disagree Strongly on Excess Earnings Methodology." *Shannon Pratt's Business Valuation Update*, April 1997, pp. 1–3.

Pratt, Shannon P. "The Excess Earnings Method: How to Get a Defensible Result." *Shannon Pratt's Business Valuation Update*, October 1996, p. 1, 20–21.

Shayne, Mark. "A Reexamination of Revenue Ruling 68-609." *FAIR$HARE: The Matrimonial Law Monthly*, July 1992, pp. 5–8.

Summers, S. Chris. "The Excess Earnings Method," Chapter 15. In Thomas L. West and Jeffrey D. Jones, eds. *Handbook of Business Valuation*. New York: John Wiley & Sons, 1992, pp. 167–76.

Trugman, Gary R. "Crossfire: Should You Use the Excess Earnings Method? Trugman Says No!" *Proceedings of the American Institute of Certified Public Accountants National Business Valuation Conference*, New Orleans, December 5, 1995.

Zipp, Alan S., and Sharon M. Stouffer. "Using the Excess Earnings Method of Business Valuation." *Proceedings of the American Institute of Certified Public Accountants 1995 National Business Valuation Conference*, New Orleans, December 5, 1995.

Chapter 24

Discount for Lack of Control

This chapter deals with the valuation of noncontrolling—or minority—ownership interests in small businesses and professional practices. In the vernacular, this type of ownership interest is often referred to as a *minority interest*. To be more technically correct, this type of ownership interest should be referred to as a noncontrolling ownership interest. For purposes of this chapter, we will interchangeably refer to minority ownership interests and to noncontrolling ownership interests. Readers should be aware that these two terms mean exactly the same thing as what courts (and others) simply refer to as a *minority interest*.

This chapter discusses one aspect of the phenomenon that occurs when a particular ownership interest in a business is worth less than its pro rata percentage of the overall business enterprise value. That is, this chapter will explore why a 20 percent ownership interest in a small business may be worth less (and in some cases, much less) than 20 percent of the overall enterprise value of that very business. The aspect that will be discussed in this chapter is the decremental effect on the value of an equity investment due to fact that its owner is not able to personally control the financial, operational, or legal aspects of the subject business.

This decremental effect on the pro rata value of an ownership interest is interchangeably called the lack of control discount or the minority interest discount. In this chapter, we will investigate how to identify and quantify the minority ownership interest discount. Again, to be more technically correct, this valuation adjustment should be referred to as the lack of control discount.

There is a technical reason for this preferred nomenclature. This economic phenomenon—that is, a valuation adjustment—is caused by the fact that the subject equity investment is a noncontrolling ownership interest, not because it is a minority ownership interest. What's the difference? Let's consider two fairly common scenarios where a lack of control discount applies even when the appraisal subject is not a minority ownership interest. And for purposes of this discussion, let's define a minority ownership interest as being less than a 50 percent equity ownership of a business.

In the first scenario, let's assume there are two stockholders: Joe and Joan. Each stockholder owns exactly 50 percent of the company's common stock: 100 shares each out of a total of 200 shares outstanding. Further, let's assume that these two stockholders do not get along. In fact, Joe and Joan cannot agree on anything, including compensation policy, hiring and firing of employees, dividend policy, what contracts to enter into, and the sale of the company itself. What's more, each shareholder is suspicious of the other, attempts to (and does) block the actions of the other, and regularly threatens litigation against the other. To simplify this example, let's also assume that there are no buy-sell or other shareholder agreements between Joe and Joan.

If the appraisal assignment is to value Joe's 50 percent equity interest, a substantial lack of control discount may be appropriate in this case. That is so even though Joe does not own a minority ownership interest.

In the second scenario, let's assume the same two stockholders, Joe and Joan, and add a third stockholder, Jim. Joe and Joan each own 100 shares of common stock. Jim has invested in this company by buying 800 shares of common stock. However, Jim's stock is nonvoting common stock. Joe and Joan own all of the voting common stock. While Jim owns 80 percent of the 1,000 shares outstanding, a lack of control valuation discount would be appropriate. Jim is not a minority stockholder (by virtue of the fact that he owns 80 percent of all outstanding shares). However, Jim is not a controlling stockholder since his nonvoting shares cannot affect any of the aspects of the subject business.

There are other scenarios when a lack of control valuation adjustment should be applied to something other than a minority ownership interest. We will introduce these scenarios later in the chapter.

As a final introductory comment, some analysts refer to minority ownership interests as fractional ownership interests. They define a fractional ownership interest as anything less than a 100 percent ownership interest. Readers should be aware of the term *fractional ownership interest*. However, with regard to small business valuation, this term is not as commonly used in the appraisal literature, in the appraisal standards, and in the judicial precedent as the term *minority interest*. Rather, the term *fractional interest* is more commonly used in the appraisal of less than a 100 percent ownership interest in real estate.

Elements of Ownership Control

The following is a list of some of the more common prerogatives of ownership control with regard to a small business or professional practice:

1. Appoint management.
2. Determine management compensation and perquisites.
3. Set policy and change the course of business.
4. Acquire or liquidate assets.
5. Select people with whom to do business and award contracts.
6. Make acquisitions.
7. Liquidate, dissolve, sell out, or recapitalize the company.
8. Sell or acquire treasury shares.
9. Register the company's stock for a public offering.
10. Declare and pay dividends.
11. Change the articles of incorporation or bylaws.

From the above list, it is apparent that the owner of a controlling ownership interest in a business enjoys some very valuable rights that an owner not in a controlling position does not enjoy.

Degree of Ownership Control

The matter of a controlling ownership position versus a noncontrolling ownership position is not an either/or proposition. Relevant state statutes, the subject company's articles of incorporation and bylaws, and the way the overall ownership of the subject company is distributed have a bearing on the relative rights of the noncontrolling and of the controlling stockholders.

Effect of State Statutes

Statutes affecting the relative rights of controlling versus noncontrolling stockholders vary from state to state.

Supermajority Vote Requirements. In some states, a simple majority can approve major actions such as a merger, sale, or liquidation of the company. Other states require a two-thirds or an even greater majority vote in order to approve such actions. In these instances, a stockholder with just over a one-third ownership interest in the company (and in a few states, even less) has the power to block such actions.

State Dissolution Statutes. Under the statutes of California, New York, Delaware, Rhode Island, and some other states, minority stockholders enjoy certain legal rights under some circumstances that minority stockholders in other states generally do not enjoy. For example, under certain circumstances, minority stockholders can bring suit to dissolve the corporation. If the suit is successful and if the controlling stockholders wish to avoid dissolution, the remedy is to pay the minority stockholders the "fair value" for their stock. The variations in state law concerning legal rights attributable to various equity ownership percentage interests have an important bearing on the valuation.

Effect of Articles of Incorporation and Bylaws

As with state statutes, a company's articles of incorporation or bylaws may require supermajorities for certain actions. Also, the company's articles of incorporation or bylaws may confer special rights to minority stockholders under certain conditions. The possibilities are almost without limit. The analyst should be sure to read the articles of incorporation and the bylaws (and all amendments thereto) in order to understand any factors affecting the minority stockholders' degree of ownership control.

Effect of Distribution of Equity Ownership

If one person owns 49 percent of the stock and another person owns 51 percent, the 49 percent holder typically has little or no control of the company. However, if two stockholders each own 49 percent and a third stockholder owns 2 percent, the 49 percent stockholders may be on a par with each other—depending on who owns the other 2 percent. The 2 percent stockholder may be able to command a considerable price premium over the pro rata value for that particular block of stock because of its "swing vote" power.

If each of three stockholders (or partners) owns a one-third ownership interest, no one has complete control. On the other hand, no one owner is in a relatively inferior position to the other two. This is true unless two of the three owners have close ties with each other (that are not shared by the third).

Normally, equal individual ownership interests are each worth less than a pro rata proportion of what the total business enterprise is worth. What this means is the sum of the values of the individual ownership interests normally is less than what the total business enterprise could be sold for to a single buyer. However, the percentage valuation adjustment from pro rata value for each of such equal ownership interests would not normally be as great as for a minority ownership interest that had no control whatsoever.

Each situation has to be analyzed individually with respect to (1) the degree of control, or lack of it, and (2) the implications for the value of the subject minority ownership interest.

Distinction between Discount for Lack of Control and Discount for Lack of Marketability

Much confusion has been created because some analysts have failed to distinguish between (1) a discount for lack of ownership control (also called a minority interest discount) and (2) a discount for lack of marketability. These are two separate concepts, although there is some interrelationship between them.

The concept of *minority ownership interest* deals with the relationship between the ownership interest being valued and the total business enterprise. This relationship is based on the factors discussed in the first two sections of this chapter. The primary factor bearing on the value of the subject minority ownership interest in relation to the value of the total entity is how much ownership control the minority ownership interest does—or does not—have over the particular entity.

The concept of *marketability* deals with the liquidity of the subject ownership interest—that is, how quickly and certainly it can be converted to cash at the owner's discretion.

Analysts sometimes overlook the fact that valuation adjustments (and in this case, discounts) are meaningless until the base from which the adjustment is to be taken has been clearly defined. Since a minority ownership interest discount reflects lack of control, the base from which the minority ownership interest discount should be subtracted is its proportionate share in the total entity value (including all of the rights of ownership control). Since a discount for lack of marketability reflects lack of liquidity, the base from which the discount should be subtracted is the value of an entity or ownership interest that is otherwise comparable but that enjoys higher liquidity.

Even controlling ownership interests suffer to some extent from a lack of marketability. For example, it usually takes several months—and a significant amount of expense and effort on the part of the owners—to sell a company. The relationship between the discount for lack of marketability and the discount for lack of control lies in the fact that, even after discounting a minority ownership interest for its lack of control, it still is usually much harder to sell a minority ownership interest than to sell a controlling ownership interest in the same closely held business.

When valuing a minority ownership interest in a closely held company by comparing it with values of publicly held stocks, the analyst should apply a discount only for lack of marketability. This is because a minority ownership interest discount is already implicit in the public stock's trading price.

Exhibit 24-1 illustrates the relationship between controlling ownership interest value, minority ownership interest value if readily marketable, and minority ownership interest value if not readily marketable.

How the Applicable Standard of Value Affects Minority Ownership Interests

As discussed in Chapter 3, the applicable standard of value for most business valuation situations falls into one of four categories: (1) fair market value, (2) investment value, (3) intrinsic value, or (4) fair value. The applicable standard of value is determined primarily by the purpose and objective of the appraisal. In some situations, the applicable standard of value is mandated by law. In other situations, the choice of the standard of value lies within the discretion of the parties involved.

Fair Market Value

We will recall from Chapter 3 that the fair market value standard implies the most likely price at which an arm's-length transaction would be expected to take place between normally motivated investors under open market conditions, without considering any special benefits that might be related to the transaction for any particular buyer or seller. Considering the relative unattractiveness of minority ownership interests in closely held companies to investors generally, under the fair market value standard, the valuation discount from a proportionate share of the subject enterprise value would normally be quite large.

Investment Value

In Chapter 3 we indicated that *investment value* takes into consideration the value to a *particular* buyer or seller. We noted that consideration could be given to (for example) the investor's cost of capital, perception or risk, and other characteristics unique to that investor.

Exhibit 24–1

EXAMPLE OF RELATIONSHIPS BETWEEN
CONTROL OWNERSHIP PREMIUMS, MINORITY OWNERSHIP
INTEREST DISCOUNTS, AND DISCOUNTS FOR LACK OF MARKETABILITY

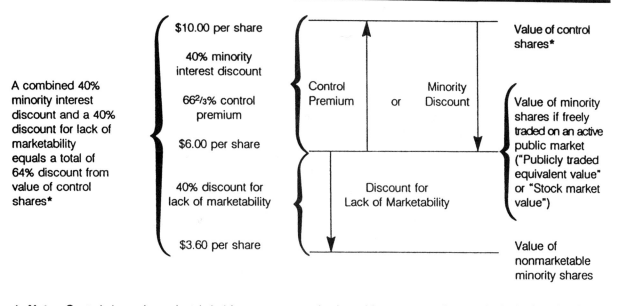

* **Note:** Control shares in a privately held company may also be subject to some discount for lack of marketability, but usually not nearly as much as minority shares.

SOURCE: Jay E. Fishman, Shannon P. Pratt, J. Clifford Griffith, and D. Keith Wilson, *Guide to Business Valuations*, 7th ed. (Fort Worth, Tex.: Practitioners Publishing Company, 1997). Reprinted with permission.

When valuing minority ownership interests, one characteristic unique to a particular investor that may be important is the investor's relationship with the other owners of the subject business. Such a relationship may give the particular minority owner some elements or benefits that would otherwise only be available to a controlling owner. It is noteworthy that some family law courts give recognition to such relationships, while the Tax Court (adhering to the standard of fair market value) does not.

Intrinsic Value

Intrinsic value, as noted in Chapter 3, arises from analysis of the characteristics of the investment, such as value of the company's assets, likely future earnings, likely future dividends, and likely future dividend rates.

The relative importance of these factors, however, may be different for minority ownership valuations than for control ownership valuations. Dividends may take on increased importance for a noncontrolling equity investor. This is because dividends are the periodic cash flow that the noncontrolling equity investor enjoys. Asset values, on the other hand, may have little or no importance to a noncontrolling equity investor unless the noncontrolling equity investor perceives that the assets will somehow translate into a real economic benefit. The same thing can be said of the expected future earnings and growth of the subject company.

Fair Value

As noted in Chapter 3, the fair value standard suffers from lack of consistent definition from one context to another. It crops up most often as the statutory standard of value applicable to appraisals under dissenting stockholders' rights. Such valuations, by their nature, are valuations of minority ownership interests. The need to interpret the meaning of this standard of value from a study of the legal precedents in dissenting stockholder actions in each of the 50 states and Canada poses a continuing challenge to the appraisal profession.

Certain state-specific precedents have suggested that fair value be interpreted to mean fair market value without a minority ownership interest discount (i.e., a proportionate share of the overall enterprise value). However, it must be reiterated that research of the specifically applicable legal precedent is very important in each context to which the fair value standard applies.

Approaches to the Valuation of Minority Ownership Interests

There are three basic ways of approaching the valuation of minority ownership interests:

1. A proportionate share of the overall enterprise value, less a valuation discount from this value.
2. A direct comparison with the values of other minority ownership interests.
3. A "bottom-up" approach of estimating the economic benefits that the minority ownership interest holder is expected to realize over the life of the investment.

Proportion of the Overall Enterprise Value less a Discount

One way to approach the valuation of a minority ownership interest is the following three-step process:

1. Estimate the value of the subject overall business enterprise.
2. Calculate the minority owner's pro rata allocation of the small business enterprise value.
3. Estimate the amount of the valuation adjustment—that is, discount (if any) applicable to the pro rata allocation of the overall business enterprise value in order to properly reflect the value of the subject minority ownership interest.

The value of the overall business enterprise should be estimated as discussed in the earlier part of this book, with certain possible variations noted in a later section. The proportionate value is normally a straightforward calculation. However, occasionally there may be calculational complications due to special rights of different classes of partners or stockholders.

The amount of the valuation adjustment—or discount—to reflect the minority ownership interest should be a matter of rigorous analysis. The degree of ownership control or lack of it, as discussed in an earlier section, definitely has a bearing on the applicable valuation discount. However, there is no simple formula to quantify this valuation adjustment.

Also, the valuation discount is generally lower for stocks that pay cash dividends or partnerships that distribute considerable cash flow, than for those that do not. However, there is no simple formula to quantify that factor, either. Some guidance with regard to typical discounts—and to typical ranges of discounts—related to noncontrolling ownership interests is presented in later sections of this chapter.

Valuation by Comparison with Other Minority Ownership Interests

If the analyst can find data on actual sales of other comparative minority ownership interests, the analyst may be able to reach a conclusion of value by direct comparison to such transactions. This analysis can be performed without ever going through the step of estimating a value for the total business enterprise. The analyst can value the subject minority ownership interest using procedures similar to those used for valuing a total company. Such procedures include, for example, the capitalization of earnings, the capitalization of cash flow, the capitalization of dividends or partnership withdrawals, a multiple of price to book value or of price to adjusted net asset value, and so on.

Guidance with regard to the quantification of the market-derived pricing multiples comes from the comparative minority ownership interest transactional data.

Sources of Comparative Data. One source of comparative data could be prior arm's-length transactions involving minority ownership interests in the subject company.

There is no generally available source of data on any broad group of minority ownership interest transactions in closely held companies.

However, there is, of course, a readily available database on daily transactions in minority equity interests in thousands of publicly traded companies. Subject to several limitations discussed earlier in the book, guidance with respect to market-derived pricing multiples for the valuation of minority ownership interests may be drawn from the prices of publicly traded stocks.

Adjustments for Risk and for Lack of Marketability. As discussed earlier in the book, if the comparison with public stock prices procedure is performed, adjustments need to be made for differences in risk and other factors. The most important of these factors is the illiquidity (or lack of marketability) of the minority ownership interest in the closely held company, compared with the virtually instant marketability of a publicly traded stock.

This difference in marketability is a more important factor with respect to value than most people who have not had experience in dealing with this issue usually realize. The fair market values of minority ownership interests in closely held companies average between 35 to 50 percent less than prices of comparative minority equity interests in very liquid, publicly traded companies, all other things being equal. See the following chapter, Discounts for Lack of Marketability, for more discussion on this topic.

"Bottom-Up" Approach

In the two previous sections, we started with an estimated value and, in some cases, applied a valuation discount (or two) in order to estimate the value of the minority ownership interest. In the bottom-up approach, we start with a clean slate and estimate what the minority equity interest owner might sometime realize.

In most cases, the economic benefits the minority ownership interest holder may realize fall into two categories:

1. Dividends or partnership withdrawals (i.e., current economic income).
2. Proceeds realized on sale of the interest (i.e., including any long-term capital appreciation).

What this really boils down to is an application of the discounted economic income method of the income approach to valuation, as discussed in Chapter 14. The general procedures in the bottom-up approach are as follows:

1. Project the expected distributions (i.e., dividends or partnership withdrawals).
2. Project a time and a price at which the subject ownership interest can be expected to be sold.

3. Estimate an appropriate present value discount rate, using the methods and information discussed in Chapter 13.

4. Discount the projected distributions and the projected sale price to a present value, using the formula presented in Chapter 14.

Errors to Avoid

The following points should help the reader (1) avoid certain common errors when estimating the value of minority ownership interests and (2) identify such errors when they appear in someone else's minority ownership interest valuation.

The Public Offering Myth

We have occasionally seen authors and analysts use the estimated cost of a public offering as a method for quantifying the discount for lack of marketability for a minority ownership interest in a closely held company. The stated rationale for such a procedure is that if the difference in value compared to a publicly traded minority interest is lack of marketability, the discount should be no more than the cost of overcoming that deficiency.

The fallacy in this procedure is the basic fact that a minority stockholder does not have the legal right to register the company's stock for a public offering. Since the registration for public offering is not an alternative available to a minority stockholder, the matter of what it would cost him to do so is not relevant.

Irrelevant Financial Statement Adjustments

In Part II, "Analyzing the Company," we suggested that when developing the company's earnings capacity, the analyst may remove from expenses such discretionary items as shareholders' consulting fees and the cost of a shareholder's chauffeured Cadillac. At that time, we were discussing the valuation of the entire company. And we were assuming that it was within the controlling owner's discretion to remove such expenses with no significant impairment to company revenues. The minority stockholder, however, has no such power to eliminate these discretionary expenses. Therefore, these adjustments may not be relevant in estimating an earnings base for the valuation of minority ownership interests. That is true unless there is reason to believe that the changes actually are going to be made.

The same general concept applies to adjustments to the balance sheet to reflect the values of excess or nonoperating assets. Unless the controlling business owner is expected to take some immediate action to liquidate these assets, their value to the minority stockholders are remote.

Comparison with Real Estate Minority Discounts

Discounts for minority ownership interests (i.e., fractional interests) in direct investment in real estate, when estimated at all, usually are only about 10 to 20 percent below a pro rata proportion of the value of the total parcel. Sometimes analysts more familiar with direct investments in real estate than with direct investments in businesses impute similarly low minority ownership interest discounts to investments in business interests.

There are at least two reasons for a disparity in the amount of valuation discounts for minority ownership interest between businesses and direct real estate investments.

The first reason is that direct fractional owners of real estate normally have the right to partition. That means that if they are dissatisfied with the investment, they can initiate an action to divide the property (but incur a cost to do so) and to ultimately own 100 percent of the fractional proportion of the property.

The second reason for the disparity in minority ownership interest discounts is the greater diversity of options available to the controlling owners of most operating businesses, as compared to the generally narrower range of options available to the controlling owners of most parcels of real estate.

Data on Sales of Minority Ownership Interests

Very few reliable data exist regarding sales of minority interests in closely held businesses. The market for publicly traded stocks, on the other hand, provides thousands of reported transactions every day.

Trust and Estate Sales

Some of the most convincing evidence with respect to actual sales prices of minority ownership interests in closely held businesses were compiled by a bank trust officer responsible for administering estates that owned all or portions of closely held businesses. For openers, he offers the following generalities:

> A number of years of experience has demonstrated that it is extremely difficult to find any market for minority interests . . . despite efforts to do so. . . . . On the relatively rare occasions when an offer is made to buy a minority interest, it is almost always for an amount far less than the fiduciary and the beneficiary expect to get.[1]

---

[1]H. Calvin Coolidge, "Fixing Value of Minority Interest in a Business: Actual Sales Suggest Discount as High at 70 Percent," *Estate Planning*, Spring 1975, p. 141.

The trust officer compiled data on 30 actual sales of minority ownership interests. He found that the average transaction price was 36 percent below the accounting book value of the subject ownership interest. He concludes with the following observations:

> Only 20 percent of the sales were made at discounts less than 20 percent. A little more than half the sales (53 1/3 percent) were made at discounts that ranged from 22 percent to 48 percent, and 23 1/3 percent of the sales were made at discounts of from 54.4 percent to 78 percent.
>
> It would be dangerous to draw too many generalizations from the survey, but those sales where the discounts were below 20 percent involved, with one exception, purchases from close relatives where friendly relations existed. The exception was the sale by a holder of swing shares who used his leverage well, but still took a 4.3 percent discount. At the other end of the spectrum was the settlement of a three year bitter dispute between two families; the majority family raised its token offer only after threat of a lawsuit, but the price the minority interest took nonetheless represented a 78 percent discount.[2]

It is noteworthy that the valuation discounts in the foregoing surveys were from accounting book value, not from the value of the business enterprise as a whole. Accounting book value, of course, recognizes no appreciation in assets above depreciated net asset value. However, in a very few cases in the survey referenced above, the discounts were computed from an adjusted book value reflecting appreciation in real estate values. One would expect that the total business enterprise value would be above the company's accounting book value in most cases. If that was true in the survey, the valuation discounts from the owners' proportionate shares of the total enterprise values were even greater than the valuation discounts quantified in the survey (which were from accounting book value).

An update published in 1983 indicates a trend toward even larger discounts when selling minority ownership interests in closely held corporations. In the update, a much higher concentration of discounts from accounting book value was at the high end of the range, and the average valuation discount for the two studies combined was approximately 40 percent. The updated study concludes as follows:

> Each of the sales used in the survey involved a combination of factors that made it somewhat unique. To use any of the data, or any classification of the data, as definitive proof of the discount to be applied in a prospective valuation would be dangerous. This should not, however, obscure the true significance of the data, which is that in the actual marketplace, the typical discount is not of token size, but of substantial magnitude.[3]

---

[2]Ibid., p. 141.

[3]H. Calvin Coolidge, "Survey Shows Trend towards Larger Minority Discounts," *Estate Planning*, September 1983, p. 282.

To the best of our knowledge as of this writing, no comparable studies have been published since the above.

Public Stock Market Data

The thousands of daily stock transactions on stock exchanges and in the over-the-counter market are, of course, minority equity interest transactions. The prices per share at which these transactions take place usually are significantly below the prices stockholders receive when an entire company or a controlling ownership interest is purchased.

The following table presents examples that show how buyout prices for minority interests significantly exceed pre-buyout prices for minority interests. These examples involve companies that probably are familiar to many readers.

Name of Company Interest Acquired	Date of Buyout	Price Premium Paid over Previous Market Price[a]	Implied Minority Ownership Price Discount[b]
Helene Curtis Industries	03/19/96	27.9%	21.8%
The Circle K Corp.	05/30/96	34.1	25.4
Uniroyal Chemical Corp.	08/21/96	36.1	26.5
Caremark International Inc.	09/05/96	16.0	13.8
Thrifty PayLess Holdings	12/12/96	28.6	22.2
Bally Entertainment Corp.	12/18/96	20.0	16.7
Duracell International Inc.	12/31/96	51.7	34.1

a. The premium paid over market is a percentage based on the buyout price over the market price of the seller's stock five business days prior to the announcement date.
b. Formula: 1 - [1 ÷ (1 + Premium paid)], for example, 1 - (1 ÷ 1.361) = 1 - .735 = .265.
Source: *Mergerstat Review 1997* (Los Angeles: Houlihan Lokey Howard & Zukin, 1997) and Willamette Management Associates' calculations.

The average percentage price discount from the buyout (or control transaction) price at which stocks were selling immediately prior to announcements of acquisitions (i.e., the control transaction) for the years 1980-96 are as follows.

Year	Pre-Acquisition Price Discount Compared to Control Transaction Price
1980	33.3%
1981	32.4
1982	32.2
1983	27.4
1984	27.5
1985	27.1
1986	27.6
1987	27.7
1988	29.5
1989	29.1
1990	29.6
1991	26.0
1992	29.1
1993	27.9
1994	29.5
1995	30.9
1996	26.8

Source: *Mergerstat Review 1997*. Average price discount calculated by Willamette Management Associates.

Other Influences Related to a Minority Ownership Interest Discount

As mentioned earlier, there are additional instances when a lack of control discount applies even when the appraisal subject is not a minority ownership interest. And there are several additional influences that affect the applicability of—and the magnitude of—lack of control discounts. Some of these additional influences will be discussed in this section.

Highly Regulated Industries

With respect to companies in highly regulated industries, a lack of control discount may apply even if the appraisal subject is a 100 percent equity ownership interest. This is because the controlling stockholders of a highly regulated business do not have all of the perquisites of control that owners of less regulated businesses have. In some industries, governmental authority is needed to buy, sell, or merge a company. In some industries, government authority is needed to liquidate or otherwise shut down a company (or a part of a company)—even when company operations have turned unprofitable. And in some industries, government authority is needed to open a new branch (or sell a new product or provide a new service).

For these highly regulated companies, a lack of control discount may be applicable to the overall business value. This is because the government —not the 100 percent stockholder—enjoys some of the prerogatives of ownership control. In such instances, there may be a greater discount for lack of control applicable to a minority block of stock than to a controlling block of stock. But the difference in the two levels of lack of control discounts would not be as great as in a less regulated industry. This is because in a highly regulated industry, neither the minority stockholder nor the majority stockholder enjoys absolute control.

Buy-Sell and Other Shareholder Agreements

In some companies, all shareholders have entered into buy-sell agreements or into other shareholder agreements. The provisions of such agreements usually dictate the valuation of the company stock for purposes of transactions between the company and shareholders and among shareholders.

If the language of the relevant agreements indicates that minority blocks of stock will be valued on a controlling ownership interest level of value, a lack of control discount will not apply to the transactions to which the provision is applicable. For example, the agreement may say that the subject shares will be valued "on an enterprise basis" or as "a per share portion of the overall company value." In such instances, the company stockholders have agreed to deal with each other on a controlling ownership interest basis—according to the terms of the agreements.

Fiduciary Duties

Sometimes, controlling stockholders cannot or do not exercise all of the prerogatives of ownership control. This may occur when the controlling stockholder has a fiduciary or other special duty to the minority stockholders. In such cases, controlling stockholders and noncontrolling stockholders could be treated equally with regard to economic benefits of equity ownership.

In such instances, the lack of control discount may not be so great as it otherwise would be. This is because the base to which the discount would apply—that is, the overall business enterprise value—may not be inflated due to the influences of ownership control. And this is because all stockholders—minority and controlling—would expect to share equally in the fruits of the company's commercial success. However, there are very few situations in which a fiduciary obligation would require treating a minority stockholder on a basis equivalent to a control stockholder. Under most state laws, a controlling stockholder can even sell the control stock without requiring that any offer be made to purchase minority stock.

Private Company with Public Securities

Some privately owned companies have publicly traded securities that are subject to the Securities and Exchange Commission (SEC) registration process. This situation generally occurs when all of the company's common stock is closely held but some of the company's bonds are publicly traded. In this circumstance, the company is generally subject to all of the periodic disclosure requirements of other "public" companies.

In such instances, the discount for lack of control may be less than it would otherwise be. Due to the SEC public reporting requirements, the controlling stockholder would have to disclose information not normally available to minority stockholders, such as detailed financial statements, officers' compensation, transactions between the company and shareholders, and so forth. Therefore, some of the benefits of ownership control are lost due to these public disclosure requirements. Also, the controlling stockholder would always be aware of the applicable regulatory authority of the SEC. Accordingly, the controlling stockholder may not always "act" like a controlling stockholder would in a company not subject to SEC scrutiny.

Private Company that Operates Like a Public Company

Even if they don't have public debt outstanding, some closely held companies operate very much like publicly owned companies. They follow the business, accounting, and legal formalities of public companies. They have independent directors on their boards of directors. And they believe in full disclosure to all stockholders.

In such an instance, the lack of control discount is usually less than it would otherwise be. One reason is that in such a case the controlling stockholder is (presumably on a voluntary basis) not exercising all of the prerogatives of control.

Control Has Already Been Dissipated

Earlier, we mentioned the case of three equal shareholders. Let's consider slightly more extreme cases. What happens if there are 10 or 20 equal (or relatively equal) stockholders? Such a scenario may not be uncommon at all in many professional practices. For example, consider a medical practice with five physicians, a dental practice with 10 dentists, an accounting practice with 15 CPAs, or a legal practice with 20 lawyers. In such instances, ownership control may have already been dissipated.

In such circumstances, the lack of control discount is often less than it would otherwise be. That is because when all owners are sharing (relatively) equally in the wealth of the business, the overall business value may not be affected by the actions of a controlling owner. Consequently, the base to which the lack of control discount is applied is lower than it would otherwise be. And with all owners sharing (relatively) equally in the wealth of the business, there is no significant disparity between the economic benefits available to minority owners and to majority owners.

Summary

Minority ownership interests in small businesses and professional practices are not usually worth their pro rata allocation of the value of the total business. They usually are worth less than that because there are many decisions over which the majority owner has control and the minority owner does not. The many factors affecting the rights and powers of the minority ownership interest holder should be analyzed and evaluated in each individual case.

The concepts of (1) minority ownership interest versus controlling ownership interest and (2) ready marketability, or lack of it, are two different concepts. Minority ownership interest deals with lack of control. Marketability deals with the degree of ready liquidity (or lack of it) to sell the subject ownership interest. These two factors should be separately recognized and individually analyzed.

The applicable standard of value (e.g., fair market value, investment value, and so on) may affect the procedures used and the factors considered in the valuation of minority ownership interests.

There are three broad ways to approach the value of minority ownership interests:

1. Overall business enterprise value less appropriate lack of control valuation discounts.
2. Comparison with the market-derived value of other minority ownership interests.

3. Present value of the expected economic income distributions and of the eventual equity interest sale proceeds.

The chapter discussed some errors frequently encountered in minority ownership interest valuations. It also discussed some sources of empirical data with regard to minority ownership interest valuations. The chapter concluded with a discussion of other considerations with respect to the identification and quantification of the lack of control discount.

Bibliography

Becker, Brian C. "Minority Interests in Market Valuation: An Adjustment Procedure." *Business Valuation Review*, March 1997, pp. 27–31.

Bogdanski, John A. "The Outer Limits of Minority Discounts." *Estate Planning*, October 1996, pp. 380–84.

Bolten, Steven E. "Discounts for Stocks of Closely Held Corporations." *Trusts & Estates*, December 1990, pp. 47–48.

Curtis, Andrew M. "Discounting Minority Stock Interests in Closely Held Corporations: When and How Much?" *Journal of Taxation of Estates and Trusts*, Spring 1991, pp. 26–30.

Fiore, Nicholas J. "All in the Family: Determining the Value of a Minority Interest in Stock in a Closely Held Corporation." *Journal of Accountancy*, September 1991, p. 14.

Fishman, Jay E., Shannon P. Pratt, J. Clifford Griffith, and D. Keith Wilson. "Premiums and Discounts in Business Valuations." Parts I and II. *FAIR$HARE: The Matrimonial Law Monthly*, May and June 1992, pp. 11–17, 14–16.

Hall, Lance S., and Timothy C. Polacek. "Strategies for Obtaining the Largest Valuation Discounts." *Estate Planning*, January/February 1994, pp. 38–44.

Harper, John S. "Minority Shareholders: It's the Cash You Get that Counts: Discounting Expected Future Cash Distributions to Determine the Fair Market Value of a Minority Ownership Interest in a Partnership or Corporation." *Tax Management Estates, Gifts, and Trusts Journal*, November/December 1990. pp. 215–21.

Harris, James Edward. "Minority and Marketability Discounts: Are You Taking Enough?" *Probate and Property*, January/February 1990, pp. 6–11.

Herpe, David. A., and Carter Howard. "Minority Discounts Revisited: The Estate of Murphy." *Trusts & Estates*, December 1990, pp. 35–38.

Hitchner, James R., and Kevin J. Rudd. "The Use of Discounts in Estate and Gift Tax Valuations." *Trusts and Estates*, August 1992, pp. 49–56, 60.

Hopson, James F., and William J. Sheehy. "Valuation of Minority Discounts in Closely-Held Corporations." *The National Public Accountant*, December 1993, pp. 30–33.

Janiga, John M., and Louis S. Harrison. "Valuation of Closely Held Stock for Transfer Tax Purposes: The Current Status of Minority Discounts for Intrafamily Transfers in Family-Controlled Corporations." *TAXES*, May 1991, pp. 309–317.

Lauer, Eliot, and Benard V. Preziosi. "A Fair Share for Minority Shareholders." *New York Law Journal*, June 1, 1992, p. 7.

Mercer, Z. Christopher. "A Brief Review of Control Premiums and Minority Interest Discounts." *Proceedings of the 12th Biennial Business Valuation Conference of Canadian Institute of Chartered Business Valuators.* Toronto: Canadian Institute of Chartered Business Valuators, 1997, pp. 365–87.

Nath, Eric W. "Control Premiums and Minority Interest Discounts in Private Companies." *Business Valuation Review*, June 1990, pp. 39–46.

Radom, Carl C., and Michael A. Yuhas. "Disputes over Minority Discounts Continue." *The Practical Accountant*, January 1996, pp. 30–37.

Schilt, James H. "Discounts for Minority Interests." *Business Valuation Review*, December 1996, pp. 161–66.

Schlenger, Jacques T., Robert E. Madden, and Lisa H.R. Hayes. "Minority Discount Was Applied to Determine FMV Before Special-Use Valuation Was Calculated." *Estate Planning*, March/April 1996, pp. 129–30.

Trieschmann, James S., E.J. Leverett, and Peter J. Shedd. "Valuating Common Stock for Minority Stock and ESOPs in Closely Held Corporations." *Business Horizons*, March/April 1988, pp. 63–69.

Chapter 25

Discount for Lack of Marketability

In the absence of an effective exit vehicle, private placements normally sell at a significant discount—often 30%-60% or even more—from freely traded securities.[1]

All other things being equal, an ownership interest in a small business or professional practice is worth more if it is readily marketable. An ownership interest in a small business or professional practice is worth less if it is not readily marketable. This is because business owners prefer liquidity to illiquidity. Ownership interests in closely held businesses are illiquid relative to most other investments. This phenomenon is often further compounded by restrictions on the transfer of ownership interests found in buy-sell agreements or shareholder agreements. Therefore, analysts have to identify and quantify the valuation adjustment associated (1) with the illiquidity of the subject business and (2) with the lack of marketability in the subject business ownership interest.

The quote above suggesting a range of 30 percent to 60 percent for the valuation adjustment for lack of marketability is based largely on the data on restricted public company stock transactions that were available in the 1970s and early 1980s. This range is consistent with the more recent series of data (which began to become available in the late 1980s) on closely held stock transactions before initial public offerings (IPOs) cited in this chapter. Actual valuation adjustments for lack of marketability are larger than many analysts realize. This chapter presents evidence of the market realities of this issue.

Concept and Importance of Marketability

The concept of *marketability* deals with the liquidity of the subject ownership interest. That is, how quickly can the ownership interest be converted to cash at the business owner's discretion?

For this text, we will define *marketability* as the ability to convert the property to cash quickly, with minimum transaction and administrative costs in so doing and with a high degree of certainty of realizing the expected amount of net proceeds.

---

[1]Daniel W. Bielinski, "The Comparable-Company Approach: Measuring the True Value of Privately Held Firms," *Corporate Cashflow Magazine*, October 1990, p. 68.

Our definition is consistent with the definition offered by the *Encyclopedia of Banking & Finance*, which focuses on securities for which *some* public market already exists:

> **Marketability.** The relative ease and promptness with which a security or commodity may be sold when desired, at a representative current price, without material concession in price merely because of the necessity of sale. Marketability connotes the existence of current buying interest as well as selling interest and is usually indicated by the volume of current transactions and the spread between the bid and asked price for a security—the closer the spread, the closer are the buying and selling interests to agreement on price resulting in actual transactions. To look at it from the standpoint of a dealer maintaining the MARKET, the closer his bid to current transactions and the smaller his markup is to asking prices, the larger the volume will be. By contrast, inactive securities that rarely trade or for which buyers have to be located or sales negotiated are characterized by large spreads between the bid and asked prices.[2]

With respect to the ownership characteristics of assets, the terms *marketability* and *liquidity* are sometimes interchangeable. The *Encyclopedia of Banking and Finance* offers the following:

> **Liquidity.** The amount of time required to convert an asset into cash or pay a liability. For noncurrent assets, liquidity generally refers to marketability . . . .
>
> In economics, liquidity is the desire to hold assets in the form of cash. Common elements often included in the concept of liquidity include marketability, realizability, reversibility (as to the difference between buying and selling prices), divisibility of the asset, predictability or capital certainty, and plasticity (ease of maneuvering into and out of various yields after the asset has been acquired). Firms and individuals often prefer to hold money for the sake of holding money. Liquidity may be desired for the following reasons: (1) the transactions motive, (2) the precautionary motive, and (3) the speculative motive. Money is desired to carry out future monetary transactions, to save for a rainy day, or to take advantage of movements in the price level.[3]

Barron's Dictionary of Business Terms defines marketability and liquidity as follows:

> **Marketability.** Speed and ease with which a particular product or investment may be bought and sold. In common use, *marketability* is interchangeable with *liquidity*, but *liquidity* implies the preservation of value when a security is bought or sold.[4]

---

[2]Charles J. Woelfel, *Encyclopedia of Banking & Finance*, 10th ed. (Chicago: Probus Publishing Company, 1994), p. 729.

[3]Ibid., p. 703.

[4]Jack P. Friedman, ed., *Barron's Dictionary of Business Terms*, 2d ed. (Hauppauge, NY: Barron's, 1994), p. 363.

The market for securities in the United States is the most liquid market for any kind of property anywhere in the world. This is one of the reasons that companies are able to raise investment capital from both institutional and individual investors: the ability to liquidate the investment immediately, at little cost, and with virtual certainty as to realization of the widely publicized market price. Empirical evidence suggests that investors are willing to pay a high premium for this level of liquidity. Conversely, investors extract a high discount relative to actively traded securities for stocks or other investment interests that lack this high degree of liquidity.

Adjustment for Lack of Marketability for Minority Ownership Interests

For a valuation "adjustment" to have a precise meaning, there must be a precise definition of the level of value from which the adjustment is taken. When small business minority ownership interests are valued by reference to the prices paid for guideline actively traded securities, the benchmark for the lack of marketability of the minority ownership interests is the active public securities markets. This publicly traded counterpart value is often called the *publicly traded equivalent value* or the *freely traded value.*

In the U.S. public markets, a security holder is able to sell a security over the telephone in seconds, usually at or within a small fraction of a percent of the last price at which the security traded, with a relatively small commission cost, and receive the cash proceeds within three working days.

By contrast, the universe of realistically potential buyers for most small business minority ownership interests is an infinitesimal fraction of the universe of potential buyers for publicly traded securities.

Besides the problems of actually trying to sell the subject ownership interest, the liquidity of small business ownership interests is further impaired by banks and other lending institutions' unwillingness to accept them as loan collateral as they would accept public stock.

Because of these extreme contrasts between the ability to sell or hypothecate small business ownership interests as compared with publicly traded stock, empirical evidence suggests significant valuation discounts for lack of marketability. These lack of marketability discounts for small business minority ownership interests tend to cluster in the range of 35 to 50 percent from their publicly traded counterparts. Naturally, each valuation should be analyzed on the basis of the individual facts and circumstances. Accordingly, individual small business valuations may justify a discount for lack of marketability above or below this typical range.

Evidence for the Quantification of Discount for Lack of Marketability

There are two general types of empirical studies designed to quantify the valuation adjustments associated with the lack of marketability of minority ownership interests in closely held businesses:

1. Discounts on the sale of restricted shares of publicly traded companies.
2. Discounts on the sale of closely held company shares—compared to prices of subsequent initial public offerings of the same company's shares.

As noted earlier, the above empirical studies indicate that the base from which to take the indicated lack of marketability discount is the actual (or estimated) price at which the shares would sell if registered and freely tradeable in a public stock market.

The immediately following sections of this chapter summarize the findings of these two extensive lines of empirical evidence. The second line of empirical studies is more recent. More importantly, the transactions are more similar to closely held business minority transactions because that is what they are, even though the company may have contemplated a public offering at the time of the transaction. Therefore, it may be more relevant in the estimation of the discount for lack of marketability for most closely held business interests.

The data presented in this chapter relate to the quantification of the discount for lack of marketability only. This discount for lack of marketability is separate and distinct from the discount for minority ownership interest. The discount for minority ownership interest is discussed in the previous chapter.

The body of evidence to quantify discounts for lack of marketability for small business controlling ownership interests is much less extensive and of a somewhat different nature. This subject will be covered later in the chapter.

Marketability Discounts Extracted from Prices Of Restricted Stocks

One body of empirical evidence specifically isolates the pricing implications of marketability from all other valuation-related factors: the body of data on transactions in letter stocks. A *letter stock* is identical in all respects but one to the freely traded stock of a public company: It is restricted from trading on the open stock market for a certain period. The duration of the restrictions varies from one situation to another. Since marketability is the only difference between the letter stock and its freely tradable counterpart, the analyst may quantify differences in the price at which letter stock transactions take place compared with open market transactions in the same stock on the same date. This difference will provide some evidence of the price spread between (1) a readily marketable security and (2) one that is otherwise identical but subject to certain restrictions on its marketability.

Publicly traded corporations frequently issue letter stock in making acquisitions or in raising capital. This is because the time and cost of registering the new stock with the SEC would make registration at the time of the transaction impractical. Also, company founders or other insiders may own portions of a publicly traded company stock that has never been registered for public trading. Even though such stock cannot be sold to the public on the stock market, it may be sold in private transactions under certain circumstances. Such transactions usually must be reported to the SEC. Therefore, these private transactions become a matter of public record. Accordingly, empirical data on the prices of private transactions in restricted securities—or letter stocks—can be used for comparison with prices of the same but unrestricted securities eligible for trading on the open market.

Since these data represent hundreds of actual arm's-length transactions, anyone who is considering a deal involving such securities (for example, receiving letter stock in connection with selling out to a public company) would be well advised to become familiar with the information. Furthermore, courts frequently reference the data on letter stock price discounts when estimating the discount for lack of marketability appropriate to ownership interests in closely held companies.

It is particularly noteworthy that the restrictions on the transfer of letter stock eventually lapse, usually within 24 months. At that point, the holder can sell the shares into the existing market, subject to whatever volume and other restrictions may be imposed by SEC Rule 144. Consequently, all other things being equal, shares of closely held stock —which may never have the benefit of a public market—would be expected to require a higher discount for lack of marketability than that applicable to restricted stock of a public company. In fact, the market does impose a higher discount on closely held ownership interests than on restricted stock of a public company, as we will see in a later section.

SEC Institutional Investor Study

In a major SEC study of institutional investor actions, one topic was the amount of discount at which transactions in restricted stock (or letter stock) occurred compared to the prices of identical but unrestricted stock on the open market.[5] The most pertinent summary tables from that study are reproduced in Exhibits 25-1 and 25-2.

Exhibit 25-1 presents the price discount from stock market prices on letter stock transactions broken down by the market in which the unre-

---

[5]"Discounts Involved in Purchases of Common Stock," in U.S. 92nd Congress, 1st Session, House, *Institutional Investor Study Report of the Securities and Exchange Commission* (Washington, DC: Government Printing Office, March 10, 1971, 5:2444B2456, Document No. 92-64, Part 5).

Exhibit 25–1

TABLE XIV-45 OF SEC INSTITUTIONAL INVESTOR STUDY: DISCOUNT BY TRADING MARKET

Trading Market	-15.0% to 0.0% No. of Transactions	-15.0% to 0.0% Value of Purchases	0.1% to 10.0% No. of Transactions	0.1% to 10.0% Value of Purchases	10.1% to 20.0% No. of Transactions	10.1% to 20.0% Value of Purchases	20.1% to 30.0% No. of Transactions	20.1% to 30.0% Value of Purchases	30.1% to 40.0% No. of Transactions	30.1% to 40.0% Value of Purchases	40.1% to 50.0% No. of Transactions	40.1% to 50.0% Value of Purchases	50.1% to 80.0% No. of Transactions	50.1% to 80.0% Value of Purchases	Total No. of Transactions	Total Value of Purchases
Unknown	1	$ 1,500,000	2	$ 2,496,583	1	$ 205,000	0	$ 0	2	$ 3,332,000	0	$ 0	1	$ 1,259,995	7	$ 8,793,578
New York Stock Exchange	7	3,760,663	13	15,111,798	13	24,503,988	3	17,954,085	3	11,102,501	1	1,400,000	4	5,005,068	51	78,838,103
American Stock Exchange	2	7,263,060	4	15,850,000	11	14,548,750	20	46,200,677	7	21,074,298	1	44,250	4	4,802,404	49	109,783,439
Over-the-Counter (reporting companies)	11	13,828,757	39	13,613,676	35	38,585,259	30	35,479,946	30	58,689,328	13	9,284,047	21	8,996,406	179	178,477,419
Over-the-Counter (nonreporting companies)	5	8,329,369	9	5,265,925	18	25,122,024	17	11,229,155	25	29,423,584	20	11,377,431	18	13,505,545	112	104,253,033
Total	26	$34,681,849	67	$52,337,982	78	$102,965,021	77	$110,863,863	67	$123,621,711	35	$22,105,728	48	$33,569,418	398	$480,145,572

Exhibit 25–2

TABLE XIV-47 OF SEC INSTITUTIONAL INVESTOR STUDY: DISCOUNT BY SIZE OF TRANSACTION AND SALES OF ISSUER

Sales of Issuer (Thousands of Dollars)	0.1% to 10.0% No. of Transactions	0.1% to 10.0% Size of Transactions	10.1% to 20.0% No. of Transactions	10.1% to 20.0% Size of Transactions	20.1% to 30.0% No. of Transactions	20.1% to 30.0% Size of Transactions	30.1% to 40.0% No. of Transactions	30.1% to 40.0% Size of Transactions	40.1% to 50.0% No. of Transactions	40.1% to 50.0% Size of Transactions	50.1% or More No. of Transactions	50.1% or More Size of Transactions	Total No. of Transactions	Total Size of Transactions
Less than 100	9	$12,566,000	6	$ 12,267,292	16	$ 12,197,394	17	$ 19,642,364	7	$ 2,554,000	11	$ 2,894,999	66	$ 62,122,049
100-999	2	3,877,500	1	1,018,500	1	500,000	0	0	2	1,221,000	7	474,040	13	7,091,040
1,000-4,999	3	2,295,200	10	9,351,738	15	9,865,951	12	10,675,747	13	8,170,747	8	4,605,505	61	44,964,291
5,000-19,999	47	12,750,481	24	21,441,347	25	27,238,210	13	25,986,008	4	1,147,305	6	1,620,015	119	90,183,366
20,000-99,999	17	36,481,954	18	22,231,737	8	11,817,954	6	11,499,250	3	4,372,676	3	605,689	55	87,009,260
100,000 or More	7	10,832,925	10	24,959,483	3	7,903,586	2	2,049,998	0	0	2	1,805,068	24	47,551,060
Total	85	$78,804,060	69	$91,270,097	68	$69,523,095	50	$69,852,770	29	$17,465,728	37	$12,005,316	338	$338,921,066

SOURCE: Institutional Investor Study Report of the Securities and Exchange Commission, Chapter XIV, Section F.8., "Discounts Involved in Purchases of Common Stock," H.R. Doc. No. 64, Part 5, 92d Cong., 1st Sess. (1971), pp. 2444-56.

stricted stock trades. The four categories are the New York Stock Exchange, American Stock Exchange, over-the-counter (OTC) reporting companies, and over-the-counter nonreporting companies. A *reporting company* is a publicly traded company that must file Forms 10-K, 10-Q, and other information with the SEC. A *nonreporting company* is one whose stock is publicly traded OTC but is not subject to the same reporting requirements. A company whose stock is traded OTC can avoid becoming a SEC reporting company either by maintaining its total assets under $1 million or by keeping its number of stockholders under 500.

Because most small businesses and professional practices are much smaller than typical well-known public companies, the smaller nonreporting public companies may have characteristics that are more comparable to the subject small business. However, since these nonreporting public companies need not report to the SEC, the analyst may have trouble obtaining annual and interim reports for them.

Exhibit 25-1 indicates that, compared to their free-trading counterparts, the price discounts on the letter stocks were the least for NYSE-listed stocks and increased, in order, for AMEX-listed stocks, OTC reporting companies, and OTC nonreporting companies. For OTC nonreporting companies, the largest number of observations fell in the 30 to 40 percent price discount range. Slightly over 56 percent of the OTC nonreporting companies had price discounts greater than 30 percent on the sale of their restricted stock—compared with the stock market price of their free-trading stock. A little over 30 percent of the OTC reporting companies were discounted over 30 percent, and over 52 percent had price discounts over 20 percent.

Using midpoints of the price discount range groups from Exhibit 25-1 —and even including those that sold at premiums for one reason or another—the overall mean average price discount was 25.8 percent and the median price discount was about the same. The study also noted, "Average discounts rose over the period January 1, 1966, through June 30, 1969," and average discounts were "27.9 percent in the first half of 1969."[6] For nonreporting OTC companies (which are more comparative to smaller businesses), the average price discount was 32.6 percent, and the median price discount again was about the same.

Since the time of the SEC study, the efficiency of the OTC market has improved considerably. This has been aided by the development of inexpensive and virtually instantaneous electronic communications and the advent of the Nasdaq system. Since the market in which restricted OTC shares will eventually trade once the restrictions expire (or are removed) is now somewhat more efficient, one would expect the differential in price discounts for restricted listed versus OTC stocks to be less pronounced. And this generally has been the case.

Exhibit 25-2 presents the discounts from open market prices on letter stock transactions, disaggregated into six groups, by the subject companies' annual sales volume. Companies with the largest sales volumes tend to receive the smallest discounts, and companies with the smallest

---

[6]Ibid., p. 2452.

sales volumes tend to receive the largest discounts. Well over half the companies with sales under $5 million (the three smallest of the six size categories used) had price discounts of over 30 percent. However, this may not be a size effect but just further evidence of the influence of the trading market. This is because most of the largest companies were listed on the NYSE, by far the most liquid market at that time.

Gelman Study

In 1972, Milton Gelman published the results of his study of prices paid for restricted securities by four closed-end investment companies specializing in restricted securities investments.[7] From 89 transactions between 1968 and 1970, Gelman found that (1) both the arithmetic average and median price discounts were 33 percent and that (2) almost 60 percent of the purchases were at price discounts of 30 percent and higher. The distribution of price discounts found in the Gelman study is presented in Exhibit 25-3.

Trout Study

In a study of letter stocks purchased by mutual funds from 1968 to 1972, Robert Trout attempted to construct a financial model that would provide an estimate of the price discount appropriate for a private company's stock.[8] His multiple regression model involved 60 purchases and found an average price discount of 33.45 percent for restricted stock from freely traded stock. As the SEC study previously showed, Trout also found that companies with stock listed on national exchanges had lower discounts on their restricted stock transactions than did companies with stock traded over-the-counter.

Exhibit 25–3

| | Price Discounts From Gelman Study | |
Size of Price Discount	Number of Common Stocks	Percent of Total
Less than 15.0%	5	6
15.0–19.9	9	10
20.0–24.9	13	15
25.0–29.9	9	10
30.0–34.9	12	13
35.0–39.9	9	10
40.0 and Over	<u>32</u>	<u>36</u>
Total	89	100

Source: Milton Gelman, "An Economist-Financial Analyst's Approach to Valuing Stock of a Closely Held Company," *Journal of Taxation*, June 1972, p. 354.

---

[7]Milton Gelman, "An Economist-Financial Analyst's Approach to Valuing Stock of a Closely Held Company," *Journal of Taxation*, June 1972, pp. 353–54.

[8]Robert R. Trout, "Estimation of the Discount Associated with the Transfer of Restricted Securities," *Taxes*, June 1977, pp. 381–85.

Moroney Study

In an article published in the March 1973 issue of *Taxes*, Robert E. Moroney presented the results of a study of the prices paid for restricted securities by 10 registered investment companies.[9] The study reflected 146 purchases. The average price discount for the 146 transactions was 35.6 percent, and the median price discount was 33.0 percent.

Moroney points out:

> It goes without saying that each cash purchase of a block of restricted equity securities fully satisfied the requirement that the purchase price be one, "at which the property would change hands between a willing buyer and a willing seller, neither being under any compulsion to buy or to sell and both having reasonable knowledge of relevant facts." Reg. Sec. 20.2031-1(b)[10]

Moroney contrasts the evidence of the actual cash deals with the lower average price discounts for lack of marketability adjudicated in most prior court decisions on gift and estate tax cases. He points out, however, that the empirical evidence on the prices of restricted stocks was not available as a benchmark for quantifying lack of marketability discounts at the time of the prior cases. And he suggests that higher price discounts for lack of marketability be allowed in the future now that the relevant data are available.

Maher Study

Another well-documented study on lack of marketability discounts for closely held business ownership interests was performed by J. Michael Maher and published in the September 1976 issue of *Taxes*.[11] Maher's analytical method was similar to Moroney's in that it compared prices paid for restricted stocks with the market prices of their unrestricted counterparts. Maher found that mutual funds were not purchasing restricted securities during 1974 and 1975, which were very depressed years for the stock market. Therefore, the data actually used covered the five-year period from 1969 through 1973. The study showed, "The mean discount for lack of marketability for the years 1969–73 amounted to 35.43 percent."[12] Maher further eliminated the top and bottom 10 percent of purchases in an effort to remove especially high- and low-risk situations. The result was almost identical with the outliers removed, with a mean price discount of 34.73 percent.

---

[9]Robert E. Moroney, "Most Courts Overvalue Closely Held Stocks," *Taxes*, March 1973, pp. 144–54.

[10]Ibid., p. 151.

[11]J. Michael Maher, "Discounts for Lack of Marketability for Closely-Held Business Interests," *Taxes*, September 1976, pp. 562–71.

[12]Ibid., p. 571.

Standard Research Consultants Study

In 1983, Standard Research Consultants analyzed recent private placements of common stock to test the current applicability of the SEC study.[13] Standard Research Consultants studied 28 private placements of restricted common stock from October 1978 through June 1982. Price discounts ranged from 7 percent to 91 percent, with a median of 45 percent.

Willamette Management Associates Study

Willamette Management Associates analyzed private placements of restricted stocks for the period January 1, 1981, through May 31, 1984. The early part of this study overlapped the last part of the SRC study, but few transactions took place during the period of overlap. Most of the transactions in the Willamette Management Associates study occurred in 1983.

Willamette Management Associates identified 33 transactions during that period (1) that could reasonably be classified as arm's length and (2) for which the price of the restricted shares could be compared directly with the price of trades in identical but unrestricted shares of the same company at the same time. The median price discount for the 33 restricted stock transactions compared to the prices of their freely tradable counterparts was 31.2 percent.

The slightly lower average percentage price discounts for private placements during this time may be attributable to the somewhat depressed pricing in the public stock market. This, in turn, reflected the recessionary economic conditions prevalent during most of the period of the study. This study basically supports the long-term average price discount of 35 percent for transactions in restricted stock compared with the prices of their freely tradable counterparts.

Silber Study

In a 1991 article in the *Financial Analysts Journal*, William L. Silber presented the results of analysis of 69 private placements of common stock of publicly traded companies between 1981 and 1988.[14] He found that the average price discount was 33.75 percent, very consistent with earlier studies.

Silber also found that the size of the price discount tended to be higher for private placements that were larger as a percentage of the shares outstanding. He found a small effect on the price discount on the basis of the size of the company as measured by revenues.

---

[13]William F. Pittock and Charles H. Stryker, "Revenue Ruling 77-287 Revisited," *SRC Quarterly Reports*, Spring 1983, pp. 1–3.

[14]William L. Silber, "Discounts on Restricted Stock: The Impact of Illiquidity on Stock Prices," *Financial Analysts Journal*, July–August 1991, pp. 60–64.

FMV Opinions, Inc., Study

An article in the January/February 1994 issue of *Estate Planning* referenced a study by FMV Opinions, Inc., that "examined over 100 restricted stock transactions from 1979 through April 1992."[15] The FMV study found a mean price discount of only 23 percent.

Management Planning, Inc., Study

Management Planning performed a study titled "Analysis of Restricted Stocks of Public Companies: 1980–1995," which covered a total of 49 transactions after eliminations for various factors.[16] The elimination factors included the following:

- Any company that suffered a loss in the fiscal year preceding the private transaction.
- Any company defined as a "start-up" company (defined as having revenues of less than $3 million).
- Any transactions that were known to have registration rights.

There was clear size effect, with smaller companies tending to have larger discounts, as shown in Exhibit 25-4.

Summary of Empirical Studies on Restricted Stock Transactions

The ten empirical studies of restricted stock transactions reported above cover several hundred transactions spanning the late 1960s through 1995. Considering the number of independent researchers and the very long time span encompassing a wide variety of market conditions, the results are remarkably consistent, as summarized in Exhibit 25-5.

In many of the cases of restricted stock transactions tabulated in Exhibit 25-5, the purchaser of the stock had the right to register the stock for sale in the existing public market. Sometimes investors get a commitment from the issuer to register the securities at a certain future date; sometimes investors have "demand" rights, where they can force the issuer to register the securities at a time of their choosing. Sometimes investors get "piggyback" rights where there is no obligation other than to include the securities on any future registration that the issuer undertakes. And sometimes the purchaser has to rely on SEC Rule 144, where they can sell after two years if other parts of the rule are followed. In recent years, more transactions have occurred under

---

[15]Lance S. Hall and Timothy C. Polacek, "Strategies for Obtaining the Largest Valuation Discounts," *Estate Planning*, January/February 1994, pp. 38–44.

[16]See Chapter 12 in Z. Christopher Mercer, *Quantifying Marketability Discounts* (Memphis: Peabody Publishing, 1997).

Exhibit 25–4

ANALYSIS OF RESTRICTED STOCK DISCOUNTS BY REVENUE SIZE
BASED UPON DATA FROM THE MANAGEMENT PLANNING STUDY

Revenues	Percent of Sample	Average Revenues ($ Millions)	Average Discounts	Standard Deviations	Range of Discounts	
					Low	High
Under $10 million	28.6%	6.6	32.9%	15.6%	2.8%	57.6%
$10-$30 million	22.4%	22.5	30.8%	11.2%	15.3%	49.8%
$30-$50 million	20.4%	35.5	25.2%	15.1%	5.2%	46.3%
$50-$100 million	16.3%	63.5	19.4%	7.3%	11.6%	29.3%
Over $100 million (adjusted) *	8.2%	224.9	14.9%	10.5%	0.0%	24.1%
Overall sample averages	95.9%	47.5	27.7%	14.1%	0.0%	57.6%
*Over $100 million (actual calculation)	4.1%	187.1	25.1%	17.9%	0.0%	46.5%

Note: Excludes Sudbury Holdings, Inc. whose private placement consisted of 125% of the pre-transaction shares outstanding. Excludes Starrett Housing Corp. which is one of the five most thinly traded companies in the sample.

Exhibit 25–5

SUMMARY OF RESTRICTED STOCK EMPIRICAL STUDIES

Empirical Study	**Years Covered in Study**	**Average Price Discount (%)**
SEC Overall Average[a]	1966–1969	25.8%
SEC Nonreporting OTC Companies[a]	1966–1969	32.6
Gelman[b]	1968–1970	33.0
Trout[c]	1968–1972	33.5[l]
Moroney[d]	[k]	35.6
Maher[e]	1969–1973	35.4
Standard Research Consultants[f]	1978–1982	45.0[l]
Willamette Management Associates[g]	1981–1984	31.2[l]
Silber[h]	1981–1988	33.8
FMV Opinions, Inc.[i]	1979–April 1992	23.0
Management Planning, Inc.[j]	1980–1995	27.7

a. From "Discounts Involved in Purchases of Common Stock (1966-1969)," *Institutional Investor Study Report of the Securities and Exchange Commission*, H.R. Doc. No. 64, Part 5, 92nd Congress, 1st Session, 1971, pp. 2444–2456.

b. From Milton Gelman, "An Economist-Financial Analyst's Approach to Valuing Stock of a Closely Held Company," *Journal of Taxation*, June 1972, pp. 353–354.

c. From Robert R. Trout, "Estimation of the Discount Associated with the Transfer of Restricted Securities," *Taxes*, June 1977, pp. 381–385.

d. From Robert E. Moroney, "Most Courts Overvalue Closely Held Stocks," *Taxes*, March 1973, pp. 144–154.

e. From J. Michael Maher, "Discounts for Lack of Marketability for Closely-Held Business Interests," *Taxes*, September 1976, pp. 562–571.

f. From "Revenue Ruling 77-287 Revisited," *SRC Quarterly Reports*, Spring 1983, pp. 1–3.

g. From Willamette Management Associates study (unpublished).

h. From William L. Silber, "Discounts on Restricted Stock: The Impact of Illiquidity on Stock Prices," *Financial Analysts Journal*, July-August 1991, pp. 60–64.

i. From Lance S. Hall and Timothy C. Polacek, "Strategies for Obtaining the Largest Valuation Discounts," *Estate Planning*, January/February 1994, pp. 38–44.

j. From Z. Christopher Mercer, *Quantifying Marketability Discounts* (Memphis, TN: Peabody Publishing, 1997), pp. 345–67. Also available on Business Valuation Update Online, www.nvst.com/bvu.

k. Although the years covered in this study are likely to be 1969–1972, no specific years were given in the published account.

l. Median discounts.

SEC Rule 144(a), which relaxes some of the restrictions on such transactions, thus making the restricted securities more marketable. In any case, investors generally expect to be able to resell the stock in the public market in the foreseeable future.

The Internal Revenue Service specifically recognized the relevance of restricted stock transaction data as evidence for quantification of the discount for lack of marketability in Revenue Ruling 77-287.

Studies of Private Transactions Before Initial Public Offerings

Before the 1980s, virtually all the empirical research directed at quantifying the value impact of marketability (or the discount for lack of marketability) focused on comparisons between the prices (1) of freely tradable shares of stock and (2) of restricted but otherwise identical shares of stock. Observers agreed that price discounts for lack of marketability for ownership interests of closely held companies were greater than those for restricted shares of publicly held companies. This is because the closely held ownership interests had no established market in which they could eventually sell following the removal of certain trading restrictions. However, data for quantifying how much greater this price discount should be had not yet been developed and analyzed.

During the 1980s, an investment banking firm and a valuation consulting firm independently undertook development of data with which to address this question. The research proceeded along basically parallel lines, although each firm was unaware of the other's efforts until their respective research was far along and each had enough data to reach some conclusions.

Both firms used data from *registration statements*, forms that companies must file with the SEC when they sell securities to the public. Each of the series of studies reported in the following sections used data from these forms in order to analyze prices of the private transactions relative to the public offering prices and market prices following initial public offerings.

Robert W. Baird & Company Studies

Eight studies were conducted under the direction of John D. Emory, first vice president of appraisal services at Robert W. Baird & Company, a regional investment banking firm headquartered in Milwaukee.[17] The studies covered various time periods from 1981 through 1997.

---

[17]John D. Emory, "The Value of Marketability as Illustrated in Initial Public Offerings of Common Stock—January 1980 through June 1981," *Business Valuation News*, September 1985, pp. 21–24, also in *ASA Valuation*, June 1986, pp. 62–66; "The Value of Marketability as Illustrated in Initial Public Offerings of Common Stock, January 1985 through June 1986," *Business Valuation Review*, December 1986, pp. 12–15; "The Value of Marketability as Illustrated in Initial Public

The basic methodology for the eight studies was identical. The population of companies in each study consisted of initial public offerings during the respective period in which Baird & Company either participated in or received prospectuses. The prospectuses of these over 2,200 offerings were analyzed to determine the relationship between (1) the price at which the stock was initially offered to the public and (2) the price at which the latest private transaction occurred up to five months prior to the initial public offering. Emory gives the following explanation regarding the studies:

> In order to provide a reasonable comparison of prices before and at the IPO, I felt it necessary both for the company to have been reasonably sound, and for the private transaction to have occurred within a period of five months prior to the offering date.
>
> The transactions primarily took one of two forms: (1) the granting of stock options with an exercise price equal to the stock's then fair market value; or (2) the sale of stock. . . . In most cases, the transactions were stated to have been, or could reasonably be expected to have been, at fair market value. All ultimately would have had to be able to withstand SEC, IRS or judicial review, particularly in light of the subsequent public offering.[18]

Following the above guidelines, and after eliminating development-stage companies (i.e., companies with a history of operating losses) and companies with no transactions within the five months before the initial public offering, 310 qualifying transactions remained in the eight studies.

The mean price discount for the 310 transactions was 44 percent, and the median price discount was 43 percent. The fact that these averages are a little more than 10 percentage points greater than those shown in restricted stock studies is about what one might reasonably expect. This is because the transactions occurred when there was not yet any established market for the stocks at all. A summary of the results of each of the eight Baird studies is presented as Exhibit 25-6.

Willamette Management Associates Studies

Over the last several years, Willamette Management Associates has conducted a series of studies on the prices of private stock transactions

Offerings of Common Stock (August 1987–January 1989)," *Business Valuation Review*, June 1989, pp. 55–57; "The Value of Marketability as Illustrated in Initial Public Offerings of Common Stock, February 1989–July 1990," *Business Valuation Review*, December 1990, pp. 114–16; "The Value of Marketability as Illustrated in Initial Public Offerings of Common Stock, August 1990 through January 1992," *Business Valuation Review*, December 1992, pp. 208–212; "The Value of Marketability as Illustrated in Initial Public Offerings of Common Stock, February 1992 through July 1993," *Business Valuation Review*, March 1994, pp. 3–5; "The Value of Marketability as Illustrated in Initial Public Offerings of Common Stock, January 1994 through June 1995," *Business Valuation Review*, December 1995, pp. 155–160; "The Value of Marketability as Illustrated in Initial Public Offerings of Common Stock, November 1995 through April 1997," *Business Valuation Review*, September 1997, pp. 123–131.

[18]Emory, "The Value of Marketability as Illustrated in Initial Public Offerings of Common Stock, November 1995 through April 1997," *Business Valuation Review*, September 1997, p. 124.

relative to those of subsequent public offerings of stock of the same companies. The studies covered the years 1975 through 1993.

The Willamette Management Associates studies differed from the Baird studies in several respects. One important difference was that the source documents for the Willamette Management Associates studies were complete SEC registration statements primarily on Form S-1 and Form S-18. By contrast, the source documents for the Baird studies were prospectuses. Although the prospectus constitutes a portion of the registration statement, it is required to disclose only transactions with affiliated parties. Form S-1 and Form S-18 registration statements require disclosure of *all* private transactions in the stock within the three years before the public offering, in a section of the registration statement separate from the prospectus portion. The Willamette Management Associates studies attempted to include only transactions that were on an arm's-length basis. The data analyzed included sales of stock in private placements and repurchases of treasury stock by the companies. All stock option transactions and sales of stock to corporate insiders were eliminated unless there was reason to believe they were bona fide transactions for full value. In some cases, the companies were contacted by telephone to either validate the arm's-length nature of the transaction or eliminate the transaction from the study.

The Willamette Management Associates studies considered all public offerings in the files of the *IPO Reporter*. According to the *IPO Reporter*, they included all public offerings during the respective period except for offerings of closed-end fund companies. Eliminated from each of the studies were financial institutions, natural resource companies, offerings priced at $1 or less per share, and offerings that included units or warrants since such offerings might be thought to have unique characteristics. The private transactions analyzed took place from 1 to 36 months before the initial public offering. If a company had more than one transaction that met the study's criteria, all such transactions were included.

Exhibit 25–6

THE VALUE OF MARKETABILITY AS ILLUSTRATED IN INITIAL PUBLIC OFFERINGS OF COMMON STOCK

Study	Number of IPO Prospectuses Reviewed	Number of Qualifying Transactions	Discount	
			Mean	Median
1995-97	732	91	43	42
1994-95	318	46	45	45
1991-93	443	54	45	44
1990-92	266	35	42	40
1989-90	157	23	45	40
1987-89	98	27	45	45
1985-86	130	21	43	43
1980-81	97	13	60	66
All 8 studies	2,241	310	44%	43%

SOURCE: John D. Emory, "The Value of Marketability as Illustrated in Initial Public Offerings of Common Stock, November 1995 through April 1997," *Business Valuation Review*, September 1997, p. 125. Also available on *Business Valuation Update Online*.

For each transaction for which meaningful earnings data were available in the registration statement as of both the private transaction and public offering dates, the price earnings multiple of each private transaction was compared with the subsequent public offering price earnings multiple. Companies that had no meaningful earnings as of the private transaction date and/or the public offering date were eliminated.

Because the private transactions occurred over a period of up to three years prior to the public offering, Willamette Management Associates made adjustments to reflect differences in market conditions for stocks of the respective industries between the time of each private transaction and the time of each subsequent public offering. Price/earnings multiples were adjusted for differences in the industry average price/earnings multiple between the time of the private transaction and that of the public offering.

The formula used to derive the discount for the private transaction price from the public offering price was as follows:

$$\frac{P/E_o - P/E_p\left(\frac{IP/E_o}{IP/E_p}\right)}{P/E_o}$$

where:

P/E_o = Price/earnings multiple of the public offering
P/E_p = Price/earnings multiple of the private transaction
IP/E_o = Industry average price/earnings multiple at time of offering
IP/E_p = Industry average price/earnings multiple at time of private transaction

The results of the Willamette Management Associates studies described above are summarized in Exhibit 25-7. As the exhibit indicates, the average discounts varied from period to period. However, in all cases, the concluded discounts were higher than the average discounts presented in the studies for restricted stocks of companies that already had an established public trading market—which is the result one would expect. As we go to press, the studies are being updated through 1996. Although we do not have final figures, we are advised that the general results continue to be consistent with those shown.

Summary of Conclusions from Private Transaction Studies

The evidence from the Baird and Willamette Management Associates studies, taken together, are compelling. The studies covered hundreds of transactions over 19 years. Average differentials between private transaction prices and public market prices varied under different market conditions, ranging from about 40 to 63 percent, after eliminating the outliers. This is very strong support for the hypothesis that the fair market values of minority ownership interests in privately held businesses are greatly discounted from their publicly traded counterparts.

Exhibit 25–7

SUMMARY OF DISCOUNTS FOR PRIVATE TRANSACTION P/E MULTIPLES
COMPARED TO PUBLIC OFFERING P/E MULTIPLES
ADJUSTED FOR CHANGES IN INDUSTRY P/E MULTIPLES

Time Period	Number of Companies Analyzed	Number of Transactions Analyzed	Mean Discount	Trimmed Mean Discount*	Median Discount	Standard Deviation
1975–7	17	31	34.0%	43.4%	52.5%	58.6%
197	9	17	55.6%	56.8%	62.7%	30.2%
1980–8	58	113	48.0%	51.9%	56.5%	29.8%
1983	85	214	50.1%	55.2%	60.7%	34.7%
1984	20	33	43.2%	52.9%	73.1%	63.9%
1985	18	25	41.3%	47.3%	42.6%	43.5%
1986	47	74	38.5%	44.7%	47.4%	44.2%
1987	25	40	36.9%	44.9%	43.8%	49.9%
1988	13	19	41.5%	42.5%	51.8%	29.5%
1989	9	19	47.3%	46.9%	50.3%	18.6%
1990	17	23	30.5%	33.0%	18.5%	42.7%
1991	27	34	24.2%	28.9%	31.8%	37.7%
1992	36	75	41.9%	47.0%	51.7%	42.6%
1993	51	110	46.9%	49.9%	53.3%	33.9%

* Excludes the highest and lowest deciles of indicated discounts.

SOURCE: Willamette Management Associates.

Other Analysis of Discounts for Lack of Marketability for Minority Interest

Ultimately, of course, the value of the nonmarketable, minority interest is the present value of the benefits it will produce for its owner. This fact is recognized in the *Quantitative Marketability Discount Model* developed by Chris Mercer.[19] In the model, Mercer simply estimates a time horizon at which the interest will be liquidated, a liquidating price based on annual percentage growth in value from the valuation date, and interim cash flows to the holder. He discounts these estimated values back to a present value at a discount rate that is higher than the normal discount rate for cash flows for the subject company to reflect the illiquidity and extra uncertainty of being "locked up" for an indeterminate time. His book gives examples of factors to consider and approximate percentage points to accord to each in adding to the discount rate.

The model is totally sound, but the inputs require substantial subjective estimation. It is useful for identifying situations where the discount should be significantly above or below the averages shown by the restricted stock or pre-IPO studies.

The book also gives a much more complete analysis of some of the studies discussed in this chapter.

---

[19]Z. Christopher Mercer, *Quantifying Marketability Discounts* (Memphis: Peabody Publishing, 1997).

Discounts for Lack of Marketability for Controlling Ownership Interests

It is often necessary to agree on the cash equivalent value today (or as of some date certain) for a controlling ownership interest in a small business or professional practice. This is true whether or not the business will actually be sold. Examples of this cash equivalency analysis include *federal estate taxes* (in the case of a death of the controlling business owner) or the value of a closely held business as *marital property* (in the case of a marital dissolution).

Federal estate taxes, by law, require a cash equivalency value as of a date certain. The estate taxes themselves are paid in cash, not in kind by tendering shares of stock. Therefore, it seems reasonable to make an adjustment from the estimated (but uncertain) sale value of the subject controlling business interest at some undetermined time in the future to a cash equivalency value as of the valuation date, reflecting the time, costs, and risks attendant to achieving such a sale. This valuation adjustment, or discount, is often referred to as a discount for illiquidity, or the discount for lack of marketability of the controlling ownership interest.

In many reported decisions, the U.S. Tax Court has recognized that discounts for lack of marketability for controlling ownership interests in closely held companies are appropriate. The courts have used language such as the following:

> Even controlling shares in a nonpublic corporation suffer from lack of marketability because of the absence of a ready private placement market and the fact that flotation costs would have to be incurred if the corporation were to publicly offer its stock.[20]

Similarly, in the marital dissolution situation, the spouse most actively involved in the small business usually gets the controlling ownership interest in the business. And the nonoperating spouse usually gets much more liquid assets, such as cash, marketable securities, and real estate.

A rational argument can be made that the same factors discussed above should be reflected in the value of the illiquid controlling ownership interest in the small business or professional practice for marital dissolution valuation purposes.

Illiquidity Factors Affecting Controlling Ownership Interests

Unlike the owner of publicly traded securities, the owner of a controlling ownership interest in a small business cannot call up a securities broker, sell that controlling ownership interest in seconds at a predeter-

---

[20]*Estate of Woodbury G. Andrews*, 79 T.C. 938 (1982).

mined price and with a nominal transaction commission, and realize the cash proceeds of the sale in three business days. Rather, selling a controlling ownership interest in a small business is a lengthy, expensive, and uncertain undertaking.

The typical means of liquidating a controlling ownership interest in a small business are as follows:

1. Consummate a public offering of the controlling block of stock.
2. Sell the company in a private transaction:
    a. Sell the overall business enterprise (and equitably allocate the sale proceeds to all of the business owners).
    b. Sell the controlling ownership interest only (to the other minority ownership stockholders or to an independent third-party buyer).

Under various conditions in the public capital markets for stocks and the merger/acquisition markets for companies, one or more of the above transactional alternatives may be clearly more or less attractive —at any point. The values realizable from these transactional alternatives usually have some relationship to each other. This is because potential small business acquirers may themselves be public companies. And there is a tendency for public company acquirers to avoid stock price dilution by paying a higher price/earnings multiple for an acquisition target than the multiple at which their own stock is selling. In the highly valued public markets of 1994 and 1995, public market minority ownership interest valuation multiples were as high or higher than those attainable by selling a controlling ownership interest in many industries.[21]

The controlling owner of a small business who wishes to liquidate a controlling ownership interest generally faces the following transactional considerations:

1. Uncertain time horizon to complete the offering or sale.
2. Cost to prepare for and execute the offering or sale.
3. Risk concerning eventual sale price.
4. Form of the transaction proceeds.
5. Inability to hypothecate.

Time Horizon.   It takes many months, and in some cases years, to complete either an offering or a sale of a small business or professional practice. To some extent, the time factor may be offset by cash flows available to the owner awaiting sale, if they are equal to or greater than the company's cost of capital on a stand-alone basis.

---

[21]*Mergerstat Review 1997* (Los Angeles: Houlihan, Lokey, Howard & Zukin, 1997), p. 25.

Costs. There will be many costs attendant to the sale:

1. Auditing and accounting fees, to provide potential buyers the financial information and assurances they demand.
2. Legal costs, at a minimum to draft all the necessary documents and often to clear away potential perceived contingent liabilities and/or to negotiate warranties.
3. Administrative costs on the part of business owners to deal with the accountants, lawyers, potential buyers, and/or their representatives.
4. Transaction and brokerage costs if a business broker, investment banker, or other transactional intermediary is involved.

Risk. There is a high degree of risk concerning the amount of the actual sale price that will be realized relative to the estimated sale price. This is (1) partly because business valuations are only estimates and (2) partly because internal and/or external factors may influence the business value during the sale negotiation period.

Furthermore, in many cases, there is substantial risk concerning whether the business can be sold at all. There is always considerable risk as to whether an initial public offering can actually be completed at any given stock price. The capital markets are more or less receptive to stocks of companies in different industries at different points. And some small companies will not be accepted by the public markets at all.

Form of the Proceeds. Even when a sale is completed, the business sale proceeds may not be all in cash. Often, the seller may receive part of the business sale proceeds in a note or contingent compensation, or in stock of the acquiring company (and usually restricted stock if the acquiring company is a publicly traded company).

As presented in Exhibit 25-8, the trend over the last 20 years has been away from straight cash for assets or cash for stock acquisition structures. From 1975 to 1979, almost half the reported business acquisitions were for all cash. In 1996, only about 34 percent of the business acquisitions were all cash, 37 percent were all stock, and 29 percent were some combination of cash, debt, and stock. In most of these cases, the stock (in the stock for assets or stock transfer) is restricted stock. Accordingly, the cash equivalency value of a small business sale transaction may be substantially lower than the announced deal price.

For smaller company sales through business brokers, seller financing through a note is involved in the vast majority of transactional cases. Usually, these seller paper notes are at interest rates below market rates for notes of comparable risk. Furthermore, many smaller "deal prices" have a portion of the payments contingent on given levels of revenues or earnings, further reducing the cash equivalency value.

In the initial public offering transaction scenario, normally it is not possible to sell 100 percent of the company's stock at one time. Underwriters generally are not willing to sell an offering in which insiders are bailing out of all their stock. Thus, the business seller usually

Exhibit 25–8

PAYMENT TRENDS
1975-1996

Year	Total Number Disclosing Method of Payment	Cash		Stock		Combination		Debt & Other	
1975	1,225	585	48%	325	27%	285	23%	30	2%
1976	1,255	656	52%	327	26%	250	20%	22	2%
1977	1,238	663	54%	322	26%	224	18%	29	2%
1978	1,182	539	46%	353	30%	273	23%	17	1%
1979	1,233	654	53%	323	26%	247	20%	9	1%
1980	1,121	522	47%	345	31%	237	21%	17	1%
1981	1,309	542	42%	448	34%	301	23%	18	1%
1982	1,083	405	38%	317	29%	338	31%	23	2%
1983	1,108	350	32%	387	35%	362	33%	9	0%
1984	1,079	465	43%	281	26%	320	30%	13	1%
1985	1,468	742	51%	344	23%	377	26%	5	0%
1986	1,303	545	42%	411	32%	345	26%	2	0%
1987	724	298	41%	248	34%	176	24%	2	1%
1988	777	437	56%	166	21%	170	22%	4	1%
1989	664	307	46%	199	30%	153	23%	5	1%
1990	657	260	40%	207	31%	186	28%	4	1%
1991	645	221	34%	221	34%	197	31%	6	1%
1992	818	178	22%	328	40%	303	37%	9	1%
1993	929	236	25%	369	40%	321	35%	3	0%
1994	1,202	317	26%	466	39%	412	34%	7	1%
1995	1,540	413	27%	566	37%	557	36%	4	0%
1996	2,433	830	34%	900	37%	687	28%	16	1%

SOURCE: *Mergerstat Review 1997* (Los Angeles: Houlihan Lokey Howard & Zukin, 1997), p. 14.

is left with some unregistered (restricted) stock. This stock would still be subject to the discount for lack of marketability for restricted stocks as discussed in an earlier section.

Inability to Hypothecate. Ownership interests in closely held businesses, even controlling ownership interests, generally do not make satisfactory bank collateral. If, while awaiting a sale, an owner of a controlling ownership interest wants cash for an emergency or an opportunity or whatever, it will be time-consuming—and may be impossible—to borrow against the estimated value of the business interest.

Benchmark for the Discount for Lack of Marketability for Controlling Ownership Interests

If the appropriate standard of value is fair market value, the price ultimately expected to be reached between "a willing buyer and a willing seller"—before the costs and risks listed above are considered—is a benchmark from which the discount for lack of marketability could be taken. Other possibilities concerning the appropriate base from which a discount for lack of marketability on a controlling ownership interest basis should be taken are:

1. The price one might get in an initial or secondary public stock offering (i.e., the publicly traded equivalent value).
2. The price achievable in the private sale of the entire closely held business, which itself may be estimated in a variety of ways.

In addition to the underwriting commissions and the direct expenses, underwriters frequently receive stock warrants, especially in connection with smaller initial public offerings. Although this is not an immediate cash expense, it is a very real cost of the transaction if the company is successful, possibly amounting to several percentage points of dilution. There are also other indirect transaction costs, such as a large commitment of top management's time to negotiate and to carry out a successful stock offering. If the lack of marketability discount is a critical issue in the subject small business valuation, it may be appropriate to obtain more current data with regard to the cost of a public flotation.

Many of the same or similar costs are involved in preparing a company for a private sale. In addition, the cost of an intermediary to effect the sale may need to be considered. Also, if the benchmark for the estimated sale price is valuation multiples observed in acquisitions of public companies, data indicate that valuation multiples for acquisitions of private companies tend to be lower. This phenomenon is discussed in the following section.

Differences between Private and Public Company Acquisition Price/Earnings Multiples

Every year, *Mergerstat Review* publishes a table presenting the average price/earnings multiples for the acquisitions of private companies for which they have data—compared with the average price/earnings multiples for the acquisitions of companies that had been publicly traded. Every year, the average price/earnings multiple for the acquisitions of private companies is significantly lower than the average price/earnings multiple for the acquisitions of public companies. The public versus private acquisition price/earnings multiple table from the 1997 *Mergerstat Review* is presented in Exhibit 25-9.

Only in 1993 and 1994 were private company acquisition price/earnings multiples higher than public company acquisition price/earnings multiples. And these results could well be an anomaly because only 14 such private company acquisitive transactions were analyzed by *Mergerstat Review* in 1993 and only 18 in 1994.

Observers have hypothesized a number of reasons for this consistent and significant acquisition pricing differential. The most common reasons for this phenomenon are as follows:

1. Exposure to the market.
2. The quality of financial accounting and other information.
3. The size effect.

Exhibit 25–9

**MEDIAN P/E OFFERED
PUBLIC VERSUS PRIVATE
1985-1996**

Year	Acquisitions of Public Companies	(Base)	Acquisitions of Private Companies	(Base)
1985	16.4	(240)	12.3	(187)
1986	24.3	(259)	16.5	(105)
1987	21.7	(191)	15.2	(25)
1988	18.3	(309)	12.8	(50)
1989	18.4	(222)	12.7	(42)
1990	17.1	(117)	13.2	(36)
1991	15.9	(93)	8.5	(23)
1992	18.1	(89)	17.6	(15)
1993	19.7	(113)	22.0	(14)
1994	19.8	(184)	22.0	(18)
1995	19.4	(239)	15.5	(16)
1996	21.7	(288)	17.7	(31)

SOURCE: *Mergerstat Review 1997* (Los Angeles: Houlihan Lokey Howard & Zukin, 1997), p. 19.

Exposure to the Market. The names and stock prices of publicly traded companies are published in hundreds of newspapers throughout the world every day. Publicly traded companies also issue many press releases every year with quarterly earnings and other information; these press releases are also published in hundreds of newspapers. Many computer databases have financial information on thousands of publicly traded companies, including SIC codes, which anyone can access on-line. Publicly traded companies are required to file Forms 10-K, 10-Q, and 8-K, as well as other detailed financial information, with the SEC, which anyone can obtain copies of. Any company, or financial intermediary, interested in an acquisition in any industry has this list of publicly traded companies and the detailed financial information on them at its fingertips.

By contrast, there is no such comprehensive and reliable listing of small businesses and professional practices. And privately owned businesses normally do not disclose financial data. Many privately owned businesses do not even disclose gross revenues. Therefore, acquisition seekers do not have privately owned businesses constantly exposed to them. Business buyers have difficulty making a comprehensive list of available closely held businesses even if they decide to attempt to do so. Generally, business buyers cannot get financial inform1ation regarding closely held businesses—short of a direct approach to the subject business, which they are often reluctant to take.

Quality of Financial Accounting and Other Information.
The SEC requirements for accounting information and other disclosures

are far more stringent and extensive than what is required for an un-qualified audit opinion under normal GAAP rules. Many analysts believe that this difference in the quantity and reliability of financial data has an impact on the differential in average price/earnings multiples paid for the acquisition of public companies versus the acquisition of private companies.

Size Effect. Empirical studies have proven that larger companies tend to be less risky than smaller companies. This phenomenon would generally result in a lower present value discount rate and a higher price for larger companies. On average, the privately owned companies reported in *Mergerstat Review* are smaller in size than the publicly traded companies reported in *Mergerstat Review*.

This appears to be a contributing factor to the price/earnings multiple differential between privately owned and publicly traded company acquisitions reported in the *Mergerstat Review*. However, it is highly questionable whether this difference in average acquisition size is significant enough to account for the large magnitude of difference between privately owned and publicly traded company acquisition price/earnings multiples.

It is not possible, with the data currently available, to completely explain the relative impact of the various influences that cause privately owned business acquisitions to trade at much lower price/earnings multiples than publicly traded company acquisitions. In any case, the data are clear that privately owned businesses realize lower acquisition price/earnings multiples, on average, when compared to publicly traded companies. Additional research on this point is clearly warranted. Nonetheless, the three factors listed above (i.e., exposure to market, quality of financial accounting, and size effect) generally explain this phenomenon.

If the analysis of the value of a controlling ownership interest in a privately owned business is based on market prices for the acquisitions of publicly traded companies, these data suggest that some amount of valuation adjustment is applicable. For convenience, we may refer to this valuation phenomenon as a part of the discount for the lack of marketability of a controlling ownership interest in a closely held business. Or, to distinguish it from the lack of marketability of minority ownership interests, we may refer to this phenomenon as the discount for the illiquidity in the overall closely held business. Regardless of what we call this phenomenon, empirical data clearly suggest that a valuation discount is appropriate for controlling ownership interests (and, for that matter, 100 percent ownership interests) in closely held businesses. This lack of marketability discount (or illiquidity discount) applies— although to varying degrees—regardless of whether the subject business is valued by reference to discounted or capitalized economic income analyses, to guideline publicly traded companies, to consummated guideline acquisitions, or to an asset-based valuation method.

Factors That Affect the Discount for Lack of Marketability

It is important to recognize that the discount for lack of marketability is not a black and white issue. That is, an ownership interest is not necessarily simply "marketable," freely tradable in a public market, or "nonmarketable," not freely tradable. There are *degrees* of marketability. These degrees of marketability depend on the circumstances in each case. The following are some of the factors that affect the degree of marketability. Although there is no empirically supported formula to assess the impact of each, consideration of these factors should guide the analyst's judgment about where the subject ownership interest should fall within the reasonable range of discounts for lack of marketability.

"Put" Rights

Generally, the most powerful factor that could reduce or eliminate a discount for lack of marketability would be the existence of a "put" right. A put is a contractual right that entitles the holder, at his or her option, to sell the ownership interest to a specified party at some time or under some specified circumstances, at the price or mechanism for determining the price specified in the contract. In other words, a put *guarantees* a market under specified circumstances. Puts are most commonly found in connection with ESOP-owned stock.

Dividend Payments

Stocks with no or low dividends suffer more from lack of marketability than stocks with high dividends. Besides being empirically demonstrable, this makes common sense. If the stock pays no dividend, the holder is dependent *entirely* on some future ability to sell the stock to realize any return. The higher the dividend, the greater the return the holder realizes without regard for sale of the stock. For this reason, dividend-paying preferred stocks would typically be subject to a lower discount for lack of marketability than non-dividend-paying common stocks.

Potential Buyers

The existence of a reasonable number of potential buyers or even one strong potential buyer (often as demonstrated by past activity in the company's stock) could dampen the discount for lack of marketability. For example, if an ESOP regularly purchases shares, the possibility of sometime selling shares to the ESOP may cause the discount for lack of marketability to be less than if the ESOP did not exist.

Size of Interest

Strictly from a marketability perspective, the empirical evidence cited in earlier sections suggests that larger blocks may tend to have larger discounts for lack of marketability than do smaller blocks. There may be fewer potential buyers for a large block, and a large block transaction may be more difficult to finance.

One might logically note that a larger ownership interest may have higher value because of possible elements of ownership control, such as a swing vote position or a seat on the board of directors. However, this is a discount factor different from lack of marketability, discussed in the previous chapter.

Prospect of Public Offering or Sale of the Business

An imminent public offering or sale of the business could decrease the discount for lack of marketability. However, such prospects are almost never certain, and the degree of offset to the discount for lack of marketability is problematic since much of the empirical evidence that illustrates the discount is taken from companies that subsequently went public. In some cases, even if such an event were to occur, all minority shareholders might not necessarily have the right to participate.

Conversely, a business being absolutely committed to remaining private and in the hands of current control owners for the foreseeable future would tend to increase the discount for lack of marketability.

Information Access and Reliability

The degree to which information is or is not made available to minority owners and the reliability of that information affects the discount for lack of marketability. For example, a recent article on partnership interest valuations states, "An important basis for illiquidity discounts is the difficulty faced by prospective purchasers in obtaining information."[22]

Restrictive Transfer Provisions

Many closely held stocks are subject to provisions that severely restrict the right of the holder to transfer stock. Any provision that limits the

---

[22]Mark S. Thompson and Eric S. Spunt, "The Widespread Overvaluation of Fractional Ownership Positions," *Trusts & Estates*, June 1993, pp. 62–66. See also Michael J. Bolotsky, "Adjustments for Differences in Ownership Rights, Liquidity, Information Access, and Information Reliability: An Assessment of 'Prevailing Wisdom' versus the 'Nath Hypotheses,'" *Business Valuation Review*, September 1991, pp. 94–110. Bolotsky's position is that, conceptually, this is a factor separate from marketability, but he recognizes the reality that we have no good way to measure this factor separately.

right of the holder to transfer the stock would tend to increase the amount of the discount for lack of marketability. In some cases, the restrictive provision may fix the value or put a ceiling on it. The impact of such restrictions is a matter of judgment that must be analyzed in light of the provisions in each case, in some cases with the advice of legal counsel regarding enforceability.

Court Decisions on Discounts for Lack of Marketability

There is a substantial body of judicial precedent with regard to the identification and quantification of the discount for lack of marketability. It is particularly noteworthy that each of these judicial decisions depends on the facts and circumstances of the particular case in point. Therefore, it is difficult for the analyst to extract lack of marketability discount data from judicial precedent—except in the rare instances when the facts and circumstances of the subject valuation are identical to the facts and circumstances of the litigated case.

However, it may be useful for analysts to review published judicial precedent with regard to lack of marketability discounts. This review should *not* be used to extract a particular discount percentage. Rather, it may be used to better understand the various factors that the courts have considered in their estimates of the lack of marketability discounts.

There is a substantial amount of precedent related to lack of marketability discounts with respect to federal gift taxes, estate taxes, and income taxes. These cases are summarized in the *Federal Tax Valuation Digest*, published annually. [23] We highly recommend this publication for its organized summaries of valuation-related federal tax cases. Chris Mercer's new book (discussed earlier) offers an overview of marketability discounts in the tax court and detailed analysis of four interesting cases. [24]

The topic of lack of marketability arises in many other litigation contexts, including shareholder disputes, marital dissolution cases, and damages matters. One report, *Marketability Discounts in the Courts, 1991–1996*, covers (in addition to gift and estate tax cases) other federal and state cases where discounts were an issue in marital dissolutions, corporate disagreements, ESOPs, bankruptcy cases, income tax cases, dissenting stockholder cases, and other litigation. [25]

---

[23]Idelle A. Howitt, ed., *Federal Tax Valuation Digest* (New York: Warren, Gorham & Lamont, 1997).

[24]Z. Christopher Mercer, *Quantifying Marketability Discounts.*

[25]Janet Hamilton, "Marketability Discounts in the Courts, 1991–1996," *Shannon Pratt's Business Valuation Update*, March 1997.

Summary

This chapter presented a substantial amount of evidence to assist in estimating appropriate discounts for lack of marketability for both minority ownership interest and controlling ownership interests in small businesses and professional practices. In the final analysis, however, as with many other valuation issues, the estimation must be made in light of a studied examination of the facts and circumstances of each case. The specific data that the analyst collects and relies on for each valuation should relate as closely as possible in time and other characteristics to the valuation subject.

Ownership interests in closely held businesses, most of which will never be freely tradable, suffer much more from lack of marketability than do restricted shares of publicly traded companies. In general, they also have fewer prospects of being marketable than do shares of companies that are considering (or are already in the process of attempting) an initial public offering.

Courts have tended to recognize higher discounts for lack of marketability in recent years. The trend toward higher discounts for lack of marketability has continued since publication of the second edition of this book. However, the levels of discounts for lack of marketability allowed in most court decisions still seem to be below what the empirical evidence related to arm's-length transactions tends to suggest.

We hope that appraisers, attorneys, and small business owners will use the types of data presented in this chapter, along with continuing related research, to reduce the disparity between the (often low) lack of marketability discounts found in court decisions and the lack of marketability discounts empirically evidenced in actual market transactions.

Bibliography

Abrams, Jay B. "Discount for Lack of Marketability: A Theoretical Model." *Business Valuation Review,* September 1994, pp. 132–39.

Arneson, George S. "Nonmarketability Discounts Should Exceed Fifty Percent." *Taxes,* January 1981, pp. 25–31.

Barron, Michael S. "When Will the Tax Court Allow a Discount for Lack of Marketability?" *Journal of Taxation*, January 1997, pp. 46–50.

Bogdanski, John A. "Dissecting the Discount for Lack of Marketability." *Estate Planning*, February 1996, pp. 91–95.

Bolten, Steven E. "Discounts for Stocks of Closely Held Corporations." *Trusts & Estates,* December 1990, pp. 47–48.

Budyak, James T. "Estate Freeze Rules Affect Partnership Valuation Discounts." *Taxation for Accountants*, December 1996, pp. 340–47.

Cavanaugh, James C. "Valuation Discounts Are Available in an Estate Plan." *Taxation for Accountants*, July 1995, pp. 31–37.

Chaffe, David B.H. III. "Option Pricing as a Proxy for Discount for Lack of Marketability in Private Company Valuations." *Business Valuation Review,* December 1993, pp. 182–88.

Emory, John D. "The Value of Marketability as Illustrated in Initial Public Offerings of Common Stock—November 1995 through April 1997." *Business Valuation Review*, September 1997, pp. 123–131.

Fowler, Bradley A. "How Do You Handle It?" *Business Valuation Review*, September 1995, pp. 130–33.

Garber, Steven. "A Proposed Methodology for Estimating the Lack of Marketability Discount Related to ESOP Repurchase Liability." *Business Valuation Review,* December 1993, pp. 172–81.

Hall, Lance S., and Timothy C. Polacek. "Strategies for Obtaining the Largest Valuation Discounts." *Estate Planning,* January/February 1994, pp. 38–44.

Hamilton, Janet. "Marketability Discounts in the Courts, 1991–1996." (special report) *Shannon Pratt's Business Valuation Update*, March 1997.

Harris, James Edward. "Minority and Marketability Discounts: Are You Taking Enough?" *Probate and Property,* January/February 1990, pp. 6–11.

_____. "Valuation of Closely Held Partnerships and Corporations: Recent Developments Concerning Minority Interest and Lack of Marketability Discounts." *Arkansas Law Review*, 42, no. 3 (1989), pp. 649–70.

Hayes, John W., and Scott D. Miller. "Marketability Issues in the Valuation of ESOPs." *CPA Expert*, Summer 1996, pp. 7–11.

Hertzel, Michael, and Richard L. Smith. "Market Discounts and Shareholder Gains for Placing Equity Privately." *Journal of Finance,* June 1993, pp. 459–85.

Hitchner, James R. "Tax Court Reviews Nine Factors for Selecting Marketability Discounts." *CPA Expert*, Winter 1996, pp. 11–13.

Hitchner, James R., and Gary Roland. "Marketability and Control Govern Value of Family Businesses." *Taxation for Accountants,* January 1994, pp. 24–28.

Hitchner, James R., and Kevin J. Rudd. "The Use of Discounts in Estate and Gift Tax Valuations." *Trusts & Estates,* August 1992, pp. 49–56, 60.

Holthausen, Robert W., Richard W. Leftwich, and David Mayers. "The Effect of Large Block Transactions on Security Prices: A Cross-Sectional Analysis." *Journal of Financial Economics* 19 (1987), pp. 237–67.

Hopson, James F., and William J. Sheehy. "Valuation of Minority Discounts in Closely-Held Corporations." *National Public Accountant*, December 1993, pp. 30–33.

Horowitz, Steven A., and Alfred S. Scope. "IRS on Minority Interest Discounts: It Don't Mean a Thing If It Still Got That Swing." *Taxes*, February 1995, pp. 76–81.

Johnson, Richard D., and George A. Racette. "Discounts on Letter Stock Do Not Appear to Be a Good Base on Which to Estimate Discounts for Lack of Marketability on Closely Held Stocks." *Taxes,* August 1981, pp. 574–81.

Lyons, Robert P., and Michael J. Wilczynski. "Discounting Intrinsic Value." *Trusts & Estates,* February 1989, pp. 22–27.

Lyons, William P., and Martin J. Whitman. "Valuing Closely Held Corporations and Publicly Traded Securities with Limited Marketability: Approaches to Allowable Discounts from Gross Values." *Business Lawyer,* July 1978, pp. 2213–29.

Maher, J. Michael. "Discounts for Lack of Marketability for Closely Held Business Interests." *Taxes,* September 1976, pp. 562–71.

Mercer, Z. Christopher. *Quantifying Marketability Discounts.* Memphis: Peabody Publishing, 1997.

_____. "Should 'Marketability Discounts' Be Applied to Controlling Interests of Private Companies?" *Business Valuation Review,* June 1994, pp. 55–65.

Moroney, Robert E. "Why 25 Percent Discount for Nonmarketability in One Valuation, 100 Percent in Another?" *Taxes,* May 1977, pp. 316–20.

Paulsen, Jon. "Lack of Marketability and Minority Discounts for Closely-Held Stocks." *Taxes,* August 1996, pp. 491–95.

Peters, Jerry O. "Lack of Marketability Discounts for Controlling Interests: An Analysis of Public vs. Private Transactions." *Business Valuation Review*, June 1995, pp. 59–61.

Ressegieu, Matthew. "Valuation Discounts: What Is Required?" *Taxation for Lawyers*, March/April 1995, pp. 283–88.

Shenkman, Martin M., and Cal R. Feingold. "Minority, Marketability Discounts Affect Valuation of Partnership Interest." *Real Estate Finance Journal,* Summer 1993, pp. 18–25.

Silber, William L. "Discounts on Restricted Stock: The Impact of Illiquidity on Stock Prices." *Financial Analysts Journal*, July–August 1991, pp. 60–64.

Smith, Ronald C. "Leveraged Buildups, Mergers and Acquisitions." *Secured Lender,* March/April 1994, pp. 72–74.

Chapter 26

Valuation Synthesis and Conclusion

As has been presented in previous chapters, there are three generally accepted approaches to the valuation of small businesses and professional practices: (1) the income approach, (2) the market approach, and (3) the asset-based approach. Within each approach are a number of generally accepted valuation methods. And, within each method are a number of generally accepted procedures. Accordingly, valuation analyses progress from the more general to the more specific. First, the analyst selects the appropriate approaches. Second, within each approach, the analyst applies the appropriate methods. And third, within each method, the analyst performs the appropriate procedures.

As we have discussed in previous chapters, each of the three generally accepted valuation approaches has its own strengths and weaknesses. Certainly, within each unique set of facts and circumstances, each valuation approach will have its practical application limitations.

This chapter will focus on three fundamental questions:

1. How does the analyst decide which valuation approaches, methods, and procedures to use in each individual business valuation?
2. How does the analyst reconcile the differing results of alternative valuation approaches in reaching the business valuation synthesis and conclusion?
3. What does the analyst do when alternative valuation approaches indicate materially different valuation conclusions?

The Reconciliation Process

The first step in reaching the business valuation synthesis and conclusion is to perform the reconciliation process. During the reconciliation process, it is important for the analyst to review all the steps of the business valuation. The first procedure in this reconciliation process is for the analyst to review the business valuation assignment. At this point, the analyst should answer the following two questions:

1. Did I appraise the right thing?
2. Did I appraise the right thing the right way?

In other words, from an overall engagement perspective, the analyst should consider the question, "Did I accomplish what I set out to accomplish?"

A review of the business valuation assignment should consider the following:

1. The purpose and objective of the appraisal.
2. The business enterprise ownership interest subject to appraisal.
3. The bundle of legal rights subject to appraisal.

4. The ownership characteristics of the business interest subject to appraisal.
5. The date of the appraisal.
6. The standard (or definition) of value to be estimated.
7. The premise of value to be used (that is, based upon the highest and best use of the subject business ownership interest).

The business valuation engagement is performed to answer a question about the value of a business entity or business ownership interest. Even within the same valuation approach, different methods will typically result in different indications of value. For example, it is likely that different indicated values will result from two different income approach methods (e.g., the capitalized economic income method and the discounted economic income method).

The process of reconciliation is the analysis of the alternative valuation conclusions in order to arrive at a final value estimate for the subject business entity or business ownership interest. Before reaching a final value estimate, the analyst should review the entire business valuation for appropriateness and for accuracy. It is noteworthy that the definition of value sought—and its relationship to each step in the valuation process—should be carefully considered throughout the reconciliation process.

Criteria for the Selection of Valuation Approaches and Methods

As mentioned above, of the generally accepted business valuation approaches, there are no absolutely "right" or "wrong" approaches for any particular valuation engagement. Of course, this assertion deliberately excludes valuation "approaches" that are not generally accepted, such as the naive application of the accounting book value "approach."

There is also no precise guideline or quantitative formula for selecting which approach (or approaches) is most applicable in a given business valuation situation. However, the following list presents the most common and most important factors for the analyst to consider when selecting the appropriate valuation approaches and methods to apply in a particular analysis:

1. Quantity and quality of available data.
2. Access to available data.
3. Supply of industry transactional data.
4. Type of the subject business, nature of the subject business assets, and type of industry subject to appraisal.
5. The particular business ownership interest subject to appraisal.
6. Statutory, judicial, contractual, and administrative requirements and considerations.

7. Informational needs of the particular appraisal audience.
8. Purpose and objective of the appraisal.
9. Compliance with promulgated professional standards.
10. Professional judgment and technical expertise of analyst.

Each of these considerations will be explored below.

Quantity and Quality of Available Data

Practically, this may be the most important methodological selection criteria. An analyst simply can not perform a valuation approach or method (no matter how conceptually robust it is) if the requisite financial, operational, or market-derived data are not available.

Access to Available Data

In business valuations performed for litigation support, dispute resolution, and other controversy purposes, the analyst may not have unrestricted access to company data, to company management, to company facilities, and so forth. In these cases, all of the desired historical and prospective data may exist. However, the analyst may not be granted reasonable access to the existing data. Accordingly, in selecting among valuation approaches and methods, the analyst may have to consider not only what data exist but what data are readily available to the analyst.

Having said that, we should point out that, if the attorney pursues the issue vigorously with the judge, most courts will order access to the appropriate data. This statement is supported by the case law.[1]

Supply of Industry Transactional Data

In some industries, there is a large quantity of publicly available data regarding small business or professional practice sale and/or purchase transactions. When the supply of reliable industry transactional data is substantial, the analyst will more likely select and rely on market-based business valuation approaches.

Type of the Subject Business, Nature of the Subject Business Assets, and Type of Industry Subject to Appraisal

Certain industries have "rules of thumb" that may be used as quick, preliminary estimates regarding the valuation of companies in that industry. While these industry rules of thumb, guidelines, or conventions should not be exclusively relied on in a rigorous business valuation, they

---

[1]See, for example, Barth H. Goldberg and Joseph N. DuCanto, *Valuation of Divorce Assets*, 1994 Supplement (St. Paul, MN: West Publishing Co., 1994), pp. 41–45.

need not be totally ignored either. And depending upon the nature of the subject business (e.g., whether it is capital-asset intensive or intangible-asset intensive), different valuation approaches may be more or less applicable.

The Particular Business Ownership Interest Subject to Appraisal

Obviously, the valuation of a controlling ownership interest in a business enterprise is a different assignment than the valuation of a nonmarketable, noncontrolling ownership interest in the nonvoting stock of the same business enterprise. In selecting the valuation approaches and methods, the analyst should consider that some valuation methods are more appropriate for overall business enterprise valuations while other methods are more appropriate for the analysis of fractional security interests.

Statutory, Judicial, Contractual, and Administrative Considerations

For those business valuations performed for certain taxation, ESOP, and litigation purposes, the analyst should research whether certain valuation approaches and methods are required—and whether certain valuation approaches and methods are prohibited. The Internal Revenue Service has published valuation procedures and guidelines for appraisals performed for federal gift and estate tax purposes. For example, the specific Internal Revenue Code Chapter 14 guidelines apply for business valuations performed for estate planning purposes.

Certain states require some valuation methods—and prohibit others—for business appraisals performed for shareholder appraisal rights pursuant to minority squeeze-out mergers, other statutory shareholder rights or shareholder oppression cases, marital dissolution cases, and so forth. Precedential case decisions, rather than statutory law, generally provide the guidance on such issues. The analyst should be aware of whatever specific statutory requirements, administrative guidance, or judicial precedent affect the subject business valuation. The analyst should also consider whether there are any applicable contractual requirements or restrictions.

Informational Needs of the Particular Appraisal Audience

The ultimate audience for the appraisal may affect the selection of business valuation approaches and methods. These considerations include (1) the level of sophistication of the particular appraisal audience and (2) the degree of familiarity of the particular appraisal audience with the subject company. The ultimate purpose of the appraisal—as either a notational or a transactional appraisal—may also affect which valuation approaches and methods will be selected.

Purpose and Objective of the Appraisal

Overall, the purpose and objective of the business valuation may influence the selection of the valuation approaches. The various components of the appraisal objective include the description of the business ownership interest subject to appraisal, the definition (or standard) of value applied, the premise of value applied, and the valuation date. The various components of the appraisal purpose include the audience for the appraisal and the decision (or decisions) that will be influenced by the appraisal.

Compliance with Promulgated Professional Standards

Obviously, analysts who are members of professional societies and institutes should comply with the promulgated professional pronouncements of those organizations. To varying degrees, the American Society of Appraisers, the Institute of Business Appraisers, the National Association of Certified Valuation Analysts, and the American Institute of Certified Public Accountants have prepared standards and/or other professional guidance with respect to business valuation approaches and methods. These professional organizations—and their related professional guidance—were introduced in Chapter 1.

Professional Judgment and Technical Expertise of the Analyst

When all is said and done, subject to applicable legal requirements, the most important factor affecting the selection of the appropriate business valuation approaches and methods is the professional judgment, technical expertise, and practiced common sense of a competent and experienced analyst.

Criteria for the Synthesis of Multiple Valuation Indications

As with the selection of valuation approaches and methods, there are no scientific formulas or specific rules to use with regard to the synthesis, or weighting, of the results of two or more business valuation methods. In fact, the same factors or guidelines that affect the selection of the valuation methods will influence the appraiser with regard to synthesis of the indications of these valuation methods.

Some analysts use an implicit weighting scheme in their final valuation synthesis and conclusion. That is, they present the valuation indications for each method performed. Then they directly arrive at a valuation conclusion. They do not quantitatively document or qualitatively justify the valuation synthesis process.

An example of this implicit weighting scheme follows.

Professional Partnership Subject to Appraisal
Business Valuation Approaches and Methods
Valuation Synthesis and Conclusion
As of December 31, 1997

Valuation Approach	Valuation Method	Value Indication
Income approach	Capitalization of economic income method	$1,800,000
Income approach	Discounted economic income method	$2,000,000
Asset-based approach	Asset accumulation method	$2,400,000
Valuation synthesis and conclusion		$2,200,000

This valuation synthesis, of course, presents the final valuation conclusion. The valuation conclusion may be perfectly reasonable. However, the analyst has not explained (either quantitatively or qualitatively) the implicit weighting—that is, the intrinsic thought process that led to the $2,200,000 valuation conclusion.

An alternative valuation synthesis procedure is to present an explicit weighting of the several valuation methods employed in the analysis. This explicit weighting scheme allows the analyst to communicate the degree of confidence (1) in each of the several business valuation methods selected and (2) in the reasonableness of the several business value indications. In fact, a narrative description of the rationale behind the analyst's explicit weighting scheme is often included in the narrative valuation opinion report.

An example of this explicit weighting scheme follows.

Professional Partnership Subject to Appraisal
Business Valuation Approaches and Methods
Valuation Synthesis and Conclusion
As of December 31, 1997

Valuation Approach	Valuation Method	Value Indication	Weighting	Weighted Value
			Value Reconciliation	
Income approach	Capitalization of economic income method	$1,800,000	25%	$ 450,000
Income approach	Discounted economic income method	$2,000,000	25%	500,000
Asset-based approach	Asset accumulation method	$2,400,000	50%	1,200,000
Total weighted value				$2,150,000
Valuation synthesis and conclusion (rounded)				$2,200,000

Even if a narrative discussion of the weighting scheme is included in the valuation opinion report, the above explicit weighting provides important information about the analyst's thought process regarding—

and the analyst's degree of confidence in—the alternative valuation methods and the alternative valuation indications. This explicit weighting allows the appraisal reader to follow—and to reconstruct, if necessary—all of the analyst's quantitative (if not all of the analyst's qualitative) analyses.

It is noteworthy that there is no generally accepted formula or model to quantify the weighting factors. The implicit or explicit weighting will vary for each appraisal. The weighting assigned to each individual valuation method in each individual appraisal engagement is ultimately based on the experience and judgment of the analyst. If using explicit weights, the analyst should acknowledge in the written report that there are no empirical bases by which to assign weights to various methods and that the purpose of the quantitative weighting is to aid the reader in understanding the analyst's thought process.

Income Approach Methods

The following sections will discuss some of the factors that influence the weighting of the income approach methods in the valuation synthesis and conclusion.

Yield Capitalization—Discounted Economic Income Method. The primary criterion for heavy weighting of the discounted economic income valuation method is the existence of a credible business plan or financial projection. This valuation method also becomes relatively more important when it is expected that future operating results of the subject company will differ significantly enough from past operating results that reliance solely on historical results may provide a misleading indication of value.

The discounted economic income valuation method is more commonly used in the valuation of a controlling ownership interest in a business as compared to a noncontrolling ownership interest. One reason for this is that the controlling stockholder has more discretion to take those actions needed to actually realize the projected economic income. Also, the controlling stockholder has the discretion to determine the amount of the distributions of the economic income earned by the company. Of course, there are variations of the discounted economic income method that may be appropriate to the appraisal of a noncontrolling ownership interest.

In addition, this valuation method is more appropriate to the extent that asset values of the subject company tend to be more of an intangible nature than of a tangible nature.

Direct Capitalization of Economic Income Method. The validity of the direct capitalization of economic income method depends on the ability to estimate some reasonably credible level of normalized economic income (however measured) that can be considered sustainable. As with the discounted economic income method, this method is premised on the concept that future economic income capacity is important in the business valuation. Sometimes it is easier (or more reliable) to develop a "normalized" level of economic income than it is to estimate the timing of that economic income (as is necessary in the discounted economic income method).

The direct capitalization of economic income method can also work well if there is a modest and fairly sustainable expected long-term growth rate related to the company's economic income.

Asset-Based Approach Methods

The following sections will discuss some of the factors that influence the weighting of the asset-based approach methods in the valuation synthesis and conclusion.

Capitalized Excess Earnings Method.   The capitalized excess earnings method of the asset-based approach generally is most applicable when there is a high component of intangible asset value in the subject business, such as often is the case with professional practices. This valuation method is based on the conceptual premise that most of the value of the subject business derives from its expected earning power. Although adaptable to the valuation of noncontrolling ownership interests, this method is more commonly used for valuing controlling ownership interests in small businesses and professional practices. This method is also often appropriate when there is a need to allocate transaction price or value between tangible and intangible assets.

Asset Accumulation Method.   The asset accumulation method (or adjusted net asset value method) is most commonly used in the appraisal of asset-intensive businesses. Of course, to one degree or another, all businesses may be considered asset intensive. For example, a tool and die company would be considered capital-asset intensive, while most professional practices would be considered intangible-asset intensive.

The asset accumulation method is more commonly used in the valuation of controlling interests since noncontrolling interests cannot direct the disposition of the assets of the subject business.

The asset accumulation method is most applicable (and most practical) when there are detailed data available with regard to the tangible assets and the intangible assets of the business subject to appraisal.

Market Approach Methods

The following sections will discuss some of the factors that influence the weighting of the market approach methods in the valuation synthesis and conclusion.

Guideline Publicly Traded Company Method.   The primary criterion for using the guideline publicly traded company method is the existence of reasonably comparative guideline companies. This method can be especially useful for appraising smaller noncontrolling owner-ship interests. This is because most of the stock purchase/sale transactions reported on the capital market stock exchanges represent, in fact, smaller, noncontrolling ownership interests.

The application of this valuation method is expected when appraising companies for certain gift and estate tax, income tax, and ESOP purposes—given the existing regulatory authority and judicial precedent.

An experienced analyst can deal with appropriate valuation adjustments for size, marketability, and the other risk and expected return differences that need to be considered when using this method. If enough good guideline company data are available, it can provide compelling evidence of value.

Guideline Transaction Method.   As with the guideline publicly traded company method, the applicability of this method depends on the comparability of the market-derived transactional data to the subject company. However, when adequate comparative transactions are available, the application of market-derived pricing multiples is particularly relevant to the valuation of controlling ownership interests.

Gross Revenue Multiple Method.   Gross revenue pricing multiples are most commonly used when the analyst has credible data on the revenues for the subject company and/or guideline company transactions but does not have credible data on cash flow or other measures of economic income. As noted in Chapter 20, the use of gross revenue multiples for valuation purposes carries an implicit premise of homogeneity (in terms of return on sales and other risk and expected return factors) between the subject company and the guideline companies from which the pricing multiples are derived. If this is not the case, the analyst should be able to make appropriate adjustments in order to effectively apply this method.

Gross revenue pricing multiples tend to be most reliable for professional practices and service businesses, reasonably reliable for retail/service businesses such as restaurants, and least reliable for manufacturing companies. This is because most manufacturing companies are unique. In any case, a company's value ultimately is based on its ability to generate cash flow, and the validity of the gross revenue multiple method depends on the method's ability to analyze potential earning power.

Reconciling an Inconsistency of Results among Valuation Approaches and Methods

Ideally, the analyst will use several approaches and methods in the subject business valuation, and these several methods will all yield identical valuation indications. In reality, this rarely happens.

Experienced analysts expect to conclude a range of value indications when several alternative valuation methods are used. The normal situation occurs when the several valuation methods all conclude a reasonably narrow dispersion of value indications. These alternative value indications, then, indicate the reasonable range of values for the subject business. They also provide mutually supportive evidence as to the final valuation synthesis and conclusion.

Occasionally, the situation occurs when two or more valuation methods produce value indications within a reasonable range, and then one valuation method produces a value indication outlier.

An example of this value indication outlier phenomenon follows.

Professional Partnership Subject to Appraisal
Business Valuation Approaches and Methods
Valuation Synthesis and Conclusion
As of December 31, 1997

Valuation Approach	Valuation Method	Value Indication
Income approach	Capitalization of economic income method	$1,800,000
Income approach	Discounted economic income method	$2,000,000
Asset-based approach	Capitalized excess earnings method	$2,200,000
Asset-based approach	Asset accumulation method	$1,000,000
Valuation synthesis and conclusion		$2,200,000

In this example, the value indication of the asset accumulation method (i.e., the discrete application of the asset-based valuation approach) is an obvious outlier compared to the three other value indications. Accordingly, this appraisal requires further analysis and consideration before a valuation conclusion may be reached.

The question is: What is the analyst to do regarding such an outlier value indication? There are three alternatives.

First, the analyst could discard the valuation method that yields the outlier value indication. This decision is based on the rationale that the outlier valuation method simply does not provide reliable valuation information, given the subject set of facts and circumstances.

Second, the analyst could keep the outlier valuation method but assign a very low weight to the outlier value indication. This procedure is based on the rationale that if the valuation method is fundamentally sound, even an unreasonable value indication should be given some weight in the final valuation conclusion.

Third, the analyst could thoroughly investigate why one method is producing outlier value indications. The analyst could attempt to reconcile all of the value indications. The analyst could search for an answer, or at least an explanation, to this apparent anomaly. As part of this investigation and reconcilement, the analyst should recheck all of the quantitative analyses and should rethink all of the qualitative conclusions. The analyst is most likely to find that an error was made in the analysis and application of the outlier method. (An example may be that one significant intangible asset was inadvertently left out in the application of the asset accumulation method.)

After the analytical or data error is discovered, it can be corrected. Then the outlier method may produce a more reasonable, and more consistent, value indication.

This third alternative is typically preferable for handling the phenomenon of an outlier business value indication. Of course, this alternative involves additional analyses and reconciliation procedures. Only with such analysis can such a discrepancy be adequately explained and reconciled with the other indications of value.

Summary

Numerous factors affect the analyst's decision about which business valuation approaches and methods to select. Of these factors, the professional judgment and technical expertise of the individual analyst is the most important.

Numerous factors also affect the analyst's selection of a weighting scheme regarding the value indications generated by the alternative valuation methods used. The weighting scheme selected indicates the degree of confidence that the analyst has (1) in the selected valuation method and (2) in the derived value indications. Clearly, the weighting scheme used should be appropriate, given the purpose and objective of the business valuation. Typically, an explicit weighting scheme should be presented and explained (either quantitatively or qualitatively) in the final business valuation synthesis and conclusion but with careful explanation of the analyst's thought process leading to the weightings.

Finally, alternative valuation methods usually yield value indications in a reasonably tight range. These value indications, then, provide mutually supportive evidence regarding the valuation synthesis and conclusion. When a business valuation method derives an outlier value indication, the analyst should thoroughly research and reconcile this value indication, in an attempt to explain—and correct—the apparent anomaly.

Chapter 27

Trade-off between Cash and Terms

I'll pay you any price you name if you'll let me name the terms.

Deal-Makers' Credo

There is substantial evidence that the terms of sale of a small business have a significant impact on the price.[1]

Glenn Desmond

As noted in previous chapters, most sales of small businesses and professional practices are consummated on terms other than cash. In most cases, the seller "carries the paper"; that is, the seller accepts an installment payment contract for the balance of the purchase price over and above the down payment.

The principal reason for this arrangement is that the typical buyer of a small business or professional practice does not have the personal resources to pay the full purchase price in cash. And most lending institutions would not regard the subject small business or professional practice as adequate collateral to support a term loan of the balance of the purchase price. In no other broad category of transactions is it nearly as common for the seller to take an installment contract for a significant portion of the selling price. Larger businesses usually sell to larger corporations. These acquirers pay in cash or possibly in stock (if the buyer is a publicly traded company). Buyers of real estate can usually obtain conventional debt financing for a substantial portion of the total purchase price by using the real estate as collateral (thus cashing out the seller).

In a sale of a small business or professional practice on terms, the seller is, in effect, making a loan to the buyer to finance the purchase. It is, therefore, of the utmost importance to the seller to have a good contract on the sale, with adequate protective covenants.

The purpose of this chapter is to explain the difference between the face value of a transaction on terms and the equivalent cash value of that transaction. This difference is usually quite significant in the sale of small businesses and professional practices. This is because the rate of interest on contracts carried by the seller is usually far below a market rate of interest for any other comparable contract. In fact, for a large portion of the business transactions, conventional commercial financing would not be available at all.

The typical small business sale at a face value of $100,000 may have a cash equivalent value of only $80,000. This difference is probably greater than most analysts realize. Therefore, it is necessary for analysts dealing with small business and professional practice transactions to be able to convert the price of a deal on terms to an equivalent cash value (or vice versa). It is also necessary for analysts to be able to assess the differences in impact (in terms of cash equivalent value) between one set of terms and some alternative set of terms.

---

[1]Glenn M. Desmond, *Handbook of Small Business Formulas and Rules of Thumb*, 2d ed. (Camden, ME: Valuation Press, 1993), p. 20.

Converting a Price on Terms to a Cash Equivalent Value

A Typical Example

Let's start off with an example. John owns a small marina, which he sells on terms for a face amount of $100,000. The terms are as follows:

John's Marina

Sale price	$100,000
Down payment	20%

The balance of the sale price is to be paid in equal monthly installments including principal and interest at the rate of 8 percent per annum over a period of 10 years.

Let's assume that the average yield on 10-year, high-grade corporate bonds is 10 percent. The buyer's installment note, secured by the small marina, is not as high-quality a debt instrument as the high-grade corporate bond. Therefore, a reasonable market rate of interest for a note of such characteristics would have to be higher, let's say 13 percent. (We will discuss how to estimate an applicable market rate in a subsequent section.)

What is the cash equivalent value of this transaction? The first step is to compute the amount of the monthly payments that John will receive. The buyer will be paying John 120 monthly payments of principal plus interest at 0.67 percent per month (i.e., 8 percent annual rate ÷ 12 months = 0.67%) on a contract balance of $80,000. This schedule works out to monthly payments of $970.62.

The next step is to convert this stream of 120 monthly payments to a cash equivalent value using a market rate of interest. The question here is: How much cash would a lender pay for this installment contract in order for it to provide the lender a rate of return of 13 percent per year (1.08 percent per month)?

The formula for this is:

$$PV = \sum_{i=1}^{n} \frac{PMT_i}{(1 + k_d)^i}$$

where:

PV = Present value
n = Number of payments
PMT = Amount of monthly payment in dollars
i = The ith payment
k_d = Discount rate (i.e., the lender's required rate of return, or the cost of intermediate- to long-term debt for this business)

Substituting values into this formula gives us the following calculation:

$$PV = \sum_{i=1}^{120} \frac{\$970.62}{(1 + .0108)^i}$$

$$= \frac{\$970.62}{1.0108} + \frac{\$970.62}{1.0108^2} + \ldots + \frac{\$970.62}{1.0108^{120}}$$

$$= \$65,007$$

In this example, John sold his marina for $20,000 cash, plus a note with a present value of $65,007, for a total of $85,007 cash equivalent value.

Some Variations

Extending the Contract. Let's suppose that John accepted a note under the same terms and conditions but with the payments spread out over 15 years instead of 10. In this case, using similar calculations, he would receive monthly payments of $764.52 for 180 months. Also using the same formula, the present value of his contract at a 13 percent annual market rate would be $60,424.93, or a total present value of $20,000 + $60,424.93 = $80,425. In this variation, the cash equivalent value is $4,582 less than in the 10-year example.

Accepting a Lower Contract Interest Rate. Let's suppose that John had accepted a contract with an interest rate of 6.0 percent (0.5 percent per month), instead of 8 percent. Using similar calculations, on a 10-year contract, he would receive payments of $888.16 per month for 120 months. At a 13 percent market rate of interest, the present value of his contract balance would be $59,484.27. Adding this amount to his $20,000 down payment would indicate a cash equivalent value for the deal of $79,484, or $5,523 less than the value with an 8 percent interest rate.

Variations in Market Rate of Interest. Suppose that John made the same deal when the market rate of interest on his contract was about 16 percent. He would receive $970.62 per month for 120 months, as in the original example. However, the present value of his contract would have to be figured by discounting his payments back to the present time at 1.3 percent per month (i.e., 16 ÷ 12 = 1.3 percent). Using this formula, the present value of his contract would be $57,943. Adding this amount to the down payment of $20,000 would indicate a cash equivalent value for the deal of $77,943, or $7,064 less than if the market rate of interest were 13 percent.

Combining the Variations. For our last variation in this series, we'll assume that John took his $80,000 balance in the form of an installment note with equal monthly payments of principal plus a 7.2 percent annual rate of interest for 15 years (180 months), at a time when a market rate of interest on an installment note such as this would be 16 percent. In this case, he would receive 180 monthly payments of $728.04. The present value of these payments at a 16 percent annual market rate of interest would be $49,570. Adding the $20,000 down payment gives a cash equivalent value for the deal of $69,570, or about 30 percent less than the $100,000 price or face amount of the deal.

Estimating the Applicable Market Interest

All of the foregoing is simple mechanical arithmetic, which can be performed on an inexpensive pocket calculator in a few seconds. However, estimating the applicable market interest rate requires a little more data and more professional judgment. Exhibit 27-1 offers a quick listing of lending rates and other cost of capital data.

Exhibit 27–1

COST OF CAPITAL

Treasury Instrument Yields (11/17/97)		Equity Risk Premium[1]	
		Arithmetic	Geometric
30-day	4.85%	8.9%	7.0%
5-year	5.82%	7.9%	6.0%
20-year	6.18%	7.5%	5.6%
Small stock premium (< $197 million market cap)[1]			3.5%
10th decile size premium (< $94 million market cap)[1]			5.8%
Prime lending rate			8.5%
Dow Jones 20-bond yield			6.96%
Barron's intermediate grade bonds		7.05%	
High yield estimate[2]		Mean 10.19%	Median 8.60%
Dow Jones Industrials P/E multiples[3]:			
Current 19.5	On '97 estimates 17.9%	On '98 estimates 15.5%	
Long-term inflation rate estimate[4]			2.90%

1. Computed using data from *Stocks, Bonds, Bills, and Inflation 1997 Yearbook*™ (Chicago: Ibbotson Associates, 1997, annual updates work by Roger G. Ibbotson and Rex Sinquefield). Used with permission. All rights reserved. We highly recommend that analysts using Ibbotson data for cost of capital have the current year's book and thoroughly understand the derivation of the numbers used.
2. *The Wall Street Journal*, November 17, 1997, computations by *Shannon Pratt's Business Valuation Update*.
3. *Barron's*, November 17, 1997.
4. *Livingston Survey* (Philadelphia: Federal Reserve Bank of Philadelphia, June 1997).

SOURCE: Shannon Pratt's Business Valuation Update, December 1997, p. 13.

Data on Market Interest Rates

Bank Lending Rates. Bank prime lending rates (the rates that banks charge large borrowers with solid credit ratings) are published regularly in newspapers and business magazines. One can also learn the bank's current prime lending rate with a telephone call to any bank. Banks usually make short-term loans to small businesses at about 2 to 3 percentage points above their prime lending rates. This is true if the business is sound and the loan is well secured, usually by current accounts receivable and/or inventory and personal guarantees. Longer-term loans would normally carry a somewhat higher rate.

Personal Guarantees and Covenants. It is noteworthy that banks virtually always require the owner's personal guaranty for loans to small businesses and professional practices. If the seller does not get a personal guaranty from the buyer, this certainly lessens the value of the note relative to the value of a note secured by a personal guarantee as well as by business assets. Banks also impose stringent covenants requiring maintenance of certain financial ratios and limitations on owner's compensation, capital expenditures, and other actions. At least three percentage points is a reasonable estimate of the value of the personal guarantee factor in normal circumstances.

Corporate Bond Rates. Corporate bonds are rated in terms of their quality (i.e., the degree of certainty that the corporation will be able to pay the bonds' interest and principal on time) by various rating services, such as Standard & Poor's and Moody's. Moody's ratings, for example, start with Aaa as the highest and go down through a grade of C, which is very speculative. *Barron's* and other publications publish average yields for high-grade corporate bonds down through Baa. For medium-grade and lower-grade corporate bonds, *The Wall Street Journal* carries a listing of high-yield bonds weekly. Yields for additional individual bonds can be found in Standard & Poor's *Bond Guide* and Moody's *Bond Record.* Rarely do small business notes provide protection to the lender similar to that provided by the covenants and other indenture protections of even the lowest grade corporate bonds.[2]

Using Professional Judgment

An installment note receivable, secured by the stock and/or assets of a small business or professional practice, is almost always riskier than any of the foregoing debt instruments. Therefore, an installment note receivable should have a higher market interest rate. It is unlikely that an installment contract receivable on a small business sale would have

---

[2]For an explanation of how to grade and value these bonds, see Chapter 20, "Debt Securities," in Shannon P. Pratt, Robert F. Reilly, and Robert P. Schweihs, *Valuing a Business: The Analysis and Appraisal of Closely Held Companies*, 3d ed. (Burr Ridge, IL: McGraw-Hill, 1996).

a quality rating any better than grade Caa to C for corporate bonds (if that high).

Furthermore, all the foregoing debt instruments are readily marketable, while an installment contract receivable on a small business is not. Banks sell good-quality loans to other banks. Mortgage lenders sell mortgages to other mortgage lenders. Corporate bonds are traded on the public market (the New York Stock Exchange, the American Stock Exchange, and the over-the-counter market). There is no such ready market for installment contracts receivable on small businesses and professional practices.

In order to estimate an appropriate market rate for a small business installment contract, the number of percentage points that needs to be added to the benchmark rates discussed above depends on the degree of risk. If (1) there is a substantial down payment, if (2) the note is relatively short in duration (perhaps three to five years), and if (3) it is well secured and well protected by covenants in the purchase agreement, only a few percentage points need to be added in order to account for the additional risk of an installment contract. If the down payment is small, the length of the term long, and protective covenants poor or absent, no rate may be high enough.

Taking these factors into consideration, we would suggest that the payments due on a term note well collateralized by small business or professional practice assets, personal guarantees, and protective covenants should usually be discounted at an annual rate of not less than prime plus 3 percent. This is the rate to be used to convert the face value to a cash equivalent present value. Without the personal guarantee but with asset and protective covenant security, a reasonable discount rate to value the note may be prime plus 6 percent. Exhibit 27-1 presents a good summary of benchmark data used to derive capital costs for small businesses.

Converting a Cash Value to a Price on Terms

Let's say that Dusty Trail has concluded that the value of his Paperback Western Bookstore on a cash basis is $150,000. However, he expects to sell the business on terms, probably one-third ($50,000) down and the balance ($100,000 cash equivalent) on a contract, with interest at something less than a market rate. He now wants to determine the price and terms that would give him his $150,000 cash equivalent value.

The first step is to figure out a market rate of interest for the contract, probably by using one or more of the benchmark rates discussed in the previous section for guidance. Let's say the high-grade corporate bond yield is 10 percent. He thinks that the present contract should cost about 2 percent over the high-grade corporate bond rate (or about 12 percent) to obtain the credit on an arm's-length basis in the open market. (That is not a very high premium over the rate for top-quality credit; it implies that he believes there will not be a very high degree of risk associated with the credit.)

The second step is to determine what the monthly payments on the contract will be at a market rate of interest. If he assumes the contract will run for seven years (84 months), the net level payments of principal and interest on $100,000, at a 12 percent annual rate (1 percent per month) are $1,765.27 per month. The monthly payments per $100 of contract balance for various rates of interest, for various lengths of time, are shown in Exhibit 27-2.

The third and final step is to convert this stream of monthly payments back to a contract face value on the basis of the rate of interest that will be shown on the contract. Let's say that Dusty thinks the rate of interest shown on the contract will be 8 percent per annum, or the equivalent of 0.6667 percent per month. On that basis, the face value of the contract balance should be $113,258.63.

In other words, if the rate of interest on the contract is 8 percent, it takes about $113,000 of face value to have a cash equivalent value of $100,000. This is true if the market rate of interest on such a contract is 12 percent and the term of the contract is seven years. The business could be sold for $163,000, with $50,000 down and a contract balance of $113,000. The monthly payments would include interest at an 8 percent annual rate for 84 months. And the deal would have a cash equivalent value of about $150,000. Exhibit 27-3 presents the effect of different market rates on various contract terms.

Exhibit 27–2

MONTHLY PAYMENT REQUIRED PER $100 OF CONTRACT BALANCE

Contract Interest Rate	Number of Payments												
	12	18	24	30	36	48	60	72	84	96	120	144	180
6%	8.61	5.82	4.43	3.60	3.04	2.35	1.93	1.66	1.46	1.31	1.11	0.98	0.84
7%	8.65	5.87	4.48	3.64	3.09	2.39	1.98	1.70	1.51	1.36	1.16	1.03	0.90
8%	8.70	5.91	4.52	3.69	3.13	2.44	2.03	1.75	1.56	1.41	1.21	1.08	0.96
9%	8.75	5.96	4.57	3.73	3.18	2.49	2.08	1.80	1.61	1.47	1.27	1.14	1.01
10%	8.79	6.01	4.61	3.78	3.23	2.54	2.12	1.85	1.66	1.52	1.32	1.20	1.07
11%	8.84	6.05	4.66	3.83	3.27	2.58	2.17	1.90	1.71	1.57	1.38	1.25	1.14
12%	8.88	6.10	4.71	3.87	3.32	2.63	2.22	1.96	1.77	1.63	1.43	1.31	1.20
13%	8.93	6.14	4.75	3.92	3.37	2.68	2.28	2.01	1.82	1.68	1.49	1.37	1.27
14%	8.98	6.19	4.80	3.97	3.42	2.73	2.33	2.06	1.87	1.74	1.55	1.44	1.33
15%	9.03	6.24	4.85	4.02	3.47	2.78	2.38	2.11	1.93	1.79	1.61	1.50	1.40
16%	9.07	6.29	4.90	4.07	3.52	2.83	2.43	2.17	1.99	1.85	1.68	1.57	1.47
17%	9.12	6.33	4.94	4.11	3.57	2.89	2.49	2.22	2.04	1.91	1.74	1.63	1.54
18%	9.17	6.38	4.99	4.16	3.62	2.94	2.54	2.28	2.10	1.97	1.80	1.70	1.61

Exhibit 27–3

PRESENT VALUE OF A $1,000 CONTRACT
AT VARIOUS MARKET RATES

"Market Rate" 10%

Contract Interest Rate	Number of Months											
	24	30	36	48	60	72	84	96	120	144	180	240
12%	1,020	1,025	1,029	1,038	1,047	1,055	1,063	1,071	1,086	1,099	1,117	1,141
11%	1,010	1,012	1,015	1,019	1,023	1,027	1,031	1,035	1,042	1,049	1,058	1,070
10%	1,000	1,000	1,000	1,000	1,000	1,000	1,000	1,000	1,000	1,000	1,000	1,000
9%	990	988	986	981	977	973	969	965	959	952	944	932
8%	980	976	971	963	954	946	939	932	918	906	889	867
7%	970	964	957	944	932	920	909	898	879	861	836	803
6%	960	952	943	926	910	895	880	866	840	817	785	742
5%	951	940	929	908	888	869	851	834	803	774	736	684

"Market Rate" 11%

Contract Interest Rate	Number of Months											
	24	30	36	48	60	72	84	96	120	144	180	240
12%	1,010	1,012	1,015	1,019	1,023	1,027	1,031	1,035	1,042	1,048	1,056	1,067
11%	1,000	1,000	1,000	1,000	1,000	1,000	1,000	1,000	1,000	1,000	1,000	1,000
10%	990	988	986	981	977	973	970	966	959	953	945	935
9%	980	976	971	963	955	947	940	933	920	908	892	872
8%	970	964	957	945	933	921	910	900	881	864	841	810
7%	961	952	943	927	911	896	881	868	843	820	791	751
6%	951	940	929	909	889	871	853	837	806	778	742	694
5%	941	928	915	891	868	846	825	806	770	738	696	639

"Market Rate" 12%

Contract Interest Rate	Number of Months											
	24	30	36	48	60	72	84	96	120	144	180	240
12%	1,000	1,000	1,000	1,000	1,000	1,000	1,000	1,000	1,000	1,000	1,000	1,000
11%	990	988	986	981	977	974	970	967	960	954	947	937
10%	980	976	971	963	955	948	940	934	921	910	895	876
9%	970	964	957	945	933	922	911	901	883	866	845	817
8%	961	952	943	927	912	897	883	870	846	824	796	760
7%	951	940	930	909	890	872	855	839	809	783	749	704
6%	942	929	916	892	869	848	828	809	774	743	703	651
5%	932	917	902	875	848	824	801	779	739	704	659	599

Contingent Payments

Many small businesses and professional practices are sold at a "price" that is actually paid only if certain events occur. Such events may be the achievement of certain levels of revenues and/or profits.

Exhibit 27–3 continued

PRESENT VALUE OF A $1,000 CONTRACT
AT VARIOUS MARKET RATES

"Market Rate" 13%

Contract Interest Rate	Number of Months											
	24	30	36	48	60	72	84	96	120	144	180	240
12%	990	988	986	982	978	974	970	967	961	955	949	940
11%	980	976	972	963	956	948	941	935	923	912	898	881
10%	971	964	958	945	934	923	913	903	885	869	849	824
9%	961	952	944	928	912	898	884	872	848	828	802	768
8%	951	941	930	910	891	873	857	841	813	787	755	714
7%	942	929	916	893	870	849	830	811	778	748	710	662
6%	932	917	903	875	850	826	803	782	744	710	667	612
5%	923	906	890	858	829	802	777	753	710	673	625	563

"Market Rate" 14%

Contract Interest Rate	Number of Months											
	24	30	36	48	60	72	84	96	120	144	180	240
12%	980	976	972	964	956	949	942	936	924	914	901	885
11%	971	964	958	946	934	924	914	904	887	872	853	830
10%	961	952	944	928	913	899	886	874	851	832	807	776
9%	952	941	930	911	892	875	859	843	816	792	762	724
8%	942	929	917	893	871	851	832	814	781	753	718	673
7%	933	918	903	876	851	827	805	785	748	716	675	623
6%	923	906	890	859	831	804	780	756	715	679	634	576
5%	914	895	877	843	811	782	754	729	683	644	594	531

"Market Rate" 15%

Contract Interest Rate	Number of Months											
	24	30	36	48	60	72	84	96	120	144	180	240
12%	971	964	958	946	935	925	915	906	889	875	858	836
11%	961	953	944	929	914	900	887	875	854	835	812	784
10%	952	941	931	911	893	876	860	846	819	796	768	733
9%	942	930	917	894	873	852	834	816	785	758	725	683
8%	933	918	904	877	852	829	808	788	752	721	683	635
7%	923	907	891	860	832	806	782	760	720	685	642	589
6%	914	895	878	844	813	784	757	732	688	650	603	544
5%	905	884	865	827	793	762	732	705	657	616	565	501

The most common contingency is the retention of existing clients. For example, the price may be equal to 100 percent of the latest 12 months' revenues. However, it may be paid over a period of two to five years, and then only to the extent that each existing client produces revenues at or above the level of the last 12 months. To the extent that any client does not stay with the business, the contingent payments are reduced pro rata with the shortfall in revenue with that client.

Exhibit 27–3 concluded

PRESENT VALUE OF A $1,000 CONTRACT
AT VARIOUS MARKET RATES

"Market Rate" 16%

Contract Interest Rate	Number of Months											
	24	30	36	48	60	72	84	96	120	144	180	240
12%	961	953	945	929	915	901	889	877	856	839	817	791
11%	952	941	931	912	894	877	862	848	822	801	774	742
10%	942	930	918	895	874	854	836	819	789	763	732	694
9%	933	919	905	878	854	831	810	791	756	727	691	647
8%	924	907	891	861	834	808	785	763	724	691	651	601
7%	914	896	878	845	814	786	760	736	693	657	612	557
6%	905	885	865	829	795	764	736	709	663	623	575	515
5%	896	874	852	813	776	742	712	683	633	591	538	474

"Market Rate" 17%

Contract Interest Rate	Number of Months											
	24	30	36	48	60	72	84	96	120	144	180	240
12%	952	942	932	913	895	879	864	850	826	805	780	751
11%	943	930	918	896	875	856	838	822	793	768	739	704
10%	933	919	905	879	855	833	812	794	760	732	698	658
9%	924	908	892	862	835	810	787	766	729	697	659	613
8%	915	896	879	846	816	788	763	739	698	663	621	570
7%	906	885	866	830	797	766	739	713	668	630	584	529
6%	896	874	853	814	778	745	715	687	639	598	548	488
5%	887	863	841	798	759	724	692	662	610	567	514	450

"Market Rate" 18%

Contract Interest Rate	Number of Months											
	24	30	36	48	60	72	84	96	120	144	180	240
12%	943	931	919	896	876	857	840	824	796	773	745	713
11%	934	919	906	880	856	835	815	796	764	738	706	669
10%	924	908	893	863	837	812	790	769	733	703	667	625
9%	915	897	880	847	817	790	765	743	703	670	630	583
8%	906	886	867	831	798	769	742	717	673	637	593	542
7%	897	875	854	815	780	748	718	691	644	605	558	502
6%	888	864	841	799	761	727	695	666	616	574	524	464
5%	879	853	829	784	743	706	672	642	589	544	491	428

To convert a price subject to contingencies to a cash equivalent value, the analyst should use his or her best judgment to put a probability on the collection of each year's contingent payments and reduce each year's face value proceeds by the probability of actually realizing those proceeds. Then each year's probability-adjusted revenues from existing clients is discounted to a present value, as in the preceding sections.

A simple example will demonstrate the arithmetic. Let's assume a transaction price of $500,000, with nothing down, $250,000 payable at the end of the first year, $250,000 payable at the end of the second year, and each payment adjusted pro rata for any existing client revenues not retained. Let's assume that the $500,000 represents 100 percent of the last 12 months' revenues. And let's assume that there is 80 percent retention the first year and 60 percent the second year. Let's also assume a present value discount rate on the payments of 18 percent. The arithmetic is as follows:

Step 1: Probability of realization

$$Year\ 1:\ \frac{\$400,000}{\$500,000} = .80$$

$$Year\ 2:\ \frac{\$300,000}{\$500,000} = .60$$

Step 2: Multiply probability times amount paid if 100% retained

	Full Payment		Retention Probability		Expected Payment
Year 1:	$250,000	×	.80	=	$200,000
Year 2:	$250,000	×	.60	=	$150,000

Step 3: Discount expected payment to present value

$$\frac{\$200,000}{(1 + .18)} + \frac{\$150,000}{(1 + .18)^2}$$

$$= \$169,492\ 1\ 107,728$$

$$= \$277,220$$

In the above case, the estimated cash equivalent value is $277,220, or approximately 55 percent of the transaction "price" of $500,000.

Summary

A very high percentage of small businesses and professional practices are sold on some terms other than cash. The terms on the noncash portion of the price most commonly take one or both of two forms: (1) a fixed-price promissory note, usually with interest at a rate below an arm's-length market rate of interest for a promissory note of comparable risk, and/or (2) a variable price based on certain contingencies, most often retention of revenues from existing clients.

Empirical data on the sale transactions for comparative companies are often used for guidance in negotiating a price for a transaction in a similar company. This is valid if the terms on the subject company transaction are similar to the terms on the guideline company transactions. Many, but not all, of the transactions in the comparative transaction databases discussed in Chapter 21 give the sale terms for comparative purposes.

However, if transactions on noncash terms are to be used as comparative data for guidance in estimating a cash-equivalent fair market value for a subject company, the transaction price should be adjusted to a cash-equivalent fair market value. This chapter has explained the data to consider and the arithmetic to use to make that adjustment.

Furthermore, if the analyst starts with a cash equivalent value but expects that a transaction is most likely to occur on noncash terms, the chapter discussed how to convert a cash equivalent value to a price on the expected terms.

As the examples have shown, the trade-off between cash and terms can be a significant factor in negotiating business transactions and using transaction data; a cash equivalent value can be 20 to 50 percent less than the face value price under a set of terms favorable to the buyer.

Chapter 28

Making a Reality Check: Is the Value Estimate Reasonable?

Inexperienced analysts sometimes find they have applied all of the appropriate valuation approaches, methods, and procedures, only to reach an unreasonable (and incredible) value conclusion. This phenomenon occurs most commonly with the following two types of valuation practitioners:

1. *Part-time appraisers.* These are full-time (and usually quite competent) accountants, economists, and industry consultants who perform business valuation engagements on an occasional basis.
2. *Notational appraisers.* These are analysts who perform business valuations for various notational purposes (e.g., estate planning, insurance, litigation, etc.) but who do not regularly perform business valuations for transactional purposes (i.e., for the actual purchase or sale of small businesses and professional practices). Since these notational appraisers do not regularly participate in the real world of transactional "deal flow," they often are not able to recognize an unreasonable value conclusion

Inexperienced analysts may be able answer yes to the two valuation reconciliation questions below and yet may still be unable to recognize an unreasonable value conclusion.

1. Did I appraise the right thing (i.e., the correct appraisal subject)?
2. Did I appraise the right thing the right way (i.e., apply correct valuation procedures)?

However, these analysts cannot answer yes to the following question: Did I correctly apply the correct valuation procedures?

Inexperienced analysts are not always sensitive to the fact that slight errors in estimating individual valuation variables can greatly distort the value estimate—even when all of the "mechanical" valuation methodology is correctly applied. For example, small errors in measuring economic income or in estimating present value discount rates, direct capitalization rates, or expected long-term growth rates can materially distort business value estimates.

This chapter will present some of the procedures that analysts can use to test whether the value estimate is reasonable.

Cash Available for Debt Service

As was noted in earlier chapters, the large majority of sales of small businesses and professional practices are financed. Most often these transactions are financed by the seller. Sometimes they are financed by an outside lender. It is in the interest of both the buyer and the lender (whether the lender is the seller or an outside lender) to be sure that the business purchase deal is structured so that the debt service (i.e., the loan principal and interest payments) can be met.

Of course, the key phrase in the previous paragraph is "so that debt service can be met." In most cases, the source of the business acquisition debt repayment will be cash generated by the subject small business or professional practice.

To measure this ability to cover the debt service, analysts need to consider a variable not previously defined or discussed in this book. This variable is referred to as *cash available for debt service*. This phrase is descriptive; it is not a term with specific meaning that is universally accepted in the annals of finance and economics. Estimating the amount of cash available for debt service is a matter of using common sense in light of the basic facts of each case.

As a generalized framework to measure the affordability of a small business purchase, we define cash available for debt service as the following measure of economic income:

1. Before interest and principal payments (since we are measuring the coverage of those cash expenditures).
2. Before depreciation and amortization (or other noncash) expenses.
3. After reasonable compensation for the employee-related services of the owner.
4. After capital expenditures, including both fixed asset replacements and additions.
5. After federal and state income taxes (based on taxable income per the current Internal Revenue Code).

The above list assumes that the small business or professional practice itself will be the source of the funds to cover each item on the list. To the extent that funds are available from other sources for one or more of the cash flow requirements and the buyer is willing to use such sources, the list may be modified.

Amount of Debt Service Coverage Needed

The amount of debt service coverage that is required depends largely on the degree of risk in the company's expected cash flow. To the extent that the expected cash flow is highly uncertain or volatile from year to year, the amount of debt service coverage in an average year should be higher.

The important ratio to consider in this part of the analysis is the *debt service coverage multiple* (sometimes simply called the *debt coverage ratio*). For purposes of this analysis, we will define the debt service coverage ratio as follows:

$$Debt\ Service\ Coverage\ Multiple = \frac{Cash\ Available\ for\ Debt\ Service}{Annual\ Debt\ Service\ Payment}$$

where:

1. Cash available for debt service is defined as in the previous section.
2. Annual debt service payment equals the total principal and interest payments during the year.

The question becomes: What is a reasonable debt coverage multiple? Is a multiple of one times sufficient? Is a multiple of two times necessary? There is no single answer to this question. However, two factors greatly influence what is considered an adequate debt coverage multiple:

1. The industry benchmark.
2. Lenders' requirements.

First, all acquisition financing sources (both the seller and independent sources) look to industry average debt coverage multiples. They would expect the subject business to generate the industry average debt coverage multiple as a minimum benchmark.

Second, individual lenders have their own criteria. Commercial banks have different criteria than finance companies. And they both have different criteria than merchant banks. The only way to learn the criteria a particular financing source uses is to ask that financing source.

Possible Adjustments to the Purchase Contract

If the business purchase contract terms do not seem affordable by a comfortable margin, adjustments to the purchase price or adjustments to the contemplated terms—particularly with regard to debt service—may be considered. The length of the debt repayment period in the purchase contract may be extended. The debt service payments may be varied (perhaps with interest only for a time or with an increasing payment schedule if the cash available is expected to be low at first but then increasing). Also, some debt service payments may be contingent on the level of cash flow. And there may be a longer-term amortization of the business acquisition debt—with a balloon payment.

Purchase contracts with contingencies in the debt service payment schedule are not that unusual for businesses that are known to be cyclical. For example, the principal portion of the payment, or even the entire principal and interest payment, may be suspended for a year if the company's cash flow is negative. Of course, debt service is only suspended, not forgiven. The effect of the suspension is that the acquisition loan repayment schedule is extended by one year. There may also be a range of minimum and maximum debt service payments per year, depending on the amount of available cash flow generated by the acquired company.

Other factors that can be negotiated with regard to the acquisition financing include (1) the amortization period of the loan, and (2) the timing (and the existence) of a balloon payment. A 10-year acquisition loan amortization with a 5-year balloon payment means that the periodic principal and interest payments are of an amount that would pay off the acquisition loan in 10 years. However, at the end of the fifth year, the remaining unpaid acquisition loan balance becomes payable all at once.

If reasonable acquisition financing alternatives have been considered and if the purchase price cannot be amortized over a reasonable period of time, this indicates that the business value estimate is not reasonable. Arguably, the most effective reality check for a business value estimate is whether or not a buyer could afford to pay (i.e., be able to finance) the purchase price.

Protective Covenants in the Purchase Contract

From the viewpoint of either an independent lender or a seller providing acquisition financing, it obviously is important to have covenants in the purchase contract that will protect the ability of the subject business or practice to generate adequate cash flow to cover the debt service. Such covenants usually restrict such items as (1) the new owner's compensation, (2) capital expenditures above a stated amount, (3) any investments outside of the normal course of business operations, and (4) the assumption of any other indebtedness.

Example

Exhibit 28-1 presents a reality check analysis with regard to the valuation—and the proposed sale—of Simple Small Business, Inc.

Let's begin with an estimated value of $1,000,000 for the common stock of Simple Small Business, Inc. (hereinafter "Simple"). The seller of this small business has agreed to finance the acquisition under the following terms: a $400,000 down payment and a five-year term note to cover the balance of $600,000 at a 12 percent simple interest rate. The debt service on this term note would be equal annual payments of principal and interest. This means that the seller has agreed to accept a cash equivalent value of less that $1 million.

The first step in analyzing whether the subject company can cover this debt service is to calculate Simple's cash available for debt service. The company's expected pretax net income under the new owner is estimated to be $200,000. In order to calculate the company's income tax

Exhibit 28–1

SIMPLE SMALL BUSINESS, INC.
ANALYSIS OF CASH AVAILABLE FOR DEBT SERVICE

The affordability of the debt service related to the purchase of a company increases with either a decreased interest rate or an increased term of the acquisition loan.

Length of the acquisition financing	5 Years	5 Years	10 Years
Business equity value	$1,000,000	$1,000,000	$1,000,000
Purchase price down payment	400,000	400,000	400,000
Acquisition debt	600,000	600,000	600,000
Debt interest rate	12%	6%	12%
Projected pretax income	200,000	200,000	200,000
Interest expense associated with acquisition debt	72,000	36,000	72,000
Adjusted pretax income	128,000	164,000	128,000
Federal and state income taxes	51,000	66,000	51,000
Net income	77,000	98,000	77,000
Plus:			
Depreciation expense (net of assumed capital expenditures)	60,000	60,000	60,000
Interest expense	72,000	36,000	72,000
Cash available for debt service	209,000	194,000	209,000
Annual debt service	166,446	142,438	106,191
Annual debt service coverage multiple	1.26 x	1.36 x	1.97 x

expense, we need to take into consideration that Simple will receive a tax deduction associated with the increased interest expense if the $600,000 is financed as part of the purchase contract. The first year's interest expense on the term note will be $72,000 (i.e., 12% × $600,000 = $72,000). This interest expense will reduce Simple's taxable income to $128,000 (i.e., $200,000 – $72,000 = $128,000). The statutory federal and state income taxes on this amount would be approximately $51,000, assuming an effective combined income tax rate of about 40 percent. This income tax expense will result in a net income after tax of $77,000 (i.e., $128,000 – $51,000 = $77,000).

As defined above, the cash available for debt service equals net income before depreciation and interest. That is computed as follows:

Net income after tax	$ 77,000
Depreciation expense (net of assumed capital expenditures)	60,000
Interest expense	72,000
Cash available for debt service	$209,000

The next step is to determine the debt service requirements that the term note provision of this purchase contract creates. A five-year term note for $600,000 bearing a 12 percent simple interest results in annual principal and interest payments of $166,446.

Therefore, the anticipated cash available for debt service is less than 1.3 times the projected annual debt service (i.e., $209,000 ÷ $166,446 = 1.26 times). This level of available cash relative to the requirement for annual debt service is relatively low. A prospective buyer probably would not want to enter into the business purchase agreement under these terms. The uncertainty surrounding the buyer's ability to service the acquisition loan makes the business sale contract more risky from the seller's viewpoint, as well.

It is unlikely that the seller will accept less than the $1,000,000 price for Simple, assuming that the seller is under no compulsion to sell. However, if the seller is going to realize that sale price, the seller will probably have to extend more favorable acquisition financing terms to the buyer. For example, if the seller extends the length of the term note to 10 years, the annual debt service becomes $106,191. Under this scenario, the cash available to service the debt is almost twice the amount of the debt (i.e., $209,000 ÷ $106,191 = 1.97 times). This is a much more comfortable debt service level, and it is probably something the buyer could live with. Another alternative, if the seller wanted to keep the acquisition financing period at five years, is that the seller would have to accept a lower interest rate on the debt or accept the more risky debt service level.

What this example points out is that, while a value of $1,000,000 was indicated for the Simple common stock, the reality check shows that the company could just barely afford the debt service relating to the purchase of the company—that is, if the acquisition financing terms are $400,000 down with the balance payable over 5 years at a 12 percent simple interest rate. The purchase of Simple becomes more affordable (1) if the acquisition financing is extended for 10 years or (2) if a lower interest rate is charged.

Therefore, the reality check indicated that a cash equivalent valuation of $1,000,000 may be on the high side when affordability is taken into consideration. This $1,000,000 valuation means that the debt service of the company will be a strain unless (1) the acquisition financing terms are spread out over 10 years or (2) a lower interest rate is accepted.

This example is based on normalized earnings, assuming no significant fluctuations from year to year. If cash available for debt service is likely to fluctuate significantly over the years, it would be reasonable to make a discrete projection for each year over the term of the acquisition financing.

Summary

One of the last steps in the valuation process should be a "reality check." By this we mean looking at the concluded value estimate from the perspective of (1) the business purchase and (2) acquisition financing terms. In order to pass the reality check, the value estimate should result in affirmative answers to the following two questions: Is it reasonable? and Is it affordable?

"Affordable" in this sense addresses the questions, How long will it take to pay off the acquisition price? and How much cushion is there between the expected cash flow and the required debt service (principal and interest payments) in case things don't go as well as expected?

If this analysis of the proposed deal elicits discomfort on the basis of either reasonableness or affordability, the value estimate may be suspect and should be reconsidered.

Chapter 29

Common Errors

Failure to Clearly Identify and/or Adhere to the Applicable Standard of Value
Rigid Categorization of Business Valuation Methods
Reliance on Real Estate Appraisal Methods
Reliance on Rules of Thumb
The "Assets Plus . . ." Method
Indiscriminate Use of Price/Earnings Multiples
    Failure to Identify What the Buyer Gets for the Price
    Applying Price/Earnings Multiples to Earnings That Are Not Comparable
    Applying Price/Earnings Multiples When Time Periods Are Not Comparable
    Using the Reciprocal of the Price/Earnings Multiple as the Required Rate of Return
    Failure to Make Appropriate Adjustments
Other Errors in Deriving Capitalization Rates
    Using Rates from an Earlier Time Period
    Applying Rates on "Safe" Investments to Small Business Investments
    Failure to Match the Capitalization Rate with the Earnings Base
    Mistaking Historical Results for Required Rates of Return
Failure to Estimate a Realistic Normalized Earnings Base
    Reliance on Past Results without Judgment
    Failure to Recognize Any Depreciation
    Not Allowing Compensation to Owner/Operator
Failure to Consider the Full Cost of the Purchase
    Working Capital Requirements
    Deferred Maintenance
    Other Investment Needed
Failure to Understand what the Indicated Value Represents
    What Assets and/or Liabilities Are Included?
    Asset versus Stock Valuation
    Ownership Characteristics
Assuming That the Buyer Will Pay for the Now and the Hereafter
Emphasis on Items Not in Proportion to Their Relative Importance
Inadequate Documentation

It is better to know that we do not know than to know not that we know not.

Wise Man's Saying

This is a fairly long chapter. It is long because so many analysts frequently perpetrate many common errors in their attempts to estimate values of small businesses and professional practices.

By identifying some of the errors that seem to recur most frequently, we hope that this chapter will assist those who are not professional business appraisers to critically review an analyst's appraisal of a business or practice and to correct—or at least confidently call attention to—apparent errors. We also hope this chapter will help the novice analyst avoid such pitfalls. Possibly, it may even help one or two veteran but misguided analysts to mend a few of their wayward ways.

Failure to Clearly Identify and/or Adhere to the Applicable Standard of Value

We cannot count the times we have seen business appraisals go awry for failure to follow the appropriate standard of value. The analyst should ensure that the standard of value is defined at the beginning of the assignment (in the engagement letter) and again at the beginning of the written report. (For a complete discussion of this topic, please refer to Chapter 3.)

Most problems seem to arise from failure to correctly or completely specify the standard of value at the outset. The other problems seem to come from not adhering to the standard of value in the valuation work product—even after it has been defined.

This issue is especially important in controversy situations, where the standard of value is frequently mandated by statute, judicial, or other binding requirements. Examples include divorce valuations, damage cases, tax cases, dissent or dissolution cases, and valuations performed pursuant to covenants in buy-sell or arbitration agreements. We often see completed appraisals that are entirely useless because the analyst ignored or misinterpreted the governing legal context.

Rigid Categorization of Business Valuation Methods

Watch out when you hear, "There are currently five accepted methods for valuing a business," or "Three methods exist for valuing a small business," and so on. While there are three generally accepted categories of valuation approaches, there is no finite number of individual methods for valuing small businesses and professional practices. One author once listed 32 valuation methods.[1]

There are three predominate sources from which a business or practice can generate economic income for its owners: (1) earnings, (2) sales of assets, and (3) sale of the business or practice. All valuation methods attempt to measure one or a combination of these three factors, directly or indirectly, and translate them into a present value. The various valuation methods are not discrete but, rather, are variations of each other, with considerable overlap.

In our experience, viewing the problem of estimating value in terms of a finite number of specific methods tends to go hand in hand with implementing each of the methods by using some specific formula. More often than not, the formula is applied without the benefit of experienced judgment as to whether or not it conforms to the economic realities of the situation. Estimating the value of a small business or professional practice is much more than a mechanical exercise. It requires large doses of informed judgment, distilled out of years of experience and extensive continuing education on the developments in the field of small business and professional practice valuation.

Reliance on Real Estate Appraisal Methods

As discussed more extensively in Chapter 6, the world of traditional real estate appraisal has categorized the valuation methods into three approaches: (1) the cost approach, (2) the sales comparison (market) approach, and (3) the income capitalization approach. Elements of these approaches are found in generally accepted business appraisal practices. However, analysts with a real estate background tend to force business valuation methods into these three real estate valuation approaches, without a full understanding of how the dynamics and microeconomic characteristics of operating businesses and professional practices differentiate such entities from inanimate parcels of real estate.

Chapter 5 deals with differences between the valuation of large businesses (some of which may be publicly traded) and the valuation of small businesses and professional practices. Chapter 6 deals with differences between appraising real estate and appraising small businesses and professional practices. It is our opinion that small businesses and professional practices, with their dynamics of people and operations, have more in common from a valuation viewpoint with their larger brethren than with inanimate real estate. As this book points out, an analyst schooled in techniques of security analysis, but without schooling in real estate, can adapt more adequately to the discipline of

---

[1]Thomas J. Martin and Mark Gustafson, *Valuing Your Business* (New York: Holt, Rinehart & Winston, 1980), p. 23.

small business and professional practice appraisal than can a real estate appraiser without such schooling in security analysis.

Reliance on Rules of Thumb

Glenn Desmond, one of the leading proponents of the use of rules of
thumb, makes the point that they should not be relied on exclusively,
without consideration of other valuation methods:

> Rule-of-thumb valuation formulas have long been used to value small
> businesses. However, formula valuations are not substitutes for careful
> consideration of other appropriate valuation methods that are applica-
> ble to the business being appraised.[2]
>
> There is no single formula that will work for every business.
> Formula multipliers offer ease of calculation, but they also obscure de-
> tails. This can be misleading. Net revenue multipliers are particularly
> troublesome because they are blind to the business's expense and profit
> history. It is easy to see how two businesses in any given industry group
> might have the same annual net revenue (ANR), yet show very differ-
> ent cash flows. A proper valuation will go beyond formulas and include
> a full financial analysis whenever possible.[3]

Some of the problems with rules of thumb were discussed in the sec-
tion "Problems in the Application of Gross Revenue Multiples," in
Chapter 20. Other problems are discussed in the accompanying article
(Exhibit 29-1) by Jay Fishman, who, as of this writing, is an active busi-
ness appraiser and former chairman of the American Society of
Appraisers Business Valuation Committee.

For industries in which a valuation rule of thumb is widely recognized, the analyst should consider it. However, the analyst should certainly not accept it at face value.

---

[2]Glenn Desmond, *Handbook of Small Business Valuation Formulas and Rules of Thumb,* 2nd
ed. (Camden, ME: Valuation Press, 1993), p. 3.
　[3]Ibid., p. 12.

Exhibit 29–1

THE PROBLEM WITH RULES OF THUMB
IN THE VALUATION OF CLOSELY-HELD ENTITIES

by Jay E. Fishman, ASA*

Recently we completed the valuation of a pharmacy in a matrimonial matter. Our search for comparable transactions yielded insufficient information to make a direct Market Data Approach useable. Accordingly, we relied on the other traditional methods used in the valuation of closely held businesses, including a Capitalization of Income Approach. Our client reviewed the report and quickly pointed out that we failed to consider the industry rule of thumb for the valuation of pharmacies, as discussed in various pharmacy journals and trade publications. Application of that formula would have produced a negative value for the common stock of the pharmacy and was not used by our client when he purchased the pharmacy three years before. The pharmacist thought that the negative value aspect was perfectly acceptable for matrimonial purposes, but showed great reluctance to use the formula to sell his store.

The pharmacy episode was followed by our involvement in a court case relating to the valuation of a new car dealership. In this matter, the wife's expert determined goodwill grounded on a so-called industry practice which estimated goodwill based on $1,500 for new cars sold on an annual basis. Cross-examination revealed that the so-called industry practice was not derived from actual sales of automobile dealerships, but was based on yet another expert's verbal representation to this witness. Interestingly, the subject new car dealership had an average gross profit margin on the sale of new cars of approximately $500 per car.

The search for a "quick-fix" to the complex problems surrounding the valuation of a closely held enterprise has led many to rely on rules of thumb or industry formulas. The above examples illustrate the enormous potential for abuse in applying these standards to the valuation of a closely held entity.

What are the rules of thumb? Rules of thumb or industry formulas are supposedly market derived units of comparison. The multiple or percentage contained in the formula is an expression of the relationship between gross purchase price and some indicator of the operating results of an enterprise. Accordingly, the sale of a casualty insurance brokerage concern is discussed in terms of cents per retained gallon and the sale of a medical practice is referred to in terms of a multiple or percentage of the gross revenue or of the net disposable income.

The use of a rule of thumb in the valuation of a closely held entity is actually a variation of the Market Comparison Approach. The Market Comparison Approach attempts to establish value via direct comparison with exchanges of similar assets in the marketplace. The use of direct Market Comparison is contingent on the availability of sales involving reasonably comparable businesses in a free and active marketplace. Adjustments for differences between the acquired businesses and the subject entity are then calculated. Examples of adjustments include differences in market share, profitability, capital structure and management depth. These adjustments result in the production of a multiple, usually related to earnings, cash flow or equity which is applied to the subject entity resulting in an expression of value.

Since rules of thumb or industry formulas are a variation of the direct Market Comparison Approach, certain minimum criteria must exist prior to their use in the valuation process. These criteria include the following:

- The single multiple or percentage must be derived from an adequate information base.
- The expert must understand the terms and conditions of each transaction in the information base.
- The transactions should involve reasonably similar businesses.
- Adjustments should be made for differences between the acquired companies and the entity under appraisement.

Problems with industry formulas. We have found that most industry formulas or rules of thumb are not derived from actual transactions in the marketplace. Industry formulas are commonly derived from textbooks, trade publications, verbal representations or other similar sources of information. Clearly, these sources of information will not provide the expert with sufficient information to render a meaningful opinion of value for the enterprise using these formulas. There are at least three fundamental problems associated with the industry formula "quick fix" approach. All of these fundamental problems are a result of their failure to meet the above minimum criteria.

First, the lack of knowledge concerning the actual transactions that comprise the industry formulas will lead to confusion concerning the property acquired by a buyer during a particular transaction. Buyers will commonly purchase the assets or the equity of an entity. Since the objective of an appraisal for matrimonial purposes is usually the common stock or equity portion of an enterprise, reliance on an industry formula that produces a value for the assets of an entity can fundamentally misstate the value of the equity for the subject firm.

Exhibit 29–1 continued

Second, the lack of an adequate data base can lead to considerable confusion over the actual purchase price paid for a comparable entity. An opinion of Market Value presumes a 100 percent cash price at the valuation date. Without knowledge of the actual transactions underlying a given group of comparables, the experts would be unable to determine the real purchase price paid for the comparable enterprises.

For example, a gross price of $100,000 could be listed as the purchase price for a comparable entity, but this purchase price could be paid over ten years with no interest. This would further reduce the Market Value paid by the buyer due to the time value of money. If the expert is unaware of the terms of the transaction, he or she would be unable to make such a time value of money adjustment. Therefore, the gross consideration would be confused with a 100 percent cash price at the valuation date and result in a distortion in the opinion of value using the industry formula.

Alternatively, the purchase price could be augmented by a covenant not to compete given to the seller over a period of years. This covenant not to compete could actually be part of the purchase price paid for the business, but was structured in this way for tax purposes. Again, without knowledge of the actual terms of the transaction, a misstatement of value relying on formulas derived from these types of transactions would occur.

Thirdly, most industry formulas in textbooks, trade publications and other sources presume a typical or average entity. Lacking knowledge of actual transactions results in distortions due to differences in profitability, capital structure, management and other important considerations inherent in what a buyer would offer for a business entity. The insufficient information base would result in the expert's inability to make these types of adjustments. The insufficient information base would make it impossible to gauge whether the subject enterprise is typical or atypical, and accordingly, would command a price superior or inferior to the typical multiple displayed in the industry formula.

For example, an accounting firm which could be valued on a one times gross basis would have the same value whether it was profitable or unprofitable. The same would apply as to whether it had a long term lease or short term lease, whether the gross revenue was generated by 100 small clients or 3 large clients. This hypothetical situation indicates the flaws inherent in using industry formulas without sufficient information.

Summary. There are no "quick fixes" to the valuation of closely held entities. It is essential to remember that industry formulas or rules of thumb are commonly not market derived representations of actual transactions. Since most industry formulas or rules of thumb are derived from textbooks, trade publications, verbal representations, or other similar sources of information, they are poor substitutes for the Direct Market Comparison Approach.

* Mr. Fishman is President of Financial Research, Inc., in Fort Washington, Pennsylvania.

SOURCE: *FAIR$HARE: The Matrimonial Law Monthly*, December 1984, p. 13. Reprinted with permission of Aspen Law & Business, a division of Aspen Publishers, Inc.

The "Assets Plus . . ." Method

Some business brokers and others seem to think that every small business and professional practice in existence is worth at least (1) its net tangible asset value (defined as replacement cost new, less depreciation, as discussed in Chapter 7) plus (2) some amount for goodwill (and/or whatever other intangible assets may exist).

That is not always true. Many businesses do not generate enough economic income to justify their net tangible asset value.

Business owners who blindly value their operating business on the basis of an asset-based approach—without regard to the business's earning power—are likely to become too asset-intensive and eventually just go quietly out of business.

Indiscriminate Use of Price/Earnings Multiples

Valuation by the good old price/earnings (P/E) multiple has broad appeal. It seems so natural because everyone has heard of it, and it is apparently so simple. Just take the company earnings, apply a pricing multiple, and you have a value. P/E multiples for thousands of publicly traded stocks are published daily. By simply picking a P/E multiple and deciding what level of earnings for the subject company to apply it to, you can come up with almost any value you like. What could be better? It is a valuation method that is simple, widely used, and easily manipulated (albeit more frequently out of ignorance than malice aforethought). And it seems to support almost any desired value estimate.

The data used to generate the P/E multiple should be from companies that have characteristics similar to the characteristics of the subject company. Data from companies that are not comparable are unlikely to be informative.

The fundamental data used to generate the P/E multiple should be prepared on the same basis as the data to which it is being applied, including, for example, any appropriate adjustments for differences in accounting treatment and nonrecurring events.

Analysts should also understand the following characteristics of publicly traded stocks in order to use their P/E multiples for guidance in valuing small businesses and professional practices:

1. The publicly traded market prices of the stock represent minority ownership interests, not controlling ownership interests.
2. The stocks are highly liquid; they can almost always be sold in a matter of minutes with cash delivered to the seller in three business days.
3. The prices are for stock in a corporation and do not represent a direct purchase of any combination of the corporation's assets.
4. The P/E multiples apply to earnings after depreciation and amortization; after interest on all short-term and long-term debt; after compensation to all employees in the business, including stockholder/employees; and after all federal and state corporate income taxes.
5. The earnings are from audited statements prepared in accordance with generally accepted accounting principles (GAAP).
6. The price in the P/E multiple usually is the price of the last transaction on the day before the quotation was published.
7. The earnings in the P/E multiple are usually what are called "latest 12 months' trailing earnings"—that is, the earnings figure for the 12 months ending with the latest quarter for which the company has reported earnings.

Most common errors in the use of P/E multiples stem from failure to recognize one or a combination of the above characteristics of public company P/E multiples.

Failure to Identify What the Buyer Gets for the Price

For the price that becomes the numerator in the P/E multiple, the buyer receives a share of stock representing a proportionate equity interest in a total corporate enterprise. It is an indirect, residual, proportionate interest in all assets, subject to all liabilities, and with no direct claim on any assets. A common error is to use such a P/E multiple to price an asset purchase of a small business or professional practice. The error is that the use of the P/E multiple does not recognize the fact that the combination of assets actually being transferred may be quite different from the stock being bought for the price in the P/E multiple.

Applying Price/Earnings Multiples to Earnings that Are Not Comparable

The following are a few examples of applying public company P/E multiples to levels of private company earnings that are not comparable:

1. Applying the P/E multiple (based on after-tax earnings) to a private company's pretax earnings.
2. Applying the P/E multiple to a private company's net operating profit (earnings before interest and taxes).
3. Applying the P/E multiple to a private company's operating cash flow (earnings before interest and taxes plus depreciation).
4. Applying the P/E multiple to a private company's seller's discretionary cash (operating cash flow before allowance for compensation to owner).

The potential effects of the four errors above are illustrated in Exhibit 29-2, which starts with identical income statements and balance sheets for Public Corporation X and Private Corporation Y. Exhibit 29-2 also shows market data for the stock of Public Corporation X and several adjustments to the income statement of Private Corporation Y.

It can readily be seen that the aggregate market value of the outstanding shares of Public Corporation X is $3,600 (300 shares × $12 per share). If one applies the P/E multiple of 6 from Public Company X to the comparable net earnings of Private Company Y, the implied value of Private Company Y's stock is $3,600 (6 × $600 = $3,600). That is a reasonable comparative indication of value before any adjustments for differences in liquidity, for minority or controlling interests, and for any other differences.

However, the following calculations illustrate the potential effects of the four common errors listed above:

1. *P/E applied to pretax earnings:* 6 × $1,000 = $6,000.
2. *P/E applied to net operating profit:* 6 × $1,200 = $7,200.
3. *P/E applied to operating cash flow:* 6 × $1,600 = $9,600.
4. *P/E applied to seller's discretionary earnings (discretionary cash):* 6 × $2,100 = $12,600.

Exhibit 29–2

LEVELS OF ECONOMIC INCOME TO WHICH MULTIPLES MIGHT BE APPLIED

PUBLIC CORPORATION X

Sales		$10,000
Operating expenses:		
Salaries	$5,500	
Other operating expenses	2,900	
Depreciation	400	
Total operating expenses		8,800
Net operating profit (EBIT)		1,200
Interest expense		200
Net income before taxes		1,000
Federal and state income taxes		400
Net income		600
Shares outstanding		300
Net income per share		2 ($600/300 = $2)
Market price per share		12
Price/earnings ratio		6x ($12/2 = 6x)
Current assets	2,000	
Fixed assets	3,000	
Total assets	$5,000	
Current liabilities	$1,000	
Long-term liabilities (10% interest)	2,000	
Stockholders' equity	2,000	
Total liabilities & equity	$5,000	

PRIVATE CORPORATION Y

			Adjustment to Reach "Discretionary Earnings"	Discretionary Earnings (Seller's Discretionary Cash Flow)
Sales		$10,000		$10,000
Operating expenses:				
Owner's salary	$500		$500	
Other salaries	5,000			
Other operating expenses	2,900			
Total cash operating expenses		8,400		7,900
Operating cash flow		1,600		
Depreciation		400	400	
Net operating profit (EBIT)		1,200		
Interest expense		200	200	
Net income before taxes		1,000		
Federal and state income taxes		400	400	
Net income		600	1,500	
Discretionary earnings or "seller's discretionary cash"				2,100
Current assets	2,000			
Fixed assets	3,000			
Total assets	$5,000			
Current liabilities	$1,000			
Long-term liabilities (10%)	2,000			
Owner's equity	2,000			
Total liabilities & equity	$5,000			

Misguided analysts use misguided methods. One report we saw combined the above errors with the "assets plus . . ." method discussed earlier. The "six times seller's discretionary cash flow" was interpreted to represent only the goodwill or intangible value. As noted on the balance sheets presented in Exhibit 29-2, this company has a net asset value of $2,000. Adding that to the value derived from number four above would give this misguided analyst an indicated value of $14,600!

Applying Price/Earnings Multiples When Time Periods Are Not Comparable

We noted that the P/E multiples published in daily newspapers are based on the current stock prices divided by the companies' latest 12 months' actual reported earnings. Using such a P/E multiple but applying it to any other earnings base for the subject company can produce significantly misleading results. The following are a few examples of a public company's P/E multiple from one time period being applied to the subject company's earnings for a different time period.

Price/Earnings Multiple Applied to a Projection. Vassar Video, a publicly traded marketer of video cassettes, had 1997 earnings of $4 per share. Early in 1998, the stock traded at $36 per share, resulting in a P/E multiple of 9 ($36 ÷ $4 = 9). Alan Analyst (not an accredited business appraiser), who has been retained to value the stock of Yale Yuppies, a privately owned company marketing a competitive line of video cassettes, projects that Yale will earn $3 per share in 1998. Applying the comparative publicly traded company P/E multiple of 9 to Alan's projection of $3 per share for Yale gives Yale stock an indicated value of $27 per share (9 × $3 = $27), on a publicly traded equivalent basis, before adjustments for liquidity and so on.

What Alan overlooked was that analysts following Vassar stock were predicting that Vassar would earn $6 per share in 1998. Therefore, if one divided the current stock price by the projected earnings, the P/E multiple so derived would be 6 ($36 ÷ $6 = 6), rather than 9. Applying the P/E multiple of 6 on Vassar's projected earnings to Yale's projected earnings of $3 would give a publicly traded equivalent indication of value for Yale stock of $18 per share (6 × $3 = $18). Alan erred by applying a P/E multiple based on historical earnings to projected earnings in an industry that is experiencing steep earnings growth.

Failure to Match Historical Time Periods. Alan was called on to value the stock as of December 31, 1997, of Audrey's Automotive Corp., a small subcontractor to the highly cyclical automotive industry. The most comparable publicly traded company was Buddy's, another automotive subcontractor, which earned $5 per share for its latest fiscal year, ended September 30, 1997. Buddy's stock traded at $40 per share on December 31, 1997, so the *Daily Bugle* showed a P/E multiple of 8 ($40 ÷ $5 = 8). Alan applied the P/E multiple of 8 to Audrey's earnings of $4 per share for calendar 1997. This procedure results in a publicly traded equivalent indicated value of $32 ($4 × 8 = $32) per share for Audrey's stock.

What Alan overlooked was that the fourth quarter of 1997 was a big recovery quarter for the industry. During that period, Buddy earned $2 per share, compared to a loss of $1 per share in the fourth quarter of 1996 (results not dissimilar to Audrey's). Therefore, for the calendar year 1997, Buddy's stock actually earned $8 per share. And its P/E multiple at December 31, based on 1997 calendar year actual results, was really 5 ($40 ÷ $8 = 5). Applying the P/E multiple of 5, based on Buddy's calendar year 1997 earnings (instead of Buddy's fiscal year earnings), to Audrey's calendar year earnings of $4 would give a publicly traded equivalent indication of value for Audrey's stock of $20 per share (5 × $4 = $20). Alan erred by applying a P/E multiple based on earnings for an earlier time period to actual earnings for a later time period in an industry experiencing a sharp cyclical recovery.

There are numerous examples of the application of a P/E multiple derived from earnings of one time period to an earnings base of another time period.

Averaging Price/Earnings Multiples over Time.   If Alan did not like the result he got using a current P/E multiple, he had a handy solution: Just use the average price for the last five years. That way, he applied prices born out of some other set of economic conditions to earnings generated under current economic conditions. About half the time, that variation on the P/E multiple approach helped his case. Alan found that he was only rarely challenged on this anomaly. Alan gave a lot of testimony on values of small businesses and professional practices in divorce cases. And Alan believed that he needed to be flexible in his analysis. Not only was Alan not accredited, he was not a member of any professional appraisal association (all of which have codes of ethics). He felt that the constraints imposed by such professional organizations stifled his creativity.

Using the Reciprocal of the Price/Earnings Multiple as the Required Rate of Return

How often we all have heard that the reciprocal of the P/E multiple is the discount rate! For example, if a stock is selling at a P/E multiple of 12, the reciprocal would be 8.3 percent (1 ÷ 12 = 0.083). It is not reasonable to expect someone to buy a stock for an 8.3 percent total rate of return when she could get more on good grade corporate bonds. The reason the P/E multiple is 12 on historical earnings is that the market expects future earnings to be higher.

The discount rate applicable to expected earnings is the reciprocal of the public market P/E multiple only in the rare case when the earnings, on which the P/E multiple is based, are expected to be constant over time.[4]

---

[4]For a more complete discussion of this relationship, see Chapter 13.

Failure to Make Appropriate Adjustments

Public companies and transactions in publicly traded stocks differ in many ways from exchanges of interests in privately held businesses and professional practices, as discussed in Chapter 5. Unfortunately, it is common to find uninformed analysts attempting to practice the discipline of business appraisal by using P/E multiples to value small businesses and professional practices without taking account of such important factors as size or capital structure of the entity, the degree of liquidity, and the relative proportion of the total company represented by the interest being valued.

Other Errors in Deriving Capitalization Rates

As discussed in Chapters 13 and 15, the capitalization rate should be the one applicable to the measure of economic income being capitalized, both in terms of definition of the earnings base and in terms of the rate applicable at the particular time. Most errors involve some failure in matching the applicable direct capitalization rate with the economic income being capitalized.

Using Rates from an Earlier Time Period

The cost of capital varies considerably over time. As the cost of capital goes up, the value of an existing small business or professional practice goes down, and vice versa. Therefore, if the direct capitalization rate used is other than the one actually prevalent at the time of the valuation, the result will be an overstatement or understatement of value.

Incredibly, when using the capitalized excess earnings valuation method, some analysts still use the rates given as examples in Revenue Ruling 68-609 (Exhibit 23-1). Since rates have not been that low in many years, the inevitable result of using those rates is overvaluation. This common error is discussed in some detail in Chapter 23, The Capitalized Excess Earnings Method.

Applying Rates on "Safe" Investments to Small Business Investments

As discussed in Chapter 13, the biggest variable influencing the direct capitalization rate is the risk of the investment. Many analysts, however, have never been exposed to this basic economic truth. Therefore they use some virtually riskless rate, such as the prevailing money market fund or certificate of deposit rate, as a direct capitalization rate for valuing the expected earnings of small businesses and professional practices. Using too low a direct capitalization rate results, of course, in an overvaluation.

The rationale for that error is "That rate is what I can get on my money in an alternative investment." The correct rationale is "What rate can I get on my money in an alternative investment of equal risk, liquidity, and other characteristics?" The lowest rate that is reasonable to use is the rate at which the small business or professional practice can borrow the money. However, the total investment cannot be financed at that low a rate, as discussed in Chapter 13 and the following section.

Failure to Match the Capitalization Rate with the Earnings Base

It is common to find analysts applying a direct capitalization rate appropriate to bottom-line net income to other levels of earnings, such as pretax earnings, earnings before depreciation (often called cash flow), earnings before interest, and even earnings before compensation to business owners. Most of these errors seem to occur from applying too low a direct capitalization rate to too high an earnings base, resulting in an overvaluation.

A related common error is applying the company's borrowing rate to the entire equity investment. For example, if the investor thinks he can borrow from the bank at 12 percent, using accounts receivable as collateral, it is a mistake to use 12 percent as the rate at which to capitalize his entire equity investment. As discussed in Chapter 13, the equity level is where most of the risk is. An equity investment, therefore, should command a much higher rate of return. The borrowing rate should be used only as a direct capitalization rate for the percentage of the total investment that actually can be borrowed at that rate.

Mistaking Historical Results for Required Rates of Return

A common fallacy among analysts is to use a recent historical average rate of return on equity capital for an industry as a proxy for that industry's cost of equity capital. The following illustrates just how ridiculous that valuation method really is.

Suppose, for example, a representative group of publicly traded forest products companies earned an average rate of return of 6 percent per year on their equity capital from 1988 through 1992. Does that mean that the analyst developing an appropriate rate of return by which to discount a projected income stream in 1993 should use 6 percent for the equity portion of the cost of capital? Of course not! To do so would imply that investors in 1993 would have been willing to invest in stocks of that industry for a 6 percent expected return, which is far less than the return available on much safer instruments.

All that the 6 percent historical return means is that the forest products industry did not perform well financially in the 1988–1992 period. Adverse factors affected the industry far more than was anticipated.

The required rate of return is based on investor expectations. To use historical results as a proxy for future expectations can be very misleading. This is especially true when the historical results are for a single industry and for a relatively short time period.

The application of this error that we encounter most frequently is the use of historical rates of return published in Robert Morris Associates *RMA Annual Statement Studies* as required rates of return for capitalization rates. If this is used as a source for required rates of return or direct capitalization rates, the analyst needs to provide some evidence that *expected* rates of return indeed conform to the *historical* rates of return for the period selected.

Failure to Estimate a Realistic Normalized Earnings Base

Successful business owners emphasize earning power. If that earning power is not correctly assessed, the result will be an overvaluation or undervaluation of the entity.

Reliance on Past Results without Judgment

There is a mind-set that can be described as the "mechanistic mentality," for lack of a better expression. It mechanically relies on past data, without considering whether adjustments should be made or whether it is reasonable to expect future results to conform to past results.

Analysis of the earnings patterns of thousands of companies has shown that a pure extrapolation of recent past results more often leads to a poor projection than to a good one. Past results are not analyzed for their own sake but only as a guide to future expectations. The mechanistic mentality is useful for recording the past performance of the company. It lacks usefulness for appraisal purposes, however, without an explanation of why the past results of the company are reasonable predictors of future performance.

Failure to Recognize Any Depreciation

It is common simply to add back all depreciation to get a cash earnings figure. This is because depreciation is an accounting charge not requiring any cash outlay. Except for the unusual occasion when the property is not wearing out or growing obsolete at all, this practice overstates the true cash earnings of the business. As discussed in Chapter 7, the better procedure is to either (1) adjust the depreciation charge to an amount that genuinely estimates the degree of wear and tear and/or obsolescence or (2) make a separate deduction for the cash outlays that will be required for the average amount of replacements necessary to maintain the income stream. Most business valuation professionals currently favor the latter procedure. This latter procedure is one of the steps leading to net cash flow as the measure of earning power to be discounted or to be capitalized.

Not Allowing Compensation to Owner/Operator

Another common practice is to add back to the earnings all compensation to the owner(s). This results in a figure often called owner's discretionary cash, or some such appellation. This procedure is appropriate only if the multiple applied to such a figure is derived either empirically or analytically as a multiple applicable to "discretionary earnings," as presented in Chapter 19.

Any amount that a buyer pays for so-called earnings that actually include her own reasonable compensation for her services can be thought of as an employment fee. There is nothing wrong with a person buying herself a job, as long as the buyer recognizes that is what she is doing.

Failure to Consider the Full Cost of the Purchase

All too often, a prospective buyer capitalizes the alleged earning power to decide what to offer the seller, only to find that additional investment will be required in working capital, equipment, or capacity in order to achieve that earning power. When determining a purchase price for the business, any additional investment needed to generate the earnings should be deducted from the total capitalized earning power value.

Working Capital Requirements

The need for additional investment for working capital frequently is overlooked. Analysis of working capital requirements is covered in Chapter 11.

Deferred Maintenance

Property, leasehold improvements, and equipment should be inspected to determine how well they have been kept up and whether additional capital investment is needed to bring them up to standards. If so, that amount should be deducted from the purchase price.

Other Investment Needed

It would be an error in valuation to fail to deduct the cost of any investment needed to maintain the earnings stream. Such items could include the cost of relocation, the cost of replacing personnel lost in the transition, the cost of meeting various governmental compliance requirements, and a host of other things. The failure to foresee and adjust the valuation for such expenditures is a common error.

Failure to Understand What the Indicated Value Represents

All too often, the analyst ends up with an indicated value that is not directly applicable to the actual property subject to the appraisal. A common error is to fail to recognize this fact and to fail to make appropriate adjustments to the indicated value.

What Assets and/or Liabilities Are Included?

For example, when using the multiple of discretionary earnings method, the indicated multiple does *not* include some or all elements of working capital, depending on which database is used for comparative data. If the subject business being valued *has* these elements of working capital, the value thereof should be added to the value indicated by a multiple of discretionary earnings.

On the other hand, values indicated by such multiples often *do* include a covenant not to compete. If this is the case, and if the subject property does *not* include a covenant not to compete, the indicated value should be adjusted accordingly.

Asset versus Stock Valuation

It is also noteworthy that values derived from most of the small business and professional practice databases (e.g., the *IBA Market Database*, *Bizcomps*, and the smaller companies in *Pratt's Stats*[5]) are based on asset sales. If the subject property is stock, that is different than a direct investment in assets. For example, in a transaction involving the purchase of stock, the buyer is assuming whatever contingent liabilities may be inherent in the company. Also, there could be a substantial income or capital gains tax liability on the liquidation of certain assets. If asset sales data are used as guideline transactions for the purpose of valuing stock, appropriate adjustments may need to be considered.

Ownership Characteristics

It is also important to recognize whether the valuation method indicates a minority ownership interest value or a controlling ownership interest value. It is important to ensure that the indicated value relates to the assumed minority/controlling ownership characteristic of the subject property being valued. If not, appropriate valuation adjustments are called for.

---

[5] *Pratt's Stats*, in most cases, indicates whether the transaction was an asset sale or a stock sale.

Similarly, transactional data are based on actual sales that have occurred. The subject interest may not be salable instantly in its present state without incurring costs, suffering delays, or resolving uncertainties. Therefore, an adjustment for lack of marketability may be appropriate.

Assuming that the Buyer Will Pay for the Now and the Hereafter

The seller would like to be paid today for what the business could be worth in five years if a buyer brings in additional capital, manages well, and is very lucky. Some sellers seriously entertain that dream, maybe because, in unique circumstances, sellers have been paid for that investment value.

The buyer, of course, does not see it that way. He wants to pay no more than fair market value for future performance that the business has already proved it can produce with a high degree of certainty.

With respect to the two positions described above, the real world leans much more toward the buyer's perspective than the seller's. So do the divorce courts. Fair market value is based largely on what is there now, as opposed to what might be there sometime after a lot of changes are made to the business. Would-be sellers are misled when they think they should be paid now for what the business may be worth after the buyer brings his own magic show to the party.

However, note that in almost every newspaper classified section in the country, the relevant classification does not read "Businesses for Sale," but "Business Opportunities." A genuine opportunity should be worth something—certainly more to one buyer than another, depending on how good the buyer perceives the opportunity to be.

Emphasis on Items Not in Proportion to Their Relative Importance

The most common example of this error is probably the emphasis often accorded to developing the income base and the capitalization rates in the direct capitalization of economic income valuation method. The two variables are more or less equally critical to a value indication using that method. Yet many reports devote 20 pages to painstakingly developing the economic income base to be capitalized and then cavalierly capitalize that economic income base at a direct capitalization rate supported only by one or two flimsy sentences. The reader should evaluate the report in light of whether the factors that really matter in reaching the final conclusion are indeed given their due consideration.

Inadequate Documentation

Every important number used in the analysis should be justified. To the extent possible, numbers should be based on the most thorough empirical data practically available. The report should be presented so that the source of the data is clear and the reader can look it up and check it. The reader should be able to follow exactly how the computations based on the data led to each step of the result.

To the extent that the analyst is forced to rely on professional judgment in the absence of adequate empirical data, the lack of available market data for the point at hand should be noted. Then the analyst should describe in reasonable detail the reasons and analysis that led to the judgmental conclusion for which supporting empirical data were not available.

Failure to Conduct a Site Visit and/or Management Interviews

We repeatedly emphasized in Part II, Analyzing the Company, that relevant information may be gleaned from a site visit and management interview. Without this step, much perspective needed to make appropriate adjustments to historical data and to develop supportable expectations regarding future operations may not surface.

Furthermore, for valuations subject to contrarian review (which most are), courts are becoming quite sensitive to the importance of site visits and management interviews. Many clients and attorneys dismiss or downplay the importance of a site visit and/or don't want to incur the interruption or the cost of the analyst's time for it. We prefer to make site visits and conduct management interviews. In our experience—as well as in many court cases—the site visit not only helps the analyst get a better perspective, it makes a difference in the analyst's credibility in the eyes of the court.

Errors Articulated by Tax Court Judges

Collectively, the 19 judges on the U.S. Tax Court see more business valuation cases than any other single court. They often articulate their criticisms of business appraisers and appraisal methods in their written opinions. The comments could be equally applicable to almost any kind of a business valuation case. Here, for the instructive value regarding errors to avoid, are critical comments drawn from case decisions of three U.S. Tax Court judges.

The first is the criticism by Judge Wright of one appraiser's report on the fair market value of minority shares of a privately held life insurance company:

- "Troubled by the brevity of (the appraiser's) report."
- "Does not provide a discussion of the computation or model used."
- "He considered a variety of factors, but he does not elaborate to any significant degree as to what effect such consideration had on any particular variable involved in his computations."
- "Considered the stock value of several publicly traded insurance corporations, but he failed to provide any explanation of how such share values influenced his calculations."[6]

In an estate tax case involving the value of stock in a telecommunications company, Judge Laro stated that he rejected the opinion of the taxpayer's expert for several reasons, including the following:

- "Unable to explain certain parts of the analysis contained in the reports."
- "Arbitrarily applied a 35 percent marketability discount."
- "Made no mention of a hypothetical buyer or a hypothetical seller."
- "Whereas the 1989 report states that [the appraiser] toured the facilities, there is nothing in his testimony or the 1991 report to suggest that he did likewise before preparing the 1991 report."
- "Does not adequately account for the fact that [the company's] 1991 earnings increased dramatically over the years covered by the 1989 report."
- "Does not adequately take into account that [the company] began paying dividends after the time covered by the 1989 report."
- "Refers to the financial data of publicly traded companies, yet never explains how those companies were selected, or in what respects their lines of business were similar to [the subject company's]."[7]

In a case involving the value of a minority ownership interest in a manufacturer of programmable logic devices, Judge Halpern set forth several "significant concerns" regarding the taxpayer's expert report and testimony:

- "Failed to rely on identified comparable companies."
- "Ignoring recognition that future earnings might be any different from those in 1989."
- "Failure to take account of possible IPO."
- "Taking minority discount from publicly traded values, which were already discounted."

---

[6]*Rabenhorst* v. *Commissioner*, No. 23932-93, 1996 WL 86215 (U.S.T.C., Feb. 29, 1996).

[7] *Estate of Arthur G. Scanlan* v. *Commissioner*, No. 4561-95, 1996 WL 412016, (U.S.T.C., July 24, 1996).

Judge Halpern stated that the expert's "oral testimony has raised for us serious doubts as to his understanding of the approaches to valuation that he selected. That, alone, is sufficient reason for us to reject the conclusions resulting from those approaches."[8]

All of these errors are to be avoided in a valuation for any purpose, not just taxation.

Common Mistakes Made by CPAs

Exhibit 29-3 is an article by Butch Williams, a business appraiser involved in the leadership of the AICPA business valuation program and the National Association of Certified Valuation Analysts. His article is essentially a summary of the main points of his presentation at the 1996 AICPA National Business Valuation Conference. He articulates some of the points already made in this chapter, as well as others.

Summary

Most small business and professional practice appraisals that miss the mark do so for one or a combination of the following reasons:

- Failure to adequately identify and/or follow the applicable standard of value.
- Using methods and procedures not widely accepted in the professional appraisal community and/or the courts holding jurisdiction.
- Internal inconsistencies.
- Conclusions not supported by clear, rational, and convincing analysis.
- Lack of adequate empirical data.
- Lack of adequate documentation (either in the report or in supporting work papers).

It is our hope that this chapter will be useful to both the analyst and the user of the appraisal in order to evaluate the work product and to identify and correct common pitfalls.

---

[8] *Estate of Freeman* v. *Commissioner*, No. 22427-93, 1996 WL 453872 (U.S.T.C., Aug. 13, 1996).

Exhibit 29–3

Shannon Pratt's BUSINESS VALUATION UPDATE

Timely news, views and resources for better valuations   Vol. 2, No. 12, December 1996

Guest Article:

Common mistakes made by CPAs in preparing and reporting business values

By James L. "Butch" Williams
Managing Director, Williams, Taylor & Associates, P.C.

This article is condensed from a presentation by the same title at the AICPA National Business Valuation Conference held in Phoenix on November 18. (See p. 3 regarding ordering a tape of the complete presentation as well as others.) Butch is chairman of the Executive Advisory Board of the National Association of Certified Valuation Analysts (NACVA), and is also a member of ASA, IBA, and the MCS Business Valuations and Appraisals Subcommittee of the AICPA. Many of the common errors that he mentions (not always perpetrated by CPAs) have been the subject of courts' criticisms in cases that we have reported, and we've injected cites to several of those. **—SP**

"Butch" Williams

I'd like to outline a variety of mistakes that I've frequently seen made by CPAs in business valuation reports that I have reviewed. My purpose, of course, is to make you particularly conscious of these errors so that you will not fall into the same traps.

The common mistakes fall into several categories:

■ **Defining the engagement**
 ● Failure to include assumptions and limiting conditions in the engagement letter
 ● Failure to limit distribution and specific utilization of the report
 ● Using an incorrect standard of value, such as fair market value v. fair value (_See Matter of Slant Fin Corp., 12/95, p. 8,_ where one appraiser used fair market value

when statute called for fair value.)

■ **Gathering and utilization of data**
 ● Failure to do a site visit (_See Estate of Arthur G. Scanlan, 9/96, p. 7,_ where the appraiser had visited the site in conjunction with an appraisal two years earlier, but had not revisited for the current appraisal. See also **Estate of Gloeckner,** _6/96, p. 5,_ where the appraiser conducted neither an on-site inspection nor a management interview.)
 ● Relying on historical results for growth outlook (_See Davis v. Torvick, Inc., 7/96, p. 9,_ where the appraiser prepared projections "based only on past performance extended into the future.")
 ● Inadequate due diligence inquiries (_See Estate of Freeman, 10/96, p. 14,_ where the appraiser interviewed the president, but did not ask whether the company had any

plans for a public offering.)
 ● Relying on industry average data without adequate analysis of how the subject company relates to the industry.

■ **Performing valuation procedures**
 ● Applying discount and cap rates derived from after-tax data to pre-tax data
 ● Applying discount rate where capitalization rate should be used and visa versa
 ● Applying industry average price/revenue ratios without comparing profitability
 ● Dismissing consideration of the guideline public company method when valuing smaller middle market companies
 ● Dismissing the discounted cash flow method because it's either "too difficult to understand" or "too speculative" (_See Sergi v. Sergi, 9/96, p. 9,_ where the family law court adopted the conclusion of the appraiser based on the DCF method, even though it had never been used before in that court's jurisdiction. See also **Guiffrie v. Baker,** _11/96, p. 6,_ where the court accepted wife's expert's DCF method appraisal and rejected husband's expert's excess earnings method appraisal.)
 ● Adjusting for excess compensation when valuing a minority interest.

■ **Discounts and premiums**
 ● Applying a discount or premium to a level of value when it is not applicable
 ● Applying a discount without understanding the data and procedures used in compiling the underlying discount studies. **BVU**

Chapter 30

Sample Case

Rusty Metals, Inc., is a hypothetical case study developed to illustrate the application of many of the valuation methods and procedures discussed in this book. The hypothetical company is not intended to be patterned after any real-world company. The reader should not be concerned with whether any of the alternative valuation variables bear resemblance to his or her perception of reality in the metal distributing industry.

In this chapter, we describe the Rusty Metals business, its operations, and its financial condition. In the next chapter, we will illustrate the application of a variety of valuation methods on this hypothetical business.

Background of Rusty Metals, Inc.

Rusty Metals, Inc. (Rusty) is a metal distributing company located in Columbia, South Carolina. Rusty was incorporated in 1956 by its original founders, Richard and Rachel Rusty. Having owned and operated Rusty for over 40 years, Richard and Rachel Rusty wish to retire. Since the couple does not have any children or successors, they have decided to sell the business. They have asked us to express an opinion as to the fair market value of 100 percent of the equity of Rusty Metals, Inc., as of March 31, 1997. We have been asked to appraise the subject stock on a controlling ownership interest basis. On a field visit to Rusty and through interviews with the Rustys, the following information has been gathered.

Economic Outlook

The Southeastern economy continued to expand moderately in early 1997. Factory activity was mixed, with increasing payrolls and declining orders. The outlook is positive in the tourism and hospitality sectors as the expansion in the travel industry continues. Retail sales were above last year's level. Single-family home sales and construction were flat, but the commercial construction markets were showing continued strength. Wage and price pressures remained subdued, although difficulties in hiring and retaining qualified workers and higher input costs were reported.

In Spring 1997, retail sales were above those reported a year ago, and the outlook for future sales of most product lines is bright. High consumer confidence is helping to keep sales strong. Sales of apparel, shoes, and cosmetics were strong. Household goods sales, however, weakened. Prices are expected to remain unchanged over the next few months.

Single-family home sales and construction were flat during March 1997, on a year-over-year basis. Inventories of unsold homes are adequate, while second quarter 1997 construction expectations are mixed.

New industrial and office development continued to be strong, mainly because of lower vacancy and higher rental rates. The multifamily sector, although past its peak in the current expansion, still shows slight increases in the number of projects.

In the manufacturing sector, aerospace companies continue to gain new contracts and expand. New orders are increasing for some building product producers, and electrical equipment manufacturers are adding employees. Household goods producers reported healthy business activity, but apparel producers experienced continued weakness. Some furniture manufacturers are cutting back production, and paper producers are being forced to lower prices to boost sluggish sales.

Despite continuing reports of labor shortages, wage pressures and prices were generally in check in the first quarter of 1997. Part-time and "retired" employees are filling some of the positions. Companies appear to be willing to pay more for experienced employees. Although some companies reported higher input prices, they indicated their inability to pass increases on to the end user, reflecting competitive pressures from both the domestic and foreign markets.

Industry Outlook

As a metals servicing center, Rusty is a participant in, and is affected by changes in the demand for metals—primarily aluminum, copper, and galvanized steel.

The aluminum industry is cyclical in nature, being heavily influenced by the path of the economy. Aluminum prices bottomed out in 1993, at an average price of 52.7 cents per pound. In 1995, the average aluminum price was 82.5 cents per pound. However, aluminum prices began decreasing toward the end of 1995 and in the third quarter of 1996 were down to 67.0 cents per pound. Overall, financial results for aluminum companies were mixed in 1996, but have improved slightly in January 1997. Modest growth is predicted in the near future.

The copper industry has experienced drastic changes in the last two decades. The following trends are unfolding in the industry:

1. Rising capital spending will push the industry to improve its workforce.
2. Resources will need to be protected for future mining.
3. Regulatory changes will threaten the copper market.
4. Advances will be made in production technology.

Overall, caution is advised in this industry for the near term, as the supply/demand situation continues to be uncertain.

Stainless steel producers are having to modernize their facilities in order to remain competitive with the rest of the world and with changing technology. Steel inventories in service centers reached a two-year low in January 1996, but increased steadily through the remainder of

1996. The outlook for the stainless steel industry in 1997 is for moderate growth.

Operations

As a metals distributing company, Rusty retails and wholesales metal products, primarily aluminum, stainless steel, copper, galvanized sheet and coil, as well as some specialty metals. Rusty fabricates metal components on a custom basis in accordance with customer specifications. Inventories are carried in many forms, including round, hexagon, square and flat bars, plates, tubing, and sheet and coil. Rusty caters to small orders and gives high-quality service to its customers.

The following chart illustrates the composition of Rusty's sales for the fiscal year ended February 28, 1997.

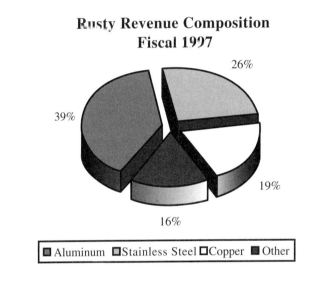

Rusty Revenue Composition Fiscal 1997

| Aluminum | Stainless Steel | Copper | Other |

Competition

Metal suppliers are in a very competitive industry. Rusty competes through its recognized quality service, which it has provided for the past 40 years. While mills can sell directly to many Rusty customers, large orders are required. Rusty primarily competes against other local metal distributors in the Southeast who cater to small custom orders.

Management and Employees

Richard Rusty, cofounder, has served as Rusty's president and chief executive officer since its inception in 1956. Mr. Rusty holds a BS in mechanical engineering as well as an MBA from the University of South Carolina.

Rachel Rusty, cofounder, has served as Rusty's chief financial officer since its inception in 1956. Ms. Rusty holds a BS in business administration, with emphasis in accounting, from the University of South Carolina. Ms. Rusty is a Certified Public Accountant in the state of South Carolina.

Harold Hott, senior vice president, joined Rusty in 1979 and has served as the company's senior vice president since 1989. Mr. Hott earned a BS in industrial management as well as an MBA from Wake Forest University.

The company's other management has extensive experience in the metal distributing industry, most of it with Rusty.

Currently, Rusty has 25 employees, some of whom have been employed for over 35 years. The average age of Rusty's employees is 30, with a wide range of ages on the production line. Rusty's employees voted against unionization due to the company's excellent benefits and retirement plan.

Customers

Rusty has developed a highly diversified customer base, with long-standing relationships. In fact, the top 10 customers represent only 29 percent of revenues, and all of the top 10 have been customers for at least five years. A majority of Rusty's customers are located in the Southeast and tend to be involved in the transportation, construction, food processing, and textile manufacturing industries. Metal needs of a wide variety of industries, subcontractors, and manufacturers are served through Rusty's Columbia, South Carolina, plant.

Financial Statements

Exhibits 30-1 through 30-4 provide information that may be used to estimate the market value of Rusty Metals, Inc. Rusty's balance sheets as of February 28, 1993, through February 28, 1997, are presented in Exhibit 30-1. Rusty's statements of operations for the fiscal years ending February 28, 1993, through February 28, 1997, are presented in Exhibit 30-2. Exhibit 30-3 presents Rusty's adjusted statements of operations, which summarize the adjustments made to the reported financial results for extraordinary and nonrecurring items that may understate or overstate the reported results of normal operations. These adjustments will be explained in the following chapter. Exhibit 30-4 presents Rusty's adjusted financial ratios.

Exhibit 30–1

RUSTY METALS, INC.
HISTORICAL BALANCE SHEETS AND COMMON SIZE ANALYSIS

	As of February 28/29,					As of February 28/29,				
	1997	1996	1995	1994	1993	1997	1996	1995	1994	1993
	$000	$000	$000	$000	$000	%	%	%	%	%
ASSETS										
Current assets:										
Cash & cash equivalents	1	26	18	9	-	0.0	1.0	0.7	0.4	-
Accounts receivable	588	738	699	574	645	22.0	28.9	26.0	28.6	26.2
Inventories	1,548	1,304	1,386	954	1,330	58.0	51.1	51.6	47.5	53.9
Other current assets	22	11	16	16	40	0.8	0.4	0.6	0.8	1.6
Total current assets	2,159	2,079	2,120	1,553	2,015	80.9	81.4	79.0	77.3	81.6
Fixed assets:										
Land & building	15	15	15	15	15	0.5	0.6	0.5	0.7	0.6
Machinery & equipment	104	104	105	77	90	3.9	4.1	3.9	3.8	3.6
Furniture, fixtures, & office equipment	322	330	317	309	298	12.1	12.9	11.8	15.4	12.1
Other fixed assets	91	82	82	82	82	3.4	3.2	3.0	4.1	3.3
Total fixed assets	532	531	519	483	484	19.9	20.8	19.3	24.0	19.6
Less: accumulated depreciation	(411)	(406)	(382)	(345)	(344)	(15.4)	(15.9)	(14.2)	(17.2)	(13.9)
Total fixed assets, net	121	125	137	137	140	4.5	4.9	5.1	6.8	5.7
Total other noncurrent assets	387	350	428	319	313	14.5	13.7	15.9	15.9	12.7
TOTAL ASSETS	2,668	2,554	2,685	2,009	2,468	100.0	100.0	100.0	100.0	100.0
LIABILITIES										
Current liabilities:										
Curr. maturities of long-term debt	1,239	1,144	1,183	945	1,158	46.4	44.8	44.1	47.0	46.9
Other short-term debt	-	-	-	-	2	-	-	-	-	0.1
Accounts payable	715	803	1,010	622	844	26.8	31.4	37.6	31.0	34.2
Accrued liabilities	25	58	25	12	25	0.9	2.3	0.9	0.6	1.0
Total current liabilities	1,979	2,005	2,219	1,580	2,029	74.2	78.5	82.6	78.6	82.2
Long-term debt	101	44	63	49	77	3.8	1.7	2.3	2.4	3.1
Total liabilities	2,080	2,048	2,282	1,629	2,106	78.0	80.2	85.0	81.1	85.3
EQUITY										
Stockholders' equity:										
Common stock	41	41	41	41	41	1.5	1.6	1.5	2.0	1.7
Retained earnings	547	465	362	339	322	20.5	18.2	13.5	16.9	13.0
Total stockholders' equity	588	506	403	380	363	22.0	19.8	15.0	18.9	14.7
TOTAL LIABILITIES AND EQUITY	2,668	2,554	2,685	2,009	2,468	100.0	100.0	100.0	100.0	100.0

SOURCE: Audited financial statements.

Exhibit 30–2

RUSTY METALS, INC.
HISTORICAL STATEMENTS OF OPERATIONS AND COMMON SIZE ANALYSIS

	Fiscal Years Ending February 28/29,					Fiscal Years Ending February 28/29,				
	1997 $000	1996 $000	1995 $000	1994 $000	1993 $000	1997 %	1996 %	1995 %	1994 %	1993 %
Net revenues	6,665	5,989	5,859	5,297	5,828	100.0	100.0	100.0	100.0	100.0
Cost of goods sold	5,236	4,641	4,670	4,155	4,635	78.6	77.5	79.7	78.4	79.5
Gross profit	1,429	1,348	1,189	1,142	1,193	21.4	22.5	20.3	21.6	20.5
Operating expenses:										
General & administrative	360	351	328	313	253	5.4	5.9	5.6	5.9	4.3
Other operating expenses	775	697	689	672	808	11.6	11.6	11.8	12.7	13.9
Selling expense	31	29	29	33	61	0.5	0.5	0.5	0.6	1.0
Total operating expenses	1,166	1,077	1,046	1,018	1,122	17.5	18.0	17.9	19.2	19.3
Net operating income	263	271	142	124	70	3.9	4.5	2.4	2.3	1.2
Other income (expenses)										
Interest income	-	-	1	-	1	-	-	0.0	-	0.0
Interest expense	(166)	(144)	(129)	(114)	(146)	(2.5)	(2.4)	(2.2)	(2.1)	(2.5)
Loss on sale of nonoperating assets	-	(50)	-	-	-	-	(0.8)	-	-	-
Litigation settlement	-	-	-	(48)	-	-	-	-	(0.9)	-
Other income (expenses), net	3	(10)	4	(3)	4	0.0	(0.2)	0.1	(0.1)	0.1
Total other income (expenses)	(163)	(204)	(124)	(165)	(141)	(2.5)	(3.4)	(2.1)	(3.1)	(2.4)
Pretax income	100	67	18	(40)	(71)	1.5	1.1	0.3	(0.8)	(1.2)
Provision for income taxes	18	39	-	-	(22)	0.3	0.6	-	-	(0.4)
Net income	82	29	18	(40)	(48)	1.2	0.5	0.3	(0.8)	(0.8)

SOURCE: Audited financial statements.

Exhibit 30–3

RUSTY METALS, INC.
ADJUSTED HISTORICAL STATEMENTS OF OPERATIONS AND COMMON SIZE ANALYSIS

	Fiscal Years Ending February 28/29,					Fiscal Years Ending February 28/29,				
	1997	1996	1995	1994	1993	1997	1996	1995	1994	1993
	$000	$000	$000	$000	$000	%	%	%	%	%
Net revenues	6,665	5,989	5,859	5,297	5,828	100.0	100.0	100.0	100.0	100.0
Cost of goods sold	5,236	4,641	4,670	4,155	4,635	78.6	77.5	79.7	78.4	79.5
Gross profit	1,429	1,348	1,189	1,142	1,193	21.4	22.5	20.3	21.6	20.5
Operating expenses:										
General & administrative	210	201	178	163	103	3.2	3.4	3.0	3.1	1.8
Other operating expenses	775	697	689	672	808	11.6	11.6	11.8	12.7	13.9
Selling expense	31	29	29	33	61	0.5	0.5	0.5	0.6	1.0
Total operating expenses	1,016	927	896	868	972	15.2	15.5	15.3	16.4	16.7
Net operating income	413	421	292	274	220	6.2	7.0	5.0	5.2	3.8
Other income (expenses)										
Interest income	-	-	1	-	1	-	-	0.0	-	0.0
Interest expense	(166)	(144)	(129)	(114)	(146)	(2.5)	(2.4)	(2.2)	(2.1)	(2.5)
Loss on sale of nonoperating assets	-	-	-	-	-	-	-	-	-	-
Litigation settlement	-	-	-	-	-	-	-	-	-	-
Other income (expenses), net	3	(10)	4	(3)	4	0.0	(0.2)	0.1	(0.1)	0.1
Total other income (expenses)	(163)	(154)	(124)	(117)	(141)	(2.5)	(2.6)	(2.1)	(2.2)	(2.4)
Pretax income	250	267	168	158	79	3.7	4.5	2.9	3.0	1.4
Provision for income taxes	97	104	65	61	31	1.5	1.7	1.1	1.2	0.5
Net income	152	163	102	96	48	2.3	2.7	1.7	1.8	0.8

SOURCE: Audited financial statements.

Exhibit 30–4

RUSTY METALS, INC.
ADJUSTED RATIO ANALYSIS

	Fiscal Years Ending February 28/29,				
	1997	1996	1995	1994	1993
LIQUIDITY					
Current ratio	1.1	1.0	1.0	1.0	1.0
Quick ratio	0.3	0.4	0.3	0.4	0.3
Working capital as a % of assets	6.8	2.9	(3.7)	(1.3)	(0.6)
ACTIVITY					
Turnover:					
Receivables	10.1	8.3	9.2	8.7	8.3
Total asset	2.6	2.3	2.5	2.4	NM
Inventory	3.7	3.5	4.0	3.6	3.7
Fixed asset	54.2	45.7	42.7	38.2	43.2
Average collection period (days)	36	43	39	41	43
Days to sell inventory	98	104	90	99	98
Operating cycle (days)	134	148	129	140	141
LEVERAGE					
EBIT/interest	2.5	2.9	2.3	2.4	1.5
Long-term debt/stockholders' equity (%)	30.5	29.9	24.4	27.7	22.7
Total debt/invested capital (%)	69.5	70.1	75.6	72.3	77.3
Total debt/total assets (%)	50.2	46.5	46.4	49.5	50.1
Total assets/stockholders' equity	4.5	5.0	6.7	5.3	6.8
PROFITABILITY (%)					
Operating margin after depreciation	6.2	7.0	5.0	5.2	3.8
Pretax profit margin	3.7	4.5	2.9	3.0	1.4
Net profit margin	2.3	2.7	1.7	1.8	0.8
Return on:					
Equity	27.9	35.9	26.1	25.9	12.5
Assets	5.8	6.2	4.4	4.3	NM
Investment	8.4	9.7	6.8	6.5	NM

SOURCES: Exhibits 30-1 and 30-3.

Chapter 31

Solution to the Sample Case

In this chapter, we present an analysis of the value of 100 percent of the common stock of Rusty Metals, Inc., as of March 31, 1997. This valuation is performed on a controlling ownership interest basis. This chapter summarizes the procedures that the analyst will perform in order to estimate a value. However, for simplification purposes, we have assumed that the clients will not require a formal, written valuation opinion report with respect to this analysis.

Financial Statement Adjustments

Before we can analyze trends in Rusty's financial condition and the results of operations over time, we need to make any necessary adjustments to Rusty's financial statements. These adjustments are made in order to account for any extraordinary or nonrecurring items that may understate or overstate the reported results of normal operations.

After reviewing Rusty's financial statements, we adjusted the company's income statements for the fiscal years ending February 28, 1993, through February 28, 1997. In fiscal 1994, we added back a $48,000 litigation expense that was incurred as the result of a lawsuit with the Environmental Protection Agency. In fiscal 1996, we added back a $50,000 loss on the sale of nonoperating assets. Since we are interested in the sustainable earning power of the company and since it is unlikely that these events will occur again, their effect was eliminated from the income statements. In fiscal 1993 through fiscal 1997, we added back $150,000 of the Rustys' annual executive compensation. This adjustment was made because Richard and Rachel Rusty were paying themselves approximately $75,000 per year more each than executives with equivalent responsibilities in similar companies. Finally, we adjusted the income tax rate to 39 percent in order to represent a normalized income tax rate after all adjustments were made.

Financial Statement Analysis

An essential step in the valuation of any company is an analysis of its operational performance over time. Past sales and earnings growth put the company's earnings in a historical context and can provide an indication of future prospects. Other things being equal, a company with rapidly rising sales and earnings is worth more than one with little or no growth.

Balance Sheets

As presented in Exhibit 30-1, the trend in the size of the asset base was relatively steady, at a level near $2.5 million. Inventories have historically accounted for the largest portion of total assets. As of February 28,

1997, Rusty's inventories totaled $1.5 million and accounted for 58.0 percent of total assets—compared to $1.3 million and 53.9 percent, respectively, in 1993. There were no significant changes in the level of fixed assets during the latest five years. Other noncurrent assets consisted of the cash surrender value for officers' life insurance. This account comprised 14.5 percent of total assets as of February 28, 1997.

Current liabilities decreased as a percent of total liabilities and stockholders' equity from 82.6 percent as of February 28, 1993, to 74.2 percent as of February 28, 1997. Long-term debt decreased from 1993 to 1996. However, long-term debt increased in 1997 due to a new note payable. Stockholders' equity increased 12.8 percent compounded annually between February 28, 1993, and February 28, 1997, due to increasing retained earnings.

Statements of Operations

As presented in Exhibit 30-3, Rusty's revenues demonstrated a material decrease between fiscal years 1993 and 1994. Since bottoming out in fiscal 1994, revenues have increased each year, reaching $6.7 million in 1997. Gross profit margins have remained fairly constant despite the fall—and then subsequent rise—of revenues over the last five years at Rusty. Operating expenses as a percent of total revenues decreased from 16.7 percent of revenues in fiscal 1993 to 15.2 percent of revenues in fiscal 1997. As a result, Rusty's net profit margins increased from 0.8 percent in fiscal 1993 to 2.7 percent in fiscal 1996, and decreased to 2.3 percent in fiscal 1997.

Financial and Operating Ratios

Rusty's adjusted financial and operating ratios are presented in Exhibit 30-4.

Liquidity ratios demonstrate the ability of a company to meet its current operations. Rusty's current and quick ratios of 1.1 and 0.3, respectively, as of February 28, 1997, have not changed significantly over the past five years.

Activity ratios measure the efficiency of Rusty's assets. The company's receivables turnover has increased from 8.3 in fiscal 1993 to 10.1 in fiscal 1997. Rusty's fixed asset turnover increased from 43.2 in fiscal 1993 to 54.2 in fiscal 1997. The company's operating cycle decreased during the observed five-year period from 141 days to 134 days.

Leverage ratios measure Rusty's use of debt and its ability to service the interest and principal charges on that debt. Rusty's EBIT/interest ratio increased from 1.5 in fiscal 1993 to 2.9 during fiscal 1996, falling to 2.5 during fiscal 1997. The company's total debt/invested capital ratio has decreased from 77.3 percent at February 28, 1993, to 69.5 percent at February 28, 1997.

Profitability ratios measure Rusty's ability to generate income and cash flow. Rusty's profitability ratios all showed signs of improvement since fiscal 1994. For example, the company's operating margin after depreciation increased from 3.8 percent in fiscal 1993 to 6.2 percent in fiscal 1997.

Guideline Publicly Traded Company Analysis

While the trend analysis performed above is particularly helpful in identifying any trends of improvement or deterioration in Rusty's financial statements, it gives no indication as to how Rusty's financial performance compares to similar companies in the industry. In this regard, a comparison of Rusty to the five selected guideline publicly traded companies is useful. It is important to note that this analysis should be performed after any adjustments have been made to the financial statements of the guideline publicly traded companies and the subject company.

The liquidity ratios presented in Exhibit 31-1 indicate that, on average, Rusty is not as liquid as the guideline publicly traded companies. The activity ratios indicate that Rusty achieves similar asset utilization levels compared to the guideline public companies. However, Rusty's operating cycle was higher than any of the guideline public companies. The leverage ratios indicate that Rusty has a higher level of debt and a lower level of interest coverage compared to the guideline public companies. In terms of profitability, Rusty's operating margin was equal to the median of the guideline public companies. However, Rusty's returns on assets and investment were below the guideline publicly traded companies on average. Overall, Rusty's performance was slightly below the guideline public companies in fiscal 1997.

Valuation Approaches

In general, the procedures and factors outlined in Internal Revenue Service Revenue Ruling 59-60 can be categorized into three general approaches for valuing the stock of closely held companies. Analysts will use one or more of these approaches to estimate the value of closely held companies. Of course, the objective of using more than one approach is to develop mutually supporting evidence as to the estimate of value.

While the specific titles of these three approaches may vary, the generic names are as follows:

1. Market approach.
2. Income approach.
3. Asset-based approach.

Exhibit 31–1

RUSTY METALS, INC.
GUIDELINE PUBLICLY TRADED COMPANIES
FINANCIAL AND OPERATING RATIOS

	Company 1 Mar-97	Company 2 Feb-97	Company 3 Dec-96	Company 4 Dec-96	Company 5 Dec-96	*Median*	Rusty Metals Feb-97
LIQUIDITY							
Current ratio	4.3	0.9	2.1	2.5	NM	*2.3*	1.1
Quick ratio	1.6	0.5	0.8	1.3	NM	*1.1*	0.3
Working capital as a % of assets	64.3	(5.7)	37.9	38.7	NM	*38.3*	6.8
ACTIVITY							
Turnover:							
Receivables	11.8	6.5	10.3	8.9	16.9	*10.3*	10.1
Total asset	3.3	2.3	2.9	2.4	0.1	*2.4*	2.6
Inventory	5.8	5.5	4.6	6.7	NM	*5.6*	3.7
Fixed asset	20.3	8.2	14.1	8.5	8.0	*8.5*	54.2
Average collection period (days)	30	55	35	40	21	*35*	36
Days to sell inventory	62	66	78	54	-	*62*	98
Operating cycle (days)	93	121	113	95	21	*95*	134
LEVERAGE							
EBIT/interest	8.0	(0.0)	15.5	25.2	14.4	*14.4*	2.5
Long-term debt/stockholders' equity	26.4	606.4	27.1	18.5	3.9	*26.4*	30.5
Total debt/invested capital (%)	24.0	241.6	23.4	17.1	3.8	*23.4*	69.5
Total debt/total assets (%)	18.9	61.2	13.8	12.8	2.7	*13.8*	50.2
Total assets/stockholders' equity	1.6	(93.5)	2.2	1.6	1.4	*1.6*	4.5
PROFITABILITY (%)							
Operating margin after depreciation	4.5	(0.4)	7.5	6.2	43.6	*6.2*	6.2
Pretax profit margin	4.0	(2.7)	7.1	6.9	40.5	*6.9*	3.7
Net profit margin	2.7	(2.7)	4.3	4.0	31.1	*4.0*	2.3
Return on:							
Equity	14.5	(479.1)	28.9	14.5	4.2	*14.5*	27.9
Assets	8.7	(6.5)	12.3	9.9	3.0	*8.7*	5.8
Investment	11.0	(24.2)	21.3	12.9	4.0	*11.0*	8.4

SOURCES: Forms 10-K and annual reports to shareholders, and Exhibit 30-4.

After carefully considering each of these generally accepted valuation approaches, we determined that the market approach and the income approach are the most appropriate valuation approaches for our analysis of the subject company.

We considered an asset-based approach, but we did not rely on this approach. This is because it is our opinion that the value of this company is best represented by the earnings that may be generated by its underlying assets, rather than the value of the underlying assets themselves.

The Market Approach

A number of valuation methods are based on market-derived pricing evidence. We considered several of these methods in performing our analysis of Rusty. Given the facts and circumstances surrounding Rusty, we believe that the most appropriate market approach valuation method is the guideline publicly traded company method.

The Guideline Publicly Traded Company Method

One of the most fundamentally sound methods of estimating the value of closely held company stock is to look to the public markets for evidence of the prices investors are willing to pay for the stock of companies in the same (or similar) lines of business.

The following are the principal procedures in the guideline publicly traded company method:

1. Identification of guideline publicly traded companies.
2. Calculation of market-derived pricing multiples based on the guideline companies' quoted trading prices and financial fundamentals.
3. Selection of appropriate market-derived pricing multiples to be applied to the company's financial fundamentals.
4. Calculation of one or more indications of value for a subject company based on the application of the selected market-derived pricing multiples.
5. Selection of the relative emphasis to be placed on each of the resulting indications of value.
6. Estimation of an overall indication of value from this method.

Invested Capital Valuation Methods

Market value of invested capital (MVIC) valuation methods are commonly used in the valuation of closely held companies. These methods are used in order to minimize capital structure differences between the subject company and the guideline publicly traded companies. The greater the differences between the capital structure of the subject company and the guideline publicly traded companies, the more important it is to use MVIC valuation methods.

For purposes of our analysis, we will define market value of invested capital as follows:

$$
\begin{aligned}
&\quad \text{Market value of short-term interest-bearing debt} \\
&+ \text{Market value of long-term interest-bearing debt, including capitalized leases} \\
&+ \text{Market value of preferred stock outstanding} \\
&+ \underline{\text{Market value of common stock outstanding}} \\
&= \text{Market value of invested capital}
\end{aligned}
$$

We considered the following MVIC valuation pricing multiples:

1. MVIC/revenues.
2. MVIC/earnings before interest and taxes (EBIT).
3. MVIC/earnings before depreciation, amortization, interest, and taxes (EBDIT).
4. MVIC/debt-free net income (DFNI).
5. MVIC/debt-free cash flow (DFCF).
6. MVIC/tangible book value of invested capital (TBVIC).

The following table summarizes the MVIC pricing multiples for the selected guideline publicly traded companies.

	Latest Twelve Months						**Five-year Average**				
	EBIT	**EBDIT**	**DFNI**	**DFCF**	**Revenues**	**TBVIC**	**EBIT**	**EBDIT**	**DFNI**	**DFCF**	**Revenues**
Company 1	6.2	5.6	9.4	8.1	0.28	1.02	11.1	10.1	17.6	14.4	0.40
Company 2	7.0	6.9	10.9	10.1	0.33	1.24	13.1	18.0	24.2	21.4	0.42
Company 3	6.1	5.7	10.2	9.1	0.53	1.87	15.3	13.4	26.8	20.0	0.66
Company 4	6.3	5.7	10.7	9.0	0.48	1.23	11.8	10.6	20.9	16.3	0.63
Company 5	5.0	5.2	8.4	8.2	0.39	1.36	10.7	9.1	15.5	13.5	0.43
Low	5.0	5.2	8.4	8.1	0.28	1.02	10.7	9.1	15.5	13.5	0.40
High	7.0	6.9	10.9	10.1	0.53	1.87	15.3	18.0	26.8	21.4	0.66
Mean	6.1	5.8	9.9	8.9	0.40	1.34	12.4	12.2	21.0	17.1	0.51
Median	6.2	5.7	10.2	9.0	0.39	1.24	11.8	10.6	20.9	16.3	0.43

MVIC/EBIT. As presented in Exhibit 31-2, the MVIC/EBIT multiples for the guideline publicly traded companies were very similar in the latest 12-month (LTM) period ranging from 5.0 to 7.0. Due to Rusty's relatively flat EBIT growth in the LTM period compared to a moderate EBIT growth by the guideline companies during the same period, we selected a multiple of 5.5. This selected multiple is at the lower end of the range. The five-year average MVIC/EBIT multiples for the guideline publicly traded companies ranged from 10.7 to 15.3. Rusty's five-year average EBIT growth was less than the guideline publicly traded company median, resulting in a selected multiple of 11.0.

MVIC/EBDIT. The MVIC/EBDIT multiples for the guideline publicly traded companies ranged from 5.2 to 6.9 in the LTM period and 9.1 to 18.0 for the five-year average. Rusty's LTM and five-year average EBDIT growth was well below the guideline publicly traded companies due to lower levels of depreciation compared to the guideline companies. As a result, we selected multiples of 5.0 and 9.5. The selected multiples were at the bottom of the range.

MVIC/DFNI. The MVIC/DFNI multiples for the guideline companies ranged from 8.4 to 10.9 in the LTM period and 15.5 to 26.8 for the five-year average. We selected multiples of 9.5 and 18.0 for the LTM period and five-year average, respectively. This is because Rusty's LTM and five-year average DFNI growth was slightly less than the guideline publicly traded company median.

Exhibit 31–2

RUSTY METALS, INC.
CAPITAL MARKET METHOD--MVIC BASIS
VALUATION SUMMARY

Financial Fundamental	Rusty Metals $000	Industry Multiples				Selected Multiples	Indicated Value $000	Emphasis		Indicated Value $000
		Low	High	Mean	Median			Horizon %	Multiple %	
EBIT										
Latest 12 months	416	5.0	7.0	6.1	6.2	5.5	2,287	50.0		
									20.0	585
5-year average	324	10.7	15.3	12.4	11.8	11.0	3,564	50.0		
EBDIT										
Latest 12 months	456	5.2	6.9	5.8	5.7	5.0	2,278	50.0		
									20.0	580
5-year average	371	9.1	18.0	12.2	10.6	9.5	3,526	50.0		
DFNI										
Latest 12 months	254	8.4	10.9	9.9	10.2	9.5	2,410	50.0		
									20.0	597
5-year average	198	15.5	26.8	21.0	20.9	18.0	3,557	50.0		
DFCF										
Latest 12 months	293	8.1	10.1	8.9	9.0	8.5	2,493	50.0		
									20.0	592
5-year average	245	13.5	21.4	17.1	16.3	14.0	3,428	50.0		
Revenues										
Latest 12 months	6,665	0.28	0.53	0.40	0.39	0.40	2,666	50.0		
									15.0	400
5-year average	5,928	0.40	0.66	0.51	0.43	0.45	2,667	50.0		
TBVIC										
Latest quarter	1,927	1.02	1.87	1.35	1.24	1.25	2,409	100.0	5.0	120

Market value of invested capital	2,875
Interest-bearing debt	1,340
Market value of equity, on a minority ownership interest basis	1,535
Add: premium for ownership control 30%	460
Market value of equity, on a controlling ownership interest basis	1,995

MVIC/DFCF. The MVIC/DFCF multiples for the guideline publicly traded companies ranged from 8.1 to 10.1 in the LTM period and from 13.5 to 21.4 for the five-year average. Once again, Rusty's LTM and five-year average DFCF growth was well below the guideline publicly traded companies. This was due to lower levels of depreciation compared to the guideline public companies. As a result, we selected multiples of 8.5 and 14.0. These multiples were at the bottom of the range.

MVIC/Revenues. The MVIC/Revenues multiples for the guideline publicly traded companies ranged from 0.28 to 0.53 in the LTM period and 0.40 to 0.66 for the five-year average. Typically, companies with higher returns on revenues sell for higher revenues multiples. In selecting our multiples, we looked at the companies with the most similar returns on revenues. Based on these relationships, we selected multiples of 0.40 and 0.45 for the LTM period and five-year average, respectively.

MVIC/TBVIC. The MVIC/TBVIC multiples for the guideline companies ranged from 1.02 to 1.87 for the latest quarter. As with returns on revenues, companies with higher returns on TBVIC typically sell for higher TBVIC multiples. In selecting our multiple, we looked at the companies with the most similar returns on TBVIC. Based on these relationships, we selected a multiple of 1.25.

Value Indication

As presented in Exhibit 31-2, after applying our selected market-derived pricing multiples to the calculated financial fundamentals, the indicated market value of invested capital is $2,875,000.

After deducting Rusty's interest-bearing debt of $1,340,000 as of February 28, 1997, Rusty's indicated market value of equity on a marketable, minority ownership interest basis, as of March 31, 1997, is $1,535,000.

Ownership Control Premium Analysis

The study of successful tender offers leading to the ownership control of publicly traded companies is convincing evidence for the incremental value of controlling ownership interests over minority ownership interests. By looking at premiums offered during a tender for ownership control, we find guidance both (1) for valuing controlling ownership interests and (2) for converting enterprise values into minority ownership interest values.

The variation in empirical control premiums is usually significant. This is because the incremental value paid over minority ownership interest value is specific to (1) the nature of the company, (2) the potential synergies between the purchaser and the acquired company, and (3) the price of the stock trading on a minority ownership interest basis prior to the acquisition announcement.

According to *Mergerstat Review*, the average premium over market price (based on market price five days prior to the initial tender announcement) paid for all companies during 1996 was 36.6 percent. This was lower than the 44.7 percent average price premium in 1995. The 1996 average price premium was calculated based on 381 acquisitions of publicly traded companies. The 1995 average price premium was based on 324 acquisitive transactions.

It is evident from this information that merger and acquisition activity increased in 1996. The empirical acquisition price premiums, however, decreased in 1996.

Somewhat more refined price premium evidence is also available through the *Mergerstat* industry compilation. One of the more relevant industry classifications and price premium evidence to Rusty is as follows:

Industry Classification of Acquired Company	Price Premium Percent (Base)			
	1996	1995	1994	1993
Primary metal processing	71.1 (3)	27.5 (3)	46.4 (2)	34.7 (2)

We analyzed the past four years of industry premiums because of the low number of transactions each year. As a result of our analysis, we estimated that the ownership control premium that would be appropriate for a business in Rusty's industry group would fall in the 25 to 35 percent range. From these values, we selected the 30 percent ownership control premium to apply to Rusty's equity value.

Value Indication

As presented in Exhibit 31-2, after recognition of a 30 percent ownership control premium, the indicated value for Rusty, on a marketable, controlling ownership interest basis, as of March 31, 1997, is $1,995,000.

The Income Approach

A number of valuation methods are based on a company's future economic income producing capacity. We considered several of these methods in the analysis of the subject company. However, given the facts and circumstances surrounding the subject company, we believe that the most appropriate income approach method in this case is the yield capitalization, or discounted cash flow, method.

Valuation Theory and Methodology

The discounted cash flow method is a generally accepted method used to value companies on a going-concern basis. It has intuitive appeal since it incorporates a risk/expected return analysis. This analysis is critical to the investment decision process.

The discounted cash flow method estimates the value of a company by (1) projecting the future cash flows a company is expected to generate and (2) discounting those cash flows to a present value using a discount rate. This method requires in-depth analyses of a company's revenues, fixed and variable expenses, and capital structure.

Valuation Calculations

We developed projected income statements for the subject company based on (1) our discussions with company management, (2) the company's historical income statements, and (3) our analysis of the industry. These projections are presented in Exhibit 31-3.

The appropriate economic income stream to discount in this valuation method is net cash flow. Net cash flow represents the maximum amount of cash available for distribution above and beyond the company's normal operational cash requirements. Net cash flow is typically calculated as follows:

> Net income
> + Interest expense, net of tax
> + Noncash charges
> − Capital expenditures
> − <u>Incremental working capital requirements</u>
> = Net cash flow

We calculated Rusty's net cash flow for projected fiscal years ending February 28, 1998, through 2002, based on the projected income statements presented in Exhibit 31-3. We estimated certain additional net cash flow components, based on (1) historical performance, (2) industry statistics, and (3) company management's estimates. The adjustment to annual compensation is due to the additional compensation that Richard and Rachel Rusty were paying themselves: $75,000 per year above executives with equivalent responsibilities in similar companies. In addition, we have calculated a normalized 2002 to reflect that depreciation and amortization expense and capital expenditures tend to offset each other in the long run.

The following table summarizes the calculation of the Rusty's projected net cash flow.

| | Projected Fiscal Years Ending February 28/29, Normalized | | | | | |
	1998[a]	1999	2000	2001	2002	2002
Net income	86.7	$100.7	$125.1	$132.4	$165.3	$165.3
Interest, net of tax	99.0	114.1	120.8	126.9	133.6	133.6
Depreciation and amortization	48.6	56.2	59.3	62.5	65.6	
Adjustment to annual compensation	137.5	150.0	150.0	150.0	150.0	150.0
Capital expenditures	(32.4)	(37.4)	(39.5)	(41.7)	(43.8)	
Working capital requirements	4.6	(85.0)	(82.0)	(87.0)	(83.0)	(83.0)
Net cash flow	$343.9	$298.4	$333.6	$343.1	$387.8	$365.9

a. Adjusted to reflect eleven months of cash flow instead of twelve.

The present value discount rate appropriate for estimating the present value of the company's projected net cash flow is its weighted average cost of capital (WACC). The WACC incorporates the present cost

Exhibit 31–3

RUSTY METALS, INC.
PROJECTED STATEMENTS OF OPERATIONS

	Projected Fiscal Years Ending February 28/29,					Projected Fiscal Years Ending February 28/29,				
	1998	1999	2000	2001	2002	1998	1999	2000	2001	2002
	$000	$000	$000	$000	$000	%	%	%	%	%
Total revenues	7,065	7,489	7,901	8,335	8,752	100.0	100.0	100.0	100.0	100.0
Revenue growth	*6.0%*	*6.0%*	*5.5%*	*5.5%*	*5.0%*					
Cost of goods sold	5,511	5,841	6,163	6,501	6,827	78.0	78.0	78.0	78.0	78.0
Gross profit	1,554	1,648	1,738	1,834	1,925	22.0	22.0	22.0	22.0	22.0
Operating expenses:										
General & administrative	382	404	415	438	438	5.4	5.4	5.3	5.3	5.0
Other operating expenses	759	805	830	875	897	10.8	10.8	10.5	10.5	10.3
Selling expense	35	37	40	42	44	0.5	0.5	0.5	0.5	0.5
Depreciation & amortization	53	56	59	63	66	0.8	0.8	0.8	0.8	0.8
Total operating expenses	1,229	1,303	1,343	1,417	1,444	17.4	17.4	17.0	17.0	16.5
Net operating income	325	344	395	417	481	4.6	4.6	5.0	5.0	5.5
Other income (expenses):										
Interest expense	(177)	(187)	(198)	(208)	(219)	(2.5)	(2.5)	(2.5)	(2.5)	(2.5)
Other income (expenses), net	7	7	8	8	9	0.1	0.1	0.1	0.1	0.1
Total other income (expenses)	(170)	(180)	(190)	(200)	(210)	(2.4)	(2.4)	(2.4)	(2.4)	(2.4)
Pretax income	155	165	205	217	271	2.2	2.2	2.6	2.6	3.1
Provision for income taxes	61	64	80	85	106	0.9	0.9	1.0	1.0	1.2
Net income	95	100	125	132	165	1.3	1.3	1.6	1.6	1.9

SOURCE: Management discussions.

of Rusty's debt capital and equity capital—as determined from empirical market evidence. These capital costs, expressed as required rates of return, were then weighted according to the company's actual capital structure, as presented below.

Cost of Equity Capital Component:		Cost of Debt Capital Component:	
Risk-free rate of return	6.8%	Average cost of debt	9.0%
Equity risk premium	7.4%	Income tax rate	39.0%
Industry beta	1.0	After-tax debt rate	5.5%
Beta adjusted equity risk premium	7.4%		
Small stock equity risk premium	3.6%		
Company-specific risk premium	1.0%		
Total required return on equity capital	18.8%		
		Debt/Invested capital	40.0%
WACC (Rounded)	13.5%	Equity/Invested capital	60.0%

It is reasonable to project that the company will have value beyond the discrete projection period of 1998–2002. Therefore, our analysis also incorporates a terminal value. The terminal value was calculated by using the standard Gordon dividend growth model. This direct capitalization model estimates the value of the company at the end of the discrete projection period by capitalizing the next period net cash flow as an annuity in perpetuity. Net cash flow for 2003 (the next period) is calculated as normalized net cash flow for 2002 multiplied by one plus the long-term growth rate of 5.0 percent. Our estimation of the Rusty's terminal value is based on an 8.5 percent direct capitalization rate. This direct capitalization rate was derived from (1) the present value discount rate of 13.5 percent and (2) an expected long-term growth rate of 5.0 percent.

The following table summarizes the results of our discounted cash flow method.

	Cash Flow	13.5 % Discount Rate[a]	Present Value
1998	$ 343.9	0.9437	$ 325
1999	298.4	0.8359	249
2000	333.6	0.7365	246
2001	343.1	0.6489	223
2002	387.8	0.5717	222
Terminal[b]	4,519.9	0.5717	2,584
Present value of invested capital			$3,848
Less: market value of interest-bearing debt			(1,340)
Indicated market value of equity			$2,508

a. Present value factor is calculated from March 31, 1998, to the middle of the year in which the cash flow is received.

b. Terminal value is calculated as normalized 2002 net cash flow ($365.9) multiplied by one plus the estimated growth rate of 5 percent, divided by the capitalization rate of 8.5 percent.

Value Indication

The indicated market value of invested capital for Rusty Metals—that is, the sum of the present value of both (1) the discrete economic income flows and (2) the terminal value—is $3,848,000.

Deducting Rusty's interest-bearing debt of $1,340,000 as of February 28, 1997, the indicated value of Rusty's equity on a marketable, controlling ownership interest basis, as of March 31, 1997, is $2,508,000.

Summary of Value Indications

The indicated values estimated for a marketable, controlling ownership interest in the equity of Rusty Metals, Inc., from each valuation method are summarized below.

Valuation Method	Indicated Values ($000s)
Guideline publicly traded company method	1,995
Discounted cash flow method	2,508

After giving equal emphasis to the respective valuation methods, we estimated the value of a 100 percent interest in the common equity of Rusty, as of March 31, 1997, on a marketable, controlling ownership interest basis, to be $2,252,000.

This represents the overall value of Rusty on a marketable, controlling ownership interest basis. However, Rusty is not a readily marketable business enterprise. That is, even on a controlling ownership interest basis, there is no ready or efficient market in which to sell the Rusty business. We therefore applied an illiquidity discount for the lack of an efficient market of 10 percent from our marketable, controlling ownership interest estimate of value. (See Chapter 25 for a discussion of discounts for lack of marketability.)

Valuation Synthesis and Conclusion

Based on the analysis and procedures described above, our estimate of the fair market value of a 100 percent interest in the equity of Rusty Metals, Inc., as of March 31, 1997, is $2,027,000.

Part IV

Valuing Professional Practices

Chapter 32

Introduction to Professional Practice Valuation

The term *professional practice* encompasses a wide variety of types of entities, including, for example, accounting firms, architecture/engineering firms, law firms, dental practices, physician practices, veterinarian practices, and professional consulting firms. This definition would include professional appraisal firms and actuarial firms.

Black's Law Dictionary describes the term *profession* as follows:

> A vocation or occupation requiring special, usually advanced, education, knowledge, and skill—e.g., law or medical professions. Also refers to whole body of such profession. The labor and skill involved in a profession is predominantly mental or intellectual, rather than physical or manual. The term originally contemplated only theology, law, and medicine, but as applications of science and learning are extended to other departments of affairs, other vocations also receive the name, which implies professed attainments in special knowledge as distinguished from mere skill.[1]

The valuation of professional practices, such as medical, dental, accounting, legal, and architecture/engineering firms, has developed into a professional discipline in its own right. Many professional practice brokers, appraisers, accountants, and consultants specialize in this valuation discipline.

This chapter discusses some of the reasons professional practices are different from other small businesses. In particular, this chapter will introduce the operational, financial, organizational, and economic characteristics of professional practices that have a direct impact on the valuation of these professional firms. While there are technical distinctions between a professional practice and a professional service firm (e.g., beauty parlor, financial advisor, tax preparer, marketing consultant), many of the valuation principles described in this chapter apply without distinction.

Reasons to Value a Professional Practice

There is an almost limitless number of individual client reasons to estimate the value of a professional practice. Most of these individual reasons may be grouped into two categories: (1) transactional and (2) controversy. Within the transactional category, the most common reasons to appraise a professional practice are (1) buy-ins and sell-offs of ownership interests and (2) structuring a buy-sell agreement. Within the controversy category, the most common reasons to appraise a professional practice are (1) disputes between equity owners and (2) marital dissolution matters.

---

[1] Henry C. Black, *Black's Law Dictionary* (St. Paul, MN: West Publishing Co., 1997), p. 1210.

Appraisals of professional practice ownership interests for estate tax reasons are less common. If the decedent practitioner is a member of a multipractitioner entity, there is usually a buy-sell agreement to set a binding value that will be paid to the estate. If the buy-sell agreement is properly drafted, the value set by that agreement may also be used in the estate tax return. If the buy-sell agreement is not as carefully prepared, the Internal Revenue Service may argue that the agreement is self-serving and should be ignored for estate tax purposes. This type of situation would call for a professional valuation of the decedent's ownership interest.

Professional practice appraisals related to bankruptcy, reorganization, and recapitalization purposes are also rare. Appraisals related to ESOPs, estate planning and intergenerational wealth transfer, and damages litigation (involving the value of the practice) are all less common with professional practices than with other businesses.

For these reasons, the focus of this six-chapter unit of the book will be a discussion of valuations for transactional and for controversy purposes. Because the factors involved in the actual sale of a practice are different from those involved in valuation for litigation (and particularly for divorce), the economic elements that create practice goodwill may be different. Therefore, the chapter on goodwill (Chapter 34) discusses the elements that are important for each valuation purpose.

A broader list of common reasons to conduct professional practice valuations is presented in Exhibit 32–1.

Characteristics of a Professional Practice

As the title of this book implies, there are both similarities and differences between a small business and a professional practice. There are numerous characteristics of a professional practice that, when taken together, distinguish it from other small businesses. These characteristics can be grouped into five categories:

1. The professional practice is primarily a service business with fewer tangible assets than most small businesses.
2. There is necessarily a relationship of trust and respect between the client and the professionals or employees of the practice. This is because the client must rely on professional expertise that the client is not fully capable of understanding or evaluating.
3. The practice or the practitioner often relies on a referral source or sources.
4. A specific college degree or graduate degree is usually required by regulatory bodies for the professional to practice in the chosen field.
5. The practitioner is licensed by a governmental or regulatory agency and/or certified by a recognized professional organization.

Exhibit 32–1

COMMON REASONS TO CONDUCT
A PROFESSIONAL PRACTICE VALUATION

There are numerous reasons—or client motivations—why a professional practice may be subject to valuation. However, all of these reasons typically can be grouped into six categories: transaction, taxation, financing, litigation, bankruptcy, and management information.

Transaction pricing and structuring motivations
- the purchase or sale of the entire practice
- the purchase or sale of an ownership interest in the practice
- the relative allocation of equity in a two-practice merger
- the relative allocation of equity in the formation of the practice (between individual practitioners)
- the equity or asset allocation during a practice dissolution

Taxation planning and compliance motivations
- estate tax planning
- estate tax compliance
- purchase price allocation
- practice asset basis adjustment

Financing collateralization and securitization motivations
- practice acquisition financing (both asset-based and cash flow–based financing)
- practice operations financing
- analysis of practice solvency
- analysis of fraudulent conveyance related to practice acquisition financing

Litigation support and dispute resolution motivations
- marital dissolution of the equity owners
- taxation disputes
- partner squeeze-outs
- claims of fraud or misrepresentation subsequent to a practice purchase or sale
- economic damages due to breach of contract, fraud, etc.

Bankruptcy and reorganization motivations
- preparing and assessing a plan of reorganization
- assessing collateral value of various creditors
- securing debtor in possession financing
- identifying spin-off opportunities

Management information and planning motivations
- long-term estate planning
- formation and operation of ownership buy-sell agreements
- partnership formation and dissolution agreements
- evaluation of practice purchase or merger offers
- evaluation of stewardship and effectiveness of practice management
- development and implementation of practice value enhancement techniques

It is apparent from this list of characteristics that the line between professional practices and certain kinds of service businesses may sometimes be a fine one.

Service Business Characteristics

Professional practices provide services of various kinds, from giving income tax advice to treating a pet's illnesses. The nature of these specialized services, in light of the professional's specialized training and the client's dependence on the professional's expertise, causes price to be a less important consideration than in the purchase of goods or of less-specialized services.

If a consumer wants to buy a refrigerator, for example, the consumer will generally shop several appliance stores to find the best price available. However, a potential patient/client is likely to be far less price-conscious in choosing a cardiologist or a defense attorney. Pricing will be important if the particular need is not critical or might be subject to an upper limit of the client's ability to pay. However, the factor that is more important to the selection of a professional than pricing is the expertise that the client or patient needs in a particular situation. A person with only wage and interest income may be completely satisfied with a book-keeping service for the preparation of a personal income tax return. However, an individual with complicated investments, capital gains income, and so forth, may want a more qualified certified public accountant (CPA) or attorney to complete the personal income tax return. People may purchase refrigerators on the basis of price. However, price is usually not the primary determining factor when selecting a physician, dentist, accountant, or lawyer.

Client Trust and Respect

The trust and respect that clients hold for the members of the practice are crucial to its success. As long as this trust is maintained, the client will generally return to the practitioner. Personal trust is an important reason professional goodwill is often strongly related to the individual practitioner.

Dependence on Referral Sources

New clients choose a professional practice primarily on the basis of referral from another source. They generally do not choose their physicians, dentists, lawyers, or accountants from ads in the Yellow Pages but rather on the recommendation of someone they know. Some types of professional practices, however, such as optometrists, veterinarians, and chiropractors, may get a substantial portion of their new patients by means of their location or by advertisements.

At the other extreme, some professional practices depend totally on new referrals to generate patient visits. An oral surgeon, for example, does not generally have continuing relationships with patients. Therefore, the surgical dental subspecialist will maintain relationships, through professional societies, social clubs, and promotional activities, with general, primary care dentists who refer patients.

Education

Individuals who make up a professional practice have graduated from institutions offering some kind of specialized education. Although some professions require a bachelor's degree or a certain number of years in a special course of study, others demand a master's degree or a doctorate degree, plus extensive on-the-job training. This requirement for extensive training affects professional goodwill in two ways: (1) The client's trust and respect are increased or generated by the long years of study involved, and (2) the long years of study represent an investment in time and money on the part of the professional, who expects a monetary return on that investment.

Licensing and Certification

Many professions require (1) licensing by a governmental or regulatory agency and/or (2) admittance to a professional organization before a professional can practice his or her specialty. This factor, when present, has the effect of limiting the number of individuals who can practice, creating a barrier to entry to that profession.

Distinctions between Professional Practice Valuations and Other Business Valuations

Type of Assets

A greater proportion of professional practice assets than is the case for other types of businesses tend to be intangible assets. To this extent, the values of professional practices tend to be even more dependent on earning capacity than are other businesses. If an asset-based valuation approach is used (which is often the case), the analyst should be well versed in the analysis and appraisal of intangible assets. In professional practices, intangible assets often derive their values primarily from their contribution to the economic income of the practice.

Dependence on the Professional

Professional practices are more dependent on one or a few individuals than is usually the case for most businesses. This has two primary implications for the practice valuation:

1. The evaluation of the contribution of the professional(s) to the practice is a key factor in the analysis.
2. In some cases, it may be important to distinguish between the elements of intangible value that are more associated with the institutional practice versus those elements that are more associated with the individual practitioner.

Professional Licenses

A license to practice a given profession usually is a valuable intangible asset. The practice license has intangible economic value. This is because it represents an independent third party's endorsement of credibility, usually to the extent of at least acknowledging demonstration of some minimum level of competence. In many cases, it also serves to limit the number of entrants (or practitioners) into the given profession.

A few states (most notably New York) have recognized professional licenses as a valuable marital estate asset in marital dissolution litigation actions. In most states, the professional license is merely recognized as one element of the practitioner's goodwill. When a number of professional licenses are amalgamated within a practice, the collection of licenses held by the practitioners can create intangible value in the nature of goodwill for the institutional practice itself.

Cash-Basis Accounting

Since most professional practices use cash-basis accounting, it usually is necessary to adjust financial statements to an accrual basis for practice valuation purposes.

However, it is noteworthy that certain comparative data for similar professional practices may be presented on a cash basis. In such a situation, the analyst may need to use cash-basis data for comparative purposes and still use accrual-basis data for other aspects of the valuation process.

Limited Life of the Practice

Professional practices are more often constrained to a limited life than are most businesses. Most businesses are regarded as having a perpetual life. While the perpetual life valuation premise may be appropriate for larger professional practices, it is not always appropriate for smaller professional practices. This is because smaller professional practices may be constrained by the limited professional working life of the individual practitioner(s). Professional practice valuations often rely heavily on income approach valuation methods. Accordingly, this limited life characteristic should be reflected in the projections underlying the income approach analyses.

Value Drivers for Professional Practice

For any kind of small business or professional practice, a few key factors are usually especially important in distinguishing the value of that business or practice from its counterparts in the same industry or profession. These key factors are sometimes referred to as *value drivers*.

Exhibit 32-2 provides an abbreviated checklist of such factors. These factors may be reflected in the valuation in a variety of ways, such as influencing the selection of practice pricing multiples, direct capitalization rates, present value discount rates, and/or a valuation discount for lack of marketability.

Exhibit 32–2

CHECKLIST OF IMPORTANT FACTORS
AFFECTING THE VALUES OF PROFESSIONAL PRACTICES

Factor	More Desirable	Less Desirable
Location and demographics	Urban High growth Affluent Stable population	Rural Mature or declining market Poor Transient population
Client persistence	Very stable	High turnover
Dependence on referrals versus direct client contact	Large direct client base	One or a few referral sources
Contractual relationships	Strong relationship(s)	Relationship(s) threatened to terminate
Supply/demand relationship (for acquisition of practice)	High demand, low supply	High supply, low demand
Reputation	Stellar, far and wide	Nonexistent or tarnished
Facilities and technology	State of the art	Antiquated
Employees	Adequate and dedicated	Inadequate and/or departing
Practitioner's work habits	Light work load	Workaholic
For medical practices, proportion of "managed care" clients (generally not assignable)	Few or none from health maintenance contracts	High proportion from health maintenance contracts
Potential vertical synergies	High propensity to be source of revenue for prospective acquiree	No synergistic revenue potential for prospective acquiree

Summary

Most professional practice valuations are performed either for transactional or controversy purposes. Nonetheless, there are many other reasons for conducting a professional practice valuation. Professional practices have certain characteristics that are unique compared to other businesses. These characteristics require the analyst to use specialized knowledge and analyses that may have little or no applicability in valuing other kinds of businesses. Professional practices also, as a broad generalization, have other distinctions from typical small businesses.

These distinctions have a bearing on the selection of the appropriate valuation methods and procedures. Finally, certain factors tend to account for a large part of the differences in value from one practice to another practice in the same professional field.

This chapter has summarized these characteristics, distinctions, and value drivers in a general sense. Subsequent chapters provide more detail about application of these general considerations in the professional practice valuation process.

Chapter 33

Adjusting the Professional Practice Balance Sheet

When valuing professional practices, as when valuing small businesses, it is important to analyze and make appropriate adjustments both to the entity's tangible and intangible assets and to its liabilities. The valuation of a professional practice differs from that of the typical small business, however. This is because the types of assets owned by a professional practice are very different from those owned by the typical small business. Perhaps the most significant difference is that intangible value in the nature of goodwill is a much more important element in the value of the professional practice compared to the typical small business. And the process of valuing both the tangible and intangible assets of a professional practice is further complicated by the cash-basis accounting method most professional practices use.

There may be a good deal of value in assets not recorded on the balance sheets of a cash-basis entity, such as accounts receivable, work-in-process inventory, and prepaid expenses. In addition, fully depreciated equipment that is still being used by the practice may have been removed from the practice's balance sheet. And leasehold improvements that would be irrelevant to the typical business may form an integral part of the operation of the professional practice. In the same context, such liabilities as accounts payable, accrued vacation time for employees, and accrued taxes may not be recorded on the cash-basis balance sheet. The analyst should use judgment to determine (1) whether these assets and liabilities are necessary to the practice operations and (2) how they affect the practice value.

Assets

The following is a discussion of the most common types of assets that the analyst will find in professional practices. The list is not all-inclusive, and the analyst should give specific recognition to the type of professional practice being appraised in order to develop a list of potential practice-specific assets.

Cash

The reliability of the cash figure on the balance sheet may depend on whether the statements were audited by an independent certified public accountant or merely compiled by the office manager or by a bookkeeping service. If there is reason to believe that the recorded cash balance may be incorrect, the analyst should request copies of bank statements and statement reconciliations. The analyst should review the deposit activity for a period just following the valuation date.

Sometimes, a professional practice will not record checks received in payment as part of the cash balance until the checks are actually deposited in the bank. Some professional practices use a system of tax deferral not authorized by the Internal Revenue Service. That is, for a certain amount of time preceding the fiscal year-end, they hold all incoming checks. The practice then deposits the checks at the beginning of the next fiscal year, enabling the practice to record the income on the following year's income tax return. The practice balance sheet should be adjusted in order to recognize these amounts as either cash or as accounts receivable.

At the other end of the spectrum of error, petty cash may be recorded incorrectly on the practice books, not to save taxes but because of poor record keeping. The incidence of such accounting anomalies is probably highest among sole practitioners.

Accounts Receivable

Accounts receivable are not recorded on the balance sheets of professional practices that operate on a cash basis of accounting. In these situations, therefore, it is necessary to estimate the value of accounts receivable, in order to include them in the value of the professional practice. There are several ways of keeping records of accounts receivable. Gross receivables at any given date are easily determined from the day sheets or accounts receivable journals of most practices.

Another type of receivable often overlooked is accounts that have been turned over to a collection agency. This is because they are often written off the accounts receivable balance when they are turned over to the agency. The value of these accounts is usually small because the collection agency deducts its fee of as much as 50 percent off the top of the amounts collected. The analyst should be aware of the value of these accounts and should include it in the overall accounts receivable amount.

Having determined the gross value of the accounts receivable, the analyst should adjust for uncollectible and slow-pay accounts. The following are the two most common methods for estimating uncollectible accounts:

1. *Accounts receivable aging.* Discounting the accounts on the basis of how long past due they are.
2. *Actual payment history.* Analyzing the payment trends of the specific practice and whether the trend is for more or fewer write-offs.

Both of these methods have positive and negative characteristics. The analyst should determine which method is more appropriate for the subject professional practice.

If the appraisal is being conducted for transaction purposes, the analyst should also take into consideration the collectability of the accounts receivable if the professional responsible for the billings will not be present to make the collection.

Aging of Receivables.   The analyst normally will either acquire or create an accounts receivable aging schedule, such as the one illustrated in Exhibit 7-1. The time periods outstanding generally run in 30-day increments, with the last category including accounts more than 180 days old. After totaling each category, the analyst applies a discount factor to each, with the further past-due balances receiving higher discounts.

This method of estimating uncollectible accounts receivable does not recognize individual payment histories or the payment procedures of the specific practice. For example, to discount by 50 percent all accounts over 180 days past due would cause an underestimation of the value if there were many accounts for which small monthly payments had been arranged and were being paid. In addition, the discount amounts are necessarily subjective. And the result may not reflect the particular payment procedures of the clients of the subject professional practice. If the practice does work for any federal agencies, it will be paid for its work eventually, but dependable private clients pay sooner. A 60-day past-due billing for the government should usually not be discounted as much as a 60-day past-due billing for a private client.

Actual Payment History.   The second method of estimating the reserve for uncollectible accounts receivable analyzes the practice's individual collection history. This method compares the accounts receivable write-offs from one period to the billings generated during the same period. The analyst requests a payment history for a 36- to 60-month period. This history would take the form of a schedule showing monthly charges, collections, credit adjustments, debit adjustments, and month-end receivable balances. From these data, the charges, collections, and net adjustments would be totaled for the entire period and for each fiscal year.

The analyst would then calculate the percentage of net adjustments to billings in order to establish an average for the period and for each fiscal year. In this way, the analyst determines the actual percentage of charges that are never collected. By analyzing trends for several fiscal years, the analyst can determine if a pattern of higher or lower write-offs is forming.

The problem with computing the percentage of historical net adjustments to the billings is that, if the practice has a significant number of clients (or patients) who pay immediately and are not billed for services, the total charges would reflect not only accounts receivable but cash transactions as well. Including accounts that were paid when incurred would tend to artificially reduce the percentage of historical write-offs. In that case, the percentage of immediate cash payments on account would need to be considered in the calculation of historical write-offs.

Many practices "houseclean" their accounts receivable at the end of the fiscal year, writing off the ones they consider uncollectible. The analyst should ascertain if the practice subject to appraisal engages in such a housecleaning. This is (1) so that the analyst does not inadvertently overadjust for uncollectible accounts and (2) so that the analyst can examine the practice's write-off method and adjust for too much or not enough estimation of uncollectible accounts.

As mentioned previously, slow-pay accounts may need to be discounted to allow for the time value of money (see Chapter 7). If the professional practice collects receivables fairly rapidly, the discount may be very small. However, if collections tend to take a long time, the accounts should be discounted accordingly, netted against any interest the practice charges on past-due amounts.

Work-in-Process Inventory

Many professional practices have unrecorded assets for work they have performed but for which they have not yet billed. Typically, work-in-process inventory is an asset that is found in practices that charge hourly for professional or staff time, such as CPA firms, consulting practices, and law firms. Work-in-process inventory is also found in practices that charge on a percentage of completion basis, such as engineering and appraisal firms. This asset may also be called *unbilled accounts receivable*.

Since work-in-process inventory is based on time spent by the professional practice's staff, there are usually (but not always) time records available from which to estimate the amount of services that are unbilled. However, it is often the case that practices can estimate unbilled receivables only at the current date. They cannot reconstruct the work-in-process inventory at any prior date. Therefore, to make a reasonable estimate of the work-in-process inventory at a prior date, the analyst should understand the billing procedures of the practice, including (1) how often the work-in-process is billed and on what day(s) of the month, and what procedures are used to compile and bill work-in-process; (2) by what criteria the accounts are determined billable; and (3) what records show work-in-process that has been written off.

It is important to remember that practices using cash-basis accounting have probably already recorded all of the expenses associated with the work-in-process inventory. For that reason, it is unnecessary to calculate the gross or net margins on their work-in-process. The amounts expensed for services that have not been billed to clients but that are expected to be billed and collected should be listed as an asset on the practice financial statements. Then, except for minor adjustments, the analyst can use the figures shown on the financial statements for the value of the work-in-process. However, under a *modified accrual system*, accounts receivable are included in revenues, but work-in-process is not recognized. In that case, goods and/or margins may become important to the analyst.

Exhibit 33-1 presents a typical method of calculating the value of work-in-process inventory for a firm using cash-basis or modified accrual-basis accounting. It is apparent in this exhibit that $32,000 worth of unbilled consulting is not equal to $32,000 of collection. Hours are often written down or written up for a variety of reasons. The analyst should calculate a historical percentage in order to estimate how much of the firm's billable time is actually billed. Then the amount is discounted for uncollectible receivables, as discussed above, in order to estimate how much is likely to be collected. If there are fixed-fee contracts, the analyst should calculate their value on the basis of the estimated percentage of completion at the valuation date.

One final adjustment may be necessary. The analyst who finds a significant number of old unbilled hours still in inventory should determine how diligently the firm has housecleaned its inventory. If there has been only haphazard housecleaning, or none at all, the analyst probably needs to age the work-in-process inventory and significantly discount (or even eliminate) the old unbilled hours.

Exhibit 33–1

SMITH & WESSON CONSULTING, INC.
CALCULATION OF VALUE OF WORK-IN-PROCESS INVENTORY
AS OF SEPTEMBER 30, 1997

	J. Smith	K. Wesson	Total
Hours in unbilled inventory	130	210	
Hourly billing rate	x $125	x $ 75	
Gross value of unbilled inventory	$16,250	$15,750	
Total gross value of unbilled inventory			32,000
Less: 3-year historical adjustment to work-in-process (amount not billed is equal to 7% of total)			(2,240)
Estimated work-in-process inventory that will be billed			29,760
Less: 3-year historical write-off on accounts receivable (amount of charges not collected is equal to 9% of total charges			(2,678)
Estimated cash value of work-in-process before calculation of discount for time to collect			$ 27,082

Some types of professional practices may have contingent work-in-process. For example, a law firm may have work-in-process for which it will collect only if it wins a litigated civil action. The value of such contingent work-in-process may be estimated on the basis of the firm's average historical realizations or on a project-by-project basis. If the practice or an interest in the practice is being sold, this may be resolved by a contingency in the purchase price based on actual realization of the contingent work-in-process.

Inventory of Supplies

The value of the supplies inventory depends on the type of professional practice. The office supplies of a CPA firm will have a small value compared, for instance, to the inventory of glasses frames in an optometric practice of comparable size. Without a detailed cataloging of inventory items, the analyst can usually estimate the amount of inventory on hand for practices that do not have substantial value in inventory. Nevertheless, the analyst normally will tour the practice offices and at least check the level of supplies kept.

A review of the prior year's history of supply purchases can aid the analyst in estimating the value of supplies on hand. If the practice generally orders supplies once a month, the total supply expense for the prior year could be divided by 12 for an estimate of the value of supplies on hand at any particular time. However, if the practice keeps a 90-day supply on hand, this method would underestimate the value of the supply inventory.

Prepaid Expenses

Two specific professional practice expenses are often prepaid: rent and insurance (including insurance policies for errors and omissions and for professional liability). However, because they are continuing, their amounts are not necessarily allocated to the periods when they are used. If they do not fluctuate significantly, the Internal Revenue Service will ignore the fact that they are improperly classified in one period. This is because over several periods, the income tax effect will net to zero. The analyst, on the other hand, is generally concerned with a specific valuation date. For that reason, prepaid expenses must be classified properly on the balance sheet to recognize the fact that future expenses have already been paid. For example, if the analyst finds that a physician has paid the annual premium on December 30 for the next year's professional liability insurance, the practice has a prepaid expense asset as of the March 30 valuation date.

Equipment

As was true of supplies, the amount and value of equipment necessary to operate any given professional practice depends very much on the type of practice. The typical dentistry practice will require significantly more valuable equipment than the typical psychiatric practice. The analyst should judge whether the equipment should be appraised by a professional equipment appraiser. For example, if there is a great deal of equipment, if the equipment is highly specialized, or if there are valuable antiques among the practice's assets, an independent analysis by a personal property appraiser should be considered. If there is very little equipment or if it consists primarily of automobiles, the analyst could estimate the value herself (for example, using the *Automotive Blue Book)*.

When needed, an equipment appraiser should be carefully selected. A qualified equipment appraiser understands standards of value and can appraise the equipment using the same standards as the business analyst. However, when the practice is being appraised under the going-concern premise of value, a used equipment dealer may give as a value only the amount he would pay for the equipment under practice liquidation conditions.

Several of the rules-of-thumb valuation methods discussed in Chapter 35 include the value of the equipment. If one of these methods is used to value a professional practice, the analyst still needs to consider the value of the equipment. The equipment may be old, unnecessary to the practice operation, or extremely specialized. Any of these characteristics alter the multiples in the rule-of-thumb method or make them useless for the specific valuation.

Finally, the analyst may examine the equipment listed on the practice's depreciation schedule. This procedure is useful, but the equipment list should be verified. This is because assets owned by the practice may have been removed or may never have been listed on the schedule.

Leasehold Improvements

Another important asset is the leasehold improvements of the practice. During the appraiser's tour of the practice office, the analyst should pay attention to the condition of the improvements—in other words, how well the office is packaged. If the leasehold improvements are in good condition and have been fully depreciated on the balance sheet, the analyst may want to adjust their value upward, considering both (1) their life expectancy and (2) the remaining term of the current lease.

Buyers may be reluctant to place much value on leasehold improvements because they will belong to the landlord and cannot be removed if the lessee vacates the premises. However, the fair market value of the leasehold improvements, as part of a going concern, may be an allocable amount of the purchase price that the buyer can depreciate for income tax purposes.

In the overall analysis of the professional practice assets, the analyst should continually ask if the asset is necessary to the operation of the practice. Assets that are unnecessary for the success of the practice should be treated as excess to the total practice value. And any income or expenses resulting from these assets should be removed from the practice income statements.

Intangible Assets

Many intangible assets may exist in the subject professional practice. Exhibit 33-2 presents a partial list of the intangible assets that may exist and that therefore should be investigated in the course of the analysis.

Exhibit 33–2

**INTANGIBLE ASSETS COMMONLY FOUND IN
VARIOUS PROFESSIONAL PRACTICES**

Computer software	Laboratory notebooks
Computerized databases	Library
Cooperative agreements	Licenses
Copyrights	Literary works
Customer contracts	Litigation awards & damages
Customer lists	Management contracts
Customer relationships	Marketing and promotional materials
Designs and drawings	Noncompete covenants
Employment contracts	Patents and patent applications
Engineering drawings	Patient charts and records
Favorable leases	Permits
Franchise agreements	Procedural manuals
Going-concern value	Royalty agreements
Goodwill	Schematics and diagrams
Government contracts	Subscription lists
Historical documents	Supplier contracts
HMO enrollment lists	Technical and specialty libraries
Insurance expirations	Technical documentation
Joint ventures	Trade secrets
Know-how	Trained and assembled workforce

For more detail on the identification and valuation of intangible assets, see Chapter 37, Examples of Practice Valuation Methods, and Chapter 42, Valuing Intangible Assets.

Liabilities

Several categories of liabilities may not typically be reflected on the books of a professional practice. On the other hand, from a valuation standpoint, some liabilities may appear there (and even be required by GAAP) that are not real debts (such as deferred rent).

Accounts Payable

Cash-basis financial statements typically do not record accounts payable. Since most professional practices sell services, their accounts payable usually relate to continuing bills, such as supplies, telephone, utilities, taxes, and so forth, rather than to materials for manufacturing or sale. There are two basic methods for estimating accounts payable. Under the first method, the analyst reviews all unpaid invoices at the valuation date. If the field work is performed substantially after the valuation date, the analyst should request all canceled checks written during a reasonable period of time after the valuation date, along with the corresponding invoices. With this information, the analyst can estimate how much money the practice owed as of the valuation date.

The second method is less accurate, but it can give a reasonable estimate with less effort. The analyst begins with the total expenses presented on the practice income statement. From that amount, the analyst subtracts expenses that do not belong with accounts payable: those payable immediately, those that were paid in advance, those not requiring cash, and those presented elsewhere on the balance sheet as payables (e.g., payroll taxes payable). The analyst considers the practice's regular bill-paying procedures, such as how often all invoices are paid and how long the practice holds them before payment, in order to calculate the estimated accounts payable at the valuation date. Exhibit 33-3 illustrates this computation.

Accrued Liabilities

Accrued liabilities are expenses, such as payroll, payroll taxes, or interest, that are allocated to a prior period but not yet due. If a note payable calls for interest payments at the end of the year and the valuation date is at midyear, the analyst should adjust for accrued interest (unless it is already presented on the financial statements). This is appropriate even though the liability is not payable for another six months.

Many firms pay employees one to five days after a payroll cycle. If the valuation takes place at the end of a payroll cycle, there could be a large payable for salaries.

Exhibit 33-3

SMITH & WESSON CONSULTING, INC.
CALCULATION OF ESTIMATED AMOUNT OF ACCOUNTS PAYABLE
AS OF SEPTEMBER 30, 1997

Total expenses shown on fiscal year-end			
September 30, 1997, income statement			$ 175,000
Less:			
Those expenses paid immediately when due:			
Salaries (officers and employees)		70,000	
Interest		500	
Those expenses paid in advance:			
Rent		57,000	
Insurance		2,500	
Dues and subscriptions		200	
Those expenses not requiring cash:			
Amortization		20	
Depreciation		1,250	
Those expenses already shown as payables on financials:			
Pension plan		10,000	
Payroll taxes		4,500	
Total of expenses not part of accounts payable			(145,970)
Total of expenses that can be part of accounts payable			29,030
Divided by payment frequency (practice normally pays bills after 30 days, once per month)			12
Estimated accounts payable at September 30, 1997			$ 2,419

One liability often overlooked is accrued employee vacation time. The analyst should consider the company's vacation policy and verify the amounts of accrued vacation held by employees. If there is a significant amount of vacation time pending, this liability should be reflected on the balance sheet or at least disclosed in the appraisal report.

Deferred Liabilities

Deferred liabilities fall into three categories:

1. Deferred revenues.
2. Deferred expenses.
3. Deferred taxes.

Deferred Revenues. Deferred revenues are amounts that have been received for services not yet performed. An obstetrician-gynecologist (OB-GYN) medical practice is likely to have this type of liability, although it may not be presented on the practice balance sheet. OB-GYN specialists often receive from expectant mothers their entire fees for prenatal care and delivery. If the specialist is on cash-basis accounting, she or he is likely to report this prepayment as current income. This is true even though, from an accounting viewpoint, there is a liability for services yet to be performed. Deferred revenues may also need to be considered in law firms and consulting firms that receive retainers before beginning work on the case.

Deferred Expenses. Deferred expenses are relatively unusual. One example is deferred rent. A landlord may offer several months of free rent in return for a tenant signing a long-term lease. This situation would warrant a liability account for deferred rent. This is because the tenant could theoretically have negotiated a lease for the same period of time at a lower monthly rent. Rather, the tenant opted to accept the free rent, even though the total payments under each option would be equal. Exhibit 33-4 illustrates the journal entries to account for a deferred rent liability.

As Exhibit 33-4 illustrates, even though the company paid only $1,000 cash toward rent during the first seven months, the financial statements show rental expense of $6,363.63. The difference between the expense and the cash paid was allocated to Deferred Rent. From the analyst's point of view, this deferral is not a real liability and should be removed. However, when calculating the expected future income, the analyst should adjust the rent expense upward by $90.91 per month.

Exhibit 33–4

SMITH & WESSON CONSULTING, INC.
ACCOUNTING ENTRIES FOR "DEFERRED RENT" ACCOUNT

Assumption:	For the signing of a 60-month lease for offices, Smith & Wesson received an additional six months' free rent--the total rent over the term of the lease would equal $60,000, or $1,000 per month over 60 months. Generally accepted accounting principles would require that the rent be charged against income over the 66-month term, or $909.09 per month.		
Month 1:	Debit, rent expense	909.09	
	Credit, deferred rent		909.09
Months 2-6 Totals:	Debit, rent expense	4,545.45	
	Credit, deferred rent		4,545.45
Month 7:	Debit, rent expense	909.09	
	Debit, deferred rent	90.91	
	Credit, cash		1,000.00
Therefore:	At the end of seven months, rent expense totaled $6,363.63, cash was decreased by $1,000, and deferred rent expense equaled $5,363.63.		

Deferred Income Taxes.   Deferred income tax is the third type of deferred liability. The purpose of deferred income taxes appearing on financial statements is to match income tax expense with the related financial accounting income for the appropriate accounting period.

Deferred income taxes usually occur because of the difference in timing between recognition of income or expense for two different accounting systems of the same practice. For example, the practice may use straight-line depreciation on its own financial statements to more accurately reflect economic depreciation. However, the practice may use accelerated depreciation on tax returns. The result of using these two procedures would be to show more income on the financial statements and less on the tax returns. The amount of deferred income taxes on the financial statements is equal to the difference between income taxes actually paid and what they would have been if based on the higher income as presented on the financial statements.

When bringing assets onto the balance sheet, the liability for deferred taxes should also be recognized. Adjusting from a cash to an accrual basis for accounts receivable is an example where recognition of the related deferred tax liability would be appropriate.

For the analyst, this account may not reflect a true liability. If the practice rarely purchases new equipment, the depreciation for income tax purposes will ultimately be less than for financial statement purposes. Consequently, the practice will report more income on its income tax returns than on its financial statements. In that case, the taxes actually paid will be higher than taxes reported due on the financial statements. This means that the deferred taxes are an actual liability.

On the other hand, if the practice continually buys new equipment, the financial statements will generally report greater income than the income tax returns. In that case, the analyst could conclude that deferred taxes will never be paid in the foreseeable future and remove them from the balance sheet liabilities.

Long-Term Debt

Long-term debt in professional practices is usually associated with equipment purchases. However, in some instances, it represents amounts due to the former owner who sold the practice to the current owner. These situations should alert the analyst to investigate the past sale. If the analyst has reason to believe that the amounts listed in long-term debt are incorrect, copies of the debt instrument(s) and payment records should be obtained. Also, the debt instrument will disclose whether the practice has an accrued interest liability that is not presented on the balance sheet.

Lease Obligations

The analyst should obtain copies of all leases of the practice whether the practice is a lessor or a lessee. The financial statements usually report capital lease obligations, under which the practice will ultimately be obliged to purchase the leased equipment. These future lease payments should be treated as long-term debt, after separating imputed interest payable.

Contingent Liabilities

Contingent obligations, as discussed in Chapter 7, are liabilities (or assets) for which there is insufficient information about the outcome to know how to account for them on the financial statements. The professional may be a defendant or plaintiff in a professional liability suit, the practice may have partner retirement obligations, or there may be disputed billings. These facts may be disclosed on the financial statement. The analyst should investigate these types of liabilities (or assets).

Summary

Balance sheet adjustments for professional practices proceed similarly to those for other small businesses, as discussed in Chapter 7. Chapter 7 should be used in conjunction with this chapter. In the case of professional practices, there generally is also a need to adjust from a cash to an accrual basis, as discussed in considerable detail in this chapter. This chapter has also discussed other balance sheet adjustments that are particularly relevant to professional practices.

Although there is a great deal of literature on the subject of professional goodwill and other professional practice intangible assets, there has been very little literature published regarding the valuation of tangible assets of professional practices. These assets may have substantial value. The analyst should not overlook them when concentrating on valuing the practice goodwill. Goodwill usually cannot exist by itself but is frequently supported by tangible and intangible assets of some kind. The reader should refer to Chapter 42 for more direction with respect to the identification and valuation of intangible assets.

One caveat: If adjusting the financial statements for comparative purposes (e.g., for comparison to other specific financial statements or some compiled composite data), adjustments should be made only to the extent appropriate in order to make the subject practice data comparable to the comparative data.

Chapter 34

Elements That Create Professional and Practice Goodwill

With respect to professional practices, intangible value in the nature of goodwill may be analyzed and quantified either (1) collectively or (2) discretely. The collective measurement of goodwill represents the total intangible value of the practice in excess of the value of the individual tangible assets of the practice. In the collective form, goodwill is often quantified using two methods: (1) residual from an actual practice sale transaction price and (2) residual from an estimated practice overall enterprise value. In the discrete form, goodwill is often quantified using two methods: (1) the present value of the economic income from the future business of the practice (i.e., future patients and clients not currently served by the practice over the expected remaining life of the practice's institutional existence) and (2) the capitalization of expected excess earnings (i.e., total practice economic income less a fair rate of return on the individual tangible and intangible assets of the practice) over the expected remaining life of the practices' institutional existence.

However it is analyzed or quantified, intangible value in the nature of goodwill is often the most important element to the overall value of a professional practice. Arguably, of all of the typical elements of a professional practice's overall value, goodwill is the most difficult to measure.

Analysts often hear professionals say that the subject practice does not have any goodwill value because "without me, its worthless." Other professionals believe there is no way to transfer their professional goodwill because it is so personal. These ideas seem plausible, but they are not necessarily true. With careful planning and cooperation between practice seller and practice buyer, at least some portion of the intangible value in the nature of goodwill can usually be transferred to the new owner.

Distinction between Practice Goodwill and Professional Goodwill

In a professional practice, there are generally two types of goodwill: practice goodwill (sometimes referred to as institutional goodwill) and professional goodwill (sometimes referred to as practitioner goodwill). *Practice goodwill* is the intangible value in the nature of goodwill that is associated primarily with the practice as an institutional entity. *Professional goodwill* is the intangible value in the nature of goodwill that is associated primarily with the individual practitioner.

In professional practice appraisals performed for many purposes, it may not be necessary to separately analyze practice goodwill versus professional goodwill. However, in professional practice appraisals performed for various transactional (e.g., sale of the practice) or controversy (e.g., marital dissolution) purposes, it may be necessary to separately identify and quantify practice goodwill as distinct from professional goodwill.

Practice Goodwill

Practice goodwill is an intangible asset of the practice as an institutional entity. Therefore, it is not really different from the type of goodwill that is owned by any other small business. A professional typically cannot sell (as in transfer) his reputation, skills, or knowledge. However, he may use these attributes to establish a successful practice and to generate substantial earnings. In doing so, he has started a successful business institution. The business institution itself will acquire many of the intangible elements, such as location, computer systems, operating procedures, a trained and assembled staff, and a patient or client base. These intangible elements are common to both a small business and a professional practice. These types of intangible elements make up the practice—or institutional—goodwill. These intangible elements (and others like them) can generate value over and above the entity's net asset value, thus producing goodwill value. A professional practice that has these intangible elements has practice goodwill, which can have significant value.

Professional Goodwill

While a professional practice does own practice goodwill in fee simple interest, the individual practitioner(s) may have personal goodwill. This professional (or practitioner) goodwill may contribute to the overall income-generating capacity of the practice.

A certain portion of the practitioner's clients or patients may come to that individual because of the practitioner's personal reputation. This personal client following or patient following generates earnings for the subject practice. If the practitioner suddenly left the practice, a large majority of the income generated from these personal clients and patients would likely leave as well.

A common misconception is that professional goodwill is not marketable because it is never transferable. Although the transfer of professional goodwill is more difficult than the transfer of practice goodwill, there are procedures by which the practitioner can facilitate the transfer of this personal goodwill, or at least a portion of this personal goodwill, to another well-qualified practitioner.

The transfer of client trust and respect from seller to buyer requires the cooperation of both parties. Their efforts would include, at least, a letter of announcement from the seller to current clients. This letter would inform them that the buyer is taking over their cases and that the buyer has the qualifications and expertise to handle their needs. In this way, the selling professional uses his or her reputation to transfer professional goodwill to the buyer.

Another means of ensuring the transfer of personal goodwill is for the seller to stay with the practice during a transition period. In this way, the clients or patients can become familiar and comfortable with the new practitioner. It requires the seller's best efforts to transfer professional goodwill to the new practitioner. Frequently, the clients will not be made aware that the buyer is other than an associate. This procedure often proves effective in increasing client retention.

It is more difficult to transfer professional goodwill if the seller depends on professional or personal contacts to refer clients. The seller cannot so easily write a letter to his or her friends at the country club and convince them that the person buying the practice should, from now on, get their referrals. Similarly, if an oral surgeon has persuaded general dentists of his expertise through presentations at professional seminars, the oral surgeon buying his practice will not necessarily have an easy time persuading them that his expertise is comparable. On the other hand, the sole cardiac surgeon in a community can usually transfer his referral base to the cardiac surgeon buying the practice. Professional goodwill is hardly ever so personal that none of it can be transferred.

Buying and Selling a Practice—Elements of Goodwill

In order for goodwill to have value transcending a transfer of ownership of the practice, the goodwill should be transferable along with the practice ownership. Many elements in a professional practice can cause transferable goodwill to exist. However, the elements that create goodwill in a buy-sell situation are somewhat different from those considered in a valuation for marital dissolution purposes. For example, one element that is very important in a buy-sell situation is the marketability of the practice. However, that factor is often irrelevant under many states' marital dissolution guidelines.

Goodwill is sometimes difficult to precisely define. This is because goodwill is generated by so many different factors and combinations of factors that it is impossible to list them all. However, several factors are dominant in determining the existence of—and estimating the value of —goodwill in professional practices:

1. Earnings levels that can be expected in the future.
2. The level of competition.
3. The referral base.
4. The types of patients or clients the practice serves.
5. Work habits of the practitioner.
6. The fees earned (compared to others in the same specialty).
7. Where the practice is located.
8. The practice's employees.
9. The general marketability of the type of practice being sold.

Expected Future Earnings

As with other business enterprises, one of the biggest factors contributing to goodwill value in a professional practice is the level of economic income. Generally, the higher the earnings, the more goodwill exists in the enterprise. However, an abundance of earnings does not inherently indicate an abundance of goodwill. Nor does a dearth of earnings inherently indicate a lack of goodwill. In judging the existence and value of goodwill based on the level of earnings, the analyst should be sure to know the causes for the economic earnings levels before concluding a value. High economic income may result from the professional's skills, reputation, and efficiencies, or from the practitioner working longer hours and seeing more clients per day. Like goodwill itself, economic income does not occur by itself, but because of other factors.

The term *economic income* does not necessarily refer to the practice net income. This is because net income is usually distributed to the practice principals in the form of salaries, perquisites, and benefits. Therefore, the net income as recorded on the books of an incorporated practice is usually close to zero.

To estimate the true economic income of the practice, the analyst should analyze several years of financial statements and income tax returns, with each account on the income statements and balance sheets compared to the other years and set out in percentages of the relevant figures. On the income statements, all accounts may be expressed as a percent of revenues. On the balance sheets, all accounts may be expressed as a percent of total assets. For comparative purposes, economic income is usually measured on a cash basis. This is because professionals generally use that accounting connection for income tax purposes. This is also because economic income surveys are generally performed on a cash basis.

Trended income statements are also helpful. In many professional firms, two types of trended statements are calculated: (1) expressing each account as a percentage of the same account in the first year considered and (2) expressing each account as a percentage of the same account in the year immediately prior.

From this information, the analyst can discover unusual year-to-year activity in specific income accounts (e.g., owners' salaries). The analyst then examines supporting documents (retirement plan payment allocations, the general ledger, various journals, check registers, invoices, etc.) in order to accurately calculate the practice's available economic income.

Level of Competition

Approximately 30 years ago, there was a shortage of physicians in this country. At that time, a physician who had met the educational requirements and received a practice license could hang up a shingle and begin seeing patients during the first week of practice. Because it was so easy to start a medical practice, the market for the sale of established practices was inactive. Medical schools responded to the shortage by graduating more physicians. The physician shortage was eliminated in most parts of the country, followed by an oversupply of physicians in many places.

It is not as easy now to start a successful medical practice as it was at that time. In fact, it is nearly impossible in many areas. For that reason, established medical practices in some areas of the country are selling at prices more attractive to the seller (compared to several years ago). This is because new physicians are seeking to associate with established practices or to buy them outright. Obviously, as the demand for established medical practices has increased, so has their value.

When appraising a professional practice, the analyst should take into account the number of other practitioners in the same profession in the area and what proportion they bear to the population at large. The census of supply of professionals has a marked bearing on the value of the professional practice.

Referral Base

Since the sources of referrals are a key characteristic of a professional practice, it is natural that they should also have a profound effect on the value of goodwill. A practice where referrals come from a large number of current patients and clients will generally have more practice goodwill value than one that relies on referrals from a relatively small client base or from other professionals. Because of the difficulty of transferring the professional goodwill associated with a base of referrals, as discussed earlier in this chapter, the referral base is an important element of the value of an entire practice.

Types of Patients and Clients

Generally, the analyst should know the types of clients who patronize the practice and why. Typically, the analyst would inquire about how many patients (or clients) are seen each day, how many new clients seek the practice's services for the first time during a time period and how many cease to do so, and whether the practice depends on any particular client or specific group of clients for a significant portion of its income.

Especially in medical and dental practices, the analyst should inquire about the percentage of patients who have private insurance, who are part of an HMO, who are part of the Medicare program, and who qualify for the government's Medicaid program. The practice with a large percentage of patients who either pay their bills themselves or who have private insurance will have a higher value than one with a preponderance of Medicare and Medicaid patients. This is because these government insurance programs generally pay later and pay less per procedure than the practitioner's usual fee.

Work Habits of the Practitioner

It's almost a cliché that professionals work long hours. However, some are willing to work longer hours than others. A practice that requires 80 hours a week of a practitioner's time will not be worth as much per dollar of income to a purchaser as one that requires only 50 hours per week.

Different work habits may also affect the value of a practice. Some dentists like to spend time with each patient. Other dentists prefer to schedule several patients at a time and to delegate more of the procedures to dental assistants or technicians. Obviously, a dentist of the more "personal" type considering purchasing a practice owned by a dentist of the "mass production" type needs to consider how her work habits will alter the earning capacity of that practice.

On the other hand, a potential purchaser may find that the selling practitioner liked to spend time on administrative duties that could have been handled by an office manager. Thus, there could be time to generate more revenue or to play more golf.

Fee Schedules

It is important that the analyst understand the practice's fee schedule. Does it charge by procedure, time spent, or some other measure? How do this practitioner's fees compare with those of others with comparable qualifications? The analyst should know how often the fees are adjusted and when the last fee adjustment occurred. If fees fall below the community's standard rate, what would happen to the income if the fees were raised, and how many patients or clients would be lost because of a fee increase? All of these questions are usually considered in the course of examining the practice's economic income.

The fee schedule also provides an index to the skill and reputation of the practitioner. A practitioner with above-average fees and a large client base may be assumed to have above-average expertise or at least a better reputation.

Practice Location

The location of a practice has a substantial impact on its value. A location that is convenient for customers can be a source of value. Some areas are perceived as more desirable than others. Some communities are good "family" communities, while others provide a fast-track lifestyle.

Like anyone else, professionals like to practice in the kind of communities in which they like to live. Therefore, areas that provide a comfortable lifestyle for the practitioner and his or her family, with a growing population or a strong and vibrant economy, will generally have professional practices that are in higher demand and are more expensive than will areas that are personally unattractive and/or economically depressed. The analyst should investigate local demographics, the economic health of the area, and the overall quality of life in the community.

Employees of the Practice

The employees of a professional practice can be very important to its value. They know the procedures, they know the clients, and the expense of training them has already been incurred. When patients come in for their first visit with the new doctor (the buyer) or when clients have their first encounter with the new lawyer or accountant, the familiar faces of the support personnel will help relieve their anxieties.

The analyst should inquire about the number of employees and their names, their job titles and job descriptions, their pay scales, and the length of time they have been with the practice. The analyst should inquire whether they plan to stay under the new management.

Particularly important are the nonowner professionals employed by the practice. They may actually hold the goodwill of some clients. And if they chose to leave the practice, their clients might go with them. The analyst should inquire as to the extent that is the case in the practice at hand. The buyer does not want to pay for professional goodwill value that is ultimately not the seller's to sell because it is owned by an employee who may or may not stay with the practice. In such a situation, an employment contract and a covenant not to compete may be negotiated with that employee, so that, in effect, the buyer purchases the employee's professional goodwill as well.

Marketability of the Practice

The marketability of the practice depends on a number of factors, some of which have been discussed throughout this chapter. Demand for the practice obviously determines marketability, but often for reasons not directly related to the specific practice itself. If there is a glut of accountants seeking to purchase accounting practices, the demand for established accounting practices is likely to rise, thus raising their practice goodwill value. If it is relatively easy to enter the specific profession, practice goodwill value will be lower.

In many parts of the country, professional practices do not sell at all because the economy is so weak. On the other hand, some professions are inherently unmarketable, such as many psychiatric practices where the trust between patient and doctor is so crucial that it is, for all practical purposes, not transferable. The analyst should examine these circumstances and use his or her judgment in estimating the market value of professional practices.

In recent years, the marketability of many kinds of professional practices, particularly in the medical and dental fields, has been significantly enhanced by consolidation into institutional groups. Several articles discussing results of this consolidation movement are included in the bibliography at the end of Chapter 35.

Valuation for Marital Dissolution Purposes— Elements of Goodwill

Valuations for marital dissolution purposes are among the most common professional engagements the appraiser of professional practices encounters. Most of the states where appellate courts have ruled on whether professional goodwill is a marital asset subject to valuation and division have held that it is indeed an asset and should be valued and accounted for in the division of property. These states consider the value of the practice in the hands of the professional spouse as part of a going concern.

All the elements that create professional goodwill discussed in the preceding section should be considered in valuing professional goodwill for marital dissolution purposes. However, some of these elements are not necessarily as important in that context as in the valuation for a sale of the practice. In a marital dissolution valuation, the marketability of the subject practice generally does not determine the existence or value of professional goodwill.

Often, the difficulty of transferring referral sources is not a consideration for value in marital dissolution valuations. This is primarily because there is no actual transfer of the professional goodwill occurring. It is more as if the "silent partner" (i.e., the nonpracticing spouse) is retiring and the practicing spouse is continuing in practice. For that reason, no diminution in professional goodwill will necessarily occur.

The various state courts have been helpful in establishing some fairly uniform guidelines to the factors that must be considered in appraising professional goodwill. The genesis of these factors is the California case *Lopez* v. *Lopez*. The *Lopez* decision is a good treatise on the valuation of professional goodwill for marital dissolution purposes. It has been widely quoted in many other states in supporting the establishment of value for professional goodwill in marital dissolution cases.

One of the primary sections of the *Lopez* opinion deals with what elements the analyst should consider before expressing an opinion of professional goodwill value. The following are the factors determined to be appropriate in that case:

1. The age and health of the professional.
2. The professional's demonstrated past earning power.
3. The professional's reputation in the community for judgment, skill, and knowledge.
4. The professional's comparative professional success.
5. The nature and duration of the professional's practice, either as a sole proprietor or as a contributing member of a partnership or professional corporation.[1]

---

[1] *In re Marriage of Lopez*, 113 Cal. Rptr. 58 (38 Cal. App. 3d 93, 1974).

As comprehensive as they seem, these factors have been the source of some confusion among analysts, attorneys, and the trial courts about how they should be measured.

Practitioner's Age and Health

It is far easier to determine the practitioner's age and health than to know how these factors affect professional goodwill value. Naturally, the practitioner's age is important. A practitioner close to retirement generally does not have a great deal of professional goodwill value, even when the historical earnings of the practice have been good. This is because those earnings cannot be expected to continue very far into the future.

For example, if the practitioner were going to retire and close the practice two years after the valuation date, any multiple of his earnings (or excess earnings) over two would normally overvalue the professional goodwill. On the other hand, a fairly young practitioner who had only recently started practice would necessarily have a lower earning potential than the "average" practitioner. Therefore, adjustments should be made before comparing those earnings to the average practitioner.

Health is another important factor. In one case, for example, the analyst retained by the nonprofessional spouse reached the opinion that the professional goodwill of the professional spouse—a heart surgeon—was very high because of his past earning power. If that analyst had inquired as to the doctor's health, he would have learned that the surgeon recently had been diagnosed as having a degenerative disease in his joints. In a very short period, that disease would cause him to curtail his surgical practice. Since the practice was not readily salable and the professional spouse could not expect continued earnings from his practice, the court dismissed the analyst's estimation of value and ruled that only a nominal amount of goodwill existed.

Demonstrated Past Earning Power

As is true in virtually all kinds of business appraisal, future earnings are a very important consideration in estimating goodwill value. Because of the peculiar circumstances of property divisions in a divorce, the discounted economic income method of valuation is not always favored by the courts. This is because the prospective economic income will result from the practitioner's efforts after the marriage is terminated. According to judicial precedent in many jurisdictions, future earnings based on future efforts are not considered a marital asset.

However, the courts have recognized that goodwill value is merely an expression of the value of expected future economic income, and the best estimate of future income is what has happened in the past. In practice valuations for marital dissolution purposes, analysts will generally consider the past five years of earnings of the practitioner as of the valuation date.

Reputation for Judgment, Skill, and Knowledge

The practitioner's reputation for judgment, skill, and knowledge is one of the most abstract factors in the measurement of goodwill. After conducting many professional practice valuations, the analyst begins to get a feel for how these elements affect value, but it is difficult to quantify.

The analyst should request a copy of the practitioner's curriculum vitae and inquire if the practitioner has received any special certifications, written any articles, taught classes, received any professional awards, or if she is a member of stature in any professional societies. Any of these activities might help quantify these elements of a favorable reputation.

On the other hand, if the professional has been judged by a court to have committed malpractice (or even been publicly accused of malpractice), that would have a negative effect on the value of her professional goodwill. An interview form listing the specific questions the analyst needs to ask can be helpful in discovering information relating to the practitioner's reputation. Experienced analysts have usually developed proprietary interview forms and valuation worksheets that can be of great assistance in the valuation process.[2]

Comparative Professional Success

Comparative professional success is a crucial factor in establishing professional goodwill. "Success" is usually measured by the amount of economic income generated. However, other factors, such as the number of patients seen, hours generally spent working, community standards of living, and so forth, must also be considered.

It is very important to attempt to compare professionals with like professionals. If the analyst is valuing the professional goodwill of a corporate attorney, it would be best to compare his earnings to other attorneys in corporate law. There are many earnings surveys, and they should be consulted. (See the bibliography at the end of Chapter 35 for a list.) But to whatever extent possible, the earnings considered should be on a golden delicious–to–golden delicious basis, not on a golden delicious–to–crab apple basis.

Nature and Duration of Practice

Goodwill is built over time. Therefore, the length of time the practice has been in existence will have a bearing on goodwill. A long-established law firm will attract more and higher-paying clients than one with wet paint on the shingle. The nature of the practice should also be considered. The following information about the practice can be relevant in estimating

---

[2]An example of such a list can be found in James G. Rabe, Charles A. Wilhoite, and Karin Zamba, "Valuation in Marital Dissolutions" (Chapter 11) in *Financial Valuation: Businesses and Business Interests*, 1997 Update, James Zukin, ed. (New York: Warren, Gorham & Lamont, 1997), pp. U11-48–U11-53.

the amount of intangible value in the nature of goodwill:

- Type of service offered.
- Type of client served.
- Length of time at the current location.
- Length of time remaining on the lease.
- How the fees are billed.
- Source of new clients.
- The individual practitioner's amount of production.
- The number of employees and their length of service.
- Economic and demographic information on the community where the practice is located.
- The number of other professionals in the community offering the same service or specialty.

Summary

Practice (or institutional) goodwill is an intangible asset that resides with the professional practice as an institutional entity rather than with the individual practitioner. Professional (or practitioner) goodwill is an intangible asset that resides with the individual practitioner apart from the attributes of the professional practice entity. Even professional goodwill, however, has some degree of transferability with some effort and cooperation by the practitioner.

A practice valuation for marital dissolution purposes is different from a practice valuation for the sale of a practice or for other purposes. The analyst needs to understand the differences. In the discussion of various valuation methods included in the next chapter, methods used primarily in marital dissolution valuations are specifically identified. Each state has slightly different statutory authority and judicial precedent concerning the valuation of professional goodwill. Any appraisal of goodwill for marital dissolution purposes should recognize that state's particular statutes and precedent in arriving at a valuation conclusion.

Chapter 35

Estimating the Value of the Professional Practice

There is no single correct method of valuing professional practices, just as there is no single correct method of valuing any other type of small business. Some methods are more common than others, however, depending on the type of practice. Of course, all of these individual analytical methods can be categorized into the three basic approaches to business valuation: the income approach, the market approach, and the asset-based approach.

This chapter examines several methods of valuing professional practices, along with rules of thumb used by some practice brokers and industry participants.

Methods of Professional Practice Valuation

Over the years, many analytical methods have been devised to appraise professional practices. Several methods, when properly used, have withstood the tests of time and reasonableness and are now the generally accepted methods for valuing professional practices. Categorized by general valuation approach, these professional practice valuation methods are as follows:

Income Approach

1. Discounted economic income.
2. Capitalization of economic income.

Market Approach

1. Multiple of revenues.
2. Comparative transactions and buy-ins (market data comparison).
3. Punitive and retirement formulas.

Asset-Based Approach

1. Capitalized excess earnings.
2. Asset accumulation.
3. Depreciating goodwill.

Each professional practice valuation method has analytical strengths and weaknesses. Not every method will be appropriate to every type of professional practice or to every type of valuation assignment.

Discounted Economic Income

The discounted economic income method for a professional practice follows the same basic procedures as presented in Chapter 14, usually focusing on the same definition of economic income—that is, net cash flow.

In some instances, the cash flows may be projected on an incremental basis rather than on an absolute basis; that is, the buyer will ask herself, "What is the *difference* between my cash flows from buying this practice and my cash flows if I just hang out my shingle and start practicing?"

Capitalization of Economic Income

Chapter 13 presents a detailed description of direct capitalization rates and of the factors that should be considered in their selection. In professional practices, two measures of economic income are typically capitalized: (1) pretax earnings after a fair salary to the owner or practitioner and (2) total earnings (including the owner's or practitioner's salary and benefits). In some cases, after-tax earnings are capitalized. Both definitions of economic income assume normalized earnings (having removed nonrecurring income and expenses and adjusting certain expenses to more accurately reflect economic reality).

Selecting a Direct Capitalization Rate. In any given professional practice, the capitalization of each measure of economic income should produce fairly consistent values, even though the economic income figures (according to the different definitions) are considerably different. When using total earnings (pretax stated earnings plus owner salary and benefits), the direct capitalization rate should be much higher than when using only pretax earnings after reasonable owner's compensation. It is not unusual to see direct capitalization rates of 100 percent or more when using total earnings as a base, compared to a 20 to 35 percent direct capitalization rate for pretax earnings after owner's compensation.

Strengths and Weaknesses of the Capitalization of Economic Income Method. The capitalization of earnings method is both one of the most common methods of appraising a professional practice and one of the most abused. Besides the difficulty of selecting an appropriate direct capitalization rate, the proper use of the method requires astute judgments concerning (1) the real economic income capacity of the subject practice and (2) the expected growth in the practice economic income.

This value generally represents the value of the entire practice business enterprise, not just the value of the practice goodwill. If a practice has excess assets or if the assets used in generating income could be replaced by less expensive items with the same function, the analyst should add the excess asset value back to the calculated value.

Multiple of Revenues

Revenue pricing multiples have been discussed elsewhere in this book, primarily in the context of emphasizing that they should not be used alone. Revenue pricing multiples serve as one of the primary rules of thumb for the valuation of businesses in several industries, particularly professional practices. It is very common to see revenue pricing multiples used in valuations for professional practices for marital dissolution purposes. The multiple of revenues method can be a useful valuation method when used in conjunction with other methods. However, it can be entirely misleading if the analyst relies on it solely. Several specific industry revenue pricing multiples are discussed in the "Rule-of-Thumb Methods" section of this chapter.

Revenue pricing multiples are sometimes used in the valuation of professional practices for several reasons:

1. The method is simple to understand.
2. Revenues are often easier to determine than the practice's other measures of economic income.
3. When looking for comparative transactions, sale price-to-revenues multiples are often the only valuation pricing data that can be found.

Proper Use of the Multiple of Revenues.   Revenue pricing multiples are sometimes used in negotiating prices for the sale of professional practices. We do not recommended relying entirely on revenue pricing multiples, however. This is because the specific practice may have certain positive and negative attributes that the pricing multiple would not take into account.

For example, if an accounting practice were appraised by the excess earnings method to be worth $100,000, the analyst may want to state this value in terms of a multiple of revenues. This restatement would be made in order to check the value estimate against an industry standard rule-of-thumb revenue multiple. If it seems out of line with the industry, the analyst may want to double-check the value estimated using the excess earnings method (and to search for and correct any error). Or this apparent anomaly may indicate that the particular practice is so different from the typical accounting practice that it does not fall in the standard revenue pricing multiple range (and that the analyst should further analyze such differences).

Strengths and Weaknesses of the Multiple of Revenues Method.   The biggest strength of this analytical method is that, being relatively easy, it is a good way of making a preliminary but educated guess at the subject practice value. By itself, on the other hand, this analytical method does not consider the essence of business value, which is the return necessary to justify the investment risk.

Comparative Transactions and Buy-Ins (Market Data Comparison)

The use of comparative transactions and buy-ins is not necessarily a set of formulas, as have been previously discussed. Rather, it is a method by which various measurements of value can be computed and compared to the subject practice.

Comparative Transactions. For example, assume that a small veterinary practice was being appraised and that the analyst found 15 comparative sales of similar practices in the same geographic area during the prior 12 months. The price of each practice was probably based on various methods, several (or all) of which were different from the others. However, if it was found that all sales occurred at a revenue multiple of between 90 and 120 percent of the latest year's net revenue, or at a multiple of the latest year's total earnings of 1.75 to 2.00, these multiples (after adjustments, if appropriate) could be applied to the subject practice. The comparative transactions are not a formula in themselves for establishing value. Rather, they can be related to previously discussed methods (revenue pricing multiples or capitalized excess earnings, for example), which can then be applied to the subject practice.

Buy-Ins. There is a situation, however, in which the comparative transaction may be based on a formula that the analyst can rely on to value the practice. Buy-in formulas may exist in the subject practice or in practices similar to it. Typically, they are designed so that a new partner or shareholder of an established practice can buy his or her interest in the partnership with before-tax dollars, offering only a small down payment, if any.

For example, suppose that Dr. Holladay's practice is expanding so rapidly that he anticipates soon reaching his maximum patient load. He therefore decides to bring in an associate who will be able to increase the number of patients the practice can handle, and to ultimately make the associate a partner. Because of economies of scale, Dr. Holladay would enjoy a higher income by practicing with the associate than he would by remaining a sole practitioner. However, Dr. Holladay realizes he has spent a long time building his practice and thinks that a new associate should be willing to purchase an interest in the practice.

Dr. Holladay could ask a new practitioner to buy a half interest in the practice immediately. However, such a purchase would require after-tax dollars from the new associate. Therefore, he decides to ask for a small down payment and to arrange a vesting schedule for the allocation of income between himself and the new associate. According to this schedule, during the early years Dr. Holladay would receive over 50 percent of total practice earnings, even though both doctors spend approximately equal time seeing approximately the same number of patients.

In other cases, the new doctor comes in as an employee. After a number of years, a buy-in is negotiated, with the associate buying the tangible assets and handling the intangible value through a salary differential over time.

Strengths and Weaknesses of Comparative Transactions and Buy-Ins. When the analyst has available comparative transaction data that provide relatively consistent measurements of value, this method is extremely helpful in establishing value. Buy-in transactions, especially in the subject practice, are also very strong evidence of value. Unfortunately, the comparative data can be very sketchy, and the prior buy-in may be too remote in time. Or the buy-ins may involve unique circumstances that cause the data to be incomplete or outdated for the current appraisal.

Punitive and Retirement Formulas

Punitive and retirement valuation formulas are established by contract in the subject practice. They do not necessarily establish the market value of the practice or of an ownership interest in the practice. Rather, they set forth a price for the practitioner's ownership interest when he or she leaves or retires. Therefore, if the standard of value calls for the analyst to value goodwill on a going-concern basis, these contractual obligations may not necessarily aid in estimating that going-concern value.

Purpose of Punitive and Retirement Formulas. A punitive formula is sometimes written into a partnership agreement to discourage partners from leaving the firm. The punitive contract offers the exiting partner a prescribed buyout formula that is lower than the fair market value of his or her partnership interest. A retirement formula, which is also often included in partnership agreements, may attempt to value the partnership interest at its fair market value. Such a retirement formula may value the practice above its fair market value, to reward the partner for many years of valuable service.

Strengths and Weaknesses of the Punitive and Retirement Formulas. Having a prescribed valuation formula for the subject ownership interest is helpful if the reason for the appraisal is the event that calls the formula into operation. However, these formulas are generally of little help if the purpose of the appraisal is some reason other than that which would cause the formula to be invoked.

Capitalized Excess Earnings.

The capitalized excess earnings method has already been described in detail in Chapter 23. We will not repeat its history or how it is calculated. The excess earnings method is used frequently in marital dissolution valuations — probably more so than in actual transactional valuations. Although most courts have held that there is no single method of valuing professional goodwill, the capitalized excess earnings method is, arguably, the most common analytical procedure for measuring goodwill.

Generally, for a professional practice, *total earnings* are defined as all economic income available to the practitioner and are computed as follows:

Net income of the practice including salary and benefits to the practitioner(s) or owner(s)

+   {Nonrecurring expenses – Nonrecurring income}

+   *Excessive expenses (not related to the generation of practice income)*

=   Total earnings

It was pointed out that a fair salary for the owner/employee should be deducted from earnings in most business valuations. In professional practices, however, earnings are counted before the owner's salary, benefits, and perquisites in most earnings surveys. This is because most professionals usually pay out most of the practice earnings in salaries, perquisites, and benefits.[1] It is important to use a similar measure of earnings when comparing the practice earnings to the industry average level, which is based on survey data.

Estimation of Net Asset Value for Return on Investment Calculation.

Chapter 33 discusses methods of valuing net assets for professional practices. The analyst valuing a practice may wonder how to treat items such as artwork owned by the practice and may be unsure whether a monetary return should be calculated on this kind of asset. Even though it is arguable that the asset is not essential to the practice operations and that operating earnings should therefore not be charged for a return on nonoperating assets, some analysts would argue that the money for this artwork could have been invested in operating equipment. Therefore, the total investment in the practice, no matter what type of asset is involved, should realize a return on investment.

Both arguments have merit. An answer is, as usual, found somewhere between the two extremes. In general, return on net asset value is calculated on operating assets less operating liabilities. However, it should give recognition to a certain portion of assets (and/or liabilities) that may not be considered operating, even though they are ordinary in the type of practice being appraised. As an example, the value of moderately priced office lithographs would probably be included in net asset value. This is because the practice's offices need to have a pleasant atmosphere for its clients. However, if the office contained 50 original M.C. Escher woodcut prints, the fair market value of these prints would most appropriately be removed from the net asset value (along with any associated debt) before calculating a return on capital. This is because such prints go far beyond the general requirements of office furnishings.

There are instances when, using the excess earnings method on professional practices, no return on capital is calculated. Sometimes earnings surveys for self-employed professionals include earnings that represent a return on capital to those practitioners. If earnings from

---

[1] The two most widely used surveys for medical practice earning data are *Medical Economics*, a semi-monthly periodical that contains an earnings survey each September (along with specific practice specialty surveys throughout the year), and the American Medical Association's *Socioeconomic Characteristics of Medical Practice* (published annually), previously known as *Profile of Medical Practice*.

such a survey are being used for comparison with earnings of a self-employed professional, it would be improper to remove from that professional's earnings an amount for a return on his or her capital. On the other hand, if the self-employed professional is being compared against salaries for nonowner professional employees, it is necessary to figure his or her return on capital because nonowner professionals have no investment at risk.

Earnings Levels. In estimating the economic income level of the practice, the analyst should consider at least five years of earnings data if they are available. A careful analysis of the practice's economic income history will provide a basis for estimating the practice's future economic income capacity. A five-year average figure may not reflect the future economic income potential of the practice. However, the five-year history will reveal trends and unusual occurrences that could be buried in an average.

Consider, for example, the partnership of Bean & Bacon, restaurant consultants. If an average earnings figure for the five-year period were routinely accepted by the analyst as indicative of future earning capacity, under the following earnings projections the analyst would calculate the average earnings at $77,400 (i.e., $387,000 ÷ 5 = $77,400) for Bacon.

	Total Earnings of Bacon	Total Earnings of Bean & Bacon
Latest Year	$100,000	$200,000
Year 4	120,000	240,000
Year 3	75,000	200,000
Year 2	52,000	175,000
Year 1	40,000	160,000
Total	$387,000	$975,000

Even though $77,400 is the mathematical average of Bacon's five-year earnings, the trend suggests that this average does not represent his future economic income capacity. In year 1, Bacon received 25 percent of the practice's total earnings. In year 2, the amount had risen to 30 percent, in year 3 to 37 percent. In years 4 and 5, Bacon received 50 percent of total practice earnings.

If the analyst had investigated, he or she would have found that partners Bean and Bacon had agreed that Bacon would take a lower percentage of profits in the first three years but that Bacon would begin to receive 50 percent in year 4 and continue at that level of earnings from then on. Therefore, Bacon's current economic income capacity is 50 percent of the practice's economic income capacity. And it should be stated at 50 percent of the five-year average of the partnership's earnings, or $97,500 (i.e., $975,000 × 50 percent ÷ 5). The analyst should consider all relevant facts before concluding current or future economic income capacity.

Earnings Surveys. A practitioner's economic income should be compared, as much as possible, to that of a like practitioner. The comparative practitioner should be in the same specific field, in the same geographic area, of approximately the same level of experience, and so on, as the professional whose practice is being valued. A psychiatrist, although a medical doctor, should not be compared to a cardiologist. This is because each specialist has different earnings expectations.

Direct Capitalization Rates.   The return expected on the professional practice's net asset value should be neither more nor less than any other small business would expect to receive. Typically, the direct capitalization rate for the professional's excess economic income depends on the positive and negative influences of the elements of value discussed in Chapter 34. Depending on the measure of economic income, direct capitalization rates for the professional's excess economic income typically range from 20 to 100 percent (or of multiples of from five to one times).

Strengths and Weaknesses of the Capitalized Excess Earnings Method.   The following are the primary strengths of the capitalized excess earnings method:

1. It is widely used and therefore recognized and understood by many people.
2. Conceptually, it quantifies the value of the practice collective intangible value in the nature of goodwill.
3. It is codified (in Revenue Ruling 68-609), and it has been approved in many court rulings with respect to the valuation of professional practice goodwill.

The following are the primary weaknesses of the capitalized excess earnings method:

1. It is easily misapplied because it requires so many subjective judgments on the part of the analyst.
2. It can overstate the value of goodwill because it does not explicitly recognize the factor of marketability.
3. It can understate the intangible value of a professional practice because it does not factor in the going-concern elements of a practice that do not create excess earnings.

Asset Accumulation

By the *asset accumulation method* in this context, we really mean *adjusted book value* (or *adjusted net worth*) including *all* practice assets, both tangible and intangible, net of all the practice liabilities.

Two examples of the asset accumulation method, including several specific identifiable intangible assets as well as goodwill, are presented in the illustrative valuations presented in Chapter 37. In a sense, this method could be viewed as a specific version of the capitalized excess earnings method. While the capitalized excess earnings method generally aggregates all the practice intangible value into a single account (often called goodwill), this method specifically identifies and values each individual component intangible asset.

Depreciating Goodwill

Goodwill is not constant. Like most other assets, it diminishes in value over time unless something is done to keep or enhance it. Goodwill should be nurtured to maintain its value. That is why the accountant may treat her client to lunch periodically and why the dentist sends out holiday greetings to his patients.

Generally, the depreciating goodwill method uses a modified version of the capitalized excess earnings formula. The analyst establishes a level of excess economic income. Instead of capitalizing those excess earnings at a constant rate, the analyst treats them as a wasting asset, depreciating to zero after a certain period. The analyst then calculates the present value of that depreciating excess economic income using a present value discount factor that reflects the risk associated with that economic income.

A good analogy might be the purchase and nurturing of a houseplant. For the houseplant to live and grow, the weekend horticulturist must water and feed the plant. However, a person with a green thumb will prune the plant, find the most ideal location for it, and probably even mist it regularly, producing a healthy and beautiful plant. Even though both plants will grow, the latter plant will have much more expansive foliage.

The concept of depreciating goodwill is soundly based. There is no argument with the general procedure of valuing depreciating excess economic income. However, there is opportunity for analysts to misuse this method.

Common Errors in Depreciating Goodwill. The first common error is that the depreciating excess economic income is generally capitalized at the same rate used in the capitalization of excess earnings method discussed earlier. Risk is one of the determining factors in selecting direct capitalization rates. The recognition of the depreciation of goodwill reduces risk. Therefore, the direct capitalization rate used in a valuation on the basis of the depreciation of excess economic income should be reduced to reflect the lowered risk, compared to a capitalized excess earnings analysis that does not factor in depreciation.

The second common error is the assumption that the date that goodwill will reach zero can be estimated. Goodwill requires maintenance to protect its value. It is difficult to measure, without the required maintenance, the rate at which goodwill's value will decline and the date it will expire.

The professional practitioner who merely goes through the motions while performing services for his or her clients or patients will see the practice goodwill diminish. However, like the weekend horticulturist, the practitioner will probably not see it depreciate to zero. In other words, goodwill, like most other assets, will generally have some "salvage value."

Strengths and Weaknesses of the Depreciating Goodwill Method. The concept of depreciating goodwill is appealing because it makes economic sense. However, it is extremely difficult to measure how much depreciation has taken place or will take place. The type of practice, location, types of clients or patients of the practice, and many other variables affect the rate at which goodwill depreciates. Considering that it is difficult to measure and value goodwill by itself, it is almost impossible to determine the life cycle of such an elusive intangible asset. Perhaps because of the extreme difficulty in developing sound bases for measurement, this method is rarely used.

Rule-of-Thumb Methods for Various Types of Professional Practices

The various methods already discussed can be applied to almost all types of professional practices. However, certain types of practices do have specific formulas (almost all based on revenue multiples) that tend to be commonly used in their respective valuations. Below is a listing of some types of professional practices that have a rule of thumb that can be applied to make a preliminary estimate of the practice value.

The analyst should be cautioned, however, that these are general rules that will be accurate only as averages, given a large number of observations. However, in any specific observation, the rule may need to be adjusted or even discarded if it is not appropriate to the situation at hand. In any case, it is highly recommended that rules of thumb be used only in conjunction with generally accepted, rigorous valuation methods.

Accounting Practices

Small accounting firms tend to sell for their net asset value plus a goodwill value, which when paid over time is equal to 75 to 150 percent of the latest year's revenues. However, this very simple formula has some complicating adjustments.

The goodwill usually is purchased when the buyer pays the seller a certain percentage of fees collected from clients who continue with the practice for a period of time. For example, at the date of sale, a list of past clients may be prepared, and buyer and seller agree that 20 percent of all fees charged to those clients (and paid by them) for the next five years will be transferred to the selling accountant immediately after those fees are paid. This agreement results in a revenue multiple of 1 (20 percent $\times$ 5 = 1). However, at the date of sale, in order to estimate a cash equivalent value for the goodwill, the analyst would need to investigate the attrition rates of clients and also apply a discount to the expected income stream for the time value of money.

Another method of valuing the goodwill of an accounting firm would be to apply a different multiple to each segment of revenue. Generally, an accountant would be willing to pay more for a continuing audit client or a write-up client than for numerous nonrecurring individual tax-return clients.

Dental Practices

The old rule was that general dental practices sold for the value of their equipment, furniture, and fixtures plus a value for goodwill of either 25 to 35 percent of revenues, or 50 to 100 percent of total earnings available to the doctor. Other analysts have used factors of all the way from 35 to 75 percent of revenues to value the goodwill and the equipment, furniture, and fixtures. There may be some upward trend in these percentages due to the current large supply of dentists.

Engineering/Architecture Practices

Architectural and engineering firms seem to have more characteristics of small businesses for valuation purposes than of professional practices. For engineering/architectural firms that are regular corporations (not professional corporations) and employ from 50 to 250 people, the adjustments made to the financial statements are more like the ones appropriate for small businesses. Architectural and engineering firms have ESOPs, stock purchase plans, and other transition vehicles that are not usually found in smaller professional practices.

Depending on the type of practice, these firms are valued at their net asset value plus 20 to 40 percent of the latest year's revenues. Practices with continuing clients would tend to sell at the high end of the multiple range. This formula should be used cautiously because many of these firms possess little, if any, goodwill.

Law Practices

In the past, a general law practice could be sold for its net asset value only. This is because legal ethics forbade the sale of clients' files or of goodwill. However, some attorneys who wish to retire refer their cases to a new attorney and then split the fee paid by the referred client with the new attorney.

In marital dissolution cases, many state courts have held that goodwill should be valued even if it can't be sold. However, no standard rule-of-thumb method exists for this type of analysis.

In recent years, state laws regarding the sale of legal practices have started to change, in many cases allowing the sale of law practices. So far, not enough data have been developed to provide meaningful generalizations.

Medical Practices

The following comments should be read with the recognition that within the broad spectrum of medical practices there are great differences in valuation depending on the specialty involved.

Fifteen years ago, medical practices were difficult to sell because the relative ease of entry into the market diminished their value. However, with the current oversupply of physicians in many parts of the country and the consolidation wave in the healthcare industry, established medical practices are selling, and they are commanding goodwill value. Generally, these practices sell in a range of 40 to 100 percent of revenues for the equipment, supplies, and goodwill. Obviously, the type of practice has a large influence on the multiple. Prices for referral practices are near the low end, and prices for practices with a continuing patient base are toward the high end of the range.

There is no general rule of thumb for valuing goodwill only. However, the *Goodwill Registry*, a publication produced annually by the Health Care Group in Plymouth Meeting, Pennsylvania, presents a compilation of medical and dental practice valuations. The *Goodwill Registry* has been published since 1981. It reports the sum total of practice intangibles under a term of convenience, *goodwill*. These intangibles can include, for example, beneficial contracts (e.g., "below market" rent), noncompete agreements, and a variety of other intangibles. As reported, for example, in the 1997 *Goodwill Registry*, the 1988–1997 average goodwill value from a total of 247 internal medicine subspecialties showed a mean average of 35 percent and a median of 30 percent of revenue.[2]

While the *Goodwill Registry* is a useful guideline source, it should be used with caution. The authors of the publication recognize that it does not represent a statistically valid sample of any particular population of practices. There are also other limitations. For example, the values reported for goodwill are not necessarily adjusted to cash equivalent value to take into account the time value of money and other factors. Also, the entries do not all represent actual arm's-length transactions; some entries represent appraisals for divorce and other purposes. Recognizing these caveats, the *Goodwill Registry*, used in conjunction with other valuation methods and data, provides some useful insight.

Optometric Practices

These practices can be more like retail businesses than professional practices. This is because location is a more important value driver than it is in other types of professional practices. Generally, the value of an optometric practice equipment, supplies, patient eye prescriptions, and goodwill can range from 40 percent to 60 percent of the latest year's revenues.

---

[2]*Goodwill Registry* (Plymouth Meeting, PA: The Health Care Group, 1997), p. iv.

Medical Laboratories

There have been many acquisitions of local laboratories by publicly traded laboratory companies. Acquisition prices as a percent of latest year's revenues have had an extremely wide range, but the vast majority fall in the range of 50 to 80 percent of latest year's revenues for the goodwill and net asset value.

Veterinary Practices

Dog and cat clinics in good locations can command premium prices. Generally, these practices sell for 75 to 125 percent of the latest year's revenues for the goodwill.

Summary

Professional practice valuation follows the basic principles and methods used to value small businesses generally. However, there are certain analytical variations arising from the general nature of professional practices. The selection of appropriate valuation methods in each instance will depend to some extent on the purpose of the valuation, the nature of the practice, and the availability of data. As with other types of businesses, rules of thumb cover such a wide range of potential value for any practice that they cannot be relied on by themselves. However, they may serve as a check for reasonableness.

Bibliography

Articles

Agiato, Joseph A. "Business Valuations: An Increasingly Important Part of a Professional Practice." *Small Business Taxation*, May/June 1990, pp. 279–85.

Becker, Scott, and John Callahan. "Physician-Hospital Transactions: Developing a Process for Handling Valuation-Related Issues." *Journal of Health Care Finance*, Winter 1996, pp. 19–31.

Brandes, Joel R., and Carole L. Weidman. "Valuation of a Professional License." *New York Law Journal*, December 24, 1996, pp. 3–5.

Cheifetz, Cary B., and Gary N. Skoloff. "Valuation of a Professional Practice." In *Valuation Strategies in Divorce*. 2d edition. Robert E. Kleeman, ed. New York: John Wiley and Sons, 1992, pp. 75–101.

Cimasi, Robert J. "Trends & Developments in the Valuation of Health Care Entities." In *The Journal of Business Valuation* (Proceedings of the Third Joint Business Valuation Conference of the CICBV and the ASA). Toronto: Canadian Institute of Chartered Business Valuators, 1995, pp. 119–48.

_____. "Valuing Medical Practices" (Chapter 24). In *Handbook of Business Valuation*, Thomas L. West and Jeffrey D. Jones, eds. New York: John Wiley & Sons, 1992, pp. 263–75.

Collier, Cindy E. "The Conversion of Nonprofit Health Care Organizations to For-Profit Entities." *Shannon Pratt's Business Valuation Update,* June 1997, pp. 1, 10.

Cosman, Madeleine Pelner, Thomas R. Lang, and Marin C. Goodheart. "Comparing Medical and Business Goodwill Components." *FAIR$HARE: The Matrimonial Law Monthly*, January 1990, pp. 3–8.

Farris, Leon W. "Valuing Accounting Firms" (Chapter 26). In *Handbook of Business Valuation*, Thomas L. West and Jeffrey D. Jones, eds. New York: John Wiley & Sons, 1992, pp. 291–97.

Fishman, Jay E., Shannon P. Pratt, J. Clifford Griffith, and D. Keith Wilson. "Valuing Professional Practices" (Chapter 11). In *Guide to Business Valuations*. 7th ed. Fort Worth, TX: Practitioners Publishing Company, 1997.

Florescue, Leonard G. "Business Value of Law License." *New York Law Journal*, August 21, 1990, p. 3.

_____. "Valuation of a Law Firm Partnership." *New York Law Journal*, September 9, 1996, pp. 3–5.

Goodman, Stanley L. "Valuing Dr. O'Brien's Medical Degree: A View from Inside." *FAIR$HARE: The Matrimonial Law Monthly*, May 1986, pp. 10–13.

Holdren, Richard C. "New Factors Affecting Medical Practice Valuation." *FAIR$HARE: The Matrimonial Law Monthly*, January 1993, p. 8.

Horvath, James L. "Valuing Management Consulting Practices" (Chapter 27). In *Handbook of Business Valuation*, Thomas L. West and Jeffrey D. Jones, eds. New York: John Wiley & Sons, 1992, pp. 299–310.

Kline, Michael E. "Law Practice Goodwill: An Evolving Concept." *FAIR$HARE: The Matrimonial Law Monthly*, April 1991, pp. 6–8. Martin, J. Thomas. "Don't Overlook These Crucial Points in a Practice Sale: Whether You're Selling or Buying, This Checklist Will Help Protect You against Financial and Tax Risks." *Medical Economics*, January 6, 1992, pp. 95–97.

Monath, Donald. "Differentiating Commercial Professional Goodwill from Personal Professional Goodwill." Parts I and II. *FAIR$HARE: The Matrimonial Law Monthly*, October and November 1990, pp. 13–15, and pp. 6–8.

Pratt, Shannon P. "The Market for Medical Practice Consolidation Hot Right Now." (interview with Rick Holdren) *Shannon Pratt's Business Valuation Update*, May 1996, pp. 1—2.

_____. "A 'New Paradigm' in Health Care—Current Trends in Medical Practice Consolidation." (interview with Bob Cimasi) *Shannon Pratt's Business Valuation Update*, October 1996, pp. 1—2.

Pratt, Shannon P., and Ralph Arnold. "Placing a Value on Your Professional Practice." *Lawyer/Manager*, May/June 1989, pp. 42–48.

_____. "Specific Methods for Determining the Value of Your Law Practice." *Lawyer/Manager*, July/August 1989, pp. 41–49.

Rabe, James G. "Estimating the Value of Your Firm." *The Oregon Certified Public Accountant*, August 1996, p. 6.

Rabe, James G., Charles A. Wilhoite, and Karin Zamba. "Valuation of Professional Practices." (Chapter 20A). In *Financial Valuation: Businesses and Business Interests*, 1997 Update. James Zukin, ed. New York: Warren, Gorham & Lamont, 1997.

Reilly, Robert F. "How Much Is Your Practice Worth." *Today's CPA*, May/June 1991, pp. 27–37.

_____. "The Valuation of Chiropractic and Similar Professional Practices" (Parts 1 and 2). *The Digest of Chiropractic Economics*, January/February 1991, pp. 17–18ff, and March/April 1991, pp. 24, 26–28.

_____. "The Valuation of a Medical Practice." *Health Care Management Review*, Summer 1990, pp. 25–34.

_____. "The Valuation of Medical, Dental, and Similar Professional Practices." *Business Valuation Review*, March 1989, pp. 7–27.

_____. "Valuation of the Professional Medical Practice." Parts 1 and 2. *Small Business Taxation*, November/December 1988, January/February 1989, pp. 107–10, and pp. 173–78.

_____. "Valuation of Accounting Practices—What's It Worth?" *National Public Accountant*, February 1991, pp. 20–29.

Reilly, Robert F., and Robert P. Schweihs. "Valuation of Accounting Practices." *Ohio CPA Journal*, Autumn 1990, pp. 19–26.

Roa, Fred. "Valuing Home Health Care Businesses." (Chapter 25). In *Handbook of Business Valuation*, Thomas L. West and Jeffrey D. Jones, eds. New York: John Wiley & Sons, 1992, pp. 277–90.

Rutkin, Arnold H. "Valuation of a Closely Held Corporation, Small Business or Professional Practice," Chapter 22. In *Valuation and Distribution of Marital Property*. New York: Matthew Bender, 1997.

Shayne, Mark. "Valuing Your Law Practice." *New York State Bar Journal*, July/August 1992, pp. 54–56.

Steiner, Erwin H., and Ronald J. Kudla. "Valuation of Professional Practices." *Law Office Economics and Management*, 1990, pp. 197–206.

Zaumeyer, David J. "The Economic Life of Professional Licenses." *FAIR$HARE: The Matrimonial Law Monthly*, March 1996, pp. 3–5.

Books

Brown, Ronald L., ed. *Valuing Professional Practices and Licenses: A Guide for the Matrimonial Practitioner*. 2d edition. Frederick, MD: Aspen Law and Business, 1993, supplemented 1997.

Domer, Larry, and Randall Berning. *Valuing a Practice: A Guide for Dentists*. Chicago: American Dental Association, 1997.

General Guidelines for Establishing the Worth of an Optometric Practice. St. Louis: American Optometric Association, 1988.

Horvath, James L. *Valuing Professional Practices*. Toronto: CCH Canadian Limited, 1990.

Jackson, James B., and Roger K. Hill. *NewTrends in Dental Practice Valuation and Associateship Arrangements.* Chicago: Quintessence Publishing, 1987.

Reilly, Robert F., and Robert P. Schweihs. *Valuing Accounting Practices.* New York: John Wiley & Sons, 1997.

_____. *Valuing Professional Practices: A Practitioner's Guide.* Chicago: CCH Incorporated, 1997.

Skoloff, Gary N., and Theodore P. Orenstein. *When A Lawyer Divorces: How to Value a Professional Practice.* Chicago: American Bar Association Press, 1986.

Unland, James J. *Valuation of Hospitals and Medical Centers,* Revised. Chicago: Health Management Research Institute, 1993.

Valuing a Medical Practice: A Short Guide for Buyers and Sellers. Chicago: American Medical Association, 1987.

Additional Sources of Information

Sources of Value Data

Comparative Performance of U.S. Hospitals: The Sourcebook. Baltimore: Health Care Investment Analysts, annual.

Financial Studies of the Small Business. Winter Haven, FL: Financial Research Associates, annual.

Goodwill Registry. Plymouth Meeting, PA: The Health Care Group, annual.

Valuation Survey of Architecture, Engineering, Planning & Environmental Consulting Firms. Natick, MA: Zweig White & Associates, annual.

Reasonable Compensation Resources for Accounting Firms

Management of an Accounting Practice Handbook. Fort Worth: American Institute of Certified Public Accountants and Practitioners Publishing Company (includes operating statistics gathered at the annual AICPA practice management and small firm conferences), annual.

Management of an Accounting Practice Survey, National Results for 1997. Dallas: Texas Society of Certified Public Accountants, annual.

Reasonable Compensation Resources for Dental Practices

The Survey of Dental Practice. Chicago: American Dental Association, Bureau of Economic and Behavioral Research, annual.

Dental Economics. Tulsa: Pennwell Publishing Company, monthly; salary survey published annually.

Reasonable Compensation for Law Firms

Small Law Firm Economic Survey. Newton Square,PA: Altman Weil Pansa, annual.

The Survey of Law Firm Economics. Newton Square, PA: Altman Weil Pansa, annual.

Reasonable Compensation Resources for Medical Practices

Medical Economics. Montvale, NJ: Medical Economics Publishing, monthly; salary survey published annually.

Physician Compensation Survey. Englewood, CO: Center for Research in Ambulatory Health Care Administration, Medical Group Management Association, annual.

Physician Marketplace Statistics. Chicago: American Medical Association, annual.

Chapter 36

Sample Professional Practice Valuation Report

Introduction

The valuation of Gateway Pediatrics is a sample case created to illustrate the application of the practice valuation methods discussed in previous chapters. It is not intended to represent a specific real-world practice. The objective of this chapter is simply to illustrate the complete valuation process regarding (1) the valuation of a medical practice and (2) the organization and presentation of the valuation in a written appraisal report.

Description of the Assignment

The objective of this appraisal is to estimate the fair market value of certain assets of Gateway Pediatrics, in fee simple interest, as of December 31, 1995.

The purpose of this appraisal is to provide an independent valuation opinion to assist Vista Hospital in its negotiations regarding the purchase of certain assets of Gateway Pediatrics.

For purposes of this appraisal, we define fair market value as the price that a business interest would change hands between a willing buyer and a willing seller, with neither being under undue compulsion to transact, with both fully cognizant of all relevant facts and circumstances, and with both seeking their maximum economic self-interests.

We appraised a marketable, controlling ownership interest in the subject assets of Gateway Pediatrics.

We appraised the assets of Gateway Pediatrics under the premise of value in continued use, as a going-concern business enterprise. Based on our analysis and in our opinion, this premise of value represents the highest and best use of the subject assets.

As part of our appraisal, we have not attributed any value to the potential referral of patients by Gateway Pediatrics to Vista Hospital.

We have appraised the subject medical practice in accordance with the *Uniform Standards of Professional Appraisal Practice* (USPAP), as promulgated by The Appraisal Foundation.

Summary Description of Gateway Pediatrics

Gateway Pediatrics is owned solely by Jeffrey D. Jones, MD. Gateway Pediatrics has operated in this manner since 1986, when Dr. Jones purchased Dr. Stan Michaels' pediatrics practice. Gateway Pediatrics is located at 111 NW 23rd Avenue in Corvallis, Oregon.

Sources of Information

We relied on the following information in performing this appraisal:

- Schedule C of Internal Revenue Service Form 1040 individual income tax returns of Dr. Jeffrey D. Jones—related to Gateway Pediatrics—for the years 1991 through 1995.

- Accounts receivable aging schedules from December 31, 1993, through January 1, 1995.
- Fixed-asset detail report as of December 31, 1995.
- Current fee schedule for services.
- 1995 ad valorem property tax assessment for the facilities occupied by Gateway Pediatrics.
- Income and expense adjustments provided by Wilstrom & Hart, CPAs.

In the course of our analysis, we visited the Gateway Pediatrics office in Corvallis, Oregon. We conducted interviews with Dr. Jeffrey D. Jones and with the other occupant of the building, Dr. Stan Olsen. We also interviewed Jill Stephens, the office manager/bookkeeper.

We obtained information regarding the Oregon and Benton County economy from the Oregon Employment Department's *Labor Trends* and from Oregon Employment Department *Regional Economic Profile, Region 4.*

We obtained information regarding the industry from *Medical Economics, S&P Industry Surveys, Physician Characteristics and Distribution in the U.S.*, and *Modern Healthcare.*

Summary and Conclusion

To estimate the fair market value of Gateway Pediatrics, we applied the following valuation approaches and methods:

1. *Asset-based approach:* The asset accumulation method.
2. *Income approach:* The discounted cash flow method.
3. *Market approach:* The comparative transaction method.

The application of these methods resulted in an indicated value range of $76,000 to $85,000 for certain assets of Gateway Pediatrics.

Based on our analysis, and on the quantity and quality of information and data supporting each method, in our opinion the fair market value of certain assets of Gateway Pediatrics in fee simple interest is $80,000, as of December 31, 1995.

Regional Economic Outlook

Overview

The outlook for the economy in the state of Oregon and in the Benton County area has an impact on the value of the subject practice. A medical practice located in a growing economic area is more valuable than a medical practice located in an area reporting decreases in economic activity. Therefore, we considered the outlook for the state and for the Corvallis area in our appraisal.

Oregon

The current economic expansion in Oregon is expected to continue. This is principally the result of the current conditions in the technology industry. Both the United States and Oregon had a peak in economic growth in 1994. However, the economic growth in Oregon is expected to be relatively steady in the coming two years.

The declining timber harvest in Oregon is being replaced by a surging production of integrated circuit chips and other technology-based products. The state's metals industry (aluminum, steel, nickel, titanium, and several other exotic metals) has turned up sharply, finally regaining its 1989 peak. Metals activity in Oregon is expected to level off due to slower growth in national markets. A decline in housing starts nationally resulted in weaker lumber prices and a drop in wood products employment in Oregon in 1995. Some improvement is expected by the second half of 1996.

The population in the state is estimated to have increased 2.4 percent in 1995, up from a 1.4 percent increase in 1994. Personal income in the state is estimated to have increased 7.9 percent in 1995, up from a 6.6 percent increase in 1994. Housing starts in the state are estimated to have increased 5.4 percent in 1995.

The state unemployment rate was 4.7 percent in December 1995, a decrease from the 5.2 percent rate in December 1994. During 1996, employment growth of 2.5 to 3.0 percent is expected, a slight decrease from 1995 levels.

Benton County

Background. The largest cities in Benton County are Corvallis and Philomath. The major industries affecting Benton County are higher education, agriculture, lumber products, electronics, and research and development. Major Benton County area employers include Hewlett-Packard, CH_2M-Hill, Oregon State University, and Linn-Benton Community College. The county seat, Corvallis, is best known as the home of Oregon State University, which enrolls 15,000 students every fall. Oregon State University enables Benton County to maintain a remarkably consistent level of employment and provides a stable economic base.

Employment. Benton County has a civilian labor force of approximately 45,560 persons. The county's current unemployment rate of 2.6 percent is lower than the state unemployment rate of 4.5 percent and is currently the lowest unemployment rate in the state. County employment trends in November 1995 followed the typical seasonal pattern, with fewer jobs in agriculture, construction, and food processing, but more jobs in education and retail trade. The lowest unemployment rate recorded in Benton County in 1995 was 2.2 percent in October 1995.

In the past year, Benton County employers added 2,490 workers to their payrolls. Over half of the new jobs have been in high tech manufacturing. That industry segment has added 3,030 new workers since

January 1993. Gains in the service sectors and in the education sector of the government have also been strong.

In July of 1994, Benton County had a population of 75,400, up from 70,811 in April 1990, for a total increase of 6.5 percent. The population of Benton County is expected to reach 81,824 by the year 2000.

Construction. Construction industry employment, a key economic indicator, totaled 950 persons in Benton County in November 1995, up from 830 persons in November 1994. This marks the highest level of construction employment for any November on record, and just 50 jobs below the all-time record of 1,000 jobs in August of 1995.

In Benton County, residential construction permits for single-family housing totaled 72 through the 10 months ending in October of 1995, down from 120 permits during the same period in 1994. New commercial construction and expansions in Corvallis—and in surrounding cities such as Millersburg, Albany, and Salem—point to continued job growth. This would result in the need for still more housing throughout the area.

Outlook. The presence of Oregon State University and Hewlett-Packard in Corvallis, along with growth in surrounding areas, point towards continued controlled growth in Benton County. Over the next 10 years, the largest job increase is expected in the services category, with only high tech manufacturing possibly having a higher percentage increase. Generally, the low unemployment rate, combined with expected moderate economic growth, indicates that the practice location is favorable.

Healthcare Industry

The outlook for the healthcare industry is an important consideration in the valuation of medical practices. This is especially true in light of the metamorphosis the healthcare system is currently experiencing. We therefore considered the outlook for this industry as of the valuation date.

Overview

The healthcare industry consists of public, private, and nonprofit providers. These providers are hospitals; offices and clinics of medical doctors; nursing homes; other specialized healthcare facilities; and managed care organizations offering prepaid and discounted plans through health maintenance organizations (HMOs), preferred provider organizations (PPOs), and independent practice associations (IPAs). The healthcare services industry includes thousands of independent medical practices and partnerships, as well as public and nonprofit institutions, and many private corporations.

According to the 1994 edition of the *U.S. Industrial Outlook* (the latest available edition as of the valuation date), expenditures on healthcare were expected to increase by approximately 12.5 percent in 1994, from an estimated $942.5 billion in 1993 (or approximately 14.0 percent of Gross Domestic Product (GDP)), to $1,060.5 billion in 1994. Over the last decade, healthcare expenditures have increased at a compound annual rate of 10 percent, compared to a 6.5 percent average annual increase in the overall economy as measured by the GDP, according to the Commerce Department. Over the next five years, healthcare expenditures are expected to increase at an average annual rate of 12 to 15 percent. The rate of increase for U.S. healthcare expenditures continues to surpass GDP growth rates due to several factors. These factors include the use of sophisticated and high-priced equipment, increases in the variety and frequency of treatments, increased longevity of the population, and increased earnings of medical professionals.

Employment in the healthcare industry has increased steadily, from 9.1 million in June 1990 to 10.2 million in June 1993. This reflects an average annual growth rate of 3.9 percent despite the 1990–1991 recession and weak economic recovery. Healthcare employment surpasses that of transportation and public utilities (5.7 million); wholesale trade (6.1 million); and finance, insurance, and real estate (6.6 million). Employment has increased in all healthcare sectors, especially in home care, nursing, and personal care facilities, offices and clinics of medical doctors and dentists, and hospitals.

Expansion in government programs, demographic changes, and technological advances have all contributed to soaring healthcare costs. However, the key factors fueling the healthcare cost increase relate to (1) the vital nature of medical goods and services and (2) the passivity of the third-party reimbursement system. Payment for healthcare is typically made by third parties, such as Medicare and Medicaid, employers, and insurance carriers. Generally, less than 20 percent is paid directly by individuals. With third parties covering the majority of healthcare expenses, the U.S. healthcare consumer is, to a large extent, insulated from the costs of care.

Physician Characteristics and Distribution in the United States

According to the 1995 edition of *Physician Characteristics and Distribution in the U.S.*, published by the American Medical Association (the latest edition available as of the valuation date), there were approximately 684,414 physicians in the United States in 1994. Of these, approximately 82 percent were involved in patient care, and 60 percent had an office-based practice. The historical rate of increase in physicians has decreased over the past five years. Over the 1985 to 1990 time frame, the number of physicians has increased by 11.3 percent. This is lower than the five-year increases of 18.2 percent for 1980–1985 and 18.8 percent for 1975-1980.

Pediatricians. Over the past 20 years, the percentage of physicians specializing in pediatrics has steadily increased. In 1994, approximately 48,113, or 7.0 percent of physicians, specialized in pediatrics, compared to 6.5 percent of physicians in 1985 and 6.2 percent of physicians in 1980.

From 1985 to 1990, the total number of practitioners specializing in pediatrics increased 13.5 percent. Between 1980 and 1994, the total number of practitioners specializing in pediatrics increased by 19,310, or a compound annual growth rate of 2.0 percent.

At the end of 1994, physicians specializing in pediatrics were the third largest physician specialty group, at 7.0 percent of physicians. Internal medicine practitioners were by far the largest physician specialty group at 16.3 percent of physicians, with the next largest being family practitioners, which represented 8.0 percent of physicians in 1994.

Physician-to-Population Ratios. The following table presents the 10 highest ranking states in terms of absolute counts of nonfederal physicians in 1990 and 1994. Also presented are physician/civilian population ratios and a ranking of ratios for both years. In addition, the totals for Oregon and the overall United States are also presented.

State	Total Non-Federal	1990 Physician Population Ratio	Ratio Rank	State	Total Non-Federal	1994 Physician Population Ratio	Ratio Rank
California	78,285	272	8	California	84,192	270	11
New York	60,744	339	4	New York	66,976	369	3
Texas	31,647	188	33	Florida	35,841	258	14
Florida	31,483	251	12	Texas	35,714	196	40
Pennsylvania	30,824	256	11	Pennsylvania	34,552	287	9
Illinois	26,603	229	19	Illinois	29,614	252	15
Ohio	23,239	213	22	Ohio	25,800	233	22
Massachusetts	21,475	364	2	Massachusetts	24,144	400	2
New Jersey	20,579	267	9	New Jersey	22,957	291	8
Maryland	16,716	360	3	Michigan	20,735	218	29
Oregon	*6,562*	*233*	*16*	*Oregon*	*7,456*	*242*	*18*

Source: *1995/96 Physician Characteristics and Distribution in the U.S.* (Chicago: American Medical Association, 1996), p. 16.

As presented, total nonfederal physicians in Oregon increased from 6,562 in 1990 to 7,456 in 1994. In addition, concentration of physicians per 100,000 civilian population has increased from 233 in 1990 to 242 in 1994, even though Oregon's rank with regard to physician concentration decreased from 16th to 18th among all states over the period. The number of nonfederal physicians per 100,000 civilian population for the entire country averaged 252 in 1994, indicating that Oregon was slightly below the national average.

Recent Industry Issues and Trends

According to Standard & Poor's *Industry Surveys*, over the past two years, the U.S. healthcare system has been bracing itself for the outcome of Congressional debate about healthcare reform. As 1994 progressed, the likelihood that Congress would pass such legislation during the year decreased. At this time, the possibility of sweeping changes in the nation's healthcare system is not an immediate concern to those who produce and provide medical products and services. Nevertheless, healthcare providers must still contend with a rapidly changing marketplace. The reins of power are shifting from traditional providers, such as hospitals and physicians, to insurance companies, employers, and others for whom cost containment is a top priority.

Both government and private third-party payers are increasingly turning to managed care providers in order to control healthcare spending through (1) more judicious utilization of medical products and services and (2) increased pricing pressure. These pressures have in turn heightened competitive conditions throughout all sectors of the healthcare universe. These pressures have resulted in a general slowing in medical inflation in recent years. Merger and acquisition activity has also accelerated, as companies pool their resources to compete more effectively in an environment where efficiency and low costs will mean the difference between success and failure.

Oregon Healthcare Reform.   The Oregon healthcare reform efforts included the Oregon Health Plan in 1994. The Oregon Health Plan includes (1) funding for the expanded Medicaid program (the state-federal health insurance coverage for approximately 90,000 low income Oregonians that began in February 1994) and (2) the employer mandate (which is scheduled to require businesses to provide health coverage for workers starting in 1997 at large companies and in 1998 at smaller ones). The Oregon Health Plan is expected to be further modified throughout 1995 by legislators.

Pediatrician Practices.   According to *Medical Economics*, physicians in rural practices are now earning more than physicians in suburban or urban practices for the first time in decades. Overall, physicians in private practices have seen their purchasing power eroded by more than eight percentage points in the last two years. [1]

According to an article in *Medical Economics*, the median gross revenues for pediatricians was $212,010 in 1994, compared to a median of $250,310 for all fields. According to the article, pediatricians experienced a 6.3 percent decline in gross revenues in 1994 and a 6.2 percent increase in net earnings, to $118,390, in 1994. [2]

Primary care physicians continue to be recruited by top hospitals. In 1994, three out of five physicians recruited were in the primary care

---

[1] *Medical Economics*, September 11, 1995, p. 192.

[2] Ibid., p. 189.

field. According to a recent survey, 41.6 percent of the hospitals surveyed are seeking pediatric physicians.[3]

Among office-based MDs and DOs in 16 fields surveyed, pediatricians were the most heavily involved in managed care. Pediatricians received approximately 32 percent of practice receipts from HMOs and 20 percent from PPOs in 1994.[4]

Impact on Intangible Value of Medical Practices.   Overall, national and state healthcare reform efforts are expected to have the beneficial effect of increasing the number of persons who will have access to healthcare services. However, these reforms will also result in (1) pressures on the pricing structures applicable to such services and (2) limitations on the number of services performed for each patient. Pricing pressures would be exerted through (1) the exclusive purchasing power of cooperatives, which would be used to hold down the prices paid to networks for reimbursement to providers; and (2) the implementation of managed care arrangements, including the imposition of limits on patient access to specialist services.

History and Description of the Practice

Practice Development and Overview

Gateway Pediatrics is a sole proprietorship operated by Jeffrey D. Jones, MD, who specializes in pediatrics. The pediatrics specialty covers the medical care of infants, children, and adolescents.

The practice is currently located at 111 NW 23rd Avenue, in Corvallis, Oregon. The practice has been at this location since its inception on January 1, 1986. Dr. Jones's employment background and medical school educational background are as follows:

- *1986–present.*   Dr. Jones purchased pediatrics practice from Dr. Steve Michaels, and in January 1986 established Gateway Pediatrics. Dr. Jones has been in solo practice since 1986.
- *1984–1986.* Dr. Jones practiced general pediatrics with Dr. Michaels in Corvallis, Oregon.
- *1981–1984.*   Internship and residency at University of Oregon Health Sciences Center.
- *1974–1981.* University of Oregon Health Sciences Center.

Dr. Jones, age 45, became board certified by the American Board of Pediatrics in January 1984. Based on Schedule C of Dr. Jones's Form 1040 individual income tax returns, a summary of the gross receipts for

---

[4] Ibid., p. 173.

[3] *Medical Economics*, October 23, 1995, p. 202.

Gateway Pediatrics for the past five calendar years is presented in the following table.

Year	Gross Receipts	% Change
1991	$172,354	6.4
1992	$160,907	(6.6)
1993	$178,801	11.1
1994	$204,440	14.3
1995	$224,884	10.0

As presented, gross receipts for the practice increased from $172,354 in 1991 to $224,884 in 1995, or at a compound annual growth rate of 6.9 percent. Based on data compiled by the American Medical Association, over the 1984 to 1994 time frame, the average pediatrician reported an annual increase in pretax income of 5.1 percent. Assuming the revenue trend for Dr. Jones would translate into a similar trend for income, the growth rate of Gateway Pediatrics parallels the national average for pediatricians over the past few years.

The following table presents Dr. Jones's gross receipts for 1994 and 1993 as compared to industry averages. These industry averages are based on data compiled and presented by the American Medical Association in *Physician Marketplace Statistics* (1995 and 1994 editions, which report 1994 and 1993 data, respectively). This is the latest data available as of the valuation date.

	Gross Receipts		Dr. Jones vs. Industry Average	
	1994 $	1993 $	1994 %	1993 %
Dr. Jones	204,440	178,801	NA	NA
Median, self-employed pediatricians	267,000	296,000	(23.4)	(39.6)
25th percentile, self-employed pediatricians	192,000	212,000	6.5	(15.7)

As presented, Dr. Jones's practice historically has generated revenues well below the national average for pediatricians. For 1994, the median gross receipts for self employed pediatricians was $267,000, compared to the reported gross receipts of $204,440 for Dr. Jones. Pediatricians at the 25th percentile reported revenues of $192,000, compared to $204,440 for Dr. Jones. The following are some of the possible explanations for the below-average revenue performance of the practice:

- *Patient visits per day.* Dr. Jones's patient visits per day were below the national average for 1994. The average pediatrician reported 25 total patient visits per day, versus 20 for Dr. Jones.
- *Fees.* Dr. Jones's fees based on the December 1995 fee schedule were somewhat lower than the fees reported by the average pediatrician. For example, the median fee for an office visit with an established patient for all pediatricians in 1994 was $45, versus $40 for a Level III visit with an established patient for Dr. Jones.

Despite the lower-than-average performance by the practice in 1994, Dr. Jones reports spending an average of 60 hours per week on all practice activities. This statistic compares to 55 hours per week for the median pediatrician, based on American Medical Association statistics.

Dr. Jones's fee schedule was last updated in January 1995. Based on discussions with Dr. Jones, this schedule is updated once annually.

Dr. Jones is reportedly in excellent health.

Facilities

The practice currently operates in a stand-alone building located at 111 NW 23rd Avenue in Corvallis, Oregon. The building is owned by Dr. Jones and has a total of approximately 2,570 square feet of office space. However, the office space in the building is occupied by both Dr. Jones's practice and by another physician, Dr. Stan Olsen, who operates a separate practice. Of the 2,570 total square feet of office space, Dr. Jones's practice occupies approximately one-half of the total.

The office space used by Dr. Jones includes four exam rooms and an office, and several rooms that are shared by Dr. Jones's practice and Dr. Olsen's practice. The shared space includes a waiting room, a reception area, and a lounge.

Dr. Jones leases office space to Dr. Olsen. The lease payments are reflected under "other income" on the income statements presented in Exhibit 36-1. (Please note that in this chapter, all exhibits are presented at the end of the chapter.)

A summary of the furniture, fixtures, and medical equipment owned by the practice is presented in Exhibit 36-5.

Office Hours

The office hours of the practice are as follows:

Monday:	9:00 AM–5:00 PM
Tuesday:	9:00 AM–5:00 PM
Wednesday:	9:00 AM–5:00 PM
Thursday:	9:00 AM–5:00 PM (closed after noon in summer)
Friday:	9:00 AM–5:00 PM
Saturday:	9:00 AM–11:00 PM (closed summer months)

The office closes an hour for lunch.

Staff

Gateway Pediatrics employed the following personnel as of the valuation date:

1. Jill Stephens, office manager/bookkeeper. Works approximately 40 hours per week and earns $12.70 per hour; has been with the practice since August 1994.
2. Sarah Wright, receptionist. Works approximately 40 hours per week and earns $8.00 per hour; has been with the practice since March 1995.
3. Tammy Hart, medical assistant. Works approximately 16 hours per week and earns $11.90 per hour; has been with the practice since August 1985.
4. Sue Johnson, medical assistant. Works approximately 24 hours per week and earns $9.50 per hour; has been with the practice since January 1995.

These four office staff members required training for their positions. Therefore, we have assigned a value to the trained and assembled workforce, presented in Exhibit 36-7.

Patients

As of December 31, 1995, Gateway Pediatrics had approximately 2,500 active patient records. Active patient records are defined as patients that have been seen by Dr. Jones in the past three years. In addition, the practice had approximately 2,800 inactive patient records, including approximately 1,500 records left at the practice by Dr. Michaels.

The following table gives a breakdown of the types of procedures Dr. Jones performed.

Service	% of Receipts
General office visits	90.0
Hospital newborn care	5.0
Other hospital visits	2.0
Consults	2.0
Miscellaneous	1.0

Dr. Jones sees an average of 19 patients in the office and 1 patient in the hospital on a typical day. He spends an average of 10 to 15 minutes with each patient.

Dr. Jones's patients include children 0 through 18 years old, with approximately 30 percent of patient visits represented by well checks (preventative healthcare) and 70 percent of visits for treatment of various illnesses.

The table below, based on discussions with Dr. Jones, indicates the sources of patient referrals.

Referral Source	% of Total Referrals
Current patients	40.0
Other doctors	30.0
Telephone book	20.0
Hospitals	10.0

As presented, a majority of the referrals to the practice result from current patients and other physicians, which is typical of the average pediatrics practice.

The practice's positive historical revenue growth rate is due to the consistent addition of new patients. Over the past three years, Dr. Jones has seen an average of over 20 to 30 new patients per month. By contrast, approximately 4 to 6 patients per month, on average, have become inactive over the past three years.

Approximately 15 percent of the practice receipts last year resulted from the treatment of Medicaid recipients.

Financial Analysis of Gateway Pediatrics

Overview

Historical financial information often provides the best indication of a practice's future performance, as trends noted are often repeated given similar industry and economic conditions. Accordingly, we have analyzed the income statements for Gateway Pediatrics for calendar years 1991 through 1995, the latest available full-year financial statements for the practice. These income statements were based on Schedule C of Dr. Jones's 1991 through 1995 individual income tax returns. Dr. Jones does not prepare annual balance sheets for the practice as part of his income tax return.

In addition, this section of the analysis summarizes the adjustments to the reported income statements of the practice. These adjustments are made in order to reflect the economic earning capacity of Gateway Pediatrics.

Income Statements. Exhibit 36-1 presents income statements for the practice for the calendar years 1991 through 1995. Over the past five years, the practice's reported gross revenues increased from $172,354 in 1991 to $224,884 in 1995, at a compound annual growth rate of approximately 6.9 percent. Revenues increased in three of the past four years. The only decrease occurred in calendar 1992, when revenues decreased 6.6 percent. For the most recent calendar year, the practice revenues increased by 10 percent. Discussions with Dr. Jones indicate that in calendar year 1995 the practice may be able to generate $235,000 in revenues.

Operating expenses for the practice have increased over the past five years at a slower rate than revenues. The practice reported operating expenses of $122,534 for calendar 1991 and $137,470 for calendar 1995, representing a compound annual growth rate of only 2.9 percent. Operating income increased from $45,784 in 1991 to $83,366 in 1995.

In addition, the practice has other income and expenses, including interest expense (related to the underlying mortgage on the building), rental income (payments from Dr. Olsen to Dr. Jones), and fees for service from third-party payers, including gatekeeper fees and risk-pool payments.

As presented in the common-size section of Exhibit 36-1, the most significant operating expenses of the practice in 1995 were employee wages (29.1 percent of revenue), depreciation (7.0 percent), taxes and licenses (6.0 percent), utilities (4.0 percent), and repairs and maintenance (3.5 percent of revenue).

Analysis of Economic Earning Capacity. Exhibit 36-2 presents the income statements of Gateway Pediatrics for calendar 1994 and 1995, adjusted to reflect the economic earning capacity of the practice. Due to (1) the recent changes in the healthcare environment and (2) the increase of Dr. Jones's practice over the past five years, we considered that the past two years of data were the most relevant for our analysis.

Several adjustments are necessary in order to estimate the economic earning capacity of the practice. Most of the adjustments related to excluding the expenses and income related to the building (owned by Dr. Jones) from the practice's reported results. These adjustments included repairs and maintenance, property taxes, insurance, depreciation, mortgage expense, utilities, and rent income. Many of these adjustments were provided by Wilstrom & Hart, CPAs, the public accounting firm for the practice.

In addition, we added back the reported pension contribution by Dr. Jones for 1994 and 1995, and we subtracted an estimated fair rental rate for the office space occupied by the Dr. Jones practice.

Exhibit 36-2 also presents data regarding normal industry compensation for a pediatrician. Comparing the profitability of a practice to an industry average is useful in estimating the intangible value associated with a practice. Since Dr. Jones's has an established practice and reported revenues are near the median, we selected the industry median profitability of a pediatrics practice to compare to Dr. Jones's profitability. Based on data reported by the American Medical Association, the median total salary and deferred compensation as a percent of total revenues for pediatricians was 42.3 percent in 1994.

The average profitability for Dr. Jones's practice for 1994 and 1995 was 45.6 percent, as presented in Exhibit 36-2. Therefore, Dr. Jones's practice was approximately 3.3 percent more profitable than the median pediatrician practice over the past two years.

Summary

Although Dr. Jones's revenues are slightly below the median for the average pediatrician, Dr. Jones has built a profitable, growing practice in a favorable location. In addition, Dr. Jones's practice is somewhat more profitable than the median pediatrics practice, as represented by American Medical Association statistics.

Medical Practice Valuation and Analysis

Overview

There are numerous generally accepted medical practice valuation methods and procedures. All of these specific methods and procedures can be generally aggregated into the following three distinct categories of medical practice valuation approaches:

1. The asset-based approach.
2. The income approach.
3. The market approach.

With regard to the appraisal of Gateway Pediatrics, we relied on an asset accumulation method, a discounted cash flow method, and a comparative transaction method under the asset-based, income, and market approaches, respectively. A brief description of each approach, as well as the particular method employed, is discussed below.

The Asset Accumulation Method

Overview. This method quantifies the fair market value of the assets of the subject medical practice as the aggregate value of all of the practice assets. Accordingly, this method requires a discrete appraisal of each category of the subject practice's assets.

Typically, medical practice assets may be grouped into four categories: (1) financial assets, (2) real estate, (3) tangible personal property, and (4) intangible assets. Each of these asset categories should be appraised in order to estimate fair market value.

Financial assets typically include cash, patient accounts receivable, prepaid expenses, and an inventory of medical and office materials and supplies. Real estate includes owned and leased land, buildings, and building improvements. Tangible personal property includes medical equipment, office furniture and fixtures, and office and computer equipment. Intangible assets typically include patient relationships and a trained and assembled workforce.

Asset Accumulation Valuation Analysis. We identified five assets of Gateway Pediatrics: (1) supplies on hand, (2) accounts receivable, (3) tangible personal property and equipment, (4) the intangible value of the patient relationships, and (5) the intangible value of the trained and assembled workforce.

Supplies on Hand. According to the practice records, for the year ending December 31, 1995, Gateway Pediatrics reported $9,920 in medical and office supplies expense.

Typically, based on our experience, supplies on hand approximate one to two months of total annual supplies expensed. Based on discussions with the office manager of the practice, a two-month supply of medical and office products is normally on hand. Projecting two months of total supplies on hand, this would indicate supplies of $1,620 (calculated as medical and office supplies expense of $9,717 for 1995, divided by 6 months, rounded).

Therefore, we estimated the value of supplies on hand to be approximately $1,600.

Accounts Receivable. Exhibit 36-3 presents the accounts receivable collection history for Gateway Pediatrics from January 1993 through December 1995, based on practice records. As presented, the average adjustment as a percent of receivables was 8.5 percent over the past three years. Since January 1994, the average adjustment as a percent of receivables increased slightly, to 9.0 percent.

Exhibit 36-4 presents our calculation of the fair market value of the patient accounts receivable, as of December 31, 1995. Based on data presented in Exhibit 36-3, we estimated the adjustment as a percent of receivables at 9.0 percent.

As presented in Exhibit 36-4, discounting the accounts receivable by 9.0 percent results in an indicated fair market value of this asset, as of December 31, 1995, of $26,000.

Tangible Property and Equipment. The tangible property and equipment of the practice includes (1) office furniture and fixtures, (2) medical equipment, and (3) office equipment. We have conducted a physical inventory and inspection of all of the tangible personal property of the practice. Based on available ad valorem personal property taxation assessment schedules, we have estimated the current depreciated replacement cost of all of the tangible personal property of the practice, as of December 31, 1995. For a value in continued use appraisal, this depreciated replacement cost represents the fair market value for the subject assets.

Exhibit 36-5 presents a listing and our valuation conclusion for all of the owned tangible personal property of the practice. The list of tangible personal property was based on Dr. Jones's individual income tax return for calendar 1995 and on our inspection. Based on our depreciated replacement cost analysis, the fair market value of the practice tangible property and equipment, as of December 31, 1995, is $24,000.

Current Patient Relationships. Exhibit 36-6 presents our analysis of the value of the current patient relationships of Gateway Pediatrics. The following is a summary of our analysis:

1. *Estimated revenue per patient chart per year.* For calendar 1995, the total revenue for the practice was $224,884. Based on a review of the active patient charts at the practice, we estimated that Gateway Pediatrics had approximately 2,500 active charts. Therefore, the average revenue per active patient chart for 1995 was $90.

2. *Estimated after-tax excess profit per patient chart per year.* Based on Exhibit 36-2, Dr. Jones's practice reported an excess economic margin of approximately 3.3 percent in 1995. Therefore, the excess before-tax profit per patient chart in 1995 equals the estimated revenue per active patient chart of $90 multiplied by 3.3 percent, or approximately $2.93. Projecting an effective income tax rate of 40 percent, the estimated after-tax excess profit per patient chart in 1995 was $1.76.

3. *Practice return attributable to patient relationships.* Multiplying the practice excess return attributable to patient relationships of $1.76 per chart by the estimated number of charts of 2,500 results in an annual practice excess return attributable to patient relationships of $4,388.

4. *Present value of patient relationships.* We estimated the average remaining useful life of the patient relationships to be six years. This estimation was based on a statistical sample of active and inactive patient charts at Dr. Jones's practice. Based on the weighted average cost of capital of 18 percent (as estimated in Exhibit 36-9), the present value of patient relationships is $15,000.

Based on the analysis presented in Exhibit 36-6, the fair market value of the current patient relationships of Gateway Pediatrics, as of December 31, 1995, is $15,000.

Trained and Assembled Workforce. Exhibit 36-7 presents our analysis of the intangible value of the trained and assembled workforce. The assembled workforce at Gateway Pediatrics is highly trained. Based on our experience, the cost of recruiting and training staff members for professional practices similar to Gateway Pediatrics is 10 percent of total salary for employees earning less than $10,000 annually, 15 percent of total salary for employees earning between $10,000 and $20,000 annually, and 20 percent of total annual salary for employees earning between $20,000 and $30,000 annually.

Exhibit 36-7 summarizes the indicated intangible value for the trained and assembled workforce, as of December 31, 1995, of $11,000.

Summary. Exhibit 36-8 presents a summary of our asset accumulation valuation method. Based on this method, the fair market value of the specified practice assets of Gateway Pediatrics, as of December 31, 1995, is $78,000.

The Discounted Cash Flow Method

Overview. The second method used to estimate the fair market value for the assets of Gateway Pediatrics was the discounted cash flow method. This method requires the quantification of the prospective net economic income associated with medical practice ownership. This quantification requires the projection of the net cash flow–generating capacity of the practice. This projection is made for a discrete period of time. The actual number of years in the projection period is determined by how long it would take for a physician to create a comparable competitive practice.

The projection of the net cash flow generation of the practice requires that the following analyses be made:

- A revenue projection.
- An economic operating margin projection.
- A cost of capital projection.
- An incremental benefit projection, based on an analysis of the earnings capacity of the subject practice incremental to the earnings that could be generated from a competitive start-up practice.

It is noteworthy that under this method, a buying entity will pay only the value of the practice represented by the incremental economic benefit generated by the established practice, as compared to the earnings available from a start-up practice opportunity. The fair market value of the medical practice is the cumulative present value of all future cash flow projections, incremental to that which would be generated by a hypothetical, competitive start-up practice.

Discounted Cash Flow Valuation Analysis. Exhibit 36-9 presents a summary of our alternative start-up practice analysis. This analysis quantifies how much a willing buyer will pay for the subject practice as compared to the alternative of starting a competitive pediatrics practice from inception. The following is a summary of our analysis projection variables:

1. *Projection period.* We selected six years. This period represents our estimate of the time required to develop a comparable practice based on (1) the historical development of Dr. Jones's practice, (2) the current healthcare environment, and (3) the location of the practice.

2. *Practice net revenues.* We estimated practice net revenues based on net revenues generated for 1995, and a projected long-term growth rate. We estimated the long-term growth rate based on (1) an analysis of the existing economic environment and (2) projections for the healthcare industry.

3. *Alternative practice net revenues.* We selected $115,000 as the first-year revenues for a start-up practice, and we increased this revenue stream at the rates presented in Exhibit 36-9. First-year revenues and the implied growth rates presented in Exhibit 36-9 for the alternative practice are based on (1) industry research regarding physician earnings expectations, (2) the historical development of similar practices, (3) the practice's location, and (4) current trends in the healthcare industry.

4. *Incremental operating expenses.* We based the incremental operating expenses on data presented in Exhibit 36-2 for the practice's

economic earning capacity. Total economic earning capacity of the practice is defined as operating income plus nonoperating and non-recurring expenses, plus owners' compensation.

5. *Present value factor.* We selected an 18 percent after-tax present value discount rate, as estimated in Exhibit 36-9. This rate reflects our best estimate of the risks associated with the anticipated returns from the practice.

Based on this method, as presented in Exhibit 36-9, the fair market value of the practice assets, as of December 31, 1995, is $76,000.

The Comparative Transaction Method

Overview. It has often been said that all values are best tested and determined in the marketplace. However, when valuing a privately held company such as a medical practice, no such marketplace exists. Often, the best alternative is to look for guidance from the prices that investors are willing to pay for the assets of similar practices.

The "willing buyer/willing seller" concept underlying this method comes from the premise that the buyer is seeking an equity participation in a particular industry and that "value" to the buyer is a function of the strength and quality of earnings, assets, dividends, and/or other relevant variables.

As we are valuing the assets of Gateway Pediatrics on an enterprise basis, market information relating to transactions involving transfers of similar practices would provide relevant information regarding the market pricing of pediatric practices.

The Health Care Group, of Plymouth Meeting, Pennsylvania, compiles annual assessments of the intangible elements of medical practice transactions. Statistics published in 1995 contain over 2,500 reports of transactions during the years 1985–95.

According to the *Goodwill Registry*, intangible value reflected in the transactions represents a combination of assets that varies on a case-by-case basis as to existence and value.

> That combination might include location, use of a practice's or individual's name, patient information (embodied in the clinical record), a favorable leasehold, a covenant not to compete, compensation for past (or future) management and entrepreneurial services, payments for referral to an associate or recommendation of a successor, patient lists, credit records, patient care and/or employee contracts, as well as assignments of future income. [5]

Because no public market exists that will provide information on market transactions involving medical practices, data provided by The Health Care Group, Inc., serves as a reasonable proxy for estimating the intangible asset value of Gateway Pediatrics.

---

[5] *Goodwill Registry 1995* (Plymouth Meeting, PA: The Health Care Group, Inc., 1995), p. v.

Combining the intangible asset value estimated based on market transactions with fair market values for all identified and discretely analyzed tangible assets provides another measure of the fair market value of the assets of Gateway Pediatrics.

Comparative Transaction Valuation Analysis. Data published in *Goodwill Registry 1995* provides information on 129 transactions involving pediatrics practices that occurred from 1985 to 1995. Of the 129 transactions, 118 (or 91.5 percent of the total) reflected transactions where some level of intangible value was reported. For the 118 transactions reported with goodwill in the pediatrics category, the mean and median intangible value percentages reported were 30.4 percent and 27.9 percent, respectively.

The data published by The Health Care Group summarizes the purpose of the valuation for each of the transactions of pediatrics practices. To estimate the appropriate level of intangible value to assign to Gateway Pediatrics, we reviewed all practices that were appraised for the purpose of the actual sale of the practice assets over the past seven years. Of the 93 total transactions since 1988, 41 (or 44 percent of the 93 transactions) were for the purpose of the actual sale of practice assets. The average intangible value as a percent of the total sale price of pediatrics practices from 1988 through 1995 was 27.2 percent, and the median was 25.0 percent.

The range of prices actually paid for the intangible assets of pediatric practices, separated by quartiles from 1988 through 1995, is as follows.

	Percentage of Actual Sale Price Paid for Intangible Asset Value	
Quartile	Mean	Median
1st	50.5%	47.5%
2nd	28.6%	28.3%
3rd	17.4%	16.2%
4th	4.4%	3.3%

As presented, there is a large range of prices that buyers are willing to pay for the intangible value of pediatric practices. This variance exists because of the numerous distinguishing characteristics among the practices, including practice location, size, growth, competition, and profitability.

Based on the changing healthcare environment, we also reviewed recent sale transactions involving pediatric practices. We focused on transactions involving practices with less than $1 million in revenues. From 1992 through 1995, the mean and median intangible value as a percent of the total sale price of pediatrics practices was 23.1 and 22.8, respectively.

We also looked at the price-to-revenue pricing multiples paid in these sale transactions. The majority of the transactions reflected revenue pricing multiples in the range of 0.20 to 0.40, with a mean multiple of 0.35. Applying the mean revenue pricing multiple of 0.35 to the

1995 net revenues of $220,836 indicates a value for Gateway Pediatrics of approximately $77,000.

As stated by the American Medical Association (AMA) Council on Ethical and Judicial Affairs in the 1986 edition of its *Current Opinions*, "In the sale of a medical practice, the purchaser is buying not only furniture and fixtures, but also goodwill, i.e., the opportunity to take over the patients of the seller." Goodwill, or intangible asset value, often represents the most significant asset in the group of assets transferred in a medical practice sale transaction. Consequently, goodwill value is generally the subject of considerable negotiation and debate.

Dictionaries define goodwill as a salable asset arising from the reputation of a business (i.e., medical practice) and its relations with its customers (i.e., patients). As stated by the AMA in *Buying and Selling Medical Practices: A Valuation Guide*:

> Goodwill incorporates such subjective factors as the 'personality' of a practice, which evolves from the physician(s) running it, the office staff, the surroundings, and the patients themselves. Goodwill is demonstrated by the fact that patients continue to seek the services of the physician(s) and that new patients are attracted as well. [6]

Many factors are considered to influence the goodwill value of a medical practice. According to the AMA, the following is a list of some of the more significant factors:

- Medical specialty.
- Referral sources.
- Practice location.
- Practice demographics.
- Amount of competition.
- Financial condition of the practice.
- Seller's reputation among colleagues.
- Collection ratio.
- Practice efficiency.
- Operational considerations.
- Hours worked.
- Medical records.
- Ease of transition, including:
  - Employee retention.
  - Patient introduction.
  - Use of seller's name.
  - Use of seller's telephone number.
  - Covenant not to compete.

---

[6] *Buying and Selling Medical Practices: A Valuation Guide* (Chicago: American Medical Association, 1990), p. 39.

With regard to the valuation of Gateway Pediatrics, we considered the above factors in arriving at our estimate of the intangible value attributable to the practice. Specifically, the following factors regarding Gateway Pediatrics were weighed and determined to result in the existence of intangible value for Gateway Pediatrics, as of the valuation date:

- Emphasis on pediatrics, or primary care medicine, rather than a referral-type specialty would generally exert a positive impact on goodwill value.
- A favorable location exerts a positive impact on goodwill value.
- Revenue below the average pediatrician exerts a negative impact on goodwill value.
- Number of patients seen per week below the average pediatrician exerts a negative impact on goodwill value.

Based on (1) the noted intangible value percentages, (2) the range of revenue pricing multiples, (3) our understanding of the operations of Dr. Jones's practice, and (4) our analysis of pertinent intangible factors relating to this practice, we estimated the fair market value of the practice intangible assets as a percent of revenues. We selected an intangible value pricing multiple for Gateway Pediatrics of 15 percent.

Exhibit 36-10 presents our analysis and indicated value for the intangible assets of Gateway Pediatrics as of the valuation date.

Based on our analysis, total intangible asset value, based on the comparative transaction method, is $33,700.

Adding the previously derived value of the tangible assets of $51,620, as presented in Exhibit 36-10, results in an indicated value of the assets of Gateway Pediatrics as of December 31, 1995, based on this method, of $85,000.

Valuation Synthesis and Conclusion

We relied on three methods within the asset-based, income, and market approaches to appraise the assets of Gateway Pediatrics: the asset accumulation method, the discounted cash flow method, and the comparative transaction method. The indicated values from each of these methods are as follows.

Valuation Method	Indicated Fair Market Value ($)
Asset accumulation method	78,000
Discounted cash flow method	76,000
Comparative transaction method	85,000

These three methods resulted in a reasonable range of valuation indications, from $76,000 to $85,000. In our final valuation estimate, we assigned slightly more weight to the asset accumulation method and to the discounted cash flow method. We assigned slightly less weight to the comparative transaction method.

Based on the analyses summarized in this report, and in our opinion, the fair market value of certain assets of Gateway Pediatrics, in fee simple interest, as of December 31, 1995, is $78,000.

Appraisal Certification

We hereby certify the following statements regarding this appraisal:

1. We have personally inspected the assets, properties, or business interests encompassed by this appraisal.

2. We have no present or prospective future interest in the assets, properties, or business interests that are the subject of this appraisal report.

3. We have no personal interest or bias with respect to the subject matter of this report or the parties involved.

4. Our compensation for making the appraisal is in no way contingent on the value reported or on any predetermined value.

5. To the best of our knowledge and belief, the statements of facts contained in this report, on which the analyses, conclusions, and opinions expressed herein are based, are true and correct.

6. Our analyses, opinions, and conclusions were developed, and this report has been prepared, in conformity with the *Uniform Standards of Professional Appraisal Practice*, as promulgated by The Appraisal Foundation.

7. No persons other than the individuals whose qualifications are included herein have provided significant professional assistance regarding the analyses, opinions, and conclusions set forth in this report.

8. The reported analyses, opinions, and conclusions are limited only by the reported contingent and limiting conditions, and they represent our unbiased professional analyses, opinions, and conclusions.

9. The reported analyses, opinions, and conclusions were developed, and this report has been prepared, in conformity with the requirements of the Code of Professional Ethics and the Standards of Professional Appraisal Practice of the Appraisal Institute, of the American Society of Appraisers, and of the other professional organizations of which we are members.

10. Disclosure of the contents of this report is subject to the requirements of the Appraisal Institute, the American Society of Appraisers, and the other professional organizations of which we are members related to review by their duly authorized representatives.

Statement of Contingent and Limiting Conditions

This appraisal is made subject to the following general contingent and limiting conditions:

1. We assume no responsibility for the legal description or matters including legal or title considerations. Title to the subject assets, properties, or business interests is assumed to be good and marketable unless otherwise stated.
2. The subject assets, properties, or business interests are appraised free and clear of any or all liens or encumbrances unless otherwise stated.
3. We assume responsible ownership and competent management with respect to the subject assets, properties, or business interests.
4. The information furnished by others is believed to be reliable. However, we issue no warranty or other form of assurance regarding its accuracy.
5. We assume no hidden or unapparent conditions regarding the subject assets, properties, or business interests.
6. We assume that there is full compliance with all applicable federal, state, and local regulations and laws unless the lack of compliance is stated, defined, and considered in the appraisal report.
7. We assume that all required licenses, certificates of occupancy, consents, or legislative or administrative authority from any local, state, or national government, or private entity or organization have been or can be obtained or reviewed for any use on which the opinion contained in this report is based.
8. Unless otherwise stated in this report, we did not observe, and we have no knowledge of, the existence of hazardous materials with regard to the subject assets, properties, or business interests. However, we are not qualified to detect such substances. We assume no responsibility for such conditions or for any expertise required to discover them.
9. Possession of this report does not carry with it the right of publication. It may not be used for any purpose by any person other than the client to whom it is addressed without our written consent, and in any event, only with proper written qualifications and only in its entirety.
10. By reason of this opinion, we are not required to furnish a complete valuation report or to give testimony or to be in attendance in court with reference to the assets, properties, or business interests in question unless arrangements have been previously made.
11. Neither all nor any part of the contents of this report shall be disseminated to the public through advertising, public relations, news, sales, or other media without our prior written consent and approval.
12. The analyses, opinions, and conclusions presented in this report apply to this engagement only and may not be used out of the context presented herein. This report is valid only for the effective date specified herein and only for the purpose specified herein.

Professional Qualifications of the Principal Analyst

Alicia Analyst, ASA, CFA

Academic and Professional Credentials

Master of Business Administration, Finance, University of Washington
Bachelor of Science, Business Administration, Finance, University of Oregon
Chartered Financial Analyst
American Society of Appraisers, Accredited Senior Appraiser, Business Valuation

Position and Experience

Senior Associate, Willamette Management Associates
Securities Analyst, Portland Investment Management Co.

Professional Affiliations

Portland Society of Financial Analysts
Institute of Management Accountants
American Society of Appraisers
Association for Investment Management and Research

Exhibit 36–1

GATEWAY PEDIATRICS
INCOME STATEMENTS

	Calendar Years Ended					Calendar Years Ended				
	1995 $	1994 $	1993 $	1992 $	1991 $	1995 %	1994 %	1993 %	1992 %	1991 %
Revenues:										
Gross revenues	224,884	204,440	178,801	160,907	172,354	101.8	101.6	102.2	102.8	102.4
Less: allowances	(4,048)	(3,147)	(3,809)	(4,448)	(4,036)	(1.8)	(1.6)	(2.2)	(2.8)	(2.4)
Net revenues	220,836	201,293	174,992	156,459	168,318	100.0	100.0	100.0	100.0	100.0
Operating expenses:										
Wages	64,263	58,174	50,029	47,296	47,862	29.1	28.9	28.6	30.2	28.4
Drugs	3,313	3,188	7,609	11,499	11,224	1.5	1.6	4.3	7.3	6.7
Lab fees	177	145	-	100	-	0.1	0.1	-	0.1	-
Bad debts	-	-	277	-	-	-	-	0.2	-	-
Advertising	155	156	-	-	-	0.1	0.1	-	-	-
Auto expenses	1,325	1,070	1,738	2,233	2,089	0.6	0.5	1.0	1.4	1.2
Depreciation	15,459	15,144	23,159	14,621	14,037	7.0	7.5	13.2	9.3	8.3
Amortization	883	650	-	-	-	0.4	0.3	-	-	-
Employee benefit programs	4,417	4,182	4,590	4,510	5,053	2.0	2.1	2.6	2.9	3.0
Insurance	4,638	4,599	4,714	4,978	4,445	2.1	2.3	2.7	3.2	2.6
Legal and professional	1,546	1,420	3,515	2,255	1,647	0.7	0.7	2.0	1.4	1.0
Office expense	1,656	1,842	1,600	1,595	7,337	0.8	0.9	0.9	1.0	4.4
Pension and profit sharing	1,767	1,550	1,632	1,852	-	0.8	0.8	0.9	1.2	-
Repairs and maintenance	7,729	8,132	5,806	9,996	5,812	3.5	4.0	3.3	6.4	3.5
Supplies	6,404	5,990	6,779	5,755	1,962	2.9	3.0	3.9	3.7	1.2
Taxes and licenses	13,250	12,063	9,748	10,488	10,335	6.0	6.0	5.6	6.7	6.1
Dues and subscriptions	1,656	1,659	1,693	1,200	2,530	0.8	0.8	1.0	0.8	1.5
Continuing education	-	-	-	524	-	-	-	-	0.3	-
Utilities	8,833	8,443	8,043	6,668	8,201	4.0	4.2	4.6	4.3	4.9
Total operating expenses	137,470	128,407	130,952	125,570	122,534	62.3	63.8	74.8	80.3	72.8
Operating income	83,366	72,886	44,040	30,889	45,784	37.8	36.2	25.2	19.7	27.2
Other income (expense):										
Interest expense	(1,767)	(1,475)	(4,434)	(7,112)	(9,535)	(0.8)	(0.7)	(2.5)	(4.5)	(5.7)
Rent	12,246	12,246	-	-	-	5.5	6.1	-	-	-
Risk pool reimbursement	3,092	2,813	-	-	-	1.4	1.4	-	-	-
Miscellaneous	-	-	40,536	31,991	20,530	-	-	23.2	20.4	12.2
Total other	13,571	13,584	36,102	24,879	10,995	6.1	6.7	20.6	15.9	6.5
Pretax income	96,937	86,470	80,142	55,768	56,779	43.9	43.0	45.8	35.6	33.7

SOURCE: Dr. Jones 1991–1995 individual income tax returns and Willamette Management Associates calculations.

Exhibit 36–2

GATEWAY PEDIATRICS
ANALYSIS OF ECONOMIC EARNING CAPACITY
As of December 31, 1995

	Year Ended 12/31/95		Year Ended 12/31/94	
	$	%	$	%
Net practice revenues [a]	220,836	100.0%	201,293	100.0%
Pretax income [a]	96,937	43.9%	86,470	43.0%
Adjustments to reflect economic earning capacity of the practice:				
Repairs and maintenance [e]	7,729	3.5%	8,132	4.0%
Property taxes [e]	4,580	2.1%	4,280	2.1%
Insurance [e]	425	0.2%	413	0.2%
Depreciation [e]	9,387	4.3%	9,881	4.9%
Amortization [e]	883	0.4%	650	0.3%
Mortgage interest [e]	1,767	0.8%	1,475	0.7%
Fair rental rate [f]	(14,000)	-6.3%	(14,000)	-7.0%
Rent income [e]	(12,246)	-5.5%	(12,246)	-6.1%
Utilities [g]	4,417	2.0%	4,222	2.1%
Pension/profit sharing [a]	1,767	0.8%	1,550	0.8%
Total adjustments	4,709	2.1%	4,357	2.2%
Economic earning capacity	101,645	46.0%	90,827	45.1%
Industry average pediatrician compensation as % of total revenue [b]	42.3%			
Economic earning (a)	96,236	45.6%		
"Excess" economic earning capacity (d)	7,183	3.3%		

a. Per Exhibit 36-1.

b. Per American Medical Association 1995 edition of *Physician Marketplace Statistics*. Reported median pediatrician net income of $113,000, divided by the median revenue for a self-employed pediatrician of $267,000.

c. Average of 1994 and 1995.

d. 1995 economic earning capacity percentage for Dr. Jones, less median pediatrician compensation as percent of total revenue, multiplied by Dr. Jones 1995 total revenue.

e. Adjusted to exclude benefits (expenses) of practice related to building ownership, per schedule provided by the practice's accountants, Wilstrom & Hart, CPAs. All reported repairs and maintenance expense was added back to reported income.

f. Based on discussions with local real estate brokers.

g. Reported utilities expense multiplied by 0.5, to reflect only half of the building is occupied by the Dr. Jones practice.

Exhibit 36–3

GATEWAY PEDIATRICS
ACCOUNTS RECEIVABLE COLLECTION HISTORY

Month	Charges $	Receipts $	Adjustments $	Accounts Receivable $	Adjustments/ Receivables %
Jan-93	11,980	13,786	1,353	26,412	5.12
Feb-93	17,719	13,338	2,155	28,638	7.53
Mar-93	23,697	17,148	2,698	32,488	8.31
Apr-93	13,987	16,547	1,913	28,015	6.83
May-93	13,272	12,693	1,390	27,205	5.11
Jun-93	17,317	16,195	3,734	24,593	15.18
Jul-93	10,265	10,463	941	23,454	4.01
Aug-93	13,700	13,062	1,894	22,198	8.53
Sep-93	13,740	9,637	1,386	24,914	5.56
Oct-93	16,685	13,056	2,108	26,435	7.97
Nov-93	21,051	15,510	2,369	29,607	8.00
Dec-93	21,929	16,407	2,864	32,265	8.88
Jan-94	14,028	14,609	2,417	29,267	8.26
Feb-94	20,588	14,708	1,896	33,251	5.70
Mar-94	26,364	22,462	4,734	32,418	14.60
Apr-94	14,322	16,576	2,278	27,886	8.17
May-94	12,602	13,401	1,903	25,184	7.56
Jun-94	21,069	16,016	2,542	27,695	9.18
Jul-94	11,083	15,126	2,245	21,406	10.49
Aug-94	14,594	13,067	2,394	20,540	11.65
Sep-94	12,054	13,722	1,743	17,128	10.18
Oct-94	16,128	10,474	1,518	21,264	7.14
Nov-94	19,170	15,485	2,268	22,681	10.00
Dec-94	17,138	15,590	1,626	22,602	7.20
Jan-95	13,480	9,038	1,530	25,514	6.00
Feb-95	27,826	16,437	3,045	33,858	8.99
Mar-95	19,516	20,534	3,250	29,589	10.98
Apr-95	15,754	16,078	2,392	26,873	8.90
May-95	13,862	14,741	1,998	23,995	8.33
Jun-95	23,176	17,618	2,466	27,088	9.10
Jul-95	12,191	14,672	2,357	22,249	10.60
Aug-95	16,053	14,374	2,322	21,607	10.75
Sep-95	13,259	14,408	1,831	18,627	9.83
Oct-95	17,740	10,997	1,594	23,776	6.70
Nov-95	21,087	16,260	2,381	26,223	9.08
Dec-95	18,851	15,430	1,594	28,051	5.68

Average adjustments as a % of receivables, total:	8.50
Average adjustments as a % of receivables from 1994 to present:	9.00

SOURCE: Monthly practice totals provided by Dr. Jones.

Exhibit 36–4

GATEWAY PEDIATRICS
ACCOUNTS RECEIVABLE
FAIR MARKET VALUE
As of December 31, 1995

Total accounts receivable balance, as of December 31, 1995	$ 28,051
Less: Discount [a]	$ 2,525
Fair market value of accounts receivable, rounded	$ 26,000

a. Per Exhibit 36-3.

SOURCE: Dr. Jones practice financial statements dated December 31, 1995, and Willamette Management Associates calculations.

Exhibit 36–5

GATEWAY PEDIATRICS
TANGIBLE PERSONAL PROPERTY
FAIR MARKET VALUE
As of December 31, 1995

Asset Description	Date Placed In Service	Original Cost $	Adjustment Factor	Estimated Fair Market Value $
Equipment	8/1/86	14,340	0.30	4,302
Toshiba copier	1/17/87	2,363	0.25	591
Calculator	2/17/87	169	0.25	42
Centrifuge	5/13/87	220	0.33	73
Pager	5/19/87	119	0.30	36
Telephones	8/15/87	1,027	0.30	308
Checkwriter	10/29/88	130	0.37	48
Audiometer	12/22/88	596	0.37	221
Computer system	6/6/90	15,950	0.10	1,595
Typewriter	10/4/90	329	0.45	148
Exam table	1/1/91	250	0.71	178
Chair	6/1/91	139	0.71	99
Wood cabinet	2/6/93	249	0.79	197
Office furniture	11/2/93	202	0.79	160
Office sign	11/6/93	560	0.74	414
Carpet	12/18/93	1,063	0.66	702
Carpet pad	1/14/94	254	0.76	193
Office furniture	1/25/94	2,122	0.83	1,761
Table/Lamp	1/25/94	237	0.76	180
Cabinets	2/11/94	9,031	0.76	6,864
Blinds	2/26/94	367	0.76	279
Computer system	1/1/95	3,551	0.58	2,060
WordPerfect software	1/1/95	645	0.58	374
Medical software	1/1/95	1,875	0.58	1,088
DOS upgrade software	1/1/95	930	0.58	539
Copier	4/3/95	1,100	0.75	825
Printer	7/22/95	275	0.58	160
Fax machine	10/3/95	337	0.75	253
Total		58,430		23,686
Rounded				24,000

SOURCE: Dr. Jeffrey D. Jones tax returns, Benton County personal property valuation schedules, and Willamette Management Associates calculations.

Exhibit 36–6

GATEWAY PEDIATRICS
CURRENT PATIENT RELATIONSHIPS
FAIR MARKET VALUE
As of December 31, 1995

Total revenue, calendar 1995 [a]	$	224,884
Total number of active patient charts in the practice [b]		2,500
Estimated revenue per patient chart per year [c]	$	90
Estimated before-tax excess profit margin [d]		3.3%
Estimated before-tax excess profit per patient per year [e]	$	2.93
Effective income tax rate [f]		40%
Estimated after-tax profit per patient chart per year [g]	$	1.76
Annual practice return attributable to patient relationships [h]	$	4,388
Average expected remaining useful life of patient relationships (years) [i]		6
Present value discount rate [j]		18%
Present value of annuity factor		3.498
Present value of patient relationships (rounded) [k]	$	15,000

a. Per Exhibit 36-1.
b. Estimated by Dr. Jones and Willamette Management Associates.
c. Total revenue divided by number of active charts.
d. Per Exhibit 36-2.
e. Revenue per chart multiplied by estimated pretax excess profit margin.
f. Willamette Management Associates estimate.
g. One minus effective income tax rate, multiplied by before-tax excess profit per patient per year.
h. Practice return attributable to patient relationships multiplied by active patient charts.
i. Willamette Management Associates estimate.
j. As presented in Exhibit 36-9.
k. Annual practice return attributable to patient relationships multiplied by present value annuity factor.

SOURCE: Dr. Jeffrey D. Jones; *Stocks, Bonds, Bills, and Inflation: 1995 Yearbook* (Chicago: Ibbotson Associates, 1996);
The Wall Street Journal ; and Willamette Management Associates calculations.

Exhibit 36–7

GATEWAY PEDIATRICS
TRAINED AND ASSEMBLED WORKFORCE
FAIR MARKET VALUE
As of December 31, 1995

Position	Hourly Wage $	Hours/ Week	Annual Pay $	Replacement Cost as % of Annual Pay	Indicated Value $
Bookkeeper/office manager	12.72	40	26,458	20.0%	5,292
Certified medical assistant	11.87	16	9,878	10.0%	988
Medical assistant	9.54	24	11,906	15.0%	1,786
Receptionist	7.95	40	16,536	15.0%	2,480
Fair market value, trained and assembled workforce					10,546
Fair market value, trained and assembled workforce, rounded					11,000

SOURCE: Dr. Jeffrey D. Jones and Willamette Management Associates calculations.

Exhibit 36–8

GATEWAY PEDIATRICS
FAIR MARKET VALUE OF PRACTICE ASSETS
ASSET ACCUMULATION METHOD
As of December 31, 1995

Practice Asset Category	Fair Market Value $
Supplies on hand	1,600
Patient accounts receivable, net	26,000
Tangible property & equipment	24,000
Current patient relationships	15,000
Trained and assembled workforce	11,000
Fair market value of practice assets (rounded)	78,000

SOURCE: Exhibits 36-1 through 36-7, and Willamette Management Associates calculations.

Exhibit 36–9

GATEWAY PEDIATRICS
FAIR MARKET VALUE OF PRACTICE ASSETS
(ALTERNATIVE START UP PRACTICE ANALYSIS)
DISCOUNTED CASH FLOW METHOD
As of December 31, 1995

Projection Variable	Year 1	2	3	4	5	6
Practice net revenues [a]	$ 228,565	$ 236,565	$ 244,845	$ 253,414	$ 262,284	$ 271,464
Less: alternative practice net revenues [b]	115,000	138,000	165,600	190,440	219,006	251,857
Implied % growth		*20.0%*	*20.0%*	*15.0%*	*15.0%*	*15.0%*
Equals: incremental practice revenues	113,565.4	98,565.1	79,244.9	62,974.5	43,278.0	19,607.0
Less: incremental operating expenses [c]	61,808.5	53,644.6	43,129.4	34,274.2	23,554.3	10,671.2
Equals: incremental practice operating income	51,756.9	44,920.6	36,115.5	28,700.3	19,723.7	8,935.8
Less: estimated taxes	(20,702.7)	(17,968.2)	(14,446.2)	(11,480.1)	(7,889.5)	(3,574.3)
Equals: net incremental practice economic earnings	31,054.1	26,952.3	21,669.3	17,220.2	11,834.2	5,361.5
Multiplied by: present value discount factor [d]	0.8475	0.7182	0.6086	0.5158	0.4371	0.3704
Equals: present value of incremental income	26,317	19,357	13,189	8,882	5,173	3,310
Present value of discrete projection	76,227					
Fair market value of practice assets (rounded)	$ 76,000					

Present value discount rate (d)	*18.0%*
Long-term growth rate	*3.5%*
Alternative growth rate	*15.0%*
Estimated income tax rate	*40.0%*

a. Assumes 1995 revenues as base revenues, increasing at a long-term rate of 3.5 percent.
b. Based on market research regarding the expected revenue-generating capacity of first-year pediatricians, the current health care environment practitioners are facing, and the practice development history of Dr. Jeffrey D. Jones.
c. Based on Dr. Jones' economic earning capacity as presented in Exhibit 36-2.
d. Assumes present value discount factor as estimated in following page of this exhibit.

Exhibit 36–9 (concluded)

GATEWAY PEDIATRICS
WEIGHTED AVERAGE COST OF CAPITAL
As of December 31, 1995

	After-Tax Cost of Capital Components
Cost of equity capital:	
Risk-free rate [a]	6.0%
Equity risk premium [b]	7.0%
Small business risk premium [b]	4.0%
Company-specific risk premium [c]	4.0%
Total	21.0%
After-tax cost of debt capital [d,f]	6.3%

Weighted Average Cost of Capital

Capital Components	After-Tax Cost of Capital	Weight [e]	Weighted Cost of Capital
Debt capital	6.3%	20.0%	1.3%
Equity capital	21.0%	80.0%	16.8%
	27.3%	100.0%	
Weighted average cost of capital			18.1%
Present value discount rate (rounded)			18.0%

a. Amount represents the yield for a 20-year, U.S. treasury note as quoted in *The Wall Street Journal* on December 31, 1995.

b. Per *Stocks, Bonds, Bills and Inflation, 1995 Yearbook* (Chicago: Ibbtoson Associates, 1996).

c. Willamette Management Associates estimate.

d. Based on estimated physician borrowing rate at the prime rate of interest plus 1 to 3 percent.

e. Debt and equity weightings are based on the debt-to-total-capital and equity-to-total-capital ratios reported by Ibbotson Associates for the SIC code 801 (Offices and Clinics of Doctors of Medicine).

f. Based on estimated effective income tax rate of 40%.

Exhibit 36–10

GATEWAY PEDIATRICS
FAIR MARKET VALUE OF PRACTICE ASSETS
COMPARATIVE TRANSACTION METHOD
As of December 31, 1995

Analysis of Intangible Asset Value:

Gross practice revenues		$ 224,884
Intangible asset pricing multiple		15.0%
Indicated total intangible asset value		33,733
Plus: fair market value of identified tangible assets:		
Supplies on hand	1,600	
Accounts receivable	26,000	
Property and equipment	24,000	
Total		51,600
Indicated fair market value of practice assets		85,333
Indicated fair market value of practice assets, rounded		$ 85,000

SOURCE: Exhibits 36-1 through 36-7, and Willamette Management Associates calculations.

Chapter 37

Examples of Professional Practice Valuation Methods

This chapter provides two illustrative professional practice valuation exercises: (1) an accounting practice valuation and (2) a veterinary practice valuation. To facilitate the brevity of the illustrations, a significant amount of background material and analysis is omitted; only the application of the selected valuation methods is presented.

Example of an Accounting Practice Valuation

The example of White, Shert & Pensle, CPAs is a hypothetical example based on a synthesis of many small accounting practices that we have analyzed over the years. This example presents one possible way of valuing an accounting practice. In this example, we selected three valuation methods, including the discounted economic income method, the asset accumulation method, and the guideline market transaction method.

Example Fact Set

We were retained by the partners of White, Shert & Pensle, CPAs (WS&P). WS&P has been approached by a large national firm to see if the six partners want to either sell or merge their practice. WS&P is an accounting, tax, and litigation consulting partnership located in Hillsboro, Oregon.

Currently, all six partners work a 40-hour week, on average, with peak time being put in during the normal tax season. All six partners have an established network of contacts in the local business community.

Because of its location, WS&P provides a majority of its accounting, tax, and litigation consulting services specifically relating to the high-technology industry. Historically, the practice has been supported by a concentration of services in the tax area. For calendar year 1996, approximately 50 percent of the firm's revenues were attributable to tax-related services (with over 60 percent of these services performed for individual taxpayers). For the same period, approximately 35 percent of latest calendar year's revenues were attributable to audit services, and approximately 15 percent were attributable to litigation consulting services.

Discounted Economic Income Method

Exhibits 37-1 through 37-4 present the valuation of 100 percent of the partners' equity capital of WS&P as of December 31, 1996, using the discounted economic income method.

Exhibit 37-1 presents the projected economic income for WS&P for calendar years ended 1997 through 2001. The projected net client revenues are based on a detailed projection of the number of partners and staff for each year, the expected billing rate for each accountant, the expected utilization for each accountant, the expected billability of the work performed, and the expected collectibility of the fees billed.

Exhibit 37–1

WHITE, SHERT & PENSLE, CPAs
STATEMENT OF PROSPECTIVE RESULTS OF OPERATIONS
AS OF DECEMBER 31, 1996
(in $000s)

| | Projected for the Calendar Years Ended December 31: | | | | |
	1997	1998	1999	2000	2001
Net client revenues	2,580	2,709	2,844	2,987	3,136
Operating expenses					
Total partner compensation	753	786	822	859	897
Staff salaries	710	741	775	810	846
Employment taxes and benefits	151	157	164	172	179
Rent expense	206	206	206	206	206
Telephone and utilities	116	121	126	131	136
Postage and stationery	108	113	119	124	131
Professional liability					
and other insurance	108	113	119	124	131
Data processing expenses	108	113	119	124	131
Depreciation expense	86	90	95	100	105
Other expenses	43	43	43	43	43
Total operating expenses	2,387	2,484	2,586	2,693	2,805
Net income	**194**	**225**	**258**	**294**	**331**

Derivation of the Normalized Economic Income to Partners:

		1997	1998	1999	2000	2001
	Net income	194	225	258	294	331
+	Partner incentive compensation	195	214	225	245	255
+	Depreciation expense	86	90	95	100	105
−	Capital expenditures	(75)	(75)	(75)	(75)	(75)
−	Increase in working capital	(6)	(6)	(7)	(7)	(7)
=	Normalized economic income	**393**	**447**	**496**	**556**	**608**

Note: Mathematical differences are due to rounding.

The projected operating expenses are based on (1) a detailed analysis of the historical levels of operating expenses, (2) the relationship between operating expenses and client revenues (or to other factors, such as number of accountants, amount of floor space, etc.), and (3) the nature of fixed costs versus variable costs of the firm's operating expense structure.

WS&P does not have any long-term, interest-bearing debt outstanding. That is, all of the capital in the WS&P capital structure is equity capital.

In addition, Exhibit 37-1 also presents the calculation of projected "normalized" economic income for the subject accounting practice. The adjustments required to estimate normalized economic income in this example include the following:

1. An adjustment was made to add back the partner compensation in excess of the amount that nonpartner staff members with similar experience and expertise would earn.
2. Depreciation expense was added back to net income since depreciation is a noncash expense item.
3. Planned capital expenditures were deducted since these capital expenditures represent necessary cash expenditures to sustain the indicated level of growth in the economic income projections.
4. Additional working capital investments necessary to fund the subject practice's growth were deducted; these investments represent decrements in the cash flow available for distribution to the equity holders.

Based on these projections, Exhibit 37-1 presents the projected "normalized" economic income available for distribution to the partners in the subject practice for the next five years.

Exhibit 37-2 presents the estimation of the appropriate present value discount rate for WS&P. In this example, the equity capital discount rate was derived through the rate build-up procedure: (1) beginning with the risk-free rate of return, (2) adding the equity risk premium, (3) adding the small company stock risk premium, and (4) adding a practice-specific risk premium. This practice-specific risk premium was derived through a detailed analysis of the various factors affecting the level of risk associated with an investment in WS&P. This discount rate build-up procedure results in a present value discount rate of 25 percent.

Exhibit 37-3 presents the estimation of the terminal value of the subject practice using the Gordon model as the terminal value estimation method. The terminal value was estimated through the following process:

1. As presented in Exhibit 37-1, the year 2001 normalized economic income of the subject accounting practice was projected at $608,000. In order to estimate the projected economic income for the year 2002, the year 2001 economic income of $608,000 was multiplied by one plus the long-term growth rate of 4 percent. This 4 percent long-term growth rate represents the appropriate nominal long-term growth rate for the subject accounting practice. This long-term growth rate was based on an analysis of the competitive position of this accounting practice (and of its industry specialization and its service line specialization). This analysis results in projected economic income in the year 2002 of $632,000.
2. Next, year 2002 economic income must be divided by (or "capitalized" by) the present value discount rate less the expected long-term growth rate. As presented in Exhibit 37-3, subtracting the expected long-term growth rate of 4 percent from the present value discount rate of 25 percent results in a terminal value direct capitalization rate of 21 percent. Dividing the projected year 2002 economic income of $632,000 by the 21 percent terminal value direct capitalization rate results in an indicated terminal value of $3,011,000.

Exhibit 37–2

WHITE, SHERT & PENSLE, CPAs
ESTIMATION OF THE APPROPRIATE PRESENT VALUE DISCOUNT RATE
AS OF DECEMBER 31, 1996

Capital Market and Money Market Data
As of December 31, 1996

	Indicated Rate	
	Risk-free rate of return [a]	5.95%
+	All common stocks equity risk premium [b]	7.50%
+	Incremental small company common stock equity risk premium [c]	5.00%
+	Practice-specific nonsystematic equity risk premium [d]	6.25%
=	Indicated present value discount rate for the subject practice equity	24.70%
	Present value discount rate (rounded)	**25.00%**

a. *The Wall Street Journal*, January 2, 1997.
b. *Stocks, Bonds, Bills and Inflation*, 1997 Yearbook (Chicago: Ibbotson Associates, 1997).
c. *Stocks, Bonds, Bills and Inflation,* 1997 Yearbook.
d. Willamette Management Associates estimate.

Exhibit 37–3

WHITE, SHERT & PENSLE, CPAs
ESTIMATION OF THE APPROPRIATE TERMINAL VALUE
AS OF DECEMBER 31, 2001
(in $000s)

	Projected economic income for year 2001 [a]	608
×	Multiplied by: the expected long-term income growth rate [b]	1.04
=	Projected economic income in year 2002	632
	The appropriate direct capitalization rate	
	Present value discount rate [c]	25.0%
	Less: the expected long-term growth rate	4.0%
	Equals: long-term direct capitalization rate	21.0%
=	Indicated terminal value of the subject practice	**3,011**

a. See Exhibit 37-4.
b. Willamette Management Associates estimate.
c. See Exhibit 37-2.

Exhibit 37-4 presents the valuation indication of the WS&P practice based on the discounted economic income method. Based on the present value discount rate of 25 percent, the present value of the discrete period cash flow projection and of the terminal value is as presented in Exhibit 37-4.

The sum of the present values of all of the prospective cash flow (i.e., both the discrete projection and the terminal value) is $2,270,000. Therefore, the indicated value of the total partners' capital of WS&P, CPAs, based on the discounted economic income method, as of December 31, 1996, is $2,270,000.

Asset Accumulation Method

Exhibits 37-5 through 37-9 present the valuation of 100 percent of the partners' equity capital of WS&P as of December 31, 1996, using the asset accumulation method.

Exhibit 37-5 presents the balance sheet for WS&P, presenting each of the assets, liabilities, and partners' capital at book value and adjusted to fair market value. Based on our analysis, no adjustments were necessary to the reported book values of WS&P's current assets and current liabilities. However, adjustments were necessary to reflect the fair market value of the net fixed assets and the intangible assets owned by the practice.

With respect to the fixed assets of WS&P, we reviewed and relied on an appraisal of the furniture, fixtures, equipment, and leasehold improvements that was conducted by the Alder Appraisal Company. Based on this appraisal, and as presented in Exhibit 37-5, the fair market value of the fixed assets of WS&P is $401,000. The identification and valuation of the intangible assets of the subject accounting practice is a complex procedure. The intangible assets are generally created by the owners of the accounting practice and are not recorded on the historical-cost-based balance sheet. Exhibit 37-5 also presents the fair market value of various intangible assets owned by WS&P, including a favorable leasehold interest, a trained and assembled workforce, client work paper files, and client relationships.

Exhibit 37-6 presents the value of the favorable leasehold interest. The value of the leasehold interest is the present value of the advantageous rent situation. This is because WS&P has a contract rent for the next seven years that is $7 per square foot below the prevailing market rental rate for similar professional office space. As presented in Exhibit 37-6, the fair market value of the leasehold interest is $266,000.

Exhibit 37-7 presents the fair market value of the WS&P trained and assembled workforce. The trained and assembled workforce is valued by consideration of the costs avoided. This is because the hypothetical willing buyer of this accounting practice would not have to incur the costs of recruiting, hiring, and training a workforce of comparable experience and expertise to the WS&P workforce. Based on the data presented in Exhibit 37-7, the fair market value of the trained and assembled workforce is $325,000.

Exhibit 37–4

WHITE, SHERT & PENSLE, CPAs
DISCOUNTED ECONOMIC INCOME METHOD
INDICATED PRACTICE VALUE
AS OF DECEMBER 31, 1996
(in $000s)

	Calendar Years Ended:					Terminal
	1997	1998	1999	2000	2001	Value
Normalized economic income	393	447	496	556	608	3,011
Present value discount factor	0.8000	0.6400	0.5120	0.4096	0.3277	0.3277
Present value of economic income	314	286	254	228	119	987
Practice valuation indication	2,268					
Indicated practice value (rounded)	**2,270**					

Note: Mathematical differences are due to rounding.

Exhibit 37-8 presents the calculations supporting the fair market value of WS&P's client work paper files. The client work paper files are valued using a similar cost-avoidance method. In this case, we estimated the cost to recreate the work paper files related to the recurring audit, bookkeeping, and tax clients. Since clients normally return to the same accounting firm, their historical and permanent accounting and tax files are valued using an estimate of the hours required to recreate the permanent file times the cost per hour that would be required of both professional staff and clerical workers to recreate the files. Based on the data presented in Exhibit 37-8, the fair market value of the client work paper files is $56,000.

We also appraised the value of the WS&P client relationships, as presented in Exhibit 37-9. The first step in estimating the value of the client relationships is estimating the average remaining life of the current client relationships. There are various "analytical" methods commonly used to estimate the remaining useful life of client relationships, including the turnover rate method, the original group method, the select and ultimate method, and the retirement rate method. Based on an analysis of historical client turnover rates, the average remaining useful life of the WS&P client relationships is estimated at five years.

The second step in the appraisal of the WS&P client relationships is a projection of the net fee revenues from the current client relationships. This projection requires consideration of expected changes in the levels of service provided, of the practice billing rates, and of the practice allowance (or charge-off) rate.

The third step in this valuation is a projection of the contribution margin (or profit margin) associated with the current clients. This con-

Exhibit 37–5

WHITE, SHERT & PENSLE, CPAs
ASSET ACCUMULATION METHOD
FAIR MARKET VALUE AS OF DECEMBER 31, 1996

	At Book Value	At Fair Market Value
ASSETS		
Current assets:		
Cash & cash equivalents	$75,000	$75,000
Client accounts receivable	150,000	150,000
Work-in-progress	200,000	200,000
Prepaid expenses	75,000	75,000
Total current assets	500,000	500,000
Fixed assets:		
Furniture & fixtures	300,000	280,000
Computer equipment	100,000	80,000
Leasehold improvements	50,000	41,000
Gross fixed assets	450,000	401,000
Less: accumulated depreciation	(405,000)	
Total fixed assets, net	45,000	401,000
Intangible assets:		
Leasehold interest (see Exhibit 37-6)	–	266,000
Trained & assembled workforce (see Exhibit 37-7)	–	325,000
Client work paper files (see Exhibit 37-8)	–	56,000
Client relationships (see Exhibit 37-9)	–	605,000
Total intangible assets	–	1,252,000
TOTAL ASSETS	**$545,000**	**$2,153,000**
LIABILITIES AND PARTNERS' CAPITAL		
Current liabilities:		
Contracts payable	20,000	20,000
Accounts payable	40,000	40,000
Salaries payable	25,000	25,000
Accrued liabilities	50,000	50,000
Total current liabilities	135,000	135,000
Partners' capital	410,000	2,018,000
TOTAL LIABILITIES AND PARTNERS' CAPITAL	**$545,000**	**$2,153,000**

tribution margin is calculated after an allowance for basic partner compensation but before consideration of any partner profit distributions. In other words, in order to calculate the contribution margin, partners are treated as fairly compensated employees, not as owners of the firm.

The fourth step is to convert the projection of net earnings into a projection of economic income. This is accomplished by subtracting any increments in net financial assets due to the projected increase in net client fees. Net financial assets are typically defined as accounts receivable plus work-in-process less accounts payable. Also, the net earnings

Exhibit 37–6

WHITE, SHERT & PENSLE, CPAs
LEASEHOLD INTEREST
FAIR MARKET VALUE AS OF DECEMBER 31, 1996

1.	Net size of leased office space	12,000	square feet
2.	Current market rent for comparable space	$ 18.00	per square foot
3.	Current contract rent	$ 11.00	per square foot
4.	Favorable leasehold advantage per square foot (#2 – #3)	$ 7.00	per square foot
5.	Total annual favorable leasehold advantage (#4 × #1)	$84,000	
6.	Number of years remaining in lease term	7.0	years
7.	Appropriate present value discount rate	25.0%	
8.	Present value of annuity factor at 25% for 7 years	3.1611	
9.	Present value of favorable leasehold advantage (#8 × #5)	$266,000	
10.	Fair market value of leasehold interest	**$266,000**	

Exhibit 37–7

WHITE, SHERT & PENSLE, CPAs
TRAINED AND ASSEMBLED WORKFORCE
FAIR MARKET VALUE AS OF DECEMBER 31, 1996

Category of Employee	Total Annual Compensation $	Recruit %	Hire %	Train %	Total %	Replacement Cost $
Professional staff	575,000	10	10	30	50	287,500
Paraprofessional staff	75,000	10	–	20	30	22,500
Support staff	75,000	10	–	10	20	15,000
Total cost to recruit, hire, & train replacement workforce						$325,000
Fair market value of trained and assembled workforce						**$325,000**

from the client relationships should be reduced by a fair return on the assets employed in the service of those clients. The fair return is often calculated as the practice-specific discount rate times the fair market value of the net assets employed in the practice on the valuation date. The discount rate typically represents the firm's weighted-average cost of capital. And the net assets employed include both the tangible assets (e.g., office furniture and fixtures) and intangible assets (e.g., client work paper files) of the practice.

The final step of this valuation is the estimation of the present value of the economic income over the average remaining useful life of the client relationships. Of course, this procedure requires the quantification of the appropriate present value discount rate. Typically, this dis-

Exhibit 37–8

WHITE, SHERT & PENSLE, CPAs
CLIENT WORK PAPER FILES
FAIR MARKET VALUE AS OF DECEMBER 31, 1996

Type of Client	Number of Clients	Hours to Recreate Permanent File	Cost Per Hour $	Cost to Recreate Each Client File $	Cost to Recreate All Client Files $
Recurring audit	60	10.0	40.00	400	24,000
Recurring bookkeeping	120	5.0	30.00	150	18,000
Recurring tax—corporate	150	2.0	30.00	60	9,000
Recurring tax—individual	250	1.0	20.00	20	5,000
Total cost to recreate client work paper files					$56,000
Fair market value of client work paper files					**$56,000**

Exhibit 37–9

WHITE, SHERT & PENSLE, CPAs
CLIENT RELATIONSHIPS
FAIR MARKET VALUE AS OF DECEMBER 31, 1996

	(in $000s)				
Projection Variable	Year 1	Year 2	Year 3	Year 4	Year 5
Net client revenues (from current clients only)	2,500	2,550	2,600	2,650	3,700
× Contribution margin	15.0%	15.0%	15.0%	15.0%	15.0%
= Contribution	375	383	390	398	405
− Increase in net financial assets	10	12	12	14	14
− Return on assets employed	150	150	150	150	150
= Economic income	215	221	228	234	241
× Present value factor at 25% present value discount rate	0.8000	0.6400	0.5120	0.4096	0.3277
= Present value of economic income	**172**	**141**	**117**	**96**	**79**
Total present value of economic income					605
Fair market value of client relationships					**$ 605**

count rate is the weighted average cost of capital for the firm. The present value of the projected economic income represents the value of the recurring client relationships to WS&P. The fair market value of the client relationships, as presented in Exhibit 37-9, is $605,000.

Under the asset accumulation method, the fair market value of the partners' capital of WS&P is equal to the difference between the fair market value of the firm's assets less the fair market value of the firm's liabilities. As presented in Exhibit 37-5, the indicated value of the partners' capital from the asset accumulation method, as of December 31, 1996, is $2,018,000.

Guideline Market Transaction Method

Exhibit 37-10 presents the market transaction analysis prepared with regard to the valuation of WS&P, as of December 31, 1996. For this method, relevant valuation pricing multiples were derived from an analysis of transactions involving accounting practices with characteristics similar to WS&P. The practice sale transactions identified and relied on are all mature accounting practices with a focus on tax services. These accounting practices are similar to WS&P. And each guideline market transaction was consummated within a reasonably recent period of time.

For this method, we focused on client revenues and pretax income as the primary financial fundamentals. Based on the guideline market transaction data available, a reasonable estimation of the fair market value of the partners' capital of WS&P, based on the guideline market transaction method, as of December 31, 1996, is $2,125,000.

Valuation Synthesis and Conclusion

We relied on the three valuation methods described above to reach our opinion of value. The indicated values from the three valuation methods are as follows.

Valuation Method	Indicated Value
Discounted economic income method	$2,270,000
Asset accumulation method	$2,018,000
Guideline market transaction method	$2,125,000

To arrive at our final opinion of the fair market value of the subject accounting practice, we assigned equal weight to each of the methods. Based on the valuation procedures described above, the fair market value of 100 percent of the partners' capital of White, Shert & Pensle, as of December 31, 1996, is $2,138,000.

This example presents an appraisal designed to quantify the value of a 100 percent equity interest. The asset accumulation method can be adjusted to accommodate the valuation of a less than 100 percent interest and the valuation of a practice with a complex capital structure. However, these adjustments are significant.

Exhibit 37–10

WHITE, SHERT & PENSLE, CPAs
GUIDELINE MARKET TRANSACTIONS METHOD
FAIR MARKET VALUE AS OF DECEMBER 31, 1996

	Guideline Practice Sale Transactional Data				
				Indicated Transactional Pricing Multiples	
		Guideline Practice			
Guideline Market Transactions	Confirmed Sale Price	Last Year Revenues	Last Year Pretax Income	Price/ Revenues	Price/ Pretax Income
1. Six-partner CPA practice in Gresham, Oregon sold in July 1996—practice is principally corporate audit and tax work	$ 1,800,000	$ 2,160,000	$ 350,000	0.83 times	5.1 times
2. Sale of three-partner CPA practice in Aloha, Oregon, sold in August 1996— practice is principally commercial tax work	1,000,000	1,100,000	200,000	0.91 times	5.0 times
3. Sale of eight-partner CPA practice in Portland, Oregon, sold in December 1996— practice is 50% (nonaudit) accounting and 50% personal and commercial tax work	2,600,000	2,800,000	540,000	0.93 times	4.8 times
Indicated valuation multiples:　Mean				0.89 times	5.0 times
Median				0.91 times	5.0 times

| | Analysis of the Subject Practice Market Transactions Method Valuation Analysis | |
White, Shert & Pensle, CPAs	Last Year Revenues	Last Year Pretax Income
Subject practice financial fundamentals	$2,500,000	$ 400,000　[a]
Selected market-derived valuation pricing multiples	.90x	5.0x
Indications of value	2,250,000	2,000,000
Overall indication of value (rounded)	**$2,125,000**	

a. Before partner incentive compensation.

In the instance when a less than 100 percent equity interest is being valued, appropriate valuation discounts and premiums should be quantified for minority ownership interests, majority (but less than 100 percent) ownership control, lack of marketability, illiquidity, and blockage. In the instance of a practice with several classes of stock outstanding, each class of stock should be valued separately: common and preferred stock, voting versus nonvoting, cumulative versus noncumulative, participative versus nonparticipative, and primary versus secondary liquidation preference. An analysis of the appropriate adjustments to the asset accumulation method—to accommodate either less than 100 percent equity interest or complex capital structures—is beyond the scope of this chapter.

Example of a Veterinary Practice Valuation

In this example, we present one possible way of valuing a veterinary practice. The example presents three valuation methods: the capitalized excess earnings method, the capitalization of economic income method, and the guideline market transaction method.

Example Fact Set

We were retained by Dan Jackson, an attorney representing Dr. John Smith. We were retained to estimate the value of 100 percent of the equity of ABC Veterinary Hospital, PC, for Dr. Smith's pending marital dissolution. ABC Veterinary Hospital has been in operation since 1983 and is located in Pastureville, Pennsylvania. Although revenues for the practice in 1983 were primarily derived from large animal work, approximately 90 percent of the revenues are currently from small animals (primarily dogs and cats), 5 percent from exotic animals, and 5 percent from large animals.

As of the valuation date, the practice was owned by Dr. Smith, and Dr. Smith employed one associate, Dr. Johnson. Dr. Smith currently works approximately 45 to 50 hours per week. Early in the practice's development, he worked approximately 80 to 100 hours per week.

According to discussions with Dr. Smith and according to our market surveys, competition in the area has increased over the past three years.

The practice's fee schedule is updated approximately every year. Based on discussions with Dr. Smith, the fee schedule is comparable to competitors.

The practice is located in an area that was primarily farmland 10 years ago. However, this area has recently been developed with several subdivisions. Dr. Smith estimates that 90 percent of his clients come from a 10-mile radius of the practice location.

Historical statements of results of operations for the practice for the last five years are presented in Exhibit 37-11.

Capitalized Excess Earnings Method

A summary of the capitalized excess earnings method is presented in Exhibit 37-12. This method requires the estimation of four variables: (1) the adjusted net tangible asset value of the practice (which is equal to the fair market value of the tangible assets less the fair market value of the liabilities), (2) the economic earnings of the practice, (3) the fair return on net tangible assets, and (4) the appropriate capitalization rate for the excess earnings of the practice.

Adjusted Net Tangible Asset Value. The adjusted net tangible asset value of the practice of $26,000 is presented on Exhibit 37-13. As presented, we have made adjustments to reported accounts receivable and reported corporate and personal net property and equipment.

Exhibit 37–11

ABC VETERINARY HOSPITAL, P.C.
STATEMENTS OF RESULTS OF OPERATIONS

| | Calendar Years Ended ($): | | | | | As a Percent of Total Revenue | | | | |
	1996	1995	1994	1993	1992	1996	1995	1994	1993	1992
Total revenue	610,000	600,000	595,000	615,000	610,000	100.0%	100.0%	100.0%	100.0%	100.0%
Total cost of professional services	127,000	116,000	124,000	112,000	115,000	20.8	19.3	20.8	18.2	18.9
Operating expenses:										
Owner's salary/bonuses	120,000	120,000	90,000	90,000	90,000	19.7	20.0	15.1	14.6	14.8
Other salaries & wages	190,000	190,000	210,000	246,000	240,000	31.1	31.7	35.3	40.0	39.3
Payroll taxes	31,000	39,000	37,000	36,000	37,000	5.1	6.5	6.2	5.9	6.1
Employee benefit programs	-	-	5,000	6,000	5,000	-	-	0.8	1.0	0.8
Practice vehicle/auto expenses	2,000	2,000	2,000	2,000	2,000	0.3	0.3	0.3	0.3	0.3
Continuing education	1,000	1,000	1,000	2,500	1,500	0.2	0.2	0.2	0.4	0.2
Building lease expense	38,000	45,000	45,000	40,000	40,000	6.2	7.5	7.6	6.5	6.6
Maintenance/service contracts	-	6,000	5,000	6,000	6,000	-	1.0	0.8	1.0	1.0
Insurance	18,000	14,000	4,000	3,000	4,000	3.0	2.3	0.7	0.5	0.7
Rent on business equipment	6,000	16,000	16,000	16,000	16,000	1.0	2.7	2.7	2.6	2.6
Dues & subscriptions	4,000	1,000	1,000	1,000	1,000	0.7	0.2	0.2	0.2	0.2
Utilities	7,000	6,000	5,000	6,000	6,000	1.1	1.0	0.8	1.0	1.0
Telephone	5,000	6,000	6,000	8,000	7,000	0.8	1.0	1.0	1.3	1.1
Advertising	2,000	3,000	2,000	2,000	2,000	0.3	0.5	0.3	0.3	0.3
Office supplies	2,000	2,000	3,000	4,000	2,000	0.3	0.3	0.5	0.7	0.3
Postage expense	1,000	1,000	1,000	1,000	1,000	0.2	0.2	0.2	0.2	0.2
Professional services	9,000	6,000	4,000	10,000	4,000	1.5	1.0	0.7	1.6	0.7
Depreciation	5,000	5,000	5,000	5,000	5,000	0.8	0.8	0.8	0.8	0.8
Bank charges	5,000	4,000	8,000	6,000	5,000	0.8	0.7	1.3	1.0	0.8
Housekeeping & janitorial	6,000	5,000	5,000	5,000	5,000	1.0	0.8	0.8	0.8	0.8
Repairs	5,000	2,000	3,000	3,000	3,000	0.8	0.3	0.5	0.5	0.5
Miscellaneous expense	2,000	4,000	3,000	3,000	3,000	0.3	0.7	0.5	0.5	0.5
Total operating expenses	459,000	478,000	461,000	501,500	485,500	75.2	79.7	77.5	81.5	79.6
Operating income (loss)	24,000	6,000	10,000	1,500	9,500	3.9	1.0	1.7	0.2	1.6
Other income (expense):										
Interest expense	(1,000)	(1,000)	(2,000)	(2,000)	(2,000)	(0.2)	(0.2)	(0.3)	(0.3)	(0.3)
Other income	14,000	3,000	6,000	4,000	4,000	2.3	0.5	0.7	0.7	0.0
Total other income (expense)	13,000	2,000	4,000	2,000	2,000	2.1	0.3	0.7	0.3	0.3
Pretax income	37,000	8,000	14,000	3,500	11,500	6.1	1.3	2.4	0.6	1.9

SOURCE: Practice financial statements and Willamette Management Associates calculations.

Accounts receivable were adjusted to exclude all receivables outstanding over 90 days. These accounts were considered uncollectible, based on discussions with the practice's office manager. In addition, we adjusted the reported net property and equipment to reflect the estimated fair market value, based on an appraisal performed by John Mackey, ASA.

Economic Earnings of the Practice. In order to estimate the economic earnings for the practice, we relied on an estimate of net cash flow normalized for industry average owner compensation, defined as follows:

Exhibit 37–12

ABC VETERINARY HOSPITAL, P.C.
CAPITALIZED EXCESS EARNINGS METHOD

Adjusted net tangible assets [a]			$ 26,000
Normalized economic earnings [b]		$ 55,000	
Less: fair return on net tangible assets			
Adjusted net tangible assets	$ 26,000		
Multiplied by: fair rate of return on net tangible assets [c]	12.0%		
Fair return on net tangible assets		3,120	
Equals: excess economic earnings		51,880	
Divided by: direct capitalization rate [c]		35.0%	
Estimated intangible asset value in the nature of goodwill			148,229
Indicated equity value			$ 174,229
Indicated equity value, rounded			$ 174,000

a. Per Exhibit 37-13.
b. Per Exhibit 37-14.
c. Willamette Management Associates estimate.

       Adjusted pretax income
+ Owners salary/bonuses
+ Depreciation
- Expected capital expenditures
- Increases in working capital
- Normalized owner compensation
= Net cash flow

Expected net cash flow is calculated in Exhibit 37-14. Adjusted income is presented on Exhibit 37-15. Adjustments to reported pretax income included the elimination of unusual professional expenses, adjusting the rent paid on business equipment by the practice to an estimated fair market rental rate, adjusting the building lease expense of the practice to an estimated fair market rental rate, and excluding other income (i.e., income not related to continuing operations of the practice).

Based on these adjustments, the adjusted income of the practice for calendar 1992 through calendar 1996 is presented on Exhibit 37-15.

In our opinion, based on results in calendar 1996 and the average from 1992 through 1996, the expected adjusted net income for the practice is $31,000, as presented in Exhibit 37-15.

Next, as presented on Exhibit 37-14, we added the expected owner's salary and bonus of $120,000. Dr. Smith is currently drawing $10,000 per month out of the corporation as salary and bonus. We then added expected depreciation expense of $5,000, based on (1) discussions with the practice's accountant, and (2) on the expected future capital expendi-

Exhibit 37–13

ABC VETERINARY HOSPITAL, P.C.
ADJUSTED NET TANGIBLE ASSETS

	At Book Value As of 12/31/96 $	Adjustments $	At Fair Market Value As of 12/31/96 $
ASSETS			
Current assets:			
Cash & cash equivalents	2,000	-	2,000
Accounts receivable [a]	15,000	(5,000)	10,000
Drugs & medical supplies inventory	25,000	-	25,000
Total current assets	42,000	(5,000)	37,000
Property & equipment:			
Equipment	26,000		
Computer & furniture	16,000		
Groom shop--remodel	6,000		
Grooming equipment	3,000		
Leasehold improvements/groom shop	7,000		
Computer software	500		
Less: accumulated depreciation	(42,000)		
Net property & equipment [b]	16,500	43,500	60,000
Other assets	-	-	-
TOTAL ASSETS	58,500	38,500	97,000
LIABILITIES & EQUITY			
Current liabilities:			
Accounts payable	32,000	-	32,000
Accrued liabilities	9,500	-	9,500
Total current liabilities	41,500	-	41,500
Long-term liabilities:			
Equipment loans	30,000	-	30,000
Total long-term liabilities	30,000	-	30,000
Total liabilities	71,500	-	71,500
Adjusted net tangible asset value			25,500
Rounded			26,000

a. Adjusted to exclude accounts receivable outstanding over 90 days based on aged receivables report.
b. Adjusted based on an appraisal performed by John Mackey, ASA.

SOURCE: Practice financial statements as of December 31, 1996, and Willamette Management Associates calculations.

tures. Next, we subtracted expected capital expenditures for the practice, equal to approximately $5,000 for calendar 1997. We then subtracted the estimated increase in working capital for the practice of $3,000.

Exhibit 37-14

ABC VETERINARY HOSPITAL, P.C.
EXPECTED NET CASH FLOW

	Projected 1997 $	Calendar 1996 $	1992-1996 Median $	1992-1996 Mean $
Adjusted income [a]	31,000	31,000	30,000	28,700
Plus: owners salary/bonuses [b]	120,000	120,000	90,000	102,000
Plus: depreciation expense [b]	5,000	5,000	5,000	5,000
Total	156,000			
Less: expected capital expenditures [c]	5,000			
Less: increased working capital [c]	3,000			
Less: normalized compensation [d]	93,000			
Expected net cash flow	55,000			

a. Per Exhibit 37-15.
b. Per Exhibit 37-11.
c. Willamette Management Associates estimate.
d. Per Exhibit 37-16.

Finally, as presented in Exhibit 37-14, we subtracted normalized compensation for Dr. Smith equal to $93,000. Exhibit 37-16 presents the calculation for normalized owner compensation. There was no available industry compensation evidence that specifically addressed the industry average compensation for a veterinarian with a background similar to Dr. Smith's (a male veterinarian with 16 years of practice experience, with one veterinarian employee). However, we were able to estimate the appropriate compensation based on certain adjustments to available industry data. The median monthly salary of private (predominantly small animal) practice owners for practices with two veterinarians was $6,000 for 1996 (or an annual salary of $72,000), based on industry sources of compensation data. Since this salary does not take into account the fact that Dr. Smith has 16 years of practice experience since graduation, we next applied an adjustment factor of 1.25 (as calculated in Exhibit 37-16). Next, since this data is for 1996, we applied an estimated inflation factor of 3 percent, to result in normalized compensation of $93,000 for 1997.

Based on these adjustments, the expected normalized economic earnings for the practice equals $55,000, as presented in Exhibit 37-14.

Fair Return on Net Tangible Assets. A 12 percent fair rate of return on net tangible assets was applied in the capitalized excess

Exhibit 37–15

ABC VETERINARY HOSPITAL, P.C.
ADJUSTED INCOME

	Calendar Years ($):				
	1996	1995	1994	1993	1992
Reported income [a]	37,000	8,000	14,000	3,500	11,500
Adjustments:					
Add: estimated unusual professional expenses [b]	-	-	-	2,500	-
Add: rent on business equipment [a]	6,000	16,000	16,000	16,000	16,000
Less: estimated rent on business equipment [c]	(6,000)	(6,000)	(6,000)	(6,000)	(6,000)
Add: building lease expense [a]	38,000	45,000	45,000	40,000	40,000
Less: estimated building lease expense [c]	(30,000)	(30,000)	(30,000)	(30,000)	(30,000)
Less: other income [d]	(14,000)	(3,000)	(6,000)	(4,000)	(4,000)
Total adjustments	(6,000)	22,000	19,000	18,500	16,000
Adjusted income	31,000	30,000	33,000	22,000	27,500

a. Per Exhibit 37-11.
b. Willamette Management Associates estimate, based on a review of historical financial statements and discussions with Dr. Smith.
c. Based on fair market rental rate.
d. Represents income not related to practice operations.

earnings method, as presented in Exhibit 37-12. This fair rate of return was based on our estimate of the risk and return expectations associated with the adjusted net tangible assets of the practice.

Excess Earnings Direct Capitalization Rate. The 35 percent direct capitalization rate applied to excess earnings was based on an analysis of the risk associated with the intangible portion of the assets of ABC Veterinary Hospital.

Based on analyses presented in Exhibit 37-12, the estimated fair market value of the equity of the practice, from the capitalized excess earnings method, is $174,000.

Capitalization of Economic Income Method

In the capitalization of economic income method illustrated in this example, we use net cash flow as the appropriate measure of economic income. This method requires the estimation of (1) net cash flow for the practice and (2) the appropriate direct capitalization rate.

Exhibit 37-17 presents the capitalization of net cash flow method. Net cash flow for the practice is defined as described earlier in this sample case. The expected net cash flow for the practice of $55,000 is presented in Exhibit 37-14.

Exhibit 37–16

ABC VETERINARY HOSPITAL, P.C.
NORMALIZED OWNER COMPENSATION

Monthly salary of private practice owners (small animal predominant practice), 1996 median [a]	$ 6,000	
Annualized		$72,000

Adjustment Factor to Reflect Number of Years in Practice and Gender:		
Professional income, male, 13 to 17 years since graduation (small animal predominant practice), 1996 [b]	$79,000	
Professional income, male (small animal predominant practice), 1996 [b]	$63,000	
Adjustment factor [c]		1.25

Estimated normalized owner compensation, 1996	$90,286
Multiplied by: one plus inflation factor, 1997 [d]	1.030
Equals: normalized compensation, 1997	$92,994
Rounded	$93,000

a. For practices with 2 veterinarians, based on industry compensation data.
b. Based on industry compensation data. Dr. Smith has 16 years of experience since graduation.
c. Calculated as $79,000 divided by $63,000.
d. Consensus 1997 inflation estimate.

Exhibit 37–17

ABC VETERINARY HOSPITAL, P.C.
CAPITALIZATION OF NET CASH FLOW METHOD

Estimated net cash flow, 1997 [a]		$ 55,000
Divided by:		
Estimated cost of capital, ABC Veterinary Hospital	30.0%	
Less: expected long-term growth rate	0.0%	
Equals: capitalization rate		30.0%
Estimated equity value		$ 183,333
Estimated equity value, rounded		$ 183,000

a. Per Exhibit 37-14.

The appropriate direct capitalization rate for the practice is estimated as 30 percent. The 30 percent direct capitalization rate represents our estimate of the rate of return that would be required for an investment in a veterinary practice exhibiting an operating structure and risk characteristics similar to ABC Veterinary Hospital, PC—less the expected long-term growth rate for the practice. Based on an analysis of historical revenue growth of the practice, and considering the increasing competitive environment that Dr. Smith is operating in, we estimated the long-term growth rate at 0 percent.

As presented in Exhibit 37-17, capitalizing $55,000 by 30 percent results in an estimated equity value, from the capitalization of economic income method, of $183,000.

Guideline Market Transaction Method

Exhibit 37-18 presents the percentage of revenue paid for intangible assets for transactions of veterinary practices, based on various industry sources. As presented, of the 20 veterinary practice transactions reported in the 1986–1996 time frame, the median pricing multiple for intangible assets as a percentage of revenue paid was approximately 29 percent, and the mean was 30 percent.

Based on our analysis of the operations of the practice, a discount from the average multiple from the transactional data is reasonable to apply to ABC Veterinary Hospital. The discount is appropriate given (1) the lack of growth of the practice over the past five years and (2) the increasing local competition. We selected an intangible asset pricing multiple of 25 percent, somewhat less than the median multiple from the transactional evidence.

Multiplying the practice's revenues of $610,000 by 25 percent results in an indicated value for the intangible assets of $152,500. Adding the net tangible asset value of $26,000 to the indicated intangible value of $152,500 results in an indicated value for the practice, from the guideline market transactions method, of $179,000 (rounded).

Exhibit 37–18

ABC VETERINARY HOSPITAL, P.C.
GUIDELINE MARKET TRANSACTIONS METHOD

Medical Specialty	Years	Number of Transactions	% of Gross Revenues Paid for Intangible Assets	
			Mean	Median
Veterinary medicine	1986 - 1996	26	42%	32%

ABC Veterinary Hospital, P.C.	
Total revenue	610,000
Selected intangible asset pricing multiple	0.25
Indicated value of intangible assets	152,500
Plus: adjusted net tangible asset value	26,000
Equals: indicated equity value	178,500
Equals: indicated equity value, rounded	179,000

SOURCE: *Goodwill Registry 1997* (Plymouth Meeting, PA: The Health Care Group, 1997) and Willamette Management Associates calculations.

Valuation Synthesis and Conclusion

We relied on the three valuation methods described above to reach our opinion of value. The indicated values from the three valuation methods are as follows:

Capitalized excess earnings method	$174,000
Capitalization of economic income method	$183,000
Guideline market transactions method	$179,000

To arrive at our final opinion of the fair market value of the subject veterinary practice, we assigned equal weight to each of the three valuation methods. Based on the valuation procedures described above, the fair market value of 100 percent of the owners' equity of ABC Veterinary Hospital, PC, as of December 31, 1996, is $178,500.

Due to space constraints, our example did not consider all of the discounts and premiums associated with professional practice valuation issues. For example, appropriate discounts should be applied for a minority ownership interest (e.g., individual partner's interest), key partner dependence, key client dependence, and so forth. In addition, appropriate premiums could be applied for majority ownership control of a practice, for significant practice diversification, and so forth. The consideration of minority ownership interest discounts, controlling ownership interest premiums, and so on are beyond the scope of this analysis.

Part V

Valuations for Specific Purposes

Chapter 38

Buy-Sell Agreements and Estate Planning

Every business or professional practice has a life cycle, with a great deal of variation from one to another. How a small business copes with unexpected ownership problems (such as the loss of a key owner-manager) or with the expected hurdles of the business life cycle (such as transfer of the company to successor owners) often makes the difference between a successful enterprise and one that falters.

In all such cases, a reasonable valuation of the business ownership interest is critical. In times of crisis, all parties should be focusing on the successful management of the business rather than being caught up in protracted valuation analysis or disputes. Every business owner should have a plan for (1) estimating the value of the ownership interest in the small business or professional practice and (2) providing the ownership transition funding that may be required.

This chapter explores these specific purposes for business appraisals. We will follow the order in which these issues are often faced during the life of the professional practice or small business owner. As will be seen, it often pays to devote time to thinking about the unthinkable in advance to uncover and solve any sticky problems.

Buy-Sell Agreements

When starting out, a professional practice or small business founder may have partners or coventurers. In addition, the departure of a founder before adequate successors are available or before the business reaches some degree of maturity can permanently cripple a business's growth.

A buy-sell agreement can effectively avoid many of the potential problems regarding disposition of a stock or partnership interest. The buy-sell agreement should be designed to accomplish the following objectives:

1. Identify those situations that will require the buy-sell agreement to be triggered. These situations include death, mental or physical disability, retirement, departure, divorce, or irreconcilable dissension among the owners.
2. Help all the equity owners by offering a definitive mechanism in order to obtain liquidity for a departing owner's interest.
3. Provide a definitive and fair provision for determining the price that the departing owner will be paid for the ownership interest.
4. Help the business continue by providing for a fair method to fund the buyout of the departing owner's equity—without unduly disrupting the financial stability of the company.
5. Prevent the ownership interest from being sold or transferred to any party not acceptable to the other owners.
6. Set a price or pricing mechanism that will be respected by taxing authorities for estate, gift, and income tax purposes or by courts for divorce or other litigation purposes.
7. Establish coordination with the personal estate planning of the owner.

Types of Agreements

The two basic types of buy-sell agreements relate to the parties that are expected to actually buy the ownership interest under the terms of the agreement.

The first type provides that the company buy back the interest from the former owner. This is often called an *entity purchase*, a *stock repurchase*, or a *redemption agreement*. The second type of buy-sell agreement allows the other owners of the company to buy the departing owner's interest. This is often called a *shareholder agreement, buy-sell agreement,* or *cross-purchase agreement*. These two concepts can be combined into a hybrid type of *wait-and-see agreement.* In a wait-and-see agreement, the company or the other owners have a right of first refusal to purchase the subject interest, with the other party being required to buy if the first refusal option is not exercised. Sometimes, key employees or other people who are not currently shareholders are given the opportunity to buy in under the terms of the buy-sell agreement.

The drafting of a buy-sell agreement should be based on the advice of an experienced attorney. In determining the appropriate type of agreement and wording, an experienced attorney will explore the following areas:

1. What are the owners' desires regarding who should be allowed to own stock in the company?
2. Does the buy-sell agreement proposed language conflict with the owners' existing wills or other estate planning objectives? Conflicts between buy-sell agreements and wills may require expensive litigation to untangle and may result in the buy-sell agreement restrictions being overturned.[1]
3. What payment terms should be made part of the buyout?
4. What will be the tax effects of such a buyout on both the company and on the individual owners?
5. What restrictions may exist in the relevant state laws on the proposed terms of the buy-sell agreement?
6. What provisions should be made for setting the value?

Provisions for Valuation

The provision for valuation is a critical element of the buy-sell agreement. Under current tax law, the parties have less flexibility than in the past with regard to structuring this provision. This is particularly true when family members are involved. Accordingly, the language of any agreement should be carefully considered in order to maintain fairness, feasibility, and tax efficiency.

The valuation provision can require the same approach under all circumstances, or it can vary for different triggering events. A voluntary

---

[1]*Globe Slicing Machine* v. *Hasner*, 333 F.2d 413 (2nd Cir. 1964), *cert. denied* 379 U.S. 969 (1965).

departure from the company may call for a different valuation approach than would be called for in the situation of a departure due to dismissal or death of the interest's owner. The vast majority of buy-sell agreements that we review call for a single value regardless of the triggering event.

If the parties intend to have the buy-sell agreement be binding for purposes other than the transfer itself (such as for estate tax purposes), the standard of value required for the appraisal (1) should be clearly spelled out and (2) should conform with what unrelated parties would be reasonably willing to agree on in arm's-length bargaining. It should be noted that courts tend to put less reliance on a buy-sell agreement that is inconsistent with the purpose for which the court is estimating value. For example, gift and estate taxes require the use of "fair market value" as the standard of value. This may not be the appropriate standard of value when, for example, three equal coventurers actually wish to specify that each other's one-third interest will be repurchased at a price that represents a pro rata one-third portion of the value of the entire company. In this case, the minority ownership interest discount that is usually appropriate under a fair market value standard is not applicable. This topic is discussed further in the following section.

The most common valuation provisions are as follows:

1. A price fixed by mutual agreement among shareholders, updated on a periodic basis, typically at least annually.
2. A formula for determining the appraised price. Such a formula may rely on guideline publicly traded company price-earnings multiples or on other market-related factors—plus a premium to reflect ownership control and/or a discount to reflect lack of marketability—or it may rely on any of many other factors.
3. A requirement for an appraisal by an independent professional appraiser, either annually or upon the occurrence of a triggering event.

Beware the Fair Market Value Standard in Buy-Sell Agreements

It is important that all parties to a buy-sell agreement—and their counsel—understand the implications of the valuation provision at the time they enter into the agreement. There are countless horror stories of expensive disputes between parties, with resolutions unsatisfactory to one party or another as a result of lack of understanding of the valuation provision. In one case, an attorney's insurance company paid a settlement of over $1 million for not incorporating language into an agreement that reflected his client's understanding and desires regarding implications for value.

The most common misconception we encounter is misinterpretation of the term *fair market value*. If an analyst or a small business owner is considering using the term *fair market value* in a buy-sell agreement, he or she should carefully read the definition and discussion of this term in Chapter 3, Defining Value, and Chapter 24, Discount for Lack of

Control. Often, a minority owner mistakenly assumes that "fair market value of the shares" means a proportionate share of the value of the equity of the small business enterprise. The chapters referenced make it clear that fair market value of a minority interest *rarely* is equal to a proportionate share of the value of the equity as a controlling interest. In fact, it is not uncommon for the fair market value of a minority ownership interest to be less than half the value of a proportionate share of a controlling interest value. This comes as a surprise to many minority interest owners who were misinformed—or uninformed—when entering into the agreement.

Such surprises—and the resulting disputes—can be avoided by ensuring that all parties to an agreement have a clear understanding of the implications for value arising from the language in the buy-sell agreement valuation provision.

A common type of valuation provision (1) calls for the parties to update the value by arm's-length negotiation at least annually and (2) provides for an independent appraisal if there has been no recent annual appraisal. Exhibit 38-1 is a sample article of a buy-sell agreement relating to valuation.

The sample in the exhibit references "fair market value of the shares," but it could also be written to reflect a pro rata portion of the value of the equity of the enterprise as a whole.

Historically, the valuation formula was sometimes arbitrary, with most parties interested in having a reasonably fair price for all involved. Accounting book value was used frequently as a quick, simple, and often inadequate proxy for fair market value.

However, in companies controlled by members of the same family, the rules under Section 2703 of Chapter 14 of the Internal Revenue Code, which apply to all buy-sell agreements created or substantially modified after October 8, 1990, require that three very specific and separate tests be met in order to have accounting book value be determinative for estate and gift tax purposes:[2]

1. It must be a bona fide business arrangement.
2. It must not be a device to transfer such property to members of the family for less than full and adequate consideration.
3. Its terms must be comparable to similar arrangements entered into by persons in an arm's-length transaction.[3]

Thus, family members are treated with particularly close scrutiny. And buy-sell agreement values should be determined on a truly arm's-

---

[2] In order for any buy-sell agreement (regardless of who owns the business) to be determinative for estate tax purposes, the general rules require that (1) the agreement must contain a determinable price, (2) it must be binding on the decedent during life as well as at death, and (3) it must be a bona fide business arrangement. Using buy-sells for nondisruptive ownership and management succession planning has been determined to be a bona fide business arrangement.

[3] Internal Revenue Code Section 2703(b). The implication of this requirement is that the agreement must reflect practices that are typical of that specific company's industry.

Exhibit 38–1

SAMPLE VALUATION ARTICLE FOR BUY-SELL AGREEMENT
(Corporation Stock Redemption Example)

As soon as practical after the end of each fiscal year, the stockholders and the corporation shall agree on the value per share of the stock that is applicable to this agreement. Such value will be set forth in Schedule A, which shall be dated, signed by each stockholder and an officer of the corporation, and attached hereto. Such value shall be binding on both the corporation and the estate of any deceased stockholder whose date of death is within one year of the last dated and signed Schedule A.

If more than a year has elapsed between the date when Schedule A was last signed and the date of death of a deceased stockholder, then the value per share shall be determined, as of the date of death of the stockholder, by mutual agreement between the corporation and the personal representative or administrator of the deceased stockholder's estate.

If the corporation and the personal representative of the deceased stockholder's estate are unable to agree upon such a value within 90 days after such personal representative or administrator has qualified to administer the estate of the deceased stockholder, then such value shall be determined by binding arbitration. Either party may give written notice of such binding arbitration pursuant to this agreement to the other party. Within 30 days of such notice of arbitration, each party shall appoint one arbitrator. Within 30 days of the appointment of the two arbitrators, the arbitrators so appointed will select a third arbitrator. The first two arbitrators will have sole discretion in the selection of the third arbitrator, except that he must be an individual or qualified representative of a firm that regularly engages, as a primary occupation, in the professional appraisal of businesses or business interests. In the event that the first two arbitrators are unable to agree on a third arbitrator within 30 days of their appointment, the Executive Director of the ABC Trade Association shall appoint the third arbitrator.

The standard of value to be used by the arbitrators shall be fair market value of the shares being valued as of the date of death, under the assumption that the stockholder is deceased and the corporation has collected the proceeds, if any, of insurance on the life of the deceased stockholder payable to the corporation.

Each arbitrator shall use his sole discretion in determining the amount of investigation he considers necessary in arriving at a determination of the value of the shares. The corporation shall make available on a timely basis all books and records requested by any arbitrator, and all material made available to any one arbitrator shall be made available to all arbitrators.

Concurrence by at least two of the three arbitrators shall constitute a binding determination of value. The value concluded by the arbitrators shall be reported to the corporation and to the personal representative or administrator of the estate of the deceased in writing, signed by the arbitrators concurring as to the concluded value, within 90 days of the appointment of the third arbitrator unless an extension of time has been agreed upon between the corporation and the personal representative of the estate.

The corporation and the estate shall each be responsible for the fees and expenses of the arbitrators they appoint. The fees and expenses of the third arbitrator shall be divided equally between the corporation and the estate.

length basis in order to have a buy-sell agreement determine the estate tax value. Adding or removing a party to a "grandfathered" buy-sell agreement in existence prior to October 9, 1990, will generally not be defined as a substantial modification to that agreement. However, this is true only if (1) this is required under the terms of the agreement and (2) the added party is not a younger generation family member.[4]

The buy-sell agreement should specify the mechanism or mechanisms not only for pricing the ownership interest but also for terms of payment.

---

[4] Treasury Regulations Section 25.2703-1(c).

Role of the Business Appraiser in Buy-Sell Agreements

A well-qualified business appraiser experienced in buy-sell agreements should be retained as a consultant to the company at the time of drafting the buy-sell agreement. The appraiser's role is to advise the company and its attorney as to the implications of the valuation provision wording. This advice includes how a business appraiser would interpret the wording (e.g., what valuation methodology might be used or rejected and what discounts or premiums might be included or rejected) and what the effect of such wording might be on valuations for other purposes, such as gift and estate taxes.

The appraiser should attend a meeting of all parties to the agreement (preferably also including their spouses) before they sign it. The appraiser should try to be sure that all parties to the agreement understand the valuation implications when a triggering event occurs, as well as implications for other situations, such as estate taxes, divorce, and so forth.

Gift and Estate Taxes

At some time, every successful small business or professional practice owner should do some serious planning in order to decide what will happen to the business as he or she grows older. Sometimes family businesses will be passed on to the next generation. Sometimes, a professional practice interest is sold, upon death or retirement, to a successor practitioner.

In any case, such transactions may give rise to income taxes or to gift and estate taxes. We will discuss below some methods for minimizing or avoiding gift and estate taxes. References for additional study on each topic are included in the bibliography.

Transfer Tax Rates and Exemptions

Estate and gift taxes are a unified transfer tax system. This system levies a tax on the fair market value of assets transferred by gift during life or by will upon death.

Many small businesses and professional practice owners will not have a significant gift or estate tax liability. This is because the current tax law provides a lifetime unified credit against gift and estate transfer taxes that allows any individual to give away $600,000 in fair market asset values before further transfers are taxed.

For estates with dates of death after December 31, 1997, the $600,000 lifetime exemption will increase as follows:

1998	$625,000
1999	$750,000
2000	$765,000
2001–04	$775,000
2005	$800,000
2006	$825,000
2007–on	$1,000,000

These amounts will be indexed to the Consumer Price Index for inflation after 1997. Qualifying family-owned business interests up to $1.3 million in value will be granted a separate (but not additional) estate tax exclusion. The requirements for obtaining this exclusion are complex.

In addition, current laws effectively provide for unlimited gifting and estate transfers between spouses. Of course, transferring a growing business interest to your spouse at your death (1) merely postpones the eventual estate tax reckoning and (2) increases the amount of taxes eventually owed.

Another useful provision of the law allows a separate annual exclusion of a maximum of $10,000 in gifts from any single donor to any single donee. Any value over $10,000 per year from any donor to any donee is charged against the $600,000 lifetime gift and estate tax exemption total.

Once the lifetime total of gifts plus the estate exceeds the exemption limit, gift and estate tax rates begin at 37 percent and increase to 55 percent, as presented below.

Amount Subject to Tax	Tax Rate (%)
Over $600,000 to $750,000	37
Over 750,000 to 1,000,000	39
Over 1,000,000 to 1,250,000	41
Over 1,250,000 to 1,500,000	43
Over 1,500,000 to 2,000,000	45
Over 2,000,000 to 2,500,000	49
Over 2,500,000 to 3,000,000	53
Over 3,000,000	55

In addition to the federal tax rates listed above, many states also impose inheritance taxes (with rates generally between 4 and 16 percent), which may apply different exemptions than the federal taxes.

A generation-skipping transfer tax is also applied to transfers by direct gift or indirect transfer (such as by trust) to persons who are two or more generations removed from the donor. An example of this would be gifts to grandchildren or great-grandchildren. The tax rate is 55 percent, which is the current maximum marginal standard rate. There is a $1 million generation-skipping tax exemption per donor.

As can be seen, gift and estate tax rates exceed most of the current levels of income tax rates. Thus, it makes sense to put together a plan while the business owner is still alive in order to minimize the impact of this largest of federal taxes.

Penalties for Undervaluation

There are also accuracy-related federal penalties for undervaluation misstatements on gift and estate tax returns. These are as shown below.

For Estate and Gift Taxes over $1,000	
Value Claimed on the Tax Return as a Percentage of the Value Finally Determined	Additional Penalty
50% or more	0%
25%–49%	20%
Below 25%	40%

Penalties are particularly onerous because they are ordinarily not deductible expenses for tax purposes. There are also other penalties for civil fraud that can be levied against the taxpayer. And there are penalties for assisting in the preparation of tax documents in order to knowingly understate tax liabilities that can be levied against tax preparers (including appraisers).

Rules for Valuation—Standard and Special

The essential guidelines for the standard valuation of closely held business interests for federal gift and estate tax purposes are contained in Revenue Ruling 59-60.[5] Revenue Ruling 59-60 is included as Appendix B at the end of the book. Most states now follow the same basic guidelines for determining inheritance tax values but are not legally bound by any federal-level interpretations for gift and estate tax issues.

In 1990, Congress added Chapter 14 to the estate and gift tax laws in the Internal Revenue Code. Chapter 14 contains four main sections that address special valuation rules to be applied to transfers of family-controlled business interests. The basic law has also been supplemented by Treasury Regulations written by the Internal Revenue Service to illustrate how the government will address key issues. As discussed above, Chapter 14 rules generally are applied to transfers made after October 8, 1990. When Chapter 14 rules are an issue, the analyst should discuss their applicability with the client's attorney.

Standard Valuation Rules. The standard of value for transfer taxes is fair market value. Fair market value is defined as the price at which the subject business interest would change hands between a willing buyer and willing seller, both having reasonable knowledge of all relevant information about the interest and neither being under any compulsion to buy or sell.

Section 2701—Preferred Interests. This section is concerned with the special valuation rules that apply (1) when senior (i.e., preferred) interests exist in a family-owned business and (2) when junior

---

[5] Rev. Rul. 59-60, 1959-1, CB 237.

(i.e., common) interests are transferred by senior generation owners to junior generations. By "preferred interests," we do not mean only preferred stock in the accounting sense, but any corporate or partnership interest that has any rights senior to the most junior equity interest. This section applies to gift tax issues only. However, it includes both incorporated or unincorporated entities (e.g., partnerships) and direct and indirect transfers. Only a few rights or features of the preferred interest will be counted as providing value for gift tax purposes. All other rights —generally optional rights that can be deferred by either the business or the preferred interest holder (such as noncumulative dividends)—are to be ignored by the appraiser.

The value of the transferred junior interests are determined by (1) subtracting this special value of the preferred interest from the fair market value of the entity owned by the family and (2) allocating this remaining value to the junior interests transferred. This is called the subtraction method, and its application can be complex in any particular situation. The technical valuation issues involved in applying this method correctly require a close reading of the law and regulations.[6] Revenue Ruling 77-287, shown in Exhibit 38-2, provides guidance on valuation of preferred equity interests.

Section 2702—Retained Interests in Trusts. This section is concerned with the valuation of time-based fractionalization of ownership interests, such as grantor-retained income trusts. No substantial changes are made in the standard valuation methods for family-owned business interests in this section.

Section 2703—Options. The application of this section was discussed above under buy-sell agreements.

Section 2704—Lapsing Rights and Liquidation Restrictions. This section deals with two primary issues: (1) the treatment of lapsing rights and (2) the treatment of liquidation restrictions when a family owns 50 percent or more of the vote or value of an entity. The special valuation rules of this section require the analyst to include certain rights, even if they lapse in conjunction with a transfer by gift or death (such as voting rights that lapse if the original holder sells or transfers her shares). These special valuation rules also require the analyst to ignore certain "applicable restrictions" on the right of an interest holder to liquidate the entity (in whole or in part) when an interest is transferred for the benefit of a family member. These types of applicable restrictions are generally provisions that are more restrictive than those found under the basic state laws for the entity.

---

[6] See the Final Regulations issued by the IRS, effective January 28, 1992; Treasury Regulations, sections 25.2701-2704 (Treasury Decision 8395).

Exhibit 38–2

Revenue Ruling 77-287

SECTION 1. PURPOSE.

The purpose of this Revenue Ruling is to amplify Rev. Rul. 59-60, 1959-1 C.B. 237, as modified by Rev. Rul. 65-193, 1965-2 C.B. 370, and to provide information and guidance to taxpayers, Internal Revenue Service personnel, and others concerned with the valuation, for Federal tax purposes, of securities that cannot be immediately resold because they are restricted from resale pursuant to Federal securities laws. This guidance is applicable only in cases where it is not inconsistent with valuation requirements of the Internal Revenue Code of 1954 or the regulations thereunder. Further, this ruling does not establish the time at which property shall be valued.

SEC. 2. NATURE OF THE PROBLEM.

It frequently becomes necessary to establish the fair market value of stock that has not been registered for public trading when the issuing company has stock of the same class that is actively traded in one or more securities markets. The problem is to determine the difference in fair market value between the registered shares that are actively traded and the unregistered shares. This problem is often encountered in estate and gift tax cases. However, it is sometimes encountered when unregistered shares are issued in exchange for assets or the stock of an acquired company.

SEC. 3. BACKGROUND AND DEFINITIONS.

.01 The Service outlined and reviewed in general the approach, methods, and factors to be considered in valuing shares of closely held corporate stock for estate and gift tax purposes in Rev. Rul. 59-60, as modified by Rev. Rul. 65-193. The provisions of Rev. Rul. 59-60, as modified, were extended to the valuation of corporate securities for income and other tax purposes by Rev. Rul. 68-609, 1968-2 C.B. 327.

.02 There are several terms currently in use in the securities industry that denote restrictions imposed on the resale and transfer of certain securities. The term frequently used to describe these securities is "restricted securities," but they are sometimes referred to as "unregistered securities," "investment letter stock," "control stock," or "private placement stock." Frequently these terms are used interchangeably. They all indicate that these particular securities cannot lawfully be distributed to the general public until a registration statement relating to the corporation underlying the securities has been filed, and has also become effective under the rules promulgated and enforced by the United States Securities & Exchange Commission (SEC) pursuant to the Federal securities laws. The following represents a more refined definition of each of the following terms along with two other terms—"exempted securities" and "exempted transactions."

(a) The term "restricted securities" is defined in Rule 144 adopted by the SEC as "securities acquired directly or indirectly from the issuer thereof, or from an affiliate of such issuer, in a transaction or chain of transactions not involving any public offering."

(b) The term "unregistered securities" refers to those securities with respect to which a registration statement, providing full disclosure by the issuing corporation, has not been filed with the SEC pursuant to the Securities Act of 1933. The registration statement is a condition precedent to a public distribution of securities in interstate commerce and is aimed at providing the prospective investor with a factual basis for sound judgment in making investment decisions.

(c) The terms "investment letter stock" and "letter stock" denote shares of stock that have been issued by a corporation without the benefit of filing a registration statement with the SEC. Such stock is subject to resale and transfer restrictions set forth in a letter agreement requested by the issuer and signed by the buyer of the stock when the stock is delivered. Such stock may be found in the hands of either individual investors or institutional investors.

(d) The term "control stock" indicates that the shares of stock have been held or are being held by an officer, director, or other person close to the management of the corporation. These persons are subject to certain requirements pursuant to SEC rules upon resale of shares they own in such corporations.

(e) The term "private placement stock" indicates that the stock has been placed with an institution or other investor who will presumably hold it for a long period and ultimately arrange to have the stock registered if it is to be offered to the general public. Such stock may or may not be subject to a letter agreement. Private placements of stock are exempted from the registration and prospectus provisions of the Securities Act of 1933.

(f) The term "exempted securities" refers to those classes of securities that are expressly excluded from the registration provisions of the Securities Act of 1933 and the distribution provisions of the Securities Exchange Act of 1934.

(g) The term "exempted transactions" refers to certain sales or distributions of securities that do not involve a public offering and are excluded from the registration and prospectus provisions of the Securities Act of 1933 and distribution provisions of the Securities Exchange Act of 1934. The exempted status makes it unnecessary for issuers of securities to go through the registration process.

SEC. 4. SECURITIES INDUSTRY PRACTICE IN VALUING RESTRICTED SECURITIES.

.01 *Investment Company Valuation Practices.* The Investment Company Act of 1940 requires open-end investment companies to publish the valuation of their portfolio securities daily. Some of these companies have portfolios containing restricted securities, but also have unrestricted securities of the same class traded on a securities exchange. In recent years the number of restricted securities in such portfolios have increased. The following methods have been used by investment companies in the valuation of such restricted securities:

(a) Current market price of the unrestricted stock less a constant percentage discount based on purchase discount;

(b) Current market price of unrestricted stock less a constant percentage discount different from purchase discount;

(c) Current market price of the unrestricted stock less a discount amortized over a fixed period;

(d) Current market price of the unrestricted stock; and

(e) Cost of the restricted stock until it is registered.

The SEC ruled in its Investment Company Act Release No. 5847, dated October 21, 1969, that there can be no automatic formula by which an investment company can value the restricted securities in its portfolios. Rather, the SEC has determined that it is the responsibility of the board of directors of the particular investment company to determine the "fair value" of each issue of restricted securities in good faith.

.02 *Institutional Investors Study.* Pursuant to Congressional direction, the SEC undertook an analysis of the purchases, sales, and holding of securities by financial institutions, in order to determine the effect of institutional activity upon the securities market. The study report was published in eight volumes in March 1971. The fifth volume provides an analysis of restricted securities and deals with such items as the characteristics of the restricted securities purchasers and issuers, the size of transactions (dollars and shares), the marketability discounts on different trading markets, and the resale provisions. This research project provides some guidance for measuring the discount in that it contains information, based on the actual experience of the marketplace, showing that, during the period surveyed (January 1, 1966, through June 30, 1969), the amount of discount allowed for restricted securities from the trading price of the unrestricted securities was generally related to the following four factors.

(a) *Earnings.* Earnings and sales consistently have a significant influence on the size of restricted securities discounts according to the study. Earnings played the major part in establishing the ultimate discounts at which these stocks were sold from the current market price. Apparently earnings patterns, rather than sales patterns, determine the degree of risk of an investment.

(b) *Sales.* The dollar amount of sales of issuers' securities also has a major influence on the amount of discount at which restricted securities sell from the current market price. The results of the study generally indicate that the companies with the lowest dollar amount of sales during the test period accounted for most of the transactions involving the highest discount rates, while they accounted for only a small portion of all transactions involving the lowest discount rates.

Exhibit 38–2 (concluded)

(c) *Trading Market.* The market in which publicly held securities are traded also reflects variances in the amount of discount that is applied to restricted securities purchases. According to the study, discount rates were greatest on restricted stocks with unrestricted counterparts traded over-the-counter, followed by those with unrestricted counterparts listed on the American Stock Exchange, while the discount rates for those stocks with unrestricted counterparts listed on the New York Stock Exchange were the smallest.

(d) *Resale Agreement Provisions.* Resale agreement provisions often affect the size of the discount. The discount from the market price provides the main incentive for a potential buyer to acquire restricted securities. In judging the opportunity cost of freezing funds, the purchaser is analyzing two separate factors. The first factor is the risk that underlying value of the stock will change in a way that, absent the restrictive provisions, would have prompted a decision to sell. The second factor is the risk that the contemplated means of legally disposing of the stock may not materialize. From the seller's point of view, a discount is justified where the seller is relieved of the expenses of registration and public distribution, as well as of the risk that the market will adversely change before the offering is completed. The ultimate agreement between buyer and seller is a reflection of these and other considerations. Relative bargaining strengths of the parties to the agreement are major considerations that influence the resale terms and consequently the size of discounts in restricted securities transactions. Certain provisions are often found in agreements between buyers and sellers that affect the size of discounts at which restricted stocks are sold. Several such provisions follow, all of which, other than number (3), would tend to reduce the size of the discount:

(1) A provision giving the buyer an option to "piggyback", that is, to register restricted stock with the next registration statement, if any, filed by the issuer with the SEC;

(2) A provision giving the buyer an option to require registration at the seller's expense;

(3) A provision giving the buyer an option to require registration, but only at the buyer's own expense;

(4) A provision giving the buyer a right to receive continuous disclosure of information about the issuer from the seller;

(5) A provision giving the buyer a right to select one or more directors of the issuer;

(6) A provision giving the buyer an option to purchase additional shares of the issuer's stock; and

(7) A provision giving the buyer the right to have a greater voice in operations of the issuer, if the issuer does not meet previously agreed upon operating standards.

Institutional buyers can and often do obtain many of these rights and options from the sellers of restricted securities, and naturally, the more rights the buyer can acquire, the lower the buyer's risk is going to be, thereby reducing the buyer's discount as well. Small buyers may not be able to negotiate the large discounts or the rights and options that volume buyers are able to negotiate.

.03 *Summary.* A variety of methods have been used by the securities industry to value restricted securities. The SEC rejects all automatic or mechanical solutions to the valuation of restricted securities, and prefers, in the case of the valuation of investment company portfolio stocks, to rely upon good faith valuations by the board of directors of each company. The study made by the SEC found that restricted securities generally are issued at a discount from the market value of freely tradable securities.

Sec. 5. Facts and Circumstances Material to Valuation of Restricted Securities.

.01 Frequently, a company has a class of stock that cannot be traded publicly. The reason such stock cannot be traded may arise from the securities statutes, as in the case of an "investment letter" restriction; it may arise from a corporate charter restriction, or perhaps from a trust agreement restriction. In such cases, certain documents and facts should be obtained for analysis.

.02 The following documents and facts, when used in conjunction with those discussed in Section 4 of Rev. Rul. 59-60, will be useful in the valuation of restricted securities:

(a) A copy of any declaration of trust, trust agreement, and any other agreements relating to the shares of restricted stock;

(b) A copy of any document showing any offers to buy or sell or indications of interest in buying or selling the restricted shares;

(c) The latest prospectus of the company;

(d) Annual reports of the company for 3 to 5 years preceding the valuation date;

(e) The trading prices and trading volume of the related class of traded securities 1 month preceding the valuation date, if they are traded on a stock exchange (if traded over-the-counter, prices may be obtained from the National Quotations Bureau, the National Association of Securities Dealers Automated Quotations (NASDAQ), or sometimes from broker-dealers making markets in the shares);

(f) The relationship of the parties to the agreements concerning the restricted stock, such as whether they are members of the immediate family or perhaps whether they are officers or directors of the company; and

(g) Whether the interest being valued represents a majority or minority ownership.

Sec. 6. Weighing Facts and Circumstances Material to Restricted Stock Valuation.

All relevant facts and circumstances that bear upon the worth of restricted stock, including those set forth above in the preceding Sections 4 and 5, and those set forth in Section 4 of Rev. Rul. 59-60, must be taken into account in arriving at the fair market value of such securities. Depending on the circumstances of each case, certain factors may carry more weight than others. To illustrate:

.01 Earnings, net assets, and net sales must be given primary consideration in arriving at an appropriate discount for restricted securities from the freely traded shares. These are the elements of value that are always used by investors in making investment decisions. In some cases, one element may be more important than in other cases. In the case of manufacturing, producing, or distributing companies, primary weight must be accorded earnings and net sales; but in the case of investment or holding companies, primary weight must be given to the net assets of the company underlying the stock. In the former type of companies, value is more closely linked to past, present, and future earnings while in the latter type of companies, value is more closely linked to the existing net assets of the company. See the discussion in Section 5 of Rev. Rul. 59-60.

.02 Resale provisions found in the restriction agreements must be scrutinized and weighted to determine the amount of discount to apply to the preliminary fair market value of the company. The two elements of time and expense bear upon this discount; the longer the buyer of the shares must wait to liquidate the shares, the greater the discount. Moreover, if the provisions make it necessary for the buyer to bear the expense of registration, the greater the discount. However, if the provisions of the restricted stock agreement make it possible for the buyer to "piggyback" shares at the next offering, the discount would be smaller.

.03 The relative negotiation strengths of the buyer and seller of restricted stock may have a profound effect on the amount of discount. For example, a tight money situation may cause the buyer to have the greater balance of negotiation strength in a transaction. However, in some cases the relative strengths may tend to cancel each other out.

.04 The market experience of freely tradable securities of the same class as the restricted securities is also significant in determining the amount of discount. Whether the shares are privately held or publicly traded affects the worth of the shares to the holder. Securities traded on a public market generally are worth more to investors than those that are not traded on a public market. Moreover, the type of public market in which the unrestricted securities are traded is to be given consideration.

Sec. 7. Effect on Other Documents.

Rev. Rul. 59-60, as modified by Rev. Rul. 65-193, is amplified.

SOURCE: Rev. Rul. 77-287, 1977-2, C.B. 319.

Judicial Precedent

In the nearly 40 years since Revenue Ruling 59-60 was published, hundreds of gift and estate tax cases have been decided in the courts. Accordingly, there is a body of case law concerning the valuation of small businesses and professional practices. Disputes between taxpayers and the Internal Revenue Service regarding Chapter 14 special valuation issues are just now being litigated.

In most situations, the courts will give the most weight to well-documented appraisal reports prepared contemporaneously with the gift or date of death by an appraiser familiar with the applicable regulations and existing case law issues. Certainly, having a qualified, well-thought-out appraisal report provides the taxpayer and the tax preparer with a reasonable basis for establishing their position against any subsequent inquiry from the Internal Revenue Service.

Methods Used to Minimize Gift and Estate Taxes

In general, most modern estate planning has the primary aim of avoiding the application of the special valuation rules under Chapter 14 outlined above. This is due to the adverse estate and gift tax results that usually impact family member shareholders. The following types of transactions are methods typically used to minimize the impact of gift and estate taxes for the small business and professional practice owner.

Estate-Freezing Recapitalizations. Often, the owner of a rapidly growing business wishes his children to receive the value of the business's future appreciation, while retaining an interest that will provide him with some income for retirement. One available estate planning method to accomplish this is the estate-freezing recapitalization.

In essence, the estate freeze involves dividing the ownership of the business into two or more classes of senior preferred and junior common interests—either corporate stock or partnership interests. The senior interest will have a nondiscretionary cumulative right to receive cash distributions (e.g., preferred dividends) and other preferences senior to the rights of the junior common interests. The relatively steady return on the distributions will provide a base for the value of the senior preferred interest to be, in effect, "frozen." As the result of this recapitalization, any appreciation in the value of the entire business is diverted to the junior class(es) of equity. The junior equity interests are then transferred out of the estates of the senior family members to the younger generation of family members.

The special valuation rules set forth in Chapter 14 discussed above will often apply. The rules are somewhat complex. Basically, they are designed to force the payment of a market rate of cumulative distributions/dividends to the senior preferred securities and to prohibit the use of liquidation, conversion, put rights, or other rights and features to unrealistically alter the value of the senior securities.

In most of the newer estate-freezing transactions we have seen, the critical issue limiting the amount of value that can be "frozen" is the available level of the distribution/dividend payout. Because preferred stock dividends are not deductible expenses for corporate income tax purposes, it would appear that better overall income and estate tax efficiency will be achieved with a partnership freeze. If an estate-freezing transaction is contemplated, we recommend retaining at the outset—as part of the estate planning team—a business appraiser who is experienced in recapitalizations. The business appraiser can help determine what the feasible freeze limits are for any particular company under the current market conditions, laws, and regulations.

Revenue Ruling 83-120, included as Exhibit 38-3, provides the view of the Internal Revenue Service with regard to guidelines for valuing preferred interests.

Minority Ownership Block Gifting.   Many family-owned businesses can be transferred slowly over a period of time as the next generation of family managers (1) gains experience and (2) demonstrates its ability to succeed the senior generation managers. Succession in management can be accompanied by having senior family members gift a series of minority ownership blocks of shares to junior family members, thereby increasing ownership in the younger generation. The advantage in gifting away control over a period of time by this method is that appraisals of such minority ownership blocks can take full advantage of whatever minority ownership interest discount and lack of marketability discount is appropriate for such blocks. These discounts are usually considerably larger for minority ownership interest blocks than for an interest that represents outright ownership control. We also find that senior generation family owners are often reluctant to part with ownership control of the business in a single transaction but are more comfortable with transferring control over time.

When these factors exist, a family limited partnership may be effective in allowing the entity to continue to be controlled by a relatively minor percentage ownership interest held by the senior family member, while the large majority of value and future growth of the entity can be gradually gifted away to the junior family members at current prices.

The advent of the family limited partnership as the estate planner's tool of choice has rapidly advanced in the last few years, and its use is accelerating. As of this writing, the most up-to-date discussion of the use of family limited partnerships is an interview with estate planning attorney Owen Fiore, shown as Exhibit 38-4. In-depth treatment of the topic is beyond the scope of this book, but the most comprehensive written treatise available at this time is a 146-page paper by another nationally known estate tax attorney, Stacy Eastland.[7]

---

[7] Stacy Eastland, "The Art of Making Uncle Sam Your Assignee Instead of Your Senior Partner: The Use of Family Limited Partnerships in Estate Planning," presented at the American Society of Appraisers Conference in Houston, June 1997, and available on-line from *Business Valuation Update Online*, an enhanced service for subscribers of *Shannon Pratt's Business Valuation Update*. For information on this on-line service, call (206) 369-2000 or email loriking@nvst.com. Website address is http://www.nvst.com/bvu.

Exhibit 38–3

Rev. Rul. 83-120

SECTION 1. PURPOSE

The purpose of this Revenue Ruling is to amplify Rev. Rul. 59-60, 1959-1 C.B. 237, by specifying additional factors to be considered in valuing common and preferred stock of a closely held corporation for gift tax and other purposes in a recapitalization of closely held businesses. This type of valuation problem frequently arises with respect to estate planning transactions wherein an individual receives preferred stock with a stated par value equal to all or a large portion of the fair market value of the individual's former stock interest in a corporation. The individual also receives common stock which is then transferred, usually as a gift, to a relative.

SEC. 2. BACKGROUND

.01 One of the frequent objectives of the type of transaction mentioned above is the transfer of the potential appreciation of an individual's stock interest in a corporation to relatives at a nominal or small gift tax cost. Achievement of this objective requires preferred stock having a fair market value equal to a large part of the fair market value of the individual's former stock interest and common stock having a nominal or small fair market value. The approach and factors described in this Revenue Ruling are directed toward ascertaining the true fair market value of the common and preferred stock and will usually result in the determination of a substantial fair market value for the common stock and a fair market value for the preferred stock which is substantially less than its par value.

.02 The type of transaction referred to above can arise in many different contexts. Some examples are:

(a) *A* owns 100% of the common stock (the only outstanding stock) of *Z* Corporation which has a fair market value of 10,500x. In a recapitalization described in section 368(a)(1)(E), *A* receives preferred stock with a par value of 10,000x and new common stock, which *A* then transfers to *A*'s son *B*.

(b) *A* owns some of the common stock of *Z* Corporation (or the stock of several corporations) the fair market value of which stock is 10,500x. *A* transfers this stock to a new corporation *X* in exchange for preferred stock of *X* corporation with a par value of 10,000x and common stock of corporation, which *A* then transfers to *A*'s son *B*.

(c) *A* owns 80 shares and his son *B* owns 20 shares of the common stock (the only stock outstanding) of *Z* Corporation. In a recapitalization described in section 368(a)(1)(E), *A* exchanges his 80 shares of common stock for 80 shares of new preferred stock of

Z Corporation with a par value of 10,000x. *A*'s common stock had a fair market value of 10,000x.

SEC. 3. GENERAL APPROACH TO VALUATION

Under section 25.2512-2(f)(2) of the Gift Tax Regulations, the fair market value of stock in a closely held corporation depends upon numerous factors, including the corporation's net worth, its prospective earning power, and its capacity to pay dividends. In addition, other relevant factors must be taken into account. *See* Rev. Rul. 59-60. The weight to be accorded any evidentiary factor depends on the circumstances of each case. *See* section 25.2512-2(f) of the Gift Tax Regulations.

SEC. 4. APPROACH TO VALUATION—PREFERRED STOCK

.01 In general the most important factors to be considered in determining the value of preferred stock are its yield, dividend coverage and protection of its liquidation preference.

.02 Whether the yield of the preferred stock supports a valuation of the stock at par value depends in part on the adequacy of the dividend rate. The adequacy of the dividend rate should be determined by comparing its dividend rate with the dividend rate of high-grade publicly traded preferred stock. A lower yield than that of high-grade preferred stock indicates a preferred stock value of less than par. If the rate of interest charged by independent creditors to the corporation on loans is higher than the rate such independent creditors charge their most credit worthy borrowers, then the yield on the preferred stock should be correspondingly higher than the yield on high quality preferred stock. A yield which is not correspondingly higher reduces the value of the preferred stock. In addition, whether the preferred stock has a fixed dividend rate and is nonparticipating influences the value of the preferred stock. A publicly traded preferred stock for a company having a similar business and similar assets with similar liquidation preferences, voting rights and other similar terms would be the ideal comparable for determining yield required in arms length transactions for closely held stock. Such ideal comparables will frequently not exist. In such circumstances, the most comparable publicly-traded issues should be selected for comparison and appropri-

ate adjustments made for differing factors.

.03 The actual dividend rate on a preferred stock can be assumed to be its stated rate if the issuing corporation will be able to pay its stated dividends in a timely manner and will, in fact, pay such dividends. The risk that the corporation may be unable to timely pay the stated dividends on the preferred stock can be measured by the coverage of such stated dividends by the corporation's earnings. Coverage of the dividend is measured by the ratio of the sum of pre-tax and pre-interest earnings to the sum of the total interest to be paid and the pre-tax earnings needed to pay the after-tax dividends. *Standard & Poor's Ratings Guide, 58* (1979). Inadequate coverage exists where a decline in corporate profits would be likely to jeopardize the corporation's ability to pay dividends on the preferred stock. The ratio for the preferred stock in question should be compared with the ratios for high quality preferred stock to determine whether the preferred stock has adequate coverage. Prior earnings history is important in this determination. Inadequate coverage indicates that the value of preferred stock is lower than its par value. Moreover, the absence of a provision that preferred dividends are cumulative raises substantial questions concerning whether the stated dividend rate will, in fact, be paid. Accordingly, preferred stock with noncumulative dividend features will normally have a value substantially lower than a cumulative preferred stock with the same yield, liquidation preference and dividend coverage.

.04 Whether the issuing corporation will be able to pay the full liquidation preference at liquidation must be taken into account in determining fair market value. This risk can be measured by the protection afforded by the corporation's net assets. Such protection can be measured by the ratio of the excess of the current market value of the corporation's assets over its liabilities to the aggregate liquidation preference. The protection ratio should be compared with the ratios for high quality preferred stock to determine adequacy of coverage. Inadequate asset protection exists where any unforeseen business reverses would be likely to jeopardize the corporation's ability to pay the full liquidation preference to the holders of the preferred stock.

.05 Another factor to be considered in valuing the preferred stock is whether it

Exhibit 38–3 (concluded)

has voting rights and, if so, whether the preferred stock has voting control. See, however, Section 5.02 below.

.06 Peculiar covenants or provisions of the preferred stock of a type not ordinarily found in publicly traded preferred stock should be carefully evaluated to determine the effects of such covenants on the value of the preferred stock. In general, if covenants would inhibit the marketability of the stock or the power of the holder to enforce dividend or liquidation rights, such provisions will reduce the value of the preferred stock by comparison to the value of preferred stock not containing such covenants or provisions.

.07 Whether the preferred stock contains a redemption privilege is another factor to be considered in determining the value of the preferred stock. The value of a redemption privilege triggered by death of the preferred shareholder will not exceed the present value of the redemption premium payable at the preferred shareholder's death (i.e., the present value of the excess of the redemption price over the fair market value of the preferred stock upon its issuance). The value of the redemption privilege should be reduced to reflect any risk that the corporation may not possess sufficient assets to redeem its preferred stock at

the stated redemption price. *See* Section .03 above.

SEC. 5. APPROACH TO VALUATION— COMMON STOCK

.01 If the preferred stock has a fixed rate of dividend and is nonparticipating, the common stock has the exclusive right to the benefits of future appreciation of the value of the corporation. This right is valuable and usually warrants a determination that the common stock has substantial value. The actual value of this right depends upon the corporation's past growth experience, the economic condition of the industry in which the corporation operates, and general economic conditions. The factor to be used in capitalizing the corporation's prospective earnings must be determined after an analysis of numerous factors concerning the corporation and the economy as a whole. *See* Rev. Rul. 59-60, at page 243. In addition, after-tax earnings of the corporation at the time the preferred stock is issued in excess of the stated dividends on the preferred stock will increase the value of the common stock. Furthermore, a corporate policy of reinvesting earnings will also increase the value of the common stock.

.02 A factor to be considered in determining the value of the common stock is whether the preferred stock also has voting rights. Voting rights of the preferred stock, especially if the preferred stock has voting control, could under certain circumstances increase the value of the preferred stock and reduce the value of common stock. This factor may be reduced in significance where the rights of common stockholders as a class are protected under state law from actions by another class of shareholders, *see Singer v. Magnavox Co.,* 380 A.2d 969 (Del. 1977), particularly where the common shareholders, as a class, are given the power to disapprove a proposal to allow preferred stock to be converted into common stock. See ABA-ALI Model Bus. Corp. Act, Section 60 (1969).

SEC. 6. EFFECT ON OTHER REVENUE RULINGS

Rev. Rul. 59-60, as modified by Rev. Rul. 65-193, 1965-2 C.B. 370 and as amplified by Rev. Rul. 77-287, 1977-2 C.B. 319, and Rev. Rul. 80-213, 1980-2 C.B. 101, is further amplified.

SOURCE: Rev. Rul. 83-120, 1983-2 C.B. 170.

When the value of the enterprise is growing rapidly, however, periodic gifting of family limited partnership interests may not reduce the overall dollar amount of value in the company held by the senior generation quickly enough, even though the senior generation owns a smaller and smaller percentage of the company's equity. Even in this situation, however, having an estate plan is better than not having a plan.

Revenue Ruling 93-12 deals with the issue of minority ownership interest discounts being applied to gifts of stock where control is held by a family. Previously, Revenue Ruling 81-253 held that no minority interest discounts could be applied to minority ownership interests gifted to members of the family that controlled the business. Revenue Ruling 93-12 reversed this position and states that "the shares of other family members will not be aggregated with the transferred shares to determine whether the transferred shares should be valued as part of a controlling interest." Revenue Ruling 93-12 is presented in Exhibit 38-5.

Private Annuities and Other Sale Methods. Often, if no clear family successor is available or if the owner wishes to completely terminate her direct equity interest in the company, a sale of the interest back to the company may be the best method. Such a sale could be made

Exhibit 38–4

Partnership between appraiser and tax attorney

A leading national tax attorney discusses working with appraisers on FLPs and LLCs

Owen G. Fiore, JD, CPA, is a Certified Specialist in Taxation Law, California State Bar Board of Legal Specialization, and founder of the San Jose-based law firm, The Fiore Law Group. He has 36 years of experience in advising families and their businesses on family wealth planning, wealth succession, valuation strategies and both income and transfer tax litigation. His recent tax litigation experience includes an FLP valuation case tried in Tax Court in late 1996, which is discussed below. A Fellow of the American College of Trust and Estate Counsel and the American College of Tax Counsel, Mr. Fiore is a frequent author of taxation and estate planning articles and faculty member for numerous tax conferences. A substantial amount of backup material relative to this interview has been made available on Business Valuation Update Online *(see footnote for listing). --SP*

Owen G. Fiore

SP: Owen, I heard you say recently, "The IRS has adopted the 'hyena pack' approach to transfer tax audits and tax litigation," believing there is tax abuse in the FLP area. What do you mean by that?

OF: IRS National Office technical and litigation personnel, as well as field personnel, like a pack of animals in a frenzy, are attacking transfers involving family members, especially where a family limited partnership is involved. It's clear from my Schauerhamer case[1], as well as cases recently handled by **Stacy Eastland** in Texas[2], that the IRS is trying every possible way to destroy entity viability, especially Family Limited Partnerships (FLPs), directly or indirectly. This is the case in spite of clear state and federal tax law to the contrary.

SP: How do they think they can do that?

OF: The service is taking the position that the partnership entity should be ignored in many fact patterns, such as FLP formation and gifting of partnership interests shortly prior to a donor's death. That is, ignore the fact that the property actually being transferred is a partnership interest, and just value the underlying assets as if direct ownership of the underlying assets is what is being transferred.

SP: Is their position articulated in writing where our readers can see exactly what they're saying?

OF: Absolutely. There are the IRS' briefs in the Schauerhamer case[3], and they've issued two Tax Advice Memoranda[4].

SP: Do you think the IRS' position will prevail?

OF: No, not ultimately. The Service's position that is termed "the partnership wrapper should be ignored" flies straight in the face of a person's constitutional right to deal with his or her property as the person sees fit, where such action is within legal alternatives. Long ago, in *Gregory v. Helvering*, 293 U.S. 465 (1935), it was established that tax avoidance by legal means is permissible and, more recently, in *Estate of Frank*, T.C. Memo, 1995-132, the Tax Court rejected IRS challenge of gifts shortly before death as being tax-avoidance motivated. In addition, as to FLPs, we should remember that Congress, as part of the Revenue Act of 1951, over 45 years ago, provided a "safe harbor" for

FLPs as an income tax savings technique with no requirement for "business purpose," clearly recognizing that partnership interests can be owned as the result of gift transfers.

SP: How have these issues played out in your Schauerhamer case?

OF: The parties to the case, which was tried in San Francisco before Tax Court Judge **Maurice Foley**, completed filing Reply Briefs on April 9th, having in February filed the Opening Briefs. A number of issues were disputed, including those relating to continued control of the partnership property from the date of partnership unit gifts to the date of the donor's death, 11 months later, albeit, per our view, when he was managing general partner.

However, of greatest significance is that a tentative settlement of gift and estate tax FLP unit values failed because the IRS insisted on preserving the issue of using IRC Sec. 2703 to eliminate the entity, leaving only NAV-based valuation for transfer tax purposes. Ignoring the statutory history and any reasonable statutory interpretation, the Commissioner asserted that the entity itself is a "testamentary device" and partnership provisions can be totally ignored since they all are part of a family-controlled "restrictive arrangement."

Therefore, you can see why I believe strongly in the role of the tax counsel working with the appraiser in the valuation process. A decision in this case, likely the first to deal with 2703 directly, cannot be expected before late 1997, and we are hopeful the taxpayer's estate will prevail.

The increased audit and litigation visibility of FLP-based discounts has increased planning, compliance and litigation costs (difficult to deduct for income tax purposes in gift tax cases). The Service is not above using the "cost issue"

---

[1] *Estate of Dorothy Morganson Schauerhamer v. Commissioner*, TC Docket No. 25058-95.

[2] See "Family limited partnership interests enjoy 40 to 85% discounts from NAV," *Business Valuation Update*, January 1997, pp. 1-3.

[3] *Estate of Schauerhamer*, op. cit.

[4] National Office Technical Advice Memoranda nos. 50127-96 and 246145-96. For the convenience of our readers we will have the Schauerhamer brief language and both of these TAMs on *Business Valuation Update Online* in June. (See accompanying article starting on page 1 regarding these additions to the online service.)

[5] See, for example, *Estate of Bright v. United States*, 658 F.2d 999 (1981), *Propstra v. United States*, 680 F.2d 1248 (1981), and *Estate of Woodbury G. Andrews*, 79 T.C. 938 (1982).

---

against taxpayers - this may intimidate taxpayers by making it costly and, if taxpayers are not careful, risky to stand up for their rights.

SP: This sounds like deja vu - they clung to the "family attribution" revenue ruling, 81-253, for 12 years, even though they lost every time they went to court on the issue[5]. They finally capitulated with Revenue Ruling 93-12, recognizing that minority interests do not have to be valued as part of a control block, even though other family members own control. What tactics do you expect the IRS to use?

OF: I think that they'll select what they regard as the most egregious cases to attack, those with bad fact patterns:

- Timing in contemplation of death, suggesting tax-avoidance motivation
- Failure to have a professional valuation by a qualified appraiser at the time of the transaction
- Valuation reports that do not comply with USPAP [Uniform Standards of Professional Practice].

SP: Do you see the December 1996 revision of the U.S. Gift Tax Return (Form 709) and its related instructions regarding valuation discount disclosures as a part of the IRS tactics? (See sidebar for wording of new valuation discount instructions.)

OF: Sure. New Form 709 alerts them to each situation where the value is less than dollar for dollar relative to the underlying assets. And I'll bet that the same instruction will be added the next time the IRS revises the estate tax return (Form 706).

SP: Does all this furor mean that you've suspended recommending FLPs to you clients?

OF: Not at all. I believe that FLPs, and also LLCs, can be ideal wealth-preservation vehicles. But if the client is not willing to invest the requisite time and money to set up the partnership or LLC correctly, don't be surprised if the IRS comes along and upsets the applecart. The key to success is careful analysis in planning situations, development of a valid multipurpose partnership entity, complete documentation and operational follow-up. And, of course, the business valuation appraiser is a necessary team player.

SP: So what is involved in setting it up correctly?

OF: The essential concept is to have a valid entity to split up the ownership for a purpose or purposes other than solely for tax avoidance. Setting it up properly requires a working partnership between the

Exhibit 38–4 (concluded)

attorney and a well-qualified appraiser who is knowledgeable about transfer-tax valuations for FLPs from the outset.

SP: Let's pause for a moment on nontax reasons for these family entities. What reasons would you normally think would qualify?

OF: There are lots of good reasons that have substance. For example:

● Sharing the equity on one basis and concentrating the management and control on another basis
● Protection of assets against outside creditors
● Avoidance of liability for limited partnership interests and LLC members. Having an LLC as a general partner in a FLP also avoids the personal liability of a general partner.

The nontax reasons should be spelled out in the partnership agreement and have real substance.

SP: Can you elaborate on the concept of the attorney/appraiser partnership?

OF: The appraiser needs to be a consulting expert at the time of structuring the entity and the gifts. The appraiser will opine on valuation implications of various structural features and provisions, but these opinions necessarily are based on legal assumptions provided by the attorney.

SP: What are the relevant legal assumptions that the appraiser needs to glean from the attorney?

OF: The most critical is the tax lawyer's opinion as to what property is being transferred - is it assets, partnership interests, assignee interests or what? The attorney needs to opine that the partnership or LLC will be recognized as an entity both under state law and also for tax law purposes.

The attorney needs to provide the appraiser the fundamental interpretation of the relevant state law and tax law, and an analysis of the partnership or LLC agreement provisions. Thus, now IRC Sec. 2703 needs to be factored into the analysis by competent tax counsel. The appraiser absolutely must know what assumptions in these respects the valuation opinion will be based on.

SP: Then what is the appraiser's role in this process?

OF: Based on the assumptions provided by the attorney, the appraiser will develop a full report that is reasonable, well documented, and can be used in tax litigation. This requires, of course, an understanding between the attorney and the appraiser as to Federal Rules of Evidence and Tax Court Rules respecting experts' reports and testimony, as well as issues on attorney-client privilege.

You should look at it as if any potential tax litigation begins with filing the return, and I like to attach the whole appraisal. The business valuation report should contain within its four corners all the major points, including expanded presentations of the assumptions underlying the report. The report must stand on its own legs, not a letter report with the rest of the material in the work papers. In short, the report should conform to USPAP.

SP: Can you give us a few summary concluding comments?

OF: There is no requirement that families maximize taxes, as long as what they do is real and done in a legally acceptable way. Discounts of various kinds will be based on state laws regarding the entities as well as tax-law principles, so the partnership between the appraiser and the tax attorney must fully reflect the relevant legal context in the valuation analysis.

There is nothing in the IRS's stepped-up-scrutiny to say that families can't engage in legitimate transactions. However, legal costs will go up, and we won't see the "cookie cutter" entity structures and valuations that have been propounded in some popular seminars.

I'm glad that you're putting back-up materials relative to this interview online for your subscribers. If they set up FLP-based valuation discount planning for clients, I think your readers will find the materials very helpful.

The following items are being put on **Business Valuation Update Online** *for those interested in more details relative to the Owen Fiore interview:*

● Fiore, Owen G., "Valuation Discount Planning - Especially FLP & IRC 2703," April, 1997, 19-page unpublished paper.
● Fiore, Owen G., "FLPs/LLCs - Ideal Wealth Preservation Vehicles - Management & Equity Succession and the Confiscatory Estate Tax," June, 1996, nine-page unpublished paper.
● National Office Technical Advice Memorandum 50127-96.
● National Office Technical Advice Memorandum 246145-96.
● Selected pages from IRS brief in case of Estate of Dorothy Morganson Schauerhamer v. Commissioner, T.C. Docket No. 25058-95. **BVU**

IRS attorney confirms close scrutiny of FLPs

As a supplement to the **Owen Fiore** interview, I also interviewed **Martin Basson,** supervisory attorney for gift and estate tax for the IRS South Florida district, and an adjunct professor at the University of Miami. He is also a member of the eight-person IRS National Gift and Estate and Gift Tax Advisory Panel.

Basson confirmed that the IRS is taking a close look at Family Limited Partnerships (FLPs), especially those holding passive assets. He also confirmed that one of several theses the IRS is currently exploring would be to disregard the partnership entity where the primary reason for creation was tax avoidance. At the same time, they don't want to penalize FLPs where they're legitimate, "but sometimes it's a close call." —SP **BVU**

SOURCE: *Shannon Pratt's Business Valuation Update,* May 1997, pp. 1–3. For a more comprehensive treatment, see Owen Fiore, "New Partnership between Appraiser and Tax Attorney," *Business Valuation Update Online,* http://www.nvst.com/bvu, originally presented at the 1997 American Society of Appraisers Advanced Business Valuation Conference.

Exhibit 38–5

Revenue Ruling 93-12

Issue

If a donor transfers shares in a corporation to each of the donor's children, is the factor of corporate control in the family to be considered in valuing each transferred interest, for purposes of section 2512 of the Internal Revenue Code?

Facts

P owned all of the single outstanding class of stock of *X* corporation. *P* transferred all of *P*'s shares by making simultaneous gifts of 20 percent of the shares to each of *P*'s five children, *A, B, C, D*, and *E*.

Law and Analysis

Section 2512(a) of the Code provides that the value of the property at the date of the gift shall be considered the amount of the gift.

Section 25.2512-1 of the Gift Tax Regulations provides that, if a gift is made in property, its value at the date of the gift shall be considered the amount of the gift. The value of the property is the price at which the property would change hands between a willing buyer and a willing seller, neither being under any compulsion to buy or to sell, and both having reasonable knowledge of relevant facts.

Section 25.2512-2(a) of the regulations provides that the value of stocks and bonds is the fair market value per share or bond on the date of the gift. Section 25.2512-2(f) provides that the degree of control of the business represented by the block of stock to be valued is among the factors to be considered in valuing stock where there are no sales prices or bona fide bid or asked prices.

Rev. Rul. 81-253, 1981-1C.B. 187, holds that, ordinarily, no minority shareholder discount is allowed with respect to transfers of shares of stock between family members if, based upon a composite of the family members' interest at the time of the transfer, control (either majority voting control or de facto control through family relationships) of the corporation exists in the family unit. The ruling also states that the Service will not follow the decision of the Fifth Circuit in *Estate of Bright v. United States*, 658 F.2d 999 (5th Cir. 1981).

In *Bright*, the decedent's undivided community property interest in shares of stock, together with the corresponding undivided community property interest of the decedent's surviving spouse, constituted a control block of 55 percent of the shares of a corporation. The court held that, because the community-held shares were subject to a right of partition,

the decedent's own interest was equivalent to 27.5 percent of the outstanding shares and, therefore, should be valued as a minority interest, even though the shares were to be held by the decedent's surviving spouse as trustee of a testamentary trust. *See also, Propstra v. United States*, 680 F.2d 1248 (9th Cir. 1982). In addition, *Estate of Andrews v. Commissioner*, 79 T.C. 938 (1982), and *Estate of Lee v. Commissioner*, 69 T.C. 860 (1978), *nonacq.*, 1980-2C.B. 2, held that the corporation shares owned by other family members cannot be attributed to an individual family member for determining whether the individual family member's share should be valued as the controlling interest of the corporation.

After further consideration of the position taken in Rev. Rul. 81-253, and in light of the cases noted above, the Service has concluded that, in the case of a corporation with a single class of stock, notwithstanding the family relationship of the donor, the donee, and other shareholders, the shares of other family members will not be aggregated with the transferred shares to determine whether the transferred shares should be valued as part of a controlling interest.

In the present case, the minority interests transferred to *A, B, C, D*, and *E* should be valued for gift tax purposes without regard to the family relationship of the parties.

Holding

If a donor transfers shares in a corporation to each of the donor's children, the factor of corporate control in the family is not considered in valuing each transferred interest for purposes of section 2512 of the Code. For estate and gift tax valuation purposes, the Service will follow *Bright, Propstra, Andrews*, and *Lee* in not assuming that all voting power held by family members may be aggregated for purposes of determining whether the transferred shares should be valued as part of a controlling interest. Consequently, a minority discount will not be disallowed solely because a transferred interest, when aggregated with interest held by family members, would be a part of a controlling interest. This would be the case whether the donor held 100 percent or some lesser percentage of the stock immediately before the gift.

Effect on Other Documents

Rev. Rul. 81-253 is revoked. Acquiescence in issue one of *Lee*, 1980-2 C.B. 2.

SOURCE: Rev. Rul. 93-12, 1993-1, C.B. 202.

in exchange for a private annuity, for a self-canceling installment note, or as some other type of sale transaction. The remaining shareholders then become the owners of the outstanding common equity of the company. Sometimes an employee stock ownership plan is the best option (see Chapter 39).

Charitable Contribution. Another method of reducing a senior generation owner's interest in the business is to make a charitable contribution of at least part of the interest and thus receive an income tax deduction. When the charity later redeems this holding (charities rarely wish to continue to own interests in private companies over long periods of time), the remaining junior generation owners will see an increase in their ownership percentage in the company. The senior owner gets to take a charitable income tax deduction for the full fair market value of the shares contributed. Of course, this deduction is subject to the limits of the current tax law for alternative minimum tax and other rules. Another charitable gifting technique involves the use of a charitable remainder trust to remove closely held business interests from the senior generation's estate but provide for income during life (see also the subsequent section on Appraisals for Charitable Contributions).

Funding with Life Insurance. A popular method of assuring that the financial impact of estate taxes on the beneficiaries of the deceased owner and on the business is minimized is to provide for adequate levels of life insurance to do the following:

1. Repurchase the owner's interest from the estate. Often, life insurance funding will be coupled with a buy-sell agreement in order to provide for a smooth and certain transition and valuation. The previous section discusses buy-sell agreements in greater detail.
2. Provide liquidity to the estate in order to pay estate taxes, even if the shares will not be repurchased by the company or by the other owners.
3. Provide liquidity for continuity of the company if the deceased owner was a key executive whose departure would disrupt business operations.

The last decade has seen an explosion of new insurance products designed to address all of these issues and more. It is not within the scope of this book to adequately discuss all of the current policy permutations generated by the creativity of the life insurance industry. We recommend that a good life insurance agent be part of the small business owner's estate planning team.

However, one clear issue should be kept in mind with regard to life insurance funding for small businesses and professional practices. As one practitioner put it:

> In each case the right result can only occur if planning determines the product and not vice versa. It is the planning that draws out the client's design specifications and lays the foundation for selection of an appropriate, competitive (insurance) product. [8]

Often, a combination of these estate planning tactics is necessary to transfer interests at the lowest sustainable value with the least possible impact on the future growth of the smaller business.

---

[8] Charles Ratner, "Life Insurance Planning: How to Help Clients Get a Perfect Fit," *Probate & Property*, November/December 1991, p. 22.

Appraisals for Charitable Contributions

The current tax laws require individuals, closely held corporations (other than S corporations), and personal service corporations (not including S service corporations) to obtain a qualified appraisal for non-cash property contributions having a claimed value of more than $5,000. In the case of securities not traded publicly, a qualified appraisal is required if the claimed value of the securities donated to one or more donees is greater than $10,000. The statute stipulates that the appraisal must include a description of the property or security; a statement of its fair market value; the specific basis of the valuation; a statement that the appraisal was prepared for income tax purposes; and the qualifications of the appraiser, his or her signature, and tax identification number. The following are some of the most salient points:

1. No appraisal will be accepted if all or part of the appraisal fee is based on a percentage of the appraised value of the property.
2. The appraisal must be made by a person qualified to appraise the donated property.
3. The appraisal must be received by the donor before the due date (including extensions) of the return on which the deduction is claimed. The donor must attach to the return on which the deduction is claimed a summary of the written appraisal (IRS Form 8283), also signed by the appraiser.
4. *Appraisers beware:* The new requirements include sanctions against appraisers submitting overstated valuations. Appraisers are subject to a civil tax penalty for aiding and abetting an understatement of tax liability (Section 6701). A $1,000 penalty can be imposed against the appraiser, and the appraiser may be barred from presenting evidence in administrative proceedings, causing the appraisal to be disregarded. (Note also, if the property contributed to the charity is sold within two years, the charity must report the selling price to the IRS.)

Summary

Businesses have life cycles just as people do. Unlike people, however, the lives of businesses can be extended if their owners plan properly. The owners of a small business or professional practice can protect their ownership interests (and those of their families) by planning for the smooth transfer of their interests during life or at death. Part of the planning process includes an awareness of (1) the value of the business ownership interest and (2) the owner's objectives for the interest. The general objectives are (1) liquidation of the interest, or at least liquidity at death, disability, or departure from the company; (2) minimization of gift and estate taxes; and (3) continuity of the business. These objectives can be accomplished on a basis that is fair to all concerned and that will avoid unnecessary crises by having the owners (1) carefully consider a buy-sell agreement, (2) implement a gift and estate tax plan, and (3) provide for funds to cover eventualities.

In any case, we highly recommend the use of a business appraiser as a consultant on the implications of the valuation provisions in the buy-sell agreement. We also recommend that the appraiser meet with all parties to the agreement (preferably including spouses) to be sure they understand the implications of the agreement before they sign off on it.

Bibliography

Abatemarco, Michael J., and Alfred Cavallaro. "The Importance of Buy-Sell Agreements for Closely Held Corporations." *CPA Journal,* February 1992, pp 57–59.

Abbin, Byrle M. "IRS Valuation Process Receives a Billion Dollar Setback." *Journal of Taxation,* May.1990, pp. 260–65.

Adams, Roy M. "Buy-Sell Agreements." *Trusts & Estates*, January 1996, pp. 67–68.

Adams, Roy M., David A. Herpe, and Thomas W. Abendroth. "Highlights of the Chapter 14 Final Regulations." *Trusts & Estates,* April 1992, pp. 35–49.

August, Jerald D. "Artificial Valuation of Closely Held Interest: Sec. 2704." *Estate Planning,* November/December 1995, pp. 339–344.

Blatt, William S. "The Effect of Sec. 2701 on Preferred Interest Freezes." *Trusts & Estates,* March 1991, pp. 8–14.

Blattmachr, Jonathan G. "Don't Be Driven by Tax-Driven Formula Clauses." *Probate & Property,* September/October 1991, pp. 34–38.

Bogdanski, John A. *Federal Tax Valuation.* Boston: Warren, Gorham & Lamont, 1997.

Brier, Kenneth P. and Joseph B. Darby III. "Family Limited Partnerships: Decanting Family Investment Assets into New Bottles." *The Tax Lawyer,* Fall 1995, pp. 127–164.

Budyak, James T. "Estate Freeze Rules Affect Partnership Valuation Discounts." *Taxation for Lawyers,* January/February 1997, pp. 228–234.

Cooper, Scott J. "A Guide through the Estate Freeze Maze." *Journal of Taxation of Estates and Trusts,* Winter 1992, pp. 5–10.

Drake, Dwight J., Kent Whiteley, and Timothy J. McDevitt. "The Ten Most Common Mistakes of Buy-Sell Agreements." *Journal of Financial Planning,* July 1992, pp. 104–12.

Eastland, S. Stacy (interview). "Family Limited Partnership Interests Enjoy 40 to 85% Discounts from NAV." *Shannon Pratt's Business Valuation Update*, January 1997, pp. 1–3.

Eastland, S. Stacy, and Margaret W. Brown. "New Attack on Family Business." *Trusts & Estates,* March 1991, pp. 48–56.

Eastland, S. Stacy, and Stephen L. Christian. "Proposed Valuation Regulations Provide Harsh Results under Adjustment and Lapse Rules." *Journal of Taxation,* December 1992, pp. 364–72.

Fiala, David M. "Business Success Planning." *National Public Accountant,* August 1991, pp. 22–27.

Fiore, Nicholas J. "Buy-Sell Agreements and Estate Planning." *Journal of Accountancy*, October 1995, p. 40.

Fiore, Owen G. "Chapter 14 Special Valuation Renewed Estate Tax Savings Opportunities via Inter-Vivos Family Wealth Planning." USC Institute on Federal Taxation, January 29, 1992.

Fodor, Gerald M., Benjamin M. Lash, and Edward J. Mazza. "Family Business Valuations and Chapter 14 of the Internal Revenue Code." *Journal of the American Society of CLU & ChFC*, January 1995, pp. 62–68.

Fowler, Bradley A. "How Do You Handle It? Family Partnership Valuations." *Business Valuation Review*, March 1997, pp. 41–44.

Freund, Susan M., and Gregory V. Gadarian. "Buy-Sell Agreements May Have Far-Reaching Tax Consequences." *Journal of Taxation of Estates & Trusts,* Summer 1990, pp. 12–17.

Fross, Roger R. "Estate Tax Valuation Based on Book Value Buy-Sell Agreements." *Tax Lawyer*, Winter 1996, pp. 319–40.

Gamble, E. James. "How Do We Handle Buy-Sell Agreements under Chapter 14?" *Trusts & Estates,* March 1991, pp. 38–46.

Gardner, John H., and Brent Lipschultz. "Estate and Gift Tax Update." *Business Valuation Update Online,* http://www.nvst.com/bvu, originally presented at AICPA Business Valuation Conference, November 1997.

Grassi, Sebastian V., Jr. "Business Problems and Planning— Shareholder Buy-Sell Agreements and the Revenue Reconciliation Act of 1990." *Michigan Bar Journal,* May 1991, pp. 447–49.

Hall, Lance. "Corporate Structure Discount and Valuation of Asset-Holding C Corps." *Trusts & Estates,* September 1996, pp. 45–48.

Herpe, David A. "Climate for Valuation Discounts Remains Good Despite IRS Obstinancy." *Trusts & Estate,* January 1995, pp. 66–76.

Hitchner, James A. "Landmark Cases." *Business Valuation Update Online*, http://www.nvst.com/bvu, originally presented at AICPA Business Valuation Conference, November 1997.

_____. "The Use of Discounts in Estate and Gift Tax Valuations." *Trusts & Estates*, August 1992, pp. 49–56, 60.

_____. "Valuation of a Closely Held Business." *Tax Adviser*, July 1992, pp. 471–79.

Hudson, Boyd D. "Substantial Modifications of Buy-Sell Agreements." *Tax Adviser*, October 1996, pp. 598–599.

Hunsberger, Donald A. "Owners and Estates: A Buy-Sell Primer." *Journal of the American Society of CLU & ChFC,* September 1991, pp. 48–52

IRS Valuation Guide for Income, Estate and Gift Taxes: Valuation Training for Appeals Officers. Chicago: Commerce Clearing House Inc., 1994.

Jeffries, Spencer, and Bruce A. Johnson. "Publicly Registered Limited Partnership Interests." *Business Valuation Review*, December 1996, pp. 155–56.

Johnson, Linda M., and Brian R. Greenstein. "Using Buy-Sell Agreements to Establish the Value of a Closely Held Business." *The Journal of Taxation*, December 1994, pp. 362–369.

Jones, John R., Jr., and Robert W. Fisher. "Income Tax Considerations of Buy-Sell Agreements." *Taxation for Accountants*, January 1991, pp. 34–42

Jurinski, James John, and W. Ron Singleton. "New Estate Freeze Rules Require Heating up of Planning Tactics." *Practical Accountant*, May 1991, pp. 21–33.

Kasner, Jerry A. "Valuation of Family Partnership Interests." *Tax Analysts—Special Reports*, 97 TNT 50-47 (March 14, 1997).

Kelly, James P., III. "Waiving Rights under Buy-Sell Agreement Affects Stock Value." *Estate Planning*, September/October 1991, pp. 284–291.

Kimball, Curtis R. "Valuation of Fractional Interests in Real Estate," Chapter 10A in *Financial Valuation: Businesses and Business Interests*, 1997 Update, James H. Zukin, ed. New York: Warren Gorham & Lamont, 1997.

————. "Valuation in Estate Planning," Chapter 11A in *Financial Valuation: Businesses and Business Interests*, 1997 Update. James H. Zukin, ed. New York: Warren Gorham & Lamont, 1997.

Kimball, Curtis R., and Robert F. Reilly. "Kinder, Gentler Gift and Estate Tax Valuation Rules Offer Planning Possibilities." *Journal of Taxation of Estates and Trusts*, Fall 1991, pp. 27–33.

King, Hamlin C. "Final Estate Freeze Rules Simplify Subtraction Method." *TAXES*, July 1992, pp. 460–90.

Kuenster, Richard A. "Estate Planning, Family Businesses and Divorce." *FAIR$HARE*, October 1991, pp. 7–9

Laro, David. "Business Valuation: A View from the United States Tax Court." *Proceedings of the American Society of Appraisers International Appraisal Conference*, Denver, Colorado, June 20, 1995.

Lusby, Roger W. "Recognizing Built-in Capital Gains for Valuation Purposes." *Business Valuation Update Online*, http://www.nvst.com /bvu, originally presented at AICPA Business Valuation Conference, November 1997.

Marcus, Fred J., and Douglas K. Freeman. "Valuation of Closely-Held Stock." *Journal of the American Society of CLU & ChFC*, September 1993, pp. 24–25.

Margulis, Marc S. "Valuing a Decedent's Legal Claims, Lawsuits, and Choses in Action." *Valuation Strategies*, January/February 1998, pp. 5–9.

Mazza, Edward J. "Business Valuations: A Clear Path to Large Cases." *Life Association News*, March 1995, pp. 124–127.

Mezzullo, Louis A. "Buy-Sell Agreements after Chapter 14." *Trusts & Estates*, June 1994, pp. 49–59.

_____. "New Valuation Rules Affect Buy/Sell Agreements." *Life Association News*, June 1996, pp. 94–98.

_____. "Special Valuation Rules Affect Buy-Sell Agreements." *National Underwriter (Life/Health/Financial Services)*, April 1, 1996, pp. 8, 12.

Miller, Kenneth C., and Joseph M. Kuznicki. "New IRS Position Shows How Buy-Sell Agreements Can Avoid Anti-Estate Freeze Rules of 2036(c)." *Estate Planning*, July/August 1990, pp. 194–200.

Moore, M. Read "Honey, Who Shrunk My Deduction?" *Probate & Property*, January/February 1997, pp. 9–14.

Mulligan, Michael D. "Estate Freeze Rules Eased by New Tax Law but Other Restrictions are Imposed." *Estate Planning*, January/February 1991, pp. 2–7.

Nager, Ross W. "Estate Freeze Rules Repealed, but Uncertainty Remains." *Journal of Taxation of Estates and Trusts*, Winter 1991, pp. 4–7.

Owens, Thomas. "Buy-Sell Agreements." *Small Business Reports*, January 1991, pp. 57–61.

Painter, Andrew D., and Jonathan G. Blattmachr. "How the Final Chapter 14 Anti-Freeze Regulations Affect Estate Planning Strategies." *Journal of Taxation of Estates and Trusts*, Spring 1992, pp. 5–14.

Pennell, Jeffrey N. "Valuation Discord: An Exegesis of Wealth Transfer Tax Valuation Theory and Practice." In James A. Kasner and Jeffrey N. Pennell, *Estate Planning*, 6th ed. Boston: Little Brown, 1995.

Peterson, James. "Ducking the Cross Fire: Avoiding Disputes in Buy-Sell Agreements." *Journal of Accountancy*, January 1991, pp. 65–69; 71.

Rapkin, Stephanie. "The Basics of the S Corporation for the Estate Planner." *Trusts & Estates*, September 1996, pp. 38–44.

Reilly, Robert F. "Valuation Requirements for Charitable Contribution Deductions." *CPA Expert*, Winter 1997, pp. 7–10.

Reilly, Robert F., and Robert P. Schweihs. "How the Buy/Sell Agreement Smooths a Shift in Control." *Mergers & Acquisitions*, January/February 1991, pp. 52–57.

_____. "Valuation Aspects of Buy/Sell Agreements Subsequent to the Repeal of Section 2036(c)." *Ohio CPA Journal*, January–April 1991, pp. 38–43.

Robinson, Debra A., and Edward J. Rappaport. "Impact of Valuation Discounts on Estate and Income Tax Basis." *Estate Planning*, June 1997, pp. 223–30.

Rothberg, Richard S. "Valuation of Interests in Family Businesses after *Newhouse*." *Journal of Taxation of Investments*, Winter 1991, pp. 161–65.

Schneider, Pam H., and Lloyd Leva Plaine. "Proposed Valuation Regulations Flesh out Operation of the Subtraction Method." *Journal of Taxation*, August 1991, pp. 82–90.

Segal, Mark A. "Buy-Sell Agreements—A Valuable Estate Planning Tool." *National Public Accountant*, February 1990, pp. 14–17.

Shore, H. Allen and Craig T. McClung. "Beyond the Basic SUPER-FREEZE—An Update and Additional Planning Opportunities." *Taxes,* January 1997, pp. 41–55.

Soled, Jay A., P.V. Viswanath, and Patrick I. McKenna. "Almost Two Decades Later, *Buffalo Tool* Admonishments Still Largely Ignored." *Taxes,* January 1997, pp. 65–73.

Stoneman, Christopher. "Buy-Sell Agreements: Accomplishing Planning Objectives with Optimal Tax Consequences." *Tax Management: Estates Gifts & Trusts Journal*, July 9, 1992, pp. 99–112.

Strauss, Benton C., and James K. Shaw. "Final Chapter 14 Regs. Clarify GRATs, Business Planning." *Estate Planning,* September/October 1992, pp. 259–66.

Strouse, Jonathan E. "Redemption and Cross-Purchase Buy-Sell Agreements: A Comparison." *Practical Accountant,* October 1991, pp. 44–53+.

Thornton, D. John, and Gregory A. Byron. "Valuation of Family Limited Partnership Interests." *Valuation Strategies,* September/October 1997, pp. 10–17; 37–43.

Willens, Robert. "Buy-Sell Agreements: Constructive Dividend Dangers Lurk." *Journal of Accountancy,* February 1992, pp. 49–52.

Wise, Richard M. "Practice Standards, Tax Valuations and Valuation Methodologies—CICBV vs. ASA." *Proceedings of the 12th Biennial Conference of the CICBV*. Toronto: Canadian Institute of Chartered Business Valuators, 1997, pp. 235–58.

Chapter 39

Employee Stock Ownership Plans in Small Companies

Employee stock ownership plans (ESOPs) are an increasingly advantageous and popular means of transferring all, or any part, of a company's ownership to its employees. An owner may sell all, or any portion, of his or her stock to employees through an ESOP, through one or a series of transactions. An ESOP can be used effectively for financing and can result in significant income tax savings—to both the selling shareholder and the company. ESOPs continue to grow in popularity among smaller companies and professional practices.

What Is an ESOP?

The concept of an ESOP is to allow employees to have an ownership interest in a company. An ESOP is a tax-qualified employee benefit plan designed to invest primarily in the sponsoring company's securities. An ESOP, therefore, is subject to the Employee Retirement Income Security Act of 1974 (ERISA), similar to most pension or profit-sharing plans The company may contribute cash to the ESOP, and the ESOP may use the cash to buy stock from one or more current stockholders. Alternatively, the company may issue additional shares of stock and contribute such shares to the ESOP. In that case, the fair market value of the contributed stock is a tax-deductible expense to the company. The ESOP's ownership interests are allocated among employee participants on a basis similar to that used by pension and profit-sharing plans.

An ESOP may also borrow money and enter into transactions with related parties to acquire the employer's securities in what would otherwise be prohibited transactions under ERISA and the Internal Revenue Code.

Leveraged ESOPs

A leveraged ESOP is one that uses borrowed funds to purchase stock from one or more existing owners or the company. The company borrows the funds from an external lending source and lends the funds to the ESOP, generally under the same terms as a conventional bank loan. The company then makes annual cash contributions to the ESOP, which the ESOP returns to the company to pay off the loan. Since the contribution to the ESOP is tax deductible, the bank loan (both principal and interest) is effectively repaid with pretax dollars.

The Leveraged Buyout

When an ESOP borrows money to buy all or part of the company's stock from the current owner or owners and uses the company's assets as collateral, the transaction is referred to as a leveraged buyout. This type of transaction is becoming increasingly available to small businesses.

This is partly because of the low interest-rate environment and banks' willingness to make such loans. This is also partly because of the excellent income tax advantages of such transactions, as discussed in the next section.

The ESOP as a Financing Vehicle

An ESOP can also borrow money to buy newly issued stock or treasury stock from the company. In this situation, the ESOP is used as a vehicle to provide new equity financing to the company, as opposed to providing liquidity to one or more of the company's shareholders.

Advantages of ESOPs

Tax-free Rollover of Sale Proceeds

One of the biggest advantages underlying ESOP transactions is the income tax benefits available to the selling shareholder. Under Internal Revenue Code Section 1042, a shareholder will be able to indefinitely defer all capital gains taxes otherwise due on the sale of stock to an ESOP, so long as three conditions are met:

1. The shareholder must have held the stock for at least three years prior to the sale to the ESOP.
2. The ESOP must own at least 30 percent of the company's stock immediately after the sale.
3. The sale proceeds must be reinvested, within a year after the sale, in qualified replacement property (QRP). QRP generally refers to the securities of a domestic operating company.

Recent studies by The ESOP Association have identified this Section 1042 income tax treatment to be the single largest motivating factor underlying ESOP transactions.

Tax-Deductibility of ESOP Dividends

Dividends paid to ESOP participants will be deducted from the employer company's taxable income (although the deductions are subject to alternative minimum tax limitations). The company may also deduct dividends used to make loan repayments in the case of a leveraged ESOP.

Improve Employee Morale and Productivity

There is evidence, at least in the United States, that ESOP companies tend to be more efficient than their competitors. This is particularly true if there are meaningful efforts to promote employee participation.

As owners, employees tend to appreciate the need for operating efficiently and are likely to be more aware of how their activities affect the
bottom line.

Achieve Other Corporate Objectives

An ESOP can also provide a means for achieving other corporate objectives:

- Facilitate the sale of a division of the company to employees.
- Facilitate a management buy-out of the company.
- Increase a company's capital by selling stock to the ESOP, which
  uses funds provided by tax-deductible contributions.
- Enhance employee retirement benefits.

When Does An ESOP Make Sense?[1]

Not every company is a good ESOP candidate. The following are some
factors to consider in determining whether or not an ESOP is feasible
for a particular company:

- Value of the company.
- Borrowing capacity.
- Corporate form.
- Adequacy of payroll.
- Level and stability of cash flow.
- Dependence on the continuation of current ownership.
- Corporate culture.

Value of the Company

Where an ESOP is being used as a vehicle to buy out existing shareholders, the first step in this process is to determine how much of the
ownership of the company the shareholders want to sell and over what
period of time. From there, a preliminary estimate of the value of the
shares to be purchased by the ESOP should be estimated. With this information, the selling shareholder can decide if the price is acceptable,
and the parties can explore whether the deal is financable.

If an ESOP is to be used primarily as an employee benefit plan, the
determination of transaction feasibility is fairly straightforward. The

---

[1]Much of this discussion was drawn from articles appearing in *Employee Ownership Report*,
published by The National Center for Employee Ownership, Inc. (NCEO). The NCEO is a private,
nonprofit information and research organization headquartered in Oakland, California. They can
be contacted by telephone at (510) 272-9461.

costs of the ESOP plan should be compared with other potential employee benefit plans. While ESOPs can be more expensive to administer than other plans, the tax deductibility of dividends and principal payments and noncash contributions can increase a company's cash flow.

Corporate Form

Effective January 1, 1998, ESOPs may be installed in S corporations. Prior to that date, only C corporations have been allowed to sponsor ESOPs. As of this writing, the proposed rules regarding S corporation ESOPs are more restrictive than C corporation ESOPs. However, these rules may be subject to change.

Adequacy of Payroll

In leveraged ESOPs, companies can generally contribute up to 25 percent of eligible payroll of plan participants, so long as the contributions are used to repay the principal portion of an ESOP loan. Under Internal Revenue Code Section 133, the annual limitation on contributions is generally 15 percent in nonleveraged ESOPs, although this can be as high as 25 percent under certain limited circumstances. Often, companies can use dividends to expand these limits. Generally, the amount of the company contribution made to buy the targeted number of shares must fall within these limits, or an ESOP will not be feasible.

Eligible payroll may not be the same as total payroll. For example, new employees would probably not be participating in the ESOP immediately. Some highly compensated employees may have to be excluded or limited under some circumstances. And some union groups may not be eligible for participation. These factors will serve to reduce the overall level of eligible payroll and, thus, allowable contributions.

The above limitations can also be reduced by contributions to other existing qualified employee benefit plans, such as profit sharing, 401(k), and defined benefit plans.

If it is determined that a particular company does not have sufficient eligible payroll, consideration may be given to reducing contributions to existing plans or transferring funds from an existing plan to help fund a portion of the shares to be purchased by an ESOP.

We are familiar with situations where ESOPs have been successfully (and cost-effectively) implemented in companies with as few as 9 or 10 employees and with eligible payroll of as little as $400,000.

Cash Flow

An ESOP impacts cash flow in two ways. First, cash is needed to make contributions to fund purchases of shares (unless the contributions are made in newly issued stock) or to pay off the loan incurred to purchase the stock. Second, cash is needed to fund the repurchase of shares allocated to participants' accounts when they leave the company. In short, companies need to analyze the cash available to fund these obligations.

If the company's cash flow is shaky to begin with, it is unlikely that it can afford an ESOP without major changes and/or sacrifices.

On the other hand, if the contribution to the ESOP is in newly issued stock, the noncash expense (fair market value of shares issued) is tax deductible, thus enhancing cash flow.

Dependence on the Primary Shareholder(s)

Some companies are heavily dependent on the existing owner's skills, contacts, and reputation. An abrupt departure of such a key person can have serious implications for a company that is not prepared for such a departure. A management succession plan should be in place, and the new managers/owners should be given the opportunity to develop their own relationship with customers, employees, lenders, and others before the existing owner leaves. Typically where such dependence exists, the financial institution lending funds to the ESOP will likely require that the selling owner stay on in a consulting capacity or as a corporate officer for a couple of years.

Corporate Culture

Before installing an ESOP, existing management/owners need to determine if they are really comfortable with the employees being business owners. Employees as owners are typically involved to some extent with corporate decision making and often share in the company's financial information to some degree. An ESOP is probably inappropriate in a company where management is not willing to share such responsibilities and financial information with employee shareholders despite the financial benefits associated with an ESOP.[2] The most important action necessary to ensure that ESOP benefits are maximized, including increased productivity, is (1) to facilitate and encourage employee participation and (2) to effectively communicate the ESOP's purpose and benefits to the employees.

Issues in the Valuation of ESOP Stock

Government Regulation

Annual valuations of ESOP stock by a qualified, independent financial advisor became mandatory with the Tax Reform Act of 1986.

Valuation of ESOP shares in privately held companies must meet the requirements of the Internal Revenue Service, the Department of Labor (DOL), and ERISA. The IRS points to Revenue Ruling 59-60 (the

---

[2]However, a court ruling has held that companies are *not* required to provide the annual ESOP valuation report to ESOP participants. See *Faircloth* v. *Lundy Packing Company*, 91 F.3d 640 (4th Cir. Aug. 2, 1996), *cert. denied* Jan. 13, 1997.

general guidelines for gift and estate tax valuations) as guidance for ESOP valuations as well. As of this writing, the IRS has not issued any supplemental revenue ruling or other guidance specifically applicable to ESOPs. Section 3(18) of ERISA refers to fair market value determined in good faith "and in accordance with regulations promulgated by the Secretary (of Labor)."

The DOL has published a *proposed* regulation for guidance in valuing ESOP stock. As of this writing, these guidelines have not been finalized. Nonetheless, they represent the "industry standard" for ESOP valuation guidelines.[3] However, the proposed guidelines do embrace Revenue Ruling 59-60 and add provisions specifically applicable to ESOPs.

The appraiser of ESOP shares should be intimately familiar with the guidelines set forth in these two documents and should rely on generally accepted appraisal practices and the case law that has developed to date.[4]

Requirements for Valuation Analyses

A valuation of a company's ESOP stock is required when:

1. The ESOP makes its first acquisition of stock.
2. Annually thereafter.
3. When there is a transaction with a related party (i.e., a "prohibited transaction").
4. If the ESOP is selling out.

While typically only an annual valuation is required, many (usually larger) companies have their ESOP stock valued twice a year or even on a quarterly basis. These periodic valuations are performed in order to have a more current value for transactions several times during the year.

Qualified and Independent Financial Advisor

The financial advisor selected by the ESOP fiduciary must, at a minimum, meet two basic criteria:

1. The financial advisor should be a company or person who regularly engages in the valuation of businesses or business interests.
2. The financial advisor must be independent with respect to the company and other parties to an ESOP transaction.

---

[3] Proposed Regulation Relating to the Definition of Adequate Consideration, 53 Fed. Reg. 17, 632 (1988) (to be codified at 29 C.F.R. Part 2510).

[4] For a discussion of the most recent ESOP-related court cases, see Shannon P. Pratt and Robert F. Reilly, "ESOP Valuation Controversies and Court Cases" (Chapter 9) in Robert W. Smiley Jr., Ronald J. Gilbert, and David M. Binns, eds. *Employee Stock Ownership Plans*, 1997 Yearbook (New York: Warren, Gorham & Lamont, 1997).

Treasury Regulation Section 54.4975-ll(d)(5) states:

> An independent appraisal will not in itself be a good faith determination of value in the case of a transaction between a plan and a disqualified person. However, in other cases, a determination of fair market value based on at least an annual appraisal independently arrived at by a person who customarily makes such appraisals and who is independent of any party to a transaction under Section 54.4975(b)(9) and (12) will be deemed to be a good faith determination of value.[5]

In order to be considered independent, a financial advisor should generally be a company or person who does not perform any other services for a party whose interest may be adverse to the ESOP and who would meet an objective standard of impartiality.[6] The regulations make it clear that a financial advisor needs to be retained by the ESOP and act in the sole best interest of the ESOP. It is also extremely important for the ESOP to be represented by competent legal advisors with experience in ESOPs. With both competent financial and legal advisors, any ESOP transaction is much more likely to pass the scrutiny of the various regulatory authorities.

A financial advisor should also be experienced in performing ESOP valuations. This is because the special features of an ESOP—such as the put option—impact the valuation of the shares held by the plan.

Common Problems in ESOP Valuation

Based on our analysis of ESOP court decisions and our own experience, most of the problems with ESOP valuations tend to be of an administrative nature rather than specifically focused on the particular valuation conclusion. Valuation problems have occurred in the following situations:

- The financial advisor was not independent.
- The financial advisor used unconventional procedures not acceptable to the IRS or DOL.
- The valuation report was not thoroughly documented.
- The valuation was out of date at the time of the transaction.

Summary

In order to avoid problems with these regulatory authorities with respect to an ESOP valuation, we recommend the following:

---

[5] *Valuing ESOP Shares* (Washington, DC: The ESOP Association, 1989), p. 6.

[6] Jared Kaplan and Jack Curtis, "ESOPs," *Tax Management*, 1991, p. A 4.

- Retain a reputable independent financial advisor with a good proven track record with regulatory authorities and courts.
- Bring an independent and qualified financial advisor into the professional advisory team at the earliest possible time.
- Allow adequate time and budget to do the job right.
- Allow the ESOP's financial advisor to reach an independent conclusion without undue pressure from either the selling shareholder or the ESOP fiduciaries.

As discussed above, in addition to providing for an employee's retirement, ESOPs, if appropriately considered and implemented, can provide numerous financial advantages, boost employee morale and productivity, and provide a viable means for transferring ownership.

We would encourage any company considering the formation of an ESOP to contact one of the following nonprofit groups:

- The ESOP Association, 1726 M Street, NW, Suite 501, Washington, DC 20036, telephone (202) 293-2971, fax (202) 293-7568. This association is composed of companies that have ESOPs as well as companies that provide services to ESOP companies, such as firms that specialize in installing and administering ESOPs, firms that specialize in valuing ESOP shares, and firms that provide legal advice to ESOPs. The ESOP Association sponsors conferences several times a year and offers a variety of informative publications.[7]
- The National Center for Employee Ownership (NCEO), 1201 Martin Luther King Jr. Way, Oakland, CA 94612-1217, telephone (510) 272-9461, fax (510) 272-9510. The NCEO was founded in 1981 to provide reliable, objective, comprehensive information about employee ownership. The NCEO is a private, nonprofit, membership and information organization whose members receive a bimonthly newsletter, consultant listings, and discounts on events and on dozens of publications and videos.[8]

Bibliography

Articles

Abrams, Jay B. "An Iterative Procedure to Value Leveraged ESOPs." *ASA Valuation,* January 1993, pp. 76–103.

Ackerman, David. "Innovative Uses of Employee Stock Ownership Plans for Private Companies." *DePaul Business Law Journal,* Spring 1990, pp. 227–54.

---

[7] Note especially, *Valuing ESOP Shares.*

[8] Note especially, *The Journal of Employee Ownership Law and Finance.*

Ackerman, David, and Idelle A. Howitt. "Tax-Favored Planning for Ownership Succession via ESOPs." *Estate Planning*, November/December 1992, pp. 331–37.

Akresh, Murray S., and Barry I. Cosloy. "New Math for ESOPs." *Financial Executive*, May/June 1994, pp. 45–48.

Berkery, Peter M., Jr. "High Court OKs Retroactive Amendment of Estate Tax ESOP Deduction." *Accounting Today*, July 11, 1994, p. 8.

Blasi, Joseph R., and Douglas L. Kruse. "Employee Ownership and Participation: Trends, Problems, and Policy Options." *Journal of Employee Ownership Law and Finance*, Spring 1993, pp. 41–73.

Block, Stanley B. "The Advantages and Disadvantages of ESOPs: A Long-Range Analysis." *Journal of Small Business Management*, January 1991, pp. 15–21.

Braun, Richard S. "The ESOP Lifecycle." *ESOP Report* (official newsletter of The ESOP Association), December 1991, pp. 4–5.

Brockhardt, James, and Robert Reilly. "Employee Stock Ownership Plans after the 1989 Tax Law: Valuation Issues." *Compensation and Benefits Review*, September-October 1990, pp. 29–36

_____. "ESOPs Are Becoming Popular Corporate Financial Tools." *Trusts & Estates*, February 1990, pp. 40–43.

Bromberg, Alan R. "The Employee Investor: ESOPs and Other Employee Benefit Plans as Securities." *Securities Regulation Law Journal*, Winter 1992, pp. 325–40.

Brown, Gregory K., and Kim Schultz Abello. "ESOPs and Security Design: Common Stock, Super Common, or Convertible Preferred?" *Journal of Pension Planning & Compliance*, Summer 1997, pp. 99–105.

Brown, Karen W. "Payment of Control Premiums by ESOPs." *ESOP Report*, November/December 1993, pp. 6–8.

Buxton, Dickson C. "ESOP and Business Perpetuation Plans." *Journal of the American Society of CLU & ChFC*, November 1990, pp. 34–44.

Cahill, Kathleen. "Accounting for ESOPs." *CFO: The Magazine for Senior Financial Executives*, February 1993, p. 12.

Cefali, Sheryl L., and Sandra M. Wimsat. "An ESOP Valuation Case Study." *Journal of Employee Ownership Law and Finance*, Winter 1995, pp. 67–88.

Chaplinsky, S., and G. Niehaus. "Leveraged ESOP Financing and Risk." *Financial Analysts Journal*, March-April 1990, pp. 10–13.

Curtis, John E., Jr. "Use of 'Enterprise Value' When an ESOP Purchases Less than a 'Majority' of a Company's Outstanding Stock." *Tax Management Compensation Planning Journal*, March 5, 1993, pp. 43–45.

Dema, Robert J., and Duncan Harwood. "Tapping the Financial Benefits of an ESOP." *Journal of Accountancy*, April 1991, pp. 27–28ff.

Elgin, Peggie R. "Accounting Change Removes Advantages of Leveraged ESOPs." *Corporate Cashflows*, April 1994, pp. 12–14.

"Employee Ownership (Special Report)." *Employee Benefit Plan Review*, July 1992, pp. 14–26.

"ESOP Conference Addresses Whether Appraiser May Be a Fiduciary." *Shannon Pratt's Business Valuation Update*, June 1997, p. 6.

Flesher, Dale L. "Using ESOPs to Solve Succession Problems." *Journal of Accountancy*, May 1994, pp. 45–48.

Freiman, Howard A. "Understanding the Economics of Leveraged ESOPs." *Financial Analysts Journal*, March–April 1990, pp. 51–67.

Garber, Steve. "A Proposed Methodology for Estimating the Lack of Marketability Discount Related to ESOP Repurchase Liability." *Business Valuation Review*, December 1993, pp. 172–81.

Gilbert, Ronald J. "Considerations for Initial Public Offerings Involving Employee Stock Ownership Plans." *Journal of Employee Ownership Law and Finance*, Fall 1992, pp. 77–84.

Griswold, Terence L. "Some Thoughts on Dividend Reasonableness and Related Valuation Issues." *Journal of Employee Ownership Law & Finance*, Summer 1995, pp. 45–58.

Gross, Robert J. "ESOP Valuation Issues." *Journal of Employee Ownership Law & Finance*, Winter 1991, pp. 53–62.

Heermance, Paul F. "A Valuation Approach for ESOP Convertible Stock." *ESOP Report,* February 1992, pp. 4–6.

Hess, Eric G. "The Valuation Implications of the ESOP Repurchase Obligation." *Journal of Employee Ownership Law & Finance*, Summer 1995, pp. 73–92.

Hill, R. Bradley. "Why Stock Ownership Is a Better Incentive than Stock Options." *Journal of Compensation & Benefits,* November–December 1992, pp. 24–27.

"How Valuation Techniques Can Impede Corporate Growth and Long-Term Employee Ownership." *Employee Ownership Report*, September/October 1995, pp. 1, 3.

Huffaker, John B. "Retroactive Change for Stock Sales to ESOPs Upheld." *Journal of Taxation*, August 1994, p. 199.

Lannom, Allan L. R. "Valuing Non-ESOP Shares in ESOP Companies—Some Empirical Evidence." *Business Valuation Review*, March 1994, pp. 19–21.

Levitske, John, Jr. "ESOP Valuation: The 'Quality' of All Earnings Is Not the Same." *Journal of Pension Planning & Compliance*. Fall 1994, pp. 76–85.

Lint, Ron J. "ESOP Power." *Management Accounting*, November 1992, pp. 38–41.

Maldonado, Kirk F. "Special Issues Affecting Termination of ESOPs." *Tax Management Memorandum*, August 23, 1993, pp. 247–56.

Mano, Ronald M., E. DeVon Depe, and Jerry L. Jorgensen. "The ESOP Fable: ESOPs and Pre-ERISA Problems." *Ohio CPA Journal*, February 1993, pp. 9–12.

May, Richard C., Robert L. McDonald, and Brad Van Horn. "Valuation Issues in Leveraged ESOPs." *Journal of Employee Ownership Law and Finance*, Summer 1994, pp. 61–82.

McBreen, Maura Ann. "Retirement Plan Investments in Company Stock." *Journal of Corporate Taxation*, Spring 1993, pp. 87–93.

Merton, William W. "How to Sell Stock to ESOP Tax-Free." *Business Valuation Update Online*, http://www.nvst.com/bvu.

Mueller, Susan L., and Judith C. Gehr. "Valuation Issues in Multi-Investor ESOP LBOs." *Journal of Employee Ownership Law and Finance*, Winter 1995, pp. 27–46.

Murphy, John W., and John P. Murphy. "An Introduction to ESOP Valuation." *Journal of Employee Ownership Law and Finance*, Winter 1995, pp. 3–26.

Napier, Brian T. "Valuation for ESOP Purposes" (Chapter 36). In *Handbook of Business Valuation,* Thomas L. West and Jeffrey D. Jones, eds. New York: John Wiley & Sons, 1992, pp. 389–401.

Paone, Louis A., and Donna J. Walker. "ESOP Case Law–Valuation." *Journal of Employee Ownership Law and Finance*, Spring 1992, pp. 37–60.

Pratt, Shannon P. "Court Cases Involving ESOP Valuation Issues." *Journal of Pension Planning & Compliance*, Fall 1990, pp. 245–60.

Reilly, Robert F. "Current Issues in the Valuation of ESOP-Owned Securities." *Journal of Pension Planning & Compliance*, Winter 1996, pp. 47–60.

_____. "ESOPs are Becoming Popular Financial Planing Tools." *Trusts & Estates*, February 1990, pp. 22–24.

_____. "An Overview of ESOP Case Law." *Journal of Employee Ownership law and Finance*, Spring 1992, pp. 3–10.

_____. "Performing ESOP Valuations that Meet Tough Tests." *Mergers & Acquisitions*, March/April 1994, pp. 27–33.

Rosen, Corey. "A Primer on Leveraged ESOPs." *Journal of Employee Ownership Law and Finance*, Summer 1994, pp. 3–22.

Ryterband, Daniel J. "The Decision to Implement ESOPL Strategies and Economic Considerations." *Employee Benefits Journal*, December 1991, pp. 19–25.

Searfoss, D. Gerald, and Dionne D. NcNamee. "Employers' Accounting for Employee Stock Ownership Plans." *Journal of Accountancy*, February 1993, pp. 53–60.

Schendt, Thomas G., H. Douglas Hinson, and David A. Benoit. "Use of Experts: Implications of *Howard v. Shay* for Fiduciary Duties in ESOP Transactions." *Journal of Pension Planning & Compliance*, Summer 1997, pp. 64–87.

Szabo, Joan C. "Using ESOPs to Sell Your Firm." *Nation's Business*, January 1991, pp. 59–60.

Theisen, Barbara A., and Robert T. Kleiman. "Employee Stock Ownership Plans: The Right Choice for Closely Held Corporations?" *Tax Advisor*, January 1991, pp. 40–49.

Thomas, Paula B., and Barbara Sutton. "The AICPA Tackles ESOP Accounting: What You Need to Examine." *Journal of Corporate Accounting & Finance*, Winter 1993/1994, pp. 255–63.

Urcinoli, Arthur. "A Piece of the Pie." *Executive Female*, May–June 1991, p. 72.

Vosti, Curtis. "The Haunting Side of ESOPs." *Pensions & Investments*, March 2, 1992, p. 30.

Wagner, William J. "ESOPs and Chapter 14 Valuation Rules." *Taxline*, April 1993, pp. 5–6.

Walter, Ira S. "Using Incentive Compensation to Create Shareholder Value." *Journal of Compensation & Benefits*, January–February 1992, pp. 40–45.

"What's It Worth?" *Employee Ownership Report* (official newsletter of the National Center for Employee Ownership), March/April 1991, p. 9.

Willlens, Robert W. "ESOPs Provide Unique Tax Benefits." *Journal of Accountancy*, June 1994, pp. 28–29.

Wise, Richard M., Line Racette, and Perry Phillips. "ESOPs Change the Rules." *CA Magazine*, September 1992, pp. 28–33.

Wood, Robert W. "ESOP Stock Sales May Incur Gift Tax Liability." *Taxation of Mergers & Acquisitions*, February 1992, pp. 24–27.

Wynne, Kevin C. "The Forgotten Fiduciary Duty of ESOP Trustees." *Journal of Compensation & Benefits*, September–October 1991, pp. 34–40.

Books

Blasi, Joseph R. *Employee Ownership: Revolution or Ripoff?* Cambridge, MA: Ballinger, 1988.

Blasi, Joseph R., and Douglas Lynn Kruse. *The New Owners: The Mass Emergence of Employee Ownership in Public Companies and What It Means to American Business.* New York: HarperCollins, 1991.

Braun, Warren L. *On the Way to Successful Employee Stock Ownership.* Harrisonburg, VA: Dr. Warren L. Braun, P.E., 1992.

Employee Benefit Plans in Mergers and Acquisitions. Chicago: American Bar Association, 1987.

Frisch, Robert A. *The ESOP Handbook: Practical Strategies for Achieving Corporate Financing Goals.* New York: John Wiley & Sons, 1995.

_____. *The Magic of ESOPs and LBOs.* New York: Farnsworth Publishing Co., 1985.

Kalish, Gerald I., ed. *ESOPs: The Handbook of Employee Stock Ownership Plans.* Burr Ridge, IL: Richard D. Irwin, 1989.

Kaplan, Jared, John E. Curtis, Jr., and Gregory K. Brown. *ESOPs (Tax Management Portfolio),* Washington, DC: Tax Management Inc., 1991.

Manson, Veronica. *International Employee Stock Ownership Plans (ESOPs) for Multinational Corporations.* Oakland, CA: National Center for Employee Ownership, 1993.

McWhirter, Darien A. *Sharing Ownership: The Business Manager's Guide to ESOPs & Other Ownership Incentive Plans.* New York: John Wiley & Sons, 1993.

Quarrey, Michael. *Employee Ownership and Corporate Performance.* Oakland, CA: National Center for Employee Ownership, 1986.

Quarrey, Michael, Joseph R. Blasi,and Corey Rosen. *Taking Stock: Employee Ownership at Work*. Cambridge, MA: Harper Business Publications, 1986.

Rosen, Corey, Katherine J. Klein, and Karen M. Young. *Employee Ownership in America: The Equity Solution*. Lexington, MA: Lexington Books, 1986.

Smiley, Robert W. Jr., Ronald J. Gilbert, and David M. Binns. *Employee Stock Ownership Plans*, 1997 Yearbook. New York: Warren, Gorham & Lamont, 1997 (updated annually).

Valuing ESOP Shares, rev. ed. Washington, DC: The ESOP Association, 1994.

Young, Karen M., ed. *The Expanding Role of ESOPs in Public Companies*. New York: Quorum Books, 1990.

Chapter 40

Corporate and Partnership Buyouts and Dissolutions

Two of the important reasons that owners need to know the value of their closely held business are (1) for corporate or partnership dissolution purposes and (2) for buyout purposes. Dissolutions and buyouts can be voluntary or involuntary. When these events take place, the business owner should recognize some of the specific factors that affect the value of the company.

There are numerous circumstances in which dissolutions and buyouts take place. Each of these situations is unique and specific to the nature of the case and to the property involved in the action. Several examples of such circumstances are unsolicited offers to buy a business interest, corporate tender offers, bankruptcy, eminent domain, property damage, infringement, squeeze-out transactions, and breach of contract.

This chapter discusses some of the important factors affecting the value of a business that is the subject of a voluntary or involuntary dissolution or of a buyout. These important factors include the purpose and objective of the appraisal, the appropriate standard (or definition) of value, the appropriate premise of value, the actual valuation approaches and methods used, and the presentation of the appraisal work product.

Of course, the standard of value used and the valuation procedures performed will be directly influenced by the statutory authority, judicial precedent, and administrative rulings of the jurisdiction in which the dissolution or buyout is taking place.

Buyouts

Buyouts of business interests are usually voluntary. The owner decides that the price offered is adequate—or more than adequate—in order to compensate the owner for giving up his rights of ownership. If the price offered is not considered adequate, the owner will not accept the buyout offer.

There are involuntary buyouts, however. These are often referred to as *squeeze-outs or freeze-outs*.[1] These situations often lead the shareholder to exercise his "appraisal rights." Every state provides protection to minority ownership shareholders by giving them the legal right to dissent from certain corporate actions. When a minority ownership shareholder exercises his or her right to dissent from a qualified corporate action, the corporation must purchase the stock at the judicially determined value. This appraisal remedy is available only under the specific terms and conditions of that state's statutes.

---

[1]*O'Neal's Oppression of Minority Shareholders*, 2d ed. (Deerfield, IL: Clark Boardman Callaghan, 1991, supplement May 1996), defines the term *squeeze-out* as "the use by some of the owners or participants in a business enterprise of strategic position, inside information, or powers of control, or the utilization of some legal device or technique, to eliminate from the enterprise one or more of its owners or participants." The term *freeze-out* is used as a synonym for *squeeze-out* in this text (see page 1·1–1·3).

Dissolutions

In some situations, the dissolution is voluntary. Examples include (1) a transfer of a business interest to a new owner, whereby that transfer (according to the company's bylaws) triggers the dissolution of the business and (2) a transaction that leads to the dissolution of the former organization. A transaction structure such as a cash purchase of all of the assets of a corporation often leads to (1) the dissolution of the selling corporation and (2) the distribution of any remaining assets and liabilities.

Some bankruptcy filings are voluntary to the extent they are "prepackaged." Prepackaged bankruptcies have a reorganization plan that has been agreed to by most of the company's capital holders. In these situations, the creditors have agreed to accept modifications to their original loans in order to protect a majority of their original investment.

Deprivation

When the dissolution or buyout is involuntary, it is often referred to as a "deprivation." A deprivation occurs when the owner of an asset, property, or business interest is involuntarily deprived of the ownership (or other legal or economic rights) of her property. As a result of the deprivation, the property owner is typically eligible for compensation for the economic loss suffered. The measurement of the economic loss often requires an appraisal. The appraisal may include the valuation and economic analysis of a variety of properties, such as business entities and securities, intangible assets and intellectual properties, real estate and real property interests, tangible personal property, and so forth.

Typically in a deprivation, the party subject to the deprivation loses some portion (or all) of the bundle of legal rights related to the property. The party subject to the deprivation also loses some portion (or all) of the economic value attendant to those legal rights. The party responsible for the deprivation receives some portion (or all) of the economic value attendant to those legal rights. In other words, the party being deprived is economically disadvantaged, and the party responsible for the deprivation is economically advantaged.

The typical objective of the deprivation analysis is to quantify the amount of fair and just compensation that achieves a balance between (1) the economic value lost by the party who was deprived of the bundle of rights and (2) the economic value gained by the party who succeeded to those rights. Normally, this balance is to be reached based on the circumstances affecting the parties immediately before the deprivation took place, without consideration of any of the potential subsequent consequences of the deprivation.

Perhaps the most obvious situation of deprivation is eminent domain. In an eminent domain action, the government exercises its right to take a portion of real estate from its private owner in order to achieve a "greater good" for the citizens at large (such as to widen a dangerous intersection). However, deprivation situations may involve property other than real estate, such as tangible personal property, intangible personal property, intangible real property, or an entire business or security interest.

Dissenting Shareholder Actions

In the early part of the 20th century, unanimous approval of shareholders was required before any significant corporate action could take place. This put minority shareholders in a position to veto important corporate strategic initiatives. This unanimity requirement often prevented companies (1) from establishing larger and more complex business entities and (2) from more effectively participating in the industrial revolution.

Later, in order to facilitate economic growth, state statutes permitted majority rule. In order to protect minority shareholders, dissenting shareholder statutes were enacted. These statutes provide for the minority shareholders (1) to dissent from certain corporate actions and (2) to receive the judicially determined value for their shares.

In most states, shareholders are entitled to receive *fair value* for their shares from the corporation. The various statutory definitions and legal precedents regarding the interpretation of fair value create uncertainty regarding (1) how business valuation methods should be implemented and (2) how the indications of value should be adjusted for factors such as marketability and control. The analyst should not assume there is a clear and concise definition of fair value. Rather, the analyst should seek the advice of legal counsel in the jurisdiction where the case would be heard. The specific facts and circumstances should be considered when selecting a relative level of value to assume in the analysis.

The primary arguments made by proponents of the position that a dissenting stockholder should receive a pro rata share of the marketable, control value of the company are as follows: (1) The statutory requirement that corporations purchase dissenters' shares creates the economic environment of a market, and (2) shareholders should be compensated for the compulsory nature of the transaction. The proponents of this position argue that a dissenting shareholder is required to tender, and the corporation is required to purchase, all stock held by the dissenting shareholder. Therefore, the fact that the dissenter's shares do not control the company—and are otherwise not immediately marketable—should be ignored for this purpose.

Those who proffer the position that dissenting shareholders should not receive the marketable, control value for their shares argue that these shareholders should receive the equivalent of what they give up and no more. They suggest that the purpose behind the enactment of dissenter's appraisal statutes was to compensate shareholders fully for having to sell their shares back to the corporation as if the corporate action had not taken place. They suggest that it is fair to exchange their interests for payment of fair value after applying the same discounts that the shares were subject to immediately prior to the corporate action. After all, they assert, these were the conditions under which the minority interest shareholder acquired their interest. Paying a dissenter any amount greater than that would provide the dissenter with an unintended and unfair advantage.

The facts and circumstances involved in the corporate action and the ownership characteristics of the subject block of stock are important to consider when concluding an equitable treatment of the shareholders.

Bankruptcy

In a bankruptcy appraisal, the most common value estimated is *market value*. The following subtle ambiguities in the definition of market value may affect the valuation conclusion:

- *Value on an all-cash basis or value with noncash-equivalent financing terms.* Many distressed businesses or businesses sold out of bankruptcy are sold with financing terms. If such financing terms are the norm for distressed properties or properties sold out of bankruptcy, including the effect of these terms is appropriate to ascertaining market value.
- *Value of specified property rights versus fee simple estate.* The fee simple estate may not be the bundle of rights that exists with a property in bankruptcy. If the specified rights that are transferable from the bankruptcy estate are the as-leased estate, the as-mortgaged estate, or some other interest in the real estate, these should be encompassed in market value.
- *Value as the most probable price or as the highest price.* Bankruptcy appraisal users are often concerned with the highest price the subject property will sell for, not the most probable price that the subject property may sell for, under a set of specific conditions. The highest price is often considered to be market value in a bankruptcy appraisal.
- *Value in an equilibrium market versus value in a depressed market.* Value in use as part of a going concern is not necessarily a meaningful premise of value in bankruptcy appraisals. In a bankruptcy environment, business owners, investors, and their advisors are usually concerned with the premise of value that is representative of the most likely disposition of the business and its property.

The three traditional approaches to value are the starting point for the bankruptcy appraisal. However, in a bankruptcy environment, there are several specific factors the analyst should consider regarding the application of the asset-based approach, the market approach, and the income approach.

The asset-based approach implicitly assumes that the owner can earn a fair return on the cost of the investment. But this premise is not always valid for a business in bankruptcy. In bankruptcy, the analyst should carefully identify and quantify all elements of functional obsolescence and economic obsolescence that relate to the subject assets. Functional obsolescence may be one reason why the subject business is in bankruptcy. Almost by definition, a company in bankruptcy is not generating an adequate return to its owner. This would indicate that a substantial amount of economic obsolescence may exist. In categorizing obsolescence, the appraiser should distinguish between (1) those factors that are intrinsic to the business and (2) those factors that are directly related to the current ownership of the company. The asset-based approach to value is not normally penalized due to the bankruptcy of the owner. This is because new owners and management will be the successors.

The market approach assumes willing buyers and sellers not under duress who are operating at arm's length with adequate information. These conditions are rare in bankruptcy situations. Focusing on likely buyers and on the dynamics of the distressed property market will lead the analyst to guideline company transactional data. This process may require adjustments after an analysis of guideline transactions. These adjustments may relate to (1) special financing terms and conditions, (2) the allocation of purchase price among the assets acquired, (3) granting of a noncompetition agreement as a condition of the sale, (4) commitment of third-party guarantees or concessions, and (5) any special transaction conditions imposed by the bankruptcy court or creditors' committee. The analyst should consider whether special financing terms are a characteristic of the normal market value.

The income approach requires an identifiable economic income stream. A company in bankruptcy may be generating a negative level of economic income. Identifying an economic income stream for the business should take into account any detrimental income effects associated with current inefficient or ineffective management or ownership. This assessment may filter out incremental costs (e.g., legal, accounting, administrative) and detrimental effects on value associated with the bankruptcy filing itself. After analyzing where the subject company is in its business cycle, the length of the projection period for a yield capitalization will follow. Also, in order to estimate the required direct capitalization rate or present value discount rate, the analyst should consider and quantify the risk premiums that holders of capital (both debt and equity) will require for investing in this distressed property.

In a bankruptcy environment, business owners, investors, and creditors are not so much interested in what a willing buyer would pay to a willing seller for a similar property. Rather, they are interested in the expected current selling price for the particular business in its particular market.

Standard of Value

To conduct an appraisal assignment, the analyst does not have to judgmentally decide the appropriate standard of value, premise of value, description of property subject to appraisal, or the valuation date. These fundamentals are part of the instructions given to the analyst at the outset of the project. In dissolutions and buyouts, these factors often are central to the controversy. Therefore, the analyst and the attorney must work very closely together to insure that they are properly specified within the relevant legal context.

Fair Market Value

The standard of value answers the question Value to whom? The most commonly used standard of value is fair market value. Fair market value is generally recognized to mean the amount of money that a hypothetical willing buyer would pay for a property to the hypothetical willing seller, each being knowledgeable about the property and its prospects, and neither being under duress to enter into the transaction. In voluntary, or friendly, buyout situations, fair market value is usually the standard that the parties to the transaction employ.

Analysts realize that numerous alternative standards of value can be assigned to the same property. These different standards may result in different, but valid, estimates of value. Usually, the standard of value is determined by the judicial, statutory, or regulatory authority surrounding the action that resulted in the deprivation. In the case of appraisals for corporate or partnership dissolution purposes, some judicial and statutory authorities require fair market value as the appropriate standard of value. It is more common, however, for the judicial, statutory, or regulatory authority to require fair value as the appropriate standard of value.

Fair Value

Fair value is generally considered to result in the most fair and equitable treatment of the property owner in the case of an involuntary transaction, taking, or conversion of the property. The specific definitions of fair value are as numerous as the number of court cases and governmental statutes in which the term is mentioned. However, there are a number of basic tenets universal to the concept of fair value (at least in terms of how they affect the appraisal).

In deprivation situations, a willing buyer/seller transaction is not contemplated. Generally, the "seller" is not in a position to sell the property to anyone other than the party responsible for the deprivation.

The objective of a deprivation valuation analysis is not to estimate the likely activity of a hypothetical marketplace but to restore the property owner to his economic status before the deprivation occurs. As the word *fair* implies, fair value quantifies the (fair and) just compensation to the property owner who was involuntarily deprived of the economic enjoyment of the property.

Premise of Value

In deprivation appraisals, the analyst should apply the premise of value that would have been appropriate immediately before the deprivation occurred. If the business was an operating going concern, it should be appraised under the fundamental premise of value in continued use. If the business was not a going concern, it should be appraised under a fundamental premise of value in exchange.

The analyst will select the appropriate premise of value (1) based on the purpose and objective of the appraisal and (2) based on the actual physical and functional status of the subject property. Applying an inappropriate premise of value would not achieve a fair value (meaning a balance between the opposing parties).

Summary

Dissolutions and buyouts can be voluntary or involuntary. Dissolutions and buyouts normally take place at fair market value.

An involuntary dissolution or buyout is called a deprivation. Before performing a deprivation appraisal, the analyst should understand (1) the purpose and objective of the appraisal (within the deprivation context), (2) the nature of the deprivation action, and (3) the type of property subject to the deprivation. The analyst should consider (1) the appropriate definition of value and (2) the appropriate premise of value in order to conclude the compensatory value of the subject property. Such a definition of value (and the corresponding valuation approaches and methods) will be different from the traditional hypothetical willing buyer/seller concept. Since the deprivation appraisal relates to an involuntary transaction, the analysis should conclude an economic value that represents a fair and just measure of compensation for the economic damage suffered by the deprived property owner.

Chapter 41

Marital Dissolution

In increasing numbers, attorneys and clients are turning to the expertise of valuation analysts as part of the matrimonial dissolution process. The analyst's expertise is generally required pursuant to property distribution laws. These laws are enacted by each state. Therefore, the rules and guidelines are state-specific.

A term of art employed in the matrimonial field is *marital estate*. This entity comes into being upon the filing for divorce. The marital estate represents the assets that must be divided according to the property distribution laws of the state. These assets often include ownership interests in small businesses and professional practices. Currently, each state adheres to either (1) the *community property* standard or (2) the *equitable distribution* standard with regard to the division of the assets included within the marital estate.

In states adhering to the community property standard, distributable property is referred to as community property. The community property standard is based on the premise of joint and equal ownership of the marital estate. In a community property standard state, all assets acquired during a marriage are assumed (1) to be acquired by the marital community and (2) to be owned jointly by the community. These states generally follow the practice of an equal division of the marital estate upon divorce.

However, most states follow the standard of equitable distribution. Under this concept, equitable distribution of the marital estate may mean equal distribution, or it may not. The court may make adjustments and decisions related to the allocation process based on the specific facts and circumstances.

The task of the analyst in matrimonial cases is complicated by the fact that statutes that mandate most aspects of the divorce valuation are adopted on a state-by-state basis. In addition, most statutes are general. Therefore, judicial precedent may be a determinative factor in the finer points of valuation methodology. The courts may take considerable freedom in affirming or modifying an independent opinion of value. Often, a judge may rely on spousal maintenance remedies to compensate for any perceived inequity resulting from the marital estate valuation. As a result, fundamental valuation issues are more nebulous in marital dissolution matters than in other areas of valuation practice.

Standard of Value

The key to defining the scope of any valuation engagement is the definition of the standard of value to be adopted in the appraisal. However, in marital dissolution proceedings, virtually all state statutes are silent with regard to the standard of value. And judicial precedent is often contradictory as to the appropriate standard of value. Therefore, it is incumbent on the analyst to review the judicial precedent in the state in which the divorce is taking place. In general, however, the standards of value adopted by the family law courts are *fair market value*, *intrinsic value*, and *investment value*.

Many states have adopted fair market value as the relevant standard of value. Fair market value is based on the price that would be negotiated between an informed hypothetical buyer and an informed hypothetical seller, as discussed in Chapter 3. The fair market value concept is more thoroughly defined in Internal Revenue Service Revenue Ruling 59-60. The appraiser should be aware, however, that many marital dissolution decisions *say* fair market value but then appear to depart from that standard in reaching their value conclusion.

Intrinsic value is a concept of value based on the fundamental or real value of the asset. Intrinsic value assumes a higher level of insight and knowledge about the asset than a typical investor may possess. For example, for a publicly traded company, the intrinsic value would represent someone's estimate of the "true" value of the stock of the company versus the published stock price.

Investment value is a value standard that may be appropriate in certain circumstances. Investment value is the value of a small business (or business interest) or a professional practice to a specific owner. Unlike the fair market value standard, this standard considers (1) the specific owner's expectation of risks, (2) the potential synergy associated with ownership of the subject business, and (3) the specific earnings expectations resulting from the subject ownership.

Valuation Date

Selecting the appropriate valuation date is a critical step in the valuation process. In a marital dissolution valuation, relevant state-specific statutory authority and judicial precedent sometimes specifies the appropriate valuation date or dates. In many instances, however, the appropriate valuation date is unclear based on the state-specific judicial precedent. Accordingly, the appropriate valuation date for the ownership interest included in the marital estate is a question most appropriately answered by legal counsel, not by the valuation analyst.

Based on judicial precedent in numerous states and jurisdictions throughout the country, and based on the specific circumstances of the particular marital dissolution, the valuation date is generally one or more of the following dates:

1. The date of marriage.
2. The date of separation.
3. The date of filing.
4. The date of the trial.

Since the selection of the appropriate valuation date can impact the value of the subject business, it is important that the attorney instruct the analyst regarding the applicable valuation date (or dates) early in the valuation process. However, the appraiser may have to go to court prepared to testify as to the value on several different dates if the court does not address that issue beforehand.[1]

Discovery

There are often obstacles in the discovery process for the analyst in a divorce proceeding. In the case where the analyst is working for a nonowner spouse, information regarding the subject small business or professional practice may be difficult to obtain. Also, the owner spouse may not readily share strategic and financial information with the analyst.

In these cases, it is advisable for the analyst to prepare a comprehensive data and document request to give to the client or to the client's attorney. Often, it is difficult to add to or amend an initial document request. Therefore, the analyst is advised to prepare as comprehensive a document request list as possible for submission. Exhibit 44-3 (in Chapter 44) presents a checklist that may be useful to practitioners in preparing a document request. Some of these documents may be accessible from the subject company's accountants, attorneys, or bankers.

Valuation Methods

As noted previously, the courts often take considerable latitude in their reliance on valuation methods and value conclusions. This situation makes it even more important for the analyst to consider any applicable state statutes and relevant judicial precedent when concluding which valuation approaches and methods are most appropriate.

The methods used for the valuation of small businesses and professional practices for marital dissolution purposes fall within three general categories: the income approach, the market approach, and the asset-based approach. In addition, courts may recognize the use of hybrid methods. Within each of these approaches, are specific methods that have had acceptance in the various states.

Income Approach

The commonly used income approach valuation methods (especially for valuing operating companies) are the discounted cash flow method and the capitalization of earnings method. The trend in many family law

---

[1]The date of valuation is a frequent issue. See, for example, *Else* v. *Else*, No. A-95-488, 1997 WL 22615 (Neb. App. Jan. 14, 1997), where the appellate court decided that the trial court erred by using the date of trial rather than the date of separation. See also *Quillen* v. *Quillen*, No. 29502-9608-CV-531, Sup. Ct. Ind. (Aug. 6, 1996), where the court decided the date should be *before* the husband lost financing capacity for his construction company because of sex offences against his daughter since he brought it on himself.

courts is to emphasize income approach methods more than asset-based approach and market approach methods of valuation.

The capitalized economic income method (discussed in Chapter 15) is one of the more frequently used methods in marital dissolution valuations.[2] However, recent family law court cases have indicated that the courts are turning more frequently to other valuation methods. This is because these other methods (such as the discounted cash flow method) have achieved wide acceptance in the valuation community at large.

In the capitalized economic income method, the value of the company is estimated by dividing the expected economic income of a company by an appropriate direct capitalization rate. If the economic income measure is net cash flow, this direct capitalization rate is generally equal to the present value discount rate less the expected long-term growth rate for the cash flow stream.

In the discounted cash flow method (one version of the discounted economic income method, discussed in Chapter 14), the value of a company is based on the present value of the future economic income (measured as cash flow), discounted at a yield capitalization rate appropriate to the level of risk associated with an investment in the subject company. This valuation method is gaining more widespread acceptance by the family law courts.[3]

Market Approach

The market approach valuation methods rely on prices paid for guideline publicly traded companies (discussed in Chapter 16) or for guideline acquired companies (discussed in Chapter 18) as the basis for estimating the value of a small business or professional practice. The multiple of discretionary earnings method (Chapter 19) and the multiple of gross revenue method (Chapter 20) are other market-approach methods used. The market-approach methods are used somewhat less frequently than other valuation methods, especially in the valuation of smaller enterprises or professional practices, because of the lack of an active market for spousal interests in a privately held company.

Asset-Based Approach

Asset-based approach methods (discussed in Chapters 22 and 23) are often recognized by courts in marital dissolution valuations. These methods rely on the adjusted balance sheet of the subject company in order to estimate the value of the subject ownership interest in the subject company. This method, although widely used, is often incorrectly performed.

---

[2]See, for example, *DeLucia* v. *DeLucia*, No. FA 950249319S, 1997 WL 16832, Conn. Super. Ct. (Jan. 10, 1997), and *Giuliani* v. *Giuliani*, No. CA 930526886S, 1996 WL 409324, Conn. Super. Ct. (June 19, 1996).

[3]See, for example, *Guiffre* v. *Baker*, No. 95-G-1904, 1996 WL 535254, Ohio Ct. App. 11th Dist. (Aug. 30, 1996), and *Sergi* v. *Sergi*, No. 17476, 1996 WL 425914, Ohio Ct. App. 9th Dist. (July 31, 1996). In both these cases, the courts rejected the excess earnings method and accepted the discounted cash flow method.

Often—and inappropriately—the net book value of the business assets less the book value of the liabilities is used to value the subject ownership interest. Rather, an asset-based method should be used to value the subject ownership interest by appraising all of the assets and all of the liabilities of the subject business. This appraisal should include adjustments for off-balance-sheet items as well. Such items may include unrecorded liabilities, unrecorded intangible assets, and unrecorded (or nonoperating) assets. The net difference in the value of all of the assets and all of the liabilities will indicate the value of the subject business equity. Adjustments to that business value in order to appraise the subject ownership interest will depend on the individual facts and circumstances.

Another asset-based method that is used in marital dissolution valuations is the *capitalized excess earnings method* (see Chapter 23). Although this method is sometimes disparaged in valuation texts, it remains a common valuation method in analyses performed for marital dissolution purposes.

Under this method, the value of the subject business is the sum of the value of the tangible assets and the intangible assets less the value of the outstanding liabilities. The method takes its name from the fact that the intangible asset value is estimated based on the direct capitalization of the economic income earned by the business in excess of a fair return on its tangible assets.

Other valuation methods have been used in divorce cases. However, the above paragraphs describe the most common valuation methods. The selection of the appropriate valuation method will depend on the facts and circumstances of the particular case. However, the latitude afforded judges in the divorce process should persuade the analyst to adopt more than one valuation method—in order to provide mutually supportive evidence as to the valuation conclusion.

In general, once the valuation method has been selected, implementing it in the divorce context is similar to implementing it outside of the divorce context. However, certain issues are dealt with differently or assume unique significance in a divorce proceeding.

Goodwill

One issue of particular significance to the marital dissolution valuation is the consideration of intangible value in the nature of goodwill. In general, goodwill is defined as the ability to earn a rate of return in excess of a normal rate of return on the net assets of the business. In marital dissolution cases, this goodwill may require allocation between two types of goodwill: (1) institutional (or practice) goodwill and (2) professional (or personal) goodwill. Professional or personal goodwill may be described as the intangible value attributable solely to the efforts of or reputation of an owner spouse of the subject business. Institutional or practice goodwill may be described as the intangible value that would continue to inure to the small business or professional practice without the presence of that specific owner spouse.

As with many matters related to divorce valuations, the consideration of goodwill varies between states. In general, the various judicial precedent follow one of three positions regarding the consideration of goodwill:

1. Goodwill is never a distributable marital asset.
2. Institutional or practice goodwill *only* is a distributable marital asset.
3. All intangible value in the nature of goodwill (both personal and practice goodwill) related to the small business or professional practice is distributable.

The analyst should consult the attorney regarding the appropriate treatment of goodwill early in the assignment. This consultation procedure should be performed in order to determine what information should be requested and what valuation methods should be used. The appraiser also should carefully study the relevant case law. There are literally hundreds of cases dealing with goodwill as a marital asset (far too many to cite here).[4]

Compensation

Another area in which the analyst may perform procedures of particular significance to the marital dissolution assignment is in the area of adequate compensation. In certain cases, the court may want to establish whether or not the amount paid to an owner spouse in salary and benefits has adequately compensated the marital estate for the owner spouse's efforts. This issue usually arises in the case of a spouse who is the owner of a business that is arguably a nonmarital asset. Using "marital income" that is not paid in the form of compensation may be considered an investment in the nonmarital asset. An attorney may want to discern whether the value of a nonmarital business has been enhanced because the owner spouse has not withdrawn adequate compensation from the company. This issue could trigger some argument as to the extent of the exclusion of the enterprise from the marital estate. Thus, the analyst in a valuation for divorce purposes should be familiar with compensation issues and with sources of information regarding reasonable compensation.

---

[4]See, for example, *Potter v. Potter*, No. 36005-1-I, 1996 WL 511050, Wash. Ct. App. (Sept. 9, 1996), which addresses factors to consider in valuing personal goodwill, and *Alsup v. Alsup*, No. 01A01-9509-CH-00404, 1996 WL 411640, Tenn. Ct. App. (July 24, 1996); *Skrabak v. Skrabak*, No. 674, 1996 WL 143345, Md. Ct. App. (Mar. 28, 1996); and *Utter v. Utter*, No. A-94-984, 1996 WL 169911, Neb. Ct. App. (Apr. 9, 1996), which reject the inclusion of personal goodwill.

Noncompete Covenants

Noncompete covenants require special attention in a marital dissolution proceeding. If the sale of the marital asset business occurs, a noncompete covenant may be required of the owner spouse. This issue may trigger argument over whether the value of the proceeds attributable to the noncompete covenant are part of the marital estate. In addition, in the case of a jointly owned business, one spouse may be required to buy out the other—and some form of a noncompete agreement could be required. The value assigned to this noncompete agreement may have special significance in the divorce valuation.

Generally speaking, the value of the noncompete covenant would *not* be a marital asset because it restricts the postmarital activity of the spouse. However, the covenant may need to be valued to ascertain whether the amount allocated to it is the fair market value of the covenant.[5]

Valuation Discounts and Premiums

The applicability of valuation discounts and premiums offers further challenges in a marital dissolution valuation. The size of valuation discounts and premiums is often a matter of informed professional judgment on the part of the analyst. The situations in which discounts and premiums are applicable—and the reasonable range of these valuation adjustments—are fairly well addressed within most legal contexts, such as federal income, gift, and estate tax and ESOP transactions. In a valuation for divorce, however, the state-specific nature of the statutes and judicial precedent encourage the analyst to become familiar with both (1) the types of valuation adjustments and (2) the circumstances under which each has been accepted within each state. The analyst should form an independent opinion regarding the appropriate application of discounts and premiums. This includes valuation adjustments that are fairly common, such as the discount for lack of marketability, the discount for lack of ownership control or the ownership control premium, and the discount for key person dependence.

Capital Gains Tax

Another issue that may be important in the marital dissolution analysis is the inclusion of the capital gains tax effect with regard to the value conclusion. This influence is often considered in the valuation of busi-

---

[5]See, for example, *In re Marriage of Monaghan*, 899 P2d 841 (Wash. App. Aug. 9, 1995) and *Sweere* v. *Gilbert-Sweere*, 534 NW2d 294 (Minn. App. July 18, 1995).

ness ownership interests using asset-based methods. This influence is intended to reflect the contingent tax liability for the unrealized capital gains on appreciated business assets. In concluding whether this adjustment is appropriate, it is noteworthy that the repeal of the General Utilities doctrine (by the Tax Reform Act of 1986) makes it virtually impossible for a corporation to sell or distribute appreciated assets without incurring a taxable gain.

In marital dissolution proceedings, however, courts have generally found that consideration of tax consequences is appropriate only (1) when the tax liability is imminent or (2) when the tax will arise directly from the court's property disposition. In situations where there is some speculation as to when (or if) the assets will be sold and the magnitude of the associated tax liability, family law courts have generally found that it is inappropriate to consider the tax consequences related to the sale.[6] However, it often falls to the analyst to determine—and to defend—an independent opinion regarding the appropriate consideration of capital gains taxes.

The Role of the Analyst

The valuation of small businesses and professional practices for marital dissolution purposes is a complex and challenging task due to the diverse jurisdictions and unique issues in these cases. In addition, the analyst in a divorce engagement may often assume an expanded role. In addition to performing a valuation, the analyst may often assume a more forensic accounting or forensic economics role, by assisting attorneys in identifying distributable assets and tracing their origins. The valuation process may require the analysis of the flow of financial resources into and out of the subject business enterprise. However, in some instances, the appraiser will defer such investigative analysis to a forensic accountant.

Since many divorce valuations are performed within a litigation environment, the analyst should function effectively and should offer several services to legal counsel. These services should begin with assisting counsel in the discovery process. In addition, the analyst may be asked to analyze and evaluate settlement offers that occur frequently during the marital dissolution process. In this capacity, the analyst would be called upon to evaluate the reasonableness of a settlement offer in light of the value or estimated value of the assets in the marital estate.

As with most litigation support assignments, the analyst may be called upon to assist legal counsel in the deposition and subsequent examination of opposing experts. This may involve assessing the strengths and weaknesses of the opposing expert's position in terms of both factual interpretation and valuation methodology.

---

[6]See, for example, *In re the Marriage of Hay*, No. 14368-6-111, 1995 WL 757772, Wash. Ct. App. (Dec. 26, 1995).

Most importantly, the analyst should present his or her opinions credibly and persuasively in deposition and in testimony. The analyst should be able to effectively explain complicated financial issues to a judge or attorney whose expertise is not accounting or finance. The analyst should be experienced in the application of valuation procedures within a contrarian environment.

We cannot stress enough the importance of the expert and the attorney working together to build an adequate record at trial. On appeal, courts look to the question of whether or not the lower court had adequate evidence on which to base its decision. If so, the decision normally is upheld. If not, the decision often is remanded for further proceedings.[7]

Summary

The applicable standard of value is generally less clear in the context of marital dissolution than for practically any other appraisal purpose. The expert needs to study the relevant case law and interpret it from a valuation point of view. Often, family law courts lean toward *investment value* (value to the particular spouse), even though they may use the phrase *fair market value*.

The date of valuation is critical, and the expert may have to prepare valuations for more than one effective date. However, sometimes the court will bifurcate the matter and rule on the valuation date ahead of the trial addressing the property settlement.

Methodology varies greatly, with much discretion on the part of the court. Family law courts gradually are moving toward acceptance of methods typically used in the financial community, such as discounted cash flow.

Owners' compensation adjustments often are a major issue. Treatment of goodwill varies greatly from state to state, with some recognizing only practice (or institutional) goodwill as a marital asset, while others recognize all goodwill as a marital asset, even though it may be entirely personal in nature.

The role of the appraiser is critical. It is important to bring in a competent, experienced appraiser at the outset and to have the appraiser involved at every step. It is essential for the attorney and appraiser to work together to build a complete evidentiary record at trial that will be upheld in case of an appeal.

---

[7]See, for example, *Crosetto v. Crosetto*, No. 17911-3-11, 1996 WL 389337, Wash. Ct. App. (July 12, 1996), remanded for lack of an adequate trial court record.

Bibliography

Articles

Brandes, Joel R., and Carole L. Weidman. "Valuation of a Professional License." *New York Law Journal*, December 24, 1996, pp. 3–5.

Broeker, H. W. "Cross-Examination of a Business Valuation Expert Witness." *American Journal of Family Law*, Fall 1989, pp. 213–21.

Brown, Ronald L., ed. "Valuing and Distributing Businesses." Chapter 10 in *Encyclopedia of Matrimonial Practices*. 2d ed. Englewood Cliffs. NJ: Prentice-Hall Law and Business, 1991, pp. 637–856.

Cenker, William J., and Carl J. Monastra. "The Basics of Business Valuation in Divorce Settlements." *Practical Accountant*, January 1991, pp. 18–26.

Chiefetz, Carl B. "Direct Testimony of the Accounting Expert." *FAIR$HARE: The Matrimonial Law Monthly*, May 1990, pp. 3–5.

Cohen, Harriet N., and Patricia Hennessey. "Valuation of Property in Marital Dissolutions." *Family Law Quarterly*, September 1989, pp. 339–81.

Cohen, Robert S., and Arthur H. Rosenbloom. "The Whole May Be Worth Less Than the Sum of Its Parts." *New York Law Journal*, December 18, 1995, pp. 1–4.

Connell, John R., and William H. Vincent. "Valuing Pension Benefits in Divorce: Look before You Leap." *Journal of Accountancy*, January 1994, pp. 98–100.

Cowhey, Gregory J., Lester Barenbaum, and Sandra R. Klevan. "Putting a Price Tag on the Company." *Family Advocate*, Spring 1995, pp. 44–52.

Dennis, Stephen G. "Selecting and Using a Financial Expert in Dissolution Practice." *Family Law Quarterly*, Spring 1992, pp. 17–25.

Felder, Myrna. "A Blueprint for a 'McSparron' Evaluation." *New York Law Journal*, October 29, 1996, pp. 3–5.

Feder, Robert D. "Direct Examination of a Business Appraiser in a Divorce Action." *American Journal of Family Law*, Spring 1993, pp. 1–11.

Field, Harold G. "Direct Examination of a Business Valuator." *American Journal of Family Law*, Fall 1989, pp. 223–32.

Fishman, Jay E., Shannon P. Pratt, et al. "Premiums and Discounts in Business Valuation." *FAIR$HARE: The Matrimonial Law Monthly*, June 1992, pp. 14–16.

Gitlin, Gunnar J. "Business Valuation in Divorce—What Is Double-Dipping and How Is it Quantified?" *American Journal of Family Law*, Summer 1997, pp. 109–18.

Goodman, Beverly. "Appraisers Find Band of Gold in Dissolving Ties That Bind." *Accounting Today*, August 7, 1995, pp. 3–4.

Goodman, Stanley L. "The Three Big Issues in Business and Professional Practice Valuation." *FAIR$HARE: The Matrimonial Law Monthly*, April 1996, pp. 2–3.

Jimmerson, James J. "Celebrity Goodwill: Is it Real or Is it a Mirage?" *American Journal of Family Law*, Summer 1997, pp. 145–51.

Kendig, Robert E. "Discovery Issues in Valuation Cases." *American Journal of Family Law*, Spring 1992, pp. 55–74.

Kinser, Katherine A. "Practical Approaches to the Presentation of Business Values in Divorce." *FAIR\$HARE: The Matrimonial Law Monthly*, August 1992, pp. 3–5.

Klein, Ronald. "The Role of the Expert in Divorce Valuation." *FAIR\$HARE: The Matrimonial Law Monthly*, May 1986, pp. 3–6.

Krauskopf, Joan. "Compensation for Supporting the Student Spouse." Chapter 17 in *Valuing Professional Practices and Licenses: A Guide for the Matrimonial Practitioner*. 2d ed. Ronald L. Brown, ed. Englewood Cliffs, NJ: Prentice-Hall Law & Business, 1996, pp. 17·1–17·5.

Lieber, Frederick E. "Adjusting the Income Statement in Business Valuations." *FAIR\$HARE: The Matrimonial Law Monthly*, November 1992, pp. 3–5.

Mastracchio, James N, and Nicholas J. Mastracchio. "Professional License Value in a Divorce." *CPA Journal*, December 1996, pp. 34–39+.

Mitchell, Marvin. "Cross-Examining an Opponent's Business Valuation Expert." *FAIR\$HARE: The Matrimonial Law Monthly*, May 1990, pp. 13–19.

Oldham, J. Thomas. "The Closely Held Business." Chapter 10 in *Divorce, Separation and the Distribution of Property*. New York: Law Journal Seminars Press, 1996, pp. 10·1–10·51.

Person, Stanley. "Reasonable Compensation." *Journal of Accountancy*, October 1995, pp. 37, 127.

Pia, Kenneth J. "Who Is Qualified to Value a Business?" *Family Advocate*, Spring 1995, pp. 22–24.

Pratt, Shannon P. "What Is Value?" *Family Advocate*, Spring 1995, pp. 28–33.

Raymond, Richard. "A Biased Valuation: The Treatment of a Professional Degree in Divorce Actions." *American Journal of Economics and Sociology*, July 1995, pp. 268–87.

Reilly, Robert F. "The Differences in Valuing Big and Small Businesses for Divorce." *FAIR\$HARE: The Matrimonial Law Monthly*, September 1995, pp. 3–8.

_____. "The Identification and Qualifications of Business Valuation Discounts and Premia." *FAIR\$HARE: The Matrimonial Law Monthly*, July 1996, pp. 2–5.

Riesebell, H.F. "Divorce of a Closely Held Business Owner." *FAIR\$HARE: The Matrimonial Law Monthly*, May 1992, pp. 3–8.

Rooney, David A. "Divorce Taxation Update." *Business Valuation Update Outline*, http://www.nvst.com/bvu, orginally presented at AICPA Business Valuation Conference, November 1997.

Skoloff, Gary N., and Cary B. Cheifetz. "Direct Examination of Marital Property Valuation Experts." *The Practical Litigator*, May 1992, p. 25.

Shayne, Mark. "The Role of the Business Valuator in Marital and Family Business Litigation," *American Journal of Family Law*, Fall 1991, pp. 239–49.

Shenkman, Martin M. "When Should Professional Goodwill Be Valued?" *The Matrimonial Strategist*, March 1997, pp. 1–3.

Sziklay, Barry S. "Divorce Valuation." *Business Valuation Update Online*, originally presented at AICPA Business Valuation Conference, November 1997.

Trugman, Gary R. "An Appraiser's Approach to Business Valuation." Parts I and II. *FAIR$HARE: The Matrimonial Law Monthly*, July 1991, pp. 3–8 and August 1991, pp. 8–13.

Weinstein, Jeffrey P. "The Use and Abuse of Economic Experts in Divorce Litigation." *FAIR$HARE: The Matrimonial Law Monthly*, February 1995, pp. 3–6.

Books

Barson, Kalman A. *Investigative Accounting in Divorce.* New York: John Wiley & Sons, 1996.

Bateman, Tracy A. Annotation. *Divorce and Separation Consideration of Tax Consequences in Distribution of Marital Property*, 9 A.L.R. 5th (1993).

Brown, Ronald L., ed. *Valuing Professional Practices and Licenses: A Guide for the Matrimonial Practitioner*, 2d ed. Englewood Cliffs, NJ: Prentice-Hall Law and Business, 1996.

Executive Compensation. Alexandria, VA: National Institute of Business Management, June 1995.

Feder, Robert D. *Valuation Strategies in Divorce,* 4th ed. New York,: John Wiley & Sons, 1997.

Fishman, Jay E., Shannon P. Pratt, J. Clifford Griffith, and D. Keith Wilson. *Guide to Business Valuations*, 7th ed. Fort Worth, TX: Practitioners Publishing Company, 1997.

Goldberg, Barth H. *Valuation of Divorce Assets.* St. Paul: West Publishing Company, 1984.

Goldberg, Barth H. and Joseph N. DuCanto. *Valuation of Divorce Assets*, 1994 Supplement. St. Paul: West Publishing Company, 1994.

Kleeman, Robert E., ed. *Valuation Strategies in Divorce*, 2d ed. New York: John Wiley & Sons, 1992.

Meltzer, Stanton L., David A. Rooney, et al. *Guide to Divorce Engagements*, 6th ed. Fort Worth: Practitioners Publishing Company, 1997.

Moriarty, Robert B., and David J. Zaumeyer. *The Valuation Expert in Divorce Litigation: A Handbook for Attorneys and Accountants.* New York: American Bar Association, 1992.

Oldfather, Ann, Janice E. Kosel, et al. *Valuation and Distribution of Marital Property.* New York: Matthew Bender & Co., January 1996.

Orenstein, Theodore P., and Gary N. Skoloff. *When a Professional Divorces: Strategies for Valuing Practices, Licenses, and Degrees,* 2d ed. Chicago: American Bar Association, 1994.

Periodicals

American Journal of Family Law, quarterly. John Wiley & Sons, 1320 Edgewood Drive, Altoona, WI 54720, (715) 835-3338.

CPA Litigation Services Counselor, monthly. Harcourt Brace Professional Publishing, 6277 Sea Harbor Drive, Orlando, FL 32887, (800) 831-7799.

Fair$hare: The Matrimonial Law Monthly, monthly. Aspen Law & Business, 7201 McKinney Circle, Frederick, MD 21704, (800) 901-9075.

Family Advocate, quarterly. American Bar Association, PO Box 10892, Chicago, IL 60610, (312) 988-5522.

The Matrimonial Strategist, monthly. Leader Publications, 345 Park Avenue South, New York, NY 10010, (800) 888-8300.

Shannon Pratt's Business Valuation Update, monthly. Business Valuation Resources, 4475 S.W. Scholls Ferry Road, Suite 101, Portland, OR 97225, (888) BUS-VALU.

Part VI

Topics Related to Valuation

Chapter 42

Valuing Intangible Assets

This chapter will discuss the identification and valuation of intangible assets and intellectual properties. We discussed valuation of an assemblage of intangible assets (all intangible assets as a group) as part of the appraisal of a small business or professional practice in Chapter 23, The Capitalized Excess Earnings Method. This chapter focuses on the valuation of a single intangible asset (or of a portfolio of intangible assets) appraised separately and independently from the ownership of a small business or professional practice.

It is important to emphasize that these concepts will be developed within our overall framework of small businesses and professional practices. As we will see, there are numerous reasons why the intangible assets of a small business may be analyzed. Certainly, the existence and value of the intangible assets is an important consideration with regard to the valuation of any small business or professional practice. And the identification and valuation of individual intangible assets is an integral part of the asset accumulation method to the valuation of small businesses and professional practices.

The subject of this book is the valuation of small businesses and professional practices. Therefore, we will not present a comprehensive treatise on intangible asset valuation. However, the basics of intangible asset analysis will be developed adequately to allow for the valuation of the typical small business. The technical development of some of the more esoteric issues regarding intangible asset analysis (e.g., the quantification of the remaining useful life of specific intangibles) is reserved for other books (see the bibliography at the end of this chapter).

In terms of the outline of this chapter, we will first discuss the fundamentals of any appraisal of the intangible assets related to small businesses and professional practices. Second, we will discuss the legal and economic attributes associated with the identification of the existence of intangible assets. Third, we will discuss the three generally accepted analytical approaches with regard to the valuation of intangible assets and intellectual properties. Finally, we will discuss general concepts regarding the remaining useful life analysis of intangible assets. We will also explain the impact of the remaining useful life analysis on the estimation of intangible asset value.

Fundamentals of the Appraisal

Before conducting an appraisal of intangible assets, the analyst should document certain fundamental issues regarding the valuation assignment. This documentation should be in writing and should be clear and complete with regard to each fundamental issue. This documentation should be agreed upon by the analyst and the client before the analyst begins any quantitative or qualitative valuation analyses.

The documentation of an intangible asset valuation assignment includes the following:

1. A detailed description of the intangible assets subject to analysis.
2. A description of the specific bundle of legal rights of intangible asset ownership subject to analysis.
3. A specification of the valuation "as of" date.
4. A description of the definition of value—or standard of value—that is being estimated.
5. A description of the premise of value under which the subject intangible assets are being analyzed.
6. The audience for the valuation report and the use to which the valuation is to be put.

Exhibit 42-1 presents a listing and description of the alternative premises of value with respect to the analysis of intangible assets. The premise of value is the set of transactional circumstances in which the buyer will interact with the seller with regard to the subject intangible assets. The premise of value answers the question: "In what type of market transaction will these two willing parties interact?" The selection of the appropriate premise of value is usually a function of the highest and best use of the subject intangible assets. In other words, the conclusion as to the highest and best use of the subject intangible assets typically will dictate the appropriate premise of value to use in the analysis.

The statement of the objective of an intangible asset valuation answers the following questions:

1. What particular intangible assets are the subject of the appraisal?
2. With which particular legal and ownership rights are the subject intangible assets associated?
3. What is the effective valuation date?
4. To whom are we estimating the value of the subject intangible assets?
5. How, or under what set of transactional conditions, will the transfer of ownership of the assets take place?
6. For what use will the valuation be valid?

There are numerous individual reasons for conducting an intangible asset analysis. However, all of these individual reasons may be grouped into the following categories of client motivations:

1. Transaction pricing and structuring, for either the sale or the license (i.e., transfer pricing) of intangible assets.
2. Financing securitization and collateralization, for both cash flow–based financing and asset-based financing.
3. Taxation planning and compliance, with regard to amortization, abandonment, charitable contribution, gifting, intercompany transfer pricing, basis adjustment and other federal taxation matters, and with regard to state and local ad valorem taxation matters.

Exhibit 42–1

VALUATION OF INTANGIBLE ASSETS
ALTERNATIVE PREMISES OF VALUE

There are several premises of value that may apply in the valuation of intangible assets. A premise of value states an assumption as to the overall conceptual framework within which the analyst applies quantitative analysis and qualitative judgment to ultimately reach an estimation of the definition of value sought. An intangible asset analysis may result in materially different valuation estimates for the same asset—using the same definition of value—depending on which premise of value is applied.

The alternative premises of value for an intangible asset valuation are as follows:

Value in use, as part of a going concern.   This premise contemplates the contributory value of the intangible asset, as part of a mass assemblage of tangible and intangible assets, to an income-producing, going-concern business enterprise.

Value in place, as part of an assemblage of assets.   This premise contemplates that the intangible asset is fully functional, is part of an assemblage of assets that is ready for use, but is not currently engaged in the production of income as part of a going-concern business.

Value in exchange, in an orderly disposition.   This premise contemplates that the intangible asset will be sold, in its current condition, with normal exposure to its appropriate secondary market, but without the contributory value of any associated tangible or intangible assets.

Value in exchange, in a forced liquidation.   This premise contemplates that the intangible asset will be sold piece-meal (i.e., independent of all other tangible and intangible assets), in an auction environment, with an artificially abbreviated exposure to its appropriate secondary market.

---

4. Management information and planning, including business value enhancement purposes, exploitation of licensing and other commercialization opportunities, estate planning, and other long-range strategic planning issues.

5. Bankruptcy and reorganization analysis, including the value of the estate in bankruptcy, debtor-in-possession financing, traditional refinancing, restructuring, identification of licensing or other spin-off opportunities, and assessment of the impact of proposed reorganization plans.

6. Litigation support and dispute resolution, including infringement, shareholder and/or joint venture disputes, breach of contract, fraud, lender liability, and a wide range of deprivation-related reasons.

In particular, intangible asset analyses are often called for in the purchase price allocation with regard to the sale of a small business or professional practice. Also, intangible asset analyses are often an integral part of the valuation of a small business or professional practice for marital dissolution purposes. This is because the total business value may include the economic value of employment agreements and noncompete agreements. These agreements are discrete intangible assets. In marital dissolution cases, the value of the family-owned operating business may be part of the marital estate. However, in some jurisdictions, the incremental business value associated with employment agreements and noncompete agreements may not be considered part of the marital estate.

Clearly, there are many reasons to conduct an intangible asset appraisal. Of these six categories of reasons, many are for litigation support and dispute resolution. Within this category of reasons, a common subcategory relates to deprivation analyses. And within this subcategory, there are the following general types of intangible asset deprivation analyses:

1. *Eminent domain*—including municipal condemnations, nationalization of properties and industries, and expropriation.
2. *Property damages*—including slander, libel, and other forms of damage to a party's name, reputation, or goodwill.
3. *Infringement*—including the unauthorized use of (and resulting damage to) patents, trademarks, copyrights, and other intellectual properties.
4. *Squeeze-out transactions*—including any involuntary deprivation of the minority ownership party in an asset, property, or business interest by the majority ownership party (and the associated loss of economic satisfaction by the minority owners).
5. *Breach of contract*—including the loss of economic satisfaction realized by a party suffering from the breach of a contract to buy, sell, license, lease, use, forgo using, or otherwise transact in the subject intangible asset.

In all of these cases, an intangible asset analysis is usually called for. That intangible asset analysis will be performed more effectively and efficiently if the analyst begins the assignment with a clear and complete statement of the purpose of the appraisal.

Identification of Intangible Assets

Analysts experienced in intangible asset valuations could easily create a list of over a hundred intangible assets commonly found in the industrial and commercial environment. For an intangible asset to exist from a valuation, accounting, and legal perspective, it should possess certain attributes. The following are some of these intangible asset identification attributes:

- It should be subject to specific identification and recognizable description.
- It should be subject to legal existence and protection.
- It should be subject to the right of private ownership, and this private ownership must be legally transferable.
- There should be some tangible evidence or manifestation of the existence of the intangible asset (e.g., a contract, a license, a document, or a registration document).
- It should have been created or have come into existence at an identifiable time or as the result of an identifiable event.
- It should be subject to being destroyed or to a termination of existence at an identifiable time or as the result of an identifiable event.

In other words, there should be a specific bundle of legal rights (and/or other natural properties) associated with the existence of an intangible asset.

For an intangible asset to have a quantifiable value from an economic perspective, it should possess certain additional attributes. Some of these additional economic value attributes include the following:

- It should generate some measurable amount of economic income to its owner. This economic benefit could be in the form of an income increment or of a cost decrement. This economic income may be measured in any of several ways, including present value of net income, net operating income, net cash flow, and so on.
- It should enhance the value of other assets with which it is associated; the other assets may include tangible personal property, real estate, or other intangible assets.

Accordingly, based on these criteria, there may be a substantial distinction between the legal existence of an intangible asset and the economic value of that intangible asset.

Categorization of Intangible Assets

Generally, analysts will categorize all discrete (or individual) intangible assets into several distinct categories. This categorization of intangible assets is used for general asset identification and classification purposes.

Intangible assets in each category are generally similar in nature and function. Also, intangible assets are grouped in the same category when similar valuation and economic analysis methods apply to that group of assets. A common categorization of intangible assets follows:

- *Technology-related* (e.g., engineering drawings and technical documentation).
- *Customer-related* (e.g., customer lists and customer relationships).
- *Contract-related* (e.g., favorable supplier or other product/service contracts).
- *Data processing–related* (e.g., computer software, automated databases).
- *Human capital–related* (e.g., employment agreements, a trained and assembled workforce).
- *Marketing-related* (e.g., trademarks and trade names).
- *Location-related* (e.g., leasehold interests, certificates of need).
- *Goodwill-related* (e.g., going-concern value).
- *Engineering-related* (e.g., patents, trade secrets).
- *Literary-related* (e.g., literary copyrights, musical composition copyrights).

There is a specialized classification of intangible assets called intellectual properties. Intellectual properties manifest all of the legal existence and economic value attributes of other intangible assets. However, because of their special status, intellectual properties enjoy special legal recognition and protection.

Unlike other intangible assets that may be created in the normal course of business operations, intellectual properties are created by human intellectual and/or inspirational activity. Such activity (although not always planned) is specific and conscious. Such creativity can be attributed to the activity of identified, specific individuals. Because of this unique creation process, intellectual properties are generally registered under, and protected by, specific federal and state statutes.

Like other intangible assets, intellectual properties may be grouped into like categories. The intellectual properties in each category are generally similar in nature, feature, method of creation, and legal protection. Likewise, similar valuation and economic analysis methods would apply to the intellectual properties in each category.

Commonly, intellectual properties are assigned to one of two categories:

- Creative (e.g., copyrights).
- Innovative (e.g., patents).

It is noteworthy that these intellectual properties are themselves part of the 10 categories of intangible assets listed above.

Listing of Intangible Assets

There is no such thing as a complete or comprehensive listing of all intangible assets that may be subject to analysis. As industries and businesses evolve, new intangible assets are periodically created in the normal course of business operations. Also, as economic analysis procedures develop over time, analysts become better equipped to identify and appraise previously ignored intangible assets.

Exhibit 42-2 presents a listing of over one hundred industrial and commercial intangible assets commonly subject to analysis. This listing is presented to illustrate the variety of intangible assets subject to analysis. It is not intended to present a comprehensive listing or checklist of all intangible assets found in small businesses and professional practices.

Valuation of Intangible Assets

There are three fundamental approaches with regard to the valuation of all assets or properties: the market approach, the income approach, and the cost approach. These three valuation approaches apply equally to tangible assets and to intangible assets. Of course, within each category of valuation approach, different methods and procedures may be used to appraise individual intangible assets.

All individual methods and procedures used with regard to intangible asset valuation are derived from these three approaches. For each intangible asset analysis, one or more of these approaches will prove more or less relevant. Therefore, the analyst should consider and (if possible) use all three approaches during the valuation of individual intangible assets. Each procedure results in a preliminary and (ultimately) a final indication of intangible asset value. In the valuation synthesis and conclusion procedure of the valuation process, the analyst integrates the results of applying the various analytical methods. This reconciliation considers all of the valuation approaches and methods used, resulting in a synthesis of value that indicates the analyst's conclusion about the value of the subject intangible asset.

We will first describe the three approaches to intangible asset valuation. Then we will discuss several specific methods within each approach. Finally, we will present several caveats that analysts should be mindful of when reaching a valuation synthesis and conclusion.

Exhibit 42–2

ILLUSTRATIVE LISTING OF INTANGIBLE ASSETS AND INTELLECTUAL PROPERTIES COMMONLY SUBJECT TO VALUATION AND ECONOMIC ANALYSIS

Advertising campaigns and programs
Agreements
Airport gates and slots
Appraisal plants
Awards and judgments
Bank customers—deposit, loan, trust, and credit card
Blueprints
Book libraries
Brand names
Broadcast licenses
Buy-sell agreements
Certificates of need
Chemical formulations
Claims
Computer software
Computerized databases
Contracts
Cooperative agreements
Copyrights
Credit information files
Customer contracts
Customer lists
Customer relationships
Designs
Development rights
Distribution networks
Distribution rights
Drilling rights
Easements
Employment contracts and agreements
Engineering drawings
Environmental rights
FCC licenses
Favorable financing
Favorable leases
Film libraries
Food flavorings and recipes

Franchise agreements
Franchise ordinances
Going concern
Goodwill—celebrity
Goodwill—institutional
Goodwill—professional
Government contracts
Governmental registrations
Historical documents
HMO enrollment lists
Insurance expirations
Insurance in force
Joint ventures
Know-how
Laboratory notebooks
Landing rights
Leasehold estates
Leasehold interests
Licenses
Literary works
Litigation awards and damages
Loan portfolios
Location value
Management contracts
Manual databases
Manuscripts
Marketing and promotional materials
Masks and masters
Medical charts and records
Mineral rights
Musical compositions
Natural resources
Newspaper morgue files
Noncompete covenants
Nondiversion agreements
Open (e.g., open to ship) orders
Options, warrants, grants, rights
Ore deposits
Patent applications
Patents—both product and process

Patterns
Permits
Personality contracts
Possessory interest
Prescription drug (customer) files
Prizes and awards
Procedural manuals
Production backlogs
Product designs
Property use rights
Proposals outstanding
Proprietary processes
Proprietary products
Proprietary (unpatented) technology
Publications
Purchase orders
Regulatory approvals
Reputation
Retail shelf space
Royalty agreements
Schematics and diagrams
Securities portfolios
Security interests
Shareholder agreements
Solicitation rights
Stock and bond instruments
Subscription lists
Supplier contracts
Technical and specialty libraries
Technical documentation
Technology
Technology sharing agreements
Title plants
Trade secrets
Trained and assembled workforce
Trademarks and trade names
Training manuals
Use rights—air, water, land
Work in process (i.e., unbilled work performed)

Market Approach

The market approach provides a systematic framework for estimating the value of an intangible asset based on an analysis of actual sale and/or license transactions of intangible assets that are reasonably comparable to the subject asset.

This approach requires comparing the subject intangible asset to guideline intangible assets that have been listed for sale/license or have been sold/licensed in their appropriate primary or secondary markets. Correlations between actual sale/license transaction prices are also examined.

The following are some of the factors considered in the selection of guideline intangible asset sale/license transactions:

- The economic income-generating capacity of the guideline intangible asset.
- The markets served by the guideline intangible asset.
- The historical and expected prospective return on investment earned by the guideline intangible asset.
- The historical age and the expected remaining useful life of the guideline intangible asset.
- The time of the sale/license transaction.
- The degree of—and the future risk of—obsolescence of the guideline intangible asset (including physical, functional, technological, and economic obsolescence).
- Special terms and conditions of the sale/license (such as special seller financing, an earn-out agreement, noncompete agreement provision, and so on).

These comparability and guideline selection factors are analyzed discretely for each guideline intangible asset transaction. Based on any differences in these factors between the subject intangible asset and the guideline intangible assets, the guideline sale/license transactional data may need to be adjusted as appropriate.

Generally, it is difficult for analysts to use the market approach to value many intangible assets. This is true for several reasons. First, discrete intangible assets are not often sold separately from other business assets. In other words, they are often (but not always) sold as part of a mass assemblage of income-producing (tangible and intangible) business assets. In these cases, the analyst faces the problem of allocating a lump-sum market transaction price among all of the assets transferred —including the subject discrete intangible asset. Second, more than in the case of transactions involving the sale of real estate or tangible personal property, buyers and sellers of intangible assets tend to keep actual transactional data very proprietary. So analysts face difficulty in obtaining, verifying, and confirming transactional data on the actual terms of arm's-length sales/licenses of intangible assets.

The analyst also faces the challenge of data purification and cash equivalency analysis. That is, even if the guideline intangible was sold/licensed without any accompanying fixed assets, there are often short-term servicing agreements and long-term noncompete agreements that accompany the transfer of the guideline intangible assets. And if there is an earn-out or other payment terms (as is often the case with the transfer of intangible assets), the analyst has to perform a cash equivalency analysis in order to estimate the actual guideline transaction price to be used for further analysis.

Nonetheless, most analysts would agree that—when they can be used—market approach methods are the best methods to use to estimate the value of an intangible asset. It is equally true for intangible assets as for tangible assets that an actual and active secondary market provides the best indicator of value for any asset, property, or business interest. It is noteworthy that an active secondary transfer market exists for the sale/license of many intangible assets. In these cases, the analyst may obtain verifiable transaction pricing data regarding the actual asset/license transfers of guideline intangible assets.

Some intangible assets do lend themselves very well to an application of the market approach. These would include situations where there are often "naked sales" of intangibles within an industry. A naked sale occurs when the subject intangible asset is sold "naked"—or separately and independently from any other tangible assets or intangible assets. For example, in the financial institution industry, bank "core deposit" accounts, loan portfolios, credit card portfolios, mortgage servicing rights, and trust customer accounts are often—in negotiated arm's-length transactions—sold separately and independently from the rest of the assets of the bank or the savings and loan institution.

In the real estate industry, leasehold interests, possessory interests, air rights, water rights, mineral rights, other development rights, easements, and other real estate–related intangible assets are often—in an active secondary marketplace—bought and sold separately from the actual underlying real estate (and separately from any other intangible assets).

In the aviation industry, airport landing rights (sometimes called "slots" at controlled airports), airline routes, airline reservation systems, FAA licenses, aircraft parking or "tiedown" rights, and airport gate positions are frequently—in negotiated arm's-length transactions—bought and sold independently from the rest of the assets of the going-concern airline business.

In fact, many licenses and permits are sold separately from other business assets. This may include Federal Communication Commission (FCC) licenses, liquor licenses, franchise agreements, territory development agreements, certificates of need, and so forth.

Income Approach

The income approach provides a systematic framework for estimating the value of an intangible asset based on economic income capitalization or on the present value of future "economic income" to be derived from the use, forbearance, license, or rental of that intangible asset.

Under the income approach to intangible asset analysis, *economic income* can be defined in many ways, including the following:

- Net income before tax.
- Net income after tax.
- Net operating income.
- Gross or net rental income.
- Gross or net royalty or license income.
- Operating cash flow.
- Net cash flow.

The income capitalization procedure can also be accomplished in several ways, including the following:

- Capitalizing current year's economic income.
- Capitalizing an average of several years' economic income.
- Capitalizing a normalized or stabilized period's economic income.
- Projecting prospective economic income over a discrete time period and determining a present value.

Quantifying the appropriate direct capitalization rate or present value discount rate is an essential element of the income approach. The appropriate direct capitalization rate or present value discount rate should reflect a fair return on the stakeholders' investment in the subject intangible asset and should consider the following:

- The opportunity cost of capital (i.e., expected return on alternative investments).
- The time value of money (including consideration of a real rate of return and the expected inflation rate over the investment time horizon).
- The term of the investment (including consideration of the expected remaining useful life of the subject intangible asset).
- The risk of the investment.

The most important factor with regard to estimating the appropriate direct capitalization rate or present value discount rate is that the selected rate must be consistent with the measurement of economic income used. For example, a before-tax capitalization rate should be applied to a before-tax measurement of economic income. An after-tax capitalization rate should be applied to an after-tax measurement of economic income. An economic income stream representing a return to stockholders only should be capitalized by a rate based on a cost of equity capital only. An economic income stream representing a return to all stakeholders (i.e., both debt holders and equity holders) should be capitalized by a rate based upon a blended—or weighted average—cost of debt and equity capital.

There are many ways to assign an economic income stream to a particular intangible asset. With regard to the analysis of intangible assets, economic income can be derived from two categories of sources: (1) increments to revenue or (2) decrements to cost. From a valuation perspective, either source of economic income is an equally valid contributor to the value of the subject intangible asset.

With regard to incremental revenue, certain intangible assets may allow the intangible asset owner or licenser to sell more products (than otherwise), sell products at a higher average selling price, gain a larger market share, enjoy a monopolistic market position, ensure a relatively sure source of recurring customers, ensure a relatively sure source of future business, generate add-on or renewal business, develop new markets, introduce new products, and so on.

With regard to decremental costs, certain intangible assets may allow the intangible asset owner or licenser to incur lower labor costs, incur lower material costs, incur lower scrap (or other waste) costs, enjoy lower rent expense, enjoy low utilities expense, enjoy lower advertising or promotional expenses, defer the costs to recruit and train employees, avoid start-up costs, avoid construction period interest, avoid interest in an otherwise greater level of receivables or inventory, avoid or defer design or development costs, supply a low-cost and dependable source of financing, avoid or defer software development or ongoing data processing costs, and so on.

Some intangible assets lend themselves very well to the application of the income approach. Such contract-related or customer-related intangible assets as favorable leases, favorable supply contracts, favorable labor agreements, customer lists, and customer contracts are likely candidates for an application of the income approach. Other technology-related, engineering-related, and marketing-related intangible assets are also likely candidates for an application of the income approach. These intangible assets may include patents, proprietary technology or processes, trademarks and trade names, copyrights, and so forth

When using an income approach valuation method, the analyst should be particularly mindful of the expected remaining useful life of the subject intangible asset. Clearly, the economic income projection associated with the subject intangible asset should not extend beyond the term of the expected remaining useful life for that intangible asset.

The analyst should be careful not to double-count the economic income associated with the subject intangible asset during the valuation process. That is, the analyst should ensure that the same stream of economic income (whether it represents a revenue increment or a cost decrement) is not assigned to more than one asset. For example, the same stream of excess earnings for a particular business should not be assigned both to the company's patent and to the company's trademark. Clearly, only one of these intangible assets deserves to be associated with that specific stream of economic income. (The other intangible asset in this example, though it has legal existence, may have little or no incremental economic value.)

The analyst should also be careful to consider only that stream of economic income that associates with the particular intangible asset in the valuation process. Regarding this caveat, the analyst should be careful to assign a fair return on the tangible assets used or used up in the production of income related to the subject intangible asset. This fair return on associated tangible assets should be subtracted from the economic income stream assigned to the subject intangible asset in order to avoid the double-counting of asset values during the valuation process.

Cost Approach

The cost approach provides a systematic framework for estimating the value of an intangible asset based on the economic principle of substitution. In other words, a prudent investor would pay no more for an intangible asset than the cost that would be incurred to replace the subject intangible with a substitute intangible of comparable utility or functionality.

Replacement Cost New

Replacement cost new typically establishes the maximum amount that a prudent investor would pay for a fungible intangible asset. To the extent that an intangible asset is less useful than an ideal replacement asset, the value of the subject intangible asset should be adjusted accordingly.

The subject intangible asset's replacement cost new is adjusted for losses in economic value due to the following causes:

* Physical deterioration (which is unusual in the case of intangible assets).
* Functional obsolescence.
* Technological obsolescence (a specific form of functional obsolescence).
* Economic obsolescence (a specific form of external obsolescence).

Physical deterioration is the reduction in the value of an intangible asset due to physical wear and tear resulting from continued use. Physical deterioration is quite rare with respect to most intangible assets.

Functional obsolescence is the reduction in the value of an intangible asset due to its inability to perform the function (or yield the periodic utility) for which it was originally designed.

Technological obsolescence is a decrease in the value of an intangible asset due to improvements in technology that make an asset less than the ideal replacement for itself. Technological obsolescence occurs when, due to improvements in design or engineering technology, a new replacement intangible asset produces a greater standardized measure of utility production than the subject intangible asset.

Economic obsolescence is a reduction in the value of the subject intangible asset due to the effects, events, or conditions that are external to—and not controlled by—the current use or condition of the intangible asset. The impact of economic obsolescence is typically beyond the control of the intangible asset's owner. For that reason, economic obsolescence is typically considered incurable.

In estimating the amounts (if any) of physical deterioration, functional obsolescence, technological obsolescence, and economic obsolescence related to the subject intangible asset, the consideration of the subject intangible asset's actual age—and its expected remaining useful life—is important to the proper application of the cost approach.

Under the cost approach, the typical formula for quantifying an intangible asset's replacement cost is as follows:

Reproduction cost new
− <u>Incurable functional and technological obsolescence</u>
= Replacement cost new

To estimate the intangible asset value, the following formula is used:

Replacement cost new
− Physical deterioration
− Economic obsolescence
− <u>Curable functional and technological obsolescence</u>
= Value

Curable versus Incurable Obsolescence

An intangible asset's deficiencies are considered curable when the prospective economic benefit of enhancing or modifying it exceeds the current cost (in terms of material, labor, and time) to change it.

An intangible asset's deficiencies are considered incurable when the current costs of enhancing or modifying it (in terms of material, labor, and time) exceed the expected future economic benefits of improving it.

Reproduction Cost

Reproduction cost is the cost to construct, at current prices, an exact duplicate or replica of the subject intangible asset. This duplicate would be created using the same materials, standards, design, layout, and quality of workmanship used to create the original intangible asset.

Therefore, an intangible asset's reproduction cost encompasses all of the deficiencies, "superadequacies," and obsolescence that exist in the subject intangible asset. Many of these conditions or characteristics are inherent in the subject intangible asset and are, therefore, incurable.

Replacement Cost

The replacement cost of an intangible asset is the cost to create, at current prices, an asset having equal utility to the intangible asset subject to appraisal. However, the replacement asset would be created with modern methods and constructed according to current standards, state-of-the-art design and layout, and the same quality of workmanship.

The difference between an intangible asset's reproduction cost and its replacement cost is typically the quantification of incurable functional and technological obsolescence. That is, in an ideal replacement intangible asset, all elements of incurable functional and technological obsolescence are removed or "reengineered" from the subject asset.

An intangible asset's replacement cost is sometimes quantified using a *green-field* approach. That is, the replacement cost of an intangible asset is the cost to redesign and reengineer an ideal replacement intangible asset on the drawing board from scratch—that is, on a green field.

With respect to both reproduction cost and replacement cost, four elements of cost should be considered in the analyses:

1. *Direct costs* (including material, labor, and overhead).
2. *Indirect costs* (including associated legal, registration, engineering, administrative, etc.)
3. *Developer's profit* (a fair return on the intangible asset creator's time and effort).
4. *Entrepreneurial incentive* (the economic benefit required to motivate the intangible asset development process).

Some intangible assets lend themselves very well to the application of the cost approach. These intangible assets are typically used—or used up—in the generation of income for the small business or professional practice. Examples of intangible assets that may be likely candidates for the cost approach include computer software and automated databases, technical drawings and documentation, blueprints and engineering drawings, laboratory notebooks, technical libraries, chemical formulations, food and other product recipes, and so forth.

Remaining Useful Life Analysis of Intangible Assets

One factor that has been mentioned in our discussion of all three valuation approaches is the estimation of remaining useful life. This estimation (sometimes called *lifing* the intangible asset) is obviously important in the market approach. This is because the analyst will want to select guideline sale/license transactions where the sold/licensed intangible asset has a similar remaining useful life to the subject intangible asset. This estimation is obviously important in the income approach. This is because the analyst will need to estimate the time period or duration over which to project (and capitalize) the economic income associated with the subject intangible asset. This estimation is also important in the cost approach. This is because the analyst will need an assessment of the remaining functionality or utility of the subject intangible asset in order to identify and quantify the elements of physical depreciation, functional obsolescence, technological obsolescence, and economic obsolescence.

There are several measures to consider when analyzing and estimating the remaining useful life for intangible assets:

1. *Remaining legal (or legal protection) life* (e.g., remaining term of trademark protection).
2. *Remaining contractual life* (e.g., remaining term on a lease).
3. *Statutory or judicial life* (e.g., some courts have allowed a "standardized" life of five years for computer software).
4. *Remaining physical life* (e.g., some intangible assets just wear out from continued use, such as blueprints or technical libraries).
5. *Remaining functional life* (e.g., some intangible assets just become dysfunctional with the passage of time, like chemical formulations that need to be continuously updated).
6. *Remaining technological life* (e.g., period until the current technology becomes obsolete, for patents, proprietary processes, etc.).
7. *Remaining economic life* (e.g., period after which the intangible asset will no longer generate income, such as a legally valid copyright on a book that's out of print).
8. *Actuarial / analytical life* (e.g., estimating the remaining life of group assets—such as customer accounts—by reference to the historical turnover—or mortality—of such accounts).

Generally, an analyst should consider all of these measures of remaining useful life in the analysis of an intangible asset. Also, the shortest resulting measurement of remaining useful life will typically be used in the valuation of each intangible asset. For example, it is not as economically relevant that the remaining legal life on a particular patent is 15 years if the expected remaining technological life on the patented technology is only 5 years.

In any event, regardless of the valuation approach used, an assessment of the remaining useful life of the subject intangible asset is an important step in the valuation process.

Covenants Not to Compete

A covenant not to compete is a unique intangible asset found in perhaps half of all small business and professional practice transactions, whether for the sale of the entire company or a partial ownership interest. A covenant not to compete is important to the buyer to protect the business's ability to grow and prosper. It is important to the seller because it defines restrictions on future personal efforts.

The tax consequences are important because the payments are tax deductible as ordinary expense to the buyer when paid. They are taxable as ordinary income to the seller when received.

The allocation to covenant also can be important when there are multiple sellers, to be sure that proceeds that should go to selling stockholders or partners are not diverted improperly to one or a few individuals involved in operations.[1]

The value of the covenant also can be important in the case of a divorce. Since the covenant restricts the future efforts of the individual party, many family law courts do not consider the value of this intangible asset to be includable in the marital estate subject to distribution (see Chapter 41, Marital Dissolutions).

While a complete dissertation on the value of covenants not to compete is beyond the scope of this book, a tax court case listed the following factors to consider:

- Ability to compete.
- Industry expertise.
- Customer and supplier relationships.
- Economic resources.
- Intent to compete.
- Potential damage posed by competition.
- Company's interest in eliminating/reducing competition.
- Duration and geographic scope of covenant.
- Intent to reside in same geographic area.[2]

Summary

Numerous small business and professional practice intangible assets may be subject to analysis. And there are numerous reasons to conduct a valuation of the intangible assets related to small businesses and professional practices.

Analysts should have a clear understanding of the purpose of the appraisal before they begin the valuation of an intangible asset. The description of the appraisal assignment should clearly specify both (1) the intangible asset subject to appraisal and (2) the bundle of legal rights subject to appraisal. The purpose of the appraisal will, in good measure, dictate (1) the appropriate definition (or standard) of value to be used and (2) the appropriate premise of value to be used.

---

[1]See, for example, *Ryan* v. *Tad's Enterprises, Inc.*, No. 10229, 11977, 1996 WL 204502, Del. Ch. (April 24, 1996), where noncompete payments of $1 million each to the two controlling selling stockholders were disallowed, and the court required the entire $2 million to be distributed pro rata among all selling stockholders.

[2]*Beaver Bolt, Inc.* v. *Commissioner*, T.C. Memo 1995-549 (Nov. 20, 1995).

Depending on (1) the definition of value specified and (2) the premise of value used, analysts may use a market approach, income approach, and/or cost approach to value the subject intangible asset. The income approach methods are often premised on the ability of the subject intangible asset to earn a fair (or, in some cases, an excess) rate of return to the business that uses the intangible asset. The market and cost approach methods recognize the independent value of discrete intangible assets—that is, a value not dependent on a rate of return to an operating business.

When selecting which valuation approach (or approaches) to use, the analyst will also consider (1) the quantity and quality of available data and (2) the nature and unique characteristics of the subject intangible asset. Some intangible assets lend themselves more to one valuation approach than to another.

Regardless of which valuation approach is used, the analyst should consider not only the legal and physical existence of the subject intangible asset but the economic validity of the intangible asset as well. Also, regardless of which valuation approach is used, an assessment of the remaining useful life is an important step in any intangible asset valuation.

Ideally, the analyst will be able to form a valuation synthesis and conclusion based on the results of two or more valuation approaches. In the valuation synthesis and conclusion, the analyst will weigh the results of the various valuation approaches based on the degree of confidence in the applicability and validity of each approach with regard to the subject intangible asset.

Bibliography

Articles

"Acquired Work Force Not Amortizable, but Contracts Were." *Journal of Taxation*, December 1991, pp. 348–49.

Anson, Weston. "Trademark/Brand Licensing and Valuations." *Journal of Business*, October 1990, pp. 213–220.

Biel, Alexander L. "How Brand Image Drives Brand Equity." *Journal of Advertising Research*, November 1992, pp. RC6–RC12.

Blackett, Tom. "Brand and Trademark Valuation—What's Happening Now?" *Marketing, Intelligence & Planning,* November 1993, pp. 28–30.

Blumberg, Grace Ganz. "Identifying and Valuing Goodwill at Divorce." *Law and Contemporary Problems*, Spring 1993, pp. 217–72.

Boose, Mary Ann, and Virginia S. Ittenbach. "Depreciation of Customer-Based Intangibles: Good News for Taxpayers." *CPCU Journal,* December 1993, pp. 232–42.

Brostoff, Steven. "Intangible Asset Treatment Seen as Critical Agent Issue." *National Underwriter (Property & Casualty / Risk & Benefits Management Edition)*, December 28, 1992–January 4, 1993, p. 4+.

Cava, Anita. "Trade Secrets and Covenants Not to Compete: Beware of Winning the Battle but Losing the War." *Journal of Small Business Management*, October 1990, pp. 99–103.

Christensen, Barbara. "Computer Software—Is It Tangible or Intangible?" *Small Business Taxation*, January/February 1990, pp. 174–76.

Cosman, Madeleine Pelner, Thomas Russell Lang, and Marin C. Goodheart. "Comparing Medical and Business Goodwill Components." *FAIR$HARE: The Matrimonial Law Monthly*, January 1990, pp. 3–7.

Dal Santo, Jacquelyn. "Valuation Concerns in the Appraisal of Covenants Not to Compete." *Appraisal Journal,* January 1991, pp. 111–14.

Dennis-Escoffier, Shirley. "Is a Solution to the Intangibles Problem on the Horizon?" *Journal of Corporate Accounting & Finance*, Winter 1992/1993, pp. 247–250.

Driscoll, Barrie K., and Stephen C. Gerard. "A Round for Buyers on Depreciation of Intangible Assets." *Mergers & Acquisitions,* July/August 1993, pp. 22–25.

Elgison, Martin J. "Capitalizing on the Financial Value of Patents, Trademarks, Copyrights and Other Intellectual Property." *Corporate Cashflow*, November 1992, pp. 30–32.

Fenton, Edmund D., Lucinda VanAlst, and Patricia Isaacs. "The Determination and Valuation of Goodwill: Using a Proven, Acceptable Method to Withstand IRS Challenge." *Tax Adviser*, September 1991, pp. 602–12.

Finkel, Sidney R. "Conflicts Continue in the Valuation of Non-competition Agreements." *Valuation Strategies*, January/February 1998, pp. 29–33.

Hall, Richard. "The Strategic Analysis of Intangible Resources." *Strategic Management Journal*, February 1992, pp. 135–44.

Hollingsworth, Danny P., and Walter T. Harrison, Jr. "Deducting the Cost of Intangibles." *Journal of Accountancy*, July 1992, pp. 85–90.

Hull, John. "Intangible Assets, Real Problems (Purchasing Insolvent Companies' Trademarks)." *Accountancy*, May 1992, p. 84.

Keller, Kevin Lane. "Conceptualizing, Measuring, and Managing Customer-Based Brand Equity." *Journal of Marketing*, January 1993, pp. 1–22.

King, Alfred M., and James Cook. "Brand Names: The Invisible Assets." *Management Accounting*, November 1990, pp. 41–45.

King, Jerry G., and Paul D. Torres. "The Purchase of a Going Concern: Planning for Intangibles." *National Public Accountant*, March 1991, pp. 32–35.

Laverde, Lorin, and Eric Knapp. "Evaluating Intangible Assets in the Sale of Technology-Based Companies." *Corporate Growth Report,* October 1990, pp. 23–25.

Martin, Michael J. "Valuing the Glamour in Brand Name Acquisitions." *Mergers & Acquisitions*, January–February 1991, pp. 31–37.

Millon, Tom. "Computer Software Valuation: Don't Be Led Astray by a Quick Approach." *National Public Accountant*, September 1992, pp. 14–17.

————. "Software Development: Cost vs. Value (Determining Fair Market Value of Internally Developed Computer Software)." *Practical Accountant,* October 1992, p. 48.

_____. "The Valuation and Amortization of Non-Compete Agreements." *CPA Litigation Service Counselor,* May 1991, pp. 1–3.

Mullen, Maggie. "How to Value Intangibles." *Accountancy,* November 1993, pp. 92–94.

_____. "What Is a Brand Name or Trademark Really Worth—How Can That Value Be Measured?" *Journal of Business,* October 1990, pp. 203–12.

Murphy, John. "A Brand New Look to Valuations." *World Accounting Report,* August/September 1992, pp. *ii–iii.*

_____. "Assessing the Value of Brands." *Long Range Planning,* June 1990, pp. 23–29.

Oswald, Lynda J. "Goodwill and Going-Concern Value: Emerging Factors in the Just Compensation Equation." *Boston College Law Review,* March 1991, pp. 283–376.

Ourusoff, Alexandra, Michael Ozanian, Paul B. Brown, and Jason Starr. "What's in a Name"—What the World's Top Brands are Worth." *Financial World,* September 1992, pp. 32–49.

Ourusoff, Alexandra, with Meenakshi Panchapakesan. "Who Says Brands are Dead?" *Financial World,* September 1993, pp. 40–50.

Parr, Russell L. "The Double-Barreled Benefits of Acquiring a Brand Name." *Mergers & Acquisitions,* March–April 1993, pp. 36–38.

Paschall, Robert H. "Measuring Functional Obsolescence at Manufacturing Plants." *ASA Valuation,* March 1994, pp. 56–62.

Rabe, James G., and Robert F. Reilly. "Looking Beneath the Surface: Valuing Health Care Intangible Assets." *National Public Accountant,* March 1996, pp. 14–17+.

_____. "Valuation of Intangible Assets for Property Tax Purposes." *National Public Accountant,* April 1994, pp. 26–28+.

_____. "Valuing Intangible Assets as Part of a Unitary Assessment." *Journal of Property Tax Management,* Winter 1994, pp. 12–20.

Rechtin, Michael D. "Intellectual Property: Ticking Time Bombs for the Unwary Buyer." *Mergers & Acquisitions,* January/February 1992, pp. 28–31.

Reilly, Robert F. "Allocation of Value between Intangible Assets and Real Estate in Location-Dependent Businesses." *ASA Valuation,* January 1993, pp. 52–66.

_____. "Appraising and Amortizing Noncompete Covenants." *CPA Journal,* July 1990, pp. 28–38.

_____. "How Buyers Value Intellectual Properties." *Mergers & Acquisitions,* January/February 1996, pp. 40–44.

_____. "How to Determine the Value and Useful Life of Core Deposit Intangibles." *Journal of Bank Taxation,* Winter 1991, pp. 10–18.

_____. "The Valuation of Computer Software." *ASA Valuation,* March 1991, pp. 34–54.

_____. "Valuation of Intangible Assets for Bankruptcy and Reorganization Purposes." *Ohio CPA Journal,* August 1994, pp. 25–30.

_____. "Valuation Standards Regarding Deprivation Appraisals." *ASA Valuation,* January 1993, pp. 10–17.

_____. "Valuing Economic Loss." *Management Accounting,* July 1993, pp. 44–48.

_____. "Valuing Intangible Assets" (Parts 1 and 2). *CPA Expert*, Winter 1996, pp. 4–6, and Spring 1996, pp. 9–11.

_____. "Valuing Intangible Assets—A Case Study." *CPA Expert*, Summer 1996, pp. 11–14.

Reilly, Robert F., and Manoj P. Dandekar. Contract-Related Intangible Asset Appraisal for Gas Processing Plants." *Journal of Property Tax Management*, Winter 1997, pp. 52–67.

Reilly, Robert F., and Daniel Lynn. "The Valuation of Leasehold Interests." *Real Estate Accounting & Taxation*, Winter 1992, pp. 24–33.

Reilly, Robert F., and Bruce L. Richman. "Identification and Valuation of Individual Intangible Assets" (Chapter 5). In Bruce L. Richman, ed. *Tax and Financial Planning Strategies in Divorce*, 2d ed. New York: John Wiley & Sons, 1996, pp. 5-1–5-53.

Russell, Lee C. "How to Value Covenants Not to Compete." *Journal of Accountancy*, September 1990, pp. 85–92.

Schlessinger, Michael R. "A Covenant Not to Compete Still Can Provide Tax Savings to a Buyer." *Taxation for Accountants*, February 1990, pp. 96–99.

Schweihs, Robert P. "The Valuation of Proprietary Technology." *Journal of Property Tax Management*, Fall 1996, pp. 34–44.

Schweihs, Robert P., and Robert F. Reilly. "The Valuation of Intellectual Properties." *Licensing Law and Business Report*, May–June 1988, pp. 1–12.

Seetharaman, Ananth, Stephen B. Shanklin, and Gregory A. Carnes. "Section 197: Methods for Treating Intangibles." *National Public Accountant*, October 1994, pp. 28–31+.

Shanda, Lawrence P. "Incorporating Intangible Assets into the Transfer Price Formula." *TAXES*, February 1991, pp. 100–05.

Shearlock, Peter. "Valuing Route Rights." *Airfinance Journal*, July 1993, pp. 4–8.

Sherwood, Stanley G., Michael Godbee, and Siv D. Janger. "The Price of Flexibility: The New Section 482 Regulations." *Tax Planning International Review*, March 1993, pp. 3–15.

Simensky, Melvin, and Lanning G. Bryer. *The New Role of Intellectual Property in Commercial Transactions*. New York: John Wiley & Sons, 1994.

Smith, Gordon V. "Trademark Valuations Run Amuck." *Business Valuation Review*, December 1992, pp. 179–82.

Tang, Roger Y.W. "Transfer Pricing in the 1990s." *Management Accounting*, February 1992, pp. 22–26.

Wacker, Raymond F. "Treasury's Proposed Regulations Allow Profit Split Method on Self-Developed Intangibles." *International Tax Journal*, Fall 1993, pp. 12–29.

Wilkins, Mira. "The Neglected Intangible Asset: The Influence of the Trade Mark on the Rise of the Modern Corporation." *Business History*, January 1992, pp. 66–95.

Woo, Michael J. "Recent Developments in the California and Federal Tax Treatment of Intangibles." *Journal of California Taxation*, Winter 1992, pp. 17–27.

Books

Battersby, Gregory J., and Charles W. Grimes. *An Insider's Guide to Royalty Rates: A Comprehensive Survey of Royalty Rates and Licensed Products*. Stamford, CN: Kent Press, 1996.

Lee, Lewis C., and J. Scott Davidson. *Managing Intellectual Property Rights*. New York: John Wiley & Sons, 1993.

Parr, Russell L. *Intellectual Property Infringement Damages*. New York: John Wiley & Sons, 1993.

_____. *Investing in Intangible Assets: Finding and Profiting from Hidden Corporate Value*. New York: John Wiley & Sons, 1991.

Parr, Russell L., and Patrick H. Sullivan. *Technology Licensing: Corporate Strategies for Maximizing Value*. New York: John Wiley & Sons, 1996.

Smith, Gordon, and Russell Parr. *Intellectual Property Licensing and Joint Venture Profit Strategies*. New York: John Wiley & Sons, 1993, supplemented annually.

_____. *Valuation of Intellectual Property and Intangible Assets*. New York: John Wiley & Sons, 1994, supplemented annually.

Periodicals

The Journal of Proprietary Rights, monthly. Published by Aspen Law & Business, 1185 Avenue of the Americas, New York, NY 10036, (212) 597-0200.

Licensing Economics Review, monthly. Published by AUS Consultants, 155 Gaither Drive, Moorestown, NJ 08057, (609) 234-1199.

The Licensing Letter, monthly. Published by EPM Communications Inc., 488 East 18th Street, Brooklyn, NY 11226, (212) 941-0099.

The Licensing Journal, ten issues per year. Published by Aspen Law & Business, 1185 Avenue of the Americas, New York, NY 10036, (212) 597-0200.

Licensing Law and Business Report, bimonthly. Published by Clark Boardman Callaghan, 125 Hudson Street, New York, NY 10014, (212) 929-7500.

Mealey's Litigation Report: Intellectual Property, semimonthly. Published by Mealey Publications, Inc., PO Box 446, Wayne, PA 19087-0446, (215) 688-6566.

Mealey's Litigation Report: Patents, semimonthly. Published by Mealey Publications, Inc., PO Box 446, Wayne, PA 19087-0446, (215) 688-6566.

Chapter 43

Buying or Selling a Business or Practice

The ultimate objective of the buyer's and seller's valuation deliberations is to arrive at a *price* and a set of *terms* acceptable to both of them. Consequently, this chapter attempts to give equal consideration to the perspectives of both the buyer and the seller. Besides the entity's *fair market value*, the following factors bear on the price determined to be mutually acceptable:

1. Special circumstances of the particular buyer and seller (which may lead to pricing on the basis of *investment value)*.
2. Trade-off between cash and terms (as discussed in Chapter 27).
3. Relative tax consequences for the buyer and seller, which depend on how the transaction is structured.

All too often, price negotiations become an exercise in futility because the specific prospective buyers and sellers never should have gotten to the point of negotiating a purchase agreement in the first place. For that reason, we first consider the decision to sell or buy, which must precede determination of the specific price.

To Sell or Not to Sell

Ideally, the business seller becomes motivated to sell his or her business ownership interest at the same time that a buyer becomes willing to pay the seller an attractive price. Unfortunately, it is usually true that the desire to sell does not coincide with the timing for the best price attainable.

The following are several common reasons to sell a business:

1. Death of an owner.
2. Ill health.
3. Retirement.
4. Desire to start a new business or alternate career.
5. Boredom (or burnout).
6. Frustration and/or disillusionment.
7. Disputes among owners.
8. Need for a parent company with the capital and resources necessary to perpetuate the business and realize its growth potential.
9. Poor financial condition and/or losing money.

Several of the reasons are so strong they may be defined as *compulsions.* These reasons are discussed under "Differing Perceptions and Circumstances of Sellers and Buyers" later in this chapter.

The following are some of the more important factors affecting price:

1. Recent profit history.
2. General condition of the company (such as condition of facilities, completeness and accuracy of books and records, morale, and so on).
3. Market demand for the particular type of business.
4. Economic conditions (especially cost and availability of capital and any economic factors that directly affect the business).
5. Ability to transfer goodwill or other intangible values to a new owner.
6. Future profit potential.

Timing of the Sell Decision

When comparing these lists of (1) reasons to sell and (2) factors affecting price, it is obvious that the reasons to sell will not necessarily occur at the same time that the business is most likely to fetch the highest price. Owners who wish to sell their business at the best possible price should consider the following suggestions:

1. Anticipate the possibility of a sale, whether or not one is imminent, and prepare accordingly.
2. Make the sale when the timing is good from a financial standpoint, rather than holding back and risking a forced sale under less advantageous circumstances.
3. Hold off on selling when the seller is convinced that significantly higher profitability is on the immediate horizon, especially if the full potential of the increased profitability would not be immediately apparent to an outsider (which is almost always the case). If this realization does not materialize, however, especially if there is a downturn, it could be a significant loss to the seller.

In some respects, there is an inherent conflict between (1) running the business the way an owner prefers and (2) preparing the business for sale. An owner typically makes a variety of discretionary expenditures that result in reduced reported profits. It may or may not be possible to convince a prospective buyer to fully adjust for these items when assessing profitability. An owner may do many things his own way when he is operating the business. But these things may not make the business most attractive to the typical potential buyer. Ideally, the efforts to sell should be made at a time when the business can put its best foot forward.

Some owners find the decision to sell emotionally difficult to reach. Sellers often procrastinate when the timing for the sale is financially opportune. They then decide to sell later, after (1) the economy or other factors have made it inopportune, and (2) it is impossible to find buyers willing to pay as much as they would have when conditions were better. If an active owner dies, business value often diminishes. This is because the owner is no longer available to facilitate the transfer of goodwill to a new owner.

If the owner is confident of a sharp rise in profits, it will almost always be financially beneficial to keep the business until the increased profitability can be demonstrated to a buyer.

Preparing the Business for Sale

The following are six suggestions for preparing the small business or professional practice for sale:

1. Have excellent records.
2. Clean up the financial statements, especially the balance sheet.
3. Have a good profit record.
4. Have the business in good general condition.
5. Have adequate personnel.
6. Have the business appraised.

Have Excellent Records

In most cases, excellent records will help a seller obtain the best possible price for her business. The most credible accounting records are five or more years of financial statements audited by an independent CPA firm. The next best are financial statements reviewed by an independent CPA firm. After that, are statements compiled by an outside CPA, including the footnoted disclosures that normally would be included in audited or reviewed statements. If using internally prepared statements, they should be prepared meticulously and should follow generally accepted accounting principles as much as possible. If the company has only tax returns, good supporting documents should be readily available.

Good supporting schedules of the details contained within line items found on the statements are very helpful. Detailed schedules of expenses are especially useful if line items are categorized in such a way that they can be compared with industry averages. The list of property and equipment, and the related depreciation schedule, should be complete and up-to-date.

Clean Up the Financial Statements

The business owner should remove items that a purchaser would consider undesirable. Such items may include any nonoperating assets. If the business owns real estate, the seller may be wise to place the real estate in a separate corporation or partnership, charging rent at a market rate to the subject business or practice. In some cases, the same course may be advantageous for machinery and equipment. Depending on the nature of the business and the potential buyer, the seller may be able to get more for the business itself by keeping the hard assets and leasing them to a new owner than by selling them in a package with the business. (If there is any question about how to handle the fixed assets, the prudent owner may seek guidance from a business broker familiar with the particulars of selling her type of business.)

Many companies keep negative balances in their cash accounts, operating on the "float" provided by checks outstanding but not yet drawn from the account. This practice appears on the balance sheet either as a negative balance in the cash account on the asset side or as an overdraft on the liability side, neither of which looks very sound to readers of balance sheets. The seller should try to have a positive balance in the cash account as of the balance sheet date, even if it means delaying a few payables. Receivables from and/or payable to owners or related parties should generally be removed from the balance sheet.

Have a Good Profit Record

A good profit record is probably the single most important factor in preparing the business for sale. The best record is one of profits increasing steadily each year, with the profitability for the period immediately prior to the offer to sell being at (or above) industry averages. This comparison to industry averages may be made based on such measures as return on equity, return on assets, and return on sales. Establishing a good profit record may require (1) careful management and (2) relinquishing some hidden perks for a time. However, it should be worthwhile to be able to produce a well-documented record of profitability at the time of the sale.

Have the Business in Good General Condition

Like a house, car, or almost anything else, a business should fetch a better price if everything is clean, neat, and in good working order. Some sellers of businesses give the plant a paint job, just like home sellers do. Inventory should be current and well balanced. Promotional material should be attractive and up-to-date. Everything should work together efficiently and harmoniously.

Have Adequate Personnel

A buyer is likely to look more favorably on a business if the personnel needed to perform the various tasks are in place, well trained, and working together with resolve. A buyer may be less enthusiastic—and may be tempted to discount the price—if he faces the chore of recruiting and training new personnel.

Have the Business Appraised

A valuation analysis will help the prospective seller determine a range of reasonable prices before exposing the business to the marketplace.

Based on the valuation analysis, the seller may be able to (1) find out at what prices similar businesses are currently selling and (2) compare their prices to their revenues, earnings, assets, and other fundamental factors. The appraiser can provide the owner with this information. A complete written appraisal is not necessary for determining a range of acceptable prices. Many financial consulting and business appraisal firms offer consulting service on an hourly basis and provide valuable guidance without having to prepare a full, formal, written report. The seller should have in mind at least an objectively determined negotiating range before her first serious conversation (1) with a potential buyer or (2) with a broker about listing the business.

A written appraisal report, however, may be useful by providing more detailed information for the buyer. In addition, the appraisal report may be useful for some potential sources of buyer financing, if the seller prefers not to carry a contract. The expense of a credible written appraisal report may be recovered many times over if the selling price increases over what would be achieved without such a report.

In any case, whether the valuation work is informal consulting or a formal report, an independent financial advisory analysis will help the owner to understand the factors that add or detract value and can help the business to achieve a better price.

Even if a lower price is indicated by the independent appraisal, it may make the seller more realistic about the selling price and therefore help facilitate the transaction.

Chapter 44 addresses the topic of working with a business appraiser, and Chapter 45 discusses working with a business broker. In recent years, many more business brokers have also started offering appraisal services. An advantage of having the appraisal done by an appraiser who is not a broker is the independence from a potential performance fee involved in a sale transaction and possible referral to one or more brokers well suited to the particular sale assignment. An advantage of having the appraisal done by a brokerage firm that also offers appraisal services is the opportunity to become better acquainted with that firm as a potential sales agent.

In either case, the competence of the person in charge of the appraisal assignment is of paramount importance. The matter of assessing the appraiser's credentials is discussed in the following chapter.

Deciding What to Buy

Some successful entrepreneurs will buy almost anything that comes along if they find it interesting and think the price is right. Most who will buy almost anything eventually go broke. This is because, sooner or later, they overextend themselves on what turns out to be a bad deal. This may happen several times. (Entrepreneurs are very resilient.) Successful potpourri buyers succeed "on balance." That is, they succeed because some good winners offset the losses from many mistakes.

The best outcomes result when a potential buyer carefully thinks out and writes down his criteria for a business he would consider buying. Then the buyer should diligently pursue only those businesses worthy of consideration. The buyer should make an offer only for a business that meets the predetermined criteria. At a minimum, the list of criteria for a potential purchase should consider the following points:

1. The type of small business or professional practice.
2. Acceptable geographic locations.
3. The minimum and maximum size the buyer considers worthwhile and that he is realistically capable of managing.
4. The amount of cash available for purchase. (If outside sources are to be used, the buyer should at least explore the availability of funds from such sources before he goes shopping for a business.)
5. Whether, and for how long, the buyer will need assistance from existing management, and/or the duration and structure of a management transition period.
6. Whether the buyer wants a smooth-running and profitable operation or a "fixer-upper" (i.e., an operation currently not doing so well).

With these and any other relevant criteria firmly in mind, the buyer should be ready to screen brokers' listings and companies advertised in newspapers and trade publications in order to develop a list of possibilities for purchase.

Preparing to Make an Offer

Once the buyer has screened potential acquisitions and identified one or a few that meet his criteria, it is time for his own valuation analysis. The buyer may perform his own analysis, consult with a business appraiser, or have the appraiser perform the entire analysis. The analysis should cover the elements discussed in this book. However, the analysis will not usually require a formal, written report.

In preparing to make an offer, the buyer and/or the analyst should have available all the documents listed in Exhibit 44-3, "Documents and Information Checklist." Moreover, they should have access to whatever records are necessary to verify any items that may be unclear or in question. If the seller is unwilling to supply enough documentation for the buyer to be totally comfortable with her offer, the buyer should walk away and consider something else. The financial and nonfinancial investment in a business is too high to buy a "pig in a poke." Naturally, however, the buyer should be willing to sign a confidentiality agreement with respect to the seller's information.

A special problem arises when the seller and prospective buyer are competitors: Should the deal fall through, the seller may be at a competitive disadvantage if the buyer had access to her financial information. We have seen buyers handling this situation by engaging an independent appraiser to analyze the information, with the independent appraiser keeping most of the details confidential from the buyer until the negotiations appeared very likely to result in a completed transaction.

Buyers almost always expect to improve the profitability of the business they are buying. They should prepare, or have someone prepare, pro forma statements, as discussed in Chapter 11, that reflect their expectations for the business under their ownership. The further into the future the buyer can prepare meaningful pro forma statements, the better. However, no benefit is derived from extending pro forma statements to the point where they are completely speculative.

The buyer's appraisal of the business as it stands probably represents the floor of a negotiating range. This is true, provided that the seller is under no compulsion to sell. A capitalization of earnings or discounted cash flow analysis, based on the buyer's pro forma statements (assuming that they are soundly conceived), should provide the top of a negotiating range.

Conditions in the market for the particular kind of small business or professional practice will determine where in the range an offer is likely to be successful without being too high. The buyer should investigate (1) recent sales of comparative companies or practices and (2) the supply and demand for the particular type of company. This investigation should be performed in order to assess how much, if any, premium should be offered over the value of the company as its stands. This analysis should be made before considering any improvement to the business profits caused by the buyer's efforts. Comparative transactions are difficult to find, but efforts in recent years have improved the availability of data. A business broker or a business appraiser may be helpful in this regard, perhaps using transactional data such as described in Chapter 21, Comparative Transaction Databases.

Differing Perceptions and Circumstances of Sellers and Buyers

Frequently, buyers and sellers use different criteria to reach conclusions about the value of a particular business. Each party has his own reasons, which are valid under his respective circumstances. Obviously, both parties must be satisfied in order for a transaction to be consummated.

Assessment of Future Profits and Risk

Obviously, different expectations of future profits logically would lead buyers and sellers to reach different conclusions of value. Both buyers and sellers tend to overestimate future profits. This condition may lead to transactions that are consummated at inflated prices compared to the values that would have resulted from accurate expectations of future profits. It seems that more businesses sell above, rather than below, the values indicated by accurate projections of future profits.

The bias toward overpricing is further exacerbated by buyers, sellers, and small-business brokers who tend to underestimate the business risk. This underestimation of risk leads to unjustifiably low capitalization rates (that is, pricing multiples that are too high). Many businesses sold with seller financing sooner or later revert back to the seller because the buyer is unable to meet the payments.

Opportunity

It is interesting that the classified ads in most newspapers do not list businesses for sale, but rather business "opportunities." Some business brokers adhere to the philosophy that a buyer should never pay more than the value of the business as it stands (which may be less than the tangible asset value). The value of any opportunity would be part of the buyer's profits that result from a judicious entrepreneurial exploitation of the opportunity. Other brokers believe that a buyer should always pay more than the tangible asset value for the opportunity that comes with the business.

The value of *opportunity* per se is a matter for each individual buyer to decide. It is not a matter that can be financially analyzed. It is not clear how much of the price premium over intrinsic or fundamental value is caused by a willingness to pay for opportunity and how much really represents a failure to analyze intrinsic or fundamental value adequately.

Personal Rewards

A buyer may be willing to pay more than the value indicated by financial analysis because of personal rewards. She may fall in love with the physical location of an operation. The business may conduct an activity the buyer enjoys as a hobby. The buyer may desire the prestige associated with ownership of a certain business. Or she may find the location and the operating hours especially convenient. It certainly can be advantageous to a seller to find a buyer who perceives extra value in the business because of intangible personal benefits, whatever they may be.

Buying a Job

In many smaller businesses, much of the price paid can be considered "buying a job." In a sense, much (or in some cases even all) of the purchase price could be regarded as tantamount to paying an employment fee. These are situations where most (or even all) of the seller's discretionary earnings (as defined in Chapter 19) are taken up by reasonable compensation to the owner/operator.

Synergy

One of the most important factors that may add to the transaction price in a sale, over and above its value on a stand-alone basis, is *synergy.* Synergy is the concept that the value of the combined operations is greater than the sum of the values of the individual operations. An example would be two pickle packers, one with substantial excess production capacity and the other without nearly enough capacity to serve the demand created by its very successful marketing.

If there really is synergy, as there often may be between potential merger candidates, how much of the value of the synergy will the seller be able to add into the selling price, and how much will be left to be reflected in the buyer's future returns? The answer, of course, is a matter of negotiation. However, the respective parties' negotiating posture depends to a great extent on supply of, and demand for, the particular type of company. If many such companies are available for sale and there is only one buyer (or a few potential buyers), very little synergy is likely to be reflected in the transaction price. On the other hand, if there is only one (or a few) company available for sale, and several active potential buyers, the seller is likely to be able to receive a price premium for a significant portion of the synergy.

Obviously, it is in the seller's interest to seek out buyers who would have synergy with the selling company. This is because such buyers might well be able to afford to pay more than anyone else for the particular company.

Compulsion

The definition of fair market value assumes that neither buyer nor seller is under any compulsion to transact. In many cases in the real world, that assumption is not met. And compulsion leads to the transfer of businesses at prices that are different from what reasonably might be considered fair market value.

The most common source of compulsion that drives owners to sell is foreclosure of credit, usually by banks. Other common sources of compulsion are illness, death of an owner or family member, and irreconcilable differences among the present business owners. These factors make it virtually impossible to operate the business effectively under current ownership.

Compulsion affecting buyers arises most often because of synergistic effects that might be lost if the deal falls through. For example, a buyer may feel compelled to buy the business of a key customer from the estate of a deceased owner in order to keep it from failing or falling into the hands of a competitor.

Structuring a Deal

Tax and other consequences of the structure of a transaction can have a significant impact on the transaction price. The following points are broadly generalized simplifications, and we recommend that both seller and buyer consult a tax attorney and/or an accountant regarding tax and legal implications of the terms of the transaction.

Stock Sale versus Asset Sale

As noted elsewhere, the smaller the business the more likely the transaction will involve a transfer of assets rather than a transfer of corporate stock. This is true, even if the selling company is a corporation.

Generally, from a tax viewpoint, an asset transaction is more favorable to the buyer, and a stock transaction more favorable to the seller. In a stock transaction, the seller receives capital gains treatment on the difference between his cost basis and the amount received. And the buyer's cost basis for the assets remains the same as the seller's cost basis. In an asset transaction, the buyer gets a new cost basis for the assets purchased. However, the seller is subject to income tax both (1) on the gain associated with the sale at the business level and (2) on the gain associated with the sale when the sale proceeds are distributed to the selling stockholders.

Selling on an Installment Contract

Most sellers would prefer to sell for cash. However, they usually sell for some combination of cash and a contract on the balance carried by the seller. This phenomenon occurs because most buyers of small businesses do not have the resources to pay the full purchase price in cash. See Chapter 27, Trade-off between Cash and Terms, for a discussion of how to price a sale on an installment contract to achieve the desired cash equivalent value.

A contract sale is typically treated as an installment sale for income tax purposes (regardless of the amount of the down payment or even if there is no down payment). This means that the seller pays taxes on the business sale proceeds in the year in which she receives them. The seller, however, has the option of electing to include all the profit in the year of sale.

When a seller accepts an installment contract, she is putting herself in the position of a lender. Therefore, the contract should contain the same kind of protective covenants that a bank or other lender would require. Such covenants usually cover such items as (1) limiting salaries and withdrawals of the new owners, (2) preventing pledging the assets as collateral for other debt, and (3) maintaining certain financial ratios and levels of working capital and net worth. There are many horror stories involving contract sales without such covenants, in which the buyer soon brings the company to such a position that he is unable to make the contract payments.

Selling for Stock of the Buying Company

If a selling corporation receives the stock of the purchasing company, the transaction may be treated as a tax-free exchange. This means that the seller does not pay income taxes on the gain until she eventually sells the stock of the buying corporation. Of course, receiving stock in another company creates the whole problem of appraising the stock of the buying company.

Also, stock of a publicly traded corporation received in exchange for another company normally is restricted from resale on the open market for a period of two years. Restricted stock usually is valued at a price discount from the equivalent freely tradable stock (See Chapter 25, Discount for Lack of Marketability).

Leveraged Buyouts

The willingness of banks and other institutions to make loans for leveraged buyouts, including leveraged buyouts of small businesses, has made this form of transaction increasingly popular the past several years. The basic concept of the leveraged buyout is to use the assets of the selling company as collateral for a loan to buy the business.

Small businesses that do not have enough assets to secure a completely leveraged deal may be able to sell on the basis of a partly leveraged buyout. The buyer could raise part of the purchase price by means of a bank loan secured by the company's assets and give the seller a contract for the balance secured by the company's stock. Naturally, it is in the interest of both the buyer and the seller to carefully analyze the company's ability to pay off both the bank loan and the seller's contract.

Employee stock ownership plans (ESOPs) have been used more frequently in recent years in the buyouts of smaller companies (see Chapter 39, ESOPs in Small Companies).

Earn-Outs

If the buyer and seller would like to make a deal but cannot agree on a fixed price (because of differing earnings expectations or different degrees of confidence in the projections), the answer sometimes is to structure the transaction as an *earn-out*. In this case, the buyer pays some amount of cash at the time of the purchase and a specified participation in earnings for a certain period of time, often three to five years. There is no limit to the variety of earn-out arrangements. For example, if earnings before interest and taxes exceed 25 percent on the buyer's investment, the seller may receive 40 percent of the excess for a specified period of time. In some cases, a minimum and/or maximum amount for the earn-out may be indicated. *Pratt's Stats* (see Chapter 21, Comparative Transaction Databases) contains many examples of various earn-out transactions. In many cases, the total deal proceeds, if the earn-out targets are met, are substantially in excess of the noncontingent asking price for the business.

Sellers contemplating an earn-out arrangement should try to retain some control of the operation for the full period of the earn-out. This procedure is recommended in order to protect the sellers from changes in personnel and policies that may diminish or eliminate the value of the earn-out.

Contingencies

Occasionally, an unresolved contingency remains at the time a transaction is contemplated. The more common contingencies include (1) the outcome of lawsuits, (2) settlements of tax liabilities or refunds from past periods, and (3) costs of compliance with regulatory requirements. In such cases, the problem of the uncertain effect of the contingency's outcome on the value of the entity can be solved by creating an escrow account. Any proceeds from collection of contingent amounts or money left over after payment of contingent liabilities can be distributed from the escrow account to the seller.

Covenants Not to Compete

Data from *Pratt's Stats* suggest that in approximately half of the sales of small businesses and professional practices, the seller provides the buyer with a covenant not to compete. The covenant usually covers certain activities within a specific geographical area for a specific period of time. It may be incorporated into the purchase agreement, or it may be a separate document. Payments over the life of a covenant not to compete are ordinary income to the seller. The value of a covenant not to compete may be amortized by the buyer over a 15-year amortization period. It is important to have the covenant professionally valued at the time of the transaction. (See Chapter 42, Valuing Intangible Assets).

Employment Contracts

The value of a business can also be enhanced by having employment contracts with one or more key employees. The value attributable to such contracts is usually amortizable for income tax purposes. Such contracts should also be valued at the time of the transaction.

Allocating the Purchase Price

Purchase price allocation is a very important step that many buyers and sellers overlook. If either the buyer or the seller is audited, the purchase price allocation—documented by justification for the various amounts—is critical. If this procedure is not performed, one can expect that the Internal Revenue Service will suggest a less favorable purchase price allocation.

From the buyer's viewpoint, the most desirable objective is to allocate as much of the purchase price as possible to those assets that can be expensed, depreciated, or amortized more quickly. The buyer normally wants to see as much of the purchase price as possible allocated to such items as inventory and fixed assets with shorter depreciation periods.

If the purchase price significantly exceeds the value of the acquired tangible assets, the remaining purchase price must be allocated to the acquired intangible assets. Chapter 42 deals the subject of identifying and valuing specific intangible assets. The justification for the allocation to various depreciable and amortizable assets should be documented in writing.

The relative income tax circumstances of the buyer and seller usually have a bearing on the eventual agreement about allocating the purchase price, and the agreement may have a measurable impact on the price finally agreed on.

In the sale of the assets of a business, the Internal Revenue Service requires that Form 8594 be completed and filed by both buyer and seller when filing their next income tax return. It requires, among other things, information on how the sale price was allocated, especially the amounts for goodwill or going-concern value, employment agreements, and covenants not to compete. Form 8594 requires that both the buyer and seller disclose the allocated amount for each asset and that they agree on these amounts.

The following are some of the items that make up the purchase price of a business and therefore are part of the allocation:

- Furniture, fixtures, equipment, and machinery.
- Leasehold improvements.
- Licenses (liquor).
- Vehicles.
- Land.
- Buildings and improvements.
- Franchise cost.
- Covenant not to compete.
- Employment or consulting agreements.
- Patents, copyrights, mailing lists.
- Training and transition period.
- Use of trade name, telephone number, and so on.
- Goodwill or going-concern value.

We strongly emphasize the importance of allocating the purchase price among the assets as part of the appraisal performed at the time of the sale of the business. A proper allocation can help avoid an unfavorable allocation performed by the Internal Revenue Service as part of the audit process.

Summary

This chapter has dealt with the entire gamut, from deciding to buy or sell to closing the deal and allocating the purchase price. Good advance planning can help smooth the way and raise the chances of making a sound deal.

Often, the terms and structure of a deal are more important than the price. Chapter 27 discussed the trade-off between cash and various sets of terms, and this chapter discussed various sale structures.

In many cases, a business broker may be instrumental in finding buyers or sellers and in negotiating a deal. Business brokers' abilities to network between cities across the country have increased significantly in recent years. Business brokers may also be helpful in preparing purchase documents. Working with a business broker is discussed in the following chapter.

If the sale is structured as an asset sale (as opposed to a stock sale), the buyer and seller should agree on the allocation of purchase price, and IRS Form 8594, Asset Acquisition Statement, should be filed.

Bibliography

Articles

Berkowitz, Richard K., and Joseph A. Blanco. "Putting a Price Tag on Your Company." *Nation's Business*, January 1992, pp. 29–31.

Cohen, Ira D. "Ten Tips When Selling Your Firm." *Small Business Reports*, August 1990, pp. 42–45.

Cosman, Madeleine Pelner. "How to Price and Sell a Practice." *Ophthalmology Management*, June 1987, pp. 22–26.

Davies, Michael. "The Practical Side of Buying and Selling Companies: Bloopers and Winners." *The Journal of Business Valuation* (Proceedings of the 3rd Joint Business Valuation Conference of the CICBV and the ASA). Toronto: Canadian Institute of Certified Business Valuators, 1995, pp. 3–20.

Hays, Charles T. "Valuation and Tax Considerations in Selling the Closely-Held Corporation." *The National Public Accountant*, January/February 1997, pp. 53–57.

Kuhn, Robert Lawrence, and David H. Troob. "When It's Time to Sell the Firm." *Nation's Business*, July 1992, pp. 47–49.

Lipman, Frederick D. "Maximizing the Sale Price of a Business." *Corporate Controller*, January/February 1997, pp. 32–37.

Mangan, Doreen. "What Is Your Company Worth?" *Executive Female*, November/December 1990, p. 74.

Martin, J. Thomas. "Don't Overlook These Crucial Points in a Practice Sale: Whether You're Selling or Buying, This Checklist Will Help Protect You against Financial and Tax Risks." *Medical Economics*, January 6, 1992, pp. 95–97.

Melcher, Albert G. "Theory vs. Reality in Appraising for Small Business Brokerage." *ASA Valuation*, January 1992, pp. 60–72.

Reilly, Robert F. "Pricing and Structuring the Sale of a Closely Held Corporation." *The Ohio CPA Journal*, December 1995, pp. 13–16.

Reilly, Robert F., and Robert P. Schweihs. "Buying & Selling Closely-Held Corporations." *The National Public Accountant*, October 1996, pp. 21–24.

Scharfstein, Alan J. "The Right Price for a Business." *CPA Journal*, January 1991, pp. 42–47.

Sliwoski, Leonard J., and Maggie Jorgenson. "Acquiring a Small Business: How Much Can Your Client Afford?" *The National Public Accountant*, October 1996, pp. 16–20.

Stollings, George D. "Selling a Dental Practice." *Dental Economics*, April 1992, pp. 31–36.

Wilkinson, Chris B. "Pricing of Small to Medium-Sized Businesses: A Business Broker's Perspective." *Proceedings of the 12th Biennial Conference of the CICBV*, 1997, pp. 301–315.

Books

Buying & Selling Medical Practices: A Valuation Guide. Chicago: American Medical Association, 1990.

Cosman, Madeleine P. *How to Value and Sell Your Medical Practice*. Englewood Cliffs, NJ: Prentice Hall, 1995.

Horwich, Willard D. *Lawyer's and Accountants' Guide to Purchase and Sale of a Small Business*. New York: Rosenfeld Launer, 1991.

Klueger, Robert. *Buying and Selling a Business: A Step-by-Step Guide*. New York: John Wiley & Sons, 1995.

Lane, Marc J. *Purchase and Sale of Small Businesses: Tax and Legal Aspects*, 2d ed. New York: John Wiley & Sons, 1991, supplemented 1994.

Nottonson, Ira N., and Erin H. Wait. *The Secrets to Buying and Selling a Business*, 2d ed. Grants Pass, OR: Oasis Press, 1997.

Stefanelli, John. *The Sale and Purchase of Restaurants*, 2d ed. New York: John Wiley & Sons, 1990.

West, Thomas L. *Complete Guide to Business Brokerage*. Concord, MA: Business Brokerage Press, 1997.

West, Thomas L., and Jeffrey D. Jones. *Mergers and Acquisitions Handbook for Small and Midsized Companies*. New York: John Wiley & Sons, 1997.

Yegge, Wilbur M. *A Basic Guide for Buying and Selling a Company*. New York: John Wiley & Sons, 1996.

Chapter 44

Working with a Business Appraiser

*In any transaction where "value" is the most important issue, a compe-
tent, experienced, and professional appraiser should be consulted on behalf of the client to determine the true value of an enterprise.*[1]

Situations that may call for a professional appraisal include the various appraisal purposes and typical assignments discussed in Chapter
4. In addition to the basic service of appraising the business or practice,
the professional appraiser may be able to provide related services.

Services Typically Offered by Business Appraisers

Although all business appraisers do not necessarily offer all services,
the following are services business appraisers typically offer:

- Preliminary appraisal opinions.
- Complete appraisals, with oral reports, opinion reports, and abbre-
  viated narrative or comprehensive narrative reports.
- Service as arbitrator in valuation disputes.
- Service as mediator in valuation disputes.
- Assistance with purchase or sale negotiations.
- Assistance in structuring purchase or sale terms.
- Estate planning assistance.
- Assistance in drafting of buy-sell agreements.
- Assistance with public offerings.
- Fairness opinion on a proposed transaction.
- Solvency opinion on a proposed transaction.
- Assistance in designing classes of business interests in corporate or
  partnership reorganizations.
- Litigation support.
  - Evaluating a case.
  - Assistance with discovery.
  - Review of opposing appraisal reports.
  - Assistance with deposition of opposing experts and fact witnesses.
  - Research.
  - Expert testimony.
  - Rebuttal testimony.
  - Evaluating settlement offers.
  - Assisting with briefs and replies to briefs.
- Allocation of purchase price among classes of assets.
- Referrals to business brokers or intermediaries.

---

[1]John E. Moye, *Buying and Selling Businesses* (Minneapolis: National Practice Institute,
1983), p. 25.

Finding and Engaging an Appraiser

The task of locating the right appraiser for the job at hand is sometimes undertaken by the owner(s) of the business or professional practice in question. More often, however, assistance in finding an appraiser is provided by the owner's attorney, accountant, insurance agent, or other professional advisor. This is because these outside advisers are usually familiar with the qualifications of one or several business appraisers, some of whom they may have worked with on past occasions. If a referral is not available, lists of members of professional organizations that are accredited in business valuation are available from the professional organizations noted in Chapter 1.

Selecting the Appraiser

The more the client or the client's advisors know about the qualifications of any financial advisory firm or individual being considered, the greater the likelihood of selecting the appraiser who is best suited for the particular assignment. An appraiser being considered usually will have available a brochure describing his firm and a resume of his own qualifications and will provide references on request. It is appropriate to interview a prospective appraiser, either on the telephone or in person. During the interview, it is proper to inquire about the appraiser's and/or his firm's specific experience relating directly to the assignment at hand. Alternatively, the appraisal firm or appraiser may be contacted in writing, with the assignment described and an inquiry made about the appraiser's qualifications to perform it.

The exact qualifications desired depend to some degree on the specific situation. Certainly, if there is litigation or potential litigation involved, experience with court testimony is an important factor. In any case, it is desirable that the appraiser be familiar with the law as it relates to the particular valuation situation.

When contacting a prospective appraiser, it is desirable to be as candid and complete as possible about such matters as the identity, nature, and size of the company, the purpose and scope of the appraisal assignment, and the desired engagement schedule. Disclosure of confidential client information to unauthorized parties is prohibited, of course, by the codes of ethics of the American Society of Appraisers and of the other professional appraisal organizations. Confidentiality of client information should not be a problem when dealing with a reputable appraisal firm.

Any potential conflicts of interest should be explored at the outset with the prospective appraiser. If the prospective appraiser has any potential conflict of interest with respect to either the client or the assignment, he or she should disclose such potential conflict immediately.

Qualifications of Business Appraisers

The primary objective is to retain someone who has a depth of knowledge and experience in the field of business appraisal. Both courts and attorneys are becoming much more sophisticated and demanding with regard to appraiser credentials and capabilities.

Credentials.   The professional credentials available to business appraisers were discussed in Chapter 1. To summarize, they are as follows:

- FASA (Fellow of the American Society of Appraisers), ASA (Accredited Senior Appraiser), AM (Accredited Member), awarded by the American Society of Appraisers.
- FIBA (Fellow of the Institute of Business Appraisers), CBA (Certified Business Appraiser), awarded by the Institute of Business Appraisers.
- CVA (Certified Valuation Analyst), awarded by the National Association of Certified Valuation Analysts.
- ABV (Accredited in Business Valuation), a specialty designation within the American Institute of Certified Public Accountants.
- CBV (Chartered Business Valuator), awarded by the Canadian Institute of Chartered Business Valuators.
- CFA (Chartered Financial Analyst), awarded by the Association for Investment Management and Research (this association is more oriented toward larger businesses and publicly traded securities but is gradually including more closely held business appraisal content in their curriculum and examinations).

In order to help the reader assess the merits of these credentials, the respective requirements to achieve each of them are listed in Chapter 1. Courts generally do not require any of the above credentials in order to qualify as a business valuation expert. However, they may recognize substantial differences in credibility when faced with one appraiser who possesses professional credentials and one who does not. It is not only holding an accreditation that counts, but continuing educational involvement, such as attendance at professional conferences, speaking, teaching, and writing. The degree and depth of business valuation experience also is of great importance.

One example of drawing a sharp distinction between experts occurred in a recent appellate court decision. The appeals court explained why it upheld the trial court's $5.5 million, based on plaintiff's expert's testimony, in a legal malpractice case:

- Defendant's expert testified that he devoted only 5 percent of his time to business valuations, while plaintiff's expert testified that he was engaged full-time in business valuations and in assisting clients in the buying and selling of companies.
- Plaintiff's expert testified that he had performed well in excess of 500 business valuations. Defendant's expert testified that in the past five years his firm had performed 31 business valuations.

- Plaintiff's expert had been engaged by the Internal Revenue Service, the Securities and Exchange Commission, and the Justice Department of the United States to assist in matters pertaining to the valuation of companies. Defendant's expert had no comparable experience.
- Plaintiff's expert had had his work in the field published. Defendant's expert could make no similar claim.
- Defendant's expert acknowledged that the American Society of Appraisers is a professional association specifically geared towards business valuations. Plaintiff's expert was a member of that association; defendant's expert was not.[2]

Industry Experience.   The consensus on the parts of both attorneys and the courts is that experience in valuing companies in the industry in question is desirable but not nearly as important as a depth of business appraisal skill. No amount of industry management or consulting experience is an adequate substitute for business valuation expertise.

In a case where the Tax Court rejected the valuation testimony of an industry expert, Judge Laro explained: "The fact that (the expert) is knowledgeable about this industry does not compel us to credit the testimony on the Transferred Assets' fair market value."[3]

In a divorce case, the husband's attorney said that the court should not have considered the testimony of the wife's expert because he had no prior experience in valuing companies in the particular industry. In upholding the trial court's conclusion of value very close to that of the wife's expert, the appellate court noted:

> [He has] testified many times regarding the valuation of companies but never concerning the value of an insurance agency. . . . A party seeking to have a witness qualified as an expert must lay a proper foundation showing the expert has some knowledge or experience in the area about which he expresses his opinion."[4]

The court cited the following seven specific factors that supported the appraiser's qualifications to testify as an expert:

1. *He testified as to the valuation of companies quite a number of times.*
2. *He reviewed all the work reports and tax documents supplied to him.*
3. *He knew what a risk manager was.*
4. *He generally understood (the subject) business.*
5. *He relied on all the documentation supplied to him.*
6. *He used a conservative multiplier.*
7. *He knew of the differences between (another company owned by husband) and its subsidiary . . . although he treated them similarly for accounting purposes.*

---

[2]*Schlesinger* v. *Herzog*, No. 95-CA-1127, 1996 WL 157382, La. Ct. App. 4th Cir. (Apr. 3, 1996).
[3]*Pabst Brewing Company* v. *Commissioner*, T.C. Memo 1996-506 (Nov. 12, 1996).
[4]*Blinderman* v. *Reib*, No. 1-94-2557, 1996 WL 454954, Ill. App. 1st Dist. (Aug. 13, 1996).

The circuit court neither abused its discretion nor committed plain error in considering (the appraiser's) testimony.[5]

An attorney's perspective on qualifications of appraisers is well articulated in an interview with one of the nation's leading gift and estate tax attorneys, Ron Aucutt, which is included in its entirety as Exhibit 44-1.

Fees and Scheduling

Besides determining that the prospective appraiser is properly qualified, the client and the appraiser should reach a mutual understanding about fees and schedule. Most appraisal firms base their fees on the amount of time that the engagement will require for one or several members of the appraisal staff, plus out-of-pocket expenses. Most appraisers have an hourly or daily billing rate, much as in a law practice. Some assignments, especially ones where the required time is difficult or impossible to estimate accurately, may be undertaken strictly on an hourly basis, usually with some estimated range of cost. If the appraiser has been furnished with sufficient information, and if the assignment can be well-defined, most appraisers are willing to commit to a fixed fee for their services, plus out-of-pocket expenses. If court testimony or arbitration may be involved, the appraiser may quote a fixed fee for the basic appraisal, with the trial preparation, depositions, and court time charged on an hourly or daily basis. This is because the amount of such time required usually is out of the appraiser's control.

The following information about a prospective appraisal assignment is helpful to an appraiser for quoting a fixed or estimated fee for an assignment, as well as for discussing the engagement schedule:

1. Line(s) of business.
2. Location(s) of operations.
3. Form of organization (C corporation, S corporation, general or limited partnership, LLP or LLC, sole proprietorship).
4. Purpose of the appraisal.
5. Ownership interest to be valued (100 percent or some partial ownership interest).
6. Applicable valuation date or dates.
7. Status of financial statements (audited, reviewed, externally compiled, internally compiled, tax returns only, records in shoe boxes, and whether on a cash or an accrual basis).
8. Any subsidiaries or financial interest in other companies.
9. Annual revenues.
10. Annual profits.
11. Approximate book value.
12. Form and extent of appraisal report desired.
13. Desired schedule.

---

[5]Ibid.

Exhibit 44–1

Guest Interview:

Criteria important to attorneys in selecting valuation experts

Ronald D. Aucutt, a member of the firm of Miller & Chevalier, Chartered, Washington, D.C., specializes in assisting clients nationwide with the transfer of wealth from one generation to another, particularly including the orderly and tax-efficient succession of family-owned businesses. Among his many leadership roles, he is a member of the Council of the Section of Taxation of the American Bar Association, a Fellow of the American College of Tax Counsel and a Fellow and Regent of the American College of Trust and Estate Counsel. He has written extensively and appears frequently at bar and estate planning forums. The Washington, D.C., Estate Planning Council recently honored Mr. Aucutt with the award of Estate Planner of the Year. In this interview he gives us candid insights about what attorneys look for in the selection of valuation experts. –SP

SP: What are the most important factors you consider in selecting a valuation expert?
RA: Broadly speaking, two things:

Ronald Aucutt

- How well the person will be received by the court, appeals officer, or other forum in which that person will appear, and
- How well I believe the chemistry will work out between the appraiser and myself.

SP: What are the most important factors in the chemistry between the appraiser and yourself?
RA: I'd say three traits are especially critical:

- **Adaptability.** Does the appraiser recognize the uniqueness of each assignment? Or does the appraiser do "cookie cutter" work, showing more interest in spouting a generic philosophy than in examining the facts of the case?
- **Ability and willingness to listen.** This is an often overlooked, but very important characteristic. If a controversy proceeds to litigation and the appraiser is called upon to give a deposition or testify in court, it is crucial that the appraiser understand and answer each question that is asked, nothing more, nothing less, and nothing else, and keep mental track of previous questions and answers, insofar as they bear on the question at hand. Loose cannons can be loose cannons.
- **Responsiveness, timeliness.** Usually, the appraiser's input is needed to support the taxpayer in meeting certain deadlines. If the case develops into litigation, there will be numerous important deadlines that must be met. If an appraiser shows difficulty providing what is needed when it is needed, from the engagement letter to returning phone calls to submitting written

work product - this could portend more serious difficulties later.

SP: Going to the matter of reception by the court or other forum, what do you consider the most important factors?
RA: Again, I would broadly group them in three categories:

- **Credentials.** How will this appraiser's written report and oral testimony be received? Is the appraiser experienced with appraising this type of asset? How has the appraiser's testimony been received and treated by the courts? (This can be explored through a computer search.) How helpful and effective has the appraiser been in other cases that have not proceeded to judgment and a written opinion? (This can be explored through networking.)

   The best appraiser to engage is one with whom the lawyer has worked before. But this is not always practical - "there's a first time for everything" - and the best alternative is to obtain copies of the appraiser's previous work product, if possible, and to talk to other lawyers who have engaged that appraiser.

   I also often solicit and certainly respect recommendations from other appraisers that I've worked with successfully. In fact, that's how I first started working with you and your colleagues at Willamette.

- **Independence.** Will the appraiser come across as an advocate for the taxpayer, rather than an objective witness whose first duty is to assist the court? If a business is involved and the appraiser is affiliated with the accounting firm that prepares and/or audits the financial statements of the business, will the appraisal seem objective? (My answer is generally no, because of the appearance of bias, even if the accounting firm keeps the audit and valuation functions completely separate.)

Exhibit 44-1

- **Understandability, credibility, and effectiveness**. Does the appraiser have the ability to communicate to an appeals officer or judge (or jury, if there is one) in a straightforward and understandable manner, both in writing and orally? Does the appraiser hem and haw, ramble, overuse aspirated pauses, like "uh," or have any other annoying habit? Does the appraiser generally use good English? Does the appraiser hold eye contact? Does it sound as if the appraiser is speaking from personal experience and judgment, rather than parroting some textbook approach or reciting what the lawyer wants to hear? In sum, does the appraiser project an image of competence, thoroughness, confidence, and sincerity?

SP: You obviously need a well-researched work product. You also mentioned good writing and good oral communication. What do you consider the relative importance of these three factors to be?

RA: Solid credentials and the facility for effective oral communication with the court or other forum are essential, and I wouldn't hire an expert without these characteristics. As for the written report, I can help work with that if I have to. I would expect to hire a firm with very good research capabilities, but the quality and comprehensiveness of the research itself is a little harder for the attorney to evaluate. Your *Valuing a Business* book is useful in that respect, but something organized more as a handbook for attorneys would be helpful.

SP: I appreciate your saying that, because we're working on exactly that, with scheduled completion early in September. Going back to the criteria for selection of experts, do you sometimes hire an expert strictly as a consulting expert, without the same emphasis on communication skills?

RA: No. Even when we hire an expert as a consultant, we want the person to have the ability to be a testifying expert.

SP: Do you often hire more than one valuation expert on a case?

RA: Yes. Sometimes an additional expert can offer a useful additional perspective. Also, having more than one expert provides the client some insurance in case we find along the way that one expert isn't working out very well.

SP: How important is experience in valuing companies in the specific industry in which the company is involved?

RA: That's way down on the list of my priorities. It's nice if it's feasible, but we need an appraiser who knows the appraisal business. That person will know where to look to find the industry information that's needed.

SP: On a related note, what's your posture on using an industry expert as a valuation witness?

RA: We wouldn't have an industry expert that's not with an appraisal firm testify on value. We might hire an industry expert as a resource for the appraiser, and might also have that person testify on what's happening in the industry, but not an opinion on value.

SP: That's certainly consistent with what we've seen in the court cases. We recently reviewed two cases in a single issue where the court said the industry expert wasn't qualified as an expert on valuation (See Pabst Brewing v. Commissioner, p. 7, and Laurel Gonzales v. Straight Arrow Publishers, Inc., p. 8, both in the January 1997 issue).

How does cost enter into your criteria for selecting an appraiser?

RA: We want the best appraiser, and we would not make a decision based on cost. That should not really be a concern. I have not seen a good appraisal that didn't have the potential to pay for itself many times over. Clients generally understand this, especially when faced with a large tax bill. I think the client is as well off investing in a good appraiser as in a good attorney. **BVU**

SOURCE: "Criteria Important to Attorneys in Selecting Valuation Experts: An Interview with Ronald D. Aucutt," *Shannon Pratt's Business Valuation Update*, February 1997, pp. 1–2.

Some clients or their attorneys wait until the last minute to contact an appraiser, failing to allow a comfortable lead time to thoroughly perform the requisite analyses. In some cases, the client has received an unexpected offer for the purchase of her company, and she needs the opinion of the expert appraiser in only a few days in order to formulate her response. Most appraisal firms have enough flexibility in their staff scheduling to accommodate such urgent needs when necessary. It is our hope, however, that those who have read this book have gained some appreciation of the complexities of business appraisal and will give their appraisers as much lead time as possible to do the job properly. In most cases, that means a matter of weeks rather than days. If litigation is involved, lead time for adequate preparation becomes even more important.

Professional Services Agreement

Once the appraiser has been selected and the assignment and fee arrangements agreed on, the engagement should be committed to writing, usually through the appraisal firm's standard professional services agreement or through an engagement letter, supplemented as necessary to provide complete details of the assignment. The professional services agreement basically should cover the definition of the valuation assignment, as discussed in some detail in Chapter 2. To summarize, the professional services agreement, engagement letter, or whatever form is used to formalize the engagement in writing should cover the following points:

1. The property to be valued.
2. The purpose(s) of the valuation.
3. The valuation date(s).
4. The applicable standard of value.
5. The form and extent of the appraisal report.
6. The engagement schedule.
7. Fee arrangements.
8. Whatever limiting conditions may be applicable.

The engagement letter should be signed by the appraiser and the client. It should be supplemented by written addenda if any of the factors are changed during the course of the engagement.

Contingent and Limiting Conditions

Exhibit 44-2 is a sample statement of contingent and limiting conditions applicable to an appraisal engagement. One of the most important conditions is that the appraisal is valid (1) only for the appraisal date and (2) only for the specific use stated in the professional services agreement. The appraisal date and the use to which the appraisal will be put are critical to the appraisal. There have been many misapplications of appraisals where they have been used for some date and/or for some use for which they were not prepared. The most certain way to prevent such misuse is to include the above limitation in the written professional services agreement, as well as in the final written report.

Exhibit 44–2

CONTINGENT AND LIMITING CONDITIONS

This appraisal is made subject to the following general contingent and limiting conditions:

1. We assume no responsibility for the legal description or matters including legal or title considerations. Title to the subject assets, properties, or business interests is assumed to be good and marketable unless otherwise stated.

2. The subject assets, properties, or business interests are appraised free and clear of any or all liens or encumbrances unless otherwise stated.

3. We assume responsible ownership and competent management with respect to the subject assets, properties, or business interests.

4. The information furnished by others is believed to be reliable. However, we issue no warranty or other form of assurance regarding its accuracy.

5. We assume no hidden or unapparent conditions regarding the subject assets, properties, or business interests.

6. We assume that there is full compliance with all applicable federal, state, and local regulations and laws unless the lack of compliance is stated, defined, and considered in the appraisal report.

7. We assume that all required licenses, certificates of occupancy, consents, or legislative or administrative authority from any local, state, or national government, or private entity or organization have been or can be obtained or reviewed for any use on which the opinion contained in this report is based.

8. Unless otherwise stated in this report, we did not observe, and we have no knowledge of, the existence of hazardous materials with regard to the subject assets, properties, or business interests. However, we are not qualified to detect such substances. We assume no responsibility for such conditions or for any expertise required to discover them.

9. Possession of this report does not carry with it the right of publication. It may not be used for any purpose by any person other than the client to whom it is addressed without our written consent, and, in any event, only with proper written qualifications and only in its entirety.

10. We, by reason of this opinion, are not required to furnish a complete valuation report, or to give testimony, or to be in attendance in court with reference to the assets, properties, or business interests in question unless arrangements have been previously made.

11. Neither all nor any part of the contents of this report shall be disseminated to the public through advertising, public relations, news, sales, or other media without our prior written consent and approval.

12. The analyses, opinions, and conclusions presented in this report apply to this engagement only and may not be used out of the context presented herein. This report is valid only for the effective date(s) specified herein and only for the purpose(s) specified herein.

SOURCE: Willamette Management Associates.

Information to Provide to the Appraiser

Exhibit 44-3 provides a generalized checklist of documents and other information that may be necessary or helpful for the appraisal. Naturally, not all of the listed items are applicable for every appraisal, and for some situations, relevant specialized information will not be included on the list. The list should be helpful to the client, however, in anticipating and preparing for the information requirements of the appraisal. The types of analysis to be done on the various data have already been discussed throughout the book, of course, so they will not be repeated in this chapter.

Financial Statements

The key phrase about the length of time for which financial statements should be provided is the "relevant period." If operations have changed significantly, financial statements may be relevant only for the period since operations have been as they are now. On the other hand, for a very cyclical business, the appraiser may require statements for a long period of time to make an assessment of normalized earning power.

For many small businesses, financial statements may be somewhat incomplete or even nonexistent. If the appraiser has to try to create the necessary financial information from original source documents (invoices, check records, and so on), the process can be time-consuming and expensive. In any case, the appraiser has to perform the best analysis possible with what data are available. The appraisal report will contain appropriate disclaimers regarding any information that is unavailable or unverifiable.

Other Financial Data

The list in Exhibit 44-3 is self-explanatory and covers a wide spectrum of data. The relative importance of the items varies from case to case, of course, and common sense should suggest which ones are most important in any given situation. Documents that can be easily copied or prepared can be provided to the appraiser prior to the field visit to the premises and interview(s) with owners and/or management. Those that are somewhat voluminous generally can be reviewed on-site by the appraiser during the field visit to the company.

Company Documents

Unless the company is a sole proprietorship, the appraiser usually will want to review the basic corporate or partnership documents and any special agreements among the parties. These documents contain information about the various rights and restrictions related to the interests and thus can have an important bearing on value. These documents can be either provided to the appraiser separately from that field visit or inspected on the premises or at the offices of the client's legal adviser.

Exhibit 44–3

DOCUMENTS AND INFORMATION CHECKLIST

FINANCIAL STATEMENTS
Balance sheets, income statements, statements of operations, and statements of stockholders' (owners') equity for the last five
    fiscal years (or other relevant period)
Income tax returns for the same years
Latest interim statements and interim statements for comparable period(s) of previous year

OTHER FINANCIAL DATA
Summary property, plant, and equipment list and depreciation schedule
Aged accounts receivable summary
Aged accounts payable summary
List of marketable securities and prepaid expenses
Inventory summary, with any necessary information on inventory accounting policies
Synopsis of leases for facilities or equipment
Any other existing contracts (employment agreements, covenants not to compete, supplier agreements, customer agreements,
    royalty agreements, equipment lease or rental contracts, loan agreements, labor contracts, employee benefit plans, and so
    on)
List of stockholders or partners, with number of shares (or units) owned by each
Schedule of insurance in force (key-person life, property and casualty, liability)
Budgets or projections, for a minimum of five years
List of subsidiaries and/or financial interests in other companies
Key personnel compensation schedule, including benefits and personal expenses

COMPANY DOCUMENTS
Articles of incorporation, bylaws, or other organizational documents, and any amendments to such documents
Any existing buy-sell agreements, options to purchase stock, or rights of first refusal
Franchise or operating agreements, if any

OTHER INFORMATION
Brief history, including how long in business and details of any changes in ownership and/or any bona fide offers recently received
Brief description of the business, including position relative to competition and any factors that make the business unique
Marketing literature (catalogs, brochures, advertisements, and so on)
List of locations where company operates, with size and recent appraisals
List of competitors, with location, relative size, and any relevant factors
Organization chart
Résumés of key personnel, with age, position, compensation, length of service, education, and prior experience
Personnel profile: number of employees by functional groupings, such as production, sales, engineering/R&D, personnel and
    accounting, customer service/field support, and so forth
Trade associations to which the company belongs or would be eligible for membership
Relevant trade or government publications (especially market forecasts)
Any existing indicators of asset values, including latest property tax assessments and any appraisals that have been performed
List of customer relationships, supplier relationships, contracts, patents, copyrights, trademarks, and other intangible assets
Any contingent or off-balance-sheet liabilities (pending lawsuits, compliance requirements, warranty or other product liabilities,
    estimate of medical benefits for retirees, and so on)
Any filings or correspondence with regulatory agencies
Information on prior transactions in the stock or any related party transactions

SOURCE: Willamette Management Associates.

Other Information

The "other information" category covers a universe of possibilities, and it is difficult to offer useful generalizations about it. The suggested list in Exhibit 44-3 should provide enough guidance to trigger the necessary thinking about the most important categories of relevant information.

Again, the extent to which various materials are provided to the appraiser, prior to the on-site visit, is largely a matter of convenience and scheduling.

If the totality of Exhibit 44-3 and other aspects of client involvement in the appraisal process seem overwhelming, the client should talk to the appraiser about what is actually required in light of the scope and purpose of the assignment. An experienced appraiser will be able to assess what data are specifically relevant to the appraisal issue at hand. Most appraisers will cooperate to the utmost to avoid making the process any more time-consuming or disruptive for the client than is absolutely necessary to get the job done properly.

Field Visit

In the vast majority of appraisal assignments, it is desirable to have the appraiser visit the operating location(s). This first-hand visit to the operating premises usually can help the appraiser gain an understanding of the operation beyond what is possible in a "desktop" appraisal (one performed entirely on the basis of telephone interviews and a study of the documents without a visit to the facilities). If expert testimony may be required, courts tend to place more credibility on testimony of an appraiser who has visited premises of the company than on testimony of one who has not.

Preparation

To the extent possible, the appraiser usually wants to review and analyze financial statements and as many documents as conveniently possible before the field trip. This way, the appraiser can (1) have an understanding of the business before arriving there and (2) be prepared with a list of general and specific questions that otherwise would have to be covered at some other time (or may even be overlooked).

Mission

The kinds of information the appraiser will want to glean through the field visit have been discussed throughout the previous chapters. The field trip can be a convenient time to review some of the documents that would be cumbersome or inconvenient to supply to the appraiser away from the premises.

The field trip usually is an excellent time to interview owners and/or managers. The appraiser's physical presence on the premises may help to trigger relevant questions that may not occur to her in the surroundings of her own conference room or office. If interviews with several people are appropriate, it usually is more convenient to conduct them on the premises than away. Also, information usually is at hand for any questions management is unable to answer completely from memory.

Generally speaking, the mission of the field trip consists of gaining a good overview of operations, getting whatever specific information is needed that has not been obtained by other means, and assessing all the qualitative factors discussed in Chapter 10. As noted elsewhere, one of the main objectives is to assess factors that might cause the future to differ from what the past record might indicate.

Confidentiality

Confidentiality is one problem that the appraiser frequently has to handle carefully on field trips. If a business is being put up for sale, the owners may not want the employees or other people to know about it. There can be many other good reasons for confidentiality. Experienced appraisers have learned to work around this problem. They can dress and act unobtrusively. If they have to be introduced or identified to someone who is not a confidant in the situation, they are "consultants," which is an accurate and adequately abstruse label.

As a last resort, the appraiser might visit the premises after working hours, when employees are not present. However, this will not give the appraiser as good a picture as if she sees the facility in operation.

Adversarial Proceedings

Another problem that the appraiser sometimes faces is opposition to an adequate facilities visit (or sometimes any facilities visit at all) in the case of an adversarial proceeding. Undoubtedly, this problem most commonly occurs in appraisals being made for the purpose of property settlements in divorces.

If this problem occurs, it is the responsibility of the client's attorney to make the necessary arrangements for the appraiser to visit the facilities and interview the necessary people. Case law generally supports the right of the parties at interest to have as much access to books and records as necessary to do the job properly.[6] The parties should understand that the field visit is a standard part of the appraiser's work. They should understand that the appraiser is not an adverse party and is not an advocate for either party. Rather, the appraiser has been retained to render an independent opinion about value, as discussed in the final section of this chapter. When using a reputable, professional appraiser, the parties should not have to be concerned with confidentiality. Furthermore, the party who is in the adversarial position to the appraiser's client should welcome the opportunity to tell his or her side of the story to the appraiser.

If all discovery has to proceed through interrogatories and court orders, the process will be much more time-consuming, costly, and disruptive to the business operation. It is usually a good business decision for

---

[6]This issue is discussed in Barth Goldberg and Joseph N. DuCanto, *Valuation of Divorce Assets,* 1994 Supplement (St. Paul: West Publishing Co., 1994), pp. 41–45.

parties on both sides of a dispute to cooperate with independent appraisers. More discussion on adversary proceedings is included in Chapter 46, Litigation.

The Appraisal Report

As noted earlier, the scope of the appraisal report should be addressed when the appraiser is engaged. The form, length, and content are dictated primarily by the purpose of the appraisal and the audience for the report. In some cases, the report format is mandated or heavily influenced by law or convention. In such cases, an experienced appraiser can give the client guidance as to the appropriate form and scope of the report. In other cases, the scope of the written report is largely or totally a matter of client preference.[7]

In some cases, only an oral report is necessary. In such an instance, it usually is best if the report can be made at a meeting, so that the appraiser can go over work papers and other materials to the extent necessary for the client to understand how the appraiser arrived at the value indication. Sometimes, however, logistics dictate that a telephone conversation will have to suffice for the oral report.

In some cases, only an opinion report is required—sometimes a single sentence. More commonly, an opinion report is one or two pages, outlining concisely the assignment, the steps taken, the approaches used, and the conclusion.

The next level would be an abbreviated narrative report that would fill in more detail on steps taken and information sources used. It usually would give specific numbers, such as earnings, capitalization rates, and asset values used in the various approaches. It may include one or more supporting tables.

A comprehensive narrative report could run from 15 to well over 100 pages, depending on the purpose of the appraisal, how complex the appraisal was, and how great the need for a comprehensive and documented written report.[8]

The purpose and the intended (or possible) audience of the report are important. Reports that are strictly for a client's internal use usually do not need to include nearly so much detail as those intended for outside use. An appraisal report for a possible sale of a business or practice, for example, may be fairly brief if it is just for the guidance of the owner. If prospective purchasers will (or may) see it, however, considerably more detail may be warranted.

Similarly, appraisal reports strictly for buy-sell agreements and to determine life insurance needs may be fairly brief. However, if the same

---

[7]Analysts are encouraged to consult professional standards regarding appraisal work product. See, for example, ASA Standard BVS-VIII, "Comprehensive, Written Business Valuation Report," available from *Business Valuation Review*, PO Box 101923, Denver, CO 80250, (303) 758-6148.

[8]A sample of a narrative report is included as Chapter 18 in Pratt, Reilly, and Schweihs, *Valuing a Business*, 3d ed., pp. 393–52.

report may also be used for gift or estate taxes, a longer report may be necessary in order to encompass all the factors contained in Revenue Ruling 59-60.

If so desired by the client or his attorney or other representative, the appraiser can be quite helpful in making suggestions as to the appropriate format, content, and length of the report, once he has a good idea of the purpose of the appraisal assignment.

Independence of the Appraiser

In most situations, the appraiser is independent of the client, which means that the appraiser (1) has no financial interest in the property being appraised, (2) is not an employee or agent of the client, and (3) neither has nor has had any financial or other dealing with the client that would prejudice his ability to render a fair and impartial opinion about the value of the subject property. Professional ethics require that disclosure be made to the extent that these conditions are not met.

Unless otherwise made clear, when a professional appraiser expresses his independent opinion about value—whether in a written report, court testimony, or some other context—he is acting neither as an agent nor as an advocate of the client. Rather, the appraiser is an advocate of his own professional opinion. This does not mean that someone who has made an appraisal cannot assume a role that is not independent (such as that of a negotiator or agent for the client in effecting a transaction). Rather, that role is different from that of an independent appraiser, and that relationship must be made clear to the parties involved. When an appraiser accepts an assignment as an *arbitrator* or *mediator,* he or she maintains the role of an independent appraiser and is not an agent of any principal (as discussed more fully in the last chapter of this book).

Summary

Business appraisers not only value businesses or business interests, but they also offer many related services. These services include arbitration, negotiation, litigation support (consultation and/or expert testimony), deal structuring, tax planning, fairness opinions, solvency opinions, assistance with drafting buy-sell and/or arbitration agreements, purchase price allocation among categories of assets, and many other services.

Qualified appraisers may be located by referrals or through professional appraisal associations. Qualifications to consider include academic and professional credentials, relevant experience, and knowledge of applicable valuation law. Referrals may be obtained from attorneys who are active in either tax planning or business purchase and sale activity. Business appraisers are much more sophisticated than they were a few years ago, due to a plethora of available business valuation professional educational programs. The courts and attorneys are increasingly aware of this and are increasingly less tolerant of unqualified people performing business appraisal services.

The chapter has covered the information that should be provided to the appraiser so that the appraiser can make a reasonable engagement proposal, including a realistic estimate of the fee and schedule. Many clients and their attorneys underestimate the time and cost required to do a proper business appraisal. It is important to allow an adequate budget and enough lead time for the appraiser to perform all of the requisite appraisal procedures. The chapter has given a summary of the general information the appraiser ultimately will need to complete the engagement. The chapter has also discussed the mission and importance of the field visit.

Generally speaking, it should be expected that the appraiser will be independent and will provide a best estimate of value according to the applicable standard of value, without bias. There may be exceptions to this when the appraiser is retained in the role of a consultant or negotiator. The role of the appraiser should be made clear at the time of the engagement. Should this role change, the change should be documented in writing.

Chapter 45

Working with a Business Broker

An analyst or client considering buying or selling a business or practice first needs to decide whether or not to use a business intermediary.[1] An increasing number of buyers and sellers are using the services of intermediaries. This is partly because both the number of intermediaries and their visibility is increasing. But perhaps more importantly, it is because the professionalism and scope of services of intermediaries have increased significantly in the last few years.

Services Offered by a Business Broker

The primary focus of business broker services has always been bringing buyers and sellers together. However, the scope of their services has increased significantly in recent years.

One of the most important services is helping to ensure a "clean" deal, where buyers and sellers will both benefit from full disclosure and understanding of the transaction. This notion carries all the way from assisting with proper due diligence to ensuring that all the appropriate documentation is completed at closing.

Most business brokers have typically represented the seller of a business through an agency relationship as the seller's sole and exclusive agent. More and more, however, brokers are being asked to represent buyers. This gives the buyer the advantage of the broker's expertise and can save the buyer considerable time that might otherwise be wasted.

Among other services offered by business brokers, is consulting for a fixed or hourly fee with buyer or seller clients who may have located a business on their own and need assistance in valuing or structuring the transaction.

A professional broker should provide sellers or buyers with practical advice on many of the following issues:

- Probability of the business being sold.
- Necessary steps, legal and otherwise, to prepare the business for sale.
- Estimate of costs involved to buyer/seller.
- Responsibilities of the parties in the sale process: broker, buyer, seller, attorney, accountant, lender.
- Estimate of total transaction time from engagement to closing.

---

[1] *Intermediaries* include the traditional business broker, normally handling transactions under $1 million and averaging around $100,000 or less, with the majority of their transactions under $200,000; merger and acquisition specialists, typically handling transactions from about $500,000 to $50 million; and investment bankers, typically handling transactions over $25 million. These divisions are by no means clear-cut. The *investment banker* typically includes the service of raising debt or hybrid capital to help finance a transaction. Such services are now available for transactions of only a few million dollars. However, many Wall Street investment bankers are typically interested in transactions starting at about $50 million.

- Confidentiality requirement.
- Timing on offers, counteroffers, escrow, closing.
- Purchaser cash requirements.
- Skills required to operate the business.
- Other listings in this range and alternate investment options.
- Suggested selling price and deal structure.
- Preclosing and post-closing responsibilities of the parties.
- Estimated net proceeds at closing.

Criteria for Selecting a Broker

A seller should select a broker whose direct sales efforts, or whose particular listing network, will be likely to reach the potential buyers for that seller's business. A buyer would be wise to make his or her interests known to several different brokers who may have access to listings that would be of interest.

The following criteria deserve consideration when selecting a broker, depending on the situation:

1. Types of businesses commonly brokered.
2. Size of businesses commonly brokered.
3. Geographical scope.
4. Overall competence of the broker.
5. Success ratio (percentage of listings actually sold).
6. Willingness of broker to spend money advertising the business for sale.

Types of Businesses

Certain brokers specialize in specific types of businesses and practices, such as radio and TV stations, magazines, beer distributorships, auto dealerships, funeral homes, hotels and motels, accounting practices, or medical practices. Others specialize in more general categories, such as wholesalers, retailers, or manufacturers. Many others do not necessarily specialize as a matter of policy. Nonetheless, they have considerable experience in transactions in one or a few industries. A broker experienced in an industry usually would have an advantage over a broker without such experience both (1) in finding buyers and sellers in that industry and (2) in negotiating a mutually satisfactory transaction.

Size of Businesses

Most brokers tend to concentrate their efforts within a certain price range. Some brokers may do very well with businesses priced under $100,000. Others find their level of comfort and success in the $100,000 to $500,000 range. And still others do most of their business in the

$500,000 and up category. Buyers and sellers should seek brokers who generally handle transactions in the appropriate size category.

Geographical Scope

Regional and national connections are not important to a seller whose business would appeal only to a local buyer, such as small retailers, taverns, and so on. However, if a buyer could conceivably come from elsewhere in the region or nation, the seller would want to contact a broker whose connections extend outside the local area. A seller should inquire whether the brokers' networks would facilitate the exposure of the seller's listing in the various markets where buyers might be located. Much more networking is available among brokers nationally now than was the case a few years ago.

A buyer seeking to locate in a particular city logically would talk to brokers in that city. If he thinks he might be interested in one of several cities, however, he should talk to (1) brokers belonging to the multiple-listing networks or to (2) one who has connections with brokers in other cities.

General Competence

Naturally, a broker's competence is an important consideration. However, competence is not easy to judge. A seller or buyer can inquire about (1) the broker's educational and professional credentials (such as CBI or CBC, see below), (2) how long he has been in the business, and (3) what his experience has been with the type of company in mind. Beyond that, sellers or buyers should ask for and contact the broker's references. Some brokers may be reluctant to give out names and addresses of previous clients as references due to the confidentiality request of both buyers and sellers. Most brokers, however, can and will give out names of their banker, accountant, attorney, and other professional references that will satisfy the purchaser's or seller's need for some comfort level with references.

Of particular note among brokers' professional credentials is the Certified Business Intermediary (CBI) designation offered by the International Business Brokers Association. The requirements are as follows:

1. A minimum of three years of recent full-time business brokerage experience. A college degree or related work experience may be submitted with the request that it be accepted as an equivalent of up to two of the three years of business brokerage experience.
2. Sixty hours of IBBA courses, including:
   a. Principles and Ethics of Business Brokerage (8 hours).
   b. Analyzing and Recasting Financial Statements (15 hours).
   c. Business Valuation (15 hours).

3. A comprehensive examination.
4. IBBA membership in good standing.

The International Business Brokers Association encompasses brokers handling all sizes and types of business. The IBBA also includes a subgroup called the M&A Source. M&A Source members generally handle businesses valued at $500,000 and up. The IBBA holds two national meetings annually, and it provides a wide variety of technical support to its members.

Another group, the Institute of Certified Business Counselors, awards the professional designation Certified Business Counselor (CBC). This group generally handles larger businesses and practices, most over $1 million. It meets once annually, with speakers on technical topics designed to increase the professionalism of its members.

Success Ratio

Naturally, a buyer or seller will want to select a broker whose track record looks good. It is prudent to investigate the ratio of sales per listings.

Willingness of a Broker to Spend Money on Advertising a Business for Sale

Unless a brokerage firm is willing to spend some money on advertising, the chances for optimum exposure to the market diminish, possibly decreasing the likelihood of a timely sale.

Locating the Broker

The *Yellow Pages* in every city offers many listings under the classification "Business Broker." However, they give little or no information to assist a prospective buyer or seller in deciding which brokers would be most suitable for any particular situation. A better locally published source in most cases is the Sunday "Business Opportunities" classified ads. They indicate which brokers are advertising businesses in which particular industries.

It is preferable to locate a business broker by referral from someone who knows the person or firm firsthand. In some cases, an attorney, accountant, banker, business appraiser, or insurance agent may be familiar with some of the local brokers either directly or through their clients.

The headquarters offices of various organizations of business brokers listed in Exhibit 45-1 can give names of member firms in the area. In some cases, these organizations can suggest which ones might be best suited to the buyer's or seller's particular needs.

Exhibit 45–1

BUSINESS BROKERAGE RESOURCES

National Business Brokers Associations

The International Business Brokers Association (IBBA)
Robert MacDicken, Executive Director
11250 Roger Bacon Drive, Suite 8
Reston, Virginia 22090-5202
(703) 437-4377

The Institute of Certified Business Counselors (CBC)
Wally Stabbert, President
P.O. Box 70326
Eugene, Oregon 97401
(503) 345-8064

State or Local Business Brokerage Associations

ARIZONA
Arizona Association of Business Brokers, Inc. (AABB)
c/o Arizona Brokers
6644 E. Paseo San Andreas
Tucson, Arizona 85710
(520) 298-0225
Contact: Tim Bathen, President
Association offers:
    Education
    Regular monthly meetings
    Annual dinner

CALIFORNIA
California Association of Business Brokers (CABB)
1608 W. Campbell Avenue
Campbell, California 95008
(408) 379-7748
Contact: Ron Johnson, President
Association offers:
    Newsletter
    Education
    Conferences
    Regular meetings
    Listing exchange
    Fax on demand services
    Association-designed forms

Business Brokers Association
of San Diego
Restaurant and Business Sales
3111 Camino Del Rio North, Suite 400
San Diego, California 92108
(619) 528-2222
Contact: Jim Pagni, President
Association offers:
    Newsletter
    Education
    Regular meetings
    Conferences

Business Brokers Associates of Southern California (BBASC)
Stan Gold & Associates
15431 Runnymede Street
Van Nuys, California 91406
(818) 994-0217
Contact: Stanley Gold, President
Association offers:
    Newsletter
    Education
    Regular meetings

Business Exchange Network (BEN)
c/o Hampton Group
480 San Ramon Valley Boulevard, Suite A
Danville, California 94526
(510) 831-9225
Contact: Peter Siegel, President
Association offers:
    Listing exchange
    Monthly newspaper
    Internet web site

Business Opportunity Council
of California (BOCC)
c/o Equis
355 South Grand Avenue, Suite 2550
Los Angeles, California 90071-1560
(213) 437-4006
Contact: Chris Paris, President
Association offers:
    Newsletter
    Education
    Conferences
    Regular meetings
    Listing exchange
    Marketing group

DISTRICT OF COLUMBIA
Washington (DC) Council of Professional Business Brokers, Inc. (WBBA)
Bostrom, Inc.
800 17th Street N.W.
Washington, D.C. 20006
(202) 223-9669
Contact: Richard W. Dodson, President
Association offers:
    Newsletter
    Education
    Regular meetings

FLORIDA
Florida Business Brokers Association (FBBA)
c/o Keystone Corporation
8120 W. Oakland Park Boulevard
2nd floor
Sunrise, Florida 33351
(954) 749-2334
Contact: Peter Louis, President

Association offers:
    Newsletter
    Education
    Conferences
    Regular meetings
    Listing exchange

GEORGIA
Georgia Association of Business Brokers (GABB)
c/o T.E.C. Enterprises, Inc.
303 Covey Court
Woodstock, Georgia 30188
(770) 442-1608
Contact: Ted Chernak, President
Association offers:
    Newsletter
    Conferences
    Regular meetings
    Listing exchange

ILLINOIS
Alliance of Business Brokers and Intermediaries
c/o Stevenson and Company
Shand Monahan Plaza
1007 Church Street, Suite 310
Evanston, Illinois 60201
(847) 866-1188
Contact: George Stevenson, President
Association was formed to deal with the Illinois State Regulations for business brokers and intermediaries

MICHIGAN
Michigan Business Brokers Association—West Chapter (MBBA-West)
c/o Jim Jilek Broker
P.O. Box 7
Freeport, Michigan 49325
(616) 945-5874
Contact: Jim Jilek, President
Association offers:
    Monthly newsletter
    Education
    Conferences
    Regular meetings
    Listing exchange
    Social

MIDWEST
Association of Midwest Business Brokers (AMBB)
c/o Purcell Associates
1020 West Mallard
Palatine, Illinois 60067-6639
(708) 358-9404
Contact: Linda Purcell, President

Exhibit 45–1 (concluded)

Association offers:
    Newsletter
    Education
    Conferences
    Regular meetings
    Listing exchange

NEW ENGLAND
The Association of New England
Business Brokers (NEBBA)
15 Walden Street
Concord, Massachusetts 01742
(508) 287-5278
Contact: Rocco Pezza, President
Association offers:
    Education
    Conferences
    Regular meetings

NEW YORK
New York Association of Business
Brokers (NYABB)
c/o Robert A. Mead, Inc.
111 Grant Avenue
Endicott, New York 13760
(607) 754-5990
Contact: Herb Cohen, President
Association offers:
    Newsletter
    Education
    Conferences
    Regular meetings
    Listing exchange in newsletter
    Marketing sessions at meetings

NORTHWEST
NW Association of Business Brokers
(NABB)
c/o Acquisition Sources, Inc.
P.O. Box 21305
Seattle, Washington 98111
(206) 624-NABB
Contact: Curtis E. Casp, President
Association offers:
    Education
    Conferences
    Regular meetings

OHIO
Ohio Business Brokers Association
c/o Commercial One Capital Corp.
1515 Bethel Road
Columbus, Ohio 43220
(614) 451-5100
Contact: Dave Goll, President

Association offers:
    Education
    Conferences
    Regular meetings
    Listing exchange
    Standard forms
    Code of ethics
    Co-operative advertising

TEXAS
Texas Association of Business Brokers
(TABB)
c/o Dailey Resources, Inc.
P.O. Box 820398
Dallas, Texas 75382
(214) 373-1560
Contact: Ron L. Payton, President
Association offers:
    Newsletter
    Education
    Conferences
    Regular meetings
    Certification (BCB)

Business Brokerage Publications

The following publications contain
buyer and seller listings—primarily of
mid-sized companies:

First List
Vision Quest Publishing, Inc.
655 Rockland Road, Suite 103
Lake Bluff, Illiniois 60044
(800) 999-0920
Robert Weicherding

Have/Want
International Business Brokers
Association (IBBA)
11250 Roger Bacon Drive, Suite 8
Reston, Virginia 22090-5202
(703) 437-4377
Robert MacDicken

World M&A Network
717 D Street, N.W., Suite 300
Washington, D.C. 20004-2807
(202) 628-6900
John Bailey

Recreation Business Exchange
Whitney Crosby-Newman
690 North Meridian Road, Suite 220
Kalispell, Montana 59901
(800) 266-5350

Riggs/Allen Report
P.O. Box 795
Southport, Connecticut 06490
(203) 254-2991
Colleen H. Adams

Business Brokerage Networks

Nation-List International
W.T. (Chip) Fuller
1660 South Albion Street, Suite 407
Denver, Colorado 80222
(800) 525-9559

Business Brokers Network, Inc.
Gerald Nance
9330 LBJ Freeway, Suite 740
Dallas, Texas 75243
(214) 680-8414

Business Brokerage Franchises

Sunbelt Business Brokers
Ed Pendarvis
1 Poston Road, Suite 190
Charleston, South Carolina 29407
(803) 769-4363

VR Business Brokers
Don Taylor
1151 Dove Street, Suite 100
Newport Beach, California 92660
(714) 975-1100

Empire Business Brokers, Inc.
Nick Gugliuzza
P.O. Box 622
Buffalo, New York 14224
(716) 677-5229

Listings On-line

NVST Investment Network
205 108th Avenue N.E., Suite 200
Bellevue, Washington 98004
(425) 454-3639
http://www.nvst.com

BizQuest
200 N. Mullan, Suite 213
Spokane, Washington 99206
(509) 928-1757
http://www.bizquest.com

SOURCE: Tom West, ed. *1997 Business Reference Guide* (Concord, Mass.: Business Brokerage Press, 1997), pp. 73–77, updated as of this writing.

Another source of broker referrals is one of the completed transaction reporting services, *Pratt's Stats*. A prospective buyer or seller may specify an industry group, a size range, and/or a geographical area, and *Pratt's Stats* will provide a list of brokers who have completed transactions that meet the criteria. *Pratt's Stats* is published by Business Valuation Resources, 4475 SW Scholls Ferry Road, Suite 101, Portland, Oregon 97225, telephone (888) BUS-VALU, fax (503) 291-7955.

A list of brokers specializing in certain industries is contained in the *Business Reference Guide*, edited by Thomas L. West, published annually by Business Brokerage Press, PO Box 247, Concord, Massachusetts 01742, telephone (508) 369-5254, fax (508) 371-1156.

Pricing and Listing a Business or Practice for Sale

The following are the essential elements of the listing agreement:

1. The property being offered for sale.
2. The offering price and terms.
3. The commission.
4. The duration of the listing agreement.

The matter of defining what is being offered for sale was discussed in Chapter 2. Commissions are discussed later in this chapter. The duration of the agreement with most brokers is usually between six months and one year on an exclusive basis. This duration is fairly standard in order for the broker to have adequate opportunity to work the listing. This is because it usually takes several months to sell a business. Most brokers will not even accept nonexclusive listings.

How the seller and the broker will set the price and terms of the listing varies a great deal from one type of business to another and, especially, from one broker to another. At one extreme, some brokers insist on doing their own appraisal and accept the listing only if the listing price approximates their appraisal. At the other extreme, some brokers have nothing to do with the pricing and simply list a property at whatever price the seller designates. Most brokers will fall somewhere in between. They will offer some practical guidance if the buyer wants it, and more brokers are offering full appraisal services.

In any case, a seller should have a pretty good idea of a reasonable price before contacting the broker. It is part of the purpose of this book to provide the seller with the guidance to develop a reasonable range of possible values. If the seller wants objective guidance before offering the business for sale, she may seek a professional appraisal from an independent fee appraiser rather than from a broker. It is a waste of both the seller's and the broker's time to start out by offering the business at a price inflated beyond a realistic range. On the other hand, a seller naturally should expect to get all she reasonably can, not leave money on the table by underpricing the business.

Since most small businesses and professional practices are sold on terms other than for cash, the listing price should be set to reflect the most generous terms the seller would be willing to accept. Chapter 27 shows how to convert a cash equivalent value to a higher price that appropriately reflects extended terms of sale. If a deal looks possible on terms more favorable to the seller (or even better, if a cash deal looks possible), the seller can negotiate to a lower price that reflects the terms more favorable to the seller. It is less psychologically appealing to list the business priced on the basis of a cash deal and then to raise the face amount to reflect the discount in value received as a result of extending terms to a buyer.

Statistics suggest that the average business sold closes at a price around 80 percent of its original listing price. However, this average varies greatly from one brokerage office to another. The more sophisticated the seller and the broker are about realistic pricing, (1) the higher the odds the business will actually be sold and (2) the more likely the price will be at or near the listing price.

Typical Fees

Brokers typically receive commissions of 10 to 15 percent of the stated sales price on sales up to about $500,000 (sometimes even up to $1 million) and somewhat lower percentages on higher amounts. Most brokers also have some minimum commission, the amount of which varies considerably from one brokerage firm to another. The broker receives his commission in cash at closing. Thus, if the down payment is 30 percent of the face amount and the commission is 10 percent, the commission amounts to one-third of the down payment.

Fees for finding financing are usually about 2.5 to 5 percent of the amount of money raised.

Business brokerage traditionally has been a strictly commission business. However, there has been a trend for some brokers to charge sellers nonrefundable retainers that usually are deducted from the commission if the business is sold.

Some brokers' retainers run several thousand dollars. However, it is more typical for a retainer for a small business to be $1,000 to $2,000. The retainer helps cover some of the broker's out-of-pocket expenses and to weed out sellers who are not serious and would merely waste the broker's time. From the seller's viewpoint, the retainer should help to get the broker's full attention and at least enhance his moral obligation to rigorously pursue the sale of the business.

Working with the Broker

The more the seller or buyer understands the functions of brokers in general—and of the broker she is working with in particular—the smoother the relationship will be. Both sellers and buyers should respect the broker's time. And both sellers and buyers should try to accomplish maximum results with a minimum amount of the broker's time.

The Seller's Role

The seller's main job is to provide the broker with business information that is as complete as possible, as discussed in Chapter 44, updating it as necessary. The seller should encourage as many of the brokerage's representatives as possible to tour the place of business so they will be familiar with it.

The seller should give the broker and other representatives of his firm a narrative account of the nature of the business and why it should be attractive to a buyer. He should make himself readily available to (1) answer the broker's questions and to (2) provide potential purchasers an opportunity to tour the premises and ask questions about the business. The information he provides should be complete and honest, not exaggerated.

The process can be broken down into three parts:

1. Business analysis and plan.
2. Broker's exhaustive search for best buyer(s) often done on a completely confidential basis.
3. Negotiate to close.

An experienced broker or M&A intermediary can work closely with the seller in all three of these phases. Brokers and buyers like to see a business plan that provides the buyer with an opportunity to increase the value of the business beyond the price being paid. The greater the detail supporting a believable plan, the more attractive the business will be.

The broker will contact relevant professional networking associates, such as attorneys, accountants, and bankers, as well as both strategic and financial buyers. More and more, strategic buyers who can realize synergistic benefits are good prospects for midsize businesses. For the smaller business, however, first-time buyers (especially early retirees) are coming to the fore as a major pool of buyers. In any case, the broker attempts to locate the "highest and best" buyer for a particular business or practice.

Having located a buyer or buyers, the seller should cooperate fully in making the buyer's due diligence process as thorough and painless as possible.

The Buyer's Role

The buyer's first step is to make clear to the broker exactly what she is looking for: the type of business, acceptable price and size range, acceptable geographical area, the cash she has available for the down payment, and any other appropriate description of what is or is not acceptable. It is not fair for a buyer to waste a broker's time on "fishing expeditions" until she has thought these things through and answered these questions in her own mind. If she has not, she should be up-front and tell the broker so, seeking the broker's guidance, if appropriate.

A buyer who is serious about a business should be entitled to full disclosure of pertinent information. She should have access to all of the information necessary to complete her due diligence, which is likely to include (at least) all the steps in the valuation process discussed in this book. Obviously, such information is confidential, and the buyer should treat it that way. It is totally appropriate for the seller to require the buyer to sign a confidentiality agreement before releasing information.

Because of the lack of multiple-listing cooperation among business brokers within virtually all cities, a buyer may need to review the listings of several brokers in order to find the most suitable business or practice.

Closing the Deal

A problem constantly facing brokers is buyers and sellers trying to make a deal excluding the broker so that the broker loses his commission. If a broker has introduced a buyer to a property, it is both unethical and illegal to avoid paying his commission if the deal is consummated. The broker is entitled to be paid for his services, and both buyers and sellers should respect this obligation.

The broker probably has offer-to-purchase and/or purchase agreement forms available. The comprehensiveness of these forms varies considerably from one brokerage firm to another, and the need for comprehensive forms varies considerably from one transaction to another.

Even if the parties choose to use the standard forms provided by the broker (or obtained elsewhere), it is appropriate for both buyer and seller to have their attorneys review the documents before finalizing the deal. However, both parties should expect their attorneys to be both expeditious and reasonable in the language they suggest in the purchase agreement. Too many deals have been killed unnecessarily by attorneys either (1) failing to act on a timely basis or (2) unreasonably demanding language that is unacceptable to the other party.

A significant proportion of the transactions put into escrow through some brokerage firms never close. Many transactions that do close take an excruciatingly long time. In fact, some brokerage firms close less than half the transactions put into escrow. Firms that close over 90 percent of the transactions put into escrow tend to be very proud of that record. High closing records come with firms that have qualified buyers with cash available and sellers that provide full and timely disclosure of all information that a buyer needs and can verify. If these conditions are met, a transaction should clear escrow on a timely basis, to the satisfaction of both buyer and seller.

Summary

The business brokerage industry has increased its professionalism greatly in recent years. Partly as a result of this increased professionalism, an increasing proportion of businesses and professional practices are being sold with the assistance of a professional intermediary.

The services provided by intermediaries have broadened. To compensate for some of these services, nonrefundable retainers, usually credited against the final transaction fee, have become more common. Some intermediaries are also offering small business and professional practice appraisal services.

In order to make the transaction process work smoothly and with maximum success, both buyers and sellers should be as complete as possible in providing the broker with a candid profile of their objectives. Once the intermediary is engaged, close cooperation is essential to consummate a "clean" deal without subsequent repercussions for the buyer or for the seller.

Part VII

Litigation and Dispute Resolution

Chapter 46

Litigation

Litigation often results when a dispute over the value of a small business or professional practice—or a fractional ownership interest in one—cannot be resolved through negotiation or arbitration. This chapter focuses on litigated controversies in which a courtroom or administrative hearing is the intended resolution vehicle. A discussion of how arbitration and mediation can be used to resolve disputes is provided in Chapter 48.

The following are the most common reasons that owners of small businesses and professional practices become involved in valuation-related litigation concerning their ownership interests:

- Marital dissolution (see Chapter 41).
- Damages (see Chapter 47).
- Dissenting stockholder actions (see Chapter 40).
- Corporate and partnership dissolutions (see Chapter 40).
- Estate, gift, and income taxes (see Chapter 38).
- Personal injury or wrongful termination.
- Bankruptcy, insolvency, and reorganization situations.
- State and local property taxes.
- Intellectual property rights infringement.

When a business owner is threatened with valuation-related litigation or is considering initiating a valuation-related lawsuit, a qualified attorney and business appraiser should be retained in order (1) to assess the merits of the case and (2) to provide a preliminary review of the valuation-related issues. Many disputes can be resolved when clients and attorneys work with a qualified analyst who is experienced in litigation matters. The analyst may be asked to (1) provide preliminary estimates of the value of the subject business interest and (2) assess the valuation merits of the opposing side. This information can be very useful in weighing the risks and potential costs associated with a courtroom trial. If the dispute cannot be resolved outside the courtroom, the preliminary analysis can be used to establish a framework for a valuation opinion report and/or expert testimony, as necessary.

The Legal Context

Appraisals performed within the litigation environment require that the analyst understand the legal context in which the appraisal is being conducted. The analyst should understand (1) the facts and circumstances of the case and (2) the relevant statutory law, administrative rulings, and judicial precedent that apply to the subject litigation. These laws—combined with relevant documentary direction and the directives and preferences of the court—define the legal context of the engagement and assist the analyst in selecting and applying appropriate valuation methods and procedures. Often the legal context can vary significantly from one valuation purpose to another and from one jurisdiction to another. Consequently, it is important for the analyst and the attorney to work closely together in order to agree on the context in which the appraisal will be applied to the subject case.

Statutory Law

Laws passed by the U.S. Congress and state legislatures are referred to as statutes. The collection of federal and state statutes makes up statutory law. Federal statutes are listed and compiled by subject in the United States Code. State statutes are included in similar state publications.

Federal statutory law may govern valuation-related issues in certain cases, such as federal gift and estate tax matters. State statutes apply to many other valuation-related disputes, such as marital dissolutions, dissenting shareholder disputes, and ad valorem (i.e., property tax) issues. Statutes governing these disputes vary considerably from state to state, and states change their statutes from time to time. Consequently, when a valuation is conducted for litigation purposes, the analyst should be aware of the legal jurisdiction and the relevant statutory law that applies to the subject case.

Administrative Rulings and Regulations

Administrative rulings and regulations define a substantial portion of the regulatory environment of business. Administrative rulings and regulations are created and based on the legislative rules and decisions of various administrative agencies, such as the U.S. Treasury Department and the Securities and Exchange Commission. Also, state agencies, such as a state department of revenue, may play an important role in the determination of applicable administrative rulings and regulations for a given litigation engagement.

Federal administrative agencies are created by Congress through "enabling legislation" that specifies the powers of the agency being created. Often, these agencies are granted the power to make legislative rules, enforce compliance, and adjudicate disputes. Administrative regulations or rules may or may not have the force of law. For example, to implement federal tax laws, the U.S. Treasury Department issues rules with the force of law. However, the Internal Revenue Service issues revenue rulings, representing the opinion of the IRS on various issues. These opinions do not have the force of law. If administrative law is an important aspect of a litigated case, the analyst should become familiar with the appropriate regulations and rulings, and with their potential impact on the matter at hand.

Administrative agencies typically conduct hearings for the purpose of adjudicating disputes. These hearings may resemble court trials in that they involve activities such as discovery, depositions, testimony, and cross-examination. Often, the evidentiary rules are considerably less stringent for an administrative hearing than for a typical courtroom trial. Decisions by administrative agencies are generally subject to judicial review once a challenger has exhausted all possible administrative remedies.

Judicial Precedent

The concept of judicial precedent—or common law—was first developed in medieval England, and it is still significantly relied upon today by the U.S. legal system. Judicial precedent is established and derived from published judicial decisions in previous legal disputes. These published decisions—generally referred to as precedent-setting cases—are reviewed by judges to gain insight into how previous judges have handled a similar set of facts and circumstances.

When the facts and circumstances dictate, judges attempt to be consistent with precedent-setting decisions within their jurisdiction. Courts will consider precedent-setting cases established in other jurisdictions as well, but they may not necessarily be heavily influenced by those decisions. When judicial precedent is an important component of a litigated valuation dispute, it is important for the analyst and attorney to be very familiar with the relevant precedent-setting cases within the subject jurisdiction.

Some analysts have studied important precedent-setting cases and maintain extensive files of court decisions involving the valuation of small businesses and professional practices. Others rely on the attorney involved in the case to research the case law and provide them with the relevant cases for their study. Either way, gaining an understanding of the relevant case law is an important area of cooperation between the analyst and the attorney in any valuation-related litigation. With the advent of electronic high-speed databases such as LEXIS-NEXIS and WESTLAW, legal research has become much more efficient and cost-effective. A research department for a law firm or a financial advisory firm should be able to identify and retrieve precedent-setting cases in any jurisdiction in the United States.

Court Directives and Preferences

Many courts prefer not to hear valuation-related cases and will try to encourage a settlement if possible. Some courts exercise considerable discretion in the handling of valuation cases, determining such matters as when or whether the retention of experts must be disclosed to the opposing side, the rules for discovery, and whether or not written valuation opinion reports must be prepared and exchanged.

Some of the foregoing items are standing matters of law or policy in certain jurisdictions, and others are left to the discretion of the judge in the particular case. When valuation-related litigation is involved, the analyst should understand the procedural ground rules and the court's preferences regarding the subject case and should plan accordingly.

Types of Litigation

The following are the common reasons that owners of small businesses and professional practices become involved in valuation-related litigation regarding their ownership interests:

- Dissenting stockholder actions.
- Corporate and partnership dissolutions.
- Marital dissolutions.
- Estate, gift, and income taxes.
- Personal injury or wrongful termination.
- Bankruptcy, insolvency, and reorganization situations.
- State and local property taxes.
- Intellectual property rights infringement.

A topical summary of important considerations regarding the litigation-related valuation of a business ownership interest is provided below.

Dissenting Shareholder Disputes

Every state in the United States and the District of Columbia has enacted statutes that provide minority shareholders with the ability to dissent from certain corporate actions. These corporate actions typically include mergers, the sale of all—or substantially all—of the corporate assets, or certain other changes in the basic organizational structure of the corporation. A minority shareholder who exercises his or her right to dissent from a qualified corporate action has the right to file suit to force the corporation to purchase the stock at the judicially determined value of the shares. This right is typically referred to as the dissenting shareholders' "appraisal right" or "appraisal remedy." It is available under the terms and conditions of specific state statutes.

In most states, the standard of value used in dissenting shareholder disputes is referred to as "fair value." Unfortunately, the conceptual definition of fair value is subject to significant variation in judicial interpretation both within and among the various states. Consequently, the judicially determined fair value of a block of stock in a dissenting shareholder dispute often involves inconsistent application of the generally accepted valuation methods. Most of the inconsistencies are attributable to the implicit or explicit use of valuation discounts and premiums in the analysis.

Fair Value as a Standard of Value. Recall from our discussion in Chapter 3 that the standard of value defines the type of value being estimated. As discussed, the standard of value estimated in the analysis can have a substantial impact on the concluded value of a business ownership interest. Accordingly, it is necessary to properly understand and define "fair value" before appraising a business ownership interest involved in a dissenting shareholder dispute.

The Revised Model Business Corporation Act (RMBCA) defines fair value as:

> The value of the shares immediately before the effectuation of the corporate action to which the dissenter objects, excluding any appreciation or depreciation in anticipation of the corporate action unless exclusion would be inequitable.

The statutory definition of fair value in most states is similar to the definition provided by the RMBCA. The definition of fair value in many other states is similar to the RMBCA definition, but without the "unless exclusion would be inequitable" clause. The definition of fair value in Delaware also excludes the "unless exclusion would be inequitable" clause and includes a clause that states "in determining such fair value, the court should take into account all relevant factors."

The various statutory definitions and judicial precedents regarding the interpretation of fair value create uncertainty regarding (1) how business valuation methods should be implemented and (2) how the indications of value should be adjusted for factors such as marketability and control. Judicial precedents may require that specific equity ownership characteristics (e.g., degree of control, degree of marketability, etc.) of the block of stock being appraised be ignored when estimating the fair value.

When estimating the value of a business ownership interest for a dissenting shareholder dispute, it is recommended that the analyst (1) consider the judicial precedents of the applicable jurisdiction and (2) obtain the opinion of counsel regarding the interpretation of fair value in the jurisdiction in which the case originates. Analysts should not assume there is a clear and concise conceptual definition of fair value.

Relative Levels of Value.   The absence of a clear definition of fair value creates controversy regarding certain valuation-related variables used to estimate the value of a dissenters' block of stock. Most of the controversy is attributable to the relative level of value considered in the valuation analysis. Typically, the relative level of value considered in an analysis of a business ownership interest is one of the following: (1) controlling ownership interest, (2) marketable noncontrolling ownership interest, or (3) nonmarketable noncontrolling ownership interest.

As previously mentioned, the analyst may be influenced by judicial precedent or authority to use a relative level of value for dissenting shareholder action purposes that is different from the level of value that the appraiser would adopt for another valuation purpose. Consequently, it is important to understand the following: (1) how different levels of control and marketability impact value, and (2) how various business valuation methods conclude different relative levels of value.

Depending on the conceptual basis of the business valuation method used, the relative level of value indicated by that method may be on a minority ownership interest basis or a controlling ownership interest basis, or on a marketable or nonmarketable basis. For instance, the guideline publicly traded company method uses stock price and earnings information (i.e., P/E multiples) from publicly traded companies in order to estimate the value of the subject stock. Consequently, the indication of value provided by the guideline publicly traded company method is on a marketable noncontrolling ownership interest basis. The reasons for this are twofold: (1) the stock of publicly traded companies trade on a minority ownership interest basis, and (2) publicly traded equity securities are relatively easy to liquidate.

Other business valuation methods provide different relative levels of value. Consequently, it is necessary to understand the conceptual support underlying the business valuation method used in order to correctly understand the relative level of value provided by that method. This is because, different business valuation methods provide different relative levels of value.

Valuation Discounts and Premiums. It may be necessary to use explicit discounts and premiums to adjust the relative level of value provided by a particular business valuation method to the relative level of value required by the valuation assignment. Therefore, it is important to understand (1) what relative level of value is provided by a particular business valuation method and (2) the relative level of value required by the valuation assignment in order to properly apply an explicit valuation adjustment. If this analysis is not correctly used, the resulting indication of value may be significantly under- or overstated.

As discussed in Chapter 24 and Chapter 25, explicit business valuation discounts and premiums typically include the following: (1) discount for lack of ownership control (i.e., minority ownership interest discount), (2) premium for ownership control (i.e., a control ownership premium), and (3) discount for lack of marketability. These valuation discounts and premiums are generally derived from empirical studies of capital market evidence. For a more complete discussion of valuation discounts and premiums, see Chapter 24 and Chapter 25.

Implications of Varying Statutory Definitions of Fair Value. The various statutory definitions of fair value provide some guidance into the selection of a relative level of value to use in the analysis. When the statutory definition of fair value excludes any appreciation or depreciation in value in anticipation of the corporate action, paying dissenting shareholders a pro rata share of the controlling ownership interest value of the company may not be appropriate. The absence of the phrase "unless such exclusion would be inequitable" or a requirement to "consider all relevant facts" suggests that the estimation of fair value should consider the ownership characteristics (e.g., lack of ownership control, lack of marketability, etc.) of the actual block of stock the dissenter owns. Before the corporate action that triggered the appraisal rights, a dissenter's block of stock in a closely held business typically suffers from both (1) a lack of ownership control and (2) a lack of ready marketability. Consequently, in states with these types of definitions, the estimated fair value may need to consider the use of discounts for lack of control and for lack of marketability.

When the statutory definition of fair value expands to consider whether the exclusion of any depreciation or appreciation of value in connection with the corporate action would be "inequitable," different relative levels of value may be appropriate. In other words, it may be "inequitable" to use discounts for lack of ownership control or lack of marketability in the analysis. The judicial precedent in the jurisdiction in which the case originates and the specific facts and circumstances should be considered when selecting a relative level of value to estimate in the analysis.

When the statutory definition of fair value requires the consideration of "all relevant factors," different relative levels of value may be considered. Again, the judicial precedent in the jurisdiction in which the case originates and the specific facts and circumstances should be considered when selecting a relative level of value to estimate in the analysis.

Summary. The concluded fair value of a block of stock in a dissenting shareholder dispute may vary substantially depending on the relative level of value estimated in the analysis. The selection of the appropriate relative level of value is influenced by (1) the statutory definition of fair value and (2) by the judicial precedent in the jurisdiction in which the dispute originates. To further complicate matters, many state courts have used inconsistent relative levels of value when deciding the judicially estimated value of a dissenters' block of stock. Typically, the inconsistencies are attributable to (1) the court's effort to reach a "fair" resolution to the dispute, (2) the unique circumstances involved in the case, and (3) misunderstandings in the following areas: (a) the different relative levels of value provided by various business valuation methods, (b) the empirical studies of valuation discounts and premiums and the appropriate base to which these adjustments should be applied, and (c) how the relative levels of value estimated in the analysis affect the concluded fair value of a block of stock. This subject is discussed further in Chapter 40, Corporate and Partnership Dissolutions.

Corporate and Partnership Dissolutions

Corporate or partnership dissolutions have many characteristics in common with marital dissolutions. People are terminating a relationship, frequently under adversarial circumstances. Generally speaking, there are no statutory laws that provide valuation-related guidance regarding corporate and partnership dissolutions. Consequently, it is necessary to research and identify the judicial precedent in the jurisdiction in which the dispute originates.

As with dissenting shareholder disputes, the appropriate standard of value and the relative level of value are important considerations. Precedent-setting cases in certain jurisdictions may use the term "fair market value" when describing the standard of value used by the court. Other cases or jurisdictions may refer to "fair value" or "market value" when estimating the value of a business ownership interest. As discussed in Chapter 3, the term "fair market value" has a generally accepted definition based on a multitude of precedent-setting cases. The terms "fair value" and "market value" are less specific and require the analyst to become familiar with (1) the facts and circumstances of the subject case and (2) the appropriate judicial precedent.

In many instances, a buy-sell provision of a shareholders' agreement may specify certain procedures to be used in the valuation of ownership interests. These provisions may contain very specific language regarding valuation formulas, arbitration or mediation requirements, the selection of an analyst, and the standard of value and premise of value to be used in case of a valuation dispute. Other buy-sell provisions may contain very general language regarding the methods and procedures to be used in case of a valuation dispute. The general language may be subject to significant differences in interpretation that can lead to a dispute over the value of an ownership interest. Even if a buy-sell agreement contains specific language designed to avoid controversy, the potential for litigation still exists. As an example, shareholders may allege that the other side of the dispute has failed to live up to its fiduciary responsibility under the terms and conditions of the shareholders agreement. When this occurs, the participants may seek to have the buy-sell provision set aside and to have an independent appraisal conducted of the value of the ownership interest in dispute. If the buy-sell provision is set aside, all of the important valuation elements (i.e., standard of value, premise of value, etc.) may become part of the analysis.

In certain states, "dissolution statutes" allow minority stockholders to force a dissolution of a corporation under specified circumstances. In these states, the company can avoid the dissolution by paying the stockholders the "fair value" of their stock. The difficulties associated with appraising the "fair value" of a corporate or partnership interest for dissolution purposes is similar to the difficulties encountered in dissenting shareholder disputes. This subject is discussed further in Chapter 40, Corporate and Partnership Dissolutions.

Marital Dissolutions

Divorce is one of the most common reasons that small business and professional practice owners end up in court. Marital dissolution cases are also the least likely to reach settlement prior to trial. There are special issues involved in valuations for marital dissolution purposes. Often, there is no clear definition of the standard of value to be used. The valuation date can be one of several different dates (e.g., date of separation, date of trial, etc.). Sometimes an appraisal must be prepared as of several dates. Because of the emotional stress and frequent bitterness associated with divorce, discovery is often hindered by the operating spouse. These issues and other issues relating to valuation for marital dissolution purposes are discussed in Chapter 41, Marital Dissolutions.

Estate, Gift, and Income Tax

When the litigated dispute involves controversy over estate, gift, and income taxes, the taxpayer is often the petitioner and the government—usually the Internal Revenue Service—is often the respondent. The basic guidelines for the appraisal of closely held businesses for federal estate, gift, and income taxes are set forth in (1) the Internal Revenue Code, (2) Treasury Regulations, and (3) various revenue rulings, technical advice memorandums, and private letter rulings. Also, there is an extensive body of judicial precedent that defines (1) the standard of value and (2) the appropriate methods and procedures to be used in the valuation.

The standard of value for estate, gift, and income tax purposes is typically fair market value. The fair market value standard requires the analyst to determine the appropriate relative level of value of the subject business interest based on its ownership characteristics (e.g., degree of control, degree of marketability, etc.). In order to correctly estimate the relative level of value of the subject ownership interest, it may be necessary for the analyst to apply valuation discounts or premiums to the indications of value provided by various valuation methods. (See Chapter 3 for a discussion of the fair market value standard, and Chapter 38 for a discussion of estate planning, using the fair market value standard.)

Bankruptcy, Insolvency, and Reorganization Situations

Creditors, debtors, judges, lawyers, and others involved in the bankruptcy and reorganization process often rely on analysts to provide a number of asset and equity valuation services. Appraisals of assets, properties, and business interests are a routine part of the bankruptcy and reorganization process. Appraisals are relied on to conclude various indications of value for such uses as debtor-in-possession financing, restructurings, reorganization financing, recapitalizations, out-of-court reorganizations, and turnarounds.

Valuation analysis can well serve the information and decision-making needs of the parties in interest to the bankruptcy. For example, the bankruptcy court may need to determine whether the company meets the legal definition of bankruptcy. An analysis may be conducted to determine (1) whether the company has the ability to meet its short- and long-term obligations and (2) whether assets exceed liabilities. Also, the court may wish to evaluate the economic feasibility of various workout plans and how these plans would impact the beneficial interests of creditors and of other interested parties.

Appraisers and economists with appropriate experience and expertise may provide a wide range of insolvency and troubled debt analyses. Often, an analyst can assist property owners before, during, and after the bankruptcy and reorganization process. This assistance may include the following services:

- Restructuring strategies for recovery of asset value.
- Creation of troubled company workout plans.
- Assessment of troubled company workout plan feasibility.
- Identification and valuation of asset or business spin-off opportunities.
- Valuation of claims for purchase or sale.
- Fraudulent conveyance analyses.
- Reorganization, recapitalization, and restructuring analyses.

The appraisal work product may be used for either notational or transactional purposes. Notational appraisals are prepared for accounting or management information purposes only. Transactional appraisals are performed in anticipation of an actual purchase or sale transaction. These appraisals may be used to establish a transaction price, to negotiate a transaction price, or to obtain transactional financing. In any event, a real transaction will be consummated based, in part, on the appraisal. Due to their transactional nature, these appraisals usually involve a greater degree of due diligence, documentation, and substantiation than do notational appraisals.

State and Local Property Taxes

When appraising assets, properties, and business interests for state and local property tax litigation, it is necessary to develop an understanding of the definitions of value, the valuation elements and methods, and the tax assessment process—all as allowed or required by the statutory authority of the relevant jurisdiction. The valuation methods and procedures, and the valuation opinion report should be consistent with the value definitions and approaches in the local jurisdiction.

Certain properties are part of interrelated and interdependent operating businesses that span numerous taxing jurisdictions. These properties may, in certain cases, be assessed state and local property taxes based on analysis using business valuation methods. Such properties may include, for example, utilities and cogeneration plants, cable television and telecommunication companies, and railroads and airlines. The reason to value certain properties using business valuation methods is based on the realization that it is not possible to accurately value, for property tax purposes, the individual property in one taxing jurisdiction simply by analyzing that property in isolation. Rather, it is more practical to value the entire operating system and to apportion some of that value to each taxing jurisdiction. This is the basic concept of unit value, sometimes referred to as unitary value or system value.

Many business valuation methods provide an indication of value that includes the going-concern value of the entire business, rather than merely the market value of the taxpayer's tangible real and personal property. Consequently, the indicated value of the business may include a variety of intangible assets. Depending on the jurisdiction, intangible assets such as franchise agreements, FCC licenses, certificates of need, licenses and permits, leasehold interests, and computer software may not be taxable assets. When these intangible assets would otherwise be grouped with the real estate and tangible personal property and be taxed as a bundle of rights, it may be appropriate to separately identify and value these assets. That way, in jurisdictions where intangible assets are not subject to state or local property taxation, their value can be separated from the value of the tangible assets.

The valuation of the intangible assets can be the subject of significant disagreement between the taxing authority and the taxpayer. If these disputes cannot be resolved through negotiation, an administrative or judicial appeal may be necessary. Administrative appeals may be conducted through quasi-judicial authorities, such as county boards or state boards of equalization. The assessment appeals process before these administrative authorities may be fairly formal and the decisions may set important precedent if the taxpayer ends up pursuing relief through judicial appeal. Obviously, administrative law is an important component of defining the legal context of a property tax dispute.

Intellectual Property Rights Infringement

As discussed in Chapter 42, intellectual property is a special classification of intangible assets. This is because the owner of the property is protected by law from unauthorized use by others. The term "intellectual property" typically refers to the following types of intangible assets:

- Patents.
- Trademarks.
- Copyrights.
- Trade secrets or know-how.
- Computer software.
- Engineering drawings.

Many business valuation theories and techniques discussed in this book can be used to quantify the impact of an infringement on such intellectual properties. Two of the more common methods are (1) decremental value of property during the infringement period and (2) present value of lost income during the infringement period.

The first method requires a comparative valuation (i.e., a valuation of the intellectual property on two different "as of" valuation dates) analysis. This method compares the value of the intellectual property before the inception of the infringement act to the value after the termination of the infringement act. The difference in the two indications of value provides an estimate of the damages caused by the infringement act.

The second method may be based on the present value of the economic income (as defined) that was foregone by the owner of the intellectual property during the infringement period. This lost economic income may be either actual lost earnings or cash flow, or the loss of hypothetical rents, royalties, or payments that would normally accrue to the ownership of such an intellectual property.

Litigation Support Services

As mentioned at the beginning of this chapter, when an owner of a small business or professional practice is threatened with imminent litigation or is considering initiating litigation, a qualified analyst should be retained in order to assess the valuation merits of the case. The selection of a qualified analyst is discussed in Chapter 44. The following sections of this chapter discuss litigation support services that an analyst may provide in connection with a valuation-related dispute.

Assessing the Case

As previously mentioned, the applicable standard of value and relative level of value are not always easily defined and readily apparent in a litigated dispute. Frequently, there is no statutorily defined standard of value or relative level of value. Also, the facts and circumstances of a particular case may be complex and subject to interpretation in a variety of ways. Often, the analyst's knowledge and expertise can be very beneficial in focusing on the relevant questions and defining the case appropriately.

Once the basic valuation aspects of the case have been defined, the analyst may be asked to (1) conduct a preliminary valuation analysis and (2) suggest a reasonable range of values within which the final conclusion may be expected to fall. The preliminary range of values can help the attorney understand the valuation merits of the case. Sometimes the most valuable service the analyst can perform is telling the clients what they do not want to hear—that the value is not what they expected it to be. The termination of financially unproductive litigation can save the client significant amounts of money. When each side of a dispute is provided with a reasonable range of values, the groundwork for a settlement is often laid. If a settlement cannot be reached, the preliminary range of values can provide comfort with respect to the decision to proceed with litigation.

Discovery

One of the most important tasks that an appraiser or economist can perform is in the area of discovery. It is extremely important that an analyst be brought in early in the case to assist in the identification and gathering of documents and information during the discovery process. The correct application of valuation methods can produce meaningless results if the data relied on is insufficient or unreliable.

Chapter 44 contains a documents and information checklist (Exhibit 44–3) that provides a general guideline to the types of information that should be sought during discovery.

Critique of the Opposition

In many valuation-related engagements, the review and critique of the opposition's position can be as important to reaching a satisfactory conclusion as preparing the valuation case in chief. If the opposing valuation analysis is found to be unsound and theoretically flawed, the strength of the opposition's position is significantly compromised.

The review and critique of the opposing expert's report may happen at various stages throughout the litigation process. If an expert's report is available early in the process of assessing the case, it is important to review it at that time and determine the reasonableness of the analysis. If the analysis is reasonable, a recommendation to negotiate a settlement may be very beneficial to the client.

If the opposing expert's report is significantly flawed, it is beneficial to know this information as soon as possible. The more sophisticated the expert is on the other side, the greater the likelihood that a reasonable settlement could be reached through negotiation. If the other side has used an inexperienced or unsophisticated expert, the likelihood of a negotiated settlement is diminished.

Expert Testimony

Obviously, one of the most important services an appraiser or economist can offer in the litigation environment is expert witness testimony. Testimony services may be provided during both deposition and trial. The testifying expert should have a collection of special personal and professional characteristics in order to practice successfully in the litigation environment. A very brief listing of the more important characteristics is provided below:

- Sufficient educational, professional, and technical credentials.
- Strong command of the subject matter.
- Ability to explain technical information in a clear and concise fashion.
- Ability to convey credibility, honesty, and integrity during testimony.
- Ability to deduce correct inferences from hypothetically stated facts.
- Ability to articulate and defend one's position quickly under pressure.

Expert witness testimony is not for everyone. Certain professionals find the work interesting and stimulating, while others wither and fade under confrontational cross-examination. An analyst interested in providing expert witness testimony in valuation-related litigation should (1) have a strong command of the theoretical and technical aspects of valuation analyses and (2) have conducted a sufficient level of due diligence and research to be very familiar with the subject case.

Rebuttal

The extent of rebuttal analysis and testimony is dependent on the nature and problems associated with the opposing expert's analysis. If the expert has made a mathematical error, the error should be disclosed to the court, and the impact on value should be discussed. If the expert has taken a position that is unsupported by the preponderance of authoritative literature on an issue, the rebuttal should cite the appropriate authoritative literature and discuss the resulting impact on value. If the expert's methods and theoretical assumptions are basically sound but the data relied on in the analysis is unreliable or incomplete, the best approach may be to use the assumptions and methods offered by the expert but to use complete and accurate data.

Summary

Any valuation performed for controversy purposes—or where potential litigation may be involved—should be conducted in conformance with the applicable legal context for the type of dispute being litigated. This legal context is based on statutes, administrative rules and regulations, judicial precedent, and directives or preferences of the court of jurisdiction. The legal context helps define the standard of value, relative level of value, and acceptable valuation methods for a particular case. Each of these factors can have a substantial impact on the indication of value provided by the valuation analysis.

Analysts can provide valuable services throughout the valuation-related litigation process. From assessing the valuation merits of the case to providing expert testimony at trial, the analyst's knowledge and expertise can be used to form the conceptual framework of the litigation. When a qualified analyst is brought into the case during the early stages, the probability of a satisfactory conclusion—for all parties involved—is substantially increased.

Bibliography

Articles

Arne, Darrell V. "The CPA as a Court-Appointed Expert: Opportunities and Challenges." *CPA Expert*, Winter 1996, pp.1–3.

Brinig, Brian P., and Michael W. Prairie. "Expert Testimony: The Business Appraiser as a Valuation Expert Witness." *The Journal of Business Valuation* (Proceedings of the Third Joint Business Valuation Conference of The Canadian Institute of Chartered Business Valuators and the American Society of Appraisers), 1995, pp. 209–224.

Brinig, Brian P., and Kenneth C. Turek. "The Art of Expert Testimony: Depositions and Trial." *The Journal of Business Valuation* (Proceedings of the Third Joint Business Valuation Conference of The Canadian Institute of Chartered Business Valuators and the American Society of Appraisers), 1995, pp. 225–29.

Field, Harold G. "Direct Examination of a Business Valuation Expert Witness." *American Journal of Family Law*, Fall 1989, p. 223.

Gibbs, Larry W. "What You Can Do if the Government Uses Rambo Tactics." *Trusts & Estates*, July 1994, pp. 57–61+.

Griffiths, David W. "Expert Witnesses—The Good, the Bad, and the Ugly." *Proceedings of the 12th Biennial Conference of the Canadian Institute of Chartered Business Valuators*, 1997, pp. 347–64.

Hitchner, James R. "Matter of Slant/Fin Corp. v. The Chicago Corp." *CPA Expert*, Spring 1996, pp. 13–15.

Hopkins, Marilee Keller. "Effectively Communicating to a Jury." *CPA Expert*, Winter 1997, pp. 4–6.

Jefferson, Mozette. "Structure of the U.S. Court System ." *Shannon Pratt's Business Valuation Update*, October 1996, pp. 11–12.

Laro, Hon. David. "A View from the Tax Court Bench: What Judges Want in Expert Reports and Testimony." *Shannon Pratt's Business Valuation Update*, October 1995, pp. 1, 4.

Livingstone, John Leslie. "Expert Testimony in the United States: Some Do's and Don'ts." *The Expert*, March 1997, pp. 8–12.

Locke, R. Christopher. "Expert Testimony in the Post-Daubert Era." *CPA Expert*, Spring 1996, pp. 3–7.

Moscarino, John M. "Expert Witness Liability: Practical Suggestions for Minimizing the Risk." *CPA Expert*, Premier Issue (Autumn 1995), pp. 1–4.

Parnie, A. David, and Steven F. Schroeder. *Expert Witness Demonstration: Let's Dig a Hole and Crawl in It* (videotape of a session of the 1997 Annual IBA Conference). Boynton Beach, FL: Institute of Business Appraisers, 1997.

Poneman, Lawrence A. "The Objectivity of Accountants' Litigation Support Judgments." *Accounting Review*, July 1995, pp. 467–488.

Pratt, Shannon P. "Criteria Important to Attorneys in Selecting Valuation Experts" (interview with Ronald D. Aucutt). *Shannon Pratt's Business Valuation Update*, February 1997, pp. 1–2.

———. "How to Be an Effective Expert Witness" (interview with Dennis Brooks). *Shannon Pratt's Business Valuation Update*, April 1996, pp. 1, 11.

———. "How to Be an Expert Witness" (interview with Gerald Nissenbaum and Elaine Lewis). *Shannon Pratt's Business Valuation Update*, November 1996, p. 1, 10.

———. "More Judicial Reaction to Valuation Testimony." *Valuation Strategies*, January/February 1998, pp. 34–36.

———. "Judicial Reaction to Valuation Testimony." *Valuation Strategies*, September/October 1997, pp. 18–22.

———. "Wanted: Better Expert Testimony" (interview with Hon. R. William Riggs). *Shannon Pratt's Business Valuation Update*, December 1995, pp. 1–2.

Reilly, Robert F. "Valuation Standards Regarding Deprivation Appraisals." *ASA Valuation*, January 1993, pp. 10–17.

Sickler, Jay. "Appraisers as Expert Witnesses—Changes to FRCP 26." *Business Valuation Review*, September 1994, pp. 130–31.

Skoloff, Gary N., and Cary B. Cheifetz. "Direct Examination of Marital Property Valuation Experts." *The Practical Litigator*, May 1992, p. 25.

Soled, Jay A., P.V. Viswanath, and Patrick I. McKenna. "Almost Two Decades Later, *Buffalo Tool* Admonishments Still Largely Ignored." *Taxes*, January 1997, pp. 65–72.

Stevens, Michael G. "Litigation Services: It Ain't What It Used to Be!" *Practical Accountant*, October 1995, pp. 20–36.

Wagner, Michael J. "Expert Problems." *Litigation*, Winter 1989, pp. 35–

38+.

Wagner, Michael J., and Bruce L. MacFarlane. "Opportunities in Litigation Services: It's a Broad Field Open to CPAs with a Wide Variety of Skills." *Journal of Accountancy*, June 1992, pp. 70–73.

Books

Bailey, Lucinda, Brian P. Brinig, and Michael G. Ueltzen. *Developing and Managing a Litigation Services Practice*. San Diego: Harcourt Brace Professional Publishing, 1996.

Dunn, Robert L. *Expert Witnesses—Law and Practice*. Westport, CT: Lawpress, 1997.

Rabinoff, Marc A., and Stephen P. Holmes. *The Forensic Expert's Guide to Litigation: The Anatomy of a Lawsuit*. Horsham, PA: LRP Publications, 1996.

Veitch, Thomas H. *The Consultant's Guide to Litigation Services: How to Be an Expert Witness*. New York: John Wiley & Sons, 1992.

Weil, Roman L., Michael J. Wagner, and Peter B. Frank. *Litigation Services Handbook: The Role of the Accountant as Expert*. 2d ed. New York: Wiley Law Publications, 1995, with annual supplement.

Chapter 47

Damages

In an economic sense, the term *damages* relates to the notion of one party experiencing a loss in value, however measured, as a result of another party's actions. In a business sense, this loss usually represents out-of-pocket costs and any other reasonably foreseeable amounts relating to increased costs, lost profits, or decreases in the value of a business or business interest. The term *damages* often brings to mind wrongful terminations, wrongful death, and permanent or total disability. This is because these circumstances often incorporate damage calculations with respect to wage and salary losses. However, the subject of this chapter will be damage analyses involving the valuation of a small business or professional practice, or the lost profits related thereto. The following are the most common types of damage analyses involving the valuation of a small business or professional practice:

1. Breach of contract.
2. Condemnation
3. Lost business opportunity.
4. Antitrust actions.
5. Personal injury.
6. Insurance claims.
7. Infringement of intellectual property.
8. Business torts.
9. Violation of securities laws.

The common thread of a damage analysis is this premise: Because of the actions of another party, the affected business did not operate as it would have absent the alleged action causing the damage. This leads to the consequential "but-for" claims of the damaged party. These claims allege that "but for" the actions of Company Z, the subject business would have realized X economic income (e.g., profits or cash flow) during this period. In the most extreme circumstance, these claims allege that the subject business would have continued to operate as a going concern "but for" the actions of the tortious party. This last allegation implies the total loss of the subject business.

Other types of damage claims include (1) the loss of a partial interest in a business, (2) the loss of an entire business, or (3) the loss of a business opportunity. Here is an example of such an allegation: "Had it not been for this wrongful action, I would own X percentage of Company Z." In performing such a damages analysis, the analyst estimates what that business interest would be worth as of a particular date. The particular date is usually (but not always) the date that the damage event occurred.

A noteworthy fact that distinguishes damage cases from other types of litigation involving business valuation is that damage cases usually are tried before a jury. Most other valuation-related litigation, such as divorce cases, dissenting stockholder suits, and tax cases, are usually tried before a judge. Preparation for a jury trial requires considerable effort to simplify the presentation of the complex subject of small business and professional practice valuation. For example, jury trial testimony may include the presentation of graphic exhibits in order to illustrate major points.

The Causation of Damages versus the Amount of Damages

From a legal standpoint, different proofs are required in order to establish whether or not damages occurred (i.e., the causation) as compared to the amount of damages (i.e., the damages). William Cerillo, a California civil litigation and antitrust attorney, explains this distinction between *causation* and *damage* as follows:

> The fact of damage relates to whether plaintiff has been injured as a result of defendant's conduct. The amount of damage involves an estimate of plaintiff's loss. These are separate proofs. The burden as to the former is more stringent than the burden as to the latter. There must be evidence of the fact of injury before a jury is allowed to estimate the amount of damage.[1]

The analyst may be called on to help prove either one—or both—of these two elements of a damages case.

Establishing the Causation of Damages

Three legal principles generally govern the establishment of the causation of damages:

1. Proximate cause.
2. Reasonable certainty.
3. Foreseeability.

Proximate Cause

The plaintiff's but-for claim raised against the defendant addresses the requirement that the defendant's wrongful actions were the proximate (or approximate) cause of the economic losses. As suggested by the term *approximate,* this does not imply that the defendant's actions were the sole cause of the plaintiff's losses. Rather, the defendant's actions were

---

[1] William A. Cerillo, *Proving Business Damages*, 2d ed. (New York: John Wiley & Sons, 1991), p. 7.

at least the major cause. Other parties or external market factors may have contributed to the economic loss. Therefore, experts on both sides of the dispute should perform sufficient analysis in order to understand (1) the subject company's position within its industry, (2) the trends in that industry, and (3) the actual—and projected—impact of external factors on the performance of participants within the industry. These analyses should be performed as of the alleged damage period. These analyses should be performed in order to sufficiently support—or refute—the plaintiff's claim of proximate cause.

Reasonable Certainty

Reasonable certainty refers to the premise that economic losses were actually experienced by the plaintiff. For example, if the subject company enjoys growth and profitability that exceeds (1) industry norms and (2) its own previous operating history *after* the alleged wrongful conduct of the defendant, the plaintiff may have difficulty recovering damages. This difficulty is due to an inability to prove that actual damages were incurred. However, a plaintiff who (1) actually incurred damages and (2) suffered significant losses after a defendant's wrongful actions may encounter similar difficulty proving actual damages if the plaintiff has failed to maintain adequate financial records—and consequently cannot provide an expert with sufficient evidential support. Thus, significant uncertainty as to the causation of—and the occurrence of—damages may be the end of any damage claim.

Foreseeability

Foreseeability is an element of contract law, *not* tort law. It relates to the idea that the damages allegedly suffered by the plaintiff were a natural result of defendant's actions at the time the wrongful acts were committed. The concept of foreseeability is relevant only in the law of contracts. With tort claims, the foreseeability of injury is not a legal requirement; that is, a tortfeasor will be held liable regardless of whether the damage was foreseeable or not.

In contract situations regarding the purchase of goods or services, the immediate effect of a breach, by either party, is generally foreseeable. This is because, for example, the buyer often has to find replacement goods or services at a higher cost, or the seller loses a sale and the related profits. Even related effects are sometimes foreseeable. For example, a buyer who is the victim of a seller's breach may not only have to acquire replacement goods at a higher cost but may also suffer the effects of lost sales while waiting for the replacement material. On the other hand, a wholesaler with many customers whose contract to sell goods to one customer was breached may have suffered total lost profits (calculated as the difference between the first contracted sale and the replacement sale *plus* the lost profits on the first sale).

In order to support or refute a plaintiff's claim of damages, analytical expertise in several areas is required. This expertise is necessary in order to (1) establish the significant factors affecting the plaintiff's success in the subject industry and (2) ascertain whether the defendant's actions were indeed the principal cause for the damage to the plaintiff's operations. Experts who understand the impact that external forces and actions would exert on the plaintiff's performance within that industry are able to estimate the foreseeable result of certain actions with a reasonable degree of certainty. For this very reason, damage cases often involve two categories of experts: (1) causation experts and (2) economics experts.

Calculating the Amount of Damages

The burden of proof regarding the presentation of damages rests with the plaintiff. However, defendants who rely on a plaintiff's inability to calculate exact damages assume significant risk. This is because the courts only require the plaintiff's presentation to be reasonable. Defendants should be prepared to provide expert evidence as to the actual amount of damages. Otherwise, a defendant may end up facing a significant liability at the conclusion of the trial, regardless of how weak the plaintiff's presentation may have been. This is because the plaintiff's case was the best (or only) proof provided (see, for example, the *Cambridge Plating* case described later in this chapter).

The circumstances surrounding different damage claims will determine the specific type of claim filed (e.g., breach of contract, antitrust, lost business opportunity, and so on). However, the methods used to quantify damage claims are fairly standard. For example, in breach of contract claims, liquidated damages and other provisions within the contract itself will often suggest a method for quantifying damages.

In other damage cases, more analysis is necessary in order to fairly quantify economic losses. The analyst endeavors to understand all of the elements of economic loss without double counting any of the elements. The analyst estimates the loss in future profits or future benefits and, perhaps, adds to that the costs incurred by the plaintiff that would not have otherwise been incurred but for the violation. Current literature suggests that most of the elements of lost profits can be estimated by applying one or more of the following methods:

1. Before-and-after method.
2. Yardstick (comparable) method.
3. Sales projection (but-for) method.

These analytical methods may appear simple in theory. However, they all encompass rigorous analysis (1) estimating the performance level for the damaged party—absent the effects of the defendant's actions—and (2) comparing these projected results to the actual results that the plaintiff experienced.

The Before-and-After Method

The before-and-after method is arguably most suited to antitrust and business interruption situations. In this method, the operations of the subject company are projected as if there had been no damage to the subject company. These projected results are then compared to the actual results during the period of the effect of the alleged acts.

The success of this method depends, of course, on the ability of the plaintiff's expert to establish and support a proven historical financial record for the plaintiff's business. Based on these historical financial records, the operations preceding and succeeding the alleged damage are able to serve as damage "bookends." This comparison clearly illustrates the effects of the interruption or antitrust violation period.

Ideally, operations before and after the damage period will show similar trends. These trends will enable the analyst to estimate the company's performance during the damage period using either pre- or post-damage operations as a performance standard. The lost profits are equal to the present value of the difference between the company's expected performance and its actual performance during the period. In many cases, only the "before" period or the "after" period is available for use in predicting the "but for" performance during the damage period.

The Yardstick (Comparable) Method

The yardstick, or comparable, method requires the analyst (1) to identify companies or industries that are comparable to the subject company and (2) to plot the performance of the subject company along the performance lines of the comparable companies or industries. This method, of course, requires that the analyst perform the often difficult task of identifying guideline companies or industries. In addition, the companies or industries the analyst selects should themselves be unaffected by the acts that allegedly damaged the subject company. Applying—as a proxy—the performance of another company in a particular industry to project the performance of the subject company is a straightforward, understandable method of estimating losses. Once again, the analytical key lies in carefully identifying the most appropriate comparative companies or industry. In some instances, a comparable—but unaffected—branch or division of the subject company may provide the best yardstick.

Sales Projections (But-For) Method

The sales projections, or but-for, method entails the creation of a microeconomic model for the subject company. This microeconomic model will encompass growth rate and rate of return projections. Using the microeconomic model, operations for the subject company are projected during the damage period absent (i.e., but for) the alleged effects of the defendant's actions. The economic returns projected by the microeconomic model are then compared with the actual results realized by the subject company during the damage period. The difference between projected results and actual results is an indication of the damages.

Of the three analytical methods described above, the most common method is probably some application of the sales projection method. Typically, most businesses provide sales projections. These businesses are typically included in the many industries subject to annual, semi-annual, or even quarterly forecasts by a variety of both public and private data sources. Such circumstances often lend themselves to the development of microeconomic models designed specifically for the subject company. However, a noteworthy fact regarding the development of a sales projection (and the resulting profit projection) is that courts tend to prefer projections based on historical track records. This is true, even in light of numerous concurring industry forecasts and other published financial data regarding "normal" growth rates and rates of return for the subject industry.

Regardless of the analytical method applied, the extent that projected results exceed actual results represents the plaintiff's loss. This economic loss includes profits lost during the damage period. It also may include a decrease in the subject business value separate from lost profits. The sum total of combined lost profits and any decrease in overall business value is usually limited to the present value of total future profits anticipated by the business prior to the alleged damaging acts. This assertion is based on the fact that the maximum value of most businesses is the present value of all expected economic income. Intuitively, this fact should serve as a reasonableness check throughout the damage estimation analysis.

Some Comments on Projections

A review of the subject company's operations for a reasonable period prior to the damaging acts—typically 5 to 10 years—should provide the analyst with a reasonable basis for projecting general growth rate and rates of return patterns for the subject business. The analysts should research the subject company's industry or peer group. The analyst should then compare the subject company's historical record with the historical record of the industry or peer group for the same time period. This comparison should provide insight into whether the subject company's operations were performing historically below, at, or above industry averages.

Many times, a plaintiff will be unable to provide much historical information. This can be because the subject company's operations are in the development stage, or it may be for other reasons. In such cases, industry information will be all that the analyst will have to rely on when projecting operating results. Especially in circumstances such as these, it is important that the analyst investigate and understand the industry. A sound rationale for expecting the subject company's operations to parallel, or exceed, industry averages is needed before applying industry return and growth rates to the subject company's operations.

Armed with rate of return and growth rate analyses, the analyst is in a position to project the subject company's operations over the damage period. A simple presentation of (1) the projected, but-for operating results and (2) the actual operating results, and (3) the differences between the two projections will illustrate the alleged damages.

A cautionary note is appropriate regarding projections. Although (1) the analysis may be quite simple and (2) the final numbers may appear to speak for themselves, a reasonableness analysis of the projected results is appropriate. Implied revenue and profit growth rates during the damage period should be analyzed in order to assess if they are reasonable. Further, projected profits should be compared with initial capital investments in order to determine if the projected rates of return on investment are reasonable for businesses within the relevant industry. Unreasonable results suggest that the microeconomic model may use one or more unreasonable projections.

Particular attention should be paid to the implications of revenue growth and the resulting profits. Projections often fail to consider the limitations placed on revenue and profit growth by the capacity of the subject business at the time of the projections. Revenues projected to be enjoyed several years down the road may be unattainable without significant capital expenditures. Required investments may include additional facilities and additional equipment. Additional costs may include an increased employee base, with related labor costs. Each of these costs implies adjustments to profits and should be incorporated into projected results.

Having incorporated all relevant costs and the effects of any capital demands into the projections, the resulting summed losses represent the total loss for the plaintiff. This damage estimate has not taken into consideration any prejudgment interest that may accrue to the plaintiff. If losses have been projected past the date of adjudication, the principle of discounting (or bringing the loss to a present value) should also be considered.

Prejudgment Interest and Discounting Anticipated Returns

Let's assume a court determines that damages (1) commenced two years prior to the judgment date and (2) were projected for seven years after the judgment date. This would result in a total damage period of nine years. In order to adequately compensate the plaintiff, (1) losses prior to the judgment date would have to be compounded upward and (2) losses projected subsequent to the judgment date would have to be discounted. Though the compounding of losses incurred prior to the judgment date (known as prejudgment interest) and the discounting of future losses make sense economically, many courts do not allow prejudgment interest calculations. Some courts have refused to recognize that future losses should be discounted.

The analytical question remains: What is the correct rate to use for compounding or discounting losses? In general, most analysts agree that future profits should be discounted at an appropriate present value rate. Most analysts are reluctant, however, to state (1) what the appropriate present value rate is and (2) whether the same rate should be applied in calculating prejudgment interest. In personal injury situations, discussed below, courts have accepted both prejudgment and discount real rates (i.e., inflation-adjusted rates based on U.S. government securities). In other business applications, the courts have taken a less firm stance. Therefore, determining an acceptable discount rate requires that the analyst first estimate the degree of risk relating to the expected returns from investing in the subject business and then proceed to develop a rate implicit with inflation and other premiums that would properly reflect the risk associated with the anticipated returns.

Intuitively, most analysts agree that investing in any business is riskier than investing in U.S. securities. The extent to which risk premiums are added to the "riskless" government security rate in estimating the subject business's appropriate discount rate depends on (1) the size of the business and (2) its potential for failure (i.e., financial or default risk). The discount rate is influenced as well by the variability of returns experienced by the business and others in its industry. The key factor in estimating present value discount rates is the need to equate the expected returns from investing in a particular concern with the risk of achieving those returns.

The damage calculation is complete after the effects of any prejudgment interest and discounting have been incorporated. Statutes and case law for the particular jurisdiction should always be reviewed in order to determine the courts' views on prejudgment interest and discounting.

Common Damage Cases

As mentioned earlier, the most common types of damage cases involving small business or professional practice valuation include breach of contract, condemnation, lost business opportunity, antitrust actions, personal injury, and insurance claims. Each of these six types of damage analyses is discussed briefly below.

Breach of Contract

A variety of breach-of-contract actions can give rise to a lawsuit requiring the valuation of a business or a business fractional ownership interest as a measure of damages. A common example is a stockholder or partner's claim of a contract breach resulting in his or her removal from the company or business venture. Cancellation of an important contract between a buyer and a seller—or some other violation of its terms and conditions—is another common dispute. As mentioned earlier, substantiating or refuting the premises regarding proximate cause, reasonable certainty, and foreseeability are important in contract disputes resulting in damage claims.

The denial of a right to a business interest is usually a normal, straightforward valuation problem involving the value of whatever ownership interest was denied. However, if the breach of contract damages the business itself, this creates the need to estimate (1) the value of lost profits and (2) (often) the diminution in the total value of the business resulting from the damaging acts. In general, damage claims resulting from contract breaches should contemplate foreseeable and reasonably estimable losses reflecting a type of opportunity cost incurred by the damaged party. In other words, as a result of the breach, the damaged party was not able to enjoy economic benefits it was contractually entitled to. Further, the damaged party may even experience additional costs in the form of both (1) increased actual costs and (2) lost profits.

Condemnation

A frequent cause of damages is the taking of business premises through eminent domain proceedings. Condemnation may result in the total loss of the business if relocation is not feasible. Or condemnation may result in a temporary loss of profits plus relocation costs. These temporary costs may also be combined with some permanent loss of locational goodwill. This would occur if it is unlikely that all patrons would follow a business or practice to a new location. Ideally, the analyst would be able to document the loss of locational goodwill by the use of customer lists before and after the condemnation. However, few businesses are likely to have such customer-specific records.

Lost Business Opportunity

The most common scenario leading to a damage claim for lost business opportunity is when an employee comes upon an opportunity through contacts made through the employer company then exploits the opportunity on his own, or through another company, without offering it to the initial employer. In this case, the measure of damages is usually the value lost to the initial employer as a result of not being offered the subject business opportunity.

Antitrust Actions

Perhaps the most complicated of all categories of business damage cases is the antitrust area or those situations where certain business activities are deemed by the courts to result in the restraint of normal competition. The hard-line stance adopted by the courts in dealing with violators of antitrust laws is based primarily on the premise that most monopolistic circumstances result in consumers being forced to accept higher prices for goods and services. A victorious plaintiff under the federal antitrust laws has the right to recover treble damages in many circumstances.

In the realm of antitrust litigation, the law is the greatest ally of the party pressing suit. This is because allegations arising from clearly illegal acts of a defendant require that the plaintiff prove only that the act has occurred. The defendant's liability to the plaintiff is created by her violation of the relevant antitrust law. The plaintiff is relieved of the need to prove specific damage to competition. Below are examples and brief explanations of some such violations.

Predatory Pricing.   Horizontal price fixing results when collusive behavior among competitors within a particular market results in price stabilization. An example is situations in which larger companies (or companies with significant market share) are able to sustain a period of pricing below average unit costs long enough to drive both existing and potential competitors from the market. After such time, prices are usually raised to reap the benefits of monopolistic profits due to the absence of competitors. The difficulty in proving such behavior, known as predatory pricing, lies in establishing an appropriate cost structure for the relevant industry. This cost structure is analyzed in order to verify that the defendant is pricing below cost.

Horizontal Market Division.   As the name suggests, horizontal market division results in participants within the same industry dividing up a particular market. The end result is that each participant has a virtual monopoly in his or her particular segment of the market. Such divisions can occur on a variety of bases, including citywide, regional, and end-user classifications. The simple act of two competitors simultaneously withdrawing from a particular market area often suggests some degree of horizontal market division activity. Another example of horizontal arrangements is the group boycott, during which competitors agree to refrain from dealing with specific suppliers or customers.

Resale Price Maintenance.   Resale price maintenance is a form of vertical price fixing. This occurs when a manufacturer establishes a contract with a retailer, establishing either a maximum or minimum price at which the retailer can ultimately sell the product to the consumer. Under a maximum price arrangement, the manufacturer attempts to enhance competitiveness for its own product relative to other products. Under a minimum price-fixing arrangement, the manufacturer attempts to ensure that its product receives exposure comparable to that of its competitors' products by way of demonstration and store location. Such exposure is normally disproportionately allocated to the higher margin products. A minimum price arrangement is established to produce a margin floor for the manufacturer's product.

As in all damage situations, antitrust violations require that the analyst calculate a reasonable and supportable amount of profits that the damaged party would have realized were it not for the antitrust violations. The analyst then compares this amount with the profits that were actually generated. This may be accomplished by use of the before-and-after, yardstick, or projections analytical methods described earlier in the chapter.

Antitrust actions typically are tried in federal court for violation of either the Sherman or Clayton Acts. Each circuit of the federal court system develops its own case law. Courts usually consider case law developed in other circuits. However, they are not bound by precedents from other circuits, some of which may conflict with the local circuit. Therefore, the analyst should be aware of the local circuit case law as it affects the determination of damages in antitrust matters.

Some antitrust actions are tried in state courts under state antitrust statutes. Many states' antitrust laws are patterned after the federal statutes, but they may have some differences.

Personal Injury

Sometimes an injury impairs a person's ability to carry on his or her business or practice. In such cases, the amount of the economic loss is normally estimated by use of the discounted cash flow method. The process requires estimating the annual amount of cash flow lost, the duration of the loss period, and the appropriate present value discount rate. The discounting of future cash flows is required because the purpose of the award of damages is to provide a fund that, amortized over time, will yield the damaged party an amount equivalent to his loss. Though courts have not reached a consensus regarding the absolute need to discount future cash flows, the principle has often been accepted. Present value discount rates accepted by the courts in personal injury situations have tended to suggest that the courts continue to view individuals as risk-averse. This is because the rates normally reflect returns that could reasonably be expected by investing funds in low-risk securities.

Insurance Casualty Claims

Frequently, businesses are interrupted or destroyed by casualty losses, such as fires or storms. The discounted future cash flow method is commonly used to estimate the loss, offset by whatever value is salvaged. Other business valuation methods described in this book are often acceptable and appropriate. The but-for theory may also be applicable. In dealing with insurance claims, careful attention should be paid to the wording in the policies before a damage estimate is submitted. Inappropriate attention to coverage provisions can often result in (1) the forfeiture of potential recoveries or (2) the estimation of losses that were not insured.

Mitigation

An often crucial aspect regarding damage claims of all types, particularly contract breaches, is the principle of mitigation. This principle suggests that even victims of contract breaches have a duty to mitigate damages. That is, the victims have a responsibility to keep the damages as low as possible. Damages are not recoverable for losses that the injured party could have avoided without undue risk, burden, or humiliation. Even in fraud situations, courts have held that once a plaintiff learns of the fraud, alleged damages that accrue thereafter are not caused by the fraud. Rather, they are caused by the plaintiff's decision to continue its relationship with the defendant regardless of his or her knowledge of the fraud.

With regard to buyers and sellers of goods or services, the buyer is required by the principle of mitigation to "cover." That is, the buyer is responsible to make reasonable efforts to find replacement goods or services to purchase. A breached seller is obligated to make reasonable efforts to find an alternative purchaser for the breached goods or services. The following damages are normally recoverable: (1) excess costs incurred by the buyer in acquiring replacement goods, (2) differences between the contracted price and the resale price incurred by the seller, and (3) incidental damages, such as expenses incurred in stopping the manufacture of goods, as well as inspecting, transporting, receiving, or storing goods that resulted from the breach.

Selected Damage Cases

American Federal Group[2]

The plaintiff (a 60 percent shareholder) sought damages from the defendant (a 40 percent shareholder). The damages resulted from alleged breach of fiduciary duties, breach of a shareholder agreement, and violation of a restrictive covenant—all with regard to the demise of their wholesale insurance business. The plaintiff filed suit as a result of the defendant's resigning and establishing a competing, viable wholesale insurance business almost immediately after the demise of the first insurance business. The defendant's ability to secure the primary source of London insurance that had dealt with his previous insurance business called into question the defendant's fiduciary, shareholder, and restrictive covenant responsibilities.

The court concluded that damages were reasonably estimable based on the value of the business calculated by the defendant's analyst. The defendant's analyst used a market approach. The analyst reviewed information on completed transactions and used a multiple of earnings based on the stock trading patterns of two comparative, publicly traded insurance wholesalers. The defendant's analyst estimated the value of the initial wholesale insurance business at $860,372.

The plaintiff's analyst provided evidence regarding the alleged actual damages experienced. The *unimpaired* value of the business was

---

[2] *American Federal Group, Ltd.* v. *Rothenberg*, No. 91 CIV. 7860 (SWK) (THK), 1996 WL 282059, (S.D.N.Y. May 28, 1996).

estimated at $2 million. This value was based on the capitalization of a pro forma earnings margin (20 percent) and assumed a commission base of $1.5 million. The impaired value of the business was estimated assuming the same $1.5 million commission but with the following adjustments:

- A deduction of $600,000 in commissions assumed to have been improperly transferred to the competing firm by the defendant.
- A deduction of approximately $400,000 in commissions due to the improper displacement by the defendant of relationships with underwriters.
- A reduction of the estimated profit margin from 20 percent to 15 percent.
- An increase in the direct capitalization rate from 15 percent to 18 percent.

Based on these adjustments, the impaired business value was estimated at $420,000. This resulted in a difference, due to the alleged damaging acts, of $1,580,000. The plaintiff's loss, based on his 60 percent ownership interest, was therefore estimated at $948,000.

The court rejected the calculations of the plaintiff's analyst based on the following:

- Inadequate support of projections resulting from a failure to review the financial or tax records of the firm.
- Failure to consider normal attrition of commission business from year to year.
- Double-counting of damages based on the use of the same lost commission revenue to estimate impaired value and loss of future earnings.
- An inherent inconsistency in calculating damages based on the impaired market value of the company that assumes "the sale of the company in 1992" while, at the same time, seeking "damages for lost earnings projected forward to 1996."

The court concluded that the plaintiff was entitled to damages of $517,128. This amount represented approximately 60 percent of the company's value as estimated by the defendant's analyst.

Cooper Distributing Co.[3]

The plaintiff, Cooper Distributing Co., Inc. (Cooper), had been a distributor of Amana home appliances for approximately 30 years. Amana

---

[3] *Cooper Distributing Co., Inc., v. Amana Refrigeration, Inc.,* 63 F.3d 262 (3rd Cir., Aug. 22, 1995).

Refrigeration, Inc. (Amana), a manufacturer of home appliances, attempted to terminate its relationship with Cooper, resulting in a judgment for $9,375,000 in favor of Cooper.

Cooper asserted four claims against Amana:

1. Illegal termination of a franchise, in violation of New Jersey Franchise Practices Act (NJFPA).
2. Breach of contract.
3. Breach of implied obligation of good faith and fair dealing.
4. Tortious interference with prospective business advantage.

Cooper began operating as an independent wholesale distributor in 1931. Beginning in the late 1970s, the majority of Cooper's business (78 percent to 100 percent) was derived from the sale of Amana products. Cooper also distributed other major brands of appliances, including Hardwick, In-Sink-Erator, and Dacor. Amana occasionally subjected Cooper to competitive restraints.

During its relationship with Amana, Cooper operated a showroom/marketing center for Amana product demonstrations, dealer training in Amana products, and dealer open houses. Further, Cooper's sales managers studied the Amana product line and in turn gave Amana product training to retail dealers. Cooper also placed Amana advertisements in the yellow pages and newspapers, advertised as an authorized Amana servicer, instructed its servicemen to wear Amana uniforms, distributed promotional items bearing the Amana name, and, pursuant to an agreement (the "Agreement") with Amana, promised to "use its best efforts to promote sales" of Amana products. Based on these facts, Cooper's dealers perceived Amana and Cooper as one and the same.

As a result of industry change, resulting in the elimination of two-step distribution, Raytheon (Amana's parent company) decided to consolidate the distribution of its brands. Several of the distributors that sold one, but not all, of Raytheon's brands were eliminated. As a result, in November 1991, Amana terminated its relationship with Cooper pursuant to a provision of the Agreement that allowed either party to terminate the Agreement on 10-days written notice. At the same time, Amana terminated its relationship with 20 of the other 23 remaining Amana wholesale distributors across the country.

With regard to the franchise claim, Cooper's valuation expert in the appeal assumed that Cooper had an *exclusive right* to sell to the retail dealers in its four-state territory and "that Amana had no right to sell [to the dealers] directly." Furthermore, the analyst explained that his calculation of the value of the Cooper franchise would have been "considerably less" if "Amana did have the right to sell directly" to the dealers. The jury's award appears to have been based on the estimation of Cooper's analyst.

After a five-week trial, the jury returned a verdict of liability on all four counts and awarded damages as follows:

1. $4,375,000 on Cooper's NJFPA claim.
2. $2,000,000 on Cooper's breach of contract claim.
3. $0 on Cooper's claim for breach of the obligation of good and fair dealing.
4. $0 in actual damages on Cooper's tortious interference claim.
5. $3,000,000 in punitive damages on Cooper's tortious interference claim.

Cambridge Plating Co.[4]

At the end of an 11-day trial, the jury returned verdicts for the plaintiff, Cambridge Plating Co., Inc. (Cambridge) on three counts: (1) breach of contract, (2) intentional misrepresentation, and (3) negligent misrepresentation, and assessed damages in the amount of $12,183,120. Further, the jury returned an advisory verdict for the plaintiff on a fourth count, finding that the defendant, NAPCO, had violated M.G.L. c. 93A, with the judge rendering an opinion in the amount of $6,726,240.

Cambridge is an electroplating and metal finishing business located in Belmont, Massachusetts. Cambridge plant operations require the use of large quantities of water for bath solutions, to rinse plated parts, and to perform other functions. Under environmental laws, this water, which is contaminated by various chemicals employed in the plating and finishing processes, must be treated before it may be discharged into the sewer system.

In January 1984, Cambridge entered into a contract with NAPCO, a company from Terryville, Connecticut. According to the contract, NAPCO would design, sell, and install a precipitation wastewater treatment system (the "System") in the Cambridge Belmont plant. In addition to the actual physical installation, NAPCO agreed to provide engineering assistance during the first year of operation without extra cost. The contract also contained a performance warranty, guaranteeing that the discharge would meet the latest discharge limits set by the Environmental Protection Agency (EPA) and the Metropolitan District Commission (MDC), the regional regulatory agency later succeeded by the Massachusetts Water Resources Authority (MWRA).

The contract also contained the following provision purporting to bar any claim for consequential damages:

> No claim will be allowed for damages or delays caused by defective materials, or operating failures, including delays in production, whether or not related to the use of, or delivery of any equipment, or for any consequential damage or business loss incurred by the Buyer.

---

[4] *Cambridge Plating Co., Inc.* v. *NAPCO, Inc.,* 876 F.Supp. 326 (D. Mass. Feb. 7, 1995).

The purchase price for the System was $398,000. In addition, Cambridge made costly modifications to its Belmont facility in order to accommodate the tanks and equipment for the System and to pipe the wastewater from its plating tanks.

The parties originally anticipated that the System would be completely installed by June 15, 1984, and that it would commence operating on July 1. The System was only partly operational by October 30, 1984. From March 1985 to September 1985, the System still suffered from faulty parts and incomplete installation. NAPCO sent technicians to the site to address the mechanical problems and advised Cambridge on correct operational procedures. During this time, Cambridge forwarded six discharge reports to the MWRA. All of these reports indicated that the Company was meeting applicable discharge limits.

After September 1985, Cambridge continued to submit reports to the state regulatory agency. These reports show that it often exceeded the applicable discharge limits.

Cambridge made its final payment to NAPCO for the System in December 1985.

After 1985, Cambridge sales declined steadily, from record sales of $6,164,000. Lost sales were attributed to Cambridge's inability to deliver rapid service in order to meet the timetables for production demanded by its customers. Further, "the ability to meet pollution control standards" was used by a former large customer, General Electric, as one factor in determining the qualifications of a company to bid on GE work.

Complaints directed at potential flaws in the NAPCO System by Cambridge were redirected by NAPCO to operator error. Later, operator requests for field representatives from NAPCO were responded to with telephone advice. Further, Cambridge was not informed by NAPCO of the fact that the System did not contain a static mixer—a necessary component, according to original blueprints and drawings.

As a result of lost revenues, and a consistent inability to meet the MWRA discharge limits for zinc, Cambridge experienced declining operations. In March 1988, Cambridge terminated its zinc plating operations and ceased operations in its paint shop. On December 28, 1988, the MWRA, in a widely publicized move, issued a penalty assessment in the amount of $682,250 against Cambridge for discharging excessive levels of contaminants. By August 12, 1991, Cambridge was forced to file a voluntary Chapter 11 bankruptcy petition.

Cambridge's analyst produced a damage analysis based on extending the company's recent historical sales increases and related gross profits and net profits over a projected damage period, 1985 through 1993. While the court did not accept the entire damage period (1992 and 1993 were excluded), and revised certain assumptions made by Cambridge's analyst, the court did rely on the analysis prepared by Cambridge's analyst as a "road map." This was because the defendant opted to attack the analysis of Cambridge's analyst rather than present its own expert analysis.

Summary

In general, damage cases require a creative, but realistic, approach to calculating "hypothetical" values absent the alleged effects of the damaging party's actions. A broad understanding of the damaged party's industry is an important first step in any damage calculation. If it is available, a historical record of the damaged party's results of operations generally proves beneficial. Knowledge of judicial precedent will provide the analyst with important guidance regarding approaches and methods that the courts will (and will not) accept in the estimation of damages within the specific legal context in question.

Bibliography

Articles

Bagby, John W., Norman G. Miller, and Michael E. Solt. "The Determination of Compensatory Damages: A Valuation Framework." *American Business Law Journal*, Spring 1984, pp. 1–29.

Bjorklund, Paul R. "Calculating Lost Earnings for Damage Awards." *Practical Accountant*, June 1991, pp. 62–70.

Blair, Roger D. "Measuring Damages for Lost Profits in Franchise Termination Cases." *Franchise Law Journal*, Fall 1988, pp. 3–12.

Bongiorno, Anthony A. "Recovery of Damages for Lost Profits." *The Best of MCLE*, August 1996, pp. 27–30.

Budge, Bruce. "Damage Control." *Washington Law*, December 1990, pp. 26–27.

Goldsheider, Robert. "Measuring the Damages: ADR and Intellectual Property Disputes." *Dispute Resolution Journal*, October-December 1995, pp. 55–63.

Jarosz, John C. "Damages in Patent and Trademark Infringement." *The Journal of Business Valuation* (Proceedings of the Third Joint Business Valuation Conference of the Canadian Institute of Chartered Business Valuators and the American Society of Appraisers), 1995, pp. 161–74.

Lansche, James M. "Business Damages: What Are They Worth?" *Washington State Bar Association Business Law Newsletter*, October 1990, pp. 1–3.

Lanzillotti, R. F., and A. K. Esquibel. "Measuring Damages in Commercial Litigation: Present Value of Lost Opportunities." *Journal of Accounting, Auditing & Finance,* Winter 1990, pp. 125–44.

Love, Vincent J., and Steven Alan Reiss. "Guidelines for Calculating Damages." *CPA Journal*, October 1990, p. 36.

McCarter, W. Dudley. "Economic Loss Doctrine: Is Privity Required?" *Journal of The Missouri Bar*, January-February 1997, pp. 23–30.

Meyer, James E., Patrick Fitzgerald, and Mostafa Moini. "Loss of Business Profits, Risk, and the Appropriate Discount Rate." *Journal of Legal Economics*, Winter 1994, pp. 27–42.

O'Brien, Vincent E., and Joan K Meyer. "A Guide to Calculating Lost Profits." *National Law Journal*, January 29, 1990, pp. 17–19.

Paulsen, Jon. "Valuation of Patent Infringement Damages." *ASA Valuation*, March 1994, pp. 18–23.

Rainer, J. Marbury. "Recovery of Lost Profit Damages for Business Interruption or Destruction." *Georgia State Bar Journal*, August 1991, pp. 63–67.

Reilly, Robert F. "Tackling a Common Appraisal Problem." *Journal of Accountancy*, October 1992, pp. 86–92.

_____. "Valuing Economic Loss." *Management Accounting*, July 1993, pp. 44–47.

_____. "Valuation Factors Regarding Deprivation Analyses." *The National Public Accountant*, November 1992, pp. 32–36.

_____. "Valuation Standards Regarding Deprivation Appraisals." *ASA Valuation*, January 1993, pp. 10–17.

Rosenblatt, David P., and Joseph J. Floyd. "Measuring Economic Losses in Environmental Cases." *Massachusetts CPA Review*, Summer 1992, pp. 23–25.

Schalow, David, and Christine Shalow. "Determination of Settlement Values in Loss of Earnings Litigation." *National Public Accountant*, June 1995, pp. 29–32+.

Sliwoski, Leonard J. "Reconciling Discount Rates: Personal Injury/Wrongful Death Cases, Commercial Damage Cases, Business Appraisal Engagements." *Business Valuation Review*, December 1996, pp. 167–70.

Smith, James B. Jr., and Jack A. Taylor. "Injuries and Loss of Earnings." *The Alabama Lawyer*, May 1996, 176–78.

Wagner, Michael J. "Experience Enhances Objectivity of Damage Estimates." *CPA Expert*, Winter 1997, pp. 12–13.

Wagner, Michael J., and Bruce McFarlane. "Court Expands Lost Profits Damages from Patent Infringement." *CPA Expert*, Summer 1996, pp. 1–3.

_____. "How Do You Measure Damages? Lost Income or Lost Cash Flow?" *Journal of Accountancy*, February 1990, pp. 28–31.

_____. "The Accountant's Role in the Process of Damage Measurement." *Practical Accountant*, July 1990, pp. 52–60.

Books

Brookshire, Michael L., and Stan V. Smith. *Economic/Hedonic Damages: The Practice Book for Plaintiff and Defense Attorneys*. Cincinnati: Anderson Publishing Co., 1990.

Cerillo, William A. *Proving Business Damages*. New York: John Wiley & Sons, Inc., 1991.

Dunn, Robert L. *Recovery of Damages for Lost Profits*. 4th ed. Westport, CN: Lawpress Corporation, 1992, supplemented 1997.

Frank, Peter B., Michael J. Wagner, and Roman L. Weil. *Litigation Services Handbook: The Role of the Accountant as Expert Witness.* New York: John Wiley & Sons, 1990.

Gaughan, Patrick A., and Robert J. Thornton, eds. *Litigation Economics.* Greenwich, CN: JAI Press, 1993.

Kaufman, Michael J. *Securities Litigation: Damages.* New York: Clark Boardman Callaghan, 1990, supplemented annually.

Link, Albert N. *Evaluating Economic Damages: A Handbook for Attorneys.* Westport, CN: Greenwood Press, 1992.

McCarthy, John C. *Recovery of Damages for Bad Faith.* 5th ed. Kentfield, CA: Lawpress Corporation, 1992.

Page, William H., ed. *Proving Antitrust Damages: Legal and Economic Issues.* Chicago: American Bar Association, 1996.

Parr, Russell L. *Intellectual Property Infringement Damages: A Litigation Support Handbook.* New York: John Wiley & Sons, 1993, supplemented in 1997.

Schwartzkopf, William, John J. MacNamara, and Julian F. Hoffar. *Calculating Construction Damages.* New York: John Wiley & Sons, 1992.

_____ Chapter 48

_____ Arbitrating or Mediating Disputed Valuations

_____

_____

Disputes over the value of small businesses and professional practices arise from a variety of circumstances, including divorce, corporate or partnership dissolution, dissenting stockholder actions, and assorted damage cases. There has been a growing trend in recent years to resolve such disputes through arbitration rather than through litigation (i.e., taking them through a court trial). While not all situations are suitable for arbitration, and the decision to arbitrate should be made on the advice of the principal's attorney in each case, parties involved in controversies frequently find that arbitration is a preferable alternative to a court trial.

There can be much potential grief, however, for both the principals and the arbitrators if the essential elements of the arbitration process are not anticipated, understood, and agreed on by the parties involved. We hope that the following discussion will help principals, their attorneys, other advisors, and those who may act as arbitrators use the arbitration process efficiently and obtain results that are fair to all.

In the last few years, mediation has also been used successfully to resolve business valuation disputes. Mediation differs from arbitration in that a final resolution of the disputed matter is not assured—the matter is concluded only if the parties can be convinced to reach a settlement. A section describing the mediation process and its advantages and disadvantages is included at the end of this chapter.

Advantages of Arbitration versus Litigation

The following are the primary advantages of arbitration over litigation (i.e., a court trial):

1. Usually takes less elapsed time from start to finish.
2. Usually costs less. Attorneys' time is reduced considerably, and experts' fees usually are less than for a court trial. The appraisal process itself, however, may not be less expensive.
3. Scheduling usually can be made more convenient for all parties involved.
4. Usually less formal and less taxing on all participants, especially the principals to the controversy.
5. Less likelihood of an outlandish result in favor of one side over the other, assuming that the arbitrators are qualified valuation professionals.
6. The award of the arbitrators in most situations is final and binding, and it and can be confirmed in court on motion.

Independent Role of Arbitrators

The most important point to understand about the arbitration process is that, at least from the arbitrators' viewpoint, it is not an adversarial proceeding. Rather, it is a cooperative effort to reach a fair and equitable conclusion. All the parties should realize that each arbitrator, regardless of who appointed him or her, is not an agent of any principal (as might be the case in a negotiation for a sale). Rather, the arbitrator is acting independently in using his or her expertise and judgment to reach a conclusion that is fair to all parties. The neutrality of party-appointed arbitrators should be established at the outset.

This attitude of cooperation should be evidenced in the way the valuation professionals appointed as arbitrators normally interact during the arbitration process. Such professional cooperation can be contrasted to the type of interaction that occurs when experts are presenting testimony in a court proceeding. In a court proceeding, there is normally no direct communication between the experts. Expert testimony is limited to answering the questions posed by attorneys on direct or cross-examination, or to answering questions posed by the court. In an arbitration proceeding, on the other hand, maximum communication among the valuation analysts normally is expected from the outset. Discussion is expected to cover all points thoroughly and impartially. It should not be limited to answering questions posed by opposing attorneys (each of whom are acting from the perspective of advocacy).

Situations Giving Rise to Arbitration

Almost any dispute over the value of a small business or professional practice (or over an ownership interest in one) can lend itself to resolution by arbitration, rather than by trial. The following situations are examples of controversies that are often resolved through arbitration.

In marital dissolution matters and in corporate or partnership dissolution matters, a decision ahead of time to determine any valuation issues by arbitration may prevent these issues from ever reaching the point of dispute.

Marital Dissolution

Of all situations involving disputed small business or professional practice valuations, those arising from marital dissolutions are the most difficult for the parties to resolve by amicable negotiation. Disputed valuation issues can become a major element in the already intense emotional strain accompanying divorce proceedings. Frequently, the valuation for the marital estate property settlement is the major, if not the only, disputed issue. Besides the time and cost advantages, arbitration spares the parties the tension and added antagonism associated with litigating these issues.

Corporate and Partnership Dissolutions

A corporate or partnership dissolution is somewhat akin to a marital dissolution. We would also include in this general category the buyout of a minority stockholder or partner pursuant to a buy-sell agreement. By arbitrating the valuation issue, the principals can part on as friendly a basis as possible, whatever the circumstances of the dissolution may be.

Dissenting Stockholder Actions

A merger, sale, or other major corporate action can give rise to dissenting stockholders' appraisal rights under all state statutes. The factors of expediency and lower cost make the arbitration process an attractive alternative to a trial in such cases. This is especially true for smaller controversies for which prolonged and expensive court proceedings can result in a no-win situation for everyone.

Damage Cases

Damage cases, where the valuation of a business or practice often is the central issue in determining the amount of equitable relief, include the following:

1. Breach of contract.
2. Condemnation.
3. Antitrust.
4. Lost profits.
5. Lost business opportunity.
6. Amount of casualty insurance proceeds or allocation of proceeds among parties at interest.
7. Infringement of intellectual property.
8. Business torts.
9. Violation of securities laws.

The risk of an extreme decision regarding value by a court is greater in damage cases than in any other major category of disputed valuation cases. This inclination toward an extreme decision—one way or the other—may result from a tendency of some juries or courts to allow the damage event to affect their objective view of the valuation issue. This risk can be reduced significantly through the use of an arbitration process when qualified valuation analysts serve as the arbitrators.

Selection of Arbitrators

Two factors to delineate regarding the selection of arbitrators are (1) the criteria for selection and (2) the procedure for selection.

Criteria for Selection

The arbitration process produces the most equitable results for all parties if all of the arbitrators (or if the sole arbitrator) are experienced, qualified valuation professionals. If there are three arbitrators, it is most desirable if all three are full-time valuation professionals.

In some cases, if the business or profession is highly specialized, it may be desirable to seek as arbitrators one or more analysts who have experience in appraising the specific line of business or professional practice. It generally is not desirable to gain the desired industry expertise by using (1) an arbitrator who is an active or retired participant in the subject industry or profession or (2) an arbitrator who has performed ancillary functions (such as accounting or economic analysis) in the subject industry or profession. Many of these industry experts lack the requisite technical training to deal professionally with the esoteric valuation issues. Also, there is the risk that the industry expert's biases toward the industry or profession could prevent objective valuation. The expertise of industry experts can be gained (1) through informal discussion with the arbitrator(s) or (2) through formal testimony presented to the arbitrator(s). This alternative is preferable to having industry experts act as the arbitrators themselves.

Certainly, it is possible to have reasonable valuation conclusions reached by arbitration panels composed of industry experts who are knowledgeable in finance, along with attorneys who are knowledgeable in both the industry and in valuation matters. However, in these instances, costs are usually incurred, not only for the three arbitrators, but also for expert testimony to be presented to the arbitration panel by the appraisers for each principal. Of course, it is also possible to have nonappraiser arbitration panels reach value conclusions that a consensus of professional appraisers would consider insupportable.

Obviously, one practical criterion for selection is the availability of the desired arbitrator(s). This is important so that the arbitration can take place promptly.

Procedure for Selection

The most typical procedure is that (1) each party selects one arbitrator, and (2) the two arbitrators select the third. It is preferable for the two arbitrators appointed by the parties to have complete authority to select the third arbitrator (rather than having the selection of the third arbitrator subject to the approval of the principals). This avoids delays and the need to deal with pressures arising from the principals' biases.

It is important that there be an alternative procedure for the selection of a third arbitrator in case of a deadlock. A contingency procedure should be planned in advance or in conjunction with entering into the arbitration agreement. There should be a deadline, at which time the alternate selection process takes effect if the first two arbitrators have failed to reach agreement on a third arbitrator. In case of a deadlock, the procedure should call for the appointment of the third arbitrator (who is a qualified appraiser) by (1) some predetermined entity, such as the American Arbitration Association, (2) a court, or (3) some designated official in the industry or profession.

Another possibility is to establish the procedure whereby the two arbitrators attempt to reach agreement, bringing in the third arbitrator only if the first two arbitrators are unable to reach agreement. In that case, we recommend that the first two arbitrators agree on the prospective third arbitrator at the outset, before they get involved in other aspects of interaction with each other in the arbitration process. This procedure could be established as part of the language in a buy-sell agreement.

If a court appoints an arbitrator, the arbitrator may be an equal part of a three-member arbitration panel or may be a *special master*. In the case of a special master, the master's conclusion does not require the concurrence of any other arbitrator. Nonetheless, normally the court special master would be expected to take the respective positions of the other arbitrators into consideration.

American Arbitration Association Procedure

The American Arbitration Association (AAA) procedure for appointing arbitrators is different than that described in the foregoing section. When parties agree to submit a disputed matter to arbitration through the AAA, the association sends the parties a list of suggested arbitrators from the association's panel of arbitrators. Each party may veto nominees and indicate its preferences. However, the AAA makes the final decision.

In a letter discussing an early draft of this chapter in the first edition of this book, Robert Coulson, president of the American Arbitration Association, made the following observation:

> Although you encourage parties to use the party-appointed system, many arbitration experts have come to believe that using neutral arbitrators is more reliable and less subject to a concern that one of the party-appointed arbitrators might be prejudiced in favor of the party that appointed him.

Mr. Coulson also said, "I, too, believe that experts are the best arbitrators for such valuation questions." However, there is no assurance that a panel appointed by the AAA will be composed of appraisers unless the arbitration clause so provides or unless the parties so agree.

In many AAA arbitrations, each party will retain its own expert who will present testimony before the arbitration panel, rather than having the expert actually participate as an arbitrator. In this sense, the preparation and presentation of expert testimony is similar to a court trial although slightly less formal. For additional information, the address of the American Arbitration Association is 140 West 51st Street, New York, NY 10020.

The next few sections of this chapter discuss the type of situation where the appraiser is acting as a member of the arbitration panel rather than as a presenter of expert testimony.

Engagement and Compensation of Arbitrators

Once the arbitrators have been appointed, the engagement should be committed to writing. The description of the engagement may take the form of an engagement letter or a professional services agreement initiated either by one of the attorneys or parties, or by an appraiser serving as arbitrator. All aspects of the engagement should be adequately covered. Sometimes, addenda to the initial engagement document(s) may be necessary since decisions on some items, such as schedules and some expenses, may be made or changed as the engagement progresses.

The engagement document(s) should include by reference the document(s) giving rise to the arbitration (e.g., a buy-sell agreement) and should cover compensation of the arbitrator and all necessary instructions not addressed or not made clear in the arbitration document(s).

All documents relating to the engagement of an arbitrator should be signed both by the arbitrator and by whoever is responsible for compensating the arbitrator for her or his services. The most common compensation arrangement is that each party assumes responsibility for the compensation and expenses of the arbitrator it has nominated or appointed, with the parties sharing equally the compensation and expenses of the third arbitrator. Such arrangements vary, however, from case to case.

The amount of compensation usually is based on each arbitrator's normal professional hourly or daily billing rate (or some mutually agreed-upon rate) plus out-of-pocket expenses. It is much less common for an arbitrator's compensation to be based on a fixed fee. This is because it is very difficult to estimate in advance just how much time the total appraisal and arbitration process will require. However, it is reasonable to expect to discuss some estimate of probable fees and the daily rate or other basis for the fees. Under the procedures of the American Arbitration Association, these arrangements are carried out by a representative of that organization.

Establishing the Ground Rules for Arbitration

The ground rules by which the arbitration will proceed are critical. They start with a document mandating certain elements of the arbitrators' assignment. This document may be, for example, a buy-sell agreement, a prenuptial agreement, or an agreement drawn up specifically for the purpose of the arbitration. Sometimes, an agreement such as a buy-sell agreement will be supplemented by written instructions agreed on by the attorneys involved. It is important that the written agreement directing the arbitration specify what factors are mandated by the agreement and what factors are left to the discretion of the arbitrators.

Factors Specified in the Arbitration Agreement

The following are factors that are typically mandated by the agreement:

1. The procedure for selection of arbitrators.
2. The definition of the property to be appraised.
3. The valuation date.

4. The standard of value and premise of value to be used (as discussed in Chapter 3 and elsewhere in the book).
5. What constitutes a conclusion by the arbitrators, such as:
   a. Agreement by at least two out of three.
   b. Average of the two closest to each other.
   c. The conclusion of the third (neutral) arbitrator, such as in a "special master" situation.
6. The format and procedure for the arbitrators to render their conclusion.
7. The terms of payment of the amount determined by the arbitrators, including interest, if any.
8. The time schedule for the various steps in the arbitration process, at least the selection of arbitrators and some outside time limit for the total process.

Failure to specify any of the matters above may leave the door open for costly and extensive legal battles. Most state statutes specify that the standard of value for dissenting stockholders' appraisal rights is fair value, although a minority of states specify fair market value. In other cases, the arbitrators usually must look to the arbitration document to establish the standard of value.

Some buy-sell agreements specify fair market value as the appropriate standard of value. In cases of minority ownership interests, this standard of value implies a valuation discount from a proportionate share of the fair market value of the total entity. This fact is often overlooked by many business owners (and even some attorneys) when drafting the agreement. Some buy-sell agreements specify that the valuation is to be a proportionate share of the fair market value of the total enterprise, with no minority ownership interest discount. We recommend that the drafter of the agreement discuss this with the parties to the agreement (see the Chapter 38, Buy-Sell Agreements and Estate Planning, for sample wording).

A reporting deadline may be specified in the agreement, or a reporting schedule may be worked out in conjunction with the process of engaging the arbitrators.

Because of the many ramifications inherent in the wording of the arbitration agreement, an appraiser experienced in arbitration should be consulted when drafting the agreement. This consultation will help to avoid both important omissions and unintentional implications of the wording discussing the valuation (such as the standard of value to be used).

Factors Left to the Arbitrators' Discretion

The following are factors that are typically left to the arbitrators' discretion:

1. Whether or not each arbitrator is expected or required to make a complete, independent appraisal, or the extent to which each arbi-

trator considers it necessary to perform independent analyses, as opposed to relying on certain data or analyses furnished by other arbitrators and/or appraisers.

2. The procedures for the arbitrators to communicate with each other (writing, telephone calls, personal meetings) and the rules for sharing information.

3. Scheduling of the arbitrators' work and meetings within the constraint of the agreed-upon reporting schedule.

4. The valuation approaches and criteria to be taken into consideration, within the constraints of any legally mandated criteria.

5. The facts, documents, and other data on which to rely (although the principals may agree to stipulate certain facts or assumptions that could make the arbitrators' job easier with respect to some matters of possible uncertainty).

The Arbitration Process

One of the major variables in the arbitration process is the extent to which each arbitrator is expected or required to carry out an independent appraisal analysis. Some arbitration documents specify that each expert on the arbitration panel do a complete, independent appraisal. More commonly, however, the extent of the independent appraisal analyses is left to the judgment of each individual arbitrator or to the arbitration panel as a group.

Review of Arbitration Document

Each arbitrator should begin with a careful review of the document(s) giving rise to the arbitration. If there is any confusion or disagreement about any details of the assignment—such as the exact definition of the property, the effective date of the valuation, or the applicable standard of value—the arbitrators should seek clarification immediately. This clarification procedure should be performed in writing to avoid any possible disputes later.

Initial Communication among Arbitrators

It is customary that the arbitrators establish communication among themselves at the earliest possible time after their appointment. A face-to-face meeting is ideal if geographic proximity to each other makes such a meeting feasible, but a conference call (or a series of conference calls) is a reasonable substitute, perhaps supplemented by correspondence. While each case is unique, the following is a generalized list of issues to try to resolve early:

1. The status of analyses already performed, if any (who has performed what analysis up to that point).

2. An agreement about sharing of information. (A common procedure is to agree that all information gathered or developed by one arbitrator will be shared with the other arbitrators as quickly as possible.)

3. An agreement, if possible, about the relevant valuation approaches to consider. (Where this becomes an issue, it seems fair to allow the parties' representatives to be heard as to their preferences. However, this often results in highly biased supplications by parties' representatives who have no technical knowledge of relevant valuation approaches.)

4. A list of documents and data needed, and assignment of responsibility for obtaining each and seeing that the necessary distribution to other arbitrators is made. (It should be agreed up front that any such documents in the possession of the parties will be provided as evidence to the arbitrators promptly and completely.)

5. Any other possible division of the research effort, such as searches for guideline transactions, development of economic and/or industry data, and routine financial statement analysis (spread sheets, ratio analysis, comparison with industry averages, and so on). The division of research effort, of course, should depend on each arbitrator's willingness to accept certain efforts of another. This willingness will be based on a judgment of professional ability and unbiased presentation of data and analysis.

6. Scheduling.

Field Visit

In most cases, arbitrators will want to visit the operating premises and interview relevant principals and/or management. It works out best if the arbitrators can conduct this field trip together rather than separately so that they will see the same things at the same time and benefit from hearing each other's questions and answers firsthand. A joint field trip also gives the arbitrators an opportunity to address any items not fully covered in their previous communications and gives any previously unacquainted arbitrators an opportunity to get to know each other and to form a basis for working together.

Hearings

The arbitrators should offer each party the opportunity to present oral and written information and opinions if they so desire. It frequently is convenient to hold a meeting to accommodate such input in conjunction with the field trip.

The Valuation Meeting

Usually, the arbitrators will meet in person to reach the valuation conclusion. In some instances, this meeting may be replaced by a conference call. In either case, all should be as prepared as possible, having exchanged and assimilated as much information as possible prior to the meeting.

In the meeting, it is usually most productive to come to agreements issue by issue, identifying and keeping track of each point of agreement and disagreement. Good notes should be kept so it is clear exactly what points have been agreed on and what the respective positions are on points that have been addressed but not yet agreed on. Each arbitrator should be receptive to the others' information and viewpoints, and the arbitrators should attempt to reach compromises on points where reasonable judgments may differ.

It is most desirable to come to a conclusion that can be endorsed as fair by all members of the arbitration panel. This agreement usually can be achieved if all of the arbitrators are qualified professional business appraisers. If unanimous agreement cannot be reached, the arbitrator in the minority position may render a dissenting opinion for the record, if he or she so desires.

Reporting the Results of the Arbitration

The formal report of the valuation conclusion reached by the arbitrators usually is contained in a very brief letter that does no more than reference the arbitration agreement, state that the arbitrators have completed their assignment in accordance with the agreement, and state the conclusion reached. The letter is signed by the arbitrators concurring in the conclusion. In the parlance of arbitration, this is called an *award*. In some cases, the letter must be notarized as well as signed.

In a significant proportion of cases, the principals on both sides would like to have a brief report explaining how the valuation conclusion was reached. In arbitration parlance, this is called an *opinion*. In such situations, such an advisory report may be the sole responsibility of the third appraiser. To make such a report, a joint task of two or more arbitrators, each of whom probably judged various factors a little bit differently—though they were able to agree on a conclusion—would usually be an unnecessarily complicated and costly exercise.

If the valuation conclusion is reached unilaterally by a special master, normally he or she would be the only one to sign the report. An explanation of the procedures and criteria used is usually included.

Mediation

While an arbitrator's role is to reach a conclusion that is binding on the parties, the mediator's role is to reach closure by convincing the parties to come to a settlement. The Internal Revenue Service authorized mediations to resolve gift and estate tax matters starting late in 1995, and at least two successful tax mediations have been concluded since then.

Exhibit 48–1 is a firsthand account of one of those mediations, with quite a bit of detail on the process itself and elements for a successful mediation.

Exhibit 48–1

Editor's Column:

Gift tax mediations reach settlements

The purpose of IRS Office of Chief Counsel Notice N(35)000-135 dated October 13, 1995, was "to outline general considerations for the use of mediation to resolve Tax Court cases." The IRS and taxpayers have engaged in two such mediations, both of which were concluded successfully.

Mediations gaining favor

Mediations are also gaining favor in other business valuation dispute contexts. As a result of a recent experience, I have gained a new-found respect for the mediation process, and I'm pleased to share my observations with our readers.

Even after a case has been calendared for trial in the U.S. Tax Court, the court may grant an extension based on an agreement between the taxpayer and IRS District Counsel to submit the matter to nonbinding mediation.

Each side has valuation expert(s)

In such cases, normally both the taxpayer and the IRS will have retained one or more independent business valuation experts. Often, the role of the second expert on each side is to review the work of the first expert and the other side's expert(s), and to provide support, critique, and/or rebuttal as appropriate to the specific case.

The following account describes the basic mediation process in a typical tax dispute context. The process would be similar in other valuation mediation contexts.

Issues often stipulated before mediation

Usually each side will have developed at least one written expert valuation report, and the IRS District Counsel and taxpayer will have engaged in settlement negotiations. Often certain issues, such as underlying real estate values, will be resolved and stipulated during the negotiations, bringing the parties closer together that

they were at the time of the IRS Notice of Deficiency. (Such stipulations are desirable regardless of whether the matter is headed to court or mediation.)

Need skilled mediator and business valuation expert

The parties must agree on one or more mediators. It is important that at least one have mediation experience with demonstrated mediation skills. For a business valuation matter, I believe it is also essential that there be a mediator with strong business valuation expertise.

Since there are few business valuation experts with mediation experience, the logical solution is a two-person mediation team. This would consist of an experienced mediator (often an attorney) and a senior business valuation expert.

Prior to the mediation, the attorneys should provide both mediators with the expert reports and legal briefs of both parties. One would expect the mediators, especially the business valuation expert, to arrive at the site of the mediation proceeding well-versed in the details of these documents.

Participants include clients, attorneys and experts

Participants in the mediation process itself, in addition to the mediators, include the parties to the dispute, the attorneys representing each side, and each side's experts. It is important that both parties approach the mediation seriously committed to reaching an agreement and that they recognize that some compromise will be necessary to reach that goal.

The mediation process typically opens with all participants in one room. One of the mediators takes the lead in chairing the proceeding, which is quite informal. The lead mediator emphasizes the necessity for movement toward an agreement at every stage of the process.

No written record of the proceedings

There is no court reporter and no official record of the meetings. The rule is that, if the process fails, nothing said or conceded

during the mediation process can later be used in litigation.

While the participants are all together, each side presents opening statements. For example:

- The taxpayers describe their perspectives on the company and the philosophy and details of the transaction.
- The Company's CFO and outside CPA describe financial details.
- The taxpayer's attorneys describe the legal aspects of their position.
- The valuation experts retained by the taxpayers present their views on valuation issues.
- The IRS attorney describes the legal aspects of their position.
- The valuation experts retained by the IRS present their views on valuation issues.

Parties make "offer" and "demand"

All this should take two to three hours. The mediators again emphasize the critical importance of moving toward a settlement at every phase of the process. They ask each side for an opening settlement number (an "offer" and a "demand"). The taxpayer and IRS make their "offer" and "demand," respectively, perhaps somewhere near where the latest settlement negotiations had broken off.

From this point forward, the parties adjourn to separate rooms, and the mediators engage in "shuttle diplomacy, " moving back and forth from one room to the other. Each time the mediators present a higher "offer" or a lower "demand," interpreting rationale of the offering or demanding party, and exhorting the other to consider the rationale and move closer toward an agreement.

Major issues in the case could include, for example:

- Differences in projections for the DCF method
- Differences in appropriate discount and/or capitalization rates
- Whether or not certain assets were "excess" and should be added to the value of the operating company

Exhibit 48–1 (concluded)

- Whether or not there was "blue sky" (intangible value over and above the tangible asset value)
- Whether or not trapped in capital gains taxes should be considered when adjusting certain asset values
- Relative weightings of income and asset approaches
- Whether or not there should be a discount for lack of marketability

Agreement not on issue-by-issue basis

Unlike an arbitration or other type of negotiation, the parties may not reach agreement issue by issue. However, it may be apparent from the mediators' presentations of the opposing parties' positions that some issues seemed to become moot, and others held steadfastly or subject to varying degrees of compromise. The "rationale" presented by the parties would be largely (although not totally discreetly) in two categories:

- The experts' reasons why their positions on various points represent the realities of the market in the particular set of facts and circumstances.
- The attorneys' rationale as to the probability of winning in court on various issues based on their interpretations of statutory law and past case precedent.

Gap narrows as process goes on

As the process wears on (and the gap hopefully has narrowed significantly), the presentations of the opposing parties' rationale for their positions may begin to take a back seat to costs and risks of litigation, and the process may take on more of the characteristics of a negotiation. Each party, however, hopefully genuinely sensing and desiring a settlement, may be reluctant to put forward a final hard and fast walkaway number. In each round the mediators convey some sense of the extent of the other party's willingness to negotiate from their latest offer.

Throughout the mediation process, the mediators generally refrain from expressing positions of their own, but in a sense play "devil's advocate" in conveying the strengths of the other party's position and the weaknesses of the positions of the parties they are addressing. As one mediator stated, "We have to focus on the weakest points of each side's position in order to bring them together."

Optimism increases during process

In the early stages of the process there may be intransigence that some may feel dooms the possibility of success. Optimism for success tends to increase over time, and eventually one may feel that the remaining differences are too small to result in either party walking away. Ultimately, an agreement is reached, perhaps significantly closer to one party's end of the opening range than the other.

I have been involved as an arbitrator or expert in about 30 business valuation arbitrations. As readers of my books know, I am a real fan of the arbitration process to resolve business valuation disputes, provided that the arbitrators, or at least a majority of the arbitration panel, are competent business valuation experts.

New appreciation for mediation

I emerged from this experience with a new-found appreciation for mediation as an alternative dispute resolution mechanism in business valuation disputes. One mediator said, "If your case is well-prepared on both sides, the process has quite a bit of merit. I think it was a positive experience for everyone. You do need to be prepared to settle, and not necessarily in the middle." He noted that it was hard work, encompassing 23 hours over two days.

I believe that both excellent mediation skills and business valuation expertise are necessary. The two-person mediation team approach is essential to a successful conclusion, unless there is an experienced business valuer with strong mediation skills available. Excellent lawyering skills, including a real understanding of the valuation issues, also contributes positively to the success of the process.

Best Wishes,

Shannon Pratt

SOURCE: *Shannon Pratt's Business Valuation Update*, July 1996, pp. 1, 3–4

Summary

The two most critical elements for an expeditious and successful arbitration are (1) a definitive arbitration agreement that provides the arbitrators with unambiguous instructions on the key matters listed above and (2) the appointment of independent arbitrators who will be both fair and competent in reaching a conclusion about the value of the subject property. If these two elements are properly addressed, the arbitration process can be a very efficient and fair way of resolving small business or professional practice valuation matters.

Bibliography

Berman, Peter J. "Resolving Business Disputes through Mediation and Arbitration." *CPA Journal*, November 1994, pp. 74–77.

Block, Jerome N. "The Process of Arbitration." *The Appraisal Journal*, April 1993, pp. 234–38.

Brief, Matthew, and Vincent Love. "Alternative Dispute Resolution: The Pros and Cons." *CPA Expert*, Summer 1996, pp. 3–7.

Brinig, Brian P., et al. "Alternative Dispute Resolution" (Chapter 12). In *Guide to Litigation Support Services*, 2d ed. Fort Worth, TX: Practitioners Publishing Company, 1996.

Carper, Donald L. "Remedies in Business Arbitration." *Arbitration Journal*, September 1991, pp. 49–58.

Coulson, Robert. "Using Arbitration to Resolve Valuation Issues" (Chapter 39). In Thomas L. West and Jeffrey D. Jones, eds. *Handbook of Business Valuation*. New York: John Wiley & Sons, 1992, pp. 415–22.

Demery, Paul. "Is Mediation in Your Future?" *Practical Accountant*, January 1996, pp. 48–55.

Diana, James C. "The New Mediation Procedure in Appeals: The Latest Development in the IRS' ADR Initiative." *Tax Management Memorandum*, November 13, 1995, pp. 331–339.

Fiore, Nicholas. "Pros and Cons of the New IRS Mediation Program." *Journal of Accountancy*, May 1996, p. 36.

Goldsheider, Robert. "Measuring the Damages: ADR and Intellectual Property Disputes." *Dispute Resolution Journal*, October–December 1995, pp. 55–63.

Kaufman, Steve. "See You Out of Court: Mediation Used in Resolving Business Disputes." *Nation's Business*, June 1992, pp. 58–60.

Klinefelter, Stanard T., and Sandra P. Gohn. "Alternative Dispute Resolution: Its Value to Estate Planners." *Estate Planning*, May/June 1995, pp. 147–154.

Koritzinsky, Allan R., Robert M. Welch Jr., and Stephen W. Schlissel. "The Benefits of Arbitration." *Family Advocate*, Spring 1992, pp. 45–52.

Kratchman, D. Michael, and William P. Walsh. "Mediation Instead of Litigation for Resolution of Valuation Disputes." *Michigan Business Law Journal*, Winter 1995, pp. 15–17.

Lore, Martin M., and L. Paige Marvel. "IRS Willing to Try Mediation in Docketed Tax Court Cases." *Journal of Taxation*, March 1996, p. 186.

Miller, Seymour W. "Mediation—An Alternate Dispute Resolution Methodology Whose Time Has Come." *CPA Journal*, July 1994, pp. 54–55.

Nicolaisen, Donald T., and Albert A. Vondra. "How Arbitration Can Reduce the Cost of Disputes." *CPA Journal*, September 1991, p. 10.

Pearson, Claude M. "Using Streamlined Arbitration to Resolve Valuation Disputes for an Accounting Partnership." *Practical Accountant*, September 1987, pp. 116–17.

Saltzman, Michael I. "Tax Court Mediation: A Case Study." *Tax Executive*, November/December 1996, pp. 449–453.

Wilburn, Kay O., Lowell S. Broom. "Alternative Strategies for Litigation Battles." *Journal of Accountancy*, March 1994, pp. 77–80.

Wilburn, Kay O., and Frank M. Messina. "IRS Has Now Begun to Open the Door of Opportunity for Resolving Disputes in a More Effective Way." *CPA Journal*, July 1996, pp. 52–54.

Zimmerman, Philip. "A Practical Guide to Mediation for CPAs." *CPA Journal*, June 1995, pp. 42–46.

Appendix A

General Resource List

General References

Basic Business Appraisal, 1984, by Raymond C. Miles (New York: John Wiley & Sons). Available from IBA, PO Box 1447, Boynton Beach, FL 33425, (407) 732-3202.

Conducting a Valuation of a Closely Held Business, 1993, by Gary R. Trugman. AICPA Management Consulting Services Division, PO Box 2209, Jersey City, NJ 07303-2209, (800) 862-4272.

Financial Valuation: Businesses and Business Interests, 1998 Update, James H. Zukin, et al., editors. Warren, Gorham & Lamont, 31 St. James Avenue, Boston, MA 02116, (800) 950-1205.

Guide to Business Valuations, 7th edition, 1997, by Jay E. Fishman, Shannon P. Pratt, J. Clifford Griffith, and Mark Wells. Practitioners Publishing Company, PO Box 966, Fort Worth, TX 76101-9940, (800) 323-8724.

Handbook of Business Valuation, 1992, Thomas L. West and Jeffrey D. Jones, eds. John Wiley & Sons, 7222 Commerce Center Drive, Suite 210, Colorado Springs, CO 80919, (800) 825-8763.

Mergers and Acquisitions Handbook for Small and Midsize Companies, 1997, Thomas L. West and Jeffrey D. Jones, eds. John Wiley & Sons (see above).

Valuing a Business: The Analysis and Appraisal of Closely Held Companies, 3d ed., 1996, by Shannon P. Pratt, Robert F. Reilly, and Robert P. Schweihs. McGraw-Hill, 1333 Burr Ridge Parkway, Burr Ridge, IL 60521, (800) 634-3966, ext. 2318.

Periodicals

Business Valuation Review, quarterly publication (40-50 pages) of the Business Valuation Committee of the American Society of Appraisers. Subscriptions are available from the publisher: PO Box 24222, Denver, CO 80224, (303) 758-6148.

CPA Expert, quarterly publication (12-16 pages) of the AICPA, Management Consulting Services (MCS) section for professionals engaged in business valuation and litigation services. Subscriptions available from AICPA, Harborside Financial Center, Circulation Department, 201 Plaza Three, Jersey City, NJ 07311, (800) 862-4272.

CPA Litigation Services Counselor, monthly publication (8 pages). Provides background information, practice management techniques, marketing help, case studies, and technical data to help prepare for a valuation or other litigation support engagement. Subscriptions available from Harcourt Brace Professional Publishing, Periodicals, 6277 Sea Harbor Drive, Orlando, FL 32877, (800) 831-7799.

Fair$hare: The Matrimonial Law Monthly, monthly publication (16 pages). Approaches, techniques, and precedents used by lawyers to solve financial and economic questions of equitable distribution in divorce practice. Subscriptions available from 7201 McKinney Circle, Frederick, MD 21701, (800) 638-8437.

Family Advocate, quarterly publication (40+ pages). Assists and educates nonprofessionals in family litigation matters. Subscriptions available from American Bar Association, Order Fulfillment, PO Box 10892, Chicago, IL 60610, (312) 988-5522.

Shannon Pratt's Business Valuation Update, monthly newsletter (12–24 pages plus supplements). Departments include current court case decision summaries, new data and publications available, news update, calendar of forthcoming meetings, current cost of capital, and reader/editor exchange. Each issue also has an editor's column and articles or interviews by or with leading authorities on business valuation topics. Subscription also includes "Where to Find It: 1998 Business Valuation Data Directory." Subscriptions available from Business Valuation Resources, 4475 S.W. Scholls Ferry Road, Suite 101, Portland, OR 97225, (888) BUS-VALU.

The Valuation Examiner, bimonthly publication published by NACVA. Subscriptions available from NACVA, 1245 East Brickyard Road, Suite 110, Salt Lake City, UT 84106-2563, (801) 486-0600.

Valuation Strategies, bimonthly publication (48+ pages), published by Warren, Gorham & Lamont, RIA Group, 117 East Stevens Avenue, Valhalla, NY 10595, (800) 431-9025.

Video Courses

Business Valuation Videocourse, 1993 (accompanying handbook updated in 1997), moderated by Shannon P. Pratt, with Robert F. Reilly, Robert P. Schweihs, and Jay E. Fishman. AICPA, PO Box 2209, Jersey City, NJ 07303-2209, (800) 862-4272.

Valuation of Closely-Held Businesses, 1995, James R. Alerding. Research Institute of America, 117 East Stevens Avenue, Valhalla, NY 10595, (800) 431-9025, ext. 4.

Appendix B

Revenue Ruling 59–60

REVENUE RULING 59-60

SECTION 2031.—DEFINITION OF GROSS ESTATE

26 CFR 20.2031-2: Valuation of stocks and bonds. Rev. Rul. 59-60
(Also Section 2512.)
(Also Part II, Sections 811(k), 1005, Regulations 105, Section 81.10)

In valuing the stock of closely held corporations, or the stock of corporations where market quotations are not available, all other available financial data, as well as all relevant factors affecting the fair market value must be considered for estate tax and gift tax purposes. No general formula may be given that is applicable to the many different valuation situations arising in the valuation of such stock. However, the general approach, methods, and factors which must be considered in valuing such securities are outlined.
Revenue Ruling 54-77, C.B. 1954-1, 187, superseded.

SECTION 1. PURPOSE.

The purpose of this Revenue Ruling is to outline and review in general the approach, methods and factors to be considered in valuing shares of the capital stock of closely held corporations for estate tax and gift tax purposes. The methods discussed herein will apply likewise to the valuation of corporate stocks on which market quotations are either unavailable or are of such scarcity that they do not reflect the fair market value.

SEC. 2. BACKGROUND AND DEFINITIONS.

.01 All valuations must be made in accordance with the applicable provisions of the Internal Revenue Code of 1954 and the Federal Estate Tax and Gift Tax Regulations. Sections 2031(a), 2032 and 2512(a) of the 1954 Code (sections 811 and 1005 of the 1939 Code) require that the property to be included in the gross estate, or made the subject of a gift, shall be taxed on the basis of the value of the property at the time of death of the decedent, the alternate date if so elected, or the date of gift.

.02 Section 20.2031-1(b) of the Estate Tax Regulations (section 81.10 of the Estate Tax Regulations 105) and section 25.2512-1 of the Gift Tax Regulations (section 86.19 of Gift Tax Regulations 108) define fair market value, in effect, as the price at which the property would change hands between a willing buyer and a willing seller when the former is not under any compulsion to buy and the latter is not under any compulsion to sell, both parties having reasonable knowledge of relevant facts. Court decisions frequently state in addition that the hypothetical buyer and seller are assumed to be able, as well as willing, to trade and to be well informed about the property and concerning the market for such property.

.03 Closely held corporations are those corporations the shares of which are owned by a relatively limited number of stockholders. Often the entire stock issue is held by one family. The result of this situation is that little, if any, trading in the shares takes place. There is, therefore, no established market for the stock and such sales as occur at irregular intervals seldom reflect all of the elements of a representative transaction as defined by the term "fair market value."

SEC. 3. APPROACH TO VALUATION.

.01 A determination of fair market value, being a question of fact, will depend upon the circumstances in each case. No formula can be devised that will be generally applicable to the multitude of different valuation issues arising in estate and gift tax cases. Often, an appraiser will find wide differences of opinion as to the fair market value of a particular stock. In resolving such differences, he should maintain a reasonable attitude in recognition of the fact that valuation is not an exact science. A sound valuation will be based upon all the relevant facts, but the elements of common sense, informed judgment and reasonableness must enter into the process of weighing those facts and determining their aggregate significance.

.02 The fair market value of specific shares of stock will vary as general economic conditions change from "normal" to "boom" or "depression," that is, according to the degree of optimism or pessimism with which the investing public regards the future at the required date of appraisal. Uncertainty as to the stability or continuity of the future income from a property decreases its value by increasing the risk of loss of earnings and value in the future. The value of shares of stock of a company with very uncertain future prospects is highly speculative. The appraiser must exercise his judgment as to the degree of risk attaching to the business of the corporation which issued the stock, but that judgment must be related to all of the other factors affecting value.

.03 Valuation of securities is, in essence, a prophesy as to the future and must be based on facts available at the required date of appraisal. As a generalization, the prices of stocks which are traded in volume in a free and active market by informed persons best reflect the consensus of the investing public as to what the future holds for the corporations and industries represented. When a stock is closely held, is traded infrequently, or is traded in an erratic market, some other measure of value must be used. In many instances, the next best measure may be found in the prices at which the stocks of companies engaged in the same or a similar line of business are selling in a free and open market.

SEC. 4. FACTORS TO CONSIDER.

.01 It is advisable to emphasize that in the valuation of the stock of closely held corporations or the stock of corporations where market quotations are either lacking or too scarce to be recognized, all available financial data, as well as all relevant factors affecting the fair market value, should be considered. The following factors, although not all-inclusive are fundamental and require careful analysis in each case:

(a) The nature of the business and the history of the enterprise from its inception.

(b) The economic outlook in general and the condition and outlook of the specific industry in particular.

(c) The book value of the stock and the financial condition of the business.

(d) The earning capacity of the company.

(e) The dividend-paying capacity.

(f) Whether or not the enterprise has goodwill or other intangible value.

(g) Sales of the stock and the size of the block of stock to be valued.

(h) The market price of stocks of corporations engaged in the same or a similar line of business having their stocks actively traded in a free and open market, either on an exchange or over-the-counter.

.02 The following is a brief discussion of each of the foregoing factors:

(a) The history of a corporate enterprise will show its past stability or instability, its growth or lack of growth, the diversity or lack of diversity of its operations, and other facts needed to form an opinion of the degree of risk involved in the business. For an enterprise which changed its form of organization but carried on the same or closely similar operations of its predecessor, the history of the former enterprise should be considered. The detail to be considered should increase with approach to the required date of appraisal, since recent events are of greatest help in predicting the future; but a study of gross and net income, and of dividends covering a long prior period, is highly desirable. The history to be studied should include, but need not be limited to, the nature of the business, its products or services, its operating and investment assets, capital structure, plant facilities, sales records and management, all of which should be considered as of the date of the appraisal, with due regard for recent significant changes. Events of the past that are unlikely to recur in the future should be discounted, since value has a close relation to future expectancy.

(b) A sound appraisal of a closely held stock must consider current and prospective economic conditions as of the date of appraisal, both in the national economy and in the industry or industries with which the corporation is allied. It is important to know that the company is more or less successful than its competitors in the same industry, or that it is maintaining a stable position with respect to competitors. Equal or even greater significance may attach to the ability of the industry with which the company is allied to compete with other industries. Prospective competition which has not been a factor in prior years should be given careful attention. For example, high profits due to the novelty of its product and the lack of competition often lead to increasing competition. The public's appraisal of the future prospects of competitive industries or of competitors within an industry may be indicated by price trends in the markets for commodities and for securities. The loss of the manager of a so-called "one-man" business may have a depressing effect upon the value of the stock of such business, particularly if there is a lack of trained personnel capable of succeeding to the management of the enterprise. In valuing the stock of this type of business, therefore, the effect of the loss of the manager on the future expectancy of the business, and the absence of management succession potentialities are pertinent factors to be taken into consideration. On the other hand, there may be factors which offset, in whole or in part, the loss of the manager's services. For instance, the nature of the business and of its assets may be such that they will not be impaired by the loss of the manager. Furthermore, the loss may be adequately covered by life insurance, or competent management might be employed on the basis of the consideration paid for the former manager's services. These, or other offsetting factors, if found to exist, should be carefully weighed against the loss of the manager's services in valuing the stock of the enterprise.

(c) Balance sheets should be obtained, preferably in the form of comparative annual statements for two or more years immediately preceding the date of appraisal, together with a balance sheet at the end of the month preceding that date, if corporate accounting will permit. Any balance sheet descriptions that are not self-explanatory, and balance sheet items comprehending diverse assets or liabilities, should be clarified in essential detail by supporting supplemental schedules. These statements usually will disclose to the appraiser (1) liquid position (ratio of current assets to current liabilities); (2) gross and net book value of principal classes of fixed assets; (3) working capital; (4) long-term indebtedness; (5) capital structure; and (6) net worth. Consideration also should be given to any assets not essential to the operation of the business, such as investments in securities, real estate, etc. In general, such nonoperating assets will command a lower rate of return than do the operating assets, although in exceptional cases the reverse may be true. In computing the book value per share of stock, assets of the investment type should be revalued on the basis of their market price and the book value adjusted accordingly. Comparison of the company's balance sheets over several years may reveal, among other facts, such developments as the acquisition of additional production facilities or subsidiary companies, improvement in financial position, and details as to recapitalizations and other changes in the capital structure of the corporation. If the corporation has more than one class of stock outstanding, the charter or certificate of incorporation should be examined to ascertain the explicit rights and privileges of the various stock issues including: (1) voting powers, (2) preference as to dividends, and (3) preference as to assets in the event of liquidation.

(d) Detailed profit-and-loss statements should be obtained and considered for a representative period immediately prior to the required date of appraisal, preferably five or more years. Such statements should show (1) gross income by principal items; (2) principal deductions from gross income including major prior items of operating expenses, interest and other expense on each item of long-term debt, depreciation and depletion if such deductions are made, officers' salaries, in total if they appear to be reasonable or in detail if they seem to be excessive, contributions (whether or not deductible for tax purposes) that the nature of its business and its community position require the corporation to make, and taxes by principal items, including income and excess profits taxes; (3) net income available for dividends; (4) rates and amounts of dividends paid on each class of stock; (5) remaining amount carried to surplus; and (6) adjustment to, and reconciliation with, surplus as stated on the balance sheet. With profit and loss statements of this character available, the appraiser should be able to separate recurrent from nonrecurrent items of income and expense, to distinguish between operating income and investment income, and to ascertain whether or not any line of business in which the company is engaged is operated consistently at a loss and might be abandoned with benefit to the company. The percentage of earnings retained for business expansion should be noted when dividend-paying capacity is considered. Potential future income is a major factor in many valuations of closely held stocks, and all information concerning past income which will be helpful in predicting the future should be secured. Prior earnings records usually are the most reliable guide as to the future expectancy, but resort to arbitrary five- or ten-year averages without regard to current trends or future prospects will not produce a realistic valuation. If, for instance, a record of progressively increasing or decreasing net income is found, then greater weight may be accorded the most recent years' profits in estimating earning power. It will be helpful, in judging risk and the extent to which a business is a marginal operator, to consider deductions from income and net income in terms of percentage of sales. Major categories of cost and expense to be so analyzed include the consumption of raw materials and supplies in the case of manufacturers, processors and fabricators; the cost of purchased merchandise in the case of merchants; utility services; insurance; taxes; depletion or depreciation; and interest.

(e) Primary consideration should be given to the dividend-paying capacity of the company rather than to dividends actually paid in the past. Recognition must be given to the necessity of retaining a reasonable portion of profits in a company to meet competition. Dividend-paying capacity is a factor that must be considered in an appraisal, but dividends actually paid in the past may not have any relation to dividend-paying capacity. Specifically, the dividends paid by a closely held family company may be measured by the income needs of the stockholders or by their desire to avoid taxes on dividend receipts, instead of by the ability of the company to pay dividends. Where an actual or effective controlling interest in a corporation is to be valued, the dividend factor is not a material element, since the payment of such dividends is discretionary with the controlling stockholders. The individual or group in control can substitute salaries and bonuses for dividends, thus reducing net income and understating the dividend-paying capacity of the company. It follows, therefore, that dividends are less reliable criteria of fair market value than other applicable factors.

(f) In the final analysis, goodwill is based upon earning capacity. The presence of goodwill and its value, therefore, rests upon the excess of net earnings over and above a fair return on the net tangible assets. While the element of goodwill may be based primarily on earnings, such factors as the prestige and renown of the business, the ownership of a trade or brand name, and a record of successful operation over a prolonged period in a particular locality, also may furnish support for the inclusion of intangible value. In some instances it may not be possible to make a separate appraisal of the tangible and intangible assets of the business. The enterprise has a value as an entity. Whatever intangible value there is, which is supportable by the facts, may be measured by the amount by which the appraised value of the tangible assets exceeds the net book value of such assets.

(g) Sales of stock of a closely held corporation should be carefully investigated to determine whether they represent transactions at arm's length. Forced or distress sales do not ordinarily reflect fair market value nor do isolated sales in small amounts necessarily control as the measure of value. This is especially true in the valuation of a controlling interest in a corporation. Since, in the case of closely held stocks, no prevailing market prices are available, there is no basis for making an adjustment for blockage. It follows, therefore, that such stocks should be valued upon a consideration of all the evidence affecting the fair market value. The size of the block of stock itself is a relevant factor to be considered. Although it is true that a minority interest in an unlisted corporation's stock is more difficult to sell than a similar block of listed stock, it is equally true that control of a corporation, either actual or in effect, representing as it does an added element of value, may justify a higher value for a specific block of stock.

(h) Section 2031(b) of the Code states, in effect, that in valuing unlisted securities the value of stock or securities of corporations engaged in the same or a similar line of business which are listed on an exchange should be taken into consideration along with all other factors. An important consideration is that the corporations to be used for comparisons have capital stocks which are actively traded by the public. In accordance with section 2031(b) of the Code, stocks listed on an exchange are to be considered first. However, if sufficient comparable companies whose stocks are listed on an exchange cannot be found, other comparable companies which have stocks actively traded in on the over-the-counter market also may be used. The essential factor is that whether the stocks are sold on an exchange or over-the-counter there is evidence of an active, free public market for the stock as of the valuation date. In selecting corporations for comparative purposes, care should be taken to use only comparable companies. Although the only restrictive requirement as to comparable corporations specified in the statute is that their lines of business be the same or similar, yet it is obvious that consideration must be given to other relevant factors in order that the most valid comparison possible will be obtained. For illustration, a corporation having one or more issues of preferred stock, bonds or debentures in addition to its common stock should not be considered to be directly comparable to one having only common stock outstanding. In like manner, a company with a declining business and decreasing markets is not comparable to one with a record of current progress and market expansion.

SEC. 5. WEIGHT TO BE ACCORDED VARIOUS FACTORS.

The valuation of closely held corporate stock entails the consideration of all relevant factors as stated in section 4. Depending upon the circumstances in each case, certain factors may carry more weight than others because of the nature of the company's business. To illustrate:

(a) Earnings may be the most important criterion of value in some cases whereas asset value will receive primary consideration in others. In general, the appraiser will accord primary consideration to earnings when valuing stocks of companies which sell products or services to the public; conversely, in the investment or holding type of company, the appraiser may accord the greatest weight to the assets underlying the security to be valued.

(b) The value of the stock of a closely held investment or real estate holding company, whether or not family owned, is closely related to the value of the assets underlying the stock. For companies of this type the appraiser should determine the fair market values of the assets of the company. Operating expenses of such a company and the cost of liquidating it, if any, merit consideration when appraising the relative values of the stock and the underlying assets. The market values of the underlying assets give due weight to potential earnings and dividends of the particular items of property underlying the stock, capitalized at rates deemed proper by the investing public at the date of appraisal. A current appraisal by the investing public should be superior to the retrospective opinion of an individual. For these reasons, adjusted net worth should be accorded greater weight in valuing the stock of a closely held investment or real estate holding company, whether or not family owned, than any of the other customary yardsticks of appraisal, such as earnings and dividend paying capacity.

SEC. 6. CAPITALIZATION RATES.

In the application of certain fundamental valuation factors, such as earnings and dividends, it is necessary to capitalize the average or current results at some appropriate rate. A determination of the proper capitalization rate presents one of the most difficult problems in valuation. That there is no ready or simple solution will become apparent by a cursory check of the rates of return and dividend yields in terms of the selling prices of corporate shares listed on the major exchanges of the country. Wide variations will be found even for companies in the same industry. Moreover, the ratio will fluctuate from year to year depending upon economic conditions. Thus, no standard tables of capitalization rates applicable to closely held corporations can be formulated. Among the more important factors to be taken into consideration in deciding upon a capitalization rate in a particular case are: (1) the nature of the business; (2) the risk involved; and (3) the stability or irregularity of earnings.

SEC. 7. AVERAGE OF FACTORS.

Because valuations cannot be made on the basis of a prescribed formula, there is no means whereby the various applicable factors in a particular case can be assigned mathematical weights in deriving the fair market value. For this reason, no useful purpose is served by taking an average of several factors (for example, book value, capitalized earnings and capitalized dividends) and basing the valuation on the result. Such a process excludes active consideration of other pertinent factors, and the end result cannot be supported by a realistic application of the significant facts in the case except by mere chance.

SEC. 8. RESTRICTIVE AGREEMENTS.

Frequently, in the valuation of closely held stock for estate and gift tax purposes, it will be found that the stock is subject to an agreement restricting its sale or transfer. Where shares of stock were acquired by a decedent subject to an option reserved by the issuing corporation to repurchase at a certain price, the option price is usually accepted as the fair market value for estate tax purposes. See Rev. Rul. 54-76, C.B. 1954-1, 194. However, in such case the option price is not determinative of fair market value for gift tax purposes. Where the option, or buy and sell agreement, is the result of voluntary action by the stockholders and is binding during the life as well as at the death of the stockholders, such agreement may or may not, depending upon the circumstances of each case, fix the value for estate tax purposes. However, such agreement is a factor to be considered, with other relevant factors, in determining fair market value. Where the stockholder is free to dispose of his shares during life and the option is to become effective only upon his death, the fair market value is not limited to the option price. It is always necessary to consider the relationship of the parties, the relative number of shares held by the decedent, and other material facts to determine whether the agreement represents a bonafide business arrangement or is a device to pass the decedent's shares to the natural objects of his bounty for less than an adequate and full consideration in money or money's worth. In this connection see Rev. Rul. 157 C.B. 1953-2, 255, and Rev. Rul. 189, C.B. 1953-2, 294.

SEC. 9. EFFECT ON OTHER DOCUMENTS.

Revenue Ruling 54-77, C.B. 1954-1, 187, is hereby superseded.

Index

B